Advancing Develop.

Core Themes in Global Economics

Edited by

George Mavrotas and Anthony Shorrocks

Foreword by Amartya Sen

in association with the United Nations University –
World Institute for Development
Economics Research

First published 2007 by
PALGRAVE MACMILLAN
Houndmills, Basingstoke, Hampshire RG21 6XS and
175 Fifth Avenue, New York, N.Y. 10010
Companies and representatives throughout the world

PALGRAVE MACMILLAN is the global academic imprint of the Palgrave
Macmillan division of St. Martin's Press, LLC and of Palgrave Macmillan Ltd.
Macmillan® is a registered trademark in the United States, United Kingdom
and other countries. Palgrave is a registered trademark in the European
Union and other countries.

ISBN-13: 978–0–230–01902–7   hardback
ISBN-10: 0–230–01902–1   hardback
ISBN-13: 978–0–230–01904–1   paperback
ISBN-10: 0–230–01904–8   paperback

This book is printed on paper suitable for recycling and made from fully
managed and sustained forest sources.

A catalogue record for this book is available from the British Library.

Library of Congress Cataloging-in-Publication Data
    Advancing development : core themes in global economics / edited by George
Mavrotas and Anthony Shorrocks.
        p. cm.
    Selected papers from a June 17–18, 2005 conference held in Helsinki on the
    occasion of the jubilee anniversary of the World Institute for Development
    Economics Research (UNU-WIDER), and dedicated to the memory of Lal
    Jayawardena, the first Director of UNU-WIDER.
    Includes bibliographical references and index.
    ISBN 0–230–01902–1 (cloth) – ISBN 0–230–01904–8 (pbk.)
        1. Development economics – Congresses. 2. Economic development – Congresses.
    3. World Institute for Development Economics Research – Congresses. I. Mavrotas,
    George. II. Shorrocks, Anthony F. III. World Institute for Development Economics
    Research.
HD73.A33 2007
338.9—dc22   2006048540

10 9 8 7 6 5 4 3 2
16 15 14 13 12 11 10 09 08 07

Printed and bound in Great Britain by
Antony Rowe Ltd, Chippenham and Eastbourne

Contents

List of Tables

List of Boxes

List of Figures

Preface

George Mavrotas and Anthony Shorrocks

The 20 years since the World Institute for Development Economics Research (UNU-WIDER) began work in 1985 have witnessed major changes in the world economy that have profound implications not only for the developing world but also for development economics itself. In June 2005, leading researchers and policy-makers met in Helsinki on the occasion of WIDER's jubilee anniversary, to reflect upon current thinking in development economics and on what the next two decades might hold. The conference sought to highlight new and emerging issues in development, to consider how research can best address these issues and to identify promising methodologies that could advance the frontiers of research and practice. The two-day conference (17–18 June 2005) covered a broad range of development topics including growth, trade and finance; poverty and inequality; strategies for poverty reduction; conflict; and economic policy making. In addition to current research issues, the presentations focused on the challenges and dilemmas which are likely to engage researchers and policy-makers over the next 20 years. The present volume entitled *Advancing Development: Core Themes in Global Economics* contains a selection of papers from the jubilee conference and is dedicated to the memory of Lal Jayawardena, the first director of UNU-WIDER.

The world as we know it is one in which there is a great deal of deprivation, disparity and strife. Globalization may have shrunk distances among countries, but it has not succeeded in bridging the yawning gap between the rich and the poor of this world. One consequence is a growing imbalance in trade and power relations. The ability of poorer countries to cope with and benefit from globalization has been impeded by dwindling international aid flows, volatile private capital movements, a lack of attention to human security and the causes of conflict, as well as the social costs of market liberalization. The deep poverty that is still widespread – especially in Africa – is a stark reminder that all is not well with the world, even if some parts of it have experienced regular improvement in their level of prosperity. Pessimism, resignation, indifference, or recourse to looking the other way, are all possible responses to the state of the global order. But engagement is also on the menu, and it is this option that WIDER, in furtherance of its mandate, has pursued. By drawing on the expertise and commitment of a broad international body of researchers, WIDER has endeavoured to come to grips with the reality of the world's problems, to understand the nature of the processes at work, to describe and evaluate the vicissitudes of global development, to provide sound empirical and conceptual bases for policy analysis and to hold out hope for solutions to problems which might otherwise be regarded as intractable. In the process, WIDER has presided over a body of research which can claim in parts to be genuinely seminal, policy-rich and path-breaking.*

---

* See T. Addison, A. Shorrocks and A. Swallow (eds) (2005), *Development Agendas and Insights: 20 Years of UNU-WIDER Research* (Geneva: UN Publications), for a discussion of WIDER's history and research activities.

The present volume seeks to continue this tradition. As suggested by the title, one aim is to document the way that development economics has advanced, by reviewing the evolution of past thought on the subject and anticipating possible future directions. 'Advancing Development' is also an appropriate description of the role that WIDER has set itself as an institution dedicated to the promotion of policies for improving the lot of those living in the developing world. The volume may therefore be viewed as a reflection of WIDER's interests and a celebration of WIDER's achievements during its first two decades of existence. Finally, 'Advancing Development' is a fitting epitaph for Lal Jayawardena, whose energy and vision laid the foundation for WIDER's success, and whose considerable personal contributions to development thinking continue to inspire the work of the Institute.

The volume consists of eight parts, each of which deals with a core area of development economics. The authors of the 36 chapters have striven to address key issues in a non-technical manner in order that the volume is accessible to readers who are not accustomed to the technical language of academic journals. However, rigorous analysis and in-depth discussion of the issues have not been compromised. A few of the chapters provide comprehensive and critical reviews of the relevant topic. But most of the contributions are not intended to be surveys, aiming instead to present thoughtful views on important and timely issues in development economics.

Part I, entitled *Development Economics in Retrospect*, offers a fascinating tour of the history of thought on development economics, illuminating its evolution into a significant and dynamic area within economics. In this regard, **Erik Thorbecke** classifies the body of knowledge into four interrelated components: the prevailing development objectives; the conceptual state of the art relating to development theories, models, techniques and applications; the underlying data system; and the resulting development strategy. The main contributions and changes to these four components are traced, decade by decade, starting from the 1950s. **Louis Emmerij** asks a number of questions regarding development thinking and practice, such as why and when turning points occur; what options are available when it comes to economic and social development policies; and what is the notion of culture in development. He also compares the merits and disadvantages of global development theories with regional and local development policies that place more emphasis on the role of culture in economic development. E. **Wayne Nafziger** compares alternative conceptions of the meaning of development over the past 30 years, with special reference to the work of Dudley Seers and Amartya Sen. Nafziger argues that both thinkers were critical of the development literature of their times, and that one of the challenges for future work is for development economists to be more holistic, integrating economic development, human rights and conflict reduction. In his contribution, **Richard Jolly** claims that global inequality (the gap between the rich and the poor) has grown substantially by almost every measure since it was identified as an issue in the influential works of Adam Smith, Tom Paine, John Stuart Mill and Karl Marx. Over the last two or three decades, national income inequality has also grown. Jolly recommends more attention be given to the extremes of inequality, especially the sources of extreme wealth and poverty, and how these sources are linked to injustices in the past.

The historical perspective on inequality provided by Jolly leads conveniently to the theme of *Inequality and Conflict* covered by four chapters in Part II. A concern with inequality is central to development strategies. At the same time, the nature of conflict has undergone profound change in recent years and violent conflict can further aggravate inequality problems in the developing world. **Giovanni Andrea Cornia** and **Leonardo Menchini** juxtapose changes over the last 40 years in income growth and distribution with the mortality changes recorded at the aggregate level in about 170 countries and at the individual level in 26 countries. They highlight the similarities and linkages between changes in income inequality and health inequality, and offer some tentative explanations of the trends. The chapter by **Eric M. Uslaner** argues that economic inequality provides a fertile breeding ground for corruption which in turn leads to further inequalities. Uslaner uses Romanian data to estimate a simultaneous equation model of trust, corruption, perceptions of inequality, confidence in government and demands for redistribution, and shows that perceptions of rising inequality and corruption lead to lower levels of trust and demands for redistribution. The following chapter by **S. Mansoob Murshed** discusses the problems of achieving lasting peace. One important aspect is an equitable division of the post-war economic and political settlement (the 'peace dividend'). Murshed also discusses how perceived injustices can lead to a deep sense of humiliation, an important factor in acts of transnational terrorism and one not easily deterred by force alone. **Marcia Byrom Hartwell** examines the reasons for the escalation of violence following peace agreements in early post-conflict transitions and the implications for development. She describes the underlying dynamics, including the relationship between perceptions of justice as fairness, the formation of post-conflict identity, the political processes of forgiveness and revenge and the policy implications for development.

Issues related to *Human Development and Wellbeing* (Part III) have been for many years at the heart of the research and policy agenda in development economics, and have more recently received considerable attention in connection with the Millennium Development Goals (MDGs). **Farhad Noorbakhsh** examines differences in the human development index across countries, and finds some evidence that these differences narrowed over the period 1975–2002. While country positions remained relatively stable during the early part of the period, this was followed by considerable upward and downward movement, indicating a possible example of the 'twin peaks' type of polarization. In recognition of the importance of health, both as a source of human welfare and as a determinant of overall economic growth, **Nora Lustig** examines the impact of the Popular Health Insurance programme in Mexico, which was first introduced as a pilot programme in 2001, and became part of the formal legislation in 2003. Lustig reviews some of the early results of the programme, along with the improvements made so far to public health coverage in Mexico. **David Fielding**, **Mark McGillivray** and **Sebastian Torres** discuss the findings of research into the impact of foreign aid on human development. Instead of looking at per capita income, as is common, they look at how aid affects a range of human development indicators, including health, education and fertility, and allow for the fact that these different dimensions of wellbeing are likely to interact with each other. **Stephen Knowles** points out that the literatures on social capital and on institutions rarely acknowledge the existence of each other. He believes that cross-country evidence on both subjects could be enriched by empirically modelling social capital as a fundamental determinant of development.

During the last two decades the world economy has experienced an intense evolution of economic policy, particularly in the area of international trade. At the same time economic integration has increased, as reflected in higher trade and financial flows. This process – *Globalization* – has also affected the movement of people and knowledge across international borders. These issues are the subject of Part IV, along with the cultural, political and environmental dimensions of globalization that go beyond international trade. **Nancy Birdsall** argues that openness is not necessarily good for the poor. Reducing trade protection has not brought growth to today's poorest countries, and open capital markets have not been good for the poorest households in emerging market economies. Birdsall presents evidence on these issues and also discusses the asymmetries that help explain why countries and people cannot always compete on equal terms on the 'level playing field' of the global economy. **Machiko Nissanke** and **Erik Thorbecke** stress that globalization offers participating countries new opportunities for accelerating growth and development but, at the same time, also poses challenges to, and imposes constraints on, policy-makers in the management of national, regional and global economic systems. They discuss the various relationships embedded in the openness-growth-inequality-poverty nexus and analyse how globalization affects poverty, concluding with some thoughts on formulating a set of measures to make globalization more pro-poor. **Arjan de Haan** explores the role that migration has played in development studies and in debates on economic growth and poverty. Highlighting the importance of interdisciplinarity and of an institutional understanding of the processes of economic growth, he argues that development economics needs to draw more strongly on the insights and approaches of social scientists outside economics.

Despite the rapid and large increase in flows of trade, finance and technology across the global economy, most developing countries have limited access to the finance deemed necessary for development; and lack of finance limits the ability of many countries to diversify their trade, to access new technologies and to reduce poverty. *Development Finance* issues are the subject of Part V in this volume. **Valpy FitzGerald** examines the linkages between international risk tolerance, capital market failure and capital flows to emerging markets. The microeconomic roots of home bias and demand instability are explained in terms of investor risk perception and credit rationing, exacerbated by the behaviour of traders. FitzGerald concludes by examining the implications of his findings for the future of development economics in general and for policy response in particular. **Silvia Marchesi** and **Laura Sabani** review the literature dealing with the failure of conditional lending and propose a novel explanation: the repeated nature of IMF involvement, together with the fact that the IMF acts simultaneously as a lender and as a monitor (and as an advisor) of economic reforms, weakens the credibility of the IMF threat. They conclude that prolonged use of IMF resources is not only a consequence of the ineffectiveness of conditional lending but may itself be a determinant of conditionality failure. **Tony Addison** identifies five broad topics in international finance that may become prominent over the next 20 years: the flow of capital from ageing societies to the more youthful economies of the South; the growth of the financial services industry in emerging economies and the consequences for their capital flows; the current strength in emerging market debt; the impact of globalization in goods markets in lowering inflation expectations; and the implications of the adjustment in global imbalances between Asia (in particular China) and the United States for emerging bond markets as a whole.

The chapters included in Part VI, *Growth and Poverty*, cover various aspects of the growth process in developing countries and the formulation of pro-poor policies. **Mark Blackden**, **Sudharshan Canagarajah**, **Stephan Klasen** and **David Lawson** examine the issues related to gender and growth in sub-Saharan Africa. By identifying some of the key factors that determine the ways in which men and women contribute to, and benefit (or lose) from, growth in Africa, they argue that looking at such issues through a gender lens is an essential step in identifying how policy can be shaped in a way that is explicitly gender-inclusive and beneficial to growth and to the poor. Focusing on cross-country differences in output per worker between 1980 and 2000, **Pertti Haaparanta** and **Heli Virta** decompose changes in the distribution of labour productivity into changes in productive efficiency, changes in best practice technology, accumulation of physical capital and accumulation of human capital. The study focuses on low-income countries, and especially on highly indebted poor countries (HIPCs), which could not be done in earlier studies. **Nanak Kakwani** and **Hyun H. Son** discuss how the targeting efficiency of government programmes may be better assessed. Using their own 'pro-poor policy' index, they investigate the pro-poorness of not only government programmes aimed at the poorest segment of the population, but also basic service delivery in education, health and infrastructure. **Lakhwinder Singh** focuses on the long-term innovation strategy of industrial and technological progress in developing countries. Growth theory, empirical evidence and several indicators of innovation are used to draw lessons from the historical experience of the developed and newly industrializing countries for the industrial development of the poorest economies. **Sukti Dasgupta** and **Ajit Singh** use a Kaldorian framework to examine the evidence of deindustrialization in developing countries at low levels of income, the jobless growth in these economies and the fast expansion of the informal sector. These questions are specifically examined for the Indian economy using state-level data, but the analysis can be applied more broadly to economic policy in developing countries.

Part VII focuses on the core theme of *Development Strategies* in the developing world. **Guillermo Rozenwurcel** explains why all development strategies have failed in Latin America, arguing that after the Great Depression and throughout the rest of the twentieth century, Latin American countries followed two successive and contradictory strategies, namely import substitution industrialization and the Washington Consensus approach. However, neither managed to deliver sustained economic development due to the failure of the state and the inability to achieve mature integration into the world economy. **Álvaro García Hurtado** draws more positive conclusions from the experience of Chile over the period 1990–2005. García Hurtado argues that Chile has shown remarkable results in terms of growth, poverty reduction and democratic governance. He stresses that Chile did better in terms of growth than social integration, and that this is related to the weak representation and participation of a large portion of the population in the national debate and decision-making process. **Annelies Zoomers** extends the geographical coverage by examining successes and failures in three decades of rural development projects in Africa, Asia and Latin America, using the evidence to suggest how development interventions can be made more effective. **Justin Yifu Lin**, **Mingxing Liu**, **Shiyuan Pan** and **Pengfei Zhang** examine the linkages between development strategy, viability and economic institutions in China, arguing that the distorted institutional structure in many developing countries after the Second World War can be largely explained by government adoption of inappropriate development strategies. They also examine the evolution of economic institutions and government development strategies in China from the 1950s–1980s. **Grzegorz W. Kolodko** explores the crucial nexus between institutions, policies and economic development. According to Kolodko, progress in market-economy institution building is not itself sufficient to ensure sustained growth: another indispensable component is an appropriately designed and implemented economic policy which must not confuse the means with the aims. **Richard M. Auty** identifies two basic trajectories to a high-income democracy linked to the scale and deployment of rents in developing countries. Low-rent countries tend to generate developmental political states that competitively diversify the economy and sustain rapid per capita GDP growth. This strengthens three key sanctions against anti-social governance: political accountability, social capital and the rule of law. In contrast, rent-rich countries are likely to experience a slower and more erratic transition. In his chapter on the role of credit co-operatives in locally financed economic development, **Robert J. McIntyre** stresses transitional and developing countries often fail to produce institutions capable of supporting economic development with localized saving-investment cycles. The advantages of credit co-operatives in mobilizing and financing local economic development are contrasted with the disadvantages of both conventional microcredit and the most recent neoliberal fashion of so-called 'new wave financial institutions'.

The chapters in the concluding part, *Development Economics in Prospect*, expand and enrich the preceding discussion by looking forward to the crucial issues and policy dilemmas which are likely to preoccupy policy-makers and scholars over the next two decades. **Deepak Nayyar** examines the prospects for development in a changed international context, where globalization has diminished the policy space so essential for countries that are latecomers to development. Nayyar emphasises the importance of initial conditions, the significance of institutions, the relevance of politics in economics and the critical role of good governance. Even if difficult, there is a clear need to create more policy space for national development. Building on Karl Polanyi's work on 'The Great Transformation', **Frances Stewart** considers whether, in the light of the consequences of the unregulated market, a new 'Great Transformation' is needed in contemporary developing countries. Stewart also examines whether such a transformation is likely, reviewing moves towards increased regulation of the market, and also the constraints faced by any contemporary great transformation arising from globalization and the nature of politics. **François Bourguignon** and **Mark Sundberg** focus on the issue of building absorptive capacity to meet the Millennium Development Goals, addressing absorptive capacity in low-income countries from both a theoretical and empirical perspective. They also present a framework (with an application to the case of Ethiopia) for undertaking country-specific analysis, which relates the macroeconomic environment and economic growth on the one hand, and sector-specific micro-constraints affecting implementation of the social MDGs on the other. Discussing the pros and cons of applying behavioural economics to international development policy, **C. Leigh Anderson** and **Kostas Stamoulis** note that many development policies are premised on a traditional economic model of rationality to predict how individuals will respond to changes in incentives. Despite the focus on poverty reduction, economists and others in the development community are still unable to fully understand how the poor make decisions, especially under uncertainty and over time. Behavioural economics may provide more helpful answers. **Mihály Simai** examines critical trends and new challenges affecting the human dimensions of global development. Simai argues that the new state and non-state actors make the system of interests and values more diverse, and that all of these have a major influence on the future of the development process. Developing societies do not need old textbook models, neoliberal, or other utopias as there is a widespread demand for a new scientific thinking on development, with realistic and humanistic alternatives helping collaborative national and global actions. In the final chapter in the volume, **Lance Taylor** reviews the recent growth experience in developing countries with an emphasis on structural change and the sources of effective demand. The means by which policy influences such outcomes is also analyzed in light of historical experience, alongside the options for macro and industrial/commercial policy, and how they influence the growth process. Taylor argues that the recent 'institutional turn' in development theory may obscure serious policy analysis.

The process of preparing this volume has been particularly challenging and rewarding. We are grateful to all of the authors for their enthusiastic commitment to the overall project, and to the referees of individual chapters for their helpful comments and suggestions. Special thanks are due to Lorraine Telfer-Taivainen, who shouldered most of the administrative work for the jubilee conference and was responsible for assembling the complete manuscript. Thanks are also due to Adam Swallow for his advice on editorial issues and to Amanda Hamilton,

Economics Publisher at Palgrave Macmillan, for enthusiastically embracing the project from its inception. Finally, we express our gratitude to the governments and other donors who have generously supported the activities of WIDER over the past 20 years; this book and the other outputs and achievements of WIDER would not have been possible without their support and financial backing.

Foreword

Amartya Sen

As the World Institute for Development Economics Research reaches adulthood – it was established 21 years ago in 1985 – there are good reasons to celebrate what has been achieved in what must be seen as rather a short time. The impressively broad range of issues in global economics that are covered in this conference volume, edited by George Mavrotas and Anthony Shorrocks, bring out not only the diversity of problems that are all quite important for development in the contemporary world, but also the fact, in which there is reason to take some pride, that WIDER, as a new institute of research, has been able to contribute substantially to such a variety of fields, informed by a good understanding of the need for coverage as well as quality.*

It is a great pity that the founding director of WIDER, Lal Jayawardena, who set the institute firmly on course and jump-started it from nothing, is no longer with us. The fact that this book is being dedicated to Lal's memory is a small indication of the recognition of what he did for WIDER. Ajit Singh's excellent essay on Lal Jayawardena's remarkable qualities, gifts and accomplishments will give the reader a flavour of the kind of intellectual background and commitment that he brought to WIDER. The reaching of maturity is not, however, only an occasion for celebration and champagne, but also for reflection on the history of this institution, especially since the people originally involved with WIDER are not any less afflicted by mortality than normal human beings are at their respective ages.

The time may not have come yet for an official history of WIDER (but that time cannot be far off), but the ideas, aspirations and commitments of those early years are worth putting on record. In this Lal Jayawardena's leadership was, of course, pivotal, but it was strongly backed by the exceptional cluster of creative and innovative people who made research at WIDER proceed with the speed and understanding that a new research institution badly needs but often does not get. I personally felt immensely privileged to be able to work with such original, communicative and friendly people. Collaborative relations with Finnish and other Scandinavian research and teaching institutions were gradually developed, benefiting WIDER from the presence of rich intellectual traditions in Helsinki and elsewhere. Finnish presence was strong, not only in research collaboration but also in overcoming institutional difficulties in developing an organizational system that could sustain the ambitious research programmes that were planned and gradually implemented.

---

* In writing this Foreword, I have been greatly helped by the counsel – and shared memory – of Lorraine Telfer-Taivainen, who runs the Office of the Director of WIDER and who has had an active presence at this institution right from its early days which I talk about in this introductory essay.

The nature of the interactions is, for me personally, well illustrated by the extensive benefit that my part of the research programme, connected with poverty, hunger, nutrition, and quality of life, received from the extraordinary intellectuals who came to the new WIDER. I think of those who joined me to lead these projects, in addition to doing their own research, including Jean Drèze, Siddiqur Osmani, and Martha Nussbaum, but also the remarkable researchers who made it possible for WIDER to do so much so quickly, including Peter Svedberg, Nanak Kakwani, V.K. Ramachandran, and others. I also think of Frédérique Appfel Marglin and Stephen Marglin, who co-directed a different project at WIDER but worked jointly with us often enough. I also recollect with much joy – and appreciation – the contributions that came to WIDER from collaboration with Martti Ahtisaari, Erik Allardt, Sudhir Anand, Michael Bruno, Partha Dasgupta, Robert Dorfman, Robert Erickson, Roderick Flood, Robert Fogel, John Harsanyi, Eric Hobsbawm, Seppo Honkapohja, Janos Kornai, Pentti Kouri, Val Moghadam, Jeffrey Sachs, Thomas Schelling, Ajit Singh, Rehman Sobhan, Gareth Steadman-Jones, Frances Stewart, Marja Liisa Swantz, Lance Taylor, Bernard Williams, Stefano Zamagni, among many others. There was a general sense of confidence that research at WIDER could make a difference to the world, and it was thrilling to see how determined the early workers at WIDER were to make a substantial change in the world of developmental thinking.

Since I had a hand in choosing the name (World Institute for Development Economics Research) that led us to that energizing acronym, WIDER, it was very pleasing for me to see that in its research work, the new institute was indeed taking a very broad view of development – including developmental economics – and was living up to the counsel of that acronymal admonishment. I must, however, acknowledge that in those early days not only was I privileged to observe closely the exceptional work that was going on in the new WIDER, I also had the opportunity of witnessing some of the difficulties that WIDER went through as it got started in Helsinki. The initial problems were particularly manifest in the sometimes troubled public relations through which WIDER went.

During 1983–84, before WIDER got started, Finland's offer to host the soon-to-be-set-up new institute was one of the two proposals that the United Nations University (UNU) was considering when the choice of location and collaboration was finalized. The other 'final round' proposal was from the Netherlands, complete with a plan to base the new organization in Maastricht (some other proposals had been turned down by UNU by then).

The UNU dispatched Alex Kwapong (a distinguished classicist who was Vice-Rector of UNU and a former Vice-Chancellor of the University of Ghana) and me, along with a sizeable team of UNU experts, to both the Netherlands and Finland to talk, assess and advise. It was not altogether an easy decision. The pro-Netherlands school pointed to the well-established fact that it was a country with tremendous experience of international institutions, and also quite importantly, it had a very broad and cosmopolitan media. Those of us who wanted to take up the Finnish offer, despite our admiration for the Netherlands and its experience in international collaboration and communication, saw in Finland a remarkable country of rapidly growing importance, with a deep commitment to global development – and also a country that was, we felt, already firmly on the way to becoming a major player in international thinking. Our arguments for going to Finland did ultimately prevail, and Helsinki welcomed the new WIDER in 1985.

As I think about how WIDER's founding years went, the arguments on both sides, about the comparative merits of different locations, proved to be substantially correct. WIDER's public relations had several problems, but they were made much more arduous by the fact that Finland was then a country effectively of one principal newspaper – with immense influence – and if its reporter took a dislike to something in the new institution it would be extremely hard to generate any different public perception, especially when the news coverage about WIDER got thoroughly linked up with Finland's electoral politics. For quite a few years, the appreciation of WIDER in the international world was immensely higher than its standing in Finland itself. Yet, ultimately, WIDER's work did receive the recognition even within Finland that it was receiving, right from the beginning, across the world. And Finland's deep commitment to global development, which influenced the Finns, from the President of the country to ordinary citizens, did eventually come through loud and clear, and provided the supportive environment in which WIDER's work could flourish and broaden even further.

The early intellectual departures, led by Lal Jayawardena, in the research undertaken in WIDER have been further enriched by the new challenges that Jayawardena's successors have perceptively identified as problems of growing importance. I think particularly of the second director Mihaly Simai's insightful diagnosis that globalization as a problem as well as an opportunity would speedily become a major focus of attention in the contemporary world – a theme that would be further pursued by the next director, Giovanni Andrea Cornia, who also initiated major studies on interregional and intertemporal disparities in living conditions, including morbidity, mortality and life expectancy. WIDER's research work has been further strengthened by the present director Anthony Shorrocks' far-reaching understanding that the centrality of inequality as a contentious issue cannot but influence development work in every field in the world. This has, of course, been helped by the fact that Shorrocks is himself one of the leading experts in the world on the economics of inequality. I have viewed these later initiatives, and others, at WIDER with interest and admiration from a distance, but I had myself, by then, moved on to other commitments. It is, however, extremely satisfying to see that the tradition of breaking fresh ground, which has characterized WIDER's research from the beginning, is continuing to flourish so well, through the leadership of Lal Jayawardena's impressive successors.

The history of WIDER will certainly be written before long in some detail to make the story of that remarkable intellectual initiative more fully understood and assessed. I have pointed to some issues that will, I hope, receive fuller attention then. But having done my little piece here, I can now move on to the champagne moment of celebration and commemoration. So I end by applauding the memory of the remarkable Lal Jayawardena, the achievements of the wide-ranging study for which this foreword is being written, and the continuing rich tradition of 'research for action' that has inspired WIDER from its very beginning. There is indeed something to celebrate here.

Acknowledgements

Reprinted here with some amendments, 'Legacies – Lal Jayawardena: Crafting Development Policy', by Ajit Singh was published in *Development and Change*, 36, 6: 1219–23 (2005) by Blackwell Publishing and is reproduced with permission.

UNU-WIDER gratefully acknowledges the recent financial contributions to the research programme from the governments of Australia (Australian Agency for International Development – AusAID), Denmark (Royal Ministry of Foreign Affairs), Finland (Ministry for Foreign Affairs), Italy (Directorate General for Development Cooperation), Norway (Royal Ministry of Foreign Affairs), Sweden (Swedish International Development Cooperation Agency – Sida) and the United Kingdom (Department for International Development).

Notes on the Contributors

Tony Addison is Deputy Director of UNU-WIDER, Helsinki.

C. Leigh Anderson is an associate professor at the Daniel J. Evans School of Public Affairs, University of Washington.

Richard M. Auty is Emeritus Professor of Economic Geography at Lancaster University.

Nancy Birdsall is President of the Center for Global Development, Washington, DC.

Mark Blackden is Senior Operations Officer and Regional Gender Co-ordinator in the Poverty Reduction and Social Development Group, World Bank, Washington, DC.

François Bourguignon is Chief Economist and Senior Vice-President at the World Bank, Washington, DC.

Sudharshan Canagarajah is a country economist for Tajikistan at the World Bank, Washington, DC.

Giovanni Andrea Cornia is a professor of economics at Florence University.

Sukti Dasgupta conducts research on employment and labour market policy at ILO, Delhi.

Arjan de Haan is a visiting professor at the University of Guelph, on special leave from the UK Department for International Development.

Louis Emmerij is a co-director of the UN Intellectual History Project, City University of New York.

David Fielding is a lecturer and researcher at the University of Otago, Dunedin.

Valpy FitzGerald is at the Finance and Trade Policy Centre, University of Oxford.

Álvaro García Hurtado is Chile's ambassador to Sweden, Stockholm.

Pertti Haaparanta is a professor of economics at the Helsinki School of Economics.

Marcia Byrom Hartwell is a PhD student at the Refugee Studies Centre, Queen Elizabeth House, University of Oxford.

Sir Richard Jolly is an honorary professor and research associate of the Institute of Development Studies at the University of Sussex, Brighton.

Nanak Kakwani is a principal researcher at the International Poverty Centre, UNDP, Brasilia.

Stephan Klasen is professor of development economics and empirical economic research at the University of Göttingen.

Stephen Knowles is a lecturer and researcher at the University of Otago, Dunedin.

Grzegorz W. Kolodko is Director of TIGER, Kozminski School of Business, Warsaw.

David Lawson is a lecturer at the Institute for Development Policy and Management, University of Manchester.

Justin Yifu Lin is at Peking University and Hong Kong University of Science and Technology.

Mingxing Liu is at the School of Government, Peking University.

Nora Lustig is Director of the Poverty Group, UNDP, New York.

Silvia Marchesi is an economics lecturer at the University of Siena.

George Mavrotas is a research fellow at UNU-WIDER, Helsinki.

Mark McGillivray is a senior research fellow at UNU-WIDER, Helsinki.

Robert McIntyre is affiliated with Local Development in Transition (LdiT), and the Institute for International Economic and Political Studies, Russian Academy of Sciences, Moscow.

Leonardo Menchini is a project officer at UNICEF Innocenti Research Centre, Florence.

S. Mansoob Murshed is affiliated with the Birmingham Business School, the Institute of Social Studies, The Hague, and the Center for the Study of Civil War, Oslo.

E. Wayne Nafziger is University Distinguished Professor of Economics at Kansas State University, Manhattan.

Deepak Nayyar is a professor of economics at the Centre for Economic Studies and Planning, Jawaharlal Nehru University, New Delhi.

Machiko Nissanke is Head of Economics Department, School of Oriental and African Studies (SOAS), University of London.

Farhad Noorbakhsh is Head of Economics Department, University of Glasgow.

Shiyuan Pan is at Peking University and Zhejiang University.

Guillermo Rozenwurcel is a professor and senior researcher at the School of Politics and Government, University of San Martín, Buenos Aires.

Laura Sabani is an associate professor of economics at the University of Florence.

Anthony Shorrocks is Director of UNU-WIDER, Helsinki.

Mihály Simai is a research professor at the Institute for World Economics, Hungarian Academy of Sciences, Budapest.

Ajit Singh is a professor of economics at the University of Cambridge.

Lakhwinder Singh is an economics lecturer at Punjabi University, Patiala.

Hyun H. Son is at the International Poverty Centre, UNDP, Brasilia.

Kostas Stamoulis is Chief of Agricultural Sector in Economic Development, United Nations Food and Agriculture Organization (FAO), Rome.

Frances Stewart is Director of the Centre for Research on Inequality, Human Security and Ethnicity (CRISE) at Queen Elizabeth House, University of Oxford.

Mark Sundberg is Lead Economist, Development Economics Department of the World Bank, Washington, DC.

Lance Taylor is Arnhold Professor of International Co-operation and Development, Center for Economic Policy Analysis, New School for Social Research, New York.

Erik Thorbecke is H.E. Babcock Professor of Economics and Food Economics Emeritus at Cornell University, Ithaca.

Sebastian Torres is a PhD student in economics at the University of Leicester.

Erik M. Uslaner is a professor of government and politics at the University of Maryland, College Park.

Heli Virta is a researcher at the Helsinki School of Economics.

Pengfei Zhang is at the China Centre for Economic Research, Peking University.

Annelies Zoomers is an associate professor in human geography at the Centre for Latin American Research and Documentation, University of Amsterdam.

List of Abbreviations

AEA	American Economic Association
AIDS	Acquired Immune Deficiency Syndrome
BEEPS	Business Environment and Enterprise Performance Survey
CAD	comparative advantage defying
CEE	Central and Eastern Europe
CGE	computable general equilibrium
CIDA	Canadian International Development Agency
CIM	competitive industrialization model
CIS	Commonwealth of Independent States
CMH	Commission on Macroeconomics and Health
CSOs	civil society organizations
CSR	corporate social responsibility
DGIS	Directorate-General for International Co-operation (Netherlands)
DHS	demographic and health survey
ECLAC	Economic Commission for Latin America and Caribbean
ECOSOC	(UN) Economic and Social Council
EFF	extended fund facility
FDI	foreign direct investment
FSU	former Soviet Union
FTA	free trade agreement
GSC	global civil society
HDI	human development index
HIPC	highly indebted poor country
HRC	Human Rights Convention
ICT	information and communications technology
IDEA	International Institute for Democracy and Electoral Assistance
IFC	International Finance Corporation
IFI	international financial institution
IFPRI	International Food Policy Research Institute
IMD	Institute for Management Development
IMR	infant mortality rate
INGO	international non-governmental organization
IQR	interquintile ratio
ISI	import substitution industrialization
IT	information technology
LDC	least developed country
LEB	life expectancy at birth
MDG	Millennium Development Goal
MFI	microfinance institution
MFN	most favoured nation

MNC	multinational corporation
NGO	non-governmental organization
NIEO	New International Economic Order
ODA	official development assistance
OLS	ordinary least squares
PCGDP	per capita GDP
PCI	per capita income
ppp	pro-poor policy (Kakwani and Son)
PPP	purchasing power parity
PPS	purchasing power standard
PREM	Poverty Reduction and Economic Management
PRI	Institutional Revolutionary Party, Mexico
PRSP	Poverty Reduction Strategy Paper
PSD	Social Democratic Party, Romania
PTA	preferential trading arrangements
SITC	Standard International Trade Classification
SME	small- and medium-sized enterprises
SOE	state-owned enterprise
SPA	Special Programme of Assistance for Africa
SSA	sub-Saharan Africa
STM	staple trap model
TFP	total factor productivity
TNC	transnational corporation
TOT	terms of trade
TRIP	trade-related intellectual property
TVE	township and village enterprise
UNCED	United Nations Conference on Environment and Development
UNCTAD	United Nations Conference on Trade and Development
UNDP	United Nations Development Programme
UNECA	United Nations Economic Commission for Africa
UNFPA	United Nations Population Fund
UNSC COMTRADE	United Nations Statistics Division
UNU-WIDER	United Nations University–World Institute for Development Economics Research
U5MR	under five mortality rate
WDI	World Development Indications
WIEGO	Women in Informal Employment: Globalizing and Organizing
WIID	World Income Inequality Database

Legacy – Lal Jayawardena: Crafting Development Policy

Ajit Singh*

Dr Lal Jayawardena, who died in Colombo in April 2004, was an intellectual, a lover of life and a humane and gifted leader. He was a top Sri Lankan civil servant of the post-independence era and an influential policy-maker. Lal was educated in Sri Lanka and at King's College, Cambridge, where he graduated with a double first in the Economics Tripos. He later did research for his PhD degree, also in Cambridge. He not only excelled academically, but was by all accounts a popular figure among his contemporaries, who included Amartya Sen, Richard Layard, Tam Dalyell, Mahbub ul Haque, Jagdish Bhagwati, Manmohan Singh and Geoff Harcourt. He was an 'apostle' (a member of the famous, select club of undergraduates and dons). He is well remembered by his teachers, particularly Robin Marris and Ken Berrill. He also remained close to one of his Cambridge mentors, the late Nicholas Kaldor, with whom he shared an abiding interest in economic policy making. Lal's contributions were recognized by his college, which bestowed on him an Honorary Fellowship.

He was his country's ambassador to the European Community and to Belgium and the Netherlands between the late 1970s and the early 1980s, and High Commissioner to the UK 1999–2000. During the 1990s he was the principal economic advisor to the President of Sri Lanka and deputized for her as Chair of the National Development Council. Indeed, at one time or another, Lal Jayawardena held almost all the top economic posts in Sri Lanka, having become Treasury Secretary at the very young age of 41. He also had spells as an international civil servant. In this and related capacities he was a serious contributor to the concept of the Third World and he helped create collective organizations to realize the poor countries' demands for a more just international economic order, such as the Group of 77 at the United Nations and the Group of 24 at the IMF, where he served for many years as either Deputy Chairman or Chairman.

Lal Jayawardena was typical of his generation of senior civil servants in many (alas, not all) developing countries: they normally came from the upper crust of their nations but were deeply committed to equity; they were thoroughly professional, proud of their countries but very conscious of the backwardness of their economies. Their forebears may have learned the art of sound civil service from their colonial masters, but Lal and his peers from other developing countries were

* Several people have helped me with the preparation of this article. I am particularly grateful to Andrea Cornia, Vincent Massaro and Amartya Sen for many helpful discussions. However, I alone am responsible for the views expressed and for any errors made.

Reprinted with some amendments from 'Legacies – Lal Jayawardena: Crafting Development Policy', by Ajit Singh, published in *Development and Change*, 36, 6: 1219–23 (2005) with the permission of Blackwell Publishing.

critical of colonialism. They had the self-confidence to believe that they could carry out the tasks of reducing poverty and promoting economic development much better than the colonial governments had done. Over the last 40 years, these diplomats and policy-makers have been deeply involved in fighting for a global regime, which would provide space for developing countries in the world economy.

As a young economist at UNCTAD, Lal was an early and extremely active member of Sydney Dell's study group on the international financial system, which for the first time paid attention to the views and interests of developing countries, as well as the socialist countries of Eastern Europe and Asia. Lal and his colleagues wrote papers which undertook rigorous analyses of international economic issues from a Third World perspective. At the Memorial meeting for Lal in New Delhi in April 2005, Dr Manmohan Singh, the Indian Prime Minister, who was Lal's contemporary at UNCTAD, recalled with pleasure the important work of this group in relation to the establishment of Special Drawing Rights at the IMF. Dr Singh also referred to the setting up of the aid target for advanced countries at 0.7 per cent of GDP. Why 0.7 per cent? The answer, which is buried in the deliberations of this group, is that 0.7 per cent was regarded as being a target for public aid and 0.3 per cent represented private investment (which was the then current level of such investments), giving a total of 1 per cent.

Later, this experience led Lal to become an 'eminent advisor' to the Brandt Commission and a member of his country's delegation to periodic conferences of UNCTAD. Although the credit for creating the entity of the Third World usually goes to the political leaders of the time – Nehru, Nasser, Sukarno, Tito and others – its real architects were dedicated professionals like Lal Jayawardena, Manmohan Singh of India, Mahbub ul Haque of Pakistan, the legendary Raul Prebisch from Argentina, Ken Dadzie from Ghana, Gamani Corea, also from Sri Lanka, as well as many others from around the developing world.

In 1985, Lal was appointed as the first Director of the UN University's World Institute for Development Economics Research (UNU-WIDER) in Helsinki. He was outstandingly successful as Director, helping build within a few years a world-renowned policy think tank focused on the development of poor countries. Under Lal's leadership, WIDER gained rapidly in reputation and compared favourably with scholarly institutions in both international organizations and the academic world. He did this with his unique mixture of intuition, dedication, flair and professional competence. Under Lal, WIDER represented serious, independent and high-quality research. It attracted well-known scholars, including several existing and prospective Nobel Prize winners, as well as top policy-makers from both rich and poor countries. During Lal's tenure as Director, UNU-WIDER published numerous books in the series WIDER Studies in Development Economics, which was established with Oxford University Press (OUP).

Lal was very much a hands-on director in terms of organizing the research agenda and he was a fully engaged academic participant in the research programme. As an economist, Lal continued to work in the international Keynesian tradition and a part of WIDER's research programme was concerned with the renewal and revitalization of this school of thought so as to be of greater relevance to the policy needs of developing countries. This is evident from Lal's own publications, as well as from the invariably thoughtful prefaces he wrote to the many books coming out of WIDER. His own research, as would be expected, was very much concerned with policy issues and specifically the problems of imbalances and asymmetries (both monetary and real) in the international economy. His policy proposals for using the Japanese surpluses in the 1980s for resolving the Third World debt problem and for advancing economic development were widely acclaimed in developing country policy circles, but of course did not win him many friends in the newly converted neoliberal citadels of the Bretton Woods institutions. His 1991 WIDER Research for Action publication, *A Global Environmental Compact for Sustainable Development*, provided the basis for the proposal presented by the United Nations Secretariat to the Rio Earth Summit. Lal also sponsored research at WIDER on Indo-Sri Lanka economic co-operation and in 1993 he co-authored an analysis of the issues and policy proposals for enhancing such co-operation, including a reciprocal preference scheme for promoting trade between the two countries. This scheme was accepted by the two governments and came into effect at the end of 1998 with the signing of the relevant agreements by the prime ministers of India and Sri Lanka.

To sum up, Lal's close friend, the Nobel laureate Amartya Sen, has aptly described him as having the 'rare ability to be energetically sensitive to the predicament of people everywhere in the world' and someone who was 'deeply sympathetic to radical changes and wanted to build a society that would be foundationally more just'.* In Lal's death the world has lost an extraordinary human being.

Appendix

Listed below, in References, are Lal Jayawardena's publications during his tenure as Director of WIDER. Much of his writing during his career was done either for the Sri Lankan government or the international organizations he was working with. For example, he served on groups which advised the UN Secretary General on the Re-structuring of the United Nations system (1975) and on the Re-structuring of Regional Training and Research Institutions in Asia (1978). He also contributed extensively to the work of several important commonwealth study groups, including Reforming the Bretton Woods System (1983) and on the International Debt Crisis and the World Economy (1984). Dr Jayawardena's PhD dissertation was on the subject 'The Supply of Sinhalese Labour to Ceylon Plantations (1830–1930): A Study of Imperial Policy in a Peasant Society' (Cambridge University, 1963). The dissertation was awarded the coveted Ellen McArthur Prize; it has, however, not been published.

---

* 'Amartya Sen on Lal Jayawardena'. Address prepared for a colloquium organized by the Global Development Network in memory and honour of Lal Jayawardena. The memorial meeting was inaugurated by Manmohan Singh in April 2005. A summary of the proceedings is forthcoming in *Economic and Political Weekly*.

References

Berrill, Sir K., L. Jayawardena, Y. Kurosawa, A.L. Resende, J.M. Mobius, H.T. Parekh and S. Unakul (1990) *Foreign Portfolio Investment in Emerging Equity Markets*, Study Group Series No. 5, Helsinki: UNU-WIDER.

Berrill, Sir K., L. Jayawardena, C. Massad and F. Vibert (1992) *Private Investment in Infrastructure: The Mobilization of Equity Capital*, Study Group Series No. 6, Helsinki: UNU-WIDER.

Dasgupta, P., L. Jayawardena, K.-G. Mäler and P. N. Radhakrishnan (1992) *The Environment and Emerging Development Issues*, Study Group Series No. 7, Helsinki: UNU-WIDER.

Furtado, C., L. Jayawardena and M. Yoshitomi (1989) *The World Economic and Financial Crisis*, Research for Action Series No. 4, Helsinki: United Nations University Press.

Jayawardena, L. (1991) *A Global Environmental Compact for Sustainable Development: Resource Requirements and Mechanisms*, Research for Action Series No. 9, Helsinki: UNU-WIDER.

Jayawardena, L. (1993) *The Potential of Development Contracts and Conditionality: Towards Sustainable Development Compacts*, Research for Action Series No. 12, Helsinki: UNU-WIDER.

Jayawardena, L. (1996) 'Developing Country Cooperation in International Financial Institutions', in G.K. Helleiner (ed.), *The International Monetary & Financial System: Developing Country Perspectives*, London: Macmillan.

Jayawardena, L., L. Ali and L. Hulugalle (1993) *Indo-Sri Lanka Economic Cooperation: Facilitating Trade Expansion through a Reciprocal Preference Scheme*, Study Group Series No. 9, Helsinki: UNU-WIDER.

Okita, S., L. Jayawardena and A.K. Sengupta (1986) *The Potential of the Japanese Surplus for Economic Development*, Study Group Series No. 1, Helsinki: UNU-WIDER.

Okita, S., L. Jayawardena and A.K. Sengupta (1987) *Mobilizing International Surpluses for World Development: A WIDER Plan for a Japanese Initiative*, Study Group Series No. 2, Helsinki: UNU-WIDER.

Sukhamoy, C., E. Iglesias, L. Jayawardena, S. Marris, R. McNamara, P. Ndegwa, S. Okita, Soedjatmoko, B. Urquhart and J. Witteveen (1989) *World Economic Summits: The Role of Representative Groups in the Governance of the World Economy*, Study Group Series No. 4, Helsinki: UNU-WIDER.

Witteveen, J., R. Barre, L.C. Bresser Pereira, S. Chakravarty, L. Jayawardena, F. Leutwiler, O. Obasanjo, R.V. Roosa, J. Sachs, R. Solow and M. Yoshitomi (1988) *Debt Reduction*, Study Group Series No. 3, Helsinki: UNU-WIDER.

Part I

Development Economics in Retrospect

1
The Evolution of the Development Doctrine, 1950–2005

Erik Thorbecke

Introduction

The economic and social development of the Third World, as such, was clearly not a policy objective of the colonial rulers before the Second World War.[1] Such an objective would have been inconsistent with the underlying division of labour and trading patterns within and among colonial blocks. It was not until the end of the colonial system in the late 1940s and 1950s, and the subsequent creation of independent states, that the revolution of rising expectations could start. Thus, the end of Second World War marked the beginning of a new regime for the less developed countries involving the evolution from symbiotic to inward-looking growth and from a dependent to a somewhat more independent relation vis-à-vis the ex-colonial powers. It also marked the beginning of serious interest among scholars and policy-makers in studying and understanding better the development process as a basis for designing appropriate development policies and strategies. In a broad sense a conceptual development doctrine had to be built which policy-makers in the newly independent countries could use as a guideline to the formulation of economic policies.

The selection and adoption of a development strategy – that is, a set of more or less interrelated and consistent policies – depend upon three building blocks: (1) the prevailing development objectives which, in turn, are derived from the prevailing view and definition of the development process; (2) the conceptual state of the art regarding the existing body of development theories, hypotheses, models, techniques and empirical applications; and (3) the underlying data system available to diagnose the existing situation, measure performance and test hypotheses.

Figure 1.1 illustrates the interrelationships and interdependence which exist among (i) development theories and models, (ii) objectives, (iii) data systems and the measurement of performance and (iv) development policies, institutions and strategies, respectively. These four different elements are identified in four corresponding boxes in Figure 1.1. At any point in time or for any given period these four sets of elements (or boxes) are interrelated. Thus, it can be seen from Figure 1.1 that the current state of the art, which is represented in the southwest box embracing development theories, hypotheses and models, affects and is, in

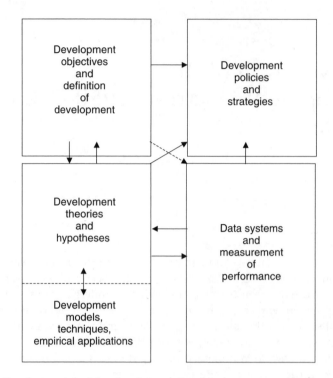

Figure 1.1   Development doctrine: key interrelationships

turn, affected by the prevailing development objectives – hence the two arrows in opposite directions linking these two boxes. Likewise, data systems emanate from the existing body of theories and models and are used to test prevailing development hypotheses and to derive new ones. Finally, the choice of development policies and strategies is jointly determined and influenced by the other three elements – objectives, theories and data, as the three corresponding arrows indicate.[2]

The analytical framework presented above and outlined in Figure 1.1 is applied to describe the state of the art that prevailed in each of the last six decades to highlight in a systematic fashion the changing conception of the development process. The choice of the decade as a relevant time period is of course arbitrary and so is, to some extent, the determination of what should be inserted in the four boxes in Figure 1.1 for each of the six decades under consideration.[3]

Figures 1.2 to 1.7 attempt to identify for each decade the major elements that properly belong in the four interrelated boxes. In a certain sense it can be argued that the interrelationships among objectives, theories and models, data systems and hypotheses and strategies constitute the prevailing development doctrine for a given time period. A brief sequential discussion of the prevailing doctrine in each of the last five decades provides a useful way of capturing the evolution that development theories and strategies have undergone. A final section sums up and concludes.

The development doctrine during the 1950s

Economic growth became the main policy objective in the newly independent less developed countries. It was widely believed that through economic growth and modernization per se, dualism, and associated income and social inequalities that reflected it, would be eliminated. Other economic and social objectives were thought to be complementary to, if not resulting from, GNP growth. Clearly, the adoption of GNP growth as both the objective and yardstick of development was directly related to the conceptual state of the art in the 1950s. The major theoretical contributions that guided the development community during that decade were conceived within a one-sector, aggregate framework and emphasized the role of investment in modern activities. The development economists' tool kit in the 1950s contained such theories and concepts as the 'big push' (Rosenstein-Rodan 1943), 'balanced growth' (Nurkse 1953), 'take-off into sustained growth' (Rostow 1956) and 'critical minimum effort thesis' (Leibenstein 1957) (see Figure 1.2).

What all of these concepts have in common, in addition to an aggregate framework, is equating growth with development and viewing growth in less developed countries as essentially a discontinuous process requiring a large and discrete injection of investment. The 'big push' theory emphasized the importance of economies of scale in overhead facilities and basic industries. The 'take-off' principle was based on the simple Harrod-Domar identity that in order for the growth rate of income to be higher than that of the population (so that per capita income growth is positive) a minimum threshold of the investment to GNP ratio is

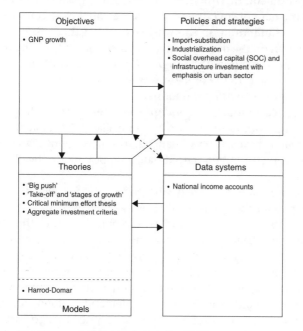

Figure 1.2   Development doctrine during the 1950s

required given the prevailing capital–output ratio. In turn, the 'critical minimum effort thesis' called for a large discrete addition to investment to trigger a cumulative process within which the induced income-growth forces dominate induced income-depressing forces. Finally, Nurkse's (1953) 'balanced growth' concept stressed the external economies inherent on the demand side in a mutually reinforcing and simultaneous expansion of a whole set of complementary production activities which combine together to increase the size of the market. It does appear, in retrospect, that the emphasis on large-scale investment in the 1950s was strongly influenced by the relatively successful development model and performance of the Soviet Union between 1928 and 1940.

The same emphasis on the crucial role of investment as a prime mover of growth is found in the literature on investment criteria in the 1950s. The key contributions were (i) the 'social marginal production' criterion (Kahn 1951; Chenery 1953), (ii) the 'marginal per capita investment quotient' criterion (Galenson and Leibenstein 1955) and (iii) the 'marginal growth contribution' criterion (Eckstein 1957).

It became fashionable to use as an analytical framework one-sector models of the Harrod-Domar type which, because of their completely aggregated and simple production functions, with only investment as an element, emphasized at least implicitly investment in infrastructure and industry. The one-sector, one-input nature of these models precluded any estimation of the sectoral production effects of alternative investment allocations and of different combinations of factors since it was implicitly assumed that factors could only be combined in fixed proportions with investment. In a one-sector world GNP is maximized by pushing the investment-ratio (share of investment in GNP) as high as is consistent with balance-of-payments' equilibrium. In the absence of either theoretical constructs or empirical information on the determinants of agricultural output, the tendency was to equate the modern sector with high productivity of investment and, thus, direct the bulk of investment to the modern sector and to the formation of social overhead capital – usually benefiting the former.

The reliance on aggregate models was not only predetermined by the previously discussed conceptual state of the art but also by the available data system which, in the 1950s, consisted almost exclusively of national income accounts. Disaggregated information in the form of input–output tables appeared in the developing countries only in the 1960s.

The prevailing development strategy in the 1950s follows directly and logically from the previously discussed theoretical concepts. Industrialization was conceived as the engine of growth that would pull the rest of the economy along behind it. The industrial sector was assigned the dynamic role in contrast to the agricultural sector which was, typically, looked at as a passive sector to be 'squeezed' and discriminated against. More specifically, it was felt that industry, as a leading sector, would offer alternative employment opportunities to the agricultural population, would provide a growing demand for foodstuffs and raw materials, and would begin to supply industrial inputs to agriculture. The industrial sector was equated with high productivity of investment – in contrast with agriculture – and, therefore, the bulk of investment was directed to industrial activities and social overhead projects.[4] To a large extent the necessary capital resources to fuel industrial growth had to be extracted from traditional agriculture.

Under this 'industrialization-first' strategy the discrimination in favour of industry and against agriculture took a number of forms. First, in a large number of countries, the internal terms of trade were turned against agriculture through a variety of price policies which maintained food prices at an artificially low level in comparison with industrial prices. One purpose of these price policies – in addition to extracting resources from agriculture – was to provide cheap fuel to the urban workers and thereby tilt the income distribution in their favour. Other discriminatory measures used were a minimal allocation of public resources (for both capital and current expenditures) to agriculture and a lack of encouragement given to the promotion of rural institutions and rural off-farm activities. In some of the larger developing countries, such as India and Pakistan, the availability of food aid on very easy terms – mainly under US Public Law 480 – was an additional element which helped maintain low relative agricultural prices.[5]

A major means of fostering industrialization, at the outset of the development process, was through import substitution – particularly of consumer goods and consumer durables. With very few exceptions the whole gamut of import substitution policies, ranging from restrictive licensing systems, high protective tariffs and multiple exchange rates to various fiscal devices, sprang up and spread rapidly in developing countries. This inward-looking approach to industrial growth led to the fostering of a number of highly inefficient industries.

It should not be inferred that the emphasis on investing in the urban modern sector in import-substituting production activities and physical infrastructure was undesirable from all standpoints. This process did help start industrial development and contributed to the growth of the modern sector. It may even, in some cases, have provided temporary relief to the balance-of-payments constraint. However, by discriminating against exports – actual and potential – the long-run effects of import substitution on the balance of payments may well turn out to have been negative.

The development doctrine during the 1960s

Figure 1.3 captures the major elements of the development doctrine prevailing in the 1960s. On the conceptual front, the 1960s was dominated by an analytical framework based on economic dualism. Whereas the development doctrine of the 1950s implicitly recognized the existence of the backward part of the economy complementing the modern sector, it lacked the dualistic framework to explain the reciprocal roles of the two sectors in the development process. The naive two-sector models à la Lewis (1954) continued to assign to subsistence agriculture an essentially passive role as a potential source of 'unlimited labour' and 'agricultural surplus' for the modern sector. It assumed that farmers could be released from subsistence agriculture in large numbers without a consequent reduction in

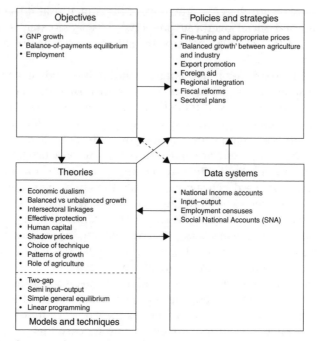

Figure 1.3   Development doctrine during the 1960s

agricultural output while simultaneously carrying their own bundles of food (i.e. capital) on their backs or at least having access to it.

As the dual-economy models became more sophisticated, the interdependence between the functions that the modern industrial and backward agricultural sectors must perform during the growth process was increasingly recognized (Fei and Ranis 1964). The backward sector had to release resources for the industrial sector, which in turn had to be capable of absorbing them. However, neither the release of resources nor the absorption of resources, by and of themselves, were sufficient for economic development to take place. Recognition of this active interdependence was a large step forward from the naive industrialization-first prescription because the above conceptual framework no longer identified either sector as leading or lagging.

A gradual shift of emphasis took place regarding the role of agriculture in development. Rather than considering subsistence agriculture as a passive sector whose resources had to be squeezed in order to fuel the growth of industry and to some extent modern agriculture, it started to become apparent in the second half of the 1960s that agriculture could best perform its role as a supplier of resources by being an active and co-equal partner with modern industry. This meant in concrete terms that a gross flow of resources from industry to agriculture may be crucial at an early stage of development to generate an increase in agricultural output and productivity which would facilitate the extraction of a new transfer out of agriculture and into the modern sector. The trouble with the alternative approach, which appears to have characterized the 1950s, of squeezing agriculture too hard or too early in the development process was described in the following graphic terms: 'The backwards agricultural goose would be starved before it could lay the golden egg' (Thorbecke 1969: 3).

The 'balanced' versus 'unbalanced' growth issue was much debated during the 1960s. In essence, the balanced growth thesis (Nurkse 1953) emphasized the need for the sectoral growth of output to be consistent with the differential growth of demand for different goods as income rises. Unbalanced growth, on the other hand, identified the lack of decision-making ability in the private and public sectors as the main bottleneck to development (Hirshman 1958). The prescription for breaking through this bottleneck was to create a sequence of temporary excess capacity of social overhead facilities which, by creating a vacuum and an attractive physical environment, would encourage the build-up of directly productive activities. Alternatively, the process could start by a build-up of directly productive activities ahead of demand, which, in turn, would generate a need for complementary social overhead projects.

The similarities between the balanced and unbalanced growth theses are more important than their apparently different prescriptions. Both approaches emphasized the role of intersectoral linkages in the development process. In a certain sense they extended the dual-economy framework to a multisectoral one without, however, capturing the essential differences in technology and form of organization between modern and traditional activities. This was at least partially due to the type of sectoral disaggregation available in the existing input–output tables of developing countries during the 1960s. Except for the various branches of industry, the level of sectoral aggregation tended to be very high, with agricultural and service activities seldom broken down in more than two or three sectors. Consequently, any attempt at distinguishing traditional, labour-intensive activities from modern, capital-intensive activities in either agriculture or in service, could not be performed given the classification criteria underlying input–output tables. This example illustrates the interdependence that exists between the prevailing data systems and the conceptual framework in the actual formulation of development plans and strategies. This is an issue that is returned to subsequently.

Another contribution of the late 1960s that was imbedded in intersectoral (input–output) analysis is the theory of effective protection, which clarified and permitted the measurements of the static efficiency cost of import substitution when both inputs and outputs are valued at world prices. Still another important set of contributions that appeared in the 1960s relates to the intersectoral structure and pattern of economic growth. Two different approaches provided important insights into the changing intersectoral structure of production and demand throughout the process of economic development. The first approach, based largely on the work of Kuznets (1966), relied on a careful and painstaking historical analysis of a large number of countries. The second approach was pioneered by Chenery and based on international cross-sectional analysis which was subjected to regression analysis to derive what appeared to be structural phenomena in the process of growth (Chenery 1960; Chenery and Taylor 1968).

The models that were designed in the 1960s can be divided into three types: (i) two-gap models, (ii) semi-input–output models and (iii) simple general equilibrium models. The first type tried to incorporate into a macroeconomic model the role of foreign aid (Chenery and Strout 1966). The underlying logic of these models is that two independent constraints may limit economic growth. The first constraint on skills and savings, if it were the binding one, is described as the investment-limited growth. Alternatively, when the balance-of-payments constraint is effective, trade limited growth would follow. This is a disequilibrium-type model which assumes that developing countries are characterized by limited structural flexibility – with either the investment-savings gap or the balance-of-payments gap binding at any one point in time.

The other types of models (ii and iii above) rely on an intersectoral input–output framework. The semi-input–output method initiated by Jan Tinbergen distinguishes between international sectors, which produce tradable goods, and national sectors, which produce non-tradable goods (Kuyvenhoven 1978). Hence, the required capacity expansion throughout the growth process can be computed for, at least, the non-tradable sectors. The general equilibrium models which appeared in the 1960s were either of a consistency or linear programming type. The main purpose of these models was to throw more light on the intersectoral linkages and the effects of alternative sectoral investment allocations on economic growth (Fox *et al.* 1972; Manne 1974).

The conception of economic development in the 1960s was still largely centred on GNP growth as the key objective. In particular, the relationship between growth and the balance of payments was made clearer. Towards the end of this decade the increasing seriousness of the under- and unemployment problem in the developing world led to a consideration of employment as an objective in its own right next to GNP growth. The most noteworthy change in the conception of development was the concern for understanding better the intersectoral structure and physiology of the development process – as the preceding review of the conceptual state of the arts revealed.

The development policies and strategies that prevailed in the 1960s flowed directly from the conceptual contributions, development objectives and the data system. These policies fall into a few categories, which are reviewed briefly below. The first set embraces the neoclassical prescription and can be expressed under the heading of 'fine-tuning' and 'appropriate prices'. In a nutshell the 'fine-tuning' instruments embrace the use of an appropriate price system (including commodity, tax and subsidy rates), the removal of market imperfections, and appropriate exchange rate and commercial policies. It was expected that these measures would lead to a more appropriate output mix between production activities and input mix, or choice of technique, and thereby generate increased employment.

A second set of policies can be classified as essentially structural, emphasizing the importance of intersectoral linkages. They include the allocation of investment and current public expenditures among sectors, so as to achieve a process of intersectoral balanced (or, in some instances, unbalanced) growth. More specifically, by the late 1960s agriculture was assigned a much more active role in the development process. The provision of a greater level of public resources to that sector – combined with less discriminatory price policies – were expected to result in a growth of output and productivity which would facilitate a net transfer back to the rest of the economy. The success of South Korea and Taiwan in nurturing their agricultural sector and using the agricultural surplus to achieve a successful industrial take-off was starting to resonate.

The development doctrine in the 1970s

Figure 1.4 summarizes the major development objectives, theories, data sources and policies prevailing in the 1970s. By the 1970s the failure of a GNP-oriented development strategy to cope successfully with increasingly serious development problems in much of the Third World led to a thorough re-examination of the process of economic and social development. The major development problems that became acute and could no longer be ignored during this decade can be summarized as:

 (i) the increasing level and awareness of under- and unemployment in a large number of developing countries;
 (ii) the tendency for income distribution within countries to have become more unequal or, at least, to have remained as unequal as in the immediate post-Second World War period;
 (iii) the maintenance of a very large, and perhaps rising, number of individuals in a state of poverty; for instance, below some normative minimum income level or standard of living;
 (iv) the continuing and accelerating rural-urban migration and consequent urban congestion; and, finally,
 (v) the worsening external position of much of the developing world reflected by increasing balance-of-payments pressures and rapidly mounting foreign indebtedness and debt servicing burdens. Largely as a consequence of these closely interrelated problems a more equal income distribution, particularly in terms of a reduction in absolute poverty, was given a much greater weight in the preference function of most developing countries compared to the objective of aggregate growth per se. Furthermore, this reduction in absolute poverty was to be achieved mainly through increased productive employment (or reduced underemployment) in the traditional sectors.

By the mid-1970s, GNP as a dominant all-encompassing objective had been widely, but by no means universally, dethroned. The presumption that aggregate growth is synonymous with economic and social development or, alternatively, that it will ensure the attainment of all other development objectives, came under critical scrutiny and was rejected in many circles. The launching of the World Employment Programme by the ILO in 1969 signalled that the primary objective should be to raise the standard of living of the poor through increased employment opportunities. The generation of new or greater productive opportunities was considered a means towards the improvement of the welfare of the poor.

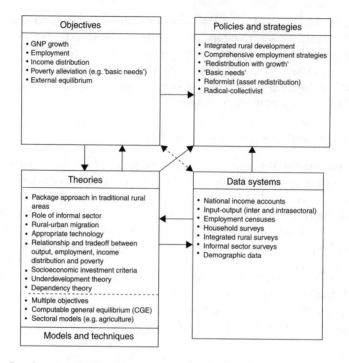

Figure 1.4   Development doctrine during the 1970s

The changing meaning of development as a process that should have as simultaneous objectives growth and poverty alleviation, both influenced and was influenced by a number of conceptual and empirical contributions. The first set of contributions comes under the rubric of integrated rural and agricultural development. A whole series of empirical studies at the micro and macro levels combined to provide an explanation of the physiology and dynamics of the transformation process of traditional agriculture. This body of knowledge provided a rationale for a unimodal strategy in the rural areas, which is discussed subsequently under the strategy box.

A second type of conceptual breakthrough which appeared in the 1970s were those of the informal sector and the role of employment in furthering the development process. Even though the informal sector concept had been around a long time and taken a variety of forms such as Gandhi's emphasis on traditional cottage industries, it became revitalized in a more general and formal sense in the Kenya Report of International Labour Organization (ILO 1972). A number of case studies undertaken by ILO focusing specifically on the role of the informal sector concluded that it was relatively efficient, dynamic and often strongly discriminated against as a result of market imperfections or inappropriate national or municipal regulations. These studies suggested that the informal activities represent an important potential source of output and employment growth. The ILO's World Employment Programme and the World Bank generated much useful empirical research focused on such issues as the relationship between population growth and employment; appropriate labour-intensive technologies; the educational system–labour market–employment–income distribution nexus; the informal sector; the determinants of rural–urban migration and the role of traditional agriculture in the development process.

A third contribution that surfaced in the 1970s includes the interdependence between economic and demographic variables and the determinants of the rural–urban migration. A number of empirical studies, mainly at the micro level, attempted to throw some light on the relationship between such sets of variables as (i) education, nutrition and health and (ii) fertility, infant mortality and, ultimately, the birth rate. The hypotheses that were generated by these studies highlighted the complex nature of the causal relationship between population growth and economic development.

With regard to the determinants of migration, the initial Harris-Todaro (1970) formulation triggered a series of empirical studies and simple models of the migration process. In general, migration was explained as a function of urban–rural wage differentials weighted by the probability of finding urban employment. A somewhat parallel set of contributions at the micro level consists of the attempt at incorporating socioeconomic objectives – such as employment and income distribution – among investment (benefit–cost) criteria and in the appraisal and selection of projects (Little and Mirrlees 1974).

A review of contributions to the state of the art in development economics would not be complete without at least a reference to the neo-Marxist literature on underdevelopment and dependency theories. The essence of these theories is that underdevelopment is intrinsic in a world trading and power system in which the developing countries make up the backward, raw material-producing periphery, and the developed countries the modern industrialized centres (Hunt 1989). A neo-colonial system of exploitation by indigenous classes associated with foreign capital (for example, multinational corporations) is considered to have replaced the previous colonial system. After this review of major contributions to development theory, only a few words need be said about the nature of models which appeared in the 1970s. A major characteristic of these models was to explain, at the sectoral and multisectoral levels, the simultaneous determination of output, employment and income distribution. Most of these models were partial in the sense that they did not capture the complete interdependence among these variables.

The coverage and quality of the data available improved substantially in the 1970s as compared to the previous decades. By the mid-1970s, survey-type information on variables such as employment, income, consumption and saving patterns were becoming available. A variety of surveys covering such diverse groups as urban, informal and rural households started to provide valuable information on the consumption and savings behaviour of different socioeconomic groups. In a number of developing countries it became possible, for the first time, to estimate approximately the income distribution by major socioeconomic groups.

After having reviewed the changing development objectives, conceptual contributions and data sources that marked the 1970s, the next logical step is to describe and analyze briefly the new development strategies that emerged. From a belief that growth was a necessary and sufficient condition for the achievement of economic and social development, it became increasingly recognized that even though necessary, growth might not be sufficient. The first step in the broadening process of moving from a single to multiple development objectives was a concern with, and incorporation of, employment in development plans and in the allocation of foreign aid to projects and technical assistance.

One possible attraction of using employment as a target was that it appeared, on the surface, to be relatively easily measurable, in somewhat the same sense as the growth rate of GNP had provided previously a simple scalar measure of development. The real and fundamental issue was an improvement in the standards of living of all groups in society and, in particular, that of the poorest and most destitute groups.

Two partially overlapping variants of a distributionally oriented strategy surfaced during this decade. These were 'redistribution with growth' and 'basic needs'. The first one was essentially incremental in nature, relying on the existing distribution of assets and factors and requiring increasing investment transfers in projects (mostly public but perhaps even private) benefiting the poor (Chenery *et al.* 1974). The first step in this strategy was the shift in the preference (welfare) function away from aggregate growth per se towards poverty reduction. This strategy, which was favoured by the World Bank, focused on the redistribution of at least the increments of capital formation in contrast with the initial stock of assets. Since the bulk of the poor are located in the rural sector and the informal urban sector, this strategy had to be directed towards increasing the productivity of the small farmers and landless workers and making small-scale producers (mainly self-employed) in the informal urban sector more efficient.

The second alternative strategy inaugurated during the 1970s was the basic needs strategy, which was particularly advocated by the ILO.[6] It entailed structural changes and some redistribution of the initial ownership of assets – particularly land reform – in addition to a set of policy instruments, such as public investment. Basic needs, as objectives defined by ILO, included two elements: (i) certain minimal requirements of a family for private consumption, such as adequate food, shelter and clothing and (ii) essential services provided by and for the community at large, such as safe drinking water, sanitation, health and educational facilities.

A complementary policy within the agricultural sector was that of integrated rural development. In a nutshell, the new approach centred on lending and technical activities benefiting directly the traditional sector. This strategy conformed to a broader so-called unimodal agricultural development strategy (Johnston and Kilby 1975). The latter relied on the widespread application of labour-intensive technology to the whole of agriculture. In this sense, it was based on the progressive modernization of agriculture 'from the bottom up'. This strategy can be contrasted with a bimodal strategy, which encourages the growth of the modern, commercial, large-scale, relatively capital-intensive subsector of agriculture while ignoring for all practical purposes the traditional subsistence subsector. Under the unimodal approach, agricultural development was spread relatively evenly over the mass of the people through a combination of appropriate agricultural research and technology, land redistribution, the provision of rural infrastructure, the growth of rural institutions and other measures. This approach was successful in accelerating the output of cereals and invigorating small-scale farms as it was linked to the dissemination of the green revolution technology.

A third type of development strategy follows from the neo-Marxist underdevelopment and dependency theories, which have been previously touched upon. This approach was radical, if not revolutionary, in nature. It called for a massive redistribution of assets to the state and the elimination of most forms of private property. It appeared to favour a collectivistic model – somewhat along the lines of the Chinese regime in power at that time – based on self-reliance and the adoption of indigenous technology and forms of organization.

The development doctrine in the 1980s

A combination of events, including an extremely heavy foreign debt burden – reflecting the cumulative effects of decades of borrowing and manifested by large and increasing balance-of-payments and budget deficits in most of the developing world – combined with higher interest rates and a recession in creditor countries, radically changed the development and aid environment at the beginning of the 1980s. The Mexican financial crisis of 1982 soon spread to other parts of the Third World. The magnitude of the debt crisis was such that, at least for a while, it brought into question the survival of the international financial system.

Suddenly, the achievement of external (balance-of-payments) equilibrium and internal (budget) equilibrium became the overarching objectives and necessary conditions to the restoration of economic growth and poverty alleviation. The debt crisis converted the 1980s into the 'lost development decade'. Before the development and poverty alleviation path could be resumed, the Third World had to put its house in order and implement painful stabilization and structural adjustment policies.

Notwithstanding the fact that the development process was temporarily blocked and most of the attention of the development community was focused on adjustment issues, some important contributions to development theory were made during this decade (see Figure 1.5).

The first one greatly enriched our understanding of the role of human capital as a prime mover of development. The so-called endogenous growth school (Lucas 1988; Romer 1990) identifies low human capital endowment as the primary obstacle to the achievement of the potential scale economies that might come about through industrialization. In a societal production function, raw (unskilled) labour and capital were magnified by a term representing human capital and knowledge, leading to increasing returns. This new conception of human capital helped convert technical progress from an essentially exogenously determined factor to a partially endogenously determined factor. Progress was postulated to stem from two sources: (i) deliberate innovations, fostered by the allocation of resources (including human capital) to research and development (R&D) activities, and

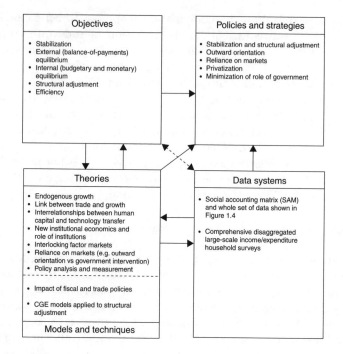

Figure 1.5   Development doctrine during the 1980s

(ii) diffusion, through positive externalities and spillovers from one firm or industry to know-how in other firms or industries (Ray 1998). If investment in human capital and know-how by individuals and firms is indeed subject to increasing returns and externalities, it means that the latter do not receive the full benefits of their investment resulting, consequently, in underinvestment in human capital (the marginal social productivity of investment in human capital being larger than that of the marginal private productivity). The market is likely to under-produce human capital and this provides a rationale for the role of the government in education and training.

   A second contribution based on a large number of quantitative and qualitative empirical studies – relying on international cross-sectional and country-specific analyses of performance over time – was the robust case made for the link between trade and growth. Outward orientation was significantly and strongly correlated with growth. Countries that liberalized and encouraged trade grew faster than those that followed a more inward-looking strategy. The presumed mechanism linking export orientation to growth is based on the transfer of state of the art technology normally required to compete successfully in the world market for manufactures. In turn, the adoption of frontier technology by firms adds to the human capital of those workers and engineers through a process of 'learning-by-doing' and 'learning-by-looking' before spilling over to other firms in the same industry and ultimately across industries. In this sense, export orientation is a means of endogenizing and accelerating technological progress and growth.

Furthermore, to the extent that outward orientation in developing countries normally entails a comparative advantage in labour-intensive manufactures, there is much evidence, based on the East and Southeast Asian experience, that the growth path that was followed was also equitable – resulting in substantial poverty alleviation (for a recent survey of the evidence linking trade to growth see Winters 2004).

A third set of contributions that surfaced in the 1980s can be broadly catalogued under the heading of the 'new institutional economics' and collective action (North 1990; Williamson 1991; Nabli and Nugent 1989). As de Janvry *et al.* (1993: 565) noted,

> The main advance was to focus on strategic behaviour by individuals and organized groups in the context of incomplete markets. The theories of imperfect and asymmetrical information and, more broadly, transaction costs gave logic to the role of institutions as instruments to reduce transaction costs.

The neo-institutional framework, in addition to reminding the development community that appropriate institutions and rules of the game are essential to provide pro-development and anti-corruption incentives, also suggested broad guidelines in building institutions that reduced the scope for opportunistic behaviour.

Another contribution of this approach was to provide a clear rationale for the existence of efficient non-market exchange configurations, particularly in the rural areas. Proto-typical examples of such institutions include intra-farm household transactions; two-party contracts (sharecropping and interlinked transactions, for example), farmers' co-operatives and group organizations, mutual insurance networks and informal credit institutions (Thorbecke 1993). Those exchange non-market configurations – called agrarian institutions by Bardhan (1989) – owe their existence to lower transaction costs than those that would prevail in an alternative market configuration providing an equivalent good, factor or service. In most instances market imperfections or, at the limit, market failure (in which case there is no alternative market configuration and transaction costs become infinite) are at the origin of non-market configurations.

The 1980s witnessed some seminal contributions to a better understanding of the concept of poverty and its measurement. A comprehensive and operationally useful approach to poverty analysis was developed by Sen (1985) in his 'capabilities and functioning' theoretical framework. According to this framework what ultimately matters is the freedom of a person to choose her functionings. In order to function, an individual requires a minimum level of wellbeing brought about by a set of attributes. In turn, the Foster-Greer-Thorbecke (1984) class of decomposable poverty measures allowed poverty to be measured while satisfying most important welfare axioms.

A final contribution worth noting – which can be subsumed under the 'new institutional economies' heading – is that of interlinked transactions (Bardhan 1989). An interlinked contract is one in which two or more interdependent exchanges are simultaneously agreed upon (for instance, when a landlord enters into a fixed-rent agreement with a tenant and also agrees to provide credit at a given interest rate). In a more general sense, this type of contract leads to inter-locking factor markets for labour, credit and land. In retrospect it is somewhat ironical that during a decade dominated by a faith in the workings of markets – as is discussed subsequently – important theoretical contributions were made that highlighted market imperfections and failures.

Some important contributions to general equilibrium modelling appeared during the 1980s (Dervis *et al.* 1982). These models – calibrated on a base year social accounting matrix (SAM) reflecting the initial (base year) socioeconomic structure of the economy – proved particularly useful in tracing through the impact of a variety of exogenous shocks and policies (such as a devaluation, trade liberalization and fiscal reforms) on the income distribution by socioeconomic household groups. Computable general equilibrium (CGE) models became an important tool to simulate the disaggregated impact of structural adjustment policies on growth and equity. In fact, these models provided the only means to compare the impact of adjustment scenarios to the counterfactual of no- or limited-adjustment scenarios. Since most applied CGEs were built in the 1990s, they are discussed in the next section.

The 1980s witnessed a proliferation of statistical information on a variety of dimensions of development and the welfare of households. Besides more elaborate and disaggregated employment, manufacturing, agricultural and demographic surveys and censuses, large-scale household income and expenditure surveys produced by statistical offices of most developing countries – and often designed and funded by the World Bank (for example, the Living Standard Measurement Surveys) – became available to analysts and policy-makers. Perhaps for the first time, reasonably reliable and robust observations could be derived relating to the magnitude of poverty, the characteristics of the poor and the inter-household income distribution. In turn, the various data sources could be combined to build SAMs of a large number of countries.

The development strategy of the 1970s – centred on redistribution with growth and fulfilment of basic needs – was replaced by an adjustment strategy. The magnitude of the debt crisis and the massive internal and external disequilibrium faced by most countries in Africa and Latin America and some in Asia, meant that adjustment became a necessary (although not sufficient) condition to a resumption of development. The main policy objective of Third World governments became macroeconomic stability, consisting of a set of policies to reduce their balance-of-payments deficits (for example, devaluation) and their budget deficits (through retrenchment). Whereas stabilization per se was meant to eliminate or reduce the imbalance between aggregate demand and aggregate supply, both externally and internally, structural adjustment was required to reduce distortions in relative prices and other structural rigidities that tend to keep supply below its potential. A typical adjustment package consisted of measures such as a devaluation, removal of artificial price distortions, trade liberalization and institutional changes at the sector level.

Complementary elements of the prevailing adjustment strategy of the 1980s included outward orientation, reliance on markets and a minimization of the role of the government. The outward orientation was meant to encourage exports and industrialization in labour-intensive consumer goods. In turn, to achieve competitiveness in exports, vintage technology would have to be imported, which would trigger the endogenous growth processes described previously – investment in the human capital and knowledge of workers and engineers employing those technologies and subsequent spillover effects.

Under the influence of ideological changes in the Western world (for example, the Reagan and Thatcher administrations) developing countries were strongly encouraged, if not forced, to rely on the operation of market forces and in the process to minimize government activities in most spheres, not just productive activities. Inherent contradictions and conflicts arose among the elements of the broad adjustment strategy of the 1980s. The successful implementation of adjustment policies called for a strong government. Likewise, the rationale for a larger role of government in the education sphere to generate the social spillover effects and counteract the under-investment in education by private agents, which do not capture the positive externalities of their investment, ran counter to the objective of a minimalist state. Another conflict was caused by the stabilization goal of reducing the balance-of-payments disequilibrium, while simultaneously liberalizing trade – mainly through elimination of quantitative restrictions and reduction and harmonization of tariff rates. The latter measures would invariably lead to a significant rise in imports that would make it more difficult to restore balance-of-payment equilibrium. Here again, the successful implementation of somewhat conflicting measures called for a strong state.

In this decade, characterized by pro-market and anti-government rhetoric, there was strong sentiment to do away with aid altogether and have private capital flows substitute for it. Thus, in the early 1980s, the Reagan administration created a fertile environment for conservative critics of foreign aid who felt that 'economic assistance distorts the free operation of the market and impedes private sector development' (Ruttan 1996: 143). Clearly, the debt overhang put a damper on going too far in eliminating aid. Both public and private creditors in the industrialized world had too much at stake.

The development doctrine in the 1990s

In the first half of the 1990s, stabilization and adjustment were still the dominant objectives (see Figure 1.6). While most of the Latin American countries (and the few Asian countries affected by the debt crisis) had gone through a painful adjustment process and were back on a growth path, the overall situation was still one of stagnation – largely caused by poor governance in sub-Saharan Africa and most transition economies in Eastern Europe. It was becoming increasingly clear to the development community that fundamental and deep-rooted institutional changes to reduce corruption and facilitate a successful transition from socialism and command economies to market economies were a precondition to successful adjustment and a resumption of development in Eastern Europe and sub-Saharan Africa. Potentially the

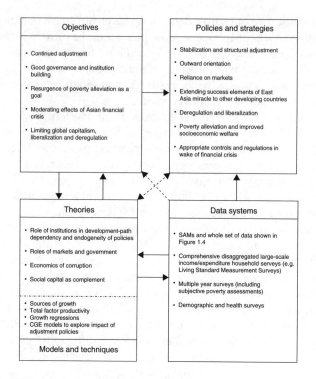

Figure 1.6   Development doctrine during the 1990s

institutions and policies at the root of the East Asian 'miracle' could provide the model to follow.

In the second half of the 1990s the Asian financial crisis hit East and Southeast Asia with a vengeance, resulting in a sharp reversal of the long-term poverty-reduction trend. Simultaneously socioeconomic conditions deteriorated so drastically in the former Soviet republics that poverty alleviation in its broadest sense – including improvements in health, nutrition, education, access to information and to public goods and a participation in decision making – resurfaced as the major, if not overarching, objective of development.

Another consequence of the financial crisis was to bring into question the Washington and IMF consensus of unbridled capital and trade liberalization and complete deregulation of the financial system. A number of East and Southeast Asian countries are still suffering from the extreme deregulation of the banking sector and capital flows that weakened the supervisory and monitoring functions of central banks and other institutions. The international monetary and financial system that still relies on the outdated Bretton Woods 'rules of the game' needs major revamping and a new set of rules befitting the contemporaneous environment. In the meantime, a number of affected countries were restoring controls on an ad hoc basis.

The conceptual contribution to development theory in the 1990s, in general, extended and further elaborated on earlier concepts. Perhaps the most fundamental issue that was debated during the 1990s is the appropriate roles of the state and the market, respectively, in development. An inherently related issue is to identify the set of institutions most conducive to the acceleration of the process of economic growth and socioeconomic development. Prior to the onset of the Asian financial crisis it was felt that the mix of institutions and policies adopted by the East Asian countries that gave rise to the East Asian miracle (World Bank 1993) provided a broad model, with parts of it potentially transferable to other developing countries. The financial crisis led to a more sceptical appraisal – even whether the miracle, after all, was not a 'myth'. In any case, the reliance on government actions in the previous decades to promote industrial growth on the part of East Asian countries (particularly South Korea) appeared suspect and came under heavy criticism. Some critics argued that the already impressive growth performance would have been even better with less government intervention – and that even if those industrial policies had contributed to growth they required a strong state, an element sorely missing in other parts of the Third World.

While the debate on the proper mix between the degree of government intervention and reliance on markets is still very much alive, the neo-institutional and public choice schools have helped clarify how the state can affect development outcomes. This can be done in a number of ways: (i) by providing a macroeconomic and microeconomic incentive environment conducive to efficient economic activity; (ii) by providing the institutional infrastructure – property rights, peace, law and order and rules – that encourages long-term investment; and (iii) by insuring the delivery of basic education, healthcare and infrastructure required for economic activity (Commander *et al.* 1996). Institutional capability as evaluated from the standpoint of entrepreneurs depends, in turn, on such indicators as predictability of rule making, perception of political stability, crime against persons and property, reliability of judicial enforcement and freedom from corruption (Brunetti *et al.* 1997; Chibber 1998).

The role of institutions as a precondition to following a successful development path becomes even more critical if one subscribes to the new approach to political economy that takes institutions as largely given exogenously and argues that policies tend to be determined *endogenously* within a specific institutional context (Persson and Tabellini 1990). Thus, for example, if the central bank and the finance ministry are not independent or are operating under loose discretionary rules, the monetary and fiscal policies that result will depend on political and social factors (or according to the political power of the different lobbies in society and the public choice formulation).

Two additional contributions worth highlighting in this decade are the concept of social capital and a better understanding of sources of growth (total factor productivity) and the need to explain the residual. Social capital was devised as a concept to complement human capital. If individuals are socially excluded, or marginalized, or systematically discriminated against, they cannot rely on the support of networks from which they are sealed off. Alternatively, membership of group organizations brings about benefits that can take a variety of forms (the provision of informal credit and help in the search for employment, for example). The acquisition of social capital by poor households is particularly important as a means to help them escape the poverty trap.

The spectacular growth of East Asian countries prior to 1997 renewed the interest in identifying, explaining and measuring the sources of growth. Recent studies tended to demystify the East Asian miracle by suggesting that the rapid growth of these economies depended on resource accumulation with little improvement in efficiency and that such growth was not likely to be sustainable (Krugman 1994; Kim and Lau 1994; Young 1995). This conclusion was based on estimates of total factor productivity (TFP) growth and depends crucially on the form of the production function used and on an accurate measurement of the capital and labour inputs. Whatever residual is left over is ascribed to technological progress. Some critics argue that typical TFP calculations significantly underestimate organizational improvements within firms or what Leibenstein called x-efficiency (1957).

The 1990s witnessed an increased interest in CGE models used to simulate the impact of exogenous shocks and changes in policies on the socioeconomic system and particularly income distribution. A key issue explored in those models was that of the impact of adjustment policies on income distribution and poverty. General equilibrium models provide the only technique to compare the impact of alternative (counterfactual) policy scenarios, such as a comparison of the effects of an adjustment programme versus a counterfactual non-adjustment programme (Thorbecke 1991 for Indonesia; Sahn *et al.* 1996 for Africa).

This decade was marked by a proliferation of statistical information relating particularly to the socioeconomic characteristics and welfare of households – in addition to the more conventional data sources previously collected (see data box in Figure 1.6). A large number of quantitative poverty assessments based on household expenditure surveys were completed, as well as more qualitative participatory poverty assessments. Furthermore the availability of demographic and health surveys for many developing countries provided micro-level information on health and nutritional status, assets and access to public goods and services to supplement information on household consumption. Also, perhaps for the first time, the availability of multiple-year surveys and panel data for many countries allowed reliable standard of living and welfare comparisons to be made over time.

In many respects, the development strategy of the 1990s was built upon the foundations of the preceding decade and retained most of the latter's strategic elements – at least in the first half of the decade. However, as the decade evolved, the adjustment-based strategy of the 1980s came under critical scrutiny that led to major changes – particularly in the wake of the Asian financial crisis. In sub-Saharan Africa, the great majority of the countries were still facing serious adjustment problems. A widely debated issue was whether adjustment policies per se without complementary reforms – within the context of Africa – could provide the necessary initial conditions for a take-off into sustained growth and poverty alleviation. Two conflicting approaches to adjustment and diagnoses of its impact on performance were put forward. The 'orthodox' view, best articulated by the World Bank (at the beginning of the decade but subsequently modified), argued that an appropriate stabilization and adjustment package pays off. Countries that went

further in implementing that package experienced a turnaround in their growth rate and other performance indicators.

In contrast, the 'heterodox' approach – best articulated by the concept of 'adjustment with a human face', embraced by UNICEF (see Cornia *et al.* 1987) – while supporting the need for adjustment, argued that the orthodox reforms focus extensively on short-term stabilization and do not address effectively the deep-rooted structural weaknesses of African economies that are the main causes of macro instability and economic stagnation. Accordingly, major structural changes and institutional changes are needed to complement adjustment policies to induce the structural transformation (such as industrialization, diversification of the export base, the build-up of human capital and even land reform) without which sustainable long-term growth in Africa (and by extension in other developing countries facing similar initial conditions) is not possible.

The UNICEF and heterodox critical evaluation of the impact of adjustment policies on long-term growth and poverty alleviation – even when it was not appropriately justified on empirical grounds – sensitized multilateral and bilateral donors to the need to focus significantly more on the social dimensions of adjustment. It made a strong case for the implementation of a whole series of complementary and reinforcing reforms, ranging from greater emphasis on and investment in human capital and physical infrastructure to major institutional changes – particularly in agriculture and industry – benefiting small producers. In turn, the orthodox approach has made a convincing case that appropriately implemented adjustment policies are not only a necessary condition to the restoration of macroeconomic equilibrium but can also contribute marginally to economic growth and poverty alleviation, in the short run.

In 1993, the World Bank published a very influential report on the East Asian miracle (World Bank 1993). The report analyzed the success elements of the high performing Asian economies and argued that many of them were potentially transferable to other developing countries. In brief, these success elements consisted of:

   (i)   sound macroeconomic foundations and stable institutions aiming at a balanced budget and competitive exchange rates;

  (ii)   technocratic regimes and political stability that provided policy credibility and reduced uncertainty – an important factor for foreign investors;

 (iii)   an outward (export) orientation;

 (iv)   reliance on markets;

  (v)   a more controversial set of industrial policies with selective government interventions often using 'contests' among firms as proxy to competition;

 (vi)   high rates of investment in building human capital;

(vii)   high physical investment rates;

(viii)   a process of technology acquisition consistent with dynamic comparative advantage; and

 (ix)   a smooth demographic transition.

In particular, the outward orientation, encouraging exports, was applauded as a means of acquiring state of the art technology which in turn would trigger a 'learning-by-doing' and 'learning-by-looking' (reverse engineering) process that would lead to spillover effects on human capital and positive externalities among firms within an industry and among industries.

The East Asian miracle also provided a convincing example of the essential importance of sound institutions (such as the balanced budget presidential decree in effect in Indonesia between 1967 and 1997) as preconditions to a sustainable process of growth with equity. The absence of institutions appropriate to a smooth transition from command to market economies in much of Eastern Europe and the fragility of existing institutions in much of sub-Saharan Africa provide painful counter-examples of the enormous human costs of a weak institutional framework.

The Asian financial crisis that wrought havoc in much of East and Southeast Asia in 1997 forced a critical re-examination of an international trade and financial system based on excessive trade and capital liberalization and financial deregulation. The large increase in the incidence of poverty that followed in the wake of the crisis sensitized the development community to again focus on poverty alleviation and improvements in the socioeconomic welfare of vulnerable households as the overarching objective of development. Thus, at the end of the decade, the World Bank made it clear that poverty reduction – in its broadest sense – measured in terms of outcomes (health, education, employment, access to public goods and services and social capital) rather than inputs was the primary goal to strive for.

The crisis also triggered a re-examination of the role of government in protecting the economy from major shocks originating abroad. In particular, it pointed towards strengthening financial institutions and the provision of the minimum set of rules and regulations (for example, improved monitoring and supervision of the banking sector) to reduce corruption and speculative borrowing from abroad; and the establishment of institutional safety nets that could act as built-in stabilizers following a crisis.

The decade of the 1990s was marked by a strong and lingering case of 'aid fatigue' evidenced by the absolute decline in net disbursements of official development assistance (ODA) after 1992. This downward trend reflected the strong faith in the operation of markets and scepticism regarding governments' (both aid donors and recipients) involvement in productive sectors such as agriculture and industry. Fatigue was also influenced by the rising fear that foreign aid was generating aid dependency relationships in poor countries and, as such, would have the same type of negative incentive effects that welfare payments have on needy households whose recipients might be discouraged from job searching.

A related issue that was critically debated in the 1990s was that of the effectiveness of aid conditionality. First of all, given fungibility, is it really possible to use aid to 'buy' good policies, or even a sound programme of public (current and capital) expenditures from aid recipients? From the standpoint of the political economy of external aid, structural adjustment can be looked at as a bargaining process between bilateral and multilateral donors, on the one hand, and debtor governments, on the other. Both sides may have a vested interest in following soft rules in their lending and borrowing behaviour, respectively. This tends to foster and continue a dependency relationship that may well be fundamentally inconsistent with a viable long-term development strategy for the recipient countries (particularly in sub-Saharan Africa).

The conditionality debate fuelled a number of econometric studies of aid's effectiveness based on international cross-sectional data. Perhaps the most influential one was that of Burnside and Dollar (2000) which concluded that aid can be a powerful tool for promoting growth and reducing poverty but only if it is granted to countries that are already helping themselves by following growth-enhancing policies. In contrast, Guillaumont and Chavet (2001) find that aid effectiveness depends on exogenous (mostly external) environmental factors such as the terms of trade trend, the extent of export instability and climatic shocks. Their results suggest that the worse the environment, the greater the need for aid and the higher its productivity. Hansen and Tarp (2001), using essentially the same cross-sectional dataset as do Burnside and Dollar, argue that when account is taken of unobserved country-specific fixed effects and the dynamic nature of the aid–growth relationship, the Burnside-Dollar conclusion fails to emerge. Country-specific characteristics of aid recipient countries – aside from the policy regime followed by those countries – have a major impact on aid's effectiveness.

The socioeconomic havoc created by the Asian financial crisis engendered a fundamental re-examination of the role of aid and the uncritical acceptance of rules of the game, based on the outdated international trade and monetary system designed at Bretton Woods and the Washington Consensus no longer consistent with the contemporaneous conditions. Reflective of the trend towards using aid as an instrument to fight poverty is the recent study by Collier and Dollar (1999) that develops criteria for allocating aid when the objective is to maximize poverty alleviation.

Development doctrine in the present decade

It has been claimed with some justification that the development community has run out of 'big ideas' at the beginning of this new millennium. Lindauer and Pritchett (2002), comparing the state of the art in 1962 and 1982 show the amazing reversal of big ideas between the two periods. In 1962 government played a central role and was the driving force behind development, while in 1982 the government was considered to be the main obstacle to development. Similar reversals are noted with respect to the accepted roles of accumulation, trade, foreign capital and foreign aid, respectively, over these two decades. Fast forward to 2002, how would one advise, say, a president of a Latin American country? To quote Lindauer and Pritchett (2002: 2):

> Any push toward deepening market reforms will be seen as a continuation of the failed strategies of the present, while any strategy that calls for government intervention and leadership ... will be seen as a reversion to the failed strategies

of the past. What is of even deeper concern than the lack of an obvious dominant set of big ideas that command (near) universal acclaim is *the scarcity of
theory and evidence-based research on which to draw*. (Emphasis added)

It can be argued that the last few years have been marked by a critical re-evaluation
and consolidation of previous concepts and techniques as opposed to the formulation of brand new ideas per se. Figure 1.7 summarizes the main development
characteristics of this decade. Arguably the most important contribution to development doctrine in this decade is a technique rather than a theory, for instance,
the use of randomized and controlled experiments in the evaluation of development effectiveness (Duflo and Kremer 2003). As they argue, 'Any impact evaluation attempts to answer an essentially counterfactual question: how would
individuals who participated in the programme have fared in the absence of the
programme?' Perhaps the best example of impact analysis is the quasi-experimental
design used in evaluating the redistributive PROGRESA programme in Mexico that
relied on the selection of target villages (receiving benefits) and control villages
(not presently receiving benefits but eligible for benefits in future rounds).
Programme effects are estimated by comparing treated individuals or communities
to control individuals or communities. There is no question that this new methodology has revolutionized the evaluation of social programmes in such areas as

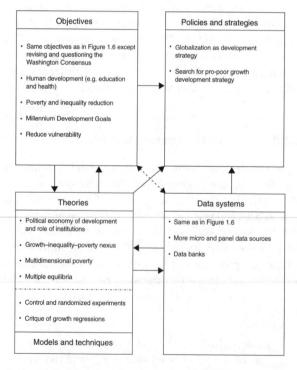

Figure 1.7   Development doctrine during present decade (2000–05)

education and health by providing a scientific base for the recommendations comparable to the design of drug and medical trials. On the other hand the limitation of this approach is that it only provides a precise and robust answer to a very narrow question, 'What is the effect of a specific programme within a specific context?'

Researchers today appear consumed, if not overwhelmed, by what can be called the endogeneity curse or dragon. The emphasis is on combating the econometric biases and problems often to the exclusion of the importance of larger structural and conceptual issues. Controlled experiments have not enlightened us on the underlying mechanisms generating the outcomes. As Mookherjee (2004) points out 'The purpose is not to understand the underlying structure of the system of relationships generating the outcomes, only the statistical outcome impact of certain policy treatments.' Relying on reduced form relations without explicitly identifying and presenting the structural (and behavioural) model yielding the reduced form allows the researchers to by-pass what some would consider a fundamental prior step, namely, the theoretical foundation of the tested hypotheses. Another limitation of impact analysis is that it ignores entirely the general equilibrium effects of an intervention. Given those qualifications, this new methodology has generated a large number of excellent empirical studies of the impact of educational, health and other social interventions in a variety of different settings in poor countries. A recent survey (Glewwe 2002) concludes that this new methodology in the field of education provides an opportunity to make significant progress in understanding what to do in specific situations.

Randomized and controlled experiments appear to have largely replaced structural and behavioural models in the toolkit of development economists. The latter rely heavily on imposed assumptions regarding individual behaviour and rationality and even when econometric results suggest that the imposed structure cannot be rejected, there is no guarantee that a better and still more general model might not exist and reflect observed behaviour more accurately. At the same time the potential strength of those models is that they capture explicitly the underlying structure and behaviour of the agents. It seems that a blending of those two approaches might be quite fruitful as long as it could be done in a fair way consistent with the existing norms and political economy setting. Combining programmes that use some randomization in selecting eligible recipients while also gathering sample survey data on both target and control groups to build structural models could relax somewhat the non-transferability of purely randomized experiments to other settings. Greater use of theory could help explain and clarify the (causal) mechanisms underlying findings generated by controlled experiments and permit a wider range of policy assessments (Mookherjee 2004).

Growth regressions, an important and popular tool of development economists ever since the days of Hollis Chenery, have recently come under heavy criticism. In fact, in an 'obituary for growth regressions' Lindauer and Pritchett (2002) provide many convincing technical reasons for rejecting growth regressions. Their basic flaw is that 'they confuse partial correlations with (stable) parameters and confuse empirical variables (that might be associated with policies) with feasible actions to promote growth'. The right-hand side variables appearing in the reduced form equations – in the absence of an underlying structural and behavioural model actually yielding the reduced form – can be selected on spurious grounds simply because they are correlated with growth. Without an explicit model reflecting the underlying assumed theoretical mechanisms affecting the dependent variable (growth), some critics have dismissed those reduced form regressions as 'right hand side fundamentalism'. The popularity of this approach reflects again a relative lack of theoretical models capable of explaining convincingly the contemporaneous growth process.

On the positive side some important conceptual contributions are flourishing today. The first one can be categorized under the broad theme of the political economy of development and the role of institutions. One of its major tenets is that a more equal initial income and wealth distribution is consistent with and conducive to growth. The new political economy theories linking greater inequality to reduced growth operate through the following channels:

(1) unproductive rent-seeking activities that reduce the security of property;
(2) the diffusion of political and social instability leading to greater uncertainty and lower investment;
(3) redistributive policies encouraged by income inequality that impose disincentives on the rich to invest and accumulate resources;
(4) imperfect credit markets resulting in under-investment by the poor, particularly in human capital; and
(5) a relatively small income share accruing to the middle class – implying greater inequality – has a strong positive effect on fertility which, in turn, has a significant and negative impact on growth.

This new approach turns on its head the prevailing view under the classical framework that an unequal income distribution is a prerequisite to growth, based on the argument that the rich (the capitalists) save a larger proportion of their income than the poor (the workers). Hence, for a given level of total income a more unequal income distribution would generate a larger flow of aggregate savings that could be channelled into investment to yield a higher growth rate of GDP. In this sense the desirability of an unequal income distribution could be rationalized on economic grounds while clashing with the ethical concern for more equality, equity and egalitarianism. More poverty today was a precondition to more economic growth and less poverty in the future. As the Cambridge School baldly put it, impoverishment of the masses is necessary for the accumulation of a surplus over present consumption. If indeed equality is conducive to growth then it becomes a means towards economic development and future poverty alleviation and the conflict between the ethical objective (norm) of egalitarianism and the economic conditions required for growth disappears (Thorbecke 2006).

The new political economy of development approach relies extensively on the role of institutions. In an extremely influential article Acemoglu *et al.* (2001) made a strong case that development depends on institutional quality. They selected an instrumental variable, colonial settler mortality, that affects institutions exoge-nously but not income directly and were able to explain inter-country differences in per capita income as a function of predicted quality of institutions. Their hypothesis is that mortality rates among early European settlers in a given colony determined whether they would decide to establish resource-extractive or plun-dering institutions or to settle and build European institutions and, in particular, those protecting property rights. However, as Bardhan (2005) has argued, there are other types of institutions that matter for development such as participatory and accountability institutions and institutions that facilitate investment co-ordination.

A second and related contribution is to understand and explain the growth–inequality–poverty nexus as an essentially indivisible process. Growth is a necessary (but not sufficient) condition for development to occur. If the initial income and wealth distribution is uneven then growth may not only be lower (as proponents of the new political economy of development would argue) but the impact of a given aggregate (GDP) growth rate on poverty reduction will also be significantly smaller (the elasticity of poverty reduction with respect to growth varies within a wide range, between -0.2 and 3.0 depending on the initial condi-tions). Inequality can be thought of as the filter between growth and poverty.

In addition to the initial income distribution, the pattern and structure of growth play a fundamental role in their impact on poverty. Given the initial con-ditions, including the institutional framework in place at the time, the outcomes of the nexus of growth, inequality and poverty are jointly determined. This is essentially the theme of the *World Development Report* for 2006 (World Bank 2005) which argues convincingly that there need not be any tradeoff between growth (efficiency) and poverty reduction (equity). The key issue is to identify institutions and policies that are conducive to a pro-poor growth pattern.

A third recent contribution, also interrelated with the above two themes, is a much more comprehensive and multidimensional definition of human welfare than prevailed previously. Building on the foundations of Sen's functioning and capabilities concepts, human development, as opposed to the narrower concept of poverty reduction, has taken over centre-stage as the ultimate goal of develop-ment. Human development consists of a plethora of dimensions and aspects as they relate to health, education, nutrition, shelter, access to information, partici-pation, nature of regime (degree of democracy and liberty) and many others. Conceptually, one can think of a human development profile over n dimensions. An individual profile would consist of the specific values or scores of that individ-ual on each of the indicators proxying the n dimensions. Likewise, one could com-pute average regional and national profiles. Instead of deriving a scalar value by weighing each of the dimensions (as the UNDP Human Development Index does), complete profiles would be compared.

In some, probably unusual circumstances, one profile could reveal higher (better) values on each of the indicators of the n dimensions. In this case the equivalent of first order stochastic dominance would obtain and it could be stated unambiguously that the level of human welfare was higher in the dominant pro-file. When one profile scores higher on some dimensions but lower on others, no unambiguous ranking can be established without linking each dimension of human welfare to some utility function. It is very difficult if not impossible to imagine that this mapping from dimension to utility can be done totally objectively in a non-arbitrary fashion. In this case, as two profiles intersect, one can check whether second or higher order (stochastic) dominance obtains. Until now the theoretical and empirical work on multidimensional welfare has been focused on and limited to the measurement of multidimensional poverty as opposed to the even broader concept of human development (Bourguignon and Chakravarty 2003; Tsui 2002; Duclos *et al.* 2006). In many respects, this approach goes back to, and represents a much more sophisticated version of the basic needs doctrine of the 1970s. A complementary approach also meant to broaden the concept and measurement of poverty is the attempt at blending objective and quantitative (essentially money-metric) indicators and more subjective and qualitative indicators (à la Sussex School) based on focus groups and interviews (Kanbur 2004).

A final theoretical construct that is presently in vogue and that appears promising in exploring a variety of issues in development economics is that of multiple equilibria. Ray (2000) provides a vivid example drawn from Rosenstein-Rodan's (1943) 'big push' notion and Hirschman's (1958) backward and forward linkages concept. These pioneers argued that economic development could be thought of as a massive co-ordination failure, in which several investments do not occur simply because of the absence of other complementary investments and, similarly, these latter investments are not forthcoming because the former are missing. To quote Ray (2000: 5):

> Thus one might conceive of two equilibria under the very same fundamental conditions, one in which active investment is taking place, with each industry's efforts motivated and justified by the expansion of other industries, and another equilibrium involving persistent stagnation, in which the inactivity of one industry seeps into another. This serves as an explanation of why similar economies may behave very differently.

Institutions and policies might be viewed as tools for moving an economy out of one (bad) equilibrium into another (good) one. In a dynamic sense this process corresponds to a phase transition. If economic development is conceived as one of phase transitions, it carries far-reaching implications for the role of government. Institutions have to be established and policies designed and implemented that facilitate the phase transition. One implication is that the emphasis on temporary, one-time interventions is likely to be much greater and if successful will not have to be repeated. If and once the new (good) equilibrium is reached it is presumably sustainable within the new institutional and policy framework. It would be like jump-starting a car whose battery had run down.

The objectives and definition of development have been further broadened in this decade. As discussed above, improvement in human development is increasingly seen as the ultimate goal to strive for. Since a case has been made that less inequality in the income and wealth distribution can be conducive to growth and future development, greater equality has taken its place along with poverty reduction as joint objectives to be reached through a pattern of growth sensitive to the needs of the poor. The Millennium Development Goals provide a general framework to monitor the progress of the Third World in its search for improving its level of human welfare. Although it is too early to predict confidently, it appears that most of the Millennium Goals have been set at an unrealistically high level and are therefore very unlikely to be attained. There is one more objective that has surfaced recently, namely reduced vulnerability. Since the poor in an era of globalization tend to be more vulnerable to external (essentially macroeconomic shocks) as the Asian Financial Crisis of 1997 demonstrated, it is important to design and implement a set of safety nets and structural measures that would reduce their vulnerability.

The datasets available to the development community are essentially the same as in the previous decade except for the availability of more panel data information useful in tracing the dynamics of poverty and many new cross-country databases on inequality and many other micro and macro variables. Increasingly, data banks are being created by different institutions that can be easily accessed by researchers worldwide.

The formulation of development strategy in this decade has to be scrutinized within the context of a world economy that is globalizing at a very fast rate. A key issue is whether the present form of globalization/integration is conducive to a process of growth-cum-structural transformation, which is capable of engendering and sustaining pro-poor economic growth and favourable distributional consequences. It is possible, contrary to the income convergence thesis, that globalization could generate, both at the national and global levels, adverse distributional consequences that could slow down the present poverty alleviation trend (Nissanke and Thorbecke 2006).

Hence, policy-makers need to design and implement an active development strategy not only to benefit from, but also to help counteract some of the negative effects of the immutable forces of globalization. Globalization should not be viewed as a reliable substitute for a domestic development strategy. It is not enough for governments to assume an active role in liberalizing trade and capital movements and deregulating their economies, while passively waiting for the fruits of the Washington Consensus and the market forces of globalization to pull them on a fast development track. Instead, governments need to pursue both active liberalization and active domestic development policies.

Globalization offers large potential benefits for those countries that decide to engage strategically and actively in the globalization process. Benefits are neither automatic nor guaranteed. Passive liberalization may lead to marginalization. At the same time those countries that are still stagnating (most of sub-Saharan Africa) need to strengthen institutions as well as to invest in agriculture in order to reach the take-off point for structural transformation of their economies to proceed.

Conclusions

The retrospective appraisal revealed the close interdependence and evolution among development objectives, the conceptual framework and models, data and information systems, and development strategies throughout the last six decades. In each period the nature and scope of the prevailing development strategy was influenced, and sometimes predetermined, by the conceptual state of the art and the available data systems. The interdependent evolution among the four elements of the development doctrine can perhaps best be brought to light by the gradual progression which these elements underwent through time. The definition of development broadened from being tantamount to GNP growth, as both an objective and a performance criterion, to growth and employment, to the satisfaction of basic needs and, ultimately, to the enhancement of human welfare and the reduction of multidimensional poverty to be achieved through a pattern of pro-poor growth. Thus, development evolved from an essentially scalar concept to a multidimensional one entailing the simultaneous achievement of multiple objectives.

A parallel progression occurred in development theory. During the 1950s the analytical framework was completely aggregative and relied on one-sector models. In the 1960s the prevailing framework became dualistic, distinguishing between an urban, modern-industrial sector and a rural, traditional-agricultural sector. Gradually, as distributional issues became paramount major breakthroughs in the analysis and measurement of poverty occurred. A concern for structural issues early on gave way to a concern with the role of institutions and the market in the development process. The somewhat idealized and misplaced faith in planning which characterized the early decades was replaced by an arguably controversial over-reliance in the effectiveness of markets as an engine of development and as a corollary the minimization of the role of governments. Endogenous growth requires governments capable of intervening in areas such as education and health to yield the spillover effects of investment in human capital on overall development. In the present era of globalization the appropriate roles of governments and markets is one of the most debated issues.

The advance in the coverage and quality of the data and data systems needed for development analysis and policy over the last half century as been remarkable. Until the 1970s the statistical information available to researchers and government offices consisted almost exclusively of national accounts, population, agricultural and manufacturing censuses and, in a few instances, simple input–output tables. Survey-type information on variables such as employment, income, consumption and savings patterns tended to be scarce and not very representative. Thus, in general, the existing data systems were not conducive to empirical studies that could illuminate such fundamental issues as the state of income distribution and the incidence of poverty. From the 1980s on, the coverage of household survey data expanded enormously and allowed a plethora of microeconomic studies to be conducted on a large variety of issues related to human welfare such as health and education. In turn, the evolution in the quality and comprehensiveness of social accounting matrices worldwide provided a necessary bridge between the macro- and the microeconomic settings. Computable general equilibrium models and macro–micro simulation models made it possible, within limits, to estimate the impact of macroeconomic policies and shocks on the earnings and incomes of different socioeconomic household groups and even, in some instances, on individual households. The parallel progress in theoretical concepts and in data systems opened up the domain of distributional issues to more rigorous investigation.

Notwithstanding a possible shortage of 'big ideas' in the present decade, we can agree with Bardhan's (1993: 139–40) conclusion, in his assessment of the state of development economics, that

> While the problems of the world's poor remain as overwhelming as ever, studying them has generated enough analytical ideas and thrown up enough challenges to the dominant paradigm to make all of us in the profession somewhat wiser, and at least somewhat more conscious of the possibilities and limitations of our existing methods of analysis.

Notes

1. This chapter is based on and updates an earlier study by Thorbecke (2000).
2. There are two additional reciprocal relationships denoted by arrows in Figure 1.1. The first one is the interaction between development theories and hypotheses and development models. Models are typically based on theoretical hypotheses, which often are of a partial nature. By integrating various hypotheses into a consistent framework, which the model provides, some new insights may be derived which could lead to a modification of the initial hypotheses. The second bi-directional arrow is the one linking development objectives and data systems. Clearly, the choice of development goals both predetermines the kind of data system that is required and is affected by it. Many concrete examples of these interrelationships are described and analyzed next in the application of the conceptual framework in Figure 1.1 to the five decades spanning the period 1950–2005.
3. In particular, certain conceptual and theoretical contributions may have been formulated before they became part of the conventional wisdom. An example of this is the seminal article of Lewis (1954), which triggered the economic dualism concept that became a major element of the development paradigm of the 1960s rather than of the 1950s.
4. Here again the emphasis on industrialization was greatly influenced by the Soviet model.
5. Public Law (PL) 480 refers to the Agricultural Trade Development and Assistance Act passed in the United States in 1954, marking the inception of food aid programmes.
6. Far from originating with ILO, the concept of basic needs and planning for poverty alleviation had already been expressed and formulated very clearly by the Indian planner Pitambar Pant as early as 1962 (see Pant 1974).

References

Acemoglu, D., S. Johnson and J.A. Robinson (2001) 'The Colonial Origins of Comparative Development: An Empirical Investigation', *American Economic Review*, 91, 5: 1369–401.

Bardhan, P.K. (1989) *The Economic Theory of Agrarian Institutions*, Oxford: Clarendon Press.

Bardhan, P.K. (1993) 'Economics of Development and the Development of Economics', *Journal of Economic Perspectives*, 7, 2: 129–42.

Bardhan, P.K. (2005) 'Theory of Empirics in Development Economics', *Economic and Political Weekly*, 1 October.

Bourguignon, F. and S.R. Chakravarty (2003) 'The Measurement of Multidimensional Poverty', *Journal of Economic Inequality*, 1: 25–49.

Brunetti, A., G. Kisunko and B. Weder (1997) 'Economic Growth with "Incredible" Rules: Evidence from a Worldwide Private Sector Survey', background paper for *World Development Report* (1997), World Bank, Washington, DC.

Burnside, C. and D. Dollar (2000) 'Aid, Policies, and Growth', *American Economic Review*, 90, 4: 847–68.

Chenery, H.B. (1953) 'Application of Investment Criteria', *Quarterly Journal of Economics*, 67: 76–96.

Chenery, H.B. (1960) 'Patterns of Industrial Growth', *American Economic Review*, 50, 4: 624–54.

Chenery, H.B. and A.M. Strout (1966) 'Foreign Assistance and Economic Development', *American Economic Review*, 56, 4: 679–733.

Chenery, H.B. and L. Taylor (1968) 'Development Patterns: Among Countries and Over Time', *Review of Economics and Statistics*, 50, 4: 391–416.

Chenery, H.B., M.S. Ahluwalia, C.L.G. Bell, J.H. Duloy and R. Jolly (eds) (1974) *Redistribution with Growth: Policies to Improve Income Distribution in Developing Countries in the Context of Economic Growth*, Oxford and New York: Oxford University Press.

Chibber, A. (1998) 'Institutions, Policies and Development Outcomes', in R. Picciotto and E. Wiesner (eds), *Evaluation and Development: The Institutional Dimension*, New Brunswick and London: Transaction.

Collier, P. and D. Dollar (1999) 'Aid Allocation and Poverty Reduction', Policy Research Working Papers 2041, Development Research Group, World Bank, Washington, DC.

Commander, S., H. Davoodi and U.J. Lee (1996) 'The Causes and Consequences of Government for Growth and Wellbeing', background paper for *World Development Report* (1997), World Bank, Washington, DC.

Cornia, G., R. Jolly and F. Stewart (1987) *Adjustment with a Human Face: Protecting the Vulnerable and Promoting Growth*, Oxford: Clarendon Press.

de Janvry, A., E. Sadoulet and E. Thorbecke (1993) 'Introduction to State, Market, and Civil Organizations: New Theories, New Practices, and Their Implications for Rural Development', *World Development*, 21, 4: 565–75.

Dervis, K., J. de Melo and S. Robinson (1982) *General Equilibrium Models for Developing Countries*, London: Cambridge University Press.

Duclos, J.-Y., D. Sahn and S. Younger (2006) 'Robust Multidimensional Poverty Comparisons', *Economic Journal*, 116, 514: 943–68.

Duflo, E. and M. Kremer (2003) 'Use of Randomization in the Evaluation of Development Effectiveness', paper prepared for the World Bank Operations Evaluation Department Conference, World Bank, Washington, DC.

Eckstein, A. (1957) 'Investment Criteria for Economic Development and the Theory of Intertemporal Welfare', *Quarterly Journal of Economics*, 71, 1: 56–85.

Fei, J.C.H. and G. Ranis (1964) *Development of the Labor Surplus Economy: Theory and Policy*, Homewood, IL: Irwin.

Foster, J., J. Greer and E. Thorbecke (1984) 'A Class of Decomposable Poverty Measures', *Econometrica*, 52, 3: 761–66.

Fox, K., J.K. Sengupta and E. Thorbecke (1972) *The Theory of Quantitative Economic Policy*, Amsterdam: North Holland.

Galenson, W. and H. Leibenstein (1955) 'Investment Criteria, Productivity and Economic Development', *Quarterly Journal of Economics*, 69, 3: 343–70.

Glewwe, P. (2002) 'Schools and Skills in Developing Countries: Education Policies and Socioeconomic Outcomes', *Journal of Economic Literature*, 40, 2: 436–82.

Guillaumont, P. and L. Chavet (2001) 'Aid and Performance: A Reassessment', *Journal of Development Studies*, 37, 6: 66–92.

Hansen, H. and F. Tarp (2001) 'Aid and Growth Regressions', *Journal of Development Economics*, 64, 2: 547–70.

Harris, J. and M. Todaro (1970) 'Migration, Unemployment and Development: A Two-Sector Analysis', *American Economic Review*, 60, 1: 126–42.

Hirschman, A. (1958) *The Strategy of Economic Development*, New Haven, CT: Yale University Press.

Hunt, D. (1989) *Economic Theories of Development*, London: Harvester Wheatsheaf.

ILO (1972) *Employment, Incomes and Equality: A Strategy for Increasing Productive Employment in Kenya*, Geneva: International Labour Organization.

Johnston, B.F. and P. Kilby (1975) *Agriculture and Structural Transformation*, London: Oxford University Press.

Kahn, A.E. (1951) 'Investment Criteria in Development Programmes', *Quarterly Journal of Economics*, 65: 38–61.

Kanbur, R. (ed.) (2004) *Q-Squared: Qualitative and Quantitative Methods of Poverty Appraisal*, New Delhi: Permanent Black.

Kim, J.I. and L.J. Lau (1994) 'The Sources of Economic Growth of East-Asian Newly Industrialized Countries', *Journal of the Japanese and International Economies*, 8, 3: 235–71.

Krugman, P.R. (1994) 'The Myth of Asia's Miracle', *Foreign Affairs*, 73, 6: 62–78.

Kuyvenhoven, A. (1978) *Planning with a Semi-input–output Method*, Mimeo, Leiden.

Kuznets, S. (1966) *Modern Economic Growth: Rate, Structure and Spread*, New Haven, CT: Yale University Press.

Leibenstein, H. (1957) *Economic Backwardness and Economic Growth*, New York: Wiley.

Lewis, W.A. (1954) 'Economic Development with Unlimited Supplies of Labour', *Manchester School of Economic and Social Studies*, 22, 2: 139–91.

Lindauer, D.L. and L. Pritchett (2002) 'What's the Big Idea? The Third Generation of Policies for Economic Growth', *Economia*, 3, 1: 1–39.

Little, I.M.D. and J. Mirrlees (1974) *Project Appraisal and Planning for Developing Countries*, New York: Basic Books.

Lucas, R.E. (1988) 'On the Mechanics of Economic Development', *Journal of Monetary Economics*, 22, 1: 3–42.

Manne, A.S. (1974) 'Multi-Sector Models for Development Planning, A Survey', *Journal of Development Economics*, 1, 1: 43–69.

Mookherjee, D. (2004) 'Is There Too Little Theory in Development Economics Today?', *Economic and Political Weekly*, 1 October.

Nabli, M.K. and J.B. Nugent (1989) 'The New Institutional Economics and Its Applicability to Development', *World Development*, 17, 9: 1333–48.

Nissanke, M. and E. Thorbecke (2006) 'Channels and Policy Debate in the Globalization–Inequality–Poverty Nexus', *World Development*, 34, 8.

North, D.C. (1990) *Institutions, Institutional Change and Economic Performance*, Cambridge and New York: Cambridge University Press.

Nurkse, R. (1953) *Problems of Capital Formation in Underdeveloped Countries*, New York: Oxford University Press.

Pant, P. (1974) 'Perspective of Development: 1961–1976. Implications for Planning for a Minimum Level of Living', in T.N. Srinivasan and P.K. Bardhan (eds), *Poverty and Income Distribution in India*, Calcutta: Calcutta Statistical Publishing Society.

Persson, T. and G. Tabellini (1990) *Macroeconomic Policy, Credibility, and Politics*, New York and Melbourne: Hardwood Academic.

Ray, D. (1998) *Development Economics*, Princeton: Princeton University Press.

Ray, D. (2000) 'What is New in Development Economics?', *American Economist*, 44: 3–16.

Romer, P. (1990) 'Endogenous Technological Change', *Journal of Political Economy*, 98: S71–102.

Rosenstein-Rodan, P.M. (1943) 'Problems of Industrialization of Eastern and South-Eastern Europe', *Economic Journal*, 53, 210: 202–11.

Rostow, W.W. (1956) 'The Take-Off into Self-Sustained Growth', *Economic Journal*, 66: 25–48.

Ruttan, V.W. (1996) *United States Development Assistance Policy: The Domestic Politics of Foreign Economic Aid*, Baltimore: Johns Hopkins University Press.

Sahn, D.E., P. Dorosh and S. Younger (1996) 'Exchange Rate, Fiscal and Agricultural Policies in Africa: Does Adjustment Hurt the Poor?', *World Development*, 24, 4: 719–47.

Sen, A.K. (1985) *Commodities and Capabilities*, Amsterdam: North Holland.

Thorbecke, E. (ed.) (1969) *The Role of Agriculture in Economic Development*, New York: Columbia University Press.

Thorbecke, E. (1991) 'Adjustment, Growth and Income Distribution in Indonesia', *World Development*, 19, 11: 1595–614.

Thorbecke, E. (1993) 'Impact of State and Civil Institutions on the Operation of Rural Market and Non-Market Configurations', *World Development*, 21, 4: 591–605.

Thorbecke, E. (2000) 'The Evolution of the Development Doctrine and the Role of Foreign Aid, 1950–2000', in F. Tarp (ed.), *Foreign Aid and Development*, London: Routledge.

Thorbecke, E. (2006) 'Economic Development, Equality, Income Distribution and Ethics', in M. Altmann (ed.), *Handbook of Contemporary Behavioural Economics: Foundations and Developments*, Armonk, NY: Sharpe.

Tsui, K.Y. (2002) 'Multidimensional Poverty Indices', *Social Choice and Welfare*, 19: 69–93.

Williamson, O. (1991) 'Comparative Economic Organization: The Analysis of Discreet Structural Alternatives', *Administrative Science Quarterly*, 36, 2: 269–96.

Winters, L.A. (2004) 'Trade Liberalization and Economic Performance: An Overview', *Economic Journal*, 114: F4–F21.

World Bank (1993) *The East Asian Miracle*, Washington, DC: World Bank.

World Bank (2005) *World Development Report; Equity and Development*, Washington, DC: World Bank.

Young, A. (1995) 'The Tyranny of Numbers: Confronting the Statistical Realities of the East-Asian Growth Experience', *Quarterly Journal of Economics*, 110, 3: 641–80.

2
Turning Points in Development Thinking and Practice

Louis Emmerij

A turning point in the balance of thinking and influence

In this study, I first examine why and how the balance of development thinking and practice changed around 1980. This turning point coincided with a change of influence at the level of strategic thinking from the UN to the Bretton Woods institutions. Second, I look into the possibility of future turning points in development thinking and practice. In doing so, I describe, first, what could well become (and is already becoming) a new and expanded general concept of development and, second, the very opposite, namely development not as a global but as a regional and local strategy. Thus, having examined the future at the global, regional and national levels of development thinking, the study ends with reflections about the interests that lie behind the ideas that help to explain why they get implemented or not, why there are turning points or not.

During the 1940s and 1950s the UN was *the* place where big ideas about economic and social development policies were initiated. This continued during the 1960s and 1970s with the initiation of the UN Development Decades, the unified approach of the United Nations Research Institute for Social Development (UNRISD) and the elaboration of employment and basic needs-oriented development strategies by the ILO. It was in this connection that Hans Singer discovered the concept of 'redistribution from growth' during the Kenya High-Level Comprehensive Employment Mission (ILO 1972). During the 1970s the World Bank entered the scene of alternative thinking about development thanks to Hollis Chenery who elaborated and systematized the Singer analysis setting it into a broader statistical framework using data banks and analytical resources from the World Bank. He changed the title in the process from redistribution *from* growth to redistribution *with* growth (Chenery *et al.* 1974).

All this changed at the end of the 1970s with a harsh reversal of economic policies followed hitherto and a move towards neoliberal and neoclassical policies that emphasized privatization and liberalization. This policy reversal was soon followed in all OECD countries and became the conventional wisdom of the West. Contrary to what the innocent bystander might have thought at the time, this 'new' orthodoxy did not come out of the blue. Turning points rarely come out the blue. It had been prepared carefully over time by a core of neoclassical economists. Indeed, the 1970s saw the emergence of two opposing trends in development thinking. One trend consisted in widening the scope of the development strategies pursued by explicitly including social considerations, such as education, health, nutrition, employment, income distribution, basic needs, poverty reduction, environmental considerations, gender and so on. The other trend was represented by a return to neoclassical thinking. And so, as development thinking during the 1970s became more comprehensive and more poverty- and income distribution-oriented, the groundwork was laid by the followers of the neoclassical and neoliberal approach that was to become the 'new' paradigm of the 1980s and beyond. For example, the criticism of import substitution became more precise, technical and empirical (Little *et al.* 1970). This early work was followed by other studies that represented an important strengthening of the theoretical framework of the open-economy model. The same reasoning applies to the monetarist strand of the neoclassical resurgence.

This new paradigm was of course a recycled version of trickle-down economics, with growth given greater weight than income distribution and social objectives. The underlying hypothesis was that policy reforms designed to achieve efficiency and growth would also promote better living standards, especially for the poorest. The social costs of structural adjustment were inconvenient but temporary; in any case they were inevitable in order for countries to return to more rational and viable economic structures. Not only did this 'new' orthodoxy become the economic strategy of the West but, through its adoption by the World Bank and the IMF it became the conventional wisdom of practically the entire globe, whether voluntarily or not. The (important) exception here were the East Asian countries that went under a variety of labels, such as the Asian Tigers, the Flying Geese, etc.

The Bretton Woods institutions adopted the reversal of policies because the Western countries could impose their will in the Board, given the weighted voting system. Once adopted, they (that is, the Bretton Woods institutions and Western countries) could impose it on the rest of the world – also in the light of the international debt crisis. It was a typical case of the power of the purse versus the power of ideas. The purse won mainly, we contend, because of the absence of ideas on the part of the UN and the rest of the world during this period, with the exception, once again, of East Asia.

But, it can be asked, where had all the Nobel laureates gone who had been so instrumental in the early years to shape development thinking both in the UN and in the world at large? In 1980 most of them were still very much alive. Jan Tinbergen, Gunnar Myrdal, W. Arthur Lewis, Richard Stone, James Meade, Amartya Sen and others were still very active. But no consistent counter-offensive was mounted in the early 1980s. True enough, hundreds of British economists[1] signed their rejection of Thatcherite economics, but with little effect on practical policy or ideological stance. And so the purse won mainly because the existing ideas of the 1970s were not defended and adapted strongly and carefully enough and no alternative ideas were brought forward in a sufficiently authoritative fashion. We had to wait until the 1990s for this to happen – in terms of thinking rather than of practice – when the series of *Human Development Reports* were launched by Mahbub ul Haque and his small team at the United Nations Development Programme (UNDP).[2]

The future of development as a global concept

What is amazing when it comes to development thinking is the dominance of Western ideas. Starting with modernization theory, all the development approaches are 'Western' and are dominated by economists. This remains true even with strategies conceived by thinkers from the South or the East.

The classicists and the other great names in development thinking were all from Europe and secondarily from the United States. Development thinking in the modern era, since 1945, saw a wider cast of characters come to the fore, but it remained a global concept that was not 'deconstructed', to use Escobar's (1995) terminology. The labour-surplus model, the 'big push', balanced and unbalanced growth, great spurt and stages of economic growth doctrines were all of European and American extraction. The only person from a developing country – W. Arthur Lewis – did not depart from his neoclassical upbringing.

The same applies to the Marxist school of thought, although to a lesser degree. For instance, Paul Baran saw European colonialism interfering not only with development in the pre-capitalist colonies but modifying their future development path as well. His analysis points to the asymmetrical power and political relations – rather than God-given 'natural endowments' and free market-determined 'comparative advantages' – in determining the growth path followed by many underdeveloped countries. Baran (1957) concluded that 'far from serving as an engine of economic expansion, of technological progress, and of social change, the capitalist order in these countries has represented a framework for economic stagnation, for archaic technology and for social backwardness'. Baran and Sweezy (1966) inverted the law of uneven development on a worldscale relative to the formulations of the classical Marxist analysis of imperialism: rather than slowing down the accumulation in the advanced countries, imperialism blocked development in the less developed economies. The internal dynamics of underdeveloped societies came to be seen as fundamentally determined by their insertion into the world capitalist system. Although their analysis was pertinent and interesting, their suggestions for setting up an alternative development approach remained highly tentative and defensive and not really departing from its Western origins.

What is 'Western' about all this is that no account is taken of local thinking in and local theorists of developing countries. A possible exception is Raul Prebisch and the Latin American Structuralist school that emerged in the late 1940s. Here development and underdevelopment are seen as related processes occurring within a single, dynamic economic system. Development is generated in some areas – the centre defined as those countries whose economies were first penetrated by capitalist production techniques – and underdevelopment is generated in others – the periphery. Modern underdevelopment is therefore seen as a result of a process of structural change in the peripheral economies that occurs in conjunction with – is conditioned by, but not caused unilaterally by – their relations with the centre (Prebisch 1950). So even here the Western influence is important, as it is in the writings of Cardoso and Faletto (1979), Samir Amin and others of the *dependencia* school.

The neoclassical resurgence we have observed since 1980 is of course totally Western bred, but so were the redistribution with growth and the basic needs development strategies of the 1970s. Although the latter did explicitly take into consideration the specific circumstances of the developing countries, they remained embedded in Western concepts and thinking.

The events of the past decades challenge much of the validity of these Western development theories, whether liberal or Marxist, neoclassical or post-Keynesian. They did not anticipate turning points, collapses or failures; neither did they explain them ex post. They do not explain why so many countries do not seem to be able to take off economically or are regressing to previous levels of economic development. They do not explain either the 'ennui' in the apparently successful countries. Examples are the totally unanticipated collapse of communism and the reintegration of Central and Eastern Europe and the former Soviet Union into the capitalist world economy. Nor do they give an explanation of the reappearance of virulent nationalism and ethnic conflicts as well as the rapid growth of militant religious fundamentalism in both Western and non-Western societies. The economic stagnation and decline in African and Latin American countries; the imposition and the lack of success of structural adjustment programmes, especially in Africa, the rapid state-led industrialization of the East Asian countries cannot be explained by any rational criteria of the Washington Consensus school. Hence, all of those were on the whole not anticipated by either mainstream or more radical theories of development. In the face of such a failure to foresee major changes it can be maintained that we are witnessing a crisis in development theory even if in practice many stress the average progress achieved.

None of the theories – whether of the modernization, dependency, neoliberal or Marxist variety – seems to be working in the sense that each one runs into trouble, even if initial successes were secured. During the 1980s and 1990s these theories have been supplanted by a hegemonic neoliberal view of development based on 'globalization', 'free markets' that effectively dismiss questions of ethnicity, of culture, and does not try to understand nationalism, fundamentalism and terrorism. It can be maintained that the whole Western model of development, the 'paradigm of modernity', of a secular, industrial nation-state, is now in question and that a coherent and persuasive alternative model is yet to be found.

It would appear obvious that within the global economy enough flexibility must be created to make room for regional and national variations towards development policies, given the specific situation of the region or country in question. For instance, it can hardly be maintained that the Washington Consensus has been a success story in Latin America. In 1996, Ajit Singh challenged his Latin American colleagues to say how much more time they needed before being able to say that the Washington Consensus has been a failure. 'Five more years', they answered.[3] Five years later the picture was as follows: Argentina was in turmoil, President

Menem under house arrest, his successor and two more presidents gone by the wayside; Fujimori was in Japan and his country Peru in trouble; the Mexicans have not waited five years to oust the PRI in power for practically the entire twentieth century, although it is not all clear whether Vicente Fox has been able to find his own way; the Venezuelans sacked the traditional parties who squandered the oil revenues and replaced them by a populist Hugo Chavez; and we could go down the tragic list, from Colombia to Brazil via Ecuador. What lessons can and must be learned from all this?

Towards a new and flexible concept of development: forks in the road

There are two questions that one must ask when it comes to development theory and practice. The first is whether the approach adopted up until now is comprehensive enough or still too narrowly economistic; the second relates to the problem of homogeneity, i.e. in how far must development policies be adapted and changed according to the culture of a given region or country. In other words, the question before us is whether there is one theory and one practice for the entire world, with a little tinkering at the margins to take account of regional differences, or whether there should be many theories and many practices in order to tailor-make development policies according to the culture and habits of countries and regions. So far the former approach has been adopted with mixed results. This approach is now being finessed and broadened and we shall start this section presenting the state of play. The latter approach must be given more thought, as we will show. We are facing a fork in the development road.

Broadening development theory and practice

Amartya Kumar Sen, the 1998 Nobel Prize laureate, has given this problem a lot of thought and has come to the conclusion that a universal approach is desirable, as long as development thinking covers a wider surface by bringing on board political, cultural, social and human rights issues. One illustration of this belief is the importance he attaches to tolerance and pluralism, of democratic procedures in short: 'To see political tolerance merely as a "Western liberal" inclination seemed to me a serious mistake.'[4] Sen has always adopted a broad approach to development, including work on economic inequality, poverty, employment, technology, investigating the principles and implications of liberty and rights, assessing gender inequality, etc. In other words, his interest gradually shifted from the pure theory of social choice to more 'practical' problems (Sen 1982; 1984).

Subsequently, Sen (1985) started to explore an approach that sees individual advantage not merely as opulence or utility, but primarily in terms of the lives people manage to live and the freedom they have to choose the kind of life they have reason to value. The basic idea here is to pay attention to the actual 'capabilities' that people end up having. He elaborated his work on poverty by coming up with a universal definition, not of course in terms of purchasing power but of capabilities and functionings. The poor are poor because their set of capabilities is small, not because of what they do not have, but because of what they cannot do. This measure is universal because it entails identifying a set of capabilities, something like basic needs. A minimum list would include being able to lead a healthy and productive life, to communicate and participate in your community, to move about freely and to have a family with a partner of your choice.

Thus, Sen has elaborated a distinct agenda. Utility and income have been displaced from their primary positions in orthodox economics. Wellbeing is captured by things people can do rather than things people have. If their set of capabilities grows larger, people can do more of the things they would like to do. And so we arrive at a new and dynamic definition of freedom; choice over a larger set of capabilities (Desai 2000). Sen's (1999) emphasis on freedom of choice led him naturally to attach prime importance to democracy as a preferred political system: 'A country does not have to be deemed fit *for* democracy; rather, it has to become fit *through* democracy.'

But what exactly is democracy? Sen asserts that we must not identify democracy with majority rule. Democracy does, of course, include voting and respect for election results, but it also requires the protection of liberties and freedoms, respect for legal entitlements, and the guaranteeing of free discussion and uncensored distribution of news and fair comment. 'Even the idea of "needs", including the understanding of "economic needs", requires public discussion and exchange of information, views, and analysis' (*Ibid.*: 10).

Thus, Amartya Sen does not quite trust unadulterated market economics, is in favour of democratic decision making and calls for social support in development. He has been arguing in favour of softer, gentler and more humane economics and economic policies. When he was awarded the Nobel Prize in 1998, he was credited by the Royal Swedish Academy with 'having restored an ethical dimension to economics'. He points out that in the classical writings on development it was always assumed that economic development was a benign process, in the interest of the people. The view that one must ignore any kind of social sympathies for the underdog, and that you cannot have democracy, did not become the dominant thought until the beginning of modern development economics, say as of the 1950s.[5] Sen elaborates on the notion of development viewed as 'fierce' as opposed to seeing it as a 'friendly' process. The former asks for a 'needed sacrifice' in order to achieve a better future. This approach, with its emphasis on capital accumulation, is not wrong, but suffers from several handicaps mostly relating to the comparative neglect of the wellbeing and quality of life in the present and near future. Sen (1997: 537) concludes:

> Those who see in this a model to follow have continued to argue for giving priority to business ... interests so that the productive power of the nation can be radically expanded, and they warn against the spoiling of long-run benefits by the premature operation of sympathy; they are terrified of the harm that may result from the influence of 'bleeding hearts'. The 'friendly' approach, by contrast, sees development as a process where people help each other and themselves with an emphasis on human skills and human capital, and on the

role of human qualities in promoting and sustaining economic growth. Ultimately, the focus is on the expansion of human freedom to live the kind of lives people have reason to value. And, thus, the role of economic growth in expanding these opportunities has to be integrated into that more foundational understanding of the process of development.

And so we have been moving towards a global concept of development in which physical and human capital accumulation remain important ingredients, but where social objectives, freedom, democracy, ethnicity, human rights are becoming at least as crucial. It took time to realize that education is not just a consumption good that can be afforded as of a certain level of development, but that it is also an investment in human capital that is a prerequisite to *attain* that level of development. In the same way, we must now get used to the idea that social and ethnic inequalities, absence of freedom and democracy are as much reasons for lack of development as absence of investments. The concept of development not only becomes much more comprehensive and all embracing, but also the causative links and relationships are being reversed. This line of thought also underlies the concept of human development, initiated by ul Haque (with the active assistance of Sen) in the *Human Development Reports* mentioned earlier.

Obviously, it can be argued that the 'Sen approach' to development must be more formally formulated in terms of an economic and social development model. Physical and human capital investments, sector allocation, human rights, freedom, etc. must be integrated in a consistent whole in order to move away from words and towards a formal model.

Breaking down development nationally, locally and culturally

There is a growing awareness of the importance of culture in the development process and of the cultural assumptions inherent in development theory and practice. The preceding section is based on the assumption that by broadening the concept of development the range of development models becomes progressively narrower. But the question that is being asked today is whether development models are determined culturally by each region, or by the culture of one region, namely the West.[6] Culture will be defined here in a broad sense, as a way of life and living together. This relates to values people hold, to tolerance with respect to others (race, gender, foreigners), to outward versus inward orientations and inclinations, etc.

More cultural freedom leaves us free to meet one of the most basic needs, 'the need to define our *own* basic needs' (UNESCO 1995: 15). But defining one's own basic needs is one thing, the way to attain them, through which social and economic policies, for instance, is another. We must be careful to maintain a balance between universalism and localism and avoid moving from one extreme to another. The thesis of those who are in favour of more variety in development policies linked to local cultures, institutions and habits, goes somewhere along the following lines:

(i) Western culture has held an iron grip on development thinking and practice;
(ii) this influence has tended to increase further during the past twenty years; but
(iii) there do exist alternative development models based on a different cultural and institutional historical background; and
(iv) these alternatives are likely to multiply in the era of globalization that may, therefore, paradoxically witness more diversity rather than uniformity.

Examples of such variations in development policies can be given. The Japanese and other East Asian authorities have always maintained that globalization does *not* imply that a universal model or uniform set of rules – as for instance implied in the Washington Consensus, but also in Sen's much broader concept – spread to all parts of the world. According to one Japanese authority (a hard-nosed top official of the Ministry of Finance who went under the nickname Mr Yen) 'we have to recognize that what can be called localization, or an identification with local cultural values, is proceeding along with globalization' (Sakakibara 1997). As was implied earlier, most neoclassical economists tend to apply their 'universal' model unilaterally to all countries, neglecting the historical, institutional and cultural backgrounds of the countries in question. But there are doubters who recognize the plurality of economic systems or cultures and emphasize the interaction among them. For them the key concept is not universality, but diversity and interaction.

For instance, it has been argued by many economists that deregulation must be implemented as intensively as possible, simultaneously and quickly on many fronts. But such an approach implicitly assumes that Anglo-American institutions are already in place or can be quickly established by enlightened reformers with the help of consultants and international organizations. This neglect of the validity of different cultures and evolutionary processes of history has often led to confusion and the collapse of the existing order rather than to reform. How can proper macroeconomic policies be conducted if the necessary infrastructure such as a central banking system and an effectively governed enterprise system do not exist? Forcing a uniform model on diverse country and cultural situations may endanger the economic future of these countries, as well as that of the world at large.

The need for a differentiated approach has long been obvious, in view of the remarkable success of the East Asian development experience. This need is also felt because of the disquieting fact that in most countries that have adopted the current economic orthodoxy (read Washington Consensus) during the past 20 years or so, the distribution of income has worsened, poverty has tended to increase and employment trends have been very uneven. The causal linkages have not yet been well understood, but the association between the adoption of a specific uniform model and the accentuation of problems of inequality and poverty is a cause for serious concern. If one of the priorities is 'to bring the millions of dispossessed and disadvantaged in from the margins of society and cultural policy in from the margins of governance' (Council of Europe 1996: 9), then bringing these two together by adapting the development models according to the needs, institutions, history and culture of different societies is an absolute must. The margins of manoeuvre may not be huge, but wider than one might suspect at first sight. That much has become clear from the East Asian development experience. These margins refer to institutions, consumption habits, land rights, property rights in general, access to markets, distribution systems, economic democracy, etc. The growing internationalization and globalization may provoke diversity at least as much as imposing uniformity.

Participation and empowerment are, obviously, closely related to both cultural and economic rights and equality. Participation, a human right, is one of the key objects of cultural and economic policy, because it opens up both the economy and culture to as many people as possible. It is often forgotten that East Asian countries could only grow at such stupendous rates of 8–9 per cent a year over such a long time *because* there was full employment, that is, everybody participated actively in the economy. In other words, there was growth from below. One cannot expect countries to grow much beyond 3–4 per cent until the bottom half of the population is participating and contributing. 'The issue is not so much that of growth with distribution; growth with distribution can be achieved by a few cooks preparing a pie and distributing the pieces to a larger group through transfers. It is instead a matter of the poor becoming cooks too, and of more cooks preparing a bigger pie' (Birdsall: 1997: 394–9). For the 'poor' one can and must read immigrants, women, unemployed, certain ethnic groups, etc.

East Asia can be seen as a mild case of economic differentiation from the mainstream. It was less based on theory than on actual practice. There is, however, a school of thought that wants to go further. This school is best illustrated by the 'decontructionist' approach of Escobar (1995). What this school is pleading for is differentiated development policies based on the cultural, institutional and historical characteristics of a given region as determined by the participation and empowerment of the people. It is a bottom-up approach pushed to its extreme. However, if an extreme approach is discarded, what remains is an important policy alternative, namely the desirability to include local variations on the national, regional and global development theme. The 'realistic' approach here takes as a starting point the alleged fact that development policies are to a very large extent top-down, ethnocentric and technocratic that treat people and cultures as abstract concepts. They are composed of a series of technical interventions that are supposed to be universally applicable. The alternative is to be much more sensitive to local and social and cultural practice, that is producing local models of economic activity. In other words, 'the remaking of development must thus start by examining local constructions, to the extent that they are the life and history of a people, that is, the conditions of and for change' (Escobar 1995).

According to this school of thought, development theory and practice has not paid sufficient attention, if at all, to the cultural dynamics of incorporating local thinking and practice into the global orthodoxy of economic thought. Nor has it attempted to make visible the local constructions that exist side by side with the might of global forces. There is, therefore, no question of proposing grand alternatives here; alternatives that can be applied to all places and all situations. In a sense, the proponents of this version of deconstruction go further than that by introducing many local variations on the general theme (any general theme) that in turn will affect the global orthodoxy.

I have reviewed here examples of development approaches that attempt to broaden the scope in order to make them more comprehensive on the one hand, and of allowing local traditions and practice to play an important role on the other. Both approaches have the same rationale, namely to make the development policies more realistic and hence to produce better results for *all* individuals on this earth. However, both would imply a turning point in development policies at some time in the future. And once again, just like the turning point around 1980, it will not have come out of the blue.

The interests behind the ideas

'An idea whose time has come', as the saying goes. Why does the time for certain ideas come when it comes? What are the political and other interests involved? Can really important ideas that change institutions and structures only be adopted after a disaster? Why are certain periods in history pervaded by optimism and action and others by pessimism and passivity? What explains these cycles of optimism and pessimism, of action and passivity, of moving from one extreme to another?

On a personal note, I have been very much influenced in my answer to such questions by an event that happened when I was a young man in the Netherlands. On 1 February 1953 the dikes broke and a flood resulted in which more than 2,000 people drowned. During the debate that followed it became clear that warning signals had been given frequently in the past to the effect that such a disaster could happen if and when an exceptional combination of events occurred (full moon, northwestern gales of a certain force, etc.). The probability for such a constellation of factors to happen was, however, small. And so successive Dutch governments said 'Apres nous le deluge', and nothing was done. It was only after the deluge actually happened that a long-term plan was elaborated (the so-called Delta Plan) to cut off all big rivers from the sea at very considerable expense. The impressive result of dikes, bridges and other works of art can be admired by anybody driving from Antwerp to Rotterdam today.

The long-term plan and the considerable expense were only decided upon after the disaster. In the same way it took the disasters of the Great Depression and the Second World War to bring about adoption of new economic policies and a new international financial and political architecture by introducing and embracing Keynesian economics, the Bretton Woods institutions, the UN and the Marshall Plan. So one thing is quite clear. Important ideas and exceptional people get more of a chance in exceptional circumstances and when disasters are on us. This is sad but true. Cassandras are never listened to, as the Dutch experts learned at their and the population's expense, and as we can also deduce from the environmental and Kyoto saga.[7]

Can one find exceptions to this 'rule' where disasters are headed off before they strike? To a certain extent: yes. One could point to the advances in road and car safety, although the number of annual deaths on the roads continues to amount to an infinitely bigger disaster each year than the number of deaths during the 1953 flood in the Netherlands. The immunization programme as launched by UNICEF during the 1980s would come close to a real exception to the rule, although once again the number of children that died each year before the programme was dreadful. The green revolution and the new seeds are probably the clearest exception to the rule, but even here hunger and its victims has already struck many times. An intelligent policy approach to global warming would be the real exception, but we are not yet there.[8]

What makes the difference when it comes to the multitude of ideas at the second and third level of importance where millions of lives may be at stake but that do not revolutionize the existing political and institutional structure? What decides whether the time has come for them or not? There are several reasons that can be mentioned here. First, there is the question of leadership. Strong, enlightened and visionary leadership can make all the difference in order to bring an idea to the attention of national policy-makers worldwide. Courage and standing for one's convictions go with this kind of leadership.

A second reason is chance. It is like scientific research where one is looking for x and stumbles on y. John Maynard Keynes started out as a neoclassical economist and while writing the General Theory became 'Keynes'. Raúl Prebisch was a conventional central banker and, while examining the data that Hans Singer had sent to him plus those he had collected himself, became an unconventional economist and an advocate in favour of import substitution and centre–periphery analysis. It is the combination of leadership and chance that can be very powerful. A case in point is Jim Grant meeting Jon Eliot Rohde, who convinced him that more than half of all the deaths and disease among the children of the developing world was unnecessary, 'because it was now relatively easy and cheaply preventable' (Jolly 2001: 21). Other examples, like the eradication of smallpox, could be found.

A third reason is participatory decision-making. As Max Weber has remarked already, 'interaction creates ideas, imposing kills them'.[9] In the social sciences, ideas rarely come to the isolated individual shivering in the cold of his or her room in the attic. They rather come through the interaction of many individuals and groups in the warm rice fields of Asia, for instance. The green revolution is an illustration of this thesis in that it came about through a mix of high-powered research and putting one's ear to the ground. Listening to grass-root movements, to neighbourhood groups, etc., may well result in getting or sharpening ideas. It requires humility on the part of the professional to listen to those local workers, from another culture and with another mindset. It is at this point that we join what was said in an earlier section about identity and global development ideas or, as we called it, local variations on a global theme.

But let us not make a secret about it, in the end money and power count a great deal when it comes to which ideas come to the fore and which are implemented. Money, therefore, is the fourth reason. A telling illustration here is the story of the policies that were to guide the transition countries in Central and East Europe and the former Soviet Union to transform them into capitalist societies. The battle of ideas was between the 'big bang' approach and a more gradual, friendlier way of realizing this difficult transition. The idea that finally won was not necessarily the best, but rather the one with money and political clout to back it up. In the end it is obvious that an idea without the backing of money and other forms of influence will never see the light of day. Or rather it may see the light of day but it will remain sidelined.

The interests behind the ideas are a combination of the ambition of leaders, of influence, of local grass-root movements and of money, with chance thrown in for good measure. Once again, inspired leadership is of the essence and so is humility to learn from the people on the ground. There are many ideas around that can result in better development policies and hence improve the living conditions of millions of people. Identifying them takes an open mind, a lot of curiosity and the will and leadership to bring them to the attention of the world. Braudel (1985: 542) in one of his masterpieces, said it best:

> Sometimes an invention appears in isolation, brilliant but useless, the sterile fruit of some fertile brain; no more is heard of it. Sometimes there is takeoff of a kind ... there is a burst of progress, the motor seems on the point of starting, and then the whole thing comes to a halt ... A burst of progress followed by a collapse. Imperfect repetitions of each other though they may be, they are repetitions all the same and obvious comparisons practically suggest themselves.

Notes

I am grateful to my colleagues at the United Nations Intellectual History Project, Richard Jolly and Thomas G. Weiss, for continuous and stimulating discussions.

1. Three hundred and sixty-four, to be precise.
2. UNDP (various), *Human Development Report*.
3. Singh (1997: 48–61).
4. 'Autobiography of Amartya Kumar Sen', www.nobel.se/economics/laureates/1998/sen-autobio.html: 4.
5. 'Humane Development – An Interview with Amartya Sen, the Nobel Prize-winning Economist and Author of *Development as Freedom*', www/theatlantic.com/unbound/interviews/ba991215.htm: 2–3.
6. See for instance Escobar (1995).
7. See also Jenkins (2001).
8. See, for example, Lomborg (2001: chapter 24).
9. Max Weber, *Essays in Sociology*, in which he also stated that interests (material and ideal), not ideas, dominate directly the actions of men.

References

Baran, P. (1957) *The Political Economy of Growth*, New York: Monthly Review Press.

Baran, P. and P. Sweezy (1966) *Monopoly Capital*, New York: Monthly Review Press.

Birdsall, N. (1997) 'Lessons from Japan', in L. Emmerij (ed.), *Economic and Social Development into the XXI Century*, Baltimore: Johns Hopkins University Press.

Braudel, F. (1985) *Civilization and Capitalism: 15th–18th Century: The Perspective of the World*, London: Fontana Paperbacks.

Cardoso, F.H. and E. Faletto (1979) *Dependency and Development in Latin America*, Berkeley, CA: University of California Press.

Chenery, H., M.S. Ahluwalia, C.L.G. Bell, J.H. Duloy and R. Jolly (eds) (1974) *Redistribution with Growth: Policies to Improve Income Distribution in Developing Countries in the Context of Economic Growth*, Oxford and New York: Oxford University Press.

Council of Europe (1996) *In from the Margins*, Strasbourg: Council of Europe.

Desai, M. (2000) 'Portrait: Amartya Sen', *Prospect*, July: 49.

Escobar, A. (1995) *Encountering Development: The Making and Unmaking of the Third World*, Princeton: Princeton University Press.

ILO (1972) *Employment, Incomes and Equity: A Strategy for Increasing Productive Employment in Kenya*, Geneva: International Labour Organization.

Jenkins, R. (2001) *Churchill: a Biography*, New York: Farrar, Strauss & Giroux.

Jolly, R. (ed.) (2001) *Jim Grant: UNICEF Visionary*, Florence: UNICEF.

Little, I.M.D., T. Scitovsky and M.F.G. Scott (1970) *Industry and Trade in Some Developing Countries*, Oxford: Oxford University Press.

Lomborg, B. (2001) *The Skeptical Environmentalist: Measuring the Real State of the World*, Cambridge: Cambridge University Press.

Prebisch, R. (1950) *The Economic Development of Latin America and its Principal Problems*, New York: United Nations.

Sakakibara, E. (1997) 'Globalization amid Diversity', in L. Emmerij (ed.), *Economic and Social Development into the XXI Century*, Baltimore: Johns Hopkins University Press.

Sen, A.K. (1982) *Choice, Welfare and Measurement*, Cambridge, MA: Harvard University Press.

Sen, A.K. (1984) *Resources, Values and Development*, Cambridge, MA: Harvard University Press.

Sen, A.K. (1985) *Commodities and Capabilities*, Oxford: Oxford University Press.

Sen A.K. (1997) 'Development Thinking at the Beginning of the XXI Century', in L. Emmerij (ed.), *Economic and Social Development into the XXI Century*, Baltimore: Johns Hopkins University Press.

Sen, A.K. (1999) 'Democracy as a Universal Value', *Journal of Democracy*, 10, 3: 3–17.

Singh, A. (1997) 'Catching up with the West: a Perspective on Asian Economic Development and Lessons for Latin America', in L. Emmerij (ed.), *Economic and Social Development into the XXI Century*, Baltimore: Johns Hopkins University Press.

UNDP (United Nations Development Programme) (various) *Human Development Report*, New York: Oxford University Press for UNDP.

UNESCO (1995) *Our Creative Diversity*, Paris: UNESCO.

3
From Seers to Sen: The Meaning of Economic Development

E. Wayne Nafziger

Introduction

How has the meaning of economic development changed during the 20 years of UNU-WIDER's existence? This chapter compares perspectives on the meaning of development economics in the late 1970s and early 1980s, just before WIDER's inception, to contemporary perspectives. To narrow the focus from what would otherwise be an unmanageable task, I concentrate on two economists representative of these two periods. Two markers are, Dudley Seers (1969; 1979) for the earlier period, and Amartya Sen (1999) for the later. Here the meaning of development also encompasses measures and strategies of development and approaches to its study. Moreover, I examine work beyond these markers to provide more detail of the two men's views.

A thumbnail sketch of disciplinary changes during the last two decades

Before examining Seers' and Sen's approaches, I mention a few changes in the discipline of development economics during the last 20–25 years. These changes, resulting from world events or new tools and advances that have influenced the field of development, are only representative and not comprehensive. Econometric tools permit us to examine how trade liberalization reduces least developed countries' (LDCs) poverty (Cline 2004) and how financial liberalization increases LDC growth, at least in the long run (Ranciere *et al.* 2003). Recent enhanced tools, while not alleviating the imperfections of national income measures decried by Seers (1979: 14–18), expedite measuring net savings by subtracting capital depreciation, natural resource depletion and damage from carbon dioxide and particulate emissions and adding spending on education (World Bank 2003c: 119, 174–6; Arrow *et al.* 2004: 147–72). Work on national income at purchasing power parity (PPP), despite a margin of error, has improved comparisons and facilitated Maddison's (1995; 2001; 2003) comparisons of economic wellbeing across decades, centuries and epochs.

Soviet economic collapse has influenced development priorities, making much of the Lange-Taylor versus von Mises-Hayek debate on feasible socialism moot. The collapse of state socialism has consigned the stage theory of Marx to the dustbin,

but Marx's underlying premise of the inevitability of conflict between ruling and oppressed classes (even international conflict à la Lenin and Baran) still has explanatory power. Moreover, high levels of Soviet environmental pollution revived an emphasis on how market distortions give rise to environmental degradation (Panayotou 1993). Important here is the relationship between secure property and use rights, with de Soto's *The Mystery of Capitalism's* (2000) insight that most of the world's potential capital assets, outside the West and Japan, are dead capital, unusable under the legal property system and inaccessible as collateral for loans or to secure bonds. Soviet failure in collective agriculture has renewed interest in research by Berry and Cline (1979) showing an inverse relationship between the size of plot and land productivity, and that small farms have higher productivity due to fewer problems of supervision and greater incentives to invest and undertake improvements.

Negative total factor productivity (TFP) before and during the Soviet collapse gave impetus to TFP examination, with a concern about recent negative TFP in sub-Saharan Africa. The information technology (IT) revolution and a shrinking globe mean an emphasis on LDCs availing themselves of global production networks and technological transfer, adaptation, and imitation (Addison 2003: 5; World Bank 1997: 2) rather than stressing self-reliance, as Seers did.

The near-decade of falling national income in post-socialist states, together with work by North (1990) and Acemoglu *et al.* (2001), has contributed to a shift to the importance of institutions as a determinant of LDC and transitional growth among scholars and international financial institutions (IFIs), such as the International Monetary Fund (IMF). The increase in Africa's failed states, those states providing virtually no public goods and services to their citizens, has increased emphasis, even by IFIs, on the importance of governance and the analysis of rent seeking, unproductive activity to obtain private benefit from public action and resources. Other differences between the earlier and later periods result from the rise of global competition (Nayyar 1997) and its effect on the increased share of the world's middle class in Asia (especially China and India) and reduced share in the West (Bhalla 2002: 188), phenomena affecting national and global income inequality. The augmented neoclassical growth model (with an inclusion of human capital, especially health) and new endogenous growth model (with endogenous technology) increase the plausibility of numbers in recent empirical estimates of sources of growth.

Today economists are more ambivalent about the benefits of aid. Our profession has improved monetary and fiscal instruments with a concomitant deceleration of inflation. Related to this, Bruno and Easterly (1998: 3–24) discovered no negative correlation between inflation and economic growth for inflation rates under 40 per cent annually. Population growth, although still rapid by half-century periods, has decelerated from 1960 to the present (Nafziger 2006: 275). Recent empirical studies have established the negative impact of population growth on growth in GDP per capita (Barro 1997). In the last two decades, adjustment (macroeconomic stabilization, structural adjustment and economic reform) has been universal for LDCs and transitional countries, a condition required for funding by the World

Bank, the Group of Seven and the lender of last resort, the IMF. The literature has discussed the implications of adjustment and reform for economic development.

Seers and Sen as critics

Both men were critical of the development literature of their times. For Seers, neoclassical economics had a flawed paradigm and dependency theory a lack of policy realism. After the fall of state socialism in 1989–91, the ideological struggles among economists diminished. Neoclassicism's Washington Consensus of the World Bank, IMF and the USA government reigned (Williamson 1993: 1329–36; 1994: 26–8). Sen did not focus on ideological issues but, according to the Nobel Prize committee, 'restored an ethical dimension to the discussion of economic problems', such as development.

A sketch of Seers' and Sen's purposes of development

According to Seers (1979) the purpose of development is to reduce poverty, inequality and unemployment. For Sen (1999), development involves reducing deprivation or broadening choice. Deprivation represents a multidimensional view of poverty that includes hunger, illiteracy, illness and poor health, power-lessness, voicelessness, insecurity, humiliation and a lack of access to basic infrastructure (Narayan *et al.* 2000: 4–5).

Seers on neoclassicism's universal claims

For Seers, neoclassical economics' greatest error was its universalizing from the West's experience. For him, 'the abler the student has been in absorbing the current doctrine, the more difficult the process of adaptation' to the developing world (Seers 1963: 77). Calling a book that analyzes the United States and the United Kingdom 'Economic Principles' is analogous to calling a book dealing with horses 'Animals'. For Seers, development economics, in analyzing the 75–80 per cent of the world in developing countries and the past experience of industrialized economies, is closer to principles of economics (*Ibid.*: 79).

Seers on growth as the objective

Immediately after the Second World War, scholars and Third World governments were concerned with wider objectives than simply growth. However, Lewis (1955: 9) set the tone for the late 1950s and 1960s when he noted that 'our subject matter is growth, and not distribution'. But the stress of the UN's first development decade (1960–70) on LDCs' economic growth, which many alleged did not spread to the poorer half of the population, triggered widespread disillusionment. Seers (1969: 3–4) signalled the shift away from the goal of growth by asking the following questions about a country's development

What has been happening to poverty? What has been happening to unemployment? What has been happening to inequality? If all three of these have become less severe, then beyond doubt this has been a period of development for the country concerned. If one or two of these central problems have been growing worse, especially if all three have, it would be strange to call the result 'development' even if per capita income has soared.[1]

Measuring Seers' goals

Since 1969, economists have made little progress in measuring unemployment rates, at least in LDCs with a majority agricultural labour force. Poverty and inequality data have improved substantially, with efforts at the World Bank by Jain (1975), Chenery *et al.* (1974) and Ahluwalia *et al.* (1979: 299–341) to make cross-national comparisons of poverty, and subsequent contributions by such economists as Klaus Deininger, Lyn Squire, Martin Ravallion and Branko Milanovic. However, presently we have cross-national figures on poverty and inequality but few by region or community within a nation, the figures Seers considered essential for policy. Identifying and reaching the poor to enable their geographical targeting requires detailed poverty mapping, with data on poverty assessment and 'basic needs' indicators at local levels (San Martin 2003: 172–92). Few national surveys are adequate for 'guid[ing] poverty alleviation efforts aimed at attacking poverty at local levels' (*Ibid.*: 173).

Was Seers naive in setting goals that lacked policy-relevant measures in most LDCs? No. Today's scarcity of subnational poverty information would not have surprised him. 'Those who hold power rarely have much interest in such matters, still less in attention being drawn to them. It is preferable to shelter behind the "growth rates" that are commended in the reports of international agencies' (Seers 1983: 6). Seers blames LDC governments' inadequate information on a lack of will rather than competence. LDCs have:

> virtually no statistics anywhere on most of the aspects of life that really matter–the average distance people have to carry water and food; the numbers without shoes; the extent of overcrowding, the prevalence of violence; how many are unable to multiply one number by another, or summarize their own country's history ... Naturally, there are no official data anywhere on the number tortured or killed by the police, or how many are in prison for political reasons ... Many of the more important social factors are inherently unquantifiable: how safe it is to criticize the government publicly, or the chance of an objective trial, or how corruption affects policy decisions. But to say that these factors cannot be quantified, and are embarrassing subjects for those in power ... does not mean that they are unimportant or can be overlooked [when assessing] a country's development. (Seers 1983: 5–6)[2]

Seers on dependent development

According to dependency theory, global changes in demand resulted in a new international division of labour in which the peripheral countries of Asia, Africa and Latin America specialized in primary products in an enclave controlled by foreigners while importing consumer goods that were the fruits of technical progress in the central countries of the West. The increased productivity and new consumption patterns in peripheral countries benefited a small ruling class and its allies (less than a tenth of the population), who co-operated with the DCs to achieve modernization (economic development among a modernizing minority). The result is 'peripheral capitalism, a capitalism unable to generate innovations and dependent for transformation upon decisions from the outside' (Furtado 1973: 120).

Dependency theorist Andre Gunder Frank criticized the view of many development scholars that contemporary underdeveloped countries resemble the earlier stages of now-developed countries. LDCs are economic satellites of the highly developed regions of North America and West Europe in the international capitalist system. The African, Asian and Latin American countries least integrated into this system tend to be the most highly developed. For Frank, Japanese economic development after 1868 is the classic case illustrating his theory. Japan's industrial growth remains unmatched – Japan, unlike most of the rest of Asia, was never a capitalist satellite. Seers generally agrees with Frank on Japan, but emphasizes its selective borrowing, its slow pace of Westernization, and 'an elite that has remained firmly Japanese' (Seers 1983: 72).

In his economic analysis, Seers, like the *dependistas* and unlike orthodox development economics of his day, included class, power and imperialism by strong governments and economies against weak ones (*Ibid.*: 47). Seers was an admirer of Raúl Prebisch, who analyzed the world economy in terms of a core of industrial countries and a weak periphery of exporters of primary products (*Ibid.*: 52). Seers appointed him to the Institute of Development Studies' governing board, a decision reinforced for Seers when the UK's undersecretary for trade warned against Prebisch's radicalism.

Fascination with Prebisch and the dependency school did not cloud Seers' policy vision. He rejected the Prebisch-Frank policy prescription of import substitution that increased dependence on 'imports of energy, intermediate goods, sophisticated equipment and technology [and] food' and high protective barriers, which 'created monopolistic conditions [and] discourag[ed] innovation' (*Ibid.*: 53). Moreover, Seers recognized the limits of an LDC's room to manoeuvre by delinking from the world economy, given USA and Western retaliation and intervention in response to expropriation of foreign capital. For him, 'many who embark on an autonomous strategy with naïve optimism not merely lose power in a military coup and see their policies reversed, but also forfeit their liberties ... [or] even their lives'. Dependency theorists fail to recognize the constraints of too independent a policy and the importance of avoiding 'the inflow of capital ... replaced by an outflow'. His class analysis suggests that the 'decline in levels of living of the professional and managerial classes' and their possible revolt reflects what dependency entails (*Ibid.*: 53–61). While dependent governments can take advantage of the internal divisions of the dominant power, they are limited by how inflation and the reduction of foreign exchange reserves can undermine support for populism (*Ibid.*: 61, 126).[3]

Seers on development planning

Deepak Lal's *Poverty of 'Development Economics'* (1985: 70–4) contends that LDC intellectuals, nationalist leaders and politicians, in reacting to colonial capitalism, pushed for systematic state economic planning and intervention, especially in industry, to remove these deep-seated, capitalistic obstacles. Apparently Lal (*Ibid.*: 103) views Seers as a proponent of *dirigisme* (statism). But Seers is sceptical of typical LDC state planning:

> Today, 'planning' calls up memories of teams of economic graduates, who would doubtless otherwise have been unemployed, frenetically drawing up five-year plans, largely quantitative and wholly economic, to be published with a good deal of fanfare. This is often good public relations, but whether it has much impact on [policy is] a different matter. Rarely does such a team have any real authority ... Typically, after a year or two, a plan is a dead letter: by then, the ... assumptions and ... projections are clearly out of date, and the planning office is happily buckling down to prepare the next one ... It is time to move to quite a different type of planning; longer term, less economistic, not entirely quantitative. (Seers 1983: 94–5)

For Seers, LDCs should emphasize development strategy, not planning for a large part of the economy (that is, the private sector) over which government has little control. Moreover, planning needs to be well integrated, with departments communicating with each other, and planners in contact with political leaders 'on almost a day-to-day basis' (*Ibid.*: 114).

Sen's economic goals

For Sen (1999), freedom (not development) is the ultimate goal of economic life as well as the most efficient means of realizing general welfare. Overcoming deprivations is central to development. Unfreedoms include hunger, famine, ignorance, an unsustainable economic life, unemployment, barriers to economic fulfilment by women or minority communities, premature death, violation of political freedom and basic liberty, threats to the environment, and little access to health, sanitation, or clean water. Freedom of exchange, labour contract, social opportunities and protective security are not just ends or constituent components of development but also important means to development and freedom.

Sen's welfare theory relies not on individuals' attainments (of basic needs) but individuals' capabilities, an approach he believes can draw on a richer information base. From a feasible capability set, Sen focuses on a small number of basic functionings central to wellbeing. For Sen, living consists of the effective freedom of a person to achieve states of beings and doings, or a vector of functionings. He does not assign particular weights to these functionings, as wellbeing is a 'broad and partly opaque concept', which is intrinsically ambiguous. Sen focuses on a small number of basic functionings central to wellbeing, such as being adequately nourished, avoiding premature mortality, appearing in public without shame, being happy and being free. This freedom to attain, rather than the functionings themselves, is the primary goal, meaning that capability does not correlate closely to attainment, such as income. One example is life expectancy, a proxy for health, which, at 77 years, is as high for Costa Rica as for the USA, which has an income per head nine times as high. Moreover, men in the Harlem district of New York City, despite the capability sets and choices available to the US society, have less chance of living to 40 years than men in Bangladesh. This is not because Harlem has a lower GNP per capita than Bangladesh, Sen explains, but because of the high urban crime rate, inadequacy of medical attention, racism and other factors that reduce Harlem's basic attainments. Although people in Harlem have a greater command of resources than those in Bangladesh, the costs of social functionings, which include avoiding public shame and participating in the life of the community, are higher for Harlem residents (as well as USA residents generally, Sen argues) than for Bangladeshis.[4]

For Sen (1992: 102–16), poverty is not low wellbeing but the inability to pursue wellbeing because of the lack of economic means. He argues against relying only on poverty percentage or headcount approach (H) to measure poverty and deprivation, the approach of World Bank economists, Ahluwalia et al. (1979: 299–341). As Blackwood and Lynch (1994: 569) assert in their criticism of Ahluwalia et al., 'poverty does not end abruptly once an additional dollar of income raises a family's (or individual's) income beyond a discretely defined poverty line. It is more accurate to conceive of poverty as a continuous function of varying gradation.' In addition to (H), Sen contends, we need an income-gap approach (I), which measures the additional income needed to bring the poor up to the level of the poverty line, and the distribution of income or Gini coefficient (G) among the poor. Combining G, H and I, which together represent the Sen measure for assessing the seriousness of absolute poverty, satisfies Sen's three axioms for a poverty index: (1) the focus axiom, which stipulates that the measure depend only on the incomes of the poor; (2) the monotonicity axiom, which requires that the poverty index increase when the incomes of the poor decrease; and (3) the weak transfer axiom, which requires that the poverty measure be sensitive to changes in the income distribution of the poor (so that a transfer of income from a lower-income poor household to a higher-income household increases the index).

The World Bank, which became convinced of the validity of Sen's critique of Bank analyses of poverty by 1990, defines the income or poverty gap as 'the mean shortfall from the poverty line (counting the non-poor as having zero shortfall), expressed as a percentage of the poverty line. This measure reflects the depth of poverty as well as its incidence.' In 2000, Bangladesh's $1/day headcount poverty rate was 36 per cent, while its $1/day poverty gap was 8.1 per cent (World Bank 2003b: 58–61). While 36 per cent of Bangladesh's population was extremely poor, a transfer of 8.1 per cent of GNP would bring the income of every extremely poor person exactly up to the $1/day line. In China, while $1/day poverty was 16.1 per cent, the cost of bringing the income of these poor to the $1/day line was only 3.7 per cent (Ibid.: 58). For LDCs generally, 19 per cent $1/day poverty (World Bank 2003a: 30–1) could be reduced by a 1 per cent transfer from LDC consumption or a 0.5 per cent transfer from world consumption. This assumes perfect non-distortionary targeting to the extreme poor without reducing mean consumption. Alas, we do not have perfect information to identify the poor nor do we know the effect of this transfer on the income of the non-poor. Yet we have information on countries with extreme poverty and some information on the regions, classes and communities of the extreme poor.

Sen's view of gender inequality

Sen's discussion of income distribution includes intra-family and gender inequality, missing in Seers' analysis of 1979. For Sen (1993), the most obvious example of cultures' anti-female biases is the 'missing' women of India and China, their deficits of females from infanticide and anti-female health biases compared to a benchmark or norm for the ratio of females to males. In China, where the state irregularly enforced a 'one couple, one child' policy, expectant couples may use sonograms to identify the gender of the foetus, sometimes aborting female children. Moreover, a small fraction of Indian and Chinese couples practice female infanticide. Additionally, in Mumbai, India, women had to be more seriously ill than men to be taken to a hospital. India, China and the Middle East, with low female to male ratios, have a bias in nutrition and healthcare that favours males. Discrimination against women in schools, jobs and other economic opportunities lies behind the bias against the care of females within the family (Sen 1993: 40–7).

Sen's view of food entitlements, the state and famines

Econometric and case study evidence indicates that war and state violence increase nutritional vulnerability (Nafziger *et al.* 2000; Nafziger and Auvinen 2003). Relief agencies indicate 20 million deaths from severe malnutrition in 1991 in six African countries – Ethiopia, Liberia, Sudan, Somalia, Angola and Mozambique – where food trade was disrupted by domestic political conflict. Moreover, while, on the one hand, food deficits contribute to refugee problems, on the other hand, the 5 million or so refugees annually fleeing civil wars, natural disasters and political repression (including before 1990, South Africa's destabilization) added to Africa's food shortages (Daley 1992: 115; Goliber 1989: 10–11).

The conventional economic approach examines food (or total) output and its distribution, focusing on agricultural production, poverty rates and Gini indices of concentration. According to this explanation, famine arises from a decline in food availability (Ravallion 1997: 1207–8). Amartya Sen (1981; 1983b) and Drèze and Sen (1989) criticize this explanation, emphasizing that nutrition depends on society's system of entitlement. Entitlement refers to the set of alternative commodity bundles that a person can command in a society using the totality of rights and opportunities that he or she possesses. An entitlement helps people acquire capabilities (like being well nourished). In a market economy, the entitlement limit is based on ownership of factors of production and exchange possibilities (through trade or a shift in production possibilities). For most people, entitlement depends on the ability to find a job, the wage rate and the prices of commodities bought. In a welfare or socialist economy, entitlement also depends on what families can obtain from the state through the established system of command. A hungry, destitute person will be entitled to something to eat, not by society's low Gini inequality and a high food output per capita, but by a relief system offering free food. Thus, in 1974, thousands of people died in Bangladesh despite its low inequality, because floods reduced rural employment along with output, and inflation cut rural labourers' purchasing power.

Sen argues that food is 'purchased' with political pressure as well as income. Accordingly, one-third of the Indian population goes to bed hungry every night and leads a life ravaged by regular deprivation. India's social system takes non-acute endemic hunger in its stride, there are no headlines or riots. But while India's politicians do not provide entitlements for chronic or endemic malnutrition, they do so for potential severe famine through food imports, redistribution and relief. In Maoist China, the situation was almost the opposite. Its political commitment ensured lower regular malnutrition through more equal access to means of liveli-hood and state-provided entitlement to basic needs of food, clothing and shelter. In a normal year, China's poor were much better fed than India's. Yet if there was a political and economic crisis that confused the regime so that it pursued disas-trous policies with confident dogmatism, then it could not be forced to change its policies by crusading newspapers or effective political opposition pressure, as in India (Sen 1983a: 757–60; 1983b; 1986: 125–32; 1987b: 10–14).

The Nafziger-Auvinen (2003: 138–40) political economy approach analyzes the behaviour of ruling elites during periods of Darwinian pressures and food crises. This approach goes beyond Sen to examine ruling elites' deliberate withholding of entitlement, or even use of violence, to achieve their goals of acquiring or main-taining power, which often involves benefits at the expense of other segments of the population. Thus, according to this political economy analysis, Mao's effort to increase control (and reduce the influence of pragmatist Liu Shaochi) through col-lective-intensive water projects during the 1958–60 Great Leap Forward con-tributed to China's famine, in which per capita food production from 1957–59 to 1959–61 dropped 25 per cent. Indeed, amid Mao's campaign for increasing collec-tivization in 1959, the pressure of the party establishment contributed to false reports of bumper crops.[5]

Sen's (1981: 44) 'entitlement approach to starvation and famine concentrates on the ability of people to command food through the legal means available in the society' and not 'for example illegal transfers (e.g. looting)'.[6] Sen, using this approach, turns a blind eye to the possibility that the state may be the cause of famine through deliberate policy to transfer resources and food entitlements from a politically marginal group to a politically favoured one. To be sure, Jean Drèze and Amartya Sen (1989: 5–6) point out that, 'The dependence of one group's abil-ity to command food on its relative position and comparative power vis-à-vis other groups can be especially important in a market economy.' But for Sen and his co-author, famines and food shortages result from entitlement and state policy failure, and not from state action to damage the food entitlements of a group. They attribute the Soviet famines of the 1930s and the Kampuchean famines of the late 1970s to inflexible government policies that undermined the power of particular sections of the population to command food. Drèze and Sen's emphasis is on the need for public action by a benign state, making decisions about more or less food entitlements, rather than an ill-intentioned state, with much of the population facing a dog-eat-dog existence, making decisions to intervene in favour of one group at the expense of another and its food entitlement. For Drèze and Sen (1989: 17–18), avoiding famine involves the 'division of benefits [from the] differential pulls coming from divergent interest groups', not stopping the denial of groups' entitlements to food illegally or extra-legally.

As Keen (1994: 5) contends, in Drèze and Sen's view, 'There are victims of famine, but few immediate culprits or beneficiaries'. Drèze and Sen do not consider the possibility that states or politically powerful groups that control states may obstruct relief and contribute to famine for rational purposes of their own. Indeed, the Drèze and Sen conception of the state is essentially a liberal one, in which the failure to factor in the public interest is perceived as a failure of public policy. Most scholars and international agencies share the Drèze-Sen view, widely perceiving famine as relief 'blunders' and the result of poverty and market forces, and failing to see how markets are shaped or forced by state-condoned raiding, collusion and intimidation (as in Darfur in 2005). Sen's approach understates the extent to which starvation is in weak or failed states whose rulers perpetuate violence and withhold food against large numbers of their people.

Conclusion

In the last 20–30 years, changing events and new disciplinary tools have changed development economics substantially. Despite these changes, many controversies about the meaning of development remain. Yet there is an underlying consensus within the development community for the need to accelerate growth and reduce hunger, poverty, illiteracy, preventable disease, LDC debt burdens, gender inequality and unsustainable environmental damage. Perhaps development economists can become public intellectuals to stop the declining commitment to development and interest in its meaning. Can today's economists, similar to Dudley Seers (1920–83) and Amartya Sen (1933–), muster the passion, pragmatism and communication skills to lobby for development? Yes. Sen speaks frequently in the West and South Asia about the importance of development issues. I list two examples of others who have joined the public dialogue on the meaning and importance of development. Joseph Stiglitz's insights from his World Bank and US Council of Economic Advisors experience provide a platform for addressing the general public on development issues. Jeffrey Sachs, advisor to the Secretary-General of the United Nations on poverty, has popularized discussions on how to end poverty.

The goals of Seers and Sen to reduce deprivation, discrimination and conflict, and their scepticism about nations' commitments to these reductions still resonate within the development community. Seers and Sen were both interested in the nexus between development, political rights and peace but did not provide a systematic view of its interrelationships. One challenge for future work is for development economists to be more holistic in discussing the meaning of development, integrating economic development, human rights and conflict reduction.

Notes

Thanks to David Norman for comments, but I am responsible for errors.

1. See also Viner (1953: 99–100), and Chenery *et al.* (1974) for similar expressions, and Meier's (2005: 4–5) discussion of them.
2. According to Seers (1983: 45): 'Chicago-school economists are characterized by a much greater belief in quantitative techniques. They are thus more likely to restrict their analysis to variables which are quantifiable, and are particularly inclined to treat statistics as if they were facts.'
3. Seers (1983: 146) also rejects calls for the new international economic order, seeing it as an effort to maintain national elites' subjugation of the poor.
4. Sen (1973, 1981, 1987a, 1992, 1999); Sugden (1993: 1947–62); McCord and Freeman (1990). Sen was the inspiration and intellectual force behind the UN's annual *Human Development Report* (1990–2004).
5. Prybyla (1970: 264–9); Lardy (1983: 152–3); Putterman (1993: 11); Ravallion (1997: 1225–6).
6. For Drèze and Sen (1989: 22), 'It would be, particularly, a mistake to relate the causation of famines to violations of legality ... the millions that die in a famine typically die in an astonishingly "legal" and "orderly" way.'

References

Acemoglu, D., S. Johnson and J.A. Robinson (2001) 'The Colonial Origins of Comparative Development: An Empirical Investigation', *American Economic Review*, 91, 5: 1369–401.

Addison, D.M. (2003) 'Productivity Growth and Product Variety: Gains from Imitation and Education', *World Bank Policy Research Department Working Papers* 3023, Washington, DC: World Bank.

Ahluwalia, M.S., N.G. Carter and H.B. Chenery (1979) 'Growth and Poverty in Developing Countries', *Journal of Development Economics*, 6, 2: 299–341.

Arrow, K.J., P. Dasgupta, L. Goulder, G. Daily, P. Ehrlich, G. Heal, S. Levin, K.-G. Maler, S. Schneider, D. Starrett and B. Walker (2004) 'Are We Consuming Too Much?', *Journal of Economic Perspectives*, 18, 3: 147–72.

Barro, R.J. (1997) *Determinants of Economic Growth: A Cross-Country Empirical Study*, Cambridge, MA: MIT Press.

Berry, R.A. and W.R. Cline (1979) *Agrarian Structure and Productivity in Developing Countries*, study prepared for the ILO, Baltimore: Johns Hopkins University Press.

Bhalla, S.S. (2002) 'Imagine There's No Country: Poverty, Inequality, and Growth in the Era of Globalization', Institute for International Economics, Washington, DC.

Blackwood, D.L. and R.G. Lynch (1994) 'The Measurement of Inequality and Poverty: A Policymaker's Guide to the Literature', *World Development*, 22, 4: 567–78.

Bruno, M. and W. Easterly (1998) 'Inflation Crises and Long-run Growth', *Journal of Monetary Economics*, 41, 1: 3–24.

Chenery, H.B., M.S. Ahluwalia, C.L.G. Bell, J.H. Duloy, and R. Jolly (eds) (1974) *Redistribution with Growth: Policies to Improve Income Distribution in Developing Countries in the Context of Economic Growth*, Oxford: Oxford University Press.

Cline, W.R. (2004) *Trade Policy and Global Poverty*, Washington, DC: Center for Global Development.

Daley, P. (1992) 'The Politics of the Refugee Crisis in Tanzania', in H. Campbell and H. Stein (eds), *Tanzania and the IMF: The Dynamics of Liberalization*, Boulder, CO: Westview.

de Soto, H. (2000) *The Mystery of Capitalism: Why Capitalism Triumphs in the West and Fails Everywhere Else*, New York: Basic Books.

Drèze, J. and A.K. Sen (eds) (1989) *The Political Economy of Hunger: Selected Essays*, Oxford: Clarendon Press for UNU-WIDER.

Furtado, C. (1973) 'The Concept of External Dependence in the Study of Underdevelopment', in C.K. Wilber (ed.), *The Political Economy of Development and Underdevelopment*, New York: Random House.

Goliber, T. (1989) 'Africa's Expanding Population: Old Problems, New Policies', *Population Bulletin*, 44: 10–11.

Jain, S. (1975) *Size Distribution of Income: A Compilation of Data*, Washington, DC: World Bank.

Keen, D. (1994) *The Political Economy of Famine and Relief in Southwestern Sudan, 1983–1989*, New Jersey: Princeton University Press.

Lal, D. (1985) *The Poverty of 'Development Economics'*, Cambridge, MA: Harvard University Press.

Lardy, N.R. (1983) *Agriculture in China's Modern Economic Development*, Cambridge: Cambridge University Press.

Lewis, W.A. (1955) *The Theory of Economic Growth*, Homewood, IL: Richard D. Irwin.

Maddison, A. (1995) *Monitoring the World Economy, 1820–1992*, Paris: Development Centre, OECD.

Maddison, A. (2001) *The World Economy: A Millennial Perspective*, Paris: Development Centre, OECD.

Maddison, A. (2003) *The World Economy: Historical Statistics*, Paris: Development Centre, OECD.

McCord, C. and H.P. Freeman (1990) 'Excess Mortality in Harlem', *New England Journal of Medicine*, 322: 173–7.

Meier, G.M. (2005) *Biography of a Subject: An Evolution of Development Economics*, Oxford: Oxford University Press.

Nafziger, E.W. (2006) *Economic Development* (4th edn), New York: Cambridge University Press.

Nafziger, E.W. and J. Auvinen (2003) *Economic Development, Inequality, and War: Humanitarian Emergencies in Developing Countries*, Basingstoke: Palgrave Macmillan.

Nafziger, E.W., F. Stewart and R. Väyrynen (eds) (2000) *War, Hunger, and Displacement: The Origins of Humanitarian Emergencies*, Oxford: Oxford University Press for UNU-WIDER.

Narayan, D., R. Patel, K. Schafft, A. Rademacher and S.K. Schulte (2000) *Voices of the Poor: Can Anyone Hear Us?*, New York: Oxford University Press.

Nayyar, D. (1997) 'Globalisation: What Does it Mean for Development?', Rajiv Gandhi Institute for Contemporary Studies Working Papers 4, New Delhi.

North, D.C. (1990) *Institutions, Institutional Change and Economic Performance*, Cambridge and New York: Cambridge University Press.

Panayotou, T. (1993) *Green Markets: The Economics of Sustainable Development*, San Francisco: Institute for Contemporary Studies.

Prybyla, J.S. (1970) *The Political Economy of Communist China*. Scranton, PA: International Textbooks.

Putterman, L. (1993) *Continuity and Change in China's Rural Development: Collective and Reform Eras in Perspective*, New York: Oxford University Press.

Ranciere, R., A. Tornell and F. Westermann (2003) 'Crises and Growth: A Re-evaluation', *National Bureau of Economic Research Working Papers* 10073, Cambridge, MA: National Bureau of Economic Research.

Ravallion, M. (1997) 'Famines and Economics', *Journal of Economic Literature*, 37: 1205–42.

San Martin, O. (2003) 'Reaching the Poor: Fine-tuning Poverty Targeting Using a Poverty Map of Mozambique', in R. van der Hoeven and A. Shorrocks (eds), *Perspectives on Growth and Poverty*, Tokyo: United Nations University Press for UNU-WIDER.

Seers, D. (1963) 'The Limitations of the Special Case', *Bulletin of the Oxford Institute of Economics and Statistics*, 25, 2: 77–98.

Seers, D. (1969) 'The Meaning of Development', *International Development Review*, 11, 4: 3–4.

Seers, D. (1979) 'The Meaning of Development, with a Postscript', in D. Seers, E.W. Nafziger, D.C. O'Brien and H. Bernstein (eds), *Development Theory: Four Critical Studies*, London: Frank Cass.

Seers, D. (1983) *The Political Economy of Nationalism*, New York: Oxford University Press.

Sen, A.K. (1973) *On Economic Inequality*, Oxford: Clarendon Press.

Sen, A.K. (1981) *Poverty and Famines: An Essay on Entitlement and Deprivation*, Oxford: Oxford University Press.

Sen, A.K. (1983a) 'Development: Which Way Now?', *Economic Journal*, 93: 757–60.

Sen, A.K. (1983b) *On Economic Inequality*, Oxford: Clarendon Press.

Sen, A.K. (1986) 'The Causes of Famine: A Reply', *Food Policy*, 11, 2: 125–32.

Sen, A.K. (1987a) *On Ethics and Economics*, Oxford: Blackwell.

Sen, A.K. (1987b) 'Reply: Famine and Mr Bowbrick', *Food Policy*, 12, 1: 10–14.

Sen, A.K. (1992) *Inequality Re-examined*, Cambridge, MA: Harvard University Press.

Sen, A.K. (1993) 'The Economics of Life and Death', *Scientific American*, 268: 40–7.

Sen, A.K. (1999) *Development as Freedom*, New York: Alfred A. Knopf.

Sugden, R. (1993) 'Welfare, Resources, and Capabilities: A Review of *Inequality Reexamined* by Amartya Sen', *Journal of Economic Literature*, 31, 4: 1947–62.

Viner, J. (1953) *International Trade and Economic Development*, New York: Oxford University Press.

Williamson, J. (1993) 'Democracy and the "Washington Consensus" ', *World Development*, 21, 8: 1329–36.

Williamson, J. (ed.) (1994) *The Political Economy of Policy Reform*, Washington, DC: Institute for International Economics.

World Bank (1997) *Global Economic Prospects and the Developing Countries*, Washington, DC: World Bank.

World Bank (2003a) *Global Economic Prospects and the Developing Countries 2003*, Washington, DC: World Bank.

World Bank (2003b) *World Development Indicators*, Washington, DC: World Bank.

World Bank (2003c) *World Development Report*, New York: Oxford University Press for World Bank.

4
Inequality in Historical Perspective

Richard Jolly

Introduction

The magnitude of the increases in global inequality over the last two centuries are astounding, measured by both the absolute and the relative gaps between the richest and the poorest countries, and between the richest and the poorest groups of people.[1] Notwithstanding improvements in some indicators of global inequality in the last two decades due to the impressive expansion of China and India, the main indicators of global income inequality in recent years are all very high – and much higher than they appeared one or two hundred years ago. The trends can be seen in the estimates of the rise in Gini coefficients between 1820 and the 1990s, and of the increases in the gaps in per capita income between the highest 5 per cent and lowest 20 per cent of world population, shown in Tables 4.1 and 4.2.

Statistics on the trend in inequality within countries, shown in Table 4.2, reveal a more diverse picture. In the UK since the early nineteenth century, the ratio of the income shares of the richest and poorest steadily fell until about 1970, then remained level before rising sharply during 1977–89, with inequality rising more and faster than in any other OECD country.[2] In the USA, inequality rose in the second half of the nineteenth century and declined over the twentieth, until the 1970s when they started increasing again. In the Scandinavian countries, inequality also rose somewhat over the last half of the nineteenth century and declined gradually but steadily during the twentieth – and has almost always been less than in the UK or the USA.

Inequality within developing countries over the long run is more difficult to judge, because of the severe scarcity and inadequacies of data for the nineteenth and the first half of the twentieth century. But after the Second World War, the ration of the shares between the richest and poorest groups are thought to have declined somewhat in China and India until about 1980 and increased after this, not only in China and India but also in many other developing countries. Inequality within Latin American countries was already among the highest in the world and appears to have been rising in the last few decades. Although inequality in Africa (South Africa excepted) is generally not so extreme as in Latin America, the levels in many countries are high and also appear to be rising. But for

Table 4.1 Global inequality

	1820	1850	1870	1890	1910	1929	1950	1960	1970	1980	1992
World Gini	0.5	0.532	0.56	0.588	0.61	0.616	0.64	0.635	0.65	0.657	0.657
World top 5% to bottom 20%	7	7	9	10	12	12	15	14	16	18	16

Source: Bourguignon and Morrison (2002: table 1).

Table 4.2 Inequality within countries and global inequality, 1820–1992, ratios of income of top 5% to bottom 10% within selected countries

	1820	1850	1870	1890	1910	1929	1950	1960	1970	1980	1992
USA	13	13	18	25	25	20	13	13	12	12	15
UK, Ireland	40	40	35	30	30	16	10	10	7	7	10
Scandinavian countries	13	13	17	17	17	12	9	9	8	8	8
Argentina, Chile	16	16	16	16	16	16	16	16	16	22	23
Côte d'Ivoire, Ghana, Kenya	6	6	6	6	6	8	16	16	15	16	16
Egypt	16	16	16	16	16	16	16	16	15	15	15
China	14	14	14	14	14	13	9	8	8	10	12
India	12	12	12	12	12	12	10	10	10	9	8
Japan	12	12	12	12	12	14	6	6	6	6	6
Brazil	21	21	21	21	21	21	21	21	24	24	24

Source: Bourguignon and Morrison (2002).

sheer speed of increase, the rise in inequality in the countries in transition holds the record, following the collapse of the socialist model towards the end of the twentieth century.

In considering these statistical trends over the last two centuries we need to bear in mind an important point made by Champernowne and Cowell (1998: 49). They warn against contemporary investigations that span very dissimilar cultures and which take in what has happened over very long periods. We cannot interpret quantitative comparisons of inequality across widely separated time periods or within a remote era without careful reference to the underlying social order then ruling. In short, as they summarize, 'Comparing communities in terms of inequality should not be performed in a vacuum; the study of the income distribution and related issues cannot ultimately be divorced from the historical development of the social and economic system.'

Early views on inequality

What did some of the early giants of political economy and political say about the issues of inequality, national and international? In contrast to today's often bloodless statistical analysis, where changes in a few decimal points are treated with reverence and as proof, the colour and lively description of political economists writing about inequality during the late eighteenth and early nineteenth centuries shines out, vividly and sharply.

Adam Smith (1976: 232) made some powerful comments about inequality and its origins; 'Wherever there is great property, there is great inequality. For one very rich man there must be at least five hundred poor, and the affluence of the few supposes the indigence of the many.' Smith emphasized the way such inequality led on to the need for government to maintain law and order:

> The affluence of the rich excites the indignation of the poor, who are often both driven by want, and prompted by envy, to invade his possessions. It is only under the shelter of the civil magistrate that the owner of that valuable property ... can sleep at night in security ... The acquisition of valuable and extensive property, therefore, necessarily requires the establishment of civil government.

Smith had an evolutionary view of society and made clear how inequality had evolved with property. In the first period of society, the world of hunter-gatherers, there was little property, little inequality and seldom any regular administration of justice.[3] The second period of society was the 'age of shepherds' and with this 'the inequality of fortune first begins to take place and introduces among men a degree of authority and subordination which could not possibly exist before. It thereby introduces some degree of civil government which is indispensably necessary for its own preservation' (*Ibid.*: 23).

Smith though blunt, was measured. Thomas Paine (1995a: 401) writing two decades later, presented his analysis with pre-Marxian vitriol. He also focused on land as the source of inequality:

> It is very well known that in England (and the same will be found in other countries) the great landed estates, now held in descent, were plundered from the quiet inhabitants at the conquest. The possibility did not exist of acquiring such estates honestly ... That they were not acquired by trade, by commerce, by manufactures, by agriculture or by any reputable employment is certain. How then were they acquired? Blush, aristocracy, to hear your origin, for your progenitors were Thieves ... When they had committed the robbery, they endeavoured to lose the disgrace of it, by sinking their real names under fictitious ones, which they called Titles. It is ever the practice of Felons to act in this manner.

By the mid-nineteenth century, industrialization had advanced and poverty had deepened, especially in the towns in the United Kingdom. But the statistics suggest that little had changed in terms of income distribution. The income of the richest 5 per cent was still, on average, some 80 times estimated income per head. By this time, John Stuart Mill and Karl Marx had taken up the cudgels. Mill (1865: 260–1), though considering the acquisition of individual property through one's own labour as just, wrote damning indictments of the origins of the actual distribution of property in Europe at the time:

> The social arrangements of modern Europe commenced from a distribution of property which was the result, not of a just partition, or acquisition by industry, but of conquest and violence: and notwithstanding what industry has been doing for many centuries to modify the work of force, the system still retains many and large traces of its origins. The laws of property have never yet conformed to the principles on which the justification of private property rests. They have made property of things which never ought to be property, and absolute property where only a qualified property ought to exist. They have not held the balance fairly between human beings, but have heaped impediments upon some, to give advantage to others; they have purposely fostered inequalities, and prevented all from starting fair in the race.

Mill goes on with analysis of the role of law in this process, which seems to have its own parallels today:

> That all should start on perfectly equal terms is inconsistent with any law of private property; but if as much pains as has been taken to aggravate the inequality of chances arising from the natural workings of the principle, had been taken to temper that inequality by every means not subversive to the principle itself; if the tendency of legislation had been to favour the diffusion, instead of the concentration of wealth, to encourage the subdivision of the large masses instead of striving to keep them together; the principle of individual property would have been found to have no necessary connexion with the physical and social evils which almost all Socialist writers assume to be inseparable from it.

A half century later, or at least by the time of the eighth edition of his *Principles of Economics*, Alfred Marshall (1920) had considerably shifted the focus and frame of economic analysis. Although Marshall made the 'Distribution of the National Income' the title and theme of Book VI, the final part of the *Principles*, his emphasis was very different from that of Mill and Marx. His unifying approach was the new science of marginal analysis applied to land and capital, as to other factors of production. Institutions of land and property were still there and of central importance, but little attention was given to close enquiry into their distant origins.[4] Although in appendices to the *Principles*, Marshall (*Ibid.*: 647) showed himself well aware of the economic history of different parts of the world, including the role of war and conquest, he permitted himself this comment on the United States:

> Of the causes which have contributed to make the English race the chief owners of the New World, the most important is that bold enterprise which has made a man, who is rich enough to be a peasant proprietor, generally refuse to be content with the humdrum life and the narrow income of a peasant.

In spite of this paragraph being in a chapter on land tenure, there was no mention of the process under which millions of American Indians had been dispossessed of their land.

We need to jump ahead to the time of the United Nations to recover some of the blunt and colourful language of the early and mid-nineteenth-century economists. The 1951 UN report on *Measures for the Economic Development of Underdeveloped Countries* made much of the need for land reform, and reintroduced some of the early outspokenness. The expert committee included two subsequent Nobel Prize-winning economists, Arthur Lewis and T.W. Schultz. The report maintained the emphasis on how the land was owned and how it was used, not on how it was acquired. But there was quite enough to complain of in matters of landlord-peasant relationships:

> In many under-developed countries, the cultivators of the soil are exploited mercilessly by a landlord class, which perform no useful social function. This class strives to secure itself the major part of any increase in agricultural yields, and is thus a millstone around the necks of the peasants, discouraging them from making improvements in agriculture and, in any case, leaving them too little income from which they might save to invest in the land. In such countries, land reform abolishing the landlord class is an urgent pre-requisite of agricultural progress. (*Ibid.*: 21)

In its early years, the UN returned to the issues of land reform on many occasions and in many reports. But over time, the language became more temperate and the emphasis shifted from distribution to the practicalities of raising agricultural productivity.

In the 1970s, income distribution within countries was again brought into focus with the ILO's World Employment Programme. The first of the ILO country missions, led by Dudley Seers to Colombia in 1970, made income distribution the centre of its analysis (ILO 1970). Within two years, redistribution from growth became the integrating core of the ILO mission to Kenya (ILO 1972). This led in 1974 to the joint World Bank-IDS study on *Redistribution with Growth*[5] generalizing strategies for linking growth with redistribution and providing case studies of experience in India, Cuba, Tanzania, Sri Lanka, South Korea and Taiwan.

It is noteworthy that, until recently, the World Bank did very little on income distribution as is brought out in its history, *The World Bank: Its First Half Century* (Kapur *et al.* 1997). The major exception was during the presidency of Robert McNamara (1968–81), though even this was short-lived. McNamara raised the issue of income distribution on a number of occasions in the early 1970s and highlighted 'Latin America's scandalous income and wealth disparities' in a major speech in Mexico City in 1972. But after this, the emphasis was shifted away from equity and towards 'the absolute poor' (Chenery *et al.* 1974: 239). It is therefore significant and welcome that the World Bank's *World Development Report* of 2006 focused so clearly on income distribution (World Bank 2006).

Early views on international inequality

Smith is widely seen as the intellectual father of free trade and globalization and, certainly, he was a major advocate and analyst of the benefits of freer trade. But he was also careful to indicate his belief that there were losers as well as gainers in the process. For instance, he refers to the discovery of America and that of a passage to the East Indies by the Cape of Good Hope as 'the two greatest and most important events recorded in the history of mankind', and he underlines their enormously positive consequences (Smith 1976: 141); 'By uniting in some measure, the most distant part of the world, by enabling them to relieve one another's wants, to increase on another's enjoyments, and to encourage one another's industry, their general tendency would seem to be beneficial.' But Smith was totally alert to the fact that not all would benefit and he continues, 'To the natives, however, both of the East and West Indies, all the commercial benefits which can have resulted from those events have been sunk and lost in the dreadful misfortunes which they have occasioned.' Smith was careful in analyzing how the worst of the misfortunes reflected the imbalances of power of the time, adding 'At the particular time when these discoveries were made, the superiority of force happened to be so great on the side of the Europeans that they were enabled to commit with impunity every sort of injustice in those remote countries.'

Smith looked to the future, in words which should perhaps encourage broader perspectives among today's supporters of free trade:

> However, perhaps, the natives of these countries may grow stronger, or those of the Europe may grow weaker, and the inhabitants of all the different quarters of the world may arrive at that equality of courage and force which, inspiring mutual fear, can alone overawe the injustice of independent nations into some sort of respect for the rights of one another.

And for good measure he adds, 'But nothing seems more likely to establish this equality of force than that mutual communications of knowledge and of all sorts of improvements which an extensive commerce from all countries to all countries naturally, or rather necessarily, carries along with it' (*Ibid.*: 142).

Over the years of the UN, the importance accorded to global inequality has fluctuated, with periods when it has been seen as an important international issue followed by periods when it has been virtually ignored. Even in its first few years, the UN's own work on national income raised concerns about income distribution within and between countries. In 1951 in the UN Economic and Social Council (ECOSOC), for instance, the Indian delegate noted that

> the average annual per capita income of North America was $1,100, of Oceania $560, of Europe $380, of USSR $310, of South America $170, of Africa $75, and of Asia only $50. Thus, it appeared that the 65 per cent of the world's population which lived in Africa, Asia and Latin America received only about 15 per cent of the world's income.[6]

This stirred some surprising reactions. The delegate of the USSR made a strong attack on internal income distribution within the United States. More surprising, this was followed by the American delegate making supportive comments about the need to tackle global inequalities:

Everyone would agree ... that it was desirable to reduce and in due course to eliminate the existence of such large discrepancies ... that national and international action must be taken to secure a greater equality in living standards in the world. It was believed in the United States that the existing disparities in national income must be reduced by an expansion of the world's total income, an increasing share of that expanding income going to underdeveloped areas. The problem must be viewed dynamically in terms of increasing the world's volume of goods and services and in raising general well-being.[7]

The Brazilian delegate put the point with fewer qualifications: 'The problem was not to restore the old balance, but rather to create a new equilibrium by which the disparities of income and wealth throughout the world would be eliminated.'[8] When, ten years later, the First Development Decade was under preparation, the Proposals for Action prepared by the Secretariat had this to say:

It is true that the GA resolution lays down a precise quantitative target for the increase in aggregate incomes, and there is no similar quantitative target for changes in income distribution. We can, however, take it for granted that the 5 per cent growth target established by the resolution also implies that the increment in incomes thus achieved should be wisely used for the benefit of poorer sections of the population and should result in a degree of social progress which is at least in balance with the rise in aggregate national income. Normally, this would mean that the rise in aggregate income must be associated with an income distribution more equal, or at least not more unequal, than that at present. (UN 1962: 9)

In 1969, the Pearson Commission issued its report, *Partners in Development*, the first sentence of which emphasized the importance of global income distribution: 'The widening gap between the developed and the developing countries has become a central issue of our times' (Pearson 1969).

Concerns with global income distribution became more sharply focused in the 1970s with the North–South debate on the New International Economic Order (NIEO). Issues of global income distribution had been brought into sharp relief by the massive increases in oil prices, which had shifted the equivalent of about 2 per cent of global income in favour of the oil-producing countries, with about three-quarters of this coming from developed countries and the remainder from developing countries. Fundamental questions were therefore raised about the links between international trade, economic relationships and global inequality, together with hopes that further changes might be possible. But such hopes were short-lived. Debate on the NIEO met with strong opposition from the industrial countries and was effectively terminated by the end of the 1970s. Rising debt and imbalances in budgets and foreign exchange in developing countries ushered in the era of stabilization and structural adjustment.

It took until 1988 before the UN General Assembly again came out strongly on global inequality:

> Mindful that the existing inequalities and imbalances between the international economic system are widening the gap between developed and developing countries and thereby constitute of major obstacle to the development of the developing countries and adversely international relations and the promotion of world peace and security.[9]

Though in the 1990s, UNDP's *Human Development Reports* frequently drew attention to global inequality, the dominant international focus in recent years has been on poverty and the Millennium Development Goals. Though this has certainly been a move in the right direction and a big improvement on economic growth as the central preoccupation for development, it is still far from sufficient. The Millennium Declaration itself made little reference to global inequality. Cornia (2004: 3) has summarized the positives and the negatives of recent developments:

> The last decade has witnessed a blossoming of research on poverty-related topics as well as a surge in attention towards the issue of poverty reduction by governments, the international financial institutions, the United Nations and social scientists ... [but he adds] A similar shift in focus and policy stance has yet to take place in the case of income inequality. While research in the field has made considerable strides, the policy reforms inspired by the Washington consensus have broadly ignored the issues of high and rising inequality, of its impact on poverty and growth, and of the measures required to contain it.

Conclusions and recommendations

Some of the greatest economists and philosophers of two centuries ago were bold and outspoken about the injustices of extreme inequality, nationally and internationally. Their words stand in sharp contrast to the more measured descriptions of analysts today. Yet by almost every standard, global inequality has grown substantially since that period, just as national inequality has grown in most countries over the last two to three decades. There is a case today for more outspokenness. There is also a case for more outspokenness about the causes of inequality, and how these causes are linked to some of the extreme injustices of the past. Moreover, some of the inequality is *maintained* by laws of property and economic relationships which do not readily allow for investigations into the distant origins of this inequality. Several examples come to mind:

- Inequalities of land holdings, mine or forest resources, where original ownership derived from colonial times. It is conventional among politicians of developed countries to say that the colonial era is past and no longer of relevance. Often national constitutions, put in place at the time of independence, prevent reopening issues of land ownership or only allow this if there is to be full compensation. Economists should be willing to remind such persons that the ownership of inherited property, and the continuing benefits of having had such property, often serve as a link with these injustices of the colonial past.

- Inequalities related to theft or the unjust allocation of new rights influenced by political connections. A particular source of current injustice relates to the acquisition of mining royalties through support for a new government seizing power through a coup or using other undemocratic means with foreign support, as with the recent attempt in Equatorial Guinea.
- The operation of legal systems and international law in the context of great inequality of wealth and disparities of power and political influence act as a force for sustaining and sometimes for increasing inequality. Again there are many examples but those in the area of intellectual property and trade are especially important for developing countries.

For encouragement to think more courageously about international income redistribution, one can end by referring to the remarkable and bold proposal of Paine (1995b: 409–33) put forward in his pioneering pamphlet on Agrarian Justice in 1795–6. Paine began this proposal by commentating on the state of 'civilization', using language that if replaced with the word globalization could easily be applied today. He wrote that the inequalities of the time were such that 'on the one side the spectator is dazzled by splendid appearances; on the other, he is shocked by extremes of wretchedness'.

This led to Paine's remarkable proposal for income redistribution published more than two centuries ago. He proposed a plan for ameliorating the situation of young and older persons by the creation in every nation of a national fund. This would be used to pay every young man and young woman at age 21 a sum of £15 sterling to enable that person to make a start in the world. Persons reaching the age of 50 would receive an annual pension of £10. In both cases the logic was that in earlier times both groups would have had access to land to provide initial employment or security for their later years, but with the enclosure movement and dispossession of half the population from the land this was no longer available.

Paine's proposal for funding this scheme was equally remarkable. He proposed that an inheritance tax should be set at the level of 10 per cent of the value of all landed property and that this should be charged on the death of the owner, at the time the property passed to the next generation. Paine calculated that the revenue generated by this scheme would be sufficient in Britain and in France to fund the one-off payments to the young as well as the annual pensions to older persons. Some of the finer points of Paine's scheme also show him far ahead of his time: benefits would be paid equally to women and men; equally to rich as to the poor; and the scheme should apply to all countries. Moreover, in arguing for the inheritance tax, Paine kept it to 10 per cent, precisely because he recognized the important contribution that landowners had made in raising the productivity of their land, however unjustified the origins of their property. Incentives for landowners to continue to improve their land and raise productivity would remain.

If such imaginative and daring proposals could be put forward two centuries ago, when global inequality was much less and the difficulties of taking action appeared much greater, how much more should analysts today be inspired to think afresh. These bold and brave early pioneers should be today's inspiration, not only for analyzing inequality but for exploring what can be done about it.

Notes

I thank Jaideep Gupte and Josie Furness for research assistance. We are grateful for help from the librarian and staff at the UN Library in Geneva. Any errors or misinterpretations are, of course, mine.

1. As much emphasized recently, the relative gaps between the richest countries and China and India and a few other countries have narrowed in the last two decades or so, though inequality has grown within these and most other countries.
2. See, for instance, Atkinson (1999).
3. Anthropologists today would probably differ from this view.
4. Although Marshall did include an Appendix A, which traced the growth of free industry and enterprise 'from savage life to the early forms of civilization'.
5. Chenery *et al.* (1974). As made clear in the preface, it was Dudley Seers of the IDS who first proposed this collaborative effort.
6. ECOSOC, 514th meeting, 22 August 1951, paragraph 56, page 320.
7. ECOSOC, 516th meeting, 23 August 1951, paragraphs 60, 61.
8. ECOSOC, 247th meeting, 18 March 1949.
9. United Nations, General Assembly GA/RES/43/156, 8 December 1988.

References

Atkinson, A.B. (1999) 'Is Rising Inequality Inevitable? A Critique of the Transatlantic Consensus', *Wider Annual Lecture* 3, Helsinki: UNU-WIDER. Reprinted in (2005) *Wider Perspectives on Global Development*, Basingstoke: Palgrave Macmillan.

Bourguignon, F. and C. Morrison (2002) 'Inequality Among World Citizens: 1820–1992', *American Economic Review*, 92, 4: 731–44.

Champernowne, D.G. and F.A. Cowell (1998) *Economic Inequality and Income Distribution*, Cambridge: Cambridge University Press.

Chenery, H., M.S. Ahluwalia, C.L.G. Bell, J.H. Duloy and R. Jolly (1974) *Redistribution with Growth: Policies to Improve Income Distribution in Developing Countries in the Context of Economic Growth*, Oxford: Oxford University Press.

Cornia, G.A. (ed.) (2004) *Inequality, Growth, and Poverty in an Era of Liberalization and Globalization*, Oxford and New York: Oxford University Press for UNU-WIDER.

ILO (1970) *Towards Full Employment: A Programme for Colombia*, Geneva: International Labour Organization.

ILO (1972) *Employment, Incomes and Equality: A Strategy for Increasing Productive Employment in Kenya*, Geneva: International Labour Organization.

Kapur, D., J.P. Lewis and R. Webb (1997) *The World Bank: Its First Half Century*, Washington, DC: Brookings Institution Press.

Marshall, A. (1920) *Principles of Economics* (8th edn), London: Macmillan.

Mill, J.S. (1865) *Principles of Political Economy*, Vol. 1, London: Longman, Roberts and Green.

Paine, T. (1995a, first published 1792) 'Dissertations on First Principles', in *Rights of Man, Common Sense and Other Political Writings*, Oxford: Oxford University Press.

Paine, T. (1995b, first published 1792) 'Agrarian Justice', in *Rights of Man, Common Sense and Other Political Writings*, Oxford: Oxford University Press.

Pearson, L.B. (1969) *Partners in Development: Report of the Commission on International Development*, New York: Praeger.

Smith, A. (1976, first published 1776) *An Inquiry into the Nature and the Causes of the Wealth of Nations*, Vol. II, Part II, Chicago: University of Chicago Press.

UN (1951) *Measures for the Economic Development of Underdeveloped Countries: Report by a Group of Experts Appointed by the Secretary-General of the United Nations*, New York: United Nations.

UN (1962) *The United Nations Development Decade: Proposals for Action*, New York: United Nations.

World Bank (2006) *World Development Report: Equity and Development*, Washington, DC: Oxford University Press for World Bank.

Part II
Inequality and Conflict

5
Health Improvements and Health Inequality during the Last 40 Years

Giovanni Andrea Cornia and Leonardo Menchini

Introduction

The debate on the pace of improvement and convergence in levels of wellbeing between and within countries has acquired a particular relevance during the recent decades of economic liberalization and globalization. Though trends in wellbeing can be, and indeed are, affected by non-economic and non-policy factors, sustained improvements and convergence over time in wellbeing indicators across and within countries could be interpreted as an indication of the success of the liberal approach to policy making (Dollar 2001). In turn, slow progress and growing divergence might reinforce the claims of the critics who argue that globalization is inefficient and that – both globally and within each nation – it mainly benefits the upper income groups. The attention received by this debate in policy circles has substantially soared with the adoption of the Millennium Development Goals (MDGs) that have set clear targets for many indicators of wellbeing, including health wellbeing indicators such as infant mortality rate (IMR) and under-five mortality rate (U5MR). The explicit inclusion of health indicators among the MDGs is essential for various reasons. Health is a fundamental dimension of human wellbeing, good health is instrumental for improving other dimensions of wellbeing, and intertemporal and inter-country comparisons based on health wellbeing indicators are less fraught with statistical problems than comparisons effected, for instance, in the monetary space. For all these reasons, this chapter focuses on changes in the level and distribution of health wellbeing.

An analysis of changes in health wellbeing can also help shedding light on trends in income wellbeing. In this regard, while the pace of improvement of income per capita over the 1980s and 1990s shows a marked deceleration and an increase in regional variation in relation to the two preceding decades,[1] and while the distribution of within-country income per capita worsened in most countries,[2] the trends in between-country inequality are unclear, as results of alternative analyses differ considerably depending on the type of statistical assumptions on which these rest.[3] In contrast, analyses of health wellbeing are less susceptible to identification, methodological and measurement biases. While problems persist also in this approach, results of analyses of convergence in health wellbeing are less controversial than those based on income wellbeing and could therefore help to investigate overall trends in wellbeing and the distributive effects of the present development pattern.

Valuing changes in wellbeing

Traditionally, economists measure wellbeing in the monetary space. In this type of analysis, gains (losses) of wellbeing are associated with a rise (decline) in average incomes or consumption per capita, or with increases in the number of people emerging from (falling into) poverty.

While widely applied, this approach suffers from considerable theoretical and information problems and can, particularly during periods of structural transformation, lead to erroneous conclusions. To start with, unlike in the case of health indicators, which are a direct measure of wellbeing, incomes and wealth are just an input to human wellbeing. However, there are several other factors that influence health wellbeing or education wellbeing, including household assets, human capital, time use, structure and stability of the family, health practices, income inequality and instability, relative prices of essential goods, and public health expenditure. A large number of studies find a positive correlation between income level and health status, but this relation is not linear and unstable and shows a large unexplained variance around the mean. Also, changes in household income normally trigger a series of household and collective responses which can cushion it from the negative health effects of income falls. Indeed, it is not uncommon to observe improvements in health indicators concomitantly with declines in household incomes or, symmetrically, a decline in average health wellbeing and growing health inequality during periods of income growth. Finally, contrary to the common perception, income is not easily definable or measurable, especially in economies with a large subsistence or informal sector and during periods of high inflation, radical fluctuations in relative prices and rapid structural change.

Measurement of average wellbeing and of its distribution among the population, as well as cross-country comparisons, faces fewer methodological problems and does not require the adoption of arbitrary hypotheses and statistical conventions. In addition, the definition and meaning of the variables used – infant mortality rate and life expectancy at birth – is less ambiguous than that of monetary aggregates. Nevertheless, also in this case, national estimates and international comparisons can be complicated by methodological and data availability problems that are briefly reviewed hereafter. The major problem is limited data availability and quality. Vital registration coverage is complete or almost complete only in high and middle-income countries, and only one-third of all adult deaths are actually registered (WHO 2005). In most low-income countries, registration of vital statistics is incomplete, often massively so, and mortality data are estimated by means of life survival tables or by extrapolating past trends. Infant and child mortality are also estimated indirectly from censuses or demographic surveys by means of retrospective techniques (UN 2004). The stability and reliability of these estimates can, however, be affected by large sampling error, limited sample size and, in low-mortality countries, low frequency of infant and child deaths. As a result, it is not uncommon to observe large discrepancies between mortality estimates originating from surveys and register data.

The use of life expectancy at birth (LEB) as an indicator of health wellbeing poses additional problems of interpretation. Such an indicator is in fact computed on the basis of the age-specific mortality rates observed for different cohorts at a moment in time. However, as noted in Pradhan *et al.* (2001), such rates do not reflect the real life chances of a person born in the reference year, as computation of such index would require to know her future risks of death at different ages. As a consequence, LEB does not refer to any individual birth cohort but rather to a hypothetical cohort facing the age-specific death rates observed at the present time.

The chapter does not concentrate only on average aggregate changes in indicators of health wellbeing but examines, within the limitations imposed by data availability, also the changes intervened in their distribution between and within countries. Steep health differentials have been observed for a long time in many countries. In the United Kingdom, for instance, the famous Black Report (Black *et al.* 1980) focused on the marked health gradient observed among different groups of civil servants. Concern for reducing inequality in health was evident also in the WHO 'Health for All' strategy and the related target-setting exercises that in 1984 posited that 'by the year 2000, the actual differences in health status between countries and between groups within countries, should be reduced by at least 25%' (Whitehead 1990, cited in Gwatkin 2000). Meanwhile, concern for the health impact of economic policies intensified with the introduction of structural adjustment programmes that may have shifted the policy focus away from the search of 'health for all' and the achievement of the MDGs.

Finally, an emphasis on health differentials is justified by several arguments. First, according to most theories of justice, an average improvement in IMR or LEB characterized by high variation around the mean receives a lower social valuation than an equal average improvement characterized by a more egalitarian distribution. Second, targeting health intervention on the deprived groups generally permits achieving faster average gains than if it were targeted at the general population. For instance, high rates of child and adult mortality in poor rural areas can be reduced by low-cost public health interventions, while the further reduction of already low mortality rates in urban areas is costly and difficult to achieve. Greater equity in health can thus be a source of greater aggregate efficiency. Third, large health differentials, or their increase over time, may exacerbate the perception of unfairness of social relations and raise political instability. Finally, a rise in health differentials, or their persistence at high levels, collides with the emphasis placed by the Human Rights Convention (HRC) on the wellbeing of every individual. Rapid improvements limited only to a few groups and to the average do not satisfy the prescriptions of the HRC and MDGs.

Literature on changes in health wellbeing and its distribution

Pace of improvement in health wellbeing

Most of the literature in this area examines the pace of changes over the last two decades without comparing it to that realized over prior decades. In reviewing changes in IMR, LEB and life expectancy at age one, for instance, Fox (1998) emphasizes that progress continued uninterrupted for all these indicators for both developing and developed countries, but does not assess whether these gains took place at a similar, faster or slower pace than in the past. Likewise, in analyzing changes in LEB over the period 1980–2000, Goesling and Firebaugh (2004) note that the increase in LEB in the 1990s in rich countries was smaller than that recorded in the developing countries but do not compare it with that recorded over the prior two decades. In contrast, Wagstaff and Cleason (2004) note that, in the 1990s, progress in U5MR reduction was slower than in the 1980s, while Deaton (2004) points to a worldwide reduction in the rate of decline of child mortality and to slower gains in child mortality in many countries. In turn, Deaton and Drèze (2002) underscored that in India IMR declined in the 1990s by only 12.5 per cent as against 30 per cent in the 1980s. Also the *World Development Report* (World Bank 2005) points to a slowdown in the rate of increase in LEB during the 1990s.

Between-country convergence in health wellbeing

Over the past three decades, most demographers predicted growing convergence in health wellbeing between developing and developed countries. Wilson (2001), for instance, found that LEB had steadily converged across countries starting from 1950. Meyer (2001), in turn, focused on club convergence, by emphasizing that the (unweighed) distribution of LEB across countries remained twin-peaked over the period 1960–97 despite the 'migration' of several countries from the left to the right peak and the increase in the mode of the two components of this bimodal distribution. Thus, convergence towards a life expectancy of 45–50 years was evident within the low-LEB club of poor countries and 75–80 years within the high-LEB club of rich ones.

In turn, Micklewright and Stewart (1999) found that the standard deviation of the distribution of U5MR of the 15 members of the European Union declined over 1970–95 by 90 per cent as death rates in the countries of Southern Europe moved closer to those of Northern Europe. Convergence was also found, if less markedly, for the mortality rate of children of five to 14 years of age. This convergence was to a considerable extent policy-driven. Indeed, the EU Cohesion Fund has provided structural and regional funds equivalent to 3–4 per cent of the GDP of the recipient countries to help them catch up with the EU average. Participation in the EU favoured the convergence in health wellbeing also through the compulsory adoption of advanced standards – the so-called *acquis communautaire* – in the field of health services.

In contrast, the most recent analyses point to growing between-country health inequality owing to the dramatic rise in mortality rates recorded in sub-Saharan Africa (SSA) and Eastern Europe, the slow gains recorded in China despite a quadrupling of GDP/c over the period 1980–2000, and poor health performance of other countries. In this regard, Goesling and Firebaugh (2004) analyze the distribution of LEB of 169 countries for the period 1980–2000. They note that, while increasing during the 1980s in all regions, LEB declined over the period 1990–2000 in SSA and the transition economies. These divergent paths have led to a polarization of the country distribution of LEB, as confirmed by the upward trend recorded since 1992 in four synthetic indexes of the distribution of life expectancy. According to the authors, LEB inequality declined until 1992 to increase significantly between 1992 and 2000. A decomposition of this inequality rise into changes in population shares and life expectancy ratios led them to conclude that, although only one-tenth of the world's population lives in SSA, the HIV/AIDS impact on LEB (a decrease of 3.5 years on average, as opposed to a worldwide increase of 1.2 years) was the main factor in LEB divergence. When SSA was removed from the sample, the divergence in national LEB disappeared as the fall in life expectancy in the transition economies was compensated by the rapid rise recorded in populous India.

Also McMichael *et al.* (2004) also find evidence that contradicts the finding about LEB convergence. They identify in fact three sets of countries, the first (composed mainly of advanced nations) with a plateauing LEB trend, a second group of middle-income countries converging rapidly towards the LEB of the advanced nations and a third group comprising at least 42 countries (mostly from SSA and the economies in transition, but including also the Bahamas, the Dominican Republic, Fiji, Haiti, Honduras, Iraq and North Korea) that exhibited in 2001 a lower life expectancy than in 1960, 1980 or 1990. In their view, the usual explanation of health convergence – i.e., the rapid fall in deaths due to infectious diseases in poorer countries and the slower decline in mortality due to chronic diseases – has to be broadened so as to take into account new life-threatening challenges faced in the economic, social and environmental areas.

Within-country convergence in health indicators and mortality differentials

Health differentials are observed in practically all countries, including the most advanced ones. One of the most important IMR differentials is that by level of education of the mother (Caldwell 1979). Greater education among mothers is also found to reduce the IMR gender differential (Murthi *et al.* 1995). Mortality rates also correlate strongly with the region and, in particular, the type (rural or urban) of residence that offer different proximity of access to sanitation, housing, health and educational services (Sastry 1996; Jhamba 1999). Health differentials by income level are equally marked (Rutstein 2000).

Another point, central to the analysis of this chapter, is that in more egalitarian countries, mortality differentials are not as glaring as in unequal societies. A class, gender- and region-neutral development policy hardly ever is able to reduce mortality differentials, even in the presence of sizeable average improvements. For instance, an analysis of survey data on inequalities in U5MR by consumption quintiles found statistically significant inequalities in most of the nine countries analyzed (Wagstaff 2000). Such differentials were particularly pronounced in highly unequal Brazil, where an IMR concentration index of -0.322 was found. In contrast, the index was -0.016 in Vietnam and -0.028 in Ghana, that is, countries where consumption inequality was less pronounced. In turn, Wilkinson (1996) compared IMR by social class in England and Wales versus Sweden, and discovered a marked social gradient in the first countries but not in Sweden, a country strongly committed to reducing health inequality.

Growing U5MR differentials by income level are reported by Minujin and Delamonica (2003) on demographic and health survey (DHS) data for the 1980s and 1990s for 24 developing countries. In the 1980s the ratio of the U5MR of children of families belonging to the bottom 20 per cent of the household 'asset'[4] distribution to that of children of households belonging to the top 20 per cent ranged between 1.3 and 4.7, with an average of 2.2. However, over the next ten years the ratio worsened in 11 of the 24 countries studied, remained constant in ten and improved in three. Such a trend was observed not only in countries where the average U5MR worsened or stagnated, but also in half of those where it fell. In these countries, the average U5MR reduction was mostly driven by a decline in child mortality among middle- and high-income groups. Meanwhile, the reduction among the poor was lower or statistically not different from zero.

A recent analysis of IMR differentials in China making use of census and survey data by Zhang and Kanbur (2003) found that, while the nationwide IMR declined sharply from the 1960s to the 1980s, it then levelled off or was reversed in recent times due to the surge in rural IMR from 37–44.8 per thousand between 1981 and 1995. As a result, the ratio of rural to urban IMR rose from 1.5–2.1, the female to male IMR ratio rose from 0.9–1.3 and the Gini index of the regional distribution of IMR worsened. The authors explain these trends to the fiscal decentralization of 1978, the dismantling of commune-based health services, the introduction of private care in 1984 and the freedom granted to urban-based state-owned enterprises (SOEs) to lay off workers and cut health subsidies. The authors conclude by noting that, given the weakness of safety nets and social insurance arrangements and limited fiscal power of villages, it was to be expected that increases in income inequality would translate into increasing health inequality.

Trends in the pace of improvement in health wellbeing

Conscious of the methodological and data problems encountered in measuring health wellbeing, the values for the IMR, U5MR and 100-LEB (see later) were compiled for the years 1960, 1970, 1980, 1990 and 2000 for 168 countries on the basis of the *World Development Indicators* of the World Bank (2004). Missing data for several former communist countries of Europe were filled in on the basis of the data included in the UN Population Prospects 2002 revision.[5] Average, population weighted, compounded rates of change over the 1960s, 1970s, 1980s and 1990s were then computed for all main regions and country groupings, and for China and India separately. Analysis of these data points to the following results.

A widespread decline over the 1990s in the pace of improvement in 100-LEB

An analysis of changes over time in LEB risks leading to a biased conclusion as the variable LEB is upper bounded at, say, 100 years of age[6] – a fact that automatically forces smaller absolute and relative gains in countries with an already high life expectancy. Thus, barring cases of extreme deteriorations, this method of calculation is unable to provide a balanced picture of the real progress realized in overall survival. To avoid this problem, typically met in measuring progress in upper bounded variables, it was necessary to calculate the average annual compounded rate of change of the difference between 100 (the arbitrarily assumed upper bound of LEB) and its observed values. The variable 100-LEB measures the 'life years lost in relation to the maximum attainable LEB' and has the advantage of being scale-invariant, which means that rates of improvement are independent from the base value of the variable. For instance, in this framework, a two-year rise in LEB in a country with a LEB of 80 years generates a 10 per cent improvement, that is identical to that generated by a rise of six years in a country with a LEB of 40.

Table 5.1 Levels and annual population-weighted percentage average rates of change in (100-LEB) by main regions and key countries, 1960–2000

	Levels					Average annual rate of change			
	1960	1970	1980	1990	2000	60–70	70–80	80–90	90–100
High-income countries	31	29	26	24	22	−0.64	−1.04	−0.86	−0.84
Low- and middle-income countries	56	45	40	37	36	−2.14	−1.12	−0.80	−0.35
Low- and middle-income excl. China, India	51	46	41	38	38	−1.03	−1.08	−0.79	−0.14
Macro regions*									
East Asia and Pacific*	61**	41	36	33	31	−3.94**	−1.37	−0.83	−0.56
China	64**	38	33	31	30	−4.97**	−1.42	−0.63	−0.45
East Asia and Pacific excl. China	54	48	42	37	34	−1.14	−1.35	−1.30	−0.85
Eastern Europe and Central Asia	35	32	32	31	32	−0.73	0.06	−0.52	0.28
Latin America and Caribbean	44	40	35	32	30	−0.99	−1.10	−0.98	−0.78
Middle East and North Africa	53	48	42	36	32	−1.06	−1.29	−1.58	−1.05
South Asia	56	51	46	42	38	−0.92	−0.97	−1.11	−0.99
India	56	51	46	41	37	−0.94	−0.99	−1.14	−0.97
South Asia excl. India	58	53	48	44	39	−0.86	−0.91	−1.03	−1.08
SSA	60	56	52	50	53	−0.68	−0.63	−0.45	0.66
World	50*	41	37	35	34	−1.83*	−1.00	−0.74	−0.36
World excl. SSA	48*	40	36	33	31	−1.91*	−0.92	−0.86	−0.62
World excl. SSA and EECA	50*	41	37	33	31	−2.04*	−1.06	−0.88	−0.71

Notes: * High-income countries are not included in the macro regions, e.g. East Asia does not include Japan.
** These values are influenced by the famine that hit China during the 1958–62 'Great Leap Forward'. The regional averages and the measures of dispersion presented in the paper are always weighted by the appropriate populations (live births for IMR, the whole population for 100-LEB, etc.). Trends in the unweighted averages and inequality measures are mostly omitted for reasons of space. As expected, they show a greater variability than the weighted ones, though they broadly confirm the trends identified above.

Sources: Based on World Bank (2004), integrated with data from UNPD (2002).

Table 5.1 presents trends in 100-LEB and its annual compounded percentage rate of change.[7] It documents the rapid gains recorded over the 1960s and 1970s thanks to the development of national health systems and the adoption of modern health technologies in newly independent states. In the socialist countries of Europe such gains were less pronounced and indeed they stagnated in the 1970s due to 'chronic stress' (Bobak and Marmot 1996), while in the 1990s 100-LEB rose markedly because of a sharp rise in cardiovascular and violent deaths caused by 'acute stress' induced by a difficult transition to the market economy (Cornia and Paniccià 2000). As a result, in 2000 100-LEB in this region was the same as in 1970. The table documents also the massive loss of life expectancy caused in SSA by HIV/AIDS and, to a lesser degree, by economic stagnation, eroding health services, rising inequality and local conflicts. The table also show that the rate of decline in 100-LEB varies considerably across regions, and that the best results were achieved in the 1960s in Africa and Eastern Europe, the 1970s in East Asia, Latin America and the high-income group, the 1980s in MENA and India and the 1990s in the South Asian countries other than India (thanks to the rapid mortality decline recorded in Bangladesh).

The main message of Table 5.1 concerns, however, the steady and generalized decline in the rate of progress in 100-LEB, a decline that is robust to the removal of SSA and Eastern Europe from the sample and to the change of the upper bound of LEB from 100 to 90.[8] Besides the cases of Eastern Europe and SSA, a marked slowdown in relation to the prior decade is evident also in China and the East Asian economies, and a less pronounced one in Latin America, MENA and India. In contrast, the slowdown recorded in high-income countries is modest, suggesting the possibility of continued gains even at low levels of 100-LEB. The second main message is that such slowdown was most pronounced in the 1990s, possibly suggesting, with the exception of South Asia, the impact of systemic development problems or the impact of co-variant random shocks.

A fairly widespread decline over the 1990s in the rate of improvement in IMR

Table 5.2 presents the rates of change of IMR over the period 1960–2000. In many developing countries, infant deaths represent a large share of total deaths, and IMR is considered a key indicator of overall health. U5MR is an even more accurate predictor of overall health, but information on this variable is available for only 156 countries. For this reason, as well as for reasons of space, the chapter presents only the results of the analysis of IMR trends.[9]

As noted in Fox (1998), the last two decades witnessed a continuation of the improvements in child health indicators recorded over the period 1960–80. In fact, the 1980s recorded the fastest decadal rate of decline in IMR in Latin America, MENA and India, while acceptable rates of IMR decline were sustained in East Asia, Eastern Europe and the high-income countries. The fast IMR decline in Latin America and MENA during the 1980s is both remarkable and puzzling, in view of the recession experienced by both regions and of the debt, budgetary and inequality crises suffered by Latin America.[10] Continued progress was likely due to a rise in parental literacy and female education. An even greater role was played by the

Table 5.2 Levels and annual average population-weighted average percentage rates of change in IMR by main regions and key countries, 1960–2000

	Levels					Average annual rate of change			
	1960	1970	1980	1990	2000	60–70	70–80	80–90	90–100
High-income countries	36	22	12	8	6	−4.8	−5.9	−4.0	−2.8
Low- and middle-income countries	138	107	86	69	62	−2.5	−2.2	−2.2	−1.1
Low- and middle-income excl. China and India	129	111	94	75	70	−1.4	−1.7	−2.2	−0.7
Macro regions*									
East Asia and Pacific*	134**	85	56	43	34	−4.4**	−4.1	−2.6	−2.3
China	150*	85	49	38	32	−5.5*	−5.4	−2.5	−1.7
East Asia and Pacific excl. China	91	85	72	52	38	−0.7	−1.7	−3.1	−3.2
Eastern Europe and Central Asia	68	53	45	37	32	−2.5	−1.6	−1.9	−1.4
Latin America and Caribbean	102	86	61	43	31	−1.7	−3.4	−3.4	−3.2
Middle East and North Africa	163	131	94	57	46	−2.2	−3.3	−4.9	−2.1
South Asia	147	129	115	88	71	−1.3	−1.1	−2.6	−2.1
India	146	127	113	84	68	−1.4	−1.2	−2.9	−2.1
South Asia excl. India	150	135	121	99	79	−1.0	−1.1	−2.0	−2.3
SSA	164	141	116	110***	104***	−1.5	−1.9	−0.5***	−0.6***
World	122	97	79	64	57	−2.3	−2.0	−2.1	−1.2
World excl. SSA	115	91	72	54	45	−2.3	−2.2	−2.8	−1.9
World excl. SSA and EECA	119	93	75	56	45	−2.4	−2.2	−2.9	−2.0

Notes: * High-income countries are not included in the macro regions, e.g. East Asia does not include Japan. ** These values are influenced by the famine that hit China during the 1959–61 'Great Leap Forward'. *** The WDI IMR data for SSA for the 1980s and 1990s have been recently revised and describe a less dramatic trend in the 1990s. Such revision is, however, puzzling as a main factor in infant mortality has been the rise in HIV adult prevalence rate in the 1990s.

Sources: Based on World Bank (2004) and UNPD (2002).

spread of low-cost health technologies and community-based approaches to health, among which immunization and oral rehydration played an important part. As shown in Figure 5.1, the coverage of DPT3 immunization rose in Latin America from below 40 per cent in 1980 to 75 per cent in 1990. In MENA, the expansion was even more rapid. In India, progress in immunization in the 1980s was accompanied by a widespread and fairly egalitarian growth. Table 5.2, however, also shows that the rate of IMR reduction fell in the 1990s in all but two regions. In China, India, MENA and Eastern Europe the fall was sizeable. The decline is evident also at the global level, and is robust to the elimination of SSA and Eastern Europe from the sample.

It has been argued that such a widespread deceleration was due to three factors. First, the levelling of vaccination coverage at rates that do not guarantee 'herd immunity'. Second, in regions with IMR below 30–40 per thousand, the slowdown

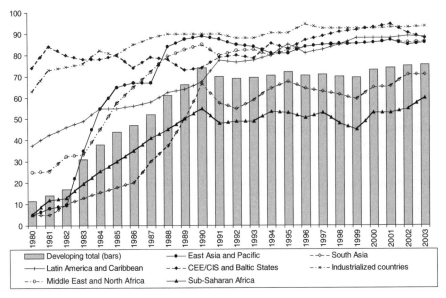

Figure 5.1   Global and regional trends in DPT3 coverage, 1980–2003
Sources: UNICEF (2004) and WHO (2004).

might be due to the elimination of all 'easy-to-remove' causes of infant death and to the difficulties faced in dealing with complex and costly peri-natal problems. Third, the quasi-stagnation (or, according to other data, the rise) of IMR in SSA was also explained by the surge in AIDS deaths among infants. Regression analysis by Cornia and Zagonari (2002), for instance, shows that a one percentage rise in HIV adult prevalence rate raised IMR by 0.88 points. This means that in countries with high HIV prevalence (say, 20 per cent) IMR rose, *ceteris paribus*, by 17 points per thousand. While pertinent, these explanations do not tell the whole story and can hardly explain the slowdown in IMR in MENA, the transition economies, China and the high-income countries. A broader set of factors is, therefore, likely to have been at play.

Trends in between-countries distribution of health wellbeing

The last decade has also witnessed a perceptible increase in between-country health inequality, as mortality declined at different rates in different nations. Growing health inequality is observed also within most regions, suggesting that the pace of progress differed also within groups of countries characterized by similar socioeconomic conditions. If continued, this polarization in health wellbeing may lead to rising spillovers of 'international public bads' (disease, refugees, drugs and illegal migration).

Rising global and regional inequality in the distribution of (100-LEB)

Table 5.3 presents the weighted and unweighted coefficient of variation and Gini coefficient[11] of the global and regional distributions of 100-LEB for the years 1960,

1970, 1980, 1990 and 2000. At the world level, both the coefficient of variation and the Gini index follow a U-shaped pattern, with the distribution of 100-LEB converging until 1990 and then diverging. However, as also suggested by Goesling and Firebaugh (2004), such divergence disappears if SSA is removed from the sample, as the fairly rapid convergence recorded in South Asia (India and Bangladesh in particular) and Central Europe (the Czech Republic and Poland) compensated the divergence registered in countries of the former Soviet Union and in nations such as Iraq, North Korea and Haiti.

Table 5.3 shows also that the intraregional dispersion in 100-LEB followed a U-shaped trend in Eastern Europe but a continuously diverging one in most other regions with the exception of East Asia and Western Europe, which registered a clear convergence. Interestingly, in SSA there was a 'downward convergence' in 100-LEB between 1990 and 2000 as the countries that suffered the biggest losses of life expectancy (South Africa, Botswana and so on) were those that had the highest LEB in the 1980s. Except for East Asia, which is dominated by China, these trends are more pronounced when the coefficient of variation and the Gini index

Table 5.3 Trend in the coefficient of variation and Gini coefficient of the intraregional and global distribution of 100-LEB, 1960–2000

	Coefficient of variation (population-weighted values)					Gini coefficient (population-weighted values)				
	1960	1970	1980	1990	2000	1960	1970	1980	1990	2000
East Asia and Pacific (22)	0.18	0.16	0.16	0.15	0.15	7.98	7.23	7.48	6.51	6.17
L. America and Caribbean (32)	0.12	0.12	0.12	0.12	0.13	6.54	6.17	6.40	6.20	6.49
Middle East and N. Africa (20)	0.10	0.10	0.10	0.12	0.14	3.61	4.06	4.99	6.06	6.78
SSA (45)	0.07	0.08	0.09	0.11	0.09	3.70	4.33	5.10	5.90	4.59
South Asia (7)	0.05	0.06	0.07	0.07	0.08	1.61	1.89	2.11	2.12	1.94
E. Europe and C. Asia (29)	0.15	0.13	0.08	0.05	0.10	6.81	5.55	4.18	2.88	5.44
W. Europe (18)	0.05	0.04	0.04	0.04	0.04	2.29	2.12	2.29	2.10	1.92
North America (2)	n.a.	n.a.	n.a.	n.a.	n.a.	n.a.	n.a.	n.a.	n.a.	n.a.
World (175)	0.27	0.24	0.24	0.23	0.27	15.2	13.32	13.19	12.86	14.18
World excl. SSA (130)	0.28	0.22	0.22	0.20	0.19	15.63	12.57	11.98	10.87	10.31
World excl. SSA & EECA (101)	0.26	0.22	0.22	0.20	0.20	14.47	12.21	12.32	11.31	10.67
Memo item: *unweighted values*										
World (175)	0.27	0.27	0.28	0.30	0.35	15.4	15.6	16.0	16.8	19.4
World excl. SSA (130)	0.25	0.24	0.23	0.23	0.24	14.2	13.3	12.5	11.8	12.5

Notes: The number of countries in each area is in parenthesis. The population of the countries included in this analysis represents over 99 per cent of the world population.

Source: Based on World Bank (2004).

Table 5.4 Decomposition of yearly changes in Gini of 100-LEB ('actual change') into the 'population effect' and 'growth effect' (% changes)

		1970–80	1980–90	1990–2000
World	Actual change	−0.10	−0.25	0.98
	Growth effect	−0.01	−0.22	0.83
	Population effect	−0.19	−0.09	0.07
World excluding SSA	Actual change	−0.48	−0.97	−0.53
	Growth effect	−0.37	−0.84	−0.51
	Population effect	−0.18	−0.11	0.02

Note: The 'growth effect' is the average yearly change in the Gini coefficient of the global distribution of 100-LEB using the countries' population weights of 1970. The 'population effect' is the average yearly change in the Gini coefficient of the global distribution of 100-LEB keeping the level of the countries' 100-LEB at its 1970 value.

Source: Based on World Bank (2004).

are computed without weighing the life expectancy data by population size. An analysis of health dispersion trends making use of the variable 90-LEB (instead of 100-LEB) shows that divergence in global health distribution starts emerging in the 1980 (rather than in 1990) but confirms the U-shaped pattern of health inequality trends and that the 1990s was the decade with the strongest rise of interregional and global health inequality.

It must finally be noted that when the coefficients of dispersion are computed without weighting country data for population size, the global divergence in health inequality persists in the 1990s even after removing SSA from the sample (bottom of Table 5.3). All this means that, in terms of countries rather than people, the derailment of long-term convergence in life expectancy predicted by Preston (1976) and Wilson (2001) is due to factors other than the spread of HIV/AIDS, stagnation and conflicts in Africa. This is a key point noted in McMichael *et al.* (2004) that should be brought to the attention of policy-makers.

Goesling and Firebaugh (2004) have suggested that rising global inequality in 100-LEB (the 'actual change') may be due more to faster population growth in regions characterized by higher values of 100-LEB (the 'population effect') than to differences in the rate of change in 100-LEB itself (the 'growth effect'). To test this hypothesis, the observed change in the Gini coefficient of the distribution of 100-LEB was decomposed into these components. The results in Table 5.4 indicate that differences in population growth explain a small part of the global changes both for the world as a whole and for the world excluding SSA. Most of the rise in the Gini coefficient is imputable to the 'growth effect'.

Increasing global and intraregional dispersion in the distribution of IMR

Table 5.5 presents the trend of the coefficient of variation and of the Gini coefficient of the population-weighted regional and global IMR distributions for the years 1960, 1970, 1980, 1990 and 2000. The table confirms that, because of country differences in rates of IMR reduction (Table 5.2), the coefficient of variation and Gini index of the global distribution of IMR have shown a clear upward trend from 1980 onward, while during the prior two decades there was only a modest increase. This trend is robust, if in a slightly attenuated way, to the removal of SSA and Eastern Europe from the sample. This means that the gains in IMR recorded during the last two decades have been distributed in an increasingly unequal way across countries and that several of them have been left behind.

Divergence in the global distribution of IMR is found also when the analysis is conducted on unweighted data. Removing SSA from the sample does not alter visibly this result (bottom of Table 5.5). Thus, also in this case, SSA accounts for part of the rise in IMR divergence but not for its entirety. Other forces are hampering the decline of IMR in several regions.

Rising inequality in the distribution of IMR since 1980 is evident also in MENA, South Asia, East Asia and Latin America. In the first three of these regions, the fastest increase in intraregional divergence in IMR took place between 1990 and 2000, a period characterized by slow and volatile growth, mounting income inequality and stagnant or declining coverage of key public health programmes in

Table 5.5 Coefficient of variation and Gini coefficient of the intraregional and global distribution of IMR

	Coefficient of variation (population-weighted values)					Gini coefficient (population-weighted values)				
	1960	1970	1980	1990	2000	1960	1970	1980	1990	2000
East Asia and Pacific (22)	0.31*	0.28	0.38	0.39	0.46	15.2*	12.5	18.4	17.1	17.8
L. America and Caribbean (27)	0.26	0.26	0.34	0.38	0.40	14.2	13.8	18.0	19.9	19.7
Middle East and N. Africa (20)	0.21	0.26	0.29	0.37	0.56	10.6	13.5	15.6	20.3	28.4
SSA (45)	0.24	0.23	0.25	0.28	0.25	12.8	13.0	13.9	15.3	13.8
South Asia (8)	0.09	0.11	0.13	0.17	0.27	2.50	4.0	4.4	5.3	8.8
Eastern Europe and C. Asia (26)	0.57	0.78	0.68	0.60	0.61	28.5	38.8	33.8	31.9	32.9
Western Europe (18)	0.37	0.35	0.26	0.14	0.18	19.0	17.5	12.6	6.5	9.4
North America (2)	n.a.	n.a.	n.a.	n.a.	n.a.	n.a.	n.a.	n.a.	n.a.	n.a.
World (168)	0.41*	0.43	0.51	0.57	0.64	22.2*	24.0	29.0	33.1	35.1
World excl. SSA (123)	0.42*	0.44	0.53	0.55	0.61	22.6*	24.3	30.1	30.5	32.6
World excl. SSA & EECA (97)	0.39*	0.41	0.51	0.54	0.60	20.4*	22.4	28.8	29.7	32.1
Memo item: *unweighted values*										
World (168)	0.54*	0.61	0.71	0.82	0.90	30.2*	35.1	39.9	44.8	48.8
World excl. SSA (123)	0.58*	0.67	0.77	0.85	0.96	32.9*	37.3	41.5	44.5	48.3

Notes: * These values are influenced by the famine that hit China during the 1958–61 'Great Leap Forward'. The number of countries in each area is in parenthesis. The population of the countries included in this analysis represents over 99 per cent of the world infants population.
Source: Based on World Bank (2004).

favour of children. The exception to this rule are the two 'crisis regions' of Eastern Europe and SSA, both of which show fluctuating trends characterized by a 'down- ward convergence' in IMR in the 1980s and 1990s, as in both regions the worst performance was recorded in countries with already fairly low IMR levels. In con- trast, the distribution of national IMRs improved steadily in Western Europe (save for a blip over 1990–2000 that disappears when using unweighted data) confirm- ing the findings about the policy-driven equalization of health wellbeing in the region (Micklewright and Stewart 1999).

To conclude, the analysis of IMR convergence confirms – more markedly than in the case of 100-LEB – that the recent global and intraregional health gains were distributed in an increasingly less egalitarian way, particularly over the 1990s. This conclusion is robust to the choice of different inequality and health indicators, and to the weighting of national indicators by means of appropriate populations.

Trends in the within-country distribution of health wellbeing

This kind of analysis is made possible by the increase in the number of countries[12] with at least two demographic and health surveys[13] over the last 20 years. These surveys permit, in principle, assessments to be carried out of changes in health dif- ferentials on the basis of several indicators. Information gaps, however, limit such choice and, for this reason, the analysis will focus exclusively on IMR[14] differen- tials for children belonging to different quintiles of the income distribution or residing in urban versus rural areas. Analysis of changes in IMR differentials by level of education of the mother is possible in principle but is biased by the under- sampling of highly educated mothers, and is thus omitted from the analysis.

Trends in IMR differentials by income level

As shown in the literature (see earlier section regarding literature on changes in health wellbeing), DHS now permit the estimation of the mortality risk of infants ranked by an 'asset index' that approximates household income. In this regard, Table 5.6 presents the values of IMR at two different points in time for 16 devel- oping countries, both for the sample's average and for the bottom and top quintile of the household asset distribution. The table provides also two measures of dis- persion, that is, the interquintile ratio (IQR), the ratio of the IMR of children belonging to the bottom and top quintiles of the asset distribution, and the concentration coefficient (CC) of the same distribution. While the former index captures changes in the tails of the IMR distribution, the latter is more sensitive to changes affecting the three central quintiles.

The evidence presented in Table 5.6 shows that average IMR fell over time in 12 of the 16 countries analyzed, stagnated in one and worsened in three. Progress in average IMR, however, was accompanied in 60 per cent of the cases by a rise in IMR inequality indexes that are used here jointly as they provide different infor- mation about health inequality.[15]

A cross-tabulation of changes in average IMR and IMR inequality (Table 5.7) fur- ther shows that in many instances an average IMR improvement was accompanied

Table 5.6 Trends in IMR and IMR differentials for 16 developing countries, 1990s and early 2000s

Country (and survey years)	First period (early 1990s)				Second period (late 1990s or early 2000s)				Change in inter quintile ratio	Change in concentration coefficient
	Total IMR	1st Q IMR	5th Q IMR	1st/5th Ratio	Total IMR	1st Q IMR	5th Q IMR	1st/5th Ratio		
Turkey (1993, 1998)	68.3	99.9	25.4	3.9	48.4	68.3	29.8	2.3	decline	decline
Kazakhstan (1995, 1999)	40.7	39.2	35.1	1.1	54.9	67.6	42.3	1.6	rise	rise
Colombia (1995, 2000)	30.8	40.8	16.2	2.5	24.4	32.0	17.6	1.8	decline	rise
Guatemala (1995, 1998)	57.2	56.9	35.0	1.6	49.1	58.0	39.2	1.5	decline	constant
Haiti (1994–95, 2000)	87.1	97.3	74.3	1.3	89.4	99.5	97.2	1.0	decline	decline
Nicaragua (1997–98, 2001)	45.2	50.7	25.8	1.9	35.3	49.6	16.3	3.0	rise	rise
Peru (1996, 2000)	49.9	78.3	19.5	4.0	43.2	63.5	13.9	4.6	rise	–
Egypt (1995, 2000)	72.9	109.7	31.8	3.4	54.7	75.6	29.6	2.6	decline	decline
Bangladesh (1996–97, 1999–2000)	89.6	96.5	56.6	1.7	79.7	92.9	57.9	1.6	decline	rise
India (1992–93, 1999)	86.3	109.2	44.0	2.5	73.0	96.5	38.1	2.5	constant	–
Nepal (1996, 2001)	93.0	96.3	63.9	1.5	77.2	85.5	53.2	1.6	rise	rise
Cameroon (1991, 1998)	80.3	103.9	51.2	2.0	79.8	108.4	55.8	1.9	decline	–
Ghana (1993, 1998)	74.7	77.5	45.8	1.7	61.2	72.7	26.0	2.8	rise	rise
Malawi (1992, 2000)	136.1	141.2	106.1	1.3	112.5	131.5	86.4	1.5	rise	rise
Mali (1995, 2001)	133.5	151.4	93.2	1.6	126.2	137.2	89.9	1.5	decline	rise
Uganda (1995, 2000–01)	86.1	109.0	63.2	1.7	89.4	105.7	60.2	1.8	rise	–

Note: The IMRs are calculated over the ten years preceding the survey.

Source: Based on data provided by the World Bank, Health, Nutrition, Population and Poverty Division (www. worldbank.org/hnp).

Table 5.7 Cross tabulation of changes in average IMR versus the interquartile ratio (IQR) and concentration coefficient (CC) for 26 inequality changes concerning 16 countries

	Falling IMR inequality	Constant IMR inequality	Rising IMR inequality
Average improvement in IMR	Turkey IQR, Turkey CC Colombia IQR Guatemala IQR Egypt IQR, Egypt CC Bangladesh IQR Mali IQR	Guatemala CC India IQR	Colombia CC Nicaragua IQR, Nicaragua CC Peru IQR, Bangladesh CC Nepal IQR, Nepal CC Ghana IQR, Ghana CC Malawi IQR, Malawi CC Mali CC
Average stagnation in IMR	Cameroon IQR		
Average worsening in IMR	Haiti IQR, Haiti CC		Kazakhstan IQR Kazakhstan CC Uganda IQR

Note: Changes of less than 4 per cent are assumed to indicate that the variable remained constant.

Source: Based on the the data report in Table 5.6.

by growing or unchanged IMR inequality. The upper right area of Table 5.7 shows, for instance, that in 12 cases concerning eight countries most of the IMR decline benefited children from higher quintiles. In three cases concerning two countries IMR inequality worsened, as expected, in parallel with a rise in average IMR, while in another three IMR inequality fell despite a rise in IMR. These results confirm the findings of Minujin and Delamonica (2003) for the mid-1980s and mid-1990s about a widespread rise in U5MR inequality despite a fall in the mean.

Trends in IMR differentials by rural vs urban residence

In this case the rural–urban IMR differentials were calculated on DHS surveys spanning the period 1985–99. DHS analysts normally compute IMR differentials over a ten-year period so as to enlarge the sample and reduce the estimation error. This procedure has the disadvantage, however, of precluding practically all analyses of changes in IMR levels and differentials for an entire decade. For this reason, the IMR differentials were computed for five-year periods so as to be able to capture the changes in IMR over the 1990s, and because when a longer period is chosen there is a higher risk that the mothers included in the sample are age-selected and that recall errors will be larger. The decision to compute IMR differentials for five-year periods, however, reduces the sample size and may affect the stability of IMR estimates. As in other cases, the data may also be affected by errors common in this kind of survey, such as omission of registrations, misreporting of age, recall error and so on. Be that as it may, the analysis was conducted assigning each survey to four sub-periods 1985–90, 1991–95, 1996–2000 and 2001–03 (Table 5.8).

Table 5.8 shows that in the mid to late 1980s, the majority of the SSA countries had fairly high average IMR but moderate rural–urban gap, ranging between 1.03 and 1.5. Differentials were somewhat more pronounced in Brazil, where the rural–urban IMR ratio exceeded 1.8. In many cases, the changes observed between the 1980s and 1990s point to an exacerbation of such differentials though in some cases the gap narrowed. Altogether, in 13 cases out of the 26 sample countries the rural–urban IMR ratio worsened between the first and last survey, in four it remained broadly unchanged and in nine it narrowed. In Indonesia the rural–urban gap worsened despite a decline in the nationwide IMR, while the opposite was true in Bangladesh and the Philippines. The three Latin American countries in the sample show moderate deterioration or stagnation between the initial and final year. As a whole, the trends observed in SSA do not permit identification of clear relations between IMR reduction and rural–urban IMR convergence. Generally speaking, rural areas continue to be disadvantaged with respect to infant health. In all cases, a greater focus on rural areas would have allowed achievement of a faster overall decline in IMR – and a more balanced distribution of health wellbeing.

Also in this case, a cross-tabulation of changes in average IMR versus the rural–urban IMR differentials in Table 5.9 shows there are many off-diagonal observations. In fact, 11 countries located above the main diagonal recorded worse-than-expected changes in IMR differentials, i.e. stable or rising IMR differential on occasion of average improvements, or a worsening of this ratio on occasion of a stagnation of average IMR. In contrast, there were only six countries below the main diagonal showing better-than-expected results. All this points to a comparatively high frequency of

Table 5.8 IMR national level and rural–urban IMR ratio in selected countries

	1985–90		1991–95		1996–2000		2001–03	
	IMR	R/U	IMR	R/U	IMR	R/U	IMR	R/U
Benin					98	1.19	94	1.55
Burkina Faso			103	1.56	114	1.79		
Cameroon			67	1.10	83	1.39		
Côte d'Ivoire			91	1.21	117	1.42		
Ghana	89	1.33	71	1.31	60	1.61	68	1.31
Kenya			65	1.22	68	1.38	80	1.31
Madagascar			98	1.47	100	1.19		
Malawi			143	1.11	110	1.62		
Mali	123	1.54			130	1.49	128	1.25
Niger			136	1.67	130	1.77		
Nigeria	96	1.25			83	1.26		
Rwanda			88	0.97	114	1.51		
Senegal			71	1.68	74	1.54		
Tanzania			95	0.76	93	1.29	103	1.05
Togo	87	1.08			84	1.32		
Uganda	108	1.03	86	1.15			92	1.78
Zambia			111	1.32	116	1.09	100	1.21
Zimbabwe	52	1.51	55	1.3	70	1.15		
Brazil	75	1.82			40	1.86		
Colombia	35	1.02	29	1.22	22	1.12		
Dominican Rep.	70	1.03	44	1.46	47	1.28	32	1.15
Egypt			64	1.73	45	1.34	39	1.41
India			81	1.52	78	1.57		
Bangladesh			91	1.52	84	1.11	68	1.07
Philippines			36	1.46	37	1.27		
Indonesia			71	1.47	47	1.52	35	1.63

Source: Based on selected DHS.

Table 5.9 Cross-tabulation of IMR changes in relation to changes in the rural–urban (r/u) IMR ratio in selected developing countries, mid–late 1980s to early 2000s

	Falling r/u IMR ratio	Constant r/u IMR ratio	Increasing r/u IMR ratio	
Average improvement in IMR	Zambia, Egypt, Bangladesh	Ghana, Nigeria, Brazil	Indonesia, Malawi, Uganda, Colombia, Dominican Rep.	11
Average stagnation in IMR	Madagascar, Mali, Philippines, Senegal, Tanzania	India	Benin, Togo, Niger	9
Average worsening in IMR	Zimbabwe		Burkina Faso, Cameroon, Kenya, Côte d'Ivoire, Rwanda,	6
	9	4	13	26

Note: Changes of less than 4 per cent are taken to indicate that the variable has remained constant.

Source: Based on selected DHS.

deterioration in the urban – rural IMR ratio explained by the faster progress realized in urban areas and revealing the limits of location-neutral policies.

Conclusions and indications for further research

The data problems mentioned throughout this chapter suggest caution in interpreting the above results. Yet, the above discussion points to a few important conclusions, some fairly robust, some still tentative. To start with, over the last 20 years the rate of improvement in health wellbeing slowed down in relation to that recorded in the 1960s and 1970s. In developing and transitional countries, the slowdown was most pronounced in the 1990s. However, there are important exceptions to this rule (such as MENA and Latin America in the 1980s) that need to be investigated in greater detail to identify the factors that permitted continuing progress in health wellbeing in spite of flat or negative growth and, in the case of Latin America, rising inequality. Yet, the slowdown in rates of progress was sufficiently general to suggest the effect of some systemic factors. Indeed, the slowdown is robust to the removal of SSA and Eastern Europe from the sample, thus invalidating the viewpoint that attributes the current slowdown to the difficulties of the transition in Eastern Europe and the spread of AIDS, civil conflicts and economic stagnation in SSA. Thus, though with some exceptions and differences in time profiles, the slowdown in aggregate rates of improvement in health wellbeing in the 1980s and 1990s seems to be fairly general.

Second, there is clear evidence that the between-country distribution of health wellbeing has become more skewed. This conclusion holds also after removing SSA and Eastern Europe from the sample. In addition, with the exception of Western Europe and East Asia (in the case of 100-LEB) and of Western Europe and Eastern Europe (in the case of IMR), the intraregional distribution of health gains has become increasingly less egalitarian. These are important conclusions as, so far, there is little agreement in the literature on the wellbeing convergence over the last two decades. The chapter also suggests that where public policy actively aimed at reducing wellbeing differentials, as in the EU, health wellbeing converged steadily.

Finally, the within-country distribution of health wellbeing by an asset index and rural–urban location appears to have worsened in about 50–60 per cent of the cases analyzed. Such trends need, however, to be confirmed on a longer time period and bigger samples but seem to corroborate the results mentioned at the beginning about the worsening of the income distribution.

What are the factors behind these changes in health wellbeing? In view of data problems and the level of aggregation of the analysis, the points made below are at times speculative and must be taken as hypotheses to be tested by detailed analyses rather than firm conclusions on causality. To start with, there is no doubt that the spread of HIV/AIDS affected in a major way trends in IMR and 100-LEB in SSA and a few Caribbean countries and that – barring new breakthroughs in medical research and drugs availability – HIV/AIDS will continue to affect negatively health wellbeing trends in these countries in the years ahead. It is important to note in this regard that, as in the 1990s, future AIDS-related mortality will be influenced by the way globalization (and in particular the TRIPS agreement) will affect the cost and transfer of health technology (anti-retrovirals in particular) in the areas affected by the pandemic. As noted by Deaton (2004), if this transfer is delayed or is too costly, mortality differentials across regions will continue to diverge because of these policies.

Yet, it is not possible to place all the blame for the unsatisfactory health performance of the last decade on HIV/AIDS, especially in countries with low HIV prevalence but a record of slow health improvements and growing health inequality. In this regard, a second possible cause of the slow health improvement and growing divergence in health wellbeing are changes in health spending and key health programmes. The debate about globalization has often highlighted the risk posed to revenue collection by liberal tax reforms, tax competition among developing countries and the globalization-driven outsourcing and informalization of the economy. Yet, the evidence on revenue collection and public expenditure is mixed. While there are examples of countries (such as China and the economies in transition) that restricted public health expenditure and access to health services, in others (from MENA and Latin America) public health expenditure increased or remained constant at relatively high levels. However, public health expenditure may be too noisy a variable to affect mortality rates. In contrast, an expansion of key public health programmes such as child immunization, oral rehydration, provision of antibiotics and pregnancy control, can deliver important health gains even during periods of stagnant health expenditure. Symmetrically, a stagnation or decline in the coverage of such programmes (as often observed in the 1990s for immunization) may have affected adversely IMR and LEB even in the presence of an expanding health budget.

Third, mortality has also been affected by a rising wave of local conflicts and natural disasters. Those of Afghanistan, Angola, Bosnia, Burundi, Cambodia, Ethiopia, Guatemala, Iraq, North Korea, Rwanda, Somalia, Sri Lanka and Sudan are just a few of the 50 or so humanitarian crises in which death rates soared markedly. Yet, only crude estimates of the health impact of such crises are available and only in few cases is it possible to fully capture the impact of these tragic events on mortality trends, as existing databases generally underreport their impact.

Fourth, changes in the structure and stability of households – and in social cohesion more generally – may have also affected, if more subtly, current health trends. The traditional family has in fact been eroded in many places, thus exposing its members to greater health risks, as suggested by micro studies that identify a greater death risk of children, elderly and adults living in incomplete families. In this regard, the last 20 years have seen a rise in the number of people living in incomplete households because of divorce, separation, lone parenthood, singlehood, migration and premature death of the parents or of a spouse. Single-parent families represent 10–15 per cent of all OECD families with dependent children and a higher percentage in Latin America, the Caribbean and parts of South East Asia. Such a trend has surfaced even in China, where traditional values usually left no space for such types of family arrangement. In turn, in the HIV-affected countries the number of orphans exposed to risk of non-AIDS-related mortality has risen well above the level that can be handled through extended family arrangements. In other countries, such as Bosnia and Ethiopia, war and ethnic conflicts have caused a sharp increase in the number of incomplete families. Meanwhile in Russia, Moldova and other economies in transition, the number of biological or social orphans has risen rapidly because of soaring parental mortality, migration and child abandonment.

Last but not least, a host of empirical data and theoretical arguments suggest that health trends have been affected by the slow or negative growth and soaring income inequality observed over the last 20 years in many developing and transition countries that adopted botched liberalization and globalization policies such as loose bank deregulation, premature external liberalization and regressive tax reforms. Indeed, both theory and empirical evidence show that slower growth, greater income inequality and rising volatility affect health and health inequality.[16] The precise extent and mechanisms of such impact remain, however, undocumented in most cases. This is a priority area for research in which existing theories linking growth and income inequality to health and health inequality have to be tested on enlarged datasets and time periods. Perhaps, this new research will help bringing about a more humane globalization, promoting faster health progress and health convergence over the next decades.

Notes

Work on this study by Giovanni Andrea Cornia was carried out in the context and with the financial support of the project 'Health and Social Upheaval' sponsored by the MacArthur Foundation. The preparation of this study also benefited from earlier research conducted by the authors at the UNICEF Innocenti Research Centre for the project 'Harnessing Globalization for Children'. The views expressed herein are those of the authors, and not their respective affiliations. The authors would like to thank Stefano Morandini for his excellent research assistance and participants to the UNU-WIDER jubilee conference, held in Helsinki on 17–18 June 2005 for useful comments on a prior version of this study.

1. The global growth rate of GDP per capita slowed from 2.6 per cent per annum over the 1960s and 1970s (the second Golden Age of Capitalism) to 1.3 per cent over the 1980s and 1990s (the second Era of Liberalization and Globalization). Growth was particularly weak in the 1990s owing to stagnation in Europe and Japan, the collapse of the European economies in transition, the persistent difficulties faced by Latin America and sub-Saharan Africa, slow growth in the Middle East and North Africa and, to a lesser extent, the Asian financial crises. In contrast, China and India recorded rapid growth following the adoption of gradual, pragmatic and selective economic reforms.

2. Cornia (2004) suggests that income inequality rose – though by different extents and with different effects on wellbeing – in 53 of the 73 countries analyzed, including China, India, Indonesia, the USA, Japan and Russia. Only in nine small and medium-sized countries inequality appears to have fallen, and only in 16 it remained constant. These country-based results are confirmed by aggregate studies (Bourguignon and Morrisson 2002).

3. Results depend crucially on the inequality index chosen, the period of analysis considered, the 'correct measurement' of the Chinese rate of growth, the weighing of results by population size, whether the comparison is carried out on the basis of GDP per capita (derived from the national accounts) or disposable income per capita (derived from household surveys), and whether the conversion of national GDP values into dollars is done by means of the market or PPP exchange rate. Results depend also on whether the country distributions of income are computed by assigning the same income per capita

to all citizens, relying on a synthetic statistic such as the Gini coefficient, or building the distribution of income on the basis of micro-data. Finally, results depend on the treatment of large dualistic countries such as China and India, and the inclusion of the 'special case' of China in the calculation of between-country inequality. In contrast, results point to a clear North – South polarization when between-country inequality is assessed not as a *ratio* of the countries' respective GDPs per capita but as their *absolute difference*. This aspect of income polarization has, however, been neglected by most of the literature.

4. The 'asset index' is used to proxy household wealth and income and is used to stratify households into quintiles. It is constructed following the procedure described in Filmer *et al.* (1998) that weights the possession of certain household durables (such as radios and bicycles), the quality of dwellings (as revealed by the type of roof and floor) and access to different kinds of water and sanitation facilities.

5. See UNPD (2002).

6. Such an upper bound is arbitrary, as the maximum attainable life duration varies over time and across countries with the development of medical technologies and other factors. Over the medium term, however, it is undeniable that we face some kind of immutable genetic maximum that cannot be changed by an increase in resources or medical services. While the choice of 100 is arbitrary, the results of the analysis would not change much if instead an upper bound of, say, 90 or 110 years had been chosen (see later).

7. The regional averages and the measures of dispersion presented in the study are always weighted by the appropriate populations (live births for IMR, the whole population for 100-LEB, etc.). Trends in the unweighted averages and inequality measures are mostly omitted for reasons of space. As expected, they show a greater variability than the weighted ones, though they broadly confirm the trends identified above.

8. The rates of improvement are sensitive to the choice of the upper bound. Yet, the conclusions do not change significantly when the arbitrary upper bound chosen is 90, so as to generate the variable 90-LEB, that is 'the life years lost in relation to the maximum attainable LEB of 90'.

9. The U5MR analysis is available from the authors. Its results support the conclusions of the IMR analysis.

10. In contrast, in MENA the public health expenditure/GDP ratio remained at a high 4–5 per cent of GDP during the entire decade. In addition, the region recorded a massive rise in female education made possible by generous allocations of public funds to education starting from the 1970s.

11. The coefficient of variation (CV) is the ratio of standard deviation to average

$$CV = \frac{\sqrt{\sum_i (y_i - \bar{y})^2 n_i}}{\sum_i y_i n_i}.$$

The Gini-type index used for the study of IMR disparity is

$$GINI_{IMR} = \left[\sum_{i=0}^{N-1} (y_{i+1} + y_i)(x_{i+1} + x_i) \right] - 1$$

where the countries (*i*) are ordered by decreasing IMR level, *y* is the cumulated proportion of infant deaths and *x* is the cumulated proportion of the infant population. These two indicators of dispersion are scale-invariant, they are easy to interpreter and are among the most used indicators in the economic literature on disparities. This is an important characteristic in the view of a multidimensional analysis of disparities in well-being. Moreover, the Gini index is increasingly used in the study of health inequalities and some adaptation to health indicators have been elaborated (e.g. for IMR).

12. The countries with at least two DHS surveys are, at this date, about 40. The 26 countries included in this analysis are Benin, Burkina Faso, Cameroon, Côte d'Ivoire, Ghana, Kenya, Madagascar, Malawi, Mali, Niger, Nigeria, Rwanda, Senegal, Tanzania, Togo, Uganda, Zambia, Zimbabwe, Brazil, Colombia, Dominican Republic, Egypt, India, Bangladesh, the Philippines and Indonesia. The size of the DHS samples vary considerably not only between countries (ranging from 92,486 households coverage by the 1998/99 DHS for India to 1,381 households of the 1999 DHS in the Dominican Republic) but also between different rounds of DHS in the same country (for example, in Malawi the households covered by the survey were 2,798 in 1996 and 14,213 in 2000).

13. DHS are large-scale nationally representative household surveys of varying sample size. This analysis used data on children based on interview of women aged 15–49 or 15–44 containing information about births and surviving children of 60 (or 36) months of age at the time of the survey.

14. The IMRs used in the analysis of differentials by rural–urban are calculated dividing the number of infant deaths under one year of age by the number of births in the five complete years preceding the survey, considering also half of the deaths occurred at age 12 months, which strictly speaking is included in the second year of life, but which probably occurred in the first year. In contrast, the mortality differentials by the asset index are computed on the ten years preceding the survey.

15. The worsening of IMR differentials was more frequent in the case of the concentration coefficient.

16. Much is known about the relation between income inequality and health inequality. To start with, it is generally accepted that, as the relation between income per capita and life expectancy is concave, an increase in income inequality will – *ceteris paribus* – cause a fall in life expectancy among the poor and middle class bigger than the gain in life expectancy among the rich. Second, high inequality reduces access to healthcare by the poor both because these have a lower income to buy it in the market and as high inequality reduces the state capacity to tax the elites and so provide subsidized health services. Third, there is evidence that high inequality raises the crime rate and the number of violent deaths. Fourth, there is initial evidence that, at least in advanced countries and transitional economies, high inequality leads to loss in social cohesion that affects the ability of communities to undertake collective action, to a hierarchal organization of work causing loss of control and worse health outcomes, and to rising psychosocial stress. Finally, there is considerable, though not universally accepted, evidence that high-income inequality affects health status via a decline in GDP growth. Indeed, most theories and empirical analyses suggest that lower growth GDP would result because of low investment in human capital, increased macroeconomic disequilibria and balance of payment instability, decreasing returns to capital, rising social instability, declining work incentives and growing policy distortions and government failures.

References

Black, D., J. Morris, C. Smith and P. Townsend (1980) *Inequality in Health: Report of a Research Working Group (The Black Report)*, London: Department of Health and Social Security.

Bobak, M. and M. Marmot (1996) 'East-West Mortality Divide and its Potential Explanations: Proposed Research Agenda', *British Medical Journal*, 312: 421–3.

Bourguignon, F. and C. Morrisson (2002) 'Inequality Among World Citizens: 1820–1992', *American Economic Review*, 92, 4: 727–44.

Caldwell, J.C. (1979) 'Education as a Factor in Mortality Decline: an Examination of Nigerian Data', *Population Studies*, 33, 3: 395–413.

Cornia, G.A. (ed.) (2004) *Inequality, Growth, and Poverty in an Era of Liberalization and Globalization*, Oxford and New York: Oxford University Press for UNU-WIDER.

Cornia, G.A. and R. Paniccià (eds) (2000) *The Mortality Crisis of Transitional Economies*, Oxford: Oxford University Press for UNU-WIDER.

Cornia, G.A. and F. Zagonari (2002) 'An Econometric Investigation of Changes in IMR and U5MR in AIDS Affected Countries During the Last Twenty Years', Mimeo, Florence: UNICEF-IRC.

Deaton, A. (2004) 'Health in an Age of Globalization', *NBER Working Papers* 10669, Cambridge, MA: National Bureau of Economic Research.

Deaton, A. and J. Drèze (2002) 'Poverty and Inequality in India: A Re-Examination', *Centre for Development Economics Working Papers* 107, Delhi: Delhi School of Economics.

Dollar, D. (2001) 'Is Globalization Good for Your Health?', *Bulletin of the World Health Organization,* 79, 9: 827–33.

Filmer, D., E.M. King and L. Pritchett (1998) 'Gender Disparity in South Asia: Comparison between and within Countries', *Policy Research Group Working Papers* 1867, Washington, DC: World Bank.

Fox, J.W. (1998) 'Gaining Ground. World Wellbeing 1950–95', *USAID Evaluation Special Study Report* 79, Washington, DC: USAID.

Goesling, B. and G. Firebaugh (2004) 'The Trend in International Health Inequality', *Population and Development Review,* 30, 1: 131–46.

Gwatkin, D.R. (2000) 'Health Inequalities and the Health of the Poor: What Do We Know? What Can We Do?', *Bulletin of the World Health Organization,* 78, 10: 3–18.

Jhamba, T. (1999) 'Regional Variation in Childhood Mortality in Zimbabwe', *Geography,* 84, 4: 319–30.

McMichael, A., M. McKee, V. Skolnikov and T. Valkonen (2004) 'Mortality Trends and Setbacks: Global Convergence or Divergence?', *The Lancet,* 363, 9415: 1155–9.

Meyer, D. (2001) 'Convergence Clubs in Cross-Country Life Expectancy Dynamics', *WIDER Discussion Paper* 2001/134, Helsinki: UNU-WIDER.

Micklewright, J. and K. Stewart (1999) 'Is the Wellbeing of Children Converging in the European Union?', *Economic Journal,* 109, 459: F692–714.

Minujin, A. and E. Delamonica (2003) 'Mind the Gap! Widening Child Mortality Disparities', *Journal of Human Development,* 4, 3: 397–418.

Murthi, M., A.-C. Guio and J. Drèze (1995) 'Mortality, Fertility and Gender Bias in India: A District-Level Analysis', *Population and Development Review,* 21, 4: 745–82.

Pradhan, M., D.E. Sahn and S.D. Younger (2001) 'Decomposing World Health Inequality', *Tinbergen Institute Discussion Paper* 01–091/2, Amsterdam: Tinbergen Institute.

Preston, S.H. (1976) *Mortality Patterns in National Populations,* New York: Academic Press.

Rutstein, S.O. (2000) 'Factors Associated with Trends in Infant and Child Mortality in Developing Countries During the 1990s', *Bulletin of the World Health Organization,* 78, 10: 1256–70.

Sastry, N. (1996) 'Community Characteristics, Individual and Household Attributes, and Child Survival in Brazil', *Demography,* 33, 2: 211–29.

UN (2004) *Handbook on the Collection of Fertility and Mortality Data,* New York: United Nations Department of Economic and Social Affairs.

UNPD (United Nations Population Division) (2002) *World Population Prospects: the 2000 Revision,* New York: United Nations.

Wagstaff, A. (2000) 'Socioeconomic Inequalities in Child Mortality: Comparison across Nine Developing Countries', *Bulletin of the World Health Organization,* 78, 1: 19–29.

Wagstaff, A. and M. Cleason (2004) *Raising to the Challenge,* Washington, DC: World Bank.

Wilkinson, R.G. (1996) *Unhealthy Societies: The Afflictions of Inequality,* London and New York: Routledge.

Wilson, C. (2001) 'On the Scale of Global Demographic Convergence', *Population and Development Review,* 27, 1: 155–71.

World Bank (2004) *World Development Indicators 2004 CD-Rom,* Washington, DC: World Bank.

World Bank (2005) *World Development Report: Equity and Development,* Washington, DC: Oxford University Press for World Bank.

WHO (2005) *World Health Report: Make Every Mother and Child Count,* Geneva: World Health Organization.

Zhang, X. and R. Kanbur (2003) 'Spatial Inequality in Education and Health in China', Mimeo, International Food Policy Research Institute, Washington, DC.

6
Inequality and Corruption

Eric M. Uslaner

Introduction

Successful (or well-ordered) democracies are marked by high levels of trust in people and in government, low levels of economic inequality, and honesty and fairness in the public sphere. Trust in people, as the literature on social capital has shown, is essential for forming bonds among diverse groups in society (Uslaner 2002). Trust in government is essential for political stability and compliance with the law. Corruption robs the economy of funds and leads to less faith in government (perhaps also to less faith in fellow citizens) and thus lower compliance with the law. And institutions seen as biased (unfair) cannot secure compliance and may exacerbate inequalities in society. Transition countries are short on both trust in people and trust in government (Badescu *et al.* 2003; Hayoz 2003). Under totalitarian regimes, there was little sense of social solidarity. The state was feared rather than legitimate (Howard 2003). Transition countries are also lacking in honest and fair institutions. And they have more than their share of corruption and an underground economy. Many citizens have little faith in their leaders or their fellow citizens.

Democratic governance is more than a set of institutional arrangements, a legislature, an executive and courts. Establishing a constitution is the easy part. 'Making democracy work' is the more difficult task (Putnam 1993). Democratic governments need legitimacy (trust in institutions and their leaders) to enforce their laws. They also need an 'underbelly' of social solidarity to foster a co-operative spirit of tolerance and compromise (*Ibid.*; Uslaner 2002). Legislators must enact laws that people will obey; courts must enforce the laws impartially; and citizens must provide the supportive culture that demands both good governance and justice. Citizens must trust the government and each other and they must support the development of a market economy.

Under communism, all citizens were theoretically equal and the overall distribution of income was, in comparison with other countries, fairly equitable.[1] Transition led to increases, often sharp, in inequality and this threatened both the social order and the legitimacy of government. I shall present some aggregate analyses of the consequences of inequality among countries in transition in

Central and Eastern Europe and the former Soviet Union. However, the availability of data for my desired measures is often rather sparse, so these analyses are merely suggestive rather than conclusive. My main focus will be the social psychology of transition economies, or how people reason about the linkage between inequality, trust (in both people and government), corruption and outlooks for the future. Drawing upon a recent survey of how people think about economic inequality in one country, Romania, I shall consider whether perceptions of inequality lead to lesser social cohesion, illegitimacy for the state, perceptions of corruption and demands for transfer of wealth from the rich to the poor. At the end of the causal chain, these demands for the transfer of wealth from the rich to the poor are likely to work *against* the reduction of poverty and inequality. Economic programmes that focus benefits on one class may lead to persistent inequality and create their own social strains. Hence there is an inequality trap.

My concerns in this chapter are to show how economic inequality and corruption inhibit political legitimacy (trust in government), social solidarity (trust in people) and support for a market economy. First, I show some aggregate results for transition countries that support my general arguments about the deleterious effects of inequality and corruption. Then I outline a more general framework that posits government performance and optimism for the future as the foundations for a more trusting citizenry. Performance and optimism in turn depend upon perceptions of corruption and rising inequality and I show support for these arguments using a survey of Romanians in October 2003. Neither confidence in government nor trust in people leads to greater support for a market economy (measured in the survey by opposition to limiting the incomes of the rich). Belief in the market is most directly tied to perceptions of corruption (and to a lesser extent to growing inequality).

I estimate a simultaneous equation model (by two-stage least squares) of government performance on the quality of life, whether the country is moving in the right or wrong direction, trust in other people and in government and whether the government should limit the incomes of the rich. I find that people who perceive increasing income inequality are less likely to approve of government performance and to trust other people and are more likely to support limits on incomes of the rich. More generally, when people see the government as corrupt and the country moving in the wrong direction, social solidarity (trust in other people) and confidence in the state will decline – and there will be increasing demands for curtailing market forces and placing limits on incomes. Most notably, people are largely inured to the petty corruption of everyday life; it is larger-scale corruption – by business people and especially government officials – that threatens social solidarity and support for the state. Rising inequality threatens economic inequality in at least two ways. First, growing inequities directly threaten the society's social fabric. Second, when people attribute growing inequality to rising corruption (as they do), this threatens the legitimacy of the state and the development of a market economy.

Rising inequality is not the only problem facing countries in transition. Persistent corruption is also problematic. Like inequality, it tears apart the social fabric and leads to a lack of confidence in government and demands for redistribution of income from the 'dishonest' rich to the powerless poor. Corruption also makes people less likely to be optimistic for the future. When elites rob the public purse and when people must help elites to line their own pockets (by extra payments for routine services), ordinary citizens will have negative views of government performance in improving the quality of life and will have less hope that the country is heading in the right direction. It is 'elite corruption' rather than dishonesty among ordinary citizens that leads people to become pessimistic about the future, government performance, and even whether to trust each other.

A puzzle: there ought to be a link between rising income inequality and corruption. Corruption transfers resources from the mass public to the elite, and generally from the poor to the rich (see especially Onishi and Banerjee 2001). It acts as an extra tax on citizens, leaving less money for public expenditures (Mauro 1997: 7; Tanzi 1998: 582–3). Corrupt governments have less money to spend on their own projects, pushing down the salaries of public employees. These lower-level staffers will be more likely to extort funds from the public purse. Government employees in corrupt societies will spend more time lining their own pockets than serving the public. Corruption leads to lower rates of economic growth.[2] Yet, in both the aggregate data and the survey, the link between inequality and corruption is minimal.[3]

Inequality, social solidarity and the transition to a market democracy

The post-communist societies in Central and Eastern Europe and the former Soviet Union all underwent severe economic shocks after transition. Most people were worse off than they were under communism. As transition countries open their markets, a growing income gap is inevitable. As the security of state employment and low-cost services vanishes and as some people get rich quickly, there will inevitably be jealousy, mistrust and a loss of confidence in public institutions. The sociopsychological foundations of trust are optimism and control, which were lacking under communism. After transition, people increasingly became convinced that it was impossible to get rich honestly. Inequality makes the transition to democracy difficult because:

- Economic equality is the foundation of social solidarity (generalized trust) and trust in government. Generalized trust leads to greater investment in policies that have longer term payoffs (education spending and transfer payments), as well as more directly leading to economic growth. A weak state with an ineffective legal system cannot enforce contracts; a government that cannot produce economic growth and the promise of a brighter future will not be legitimate (Kluegel and Mason 2000b: 201).
- Unequal wealth leads people to feel less constrained about cheating others (Mauro 1997: 12) and about evading taxes (Oswiak 2003: 73; Uslaner 2003).
- Inequality leads to unequal treatment by the courts, which leads to less legitimacy for the government.

I shall present some preliminary evidence (based upon small samples) that economic inequality makes transition rocky. Every country for which there are data on changes in economic inequality, save Slovakia, showed an increase in economic inequality from 1989 to the mid-1990s (Rosser *et al.* 2000). All but Hungary of the 17 countries for which there are data had a sharp increase (from 0.3–42 per cent) in the size of the shadow economy (Schneider 2003). The greater the share of the economy beyond the reach of the state, the more difficult it will be for a government to marshal the resources to gain public confidence that the state can provide essential services. And here we get into a vicious circle. If people have no confidence that politicians can pursue policies that will lead to prosperity and economic justice, they will hide their income from the tax collector (Uslaner 2003). Overall, the average share of the shadow economy more than doubled from 1989 to 1999–2000 (from 17–38 per cent) and the average increase in the Gini index of inequality was 33 per cent.

Corruption is similarly a plague on good government. It is associated with higher rates of crime and tax evasion, closed markets, lower economic growth and less efficient government institutions (Leite and Weidemann 1999; Mauro 1997; Tanzi 1998; Uslaner 2004). Corruption is widespread in former communist countries. The mean score on the Transparency International (TI) corruption indicator for Eastern Bloc countries is more than half the size of that for the West (with higher scores indicating greater honesty). Romania is in 69th place out of 91 countries in the 2001 TI rankings. Of the 16 transition countries TI has ranked for corruption, Romania ranks 12th.

The economic psychology of transition

My focus is on how people in one transition country (Romania, October 2003) think about inequality, trust, political institutions, corruption and hope for the future. These survey results permit a much finer test of my argument about how people reason about what makes transition a success or failure.[4] Of 21 transition countries in the World Values Survey, only Moldova ranks lower than Romania.

How inequality and corruption matter

I begin with some aggregate results on how inequality matters in transition economies. I express my results simply, through graphs, because of data limitations. For some of my analyses, limited data restricts the number of cases to as few as 12, so clearly any complicated modelling is impossible. These simple results do not represent a comprehensive theoretical argument but rather a suggestive list of the consequences (and some determinants) of inequality in transition countries. My focus here is structured by the available data; I focus on the ties between inequality and optimism for the future, the perception that courts are fair and the size of the shadow economy.

Where economic equality is lower, a larger share of the public believes that they can count on success in life (see Figure 6.1). So economic equality will provide some basis of legitimacy for the state. And where I find economic inequality, I also

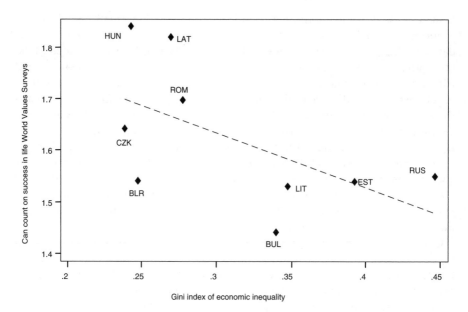

Figure 6.1   Can count on success in life by economic inequality

Note: r² = 0.326.

Source: Based on Rosser *et al.* (2000).

find a greater perception (by the elite) that courts are generally fair. In Figure 6.2, we have plotted the share of a country's business elite who believe that the courts are generally *not* fair against economic inequality. Here the relationship is stronger (r² = 0.452). Countries with more equality have stronger legal institutions that have the legitimacy to punish lawbreakers, since they are perceived as fair. Tyler (1990) argues that people obey the law when they believe that there is procedural justice. Direct experience with the courts has less to do with whether the law is obeyed than the belief of being treated fairly if brought to justice. An equal distribution of wealth goes hand-in-hand with perceptions of equal treatment before the law.[5] It is, of course, possible that the direction of the causal link could go the other way: a fair court system could lead to greater economic inequality. However, the causal chain for this argument is less clear.

There is even stronger support for the claim that a more equal distribution of wealth in transition countries leads to a lower level of flouting the law. First, I look at two related measures of the size of the unofficial economy. I find a strong relationship between Schneider's (2003) measure of the shadow economy in transition countries for 1999–2000 and the level of economic inequality in the 1990s (r² = 0.578, see Figure 6.3). For a slightly different indicator of the 'unofficial economy', I find almost as powerful a relationship – partly based upon Schneider's calculations and reported in Djankov *et al.* (2001) – (r² = 0.603, see Figure 6.4). Countries with greater disparities between the rich and the poor have larger informal sectors. This likely occurs for at least two reasons. First, the poor will find it

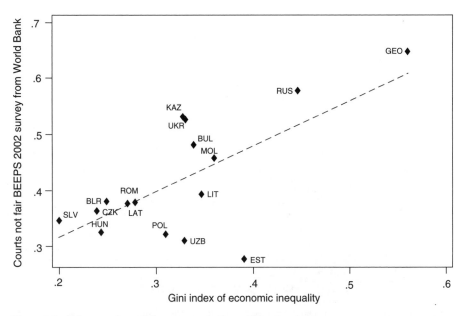

Figure 6.2 Fairness of courts by economic inequality

Note: r² = 0.452.

Source: Based on Rosser *et al*. (2000).

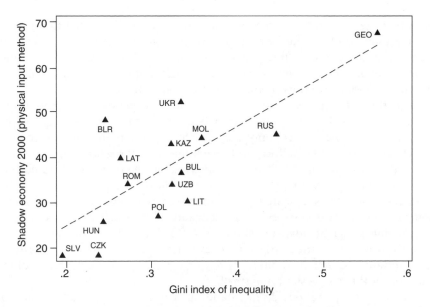

Figure 6.3 Shadow economy (physical input method) by Gini index of economic inequality

Note: r² = 0.578, N = 15.

Sources: Based on Rosser *et al*. (2000) and Schneider (2003).

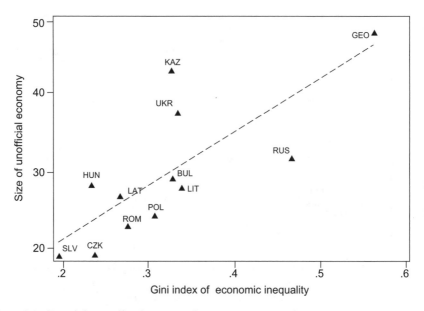

Figure 6.4   Size of the unofficial economy by economic inequality

Note: $r^2 = 0.603$.

Source: Based on Rosser *et al.* (2000).

difficult to get jobs in the formal economy and will thus be forced to forage for whatever sources of income they can get. Second, much of the unofficial economy comes from tax evasion – in countries with high levels of economic inequality, people may become wealthy (or wealthier) by evading taxation (Feld 2003). The informal economy will thus capture people at both extremes.

Most critically, changes in the level of economic inequality are strongly related to changes in the shadow economy ($r^2 = 0.356$, see Figure 6.5). As inequality has risen, so has the shadow economy. Perhaps more critical than economic inequality is the perception that political and legal influence was stacked against the ordinary citizen. Changes in the shadow economy are linked more closely to business executives' perceptions that the courts are not fair (the best surrogate for public attitudes, $r^2 = 0.580$, see Figure 6.6). We saw above that perceptions of courts not being fair are also linked to economic inequality. These views also track increases in economic inequality (data not shown, $r^2 = 0.500$, N = 16). Growing inequality clearly threatens both the ability to raise revenue and the perception that justice is tilted towards the rich. It would be nice if we could unpack the dynamics of this pattern, but the sample size is too small.

Some of my expectations do not stand up. There is no aggregate connection between inequality and generalized trust ($r^2 = 0.0006$). There is a powerful relationship between generalized trust and economic inequality over time in the USA and across nations without a legacy of communism (Uslaner 2002). I now turn to

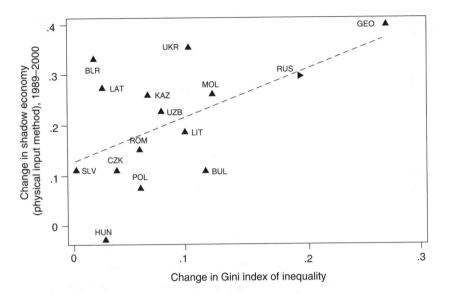

Figure 6.5 Change in shadow economy (physical input method) by change in Gini index of economic inequality

Note: r² = 0.356, N = 15.

Sources: Based on Rosser *et al.* (2000) and Schneider (2003).

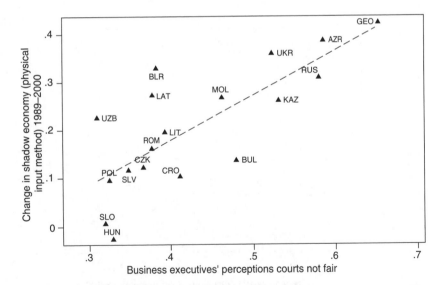

Figure 6.6 Change in shadow economy (physical input method) by business executives' perceptions of courts not fair

Note: r² = 0.580, N = 18.

Sources: Based on Schneider (2003) and BEEPS data, http://info.worldbank.org/governance/beeps/2002

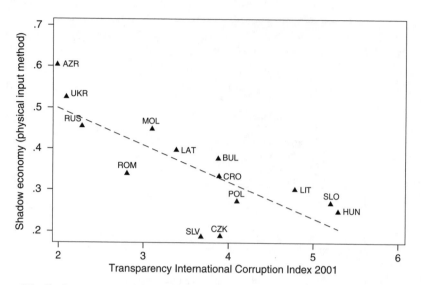

Figure 6.7 Shadow economy (physical input method) by TI Corruption Index, 2001

Note: r²=0.600, N = 14.

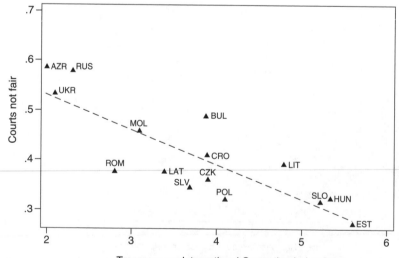

Figure 6.8 Courts not fair BEEPS 2002 survey from World Bank by TI Corruption Index, 2001

Note: r²=0.691, N = 15.

Source: Based on BEEPS data, http://info.worldbank.org/governance/keeps/2002

the survey results and here I find support for the argument that growing inequality threatens social solidarity (generalized trust) as well as for linkages with government performance and limiting the incomes of the rich.

The effects of corruption are similar (if less surprising). In societies with large unofficial economies, there is also much corruption. This link might seem trivially true, but the relationship is not as powerful as we might expect ($r^2 = 0.600$, see Figure 6.7). The shadow economy seems to be reflect activity at all levels (especially for lower-income people), while corruption points to dishonesty at the top. Corruption flourishes when the courts turn a blind eye to misdeeds, so it is hardly surprising that when corruption is strong, people believe that the courts are not fair ($r^2 = 0.691$; see Figure 6.8).

The economic psychology of transition dynamics

I use the survey[6] of the Romanian population, carried out in October 2003, to examine a complex set of relationships linking economic inequality and corruption to the success of the democratic transition. I am primarily concerned with the impacts of two of my exogenous concepts, the perceived increase (or decrease) in income inequality in 2003 compared to 1995–96 and measures of corruption on the five endogenous variables in my model. Increasing inequality and corruption are the major threats to political legitimacy, social solidarity and support for a market economy. I thus posit a causal chain from perceptions of corruption and rising inequality to less optimism for the future (country moving in the wrong direction and a negative evaluation of government performance) to governmental legitimacy (trust in political institutions), social solidarity (trust in people) and less support for a market economy (favouring limitations on incomes of the rich). In each of these models, I presume that what matters most to people is the overall performance of the economy rather than their own personal wellbeing – what political scientists call 'sociotropic' as opposed to 'pocketbook' evaluations (Kinder and Kiewiet 1979). Personal economic circumstances do have some significant effects. Yet, political legitimacy, social solidarity and support for the market depend more on overall performance than on personal wellbeing.

Perceptions of greater inequality should lead to greater pessimism for the future and less trust in others. When there is a great deal of inequality, those at the top and those at the bottom do not see the 'shared fate' that underlies the solidarity that is generalized trust (Uslaner 2002). The belief that income inequality is increasing is widespread in transition countries (Orkeny 2000: 106; Stephenson and Khakhulina 2000: 85; Vlachova 2000: 63); 91 per cent of Romanians believe that inequality increased from 1995–96 to 2003; 35 per cent believe that it has become much greater.

Corruption undermines both trust in other people and trust in government (Uslaner 2004). I distinguish between high-level corruption among people with power and money (politicians, parliamentarians, ministers, judges, local council members and business people), and low-level corruption among ordinary professionals (journalists, professors, teachers and doctors). I also differentiate between large-scale corruption (as measured by how corrupt are different groups in the survey) and more petty corruption, as reflected in gift payments that are necessary to get by in life (to doctors, banks, the police, the county, courts, the county, the city). These gift or gratitude payments are common in an economy marked by shortages and arrogant administrators. Many people see these payments as a way to ensure supply and also to establish longer-term relations with their doctors and other professionals, or to obtain even routine services from local governments.

Kornai (2000) reports that barely more than a third of Hungarians see a moral problem when doctors demand gratitude payments for medical services. This system of gift giving is so widespread that almost all doctors accept 'gratitude money'; 62 per cent of physicians' total income is off the books. A majority of public officials in the Czech Republic, Slovakia, Bulgaria and Ukraine in 1997–98 found it acceptable to receive extra payments from clients. Between 11 and 39 per cent of citizens of those countries (in that order) reported offering a 'small present' to officials and between 6 and 24 per cent offered 'money or an expensive present' (Miller *et al.* 2001: 217, 241).

In the Romanian survey, 35 per cent of respondents who had contact with doctors in the past five years admitted making gift payments to them, compared to 22 per cent for the courts (for people with contact) and 7 per cent to city or county officials (for contact over the past five years), and 9 per cent for the police (again for contact). Even though these figures may be modest, most Romanians believe that professionals and government officials are corrupt. Rothstein (2001: 491–2) presents a rationale for a close connection between strong legal institutions, corruption and trust in others:

> In a civilized society, institutions of law and order have one particularly important task: to detect and punish people who are 'traitors', that is, those who break contracts, steal, murder, and do other such non-co-operative things and therefore should not be trusted. Thus, if you think that particular institutions do what they are supposed to do in a fair and efficient manner, then you also have reason to believe ... that people will refrain from acting in a treacherous manner and you will therefore believe that 'most people can be trusted'.

I reported elsewhere that low-level corruption had little impact on generalized trust (Uslaner and Badescu 2004; Miller *et al.* 2001: 7). I extend that argument to trust in government as well. I expect that high-level corruption and to a lesser extent high-level gift payments will lead people to have less trust in each other and in governing institutions. People do not reason that dishonest doctors – or simply doctors who must supplement their income by gift payments – are a sign of a mistrusting society. Gift payments to professionals are not a sign of moral decay; apparently, not even corrupt professionals point to a failure of the social fabric or the state.

Government corruption and especially gift payments to the courts or other government officials should have greater impacts on people's optimism for the future, their evaluation of government performance, trust in both other people and in government, and on demands for redistribution of income. Different measures of corruption may shape different components of my model, but they all follow a common pattern: petty corruption (gift payments) does not shape trust; it does shape optimism and evaluations of government performance; larger-scale corruption has more pervasive effects on both forms of trust, on government performance, and on demands for redistribution of income. Whenever corruption shapes people's evaluation of their state or their society, it is high-level corruption. The misdeeds of ordinary professionals do not matter.

The endogenous variables in my model are: the successful performance of government in improving the quality of life; whether Romania is moving in the right or wrong direction; generalized trust; trust in government; and demands that the state limit the incomes of the rich. The success of government in improving the quality of life and the direction of the country are both measures of optimism for the future. Optimism in turn is the strongest determinant of both forms of trust (Uslaner 2002). My best measure in this survey is the direction of the country. Shorter-term expectations, especially government performance on the economy or quality of life, play a larger role in shaping people's support of trust in government (Kluegel and Mason 2000b: 201). There is mixed evidence on the link between generalized trust and trust in state institutions; Uslaner (2002) finds little relationship between the two types of trust, while Zmerli *et al.* (2003) argue that the two types of trust are strongly linked.

State limitations on the incomes of the rich is my best measure in this survey of the *consequences* of growing inequality. Putting a limit on the incomes of the rich taps suspicion of the market and reflects the belief that ordinary people cannot become wealthy. Almost 70 per cent of Romanians favour limits on income. Mateju (1997: 4–5) argues:

> the long-lasting presence of an egalitarian socialist ideology and a functioning 'nomenclature system' associated with various social and economic privileges mean that those countries undergoing the post-communist transformation will show a low tolerance for the growth of inequality ... individuals who feel that life-chances for their group or class are declining in relation to those of other groups or classes may tend to consider such changers as the result of social injustice.

While most Westerners believe that the path to wealth stems from hard work, 80 per cent of Bulgarians, Hungarians and Russians say that high incomes reflect dishonesty (Kluegel and Mason 2000a: 167; Orkeny 2000: 109). When Russian entrepreneur Mikhail Khorodovsky confessed his sins of relying on 'beeznissmeny' (stealing, lying and sometimes killing) and promised to become scrupulously honest in early 2003, Russians regarded this pledge as 'startling'. When he was arrested and charged with tax evasion and extortion under orders from President Vladimir Putin ten months later, the average Russian was unfazed. About the same share of people approved of his arrest as disapproved of it (Schemann 2003; Tavernise 2003).

Fifty per cent of Romanians in the survey say that people become rich by breaking the law and another 24 per cent say that wealth comes from having connections; an additional 6 per cent cite luck and just 8 per cent say that hard work brings wealth. In a companion survey in May 2003, 55 per cent proffered an 'ideal' limit averaging US$854 on wealth. There is a direct link from growing inequality to demanding limitations on income, but it is not strong (Kluegel and Mason 2000a: 184). Growing inequality threatens the social fabric (generalized trust) directly and indirectly (through its effect on government performance on the quality of life) on faith in political institutions. Corruption endangers social solidarity, but has even greater effects on government performance and (both directly and indirectly through performance) on governmental legitimacy (Kluegel and Mason 2000b: 201).

This more complex dynamic suggests that we would miss much of the story of the problems of transition were we to estimate only the simple model from increasing inequality to greater demands for limitations of income on the rich. Transition countries rank low on both trust in institutions and in generalized trust. In the World Values Surveys (using the most recent year for all countries with data), an average of 42 per cent of people in Western countries agree that 'most people can be trusted', compared to an average of 24 per cent in the former communist nations; 42 per cent of people in transition countries have confidence in their legal systems, compared to 57 per cent in the West. Both forms of trust are low because Romanians do not have faith that the future will be better than the past and because they most emphatically do not credit the government for making their lives better. Just 41 per cent of Romanians believe that their country is heading in the right direction and only 20 per cent believe that the government is doing a good job in improving the quality of life.

Inequality and corruption are the major 'unmoved movers' of all five of our endogenous variables. These models also show strong support for my thesis that optimism for the future leads to greater generalized trust and to stronger support for government. My framework posits a causal chain among my endogenous variables as follows:

- Performance of government on the quality of life: positive views lead people to believe that the country is moving in the right direction and to have more confidence in government.
- Direction of the country: believing that the country is moving in the right direction leads to greater social solidarity (generalized trust) as well as to trust in government.
- Generalized trust should lead to greater trust in government.
- Greater trust in government should lead to more optimism for the future, more generalized trust and to opposing demands to limit the income of the rich.

I picture an economic psychology where people who are satisfied with government performance will be optimistic for the country's future; greater optimism leads to more social solidarity and in turn to more support for the government. A stronger government in turn will create more social solidarity and make people sufficiently secure to oppose limits on incomes.

The economic psychology of transition in Romania

What do the data tell us about the impacts of perceived inequality change and corruption, and about the determinants of positive perceptions of governmental performance in improving the quality of life, the direction of the country (right or wrong), generalized trust, trust in government and beliefs that the government should limit the incomes of the rich?[7]

I have a lot to summarize, so I shall focus on the results that are critical to my analysis and leave other discussions to endnotes. My models include variables not of direct relevance to my theoretical concerns here since I wanted to ensure that any specification error is minimized. Table 6.1 presents the model; Figure 6.9 presents a more parsimonious summary diagram of my findings, eliminating variables not of immediate interest and aggregating variables by larger concepts (all corruption and gift-giving variables listed under corruption). I first focus on the two key exogenous variables, perceptions of rising inequality and of corruption. The most important results for my two key exogenous variables are simply stated: perceptions of rising inequality lead to the perception that government is doing a poor job in improving the quality of life and to lower levels of interpersonal trust (both significant at $p < 0.0001$ or greater). There is a lesser and barely significant effect ($p < 0.10$) of rising inequality on demands for limiting the income of the rich.

The belief that business people are corrupt ($p < 0.0001$) and whether the respondent has made a gift payment to the city ($p < 0.05$) drive demands for

Table 6.1 Simultaneous equation estimation of inequality and trust models for Romanian Survey 2003

Variable	Coefficient	Standard error	t-ratio
Performance of government on quality of life			
Inequality change	−0.106***	0.036	−2.94
Government success in controlling corruption	0.215****	0.031	6.85
Make gift payments to courts	−0.347***	0.131	−2.65
Satisfied with democracy in Romania	0.118***	0.030	3.91
Satisfied with market economy in Romania	0.161****	0.031	5.25
Wealth (can afford consumer goods)	0.020***	0.008	2.67
Constant	0.297**	0.105	2.83
Direction of country: right or wrong			
Generalized trust	0.294**	0.143	2.06
Trust in government scale	0.073*	0.051	1.45
Performance of government on quality of life	0.160***	0.063	2.54
Level of social protection increased or decreased	0.061**	0.028	2.20
State of national economy in three years	0.078***	0.024	3.24
Quality of life next year	0.041**	0.024	1.71
Number of connections you can rely upon	0.042***	0.016	2.58
Make gift payments to city	−0.088	0.101	−0.86
Hungarian ethnicity	−0.114*	0.078	−1.47
Constant	0.455	0.190	2.40

Continued

Table 6.1   Continued

Variable	Coefficient	Standard error	t-ratio
Generalized trust			
Direction of country: right or wrong	0.331***	0.117	2.82
Trust in government scale	0.024	0.050	0.47
Inequality change	−0.089***	0.031	2.86
Level of social protection increased or decreased	−0.050	0.029	1.70
Most politicians are corrupt	−0.075***	0.030	−2.47
Most teachers are corrupt	−0.032	0.026	−1.26
Constant	0.276*	10.39	1.99
Trust in government scale			
Generalized trust	−0.064	0.317	−0.20
Direction of country: right or wrong	0.427**	0.244	1.75
Performance of government on quality of life	0.221*	0.139	1.59
Performance of government on public safety	0.252****	0.060	4.23
Government success in controlling corruption	0.101**	0.046	2.18
Most politicians are corrupt	−0.136***	0.050	−2.71
Inequality change	−0.105**	0.058	−1.82
Number of contacts to public and private institutions	0.049**	0.022	2.25
State should control media and political parties	−0.049**	0.025	−1.94
Church attendance	0.035*	0.023	1.47
Support PSD	0.212****	0.027	7.89
Live in Bucharest	−0.214***	0.086	−2.48
Constant	−1.308****	0.253	−5.16
State limit incomes of rich (agree)			
Trust in government scale	0.121	0.078	1.56
Inequality change	0.091*	0.069	1.34
Satisfied with democracy in Romania	−0.138***	0.052	−2.63
Most business people are corrupt	0.155****	0.048	3.21
Make gift payments to city	0.400**	0.234	1.71
Rely on connections in court	−0.282**	0.125	−2.26
Rely on connections in foreign country	−0.246**	0.124	−1.98
Constant	−1.878****	0.253	7.41

Notes: *$p < 0.10$, **$p < 0.05$, ***$p < 0.01$, ****$p < 0.0001$, N = 610. RMSE (R^2) by equation: performance 0.560 (0.361); direction 0.426 (0.277); generalized trust 0.452 (0.129); trust in government scale 0.708 (0.471). State limits incomes of rich 1.001 (0.054). Endogenous variables in bold; endogenous dependent variables in bold italics. Inequality change in italics. Exogenous variables: gender, age, education, make gift payments to doctors, make gift payments to county, Romania needs strong leader, tolerance of gays, government performance on jobs, government performance on agriculture, government performance on privatization, maximum salary that should be allowed, economic situation of country, life satisfaction.

limiting incomes. Perceptions of high-level, especially large-scale, corruption are powerfully related to government performance, generalized trust and trust in government as well. Government success in controlling corruption is the strongest determinant of how people evaluate the state's performance in improving the quality of life ($p < 0.0001$).

People who have to make gift payments to courts are less likely to say that the government is performing well ($p < 0.01$). The belief that most politicians are

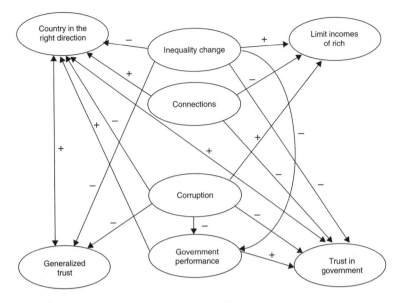

Figure 6.9 Linkages from Romanian survey models

corrupt makes someone 23 per cent less likely to trust fellow citizens compared to the (rare) expectation that no politicians are corrupt, and 15 per cent less likely compared to the more common belief that only a few politicians are corrupt ($p < 0.01$). So dishonest behaviour by leaders makes people less trusting; but when I include a measure of whether most *teachers* are corrupt (low-level corruption), the coefficient is insignificant: I get similar results for doctors, professors, journalists, police officers, or higher level officials (ministers, judges, local councilors, or even business people).

Corrupt politicians also lead people to distrust government ($p < 0.01$); government success in controlling corruption makes people *more* trusting in the state ($p < 0.05$). There are both direct and indirect (through the performance of government on the quality of life) effects for controlling corruption. But more important than how well the government improves the quality of life seems to be how well the state does in improving public safety, with a regression coefficient two and a half times the size of the endogenous quality of life measure (both measured on the same scale). With the close ties of organized crime and corruption, this measure of government success is also tapping a measure of public venality. The indicators of official dishonesty are the major determinants of trust in government.

Support for limiting incomes of the rich depend almost exclusively on perceptions of corruption and ties that most ordinary citizens would regard as less than upright – having connections in court and abroad. If you believe that most business people are corrupt or have to make gift payments to the city government ($p < 0.0001$ and < 0.05), you are likely to favour limiting the incomes of the rich.

Generalized trust is *not* a significant predictor of limiting incomes of the rich (including it yielded an insignificant t-ratio and a loss of many cases from this equation, therefore it was dropped). Trust in government has the wrong sign and a modest t-ratio. This does *not* mean that neither government legitimacy nor social solidarity shape the transition to a market economy. Support for the market, social solidarity and trust in government all depend upon the fairness of economic and political institutions (corruption and economic inequality).

If a person is well connected, using connections in dealings with the courts or having connections in a foreign country, that person will oppose limiting incomes. Relying on connections to get by in daily life – to stand in line for food, to help run errands, or to use a friend or relative to cut through the bureaucracy – was common practice under communism (Flap and Voelker 2003; Ledeneva 1998). These networks continued after the fall of communism. The only other significant predictor of support for limiting incomes is satisfaction with democracy in Romania: the happier you are, the less likely you will be to demand restrictions on income.[8] The effects of rising income inequality and corruption on satisfaction, trust and demands for redistribution are large. It is corruption at the top that matters, not from below, and even at the top it seems concentrated in politicians, business people, local officials and courts – precisely the officials most commonly cited when people discuss dishonesty in the transition countries. Lower level professionals are not held blameworthy.

I turn now to a summary of the models for my endogenous variables. When people are satisfied with governmental performance, they are more likely to believe that the country is headed in the right direction ($p < 0.0001$). Government performance on the quality of life and especially government performance on public safety lead to greater legitimacy for government ($p < 0.10$ and $p < 0.0001$, respectively). So does the belief that the country is heading in the right direction ($p < 0.05$). The direction of the country is the most powerful predictor of generalized trust: someone believing that Romania is on the right track is 33 per cent more likely to trust fellow citizens than a person who holds the country to be heading in the wrong direction. There are *no* links between generalized trust and trust in government. Performance measures (including the success of government in controlling corruption) as well as contacts with public (and private) institutions ($p < 0.05$) and especially supporters of the PSD, the governing party ($p < 0.0001$), shape trust in government but *not* faith in other people.[9]

The two measures of optimism also have different roots. The performance of government on the quality of life reflects high-level corruption and satisfaction with institutional performance (democracy and the market economy, both at $p < 0.01$). People with greater wealth also give higher marks to government performance. The direction of the country does depend to some extent on institutional performance. Government skill in improving the quality of life does shape the direction of the country ($p < 0.01$); there is a weak link ($p < 0.10$) with trust in government. There is *no* effect for any corruption measure. Making gift payments to the city is insignificant (many other forms of gift payments and corruption were tested for). The longer-term fate of the economy (three years out) is the most powerful predictor of whether the country is moving in the right direction ($p < 0.01$); there is a significant, but weaker effect, for the quality of life people expect next year ($p < 0.05$). People who believe that the level of social protection has increased are also more upbeat about the direction of the country ($p < 0.05$).[10]

The individual-level analysis also receives support from an analysis of 17 aggregated surveys conducted by the same firm from October 1996 through to October 2003.[11] Table 6.2 presents a two-stage least squares analysis of whether the country is moving in the right direction and trust in government. The aggregate models show that: (1) expectations for an improved life next year strongly shaped people's views that the country was headed in the right direction; and (2) so did perceptions that the government was handling corruption well. No impact for corruption was found in the individual-level modelling. However, only a handful of variables are available over time and the impact of corruption may be a surrogate for the trust measures or even the social safety net question. My model also shows that (3) the endogenous measure of the direction of the country strongly shapes trust in government. So does (4) the electoral cycle, a variable measuring the number of months until the next parliamentary elections. In transition countries, as in the West, governments lose popularity as their time in office increases; Downs (1957: 55–60) called this the 'coalition of minorities' effect. And I see clear evidence of this here with confirmatory evidence over time that expectations for the economy as well as perceptions of corruption shape evaluations of the country's overall democratic performance, and that strong government performance leads to greater legitimacy for political institutions. This analysis is based upon a small number of cases so it should be taken with caution, but the results are consistent with the thesis I have advanced.

Table 6.2   Simultaneous equation model of trust in government and country moving in the right direction from aggregated surveys

Variable	Coefficient	Standard error	t-ratio
Direction of country right or wrong			
Government success in controlling corruption	0.346*	0.172	2.01
Quality of life improving next year	0.836**	0.316	2.65
Constant	1.655	9.289	0.18
RMSE = 8.294 R^2 = 0.683 N = 17			
Trust in government scale			
Direction of country right or wrong	0.567***	0.150	3.78
Electoral cycle	0.351**	0.137	2.56
Constant	2.547	3.924	0.65
RMSE = 5.296 R^2 = 0.832 N = 17			

Notes: *$p < 0.05$, **$p < 0.01$, ***$p < 0.0001$. Endogenous variables in bold; endogenous dependent variables in bold italics. Exogenous variables: trust in justice, growth rate in gross domestic product for the year.

Sources: Penn World Tables (1996–2000) and www.dfat.gov.au/geo/fs/roum.pdf for (2001–03).

The demands of a successful transition

A successful transition depends upon strong institutions and a supportive civic culture (Almond and Verba 1963). A growing economy can lead people to become more supportive of their political institutions and more tolerant of each other. When the economy is expanding, people will be less likely to see the world in zero-sum terms. Sztompka (1999: 179–90) saw hope for civil society in Poland in the late 1990s as the economy revived, crime fell and young people became the vanguard of a new social order. But wealth can go only so far in restoring trust. Poland ranks 69th of 82 countries on trust and the wealthiest transition country, Slovenia, ranks 72nd.

The results so far suggests that inequality and corruption are the key factors leading to lower social solidarity and governmental legitimacy in transition countries. Corrupt elites and the failure of government to curb them lead to demands for limiting the incomes of the rich and for controlling markets more generally. Support for limiting incomes seems to reflect a critical view of government and business elites rather than social solidarity more generally. There is no significant effect of generalized trust, of increasing inequality, of the direction of the economy, or even the level of social protection on demands for restraining income. There is an insignificant (and wrongly signed) effect from trust in government, but satisfaction with democratic institutions and several measures of corruption are the major factors in shaping calls for limiting incomes.

Despite minimal correlations between the two, the data do show a more indirect connection. Public concern for corruption seems more than just a demand for honest government. If people *only* objected to official dishonesty, then we would expect that all levels of corruption should affect governmental performance, trust in both people and the state, and demands to limit incomes. However, this is not what I find. Public distress focuses on high-level corruption – in the state, the courts and in business – but not lower-level demands for bribes (the police, doctors and teachers, among others). People link corruption to larger social and political problems when they see powerful and rich people exploiting average citizens, not when they see minor officials padding their meagre salaries.

The inequality trap

Perceptions of growing inequality, corruption and a lack of confidence in government and fellow citizens lead to an inequality trap. When people believe that they have no fair chance to get a better life – and that the only way to prosper is by being corrupt – it will be difficult to escape an inequality trap. Corruption, mistrust and inequality are all sticky. They do not change easily because each breeds the other. The r^2 between generalized trust from the 1980 and 1990–95 World Values Surveys is 0.81 for the 22 nations included in both waves. Inequality similarly moves little over time. The r^2 for the most commonly used measures of economic inequality (Deininger and Squire 1996) between 1980 and 1990 is not quite as strong as the connection with trust over time, but it is still substantial at 0.676 for a sample of 42 countries. A new inequality database developed by James Galbraith extends measures of inequality further back in time and across more countries.[12] The r^2 between economic inequality in 1963 and economic inequality in 1996 is 0.706 (for 37 countries). The r^2 between the Transparency International Corruption Perceptions Index for 2003 and the ICRG measure for 1980–85 (even though they are not directly comparable) is 0.785 for 49 countries.

There is a causal spiral from inequality to corruption (and back again) and from both inequality and corruption to lower levels of trust (Uslaner 2004) and from low levels of out-group trust and high levels of in-group (or particularized) trust to corruption (Gambetta 1993). Perhaps most critical in this vicious circle is the link between inequality and trust. High levels of inequality lead to low out-group trust and high in-group trust and countries with high levels of trust enact policies that help reduce inequality; they spend more on the poor and more on programmes such as education that help equalize opportunities. The path to a successful transition must find a way to break this vicious cycle. Accomplishing this will not be easy. There are few institutional 'quick fixes' to corruption and tackling the issue of economic inequality is difficult politically, especially when there are great social strains in a society (Uslaner 2005). Unless the political and social will is found, the road to a successful transition will continue to be rocky.

Notes

This study represents joint work with Gabriel Badescu of Babes-Bolyai University, Cluj-Napoca, Romania, who is responsible for much of the material on Romanian politics and society and who directed the surveys and provided the data. I am grateful to the Starr Foundation, through the Institutional Research and Exchanges Board of the United States Department of State, for a grant in conjunction with Paul Sum of the University of North Dakota, Mihai Pisica, and Cosmin Marian, all of Babes-Bolyai University under the IREX Caspian and Black Sea Collaborative Programme (2001) to conduct a survey that formed the basis of our current work. I am also grateful to the Russell Sage Foundation and the Carnegie Foundation for a grant under the Russell Sage programme on the Social Dimensions of Inequality and to the General Research Board of the Graduate School of the University of Maryland, College Park. Some data reported here come from the Inter-University Consortium for Political and Social Research (ICPSR), which is not responsible for any interpretations. Mark Lichbach made many helpful suggestions on an earlier draft, as did an anonymous referee for this study.

1. The mean score on the Gini index of inequality for former and current (China) communist regimes in the Deininger and Squire (1996) dataset is 0.295; for the West, the mean is 0.316 and for other nations it is 0.464. The East–West differences are not significantly different from zero, but they are at $p < 0.03$ if China is excluded.
2. Using Penn World Tables data on the gross domestic product in 1993 and 2000, I calculate GDP growth; the r^2 between GDP growth and the 2001 Transparency International (TI) measure of corruption is 0.509 for 12 transition countries, but it is only 0.050 for economic inequality.
3. Across 12 nations the r^2 between the TI 2001 index of corruption and the Gini index of inequality is just 0.024 (0.048 for change in inequality). In the survey, none of the 'gift' measures has a correlation with perceived increasing inequality exceeding 0.02; the correlations for the various corruption measures are slightly higher, with the strongest being

for perceptions that the government is doing much to control corruption (0.175), but most are around 0.10 or below.

4. I focus on Romania for two reasons. The practical reason is simple: a colleague is Romanian and designed this survey to reflect our interests. Second, Romania is considered one of the more troubled new democracies. It ranks low on trust and tolerance as well as on corruption. See Badescu *et al.* (2003); Uslaner and Badescu (2004).

5. The data on business elite perceptions of justice come from the BEEPS 2002 survey of business executives in transition countries conducted by the World Bank. There are no comparable data for the mass public for more than a handful of societies.

6. The survey was carried out by the Centre for Urban Sociology (CURS) in October 2003, as part of the Public Opinion Barometer programme, sponsored by the Soros Foundation for an Open Society, Romania.

7. The measure of trust in government is a factor score from trust in the following institutions: government (generally), president, parliament, justice, the army, police, city hall and political parties. I use the overall measure because the relationships I investigate do not vary much by specific institution and, indeed, the findings are more crisp for the factor score.

8. Trust in government has the incorrect sign and, hence, is not significant even at $p < 0.10$.

9. Where one lives also plays a role. Living in Bucharest makes one less trusting of government ($p < 0.0001$); people who attend church regularly also develop a deeper faith in governmental institutions, but the effect is weak ($p < 0.10$). Support for a more authoritarian state (giving government the power to control media and political parties) leads to less support for government.

10. Hungarians, a minority that has faced discrimination, are also less optimistic, but the relationship is weak ($p < 0.10$).

11. The surveys were conducted once in 1996, three times each in 1997 and 1998, and twice annually thereafter, generally in March and October (the third surveys were conducted in June). The generalized trust question was asked in only ten surveys and government performance was asked in just 15. Government performance was not significant as a predictor of trust in government when direction of the country was endogenous, and it added little as an exogenous variable.

12. The Galbraith data can be obtained at http://utip.gov.utexas.edu/web/

References

Almond, G. and S. Verba (1963) *The Civic Culture*, New Jersey: Princeton University Press.

Badescu, G., P. Sum and E.M. Uslaner (2003) 'Civil Society Development and Democratic Values in Romania and Moldova', *Eastern European Politics and Society*, 18: 316–41.

Deininger, K. and L. Squire (1996) 'A New Data Set: Measuring Economic Income Inequality', *World Bank Economic Review*, 10: 565–92.

Djankov, S., R. LaPorta, F. Lopez-de-Silanes and A. Shleifer (2001) *The Practice of Justice*, Washington, DC: World Bank.

Downs, A. (1957) *An Economic Theory of Democracy*, New York: Harper & Row.

Feld, L.P. (2003) 'Tax Evasion in Switzerland: The Roles of Deterrence and Responsive Regulation', paper presented at the Conference on Tax Evasion, Trust and State Capabilities, 17–19 October, St Gallen.

Flap, H. and B. Volker (2003) 'Communist Societies, the Velvet Revolution, and Weak Ties: The Case of East Germany', in G. Badescu and E.M. Uslaner (eds), *Social Capital and the Transition to Democracy*, London: Routledge.

Gambetta, D. (1993) *The Sicilian Mafia: The Business of Private Protection*, Cambridge, MA: Harvard University Press.

Hayoz, N. (2003) 'Arm's-Length Relationships, Political Trust, and Transformation in Eastern and Central Europe', *Finance and Common Good*, 13/14: 35–48.

Howard, M.M. (2003) *The Weakness of Civil Society in Post-Communist Europe*, New York: Cambridge University Press.

Kinder, D.R. and R. Kiewiet (1979) 'Economic Discontent and Political Behavior: The Role of Personal Grievances and Collective Economic Judgements in Congressional Voting', *American Journal of Political Science*, 23: 495–527.

Kluegel, J.R. and D.S. Mason (2000a) 'Market Justice in Transition', in D.S. Mason and J.L. Kluegel (eds), *Marketing Democracy*, Lanham, MD: Rowman and Littlefield.

Kluegel, J.R. and D.S. Mason (2000b) 'Political System Legitimacy: Representative? Fair?', in D.S. Mason and J.L. Kluegel (eds), *Marketing Democracy*, Lanham MD: Rowman and Littlefield.

Kornai, J. (2000) 'Hidden in an Envelope: Gratitude Payments to Medical Doctors in Hungary', at www.colbud.hu/honesty-trust/kornai/pub01.PDF

Ledeneva, A. (1998) *Russia's Economy of Favours*, Cambridge: Cambridge University Press.

Leite, C. and J. Weidemann (1999) 'Does Mother Nature Corrupt? Natural Resources, Corruption, and Economic Growth?', *IMF Working Paper* WP/99/85, Washington, DC: International Monetary Fund.

Mateju, P. (1997) 'Beliefs About Distributive Justice and Social Change: Czech Republic 1991–1995', *Social Trends Working Papers* 97–6, Prague: Institute of Sociology, Academy of Sciences of the Czech Republic.

Mauro, P. (1997) 'Why Worry About Corruption?', *Economic Issues*, 6, Washington, DC: MF.

Miller, W.L., A.B. Grodeland and T.Y. Koshechkina (2001) *A Culture of Corruption: Coping with Government in Post-Communist Europe*, Budapest: CEU Press.

Onishi, N. and N. Banerjee (2001) 'Chad's Wait for Its Oil Riches May Be Long', *New York Times*, 16 May.

Orkeny, A. (2000) 'Trends in Perceptions of Social Inequality in Hungary, 1991–1996', in D.S. Mason and J.L. Kluegel (eds), *Marketing Democracy*, Lanham, MD: Rowman and Littlefield.

Owsiak, S. (2003) 'The Ethics of Tax Collection', *Finance and Common Good*, 13/14: 65–77.

Putnam, R.D. (1993) *Making Democracy Work: Civic Traditions in Modern Italy*, Princeton, NJ: Princeton University Press.

Rosser, J.B., M.V. Rosser and E. Ahmed (2000) 'Income Inequality and the Informal Economy in Transition Countries', *Journal of Comparative Economics*, 28: 156–71.

Rothstein, B. (2001) 'Trust, Social Dilemmas, and Collective Memories: On the Rise and Decline of the Swedish Model', *Journal of Theoretical Politics*, 12: 477–99.

Schemann, S. (2003) 'In Going Legit, Some Russian Tycoons Resort to Honesty', *New York Times*, 12 January.

Schneider, F. (2003) *Shadow Economies around the World: What do I know?*, Linz-Auhof: University of Linz.

Stephenson, S. and L. Khakhulina (2000) 'Russia: Changing Perceptions of Social Justice', in D.S. Mason and J.L. Kluegel (eds), *Marketing Democracy*, Lanham, MD: Rowman and Littlefield.

Sztompka, P. (1999) *Trust: A Sociological Inquiry*, Cambridge: Cambridge University Press.

Tanzi, V. (1998) 'Corruption Around the World: Causes, Consequences, Scope and Cures', *IMF Staff Paper* 45: 559–594, Washington, DC: IMF.

Tavernise, S. (2003) 'Russia Is Mostly Unmoved by the Troubles of Its Tycoons', *New York Times*, 3 November: A3 (Washington, DC, edn).

Tyler, T.R. (1990) *Why People Obey the Law*, New Haven, CT: Yale University Press.

Uslaner, E.M. (2002) *The Moral Foundations of Trust*, Cambridge and New York: Cambridge University Press.

Uslaner, E.M. (2003) 'Tax Evasion, Trust, and the Strong Arm of the Law', paper presented at the Conference on Tax Evasion, Trust and State Capabilities, 17–19 October, St Gallen.

Uslaner, E.M. (2004) 'Trust and Corruption', in J.G. Lambsdorf, M. Taube and M. Schramm (eds), *Corruption and the New Institutional Economics*, London: Routledge.

Uslaner, E.M. (2005) 'The Bulging Pocket and the Rule of Law: Corruption, Inequality, and Trust', paper presented at the Conference on the Quality of Government: What It Is, How to Get It, Why It Matters, 17–19 November, Göteborg University.

Uslaner, E.M. and G. Badescu (2004) 'Honesty, Trust, and Legal Norms in the Transition to Democracy: Why Bo Rothstein Is Better Able to Explain Sweden than Romania', in J. Kornai, S. Rose-Ackerman and B. Rothstein (eds), *Creating Social Trust: Problems of Post-Socialist Transition*, New York: Palgrave.

Vlachova, K. (2000) 'Economic Justice in the Czech Republic, 1991–1995', in D.S. Mason and J.L. Kluegel (eds), *Marketing Democracy*, Lanham, MD: Rowman and Littlefield.

Zmerli, S., J. Ramón Montero and K. Newton (2003) 'Trust in People, Confidence in Political Institutions, and Satisfaction with Democracy', unpublished manuscript, University of Mannheim.

7
Indivisibility, Fairness, Farsightedness and their Implications for Security

S. Mansoob Murshed

Introduction

It is now two decades since the founding of UNU-WIDER, an institute that commenced its activities under the leadership of the late Lal Jayawardena. Although its remit is primarily development economics research, other issues not narrowly related to economics have also been studied at WIDER. A good example, is the work of the historian Eric Hobsbawm, whose masterly analysis of contemporary world history was penned while at WIDER. The central thesis of Hobsbawm's (1995) opus is the pervasively violent nature of the twentieth century with its two world wars; something which, on a global scale, is perhaps without historical parallel.[1] Related to this notion of violence are the uncertainties and insecurities which bedevil us in the new millennium. The danger of nuclear holocaust, after which 'the living would envy the dead',[2] seem long past. Yet many insecurities still loom large. The freedoms from want and fear are still far from being realized at the present time.[3] Without the achievement of these two freedoms, human security cannot prevail, even if lip service is paid to human rights. Poverty is widespread, and vast swathes of the developing world are being marginalized in our globalized era.[4]

To a great extent, interstate wars have been largely replaced by intrastate conflict.[5] More importantly, these civil wars are closely related to poverty (the lack of the freedom from want).[6] For example, poverty makes soldiering less unattractive. Conflict also helps to perpetuate poverty.[7] This creates an interdependence between the freedoms from want and fear, as conflict (fear) and low-income (poverty) seem to go hand in hand.[8] The number of countries in civil war may be declining,[9] but their average duration during the 1990s was increasing.[10] This makes the analysis of why peace cannot be achieved or sustained an absolute imperative, if the twin freedoms and human security are to be achieved.

The second section of this chapter is concerned with the problems of *fairly* sharing the post-war economic pie or the peace dividend. Walter (2001) and Wood (2003) point out that peace agreements to end civil wars are notoriously unstable in that they are often not implemented, or break down after some time. Commitments to the peace treaty are simply not credible. One reason for that could be certain indivisibilities in perceived shares of power and income in the peace settlement, as well as the inability to infer correctly the value of path dependence (when, for example future reputation depends on present actions, but the future is heavily discounted). These matters are considered in the third section, with the subsequent section briefly discussing the role of another type of unfairness, namely a deep sense of humiliation, in determining acts of transnational terrorism. The final section of the chapter concludes.

Fairness and indivisibility

Fearon (2004) points out that of all types of civil wars, those with secessionist tendencies and 'sons of the soil' dynamics, are both the most protracted and difficult to resolve. This could be because of an attachment to the inviolability of land and territorial sovereignty by both parties to the conflict. Certainly, other causes such as the ready availability of easily lootable narcotic or gemstone revenues that help finance conflict, or misperceptions about the chances of outright military victory, are important in prolonging conflict. But the indivisibility of war aims, symbols or land can also make certain civil wars intractable.

Wood (2003) highlights *indivisibility* as a major impediment to peace deals. This arises when territory, symbols or revenue in a post-conflict situation cannot be divided up so as to achieve peace. The problem can be most acute when religious sites such as Har'm El Sharif or Temple Mount in Jerusalem are involved. Also, considerable difficulties arise when it is problematic to achieve compromise over a war aim such as land reform (Nepal and Colombia), or deep constitutional change (future of the monarchy in Nepal). There can also be seemingly irresolvable disputes over post-war power sharing, and the allocation of offices in a post-conflict government. This can lead to spoiler groups, usually but not exclusively amongst rebel groups, wrecking a peace agreement because it does not give them enough in terms of cabinet places or other lucrative positions in power. Secessionist wars where territorial sovereignty is contested can also be tricky to resolve. But in other cases, certain common territories can be dear to both sides, and the sharing rules proposed for them are not acceptable, as is the case with Har'm El Sharif or Temple Mount in Jerusalem. Compared to these, disagreements over sharing economic resources, such as oil revenues, may require less challenging solutions.[11] For example, it can be argued that separatist tendencies in Indonesia have eased following the decentralization of the fiscal system, which allows regions to keep more of locally generated natural-resource revenues. While the federal government is keen to preserve the territorial integrity of Indonesia, there are no indivisible symbols akin to Jerusalem.

The theoretical literature on sharing and division offers us several insights. For example, Brams (2005) and Brams and Taylor (1996) point out several allocation rules for a single divisible good, many divisible goods and several indivisible goods. All of these have implications for durable peacemaking involving compromises over issues and post-war economic stakes. If a peace agreement, and the divisions and compromises it entails, are perceived to be unfair then the deal itself will not be robust, as these arrangements will tend to break down. Sharing in this regard must be equitable in several senses, as well as being efficient. That is why envy-free allocative outcomes are so important. In an envy-free outcome each participant does not regard the allocation achieved by another player to be superior to what he/she has achieved. All the various allocative mechanisms considered by Brams (2005) and Brams and Taylor (1996) require design and implementation by an outside agency, a mediator and/or external power. This is all the more so in the case of allocations in a post-war situation.

In the case of a single divisible good the analogy with cake cutting is applicable. This may, for example, concern the division of the post-war peace dividend, which includes natural resource revenues and the imputed value of post-conflict overseas development assistance. Cake cutting, in a two-player situation, implies one person doing the cutting and the other player having the right to call a halt to the slicing procedure. The application of the envy-free criterion, however, may entail several slices or divisions that may be inefficient and in excess of the number of parties to the conflict. This will be all the more true if what is being divided up is not homogeneous. One can visualize situations to do with the division of the expenditure categories of post-war aid, and the dividing up of land that may require a great deal of parcelling.[12]

A second situation considered by Brams (2005) and Brams and Taylor (1996) entails several items to be divided, each of which is in principle divisible. Peace negotiations usually involve several issues, including regional autonomy, sharing of resource rents (such as oil revenues in the Sudan), constitutional changes, power sharing in the federal government and so on. Typically these issues will involve a long period of extended bargaining. The procedure behind the settlement, if reached, is described as the 'adjusted winner mechanism'. The adjusted winner mechanism not only satisfies the standard efficiency and equity criteria, but additionally has a further equitability condition, because it ensures that each player gets more than its share of the bargaining chips initially allotted to them. For example, in a two-person case, each player will get more than 50 per cent of the total value attached to all the issues and goods at stake.

Negotiations on the issues involve placing upper and lower bounds on the values of each issue, bearing in mind that assigning pecuniary values is more amenable in quantifiable matters such as resource rents rather than for non-monetary matters involving status such as who should be president. Each side will allocate weights on the different issues at hand and, given that each side has a similar number of bargaining chips, each party will win on some of the disputed issues. These will tend to be in areas most highly valued by the concerned protagonist. So if regional autonomy is more highly prized by a rebel group compared to resource rents, they will put a higher weight on it and secure that goal under the adjusted winner mechanism. In general, players will remain honest, and not risk losing on high-valued issues by undervaluing their personal bid for them out of their total allocation of bargaining chips. But one side can end up with wins on many high-valued issues, and the consequent allocation could be inequitable to the other side. So this mechanism requires an equitability adjustment. Basically, this means sharing on high valued issues where the two sides preferences are close, or the weights assigned to them out of their bargaining chip allocation are similar. So if the government and the rebels assign a close and high weight to resource rents, they must share these. In other words, if the government and the rebels both value resource rents highly, one side cannot equitably be allowed to be a sole winner. There has to be a revenue sharing mechanism on this issue. Other issues, where values diverge considerably, tend to be 'winner takes all' based on which side places the higher value. This adjusted winner mechanism gives both sides an allocation that is roughly equal and more than 50 per cent of the assigned weights from the bargaining chip pile. The problem with applying this equitability-included adjusted winner mechanism is that many issues are not easily divisible, such as which side gets to first occupy a rotating post-war presidency. A further difficulty can arise if the two sides do not have similar bargaining power, something that external actors need to engineer.

Third, and most importantly, Brams (2005) and Brams and Taylor (1996) consider allocating several indivisible issues. Once again, external intervention or mediation is required. The allocation of indivisible goods requires the application of the envy-free principle for any allocation to endure. And, a unique envy-free allocation may not be Pareto-efficient. Pareto efficiency means that one side cannot be made better off without making another side worse off.[13] One can make an envy-free allocation Pareto-efficient by improving the utility of one side without lowering the utility of the other. But such allocations may not remain envy-free as one side could have a lower allocation of relatively more highly prized items (yielding the same utility) that are being allocated, and consequently resent the other side's allocation. A similar argument can be made about a 'maximin' allocation being envy-possible. Consider an application of the envy-free principle to the elections held in Iraq in January 2005. A criticism of the method adopted in that Iraqi election, for example, could be that the electoral mechanism (one person–one vote instead of representative bodies of each community) was not envy-free for the minority Sunni community, and had therefore not enlisted their full co-operation.[14] Furthermore, the power-sharing mechanism devised does not have the properties of the equitability adjustments of the adjusted winner mechanism, which would give each side a larger share of the outcome than is strictly proportional to the bargaining chips it receives. One could even argue that the Sunnis received a smaller allocation of the total bargaining chips for negotiation than is warranted by their historical position. Despite the fact that the historical Sunni domination in Iraq was disproportionate to their (minority) population share, the present US-backed dispensation makes them feel vulnerable and disproportionately disadvantaged because of the lack of perceived constitutional safeguards for special groups. To them, there is a palpable lack of consensus and consultation.[15] The country is, consequently mired in a multifaceted civil war.

Generally speaking, allocations involving indivisible items that are more qualitative are more difficult to achieve. The answers, in the more intractable cases, must lie in *sharing*, equal user rights and other 'federal' type arrangements that eschew winner-takes-all outcomes.[16]

Wood (2003) considers non-co-operative strategies of actors in a conflict, and whether their strategies to fight or compromise are self-enforcing without third-party mediation. This is at variance with allocative rules considered by Brams (2005) and Brams and Taylor (1996) involving mediation and refereeing, making the outcome resemble co-operative solutions. The decision to compromise is based on the payoff in the peaceful state, as well as beliefs about the strategy that will be adopted by one's opponent. There also has to be bargaining over the share of the post-war pie that each side gets. The Nash equilibrium can involve either fighting or compromise; multiple equilibria are possible. If each side's expected post-war share is greater than what they can get from fighting, feasible compromise equilibria exist. But that depends upon beliefs about the other side's strategy. The feasible compromise equilibrium and the sharing it involves may not coincide with beliefs about the opponent's strategy. In general, there will be an optimal share of the post-war pie for each side that will maximize the robustness of a peaceful settlement (that is the agreement lasting or being self-enforcing) given beliefs of the two sides about each other. Within each group there may be factions or spoiler groups with more pessimistic views about their opponent's strategies. This will depress their value of any share of the post-war pie. Indivisibilities regarding the issues contested, and the post-war pie, also lower the expected worth of any share of the post-war settlement, making self-enforcing compromises difficult. In more extreme cases, as with virtually all contemporary civil wars, this may require external intervention in the form of aid to increase the total size of the potential peace dividend, so there is simply more to be shared. In the case of sites and symbols, steps have to be taken to encourage sharing and envy-free access through confederal structures. This may require diplomacy, and in some cases coercive intervention by external powers.

Indivisible periods and commitment problems

Another form of indivisibility arises when the future is heavily discounted, and when the future costs of current actions are similarly undervalued. We may describe this as the lack of recognition of path dependence. This may lead to problems of commitment to negotiated settlements even when Pareto-optimal, that is when each side is better off in a state of peace. A commitment or credibility problem implies that the signal, or treaty, establishing peace is simply 'cheap talk', and by implication the arrangement is not self-enforcing. In most situations, war is irrational and inefficient (not Pareto-optimal) as pointed out by Skaperdas (1992; 2002). Therefore, why is the credibility of the commitment to peace treaties so fragile? There could also be misperceptions about the benefits of war, or an overestimation of the prospects of military victory.

To deal with misperceptions first, the most obvious candidate that prevents peace in this category of explanations for civil war persistence is an overestimate of the probability of military victory, see Collier *et al.* (2004) in this connection.

The same authors also emphasize that the state of war may also be highly profitable for one or more of the belligerent groups. This is likely in the case of the presence of contraband substances, such as illegal drugs, and lootable minerals, such as alluvial diamonds.

The commitment problem to an agreed peace treaty is a serious one, and deserves further consideration. This difficulty arises when it is in the interest of one or either side to renege on the promise of peace, and the actions that peace involves. For example, in the model contained in Addison and Murshed (2002) one side to a peace treaty may wish to renege on its commitment to peace because it allows them then to loot valuable natural resource rents. The expropriation of these rents cannot take place without one side fooling the other, by feigning to make peace and later reneging on this undertaking. In that situation, when peace is not incentive-compatible, commitments lack credibility and acquire the characteristics of cheap talk.

Sometimes agents or groups cannot commit credibly because there are no institutions or mechanisms upon which to anchor promises. In that situation they are not believed, even when they are honest. For governments, this is more likely in the context of weak state capacity, as it is difficult for a state to guarantee pledges when its own legitimacy and power base is fragile.

An aspect of the commitment problem that has received scant attention is the very high discount rates, or the short time horizons of some of the parties involved (Addison and Murshed 2002). In situations of poverty and high uncertainty, agents may strongly prefer a dollar today to a dollar tomorrow. Although the absolute value of future peace may be much higher than that of continued warfare, the present value may be much lower when the discount rate is very high and there is an impatience to consume. The same argument can be applied to reputation, a factor that is central to the credibility of peacemaking. Breaking an agreement damages *future* reputation, but with a high enough discount rate it might pay to renege because the cost comes in the future. Each failure of the peace process raises the discount rates of the belligerents, thereby increasing the difficulty of making peace. Given the tarnished reputations of belligerents it is even harder to establish credible peace.

Solutions lie in directly increasing the cost of reneging on peace agreements and devising commitment technologies through institutional innovation, particularly at the international level. The latter is particularly important because, as noted above, many contemporary civil wars do not have self-enforcing negotiated settlements. Without external intervention, and the sanctions that entails in terms of peacekeeping, as well as the palliative effect associated with aid, peace is just not sustainable. Improving the quality of peacekeeping forces is an urgent need, as is increased commitment to bringing war criminals to trial. Peacekeeping also needs to be more legitimate and acceptable, and the current ventures involving co-operation between local peacekeepers (as in the case of African Union interventions) and major aid donors (the European Union) is a step in the right direction. More adequately mandated and efficient United Nations involvement can enhance the acceptability of peacekeeping operations.

With regard to commitment and commitment technologies there are four factors that deserve further consideration: the separation of economic life and politics, time horizons, institutional settings and the underproduction of external sanctions.

Economics and politics

When we assess why some 'post-conflict' countries returned frequently to war (Angola) while others have managed to sustain peace (Mozambique), economic motivations may lie at the root of the problem – Mozambique has few valuable minerals over which to fight while Angola has several – and this may help explain several peace commitment failures in Angola. There may be situations when conflict and business entrepreneurs are one and the same, as in many cases in Africa. That is when rulers themselves are directly engaged in appropriating lootable mineral resource rents. This makes the commitment to peace less likely to hold, compared to societies with a relatively stricter dichotomy between those who rule (politicians) and those who conduct economic affairs. This is because in the former case the political and economic interests are one, and clearly pro-war. Economic interests in this instance centre around war-contracts and the harnessing of resource or illicit drug rents. In the latter case there is some room for competition between different interests; business activities such as the exporting of manufactured goods from Sri Lanka or Nepal may be disrupted by the war. Even when there are links between the two groups, the greater the institutional separation through parliament and the political process, the better are the chances for lasting commitments to peace.

Time horizons

This turns out to be a crucial feature in individual decisions. When a future is seen to feasibly exist, this results in more peaceful attitudes, even in situations where deep-seated historical grievances are present. Generally speaking investment, which only bears fruit in the future, requires a long time horizon. More secure and affluent societies tend to have a longer time horizon and recognize the path dependence of current actions. By contrast severely war-torn, insecure and poorer societies have shorter time horizons, with a very strong preference for a dollar today compared to an uncertain prospect of more than a dollar in the future. Short-term income may be readily obtainable in a war situation, even if war destroys future earning prospects. In the language of economics, this is referred to as a high discount rate applied to future income, as opposed to the high value put on present consumption. All of this means discounting the future cost of conflict, as well as undervaluing the tarnished future reputation that arises from an excessive zeal for short-term profit. Furthermore, societies with faulty and degenerating institutions of governance and democracy tend to have a high discount rate, as the future is uncertain. New and fledgling democracies are often characterized by these high discount rates, as the future is uncertain due to the fact that the political system may collapse. The state apparatus in this situation runs the risk of descending into kleptocracy. The important point here is that many groups in these situations are also characterized by similar short-term mentalities, making them often prefer current profits in a war situation when compared to investing for a far greater income that peace might bring in the future. Also, investment in trying to bring about future peace can have substantial present-day costs in terms of foregone profit.

Institutions of commitment

Even when all parties agree to and recognize the benefits of peace they need credibly to commit to peace, and the conditions stipulated therein. Generally, this requires institutions that help parties to credibly anchor their commitment to the peace treaty. The fear of reversal in the context of poor commitment technologies, leads to a peace treaty being imperfectly credible. And if it is not credible, the peace agreement will not last. Leaders of various groups and factions will then tend to behave like roving bandits with little concern for the country, like stationary bandits who have an encompassing interest in nurturing the tax base from which they obtain rent (Olson 1996). A poor environment for commitment often arises when the government or the rebel leadership's power base is weak and/or lacks legitimacy. Solutions here lie in devising better mechanisms to engender credible commitment via institutional improvement. This includes better constitutional safeguards, greater respect for the rule of law and superior regulatory capacities. This may be even a part of a society's democratic transition.[17] Existing domestic institutions often degenerate beyond redemption in many conflict-ridden societies, making externally enforced commitment technologies imperative in the interim before domestic institutions can once again evolve.

Under-production of external sanctions

Externally devised commitment technologies could be the key to ending conflicts where the peace treaty is otherwise not self-enforceable, as is usually the case in contemporary civil wars. Sanctions, aid trade restrictions and resource redistribution, if effective, might help to eliminate conflict. But external sanctions themselves must not be perceived by potential combatants as cheap talk. In other words, the external sanctions must *also* have credibility. If the cost of effective sanctions is too high, or it yields little security benefit to the sponsor as is likely to be the case for conflicts in distant lands, there is under-production of the sanction, making it more likely that it really is cheap talk. Perhaps, that is why we do not see the end of many civil wars in Africa, where large territories as in the Congo are policed by relatively small and weakly empowered peacekeeping forces. Civil wars in Europe, such as in the Balkans, by contrast are quickly concluded, with a huge relative (to population and geographical size) commitment in peacekeeping forces and aid. The will and resources to end more distant wars by external powers may be more strictly limited. In the ultimate analysis, credible commitments to peace must be found in effective domestic constitutional restraints and delegation. These domestic commitment technologies require deep interventions in institution building, something that is notoriously difficult to achieve because of the persistence of vested interests in conflict.

Humiliation and terrorism

This section discusses transnational terrorism, which alongside the other forms of violence and insecurity considered in this chapter are also a product of injustice and unfairness. What is more relevant here is individual, rather than group behaviour. A transnational terrorist act is one that impacts on the citizenry or interests of a country not directly part of the conflict in question. It can occur anywhere, both in the country where the conflict is occurring or elsewhere. Thus, for example, if the USA or the West is a target, then its citizens may be attacked in countries where the attackers are fighting the state, such as in Egypt. Attacks, kidnappings and bombings can also occur in third countries, such as Malaysia, Bali (Indonesia) and Saudi Arabia; attacks on US interests can take place in the USA (such as against the Twin Towers), or elsewhere as with the US embassy bombings in East Africa. More recently, there have been direct attacks in the UK and Spain. Transnational terrorism may reflect the internationalization of domestic disputes (Doran 2002). So, for example, the attacks on 11 September 2001 may reflect an act of war against an external sponsor (USA) of the real enemy (the venal and apostate government of Saudi Arabia). A similar argument can be made about acts of violence against Western tourists in Egypt, where the real enemy is the pro-Western government of Egypt.

From the viewpoint of the individual perpetrator of transnational terrorism, such as a suicide bomber, intrinsic motivation, which is often the outcome of the collective sense of humiliation (Lindner 2001), plays a greater role; therefore deterrence against terrorist groups may backfire if it hardens their resolve to resist, as is modelled by Addison and Murshed (2005). Deterrence can, however, influence the choice of targets by terrorists. Depending on relative difficulty, the target may shift from sponsor interests in other lands to sponsor countries, or even to where the real enemy is located. We do see shifting targets from the Twin Towers to Bali, to Saudi Arabia, to Madrid and London. Individual terrorist groups are often relatively small, and can be very creative in terms of organizing finance for their localized cells, and evading sanctions, in order to carry out acts that are relatively much less costly and simpler than in the case of civil war.

Individual perpetrators of terrorist acts are usually not uneducated and poor (Krueger and Maleckova 2002), unlike in the case of civil wars where the soldiery is often drawn from the ranks of the impoverished whose alternative gainful employment prospects are scant. In fact, education can act as an indicator of reliability in acts such as suicide bombing. Terrorism requires individuals to express solidarity with an intrinsic cause or value, where the notion of pecuniary gain associated with greed in the case of civil wars is totally irrelevant. Individual utility functions associated with terrorism are altruistic. There is not only identification with a cause, something that can also be present in passively interested individuals, but an imperative to participate in furthering the cause. This urge to act may result in violent action, including self-destruction. From the viewpoint of individual choice, suicide bombing may be a rational act as explained by Wintrobe (2002). This is because the individual has made an all or nothing choice between solidarity with a cause and individual autonomy. An all or nothing choice involves a 'corner solution' to a utility maximization problem. In this situation, changing relative prices (increasing deterrence) has little impact on individual choice, which is another way of saying that deterring terrorism will not succeed in preventing people from committing to their cause, even if the success rate of individual acts of terrorism diminishes. Alternatively, deterrence has to be very large to prevent individuals from carrying out violent deeds in this context of deep humiliation. In many cases this implies the physical annihilation or mass deportation of 'terrorists'. Such acts of deterrence are, however, not feasible in democracies with the exception of a state like Israel. Many societies and groups are willing to go to great lengths and to sacrifice themselves out of a sense of deep humiliation.[18] Economists, in particular, are guilty of ignoring these types of preferences, which are less amenable to 'relative price' changes. Addressing the issues that cause humiliation, including those that disaffect second- or third-generation migrants in Europe are important to finding permanent solutions to terrorism.

Conclusions

Human security in the form of the freedoms from want and fear are interrelated. One of the great insecurities of the present age is the fact that there are civil wars in many low-income nations where poverty is also endemic. Indeed, as Collier *et al.* (2003) and other authors have emphasized, the most significant and robust factor in determining the risk of civil war is a low per capita income, implying that poverty and underdevelopment can result in outright violent conflict between different groups in society. In short, poverty breeds conflict, and conflict helps to perpetuate poverty. Tackling one issue without paying attention to the other is futile.

One cannot overemphasize the differing natures of the motivations behind civil war and transnational terrorism. The former is intimately linked to poverty; the latter not necessarily so, being much more connected to acts of solidarity with collective humiliation and other causes. That is why we see many of these acts of terrorism being perpetrated by relative educated and affluent individuals, including citizens (drawn from different ethnicities) of developed countries. Where mass deportation and physical extermination is not an option, as is the case in most democracies, addressing issues connected with humiliation is of utmost importance. Here, dialogue with disaffected groups may act as a palliative, just as indiscriminate criticisms of large groups (for example Muslims, who are about a fifth of humanity) have an inflammatory effect.

The message to policy-makers is clear. Most conflict-ridden countries have weakened state capacity, so that the state can no longer be regarded as an impartial actor in all of its traditional conflict prevention functions. So some external intervention is required to restore peace and security, including rebuilding state capacity. Tackling inter-group or horizontal inequalities can also be central to preventing and ending conflict. This means poverty reduction, growth, greater political participation and improved governance. As far as peace settlements are concerned, they are generally not self-enforcing without external help and commitment; peacekeeping is something that is inadequately supplied in many parts of the world. Ultimately, however, peace in any corner of the world is a public good, because of the potential costs of humanitarian intervention and managing refugee flows if there is war. Making peace settlements durable implies that sometimes the indivisible has to be made divisible through intervention in the form of diplomacy and coercion, which encourage sharing, as well as greater economic aid to make the peace dividend more palpable. It also means devising institutions that help anchor commitment. Furthermore, post-war allocations need to be envy-free in order for them to endure. In the final analysis, lasting security cannot be achieved by coercion alone; without economic development and broad-based poverty reduction the disincentive to resort violence is always small.

Notes

I am grateful to two anonymous reviewers for their comments on an earlier draft of this chapter.

1. Earlier wars may have also been just as, or more, devastating such as wars between Rome and other Italian entities in the fourth century BC, the three-year war leading to the annihilation of Carthage in 146 BC, the death and destruction wreaked by the armies of Genghis Khan in the thirteenth century, or even the English Wars of the Roses in the fifteenth century. But these wars were far more localized.
2. Commonly attributed to the erstwhile Soviet leader, Nikita Khrushchev.
3. These are the last two of the four freedoms enunciated in President Franklin Delano Roosevelt's State of the Union address to Congress on 6 January 1941. See www. Fdrlibrary.marist.edu/od4frees.html, accessed on 29 June 2005.
4. See Murshed (2002b: 1–18).
5. See Murshed (2002a) for a brief description as to their causes.
6. See the model in Addison *et al.* (2002).
7. See Collier *et al.* (2003)
8. Not all poor or low-income countries descend into conflict, but most conflict-ridden countries are poor or middle-income nations.
9. See Hegre (2004).
10. See Fearon (2004).
11. A counter-example may be in the Sudan. Although the north and south had reached agreement earlier, the discovery of oil meant that the civil war rekindled and was finally resolved via oil revenue sharing.
12. If all players are risk-averse they will follow a 'maximin' strategy; that is they will maximize the minimum allocation that they can achieve with certainty compared to uncertain prospects that yield higher returns but entail a positive probability for an outcome which is less than their maximin outcome. This is also like saying that those who dislike risk will do their best to achieve a minimum target or utility threshold.
13. This is, however, consistent with one person having everything and another person nothing in a two-person world.
14. In practice, the allocation of power in Iraq among the various communities includes several divisible and indivisible issues.
15. Shurah in Arabic.
16. As is the case in the Westminster- (and American-) style first-past-the-post electoral systems that often result in less compromise, consensus and power sharing.
17. See Haggard and Kaufman (1995).
18. See Lindner (2001) on this.

References

Addison, T. and S.M. Murshed (2002) 'Credibility and Reputation in Peacemaking', *Journal of Peace Research*, 39, 4: 487–501.

Addison, T. and S.M. Murshed (2005) 'Transnational Terrorism as a Spillover of Domestic Disputes in Other Countries', *Defence and Peace Economics*, 16, 2: 69–82.

Addison, T., P. Le Billon and S.M. Murshed (2002) 'Conflict in Africa: The Cost of Peaceful Behaviour', *Journal of African Economies*, 11, 3: 365–86.

Brams, S.J. (2005) 'Fair Division', in B.R. Weingast and D. Wittman (eds), *Oxford Handbook of Political Economy*, New York: Oxford University Press.

Brams, S.J. and A.D. Taylor (1996) *Fair Division: From Cake Cutting to Dispute Resolution*, Cambridge: Cambridge University Press.

Collier, P., L. Elliot, H. Hegre, A. Hoeffler, M. Reynal-Querol and N. Sambanis (2003) *Breaking the Conflict Trap: Civil War and Development Policy*, New York: Oxford University Press for the World Bank.

Collier, P., A. Hoeffler and M. Söderbom (2004) 'On the Duration of Civil War', *Journal of Peace Research*, 41, 3: 253–73.

Doran, M.S. (2002) 'Somebody Else's Civil War', *Foreign Affairs*, 81, 1: 22–42.

Fearon, J. (2004) 'Why Do Some Civil Wars Last So Much Longer Than Others', *Journal of Peace Research*, 41, 3: 379–414.

Haggard, S. and R.R. Kaufman (1995) *The Political Economy of Democratic Transitions*, New Jersey: Princeton University Press.

Hegre, H. (2004) 'The Duration and Termination of Civil War', *Journal of Peace Research*, 41, 3: 243–52.

Hobsbawm, E. (1995) *Age of Extremes: The Short Twentieth Century 1914–1991*, London: Abacus.

Krueger, A.B. and J. Maleckova (2002) 'Does Poverty Cause Terrorism', *The New Republic*, 24 June: 27–33.

Lindner, E.G. (2001) *The Concept of Humiliation: Its Universal Core and Culture-Dependent Periphery*, Oslo: University of Oslo.

Murshed, S.M. (2002a) 'Civil War, Conflict and Underdevelopment', *Journal of Peace Research*, 39, 4: 387–93.

Murshed, S.M. (2002b) 'Perspectives on Two Phases of Globalization' in S.M. Murshed (ed.), *Globalization, Marginalization and Development*, London: Routledge for UNU-WIDER.

Olson, M. (1996) 'Big Bills Left on the Sidewalk: Why Some Nations are Rich, and Others Poor', *Journal of Economic Perspectives*, 10: 3–24.

Skaperdas, S. (1992) 'Co-operation, Conflict and Power in the Absence of Property Rights', *American Economic Review*, 82: 720–39.

Skaperdas, S. (2002) 'Warlord Competition', *Journal of Peace Research*, 39, 4: 435–46.

Walter, B.F. (2001) *Committing to Peace: The Successful Settlement of Civil Wars*, New Jersey: Princeton University Press.

Wintrobe, R. (2002) 'Can Suicide Bombers Be Rational', paper prepared for the DIW Workshop on Economic Consequences of Global Terrorism, June, Berlin.

Wood, E.J. (2003) 'Modelling Robust Settlements to Civil War: Indivisible Stakes and Distributional Compromises', Mimeo, International Peace Research Institute, Oslo.

8
Violence in Peace: Understanding Increased Violence in Early Post-conflict Transitions and Its Implications for Development

Marcia Byrom Hartwell

Introduction

A key issue for development in the late twentieth and early twenty-first centuries has been an escalation of violence during post-conflict transitions. A long-term goal for international donor involvement is to assist in building legitimate and effective political, economic and legal institutions; however, research and observation has revealed that increased violence is commonplace during peace processes and strongly influences the ways in which these institutions are formed. In turn post-conflict violence itself is strongly influenced and motivated by the way in which peace agreements have been negotiated. Peace processes in the late twentieth century have had a mixed record of success with the results from peace agreements often more divisive than unifying. Representation in the process may be skewed so that 'after a negotiated ending to a civil war, most countries lie in the intermediate terrain' between domestic forces who backed peace accord implementation, and 'hardliners on one or more sides who would prefer a return to armed conflict over implementation of the accords' (Boyce 2002: 32).

A lack of understanding by international interveners of the underlying dynamics within post-conflict societies has exacerbated many difficulties associated with developing this co-operation. Identifying and addressing these dynamics and their effect on internal and external motivations to pursue peace and create a stable environment for development has become increasingly important.

This study addresses some of the reasons for escalation of violence following peace agreements. It describes the underlying dynamics including the relationship between perceptions of justice as fairness, formation of post-conflict identity, political processes of forgiveness and revenge; and the policy implications for development particularly in relation to peace conditionality tied to aid. The fairness and humiliation issues cited in Chapter 7 in this book by Mansoob Murshed are very relevant to this explanation. The conclusion observes that peace is an evolutionary process with some level of toleration between all groups as a goal that is necessary to prevent future conflict.

Violence in peace

Many of the problems central to recovering from conflict have focused on the process of political co-operation between former enemies. This co-operation is necessary to strike a peace agreement, to rebuild and create institutions and to lay a foundation for sustainable peace. A little understood but increasingly menacing threat to peace processes is from rank and file members of irregular forces who do not support their leaders in making deals for peace. While non-state actors within each group have been fighting for the same cause, they may have had widely differing motivations. One of the biggest threats during post-conflict transitions is from 'spoilers', often leaders of irregular combatants, paramilitaries or other non-state groups who perceive that circumstances evolving from peace negotiations may not be in their best personal or political interests, and who use violence in attempts to undermine the process.

Halliday (quoted in Cox *et al.* 2000: 286) has described four types of peace processes dominating post-Cold War conflicts throughout the 1990s that have been plagued by these types of underlying problems. One type is a process that, despite experiencing difficulties, makes progress that results in a stabilized, successful peace within a time frame of five to ten years. A second has been one where political negotiations continue but where unanticipated problems and delays have occurred. A third is where hostilities have formally ceased but where a political stalemate exists between all parties and the process becomes stalled; and a fourth is where peace breaks down completely and conflict is renewed at the previous or an escalated level of violence. These differences become clearer once a peace agreement has been struck. Stedman (1997: 7) has asserted that 'peace processes create spoilers'. During a conflict 'there are combatants, who can be identified in myriad ways – for example, rebels, bandits, pariahs, rogues, or terrorists' but 'spoilers exist only when there is a peace process to undermine'. Peace creates spoilers 'because it is rare in civil wars for all leaders and factions to see peace as beneficial. Even if all parties come to value peace, they rarely do so simultaneously, and they often strongly disagree over the terms of an acceptable peace.' As Keen (2001: 12, 18–19) noted 'the art of facilitating a transition from war to peace may lie, to a considerable extent, in ensuring that some of those benefiting from war are in a position to benefit to a greater extent from peace'.

This type of post-agreement organizational fragmentation has been consistently observed in the ease with which upper echelons of paramilitary and rebel groups have appeared to gain political legitimacy in the early phases of a peace process while the bottom half or dissident members of the organizations have failed to find dramatic improvements in their living conditions. While elite leaders of these groups often gain legitimate political power through negotiation, non-elite members often feel that their socioeconomic and political needs have not been addressed in a final settlement.

Research demonstrates that preventing the lower echelons of the former rebel/paramilitary groups that have been marginalized by peace negotiations from shifting into organized crime requires a different kind of assurance and assistance than the paramilitary elite. Their perception of equal access to economic, political and social opportunities are especially relevant to their willingness to co-operate in the early post-conflict phase and directly impacts political co-operation and formation of institutions. The bottom half of the non-state organizations, often composed of those who have fallen out of favour with rebel or paramilitary leaders or who are among the many urban and rural poor who have survived in areas of constant battles, face the type of low-paying employment available to those with their lack of qualifications, thus guaranteeing a future of grinding poverty. For them, disruptions to peace and alliances with organized crime networks are a guarantee of substantial income and elevated social status.

As has been illustrated in post-agreement paramilitary punishment beatings and intimidation in Northern Ireland; transitional violence between African political parties in South Africa; political assassinations and organized crime in post-war Serbia, violence may shift rapidly from inter- to intra-group targets. This may result in an increased number of assassinations, punishment beatings, vigilantism, coercion, forced exile and other forms of intimidation used to settle scores and jockeying for political power among one's own group.

As many non-state organizations have a youth recruitment and membership wing, this lack of hope for a better future has negative implications for long-term development strategies that do not address this problem during post-conflict transitions. If the youth do not perceive that their chances of access to a better future or life have improved, then they are likely to evolve into or join criminal organizations and gangs (Dowdney 2005).

Underlying dynamics in post-conflict transitions

No action by aid donors or peacekeepers is without consequence in a post-conflict environment, with all forms of international development, aid and peacekeeping missions under constant evaluation by internal populations. During fieldwork conducted in Northern Ireland, Serbia and South Africa over a period of three years (Hartwell 2005) and in findings of others working with adult non-state actors and youth gangs (Dowdney 2005) it has become obvious that there are common dynamics and evaluation criteria shared by both post-conflict transitions and severely unstable environments. These underlying motivations have been most accurately depicted in a framework incorporating interactions between perceptions of justice, identity and political processes of forgiveness and revenge. Perceptions of justice as fairness, where the perceived fairness of the process of arriving at a judgement has proven to be more important than the actual outcome; formation of a post-conflict identity where all groups share a common sense of victimization; and political processes of forgiveness and revenge that incorporate these motivations in enactment of or forbearance from a range of expressions of forgiveness and revenge are key influences on the process of building political co-operation and institutions (see Hartwell 2005).

Of these dynamics, perceptions of justice as fairness, also known as 'justice judgements', have been identified as a prime motivator and key to formation of identity and political processes of forgiveness and revenge. While not replacing formal legal trials and other procedures, these perceptions are formed early by all groups in order to rapidly assess their individual and group status in an unstable post-conflict transition and directly influence decisions and opinions affecting co-operation with former enemies (Hartwell 2004; 2005).

An assumption of a victim identity is common among all groups. While still focused on conflict-defined groupings, many civilians and non-state actors were less concerned with inter-group grievance than with groups' perceptions of themselves as victims of violence. In each case the formerly dominant group was especially vulnerable to assuming this identity and an articulation of victimhood has often found to have been a motivating factor for this group in initiating or prolonging the original conflict. The link between perceptions of justice and formation of post-conflict identities has been found to be of greater significance than had been previously understood. Individuals and groups were observed to renegotiate their identities utilizing their perceptions of justice as fair treatment which in turn shaped political processes of forgiveness and revenge (Hartwell 2004; 2005).

In recent work on the relationship between justice, identity and behaviour, Tyler and Blader (2003: 353–4) observed that development and maintenance of a positive individual and group identity most strongly influences co-operation and leads 'people to be internally motivated to engage in and co-operate' with groups. Attitudes and values are an important part of this process as 'to the degree that people are internally motivated, they engage in co-operative behaviours for personal reasons, and they do not need to receive incentives (rewards) or to face the risk of sanctions (punishments) to encourage their group-related behaviours'. Tyler and Blader found that social identity is formed from three interconnected areas; identification, pride and respect:

> Identification reflects the degree to which people cognitively merge their sense of self and their evaluations of self-worth with their judgments of the characteristics and status of their groups. Pride reflects the person's evaluation of the status of their group. Respect reflects their evaluation of their status within the group. (*Ibid.*)

These perceptions of justice and formation of a victimization identity are linked to a complex parallel, evolutionary and inevitably political process of forgiveness and revenge in a post-conflict transition. Although still in its infancy, the analysis of forgiveness and revenge and its relationship to political processes present in all national and international political systems raises important questions for the international community as well as the internal victims, perpetrators and bystanders:

> When considering how forgiveness unfolds for victims, the motivations underlying forgiveness decisions become important. Do people forgive to release

themselves from discomfort, or do their decisions reflect more principled motives? Are such distinctions about motives important, in terms of predicting outcomes for forgivers or offenders? (Exline *et al.* 2003: 345)

In the past decade, inspired by the South African Truth and Reconciliation Commission (TRC), intangible issues such as forgiveness, previously treated as irrelevant political concepts by most non-theologian scholars and policy-makers, began to be widely discussed in political and legal forums. Inclusion of forgiveness began to emerge in international peacemaking discussions as a new way forward in the process of promoting social reconciliation. However, examining the political dimensions of forgiveness and revenge was not new and had been previously discussed by post-Second World War philosopher Arendt (1958), who had explored the motivations of Nazi Germany, and later in the 1980s by Jacoby (1985), who examined the relationship between justice and revenge. However, it was not until the mid-1990s when studies such as Shriver (1995) appeared that a serious discussion outside of Christian theological paradigms began to take place.

Shriver, a pastor in North Carolina and participant in the 1960s civil rights marches in southern USA, concluded that the concept of forgiveness that had been 'customarily relegated to the realms of religion and personal ethics' belonged 'at the heart of reflection' in pondering ways that groups of humans could repair damage from past conflicts with each other. Because forgiveness embraced 'moral truth, history, and the human benefits' that flowed from conquering enmity, Shriver (*Ibid.*: x) defined 'forgiveness' as a 'word for a multidimensional process that is eminently political'.

Subsequent research and fieldwork has clearly underscored Shriver's interpretation and reinforced the work of Arendt and Jacoby. Both forgiveness and revenge have emerged as deeply intertwined parallel processes that directly impact political co-operation while encompassing all aspects of justice. This has been reflected in justice studies where considerable evidence has begun to mount that when confronted with serious emotional issues of justice and injustice in 'high-impact situations', individuals will give precedent to re-establishing justice over a sense of personal financial gain.

'If the justice motivation and emotional arousal are sufficiently strong, the imperative to act may narrow the focus of attention and thought' resulting in a diminished response to self-interest. Individuals may be willing to give up 'considerable economic incentives to punish a harm-doer', working instead to help those they perceive to be innocent victims rather than working to increase their own profit. In some cases they may go so far as to 'derogate their own self-worth', determined to withstand potentially severe political, economic and social costs as a consequence for their support. In this context justice assumes a counter-intuitive position as an independent and important source of motivation, overriding and separate from 'self-interested desires to maintain self-esteem and maximize profits' (see Lerner 2003: 396).

This analytical framework set against a backdrop of unstable hypersensitivity characteristic of post-conflict transitions emphasizes the relevance of the justice motive to understanding the motivation for much of the violent behaviour in the post-conflict context. Research has suggested that while unconditional forgiveness may not be necessary, or possible, in order for enemies to co-operate in the short term, a key finding has been that forbearance from revenge rather than unconditional forgiveness, directly impacts political, social and economic relationships between former enemies. Seen as a mid-phase between processes of forgiveness and revenge, this 'passive resentment', where a decision to forbear from enactment of revenge has been consciously taken, has emerged as a key factor for moving political co-operation and reforms forward (see Hartwell 2005).

Policy implications for development

In keeping with the advent of peacekeeping in post-Cold War years, a type of peace conditionality tied to donors' economic and political reform agendas has come to dominate post-conflict environments as a basic criteria for aid. In the early 1990s, a signed peace agreement was viewed as a type of investment and loan security, serving as de facto 'peace' conditionality for international financial institution (IFI) donors such as the World Bank, International Monetary Fund (IMF) and others who focused solely on goals of macroeconomic stability and economic reform. A more formal 'peace conditionality' began to evolve by the mid-1990s as the international community increasingly acknowledged that economic reform was not a neutral force and that its outcome was strongly influenced by political and social factors.

Focused on both short-term enforcement of peace agreements and long-term sustainability of peace, peace conditionality has been known by a variety of names: conflict management, peace building, conflict transformation, conflict resolution, conflict prevention, peacemaking and reconciliation (Boyce 2002: 8–9). This conditionality has been organized and implemented by governments, humanitarian aid agencies; civil society organizations (CSOs) composed of a range of institutions that includes non-governmental organizations (NGOs), faith-based institutions, professional associations, trade unions, research institutes, think tanks; IFIs such as the World Bank, IMF, European Bank for Regional Development (EBRD), large regional banks; and government donor agencies such as USAID.

Performance criteria have specified explicit targets for cuts in military spending while simultaneously creating new democratic institutions, demobilizing ex-combatants, protecting the public, and increased spending for health, education and reduction of poverty. Informal policy dialogue between aid donors and recipients has been encouraged in cases where the link between aid and conditionality has been left intentionally vague to accommodate fluctuating circumstances (see Boyce 2002: 8–9). While it has been consistently observed that peace conditionality can be a useful tool, it is not a 'magic bullet' nor does aid 'necessarily act like water on the embers of conflict' (Boyce 2004: 1032). Despite being well-meaning in most cases, it may nevertheless result in a mismatch of requirements to the reality of needs on the ground. For example, a universal and key concern expressed by all parties in previous case studies and one resonating throughout all early post-conflict transitions has been heightened anxiety regarding personal security. This climate of fear is well understood by former combatants and civilian populations especially as civil and 'ethno-national conflicts' have usually been fought in the same territory where combatants live and where civilians often assume roles as actors or as targeted bystanders (MacGinty 2001: 641–2). Aid in these unstable post-conflict transitions is ineffective unless it is framed in a way that is flexible and responsive to the changing situation on the ground. Otherwise there can be no guarantee of personal protection for any individual or group while travelling to work, to school, or conducting other daily activities.

Priorities and agendas of donors can be equally problematic and may be in direct conflict with perceptions of populations on the ground. Making invalid assumptions about situations, and/or imposing values and systems within an environment where this may provoke increased resistance may result in long-term instability that is dangerous to all parties. Demands made as explicit or implicit conditions for aid, such as badly timed international calls for specific individuals to face international tribunals, and aid linked to the formation of truth and reconciliation commissions may adversely affect internal perceptions of justice and negatively impact the co-operation necessary in forming key institutions (Hartwell 2004). For international interveners attempting to stabilize the environment by defusing short-term violence and avoiding long-term renewal of conflict, accurately identifying spoilers who are slowing or sabotaging an agreement or peace process will help to develop effective strategies to thwart them.

Overall there are three general categories of spoilers common to peace processes; total, limited and greedy. Total spoilers can be most difficult long term, as they often have fixed, inflexible goals and ideologies, are led by individuals who see the world in win/lose terms and may exhibit pathological tendencies that prevent the pragmatism necessary for compromise. Limited spoilers usually have several inflexible, specified goals accompanied by demands for protecting the security needs of their followers. Greedy spoilers are somewhere between the first two, only with more flexible demands that are tailored to the evolving circumstances.

Since the beginning of the 1990s the international community has pursued three major strategies to address spoiler-caused problems; inducement, socialization and coercion. Inducement takes a positive approach to addressing spoiler grievances that include a range of strategies incorporating fear, security, fairness, demand for greater benefits, justice and legitimization or acknowledgement of their position. Socialization relies on establishing a combination of material and intellectual norms while wielding a carrot and stick approach to a system of rewards or punishments. Normative standards can include a commitment to defined democratic standards and adherence to protecting human rights by instilling fair and appropriate standards of governance among the elites and educating citizens in democratic processes of holding elites accountable.

Coercion has ranged from the use or threat of punishment, coercive diplomacy incorporating threats and demands, the use of force and the two most common strategies – the 'departing train' and/or 'withdrawal' strategies. The departing train strategy combines the premise that a spoiler's demands and strategies are inappropriate and illegitimate and that the peace process will continue with, or without the spoiler's co-operation. Withdrawal assumes that an international presence during the peace process is desired and attempts to punish the spoiler by threatening a withdrawal of international support and peacekeepers from the peace process. A problem with this approach is that it is indiscriminately applied, potentially hurting those who have complied and rewarding spoilers who oppose international involvement (Stedman 1997: 13–14).

The most effective use of strategies is considered to be the application of either force or the 'departing train' scenario on total spoilers who 'cannot be accommo-dated in a peace settlement; they must be defeated or so marginalized that they can do little damage'; or implementation of some form of inducement that can include in some cases, a policy of socialization and/or coercion on limited spoilers who 'can be accommodated by meeting ... non-negotiable demands' (*Ibid.*: 14–15).

Greedy spoilers require a long-term socialization strategy but in the short term can be a serious problem. A controversial but somewhat common strategy has been to grant amnesty for prisoners, incurring an almost universally negative reaction among groups of all sides in countries where it has been implemented, such as Northern Ireland and South Africa. However, it has been equally clear that without prisoner co-operation in supporting peace agreements, using amnesty as a condition of their release, peace would not have occurred (Hartwell 2004; 2005).

As violence in peace processes has been continually on the increase, it is sug-gested that the following tasks be urgently undertaken and results taken on board by the international community for better understanding of ways to implement effective development programmes in violent post-conflict environments.

Formal monitoring of perceptions of recipient populations

One way to undertake a survey of perceptions would be to use a form of impact assessment that gauges the effectiveness of specific aid projects on different classes, ethnicities and regions that are the most sensitive to the previous violent conflict. This would give direct insight into how aid programmes and peacekeep-ing interventions are perceived. This could include all groups and individuals by targeting well-known and marginalized organizations and by sending emissaries with instructions to gather more information through informal networking chan-nels. Such an all-inclusive national survey strategy has been implemented in South Africa by the Institute of Justice and Reconciliation in tracking sociopoliti-cal trends for their SA Reconciliation Barometer. This data would be relatively easy to index and to quantify.

Better identification of groups at risk

In my general observation, noted in fieldwork conducted in Northern Ireland, Serbia and South Africa, and in the work of others, groups with the potential to be highly valuable indicators of instability in post-conflict environments are:

- Groups that have undergone a traumatic loss of power, usually the formerly dominant populations who feel they have the least to gain from a peace process. They are usually the ones most affected by loss of previous privilege and can belong to any socioeconomic class.

- Marginal socioeconomic groups of all sides, especially the most poverty-stricken, as they are highly reactive to change. They have often borne the brunt of the conflict and have much more in common with mirror groups on the opposite side of a conflict, than with members of middle and upper socioeconomic classes within their own groups.
- Volatile young males in formerly dominant populations. They are usually ex-combatants or members of a lower socioeconomic class who do not perceive any personal gains from peace and can often instigate and lead serious violence. This specifically emerged as a problem in Northern Ireland and South Africa.
- Pensioners and the older generation who have least to gain in future earnings and benefits from the peace, and who have lost savings and pensions during the conflict with no potential for recovery. They can become very bitter, and delay or reverse political transitions to democracy by voting to bring fundamentalist or nationalist parties to power. This was a particularly disillusioned group in Serbia as middle-class members of this age group had experienced peak career and quality of life benefits from socialism. Subsequently they saw their life savings stolen from the country's state-run banks, leaving them impoverished by the end of the Yugoslav war.
- Non-elite members of paramilitary and rebel groups from all sides of the conflict who do not have access to political power, education, good jobs, or legitimate ways of achieving greater financial success. For them a 'normal life' in peace has no advantage over continuing to engage in and expand their range of criminal activities. Their peacetime criminal activities have often expanded into lucrative non-war revenue areas and tap into formation and perpetuation of youth gangs and international criminal syndicates. This situation was noted in Northern Ireland, Serbia and South Africa.

Better understanding of language used in the public sphere

The coded use of language has been often underestimated and misunderstood by external interveners as an indicator to signal peaceful or violent intent. During conflict, social coding of language assumes hugely significant importance. Apparently neutral words and harmless questions such as: Where do you live? Where did/do you go to school? Who do you work for? can signal inclusion or exclusion, or in more serious situations, life-threatening danger.

While adversarial groups may technically speak the same language they often use common words to indicate different meanings. Decoding this language is extremely important for understanding perceptions of aid and military intervention on the ground.

Improvement in communication between internal populations and donors

Aid givers and peacekeepers often assume their intentions are clear to recipient groups. Transparency and honesty about what an international humanitarian organization and/or peacekeeping mission has to offer (including both advantages and limitations) are highly respected in post-war environments where warfare has been dependent on deception, manipulation, propaganda and misinformation. An organization that clearly states reasons for being in a place, what it has to offer and what it can and cannot accomplish will avoid tragic misunderstandings.

There is a vital need to develop effective links with local organizations below government level and to speak with diverse representatives of local populations that include qualified local actors in the process of policy making and implementation. The scope of sources can easily be widened beyond the usual 'official' range by ringing or emailing a list of secondary sources – a range of CSOs not ordinarily consulted by large international donors, for example, and requesting a list of contacts.

Improvement in deciphering transitional violence

While endemic to the peace and reconciliation process, it is the choice of targets during this time that is vital to understanding intent. Through more realistic preparation, co-operation and communication, peacekeepers and aid workers can more accurately assess risk to themselves and populations they serve for what appears to be an almost inevitable rise in violence during a post-conflict transitional period.

A review of historic patterns of violence in the area and within the recent conflict, such as the extent and pattern of police and/or military abuse, nature of violence targeted towards civilians and extent of vigilantism will help give external interveners the perspective to interpret violence as it occurs. In assessing risks of violence towards internal populations and external interveners, those intervening in post-conflict environments should ask the following questions. Is it being caused by 'spoilers' to the peace process? Is it politically motivated? Is it being used to settle internal scores? What does the timing and location reveal? Is it occurring early during the transition or later in one 'trouble' spot? Has racial or hate crime increased? If increases in crime rates are becoming problematic, then where is this occurring? What are the regions? Is there a distinct difference in types and rates of crime in urban versus rural locations?

Conclusion

Recently there has been increased recognition by many international institutions and aid givers that while post-conflict transitions share common vulnerabilities they often need to address very different combinations of problems. These are shaped and influenced by a variety of factors that include characteristics of the preceding conflict and cultural norms. The interdependence of political, security, economic and social aid activities needs to be better acknowledged and international donors and interveners should support a more integrated and unified framework for planning political, security, humanitarian, economic and development activities at a country level.

In this analysis, reconciliation has been viewed as both a short- and long-term process. In the short term, it is seen as a pragmatic co-operation between former enemies in rebuilding political, economic and social institutions; in the long term, it is a process which encompasses multiple generations. In striving for sustained peace in a society where violent conflict has created deep distrust there is a need for all sides to develop a style of personal and political toleration that a majority can accommodate and a minority can aspire to. This toleration of groups with different histories, cultures and identities is pursued not for its own sake but because many aspire to its value as justification for a 'peaceful coexistence and of the life and liberty that it serves'. This toleration of difference shifts the burden of social accountability onto those who would reject these values through acts of indiscriminate abuse such as forced removals, ethnic cleansing and other destructive deeds, to justify their actions (Walzer 1997: 2).

It is evident from the timeline of interviews and observations of others that internal reactions to important issues evolve over time. Initial elation over implementation of peace agreements almost invariably gives way to disillusionment as progress is perceived to be occurring less rapidly or not in the way originally anticipated. While an initial agreement or bargain may be struck in the short term, long-term sustainability of peace requires the international community to develop aid and peacekeeping missions with more multilevelled approaches than those currently in place (see Hartwell 2005).

Most importantly, Walzer depicts toleration as an ongoing negotiated arrangement whose goal is to strike a balance that provides a version of peaceful coexistence that is in itself 'an important and substantive moral principle'. While not necessarily a formula for harmony, it nevertheless legitimizes previously repressed or 'invisible' groups, and allows them fair access to competition for available resources. It has been found that politically engaged citizens who have a 'growing sense of their own effectiveness' in civil society are its best insurance against racist or extremist political ideologies and commitments (Walzer 1997: 6, 107).

Seeking a form of toleration that facilitates political co-operation and a will to sustain peace is a challenging but necessary achievement for societies emerging from conflict. The extent of courage and determination required by all sides to achieve this phase has been widely underestimated and misunderstood by the international community. A firm resolve is required to pursue peace by those who have had a past mired in conflict and poverty. It is even more difficult when they do not perceive access to and hope for a better future. If the international community would begin to broaden its net of those they consult when implementing development strategies, they could begin to take a bigger majority of the disenfranchised on board rather than leaving them to cause disruptions and make preparations to fight another day.

References

Arendt, H. (1958) *The Human Condition*, Chicago: University of Chicago Press.

Boyce, J.K. (2002) 'Investing in Peace: Aid and Conditionality after Civil Wars', *Adelphi Papers* 351, London: International Institute for Strategic Studies (IISS).

Boyce, J.K. (2004) 'Aid Conditionality as a Tool for Peacebuilding: Opportunities and Constraints', *Development and Change*, 33, 5: 1025–48.

Cox, M., A. Guelke and F. Stephen (eds) (2000) *A Farewell to Arms? From Long War to Long Peace in Northern Ireland*, Manchester: Manchester University Press.

Dowdney, L. (2005) *Neither War nor Peace: International Comparisons of Children and Youth in Organised Armed Violence*, Rio de Janeiro: COAV.

Exline, J.J., E.L. Worthington Jr, P. Hill and M.E. McCullough (2003) 'Forgiveness and Justice: A Research Agenda for Social and Personality Psychology', *Personality and Social Psychology Review*, 7, 4: 337–48.

Hartwell, M. (2004) 'The Concept of Justice in the Early Post-Conflict Period: A Comparative Perspective', in A. Guelke (ed.), *Democracy and Ethnic Conflict: Advancing Peace in Deeply Divided Societies*, published results of a colloquium of Research Committee (Politics and Ethnicity) of International Political Science Association, Belfast, 25–8 July 2001, Basingstoke: Palgrave Macmillan.

Hartwell, M. (2005) 'Perceptions of Justice, Identity and Political Processes of Forgiveness and Revenge in Early Post-Conflict Transitions, Case Studies: Northern Ireland, Serbia, South Africa', PhD thesis, Oxford University.

Jacoby, S. (1985) *Wild Justice: The Evolution of Revenge*, Glasgow: Collins and Bartholomew.

Keen, D. (2001) 'War and Peace: What's the Difference?', in A. Adebajo and C.L. Sriram (eds), *Managing Armed Conflicts in the 21st Century*, International Peace Academy, Oxford: Frank Cass.

Lerner, M.J. (2003) 'The Justice Motive: Where Social Psychologists Found It, How They Lost It, and Why They May Not Find It Again', *Personality and Social Psychology Review*, 7, 4: 388–99.

MacGinty, R. (2001) 'Ethno-National Conflict and Hate Crime', *The American Behavioral Scientist*, 45, 4: 639–53.

Shriver, D. (1995) *An Ethic For Enemies, Forgiveness in Politics*, Oxford: Oxford University Press.

Stedman, S.J. (1997) 'Spoiler Problems in Peace Processes', *International Security*, 22, 2: 5–53.

Tyler, T.R. and S. Blader (2003) 'The Group Engagement Model: Procedural Justice, Social Identity, and Co-operative Behavior', *Personality and Social Psychology Review*, 7, 4: 349–61.

Walzer, M. (1997) *On Toleration*, New Haven, CT: Yale University Press.

Part III

Human Development and Wellbeing

9
International Convergence or Higher Inequality in Human Development? Evidence for 1975–2002

Farhad Noorbakhsh

Introduction

This chapter is about the dynamics of inequality in development between countries. The issues of inequality along with poverty are firmly back on the agenda of most international development agencies. The Millennium Development Goals (MDGs) and targets were set at the turn of the century against a background of persistent poverty in some developing countries in order to reverse the declining trends. After a few years the hopes for reversing the trends, at least in a large number of sub-Saharan African (SSA) countries, are receding significantly (Sahn and Stifel 2003). Lack of achieving a basic threshold for education and health has been regarded as a structural impediment, among others, to sustained economic growth and welfare in poorer countries. Despite this the levels of health, education and economic growth are declining in a number of these countries mostly in SSA. During the 1990s, some 54 countries became poorer, 34 countries experienced a drop in life expectancy and the incidence of under five mortality rate (U5MR) increased in 14 countries (UNDP 2003: 34). In the table of life expectancy the bottom ten countries, mostly in SSA, have a life expectancy of below to just above 30 years, half of that of the top ten countries (WHO 2002). The most recent WHO (2003) report indicates that the increasing child mortality and decreasing life expectancy in a number of poorer countries in recent years has widened the global gap between the poor countries and the rest of the world. It seems that the large gap in life expectancy between developed and developing countries of 50 years ago has been replaced in recent years by a large gap between a group of very poor countries, mainly in SSA, and the rest of the world.

In contrast, progress in health, education and economic growth in a number of countries, mainly from Southeast Asia and Latin America, has been impressive. In between are countries that have made little progress, mainly from Asia and the Commonwealth of Independent States (UNDP 2003). In brief, the experiences of developing countries have been mixed at best. The growth rates in particular have been a mixture of take-offs, stagnation and decline. Between 1960 and 1990 fewer developed countries had wide variability in their growth rate ranging from -2.7 to $+6.9$ per cent (Pritchett 1997). This raises the question as to whether the world is becoming more polarized.

The research on income differences among countries in recent years has taken two closely related approaches: testing the hypothesis of convergence and measuring inequality and its dynamics. These are basically two sides of the same coin, both investigating whether the distribution between richer and poorer countries is moving towards equalization or more polarization. Progress in international trade and globalization has also focused the attention on international inequality. While globalization is expected to affect intra-country and inter-country inequalities there is little agreement on whether such effects are for better or worse.[1] In general, the outcome of research on world income (expenditure) inequality is controversial apparently due to the adaptation of different methodology by researchers (UNDP 2003).

A number of studies conclude that the world distribution of income has worsened over the past three to four decades. Korzeniewicz and Moran (1997) conclude that the gap between richer and poorer nations grew steadily between 1965 and 1990 and in particular intensified during the recession years of 1980s. UNDP (1999) indicates that the ratio of income in the richer countries with 20 per cent of world population to the poorest nations with 20 per cent of world population, had risen from 30 times in 1960 to 74 times in 1977. Over a longer period the ratio of per capita income of the richest country to the poorest between 1870 and 1990 increased by almost a factor of five (Pritchett 1997). While this is the case with the very richest and very poorest countries the population-weighted measures of inequality for all countries do not seem to provide a clear picture.[2]

Other studies focus on inequality between countries as well as within-country inequality by also taking into account income distribution within countries. In some cases this is done by estimating the entire distribution of income from the Gini coefficient for the country (Chotikapanich *et al.* 1997; Schultz 1998). More recently Sala-í-Martín (2002) concludes that between 1980 and 1998 world income inequality shows a decline. Dollar and Kraay (2002a; b) argue that global inequality increased significantly over the past two centuries stabilizing in 1980 and somewhat declining in more recent years. Bourguignon and Morrisson (2002) study the distribution of income among the world citizens by looking at the distribution among 11 quintiles for each country in the sample. The time span of this study is spread over two centuries, concluding that in the early nineteenth century the main contributor to inequality was the differences within countries, while in more recent years the main source was the inequality between countries. Milanovic (2002) uses country household surveys for deriving the income and expenditure distribution within countries and concludes that world income inequality increased during 1988–93 from an already very high base. The Gini coefficient of 0.63 in 1988 increased at a rather fast pace to 0.66 in 1993.

In brief, there is little agreement on whether the world inequality has declined or widened. However, the above studies, though controversial in their results, have two common features. First, they agree that most of the world inequality is driven by *between* country inequality while the within-country inequality is a low contributor to the overall inequality. Second, that they all concentrate on the inequality or convergence of income or expenditure and use no other indicator of welfare.[3] To the best of our knowledge there is no study that extends the concept of convergence to non-income indicators. Given the spread of mass communications in recent decades it seems equally likely, if not more, that convergence among countries could happen with respect to the level of education and health as compared to income. This chapter attempts to fill up this gap by studying international convergence of, and inequality in, development.

The rest of this chapter is organized as follows. The second section briefly discusses the approaches to the concept of convergence. The third section relates and tests the relevance of this concept to the human development index (HDI) and its non-income components. The fourth section tests the hypothesis of convergence for HDI. The penultimate takes into account the population concentration in deriving the measures of inequality and discusses the dynamics of change in distribution of development and the extent of upward and downward mobility. The final section concludes.

Convergence

According to the neoclassical growth model, given the fully competitive markets and the availability of similar technology, for the same rate of investment every economy would grow at a similar rate determined by the exogenous technical progress and population growth. Assuming a production function with constant returns to scale and the diminishing returns of capital, economies with lower levels of initial productivity enjoy a higher rate of growth in productivity and as such will catch up with the more developed economies. The more recent work on explaining the process of catching up is extensive and advocates three possible, and sometimes related, forms of convergence: β-convergence, conditional β-convergence and σ-convergence.

β-convergence postulates that poorer countries will tend to grow faster than the richer countries. This is because of the diminishing marginal returns to capital in the richer countries, as the level of capital per labour is relatively high in these countries. Moreover, the further down a country is below its balanced growth path and the higher the lags in access to new technology the higher would be the expected growth when the country gains access to such technology (Romer 1986). In the empirical literature, running a cross-section regression of the time-averaged per capita income growth rate on the level of per capita income in the initial period tests this. A negative sign for the respective coefficient reflects the existence of convergence.

Most of the relevant empirical literatures have attempted to test cross-country β-convergence and measure the speed of convergence.[4] The general consensus is that there exists an evidence of convergence only among the richer countries. There is little evidence of convergence on the part of low-income countries (Zind 1991). Some researchers go further by stating that, while the growth rates of income among richer countries show a historical convergence, the picture for less developed countries vis-à-vis the richer countries tells a story of divergence (Pritchett 1997). Such results provide support for the idea of 'convergence clubs' in the sense that convergence may apply to groups of countries which have similar initial conditions and structures. One such club may be the richer countries and another could be developing countries or the least developed countries (LDCs). Indeed, the inequality among such clubs may persist and may even result in further divergence (Martin and Sunley 1998; Quah 1993; 1996b). The literature considers a number of possible reasons for the lack of convergence among poor and rich countries. One such reason is mainly related to the proposition that the nature and process of convergence requires that the institutions in the poorer countries to be supportive of inward flows of foreign capital and technology. Another explanation is based on the fact that human capital is initially higher in the richer countries resulting in a higher output and hence higher saving and investment in these countries enabling them to maintain their lead over poorer countries indefinitely.[5]

The second type of convergence, conditional β-convergence, mainly takes into consideration the steady-state growth path of the country.[6] If the structural conditions of countries were different the respective long-run growth rates would be different which may result in divergence or at best a very weak convergence. This type of convergence may be tested in the same way except that the regression should also include a set of explanatory variables which would define the steady-state growth path for per capita income (Barro 1991; Barro and Sala-í-Martín 1992). A negative coefficient for the per capita income in the initial period, in the presence of the extra *conditional variables*, suggests the existence of conditional β-convergence.

The third type, σ-convergence, envisages that the cross-country dispersion of per capita income levels across economies would tend to decrease over time, implying a tendency among countries to equalization of per capita income in the long run. That is, over time the dispersion around the steady-state value decreases. β-convergence is a necessary condition for σ-convergence but not a sufficient condition (Barro and Sala-í-Martín 1995).

Convergence of human development index

The concept of convergence is mainly discussed in the literature in the context of output per capita usually measured in terms of GDP per capita. This concept was developed from the Solow model and one of its main arguments relates to the diminishing returns to capital. As HDI also has non-income components, it may be useful to explore the relevance of convergence to this index. For this purpose a brief description of HDI may be helpful.

The HDI is a composite index of four indicators. Its components are to reflect three major dimensions of development: longevity, knowledge and access to resources. These are to represent three of the essential choices in life (UNDP 1990) and are derived from the notion of human capabilities as proposed by Amartya Sen. Although this index has been criticized on a number of grounds,[7] it has been suggested that the components of the HDI together seem to provide an almost acceptable package of indicators of the level of living at an aggregate level and has been adopted frequently in recent literature.[8] The dimension of longevity is directly measured by life expectancy at birth. Knowledge is presented by a measure of educational achievement based on a weighted sum of adult literacy rate and the combined first-, second- and third-level gross enrolment ratio. Access to resources is represented by the logarithm of real per capita income (purchasing power parity).

The concept of diminishing returns would apply to the income component of HDI as discussed in the previous section. It would also seem applicable to the component of education, as the early 'units' of educational attainments are relatively easier and less costly to attain. Diminishing returns are equally applicable to the component of life expectancy as it would be much more difficult and costly to attain a higher level of life expectancy from an initially high level than a low level.

The main difference with income component is that while income in the context of diminishing returns to capital is linked to the mobility of capital, at international level for non-income components, this does not apply fully. However, the concept of diminishing returns may be linked to the point that the returns to investment in education and health diminish as the level of investment in health and education increases. Two indicators of adult literacy and combined enrolment ratios measure the dimension of education in HDI. The returns to investment in education, for improving adult literacy and increasing the combined enrolment ratio, will be higher in countries that are relatively at a lower level of initial education as measured by these indicators. Similarly, the returns to investment in health, for improving life expectancy, will be higher in countries that have a lower life expectancy as compared to those with a higher level of life expectancy. In brief, countries with lower levels of education and health will grow faster over time, in terms of education and health, than countries that initially enjoy higher levels.

More specifically, in a country that has reached a very high level of primary and secondary enrolment, only the relatively more expensive investment in tertiary education could improve the level of educational attainment used in HDI. Similarly for an equal amount of investment in health facilities in two countries with similar conditions but with low and high levels of life expectancy, relatively more life expectancy could be gained in the country with the low initial level of life expectancy.

In the light of the discussion above, the fact that the literacy and enrolment ratio components of HDI are both defined across countries regardless of differences in quality and the existence of an upper limit for these indicators, it seems plausible to suggest that the concept of convergence would be equally, if not more, applicable to education and life expectancy. Similarly it may be argued that access to technology relevant to education and health for improving the level of adult literacy, combined enrolment and life expectancy in countries that are at a lower level of these indicators is relatively more plausible as compared to access to technology required for obtaining a higher level of production in the standard neoclassical model.

We tested these suggestions empirically by estimating the parameters of the following equation, which is mainly the growth regression equation[9] for adult literacy and life expectancy:

$$\left(\frac{1}{T}\right) \log\left(\frac{x_{it+T}}{x_{it}}\right) = \alpha + \beta \log(x_{it}) + u_{it} \tag{9.1}$$

where $x_{it} = \dfrac{x_{it}}{x_t}$ is the ratio of x (adult literacy or life expectancy) in the ith

country to the average for the sample of countries under consideration. $\left(\frac{1}{T}\right) \log\left(\frac{x_{it+T}}{x_{it}}\right)$ is the annualized growth of the variable x in the ith country over the period of t and $t + T$. A negative value of β would be an evidence of β-convergence. Table 9.1 shows the results for the annualized adult literacy growth (1975–98) and life expectancy (1977–98) for a sample of 93 developing countries.

The results in Table 9.1 provide support for the suggestion that the diminishing returns to investment in education and health are indeed the case in developing countries. The β coefficient for both indicators is negative and highly significant indicating that countries with a lower initial level of adult literacy (life expectancy) grow faster in terms of these indicators. Briefly we may conclude that it is plausible to extend the concept of diminishing returns to investment to the non-income components of HDI. Consequently it would be possible that countries with a low level of development in the initial period would have a higher rate of growth in HDI in the long run than those with high level development in the initial period.

We test for the existence of β-convergence in HDI by employing the following K models:

$$\left(\frac{1}{T}\right) \log\left(\frac{hdi_{it+T}}{hdi_{it}}\right) = \alpha + \beta \log(hdi_{it}) + \sum_{j=1}^{J_k} \lambda_{ij} S_{ij} + u_{it} \quad \text{for } k = 0, 1, 2, \cdots, K \tag{9.2}$$

Table 9.1   Convergence results for adult literacy and life expectancy

Indicators	Adult literacy	Life expectancy
Constant	0.001	−0.000
	(3.15)***	(−0.23)
Log x_t	−0.020	−0.009
	(−25.44)***	(−3.00)***
N	92	92
Adjusted R^2	0.88	0.08
F statistic	647.28***	8.97***

Note: ***Significant at the 1% level. Figures in parentheses are t-ratios.

where $hdi_{it} = \dfrac{HDI_{it}}{HDI_t}$ is the ratio of HDI in the ith country to the average for the

sample of countries under consideration. $\left(\dfrac{1}{T}\right) \log\left(\dfrac{hdi_{it+T}}{hdi_{it}}\right)$ is the annualized growth

of the variable HDI in the ith country over the period of t and $t + T$. A value of β in the range of $-1 < \beta < 0$ would be an evidence of β-convergence. That is, the nearer the value of β to -1, the higher the speed of convergence and the nearer to zero the lower the speed of convergence. By implication zero means no convergence and a positive value for β indicates a divergence. S_{ij} is the jth structural condition variable and λ_{ij} is the respective parameter to be estimated. There are K different models where the structural conditional variables change and for k = 0 all S_{ij} are zeros, i.e. the absolute convergence model.

The data for HDI for the period of 1975–2002 (at intervals of five years up to 2000 and two years for the last period) has been taken from UNDP (2004). As for some countries time series start at the middle of this period; adjustment in the length of the period in equation (2) are made to reflect this for the respective countries.

The variables included for reflecting conditional convergence are selected on the grounds of contributing to the components of HDI. There are two types of variables that may take account of the external and domestic contributions to HDI. In the conditional β-convergence model it is postulated that the institutions in poorer countries should be supportive of inward flows of foreign capital and technology. While a certain amount of technology is transferred with foreign direct investment, the openness of the country to international trade also may be responsible for such a transfer. We have selected both these variables: foreign direct investment as a percentage of GDP (FDI) and trade as a percentage of GDP (TRD). Foreign aid as a percentage of GDP (AID) has also been included as a substantial amount of aid is geared to improving the health and educational status of the recipient country. These variables reflect the external sources of contribution to HDI.

We have selected three variables to reflect the domestic contributions to HDI: gross domestic investment as a percentage of GDP (GDI), the average annual growth rate of public sector expenditure on education and health as a percentage of GDP (gPEEH) and the number of telephone lines per population (TEL) to reflect the level of infrastructure.[10] Our initial sample of 93 countries includes 61 medium and 32 low human development countries. We have not included the high human development countries in the β-convergence models on the grounds of the general consensus, in the literature of growth, on the possible existence of wide-apart convergence clubs for rich and developing countries. In addition, the variables selected to represent the structural conditions would be widely different for the high human development countries.[11]

Empirical results for convergence hypotheses

We tested the hypothesis of β-convergence, in its absolute and conditional forms, through a number of models for different samples. Table 9.2 shows the results for the sample of medium and low human development countries.

Table 9.2 β-convergence models of HDI for medium and low development countries

Models/variables	1	2	3
Constant	−0.0004	0.0000	0.0003
	(−2.01)**	(0.00)	(0.08)
Log hdi_t	−0.0081	−0.0115	−0.0112
	(−5.03)***	(−3.74)***	(−3.71)***
Log GDI		0.0033	0.0036
		(1.98)**	(2.17)**
gPEEH		0.0000	0.0000
		(1.34)	(1.28)
Log TEL		0.0003	0.0005
		(0.48)	(0.80)
Log AID		−0.0003	
		(−0.61)	
Log FDI		0.0004	0.0004
		(0.76)	(0.78)
Log TRD		−0.0030	−0.0035
		(−1.97)**	(−2.86)***
N	93	75	75
Adjusted R^2	0.21	0.31	0.32
F statistics	25.28***	5.83***	6.80***

Note: *** Significant at the 1% level; ** Significant at the 5% level. Figures in parentheses are t-ratios.

Model 1 reflects the absolute convergence hypothesis. The negative sign of hdi_t is as expected and it is significant at the 1 per cent level indicating a clear tendency to convergence among the countries in the sample. However, the magnitude of the coefficient is very low reflecting a very slow speed of convergence over the period.

Model 2 introduces the conditional β-convergence. The conditions employed are of external and internal origins. Theoretically, convergence is conditional on governments being supportive of foreign capital transfer and technology. Often the literature argues that the transfer of technology and capital is through foreign direct investment, openness and sometimes aid. These variables are normally regarded as reflecting the degree of globalization in a country. Other variables are more directly of domestic origin. The gross domestic investment as a percentage of GDP is relevant to the income component of HDI, while the growth of public sector expenditure on education and health as a percentage of GDP are directly relevant to the education and longevity components of HDI. The variable reflecting the number of telephone lines per population is included as a proxy for domestic infrastructure.

In the presence of these variables in Model 2 the coefficient of hdi_t has remained negative and highly significant. GDI has a positive coefficient significant at the 5 per cent level indicating that the growth differential in HDI is a positive function of investment, which most probably works through the income component of the index. The growth rate of public sector expenditure on education and health expectedly has a positive sign but not significant. Other variables are insignificant except trade, which is significant with a negative sign. Overall Model 2 provides support for the proposition of conditional convergence in the sample over the period. However, the speed of convergence is low.

In Model 3 AID is excluded from the equation on the basis of a possible argument that aid may have been more provided to countries that have had a lower level of development, hence the question of endogeniety may arise. The results do not change and the coefficient of hdi_t remains negative and highly significant. Overall the results are robust indicating strongly that there has been a conditional convergence in HDI close to absolute convergence though in all cases the speed of convergence has been slow.

A fundamental idea behind the concept of absolute convergence is that the structural conditions in countries are similar. The literature of growth argues that there may be clubs of convergence where the members of such specific clubs have a tendency to converge. With this in mind we split the sample into medium development and low development countries to see if the results would be different. Table 9.3 provides the results for the same models for medium development countries.

The most interesting feature is that the same picture for absolute and conditional convergence emerges, as the coefficient of hdi_t remains negative and highly significant in all models. The magnitude of this coefficient once again reveals a

Table 9.3 β-convergence models of HDI for medium human development countries

Models/variables	1	2	3
Constant	0.0007	−0.0027	−0.0025
	(2.83)***	(−0.85)	(−0.82)
Log hdi_t	−0.0170	−0.0161***	−0.0159***
	(−7.42)***	(−5.06)	(−5.21)
Log GDI		0.0031**	0.0032**
		(2.23)	(2.38)
gPEEH		0.0000	0.0000
		(0.41)	(0.37)
Log TEL		−0.0002	−0.0001
		(−0.33)	(−0.24)
Log AID		−0.0001	
		(−0.31)	
Log FDI		0.0002	0.0002
		(0.37)	(0.35)
Log TRD		−0.0014	−0.0016
		(−1.13)	(−1.73)
N	61	51	51
Adjusted R²	0.47	0.62	0.63
F statistics	55.02***	12.58***	14.97***

Note: *** Significant at the 1% level; ** Significant at the 5% level. Figures in parentheses are t-ratios.

slow speed of convergence but higher than that of the full sample. In this respect the results are very robust. The globalization variables of AID, FDI and TRD are not significant in the last two models. Overall these models for the medium HDI sample seems to provide sensible results with a rather high adjusted R^2 of up to 0.63 and highly significant F statistics.

Table 9.4 shows the results for the same models of absolute and conditional β-convergence for low development countries. Once again the models are very robust as the coefficient of hdi_t remains negative and highly significant in all models. The magnitude of this coefficient is nearly one-third higher than that of the medium HDI sample though still indicating a slow speed of convergence.

The last type of convergence, σ-convergence, hypothesizes that the deviations from the long-run cross-country mean have a tendency to converge towards the mean over time (Barro 1991; Barro and Sala-í-Martín 1992). The underlying assumption for this type of convergence is that the steady-state value of the variable concerned and its time trends are the same for all countries as the constant term in equation (9.2) conceptually includes the steady-state value of the HDI variable (Barro and Sala-í-Martín 1995). In the empirical literature the standard deviation of the logarithm of the variable concerned is commonly used for investigating if this type of convergence has taken place.

Table 9.5 shows the results for three different measures of dispersion of HDI among countries over time. The first column presents the standard deviation of

Table 9.4 β-convergence models of HDI for low human development countries

Models/variables	1	2	3
Constant	−0.0032	0.0083	0.0076
	(−4.68)***	(1.06)	(0.93)
Log hdi_t	−0.0192	−0.0221	−0.0222
	(−4.97)***	(−3.72)***	(−3.59)***
Log GDI		−0.0001	−0.0009
		(−0.28)	(−0.24)
gPEEH		0.0001	0.0001
		(1.47)	(1.55)
Log TEL		0.0019	0.0025
		(1.00)	(1.28)
Log AID		−0.0020	
		(−1.57)	
Log FDI		0.0001	0.0017
		(0.65)	(1.21)
Log TRD		−0.0022	−0.0039
		(−0.69)	(−1.30)
N	32	24	24
Adjusted R^2	0.43	0.46	0.41
F statistics	24.67***	3.72***	3.62**

Note: *** Significant at the 1% level; ** Significant at the 5% level. Figures in parentheses are t-ratios.

Table 9.5 Measures of σ-convergence for HDI

Year	SD log(hdi_{it})	CV	GiniC
1975	0.1371	0.2941	0.1674
1980	0.1330	0.2792	0.1602
1985	0.1300	0.2698	0.1542
1990	0.1269	0.2643	0.1507
1995	0.1243	0.2588	0.1465
2002	0.1215	0.2554	0.1439

log(hdi). The second column depicts the results for the coefficient of variation (CV) which is the ratio of the standard deviation to the mean of distribution. The last column shows the Gini coefficient (GiniC) as a measure of dispersion among countries.[12] All measures show a convergence amongst middle and low development countries. However, considering the length of the period, the pace of convergence seems to be very slow confirming our previous results for β-convergence.

Population-weighted measures of inequality and dynamics of mobility

The measures considered so far were for investigating the possible occurrence of convergence as this particular strand of literature on inequality and convergence postulates. However, these measures assess the degree of concentration between countries without taking into account the population of the countries concerned. Furthermore as convergence is basically about poor countries catching up with rich countries, it is argued that, it should be more relevant to the cross-sectional of the distribution of the phenomena under consideration and not to the convergence of individual economies to their own individual steady state (Quah 1996a). This is to do with the dynamics of mobility in distribution.

To start with we have employed two measures of inequality, which take into account the population share of each country, for investigating the extent and dynamics of inequality among countries. These measures are the Gini coefficient and the Theil index.[13] As the concept of inequality is not constrained by the argument of clubs of convergence it would be interesting to asses both these measures for two separate samples: the medium and low development sample (ML) and for all countries including the high development countries. Furthermore, we limit our study to measuring between-country inequalities as most recent literature, which has used the decomposed measures for including the within country sources of inequality as well, concludes that the main source of inequality is the between-country component.[14] Table 9.6 shows the results for our two samples.

For the ML development sample the Gini coefficient has increased from 1975–90 with a drop in 1995 before resuming its upward trend. This indeed is showing a picture of divergence among ML development countries. Theil index for these countries shows an initial increase before coming down; its decline over the entire period is hardly considerable. This is in line with the results of weak

Table 9.6 Population-weighted measures of inequality

Time	GiniP ML	Theil index ML	GiniP all countries	Theil index all countries
1975	0.1001	0.6962	0.1887	0.6708
1980	0.1198	0.7355	0.1878	0.7059
1985	0.1220	0.7285	0.1805	0.7008
1990	0.1235	0.6827	0.1745	0.6594
1995	0.1220	0.6781	0.1678	0.6616
2002	0.1232	0.6654	0.1644	0.6588

convergence in the previous section. As for the full sample, Gini shows a steady but relatively weak decline over 28 years while the Thiel index depicts an initial increase before coming down in 2002 to just below its level in 1975. The overall picture for both samples does not show a considerable decrease in equality in development among countries.

Another way of looking at the international distribution of HDI is to focus on the degree of mobility of various regions in the world over time. Table 9.7 shows the regional composition of various quintiles of the international distribution of HDI for the period of our sample for all countries. For 1975 the first row of Table 9.7 shows the distribution of countries in various regions of the world; 85 per cent of countries in the bottom 20 per cent of HDI value were in Africa, with Asia and Pacific accounting for 15 per cent. The top 20 per cent band is exclusive to European countries and their offshoots (95 per cent) and Japan. Latin American countries dominate the middle 60 per cent band with relatively lesser presence from other regions. There is very little change in the bottom 20 per cent band in 1980, which is again dominated primarily by African and to a lesser extent by Asian countries. This is coupled with relatively little change in the middle band composition. As for the top band the dominance of Europe and its offshoots is not challenged but a relatively small presence of Latin American countries in this band is notable. A worsening of the position of African countries and an improvement in the case of Asian countries in the bottom 20 per cent band is shown in 1985, with little notable change in other bands. Fewer African and more Asian countries appear in the bottom 20 per cent band in 1990 before the worsening trend for Africa resumes its path in 1995 and 2002. For the last two periods the share of African (Asian) countries in the lower band has increased (decreased) notably. The entry of some Asian countries into the top 20 per cent band is interesting. However, despite the presence of countries from all regions (except Africa) in the top band in 2002, the European countries and their offshoots dominate this band.

The overall picture for the dynamics of human development over the period of 1975–2002 reveals little upward mobility for the poor countries of the world. The relative situation for SSA countries worsened, for some Asian countries it improved, with the top band being dominated by European countries and their offshoots.

Table 9.7 Dynamics of regional composition of HDI for selected quintiles (%)

World	Quintiles	Africa	Asia and Pacific	Japan, Hong Kong and Korea	Latin America	Eastern Europe	Europe and its offshoots	Total
1975	Total	33.0	18.0	3.0	21.0	1.0	24.0	100
	bottom 20%	85.0	15.0	0.0	0.0	0.0	0.0	100
	middle 60%	26.7	25.0	3.3	35.0	1.7	8.3	100
	top 20%	0.0	0.0	5.0	0.0	0.0	95.0	100
1980	Total	30.1	18.6	2.7	20.4	6.2	22.1	100
	bottom 20%	82.6	17.4	0.0	0.0	0.0	0.0	100
	middle 60%	22.4	25.4	3.0	32.8	10.4	6.0	100
	top 20%	0.0	0.0	4.3	4.3	0.0	91.3	100
1985	Total	32.8	19.7	2.5	18.9	5.7	20.5	100
	bottom 20%	88.0	12.0	0.0	0.0	0.0	0.0	100
	middle 60%	25.0	29.2	1.4	30.6	9.7	4.2	100
	top 20%	0.0	0.0	8.0	4.0	0.0	88.0	100
1990	Total	28.7	22.8	2.2	16.2	11.8	18.4	100
	bottom 20%	77.8	22.2	0.0	0.0	0.0	0.0	100
	middle 60%	22.0	30.5	1.2	25.6	19.5	1.2	100
	top 20%	0.0	0.0	7.4	3.7	0.0	88.9	100
1995	Total	30.0	22.9	2.1	15.7	11.4	17.9	100
	bottom 20%	85.7	14.3	0.0	0.0	0.0	0.0	100
	middle 60%	21.4	32.1	1.2	25.0	19.0	1.2	100
	top 20%	0.0	3.6	7.1	3.6	0.0	85.7	100
2002	Total	30.0	22.9	2.1	15.7	11.4	17.9	100
	bottom 20%	92.8	7.2	0.0	0.0	0.0	0.0	100
	middle 60%	18.2	33.5	1.2	25.9	20.0	1.2	100
	top 20%	0.0	3.4	7.1	3.7	0.0	85.8	100

A complementary way of reviewing the dynamics of human development disparities is to find out how countries change position over time. This approach, adopted in recent literature, investigates the degree of mobility of countries (with the size of their population taken into account) moving from one band of HDI to another over time.[15] Table 9.8 shows the results for four HDI bands relative to the mean of the sample and for various sub-periods.

For each period interval the percentage population in HDI bands in the initial year which have moved to various bands in the final year are shown. The bands are selected such that they are spread around the mean evenly. The row entitled 'total population share' shows the percentage of population in each band at the beginning of the period and the column with the same title shows the same at the end of the period. A comparison of this row and column reveals the change in inequality over the relevant period. The details of such mobility are shown in the transition matrix (figures in italics). The immobility ratio is computed as the percentage of population not changing band by the final year (the diagonal of the transition matrix). The upward and downward mobility are the shares of population moving to upper or lower bands (the upper and lower off diagonal elements of the transition matrix respectively).

Table 9.8 Relative populated HDI mobility matrix and mobility ratios (%)

HDI in final year relative to mean	More than 4/3 mean	1 to 4/3 mean	2/3 to 1 mean	Less than 2/3 mean	Total population share	Mobility ratio
1975–80						
More than 4/3 mean	99.6	0.0	0.0	0.0	19.9	
1 to 4/3 mean	0.4	100.0	0.0	0.0	17.7	
2/3 to 1 mean	0.0	0.0	99.6	5.5	53.8	
Less than 2/3 mean	0.0	0.0	0.4	94.5	8.6	
Total population share	20.0	17.7	53.4	8.9	100.0	
Immobility ratio						98.4
Upward mobility						1.4
Downward mobility						0.2
1980–85						
More than 4/3 mean	76.9	0.0	0.0	0.0	14.5	
1 to 4/3 mean	23.1	100.0	0.0	0.0	22.7	
2/3 to 1 mean	0.0	0.0	98.3	0.0	53.1	
Less than 2/3 mean	0.0	0.0	1.7	100.0	9.7	
Total population share	18.9	18.3	54.0	8.8	100.0	
Immobility ratio						93.8
Upward mobility						0.0
Downward mobility						6.2
1985–90						
More than 4/3 mean	95.0	0.0	0.0	0.0	11.3	
1 to 4/3 mean	5.0	100.0	2.2	0.0	26.0	
2/3 to 1 mean	0.0	0.0	97.8	0.0	52.4	
Less than 2/3 mean	0.0	0.0	0.0	100.0	10.3	
Total population share	11.9	24.2	53.6	10.3	100.0	
Immobility ratio						98.2
Upward mobility						0.5
Downward mobility						1.3
1990–95						
More than 4/3 mean	85.4	7.1	0.0	0.0	11.0	
1 to 4/3 mean	14.6	92.8	2.8	0.0	26.8	
2/3 to 1 mean	0.0	0.1	96.6	26.3	53.9	
Less than 2/3 mean	0.0	0.0	0.6	73.7	8.3	
Total population share	10.8	25.6	52.8	10.8	100.0	
Immobility ratio						87.1
Upward mobility						9.1
Downward mobility						3.8
1995–2002						
More than 4/3 mean	100.0	8.0	0.0	0.0	12.7	
1 to 4/3 mean	0.0	88.6	43.3	0.0	47.6	
2/3 to 1 mean	0.0	3.4	56.7	33.5	33.9	
Less than 2/3 mean	0.0	0.0	0.0	66.5	5.8	
Total population share	10.6	26.5	54.3	8.6	100.0	
Immobility ratio						77.9
Upward mobility						21.2
Downward mobility						0.9

Continued

Table 9.8 Continued

HDI in final year relative to mean	More than 4/3 mean	1 to 4/3 mean	2/3 to 1 mean	Less than 2/3 mean	Total population share	Mobility ratio
1975–2002						
More than 4/3 mean	66.6	0.0	0.0	0.0	13.4	
1 to 4/3 mean	33.4	95.3	51.9	0.0	52.5	
2/3 to 1 mean	0.0	4.7	46.3	54.8	29.0	
Less than 2/3 mean	0.0	0.0	1.8	45.2	5.1	
Total population share	20.0	17.7	53.4	8.9	100.0	
Immobility ratio						63.3
Upward mobility						26.7
Downward mobility						10.0

There is little evidence of change in distribution for the period of 1975–80. More than 98 per cent of population remained in the same bands as the initial year. There is a little more downward mobility for the period of 1980–85, though essentially there is a high degree of immobility for this period. The degree of immobility for 1985–90 is very high again. It is during the period of 1990–95 that some upward mobility takes place. This is mainly due to some populated countries moving to a higher band (among them Pakistan, Iran, Sudan and Tunisia). The downward mobility for this period is mainly due to some European countries or their offshoots dropping out of the top band due to this band not being wide enough to accommodate them all. The relatively big move takes place for the period of 1995–2002. During this period more than 21 per cent of population moved upwards. Almost all this transition is in the middle part of the distribution and is explained by the upward movement of two highly populated countries: China and Bangladesh. The change in distribution is evident in the transition matrix as well as the changes in the overall distribution at the final period as compared to the initial period (column and row of 'total population share'). For this period, and to some extent for the previous two periods, we see a movement towards the 'twin peaks' in distribution as suggested by Quah (1996a) and observed for income data in the long run by Jones (1997) and Bourguignon and Morrisson (2002).

The final section of Table 9.8 shows the mobility for the entire period of our sample, 1975–2002. The twin peak effect is clearer in this longer interval. There are clear upward and downward movements in development over the period of 28 years. The upward mobility has resulted in more than 26 per cent of population in the sample to move from the bottom two bands to the upper middle bands. There is a nearly 55 per cent movement from the bottom band to the next band coupled by nearly 52 per cent movement from the 2/3 to 1 mean band to the next upper band. The downward movement is mostly due to some European countries and their offshoots dropping to a lower band coupled with some relatively small downward movement from the second top band to the third. The overall changes in the distribution of development in 2002 as compared to 1975 (column and row of 'total population share') depict a clear picture of movement from the bottom to the lower-middle band, from the lower-middle to the upper-middle band and also from the top band towards the middle-upper band. The mobility ratios indicate that nearly 27 per cent of population moved upward as compared to a downward mobility of 10 per cent and an immobility ratio of just above 63 per cent during this period.

Conclusion and policy implications

The concepts of convergence and inequality could be usefully employed in studying the evolvement of development over time. The extension of conversion hypothesis to the non-income components of HDI could be validated conceptually and empirically. The growth regression for the medium and low development countries shows an evidence of weak absolute convergence in development over 28 years. These findings are robust and remain the same for various models of conditional convergence. The same is established for sub-samples of medium and also low development countries. The measures of σ-convergence are in line with those for weak β-convergence. When the population size of countries are taken into account the results differ. The Gini coefficient for medium and low development countries shows a worsening of inequality while in the case of all countries sample we see little change in inequality over the 28 years time span of this study. A regional breakdown of the sample over time clearly showed that in 2002 almost all countries in the bottom 20 per cent of HDI are SSA countries – a situation worse than that of 1975. During the 1975–2002 period, the Asian and Latin American countries experienced considerable progress in human development.

Regarding population mobility between mean-relative HDI bands there is little movement for the first three five-year periods from 1975–90. It is during 1990–95 that we see some upward and downward mobility with the former being higher. This is mainly driven by a number of medium population-sized countries such as Pakistan and Iran moving one HDI band up and some less populated countries moving down. During the 1995–2002 period, there is more upward mobility mainly caused by the highly populated China and Bangladesh moving up one band. This resulted in a considerable change in the middle sections of distribution. The change in distribution for the entire period of 1975–2002 shows considerable mobility again in the middle part of distribution depicting a case of 'twin peaks' with the previously dominant lower-middle band peak in the beginning of the period being replaced by an upper-middle peak at the end of the period.

All this illustrates that there have been some signs of equalization in the distribution of HDI but a few populated countries mainly drive this. There are also signs of polarization, particularly among the developing countries. While some countries, mainly in Asia and Latin America, have progressed considerably, SSA seems to have been caught in a deep trap of low human development with no signs of getting out of it. These countries are not moving in the direction of the MDG as expected and, if the current trends continue, by 2015 they would be worse off in some aspects such as poverty and nowhere near the goals for the remaining MDG. To ensure improvements in human development in poorer countries, who need this most, and a reduction in inequality far more effort under the MDG is needed.

Given that poorer countries on their own lack the required resources for this purpose, as recognized by a number of reports,[16] far more rigorous efforts are required by international aid agencies and donor countries in order to change the current trends.

Notes

I am grateful to the Helsinki conference participants for their constructive comments, in particular Giovanni Andrea Cornia, Mark McGillivray and Gustav Ranis. I am also grateful to Shadan Noorbakhsh for helping me with most of the computations.

1. See, for example, Dollar and Kraay (2002a; b); Milanovic (2003).
2. I am grateful to the anonymous referee for indicating this ambiguity of results. Firebaugh (1999); Dowrick and Akmal (2005).
3. The only partial exception to the second point is Bourguignon and Morrison (2002), which also considers the inequality in life expectancy as a wider measure of welfare. However, this measure in their study is only employed for obtaining income over the expected life of population and not as a measure of welfare in its own right.
4. See for example Baumol (1986); Romer (1986); Baumol and Wolff (1988); Mankiw *et al.* (1992); Barro and Sala-í-Martín (1995); Sala-í-Martín (1996); de la Fuente (1997).
5. These have been incorporated in the new endogenous growth models, which consider human capital and technology to be endogenous. Romer (1986; 1990); Sachs and Larrain (1993); Hossain (2000).
6. Some literature regards conditional β-convergence as a form of β-convergence and classifies it with the latter. However, the extent of empirical work on the former may warrant such typology; see for example Hossain (2000).
7. For some of the criticisms see McGillivray (1991); McGillivray and White (1993); Srinivasan (1994); Noorbakhsh (1998).
8. See, for example, Noorbakhsh (1999); Neumayer (2001); Kosack (2003).
9. For examples of the use of this type of regression see the literature referred to on pp. 157-2.
10. The data for FDI, AID, GDI and TRD are the totals over 1973-98, for gPEEH average annual for 1990-98 and TEL for 1990. The source for all is the World Development Indicators STAR disk.
11. For example, AID or TEL may be inappropriate variables for the high human development group of countries.
12. The GiniC coefficient has been computed without taking the size of the population into account. It is a measure of the concentration (dispersion) of indicator HDI among countries regardless of their population size. See Pyatt *et al.* (1980); Milanovic (1997); Noorbakhsh (2003).
13. For Gini coefficient:

$$Gini = \frac{1}{\mu} \sum_{i=1}^{N} \sum_{j=1}^{N} f(y_i) f(y_j) |y_i - y_j|$$

where for N countries y_i is the value of HDI in country i, $f(y_i)$ is the population share of country i in total population and μ is the mean value for HDI. For Theil index:

$$T = \sum_{i=1}^{N} Y_i \log \frac{Y_i}{X_i}$$

where Y_i and X_i are the HDI and population shares of country i respectively.

14. Furthermore there is a controversy in the procedure used for finding the within-country distribution and hence the within-country inequality for income. In addition, the extension of such procedures for deriving the within-country distribution of the non-income components of HDI may be even more controversial. Lastly, because education and health are more public goods in most developing countries it is more likely that their

distributions within countries are, relatively speaking, more even than that of income. Schultz (1998); Milanovic (2002); Bourguignon and Morrison (2002).
15. See Quah (1996a) and Bourguignon and Morrisson (2002) for its application to income.
16. Such as WHO (2003); UNDP (2003).

References

Barro, R.J. (1991) 'Economic Growth in a Cross Section of Countries', *Quarterly Journal of Economics*, 106: 407–43.

Barro, R.J. and X. Sala-í-Martín (1992) 'Convergence', *Journal of Political Economy*, 100: 223–51.

Barro, R.J. and X. Sala-í-Martín (1995) *Economic Growth*, New York: McGraw Hill.

Baumol, W.J. (1986) 'Productivity Growth, Convergence and Welfare: What the Long-Run Data Show', *American Economic Review*, 76: 1072–85.

Baumol, W.J. and E.N. Wolff (1988) 'Productivity Growth, Convergence and Welfare: Reply', *American Economic Review*, 78: 1155–9.

Bourguignon, F. and C. Morrisson (2002) 'Inequality Among World Citizens: 1820–1992', *American Economic Review* 92, 4: 727–44.

Chotikapanich, D., R. Valenzuela and D.P. Rao (1997) 'Global and Regional Inequality in the Distribution of Income: Estimation with Limited and Incomplete Data', *Empirical Economics*, 22: 533–46.

de la Fuente, A. (1997) 'The Empirics of Growth and Convergence: A Selective Review', *Journal of Economic Dynamics and Control*, 21: 23–73.

Dollar, D. and A. Kraay (2002a) 'Spreading the Wealth', *Foreign Affairs*, 81, 1: 120–33.

Dollar, D. and A. Kraay (2002b) 'Inequality is No Myth', *Foreign Affairs*, 81, 4: 182–3.

Dowrick, S. and M. Akmal (2005) 'Contradictory Trends in Global Income Inequality: A Tale of Two Biases', *Review of Income and Wealth*, 51, 2: 201–30.

Firebaugh, G. (1999) 'Empirics of World Income Inequality', *American Journal of Sociology*, 104, 6: 1597–630.

Jones, C.I. (1997) 'On the Evolution of the World Income Distribution', *Journal of Economic Perspectives*, 11, 3: 19–36.

Hossain, A. (2000) 'Convergence of Per Capita Output Levels across Regions of Bangladesh, 1982–97', *IMF Working Paper* WP/00/121, Washington, DC: IMF.

Korzeniewicz, R.P. and T. Moran (1997) 'World Economic Trends in the Distribution of Income, 1965–1992', *American Journal of Sociology*, 102: 1000–39.

Kosack, S. (2003) 'Effective Aid: How Democracy Allows Development Aid to Improve the Quality of Life', *World Development*, 31, 1: 1–22.

Mankiw, N.G., D. Romer and D.N. Weil (1992) 'A Contribution to the Empirics of Economic Growth', *Quarterly Journal of Economics*, 107, 2: 407–37.

Martin, R. and P. Sunley (1998) 'Slow Convergence? The New Endogenous Growth Theory and Regional Development', *Economic Geography*, 74: 201–27.

McGillivray, M. (1991) 'The Human Development Index: Yet another Redundant Composite Development Indicator?', *World Development*, 19, 10: 1451–60.

McGillivray, M. and H. White (1993) 'Measuring Development? The UNDP's Human Development Index', *Journal of International Development*, 5, 2: 183–92.

Milanovic, B. (1997) 'A Simple Way to Calculate the Gini Coefficient, and Some Implications', *Economic Letters*, 56: 45–9.

Milanovic, B. (2002) 'True World Income Distribution, 1988 and 1993: First Calculation Based on Household Surveys Alone', *Economic Journal*, 112: 51–92.

Milanovic, B. (2003) 'The Two Faces of Globalization: Against Globalization as We Know It', *World Development*, 31, 4: 667–83.

Neumayer, E. (2001) 'The Human Development Index and Sustainability: A Constructive Proposal', *Ecological Economics*, 39: 101–14.

Noorbakhsh, F. (1998) 'A Modified Human Development Index', *World Development*, 26, 3: 517–28.

Noorbakhsh, F. (1999) 'Standards of Living, Human Development Indices and Structural Adjustments in Developing Countries: An Empirical Investigation', *Journal of International Development*, 11: 151–75.

Noorbakhsh, F. (2003) 'Human Development, Poverty and Disparities in the States of India', paper presented at the UNU-WIDER conference on Inequality, Poverty and Human Well-being, 30–1 May, Helsinki.

Pritchett, L. (1997) 'Divergence, Big Time', *Journal of Economic Perspectives*, 11, 3: 3–17.

Pyatt, G., C.N. Chen and J. Fei (1980) 'The Distribution of Income by Factor Components', *Quarterly Journal of Economics*, 95, 3: 451–73.

Quah, D. (1993) 'Empirical Cross-Section Dynamics in Economic Growth', *European Economic Review*, 37: 426–34.

Quah, D.T. (1996a) 'Twin Peaks: Growth and Convergence in Models of Distribution Dynamics', *Economic Journal*, 106: 1045–55.

Quah, D.T. (1996b) 'Empirics for Economic Growth and Convergence', *European Economic Review*, 40: 1353–75.

Romer, P. (1986) 'Increasing Returns and Long-Run Growth', *Journal of Political Economy*, 94: 1002–37.

Romer, P. (1990) 'Endogenous Technological Change', *Journal of Political Economy*, 98: S71–102.

Sachs, J.D. and F. Larrain (1993) *Macroeconomics in the Global Economy*, New York: Harvester Wheatsheat.

Sahn, D.E. and D.C. Stifel (2003) 'Progress Towards the Millennium Development Goals in Africa', *World Development*, 31, 1: 23–52.

Sala-í-Martín, X. (1996) 'The Classical Approach to Convergence Analysis', *Economic Journal*, 106: 1019–36.

Sala-í-Martín, X. (2002) 'The Disturbing "Rise" of Global Income Inequality', *NBER Working Papers* 8904, Cambridge, MA: National Bureau of Economic Research.

Schultz, T.P. (1998) 'Inequality in the Distribution of Personal Income in the World: How is it Changing and Why?', *Journal of Population Economics*, 11, 3: 307–44.

Srinivasan, T.N. (1994) 'Human Development: A New Paradigm or Reinvention of the Wheel?', *American Economic Review, Papers and Proceedings*, 84, 2: 238–43.

UNDP (United Nations Development Programme) (various) *Human Development Report*, New York: Oxford University Press for UNDP.

WHO (2002) *The World Health Report 2002: Reducing Risks Promoting Healthy Life*, Geneva: WHO.

WHO (2003) *The World Health Report 2003: Shaping the Future*, Geneva: WHO.

Zind, R.G. (1991) 'Income Convergence and Divergence within and between LDC Groups', *World Development*, 19, 6: 719–27.

10
Investing in Health for Economic Development: The Case of Mexico

Nora Lustig

Introduction

Health is an asset with an intrinsic value as well as an instrumental value. Being healthy is a source of wellbeing and one of the goals most valued by human beings throughout the world.[1] Health is not only the absence of illness, but also the capacity of developing a person's potential throughout life. As the pioneer work by Nobel Prize winner Robert Fogel[2] shows, health is also an important determinant of economic growth. This author finds that between one-third and one-half of Britain's economic growth in the past 200 years is due to improvements in the population's calorific intake, which resulted in better health and higher productivity.

Given the importance of health, both as a source of human welfare and a determinant of overall economic growth, in January 2000 the World Health Organization created the Commission on Macroeconomics and Health (CMH). The Commission released its report in December 2001. This is what it had to say with respect to middle-income countries such as Mexico:

> In most middle-income countries, average health spending per person is already adequate to ensure universal coverage for essential interventions. Yet such coverage does not reach many of the poor. ... In view of the adverse consequences of ill health on overall economic development and poverty reduction, we strongly urge the middle-income countries to undertake fiscal and organizational reforms to ensure universal coverage for priority health interventions.

Additionally, the CMH suggested the creation of similar commissions on a national level. Following this suggestion, the Mexican Commission on Macroeconomics and Health (MCMH) was created on 29 July 2002. The Commission includes experts from academic institutions, the government, civil society and the private sector. Based on their professional experience, these experts have been able to analyze and reflect upon the link between health and economic development.

In this chapter, I present the main findings of the Commission in the following areas: the relationship between health, economic growth and poverty traps in Mexico; an assessment of the health status of Mexicans; and an assessment of Mexico's investment in health. In the last section, I briefly examine two pro-grammes that have been designed to reduce extreme poverty and improve the health status of the poor: *Oportunidades* (opportunities) and *Seguro Popular* (popular health insurance). As we shall see, the empirical evidence suggests that in Mexico health is an important determinant of economic growth and poverty traps. Unfortunately, the country is lagging behind in health indicators; they are below the expected level for a country with its level of development as well as, in several cases, below the rate of progress required by the Millennium Development Goals. This means that there are lost welfare-improving opportunities both for the economy as a whole as well as for the poor. Furthermore, Mexico is plagued with great disparities in health indicators across income brackets, ethnic groups and regions. Families living in extreme poverty and the poorest municipalities have indicators similar to those found in some poor countries in Africa and Asia, while the richest households and municipalities show health indicators similar to some countries in Europe.

Finally, we shall see that public health spending is at best neutral from the distributive point of view and that the health system (especially prior to the intro-duction of the Seguro Popular) leaves around 50 per cent of the population with-out access to health insurance the majority of which belong to the bottom four income deciles. In this group, out-of-pocket payments represent 40 per cent of total spending on healthcare and, as would be expected, this spending pattern is highly regressive. Given these results, there is no doubt that investing in health in Mexico can result in higher economic growth, the elimination of poverty traps and a more equitable society. It can also create more efficient health systems by pooling risks.

The main recommendation of this chapter is that the government should invest more institutional and financial resources in public policies that improve the nutrition and health status of young children of poor households and award financial protection to the poor and lower middle classes from the impact of catastrophic illness.

Health, economic growth and poverty traps

Health as human capital affects growth directly through, for example, its impact on labour productivity and the economic burden of illness. It also has an indi-rect effect since child health affects the future income of people through the impact that health has on education such as enrolment, attendance and cognitive abilities. A study on the direct relationship between health and growth in Mexico (1970–95) using life expectancy and mortality rates for different age groups as health indicators, suggests that health is responsible for approximately one-third of long-term economic growth (Mayer-Foulkes 2001). It has been shown that childhood health is an important determinant of school achievement throughout

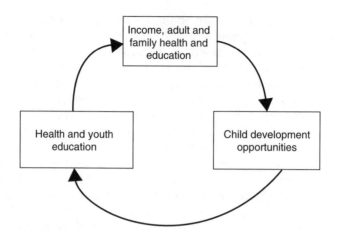

Figure 10.1   Intergenerational cycle of human capital formation
Source: Galor and Mayer-Foulkes (2004).

the cycle and that health during early childhood determines the income that child will receive on reaching adulthood. Figure 10.1 depicts this cycle in very simple terms.

In addition, due to its direct and indirect impact, health is one of the important determinants of the incidence of poverty as well as its persistence over time – the so-called poverty trap. Children from poor households are more likely to face chronic and recurrent health problems which affect their cognitive ability and cause them to miss school. In turn, their incomes as adults will be lower. Parents with low education and income will invest less in their children's human capital and the cycle gets repeated on and on. In Mexico there is evidence of a poverty trap (Mayer-Foulkes 2001). Given this, investing in health is warranted both from the growth and equity perspectives. Furthermore, given the important role played by health in the economy, protecting health assets from the impact of systemic (for example, transitional costs from economic reforms, epidemics, economic crises and natural disasters) and idiosyncratic shocks (illness, death, unemployment, or a bad harvest) is also crucial. Protection from the shocks produced by the latter is usually taken care of within a country's social insurance system.

However, despite their enormous impact, there are no systematic policies and institutions that address the impact of aggregate shocks on health. This presents us with a problem since there is increasing evidence that, for example, macroeconomic crises and natural disasters have a negative impact on investment in human capital.[3] In Mexico, for example, during the 1980s crisis, there was a slowdown in the decline of infant mortality and the mortality of pre-schoolers caused by nutritional deficiency increases. This result emphasizes the importance of having adequate social safety nets in place, and their required funding, to cope with the impact of aggregate shocks on human capital accumulation (Lustig 1995).

Health indicators

Some of the health indicators in Mexico are below those for countries with equivalent per capita income. According to one study, the expected infant mortality rate, controlling for Mexico's level of development, is 22 per cent below the actual observed rates; in other words, Mexico reported 20,000 infant deaths above the norm (Bertozzi and Gutiérrez 2003).

If we use the Millennium Development Goals (MDGs) as a benchmark to measure progress, how does Mexico fare? In what follows we will examine the actual cumulative progress for the relevant MDGs compared to the required progress, assuming a linear process with 1990 as the baseline.[4]

Goals

Goal 1: Halve the proportion of people who suffer from hunger

If we use the relationship in height according to age as an indicator of malnutrition, we will find that the decrease between 1988 and 1999 was about 22 per cent less than what was required to fulfil the Millennium Development Goal. In addition, between 1992 and 2002, 'food poverty'[5] fell by only 10 per cent, less than the required rate. That is, the rate of progress observed so far is insufficient to meet the quantitative goals set by the MDGs.

Goal 4: Reduce infant mortality rates by two-thirds and increase the proportion of children vaccinated against measles

Between 1990 and 2003, Mexico has shown a progress rate of 43.3 per cent in the reduction of infant and child mortality rates, which is satisfactory since the required rate is around 44 per cent. Also, Mexico has had a significant improvement in vaccination rates, especially against measles. In 1990 only 75.3 per cent of infants under 12 months old had been vaccinated against this disease and in 2002 the number was 96 per cent.

With respect to Goal 4, therefore, Mexico is showing progress consistent with the specific quantitative goals of the MDGs. However, as we saw above, in the case of IMR the starting point for Mexico is higher than it should be given its level of development.

Goal 5: Reduce maternal mortality rate by three quarters

The cumulative progress achieved on maternal mortality between 1990 and 2003 is 26.7 per cent, lower than the required rate to achieve the goal. Mexico also has a lower than expected proportion of births attended by trained medical personnel (only at 86 per cent). Thus, in the case of maternal health, Mexico is underperforming.

Goal 6: Combat HIV/AIDS, malaria and other serious diseases

The rate of HIV/AIDS among the adult population in Mexico is one of the lowest in Latin America and the Caribbean in proportion to its population, but it has the second highest number of people living with the disease. Also, one factor of concern is that between 1990 and 2003 the incidence of people diagnosed with HIV/AIDS per 100,000 inhabitants increased from 4.4 per cent to 8.2 per cent.

Regarding malaria, the situation in Mexico is substantially better than that of the rest of Latin America and Caribbean countries. In 2000, only eight cases occurred for every 100,000 inhabitants. In Latin America and the Caribbean, there were eight deaths caused by tuberculosis (TB) for every 100,000 inhabitants in 2002. In Mexico during that same year, only five deaths occurred for every 100,000 inhabitants.

Goal 7: Sustainable access to safe drinking water

In terms of environmental conditions and sanitation, measured through access to drinking water, on average Mexico is very close to achieving the target suggested by the Millennium Development Goals. However, it is still not adequate for a country of its level of development.

Beyond the Millennium Development Goals

Reducing inequality by setting subnational goals

In Mexico, there are enormous disparities in health indicators across states and municipalities. For example, in the poorest municipality in the state of Chiapas, infant mortality (at 66.2 per thousand live births) is similar to that of countries much poorer than Mexico, like Sudan. In contrast, the Benito Juarez district in Mexico City, with a rate of 17.2, has levels similar to Western Europe and Israel (Figure 10.2).

There are also large differences in childbirth coverage under medical supervision. Half of the states have more than 90 per cent coverage, but there are states with less than 60 per cent coverage. The percentage of childbirths attended in the 386 highly marginalized municipalities is around 36 per cent. In contrast, in the 247 least marginalized municipalities, coverage in health clinics is almost 94 per cent. Furthermore, in some indigenous communities the percentage of births attended by medical personnel is under 10 per cent. Given the low levels of health found in some regions of the country, Mexico's goals should be established at the state and municipal levels. For example, one could set as a goal that no municipality has an infant or maternal mortality rate above the national average in 1990, which were 37 (infant deaths per 1,000 born alive) and 110 (deaths per 100,000 infants less than a year born alive), respectively, even if this implies a relative reduction above that specified by the MDGs. Once the goal is chosen, one could estimate the rate of progress by municipality indicator using the following formula:

$$\text{Rate of progress indicator in } (t) = \frac{\textit{objective value in 2015} - \textit{value in } (t)}{\textit{objective value in 2015} - \textit{initial value}}$$

This rate of progress indicator has a value between 0 and 1. Using the harmonic mean, we can also define an inequality-sensitive indicator as (μ):

$$\mu = \left[\frac{1}{N} \sum_{i=1}^{N} I_i^{1-e} \right]^{\frac{1}{1-e}}$$

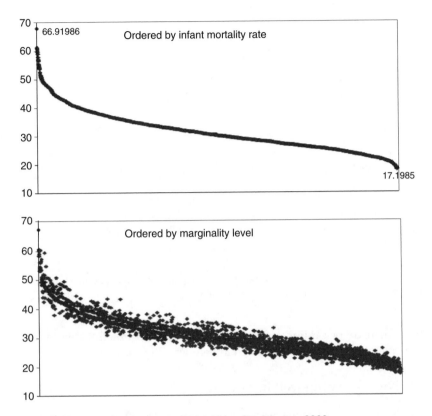

Figure 10.2   Infant mortality rate at a municipal level in Mexico, 2000
Source: Data based on CONAPO (2001).

In this expression, *e* stands for the 'inequality aversion' parameter, *I* is the indicator by municipality (or state) and N is the total number of municipalities (or states).[6]

If *e* = 0, the indicator reduces to the standard mean used for monitoring progress in the Millennium Development Goals at the national level. However, if *e* is positive, we are giving more weight to the lowest performers and the larger the parameter *e*, the more averse to inequality. The selected indicator gets smaller, as the degree of inequality aversion increases. In Figure 10.3, one can observe how the rate of progress of the infant mortality rate at a municipal level declines when we 'correct' the measure using the inequality aversion parameter.[7]

Coping with new health challenges

In addition to confronting the health challenges typical of poor countries, as a high-medium-income country Mexico is facing diseases that are more typical of wealthier countries. For example, incidence of diabetes has increased greatly in recent years; at the end of the 1970s it was the fourth cause of death but now it is considered the first, causing 12 per cent of all deaths in Mexico. Therefore, the health-related goals for Mexico should include confronting new challenges such

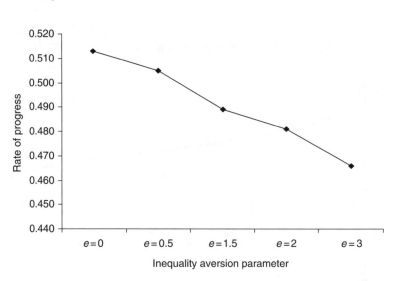

Figure 10.3   Rate of progress 'corrected' by the inequality aversion parameter for infant mortality rate at a municipal level in Mexico (2000)

as the increase of cardiovascular diseases and diabetes mellitus, both associated with changing income levels as well as demographic changes.

Is Mexico investing well in health?

In order to respond I shall try, in turn, to answer the following two questions. Are resources invested in health sufficient? Are they well allocated in terms of social equity goals? We shall see that health investment in Mexico is less than what is required or expected of a country with its level of development and needs. Also, we shall find that resources are distributed among the population in an unequal manner and not enough resources are devoted to protecting the bulk of the population, the poor in particular, from the effects of catastrophic health shocks.

Total investment in health

In 2003, Mexico's total investment in healthcare[8] was 6.1 per cent of GDP, lower than the Latin American average (6.3 per cent) and lower than other countries with similar income levels, such as Chile (7.0 per cent), Costa Rica (7.2 per cent), Brazil (7.6 per cent) and Uruguay (10.9 per cent). Furthermore, in 2001 public investment represented 44 per cent of the total investment in health, while in Latin American countries with similar or even lower income to that of Mexico had a higher percentage of public investment, such as, Argentina (48.5 per cent) and Nicaragua (53.4 per cent). That is, just based on spending figures, Mexico has been under-investing in health. It is important to note, however, that public expenditure on health as a percentage of GDP has increased 15 per cent since the year 2000, primarily as a consequence of introducing the Seguro Popular.

Progressivity of public spending in health

In Mexico there is a remarkable contrast between expenditures made in favour of the non-insured population – such as those channelled through the health ministry and the conditional cash transfer Oportunidades – which, as shown in Figures 10.4 and 10.5, is highly progressive and pro-rural, and expenditures benefiting the insured population – such as those channelled through the two largest social insurance schemes, the Mexican Institute of Social Security (IMSS) for private sector workers and Institute of Social Security Servicing State Workers (ISSSTE) for public sector workers, which is highly regressive and pro-urban (Figures 10.4 and 10.5).[9]

Fifty per cent of the population are uninsured and receive less than a third of total public health expenditures. A rigorous analysis of the incidence of public health spending reveals that the distribution of total public health expenditures is slightly regressive on a national level, although it becomes practically neutral if contributions through general taxes of beneficiaries (workers and employers) are considered.[10] Given the existing disparities in health indicators and their low level in certain parts of the country and in poor households, this is not good news.

In Figure 10.5 we show the concentration coefficients in order of increasing inequality of the most important components of public expenditures on social protection and targeted programmes. The results confirm the previous findings and indicate that most of the public spending goes to programmes that are regressive. The figure also gives us information regarding which policies and programmes are progressive.[11] Two salient ones are the conditional cash transfer programme, Oportunidades, and the social protection against health shocks programme, Seguro Popular.

Geographical inequities are also quite striking, resulting from the historical distribution of federal funds to states. For example, per capita public health

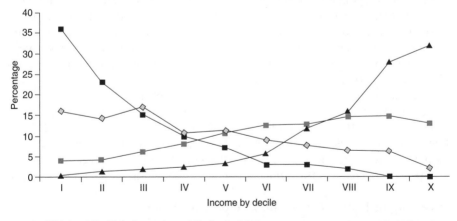

Figure 10.4 Distribution of social expenditure by income decile, 2002

Sources: Public Expenditure Report, World Bank (2004).

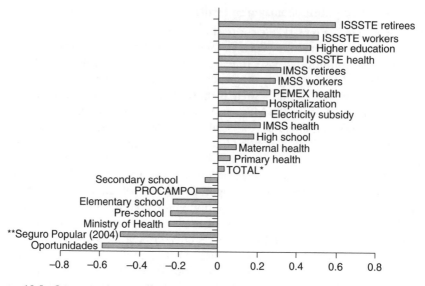

Figure 10.5 Concentration coefficients of public expenditure on health and nutrition, 2000–02

Notes: *Concentration coefficient of total public expenditure (education, health and nutrition). **The concentration coefficient that corresponds to *Seguro Popular* (−0.49) was estimated based on the policy holders distribution up to 30 June 2004, obtained from the Results Report to the First Semester of First Semester of Fiscal Year, 2004.

Sources: World Bank (2004), Public Expenditure Review, Vol. II.

expenditures are six times larger in Mexico City than in the State of Mexico despite their being right next to each other with similar health conditions and needs. Even more worrying is the fact that Baja California receives four times as much in federal health expenditures per capita than Chiapas, while the GDP per capita is 2.9 higher in the former. In general, states with a lower rate of backwardness are those receiving higher quantities of public resources. In contrast, in the poorer states, fewer public (federal) resources are allotted to health and most of their population is not protected by social security.

Public spending in health has positive returns. According to one study,[12] for countries with an institutional quality index that is equal to the mean (3.5 in a scale of 1 to 5), a 10 per cent increase in public expenditures in health as a proportion of GNP is associated with a 7 per cent reduction in maternal mortality rates, 69 per cent reduction in mortality rates for children under the age of five, and 4.14 per cent decrease in the number of underweight children under five years old.

Investing in health for the poor: Oportunidades and Seguro Popular

Oportunidades

Oportunidades is a conditional cash transfer programme designed to reduce income poverty in the short-run and at the same time induce changes in behaviour in poor households. Its main objective is to address 'parenting failures' and 'market failures' (in the credit market, for example) in human capital development faced by poor households. In order to receive the benefit, eligible households must send their children to school and have health visits. In other words, it is expected that the conditions imposed on households will result in higher investments in health, nutrition and education of their children thereby increasing the chances of the next generation.

Currently, the programme reaches about 5 million families in more than 7,500 locations in the country, in rural and urban zones, with a budget of over 25 billion pesos. This represents 100 per cent of the households living below the food poverty line in 2002. With Oportunidades, a substantial proportion of the poorest households have access to targeted health benefits as can be seen in Figure 10.6. Nevertheless, even with the programme, around 40 per cent of the poorest households do not have access to social insurance. Furthermore, as discussed below, Oportunidades is effective in terms of increasing the human capital of the poor but it does not shield them from the impact of catastrophic health shocks.[13]

Rigorous impact evaluation studies reveal that Oportunidades has been effective in improving the health and nutrition status of pregnant and lactating women and small children. Children under three who participated in the programme increased their attendance at growth monitoring check-ups between 30 and 60 per cent. Beneficiaries between zero and five years of age registered an incidence of illness 12 per cent lower than that of children who did not participate in the programme. Moreover, data suggest that children in the programme grew 1 cm more and that they face a lower probability of inadequate growth (height per age) (Gertler 2000; Behrman and Hoddinot 2000). In addition, being a beneficiary of the programme

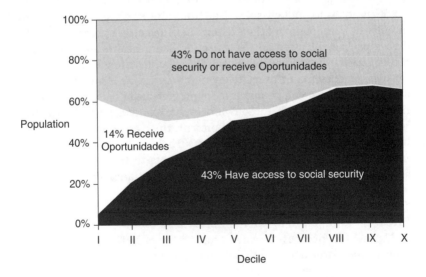

Figure 10.6   Coverage of Oportunidades and access to social security, Mexico

Source: Noriega (2004), cited in Mexican Commission on Macroeconomics and Health (2004: 39).

is associated with an 11 per cent decline in maternal mortality and 2 per cent decline in infant mortality. In the case of maternal mortality, the effect is stronger in medium and very highly marginalized municipalities, and in the case of infant mortality, in very highly marginalized municipalities (Hernandez *et al.* 2002).

Average food consumption and calorific intake in beneficiary households rose by 11 per cent and 7.8 per cent, respectively, after just one year of operation, compared to households that did not participate in the programme. This increase was due mainly to higher spending in fruit, vegetables and animal products. Associated to this is an improvement in adult health. In the 18–50-year-old group there has been a significant decrease (19 per cent) in the number of days on which the individuals had difficulty performing their daily activities due to health problems, as well as a significant (7.5 per cent) increase in the number of kilometres they can walk without getting tired.

Popular health insurance (Seguro Popular)

The other side of the lack of coverage by the formal social security system and the insufficiencies of the health ministry are large out-of-pocket expenditures. Mexico is one of the countries with the largest share of out-of-pocket payments as a proportion of total spending in health – the latter represented 53 per cent of the total. As we know, these payments are neither equitable nor efficient. There clearly was a missed opportunity of pooling risks and thereby contributing to more equitable financing and more efficient health investments. This is one of the reasons for the government to launch a programme such as the Seguro Popular.

The popular health insurance (Seguro Popular) is a new financing and health insurance model first introduced as a pilot programme by the federal government in 2001. It became part of the formal legislation of the Mexican health system in 2003. It offers access to publicly subsidized health insurance to all households that are currently not part of any of the existing social insurance programmes. It offers access to a package of essential health services and healthcare associated with ruinous illnesses. It is co-financed by the federal and state governments and the beneficiaries. The design of this relatively new programme is such that the financing of health insurance will be much more progressive because the out-of-pocket expenditures associated with ruinous illnesses in particular will be significantly reduced as the programme expands. At present, there are around 3 million families that participate in the scheme but almost all belong (or claim to belong) to the bottom of the income scale and do not contribute to the system. The government's goal is that by 2010 the popular health insurance will cover all those currently uninsured.

Reliance on out-of-pocket payments exposes families to huge expenses which can drive them further into poverty or make the non-poor poor. According to the national household income and expenditure survey of 2002, the population in the lowest decile spends around 6.3 per cent of its income on out-of-pocket healthcare payments, while households in the top decile spend 2.6 per cent.[14] The likelihood of becoming poor was quite high. The direct impact of out-of-pocket expenditures in health increased the incidence of poverty by 10 per cent, from 20.3–22.5 per cent.

This also explains the importance of launching a universal coverage social protection system in health such as the popular health insurance.[15]

Furthermore, the impact on poverty is underestimated because it does not include the indirect and intertemporal effects. It has been shown that – in the absence of formal protection mechanisms – when faced with shocks, households make decisions to smooth consumption that can lock them and their children into permanent poverty. For example, affected households tend to rely more on child labour and, hence, children's school attendance and/or achievement suffer. As we saw above, this will cause those children to be less productive and earn lower incomes when they become adults which in turn will translate into worst conditions for their own children. The vicious circle is played all over again. According to Knaul *et al.* (2005):

> Simulation results show that important impacts on the performance of the Mexican health system will occur in terms of fair financing and catastrophic expenditures, even before achieving the universal coverage goal in 2010. A reduction of 40 per cent in out-of-pocket financing and a Popular Health Insurance coverage of 100 per cent will decrease catastrophic health expenditures from 3.4 per cent to 1.6 per cent.

Furthermore, with full coverage Mexico will change its ranking position from 144 (out of 191 countries included in the study done by the World Health Organization) to 44, equal to Italy. Even before full coverage is reached, progress in fairness of health financing will be very significant. In sum, the Seguro Popular can significantly improve efficiency, by pooling risks, and equity by protecting households and individuals from the impact of catastrophic health shocks.

Concluding remarks

In Mexico, as in other countries, health as human capital is an important determinant of economic growth and poverty. Low health levels are linked to the so-called poverty traps. Health indicators and their progress in the past 15 years are below what is expected in a country with its level of development and the specific goals set within the framework of the MDGs. They are also very unequal with poorer socioeconomic groups and municipalities showing health levels similar to those found in some sub-Saharan African and South Asian countries. There is a clear imperative to focus on improving the health status of the population to unleash higher economic growth and lower poverty rates. In particular, those improvements should be concentrated in the socioeconomic groups and municipalities that are more backward. Given the large inequities in health indicators, Mexico should set its MDGs using an inequality-sensitive aggregate indicator and specific goals by municipality.

An analysis of health expenditures reveals that there is much room for improvement both in terms of efficiency and equity. First of all, Mexico spent less than comparable countries. Second, out-of-pocket spending represented a much larger share of total spending than in other countries. Third, public spending in health was at best neutral from the distributive point of view. And, fourth, more than 50 per cent of the population were not covered by social security.

With the introduction of the Seguro Popular, these problems are being corrected and the expectation is that by the time it reaches full coverage in 2010, Mexico's health system will move from 144th place to 44th place in terms of fairness in financing of healthcare. Also, the conditional cash transfer programme, Oportunidades, has been shown to be very effective in improving health and nutrition of children and mothers of beneficiary households.

Oportunidades and Seguro Popular are good examples to show that the Mexican government is committed to accelerating the improvement in health indicators, in particular for the poor. However, policy instruments should be linked to attaining some specific goals at the municipality levels. In particular, to lowering infant and maternal mortality rates to make them at least as good as the national average in 1990. If actions are not linked to outcomes at the level of municipalities, sharp contrasts are likely to continue for quite some time.

Notes

This chapter is based on the Report by the Mexican Commission on Macroeconomics and Health 2004, *Investing in Health for Economic Development. Executive Summary, Version for Consultation and Comments.* The Commission was created under the initiative of Julio Frenk, Secretary of Health in Mexico, and it is integrated by 30 members from the academic and business communities as well as government officials. I am very grateful to Juan Carlos García Fierro for his invaluable assistance.

1. See, for example, World Bank (2001).
2. See, for example, Fogel and Wimmer (1992).
3. See, for example, World Bank (2001).
4. The required rate of progress is usually defined in very simplistic terms; it is the accumulated progress one should observe if one assumes a linear process between 1990 and 2015. Although this may not be the case in reality, there are no available empirical estimates to gauge this. For details, see Organización de las Naciones Unidas para el Desarrollo (México) y Gobierno de la República de México (2005).
5. Food poverty refers to the individuals whose income is not enough to cover the cost of a pre-defined basic food basket. In Mexico food poverty is considered analogous to extreme poverty.
6. This approach is based on the methodology proposed by Foster *et al.* (2005).
7. These estimates are from Juan Carlos García Fierro (García 2005).
8. These percentages refer to spending done 'inside' the health system. Investment in health that occurs 'outside' the health system such as food production, sanitation infrastructure, potable water and housing is not included in these figures.
9. In Figure 10.4 the categories are mutually exclusive.
10. Scott (2004). It is important to note that the neutrality of net health expenditures is not observable in Figure 10.4 because the latter does not include the contributions side.
11. Public spending is assigned to individual households depending on the implied consumption of the analyzed service. For example, public spending on secondary education per household is estimated dividing the total public spending on secondary education by the number of pupils in secondary education, and then applying this amount to the number of pupils attending secondary school in the specific household.

12. World Bank (2004). The value of 3.5 corresponds to the CPIA average considered for the analyzed group of developing and industrialized countries to which the index's maximum value of 5.0 was assigned.
13. There are a number of issues raised around the suitability of conditional cash transfers. For a thorough discussion of them see de Janvry and Sadoulet (2005).
14. It is important to note that the non-insured must pay for the health services provided by the health ministry and that the amount paid is to a large extent arbitrary because it depends on the on-location assessment of the patient's ability to pay, among other factors.
15. The Seguro Popular was launched in January 2004. For a description of this reform, see Secretaría de Salud (2004).

References

Behrman, J. and J. Hoddinot (2000) *An Evaluation of the Impact of PROGRESA on Pre-School Child Height*, Washington, DC: International Food Policy Research Institute.

Bertozzi, S.M. and J.P. Gutiérrez (2003) 'The Health Gap in Mexico, Measured Through Child Mortality', *Salud Pública*, 45: 102–9.

Consejo Nacional de Población (CONAPO) (2001) *Índice de Desarrollo Humano, 2000*, Mexico: Consejo Nacional de Población.

de Janvry, A. and E. Sadoulet (2005) 'Conditional Cash Transfer Programmes for Child Human Capital Development: Lessons Derived from Experience in Mexico and Brazil', Mimeo, University of California at Berkeley.

Fogel, R.W. and L.T. Wimmer (1992) 'Early Indicators of Later Work Levels, Disease, and Death', *CPE Working Papers* 0008, Chicago: University of Chicago, Centre for Population Economics.

Foster, J., L.F. López-Calva and M. Székely (2005) 'Measuring the Distribution of Human Development: Methodology and an Application to Mexico', *Journal of Human Development*, 6, 1: 5–25.

Galor, O. and D. Mayer-Foulkes (2004) 'Food for Thought: Basic Needs and Persistent Educational Inequality', Mimeo, available from GE, Growth, Math methods 0410002 Economics Working Paper Archive at Washington University at St Louis.

García, J. (2005) 'Los ODM y la desigualdad en los indicadores de Salud en México', thesis in progress.

Gertler, P. (2000) *Final Report: The Impact of the Programa de Educación, Salud y Alimentación (Progresa) on Health*, Washington, DC: International Food Policy Research Institute.

Hernandez, B., L. Cuevas-Nasu, T. Shamah-Levy, E.A. Monterrubio, C. Ramírez-Silva, R. Garcia-Feregrino, J.A. Rivera and J. Sepúlveda-Amor (2002) 'Factors Associated with Overweight and Obesity in Mexican School-aged Children: Results from the National Nutrition Survey 1999', *Salud Pública*, 45, 4: S551–7.

Knaul, F., H. Arreola-Ornelas, O. Méndez and A. Martínez (2005) 'Fair Health Financing and Catastrophic Health Expenditures: Potential Impact of the Coverage Extension of the Popular Health Insurance in Mexico', *Salud Pública*, 47, 1: S54–65.

Lustig, N. (ed.) (1995) *Coping with Austerity, Poverty and Inequality in Latin America*, Washington, DC: The Brookings Institution.

Mayer-Foulkes, D. (2001) 'The Long-Term Impact of Health on Economic Growth in Mexico, 1950–1995', *Journal of International Development*, 13, 1: 123–6.

Mexican Commission on Macroeconomics and Health (2004) *Investing in Health for Economic Development. Executive Summary*, Mexico: Instituto de Políticas Públicas y Estudios del Desarrollo (IPD).

Organización de las Naciones Unidas para el Desarrollo (México) y Gobierno de la República de México (2005) *Los Objetivos de Desarrollo del Milenio: Informe de Avance 2005*, Mexico: UNDP.

Scott, J. (2004) 'Desigualdad en Salud y Oportunidades de Salud en México', unpublished paper prepared for the Mexican Commission of Macroeconomics and Health.

Secretaría de Salud (SSA) (2004) *Financiamiento Justo y Protección Social Universal: La Reforma Estructural del Sistema de Salud en México*, Mexico: Secretaría de Salud.

World Bank (2001) *World Development Report: Attacking Poverty*, Washington, DC: World Bank.

World Bank (2004) *The Millennium Development Goals for Health. Rising to the Challenges*, Washington, DC: World Bank.

11
A Wider Approach to Aid Effectiveness: Correlated Impacts on Health, Wealth, Fertility and Education

David Fielding, Mark McGillivray and Sebastian Torres

Introduction

The 2005 G8 summit in Scotland focused attention on the commitment of the industrialized world to promoting economic/social development in Africa and other parts of the developing world. The debates about aid delivery took place in an atmosphere of scepticism about the benefits that foreign aid might bring. For example, at the time of the summit, many newspapers reported recent IMF research casting doubt at the effectiveness of aid expenditure.[1] This pessimistic news contrasts strongly with some of the recent academic literature. The balance of evidence in the academic literature – which has not received a great deal of attention outside the academic community – is that, on average, aid does have some beneficial impact on human development (Addison *et al.* 2005; Clemens *et al.* 2004). This is not to say that aid will ever close the income gap between the northern and southern hemispheres, but rather that aid recipients experience better development outcomes, on average, than they would in the absence of aid.

The research which the newspaper reports were publicizing illustrates some of the difficulties involved in researching aid effectiveness. First of all, in producing robust estimates of the impact of aid on recipient countries, and, second, in communicating these results to a wider audience. In fact, there is a marked difference in tone between the newspaper reports above and the research paper they were quoting. This paper (Rajan and Subramanian 2005) actually states that '[a]id inflows do have systematic adverse effects on growth ... in labour intensive and export sectors', but that '[w]e have not established whether these adverse competitiveness effects offset any beneficial effects of aid'. They emphasize that '[a]id has to be spent really effectively so that the productivity improvements ... offset any dampening effects from a fall in competitiveness'. As usual, the academic research is less categorical and more hedged with doubt. But what are the reasons for uncertainty in this case? Why can economists not work out how foreign aid affects the countries to which it is directed? There are two key problems.

In the next section, we review the key difficulties in establishing empirical evidence on the effects of aid. The third section then illustrates how we might chart a way though these difficulties.

Why is it so difficult to determine the effects of aid?

First problem: identification of the treatment effect

Poor countries receive more aid (on average) than rich ones. A simple comparison of conditions in countries with aid to conditions in those without does not demonstrate the effect of aid. (Hospitals are full of sick people, but it does not mean that the hospitals made them sick.) To identify the effect of aid on an indicator of social or economic development, we need to find an *instrument*, a third variable that is independent of both, and that has a direct effect on aid only (not on the development indicator; this is an exclusion restriction). If our indicator varies systematically with this third variable, then we have demonstrated an aid effect, because, by assumption, the only way our indicator could have been affected is through aid.

But this approach relies on assumptions about how the three variables are connected; no study can ever be 100 per cent watertight. Any results from the statistical analysis are predicated on the independence of the instrument and on the exclusion restriction. Therefore, all results about the effectiveness of aid are necessarily provisional. In many cases, it is possible to question the validity of the exclusion restriction. For example, Rajan and Subramanian use information about developing countries' colonial ties as an instrument. The argument is the that former colonial powers are more inclined to give aid to their former colonies, so a developing country with a colonial tie to one of the relatively prosperous industrialized countries is likely to receive more aid, *ceteris paribus*. However, the exclusion restriction here can be questioned: colonial ties could also promote trade between the developing country and its former occupier, in which case aid is not the only route through which colonial ties impact on economic development.

Second problem: how is 'development' to be measured?

Aid might affect a wide variety of social and economic indicators. In order to identify the degree of aid effectiveness, we need to establish which indicators are important, and how the different indicators interact. A multivariate approach to the problem is a key to its solution, because there may be many virtuous spirals between different dimensions of development. It is unfortunate then that most papers examining aid effectiveness measure development only in terms of material wellbeing, specifically, in terms of average personal income in a region. In cross-country growth studies, the norm is to use PPP-adjusted per capita GDP or GNP.[2] There are a number of reasons why PPP-adjusted per capita income may be an unsatisfactory measure of material wellbeing. The price data on which PPP adjustments are based are collected only in certain countries and certain years. PPP adjustments for other countries and years, especially in the developing world, are based on extrapolations that may embody large measurement errors. Moreover, the prices used make little or no adjustment for variations in the quality of goods and services. Perhaps more importantly, many of the key goods and services that make a large difference to the utility of low-income households are consumed jointly by all the members of a single household. Examples include access to piped water and a flush lavatory, and the use of a refrigerator or radio. In this case per capita measures of prosperity may be less informative than measures based on assets per household.

There already exist empirical studies relating to the connections between different dimensions of development, not just material wellbeing, but they typically focus on a single link in the chain. There are studies of the impact of a region's education on its income (for example, Teulings and van Rens 2003), of income on education (for example, Fernandez and Rogerson 1997), of income on health (for example, Pritchett and Summers 1996), of health on income (for example, Bloom *et al.* 2004), of fertility on income (for example, Ahlburg 1996) and of income on fertility (for example, Strulik and Siddiqui 2002).[3] Many of these studies present careful and compelling evidence on their chosen area of research, but taken as a whole they embody certain limitations. The heterogeneity of statistical methodologies and datasets across these papers means that they do not shed any collective light on the relative importance of the different causal links in the overall development process. It would be useful to know, for example, if any one link is particularly strong, and hence a potential focus for development policy and expenditure.

Moreover, most existing cross-country studies use data on the average value of the development indicators in each country. The main aim of most empirical economic research has been to explain correlations in these indicators at the national level. Researchers in education and health sciences have often been more sensitive to the drawbacks of such an approach.[4] They point out that using mean income places a large weight on the income of the rich, because income distributions are left-skewed, so the mean figure reported for a country is higher than the median. Looking at the link between variations in mean income and, say, variations in infant mortality might be misleading, because high infant mortality is a consequence of the poverty of middle- and low-income groups in a developing country. One way of addressing this problem might be to include a measure of income distribution in the empirical model; however, a more direct approach would be to measure separately the income and health status of the rich and poor within a country.

A solution to these problems

In this section we illustrate how one might go about dealing with the problems listed above, drawing on the methodology and results presented in Fielding *et al.* (2005). This methodology differs from existing work on aid effectiveness in several

Table 11.1   Countries included in the analysis

	Survey year		Survey year		Survey year		Survey year
Bangladesh	2000	Dom. Rep.	1996	Madagascar	1997	Paraguay	1990
Benin	2001	Egypt	2000	Malawi	2000	Peru	2000
Bolivia	1998	Ethiopia	2000	Mali	2001	Philippines	1998
Brazil	1996	Gabon	2000	Mauritania	2001	Rwanda	2000
Burkina Faso	1999	Ghana	1998	Morocco	1992	S. Africa	1998
Cambodia	2000	Guatemala	1999	Mozambique	1997	Tanzania	1999
Cameroon	1998	Guinea	1999	Namibia	2000	Togo	1998
C.A.R.	1995	Haiti	2000	Nepal	2001	Uganda	2001
Chad	1997	India	1999	Nicaragua	2001	Vietnam	2000
Colombia	2000	Indonesia	1997	Niger	1998	Yemen	1997
Comoros	1996	Jordan	1997	Nigeria	1990	Zambia	2002
Côte d'Ivoire	1994	Kenya	1998	Pakistan	1990	Zimbabwe	1999

Source: Fielding *et al.* (2005).

ways. Most importantly, it does not use GDP as a development indicator. No reference is made to per capita income. Instead, the model employs a measure of the material assets that the household possesses, using data on material assets in 48 countries in the World Bank Health, Nutrition and Poverty (HNP) database. These countries are listed in Table 11.1. The assets recorded in the survey are basic enough for differences in quality across countries not to be a major worry. This approach also avoids any reference to PPP adjustments.

The household assets index is calculated by combining information about whether the household has the following material assets: a wooden or concrete floor, a radio, a television, electric power supply, a refrigerator or a car. The index is constructed for each household on a scale of zero to one, and then average figures are constructed for the 20 per cent of households ranked lowest by this measure, and for the four quintiles above them.[5] The household-level information is aggregated to the quintile level, and not used directly, because it is not possible to find reasonable exclusion restrictions at the household level.

In addition to this measure of material wellbeing, the model also incorporates data measuring four other dimensions of development, namely, standards of sanitation, fertility, health and education. *Sanitation* is measured in two alternative ways: first, the proportion of households within each quintile with access to piped water and, second, the proportion of households within each quintile using a 'bush latrine'.[6] *Fertility* is measured by the average number of live births per adult female in each of the five quintiles.[7] In measuring *health*, three alternatives are considered: the infant mortality rate; the child mortality rate; and life expectancy. Finally, *education* is measured by the proportion of adults in each quintile who have completed primary school. Appendix 1 lists the sample means and standard deviations of these five variables.

Illustrative statistics from Burkina Faso and Paraguay are presented in Tables 11.2 and 11.3. Burkina Faso represents one of the poorest countries in our

Table 11.2   Illustrative statistics for Burkina Faso

	Q1	Q2	Q3	Q4	Q5
Electricity %	0	0	0	0	30
Piped water %	0	0	1	4	55
Using 'bush latrine' %	100	100	99	70	12
Live births per woman	7.2	6.9	6.8	7.0	4.5
Under-five mortality %	24	25	22	23	16
Primary education %	3	4	5	9	43

Source: Fielding *et al.* (2005).

Table 11.3   Illustrative statistics for Paraguay

	Q1	Q2	Q3	Q4	Q5
Electricity %	1	10	37	96	100
Piped water %	0	2	8	45	91
Using 'bush latrine' %	2	2	1	0	0
Live births per woman	7.9	6.3	4.3	3.9	2.7
Under-five mortality %	6	5	6	4	2
Primary education %	48	71	71	83	92

Source: Fielding *et al.* (2005).

sample. All but the wealthiest households lack electricity, piped water and basic sanitation, and few have any education. Even many of the wealthiest lack basic facilities. In contrast, Paraguay represents a country at a further stage of development, with even the poorest households better off by some measures than the richest in Burkina Faso. Still, many of the poor in Paraguay lack sanitation and have higher fertility and infant mortality rates than the rich.

Each of these dimensions of human development potentially has an impact on the others. Modelling all five simultaneously facilitates identification of the linkages that are quantitatively the most important, and also the most quantitatively important channels through which aid has an effect. Moreover, in measuring development for asset quintiles within a country, rather than just the average for the country as a whole, the model gives equal weight to the development outcomes of the rich and the poor within a country.

All five development indicators are measured for each of the five quintiles in each of the 48 countries, so the dataset on which our estimates are based incorporates 240 observations on each indicator. Observations in each country are made in a single year, as noted in Table 11.1, so our dataset is not a panel in the traditional sense. Using these data, it is possible to see how the variation in development outcomes in each quintile in each country is correlated with a range of independent social and economic characteristics. With exclusion restrictions on the way in which these characteristics affect development outcomes, it is possible to measure some of the interactions between the outcomes. With further restrictions, it is possible to measure the impact of aid on each outcome. Appendix 2 provides some detail about the structure of the fitted model; the discussion that follows is a non-technical summary of this model.

A key part of the model is its identifying restrictions. Of the exogenous country characteristics that we allow for in our model of development, some might impact on all of our indicators. Among these characteristics are indicators of the countries' colonial affiliation, a measure of ethnolinguistic fractionalization[8] and a dummy for countries in Africa. However, there are some restrictions that we can plausibly impose of the effects of other exogenous variables. These restrictions, summarized in Table 11.4, are as follows. First, ethnolinguistic fractionalization and some of the geographical characteristics are unlikely to have a direct impact on anything other than material resources (measured by the assets index and sanitation) through an effect on factor productivity. These characteristics are country size and the value of the country's natural resource wealth.

Similarly, other geographical characteristics are unlikely to have a direct impact on anything other than health. These characteristics are temperature[9, 10] and the fraction of the population living in areas at risk of malarial infection. Whether a country has a coastline might affect health and wealth, but it is unlikely to affect education or fertility directly, and so it can be excluded from the equations for

Table 11.4   Model structure

Control variables	Appearing in the equations for				
Dummy = 1 if in Africa	assets	sanitation	education	fertility	health
Dummy = 1 if colonized by Britain	assets	sanitation	education	fertility	health
Dummy = 1 if colonized by France	assets	sanitation	education	fertility	health
Ethnolinguistic fractionalization index	assets	sanitation			
Log country surface area	assets	sanitation			
Log natural resource capital value	assets	sanitation			
Dummy = 1 if country has coastline	assets	sanitation			health
Fraction of the population Christian			education	fertility	
Fraction of the population Muslim			education	fertility	
Temperature (in 0.1°c)					health
Temperature squared					health
Fraction of population at risk from Malaria					health

Source: Fielding *et al.* (2005).

these two indicators. These restrictions together allow us to identify the effects of material assets, sanitation and health in each of the other four equations, except that the effects of assets on sanitation and of sanitation on assets are unidentified. The effects of fertility and education in the assets, sanitation and health equations are identified by assuming that religious adherence, as captured by the fraction of the population adhering to Christianity or Islam, has no direct effect on assets and health.[11] However, it might affect attitudes towards contraception or the value of education (especially female education), and so have a role in determining fertility and schooling. The other effects we do not attempt to identify – because of an absence of any obvious instrument – are of fertility in the education equation and of education in the fertility equation.

The exclusion restriction that is used to identify the effect of aid on all the development indicators is that the dollar value of aid per capita (and no other variable in the model) depends on the country's past ability to absorb development assistance. This is measured by the past ratio of aid actually disbursed to aid nominally committed to a country.

In the following tables we summarize the results presented in Fielding *et al.* (2005) with child mortality as a measure of health and access to piped water as a measure of sanitation. In interpreting the results, two factors must be born in mind. First, the link between two development indicators, on average, can be positive or negative. Positive links will arise because human capacity in one dimension reinforces human capacity in another dimension. For example, well-educated people might be more economically productive, and therefore wealthier; moreover, wealthier people might have more time or money to spend on education.[12] Negative links will arise when people have to make a choice about where to commit time or money. More spent on schooling might mean less spent on, for example, sanitation. (In the case of positive feedback, aid devoted to one development outcome will also benefit others indirectly. In the case of negative feedback, aid will be beneficial to the extent that it relaxes the household's resource constraint.) We need not speculate about whether the positive or negative effect dominates for any given pair of development indicators: appropriate statistical analysis will reveal which is greater on average, or whether the two more or less cancel each other out. It turns out with our data that positive feedback effects dominate more often than negative ones, on average. For example, there are mutually reinforcing positive links between material wellbeing and education, between material wellbeing and lower child mortality, and between education and lower mortality. Nevertheless, there are a few negative links, in particular between education and sanitation.

Second, we ought to distinguish between the *direct* effect of aid, on average, and the 'equilibrium' effect. Imagine a 10 per cent increase in aid in a particular country. This may have several direct effects: improved sanitation, more education, lower child mortality and so on. But this is not the end of the story: changes in one development outcome will then have knock-on effects on the others, on average. So the final effect of aid on development – the equilibrium effect – might be rather different from its direct effect.

Table 11.5   Education/health project aid as a fraction of total aid, 1995–2004 (%)

	Education	Health		Education	Health		Education	Health
Bangladesh	11.7	4.5	Ghana	7.8	5.9	Nicaragua	3.9	4.2
Benin	13.3	5.3	Guatemala	9.6	10.0	Niger	9.3	4.6
Bolivia	5.5	4.1	Guinea	12.5	4.1	Nigeria	8.6	13.6
Brazil	8.6	2.8	Haiti	9.4	9.7	Pakistan	3.0	2.6
Burkina Faso	11.4	4.6	India	7.4	6.9	Paraguay	6.6	3.7
Cambodia	7.9	8.1	Indonesia	5.8	2.5	Peru	3.2	4.1
Cameroon	11.3	2.1	Jordan	4.5	1.7	Philippines	4.5	2.3
C.A.R.	11.2	7.3	Kenya	6.7	9.7	Rwanda	6.0	6.3
Chad	11.0	7.9	Madagascar	8.2	3.4	S. Africa	17.7	5.5
Colombia	3.7	1.3	Malawi	13.0	9.0	Tanzania	7.0	9.2
Comoros	29.6	9.7	Mali	15.6	3.8	Togo	18.5	4.1
Côte d'Ivoire	7.1	2.8	Mauritania	12.0	2.9	Uganda	10.7	9.0
Dom. Rep.	8.1	8.7	Morocco	23.7	1.7	Vietnam	5.0	2.6
Egypt	5.2	1.8	Mozambique	5.9	6.4	Yemen	9.6	4.0
Ethiopia	8.3	5.9	Namibia	16.9	4.3	Zambia	11.3	9.3
Gabon	16.9	2.5	Nepal	12.4	5.9	Zimbabwe	5.9	6.2
Mean	*9.9*	*5.4*	*Standard deviation*	*5.3*	*2.9*			

Source: Fielding *et al.* (2005).

In interpreting our fitted model, we should remember that the results are conditional on the historical pattern of aid expenditure. The results show the impact of aid as it has typically been used in recent years. Our model is based on an aggregate measure of aid to each country, and we do not make use of aid figures disaggregated according to the type of development project for which they are intended. It is true that there is some variation in the proportions of aid intended for specific purposes. For example, the proportion of the total aid budget intended for education and health projects does vary somewhat from one country to another, as illustrated in Table 11.5 (in neither case is the average aid allocation to these sectors that large). However, there is not necessarily a simple correlation between the fraction of aid intended for a certain development outcome and the outcome actually observed. On the one hand, aid to a certain sector may stimulate more local investment in that sector (Gramlich 1969): evidence for this 'flypaper theory' is discussed in Devarajan and Swaroop (1998). The magnitude of the flypaper effect may vary across sectors. On the other hand, aid is at least partially fungible (see for example Devarajan *et al.* 1998). That is, the aid to a particular sector leads to a reduction in local investment in the sector. Again, the magnitude of the effect may vary across sectors.

What does the statistical analysis actually show? First, we will summarize the direct and equilibrium effects of aid (on average), without saying anything about the sizes of the different effects. Then, in order to illustrate the magnitude of the impact of aid, we will again refer to two examples drawn from our sample: Burkina Faso and Paraguay. The direct effects of aid (on average) on our five development outcomes are in Table 11.6. In indicating the direct effects, it is important to distinguish between those that are 'statistically significant' and those that are not.

Table 11.6   Direct effects of aid on the development indicators

Assets	positive and statistically significant
Sanitation	positive and statistically significant
Fertility	positive and statistically significant
Child mortality	negative (more aid reduces mortality) and statistically significant
Schooling	statistically insignificant (small but positive on average)

Source: Fielding *et al.* (2005).

Table 11.7   Equilibrium effects of aid

Assets	always positive
Sanitation	always positive
Fertility	mostly negative (that is, more aid reduces fertility)
Child mortality	always negative (that is, more aid reduces mortality)
Schooling	almost always positive

Source: Fielding *et al.* (2005).

Roughly, this is a distinction between, on the one hand, those characteristics of our data that are unlikely to have appeared at random and, on the other, those that could well be a 'fluke' telling us nothing about the likely effect of aid in countries and time periods outside our data.

Note that the direct effect of aid on fertility is positive. On average, the income stream that the aid represents encourages people to have more children. The equilibrium effects of aid are reported in Table 11.7. Here, it is important to remember that the effects of aid will vary across countries and across asset quintiles. How effective aid is depends on what level of development the households start off at.

Mostly, the direct effects of aid reinforce each other. Note that the equilibrium effect of aid on schooling is positive, even though the direct effect is small and statistically insignificant. This is because schooling responds positively to improvements in assets and child mortality. Note also that the equilibrium effect on fertility is mostly the reverse of its direct effect. The main reason for this seems to be that reductions in child mortality following an increase in aid reduce the number of births needed to achieve a family of a certain size.

Tables 11.8 and 11.9 illustrate typical predicted equilibrium effects in our sample of countries. The numbers show, in percentage terms, the equilibrium effects of a doubling of aid on each development outcome.[13] In both Paraguay and Burkina Faso (as elsewhere), aid can be expected to improve the quality of life along several dimensions. However, it can be seen that there is some variation in the size of the effects between outcomes, between countries and between quintiles. Although there is a substantial general improvement in the quality of life with an increase in aid, the effects on child mortality are typically much larger than other effects.

Table 11.8   Predicted growth, Burkina Faso (%)

	Q1	Q2	Q3	Q4	Q5
Assets increase	1.0	1.6	2.5	3.5	10.1
Sanitation increase	0.4	2.0	5.6	8.0	26.5
Fertility reduction	−3.6	−2.5	−1.0	0.8	11.6
Under-five mortality reduction	7.6	9.7	3.1	6.6	37.6
Primary education increase	1.5	2.0	2.5	3.5	7.5

Source: Fielding *et al.* (2005).

Table 11.9   Predicted growth, Paraguay (%)

	Q1	Q2	Q3	Q4	Q5
Assets increase	9.4	9.5	7.6	4.5	1.7
Sanitation increase	27.6	25.7	27.4	16.6	2.3
Fertility reduction	13.2	14.0	4.2	1.5	−3.0
Under-five mortality reduction	34.6	40.4	27.0	21.6	8.9
Primary education increase	6.3	6.4	3.4	1.3	0.9

Source: Fielding *et al.* (2005).

Conclusions

The results thus summarized show a straightforwardly positive effect of aid on development outcomes. This contrasts with an existing literature in which there are mixed results about the impact of aid on per capita GDP. One reason for this contrast may be that the results above focus on the impact of aid on human development, and how aid might promote investment in human capital. By contrast, existing studies implicitly model the impact of aid on labour productivity,[14] which will depend to a much greater degree on the extent to which aid promotes investment in physical capital. Moreover, any beneficial impact of aid on labour productivity could be offset by a Dutch Disease effect, as the inflow of foreign currency leads to a real exchange rate appreciation and a consequent reduction in export competitiveness.

The beneficial effects of aid are partly a consequence of positive interactions between different aspects of human development. For example, while higher levels of aid do not appear to be directly associated with a substantial improvement in schooling, they are associated with much better health, and there are strong positive interactions between health and schooling. Aid appears to be important in improving health outcomes, despite the fact that a relatively small fraction of aid budgets (about 5 per cent on average) is hypothecated to health expenditure. One potential explanation for this, meriting further research, is that there are relatively low fungibility and/or relatively large flypaper effects with aid to health.

It may well be the case that the effectiveness of aid in improving labour productivity does depend to a large degree on the effectiveness of domestic political institutions and macroeconomic policy. Governments need to manage the potential downsides of aid, such as Dutch Disease. Statistical analysis of the effect of institutions on development produces ambiguous results, because it is difficult to find reasonable exclusion restrictions to identify the effect of institutions. Nevertheless, there is a substantial body of evidence to suggest that institutions do matter for aid directed at industry. The Dutch Disease effect can be offset by good macroeconomic policy to promote competitiveness. These comments might apply to a much lesser degree, or not at all, when we look at the impact of aid on human capital and human development. This means that while it might make sense to restrict aid designed to promote productivity to countries with good governance, this argument does not apply when aid is designed to achieve other objectives. There is no need for industrialized nations to stop aid aimed at the alleviation of household poverty. Even with poor political institutions, it is possible that this sort of aid can be delivered with some degree of efficiency, as shown in the results summarized in this study.

Appendix 1

Table 11.A1 Summary sample statistics for the development indicators

Means	Assets	Sanitation	Education	Fertility	Health
Quintile 1	0.1595	0.0411	0.3075	6.0625	0.1781
Quintile 2	0.2511	0.1054	0.4083	5.3417	0.1682
Quintile 3	0.3379	0.1551	0.4974	4.8542	0.1556
Quintile 4	0.4481	0.2820	0.6110	4.2646	0.1294
Quintile 5	0.6534	0.5277	0.7851	3.2146	0.0876
Standard deviations	**Assets**	**Sanitation**	**Education**	**Fertility**	**Health**
Quintile 1	0.1175	0.1322	0.2224	1.3731	0.0914
Quintile 2	0.1610	0.2289	0.2592	1.4158	0.1013
Quintile 3	0.2013	0.2711	0.2691	1.5492	0.1023
Quintile 4	0.2250	0.3150	0.2580	1.5444	0.0929
Quintile 5	0.1822	0.3109	0.1642	1.1897	0.0582

Source: Fielding *et al.* (2005).

Appendix 2: The structure of the fitted model

Our dataset includes 48 countries, and in each country we measure five development outcomes in five household quintiles. Three of the outcomes (assets, sanitation, schooling) are measured on the [0,1] interval, with a substantial number of observations close to zero or unity, so these three variables are modelled in Probit form. The other two (fertility, mortality) are modelled in log-linear form.[15] Let the jth development indicator for the kth quintile in the nth country ($j = 5$,

$k = 5$, $n = 48$) be denoted y_{jkn}. Then our regression equation for the jth indicator is

$$y_{jkn} = F\left(\alpha_{jk} + \sum_{i \neq j}\beta_{ij} \cdot y_{ikn} + \sum_{p}\varphi_{jp} \cdot x_{np} + \theta_j \ln(aid_n)\right) + u_{jkn} \tag{11.A1}$$

for j = assets, sanitation, schooling and

$$\ln(y_{jkn}) = \alpha_{jk} + \sum_{i \neq j}\beta_{ij} \cdot y_{ikn} + \sum_{p}\varphi_{jp} \cdot x_{np} + \theta_j \ln(aid_n) + u_{jkn} \tag{11.A2}$$

for j = fertility, mortality.

F(.) is the Normal cumulative density function. x_{np} is the value of the pth exogenous conditioning variable (listed in Table 11.4) in the nth country, and u_{jkn} is a residual. Greek letters indicate constant parameters to be estimated. Note that the intercepts of the regression equations vary across quintiles, but the slope coefficients do not. (With only 48 countries, we do not really have enough degrees of freedom for quintile-specific regression equations.) Our aid equation is:

$$\ln(aid_n) = \alpha_{AID} + \sum_{p}\varphi_{AIDp} \cdot x_{np} + \theta_{AID} \cdot \ln(discom_n) + u_{AIDn} \tag{11.A3}$$

Identification of the model is achieved through zero restrictions on the ϕ parameters, as indicated in Table 11.4. The model is a fitted by 3SLS, allowing for non-zero correlations between all of the u_{jkn}. The fitted model is over-identified, since the assets, sanitation and health equations between them incorporate six instruments; the fitted model passes an over-identifying restrictions test. Tests of the significance of individual instruments in each equation produce results as follows. One asterisk indicates significance at the 5 per cent level, two indicate significance at the 1 per cent level; a paragraph mark indicates insignificance at the 5 per cent level.

Table 11.A2   Summary of the structure of the model

	Assets equation	Sanitation equation	Health equation
Natural resources	¶	¶	
Ethnolinguistic fractionalization	*	¶	
Size	*	**	
Coastline dummy	*	¶	**
Temperature			¶
Squared temperature			¶
Malaria			**
	Schooling equation	**Fertility equation**	
Christian population	**	**	
Muslim population	*	**	

Source: Fielding *et al.* (2005).

Omission of the insignificant instruments still leaves an over-identified model in which the regression coefficients are similar to those in the original model. Given these results, we are confident in the overall robustness of our identification structure.

Notes

We would like to express our thanks to Chris Haig for help in preparing this text. However, all remaining errors are our own.

1. With headlines such as 'Aid will not boost growth, warns IMF' (*The Age*, 4 July 2005); 'Aid will not lift growth in Africa, warns IMF' (*Financial Times*, 29 June 2005); and 'IMF: Cash Alone Won't Solve Africa's Ills' (*Iran Daily*, 2 July 2005).
2. See Summers and Heston (1991) for a description of PPP adjustment to national accounts data.
3. Briefly, the theoretical rationale for the effects is as follows. Higher standards of education and health embody human capital investments that increase productivity and so per capita income. Higher fertility entails a higher rate of population growth, and so a lower capital–labour ratio and (with decreasing returns to labour) lower productivity. Education and health are also normal consumption goods, so expenditure on them increases with per capita income. High fertility is a consequence of a low opportunity cost of labour (especially female labour), and is therefore decreasing in per capita income.
4. See for example Dean Jamison's comments at the IMF Economic Forum *Health, Wealth and Welfare*, 15 April 2004 (www.imf.org/external/np/tr/2004/tr040415.htm).
5. More details about data construction are available in Fielding and Torres (2005).
6. This is a euphemism for the complete absence of sanitary facilities.
7. One alternative measure of fertility is live births per woman aged 40–9. This alternative is free of the right-censoring present in our measure (many younger women will not have completed their fertility when surveyed). However, it is also likely that fertility patterns will change across the generations, as socioeconomic conditions change, and in many of our countries fertility rates are high among teenage girls. In this case, restricting the fertility measurement to women past childbearing age will give us out-of-date figures with a substantial measurement error.
8. This measures the probability of two randomly selected individuals in a country speaking different native languages. High fractionalization might be associated with lower social cohesion, damaging development along many dimensions.
9. Temperature might affect the value of agricultural land and so factor productivity and material wealth, but we are already using natural resource wealth to control for the value of natural resources in the assets equation.
10. Pitt and Sigle (1997) show that climatic shocks (specifically, shocks to rainfall) have a permanent impact on birth rates in rural Senegalese households. Their interpretation of this result is that a shock to rainfall represents a shock to permanent income. In this case, having conditioned fertility on household assets, we do not need a climate variable in our fertility equation.
11. We rely on the assumption that religious affiliation will affect health only through its impact on education and fertility, and not in any other way.
12. Some of these effects may occur with a substantial lag. With a cross-sectional dataset we do not have the opportunity to explore the dynamics of the interactions between the different development indicators.
13. In interpreting these figures, it is worth noting that the mean sample value of our aid variables is 0.103; the corresponding standard deviation is 0.080.
14. If the ratio of workers to non-workers in a population is constant, per capita GDP will be perfectly correlated with GDP per worker.

15. Strictly speaking, mortality is also measured on a bounded interval, but no observation is anywhere near the upper or lower bound. The sample distributions of *fertility* and *mortality* are approximately log-normal.

References

Addison, T., G. Mavrotas and M. McGillivray (2005) 'Development Assistance and Development Finance: Evidence and Global Policy Agendas', *Journal of International Development*, 17: 819–36.

Ahlburg, D. (1996) 'Population Growth and Poverty', in D. Ahlburg, A. Kelley and K. Oppenheim Mason (eds), *The Impact of Population Growth on Well-Being in Developing Countries*, Berlin: Springer-Verlag.

Bloom, D., D. Canning and J. Sevilla (2004) 'The Effect of Health on Economic Growth: A Production Function Approach', *World Development*, 32: 1–13.

Clemens, M., S. Radelet and R. Bhavnani (2004) 'Counting Chickens when they Hatch: The Short-term Effect of Aid on Growth', *Centre for Global Development Working Paper* 44, Washington, DC: Centre for Global Development.

Devarajan, S. and V. Swaroop (1998) 'The Implications of Foreign Aid Fungibility for Development Assistance', *World Bank Working Paper* 2022, Washington, DC: World Bank.

Devarajan, S., A. Rajkumar and V. Swaroop (1998) 'What Does Aid to Africa Finance?', Mimeo, Development Research Group, World Bank, Washington, DC.

Fernandez, R. and R. Rogerson (1997) 'The Determinants of Public Education Expenditures: Evidence from the States, 1950–1990', *NBER Working Paper* 5995, Cambridge, MA: National Bureau of Economic Research.

Fielding, D. and S. Torres (2005) 'Health, Wealth, Fertility, Education and Inequality', *Economics Discussion Paper* 0505, Dunedin: University of Otago.

Fielding, D., M. McGillivray and S. Torres (2005) 'Synergies between Health, Wealth, Fertility, Education and Aid and their Implications for Achieving the Millennium Development Goals', paper presented at the conference Assessing and Forecasting Progress in Millennium Development Goals, August, UNU-WIDER, Helsinki.

Gramlich, E. (1969) 'The Effects of Federal Grants on State-Local Expenditures', *Proceedings of the National Tax Association* 1969: 569–73.

Pitt, M. and W. Sigle (1997) 'Seasonality, Weather Shocks and the Timing of Births and Child Mortality in Senegal', paper presented at the 10th Anniversary Conference of the Centre for the Study of African Economies, April, Oxford University, Oxford.

Pritchett, L. and L. Summers (1996) 'Wealthier is Healthier', *Journal of Human Resources*, 31: 841–68.

Rajan, R.G. and A. Subramanian (2005) 'Aid and Growth: What Does the Cross-Country Evidence Really Show?', *IMF Working Paper* WP/05/127, Washington, DC: IMF.

Strulik, H. and S. Siddiqui (2002) 'Tracing the Income – Fertility Nexus: Nonparametric Estimates for a Panel of Countries', *Economics Bulletin*, 15: 1–9.

Summers, R. and A. Heston (1991) 'The Penn World Tables (Mark 5): An Expanded Set of International Comparisons: 1950–1988', *Quarterly Journal of Economics*, 106: 327–68.

Teulings, C. and T. van Rens (2003) 'Education, Growth and Income Inequality', *CEPR Discussion Papers* 3863, London: Centre for Economic Policy Research.

12
Is Social Capital Part of the Institutions Continuum and is it a Deep Determinant of Development?

Stephen Knowles

Introduction

There is a growing literature that analyzes, using cross-country data, whether institutions or geography is the most important deep determinant of economic development. Key contributions to this literature include Hall and Jones (1999), Acemoglu *et al.* (2001; 2002), Rodrik *et al.* (2002), Sachs (2003), Easterly and Levine (2003) and Olsson and Hibbs (2005). This literature typically cites North's (1990) definition of institutions as being 'the rules of the game in a society or, more formally, [they] are the humanly devised constraints that shape human interaction'. However, the empirical proxies for institutions that are used in this literature focus on what North (*Ibid*: 3) defined as formal institutions; informal institutions, which North argued were more important than formal institutions, are not considered. This study argues that proxies for informal institutions should be incorporated in this deep determinants literature.

This study also argues that the notion of social capital is similar to North's notion of informal institutions. Social capital can be a difficult term to pin down, but most definitions include (at least one of) the degree of trust, co-operative norms and associational memberships or networks within a society. Economists have become increasingly interested in social capital, following the seminal work of Coleman (1988) (a sociologist) and Putnam *et al.* (1993) (political scientists). Since the publication of these studies a vast quantity of research on social capital has been published by economists, as well as by researchers from other academic disciplines. Isham *et al.* (2002) report that citations for social capital in the *EconLit* database have been doubling every year since the late 1990s. Further evidence of increasing interest in social capital by economists is that a new subcategory on social norms and social capital (Z13) was recently added to the *Journal of Economic*

Literature codes. However, as noted by Fafchamps and Minten (2002), the concept of social capital is still regarded with suspicion by many economists.

Hence, this study puts forward two main arguments. The first is that in terms of its definition, and the arguments advanced as to why social capital is likely to affect economic performance, social capital is a very similar concept to what North (1990) defined as informal institutions. Social capital can therefore be viewed as part of the institutions continuum. The second argument is that ideally proxies for social capital/informal institutions should be included in deep determinants regressions. This would enrich the deep determinants literature by including information on both ends of the institutions continuum. It will also make it possible to model interactions between formal institutions and social capital, and may offer some guidance on how to deal with the problem of endogeneity in the social capital literature. Thinking of social capital as a deep determinant of development also has implications for what control variables should be included in empirical work.

The next section will briefly review the literature on defining social capital, with a view to highlighting the similarities between the concepts of social capital and informal institutions. The third section will summarize some of the key arguments in the literature as to why social capital is likely to affect economic performance. It will be argued that these arguments are consistent with viewing social capital as a deep determinant of development. The following section will discuss how social capital is measured in the existing cross-country literature, and comment on how these, or other, measures of social capital could be usefully incorporated in the institutions as a deep determinant literature. The penultimate section will summarize the potential advantages of modelling social capital in a deep determinants framework and the final section will conclude.

Social capital: is it the same thing as informal institutions?

Defining social capital is not an easy task, as social capital means different things to different people and many different definitions have been proposed in the literature. For that reason, this study will review some of the most widely cited definitions of social capital that have been proposed in the literature, without trying to make a judgement as to which definition is superior. This will make it possible to compare social capital to informal institutions, while recognizing that not everyone agrees on how social capital should be defined.

Most definitions of social capital include at least one, and in several cases two or more, of the following: trust, networks and group memberships, and a shared set of co-operative norms. The term social capital has been around for some time, with Woolcock (1998) arguing that it was first used in its modern sense by Hanifan (1920). Readers interested in the development of the term from that time are referred to Woolcock. For the purposes of this study, we will confine our attention to how the term social capital has been defined since the work of Coleman (1988), focusing on some of the most commonly cited definitions. An excellent review of how social capital is defined in the recent literature can be found in Durlauf and Fafchamps (2004). Appendix Table 12.A1 reproduces the key definitions of social capital as summarized by Durlauf and Fafchamps, with some additions. Note that Knack (2002) splits social capital into two components: government and civil, a point that is discussed more fully below.

A concept that appears in several of these definitions is that of co-operative norms. These norms may include forming orderly queues at airport check-ins, farmers helping their neighbours to harvest crops, showing respect for other drivers on the road, not parking in car parks reserved for the disabled unless you are disabled and so on. Networks and associational memberships also appear in several of these definitions. Associational memberships may include membership in sports teams, choral societies, church or religious groups etc. Networks can be thought of as the people you know or interact with, which includes informal inter-actions, in addition to associational memberships. Associations can be split into horizontal and vertical associations. Horizontal associations are those in which members relate to each other on an equal basis (a sports club, for example), whereas vertical associations are those 'characterized by hierarchical relationships and unequal power among members' (Grootaert 1999: 5). The Catholic Church is sometimes used as an example of a hierarchical association (La Porta *et al.* 1997). Associations can also be split into those which promote the interests of their members only (a revolving credit scheme) and those which aim to promote the interests of members and non-members alike (such as those formed for the purpose of charity work).

With regard to trust, it is important to note that there are different spheres of trust. At one end of the continuum is trust in people you interact with on a regular basis (such as friends and family), and at the other end is trust in those you do not know. Some researchers (Whitely 2000, for example) refer to trust in those you do not know as generalized trust. Uslaner (2002: 5) defines generalized trust slightly differently as the idea that 'most people can be trusted' and defines particularized trust as trust in one's own kind. Putnam (2000) and Holm and Danielson (2005) refer to trust in those you interact with regularly as thick trust, and trust in those you do not know as thin trust. Related to the notion of different spheres of trust is the distinction between bonding, bridging and linking social capital. Building on Granovetter's (1973) notion of weak and strong ties, Woolcock (2001) defines bond-ing social capital as links with family, friends and neighbours, bridging social capital as ties that are slightly more distant, such as with workmates and acquaintances, and linking social capital as the ability to benefit from ties with those outside one's immediate group of contacts.

It seems likely that trust and co-operation will be built up by repeated interac-tions with others; hence networks and associational memberships can be seen as a source of trust and co-operation. In fact, some researchers (Woolcock 2001, for example) prefer to define social capital as norms and networks, and see trust as being a *consequence* of social capital, rather than part of social capital per se. Uslaner (2002), on the other hand, argues that trust is the *cause*, not the consequence, of interactions with others.

Fafchamps and Minten (2002) and Bezemer *et al.* (2004) also prefer to think of social capital as networks. Fafchamps and Minten (2002: 173–4) argue that definitions of social capital fall into two camps. The first, which they argue includes those of Coleman (1988) and Putnam *et al.* (1993), sees 'social capital as a "stock" of trust and an emotional attachment to a group or society at large that facilitate the provision of public goods'. The second type of definition sees social capital as 'an individual asset that benefits a single individual or firm', which is sometimes referred to as 'social network capital' to avoid confusion. Bezemer *et al.* (2004: 3) use the term 'relational capital' to denote this individual level of social capital, defining it as 'productive contacts that individuals use in achieving sold output'. They further suggest using the terms 'social network' or 'communal social capital' to denote the membership of clubs. The most commonly cited definition from Table 12.A1 is probably Putnam *et al.* (1993), which emphasizes trust, norms and networks. These notions appear in most definitions, with norms and networks featuring the most prominently.

A key argument of this study is that there is a significant degree of overlap between the concepts of social capital and (informal) institutions. North's (1990) definition of institutions is the most frequently cited, in both the social capital and institutions literatures. North (*Ibid*: 3) defines institutions as 'the rules of the game in a society or, more formally, [they] are the humanly devised constraints that shape human interaction'. If North's definition were to end here, then it would perhaps be possible to argue that the concept of institutions is quite different to that of social capital. Perhaps the rules of the game are those imposed by the state, with social capital referring to the informal norms or conventions that have evolved over time without these being codified in statute. However, North goes further and distinguishes between formal and informal institutions.

Formal institutions are defined by North (*Ibid.*) as rules that human beings devised (a good example being laws and regulations enacted by governments), whereas informal regulations include conventions and codes of behaviour. North uses the analogy of rules in sports to make the distinction clear. The written rules of a sport are analogous to formal institutions, whereas unwritten codes of conduct, such as an acceptance that it is unacceptable to kick an opponent in the head, are analogous to informal institutions.[1] North (*Ibid.*: 36) argues that people in the Western world tend to think of life being ordered by formal rules, when in fact their actions are guided more by informal constraints, such as 'codes of conduct, norms of behaviour and conventions'. He goes on to argue that 'underlying these informal constraints/institutions are formal rules, but these are seldom the obvious and immediate source of choice in daily interactions'. The implication is that informal institutions are actually more important than formal institutions. It is also important to note that North acknowledges institutions are not always easy to classify into formal and informal, but suggests the two should be seen as opposite ends of a continuum, with taboos, customs and traditions at one end, and written constitutions at the other. North's notion of institutions, once broadened to include informal institutions, includes the concepts of norms of behaviour and social conventions, hence it seems to overlap significantly with the notion of social capital. This is especially true if it is acknowledged that North discusses the importance of co-operation. Although North says little about trust, co-operation does presuppose some degree of trust. A key theme of North (*Ibid.*) is that good institutions will encourage co-operation and reduce transactions costs, notions that also feature prominently in the social capital literature.

The above arguments suggest that the concept of social capital falls within North's definition of institutions. Interestingly, North's followers tend to focus their attention on formal institutions, with informal institutions having disappeared off the radar. In the last few years a literature has flourished examining whether institutions or geography is the most important deep determinant of income per capita. Important contributions in this area include Acemoglu *et al.* (2001; 2002), Rodrik *et al.* (2002), Sachs (2003), Easterly and Levine (2003), Olsson and Hibbs (2005), Fielding and Torres (2005) and Owen and Weatherstone (2005).

In terms of definition, deep (or fundamental) determinants of income are distinct from proximate determinants. The proximate determinants can be thought of as variables that would appear in the aggregate production function, such as labour, physical capital, human capital and technology, plus policy-related variables such as the rate of inflation or the level of government consumption. The deep determinants can be thought of as the variables that affect the proximate determinants, and are hence the underlying determinants of income per capita. Deep determinants are not necessarily exogenous, but are thought to change only slowly, if at all, over time (Glaeser *et al.* 2004). In deep determinants regressions the proximate determinants, such as the accumulation of physical and human capital and policy-type variables are not included as control variables, as this would mean the indirect effect of a deep determinant on income per capita, via the proximate determinants, would not be picked up.

Within this deep determinants literature, the focus is exclusively on formal, rather than informal, institutions. This literature typically cites North's notion of institutions defining the rules of the game, but the distinction between formal and informal institutions is not discussed. When it comes to measuring institutions, the protection of property rights and the rule of law tend to feature prominently; norms, conventions and codes of conduct do not. This is despite the fact that North (1990: 53) argued that

> a mixture of informal norms, rules, and enforcement characteristics together defines the choice set and results in outcomes. Looking only at the formal rules themselves, therefore, gives us an inadequate and frequently misleading notion about the relationship between formal constraints and performance.[2]

One exception is a recent paper by Tabellini (2005), which, although not strictly part of this strand of literature,[3] argues that institutions can be interpreted broadly to include systems of belief and social norms, which Tabellini describes as cultural variables. Rather than including formal and informal institutions as explanatory variables in the same equation, historical data on formal institutions are used as instruments for culture. This paper is discussed in more detail later.

It is also interesting to consider the extent to which the two literatures (social capital and the institutions as a deep determinant) acknowledge the existence of the other. An interesting experiment is to compare the reference lists of two recent survey papers, both of which are to appear in the *Handbook of Economic Growth*, Durlauf and Fafchamps (2004) on social capital and Acemoglu *et al.* (2004) on institutions. Of the more than 150 references cited in Acemoglu *et al.* (2004), only three of them (Durlauf and Fafchamps 2003, an ealier version of Durlauf and Fafchamps 2004; Knack and Keefer 1997; Putnam *et al.* 1993) are from the social capital literature. Durlauf and Fafchamps also cite just over 150 references, but none of them is from the deep determinants literature. They do, however, cite North (1990).

The preceding discussion begs the question of whether 'informal institutions' more accurately describes the concept being defined than 'social capital'.[4] Use of the term social capital has led to debates about whether social capital is social, and more commonly, whether it is capital, and, if it is, what this implies for how it enters the production function (see, for example, Woolcock 1998; Collier 2002; Paldam and Svendsen 2000; Narayan and Pritchett 1999; Arrow 2000; Sobel 2002).[5] Such debates could be avoided if the term 'social capital' were replaced with 'informal institutions'. An alternative would be to simply focus on the notions of trust, norms and networks as separate entities, rather than relying on an all encompassing term such as social capital. However, this is unlikely to happen. 'Social capital' rolls a little more easily off the tongue, than does 'informal institutions', and has a softer, more interdisciplinary ring to it. Which may not be a bad thing. If use of the term social capital encourages communication across academic disciplines, then more social capital has been created in the form of networks. In the words of Woolcock (1998: 188):

> [i]n social capital, historians, political scientists, anthropologists, economists, sociologists, and policymakers – and the various camps *within* each field – may once again begin to find a common language within which to engage one another in open, constructive debate, a language that disciplinary provincialisms have largely suppressed over the last one-hundred-and-fifty years.

Before ending this section on defining social capital, it should be noted that Knack (2002) splits social capital into government and civil social capital. In a definition not included in Table 12.A1, Grafton and Knowles (2004) distinguish between civic social capital and public institutional social capital, with the latter being proxied by measures of corruption and democracy. Grootaert (1999: 5), also not included in Table 12.A1, talks about a macro level of social capital which 'includes institutions such as government, the rule of law, civil and political liberties, etc.' These notions of government, public institutional and macro social capital sound identical to formal institutions. Collier (2002: 19) notes that 'many people restrict the term "social capital" to civil social capital'. Given the similarity between institutions and government, public institutional and macro, social capital, it would seem wise to restrict definitions of social capital to civil social capital.

Social capital and economic performance

This section of the study reviews the key arguments in the literature as to how social capital can affect economic performance, with a view to determining whether social capital may be considered a deep determinant of income, in the sense that it influences either the level of total factor productivity or the accumulation of labour or physical or human capital. Many arguments have been put forward in the literature as to why social capital may improve economic performance. Most of these arguments can be classified under the following headings: increasing the number of mutually beneficial trades, solving collective action problems, reducing monitoring and transactions costs (which could alternatively be referred to as solving principal-agent conflicts) and improving information flows. It is beyond the scope of this study to review every argument in the literature as to why social capital may affect economic performance; instead a small number of examples will be reviewed under each of the headings listed above.

Increasing the number of mutually beneficial trades

It has been recognized for centuries that a high degree of trust and co-operation will increase the number of mutually beneficial trades. For example, the eighteenth century Scottish philosopher David Hume (cited in Putnam *et al.* 1993: 163) discussed the importance of co-operation, and implicitly trust, using the example of two corn farmers. If two corn farmers' crops ripen at different times, but they do not have enough time to harvest their own crops, it makes sense for each farmer to assist with the other's harvest. However, this may not occur if the two farmers do not trust each other. The farmer whose crop ripens last may suspect that if she helps with her neighbour's harvest, this may not be reciprocated.

It is, of course, possible to argue that a monetary transaction could take place to overcome the lack of co-operation outlined in Hume's example of the corn farmers. If Farmer B, whose crop ripens last, suspects Farmer A will not reciprocate she could offer to work for Farmer A for a day's wages, and then hire Farmer A to help harvest her own corn in the future. However, this transaction, like all transactions, will require a degree of trust. Farmer B may fear that having worked for Farmer A for a day, she may not be paid. Anticipating this, she may demand the wages in advance, but then Farmer A will worry that Farmer B will take the money and not provide a day's labour. At some point, an element of trust is required. As noted by Arrow (1972) virtually all transactions require an element of trust, meaning that an absence of trust reduces the number of mutually beneficial trades that can take place. Arrow suggests that a lack of trust explains much of the economic backwardness observed in the world.

Another example of trust leading to a greater number of trades is the development of revolving credit schemes to overcome incomplete, or non-existent capital markets. The success of such schemes requires that members do not free ride. In a world governed by self-interest, some members may be tempted to borrow money from the scheme, and then refuse to continue to make contributions. It is also important that people have good information about those whom they are thinking of joining with in a scheme. A high degree of trust (worthiness) is required to ensure that members do not free ride, and individuals who are well networked will have good information about other potential members of the scheme (Narayan and Pritchett 1999; Grootaert, 1998). In the words of Coleman (1988: S103) 'one could not imagine a rotating-credit association operating in urban areas marked by a high degree of social disorganization – or, in other words, by a lack of social capital'. Social networks will also facilitate lending in the absence of revolving credit schemes. Grootaert (1998: 5) argues that members of a soccer team will be more likely to lend money to each other than to people they do not know. Hence the existence of networks, and the trust associated with them, are likely to increase the supply of informal credit. Informal credit is going to be especially important in LDCs where formal credit markets are typically not as well developed as in the industrialized countries.

The resolution of collective action problems

Societies with high degrees of social capital may find it easier to solve collective action problems than societies less well endowed with social capital. For example, a set of norms may evolve over time, governing the use of common property resources. A set of norms to prevent a fishery being over-fished may include not fishing during the spawning season, releasing undersized fish and not catching more fish than a family can eat. With regard to the provision of public goods, these are more likely to be provided, without recourse to government funding, in societies where co-operative behaviour is the norm. The same can be said for internalizing externalities.

Community-based institutions may also be formed to manage common property resources; several examples are given in Ostrom (1990). For example, for many centuries Spanish farmers have formed organizations to manage irrigation canals (*huertas*). The farmers elect officials, whose job it is to determine who may draw water at what time, to police the system and to settle disputes between members. Similar community-based institutions have evolved to manage irrigation schemes in many other countries including Nepal and India. It could be argued that these community-based institutions sound like a form of de facto government, but, if they are, they represent a decentralized, bottom-up form of government. The fact that it may be difficult to determine whether these community-based institutions should be classified as formal or informal institutions highlights the point that social capital (informal institutions) and formal institutions are at opposite ends of the same continuum, with, for example, community-based institutions falling somewhere in between.

The standard textbook solution to collective action problems requires some action on the part of the government: defining and enforcing property rights in the case of common property resources, public funding in the case of public goods, and taxes or subsidies in the case of externalities. However, this requires strong formal institutions. In cases where formal institutions are weak, which may well be the case in many developing countries, social capital may act as a substitute for formal institutions.

Reducing monitoring and transactions costs

In a low-trust environment, entrepreneurs will assume that workers will shirk unless closely supervised, so to reduce this risk supervisors will be hired, reducing productivity. Woolcock (1998) argues that in many developing countries hospitals and schools may exist, but the doctors and teachers are often not at work. The issue of monitoring workers may also act as a constraint on firm size in low-trust economies. Once a firm reaches a certain size, the owner operator has to delegate a degree of managerial decision making to others, especially in semi-independent parts of the company. Paldam and Svendsen (2000) argue that a lack of social capital prevents small firms growing into large firms in many parts of Africa for this very reason.

Anticipating problems with workers shirking, employers may respond by only employing people already known to them, rather than employing the person best qualified to do the job. In a society that is divided along ethnic or religious lines, preference may be given to hiring those from the same ethnic and/or religious group as the employer, in the belief that they can be trusted more. In this scenario, the most skilled workers may not be employed, which has obvious consequences for the productivity of the firm.

With regards to transactions costs, Fafchamps and Minten (2002: 175) argue that when trust is present agents can 'lower their guard and economize on transactions costs such as the need to inspect quality before buying, or the need to organize payment in cash at the time of delivery'. They go on to argue that trust 'enables agents to place and take orders, pay by check, use invoicing, provide trade credit, and offer warranty', noting that these features of markets are taken for granted in developed countries, but are often lacking in developing countries.

Improving the flow of information

The more people interact with each other, be this in choral societies, sports groups, religious or educational organizations, the better the information they will have about each other, making it easier, for example, to set up revolving credit schemes and the like. It may also improve the flow of information about best practice techniques, making the introduction of new technologies more likely, hence increasing the level of productivity. Networks and membership of groups may also help overcome the impediments to information flows due to social divergence: the phenomena whereby individuals are more likely to communicate with those with similar incomes, education, ethnicity, etc, as themselves, rather than with people from a diverse range of backgrounds (see Grafton *et al.* 2004a; b).

The negative effects of social capital

So far only the positive effects of social capital have been considered. It has to be acknowledged that there are also cases where social capital can have negative effects. It was argued above that social capital may have a positive effect on the adoption of new techniques. However, it is also possible that some customs or norms may *hinder* the introduction of new techniques. For example, Rogers (1983) discusses the example of a Peruvian village whose inhabitants largely refuse to boil their drinking water because, according to local custom, only the sick are permitted to drink boiled water. This example draws attention to the fact that social capital is not always a force for good. It is quite possible that farmers and business people may be reluctant to introduce new techniques that would improve productivity, because this would go against the established way of doing things.

It is also possible that some networks or associations may hamper the adoption of new techniques. As noted by Paldam (2000), guilds, trade organizations and unions often try to hinder change. Networks can also lead to collusion on the part of firms, at the expense of consumers (Fafchamps and Minten 2002). Social networks, such as guilds, cartels, the mafia, political organizations and lobbying groups may provide benefits for members, but this can often come at the expense of non-members (Ogilivie 2004).

Nooteboom (2005: 2) argues that in developing countries high degrees of personalized trust may actually 'lock people into closed, localized, cohesive communities that keep them from opening up to wider perspectives of development, from efficiency and innovation, in wider, more dispersed groups'. For this to occur would require that the radius of trust be limited. If people were just as likely to trust strangers as to trust those they interact with regularly, the problem would not occur. However, if the radius of trust is limited, this may impede economic development.

Bezemer *et al.* (2004: 13) argue that market-based economic development requires that 'inefficient search institutions such as informal networks and trust need to be replaced with more efficient (typically formally defined) market institutions'. Hence they argue that although informal networks and trust may reduce monitoring and search costs, compared to the alternative of their being no search devices at all, that they can only do this up to a certain point. Ultimately, sustained economic growth is going to require these informal mechanisms be replaced by more formal market-based institutions, which may not happen if this is not in the interests of the political elite. Hence high levels of social capital may hinder the adoption of the formal institutions required to promote economic development.

The interaction between social capital and formal institutions

Some of the arguments outlined above suggest that social capital can act as a substitute for formal institutions. For example, in the absence of strong formal institutions, social capital may make it easier to resolve collective action problems. The arguments regarding the provision of credit suggest that social capital can act as a substitute when formal credit markets are not well developed. In such cases, social capital may be expected to have a more marked effect on economic performance in countries where formal institutions are weak. Empirically, if an interaction term between social capital and formal institutions is included in a cross-country regressions explaining income per capita we would expect the interaction term to be negative, controlling for the level of social capital and formal institutions.

An alternative argument is that formal institutions, such as laws protecting property rights, are likely to be more effective when the level of trust is high. In addition, formal arrangements regarding the provision of public goods are also likely to be undermined in societies where cheating on your taxes is an acceptable norm. As argued by Durlauf and Fafchamps (2004: 14), '[p]ublic good delivery is best accomplished when the power of the state to tax and mobilize resources is combined with trust and community involvement'. If this argument is accepted, then formal institutions are likely to be more effective in countries with high levels of social capital. In this case, the interaction term would be expected to be positive, having controlled for the levels of social capital and institutions.

The preceding paragraphs have argued that social capital (informal institutions) and formal institutions can either be substitutes or complements. This has important implications for empirical work, as it suggests that it is important not only to control for both social capital and formal institutions, but to include an interaction term to capture interactions between the two. The only cross-country empirical study that includes proxies for both social capital and formal institutions is Knack and Keefer (1997), discussed later, but no interaction term is included. Future empirical work could be enriched by including such an interaction term.

Social capital: factor of production or deep determinant?

It is sometimes argued in the literature that social capital can be thought of as a new factor of production (for example, Paldam and Svendsen 2000), which would mean social capital is a proximate determinant of development. However, the arguments discussed above tend to suggest that social capital will affect the accumulation of *other* factors of production, or affect the level of total factor productivity, rather than social capital being a new factor of production in its own right. For example, if social capital leads to the establishment of informal credit markets, this will facilitate the accumulation of physical and human capital. If high levels of trust and co-operation lead to farmers helping to harvest their neighbours' crops, more labour is being used. When social capital helps resolve collective action problems, efficiency is increased. If social capital reduces transactions and monitoring costs, or leads to the introduction of new technologies, this will increase the level of total factor productivity. Hence, thinking of social capital as a new factor of production may not be the best way to capture the effect of social capital on output. A more useful way forward, especially in the cross-country literature, may be to think of social capital as a deep, determinant of income, in the same way it has become standard in recent times to model the effects of geography and institutions on income per capita.

Measuring social capital in cross-country studies

The previous section of the study argued that, in terms of the arguments as to why social capital will affect income, social capital should be modelled as a deep determinant of development. However, to be considered a deep determinant of development, a variable must also meet the criterion of changing only slowly over time. This section of the study will critique the social capital proxies used in past cross-country empirical work and discuss how much they vary over time. Before proceeding, it should be acknowledged that the majority of empirical studies on social capital use micro data, collected at the individual or household level, rather than cross-country data. This micro literature will not be reviewed here, given that the focus of this study is on modelling social capital as a deep determinant of economic development, in the same way formal institutions have been modelled, using cross-country data. Readers interested in a review of the micro literature are referred to Durlauf and Fafchamps (2004) and Knowles (2005, an earlier version of this study).

Social capital proxies used in the existing cross-country literature

Many definitions of social capital include at least one of: the degree of trust, co-operative norms and networks within a society. A widely cited empirical paper that proxies for all three of these variables is Knack and Keefer (1997), who use three different proxies for social capital: TRUST, CIVIC and GROUPS. These three measures of social capital are derived from the World Values Survey (Ingelhart 1994). There have been four different waves of the World Values Survey carried out at different points in time, although only two waves had been conducted at the time Knack and Keefer carried out their work.

TRUST measures the percentage of individuals in a country who answered 'most people can be trusted' to the question 'Generally speaking, would you say that most people can be trusted or that you can't be too careful in dealing with people?'. CIVIC is an index which ranges from 5–50, where respondents were asked to assign a score between 1 and 10 as to whether they agreed that certain behaviours were justified, with a 1 indicating the behaviour was never justified and a 10 indicating that the behaviour was always justified. The five behaviours are (1) claiming a government benefit to which you are not entitled, (2) avoiding a fare on public transport, (3) cheating on taxes if you have the chance, (4) buying something that you knew was stolen and (5) accepting a bribe in the course of one's duties. Knack and Keefer transform the data so that a score of 50 indicates the *highest* possible level of CIVIC and a score of 5 indicates the *lowest* possible level of CIVIC. GROUPS is the average number of groups people belong to in each country.

From the perspective of development economics, it needs to be noted that the sample of countries for which Knack and Keefer present data on TRUST, CIVIC and GROUPS is dominated by developed countries. Of the 29 countries included in their sample, only ten (South Korea, India, South Africa, Argentina, Nigeria, Chile, Portugal, Mexico, Turkey and Brazil) are developing countries. The developing countries do not fare particularly well in terms of the social capital measures, especially in the case of TRUST, with only South Korea getting an above-average score. In Brazil, only 6.7 per cent of the sample think others could generally be trusted; in Turkey the figure is only 10 per cent, compared to a sample average of 36 per cent. Two more waves of the World Values Survey have been compiled since

Knack and Keefer was published. The latest wave (Ingelhart *et al.* 2004) includes data for 33 developing countries, as well as several former communist states from Eastern Europe. For the 33 developing countries, the average value of TRUST is 23.5, whereas for the developed countries in the sample it is 42. Whether these data can be taken as reliable evidence that social capital is low in developing countries will be discussed later.

Turning to the results of empirical work using the World Values Survey data, Knack and Keefer find that TRUST and CIVIC are both positively correlated with growth in output per worker, and with the average rate of investment, across countries, when these variables are included in Barro-style regressions. The GROUPS variable is found to not have a statistically significant effect in explaining both investment and growth. Zak and Knack (2001) update the empirical work of Knack and Keefer, with a larger sample of countries, but include only TRUST as a social capital proxy, not CIVIC nor GROUPS. The empirical results obtained are broadly consistent with Knack and Keefer. La Porta *et al.* (1997) examine the effect of TRUST on a range of proxies for economic development, using cross-country data. Controlling for the level of income per capita, TRUST is found to be significantly positively correlated with the quality and adequacy of infrastructure, high school completions, the adequacy of the education system and the rate of economic growth. TRUST is found to be significantly negatively correlated with the infant mortality rate and the inflation rate. Tabellini (2005) finds TRUST to be positively correlated with income per capita, both across countries and across European regions. Helliwell (1996) finds measures of trust and associational memberships from the World Values Survey to be *negatively* correlated with growth for a sample of 17 OECD countries.

Knack and Keefer's TRUST measure is based on a question about generalized trust. The early waves of the World Values Survey also ask questions about people's trust in family and fellow nationals, as well as the more general question that Knack and Keefer focus on. Whitely (2000) combines the responses to all three questions into a social capital index using principal components analysis, and finds a significant positive correlation between this index and income per capita across countries, with social capital having a bigger influence on income per capita than does human capital.

In an often overlooked section of their paper, Knack and Keefer examine the effect of TRUST on output per worker, physical capital per worker, human capital per worker and the level of total factor productivity. TRUST is significantly positively correlated with the first three of these variables, as long as no other control variables are included. However, when measures of property rights, openness and distance from the equator are included as control variables, the only equation in which TRUST is significant is that explaining human capital per worker. Given the range of control variables included, these results could be considered a deep determinants-of-development equation. Note, however, that no attempt is made to control for endogeneity, other than arguing that, as TRUST is measured for an earlier time period than the dependent variables, it is predetermined. Neither do Knack and Keefer include an interaction term for social capital and formal institutions. Recall also that Knack and Keefer's sample is dominated by developed countries.

How valid are the social capital proxies?

It is important to acknowledge some potential problems with these measures of social capital. Whether people's answers to the TRUST question are correlated with how trusting they are of others, and/or how trustworthy they are, in economic experiments has been studied by Glaeser *et al.* (2000) for the USA and Holm and Danielson (2005) for Tanzania and Sweden. Both studies were carried out on undergraduate economics students, so the results may not be representative of the whole population. Glaser *et al.* find there is no correlation between people's answers to the TRUST question and how trusting they are of others, but that there is a positive correlation between TRUST and how *trustworthy* an individual is. Holm and Danielson find that there is no correlation between how trusting people claim to be (or how trustworthy they are) and their behaviour in experiments in Tanzania, but there is in Sweden.

The Holm and Danielson experiments also provide information on whether people are more trusting in Sweden than in Tanzania. This is an interesting comparison to make, as Sweden has one of the highest TRUST scores (66 per cent) in the fourth wave of the World Values Survey, whereas Tanzania has one of the lowest (8 per cent). In the experiment the subjects were divided into two different groups, A and B. Each individual was paired with a member of the opposite group, but they did not know the identity of the person with whom they were paired. Each person in Group A was allocated a sum of money. They then had to decide how much money they would transfer to the person they were paired with in Group B, and this amount of money was tripled. The person in Group B, then had to decide how much of the money to transfer, if any, to the person in Group A. Holm and Danielson interpret the amount of money transferred by the person in Group A as a measure of the degree of trust, and the amount of money returned by the person in Group B as a measure of trustworthiness. In Sweden 51 per cent of the money was transferred, and 35 per cent returned; in Tanzania 53 per cent of the money was sent and 37 per cent returned. These differences are not statistically significant. When participants were asked the generalized trust question from the World Values Survey, 74 per cent said others could be trusted in Sweden and 41 per cent said others could be trusted in Tanzania. The figure for Tanzania is vastly different to that reported in the World Values Survey, although it is possible this is because university students are more trusting than the population in general. Holm and Danielson's results suggest that, when evaluated on the basis of experiments, the level of trust is just as high in Tanzania as in Sweden, whereas in the World Values Survey the measure of TRUST differs by a factor of eight. This calls into question the generalization from the World Values Survey that TRUST is typically higher in developed countries than in developing countries.

Another potential problem with the trust question from the World Values Survey is that it does not really pin down who 'most people' are. Does this mean people you come into contact with regularly (thick trust), people like yourself (particularized trust) or anyone in your own village or country (thin, or general-ized, trust)? As argued by Guinnane (2005), neither does the question make it clear *how much* trust you are being expected to place in others. If you say you do trust others, does this mean you would trust them with a small sum of money or a large sum of money, or perhaps even your life?

Knack and Keefer argue that the validity of TRUST is confirmed, to some extent, by an experiment conducted by the *Reader's Digest*, who dropped a number of wallets in various countries around the world to see how many would be returned. The proportion of wallets returned was higher in countries with higher measures of TRUST, with a correlation of 0.67. With regard to the whether the question makes it clear how wide the radius of trust is, Uslaner (2002) presents evidence from a US survey that when respondents are asked to elaborate on their answers to the TRUST question, the majority of respondents include strangers in their definition of 'most people', suggesting the question is measuring generalized trust.

Knack and Keefer suggest that CIVIC is a measure of the strength of norms of civic co-operation within a society. However, this variable may be better inter-preted as a measure of civic virtue. This is because a country is assigned a low value of CIVIC if, for example, everyone thinks it is all right to cheat on their taxes. However, if *everyone* were to cheat on their taxes, this could represent a civic norm. The CIVIC variable is perhaps best interpreted as a measure of trustworthi-ness. At a more practical level, another problem with CIVIC is that it does not exhibit much variation across countries. The maximum score is 42.43 and the minimum score 34.55, with a standard deviation of 2.3. There is much more vari-ation across countries for both TRUST (range of 6.7–61.2) and GROUPS (range of 0.38–1.70). One potential weakness of the GROUPS variable is that it only takes into account the number of associations an individual belongs to, rather than taking into account how committed members are to the group.

It has been argued above that the social capital measures typically used in cross-country studies may well be measured with error. However, the same is probably true, to at least the same extent, with regard to the empirical proxies used in the formal institutions literature. Hence, if the social capital proxies are to be discounted on these grounds, so too should the proxies commonly used for formal institutions in the deep determinants literature. The two datasets most commonly used to proxy for formal institutions are the ICRG (International Country Risk Guide, also known as the Political Risk Services) measure of protection against expropriation risk (used by Hall and Jones 1999; Acemoglu *et al.* 2001; 2002), and the Kaufmann *et al.* (2002) dataset (used by Rodrik *et al.* 2002). These datasets are based on assessments by experts of, for example, the risk of expropriation in different countries, and are therefore subjective measures. Hence, there is no reason to believe these data are more reliable than, for example, survey-based measures of trust.

Glaeser *et al.* (2004) have also pointed out that the ICRG and Kaufmann *et al.* measures do not measure formal constraints on the executive, which is how North (1990) defined formal institutions. Instead, these variables tend to measure outcomes, in the sense that countries ruled by dictators who happen to choose to protect property rights are awarded a high score, despite that fact that such countries cannot be classed as having good institutions, in the sense of there being constraints on executive power. Glaeser *et al.* also point out that these commonly used measures of institutions exhibit a lot of variation over time, so don't meet the criterion for being a deep determinant of changing only slowly over time.

Hence, although the World Values Survey measures of social capital may not be ideal, they may be no worse than the proxies commonly used for formal institutions. This does not change the fact, however, that the search should continue for superior measures of social capital across countries. Possible alternatives will be discussed in later in this section.

How much does social capital vary over time?

This study has argued that social capital can be thought of as part of the institutions continuum, which suggests that social capital could be empirically modelled as a deep determinant of economic development, in the same way that formal institutions have been. For social capital to be considered a deep determinant also requires that it will change only slowly over time. Although social capital can be eroded quickly, it is often argued that social capital takes a long time to build (see, for example, Putnam *et al.* 1993; Putnam 2000). North (1990: 6) argues that informal constraints embodied in customs, traditions, and codes of conduct are more impervious to deliberate policies and will change more slowly over time than will formal institutions.

Whether or not social capital does change slowly over time will be evaluated by examining data on TRUST, from the World Values Survey, given that this is the most common proxy for social capital used in the cross-country literature. Although potential problems with the World Values Survey data have been acknowledged above, it is currently the only dataset available on social capital for a broad cross-section of countries. Whether TRUST is relatively stable over time can be assessed by comparing the TRUST data from the four different waves of the World Values Survey, for countries that have data for more than one wave. For the 60 countries that fall into this category, the average standard deviation within countries is 4.25, which does not seem particularly high. There are, however, some countries for which the measure of TRUST varies significantly over time, although this is not the norm. For example, Canada has a score of 52 in the second wave of the World Values Survey and a score of only 39 in the fourth wave. The USA has a score of 52 in the second wave and a score of only 36 in the fourth wave. This may represent a reduction in the level of trust in these countries, or alternatively, represent measurement error.

How highly correlated are formal and informal institutions?

It is important to consider how highly correlated the standard measures of informal and formal institutions are. If the correlation is high, then little new information will be introduced by including measures of informal institutions in the deep determinants literature. The correlation coefficient between TRUST and Acemoglu *et al.*'s (2001; 2002) measure of the risk of expropriation is 0.45, with

Kaufmann *et al.*'s (2002) rule-of-law index it is 0.46, and with Glaeser *et al.*'s (2004) measure of constraints on the executive it is 0.35. None of these correlations is particularly high. Examination of the dataset underlying these calculations shows there are a number of countries with high values of TRUST, but low values for the various measures of formal institutions (China, Iran and Indonesia, for example) and vice versa (Singapore and Portugal, for example). Adding proxies for social capital (informal institutions) to the deep determinants literature would, therefore, add new information. Note, however, that earlier sections of this chapter have acknowledged potential problems with the World Values Survey data. Hence, the World Values Survey data may not be the best to use for this purpose, although they are currently the only such data available for a broad cross-section of countries. The next section of the study will discuss alternative measures of social capital that could be developed in the future.

Suggestions for alternative social capital proxies

The World Bank has recently designed a social capital questionnaire, the Integrated Questionnaire for the Measurement of Social Capital (SC-IQ), which they propose incorporating into household surveys of poverty. Details of the questionnaire, which has already been piloted in Albania and Nigeria, are given in Grootaert *et al.* (2004). The questionnaire includes questions on six dimensions of social capital: (1) groups and networks, (2) trust and solidarity, (3) collective action and co-operation, (4) information and communication, (5) social cohesion and inclusion and (6) empowerment and political action. The survey is incredibly detailed, including 95 questions under the six headings. Thirty-three of the questions relate to groups and networks. Alternatively, a core questionnaire has been designed, which includes what the World Bank considers to be the 27 key questions from the longer survey.

The use of this questionnaire will hopefully lead to a rich dataset that can be used by social capital researchers. The questionnaire has been specifically designed with micro studies in mind, and there is no suggestion that the World Bank envisages aggregating these data into country measures. However, as long as the households surveyed are representative of the whole population of a specific country, and if the survey methods and questions remain consistent across countries, and if the data are collected for a large number of developing countries, the data should lend themselves to being aggregated into nationwide measures of social capital, in the same way that researchers have used the World Values Survey data. The key advantage of the World Bank dataset, from the perspective of development economists, would be that it will focus on developing countries, whereas the World Values Survey includes a large number of developed countries and East European transition economies.

Rather than relying on survey-based data, another possibility in terms of trust data is to use data collected in experiments, such as the experiment conducted by Holm and Danielson (2005) in Tanzania and Sweden, which are described earlier in the study. Such experiments do not necessarily have to involve the use of computers or other equipment, so it is feasible that they could be carried out in developing countries, even in remote areas. Researchers planning to collect survey data on social capital in different villages could potentially also use similar experiments to that of Holm and Danielson to generate a measure of village-wide trust.

The problem of simultaneity

The only papers that attempt to address the issue of simultaneity in the existing cross-country social capital literature are Knack and Keefer (1997), Zak and Knack (2001) and Tabellini (2005). Simultaneity is a potential problem as it is possible that people can afford to be more trusting, or belong to more groups, in countries where the economy is growing more quickly. Controlling for such simultaneity bias requires finding instruments that are correlated with social capital (good instruments) but which have no independent correlation with the dependent variable (valid instruments). Knack and Keefer instrument for TRUST with the percentage of a country's population belonging to the largest ethnolinguistic group and the number of law students as a proportion of all tertiary students. Whether these variables are valid instruments is questionable, given that they may well have an independent effect on the dependent variable. Rather than using the Knack and Keefer instruments for TRUST, Zak and Knack use the shares of the population that are Catholic, Muslim or Eastern Orthodox as instruments, arguing that these hierarchical religions have negative effects on trust. Again, it could be argued that these variables may have an independent effect on growth, making them invalid instruments. In critiquing these instruments, Durlauf and Fafchamps (2004: 53) argue '[w]e are not aware of any social capital study using aggregate data that addresses causality versus correlation for social capital and growth in a persuasive way. While this is a broad brush with which to tar this empirical literature, we believe it is valid.'

A useful starting point for thinking about addressing the problem of simultaneity, with regard to social capital (informal institutions), is to consider how this issue has been tackled to date with regards to formal institutions in the deep determinants literature. Hall and Jones (1999) argue that measures of the degree of Western European influence and distance from the equator can be used to instrument for institutions. The argument is that institutions that protect property rights and encourage production, rather than diversion, were first developed in Western Europe. Hence, countries more exposed to Western European influence are more likely to have adopted these institutions. The logic behind using distance from the equator as an instrument is that Europeans did not settle near the equator.

Another instrument, which has drawn much comment in the literature, has been proposed by Acemoglu *et al.* (2001), who argue that settler mortality during the colonial period can be used as an instrument for current institutions. Their argument is that the colonial powers set up one of two types of institutions in their colonies. In countries where mortality rates were low enough for Europeans to settle, institutions were established that protected the property rights of the population in general. However, in regions where mortality rates were too high for permanent settlement to be viable, the European powers were more concerned with extracting raw materials as quickly as possible, and, therefore, set up institutions geared to that end. As institutions tend to persist over time, countries where mortality rates for settlers were low have inherited institutions that protect property rights. They argue further that rates of settler mortality in the past are uncorrelated with health levels today, precluding an independent effect of settler mortality on current income per capita. Hence, they argue, settler mortality is a valid instrument. The validity of settler mortality as an instrument has been questioned on various grounds. Glaeser *et al.* (2004) argue that it is just as likely that settlers took their human capital with them, as it is that they took their institutions with them, when they emigrated. If human capital has persisted over time, and if human capital affects income per capita, instruments relying on settlement patterns are no longer valid instruments. Glaeser *et al.* also report that the correlation between settler mortality and current health levels is high, which also calls into question the validity of the settler mortality instrument.

Drawing on this literature, Tabellini (2005) uses the settler mortality variable as an instrument for TRUST in cross-country regressions explaining income per capita, and finds that TRUST is positively correlated with income per capita. However, given that the settler mortality instrument is only available for a limited number of countries, the sample size is limited to 20 countries. In his regressions examining the effect of TRUST and other cultural variables[6] on income per capita across European regions, he uses historical data on both formal institutions (data from 1600–1850) and literacy levels (data from 1880) as instruments for culture. Tabellini argues that formal institutions will shape culture, as, for example, an authoritarian regime will breed mistrust. However, past institutions will have no independent effect on income per capita across regions, once country dummies have been included, which will pick up the effect of current national institutions on income per capita.

Tabellini has shown that the settler mortality instrument used in the formal institutions literature can also be used as an instrument for variables like TRUST. As new and better instruments are found for formal institutions, it is possible they could also be used as instruments for informal institutions, given that formal institutions and informal institutions are simply different ends of the same continuum. It should be noted, however, that if formal institutions and social capital are to both be included as explanatory variables, two instruments need to be found for the purposes of identification, which may explain why Tabellini did not include formal institutions as a control variable in his cross-country equations. Another potential problem with this suggestion is that formal and informal institutions may evolve in quite different ways. If Acemoglu's argument is to be believed, institutions have typically been imposed externally. It is likely that informal institutions, on the other hand, evolve endogenously from within a country. If this is true, then a variable that is a good instrument for formal institutions may not always be a good instrument for informal institutions. Another possibility is that there may be some cultural variables that could be used as instruments for social capital, such as religious affiliation, but this requires that such variables have no independent effect on income per capita.

How will the social capital and institutional literatures be enriched by modelling social capital as a deep determinant of development?

This study has argued that social capital is a similar concept to what North (1990) defined as informal institutions. Furthermore, if social capital is considered to be part of the institutional continuum, it could be modelled empirically as a deep determinant of economic development in the same way formal institutions has been. This section of the study will summarize how the deep determinants of development and social capital literatures would be enriched if this were to happen.

The 'capital' in 'social capital' leads many to assume that it is a form of capital, to be added to the list of reproducible capitals along with physical and human capital. However, it was argued in an earlier section that social capital is best thought of as a deep determinant of economic development, which largely affects income via its affect on the accumulation of other factors of production or the level of total factor productivity (the proximate determinants), rather than as a factor of production in its own right. If social capital is not a form of capital, then the term 'informal institutions' may be a more useful descriptor. Whether social capital (informal institutions) is viewed as a proximate or deep determinant is not merely a semantic point. The framework used to analyze how social capital affects income has implications for how its effects should be analyzed empirically.

If social capital is thought of as a factor of production, then the effects of social capital on income are best modelled, as a proximate determinant of development, in a production function framework, controlling for the effects of other factors of production such as physical and human capital. This is how the effects of social capital have typically been analyzed in the existing cross-country studies on social capital. For example, Whitely (2000) controls for the accumulation of physical and human capital and Knack and Keefer (1997) and Zak and Knack (2001) control for investment in physical capital. However, if social capital (informal institutions) is thought to be a deep determinant, controlling for physical and human capital is inappropriate. This is because physical and human capital are both proximate determinants of income that are, in part, explained by the level of social capital. Including them as control variables in the regression equation means the indirect effect of social capital on income per capita, via these proximate determinants, will not be picked up. If social capital really is a deep determinant of development, then the control variables should be the other potential deep determinants of development, such as formal institutions and geographic variables, not the proximate determinants such as human and physical capital accumulation.

As was argued earlier, following the lead of the deep determinants literature may assist in the choice of instruments for social capital. Tabellini (2005) has shown that the settler mortality variable that has been used as an instrument for formal institutions can be used as an instrument for TRUST. Other variables that have been used as instruments for formal institutions could conceivably be used as instruments for social capital (informal) institutions, given that formal and informal institutions represent different ends of the same continuum.

The existing deep determinants literature will also be enriched by considering the role of social capital (informal institutions). There are a large number of studies analyzing the effect of institutions on income per capita, within a deep determinants framework. However, in these studies the focus is almost entirely on formal institutions, especially those related to property rights. Bardhan (2005: 500) criticizes this literature for having too narrow a view of institutions arguing '[t]his preoccupation of the literature with the institution of security of property rights, often to the exclusion of other important institutions, severely limits our understanding of the development process'. However, Bardhan extends this literature by including additional proxies for formal, rather than informal, institutions. North (1990) argued that informal institutions, such as co-operative norms, are more important than formal institutions, meaning that the current deep determinants literature may well suffer from omitted variables bias. Remaining true to North's definition of institutions requires including proxies for informal institutions. It is also important to control for possible interactions between formal and informal institutions. Failure to consider the role of informal institutions would not matter so much if formal and informal institutions were highly correlated, but it has been argued earlier that this is not the case.

Conclusion

This study has argued that social capital is a similar notion to what North (1990) defined as *informal* institutions. North defined *formal* institutions as rules devised by human beings, whereas *informal* institutions are codes of conduct and conventions of behaviour. Formal institutions can be considered analogous to the written rules of a sport, with informal institutions being analogous to unwritten codes of conduct generally adhered to by the players. Institutions can sometimes be difficult to categorize into formal and informal, so it can be useful to think of institutions forming a continuum, with written constitutions at one end and taboos, customs and traditions at the other. Towards the middle of the continuum will come community-based institutions, such as those that exist in many parts of the world to manage common property resources.

There are many different definitions of social capital used in the literature, but most of these definitions include at least one of the notions of trust, a shared set of co-operative norms, and networks and/or associational memberships. Hence, in terms of its definition, social capital seems similar to the notion of informal institutions. Social capital researchers often argue that social capital will improve economic performance by reducing transactions costs and encouraging co-operation, a point also made by North with regard to informal institutions. Although North (*Ibid.*) is frequently cited by researchers in both the social capital literature and the institutions as a deep determinant literature, neither group of researchers tends to acknowledge the work of the other.

This study has argued that when empirically estimating the effect of social capital on economic development across countries, social capital can be added to the list of deep determinants of economic development, along with formal institutions and geography. Deep determinants are variables that affect income per capita (or other proxies of economic development), via their effect on the proximate determinants, such as factor accumulation or total factor productivity. They are also variables that change very slowly, if at all, over time. The third section of the study reviewed a selection of the arguments as to why social capital is likely to affect economic performance. These arguments suggested that social capital is likely to affect either the level of total factor productivity, or the rate of factor accumulation, hence it seems sensible to think of social capital as a deep determinant, rather than a proximate determinant. In addition, data were presented in suggesting that social capital does not vary much across time within a given country. Thinking of social capital as a deep determinant of economic development, therefore, seems reasonable. As discussed earlier, whether social capital is a deep, or proximate, determinant of development has implications for which control variables should be included in regressions analyzing the effect of social capital on the level of income per capita.

Including measures of social capital (informal institutions) in deep determinants regressions will, of course, require that data of reasonable quality be available for a large number of countries. This study has, at times, made reference to possible measures from the World Values Survey, while acknowledging that these data are far from perfect. Over time, the ideal would be for experimental data to be collected that measure the degree of trust and co-operative norms in different countries. The literature on institutions as a deep determinant of economic development has focused exclusively on the effect of formal institutions on income per capita, despite North's suggestion that informal institutions are more important. This institutions as a deep determinant literature will be enriched by considering both ends of the institutions continuum.

Appendix

Table 12.A1   Commonly cited definitions of social capital

Author(s)	Definition
Coleman (1988: S95)	'... obligations and expectations, information channels, and social norms.'
Coleman (1990: 304)	'... social organization constitutes social capital, facilitating the achievement of goals that could not be achieved in its absence or could be achieved only at a higher cost.'
Putnam *et al.* (1993: 167)	'... features of social organization, such as trust, norms, and networks that can improve the efficiency of society.'
Fukuyama (1997: 378–9)	'... the existence of a certain set of informal rules or norms shared among members of a group that permits co-operation among them. The sharing of values and norms does not in itself produce social capital, because the norms may be the wrong ones ... The norms that produce social capital ... must substantively include virtues like truth telling, the meeting of obligations and reciprocity.'

Continued

Table 12.A1 Continued

Author(s)	Definition
Knack and Keefer (1997: 1251)	'Trust, co-operative norms, and associations within groups.'
Narayan and Pritchett (1999: 872)	'... the quantity and quality of associational life and the related social norms.'
Putnam (2000: 19)	'... connections among individuals – social networks and norms of reciprocity and trustworthiness that arise from them.'
Ostrom (2000: 176)	'... the shared knowledge, understandings, norms, rules and expectations about patterns of interactions that groups of individuals bring to a recurrent activity.'
Woolcock (2001: 13)	'... the norms and networks that facilitate collective action ... it is important that any definition of social capital focus on its sources rather than consequences ... This approach eliminates an entity such as "trust" from the definition of social capital.'
Lin (2001: 24–5)	'... resources embedded in social networks and accessed and used by actors for actions. Thus the concept has two important components: (1) it represents resources embedded in social relations rather than individuals, and (2) access and use of such resources reside with the actors.'
Bowles and Gintis (2002: 2)	'... trust, concern for one's associates, a willingness to live by the norms of one's community and to punish those who do not.'
Knack (2002: 42)	'I use the term government social capital to refer to institutions that influence people's ability to co-operate for mutual benefit. The most commonly analysed of these institutions ... include the enforceability of contracts, the rule of law, and the extent of civil liberties permitted by the state.' 'Civil social capital encompasses common values, norms, informal networks, and associational memberships that affect the ability of individuals to work together to achieve common goals.'
Sobel (2002: 139)	'Social capital describes circumstances in which individuals can use membership in groups and networks to secure benefits.'
Durlauf and Fafchamps (2004: 5)	'(1) social capital generates positive externalities for members of a group; (2) these exernalities ar achieved through shared trust, norms and values and their consequent effects on expectations and behaviour; (3) shared trust, norms and values arise from informal forms of organizations based on social networks and associations.'
World Bank (2005)	'[T]he norms and networks that enable collective action.'

Notes

In writing this study I have benefited greatly from conversations with Dorian Owen and Quentin Grafton. Thanks also to Steve Jones for getting me thinking about whether there is a difference between social capital and institutions. Earlier versions of this study have been presented at the UNU-WIDER jubilee conference (Helsinki, June 2005), the New Zealand Association of Economists' Annual Conference (Christchurch, June/July 2005) and the Roads to Riches Workshop at the Australian National University (Canberra, November 2005). I am grateful to participants and discussants for the many useful comments received. I would also like to acknowledge the useful comments made by two anonymous referees. Financial assistance from the Marsden Fund (grant number UOO 908), administered by the Royal Society of New Zealand, is gratefully acknowledged.

1. It is true, of course, that in the vast majority of sports it is against the rules to kick an opponent in the head. However, in some sports, there is an unwritten code of conduct that although it may be acceptable to punch an opponent, which is also against the rules, that kicking an opponent in the head goes beyond the pale.
2. It could be argued that measures of the extent to which property rights are protected and the rule of law prevails will be a function of both formal rules and informal institutions, hence these measures are picking up informal institutions to some extent. However, if informal institutions are omitted from the analysis, this precludes any other effect of informal institutions on income, over and above the effect via property rights and the rule of law.
3. Tabellini does not include any geographic variables, hence does not contribute to the debate as to whether institutions or geography is the most important deep determinant of development.
4. Dasgupta (2000), in reviewing the social capital literature, uses the phrase 'informal institutions', and asks in passing whether social capital is merely another name for good institutions. However, this point is not developed.
5. The standard argument against social capital being a form of capital is that the accumulation of social capital does not necessarily require sacrifice (see, for example, Arrow 2000).
6. The other cultural variables are measures of the extent to which individuals feel they have the freedom to shape their own destiny, the extent of tolerance and respect for others, and whether people view children obeying their parents as being an important quality.

References

Acemoglu, D., S. Johnson and J.A. Robinson (2001) 'The Colonial Origins of Comparative Development: An Empirical Investigation', *American Economic Review*, 91, 5: 1369–401.
Acemoglu, D., S. Johnson and J.A. Robinson (2002) 'Reversal of Fortune: Geography and Institutions in the Making of the Modern World Income Distribution', *Quarterly Journal of Economics*, 117: 1231–94.
Acemoglu, D., S. Johnson and J.A. Robinson (2004) 'Institutions as the Fundamental Cause of Long-Run Growth', Mimeo.
Arrow, K.J. (1972) 'Gifts and Exchanges', *Philosophy and Public Affairs*, 1, 4: 343–62.
Arrow, K.J. (2000) 'Observations on Social Capital', in P. Dasgupta and I. Serageldin (eds), *Social Capital: A Multifaceted Perspective*, Washington, DC: World Bank.
Bardhan, P.K. (2005) 'Institutions Matter, But Which Ones?', *Economics of Transition*, 13, 3: 499–532.
Bezemer, D.J., U. Dulleck and P. Frijters (2004) 'Social Capital, Creative Destruction and Economic Growth', Mimeo, Australian National University.
Bowles, S. and H. Gintis (2002) 'Social Capital and Community Governance', *Economic Journal*, 112, 483: F419–36.

Coleman, J.S. (1988) 'Social Capital in the Creation of Human Capital', *American Journal of Sociology*, 94: 95–120.

Coleman, J.S. (1990) *The Foundations of Social Theory*, Cambridge, MA: Harvard University Press.

Collier, P. (2002) 'Social Capital and Poverty: A Microeconomic Perspective', in C. Grootaert and T. van Bastelaer (eds), *The Role of Social Capital in Development: An Empirical Assessment*, Cambridge: Cambridge University Press.

Dasgupta, P. (2000) 'Economic Progress and the Idea of Social Capital', in P. Dasgupta and I. Serageldin (eds), *Social Capital: A Multifaceted Perspective*, Washington, DC: World Bank.

Durlauf, S.N. and M. Fafchamps (2003) 'Empirical Studies of Social Capital: A Critical Survey', Mimeo, University of Wisconsin at Madison.

Durlauf, S.N. and M. Fafchamps (2004) 'Social Capital', *NBER Working Paper* 10485, Cambridge, MA: National Bureau of Economic Research.

Easterly, W. and R. Levine (2003) 'Tropics, Germs and Crops: How Endowments Influence Economic Development', *Journal of Monetary Economics*, 50, 1: 3–39.

Fafchamps, M. and B. Minten (2002) 'Returns to Social Network Capital Among Traders', *Oxford Economic Paper*, 54: 173–206.

Fielding, D. and S. Torres (2005) 'Cows and Conquistadors: A Comment on the Colonial Origins of Comparative Development', *Economics Discussion Paper* 0504, Dunedin: University of Otago.

Fukuyama, F. (1997) 'Social Capital', Tanner Lectures on Human Values.

Glaeser, E.L., D.I. Laibson, J.A. Scheinkman and C.L. Soutter (2000) 'Measuring Trust,' *Quarterly Journal of Economics*, 115: 811–46.

Glaeser, E.L., R. LaPorta, F. Lopez-de-Silanes and A. Shleifer (2004) 'Do Institutions Cause Growth?', *Journal of Economic Growth*, 9: 271–303.

Grafton, R.Q. and S. Knowles (2004) 'Social Capital and National Environmental Performance: A Cross-Sectional Analysis', *Journal of Environment and Development*, 13, 4: 336–70.

Grafton, R.Q., S. Knowles and P.D. Owen (2004a) 'Total Factor Productivity, Per Capita Income and Social Divergence', *Economic Record*, 80, 250: 302–13.

Grafton, R.Q., T. Kompas and D. Owen (2004b) 'Bridging the Barriers: Knowledge Connections, Productivity, and Capital Accumulation', *International and Development Economics Working Papers* IDEC04–5, Canberra: Australian National University, Asia Pacific School of Economics and Government.

Granovetter, M.S. (1973) 'The Strength of Weak Ties', *American Journal of Sociology*, 78, 6: 607–31.

Grootaert, C. (1998). 'Social Capital: The Missing Link', *Social Capital Initiative Working Paper* 3, Washington, DC: World Bank.

Grootaert, C. (1999) 'Social Capital, Household Welfare, and Poverty in Indonesia', *World Bank Policy Research Working Paper* WPS2148, Washington, DC: World Bank.

Grootaert, C., D. Narayan, V.N. Jones and M. Woolcock (2004) 'Measuring Social Capital: An Integrated Questionnaire', *World Bank Working Paper* 18, Washington, DC: World Bank.

Guinnane, T.W. (2005) 'Trust: A Concept Too Many', *Economic Growth Center Discussion Paper* 907, New Haven, CT: Yale University.

Hall, R.E. and C.I. Jones (1999) 'Why Do Some Countries Produce So Much More Output Per Worker Than Others?', *Quarterly Journal of Economics*, 114, 1: 83–116.

Hanifan, L.J. (1920) *The Community Center*, Boston: Silver Burdette & Co.

Helliwell, J.F. (1996) 'Economic Growth and Social Capital in Asia', *NBER Working Paper* 5470, Cambridge, MA: National Bureau of Economic Research.

Holm, H.J. and A. Danielson (2005) 'Tropic Trust Versus Nordic Trust: Experimental Evidence from Tanzania and Sweden', *Economic Journal*, 115, 503: 505–32.

Ingelhart, R. (1994) *Codebook for World Values Survey*, Ann Arbor: University of Michigan Press.

Ingelhart, R., M. Basáñez, J. Díez-Medrano, L. Halman and R. Luijkx (2004). *Human Beliefs and Values: a Cross-Cultural Sourcebook Based on the 1999–2002 Values Surveys*, Mexico City: Siglo Veintiuno Editores.

Isham, J., T. Kelly and S. Ramaswamy (2002) 'Social Capital and Well-Being in Developing Countries: An Introduction', in J. Isham, T. Kelly and S. Ramaswamy (eds), *Social Capital and Economic Development: Well-being in Developing Countries*, Cheltenham: Edward Elgar.

Kaufmann, D., A. Kraay and P. Zoido-Lobatón (2002) 'Governance Matters II: Updated Indicators for 2000/1', *World Bank Policy Research Department Working Paper* 2772, Washington, DC: World Bank.

Knack, S. (2002) 'Social Capital, Growth and Poverty: A Survey of Cross-Country Evidence', in C. Grootaert and T. van Bastelaer (eds), *The Role of Social Capital in Development: An Empirical Assessment*, Cambridge: Cambridge University Press.

Knack, S. and P. Keefer (1997) 'Does Social Capital Have an Economic Payoff? A Cross-Country Investigation', *Quarterly Journal of Economics*, 112, 4: 1251–88.

Knowles, S. (2005) 'The Future of Social Capital in Development Economics Research', paper presented at the WIDER jubilee conference, June, Helsinki.

La Porta, R., F. Lopez-De-Silanes, A. Shleifer and R.W. Vishny (1997) 'Trust in Large Organizations', *American Economic Review Papers and Proceedings*, 87, 2: 333–8.

Lin, N. (2001) *Social Capital*, Cambridge: Cambridge University Press.

Narayan, D. and L. Pritchett (1999) 'Cents and Sociability: Household Income and Social Capital in Rural Tanzania', *Economic Development and Cultural Change*, 47, 4: 871–97.

Nooteboom, B. (2005) 'Trust, Institutions and Development', Mimeo, Tilburg University.

North, D.C. (1990) *Institutions, Institutional Change and Economic Performance*, Cambridge and New York: Cambridge University Press.

Ogilivie, S. (2004) 'How Does Social Capital Affect Women? Guilds and Communities in Early Modern Germany', *American Historical Review*, 109, 2: 325–59.

Olsson, O. and D.A. Hibbs Jr (2005) 'Biogeography and Long-Run Economic Development', *European Economic Review*, 49: 909–38.

Ostrom, E. (1990) *Governing the Commons: The Evolution of Institutions for Collective Action*, Cambridge: Cambridge University Press.

Ostrom, E. (2000) 'Social Capital: A Fad or a Fundamental Concept', in P. Dasgupta and I. Serageldin (eds), *Social Capital: A Multifaceted Perspective*, Washington, DC: World Bank.

Owen, D. and C.R. Weatherstone (2005) 'What Really Matters for Long-Term Growth and Development? A Re-Examination of the Deep Determinants of Per Capita Income', paper presented at the New Zealand Association of Economists Conference, July, Christchurch.

Paldam, M. (2000) 'Social Capital: One or Many? Definition and Measurement', *Journal of Economic Surveys*, 14, 5: 629–53.

Paldam, M. and G.T. Svendsen (2000) 'An Essay on Social Capital: Looking for the Fire Behind the Smoke', *European Journal of Political Economy*, 16: 339–66.

Putnam, R.D. (2000) *Bowling Alone*, New York: Simon & Schuster.

Putnam, R.D., R. Leonardi and R.Y. Nanetti (1993) *Making Democracy Work: Civic Traditions in Modern Italy*, New Jersey: Princeton University Press.

Rodrik, D., A. Subramanian and F. Trebbi (2002) 'Institutions Rule: The Primacy of Institutions over Geography and Integration in Economic Development', *NBER Working Paper* 9305, Cambridge, MA: National Bureau of Economic Research.

Rogers, E.M. (1983) *Diffusion of Innovations*, New York: Free Press.

Sachs, J.D. (2003) 'Institutions Don't Rule: Direct Effects of Geography on Per Capita Income', *NBER Working Paper* 9490, Cambridge, MA: National Bureau of Economic Research.

Sobel, J. (2002) 'Can We Trust Social Capital?', *Journal of Economic Literature*, 40: 139–54.

Tabellini, G. (2005) 'Culture and Institutions: Economic Development in the Regions of Europe', *CESIFO Working Paper* 1492.

Uslaner, E.M. (2002) *The Moral Foundations of Trust*, Cambridge and New York: Cambridge University Press.

Whitely, F. (2000) 'Economic Growth and Social Capital', *Political Studies*, 48: 443–66.

Woolcock, M. (1998) 'Social Capital and Economic Development: Toward a Theoretical Framework', *Theory and Society*, 27: 151–208.

Woolcock, M. (2001) 'The Place of Social Capital in Understanding Social and Economic Outcomes', *Canadian Journal of Policy Research*, 2, 1: 11–17.

World Bank (2005) Social Capital Home Page, www1.worldbank.org/ prem/poverty/scapital/ index.htm, accessed 2 May 2005.

Zak, J. and S. Knack (2001) 'Trust and Growth', *Economic Journal*, 111, 470: 295–321.

Part IV
Globalization

13
Stormy Days on an Open Field: Asymmetries in the Global Economy

Nancy Birdsall

Introduction

Openness is not necessarily good for the poor. Reducing trade protection has not brought growth to today's poorest countries, including many in Africa, and open capital markets have not been particularly good for the poorest households within many developing countries, including many of the emerging market economies of Asia and Latin America. Too often, the word 'openness' has been used to embrace the entire scope of policies and outcomes that characterize a healthy economy. But this makes 'openness' unachievable from a policy point of view. Here, I use the word to refer narrowly to an open trade policy stance, the opposite of protectionism. Defined this way, 'openness' does not in itself guarantee growth, and in some circumstances it makes poverty reduction more difficult.

Many students of globalization have remarked that certain countries and groups have been 'marginal' to the process.[1] It is less often remarked that many have remained marginal despite being, by some measures, 'open'. That this is so is of course perfectly consistent with the evidence that trade is good for growth and growth is good for the poor, since what is true on average need not be true for every country.[2] But it does put a different spin on that evidence, one that raises concerns about the way the global economy is working that market fundamentalists have tended to overlook. The point I want to illustrate is that globalization, as we know it today, is fundamentally asymmetric. In its benefits and its risks, it works less well for the currently poor countries and for poor households within developing countries. Domestic markets also tend to be asymmetric, but modern capitalist economies have social contracts, progressive tax systems and laws and regulations to manage asymmetries and market failures. At the global level, there is no real equivalent to national governments to manage global markets, though they are bigger and deeper, and if anything more asymmetric. They work better for the rich; and their risks and failures hurt the poor more.

In fact, we think of globally integrated markets as generally open and competitive, providing the paradigmatic level playing field. In the series of contests on this level playing field, there is plenty of room for disagreement and wrangling among teams (countries) about the rules and their interpretation and implementation. But the team owners constitute themselves members of a league (as in the World Trade Organization, the Bank of International Settlements and so on) and in the interests of the game they get together often to agree on the rules, adjust them to changing times and manage their application. The problem is that a level playing field and good rules are not sufficient to ensure competitive games. If some teams have better equipment, more training and a long and successful history with money in the bank to sustain the investments that help them retain their advantages, then they are likely to win the league year after year. In soccer the big, powerful and wealthy teams tend to stay year after year in the premier division, and the teams in the third or lower divisions rarely move up. In US baseball the richer, big city teams, such as the New York Yankees, tend to dominate year after year. In sports leagues, however, a lack of competition cannot persist for long. If the spectators lose interest the team owners lose money, so the team owners collaborate to implement rules that minimize the problem – such as the order of draft picks or caps on teams' spending on salaries. Of course 'competition' between countries is not like soccer; it is not a zero-sum game. But for the global economy as a whole, we might think of the global system (of institutions, rules, customs) as playing a role closer to that of the league owners – to collectively maximize overall gains while agreeing on the long-run sharing of the gains. But here the analogy to the global market system breaks down because national governments face much greater obstacles to the kind of co-ordination and collaboration that team owners can manage.

In addition, a level playing field is insufficient to ensure competitive games if the rules of the game have been designed to favour one type of team over the other, or if the referee in implementing sensible rules favours one side over another.[3] The protection of agriculture and textiles by rich countries is a good example of an existing set of rules that favours one type of team over another. Sometimes it is the interpretation or implementation of WTO rules that favours one side. The interpretation of TRIPs (the trade-related intellectual property regime agreed at the Uruguay Round) as limiting the use of compulsory licensing in developing countries, even in public health emergencies, for a while reflected backdoor pressure of the United States on the referees. After a contentious negotiation, the interpretation and rules have been made somewhat less unfriendly to poor countries coping with AIDS and other public health problems, but the TRIPs arrangement still reflects much more the interests of rich-country producers of innovations relative to poor-country consumers. Then there is the case of anti-dumping. A few of the bigger teams have players who are prepared to interrupt the game (crying injury!) when they are beginning to lose their advantage. Smaller teams are learning the trick too, but will never have the same resources to make their interruptions stick.[4] In this note, however, I do not focus on the unfair rules and their imperfect interpretation and implementation (though that subject merits considerable discussion in itself).[5] Instead I concentrate on two more subtle shortcomings of open global markets for the poor. I state them here, continuing with the sports league metaphor, and in two subsequent sections discuss and document them.

First, openness in open global markets does not necessarily lead countries to grow (and growth is necessary if not always sufficient for reducing poverty). Like sports teams, countries without the right equipment are in trouble from the start – even on a perfectly level playing field with fair rules fairly implemented. Countries highly dependent on primary commodity exports two decades ago provide a convincing example. Their particular training and equipment, in retrospect, seems to have condemned them to the lowest division in the globalization league.

Second, for weaker teams with the wrong equipment and inadequate training, openness may actually be dangerous. For them, bumps in the level playing field (market failures/negative externalities) are hard to handle. The example in this case is that of emerging market economies that entered this latest globalization era with high debt. For them, a stormy day or a rough soccer field can easily provoke a ruined pass or a twisted ankle. Among their players, those with less training and experience, like the poor in growing but volatile emerging markets, are vulnerable to injuries that can handicap them permanently.

Openness does not necessarily lead to growth

Consider the situation of many of the world's poorest countries, including most of the poor countries of sub-Saharan Africa. Many are highly dependent on primary commodity and natural-resource exports. In Birdsall and Hamoudi (2002), we define a group of countries in terms of the composition of their exports in the early 1980s, when the terms of trade for commodity exporters were in the early stages of a subsequent long decline. Using data on exports for 115 developing and 22 developed countries for each year between 1980 and 1984, we classified all exports (except those in SITC 9 'unspecified' products) as primary commodities or manufactures. For each country in each year we then calculated the share of primary commodities in total (specified) exports. Developing countries that fell into the top third of primary commodity exporters for at least four of the five years we labelled as 'most commodity dependent' (34 countries), and those that fell into that category for zero or one year we labelled as 'least commodity dependent' (72 countries). All the developing countries were, in fact, highly commodity dependent, with the average share of primary commodities in total exports for the least and most commodity-dependent groups at 62 and 98 per cent respectively. More to the point of this chapter, the most commodity-dependent countries (defined as of the early 1980s) have not been any more reticent than the least commodity-dependent countries about participating in international trade. They:

- generally traded as much as countries in the category of 'least commodity dependent' between 1960 and 1980, if the level of trade is measured in terms of the ratio of exports plus imports to GDP (Figure 13.1a);[6]
- continued to participate in global markets in the period 1980–2003 by this definition, and have had a higher export/GDP ratio than the 'least commodity dependent' countries for the entire period 1960–2003 (Figure 13.1b);

- have been nearly as open from a policy point of view as the 'least commodity-dependent' group.[7] For example, their tariff rates have been comparable to the rates of the least commodity-dependent group. For countries in the two groups for which we have data on tariff rates, the most commodity-dependent group cut their tariffs from an average of 25 per cent in the late 1980s to 18 per cent in the late 1990s; the least commodity-dependent countries cut their tariffs from almost 26 per cent to 15 per cent, so they have had only slightly lower rates (see Table 13.1).[8,9]

But despite their substantial engagement in trade and the decline in their tariff rates, the most commodity-dependent countries have failed to grow, especially after 1980. They grew at lower rates than the least commodity-dependent group in the 1970s and 1980s, and have not grown at all since 1980 (Table 13.2).

What happened? The countries that were most commodity dependent in the early 1980s entered that decade as relatively successful exporters of goods whose relative prices had been steady in the 1960s increased rapidly during the 1970s and then declined dramatically in the 1980s. In the 1980s, when the prices of their principal exports began to decline, their export revenue and capacity to import fell. Despite the large decline in their terms of trade, almost 30 per cent in the most

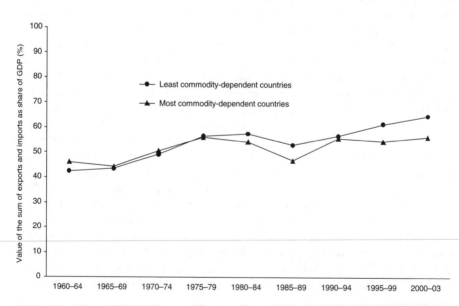

Figure 13.1a The 'most commodity-dependent' countries have participated in global trade since the 1960s: trade to GDP ratios

Notes: Indicates the simple unweighted average ratio of the value of the sum of exports and imports to GDP for the most commodity-dependent and least commodity-dependent countries between 1960 and 2003. The most commodity-dependent and least commodity-dependent countries are as defined in table 2 of Birdsall and Hamoudi (2002). There are 72 least commodity-dependent countries and 34 most commodity-dependent countries.

Source: *World Development Indicators* (2005).

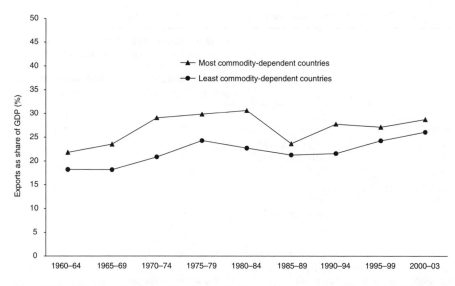

Figure 13.1b The 'most commodity-dependent' countries have participated in global trade since the 1960s: exports to GDP ratios

Notes: Indicates the simple unweighted average ratio of the value of exports to GDP for the most commodity-dependent and least commodity-dependent countries between 1960 and 2003. The most commodity-dependent and least commodity-dependent countries are as defined in table 2 of Birdsall and Hamoudi (2002). There are 72 least commodity-dependent countries and 34 most commodity-dependent countries.

Source: *World Development Indicators* (2005).

Table 13.1 The 'most commodity-dependent' countries have not eschewed global trade

		Average tariff rates (unweighted, %)	
		Least commodity-dependent countries	Most commodity-dependent countries
1986–89	mean	26	25
	median	19	27
	standard deviation (across countries)	19	12
	N	50	26
1996–99	mean	15	18
	median	14	15
	standard deviation (across countries)	7	9
	N	50	26

Source: World Bank (2006).

Table 13.2 The 'most commodity-dependent' countries have not grown

		Average annual rate of growth of real PPP adjusted GDP per capita (%)	
		Least commodity-dependent countries	Most commodity-dependent countries
Growth during the 1980s	mean	1.1	−0.09
	median	0.5	−1.3
	25th percentile	−0.7	−2.4
	75th percentile	3.0	0.4
	N	65	32
Growth during the 1990s	mean	1.5	0.0
	median	1.7	0.4
	25th percentile	0.0	−1.6
	75th percentile	3.2	1.6
	N	68	28

Notes: All statistics are unweighted. The classification of countries is as shown in table 2 of Birdsall and Hamoudi (2002). Average annual rates of growth of real PPP adjusted GDP per capita during the 1980s and during the 1990s are taken from the dataset underlying Dollar and Kraay (2001), which the authors were generous to share. The samples do not include all 34 most commodity-dependent and 72 least commodity-dependent countries because some countries had to be dropped due to the lack of income data. These data on growth rates are far from perfect, though the overall differences between the two groups are sufficient to buttress the point. The low growth rates reflect the arithmetic influence of many slow-growing (but small) countries, and so are lower than population-weighted averages would be.

Source: Birdsall and Hamoudi (2002).

commodity-dependent countries from 1980–90 to 1991–2002 and nearly 8 per cent for the least commodity-dependent countries (Figure 13.2), they for the most part failed to diversify their exports. The problem may have been that producers and investors believed that relative prices would recover. One result is that imports as a proportion of GDP (which was itself not growing, see Table 13.2) never rose (Figure 13.3).

For countries highly dependent on commodities for export income the problem of declining terms of trade persisted in the 1990s. For example, declines in cotton prices (and increases in oil prices) hurt Mali (Figure 13.4), and in Ethiopia an increasing volume of coffee exports failed to compensate for declining prices (Figure 13.5). Diversification of exports is obviously key for these countries, but their infrastructure, governance, human capital and overall institutional setting are not propitious for diversification.[10] Whatever the reason, the fact remains that these countries have been 'open' for more than two decades – in the sense that they have been clearly engaged in global markets, and have reduced their own tariff rates. But with the value of their exports stagnating over the past two decades, their capacity to increase imports has been constrained. As a result, the amount of trade that occurs between these countries and the rest of the world has failed to increase relative to their GDP.

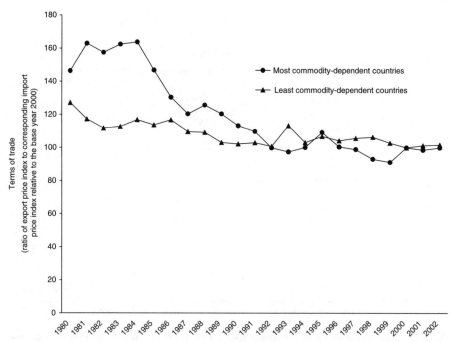

Figure 13.2 The terms of trade of commodity-producing countries have declined since the early 1980s

Source: *World Development Indicators* (2005).

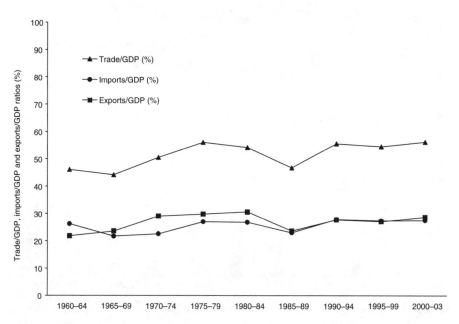

Figure 13.3 Trade ratios in the most commodity-dependent countries

Note: Unweighted average ratios.

Source: *World Development Indicators* (2005).

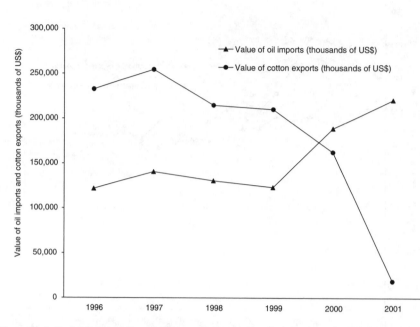

Figure 13.4 In Mali, the value of cotton exports declined while the value of oil imports rose
Source: UNSD COMTRADE Database 2005.

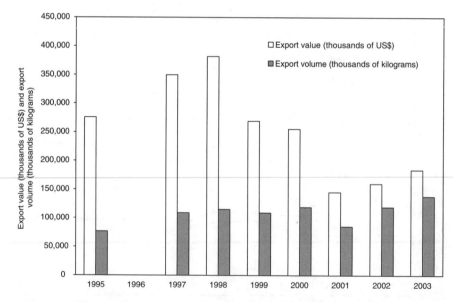

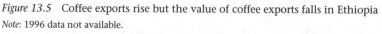

Figure 13.5 Coffee exports rise but the value of coffee exports falls in Ethiopia
Note: 1996 data not available.
Source: UNSD COMTRADE Database 2005.

In short, their initial and continuing relatively high degree of openness has not bought them subsequent healthy rates of growth. Their lack of growth is apparently due to factors that have little to do with whether they are open, and much to do with other factors associated with their continuing dependence on commodity exports.[11] In addition to the direct fiscal and import constraints, it seems likely that they are trapped in some sort of bad equilibrium, in which commodity dependence is associated with institutional failures that have made escape from commodity dependence difficult.[12] In settings where initial political and economic institutions are relatively weak, production based on natural resources appears to encourage predatory government behaviour and rent-seeking and to discourage development of the predictable, stable, democratic institutions that are conducive to growth. It also provides poor incentives for human capital investment, and discourages learning by doing, knowledge spillovers and increasing use of technology, at least compared to production of manufactured goods.[13] Of course there are other possible traps besides heavy dependence on commodity exports in the early 1980s (though they may well be highly correlated with and reinforced by such dependence).[14] Frankel and Romer (1999) present evidence of the effect of what might be called trade-enhancing geography (or conversely trade-reducing geography) on growth, including the effects of country size (small size is bad for growth) and landlocked status (bad). The impact of trade-enhancing geography on growth is large and positive, perhaps because good geography enhances not only trade itself but also other 'income-enhancing interactions' such as the spread of ideas.

To return to the sports metaphor, success in global markets depends on arriving at the game with the right equipment and training. Most of the countries with a comparative advantage in primary goods in the early 1980s (unless they already had developed good institutions) have not done well – no matter how open they have been – on the level playing field.[15] At least for the last two decades, their resources have turned out to provide the wrong equipment for the globalization game.[16] This does not imply that these countries would have been better off with more protectionism – only that lack of policy openness is not necessarily the key constraint to their future growth.[17]

Openness can be dangerous for the poor

Developing countries have had lower overall growth and higher volatility of growth rates compared to advanced economies in every decade including and since the 1960s.[18] There seems little questions that the deeper financial integration, greater trade diversification and more effective macroeconomic management in the latter group all contribute to lower volatility. For example, a deep domestic financial sector though not causally linked to growth (Prasad *et al.* 2004), is associated with reduced growth volatility (Frankel and Cavallo 2004). But that is the case mainly for developed economies; indicators of financial depth such as the ratio of credit to the private sector to GDP are much lower in developing countries (25 per cent in the Easterly *et al.* 2000 sample, compared to 64 per cent). Indeed volatility can be thought of in general as a natural outcome of the less effective institutions that distinguish developing countries from their more advanced and richer counterparts. Similarly with trade integration, there is some evidence that though greater trade integration reduces volatility on average across all countries that is not true or at least is less the case for developing economies (*Ibid.*).[19]

The key point I want to emphasize, however, is that open markets, especially open capital markets, can be associated with greater volatility, and the resulting volatility is bad for the poor *within* countries. That open markets may increase volatility is almost certainly due to the interaction of openness with the institutional and policy shortcomings referred to above. Thus, though openness is dangerous for the poor within countries, the solution is not necessarily to reduce openness itself but to address the other shortcomings which, interacting with openness, attenuate or even reverse its benefits for the poor.

Volatility and the poor

Figure 13.6 uses data from Dollar and Kraay (2001) to plot the annual growth rate of the poor on the average annual overall per capita growth rate for a sample of developing countries during various growth spells. It suggests that growth is indeed shared proportionately by the poor. Figure 13.7 shows the results of using the same data to regress the income growth of the bottom quintile on overall

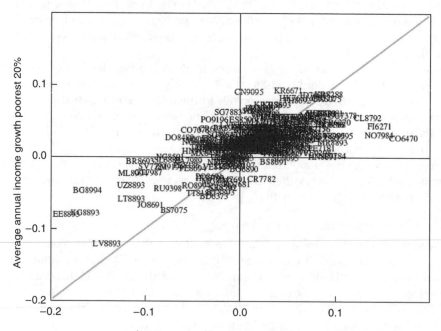

Figure 13.6   On average, economic growth is probably being distributed proportionately across income groups

Note: Data on average annual income growth of the total population and average annual income growth of the poorest quintile. The 45-degree line is drawn for reference.

Source: Reproduced using date from Dollar and Kraay (2001).

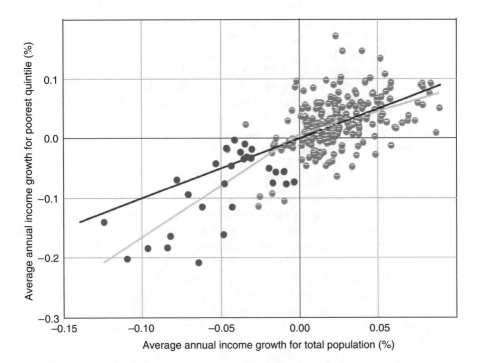

Figure 13.7   But *contractions* may take disproportionately from the poor

Notes: Graphical representation of the results of a regression of income growth in the total population against income growth in the poorest quintile, with an interaction term to allow for differential effects of contractions as opposed to expansions. The regression includes 258 observations, and produces an R-squared of 0.54; the coefficient on average income growth is 0.78 (s.e. 0.12), plus an additional 0.94 (s.e. 0.24) in times of contraction. The intercept term is nearly at the origin (0.006, s.e. 0.004). The standard errors given use the Huber/White/Sandwich estimator of the variance in order to be robust to heteroskedasticity, but are not corrected for possible serial correlation. The coefficient on income in times of contraction is significantly greater than one, implying that there may be a systematic correlation between contractions in average income and declines in the income share of the poorest quintile. The 45-degree line is drawn (solid black line) for reference.

Source: Birdsall and Hamoudi (2002).

growth, but adding an interaction term to distinguish the effect of contractions on the poor from the effect of expansions. The slope of the best-fit line in the southwest quadrant is about 1.6; in the northeast quadrant, it is about 0.8. Though expansions are good for the poor, contractions are more than proportionately bad for them.[20] This suggests an important qualification to Dollar and Kraay's findings about the *general* relationship between average growth and the share of the poor.[21] Of course, we must be mindful of the fact that the countries and time periods in the southwest quadrant are different from the countries and time periods in the northeast quadrant,[22] and it may be that contractions and expansions in different places have very different effects on the poor. The observations in the southwest quadrant include negative growth spells in transition economies of Eastern Europe and the former Soviet Union, but also spells in Mali, Peru, Brazil, Guatemala, Zambia, Jordan, Mexico, Honduras, Nigeria and others.

Consistent with the possibility that openness, because it increases the likelihood of volatility, may indirectly hurt the poor within developing countries, Lundberg and Squire (2003), using country data on changes in income for different quintiles of the income distribution, report that the negative consequences of terms of trade changes are 'far greater' for the poorest 40 per cent than for the middle 60 per cent and wealthiest 40 per cent of households (overlapping groups), with that vulnerability exacerbated by a country's openness.[23,24]

Volatility, capital markets and the poor

The global financial crises of the 1990s were only the most recent in a long history of financial bubbles that have burst. Financial crises are not special to poor and emerging markets; but the crises of the last decade suggest that whether induced by domestic policy problems or global contagion (or the combustible mix of both), the same crisis can be more costly for relatively poorer countries, if only because their local financial markets are thinner and less resilient and local and foreign creditors more skittish than in deeper markets.[25] Indeed, one of the ironies of globalization may be that emerging market economies, if they are to exploit the benefits of a global market, simply cannot afford the policy errors and institutional weaknesses that are characteristic of being 'emerging'.

Despite those risks, the trend among developing countries over the past three decades has been towards greater capital market openness; the number of developing countries declaring their currencies convertible on capital account transactions increased from 34 (30 per cent of IMF member countries) to 143 (77 per cent) between 1970 and 1997.[26] It makes sense for countries that are capital-scarce to open their capital accounts, and in principle an open capital account could make it easier for a country to manage shocks. On the other hand, an open capital account in good times invites inflow surges creating pressure on exchange rates that can hurt exports and/or if sterilized, keep interest rates high. In bad times there is the risk of panicked outflows over which authorities have little control – for example because of a liquidity crisis provoked elsewhere in the global market.[27] In some emerging market economies, resulting crises have led to an accumulation of debt, higher interest rates (reducing investment and growth), and the risk of future self-fulfilling losses of confidence.[28] The problem for the poor is compounded because to restore confidence, emerging markets are forced to abstain from otherwise sensible countercyclical fiscal and monetary policy – and therefore have difficulty sustaining a social safety net to protect the poor during downturns.[29]

We cannot conclude that openness is a principal cause of volatility, and certainly not that closing trade markets and the capital account would in themselves reduce volatility or increase growth. Indeed, growth in the developing world could well have been even lower than it has been with less open trade and capital markets (though China and India have remained relatively closed they are large enough economies to have large internal markets). But neither can we deny that with greater average dependence on exports whose prices are volatile and on domestic financial sectors that are smaller and less resilient, openness poses greater risks than it does for the richer economies, and is particularly risky for the poor within developing countries, increasing the risks of negative growth spells and compounding the difficulty of managing a countercyclical social safety net.[30]

Open capital markets and inequality

An additional problem is that open capital markets may not only slow poverty reduction, but contribute to an increase in the concentration of income within developing countries, i.e. increasing the income gap between the rich and other households. To the extent that open capital markets contribute to income concentration, they may indirectly reduce growth. That is because in developing countries inequality of income combined with weak capital markets appears to reduce growth, and may contribute to social and ethnic tensions that make good management of the economy politically difficult.[31]

Why would open capital markets be associated with income inequality? Theory, after all, predicts the opposite – that better access to capital would reduce the domestic return to capital relative to the return to labour. One explanation may be that capital and skilled labour are complementary, so that increased access to capital raises the returns to highly skilled labour and increases the wage gap between the skilled and unskilled. Behrman *et al.* (2003) report dramatic increases in the return to higher (post-secondary) education in most countries of Latin America, especially compared to secondary education. They test the effects of various liberalizing economic reforms on the wage differential between the skilled and unskilled, using household survey data combined with country- and year-specific indices of policy, across 28 countries of Latin America over several decades.[32] Their results indicate that capital account liberalization (and domestic financial market liberalization) are associated with an increase in the wage differential which is substantial for several years and then diminishes.[33] This market-led effect is not small, but in principle it should increase the demand for higher education as an equilibrating mechanism, and indeed that may be happening in Latin America and worldwide.[34]

More disturbing is the evidence of more patently non-market and 'unfair' disadvantages for lower income groups associated with open capital markets. In Turkey, Argentina and Mexico, with repeated bouts of inflation and currency devaluations in the last two decades, the ability of those with more financial assets to move those assets abroad, often simultaneously acquiring bank and corporate debt that is then socialized and paid by taxpayers, has almost certainly increased inequality.[35] In South East Asia, inequality of income increased (in Thailand and Malaysia and probably in Indonesia) during the boom years of high capital inflows in the mid-1990s; as portfolio inflows and high bank lending fuelled demand for assets such as land and stocks, inequality of wealth no doubt increased even more, though data on the distribution of wealth are not reliable (due mostly to underreporting) and many of those who accumulated wealth no doubt lost much of it when the crisis hit. Still, some evidence suggests that the lower-middle and working classes in those countries were hit hardest by the crisis, especially in terms of lost employment,[36] and to the extent the poor also lost out, their losses in welfare terms would be particularly great. In addition, there is the likelihood that the high interest rates to which the affected countries resorted to stabilize their currencies – both in East Asia and then in 1998–99 in Brazil – also had a redistributive effect, hurting most capital-starved enterprises and their low-wage employees.

Table 13.3 shows changes in the income shares of the richest 20 per cent of households and the 'other' 80 per cent, pre- and post-crisis, for selected countries. Given the fragility of the income data, the consistency of the changes is noteworthy. The richest 20 per cent may well lose in absolute terms during crises but they lose relatively less than the rest. The Gini coefficient, similarly, rose after financial crises in Korea, the Philippines, Thailand, Brazil and Mexico (Table 13.4). (Of course these before and after comparisons cannot establish causation.) Opening of the capital account is usually one aspect of liberalization of the domestic financial sector, which is also associated with reduction of the income share of the non-rich (Figure 13.8).

In addition, the bank bailouts that generally follow financial crises tend to create substantially more public debt relative to GDP in developing than in

Table 13.3   Financial crises and changes in income shares

	Pre-crisis		Post-crisis	
	Income share *poorest 80%* of population (%)	Income share *richest 20%* of population (%)	Income share *poorest 80%* of population (%)	Income share *richest 20%* of population (%)
Korea	61.2	38.8	58.3	41.7
Philippines	48.0	51.9	45.3	54.8
Thailand	39.2	60.8	38.2	61.8
Brazil	35.1	64.8	34.4	65.6
Mexico	42.0	58.0	41.5	58.5
	Income share *poorest 40%* of population (%)	Income share *richest 20%* of population (%)	Income share *poorest 40%* of population (%)	Income share *richest 20%* of population (%)
Korea	19.3	38.8	15.9	41.7
Philippines	13.7	51.9	12.3	54.8
Thailand	8.2	60.8	7.8	61.8
Brazil	8.2	64.8	8.0	65.6
Mexico	11.2	58.0	10.7	58.5

Note: East Asian financial crisis 1997–98, Brazil crisis 1999 and Mexico crisis 1994–95. Pre-crisis data for Thailand, Korea and Brazil are from 1996, for the Philippines from 1994 and Mexico 1992. Post-crisis data are from 1996 for Mexico, 1998 for Korea, 1999 for Thailand, 2000 for the Philippines and 2001 for Brazil.
Source: WIDER WIID 2.0a (www.wider.unu.edu).

Table 13.4 Financial crises and inequality

	Pre-crisis	Post-crisis
	Gini	Gini
Korea	32.6	37.2
Philippines	46.2	49.5
Thailand	57.5	58.5
Brazil	60.2	61.2
Mexico	52.9	53.7

Note: East Asian financial crisis 1997–98, Brazil crisis 1999 and Mexico crisis 1994–95. Pre-crisis data for Thailand, Korea and Brazil are from 1996, for the Philippines from 1994 and Mexico 1992. Post-crisis data are from 1996 for Mexico, 1998 for Korea, 1999 for Thailand, 2000 for the Philippines and 2001 for Brazil.

Source: WIDER WIID 2.0a (www.wider.unu.edu).

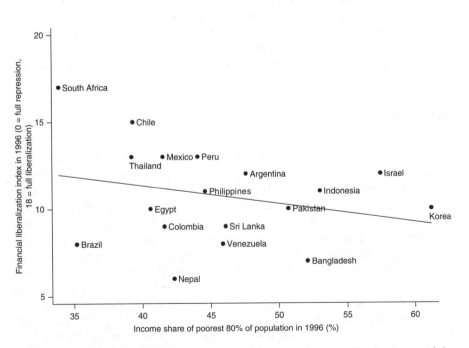

Figure 13.8 Financial liberalization and the income share of 'non-rich' 80 per cent of the population in 1996

Sources: Abiad and Mody (2003) and WIDER WIID 2.0a (www.wider.unu.edu).

developed countries. Indonesia's 1998–99 financial crisis cost it an astonishing 45 per cent of GDP.[37] The cost of crises in developing countries is usually over 10 per cent of GDP compared to below 5 per cent in the OECD. The USA savings and loan crisis of the early 1990s cost an estimated 2–3 per cent of GDP (Norton 1997). The resulting high public debt in developing countries helps sustain high-income inequality, since public debt generally implies a transfer from taxpayers to rentiers.[38] Even when depositors are protected, the distributive effect is probably perverse, as long as depositors are on average from higher-income households than taxpayers. That seems a good possibility in many developing countries, since they tend to rely heavily on indirect trade taxes and the value-added tax, which are not progressive.[39] There is also the point that the poor benefit more from higher public expenditures, and the medium-term effect of the public financing of bailouts is to reduce public expenditures from whatever they might have been.[40]

Consistent with the story above, Diwan (2001) finds, using a panel of country data that the share of labour in GDP usually falls sharply following a financial crisis, and recovers only partially in subsequent years. He suggests that the declining labour share reflects not only the relatively automatic asymmetry in the effects of crises to which I have referred, but also a 'change in the distribution rules' with crises. If the state feels compelled to bail out the banking sector (to avoid a run on deposits and a collapse in output), it is likely to be labour that in the short run finances the bailout through reduced employment and real wage cuts.[41] With capital able to shield itself more easily from the costs of adjustment, labour takes the brunt of the adjustment. His results are also consistent with the apparent disproportionate effect of contractions on the income of the poor shown above, assuming there is a correlation between effects on the labour share and effects on the poor.

Implications

That openness is not necessarily good for the poor does not imply that it is necessarily bad for the poor. Only that it all depends. It depends on the resolution of two existing asymmetries in the way the global economy operates. (In addition to these two asymmetries there is the problem that the powerful make and implement the rules, as the limited access of developing countries to certain rich-country markets suggests. That problem, though politically difficult to fix, is conceptually straightforward, and even avid globaphiles agree that change is needed.)

First, some teams are trying to play without the right equipment. On a level playing field, participation in the game by ill-equipped teams does not provide an equal opportunity to win. Open markets (a level playing field) naturally reward most those who are well equipped and trained – in economic terms those who already have the most productive assets. At the individual level, those with land, financial assets and human capital naturally have a leg up. The analogue of these individual assets at the country level seems to be effective and stable political and social institutions, particularly deep financial markets – a characteristic still confined almost completely to the OECD economies. Countries that are already ahead, with deep financial markets, stable political systems, secure property rights, adequate banking supervision, reasonable public services and so on, have a much higher probability of staying ahead. They are able not only to adjust and diversify their economies in the face of changing global opportunities, but to attract more local and foreign investment, better exploiting their own people's entrepreneurial energy and skills. Though it is true that, all other things the same, capital will flow to places where it is most scarce because those are the places where its return will be highest, and that therefore convergence in income across countries ought to happen, it is also true that all other things are not the same. Because they are not the same, as much as 80 per cent of all foreign investment occurs among the industrialized countries, and just 0.1 per cent of all USA foreign investment went to sub-Saharan Africa in 2001.[42]

Second, the global market is far from perfect. Its market failures create risks for all countries, but the risks are asymmetric – greater for the more vulnerable developing countries. The evidence is clear in their greater growth volatility, the higher cost to them of financial crises and the special risk that their government and institutional failures will combine with weak markets to exacerbate and perpetuate high inequality.

These two asymmetries help explain the lack of convergence between the income and welfare of rich and poor countries in the last 50 years and, within many countries, between rich and poor individuals.[43] The status quo of the global economy does not produce the equal economic opportunities for all that would justify the mainstream view that the current global regime will more or less automatically bring growth and poverty reduction to everyone – if only all countries would get 'globalized'. Like domestic economies, the global economy needs the civilizing hand of appropriate intervention if we are to see a reduction in global poverty and increased income convergence across countries. What that appropriate intervention would be is too large and complex a topic to tackle here. But it would surely include more transfers from rich to poor countries than the current 0.3 per cent of the formers' combined GDPs (compared to transfers from rich to poor in the USA more than ten times as great), and more active management of such global problems as money laundering, tax evasion, sovereign bankruptcy and capital flight, not to speak of global health and environmental issues. Because the market works and rewards more highly the more able and productive, the global economy would be enriched in the long run by a global social contract that financed equal opportunity investments in the initially weak and disadvantaged.[44] And because the global market is ridden with the usual market failures, we need global arrangements that, via some mechanisms equivalent to the usual taxes, subsidies and regulatory arrangements we have in modern capitalist economies, reduce the difference between individual country returns and the social return to the global economy and all its players.

Thus, the discussion of whether globalization and openness are good or bad for the poor should move on to a discussion of the appropriate global social contract and appropriate global arrangements for minimizing the asymmetric risks and costs of global market failures.

Appendix

Table 13.A1   Definitions of country groups

	Least commodity dependent (1980–84)	Most commodity dependent (1980–84)	Neither most nor least commodity dependent
Non-globalizers	Benin; Burkina Faso; Egypt; El Salvador; Fiji; Guatemala; Honduras; Indonesia; Israel; Kenya; Madagascar; Mauritius; Morocco; Pakistan; Peru; Senegal; South Africa; Sri Lanka; Syria; Togo; Trinidad and Tobago; Tunisia	Algeria; Burundi; Cameroon; Central African Republic; Rep. Congo; DR Congo; Ecuador; Gambia; Ghana; Iran; Mauritania; Myanmar; Nigeria; Papua New Guinea; Sierra Leone; Venezuela; Zambia	Chad; Gabon; Guinea-Bissau; Malawi; Niger
Globalizers	Argentina; Bangladesh; Brazil; China; Colombia; Costa Rica; Côte d'Ivoire; Dominican Rep.; Haiti; Hungary; India; Jamaica; Jordan; Malaysia; Mexico; Nepal; Nicaragua; Philippines; Thailand; Uruguay; Zimbabwe	Mali; Rwanda	Paraguay
Not included in Dollar and Kraay	Afghanistan; Albania; Barbados; Belize; Bhutan; Bulgaria; Cambodia; Comoros; Cyprus; Djibouti; Guyana; Hong Kong; Kiribati; South Korea; Kuwait; Laos; Lebanon; Maldives; Malta; Mongolia; Mozambique; New Caledonia; Panama; Poland; Romania; Seychelles; St. Kitts and Nevis; Tanzania; Vietnam	Angola; Bahamas; Bolivia; Ethiopia; Guinea; Liberia; Libya; Oman; Saudi Arabia; Solomon Islands; Somalia; Sudan; Suriname; Uganda; United Arab Emirates	Bahrain; Equatorial Guinea; Yemen
Total	72 countries (of which 43 are included in Dollar and Kraay)	34 countries (of which 19 are included in Dollar and Kraay)	9 countries (of which 6 are included in Dollar and Kraay)

Source: Reproduction of table 2 from Birdsall and Hamoudi (2002).

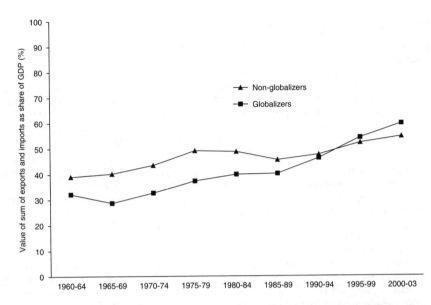

Figure 13.A1   Non-globalizers have participated in global trade as much as globalizers

Notes: There are 24 globalizers and 44 non-globalizers. Trade GDP ratios are unweighted averages. See Note 6.

Source: *World Development Indicators* (2005).

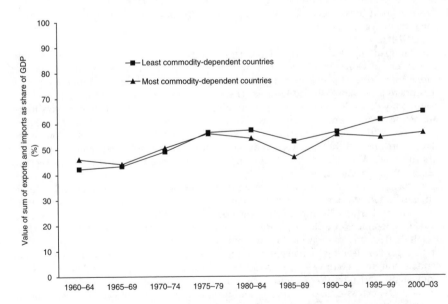

Figure 13.A2   Similarly, the most commodity-dependent group of countries has participated in global trade as much as the least commodity-dependent group

Note: There are 72 least commodity-dependent countries and 34 most commodity-dependent countries. Trade to GDP ratios are unweighted averages.

Source: *World Development Indicators* (2005).

Notes

This chapter is an update of a paper originally presented at the 2002 G-20 Workshop on Globalization, Living Standards and Inequality in Sydney, Australia. I am grateful for the comments of participants in that workshop, especially Edward Gramlich, and to Michael Clemens, William Cline, Benoit Coeure, David Dollar, William Easterly, Carol Graham, Jenny Lanjouw, Guy Pfeffermann and John Williamson. I am particularly grateful to Amar Hamoudi who co-authored the commodities paper on which much of one part of this chapter is based, and to Gunilla Pettersson who was particularly imaginative in suggesting good use of available data on the relationship between volatility and changes in the poor's income.

1. A stronger statement is that the poor have been 'marginalized'. That word suggests or at least allows for some effort by some party to push the poor to the margin. My point in this chapter is that the poor often end up at the margin for reasons reflecting larger structural forces, not explicit efforts of the non-poor to marginalize them.
2. On growth is good for the poor, the recent study of Dollar and Kraay (2001) has been widely cited. Ravallion (2001) shows that what is true on average is not true for every country or time period.
3. Referring to unfair interpretation of trade rules, then-President Jorge Quiroga of Bolivia said in a 2002 speech at the Center for Global Development: 'We were out of shape, high deficits, ... high tariffs ... We got in shape. ... we start practicing ... So we come in and score a goal with our foot and they say "No, no, you can't do that, you can only score with your head." And we're not very tall to begin with, so it's kind of tough ... Then we score a goal from 18 yards away and they say, "No, no, you can only score from 35 yards away"... huge agricultural subsidies that keep you out ... And if you have a good mid-fielder, oops, red card, anti-dumping, he's selling too much, take him out.'
4. At some point the owners may have to tighten up the injury rule if they want to preserve the integrity of the game.
5. See UNDP (2005).
6. Our group of most commodity-dependent countries overlaps closely with the 'non-globalizers' in Dollar and Kraay's now well-known classification, as shown in Appendix Table 13.A1 (see Dollar and Kraay 2001). The only 'globalizers' in our commodity-dependent group are Mali and Rwanda. Their 'non-globalizers' were in fact, like our set of commodity-dependent countries, 'open' in the early 1980s. However, their 'non-globalizers' are defined not in terms of countries' levels of openness but in terms of their change in openness in the subsequent two decades. Non-globalizers are those where 'openness' did not increase in the last two decades (in comparison to globalizers where 'openness' did increase). Appendix Figures 13.A1 and 13.A2 compare the initial levels and trends using the two classifications.
7. It is worth making a distinction between trade policies and what could be called 'trade infrastructure'. Winters (2001) notes that low tariff rates are misleading if they are unevenly and artificially applied as in Uganda in the 1980s, when there was dire conflict and considerable corruption by border and customs officials. But these kinds of barriers usually reflect not 'trade policy' or any policy intent, but poor governance and a weak state in general, leading to inadequate 'trade infrastructure', best thought of as a result of (endogenous to) a country's poverty and lack of growth. See Rodriguez and Rodrik (1999).
8. Equivalent tariff rates do not imply equivalent protection, as Clemens and Williamson (2004) note, across time or countries, and need not generate equivalent growth effects. Countries that export mostly commodities and import mostly manufactures face a higher cost of capital and lower effective investment rates, which will affect growth (Hsieh and Klenow 2002; Jones 1994).
9. The standard deviations in Table 13.1 suggest there is no marked difference between the two groups in the variances of their rates. The more commodity-dependent countries do not protect their industrial products more; their protection of these products in the late 1990s

was only slightly higher in the most commodity-dependent group. Average industrial and agricultural tariffs by country available from the World Bank, http://web. worldbank.org/WBSITE/EXTERNAL/TOPICS/TRADE/0,,contentMDK:20103740~menuP K:167374~pagePK:148956~piPK:216618~theSitePK:239071,00.html

10. Rodrik (1999) shows the relevance of institutions to growth – in contrast to any simple relation between trade policy and growth – and discusses the implications for the global governance of trade (Rodrik 2001).

11. Most of these countries in the late 1990s still had more than 80 per cent of their exports being commodities (WTO Trade Database, see http://stat.wto.org/StatisticalProgram/ WSDBStatProgramHome.aspx?Language=E).

12. Highly commodity-dependent countries' difficulty in increasing their trade share may itself be bad for their governance. Krueger (1990) suggested that openness is likely to reduce rent-seeking; Ades and di Tella (1999) show that a higher ratio of imports to GDP is associated with less corruption, and that a high proportion of fuels and minerals in exports is associated with more corruption. Wei (2000) shows that countries that are 'naturally open', including due to good geography, have better government institutions; corruption is negatively correlated with the difference between actual and predicted openness.

13. Birdsall and Hamoudi (2002) include a brief review of the relevant literature.

14. Recent calls for a doubling of aid to Africa have been based in part on the need for a 'big push' of new investments on multiple fronts (health, education, agriculture, infrastructure), to enable countries to escape the poverty trap, harking back to the ideas of Rostow (1960); see Sachs *et al.* (2004), UN (2004). Easterly (2005) and Kraay and Raddatz (2005) present historical and other evidence inconsistent with the existence of poverty traps.

15. This is obviously not true for all commodity-dependent countries – Botswana, Chile and Indonesia have had high average growth rates since 1980. But it does appear to be true for our 'most' commodity-dependent countries – those for which in the early 1980s more than 90 per cent of exports were primary commodities.

16. Moreover, their failure to grow has apparently made it tough to acquire better equipment. This is the case even though some of the poorest countries have been receiving net annual transfers amounting to as much as 10 per cent of their GDP. Even discounting the value of net transfers to take into account that much of the aid has been tied and has come in the unco-ordinated and sometimes unpredictable form of multiple projects financed by multiple donors, the failure to grow suggests that institutional problems have been paramount, and that dependence on commodity exports, if it has constrained growth, has done so for reasons beyond its disadvantages from a financial point of view.

17. On this particular point, see Birdsall *et al.* (2005), who suggest that lack of infrastructure and other domestic factors are likely to limit the benefits of agricultural and other Doha-negotiated liberalizations, at least in the short run, for many poor countries.

18. See Kose *et al.* (2004: table 1). Easterly *et al.* (2000) report that growth volatility in developing countries was twice that in OECD economies in the periods 1960–78 and 1979–97.

19. Kose *et al.* (2004) report a mitigating effect of 'trade integration' on the negative effect of volatility on growth, but they use the Sachs–Warner measure of 'trade integration', which incorporates measures that reflect institutional and macro management problems (such as the black-market premium), which are not necessarily directly controlled by policy-makers, especially in the short run.

20. This is the case within countries independent of the absolute level of income of the poor – which is much higher in Poland, for example, than in most countries of sub-Saharan Africa.

21. Similarly, a regression of the average annual proportional change in the poverty headcount against average annual income growth (along the lines of Ravallion 2001) indicates that the effects of contractions increase the number of poor more than the

effects of expansions increase their numbers. The poverty headcount is about twice as sensitive to income contractions as it is to income expansions, though that may simply reflect the larger number of people above compared to below the poverty line (in, for example, a log-normal distribution of income).

22. In addition, the 'poor' at the beginning and end of each spell need not be the same people.

23. Lundberg and Squire (2003) also conclude that the costs of adjusting to 'openness' have been borne *'exclusively'* (their italics) by the poorest 40 per cent of households. Their results are suggestive but not definitive since they use the Sachs–Warner index of openness, which includes country characteristics such as the black-market premium that reflect outcomes of many policies and not just of trade policy itself.

24. Of course we cannot be sure that the right counterfactual is not a closed economy growing so slowly or not growing at all that would make the poor even worse off. Technically, one could make the following argument about variability and volatility. If the marginal utility of consumption is higher at low income levels, as we expect, then the change in utility from a given degree in volatility will be more severe for the poor than for the non-poor. So there is some amount of sacrifice in the plateau of average income that could be made in exchange for reduced volatility that would leave the utility of the poor unchanged. The question is whether openness increases growth enough that this tradeoff is unattractive, because the sacrifice in average income from closedness is greater than the amount that just offsets the utility loss from greater volatility. I am grateful to Bill Cline for elaborating on this point.

25. Countries with a history of inflation, as is the case in the emerging market economies of Latin America, have the particularly grim problem that their bad history leads the markets to demand procyclical fiscal austerity during crises.

26. Dailami and ul-Haque (1998).

27. High inflows can also create dangerous asset bubbles etc. The crisis in Russia in 1998 precipitated the crisis in Brazil that led to Brazil's devaluation of the real – in turn contributing to Argentina's crisis (by undermining the latter's export competitiveness). Chile-type disincentives to restrain short-term capital inflows, along with high reserves to protect economies during global crises can help, but these also imply costs to emerging markets that the 'emerged' economies need not bear.

28. Rojas-Suarez (2005) notes that the ratio of deposits to GDP remained highly volatile in developing countries in the 1990s (her table 1), along with high real interest rates (her table 2), reflecting investors' concerns.

29. Dervis and Birdsall (2006) propose a new facility at the IMF or the multilateral banks, among other things, to help address the problem of high-debt emerging market economies finding it difficult to sustain social spending during downturns.

30. Regressions of spells of income growth for the poorest quintile across countries in the 1990s, on the openness of countries' capital account and other standard variables suggested no obvious association between capital openness and the changing income shares of the poor. However, the measure of countries' capital openness, available from the IMF, exists for only a single year late in the 1990s; there is no measure that I could find of the change in capital openness. And the measure used is probably crude. There has been much less effort to quantify openness of the capital account than of the trade regime.

31. For evidence that income inequality reduces growth in developing countries though not in developed countries (presumably because government and market failures are lesser in the latter), see Barro (2000). Birdsall (2001) discusses why inequality matters. Birdsall and Londono (1997) emphasize that it is asset inequality not necessarily income inequality itself that is associated with low growth; they show that inequality of education and of land are associated with reduced growth across countries. See also Deininger and Olinto (2000). Aghion *et al.* (2000) suggest how unequal access to credit markets can reduce aggregate investment returns.

32. They estimate differences in differences; the dependent variable is the difference between two survey points in the private rate of return to education for males aged 20–55. Their results demonstrate the relevance, and the limits, of Stolper-Samuelson.

33. Other reforms, including trade liberalization and privatization, have a zero (trade) or negative (i.e. beneficent, for privatization) effect. The short-term 'bad' effects of the financial and capital account variables are sufficient to ensure an overall 'bad' effect of an aggregate country and year-specific reform index. Morley (2001) reports the opposite effect of more open capital markets for his urban and nationwide samples, but not for his, combined sample (nationwide plus urban sample). He reports a positive and statistically significant relationship between more open capital markets and equality. So there is no clear story – only some evidence that the textbook theory may not apply in all circumstances.

34. Only if the distribution of education improves very rapidly, however, is it likely to outpace growing demand for the highly skilled. At least, that is the record of recent decades: demand for the highly skilled has been outpacing supply, raising the relative returns to skills worldwide. Milanovic and Squire (2005) emphasize the resulting anomaly in developing countries, where globalization should favour their plentiful unskilled.

35. Pfeffermann (2002) puts together the relevant pieces of data on crises and devaluations for Latin America, suggesting that if the rich can manage capital flight, they can exploit the crises.

36. Birdsall and Haggard (2000) present evidence on this point. Consumption levels of these groups were mostly preserved, presumably by their using savings and otherwise reducing their assets.

37. Author's calculations from *World Development Indicators Database* (2002).

38. In particular, interest rate increases are assumed to hurt the poor more. Agénor *et al.* (2006) simulate the effect of a 10 percentage point increase in the interest rate in a model of the Brazilian economy. Their results include increases in the poverty headcount and the Gini coefficient.

39. Honohan (2005) notes that banking crises sometimes reduce income inequality because the rich suffer substantial losses. The exceptions he reports are in Latin America (where concentration of income is very high and the rich may be better able to protect their assets).

40. Take the case of Argentina. The public sector assumed substantial debt in the early 1990s when the convertibility policy was introduced, and this reduced its ability to finance greater spending on social programmes throughout the decade; the same phenomenon is likely to repeat itself given the 2002 crisis.

41. The trigger can be a loss in public sector creditworthiness with confidence in the value of deposits eroding, as in Argentina recently, or private sector losses which the public sector ends up having to assume, as during the East Asian crisis.

42. UNCTAD (2001). A reader might ask: 'What about South Korea's convergence on Japan's income, and China's several decades of growth?' The answer is, I am describing a tendency, not a predictable, definitive, generalizable outcome.

43. See Pritchett (1997).

44. Thus, we have such institutions as the World Bank and bilateral development assistance programmes. They tend to operate more in the spirit of charity, however, than as part of a global social contract in which both 'sides' benefit.

References

Abiad, A. and A. Mody (2003) 'Financial Reform: What Shapes It? What Shakes It?' *IMF Working Papers* 03/70, Washington, DC: IMF.

Ades, A. and R. Di Tella (1999) 'Rents, Competition, and Corruption', *American Economic Review*, 89, 4: 982–93.

Agénor, P.-R., R. Fernándes, E. Haddad and H. Tarp Jensen (2006) 'Adjustment Policies and the Poor in Brazil', in P.-R. Agénor, A. Izquierdo and H. Tarp Jensen (eds), *Adjustment Policies, Poverty and Unemployment: The IMMPA Framework*, Oxford: Blackwell.

Aghion, P., P. Bacchetta and A. Banerjee (2000) 'A Simple Model of Monetary Policy and Currency Crises', *European Economic Review*, 44, 4/6: 728–38.

Barro, R.J. (2000) 'Inequality and Growth in a Panel of Countries', *Journal of Economic Growth*, 5, 1: 5–32.

Behrman, J.R., N. Birdsall and M. Székely (2003) 'Economic Policy and Wage Differentials in Latin America', *CGD Working Paper* 29, Washington, DC: Center for Global Development.

Birdsall, N. (2001) 'Why Inequality Matters: Some Economic Issues', *Ethics and International Affairs*, 15, 2: 3–28.

Birdsall, N. and S. Haggard (2000) *After the Crisis: the Social Contract and the Middle Class in East Asia*, Washington, DC: Carnegie Endowment for International Peace.

Birdsall, N. and A. Hamoudi (2002) 'Commodity Dependence, Trade, and Growth: When 'Openness' is Not Enough', *CGD Working Paper* 7, Washington, DC: Center for Global Development.

Birdsall, N. and J.L. Londono (1997) 'Asset Inequality Matters: An Assessment of the World Bank's Approach to Poverty Reduction', *American Economic Review Papers and Proceedings*, 87, 2: 32–7.

Birdsall, N., D. Rodrik and A. Subramanian (2005) 'How to Help Poor Countries', *Foreign Affairs*, 84, 4: 136–52.

Clemens, M.A. and J.G. Williamson (2004) 'Why Did the Tariff-Growth Correlation Change after 1950?', *Journal of Economic Growth*, 9, 1: 5–46.

Dailami, M. and N. ul-Haque (1998) 'What Macroeconomic Policies Are "Sound"?', *World Bank Macroeconomics and Growth Group Working Paper* 1995, Washington, DC: World Bank.

Deininger, K. and P. Olinto (2000) 'Asset Distribution, Inequality and Growth', *World Bank Policy Research Working Paper* 2375, Washington, DC: World Bank.

Dervis, K. and N. Birdsall (2006) 'A Stability and Growth Facility', in E.M. Truman (ed.), *Reforming the IMF for the 21st Century*, Washington, DC: Institute for International Economics.

Diwan, I. (2001) 'Debt as Sweat: Labour, Financial Crises, and the Globalization of Capital', Mimeo.

Dollar, D. and A. Kraay (2001) 'Trade, Growth, and Poverty', *World Bank Policy Research Working Paper* 2615, Washington, DC: World Bank.

Easterly, W. (2005) 'Reliving the 50s: the Big Push, Poverty Traps, and Takeoffs in Economic Development', *CGD Working Paper* 65, Washington, DC: Center for Global Development.

Easterly, W., R. Islam and J. Stiglitz (2000) 'Shaken and Stirred: Explaining Growth Volatility', paper presented at Annual World Bank Conference on Development Economics, Washington, DC.

Frankel, J.A. and D. Romer (1999) 'Does Trade Cause Growth?', *American Economic Review*, 89, 3: 379–99.

Frankel, J.A. and E.A. Cavallo (2004) 'Does Openness to Trade Make Countries More Vulnerable to Sudden Stops, or Less? Using Gravity to Establish Causality', *NBER Working Paper* 10957, Cambridge, MA: National Bureau of Economic Research.

Honohan, P. (2005) 'Banking Sector Crises and Inequality', *World Bank Policy Research Working Paper* 3659, Washington, DC: World Bank.

Hsieh, C.-T. and P.J. Klenow (2002) 'Relative Prices and Relative Prosperity', *NBER Working Paper* 9701, Cambridge, MA: National Bureau of Economic Research.

Jones, C.I. (1994) 'Economic Growth and the Relative Price of Capital', *Journal of Monetary Economics*, 34, 3: 359–82.

Kose, M.A., E.S. Prasad and M.E. Terrones (2004) 'How Do Trade and Financial Integration Affect the Relationship between Growth and Volatility?', www.sf.frb.org/economics/conferences/0406/Kose.pdf

Kraay, A. and C. Raddatz (2005) 'Poverty Traps, Aid, and Growth', *World Bank Policy Research Working Paper* 3631, Washington, DC: World Bank.

Krueger, A.O. (1990) 'Asian Trade and Growth Lessons', *American Economic Review*, 80, 2: 108–12.

Lundberg, M. and L. Squire (2003) 'The Simultaneous Evolution of Growth and Inequality', *Economic Journal*, 113, 487: 326–44.

Milanovic, B. and L. Squire (2005) 'Does Tariff Liberalization Increase Wage Inequality? Some Empirical Evidence', *World Bank Policy Research Working Paper* 3571, Washington, DC: World Bank.

Morley, S.A. (2001) *The Income Distribution Problem in Latin American and the Caribbean*, Santiago: ECLAC.

Norton, R. (1997) 'The Big Costs of Policy Mistakes', *Fortune*, 29 September.

Pfeffermann, G. (2002) 'Why Latin America Stays Trapped', *The Globalist*, 21 November, www.theglobalist.com/research/papers/pfeffermann2.shtml

Prasad, E., K. Rogoff, S.-J. Wei and A. Kose (2004) 'Financial Globalization, Growth and Volatility in Developing Countries', *NBER Working Paper* 10942, Cambridge, MA: National Bureau of Economic Research.

Pritchett, L. (1997) 'Divergence, Big Time', *Journal of Economic Perspectives*, 11, 3: 3–17.

Ravallion, M. (2001) 'Growth, Inequality and Poverty: Looking Beyond Averages', *World Development*, 29, 11: 1803–15.

Rodriguez, F. and D. Rodrik (1999) 'Trade Policy and Economic Growth: A Skeptic's Guide to the Cross-National Evidence', *CEPR Discussion Paper* 2143, London: Centre for Economic Policy Research.

Rodrik, D. (1999) 'Institutions for High-Quality Growth: What They Are and How to Acquire Them', paper presented at the International Monetary Fund Conference on Second-Generation Reforms, 8–9 November, Washington, DC.

Rodrik, D. (2001) 'The Global Governance of Trade As If Development Really Mattered', background paper to the UNDP project on Trade and Sustainable Human Development, UNDP, New York.

Rojas-Suarez, L. (2005) 'Domestic Financial Regulations in Developing Countries: Can they Effectively Limit the Impact of Capital Account Volatility?', *CGD Working Paper* 59, Washington, DC: Center for Global Development.

Rostow, W.W. (1960) *The Stages of Economic Growth. A Non-Communist Manifesto*, Cambridge: Cambridge University Press.

Sachs, J.D., J.W. MacArthur, G. Schmidt-Traub, M. Kruk, C. Bahadur, M. Faye and G. McCord (2004) 'Ending Africa's Poverty Trap', www.cefe.net/forum/EndingAfricasPovertyTrap.pdf

UNCTAD (United Nations Conference on Trade and Development) (2001) *World Investment Report. Promoting Linkages*, New York: United Nations.

UNDP (United Nations Development Programme) (2005) *Human Development Report. International Co-operation at a Crossroads: Aid, Trade and Security in an Unequal World*, New York: Oxford University Press for UNDP.

United Nations Millennium Project (2004) *Investing in Development: A Practical Plan to Achieve the Millennium Development Goals*, www.unmillenniumproject.org/documents/MainReportComplete-lowres.pdf

Wei, S.-J. (2000) 'Natural Openness and Good Government', *NBER Working Paper* 7765, Cambridge, MA: National Bureau of Economic Research.

Winters, A. (2001) 'Trade Liberalization and Growth: Implementation and Complementary Policies', paper presented at the International Economic Study Group 26th Annual Conference, 15–17 September, London.

World Bank (2001) *Global Economic Prospects and the Developing Countries*, Washington, DC: World Bank.

World Bank (2006) 'Trends in Average Tariff Rates for Developing and Industrial Countries', available at http://web.worldbank.org/WBSITE/EXTERNAL/TOPICS/TRADE/ 0,,content MDK:20103740~menuPK:167374~pagePK:148956~piPK:216618~theSitePK:239071,00.html

World Bank (various years) *World Development Indicators Database*, Washington, DC: World Bank.

14
A Quest for Pro-poor Globalization
Machiko Nissanke and Erik Thorbecke

Introduction

Globalization offers participating countries new opportunities for accelerating growth and development but, at the same time, it also poses challenges to, and imposes constraints on policy-makers in the management of national, regional and global economic systems. While the opportunities offered by globalization can be large, the question is often raised whether the actual distribution of gains is fair and, in particular, whether the poor benefit proportionately less from globalization and could under some circumstances actually be hurt by it. The risks and costs brought about by globalization can be significant for fragile developing economies and the world's poor.[1] The fear that the poor have been by-passed or actually hurt by globalization has been highlighted by the findings from a number of recent studies, which point towards a continuing high inequality in world income distribution and limited, if not a lack of, convergence among participating national economies and across regions as globalization has proceeded.[2] There is much empirical evidence that openness contributes to more within-country inequality. China is a good example, with coastal provinces benefiting but not inland provinces.

The progress on poverty reduction has also been uneven. The share of the population of the developing countries living below US$1 per day declined from 40–21 per cent between 1981 and 2001, but this was mainly achieved by the substantial reduction of the poor in Asia, in particular in China (Chen and Ravallion 2004). Furthermore, the total number of people living on under US$2 per day actually increased worldwide. In particular, poverty has increased significantly in Africa in terms of poverty incidence as well as the depth of poverty.[3] Though any trend in poverty and income inequality observed so far cannot be exclusively or even mainly attributed to the 'globalization' effect, as such, these various estimates, even the most optimistic ones, cannot dismiss the concerns raised that globalization as it has proceeded so far may have had at least some adverse effects on poverty and income distribution.[4] Indeed, globalization has created winners and losers at numerous levels throughout modern history.[5] The losers include many of those who have keenly participated in the process of globalization. These concerns have generated a passionate debate worldwide as well as a powerful anti-globalization movement.

The globalization–poverty relationship is complex and heterogeneous, involving multifaceted channels. It is highly probable that globalization–poverty relationships may be non-linear in many aspects, involving several thresholds effects. Indeed, each subset of links embedded in the *globalization (openness)–growth–income distribution–poverty* nexus can be contentious and controversial. Besides the 'growth' effects of globalization on poverty (that is, the effects of globalization on poverty filtered through economic growth), globalization/integration is known to directly create winners and losers through other channels, affecting both vertical and horizontal inequalities (Ravallion 2004a). Because these multifaceted channels interact dynamically over space and time, the net effects of globalization on the poor can only be judged on the basis of context-specific empirical studies. Cross-country studies requiring precise measurements and definition of the two key concepts – globalization and poverty – tend to fail to give a deeper insight into this critical nexus. Both concepts are multidimensional, and not easily captured in a composite index to be used in a meaningful manner in cross-country comparative studies.

Building on earlier research projects, UNU-WIDER initiated a project on 'The Impact of Globalization on the World's Poor' in 2004. The project aims at producing a set of rigorous theoretical and empirical economic analyses, which could allow us: (i) to deepen our understanding into how conditions facing the world's poor have been evolving under globalization; and (ii) to provide a framework yielding the elements of a strategy for 'pro-poor globalization'.

This chapter brings out some of the highlights from the papers presented at the first project conference in Helsinki, October 2004.[6] That conference focused on conceptual and methodological issues with a view of identifying and discerning channels and transmission mechanisms through which the process of globalization affects different aspects and dimensions of poverty in the developing world. In this study we examine how these numerous channels interact, as the net effects on poverty depend on the relative strength of the positive and negative forces of globalization. On the basis of our analysis of these transmission mechanisms from globalization to the world's poor, we also discuss what may constitute a policy framework for encouraging globalization to be more pro-poor.

In Nissanke and Thorbecke (2006b), we identified and explored various transmission mechanisms in detail. The first and most important of these mechanisms is the growth–inequality–poverty channel. Other channels in the globalization–poverty nexus operate, respectively, through changes in relative factor and goods prices, factor movements, the nature of technological change and technological diffusion, the impact of globalization on volatility and vulnerability, the worldwide flow of information, global disinflation, and institutions. Following this approach, the chapter is structured as follows: in the second secton, we discuss various relationships embedded in the openness–growth–inequality–poverty nexus. Then the chapter goes on to analyze how globalization affects poverty through the various other channels listed above. In the concluding section, some preliminary thoughts are presented aimed at formulating a set of measures to make globalization more pro-poor.

The openness–growth–inequality–poverty nexus and channel

The 'growth' channel, through which globalization affects the poor, is examined by scrutinizing the causal chain in the *openness–growth–inequality–poverty* nexus link by link.

The openness–growth link

Policies of openness through liberalization of trade and investment regimes, and capital movements have been advocated worldwide for their growth- and welfare-enhancing effects on the basis of the propositions embedded in the economic theories of international trade and investment (for instance, the Ricardian comparative advantage theory, the Heckscher-Ohlin-Samuelson model, the new trade theories à la Krugman, and the model of intertemporal international borrowing/lending). In these models, the main growth-enhancing effects of openness are assumed to filter through: (i) static efficiency gains associated with improved resource allocation for national economies as well as for the world economy due to increased specialization; (ii) dynamic efficiency gains from such factors as economies of scale, diffusion of information, technology transfers, knowledge spillover effects as well as intertemporal trade gains from cross-border borrowing/lending for increased investment and consumption smoothing and portfolio risk diversification.

Indeed, openness through trade, foreign direct investment (FDI) and financial markets could increase the flow of goods and capital across national borders and could contribute significantly to economic growth (the openness–growth link). However, the direction of causality in this link is still being debated as well as how trade and capital flows could be interlinked into a virtuous circle. Furthermore, the positive openness–growth link is neither automatically guaranteed nor universally observable. The growth-enhancing effect of trade openness depends critically on the way a country is integrated into the global economy, as discussed below. Similarly, the transfer of technology, skills and management know-how that is assumed to accompany FDI is not necessarily automatic or guaranteed. Further, the postulated positive effects of portfolio and other capital flows (hot money) on growth have been questioned increasingly in recent years. The recent IMF study (Prasad *et al.* 2003) acknowledges that it is difficult to establish a strong positive causal relationship between financial globalization and economic growth.[7] Furthermore, these short-term capital flows contribute to the increased vulnerability to external shocks of the recipient developing countries. A large number of empirical studies based on cross-country regressions have been conducted to show the beneficial effects of an open economy regime on growth; for example, Dollar (1992); Sachs and Warner (1995); Dollar and Kraay (2001a; b).[8] However, the validity of these empirical exercises has been contested on technical grounds by many researchers.[9]

The growth–inequality–poverty interrelationship

The second link in the causal chain from openness to poverty is the interrelationship between growth and inequality. There are two conflicting theoretical strands relating income inequality and wealth inequality to growth. The classical approach best reflected by Kaldor (1956) argues that a higher marginal propensity among the rich to save than among the poor implies that a higher degree of initial income inequality will yield higher aggregate savings, capital accumulation and growth. Additional arguments in favour of the growth-enhancing effect of inequality are based on the existence of investment indivisibilities and incentive effects.[10] From this theoretical perspective, the desirability of an unequal income distribution is thus rationalized on economic grounds, that is on the basis of the claim that 'more poverty today is a precondition to more economic growth and less poverty in the future' (Thorbecke 2004).

The contrasting new political economy theories linking greater inequality to reduced growth operate through a number of subchannels (Thorbecke and Charumilind 2002). These subchannels are, respectively:

(i) unproductive rent-seeking activities that reduce the security of property;
(ii) the diffusion of political and social instability leading to greater uncertainty and lower investment;
(iii) redistributive policies encouraged by income inequality that impose disincentives on the rich to invest and accumulate resources;
(iv) imperfect credit markets resulting in underinvestment by the poor, particularly in human capital; and
(v) a relatively small income share accruing to the middle class – implying greater inequality – has a strong positive effect on fertility, and this, in turn, has a significant and negative impact on growth.

In addition, wide income and wealth disparities can impact on education, health and crime, through such manifestations as underinvestment in human capital, malnutrition leading to low worker productivity, stress and anxiety. In turn these manifestations may contribute to lower long-term growth. With particular reference to capital market imperfections and the role of resultant credit constraints, Aghion *et al.* (1999: 1617) make a similar point, emphasizing that 'wealth inequality determines investment in physical or human capital, which in turn affects the long-run growth rate'.

The rejection of the Kuznets hypothesis of the inverted U-shaped relationship between growth and inequality (as per capita income increases) by a number of empirical studies provided much impetus to the new political economy literature that postulates that high initial inequality is detrimental to economic growth.[11] The proponents of this approach, while rejecting the immutability of the Kuznets curve, argue that growth patterns yielding more inequality in the income distribution would, in turn, engender lower future growth paths.

In the light of the new literature that emphasizes the impact of inequality on incentives, social conflicts, transaction costs and property rights, the possible link between growth and poverty is examined in the previous UNU-WIDER studies on growth–inequality–poverty interrelationships (Addison and Cornia 2001; Cornia 2004, Shorrocks and van der Hoeven 2004). They argue that the widespread increase in inequality has been detrimental to the objective of poverty reduction, because large rises in inequality have stifled growth, and because poverty, at any given growth rate of GDP, falls less rapidly in the case of a more unequal distribution than in the case of a more equitable one. The obvious policy implication following from these studies is that successful poverty alleviation depends not only on favourable changes in average GDP per capita growth but also on favourable changes in income inequality.

The conclusions drawn from these recent studies challenge the dominant mainstream views derived from a number of World Bank studies such as Deininger and Squire (1996); Li *et al.* (1998); Dollar and Kraay (2001a; b). The conventional views argue that there is no clear association between inequality and growth and that growth is distribution-neutral, hence growth is the only realistic option. For example, Dollar and Kraay (2001a; b) state that 'since the share of income going to the poor does not change *on average* with growth, the poor benefit from growth', and 'trade is good for growth and growth is good for the poor'. However, the methodology used in yielding these results has since then been challenged. Ravallion (2002) argues, for example, that average neutrality found in the Dollar and Kraay study and other studies is not inconsistent with strong distributional effects at the country level. A critical question, according to Ravallion, is whether or not inequality is an impediment to poverty reducing growth, or in other words, whether high inequality attenuates the growth elasticity of poverty. His analysis confirms that the elasticity of poverty with respect to growth is found to decline with the extent of inequality.

Thus, we argue that while it is most likely that the poor will benefit from growth, the ultimate poverty reduction effects will depend on how the growth pattern affects income distribution. Inequality is the filter between growth and poverty reduction.[12] If growth leads to an increase in income inequality the poor may benefit only slightly or, in some instances, actually be hurt by the globalization process. We argue specifically that the *pattern* of economic growth and development, rather than the rate of growth per se, may have significant effects on a country's income distribution and poverty profile. Indeed, the recent debate on the meaning of pro-poor growth is related to the complex triangular relationships among poverty, growth and inequality. Clearly, poverty reduction would require some combination of higher growth and a more pro-poor distribution of the gains from growth. Hence what is relevant for poverty reduction is a 'distribution corrected' rate of growth, as Ravallion notes (2004b), and in our view, growth is considered pro-poor if in addition to reducing poverty it also decreases inequality.

Diverse approaches for examining the globalization–poverty relationships

Given the complex relationships embedded in the globalization–poverty nexus, as discussed above, it is not surprising to see the diversity in approaches adopted by researchers in examining the physiology of the causal chain in the openness–growth–inequality–poverty.

Taking an aggregate approach, Heshmati (2006) computes two composite indices of globalization and examines how poverty and inequality are affected by four globalization components. His results generally confirm that initial endowments and the degree and nature of integration into the international economy largely determine the distributional effects of globalization. The importance of regional variations in understanding the globalization–inequality–poverty nexus is further taken up by Kalwij and Verschoor (2006). They examine the impact of globalization on poverty, focusing on the responsiveness of poverty to aggregate changes in income distribution. On the basis of region-specific analysis, they challenge the dominant mainstream view that globalization is good for the poor by generating approximately distribution-neutral income growth, as argued by Collier and Dollar (2001). They reaffirm instead the position emphasized by Ravallion (1997) and Bourguignon (2003: 3–26) that inequality, in particular the initial income distribution, has an important indirect effect on poverty through diminishing prospects for pro-poor growth.

Ravallion (2006) examines more specifically the relationship between trade openness and poverty, using three different lenses and techniques: (1) a macro aggregate cross-country regression of the impact of trade on poverty; (2) a macro time series analysis of China; and (3) a micro lens based on a computable general equilibrium model scrutinizing, respectively, the impacts on households of WTO accession in China and cereal deprotection in Morocco. Both the macro and micro approaches cast doubt on some widely heard generalizations from both sides of the globalization debate. In particular, he points to the inadequacy of the conventional 'macro lens' for revealing strong and robust trade–poverty relationship. Ravallion also shows that the link between trade liberalization and poverty is tenuous and that it is difficult to ascertain that trade openness is a powerful force for poverty reduction in developing countries. However, the tenuous nature of the trade–poverty relationship cannot necessarily be generalized to all cases. The data presented are more suggestive of diverse (and noisy) impacts of trade openness on poverty. Under some specific set of conditions openness to trade could clearly be very effective in alleviating poverty.

Jenkins (2006) focuses his analysis on the impact of integration within the global economy (rather than trade policies as such) on the poor in their role as producers. His central question about the impact of globalization on employment and income opportunities for poor people is addressed through case studies of three value chains – horticulture, garments and textiles – in four countries, Bangladesh, Kenya, South Africa and Vietnam. In the context of analyzing the comparative performance among case study countries, he proposes to make a clear conceptual distinction between 'non-globalizer' and 'unsuccessful globalizer' and he categorizes Kenya as a unsuccessful globalizer, while Vietnam is successful in integrating in terms of *outcome* though remaining relatively closed in terms of *policy*.

In presenting the case studies, Jenkins first emphasizes that the outcomes of globalization processes are highly context-specific, dependent both on the institutional framework and government policies that mediate global processes. Several patterns emerge from his four case studies of global value chains. For example, the growth of labour-intensive exports of manufactures and agricultural products does create employment opportunities, particularly for low-income women and migrants from rural areas, as horticulture exports in Kenya or garment exports in Bangladesh and Vietnam reveal. However, the requirements of global value chains mean that these jobs often demand a high degree of labour flexibility, long hours of work and poor working conditions, making workers vulnerable both in terms of employment and income security. Opening up to global competition has also led to job losses and deterioration in working conditions and employment conditions, as the case of textile industries in South Africa illustrates. Further, Jenkins shows how gains from globalization are likely to be more widely distributed where the initial structure of assets and entitlements is more equitable, as in Vietnam. In the latter, a strategy of building linkages between the export sector and domestic production has been more effective in creating employment and reducing poverty than trade liberalization per se. On the whole, he concludes that even in those cases that have been successful in developing labour-intensive exports, the overall impact of globalization on poverty has been relatively small. The majority of the poor are not engaged in global production and other strategies are required to reach them. Clearly, integration with the global economy is not a substitute for an anti-poverty strategy.

Other channels in the globalization–poverty relationship

How these other channels work

We suggest that in addition to the growth conduit, there are other major channels through which globalization affects poverty. They include *technology* (the nature of technological progress and the technological diffusion process); *factor mobility* and more particularly the pattern of labour migration brought about by the process of globalization; *vulnerability* (increasing world integration and openness tends to be associated with greater volatility and vulnerability of poor households to economic and financial shocks); and *the flow of information* and *institutions* in both developed and developing countries that mediate the effects of these channels on the poor (Nissanke and Thorbecke 2006b). These channels may be largely responsible for explaining why the poor have not emerged as larger beneficiaries of contemporary globalization. According to the theoretical prediction embedded in the Stolper-Samuelson theorem, developing countries well endowed with unskilled labour should experience a decline in income inequality through an increased demand for unskilled labour, while unskilled labour in developed countries would lose out when equity is adversely affected. However, the empirical evidence reveals that wage gaps between skilled and unskilled workers have been increasing in many developing countries, particularly in Latin America and Africa.

Several specific features associated with the current phase of globalization explain why the theoretical prediction does not hold. For example, the nature of technical progress and new technology is heavily biased in favour of skilled and educated labour, as technical change emanates from R&D activities in the developed (industrialized) countries in response to local conditions (Culpeper 2002).

Hence, technical change tends to be labour saving and skill-biased, and new technology is complementary to capital and skilled labour, while it is a substitute for unskilled labour. Hence, technical change tends to increase inequalities in both developed and developing countries. Furthermore, technological diffusion and access to new technology is not universal and spontaneous while intensified privatization of research, for example in biotechnology, may have adverse effects on access of developing countries and the poor to new technology. The resulting widened productivity differences explain cross-country wage/income inequality. 'Perverse' factor movements could provide another explanation. Capital and skilled labour do not migrate to poor countries as much as among developed countries. Rather, there is a tendency for skilled labour to migrate from developing countries to developed countries, while unskilled labour migration tends to be strictly controlled. With capital market liberalization, there is a propensity for capital flight to developed countries, particularly during periods of instability and crisis. Thus, Culpeper (*Ibid.*) concludes that with such perverse movements, as globalization proceeds, developed countries would see inequality fall while developing countries would experience rising inequality.

Furthermore, the differentiated degree of cross-border factor mobility (skilled labour and capital versus unskilled labour and land) affects the functional income distribution between labour and capital against the former. Wage equalization does not take place through labour migration, as was the case in the previous globalization era. Some workers are losing out as de facto labour mobility takes place through the increasingly free cross-border capital mobility and the ability of transnational corporations (TNCs) to relocate production sites in response to changes in relative labour costs. In fear of driving away TNCs, governments of developing countries are less likely to enact regulations to protect and enhance labour rights (Basu 2003). Generally, the poor and unskilled are most adversely affected by asymmetries in market power and access to information, technology, marketing and TNC activities and the dominance of TNCs in commodity and value chains.

Greater openness tends to be associated with greater volatility and economic shocks. Poor households tend to be more vulnerable to these shocks.[13] The process of global disinflation while, on the one hand, helping the poor by containing price increases might have taken place at the possible cost of slower growth and fiscal retrenchment, thereby reducing the ability of nation-states to provide adequate safety nets to those adversely affected by recurrent global financial and economic crises. Globalization has contributed to the enormous increase in the flow of information and knowledge worldwide. Internet technology and the spread of mass media transmit the most recent information almost instantaneously. At the same time, increased global flows of information can result in changing reference norms and increased frustration with relative income differences, and could increase volatility and insecurity for many cohorts. Finally, institutions act as a filter intensifying or hindering the positive and negative pass-through between globalization and poverty and can help explain the diversity, heterogeneity and non-linearity of outcomes.

Technology channel

Focusing exclusively on the technology channel, Graff *et al.* (2006) argue that the potential exists for globalization to confer dramatically higher food productivity and rural incomes on developing countries via the mechanism of North–South technology transfer. As international diffusion of technology and sustainable innovation are determined by the institutional and financial capacity and the levels of human capital in developing countries, they argue that policies to facilitate North–South and South–South technology transfer and diffusion need to recognize global complexity of innovation sources and absorption capacities, and adapt accordingly. To realize the potential positive effects of biotechnology on poverty reduction, they argue that the public and private sectors must establish institutions with local capacity for technology innovation and adaptation, reduce transaction costs in the process of international transfer of technology, and provide standardization, transparency and access to information for property rights over technologies. In addition to significant investment in higher education and research capacity in low-income countries, they argue for a new type of institution potentially capable of overcoming the lack of access to intellectual property rights, namely the Intellectual Property Rights Clearinghouse (IPRC).

The technology diffusion process by which new technologies are introduced in developing countries is analyzed by Zhao (2006). He emphasizes that technology adoption and diffusion are critical factors determining whether developing countries could truly benefit from new technologies through the globalization process. Even if a new technology can potentially increase the income level of rural farmers, its diffusion may be slow due to sunk costs of adoption and uncertainties about net payoffs of the technology in question. The lack of capital, credit and risk-sharing possibilities as well as the limited access to information about new technologies would hinder technology adoption and diffusion. An adoption of new technologies can be hindered by uncertainties about their efficiency. For example, without independent external information sources, farmers in developing countries have to rely heavily on their neighbours (so-called 'leaders', those who have already adopted the technologies) to obtain vital information about new methods.

Aggarwal (2006) analyzes the combined effects of *openness*, *technology* transfer and *institutions* on *environmental* degradation. She examines various mechanisms through which globalization may affect the wellbeing of the poor through its effects on local ecosystems on which the poor depend for their livelihood. Focusing on the concept of resilience, that is the capacity of an ecosystem to maintain its structure and pattern of behaviour in the face of disturbance, she argues that the transfer of (essentially agricultural) technology often funded by external sources may lead to a shift towards more modern resource management practices that have very short-term time horizons. Firms and even farmers expect quick results and payoffs. These changes such as, for example, mono-cropping, carried out over vast tracts of land reduce functional diversity and increase spatial uniformity in grassland ecosystems thus leading to a loss of resilience. As a consequence primary producers become more vulnerable to price volatility and shocks such as droughts. The loss of biodiversity results in a reduced number of pathways through which stress in the environment can be absorbed. An important observation of the study is that very often the governance structure of institutions (at village, state or national levels) does not overlap with the scale of ecosystems that often transcend political boundaries. Hence the closer matching of ecosystems and governance structures calls for the design of new and appropriate institutions – a key challenge for policy-makers intent on reducing some of the negative effects of globalization on the environment and the rural poor.

Vulnerability channel

Even if one accepts the argument that globalization contributes to an increase in aggregate income measures, a second consequence of globalization is increased uncertainty resulting from greater variation in income and expenditure caused by global shocks. Ligon (2006) focuses his analysis on how globalization affects poverty through this vulnerability channel. Poor households, in particular, who tend to be risk-averse may be harmed by greater volatility in their income streams. He seeks to account for variations in the consumption distribution across countries and time, and then to estimate the welfare loss associated with different types of shocks, *global shocks*, *country-specific shocks* and *globalization shocks*. Ligon finds that global shocks and globalization shocks are of minor importance relative to country-specific shocks in explaining variation in poorer quintile consumption growth. However, he finds that the total risk facing households within a country-quintile is large, with households willing to sacrifice on average 8.4 per cent of their expected consumption in exchange for eliminating all risk.

The issue of increased vulnerability, resulting from trade liberalization, as experienced by countries in Central and East Europe (CEECs) since the early 1990s, is taken up by Montalbano *et al.* (2006). Focusing on macro vulnerability, their analysis shows that the extremely high volatility of consumption observed in this region is strongly related to trade shocks and that the per capita income of the poorest quintile of the population is most vulnerable to these trade shocks. On the basis of their empirical evidence, they argue for the need to adopt, in the case of emerging and transition countries, forward-looking national policies to support their process of trade liberalization; that is, policies both to mitigate the impact of trade shocks and to enhance coping mechanisms. They also call for improvement in the governance of the globalization process by establishing a new 'culture of prevention' and designing mechanisms for limiting the size and frequency of shocks at the international level.

Information diffusion channel

The increased insecurity and vulnerability in the process of globalization is discussed by Graham (2006) with reference to 'the economics of happiness'. She observes that there are noticeable differences between standard money metric measures of poverty and inequality in assessing the effects of globalization and people's subjective assessment of some of the consequences of globalization. She explores how the economics of happiness can help explain these discrepancies between economists' assessments of the benefits of globalization for the poor and individuals' real and perceived welfare outcomes, such as vulnerability to falling into poverty among the near poor; distributional shifts at the local, cohort and sector level; and changes in the provision and distribution of public services, among others. She suggests that the latter trends play a major role in determining public perceptions about the benefits and fairness of the globalization process. Focusing on income mobility and on reported wellbeing of the poor and near poor as a way to gauge movements in and out of poverty and distributive trends across time and across cohorts within countries, she argues that while globalization is a major engine for growth in aggregate, globalization either introduces or exacerbates other trends that affect people's wellbeing as much if not more than income, for example, through the increasing flow of information about the living standards of others, both within and beyond country borders. This flow of information can result in changing reference norms and increased frustration with relative income differences, even among respondents whose own income is rising. For example, individuals in a given developing country compare their incomes increasingly with those of relatively similar individuals in developed countries rather than within their own country. Graham's analysis also illustrates how globalization can bring about increased volatility and insecurity for many cohorts, particularly those that are not well positioned to take advantage of the opportunities created by the opening of trade and capital flows. She argues that this insecurity, and the very real threat of falling into poverty for the near poor and lower-middle classes, contributes to negative perceptions of the globalization process, particularly in countries where social insurance systems are weak or where existing systems are eroding.

Graham concludes that many social and collective measures should be in place for globalization to have positive effects on poverty. These include measures such as public investments in health; institutions that can ensure adherence to basic norms of equity and fairness; and collective investments in social insurance to protect workers from the volatility that often accompanies integration into global markets. In the absence of these measures, she warns that globalization will only create opportunities for those that are best positioned to take advantage of them, leaving behind large sectors of poor and vulnerable individuals.

Institutions as a channel

Institutions mediate the various channels and mechanisms through which the globalization process affects poverty. Sindzingre (2006) suggests that institutions act as a filter: intensifying or hindering the positive and negative pass-through between globalization and poverty and can help explain the diversity, heterogeneity and non-linearity of outcomes. For example, on the one hand, the impact of globalization on the poor is intermediated by domestic political economy structures and institutions such as social polarization, oligarchic structures and predatory regimes, which may bias, confiscate or nullify the gains from globalization for particular groups of poor. On the other hand, the positive effects of globalization on growth and poverty can be found when institutional conditions are characterized by such features as political participation, social cohesion and management of social conflict arising directly from globalization effects.

In particular, Sindzingre distinguishes two causal processes in the globalization–poverty relationships. The first one is the impact of globalization on institutions. Globalization can induce institutional change, which in turn may have positive or negative effects on poverty reduction. However, the pace of change can be very different among institutions. For example, globalization as a set of flows and policies is more likely to induce transformation on the aspects of institutions that are already experiencing rapid change (for example, formal political or economic rules), and less likely on slow-changing institutions such as social institutions. The second causal process is the impact of institutions on globalization. Globalization is 'filtered' (intensified or hindered) by institutions at the country and micro levels (villages and households).

Paths towards pro-poor globalization

It should be clear from the above discussion that the globalization–poverty relationship is complex and heterogeneous, involving multifaceted channels. Hence, it is understandable why the globalization debates tend to raise many emotive issues. As Bardhan (2006: 158) notes, however, these debates often involve a clash of counterfactuals. For those against the ongoing process of globalization:

> [a] counterfactual is the world of more social justice and less dominant trading and investment companies, which gives some more breathing space to the poor producers and workers. On the other side the counterfactual for pro-globalizers is the case when there is no (or limited) trade or foreign investment, a world which may be worse for the poor (as it is in the extreme cases of the closed economies of North Korea and Burma). The way out of this clash of counter-factuals is to insist that there are policies that may attempt to help the poor without necessarily undermining the forces of globalization.

Hence, he holds the view that the distributional issue raised in the debate is not an argument against globalization (open trade and investment regimes) per se but for proactive public programmes to protect the poor. Indeed, not integrating into the global economy is not a viable or attractive development option for any nation. As noted in Deardorff and Stern (2006), countries that do not actively participate in trade liberalization are more likely to lose. They explore the impact of globalization on countries excluded from the process of globalization, that is those that have chosen (or in some cases were forced to choose) to remain relatively closed off from world markets. They use an analysis of the offer curve and a political economy model to examine the effect on countries that fail to participate in multilateral trade negotiations or preferential trading arrangements but nevertheless are engaged to some extent in international trade.

They show that the 'outsiders' are likely to be harmed, through the terms of trade effects, by multilateral most favoured nation (MFN) tariff reductions as well as preferential trading arrangements (PTAs) between insiders. In their analysis, it is the exclusion of some sectors and/or some exporting countries from the benefits of tariff cuts that creates a bias against non-participating and excluded countries. The best cure for these excluded nations is to become active participants in world markets and the world economy, in general. While there is no guarantee that the welfare gains of joining the world economy would contribute to a reduction in the large-scale poverty that reigns in those countries and particularly in Africa, their analysis suggest that it is likely to have a welfare-increasing effect by stimulating economic growth for previously excluded countries.

However, as noted in Nissanke and Thorbecke (2006b), a mere adoption of open trade and investment regimes per se does not guarantee developing countries' entry into the 'income convergence club'. Dowrick and DeLong (2001) suggest that (i) openness to the world economy does not necessarily promote convergence; (ii) many poor countries that have opened their economies since the 1980s have fallen behind, not just relatively but absolutely in terms of both income levels and structural development. The conundrum of the persistent 'non-convergence' of world income should be explicitly addressed in terms of structural features of the global economic relationships as they evolved over time and the institutional conditions found in participating countries. The income convergence trend among nation-states, to the extent that it has been observed historically, is likely to be explained more effectively by the nature of integration and specialization of subgroups of countries, rather than by the degree of openness of the trade and investment regimes per se, as is often claimed. In particular, in the current phase of globalization, developing countries have to reach a certain threshold by undergoing substantial changes in trade and production structure before they experience income convergence.

Clearly, countries need to have reached the take-off point before they can take advantage of the potential benefits of openness and globalization. One of the critical reasons why globalization may not be working for low-income developing countries lies in the fact that the effects of international trade on growth are critically dependent on the pattern of specialization and integration. By treating two sectors symmetrically, the conventional Heckscher-Ohlin trade model (consisting of two countries, two sectors and two factors) shows that two countries equally reap aggregate gains from trade through efficiency gains.[14] In reality, however, the pattern of specialization does matter for welfare implications of a trade-induced growth path on at least two accounts.

Two sectors need not be symmetrical, first, through the well-known immiserizing effect of trade à la Bhagwati – that is to say the terms of trade (TOT) effects. Though many dismiss the likelihood of such an effect in a small economy, low-income countries dependent on the exports of a limited range of primary commodities face a deterioration of TOT, in particular if the 'fallacy composition effect' is seriously taken into account. In the 1980s and 1990s, many primary commodity exporting countries, which implemented structural adjustment programmes, underwent simultaneous export drives leading to depressed prices in many export commodities (Nissanke and Ferrarini 2001). In this context, Birdsall (2002) draws attention to the fact that measured by the trade–GDP ratio or tariff rates, most commodity-dependent countries have not been more reticent than less commodity-dependent countries about participating in international trade, but the former group has failed to grow (especially after 1980) as they have remained dependent on exports of primary commodities.

Furthermore, two sectors are not necessarily symmetrical because of the possible impact of dynamic scale economies, i.e. dynamic externalities through technological spillover benefits and the accumulation of knowledge capital. As the endogenous growth theory emphasizes, it is this factor that largely accounts for diverging growth rates among countries. An application of this phenomenon to the trade model implies that a country specializing in an industry with a larger positive externality would experience a faster growth rate compared with the trading partner that specializes in an industry with a weaker externality. Thus, the growth rate of the two trading countries could differ considerably, depending on the pattern of specialization.

If a country follows the Rybczynski line dictated by static comparative advantage with given relative resource endowments, the country with an initial comparative advantage in 'non-dynamic' sectors may end up in a low equilibrium trap. Countries that have benefited from globalization and integration – such as those found in East Asia – are the ones which have successfully completed the structural transformation of the composition of their production and trade structure with continuous upgrading of their human skill endowments and technology/knowledge base. Consequently, their comparative advantages have evolved over time to maximize the benefit from dynamic externalities.

Seen from this perspective, openness per se is not sufficient to ensure that development will follow. The internal pattern of growth and forms of integration are critical for countries to benefit from globalization-induced growth. Many low-income countries could be locked in an international poverty trap through integration (UNCTAD 2002). This points to the importance of reaching the take-off stage before countries can benefit from globalization.

Policies of *strategic integration* are called for, as the effects of international trade and investment on growth are critically dependent on the pattern of specialization and integration. Whether global market forces establish a virtuous circle or vicious circle depends on the initial conditions at the time of exposure and the effective design and implementation of policies to manage the integration process.

Hence, in our view, a strategic position towards globalization cannot be equated with a mere passive adoption of free trade policy, or a simple fine-tuning of the pace and sequence of liberalization measures. At the same time, there is no place for an old-style, poorly designed and implemented protection policy, which is mired in unproductive rent seeking activities and patron–client relationships between governments and private agents. Import substitution strategy can work only when protection is granted to firms with a clearly specified 'graduation' clause. That is, protection should always be seen as temporary and 'time bound' by agents. Thus, as Kaplinsky (2000) notes, the issue confronting policy-makers is not *whether* to integrate into the global economy but *how* to integrate so as to have a stable foundation for sustainable and equitable growth. The strategic integration requires a long-term vision for upgrading a country's comparative advantages towards high-value-added activities by climbing the technology ladder step by step through learning and adaptation. To succeed, developing country governments should consciously engage in building institutional capacities for integration, including a capable nation-state that is ready to take on the enormous challenges posed by globalization. The positive benefits from globalization are neither automatic nor guaranteed and passive liberalization would risk perpetual marginalization.

In particular, national policies should be strategically designed in the light of the skewed nature of the ongoing process of globalization. First, dynamic externalities and rent-rich activities are increasingly concentrated in high-skill, knowledge-intensive sectors. In short, the skill- and technology-related divide has become wider over recent decades. This trend is clearly reflected in the continuously declining terms of trade of less skill-intensive manufactured goods relative to high-skill and technology-intensive goods over the recent decades. The markets for many labour-intensive products, consisting increasingly of internationally standard goods, have come to resemble those for primary products. The entry of China and India into global markets for these products has depressed and will continue to depress real wages and returns in these sectors.

Second, trade in the current phase of globalization is largely mediated through international production with an increasing share of intra-firm trade undertaken by TNCs, which command a lion's share of global production and marketing networks. Trade is no longer conducted in arm's length relationships, with final products being largely manufactured in a particular country and then exported. Instead, international production with vertical integration has increasingly dominated, in which production processes are sliced up and located globally (Kaplinsky 2000). There has been a tremendous growth in offshore outsourcing and global divisions of labour. Consequently, intra-firm trade within TNCs and inter-industry trade with highly differentiated products command a predominant share of global trade. At the same time, considerable asymmetries in market power and access to information, technology and other intangible knowledge assets between TNCs, on the one hand, and local farmers and traders in developing countries on the other hand, have resulted in a hugely skewed distribution of gains from trade. This is reflected in TNC dominance in commodity and value chains of international traded goods, as well as in frequently observed conditions such as the sharp decline in real wages in export processing zones. The benefits of productivity improvements, instead of going to the fragmented producers and farmers, are largely appropriated by TNCs and global supermarket chains that can exploit oligopolistic commodity markets.

This uneven distribution of market power points to the need to improve the negotiating positions of developing country governments vis-à-vis TNCs, aiming at a strategic, targeted approach to FDI, so that FDI could facilitate skill and technology transfers and generate strong positive productivity spillovers for domestic firms. In this context, Bardhan (2006) calls for a greater co-ordination of many regulations on an international scale as well as more energetic international attempts to certify codes against international restrictive business practices and to establish an international anti-trust investigation agency, possibly under WTO auspices. There is also a need for policy aiming at *structural transformation* in relation to various transmission mechanisms discussed in the study, in particular on the ground that there are critical thresholds for positive effects of globalization on poverty reduction to realize. The non-linear Laffer-type relationship between globalization and poverty, noted by both Milanovic (2002) and Agénor (2003), shows that openness helps those with basic and higher education but reduces the income share of those with no education and it is only when basic education becomes the norm, even for the poor, that openness exerts an income equalizing effect. Thus, at low-income levels, openness appears to affect equality negatively while at medium- and high-income levels it promotes equality.

Sizeable public investment in skill upgrading, as a specific pro-poor measure, is a key for ensuring positive benefits from globalization. At the same time those countries which have not yet reached the critical threshold, need (i) to invest in agriculture in order to reach the take-off point to allow the structural transformation of their economies to proceed; (ii) to build both physical and social infrastructure in conjunction with development of healthy, educated and skilled human resources; and (iii) to strengthen institutions of social protection.

Our review also raises the issue as to whether the present form of globalization/ integration is conducive to a process of growth-cum-structural transformation, which is capable of engendering and sustaining pro-poor economic growth and favourable distributional consequences. Various studies suggest that globalization indeed produces adverse distributional consequences at both the national and global levels that could slow down or even reverse the present poverty alleviation trend. Hence, globalization should not be viewed as a reliable substitute for a domestic development strategy. Designing an active development strategy should be based on a better understanding on the key issue: what structure and pattern of growth contributes most to the alleviation of poverty. However, it is clear that to address the distributional consequences of globalization a set of much more effective redistributional instruments at both national and global levels is required. This would call for exploring alternative, more equitable forms and processes of globalization to start with. However identifying such new forms would requires a much better grasp of the concept of 'pro-poor globalization' than we presently hold.

In analyzing the various processes through which *openness* to foreign trade and long-term capital movements affects the lives of the rural poor, Bardhan (2006) argues for proactive public programmes to help poor farmers adjust and co-ordinate, and suggests that international agencies that preach the benefits of free trade have an obligation to contribute to such programmes with financial, organizational and technical assistance. For the WTO and other multilateral agencies to become a true development forum, it is important to recognize explicitly the hugely asymmetrical unequal economic power relationships as observed currently among member countries. These global agencies should endeavour to create a genuine 'policy space' to allow developing countries to engage in their development agenda in the integration and globalization process. The current rules adopted by the WTO and other international agencies such as the principles of 'single undertaking' and 'reciprocity' should be critically reappraised in this light. It can be agued that a meaningful 'level playing field' could be created only if 'differential' treatments are legitimately instituted as a guiding rule governing multilateral negotiations.

For advancing our understanding of what pro-poor globalization may entail, Basu (2006) focuses his analysis more on the process of marginalization resulting from globalization. He argues that the openness channel is likely to result in international prices of goods and services somewhere between prices in industrialized nations and prices in developing countries but closer to the former. Since (a) labour is less mobile across borders than goods and services; and (b) the nature of technological progress favours capital- and skill- intensive innovations, it seems reasonable to expect for sections of the labour force in poor nations, and especially the illiterate and unskilled who are unable to take advantage of the new technology, that wages will lag behind prices. Hence some of the poorest people may be subjected to a period of hardship before the benefits of opening up trickles down.

Basu is concerned that the emphasis on maximizing per capita income in an era of fast globalization might not place sufficient weight on poverty and inequality reduction. Instead he proposes that the normative criterion which should be adopted in evaluating a country's wellbeing is that of the per capita income of the bottom quintile of the population. Such a measure would combine reducing poverty and inequality. He proceeds to build a simple model showing that the adoption of the 'bottom quintile income criterion' in addition to leading to a pro-poor growth pattern would alleviate the erosion of each national government's power to follow an equity-conscious policy – an outcome that obtains under the alternative case where income maximization is assumed to prevail. On the basis of his welfare analysis, Basu proceeds to suggest a radical distribution policy whereby workers in all firms as well as currently unemployed labourers be given a fraction of corporate equity earnings from all firms. He envisages that in today's globalizing world, such an 'equity' scheme should be extended to that of inter-country transfers. He suggests that developing rules for some inter-country transfer of equity income would ensure that the functional income distribution between capital and labour (especially unskilled labour) would not become too uneven. In order to escape from what amounts to a Prisoner's Dilemma situation, Basu also argues for a creation of a new international co-ordination organization that helps co-ordinate inter-country anti-poverty policies.

As Bardhan (2006) notes, globalization should not be allowed to be used, either by its critics or by its proponents, as an excuse for inaction on the domestic as well as the international front. On the basis of our review, we argue that what is *at minimum* called for is therefore liberalization to be accompanied by a comprehensive policy package for enhancing the capability of the poor and instituting a safety net for people who lose in the process. However, to make globalization more inclusive and truly pro-poor, we should go probably beyond this minimalist approach. We should start giving some serious consideration to more radical distributional measures such as proposed by Basu.

Birdsall (2002) also advocates the need for a global social contract to finance equal opportunity investments in the initially weak and disadvantaged as well as for appropriate global arrangements to minimize the asymmetric risks and costs of global market failures. Indeed, we should get engaged earnestly in a fresh debate on developing new governance structures of the international trade and investment regimes so that the enormous benefits that globalization promises to generate through transfer of knowledge, technology and financial resources could be more equitably shared by the world's poor.[15]

Notes

1. Birdsall (2002), for example, argues that it is the poorer countries and the poor who tend to bear the risks and costs of the higher volatility brought about by globalization.
2. See Nissanke and Thorbecke (2006b) for a review of literature and more detailed discussion on the concepts used for analyzing the trends in world inequality and empirical evidence. For historical trends towards income divergence see Pritchett (1997). Quah (1996) also discusses the twin peaks in the world's distribution dynamics, which are characterized by the tendency for stratification and polarization.
3. See Wade (2002) and Deaton (2001; 2002) for critical discussions of the World Bank's estimates of global poverty and inequality used in these studies.
4. See also Culpeper (2002) for a recent critical literature review of the effect of globalization on inequality, where a set of triangular relationships between globalization, growth and inequality is systematically discussed.
5. See Williamson (2002) for winners and losers from globalization in modern history.
6. See Nissanke and Thorbecke (2006a) for a more comprehensive summary of main findings from the papers presented at the first conference in Helsinki, October 2004. The full set of the conference papers appear in two publications: a special issue of *World Development* and in a Palgrave Macmillan volume, both published in 2006.
7. See Nissanke and Stein (2003) for a critical view on the effect of financial globalization on economic growth in emerging market economies.
8. See World Bank (2002) for a summary of these cross-country studies on the openness-growth link.
9. See Rodriguez and Rodrik (1999) for an excellent critical assessment of these cross-sectional studies. See also Pritchett (1996) for detailed discussion and comparison among various measures used in empirical analyses of outward trade orientation in least developed countries. Clearly, the simple trade intensity index (exports plus imports/GDP) – a standard variable frequently used to measure a country's outward policy orientation in cross-country regressions – is unsatisfactory and inappropriate to be used for testing the hypothesis on the trade openness–growth link.
10. See Aghion *et al.* (1999) for detailed discussion on this debate.
11. See Thorbecke and Charumilind (2002) for a comprehensive review of this new political economy literature on the subject.
12. See Naschold (2004) for empirical evidence showing that in least developed countries the distribution effect is as important as growth effects for poverty reduction, while growth effect is larger in other low-income and middle-income countries.

13. See Birdsall (2002) for a discussion of many country cases where open capital markets adversely affected inequality and the poor.
14. This two-sector model of international trade can be easily extended to N-sector model (for example, see Dornbusch *et al.* 1977).
15. See Nayyar (2002) for the debate on issues and institutional reforms required for improving the governance mechanisms over the globalization process.

References

Addison, T. and G.A. Cornia (2001) 'Income Distribution Policies for Faster Poverty Reduction', *WIDER Discussion Paper* 2001/93, Helsinki: UNU-WIDER.

Agénor, P.-R. (2002) 'Does Globalization Hurt the Poor?', Mimeo, Washington, DC: World Bank.

Aggarwal, R. (2006) 'Globalization, Local Ecosystems and the Rural Poor', *World Development*, 34, 8: 1405–18.

Aghion, P., E. Caroli and C. Garcia-Peñalosa (1999) 'Inequality and Economic Growth: the Perspective of the New Growth Theories', *Journal of Economic Literature*, 37, 4: 1615–60.

Bardhan, P. (2006) 'Globalization and Rural Poverty', in M. Nissanke and E. Thorbecke (eds), *The Impact of Globalization on the World's Poor: Transmission Mechanisms*, Basingstoke: Palgrave Macmillan for UNU-WIDER.

Basu, K. (2003) 'Globalization and Marginalization: Re-examination of Development Policy', *BREAD Working Paper* 026, London: Bureau for Research in Economic Analysis of Development.

Basu, K. (2006) 'Globalization, Poverty and Inequality: What is the Relationship? What Can be Done?', in M. Nissanke and E. Thorbecke (eds), *The Impact of Globalization on the World's Poor: Transmission Mechanisms*, Basingstoke: Palgrave Macmillan for UNU-WIDER.

Birdsall, N. (2002) 'A Stormy Day on an Open Field: Asymmetry and Convergence in the Global Economy', in D. Gruen, T. O'Brien and J. Lawson (eds), *Globalization, Living Standards and Inequality*, Sydney: Reserve Bank of Australia and Australian Treasury.

Bourguignon, F. (2003) 'The Growth Elasticity of Poverty Reduction: Explaining Heterogeneity across Countries and Time Periods', in T.S. Eicher and S.J. Turnovsky (eds), *Inequality and Growth: Theory and Policy Implications*, Cambridge, MA: MIT Press.

Chen, S. and M. Ravallion (2004) 'How Have the World's Poorest Fared since the Early 1980s?', *World Bank Policy Research Department Working Paper* 3341, Washington, DC: World Bank.

Collier, P. and D. Dollar (2001) 'Can the World Cut Poverty in Half 1/2 ? How Policy Reform and Effective Aid Can Meet International Development Goals', *World Development*, 29: 1787–802.

Cornia, G.A. (2004) 'Inequality, Growth, and Poverty: An Overview of Changes of the Last Two Decades', in G.A. Cornia (ed.), *Inequality, Growth, and Poverty in an Era of Liberalization and Globalization*, Oxford and New York: Oxford University Press for UNU-WIDER.

Culpeper, R. (2002) 'Approaches to Globalization and Inequality within the International System', paper prepared for UNRISD Project on Improving Knowledge on Social Development in International Organization, September.

Deardorff, A.V. and R.M. Stern (2006) 'Globalization's Bystanders: Does Trade Liberalization Hurt Countries that Do Not Participate?', *World Development*, 34, 8: 1419–29.

Deaton, A. (2001) 'Counting the World's Poor: Problems and Possible Solutions', *World Bank Research Observer*, 16, 2: 125–47.

Deaton, A. (2002) 'Is World Poverty Falling', *Finance and Development* 39, 2: 4–7.

Deininger, K. and L. Squire (1996) 'A New Dataset Measuring Income Inequality', *World Bank Economic Review*, 10, 3: 565–91.

Dollar, D. (1992) 'Outward-Oriented Developing Economies Really Grow More Rapidly: Evidence from 95 LDCs, 1976–85', *Economic Development and Cultural Change*, 40, 3: 523–44.

Dollar, D. and A. Kraay (2001a) 'Growth *is* Good for the Poor', reprinted in A. Shorrocks and R. van der Hoeven (eds) (2004), *Growth, Inequality, and Poverty*, Oxford: Oxford University Press for UNU-WIDER.

Dollar, D. and A. Kraay (2001b) 'Trade, Growth and Poverty', *World Bank Policy Research Working Paper* 2615, Washington, DC: World Bank.

Dornbusch, R., S. Fisher and P. Samuelson (1977) 'Comparative Advantage, Trade and Payment in a Ricardian Model with a Continuum of Goods', *American Economic Review*, 67: 829–39.

Dowrick, S. and J.B. DeLong (2001) 'Globalization and Convergence', paper presented at the NBER Conference in Historical Perspective, 4–5 May, National Bureau of Economic Research, Cambridge, MA.

Graff, G., D. Roland-Holst and D. Zilberman (2006) 'Biotechnology and Poverty Reduction in Developing Countries', *World Development*, 34, 8: 1430–46.

Graham, C. (2006) 'Globalization, Poverty, Inequality and Insecurity: Some Insights from the Economics of Happiness', in M. Nissanke and E. Thorbecke (eds), *The Impact of Globalization on the World's Poor: Transmission Mechanisms*, Basingstoke: Palgrave Macmillan for UNU-WIDER.

Heshmati, A. (2006) 'The Relationship between Income Inequality, Poverty, and Globalization', in M. Nissanke and E. Thorbecke (eds), *The Impact of Globalization on the World's Poor: Transmission Mechanisms*, Basingstoke: Palgrave Macmillan for UNU-WIDER.

Jenkins, R. (2006) 'Globalization, Production and Poverty', in M. Nissanke and E. Thorbecke (eds), *The Impact of Globalization on the World's Poor: Transmission Mechanisms*, Basingstoke: Palgrave Macmillan for UNU-WIDER.

Kaldor, N. (1956) 'Alternative Theories of Distribution', *Review of Economic Studies*, 23, 2: 83–100.

Kalwij, A. and A. Verschoor (2006) 'A Decomposition of Poverty Trends across Regions: The Role of Variation in the Income and Inequality Elasticities of Poverty', in M. Nissanke and E. Thorbecke (eds), *The Impact of Globalization on the World's Poor: The Transmission Mechanisms*, Basingstoke: Palgrave Macmillan for UNU-WIDER.

Kaplinsky, R. (2000) 'Globalization and Unequalization: What Can Be Learned from Value Chain Analysis?', *Journal of Development Studies*, 37, 2: 117–46.

Li, H., L. Squire and H. Zou (1998) 'Explaining International and Intertemporal Variations in Income Inequality', *Economic Journal*, 108, 446: 26–43.

Ligon, E. (2006) 'Poverty and the Welfare Costs of Risk Associated with Globalization', *World Development*, 34, 8: 1446–57.

Milanovic, B. (2002) 'Can We Discern the Effect of Globalization on Income Distribution? Evidence from Household Budget Surveys', *World Bank Policy Research Working Papers* 2876, Washington, DC: World Bank.

Montalbano, P., U. Triulzi, C. Pietrobelli and A. Federici (2006) 'Trade Openness and Vulnerability in Central and Eastern Europe', in M. Nissanke and E. Thorbecke (eds), *The Impact of Globalization on the World's Poor: Transmission Mechanisms*, Basingstoke: Palgrave Macmillan for UNU-WIDER.

Naschold, F. (2004) 'Growth, Distribution, and Poverty Reduction: LDCs are Falling Further Behind', in A. Shorrocks and R. van der Hoeven (eds) (2004), *Growth, Inequality, and Poverty*, Oxford: Oxford University Press for UNU-WIDER.

Nayyar, D. (2002) *Governing Globalization: Issues and Institutions*, Oxford: Oxford University Press for UNU-WIDER.

Nissanke, M. and B. Ferrarini (2001) 'Debt Dynamics and Contingency Financing: Theoretical Reappraisal of the HIPC Initiative', *WIDER Discussion Paper* 2001/139, Helsinki: UNU-WIDER.

Nissanke, M. and H. Stein (2003) 'Financial Globalization and Economic Development: Towards an Institutional Foundation', *Eastern Economic Journal*, 29, 2: 287–308.

Nissanke, M. and E. Thorbecke (2006a) 'Overview', in M. Nissanke and E. Thorbecke (eds), *The Impact of Globalization on the World's Poor: Transmission Mechanisms*, Basingstoke: Palgrave Macmillan for UNU-WIDER.

Nissanke, M. and E. Thorbecke (2006b) 'Channels and Policy Debate in the Globalization-Inequality-Poverty Nexus', in M. Nissanke and E. Thorbecke (eds), *The Impact of Globalization on the World's Poor: Transmission Mechanisms*, Basingstoke: Palgrave Macmillan for UNU-WIDER.

Prasad, E., K. Rogoff, S. Wei and M.A. Kose (2003) 'Effects of Financial Globalization on Developing Countries: Some Empirical Evidence', *IMF Occasional Papers* 220, Washington, DC: IMF.

Pritchett, L. (1996) 'Measuring Outward Orientation in LDCs: Can It be Done?', *Journal of Development Economics*, 49: 307–35.

Pritchett, L. (1997) 'Divergence, Big Time', *Journal of Economic Perspectives*, 11, 3: 3–17.

Quah, D.T. (1996) 'Twin Peaks: Growth and Convergence in Models of Distribution Dynamics', *Economic Journal*, 106: 1045–55.

Ravallion, M. (1997) 'Can High-Inequality Countries Escape Absolute Poverty?', *Economics Letters*, 56: 51–7.

Ravallion, M. (2002) 'Growth, Inequality and Poverty: Looking Beyond Averages', paper presented at World Bank Annual Bank Conference of Development Economics, 24–6 June, Oslo.

Ravallion, M. (2004a) 'Competing Concepts of Inequality in the Globalization Debate', *World Bank Policy Research Working Paper* 3243, Washington, DC: World Bank.

Ravallion, M. (2004b) 'Pro-Poor Growth: A Primer', *World Bank Policy Research Working Paper* 3242, Washington, DC: World Bank.

Ravallion, M. (2006) 'Looking beyond Averages in the Trade and Poverty Debate', in M. Nissanke and E. Thorbecke (eds), *The Impact of Globalization on the World's Poor: Transmission Mechanisms*, Basingstoke: Palgrave Macmillan for UNU-WIDER.

Rodriguez, F. and D. Rodrik (1999) 'Trade Policy and Economic Growth: A Skeptic's Guide to the Cross-National Evidence', *NBER Working Paper* 7081, Cambridge, MA: National Bureau of Economic Research.

Sachs, J.D. and A. Warner (1995) 'Economic Reform and the Process of Global Integration', *Brookings Papers on Economic Activity* 1, Washington, DC: The Brookings Institution.

Shorrocks, A. and R. van der Hoeven (eds) (2004) *Growth, Inequality, and Poverty*, Oxford: Oxford University Press for UNU-WIDER.

Sindzingre, A. (2006) 'Explaining Threshold Effects of Globalization on Poverty: An Institutional Perspective', in M. Nissanke and E. Thorbecke (eds), *The Impact of Globalization on the World's Poor: Transmission Mechanisms*, Basingstoke: Palgrave Macmillan for UNU-WIDER.

Thorbecke, E. (2004) 'Economic Development, Income Distribution and Ethics', Mimeo, Ithaca: Cornell University.

Thorbecke, E. and C. Charumilind (2002) 'Economic Inequality and Its Socioeconomic Impact', *World Development*, 30, 9: 1477–95.

UNCTAD (2002) *The Least Developed Countries Report 2002*, Geneva: UNCTAD.

Wade, R.H. (2002) 'Globalization, Poverty and Income Distribution: Does Liberal Argument Hold?', paper presented at the conference Globalization, Living Standards and Inequality, 27–8 May, Sydney.

Williamson, J.G. (2002) 'Winners and Losers over Two Centuries of Globalization', *WIDER Annual Lecture* 6, Helsinki: UNU-WIDER. Reprinted in *WIDER Perspectives on Global Development* (2005), Basingstoke: Palgrave Macmillan.

World Bank (2002) *Globalization. Growth and Poverty*, a World Bank Research Report, New York: Oxford University Press for World Bank.

Zhao, J. (2006) 'The Role of Information in Technology Adoption under Poverty', in M. Nissanke and E. Thorbecke (eds), *The Impact of Globalization on the World's Poor: Transmission Mechanisms*, Basingstoke: Palgrave Macmillan for UNU-WIDER.

15
International Migration in an Era of Globalization: Has it Come Out of its Marginality?

Arjan de Haan

Introduction

About a decade ago, many people argued that migration was receiving insufficient attention in the development studies literature, and in policy making.[1] Much has changed since, with increasing research particularly on international migration (increasingly driven by security concerns), and a growing number of research and teaching centres and conference that focus often entirely on migration. Also, in development agencies the recognition that migration is important has been growing, and practical responses to this have been emerging.[2] A key question that remains, is whether and how this increased recognition of the significance of migration has entered mainstream development studies thinking, including debates on growth and poverty reduction. This question is prompted by two observations. First, despite the flourishing of migration studies, findings particularly regarding in-country migration – by far the largest proportion of total movements – often are not reflected in mainstream reports on development topics, such as the *World Development Reports*. While data constraints are important, they do not, in my view, provide sufficient justification for the continued lack of attention.

Second, conclusions about the role of migration in development differ hugely. Recent papers from World Bank staff show the polarization in the debate. On the one hand there is an assumption that movement of labour – as part of a well-functioning integrated labour market – would lead to the elimination of disparities and equalization of development. Pritchett (2003) stresses that there are economic, technological and demographic reasons for much larger labour mobility and migration flows across borders (than exist at present), and that 'migration is the Millennium Development Goal plan B' (and this is prevented by ideas and perceptions about migration).[3] While most of world inequality is because of differences *across* countries, international population distribution has 'failed' to adjust.[4] And in one of the first attempts to quantify the impact of migration and remittances on poverty, Adams and Page (2003) conclude that an increase of 10 per cent in a country's share of international migrants leads to a 2 per cent decline in $1-a-day poverty. International remittances too are shown to have a strong impact on reducing poverty. However, in the words of Adams and Page, these estimates are made with heroic assumptions regarding data, and I believe no evidence that the correlation shows causation.

On the other hand, there are both empirical and theoretical objections against the idea that migration would lead to reducing disparities in development. Ellerman's (2003) impression is that 'much of the literature is excessively optimistic about the impact of south–north migration on the South'. For example, temporary labour migration such as by *Gastarbeiter* in Germany has not stimulated development in the sending regions. It is not impossible for such migration to be beneficial, but empirical evidence tends to show, for example, that the 'best and brightest' are over-represented among migrants, and migration often acts as a safety valve to relieve social pressures. The developmental impact of remittances has generally not been well established ('increased income is not increased development'). In an overview paper on the relationship between migration and inequality, Black *et al.* (2004) highlight that international migration carries significant risks and cost, and that it does not always reduce the inequalities as intended by the migrants. Migration and inequality exert mutual influences, the relationship depends strongly on the type of migration (as well as type of inequality), and a hierarchy of migration possibilities and opportunities and 'migration humps' exist.

What the above suggests – and polarized discussions about 'brain drain' (discussed below) suggest the same – is that the observations of Papademetriou and Martin (1991) and Appleyard (1991), and Sorensen *et al.* (2002) a decade later, that the migration–development relationship is unsettled, still appear true, despite the increased attention to migration.

In my view, the neglect of labour migration as a central phenomenon in the development process and the polarization in the debate are linked. Many serious studies ignore the existence of migration, possibly seriously influencing the results: for example, two studies on poverty reduction in India have ignored the role of remittances, possibly underestimating the poverty-reducing impact of urban-based economic growth (Ravallion and Datt 1996; Besley and Esteve-Volart 2004). At the same time, many of the studies that do try to incorporate migration findings do so at the cost of conceptual rigour and clarity, for example using 'stocks' rather than 'flows' of migrants, or using 'net migration' (which conceals movements of in- and out-migration, and movement to and fro by the same people), as an indicator for analyzing the impact of migration on economic convergence across regions.[5] While the political nature of the question will continue to provide blocks to reaching any forms of consensus, the disagreements are partly caused by the lack of care in defining the subject.

There is a possible further reason for the continued marginalization of migration: the relative lack of labour market or employment analysis in development (poverty) studies and policies.[6] Islam (2004), for example, argues that 'rigorous analysis of the role of employment in the linkage between economic growth and poverty reduction appears to be missing'. The Millennium Development Goals include no meaningful reference to labour or employment and certainly, compared to the attention that has been paid to poverty data, employment data has been mostly neglected. While discussion of the absence of labour market or employment analysis is beyond the scope of this chapter, it seems safe to assume that if labour markets and employment are not regularly included in poverty analysis, migration is even less likely to feature in that analysis.

To explore the questions about the role of migration in development studies, and the growth and poverty debates in particular, this chapter does two things. The first section argues that, in fact, we do know quite a bit about the migration–development relationship, provided we are careful with definitions, and allow for context-specificity to be a key component of our knowledge arsenal. The second part will go back to theoretical models around migration – and in their early incarnations how they were placed in mainstream development thinking – to try to understand why the movement of labour seems to be so badly represented in mainstream development thinking. The concluding section suggests what conditions need to be fulfilled for migration studies to become a more integral part of development thinking.

Migration, development, poverty reduction: what do we know?

On the basis of earlier review, joint work with Rogaly,[7] as well as a review of a recent multi-donor research project on pro-poor growth,[8] this section highlights what we *do* know about migration, and how it links to development. A key part of the argument will be around context-specificity. The problem in the migration–development question is not, I argue, that we cannot establish links. However, links are context-dependent, complex and multisectoral, assessments depend on indicator of wellbeing chosen, and different effects possibly offset each other. This section divides the migration–development relationship into a range of interactions, increasingly difficult to assess. It should be stressed that the different aspects-interact, making quantitative assessments problematic.

Who migrates? And who doesn't?

Part of the answer to the question of migration–development lies in the answer to the question: who migrates? Characteristics of migrants reflect labour demand structures, and suggest specific ways migration affects livelihoods of families, gender, social and economic relations. Labour migration is usually by young able-bodied people. They are often men, but by no means exclusively – gender patterns of migration relate to a range of political, economic and social conditions. Migrants are often not from the poorest region, usually not the poorest in the areas of origin, and often slightly better educated or skilled. Further, migration patterns are structured by social divides, such as caste in India, religion, or ethnicity in Vietnam. Evidence on landownership as determinant or correlates of migration typically varies strongly, and can change over time. Comparisons of incomes show a mixed and varied picture, with migrants often not far behind the average or non-migrants in areas of destination, making up over time – but an important finding is that the diversity of migrants is at least as large as among the non-migrant population.[9]

Different migrants also may have different motives.[10] For some it is an accumulation strategy. For the poorest it tends to be a survival strategy, often availing of the least-remunerating opportunities, and evidence exists that migration may reinforce exploitative structures like debt-bondage relationships.[11] Savings for dowries is an important motive for female migrants in western Africa, and in other cases too migration may be linked to a particular period in the life cycle. Thus, there are important variations, and the characteristics depend on economic, political as well as cultural circumstances – changing over time, partly under the influence of migration itself.

An important general finding – for understanding migration–development links – concerns the importance of networks and migration streams. Due to the segmentation of migration streams (and how they 'mature' over time), migrants tend to come from specific areas, and they are not necessarily the poorest from rural areas – particularly not when the migratory jobs are relatively attractive and have higher returns. People who are better off may pave the way for migrants with fewer resources.[12]

There is some evidence that the poorest, least skilled, least physically capable and without networks tend to migrate less. However, the types of migration the poorest engage in is also least likely to be captured in surveys and census, as may be the case in Vietnam and China where formal registration may determine being captured in surveys, but also in India where for example rural–rural migration is likely to be underrecorded (see, for example, Rogaly *et al.* 2002). Moreover, as indicated above, for the poorest migration often comes as an extreme survival strategy, suggesting that *when* they migrate, this is likely to be less beneficial than the migration by the better off.

Push and pull

Pull factors are widely relevant in explaining national as well as international migration movements (as discussed below, central elements of the classic Todaro models remain undisputed). Though there are some doubts about the responsiveness of migrants from poorer areas, and evidence of existence of a 'migration hump' (Martin 2005), most experience indicates that migrants do move in reaction to newly developing opportunities. For example, recent panel data analysis using a standard international migration model found robust 'pull effects' of improvements of mean income in host countries.[13]

There is more controversy about the relationship between migration and development in the catchment areas. Earlier migration models identified the less developed areas as likely candidates for migration. Crisis in areas of origin tends to be associated with increased migration, as the increased migration from Ecuador at the end of the 1990s indicates.[14] Many development specialists have argued for rural development to reduce migration pressures. But empirical studies (see, for example, Mosse *et al.* 2002) show a very diverse picture of reasons for out-migration. People from the poorest areas often do not have access to the most rewarding activities (e.g. Mallee 1996 for China), in urban areas (Skeldon 1997b) or abroad, though they may migrate to activities nearby, for seasonal agricultural and less rewarding work (e.g. Connell *et al.* 1976, for Indian villages).

Crucially, much evidence shows that development in areas of origin usually goes hand-in-hand with migration. Expectations that rural development will decrease out-migration may be unjustified (though it is likely to change the conditions of migration and composition of migrants); 'poverty reduction is not in itself a migration-reducing strategy' (Sorensen *et al.* 2002). For example, in the Punjab, the green revolution occurred simultaneously with both high rates of out-migration as well as in-migration from poorer Indian states, and in China the development of rural enterprises appeared to increase rates of out-migration (except among the more educated peasants; Liang and White 1997). According to Skeldon (1997a), it is impossible to envisage development without migration, and migration *is* development; for example, while Japan was urbanizing emigration was increasing.

Effects of migration

Evidence on effects of migration is controversial; the emphasis above on the closed interlinkage between development and migration already foreshadowed this. With respect to international migration and receiving countries, the consensus seems that immigration has improved economic welfare, including raising tax revenue[15] – given restrictive immigration policies this is unsurprising as receiving countries allow mainly people with skills for which there is an excess demand in the labour market. Most research, at aggregate levels, seems to contradict the popular belief that immigration contributes to unemployment, or substantial decreases in wages in host societies,[16] though there is of course micro-evidence that employers can attract migrants to reduce wages and bargaining powers of local workers.[17]

Much less clarity exists about the effect of migration on development of areas of origin, including in agriculture, even though this is perhaps the most relevant question for development studies and policies.[18] Very few studies trace the effects of migration and remittances on villages of origin, even in areas with long traditions of out-migration.[19] Leaving the question regarding remittances till the next subsection, we find much contradictory evidence and expectation. There is evidence that migrants contribute to building of schools or other community activities (Russell *et al.* 1990). For example, migration can help to alleviate unemployment (Ghosh 1992). At the same time, out-migration can lead to a shortage of labour in some contexts,[20] perhaps particularly the more skilled and, almost inevitably, entrepreneurial parts of the population. Field studies in villages of migrant origin in Jiangsu, Anhui, Sichuan and Gansu provinces in China, where out-migration was caused by land scarcity and rising costs of agriculture, showed a shortage of labour caused by migration. Supporting Ellerman's concern, while remittances benefit families, they did not contribute to village development or the establishment and maintenance of village services, including those for facilitating agricultural development (Croll and Ping 1997). The World Bank Poverty Assessment for El Salvador highlights that remittances are important for raising household incomes (and stimulating demand for goods).[21] But in assessing impact, the Assessment stresses, the counterfactual is important too: families might have increased their labour supply in local markets if migration opportunities and remittances did not exist.[22]

Not much is known, it seems, about the role of migrants and remittances on enhancing efficiency in agriculture. In England in the eighteenth century, and possibly elsewhere in Europe, migrants appear to have played important innovatory roles (Thirsk 1991). Lakshmansamy's (1990) literature review concludes that migration and remittances modernize the rural sector, both directly and indirectly, through their impact on the production-increasing technological and institutional changes in the agricultural sector.[23] Nevertheless, the positive impacts are contingent, and depend on many factors like seasonality of movement, educational levels, length of time spent away, assets and social structures and institutions, allowing women and others to pursue activities previously reserved for men and household heads.

For decades, there has been a particular concern about 'brain drain' (usually international migration by the better skilled, but equally important within countries). Recent analysis has started to look at the complexity of the issues involved, though hampered by data availability and quality. Docquier and Rapoport (2004) highlight that international migration has become increasingly selective. Detrimental effects could include increased international inequality, particularly if migrants are disconnected from those left behind. Beneficial effects could include remittances, return migration, creation of trade and business networks and incentive effects on human capital formation at home. Cross-country analysis indicates limited evidence that return migration is significant among the highly skilled, or that they contribute to technology diffusion. They find positive benefits of prospect of migration on human capital formation and GDP growth – leading to a conclusion that 'brain drain should not induce developing countries to reduce education expenditures'. However, and crucially, effects are different for different countries, bigger countries with a smaller proportion of migrants experience larger gains.

Most analysis of migration is very temporary, focusing on the top of the migration hump. Impacts, however, can be long-term, and fortunes can reverse. One important example of this is the likelihood that migration opportunities decline. There is some literature on the effects of this. On the one hand, areas of origin function as a safety valve, as seen in Indonesia during 1997 and many transition countries.[24] Other assessments, for example on the effect of changing South African policies on migrant communities in Lesotho, Malawi and Swaziland are less positive. Chirwa (1997: 650) gives a generally optimistic view about the effects of oscillating labour migration in the region, and describes the reasons for success and failure in the use of returns from migration: the 'social, economic, as well as political disruptions caused by this process are just too great for the weak economies and fragile political structures of the labour-supplying countries and local communities to effectively handle'. Leliveld (1997) describes the effects of declining migration on households in rural Swaziland: employment possibilities in Swaziland are limited, and relatively young households, with few working members and a weak economic position are among the most vulnerable in this context. Also, there is a considerable literature on the negative effects of sudden barriers to international migration, such as during the 1990–1 Gulf War which had an enormous impact on sending countries.[25]

Remittances: amounts and impact

Central in much of the thinking on impact of migration has been the question of remittances, one of the new development mantras, in the words of Kapur (2004). Economic theories tend to have rather different interpretations of remittances (insurance, bequest), as they have of migration more generally. It is generally recognized that data are difficult to interpret. Where restrictions on transfers exist official data are likely to imply underreporting (in-kind transfers and gifts are also significant). In an increasing number of household surveys remittances are captured (though in expenditure surveys remittances will be implicit), allowing in my view more analysis than often assumed.[26]

There is a large amount of literature on remittances – conclusions about both amounts and uses differ.[27] I focus here on internal migration, the more difficult question. Reardon's overview of the importance of the rural non-farm income in Africa (covering 25 case studies) is helpful to give an idea of magnitude, and how this differs across locations. This showed that on average 45 per cent of total rural income was non-farm, differing between 22 and 93 per cent. In areas not close to major cities, migration earnings constituted 20 per cent of total non-farm earnings, whereas it was as high as 75 per cent in areas close to major cities.[28]

More recent studies exist, including Ellis and Freeman's (2004) livelihood study in Uganda, Kenya, Tanzania and Malawi. They stress that reduction of dependence on agriculture is a key way out of poverty. In Tanzania, for example, about half of household income is derived from agriculture (less so for the better off) and of the other half 36 per cent was non-farm income, 11 per cent was wages and a mere 4 per cent was transfers (slightly higher for lower income groups). A similar small importance of transfers, and also higher for lower incomes, was found in Uganda (Ellis and Bahiigwa 2003). So roughly, across Africa about a quarter of total rural incomes may be derived from migration, but with wide variations, greatly depending on locations, and with different importance for different socioeconomic groups.[29]

Apart from the uncertainty in estimates of remittances, assessments of impact need to be sensitive to the complexity in which this is embedded. First, they need to take account of the fact that this counts only successful migration, and there is a possibility that many migrants have *not* remitted despite having invested heavily. Second, data on remittances need to take account of reverse flows (Lipton 1980; Findley 1997), of initial investment, but also, for example, food from villages of origin to cities. Third, as highlighted already in the discussion on brain drain, from a home country public policy perspective remittances need to be offset against the (public) investment in education and other forms of publicly funded investments.[30]

Evaluation of impact of remittances seems to have shifted since the 1970s, when there was much stress on the 'conspicuous consumption' of migrants and their relatives, towards more positive views, focusing, for example, upon the conditions needed to secure the investment of remittances and, internationally, the emphasis of increasing remittances and how they have far outstripped official aid. Authors that have emphasized the lack of productive investment include Oberai and Singh, who concluded that only 6 per cent of remittances flowing into the Indian Punjab were used for productive investment (though remittances did improve distribution of income).[31] On the other hand, literature that emphasizes productive investments include Papademetriou and Martin (1991) and various publications by Adams (1991; 1996: 149–70; 1998). Durand *et al.* (1996a; 1996b) show income from migration stimulates economic activity, both directly and indirectly, and that it leads to significantly higher levels of employment, investment and income. Finally, it needs pointing out that even very small amounts of remittances can be vital for poor people, including their food security.[32]

Thus, levels of remittances vary widely – depending on various factors such as accessibility of the home village, employment opportunities, costs of living, ease of remitting and the 'orientation' of the migrant – and estimates are usually unreliable. Evidence on the way remittances are used also shows diversity and can be modelled in rather different ways. There is no doubt that remittances can have negative and positive consequences – evidence suggests that the way remittances are used depends on the form of migration, the characteristics of the migrants and those who stay behind, and conditions for use of remittances and returning migrants. This, finally, points to one of the complexities of understanding impact of migration: the conditions that make remittances helpful for development or poverty reduction are generally the same conditions that made migrants leave in the first place.[33]

Inequality back on the agenda: and what do we know about migration?

The reappearance of inequality in the development debate should give some new impetus to the research on migration, as it already has with respect to international migration. As emphasized by Pritchett, migration has to have an impact, and has to reduce overall income inequality. However, assessments of this, too, are very varied and are very dependent on unit and indicator of analysis (Black *et al.* 2004).

The multi-donor research programme 'Operationalizing Pro-Poor Growth'[34] highlights a key dilemma in assessing migration: while it generally helps to reduce poverty and increase income of the poor, migration and remittances also lead to increased inequality within countries. A similar theme was highlighted in the Indian Village Studies project in the 1970s, which showed that rural–urban migration did not tend to equalize incomes, *between* or *within* regions, for a range of reasons: the selective nature of migration, providing higher returns to the better off and better educated, prevents equalization within areas of origin; there are costs and barriers and associated with migration, including access to information about opportunities, which tends to steer the gains of migration to the rich; absence of the most productive household members leads to a lowering of labour-intensity; the volume of net remittances was usually low; and return migrants are likely to be the old, sick and unsuccessful, and skills brought back unlikely to be of much help (Lipton 1982). Islam (1991) concluded that the negative effects of migration to the Gulf from villages in Chittagong in Bangladesh outweighed positive ones: land became concentrated in the hands of migrant families, who turned into non-farmers, which contributed to a decrease in production. Land prices went up, and so did the cost of labour, though not so high as to lead to labour-saving in agriculture.

But here too, generalizations appear meaningless. Some forms of migration lead to equalizing income within regions, though not necessarily between sending and receiving regions. In some cases migration increases income inequality, in some cases it lowers it, this relationship may change over time as has been shown in Mexico, for example. The unit of analysis matters, too, as increased male income does not necessarily translate into increased wellbeing of women. While in some cases migration and remittances have led to development, in other cases it has not. A key issue appears to be not migration itself but the condition under which people leave and conditions for development generally which determine the impact of migration.

Concluding: what do we know?

There is a point to the annoying complexity or diversity highlighted above (still only a very selective overview of the literature): it appears to me that the value of generalizing about migrants, migration and its impact is very limited. Possibly, the number of people who move is as large as those who do not, and the conditions under which they do move are as diverse as the conditions under which people stay where they are. Few straightforward conclusions or easy generalizations emerge, though some conclusions can be drawn.

First, most analysts probably tend to agree that migration emerges out of differences in opportunity, and that workers and labour markets generally are responsive to opportunities (though there will be degrees of integration of labour markets – one of the problems of migration studies is that they focus on migrants and less on the wider environment). The 'migration optimists' tend to argue that where migration does not lead to reduction in disparities, this tends to be due to barriers for migrants, such as international borders. The 'migration pessimist' emphasizes that there is very little empirical evidence that shows that migration does in fact lead to reduction in disparities. Importantly, migration will have different impacts in different contexts. While the classic Harris-Todaro model was not wrong in terms of predicting a transfer of labour from rural to urban areas, it may have been optimistic, at least implicitly, about the speed with which this would occur, and almost certainly wrong in the assumption that the migration process amounts to a lottery.

The evidence on remittances also shows that context matters greatly, in both their amount and use. I think that on balance the literature supports Ellerman's view, that the migration optimists tend to ignore the evidence on first-round effects looking for second- and third-order effects, and I have stressed that an assessment of impact of migration and remittances need to be seen in context of wider environment in which migration operates, and address contradictory and offsetting factors. The optimists' and pessimists' conclusions are not necessarily incompatible: the point is that conditions and context seem crucial for the chances that migration and remittances end up stimulating development in areas of origin. This may be of key relevance for the chances that migration leads to a reduction in disparities, as the same absent conditions that would make remittances lead to development were the reasons migrants left in the first place.

Theorizing migration: what good has this done?

Against this review of the empirical complexity of characteristics, causes and consequences of migration, this second part of the chapter will review the models in which migration has been analyzed. Like the empirical description, this will highlight a diversity in and controversy over approaches, and will tentatively answer the question how different approaches make it more or less likely that migration can be understood as an integral and often central part of development processes, and what the policy implications of the different approaches are.

Job lottery, individual motives, but only during 'transition'

While earlier theories of migration tried to explain volumes of migration, for example, by reference to distance, probably the most important theoretical starting point for migration studies since the 1960s has been the model by Harris and Todaro (1970) in the *American Economic Review* (also Todaro 1969). In this, a prospective migrant is expected to weigh the difference between the expected earnings from formal sector urban employment, an initial period of informal sector employment and the expected earnings in the village. While criticized by many, empirical analyses have shown that the model has certain predictive value. Lucas,[35] Hatton and Williamson (1992) and Larson and Mundlak (1997), all in one way or another have reaffirmed the validity of the model. More recently, Lucas (2002) provides a theoretical model of rural–urban migration based on Todaro-Harris, emphasizing the increasing skill levels in urban areas, and widening gap with agricultural workers.

It may be worth pausing at this dualistic model (two -or three-sector), and the role that dualistic thinking has had in the development studies literature. While its historical origins have been traced to the colonial Dutch economist Boeke (Breman 1980), the dualistic model draws heavily on the surplus-labour model developed by Lewis.[36] With a strong focus on modernization and agricultural transformation (perhaps foreshadowing the undue emphasis on 'formal' employment),[37] Lewis predicted that non-agricultural employment would increase without real wages rising initially, until surplus labour was absorbed. Well-functioning labour markets were thought to be key to this process of transformation. This provides some clue to the question why the Todaro and Lewis type of migration and labour market analysis has had limited value for the development debate. While it may help in analyzing labour-market developments in processes of structural (rural–urban, industrial) transformation, a priori it seems of limited value outside the contexts of such structural transformations. This seems important for four related sets of reasons.

First, the segmented market models emphasized by Todaro and others have apparent relevance in describing empirical realities that show clearly diverging wage rates in those different sectors.[38] But it may have contributed to *ignoring* forms of migration that are at least as important as those related to 'modernization', particularly (intrasectoral) rural–rural migration, which according to various observers constitutes quantitatively the most important form of migration in countries like India.

Second, it appears to have led to a conceptualization of labour markets that is restricted to, or at least focusing on, moves out of agriculture,[39] reducing the relevance of it to discussions in Africa, for example, at least the parts where urbanization has remained low, for periods where return to rural areas have dominated, and when movements within the agricultural or rural sector have been predominant.[40]

Third, the conceptualization as clearly differentiated markets makes it difficult to take account of connections of labour markets to, for example, product or output markets, which tend to be of central importance for small traders and producers.[41]

Finally, while the 1960s theories were situated in discussions of structural changes, the focus of Todaro-type of analysis has been on individual incentives (and remittances): this makes it suitable for inclusion in individualistic types of poverty analysis that have prevailed, but has arguably removed it from its origin in debates on economic and societal transformations.[42]

Beyond individual motives, but beyond 'rationality'?

At least two sets of theoretical innovations – partly related, both known under the term 'new economics of migration' – have taken migration studies beyond the individual incentives central to the Todaro type of models: one that has taken households rather than individuals as unit of analysis, the other which has focused on migration as overcoming market imperfections.

A fairly recent development in the migration literature has been the emphasis on family and family strategies as crucial elements in migration decisions. Whereas the Todaro model focuses on the individuals as rational actors, the 'new economics of migration' emphasize the family as unit of analysis:

> even though the entities that engage in migration are often individual agents, there is more to labour migration than an individualistic optimizing behaviour. Migration by one person can be due to, fully consistent with, or undertaken by a group of persons, such as the family. (Stark 1991: 3)

The family is conceptualized as a coalition *vis-à-vis* the rest of the world, family members share costs of and rewards of migration. Migration is seen as a form of portfolio diversification by families, in which they enter into chosen contractual arrangements, and remittances exemplify the 'intertemporal contractual arrangement' between migrant and family, with families investing in migrants, migrants in families and both expecting returns from that.[43]

Subsequent economic models to explain remittance behaviour have been of two types (de la Brière *et al.* 1997). First, building on the work of Rosenzweig and others, models focus on insurance contracts between the migrant and the household left behind, as a means of coping with household risk, and on migration and remittances as a form of portfolio diversification (options to receive remittances are weighed against the returns from local sources of income). The second type of model builds on literature around bequest motive: remittances as investments in household assets that the migrant will later inherit, which is supported by analysis of difference in remittance behaviour between men and women (caused by gender-differentiated inheritance rules).

Using household rather than individuals as the central unit of analysis appears appropriate, for a number of reasons. First, its sits much more comfortably with much sociological and anthropological (and livelihoods) analysis – like Krokfors' (1995: 54–64) concept of multi-active households, the emphasis on families investing in education for migration to the formal urban sector (Adepoju and Mbugua 1997: 54), or van Velsen's (1959) analysis of urban migrants' awareness of the temporary nature of their urban existence – though of course with less emphasis on context-specific and cultural factors determining household forms and interactions, and possibly biased towards the unitary household model criticized by feminist authors.[44] Second, it is much better placed to take account of the fact that much if not most migration is 'circular' – i.e. constituting continued interactions with areas of origins rather than a one-way and one-off move – taking it out of the (implicit) emphasis on 'transition' in the rural–urban model of Todaro. Third, in principle it appears that a focus on households makes it easier to incorporate findings into the dominant form of poverty analysis, with its focus on households, albeit with an inevitable sedentary bias.

However, while its unit of analysis is more promising than that of the individual in the job lottery, the new economics remains firmly grounded in a functionalistic and individualistic economic framework. Migration is seen primarily in terms of economic function (contractual arrangements) within the household,[45] without much attention to the 'non-economic' factors that drive such decisions, or the cultural determinant of household forms themselves, despite the fact that household forms and composition are key to structuring migration processes (and vice versa).[46] Further, migration is seen as a solution to market failures, such as the absence of access to insurance or, for example, to investment in education: while rightly broadening the focus from the simple job–wage consideration in the Todaro model, this emphasizes a functionality of migration that can provide only a very partial explanation of movements of people, and has little to say about the multiple and bi-directional links of migration and remittances to broader processes of development.

The structuration of migration

For a broader understanding of migration and how it links to development processes we have to move largely, it seems, outside the economics literature. Alternative conceptualizations are manifold, of course, and here I stress merely the literature that emphasizes the social institutions structuring migration, and the critical literature that has linked migration to capitalist and colonial development.[47]

There is a great amount of literature that emphasizes the way migration and social and other institutions are linked.[48] Complementing migration models like Todaro's, this emphasizes the continuity, in terms of social institutions, that marks migration processes, and sees migration decisions as part of continuing efforts, consistent with traditional values (though sometimes seen as 'unravelling social fabric')[49] to solve recurrent problems, often but not only related to resource scarcity. Migration processes are seen as embedded in social relations.[50] Gender analysis has of course contributed greatly, as indicated above in the discussion on household models of migration, not only in understanding differentiated motivations for and impacts of migration, but also more broadly in the way migration processes are structured, emphasizing power and exploitation: 'gender is an essential tool for unpicking the migration process'.[51] Finally, research focusing on migrant networks has played a very important role in helping to see movements of people as part, not only of 'traditions of migration' and interpreted in a 'cumulative migration theory',[52] but also wider processes of social and economic development.[53]

It seems that most of the literature that has made the migration–development links central to analyses, has been from critical and Marxist perspectives. Southern African academics in particular have been engaged in continued debate about migration and its relations with apartheid, uneven capitalist development and rural change. Partly in the context of urbanization and the informal sector (Safa 1982; Breman 1996), but also with focus on movement of migrant workers within rural areas (Breman 1985; Mansell Prothero and Chapman 1985), and building on historical analysis (Breman 1990), these critical studies explicitly challenged the individualistic assumptions underlying models like Todaro's, and have described migration as an inevitable part of transition towards or development of capitalism. Similarly, international migration and remittances have been conceptualized in the context of advantages for global capital and richer nations.[54]

Particularly Marxist models can be criticized for focusing exclusively on economic factors (of exploitation). It is clear that the same questions are relevant as with respect to neoclassical models, that migration processes can be understood adequately only as the outcome of interaction of a diversity of factors, including social-cultural influences as well as economic forces, gendered norms and rules, and how migration in turn alters these, and in the interaction of structures and agency. One of the keys to understand the migration process and integrate findings into broader development debates is to draw on a diversity of disciplines.

Concluding: can migration studies come out of marginality?

The key question for this chapter is not whether there are enough studies on migration. Clearly, enormous amounts of literature have been produced, with an apparent upsurge of studies during the last few years, particularly related to international migration, but also – for example, in the context of livelihoods research – on migration within countries. Neither is the key question whether we know enough about migration. Again, there is no shortage of knowledge about what drives migration, and whether migrants are able to succeed – though the review in the first part of this chapter puts a strong emphasis on context specificity, and suggests that there is a specific gap with respect to understanding the impact on or (more appropriately) interrelationship with broader development processes in areas of origin.

Further, the overview of theories in the previous session suggests there is as much complementarity as there are differences. Individual motives and push-pull considerations matter, as do the households of which migrants are a part. Social network and institution cannot be ignored in understanding processes and outcomes of migration, and historical studies have shown clearly how migration streams were created in the interest of capital and colonial powers – and in a large number of cases the effects of these can still be observed. The problem, perhaps, is not so much in what is known about migration, but that dominant debates do not fully appreciate the importance of insights from different disciplines and traditions, and different policy implications.

The key question that remains, and which relates closely to this specific gap in the literature, is whether migration studies have become an integral part of the understanding of development processes, including growth, poverty reduction, or rural development, which, as argued, does not necessarily lead to a reduction in migration. Though the burden of proof remains, my impression is that it remains difficult to integrate an understanding of mobility, labour migration in particular, in mainstream development studies texts.

To be fair, the reasons for this are manifold, and in conclusion I suggest it is worth thinking of these barriers under the following headings or reasons (not necessarily related). First, it is important to understand the political-economy of research itself – though this would take us well beyond the scope of this study. Interest in migration is to a great extent politically driven, sometimes with a main urge to reduce migration, sometimes to revalue the contribution of migration, recently of course also in the context of security concerns. The political motivation provides a partial explanation for the emphasis on international migration, in turn possibly contributing to isolation of the study of migration from that of broader development processes.

Second, apart from the fact that generalizations about migration are difficult to arrive at, data problems and scarcity continues to hamper understanding of migration, particularly its links to development in a broader sense. Though more analysis is possible, and more data (including on national migration) available than often assumed, quantitative analysis in particular is complicated by movement of people and, for example, more panel data are required than presently available in development studies.[55] Also, it is crucial to highlight the complexity of the impact of remittances on development, including possible underrecording of most vulnerable forms of migration, the counterfactual of not migrating, and offsetting gains and losses. Conversely, much migration analysis does exactly that, studying the movement of people and/or remittances, but often as isolated phenomena, rather than as integral parts of social and economic development. In particular, and perhaps reflecting the same political determination highlighted above, migration studies still tend to neglect the impact of migration on sending regions and countries.

A third point relates to the complexity of migration in the sense that, as argued above, it appears impossible and perhaps even meaningless to formulate general-izations about impacts of migration, for example on inequality, or development in areas of origin. This is not as benign as an emphasis on context-specificity sug-gests. What this highlights is exactly the need to see migration as an integral part of wider development processes, as it appears that the conditions and policies that make migration and remittances successful (e.g. as highlighted in discussion of brain drain) appear to be general conditions that make development and growth likely (and the same issues that often made migrants leave in the first place). Processes of migration, thus, can be seen as markers of wider development processes – but only as they are understood as an integral part of those rather than (as is more common) isolated phenomena.

Fourth, and discussed in the second main part of this chapter, many of the theoretical frameworks under which much migration analysis has been carried out, arguably, have hampered the understanding of migration as part of wider development processes. While household models of migration appear an appro-priate extension of the models focusing on individuals (and seem to fit in well with the dominant forms of poverty analysis), highlighting the circular nature of much migration, they continue to isolate households and their migration move-ments from wider processes of development, underestimating the importance of bi-directional linkages.

Anthropological literature, for example, on southern Africa, has portrayed much richer pictures of this complexity, and it seems important to ensure that these approaches inform strongly understanding of the role of migration. Similarly, the critical migration literature has highlighted many aspects of political economy that are key to understanding migration. However, and as a fifth possible reason for the marginality of migration analysis, the predominant development debate does often not draw sufficiently on insights from these disciplines, hence unintentionally further undermining the possibility of enriching understanding of development process by migration analysis. For future research agendas, partic-ularly (though not only) in migration and its role in development processes, it is strongly recommended that development economists look closely at anthropological and other studies.

Much of this may not come as a surprise, at present. But it may well have been a big surprise for the classical development thinkers around the 1950s, for whom labour mobility was considered a key part of processes of modernization. But in these classics, labour markets too were very important, and much of the recent development debate seems to have ignored the importance of labour markets and employment (e.g. highlighted by the absence of meaningful indicators in the MDGs). Moreover, the classics were rich in institutional details, and as argued above an institutional understanding of migration appears key to ensuring that the role of migration can be seen as part of wider development processes and, for example, to heed Ellerman's warning regarding conflating remittances with development.

Notes

The chapter draws heavily on experiences gained within DFID and conversations with colleagues in DFID and elsewhere. It has benefited greatly from comments during the UNU-WIDER jubilee conference in June 2005, and detailed suggestions made by two anonymous referees.

1. See for example McDowell and de Haan (1997).
2. Again, with much focus on international migration, and a relative neglect of national migration. See for example, Maimbo and Ratha (2005) and the discussion featured on info.worldbank.org/etools/vod/PresentationView.asp?PID=1568&EID=767. See also www.worldbank.org/socialpolicy, which highlights the role of international migration for new frontiers of social policy (all accessed December 2005).
3. See also Pritchett (2004), which emphasizes the dominance of movement within countries. Pritchett, who commented on an earlier version of this study, is currently at the World Bank but wrote his papers on migration while at the Kennedy School.
4. Moses and Letnes (2004) estimate through an applied equilibrium model that liberalization of international migration restrictions, resulting in a 10 per cent increase in international migration, would lead to an efficiency gain of US$774 billion – but in their own view with very problematic assumptions and other analytical shortcomings.
5. Cashin and Sahay (1996). There is a continued debate the question whether and why rates of labour migration are low in India, see, for example, Munshi and Rosenzweig (2005).
6. Treatment of this subject here is largely based on recent discussions with representatives of WIEGO, 'Informal Labour Markets and Pro-Poor Growth', 21–3 March 2005.
7. de Haan (1999); de Haan and Rogaly (2002).
8. de Haan (2005). Many of the case studies in this research programme provided much information about migration, and the synthesis work asked the question about the role of processes of growth and particularly increasing inequality.
9. de Haan and Dubey (2002), with NSS data for India, and review of evidence from elsewhere, including the UK.
10. As research on Ghana shows, while half of the population may be categorized as migrant, reasons are very diverse, and only a small part of this is directly related to motives to find work (Litchfield and Waddington 2003). In India the largest proportion of migration (particularly short-distance) as registered in the census may be for marriage; most women move to the house of their husband, and move outside their village of birth.
11. See Mosse *et al.* (2002) for detailed anthropological study of western India.
12. The edited volume by de Haan and Rogaly (2002) highlights, for various contexts of migration, the importance of social networks, and how social norms co-determine structures of migration, that is, who migrates, under what circumstances and potential benefits.

13. Mayda (2005). Further factors affecting migration rates are inequality in origin and destination, geographical, cultural and demographic factors, and migration policies. The theoretical model referred to is from Clark, Hatton and Williamson, on US immigrants.
14. Hall (2005). I thank one of the anonymous referees for emphasizing the links between macroeconomic factors and international migration, while my study focuses mainly on more micro factors.
15. A study in the UK on the impact of immigration on public finances showed a growing contribution (amounting to 10 per cent by 2003–04), at a substantially higher rate than the UK-born population, and a greater net contributor (Sriskandarajah *et al.* 2005).
16. For example, for the UK, Glover *et al.* (2001); this may be partly due to the fact that migration tends to occur in areas and sectors with labour scarcities.
17. For example, for western India, Breman (1985), and Rogaly *et al.* (2002) for eastern India.
18. Much emphasis has been on the integration of migrants, and the impact on host communities. A recent issue of *International Migration Review* (Autumn 2004), for example, on conceptual development in international migration studies does not pay any attention to the impact on sending areas.
19. de Haan (2002) makes an initial attempt to do this for villages in western Bihar, which has a long tradition of out-migration, which is reflected in cultural expressions too.
20. In the labour-scarce West Africa environment, absence of able-bodied men was keenly felt and led to a 'labour gap', women were working longer and harder in the compound's communal fields, and had less time to work their own land (David 1995).
21. In other contexts, the possibility of inflationary impact has been emphasized; Amjad (1989).
22. Quoted in the OPPG study on El Salvador, Marquez (2004).
23. Lakshmansamy (1990), which quotes Eames' findings that 12 per cent of the respondents' remittances were used to buy bullocks and to aid agriculture; Oberai and Singh showed that a significant proportion of remittances were used for agricultural production; and Brammer described how immigrants to Dinajpur introduced double cropping.
24. For example, the OPPG case study on Romania, Gheorghiu *et al.* (2004).
25. Connell and Wang (1992); Addleton (1991). According to a recent paper by Azam (2005), 9/11 did *not* result in a reduction of migration from Pakistan.
26. See for example information on migration highlighted in the OPPG case study on Ghana (McKay and Aryeetey, 2004); and Litchfield and Waddington (2003). Data gathered through support of the Netherlands Interdisciplinary Demographic Institute now provide insight for five sending and three receiving countries (see also Anarfi and Jagare 2005).
27. For example, Adepoju and Mbugua (1997: 54) note that African migrants often remit up to 60 per cent of their incomes, though Findley (1997: 130) in the same volume quotes research showing that migrants remit between 5 and 15 per cent of their income.
28. Reardon (1997). I am not aware of existing regional overviews elsewhere.
29. For research in India, see Deshingkar and Start (2003). Also Deshingkar and Anderson (2004) and Deshingkar (2005) for more general overviews that stress the role of migration in development. Comments by and discussions with John Farrington, ODI, have been very helpful in drafting this part of the chapter.
30. To take an example close to home: given that my education in the Netherlands may have cost the tax payer about $100,000, it would take me (who falls in the category of not remitting, and probably receiving net transfers from the home country) a long time before my remittances would become a *net* gain.
31. Oberai and Singh (1980) for India; Islam (1991) for Bangladesh; and Roberts (1997) for Mexico and China.
32. David (1995). Knowles and Anker (1981) noted that remittances are more important for poorer than richer households in Kenya, even if the rich received more.
33. The proportion of Taiwanese and Korean science PhDs trained in the US that *returned* to their home country increased significantly with the impressive growth in their home countries (quoted in Docquier and Rapoport 2004: 21).

34. This was a joint research programme of the British, German and French donor organizations, and the World Bank; see http://web.worldbank.org/WBSITE/EXTERNAL/TOPICS/EXTPOVERTY.
35. Quoted in Ghatak *et al.* (1996).
36. Lewis (1954: 400–49). Also Fei and Ranis (1964) and Ranis (2003) for a discussion of the critiques and usefulness of the dualism concept.
37. Kuznets model too incorporated labour mobility as key factor in processes of rising inequality in this structural transformation. See also, Zelinsky's transition model that linked modernization to changes in patterns of migration (Skeldon 1997a: 31).
38. See for example the Vietnam study in the OPPG research programme (Bonschab and Klump 2004).
39. This is often reflected in confusing terminology around 'mobility', which can refer to sectoral mobility *in terms of* sectoral change, and not just human mobility.
40. See the paper on Africa as part of the World Bank 'stock take' of labour market issues (Fox *et al.* 2004) which argues: 'many of the commonly used labor market concepts such as a job, employment and unemployment, participation, wage, earnings, etc. are difficult to apply in Africa'.
41. Jennifer Leavy (personal communication and her doctoral research on Northern Province, Zambia) highlights both the interrelated nature of different types of markets, and the ways markets are embedded in personal relations.
42. According to Rodgers (1996), the classic development literature of Arthur Lewis and Gunnar Myrdal was rich in institutional detail; Rodgers' article in 1996 and the volume he and others brought together provides a range of research priorities around labour institutions, in macro- and microeconomics, labour market structure, mobilization of labour, wage-setting institutions and agrarian systems.
43. Dustmann (1997) presents a life cycle model to compare the decisions of a migrant about consumption and time abroad under certainty and uncertainty in the host and home countries.
44. But see de la Brière *et al.* (1997), which emphasizes heterogeneity in explaining remittances, differences between male and female Dominican migrants to the US, and the differences in inheritance rules to explain this. The same theme has been studied in Filipino migrants, with the surprising conclusion that men send more money back than women, by Semyonov and Gorodzeisky (2005).
45. Stark's (1980) analysis of the role of urban–rural remittances in rural development sets out how migration by-passes credit and insurance markets, facilitating surplus accumulation and diversification of income sources.
46. This is a theme I tried to develop further with respect to Africa, in a background paper for the SPA report in 1999 (de Haan 1999); drawing inter alia on Findley (1997). Much earlier, Epstein's (1973) south Indian research developed the concept of 'share families', units that live separately but have agreed to share the responsibility for their incomes as well as their expenditure, emphasizing that the way family structures have evolved differs across economic classes.
47. Theories of structuration are usually associated with the work of Giddens (1979; 1984), emphasizing the importance of both human agency and social structure (http://www.theory.org.uk/giddens2.htm) and used in migration research, for example, in Chant and Radcliffe (1992) and de Haan (1994).
48. This was one of the key themes of de Haan and Rogaly (2002).
49. Adepoju, in the introduction to his edited volume on family, population and development in Africa, stated: '[m]igration is eroding day-to-day mutual support among family members' (Adepoju and Mbugua 1997: 23). Others have suggested that the negative effects might have been overstated; for example Read in Malawi (Nyasaland) in 1942 and Watson in Zambia (Northern Rhodesia) in 1958.
50. Portes and Sensenbrenner (1993); Rogaly (1997; 1998).
51. Wright (1995); also Sinclair (1998).

52. Massey *et al.* (1994). A recent critique of migration network analyses is Krissman (2005), which emphasizes the role of power relations of employers' demands and the middlemen involved within migration networks.
53. See for example Massey *et al.* (1993), regarding how international migration streams sustain themselves in cumulative fashion.
54. For example, the historical-structural framework in Rubenstein (1992) and Kritz and Zlotnik (1992).
55. Exceptions include, for example, data on Vietnam (de Brauw and Harigaya 2004).

References

Adams, R.H. (1991) 'The Economic Uses and Impact of International Remittances in Rural Egypt', *Economic Development and Cultural Change*, 39, 4: 695–722.
Adams, R.H. (1996) 'Remittances, Inequality and Asset Accumulation: the Case of Rural Pakistan', in D. O'Connor and L. Farsakh (eds), *Development Strategy, Employment and Migration*, Paris: OECD.
Adams, R.H. (1998) 'Remittances, Investment, and Rural Asset Accumulation in Pakistan', *Economic Development and Cultural Change*, 47, 1: 155–73.
Adams, R.H. and J. Page (2003) 'International Migration, Remittances and Poverty in Developing Countries', *World Bank Policy Research Working Paper* 3179, Washington, DC: World Bank.
Addleton, J. (1991) 'The Impact of the Gulf War on Migration and Remittances in Asia and the Middle East', *International Migration*, 29, 4: 509–26.
Adepoju, A. and W. Mbugua (1997) 'The African Family: An Overview of Changing Forms', in A. Adepoju (ed.), *Family, Population and Development in Africa*, London: Zed Books.
Amjad, R. (1989) 'Economic Impact of Migration to the Middle East on the Major Asian Labour Sending Countries: An Overview', in R. Amjad (ed.), *To the Gulf and Back: Studies on the Economic Impact of Asian Labour Migration*, Geneva: UNDP/ILO.
Anarfi, J. and S. Jagare (2005) 'Towards the Sustainable Return of West African Transnational Migrants: What are the Options?', paper for the World Bank conference on New Frontiers of Social Policy, 12–15 December, Arusha, Tanzania.
Appleyard, R. (1991) *International Migration: Challenge for the Nineties*, Geneva: International Organization for Migration.
Azam, F. (2005) 'Policies to Support International Migration in Pakistan and the Philippines', paper for the World Bank conference on New Frontiers of Social Policy, 12–15 December, Arusha, Tanzania.
Besley, R.B. and B. Esteve-Volart (2004) 'Operationalizing Pro-Poor Growth: A Case Study on India', paper prepared for the Operationalizing Pro-Poor Growth work programme, http://www.dfid.gov.uk/pubs/files/oppgindia.pdf
Black, R., C. Natali and J. Skinner (2004) 'Migration and Inequality', background paper for the 2006 *World Development Report*, Sussex (www.worldbank.org/wdr).
Bonschab, T. and R. Klump (2004) 'Operationalizing Pro-Poor Growth. Vietnam Case Study', paper prepared for the Operationalizing Pro-Poor Growth work programme, http://www.dfid.gov.uk/pubs/files/oppgvietnam.pdf
Breman, J.C. (1980) 'The Informal Sector in Research: Theory and Practice', *CASP* 3, Rotterdam.
Breman, J.C. (1985) *Of Peasants, Migrants and Paupers: Rural Labour Circulation and Capitalist Production in West India*, Oxford: Oxford University Press.
Breman, J.C. (1990) 'Labour Migration and Rural Transformation in Colonial Asia', *Comparative Asian Studies* 5, Amsterdam: Free University Press.
Breman, J.C. (1996) *Footloose Labour. Working in India's Informal Economy*, Cambridge: Cambridge University Press.
Cashin, P. and R. Sahay (1996) 'Internal Migration, Centre-State Grants, and Economic Growth in the States of India', *IMF Staff Papers*, 43, 1: 123–7.

Chant, S. and S.A. Radcliffe (1992) 'Migration and Development: The Importance of Gender', in S. Chant (ed.) *Gender and Migration in Developing Countries*, London: Belhaven Press.

Chirwa, W.C. (1997) 'No TEBA, Forget TEBA: The Plight of Malawian Ex-migrant Workers to South Africa, 1988–1994', *International Migration Review*, 31, 3: 628–54.

Connell, J. and J. Wang (1992) 'Distant Victims?: The Impact of the Gulf War on International Migration to the Middle East from Asia', in A.K. Tripathi and V.B. Bhatt (eds), *Changing Environmental Ideologies*, Delhi: Ashish Publishing House.

Connell, J., B. Dasgupta, R. Laishley and M. Lipton (1976) *Migration from Rural Areas: The Evidence from Village Studies*, Delhi: Oxford University Press.

Croll, E.J. and H. Ping (1997). 'Migration For and Against Agriculture in Eight Chinese Villages', *China Quarterly*, 149: 128–46.

David, R. (1995) *Changing Places: Women, Resource Management and Migration in the Sahel*, London: SOS Sahel.

de Brauw, A. and T. Harigaya (2004) 'Seasonal Migration and Improving Living Standards in Vietnam', Mimeo, Williamstown, MA: Williams College.

de Haan, A. (1994) *Unsettled Settlers: Migrant Workers and Industrial Capitalism in Calcutta*, Hilversum: Verloren.

de Haan, A. (1997) 'Migration and Poverty in Africa: Is There a Link?', background paper for the 1999 World Bank SPA Status Report on Poverty.

de Haan, A. (1999) 'Livelihoods and Poverty: the Role of Migration. A Critical Review of the Migration Literature', *Journal of Development Studies*, 36, 2: 1–47.

de Haan, A. (2002) 'Migration and Livelihoods in Historical Perspective: A Case Study of Bihar, India', *Journal of Development Studies*, 38, 5: 115–42.

de Haan, A. (2005) 'Connecting the Poor to Growth: the Role of Mobility', input paper for multi-donor research programme on Pro-Poor Growth, DFID, London.

de Haan, A. and A. Dubey (2002) 'Are Migrants Worse or Better-Off ? Asking the Right Questions', paper for conference at NEHU, Shillong, November.

de Haan, A. and B. Rogaly (eds) (2002) *Labour Mobility and Rural Society*, London: Frank Cass.

de la Brière, B., A. de Janvry, S. Lambert and E. Sadoulet (1997) 'Why Do Migrants Remit? An Analysis for the Dominican Sierra', *IFPRI Food Consumption and Nutrition Division Discussion Paper* 37, Washington, DC: International Food Policy Research Institute.

Deshingkar, P. (2005) 'Maximizing the Benefits of Internal Migration for Development', paper for Regional IOM Conference on Migration and Development in Asia, www.iom.int/chinaconference/files/documents/bg_papers/04032005_bg.pdf

Deshingkar P. and E. Anderson (2004) 'People on the Move: New Policy Challenges for Increasingly Mobile Populations', *ODI Natural Resource Perspectives* 92, London: Overseas Development Institute.

Deshingkar, P. and D. Start (2003) 'Seasonal Migration for Livelihoods in India: Coping, Accumulation and Exclusion', *ODI Working Paper* 220, London: Overseas Development Institute.

Docquier, F. and H. Rapoport (2004) 'Skilled Migration: The Perspective of Developing Countries', Mimeo.

Durand, J., W. Kandel, E.A. Parrado and D.S. Massey (1996a) 'International Migration and Development in Mexican Communities', *Demography*, 33, 2: 249–64.

Durand, J., E.A. Parrado and D.S. Massey (1996b) 'Migradollars and Development: A Reconsideration of the Mexican Case', *International Migration Review*, 30, 2: 423–44.

Dustmann, C. (1997) 'Return Migration, Uncertainty and Precautionary Savings', *Journal of Development Economics*, 52, 2: 295–316.

Ellerman, D. (2003) 'Policy Research on Migration and Development', *World Bank Policy Research Working Papers* 3117, Washington, DC: World Bank.

Ellis, F. and G. Bahiigwa (2003) 'Rural Livelihoods and Poverty Reduction in Uganda', *World Development*, 31, 6: 997–1013.

Ellis, F. and H.E. Freeman (2004) 'Rural Livelihoods and Poverty Reduction Strategies in Four African Countries', *Journal of Development Studies*, 40, 4: 1–30.

Epstein, S.T. (1973) *South India: Yesterday, Today and Tomorrow*, London: Macmillan.

Fei, J.C.H. and G. Ranis (1964) *Development of the Labor Surplus Economy: Theory and Policy*, Homewood, IL: Irwin.

Findley, S. (1997) 'Migration and Family Interactions in Africa', in A. Adepoju (ed.), *Family, Population and Development in Africa*, London: Zed Books.

Fox, L., G. Betcherman, V. Chandra, B. Eifert and A. Van Adams (2004) 'Realizing the Potential of the Labour Force in Africa: Barriers and Opportunities', Mimeo, Washington, DC: World Bank.

Ghatak, A., P. Levine and S. Wheatley Price (1996) 'Migration Theories and Evidence: An Assessment', *Journal of Economic Surveys*, 10, 2: 159–98.

Gheorghiu, R., W. Paczynski, A. Radziwill, A. Sowa, M. Stanculescu, I. Topinska, G. Turlea and M. Walewski (2004) 'Operationalising Pro-Poor Growth. A Case Study on Romania', paper prepared for the Operationalizing Pro-Poor Growth work programme, http://www.dfid.gov.uk/pubs/files/oppgromania.pdf

Ghosh, B. (1992) 'Migration – development Linkages: Some Specific Issues and Practical Policy Measures', *International Migration*, 30, 3/4: 423–52.

Giddens, A. (1979) *Central Problems in Social Theory. Action, Structure and Contradiction in Social Analysis*, London: Macmillan.

Giddens, A. (1984) *The Constitution of Society. Outline of the Theory of Structuration*, Cambridge: Cambridge University Press.

Glover, S., C. Gott, A. Loizillon, J. Portes, R. Price, S. Spencer, V. Srinivasan and C. Willis (2001) 'Migration: An Economic and Social Analysis', *RDS Occasional Paper* 67, London: Home Office, http://www.homeoffice.gov.uk/rds/pdfs/occ67-migration.pdf

Hall, T. (2005) 'Globalized Livelihoods. International Migration and Challenges for Social Policy: The Case of Ecuador', paper for the World Bank conference on New Frontiers of Social Policy, 12–15 December, Arusha, Tanzania.

Harris, J. and M.P. Todaro (1970). 'Migration, Unemployment and Development: A Two-Sector Analysis', *American Economic Review* 60, 1:126–42.

Hatton, T.J. and J.G. Willamson (1992) 'What Explains Wage Gaps between Farm and City? Exploring the Todaro Model with American Evidence, 1890–1941', *Economic Development and Cultural Change*, 40, 2: 267–94.

Islam, M.D. (1991) 'Labour Migration and Development: A Case Study of a Rural Community in Bangladesh', *Bangladesh Journal of Political Economy*, 11, 2: 570–87.

Islam, R. (2004) 'The Nexus of Economic Growth, Employment and Poverty Reduction: An Empirical Analysis', *Issues in Employment and Poverty Discussion Paper* 14, Geneva: ILO.

Kapur, D. (2004) 'Remittances: The New Development Mantra?', *G-24 Discussion Paper* 29, Geneva: UNCTAD.

Knowles, A.C. and R. Anker (1981) 'An Analysis of Income Transfers in a Developing Country', *Journal of Development Economics*, 8: 205–26.

Krokfors, C. (1995) 'Poverty, Environmental Stress and Culture as Factors in African Migrations', in J. Baker and T.A. Aina (eds), *The Migration Experience in Africa*, Uppsala: Nordiska Afrikainstitutet.

Krissman, F. (2005) '*Sin Coyote Ni Patrón*: Why the Migration Network Fails to Explain International Migration', *International Migration Review*, 34, 1: 4–44.

Kritz M.M. and H. Zlotnik (1992) 'Global interactions: Migration Systems, Processes, and Policies', in M.M. Kritz, L.L. Lim and H. Zlotnik (eds), *International Migration Systems. A Global Approach*, Oxford: Clarendon Press.

Lakshmansamy, T. (1990) 'Family Survival Strategy and Migration: An Analysis of Returns to Migration', *Indian Journal of Social Work*, 51, 3: 473–85.

Larson, D. and Y. Mundlak (1997) 'On the Intersectoral Migration of Agricultural Labour', *Economic Development and Cultural Change*, 45, 2: 295–319.

Liang, Z. and M.J. White (1997) 'Market Transition, Government Policies, and Interprovincial Migration in China: 1983–1988', *Economic Development and Cultural Change*, 45, 2: 321–39.

Leliveld, A. (1997) 'The Effects of Restrictive South African Migrant Labour Policy on the Survival of Rural Households in Southern Africa: A Case Study from Rural Swaziland', *World Development*, 25, 11: 1839–49.

Lewis, W.A. (1954) 'Economic Development with Unlimited Supplies of Labour, originally published in 1954 by the Manchester School, reprinted in A.N. Agarwala and S.P. Singh (eds) (1990), *The Economic of Underdevelopment. A series of articles and papers*, Delhi: Oxford University Press.

Lipton, M. (1980) 'Migration form Rural Areas of Poor Countries: The Impact on Rural Productivity and Income Distribution', *World Development*, 8, 1: 1–24.

Lipton, M. (1982) 'Migration from Rural Areas of Poor Countries: The Impact on Rural Productivity and Income Distribution', in R.H. Sabot (ed.), *Migration and the Labour Market in Developing Countries*, Boulder, CO: Westview.

Litchfield, J. and H. Waddington (2003) 'Migration and Poverty in Ghana: Evidence from the Ghana Living Standards Survey', *Sussex Migration Working Paper* 10.

Lucas, R.E. (2002) 'Life Earnings and Rural–Urban Migration', Mimeo.

Maimbo, S.M. and D. Ratha (eds) (2005) *Remittances. Development Impact and Future Prospects*, Washington, DC: World Bank.

Mallee, H. (1996) 'In Defence of Migration: Recent Chinese Studies on Rural Population Mobility', *China Information*, 10, 3–4: 108–40.

Mansell Prothero, R. and M. Chapman (eds) (1985) *Circulation in Third World Countries*, London: Routledge.

Marquez, J.S. (2004) 'Operationalizing Pro-Poor Growth. A Country Case Study on El Salvador', http://www.dfid.gov.uk/pubs/files/oppgelsalvador

Martin, P. (2005) 'Mexico-US Migration', www.iie.com/publications/papers/nafta-migration.pdf (accessed December 2005).

Massey, D.S., J. Arango, G. Hugo, A. Kouaouci, A. Pellegrino and J.E. Taylor (1993) 'Theories of International Migration: A Review and Appraisal', *Population and Development Review*, 19, 3: 451–4.

Massey, D.S., J. Arango, G. Hugo, A. Kouaouci, A. Pellegrino and J.E. Taylor (1994) 'An Evaluation of International Migration Theory', *Population and Development Review*, 20, 4: 699–751.

Mayda, A.M. (2005) 'International Migration: A Panel Data Analysis of Economic and Non-Economic Determinants', *IZA Discussion Papers*, 1590.

McDowell, C. and A. de Haan (1997) 'Migration and Sustainable Livelihoods: a Critical Review of the Literature', *IDS Working Paper* 65.

McKay, A. and E. Aryeetey (2004) 'Operationalizing Pro-Poor Growth. A Country Case Study on Ghana', www.dfid.gov.uk/pubs/files/oppgghana.pdf

Moses, J.W. and B. Letnes (2004) 'The Economic Costs to International Labour Restrictions: Revisiting the Empirical Discussion', *World Development*, 32, 10: 1609–26.

Mosse, D., S. Gupta, M. Mehta, V. Shah and J. Rees (2002) 'Brokered Livelihoods: Debt, Labour Migration and Development in Tribal Western India', in A. de Haan and B. Rogaly (eds), *Labour Mobility and Rural Society*, London: Frank Cass.

Munshi, K. and M. Rosenzweig (2005) 'Why is Mobility in India so Low? Social Insurance, Inequality, and Growth', *BREAD Working Paper* 97, www.ksg.harvard.edu/cid/bread/abstracts/097.htm

Oberai, A. and H.K. Singh (1980) 'Migration, Remittances and Rural Development: Findings of a Case study in the Indian Punjab', *International Labour Review*, 119, 2: 229–41.

Papademetriou, D.G. and P.L. Martin (eds) (1991) *The Unsettled Relationship: Labour Migration and Economic Development*, New York: Greenwood.

Portes, A. and J. Sensenbrenner (1993) 'Embeddedness and Immigration: Notes on the Social Determinants of Economic Action', *American Journal of Sociology*, 98, 6: 1320–50.

Pritchett, L. (2003) 'The Future of Migration: Irresistible Forces meet Immovable Ideas', paper presented to the Future of Globalization conference at Yale University, October.

Pritchett, L. (2004) 'Boom Towns and Ghost Countries: Geography, Agglomeration, and Population Mobility', Mimeo, Cambridge, MA: Kennedy School of Government, Harvard University.

Ranis, G. (2003) 'Is Dualism Worth Revisiting?', *Economic Growth Centre Discussion Paper* 870, New Haven, CT: Yale University.

Ravallion, M. and G. Datt (1996) 'How Important to India's Poor Is the Sectoral Composition of Economic Growth?', *World Bank Economic Review*, 10: 1–26.

Reardon, T. (1997) 'Using Evidence of Household Income Diversification to Inform Study of the Rural Non-farm Labour Market in Africa', *World Development*, 25, 5: 735–47.

Roberts, K.D. (1997) 'China's "Tidal Wave" of Migrant Labour: What Can We Learn From Mexican Undocumented Migration to the United States?', *International Migration Review*, 31, 2: 249–93.

Rodgers, G. (1996) 'Labour Institutions and Economic Development: Issues and Methods', in G. Rodgers, K. Foti and L. Lauridsen, *The Institutional Approach to Labour and Development*, EADI Book Series 17, London: Frank Cass.

Rogaly, B. (1997) 'Embedded Markets: Hired Labour Arrangements in West Bengal Agriculture', *Oxford Development Studies*, 25, 2: 209–23.

Rogaly, B. (1998) 'Workers on the Move: Seasonal Migration and Changing Social Relations in Rural India', *Gender and Development*, 6, 1: 21–9.

Rogaly, B., D. Coppard, A. Rafique, K. Rana, A. Sengupta and J. Biswas (2002) 'Seasonal Migration and Welfare/Illfare in Eastern India: A Social Analysis', in A. de Haan and B. Rogaly (eds), *Labour Mobility and Rural Society*, London: Frank Cass.

Rubenstein, H. (1992), 'Migration, Development and Remittances in Rural Mexico', *International Migration*, 30, 2: 127–53.

Russell, S.S., K. Jacobsen and W.D. Stanley (1990) 'International Migration and Development in Sub-Saharan Africa', *World Bank Discussion Papers* 101 and 102 (2 issues), Africa Technical Department Series, Washington, DC: World Bank.

Safa, H.I. (ed.) (1982) *Towards a Political Economy of Urbanization in Third World Countries*, Oxford: Oxford University Press.

Semyonov, M. and A. Gorodzeisky (2005) 'Labour Migration, Remittances and Household Income: A Comparison between Filipino and Filipina Overseas Workers', *International Migration Review*, 34, 1: 45–68.

Sinclair, M.R. (1998) 'Community, Identity and Gender in Migrant Societies of Southern Africa: Emerging Epistemological Challenges', *International Affairs*, 74, 2: 339–53.

Skeldon, R. (1997a) *Migration and Development. A Global Perspective*, Harlow: Longman.

Skeldon, R. (1997b) 'Rural – urban Migration and Its Implications for Poverty Alleviation', *Asia-Pacific Population Journal*, 12, 1: 3–16.

Sorensen, N., N. Van Hear and P. Engberg-Pedersen (2002) 'The Migration – development Nexus Evidence and Policy Option. State of the Art Overview', *Centre for Development Research Working Papers* 02.6, Copenhagen: Centre for Development Research.

Sriskandarajah, D., L. Cooley and H. Reed (2005) *Paying Their Way. The Fiscal Contribution of Immigrants in the UK*, London: Institute for Public Policy Research.

Stark, O. (1980) 'On the Role of Urban–Rural Remittances in Rural Development', *Journal of Development Studies*, 16, 3: 369–74.

Stark, O. (1991) *The Migration of Labour*, Cambridge, MA: Harvard University Press.

Thirsk, J. (1991) 'Rural Migration in England: The Long Historical Perspective', in J.A. Mollett (ed.), *Migrants in Agricultural Development. A Study of Intrarural Migration*, London: Macmillan.

Todaro, M.P. (1969) 'A Model of Labour Migration and Urban Unemployment in Less Developed Countries', *American Economic Review*, 59: 138–49.

van Velsen, J. (1959) 'Labour Migration as a Positive Factor in the Continuity of Tonga Tribal Society', *Economic Development and Cultural Change*, 8, 2: 265–78.

Wright, C. (1995) 'Gender Awareness in Migration Theory: Synthesizing Actor and Structure in Southern Africa', *Development and Change*, 26, 4: 771–91.

Part V
Development Finance

16
International Risk Tolerance, Capital Market Failure and Capital Flows to Emerging Markets

Valpy FitzGerald

Introduction

For the past two decades as capital market financing[1] for middle-income developing countries, now known as 'emerging markets', has expanded enormously, so has the academic literature on the explanations for the evident instability of these flows to and their allocation across these host countries. Most of this literature and the policy debate have centred on macroeconomic stability, market access and institutional arrangements in emerging market economies themselves – that is, on host 'fundamentals'. Much less attention has been paid by development economists to the nature of the demand schedule, in terms of both level and stability, or emerging market assets on the part of international investors, and in particular the role of 'home' market factors in the developed economies. In marked contrast, the professional or 'market' literature, including that written by regulators, takes these demand shifts very seriously (FitzGerald 2003).

Shifts in global demand (principally from G3 banks and institutions) for emerging market assets and accompanying characteristics of home market behaviour, account for a major part of the instability in capital flows shown in Figure 16.1. The present consensus is that about one half of flow variation is accounted for by the 'push' factors, but when market interactions are taken into account the net effect of home factors turns out to be rather higher.[2] In addition, the maturity of debt securities is generally quite short, generating large fluctuations in capital flows in response to temporary changes in home market sentiment.

What is more, emerging market securities account for less than 1 per cent of the total G3 portfolio. This low overall level of investment in the emerging market asset class as a whole cannot be simply attributed to poor risk-return characteristics. As Figure 16.2 shows, emerging market debt has a risk level lying between those of OECD bonds and equities, and a rate of return higher than either. Emerging market equity has on average better returns and lower risk than OECD equity. Indeed, it is well established that there is strong and pervasive home bias against *all* foreign assets among portfolio investors.

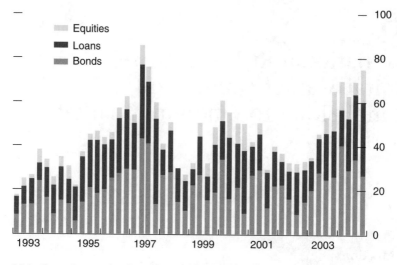

Figure 16.1   Emerging market financing (US$ billion)
Source: IMF Global Financial Stability Report, April 2005.

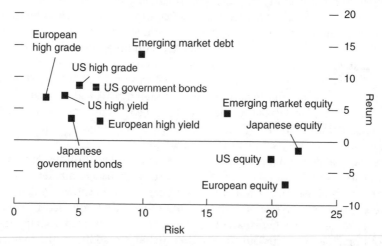

Figure 16.2   Risk–return tradeoff (%)
Source: IMF Global Financial Stability Report, April 2005.

Recent research on the determinants of capital flows and the causes of this market failure are surveyed in the second section of this chapter. Following on, the microeconomic roots of home bias and demand instability are explained in terms of investor risk perception and credit rationing, exacerbated by trader behaviour. The penultimate section demonstrates the impact of these flows on host macroeconomic balances and income distribution. Although the net impact also depends upon the host policy response, this transmission means that host 'fundamentals' are themselves strongly affected by capital flows and thus cannot be considered as to be independent of the push factors. The final section concludes by examining the implications of these findings for the future of development economics in general and for policy response in particular.

Recent research on home demand for emerging market assets

Home interest rates, home asset price volatility, covariance with emerging market assets and risk tolerance clearly affect demand for emerging market assets (Disyatat and Gelos 2001). The standard model used in the empirical literature[3] states that the portfolio capital flow from any one country of origin to a country of destination is the result of push and pull factors: two *separate* vectors for capital supply and 'country risk/return characteristics' are assumed to exist and interact to produce the observed volume (capital flow) and price (yield spread). Push factors in these models conventionally include: home country wealth (for example, GDP); home monetary policy (for example, money supply); riskless home interest rate (for example, US treasury yield); and home asset risk (for example, US bond yield spread). The empirical literature (see Montiel and Reinhart 2001) indicates that roughly half of the observed flow variance can be explained by these factors. Pull factors usually include: emerging market sovereign bond yield spreads; risk ratings as measures of creditworthiness; host country growth rates and debt levels, and so on. Montiel and Reinhart (1999) employ fixed-effects panel data analysis for 15 emerging market countries and examine the volume and composition of capital inflows. They conclude that international interest rates have an important effect on not only the volume but also the asset composition of flows. Mody *et al.* (2001) use a vector equilibrium correction model to forecast pull and push factors for inflows to 32 developing countries and conclude that in general common push factors are determinant in short-run dynamics even though pull factors are more important in the long-run allocation of aggregate flows to particular countries.[4]

Taylor and Sarno (1997) examine the determinants of US portfolio capital outflows towards Latin America and Asia using cointegration techniques. They find that global (push) and domestic (pull) factors have similar importance in explaining short-run equity flows to Asia and Latin America. However, for the short-run dynamics of bond flows, global factors (particularly USA interest rates) are found to be more important than domestic factors. Chuhan *et al.* (1998) model USA portfolio flows to Latin American and Asian markets using the panel data method. They too find that push factors are the main determinants of portfolio flows to Latin America and Asia, although equity flows are more sensitive to global factors than bond flows, which are more sensitive to credit ratings and secondary market debt prices.

Although there are good reasons to believe that the international market for emerging market assets is 'credit rationed' (see the third section), only Mody and Taylor (2002) have so far made this explicit in an innovative disequilibrium model: using a maximum likelihood estimation technique they estimate the probability of the demand for capital exceeding supply for emerging markets and find that the push effect dominates, especially in times of 'capital crunches'. A separate literature on the determination of emerging market bond spreads on primary issues justifies this approach, because it clear that home as well as host characteristics affect spreads (Fernández-Arias 1996). In consequence, FitzGerald and Krolzig (2003, 2005a) address the estimation of the aggregate international demand schedule for emerging market bonds as a single asset class, using a simultaneous-equation estimation model. We find that not only do spreads affect flows, but also that flows affect spreads (as might be expected in a rationed credit market) and that lagged spreads and flows have a similar effect – indicating that market behaviour such as investor herding and momentum trading are also significant. Our main finding is that over three-quarters of the observed variation in aggregate bond flows to emerging markets can be attributed to shifts in the demand schedule and endogenous market interactions.[5] Home market factors not only strongly influence the volatility of flows but also seem to determine their relatively low level: the proportion of foreign assets in home investment portfolios tends to be very small compared to the efficient portfolio theory prediction for observed risk (volatility) and return.[6] Administrative or regulatory barriers to international investment cannot explain this as these have been significantly lowered in recent years (Ahearne *et al.* 2001)[7] and the risk premium has not fallen to reflect diversification gains (Bekaert and Harvey 2000; Henry 2000).

An alternative approach to explaining home bias is to suggest that information is asymmetric: home investors know less about host than home stocks. It is certainly the case that foreign securities issues quoted on home markets suffer less from home bias (Ahearne *et al.* 2001). However, institutional investors who make up most of overseas investment generally do better in host markets due to scale economies in research (Grinblatt and Keloharju 2000). To attempt to redefine changing risk tolerance as variations in risk perception does not really serve, for this version of asymmetric information theory does not allow for the large fluctuations in home bias observed independently of the underlying real risk, and would make research into emerging markets extremely profitable leading in turn to rapidly decreasing home bias over time. Potentially more promising is a Bayesian approach where the investor has prior views about means and returns, updates these views as she observes new data and then makes the portfolio allocation decisions (Klein and Bawa 1977). However, numerical simulation of this process indicates that only if the investor holds implausible prior views can home bias be generated; while an investor with diffuse prior views about foreign returns would arrive an allocation not far from the optimal (Lewis 1999). An asymmetric risk function, with losses valued more highly than gains, may reflect investor behaviour better, too, but this does not explain home bias either.[8]

So the equity home bias puzzle remains and is even stronger for emerging markets than for overseas equity as a whole. Moreover, most of the literature refers to US institutional investors but this is also true of UK institutions, which are under few constraints in this regard (Blake and Timmermann 2000; Blake *et al.* 1999).

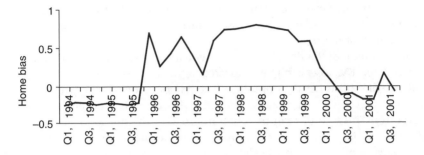

Figure 16.3 Home bias against emerging market equity by UK pension funds
Source: Babilis and FitzGerald (2005).

In consequence Babilis and FitzGerald (2005) used data on UK pension fund portfolios and the standard theoretical model (see next section) to measure home bias by UK pension funds. We find that this bias is *doubly* acute in the case of emerging market equity – a bias against overseas assets as a whole being further magnified by a bias against emerging markets within the foreign equity class as a whole. Even more interestingly, the bias varies over time as Figure 16.3 indicates, with home bias (as defined in the Technical Appendix) varying from −20 per cent to +80 per cent over a few years. Froot and O'Connell (2003) take a similar approach in comparing the equity portfolios of global and local investors, showing that relative risk tolerance of the latter varies widely and cyclically over time. There is good reason to suppose, therefore, that risk tolerance varies over time and possibly (in view of the shape of the graph in Figure 16.3 and its association with the Latin American and East Asian crises) that it is path-dependent.

Risk tolerance and credit rationing in the market for EM assets

The microeconomic foundation for the analysis of the aggregate demand for EM assets is to be found in portfolio theory. Consider a world where home investors hold assets from the home economy (h) and emerging markets (f). The stock (A_f) of these EM assets is a proportion (x^f) of the wealth (W_h) of the home portfolio holder

$$A_f = W_h x^f \tag{16.1}$$

Standard portfolio optimization theory (see Appendix) yields the efficient portfolio share (x^f) for the representative investor faced with a given set of expected returns ($E_t r_{t+1}$)

$$x_t^f = \frac{(E_t r_{t+1}^f - E_t r_{t+1}^h)/\gamma}{Var\,(r^f - r^h)} + \frac{\sigma_h^2 - \sigma_{hf}}{Var\,(r^f - r^h)} \tag{16.2}$$

where γ is the parameter of relative risk aversion, σ_h^2 is the variance of home asset returns, σ_f^2 is the variance of EM asset returns and σ_{hf} is the covariance between home and host returns.

The first term of the right hand side of equation (16.2) can be interpreted as the demand for EM assets: higher expected returns raise demand while a higher variance of returns has the opposite effect. As home investors' degree of risk aversion (γ) increases, demand falls: note that this effect is multiplicative with risk (variance). The second term in equation (16.2) is the portfolio share that minimizes the variance of the wealth portfolio. The key point here is that the demand for emerging market assets will clearly depend not only upon host 'fundamentals' that determine risk-return characteristics (that is, r_f and σ_f^2) but also upon variables in the *home* market such as risk aversion, home volatility (σ_h^2) and the covariance between home and EM assets (σ_{hf}).

Given a set of observed returns, variances and covariances home bias is the difference between x^f and the observed portfolio share, as we have seen. The only unobserved variable is risk aversion γ, which is normally set at unity in estimating home bias empirically. However, the extent and variability of home bias does seem to support the case for considering it to be a variable that changes over time in response to recent events, reinforced by endogenous market characteristics related to fund managers' behaviour. It is thus necessary to posit an explicit model of risk aversion – or its inverse, 'risk tolerance' or 'risk appetite' as it is known by market participants.

Kumar and Persaud (2001) argue that most of the indicators used to proxy risk tolerance in the literature confuse the level of risk itself with risk tolerance: asset prices (or yield spreads) are in practice a function of both underlying risk and risk tolerance, this latter containing structural components (the underlying utility function and financial market structure) and a time varying element reflecting shorter-term factors such as so-called 'wake up calls'.[9] When these result from major collapses in emerging markets (such as the 1998 Russian crash), the effect on home risk appetite then affects other emerging markets through what is known as 'pure' contagion. The sudden shifts in risk tolerance associated with these wake-up calls also reflect abrupt portfolio adjustments asset prices reach the limits of what is considered normal by the market; what De Grauwe terms a 'band of agnosticism', within which the gains from portfolio allocation are not large enough to justify the transactions costs of optimization and thus reflects 'rational behaviour in an uncertain world' (De Grauwe 1996: 181–206).

A change in risk aversion on the part of the market as a whole will, of course, affect the returns on EM assets themselves as well as the flows, as the risk premium will rise. Leaving aside covariance issues for simplicity of exposition, the 'yield spread' (s_f) of EM returns over a riskless home asset will be determined by the process of arbitrage such that asset prices adjust to the point where

$$r^f = r^h + \gamma\sigma_f^2$$

$$s_f = r^f - r^h = \gamma\sigma_f^2 \tag{16.3}$$

In other words the yield spread is equal to the risk premium. However, this in turn is the product of home risk aversion and host risk: with the additional feature that the larger the risk on any one EM asset, the more it its risk premium will rise for a given increase in risk aversion *even though the underlying risk itself has not changed*. This would help explain the 'double home bias' (against foreign assets, and within this, even more against EM assets) that we have discussed in the previous section. This also reinforces the point made in the previous section, that EM asset returns are not only determined by host fundamentals but also by home factors. In other words, pull factors cannot be fully separated from push factors.

Further, the level of risk in EM assets is essentially that of default or devaluation (if they are denominated in local currency) and this clearly increases with the level of indebtedness. In addition, higher spreads mean increased debt service costs, again increasing the probability of default. There thus emerges a process of credit rationing similar to that characterized by uncertainty in the loan market. Adverse selection arises because the two sides have different perceptions of risk and lenders cannot distinguish fully between borrowers. As in the international bank lending model of Folkerts-Landau (1985), the supply schedule for capital (that is, the demand schedule for EM assets in our case) will be backward-sloping beyond a certain point as shown in Figure 16.4[10] – in consequence, the market may not clear. In other words, the equilibrium is not the point where the demand and supply schedules intersect; and some borrowers are unsatisfied at the equilibrium interest rate.[11] Under these circumstances it is clear that a change in risk tolerance by lenders will bring about horizontal shift in the capital supply schedule. In other words, high yield spreads will be associated with low capital flows, which is in fact the case as we have seen in the previous section.

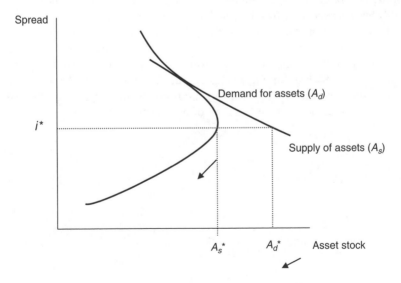

Figure 16.4 Credit rationing in emerging market assets

The implications of volatile emerging market asset demand for macroeconomic stability in developing countries

This instability in capital flows and spreads, originating in 'home' financial markets, has profound consequences for host economies themselves; particularly since small open emerging markets are increasingly driven by the capital account. This is for at least three reasons. First, because the interest rate is effectively set externally. Second, because the level of investment and the long-run capital stock is determined in relation to global capital markets. Third, because the short-run level of output is affected by the level of bank credit and import availability; and fourth because the real exchange rate (and thus both export incentives and the real wage rate) is the result of capital flows. And in each case, investor risk tolerance is crucial in determining the outcome.

With a liberalized capital account, arbitrage will ensure that uncovered interest rate parity obtains. In other words, the domestic interest rate (i_d) is necessarily equal to the sum of the world interest rate ($i_\$$), the expected rate of depreciation of the nominal exchange rate ($\dot{E}$) and the default risk premium (ρ); where of course this premium is the product of the default risk (p) itself and the risk aversion parameter (γ) as we have seen in the previous section:[12]

$$i_d = i_\$ + \dot{E} + \rho$$
$$\rho = \gamma p \tag{16.4}$$

In other words, the domestic interest rate is no longer determined by the balancing of domestic investment and domestic saving, but rather by the capital account. An important consequence is that any increase in the *home* interest rate ($i_\$$) or *home* risk aversion (γ) will immediately increase the host interest rate (i_d) and thus tighten the monetary stance in the short run and reduce the investment rate in the long. We can assess the long-run effect of this arbitrage as follows. Consider an economy with a familiar production function where output capacity (Y) depends on the stock of capital (K) and labour (L). The host rate of return on capital (r_f) must equal the rate of return in the home economy (r_h) plus the risk premium before, which solves for the level of output per worker (y):

$$Y_f = B_f K_f^\alpha L_f^{1-\alpha}$$

$$r_f = \frac{\partial Y_f}{\partial K_f} = \alpha B_f \left(\frac{K_f}{L_f}\right)^{\alpha-1} \tag{16.5}$$

$$r_f = r_h + \gamma p$$

$$y = \frac{Y_f}{L_f} = \left(\frac{\alpha B_f}{r_h + \gamma p}\right)^{\frac{\alpha}{1-\alpha}}$$

In other words, any increase in the *home* interest rate ($i_\$$) or *home* risk aversion (γ) will depress the long-run level of income per capita (y) in the host economy.

In the short run, within a given long-run capacity (which depends on investment), output (Q) will be constrained by credit supply – itself affected by bank liabilities and thus foreign borrowing – or else foreign exchange availability as the authorities regulate aggregate demand in order to ensure that reserves are not depleted. Consider a simple linear balance of payments model with exports (X), imports (M) and capital flows (F). Exports are a function of world demand (Z) and the real exchange rate (e); and imports of domestic output (Q) and the real exchange rate. Finally, reserves (R) are maintained at a target proportion (φ) of external liabilities:

$$X = x_1 Z + x_2 e$$
$$M = m_1 Q - m_2 e \qquad\qquad (16.6)$$
$$\Delta R = \varphi F$$
$$X + F \equiv M + \Delta R$$

We assume here that the government maintains a target real exchange rate (e^*) in order to maintain export competitiveness. In this case, output (Q) becomes a function of the capital flow – and by extension the home factors we have discussed before – home investor wealth, return on home assets and home risk aversion. In particular, an increase in home risk will reduce capital flows and thus emerging market output. Rearranging equation (16.6) gives Q in terms of F:

$$Q = \{F + x_1 Z + e^*(x_2 + m_2)\}/m_1 \qquad\qquad (16.7)$$
$$\partial Q/\partial F = 1/m_1 > 0$$

In other words, there is a very strong multiplier effect of capital flows on output, because the reciprocal the import coefficient (m_1) has a value between 0.2 and 0.3 for most emerging markets: so that a capital (outflow) equivalent[13] to 3 per cent of host GDP causes output to rise (fall) by up to 15 per cent.

Alternatively, if output itself is targeted by the authorities then the real exchange rate adjusts to capital flows – and by extension the same home factors mentioned above. An inflow leads to currency appreciation (that is, e falling) and *must* also mean a real wage increase and vice versa (see Appendix). The fact that overvaluation from capital inflows is politically popular among organized workers and consumers, and undervaluation resulting from outflows unpopular, is merely a reflection of this distributional logic. However, if real wages are to be stabilized, and thus the real exchange rate, then employment will fluctuate with output as in equation (16.7) and this will prejudice those at the margin of the formal sector labour force, who are likely to be the poorer ones.[14]

Moreover, whether the level of output or the real exchange rate is targeted, the implications for real investment levels as a whole are ambiguous because the former affects aggregate demand (and thus profit expectations) while the latter affects the allocation of investment between traded and non-traded sectors if the real exchange rate is allowed to fluctuate (FitzGerald and Perosino 1999). Last but not least, investment is negatively affected by output or profit rate *volatility* due to the hysteresis arising from irreversibility of fixed capital formation (FitzGerald 2001a). This is not to suggest that these capital flows necessarily have a negative effect on growth, and certainly could make a greater contribution were home bias to be less pronounced, but rather that the potential for macroeconomic instability is soundly based on economic theory.

Conclusions: international capital market failure and the future of development economics

In this study I have argued that the low level of capital flows to emerging markets and their instability are both largely due to the nature of the asset demand schedule for home investors, independently of the underlying quality of those assets ('fundamentals'). The same is undoubtedly true of the short 'tenor' of these investments, although I have not addressed this directly. Indeed the greater part of aggregate shifts in the demand emerging market assets can be attributed to events in the *home* capital markets: changes in risk tolerance and investor confidence as well as shifts in interest rates and wealth levels on the one hand, and trading behaviour in the form of herding and momentum trading on the other. This is not just a theoretical issue, because the macroeconomic and distributional consequences for emerging markets are disproportionately large: they are in effect a major externality.[15]

The practical significance of this externality results from the asymmetry in international capital markets: while these flows are relatively small in relation to home economies, they are very large relative to host markets – as Table 16.1 illustrates. Total emerging market capitalization (including all developing countries) is a very small part of the world total, and their ratio of market capitalization to GDP is far less than that for advanced economies. In consequence, a specific level of capital flow is ten times larger relative to the size of the host market compared to the home market. Thus, capital market shocks will be transferred from home to host countries in a very asymmetric fashion – shocks that the narrow and shallow host capital markets find very difficult to adsorb.

Nonetheless, the extent of home bias means that the situation in Table 16.1 is very far from equilibrium. The international version of the standard asset pricing model suggests that to maximize risk-adjusted returns investors should hold the world market portfolio of risky assets, irrespective of their country of residence. Under a number of assumptions about market efficiency (particularly that risk is fully reflected in price and thus return), the weighting of a country's assets within the portfolio should therefore reflect the weighting of the market capitalization of that country in the world market capitalization (Ahearne *et al.* 2001). From the data in Table 16.1, this implies that advanced economy investors should hold approximately one-tenth of their portfolio in emerging market assets, but in reality it is roughly one-hundredth.

There is, in consequence, a major externality to be addressed. The First Theorem of welfare economics argues that a Pareto-efficient competitive equilibrium is reached where three conditions obtain.[16] First, households and firms must act in perfect competition. Second, there is a full set of markets, particularly for futures

Table 16.1   World market capitalization (US$ billion)

	Stock market capitalization	Debt securities	Bank assets	Total	GDP	
	A	B	C	D = A+B+C	E	F = D/E
Market capitalization						
Advanced economies (AE)	27855	48236	39759	115250	27863	413.6%
Emerging markets (EM)	3947	3069	8075	15091	8457	178.4%
World total	31802	51305	47834	130341	36320	358.9%
	Equities	**Bonds**	**Loans**	**Total**		
EM financing						
Total	43	132	105	280		
% AE market capitalization	0.2	0.3	0.3	0.2		
% EM market capitalization	1.1	4.3	1.3	1.9		

Source: *IMF Global Financial Stability Report*, April 2005.

and risk bearing. Third, there is perfect information. Thus, market failure may occur even if firms and households behave in a perfectly competitive manner because the second and third conditions are unlikely to hold, and the market equilibrium, if it exists, is not welfare maximizing. The second condition usually fails to obtain in emerging markets because in many cases only spot prices exist and there are few homogeneous future options.[17] The third condition also usually fails to obtain because information is imperfect and costly to acquire, and usually proprietary in consequence. Further, the widespread presence of externalities and the public goods nature of certain investments often prevent investors in emerging markets capturing the full value of asset prices and discourage them from financing these projects.

Investors in emerging markets face a particular variant of market inefficiency: difficulties of contract enforcement (that is, debt default) and, thus, asset valuation caused by the lack of an international legal system support creditors.[18] However, at the root of two of the most discussed problems lies the problem of investor uncertainty: unobservable outcomes (for example, contractual default) and unobservable behaviour (for example, moral hazard). Banks' own limits on lending for fear of default can also promote liquidity crises as well as the credit rationing discussed in the third section, as no further lending may be available even though borrowers are solvent. Further, there are 'missing markets' for securities issued by many poor countries and for long-term bank loans to these countries. Markets for long-term bonds do not exist for most middle-income countries either.

Nonetheless, the potential gains from improved information should not be overestimated. International institutions and emerging market regulators have made considerable progress in augmenting and improving the flow of information to investors, yet there is little evidence that this information is much used. Partly this is an issue of timeliness – which is why relatively simple indicators, such as the quick ratio,[19] are still popular – but also, and more interestingly, one of the heuristic models that investors use and which determine how they process information and what information they consider relevant.[20] These models can clearly change rapidly, due to changing risk tolerance, market confidence and fads. Indeed, we do not understand how information about emerging markets is actually used by fund managers in their investment decisions. Perceptions of risk cannot reliably be based on econometric analysis of past trends, due to both the lack of data and frequent structural breaks. So asset valuation methods and portfolio composition rules used by investors in practice tend to be rather crude, being largely based on considerations of liquidity and exit possibilities (Clark *et al.* 1993) – both of which are difficult to estimate and subject to sudden shocks. Further, the incentives faced by fund managers themselves (such as quarterly performance bonuses based on performance relative to the industry average) are widely considered to exacerbate herding behaviour,[21] which in turn clearly exacerbates asset demand cycles. In addition, the risk aversion (or 'risk appetite' or 'risk tolerance') of international investors varies enormously over comparatively short periods of time – reflected in the ratio[22] of bond spreads to the volatility of returns, as Figure 16.5 indicates.

This volatility has even wider implications for development economics. Variable risk aversion is a serious difficulty for conventional economic theory because the proposition that the underlying utility function can be inferred from the financial market via the mean-variance portfolio model is a basic tenet of neoclassical economics (Levy and Markowitz 1979). The key characteristic of the constant relative risk aversion and similar utility functions is that the parameter γ must not only be constant (as it reflects basic household tastes) but also be fairly low to be consistent with other results, such as distributive fiscal.[23]

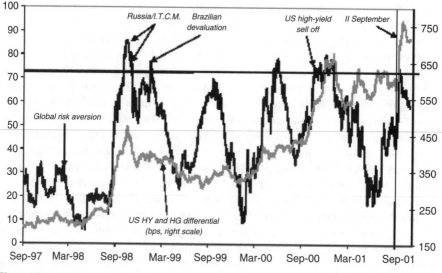

Figure 16.5   Global risk aversion

Source: J.P. Morgan (for the risk aversion index the LCPI is used).

This is no surprise from a Keynesian point of view, where uncertainty cannot be reduced to probability, but rather is related to the strength or degree of belief and where investors are strongly influenced by 'animal spirits' and 'beauty contests' that lead to wild swings in these beliefs. In terms of the psychology of decision making 'people evaluate the probability of events by the degree to which these events are representative of the relevant model or process' and perceptions of risk under circumstances that are difficult to imagine or have not been experienced before are systematically underestimated, while by extension the probability of recurrence of recent major events (particularly if themselves unexpected) is overestimated (Kahneman *et al.* 1982: 97). Indeed,

> the idea that economic agents compute a future exchange rate based on a model they believe in, then telescope it back into the present, is of little use in a world where economic agents have great difficulty in working out what the true model of the world is. (De Grauwe 1996: 189)

Further, international financial markets become 'a breeding ground for fads which, in the absence of credible alternatives, are elevated to important theories' (*Ibid.*: 202). There is, thus, a strong argument for emerging market authorities to adopt a countercyclical monetary stance in response to capital flows. This would involve real exchange rate targeting, bank credit regulation and an active fiscal stance and can be shown effective in supporting growth and investment (FitzGerald 2005b). In consequence, it is not surprising that most host governments have had to intervene (in many cases disguised as fiscal or regulatory measures) in the market in order to reduce the volatility of capital flows (FitzGerald 2005a). These controls are now usually based on price measures, particularly taxes, while quantitative instruments have become less common. Open-market operations have also proved quite successful in this regard, and can be complemented by the active use of reserve requirements and public sector deposits. Domestic regulatory systems for banks and securities markets (including corporate borrowing abroad) are also important supportive instruments.

However, the integrated nature of world capital markets means that these measures can only have a limited effect. Public intervention – by the IMF itself or by a consortium of G3 central banks – could do a great deal to reduce the externality caused by fluctuating G3 demand for emerging market assets. I do not wish to suggest that fundamentals are unimportant; but which fundamentals are considered relevant and in what way depends on home investors, not host governments. On a parallel with traditional central bank intervention in advanced economies, they could conduct open-market operations in these bonds in order to stabilize their price, and by acting as 'market makers' would encourage more home investors to enter the market. In particular, pension funds could benefit far more than they do at present from the high yields on these assets over the long run. It is of interest in this context that the Asian central banks are engaged in building a joint system of this kind based on their foreign exchange reserves built up as a crude insurance against financial crisis; but this does not address the root cause of asset demand instability.

In short, in a global economy development economists should pay far more attention to the consequences for emerging market countries of financial policies within and between advanced economies. There are major issues here for the future of development economics, which has yet to address adequately the issues raised by the externalities from international capital markets, the implications of volatile risk tolerance by international investors, and the adequacy of existing international institutions to cope with them. In recent years there have been considerable advances in this respect by trade economists concerned with the impact of global trade systems on growth and poverty in developing countries – in both the theoretical, empirical and policy dimensions – but there has been much less progress made by those working on international finance.

Technical appendix

The efficient investor portfolio with EM assets

Consider a world with two markets and two risky assets: 'home' (h) and the host emerging market (f). Home investors have access to both assets. Let x^f be the home investor's share of portfolio wealth held in the host asset, and therefore $1 - x^f$ be the share held in the domestic asset. Their objective function is given by:

$$V = V(E_t W_{t+1}, Var(W_{t+1})), \text{ where } V_1 > 0 \text{ and } V_2 < 0 \tag{16.A1}$$

Where W_t is real wealth at time t, E_t is the expectations operator conditional upon information at time t and Var is the variance–covariance matrix operator. The investors' objective function is increasing in the mean of wealth but decreasing in its variability. They maximize (16.A1) with respect to the vector of portfolio shares, $\underline{x}_t$ (x^h, x^f)' where $x^h + x^f = 1$. We define the return vector as $\underline{r}_t \equiv (r_t^h, r_t^f)'$. Then the mean and variance of wealth can be written as:

$$E_t W_{t+1} = W_t(1 + \underline{x}_t' E_t \underline{r}_{t+1}) \tag{16.A2}$$

$$Var(W_{t+1}) = W_t^2 Var(\underline{x}_t' \underline{r}_{t+1}) = W_t^2 \underline{x}_t' Var(\underline{r}_{t+1}) \underline{x}_t \tag{16.A3}$$

Substituting $E_t W_{t+1}$ and $Var(W_{t+1})$ into (16.A1) and maximizing the resulting expression with respect to x_t gives the first order condition for the efficient portfolio:

$$x_t^f = \frac{(E_t r_{t+1}^f - E_t r_{t+1}^h)/\gamma}{Var(r^f - r^h)} + \frac{\sigma_h^2 - \sigma_{hf}}{Var(r^f - r^h)} \tag{16.A4}$$

where γ is the parameter of relative risk aversion $(-2V_2 W_t / V_1)$, σ_h^2 is the variance of the home asset returns, σ_f^2 is the variance of the EM asset returns and σ_{hf} is the covariance between home and host returns.

Finally, home bias (h) is then the difference between the EM share in the efficient portfolio and in the observed portfolio (y)

$$h_t = x_t^f - y_t^f \tag{16.A5}$$

Estimating the asset demand function

A new method for joint estimation of bond flows and yield is based on this two-equation reduced form model; and tested on monthly data for US bond purchases, using the 'general to specific approach' (GETS) to find significant variables, lags and shock dummies for yield spread and bond flows separately; followed by a 'full information maximum likelihood' (FIML) estimation of the two equations together. The results shown in Table 16.A1 are robust and give a very good fit for both yields and flows (see Figure 16.A1), confirming the predictions of the theoretical model.

The backward-sloping demand curve for international bank loans to EMs

This function can be derived as follows. The lenders asset demand (A_d) schedule is similar to that in equation (16.1) above except that now the return (r_f) is the going interest rate spread (i_f) over the home riskless asset, net of the probability of default

Table 16.A1 FIML simultaneous estimates of EM bond flow and yield

Flow determinants:

$$LTBDC_t^\wedge = +0.596 \underset{(0.059)}{LTBDC_{t-1}} -0.0475 \underset{(0.011)}{Spread\_EM_t} + 3.62 \underset{(0.555)}{} + 0.163 \underset{(0.048)}{DLIIP_t}$$

$$-0.222 \underset{(0.068)}{FedFunds_t} + 0.304 \underset{(0.074)}{FedFunds_{t-2}} -0.138 \underset{(0.054)}{DSpread\_HY_{t-2}}$$

Yield determinants:

$$Spread\_EM_t^\wedge = + 6.44 \underset{(2.804)}{} + 0.836 \underset{(0.046)}{Spread\_EM_{t-1}} - 0.561 \underset{(0.278)}{LTBDC_t}$$

$$+ 0.656 \underset{(0.244)}{DSpread\_HY_t} + 7.48 \underset{(1.021)}{I1998:8_t}$$

Notes: Definitions: log of monthly flows (LTBDC), EMBI spread (Spread_EM), change in US industrial output (DLIIP), Federal Funds Rate (FedFunds), change in US high-yield spread (DSpread_HY). Adjusted R² for flows is 85%, for spreads 88%.

Source: FitzGerald and Krolzig (2003, 2005a).

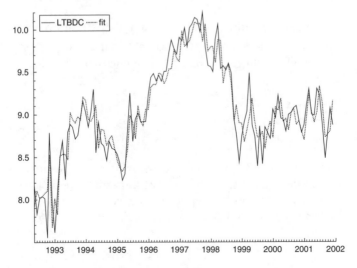

Figure 16.A1 Observed and fitted trends for bond flows

(p_f) adjusted for risk aversion (γ), and the probability of default is proportional to the square of the interest rate charged. This yields a relationship between asset demand and the interest rate of quadratic form that is depicted in Figure 16.3:

$$A_d = ar_f$$
$$r_f = i_f - \gamma p_f \qquad\qquad (16.A6)$$
$$p_f = bi_f^2$$
$$A_d = ai_f - b\gamma i_f^2$$

As in Folkerts-Landau (1985) banks are assumed to attempt to compete for market shares, so that bank lending – that is, asset demand – is maximized at the equilibrium ($\bar{A}_d$). This then corresponds to the point where

$$\frac{\partial A_d}{\partial i_f} = a - 2b\gamma i_f = 0 \qquad\qquad (16.A7)$$

$$\bar{A}_d = \frac{a^2}{4b\gamma}$$

As γ enters directly into this result, a decrease (increase) in investor risk version will lead to a rise (fall) in EM asset holdings and thus capital inflows (outflows).

There is no reason why this equilibrium point should coincide with the point of intersection of the asset demand schedule (A_d) with the asset supply schedule (A_s) except by coincidence. Of course, asset supply could be less than demand at this point, but this is not empirically plausible for EMs as an asset *class* (although it may be true of individual EMs in specific periods): so we may safely assume that in general $A_s > A_d$ at equilibrium. In other words, that the demand for loans on the part of EMs exceeds the supply of loans by the banks, and thus that the market does not clear and capital rationing exists.

Capital flows, the real exchange rate and income distribution

As an alternative to the main text, consider the case where the host economy adsorbs all the flow into the exchange rate so as to maintain the target output level (Q^*):

$$e = \frac{m_1 Q^* - F - x_1 Z}{x_2 + m_2}$$
$$\partial e/\partial F = -1/(x_2 + m_2) > 0 \qquad\qquad (16.A8)$$

in which case increased capital inflows cause the real exchange rate to appreciate, outflows lead to a depreciation. To visualize the impact of capital flows on income distribution, consider a Dornbusch-type economy with two goods and their corresponding prices foreign (P_f) and domestic (P_d), then

$$e = \frac{EP^*}{P} \qquad\qquad (16.A9)$$

and the real wage rate (ω) is expressed in terms of the nominal wage (w) and the consumer price level (P_w), which depends in turn on the proportion (θ) of the domestic good in the consumption basket:

$$\omega = \frac{w}{P_w} \tag{16.A10}$$

$$p = \theta P + (1 - \theta)EP^* \tag{16.A11}$$

Finally, the price of the non-traded domestic good (P_d) is proportional to the nominal wage rate (w):

$$P_d = \beta w \tag{16.A12}$$

We can now combine these, substituting (16.A9) and (16.A12) into (16.A11) and then plugging the result into (16.A10), so as to derive the link between the real exchange rate (e) and the real wage rate (ω), and thus the impact of capital flows (F) from (A8):

$$\omega = [\beta\{\theta + (1 - \theta)e\}]^{-1}$$

$$= \left[\beta\left\{\theta + (1 - \theta)\frac{m_1Q^* - F - x_1Z}{x_2 + m_2}\right\}\right]^{-1} \tag{16.A13}$$

$$\frac{\partial \omega}{\partial F} > 0$$

Notes

I am very grateful to colleagues at the Helsinki conference in June 2005, and to the anonymous UNU-WIDER referees, for their constructive criticism.

1. As is customary, I exclude foreign direct investment (FDI) as these are intra-firm asset/liability transactions within multinational enterprises, and thus not market flows by definition.
2. See IMF (2001) and pp. 301–3 of this chapter.
3. See Jeanneau and Micu (2002) for an excellent survey of the empirical literature. However, analytical modelling has made little progress since Dumas (1994) pointed out that international capital markets theory does not approximate the real world in a useful way.
4. However, they treat bond yields as an exogenous variable, implicitly assuming that yields are unaffected by the capital flows themselves: this may lead to an underestimation of the strength of asset demand fluctuations.
5. This model is extended in FitzGerald and Krolzig (2005b) to a two-stage procedure of portfolio allocation: first to emerging markets as an asset class and then to individual host countries according to their risk-return fundamentals. This model was successfully tested on US purchases of bonds issued by Argentina, Brazil, Korea and Mexico, using a similar econometric methodology.
6. French and Poterba (1991) and Tesar and Werner (1995) show that in the early 1990s (that is, at the start of the period considered in this chapter) stock market wealth was invested more than 90 per cent in the domestic market by the USA and Japan, and more than 80 per cent by the UK and Germany. These shares were far less than the share of

domestic equity markets in world equity markets. Indeed, in the US international equity had been less than 1 per cent of financial assets in the three post-Second World War decades. Only after 1985 holdings of foreign stocks increased sharply to roughly 10 per cent. Interestingly, this share has been relatively stable since then: 10 per cent in 1994 and 11 per cent in 2001 (Karolyi and Stulz 2002).

7. Similarly home bias might be attributed to the host withholding taxes on foreign investment income that cannot be offset against home taxes. However, Cooper and Kaplanis (1994) and French and Poterba (1991) find that the observed degree of home bias could only be explained by implausible differences in effective taxation of foreign investments.

8. For instance, Siegmann (2003) takes both a traditional risk measure and a downside risk measure and analyzes the outcomes as a function of the initial conditions. Higher uncertainty moves the optimal policy 'to the right' (that is, the minimum risk allocation is attained at higher wealth levels) and thus would reduce the overseas equity share in the efficient portfolio for any given risk tolerance.

9. Kumar and Persaud (2001) estimate risk appetite by calculating excess returns (the difference between spot rates and forward rates from the previous period) on 17 emerging market currencies over ten years. Their risk appetite index exhibits marked quarterly and annual cycles, and troughs that appear to be correlated with major market discontinuities.

10. For the derivation, see Appendix.

11. Of course, the aggregate will be made up of all emerging markets, some of which (for example, Taiwan, Chile) have permanent access and others who can only enter the market when investor sentiment permits.

12. Formally, the risk premium is only equal to the underlying default risk if the financial market is strictly risk-neutral and there is perfect information.

13. See Table 16.1 and the discussion in the final section.

14. The research literature on the economics of child welfare suggests that wages both constitute the major component of the incomes of poor families and affect the division of labour within the household. But from the viewpoint of children, the crucial aspect is whether the head of the household is in steady employment and forced to seek work away from the home; that is, in stable employment albeit at low wages (FitzGerald 2001b).

15. Interestingly, this was the position taken by the IMF in the *World Economic Outlook* for 1998 ('Financial Crises: Characteristics and Indicators of Vulnerability'), although by 2005 the *World Economic Outlook* had become much more sanguine, attributing most of emerging market volatility to domestic fundamentals.

16. See Atkinson and Stiglitz (1980).

17. Let alone the complete Arrow-Debreu set for all possible states of the world assumed in, say, Obstfeld and Rogoff (1996).

18. Default can arise for three reasons: insolvency (in the sense of insufficient trade surpluses to pay back debt); illiquidity (insufficient reserves for present debt service); and unwillingness to pay, or debt repudiation (when the cost-benefit of so doing merits it). See FitzGerald (2001c).

19. The ratio of central bank reserves to short-term external debt.

20. A good example of this is that maturity and currency mismatches in the balance sheets of Asian private banks were well known to both investors and regulators before the 1997–98 collapse, but simply not considered relevant to risk assessment.

21. Herding can be attributed to an externality where the payoff to an agent adopting an action is positively related to the number of agents adopting the same action; to principal-agent considerations where, in order to maintain or gain reputation when markets are imperfectly informed, a fund manager may 'hide in the herd' to avoid evaluation or 'ride the herd' to improve their reputation; and 'information cascades' where agents infer information from the actions of prior agents and optimally decide to ignore their own information (Devenow and Welck 1996).

22. Conventionally known as the Sharpe Ratio.

23. Formally $U(C_t) = \dfrac{C_t^{\gamma-1} - 1}{1 - r}$ where $\gamma \neq 1$, $\gamma > 0$ and $U(C_t) = \ln C_t$ where $\gamma = 1$. Conventionally, γ is assumed to lie between unity (risk neutrality) and 3.

References

Ahearne, A.G., W.L. Griever and F. Warnock (2001) 'Information Costs and Home Bias: An Analysis of US Holdings of Foreign Equities', *International Finance Discussion Papers* 691, Washington, DC: Board of Governors of the Federal Reserve System.

Atkinson, A.B. and J.E. Stiglitz (1980) *Lectures in Public Economics*, London: McGraw Hill.

Babilis, S. and V. FitzGerald (2005) 'Risk Tolerance, Home Bias and the Unstable Demand for Emerging Market Assets', *International Review of Applied Economics*, 19, 4: 459–76.

Bekaert, G. and C.R. Harvey (2000) 'Foreign Speculators and Emerging Equity Markets', *Journal of Finance*, 55, 2: 565–613.

Blake, D. and A. Timmermann (2000) 'International Investment Performance: Evidence From Institutional Investors' Foreign Equity Holdings', *Pensions Institute Discussion Paper* PI-0008, London: Birkbeck College.

Blake, D., B. Lehmann and A. Timmermann (1999) 'Asset Allocation Dynamics and Pension Fund Performance', *Journal of Business*, 72: 429–61.

Chuhan, P., S. Claessens and N. Mamingi (1998) 'Equity and Bond Flows to Latin America and Asia: The Role of Global and Country Factors', *Journal of Development Economics*, 55: 439–63.

Clark, E., M. Levasseu and P. Rousseau (1993) *International Finance*, London: Chapman and Hall.

Cooper, I. and E. Kaplanis (1994) 'Home Bias in Equity Portfolios, Inflation Hedging and International Capital Market Equilibrium', *Review of Financial Studies*, 7, 1: 45–60.

De Grauwe, P. (1996) *International Money*, Oxford: Oxford University Press.

Devenow, A. and I. Welck (1996) 'Rational Herding in Financial Economics', *European Economic Review*, 40: 603–15.

Disyatat, P. and R.G. Gelos (2001) 'The Asset Allocation of Emerging Market Funds', *IMF Working Paper* 01/11, Washington, DC: IMF.

Dumas, B. (1994) 'Partial Equilibrium Versus General Equilibrium Models Of The International Capital Market', in F. van der Ploeg (ed.), *The Handbook of International Macroeconomics*, Oxford: Blackwell.

Fernández-Arias, E. (1996) 'The New Wave of Private Capital Inflows: Push or Pull?', *Journal of Development Economics*, 48, 2: 389–418.

FitzGerald, V. (2001a) 'Short-Term Capital Flows, The Real Economy and Income Distribution in Developing Countries', in S. Griffith-Jones, M. Montes and A. Nasution (eds), *Short-term Capital Flows and Economic Crises*, Oxford: Oxford University Press for UNU-WIDER.

FitzGerald, V. (2001b) 'Financial Globalization and Child Wellbeing', Florence UNICEF at www.unicef-icdc.org/research/; also as Oxford University *QEH Working Paper* 77, Oxford: Queen Elizabeth House.

FitzGerald, V. (2001c) 'Developing Countries and Multilateral Investment Negotiations', in E.C. Nieuwenhuys and M.M.T.A. Brus (eds), *Multilateral Regulation of Investment*, The Hague: Kluwer Law International.

FitzGerald, V. (2003) 'The Instability of International Demand for Emerging Market Assets', in R. Ffrench-Davis and S. Griffith-Jones (eds), *From Capital Surges to Drought: Seeking Stability for Developing Economies*, Basingstoke: Palgrave Macmillan for UNU-WIDER.

FitzGerald, V. (2005a) 'Policy Issues in Market Based and Non-Market Based Measures to Control the Volatility of Portfolio Investment', in C.J. Green, C. Kirkpatrick and V. Murinde (eds), *Finance and Development: Surveys of Theory, Evidence and Policy*, Aldershot: Edward Elgar.

FitzGerald, V. (2005b) 'Monetary Models and Inflation Targeting in Emerging Market Economies', in P. Arestis, J. McCombie and M. Baddeley (eds), *The New Monetary Policy*, Cheltenham: Edward Elgar.

FitzGerald, V. and D. Krolzig (2003, 2005a) 'Modelling the Demand for Emerging Market Assets', *Financial Economics Working Paper* 2003-FE-10, Oxford: Said Business School. Revised version presented at the 2005 Emerging Markets Finance Conference at the Cass Business School, 5 May, London; available on www.cass.city.ac.uk/emg/seminars/Papers/Fitzgerald_Krolzig.pdf

FitzGerald, V. and D. Krolzig (2005b) 'The Simultaneous Determination of Emerging Markets Bond Flows and Yield Spreads', *Financial Economics Working Paper* 2005-FE-15, Oxford: Said Business School.

FitzGerald, V. and G. Perosino (1999) 'Trade Liberalization, Employment and Wages: A Critical Approach', in G. Barba-Navarretti, R. Faini and G. Zanalada (eds), *Labour Markets, Poverty and Development*, Oxford: Clarendon.

Folkerts-Landau, D. (1985) 'The Changing Role of International Bank Lending in Development Finance', *IMF Staff Papers*, 32: 317–63.

French, K.R. and J.M. Poterba (1991) 'International Diversification and International Equity Markets', *American Economic Review*, 81, 2: 222–6.

Froot, K.A. and P.G.J. O'Connell (2003) 'The Risk Tolerance of International Investors', *NBER Working Papers* 10157, Cambridge, MA: National Bureau of Economic Research.

Grinblatt, M. and M. Keloharju (2000) 'The Investment Behaviour and Performance of Various Investor Types: A Study of Finland's Unique Dataset', *Journal of Financial Economics*, 55: 43–67.

Henry, P.B. (2000) 'Stock Market Liberalization, Economic Reform and Emerging Market Equity Prices', *Journal of Finance*, 55, 2: 529–64.

IMF (2001) *Emerging Market Financing*, Washington, DC: IMF.

IMF (2005) *Global Financial Stability Report: Market Developments and Issues*, Washington, DC: IMF.

Jeanneau, S. and M. Micu (2002) 'Determinants of International Bank Lending to Emerging Market Countries', *BIS Working Paper* 112, Basle: Bank for International Settlements.

Kahneman, D., P. Slovic and A. Tversky (1982) *Judgement under Uncertainty: Heuristics and Biases*, Cambridge: Cambridge University Press.

Karolyi, G.A. and R.M. Stulz (2002) 'Are Financial Assets Priced Locally or Globally?', *NBER Working Paper* 8994, Cambridge, MA: National Bureau of Economic Research.

Klein, R. and V. Bawa (1977) 'The Effect of Estimation Risk on Optimal Portfolio Choice', *Journal of Financial Economics*, 3: 215–31.

Kumar, M.S. and A. Persaud (2001) 'Pure Contagion and Investors' Shifting Risk Tolerance: Analytical Issues and Empirical Evidence', *IMF Working Paper* 01/134, Washington, DC: IMF.

Levy, H. and H.M. Markowitz (1979) 'Approximating Expected Utility by a Function of Mean and Variance', *American Economic Review*, 69: 308–17.

Lewis, K. (1999) 'Trying to Explain Home Bias in Equities and Consumption', *Journal of Economic Literature* 37, 2: 571–608.

Mody, A. and M.P. Taylor (2002) 'International Capital Crunches: The Time-Varying Role of Informational Asymmetries', *IMF Working Paper* 02/43, Washington, DC: IMF.

Mody, A., M.P. Taylor and J.Y. Kim (2001) 'Modelling Fundamentals for Forecasting Capital Flows to Emerging Markets', *International Journal of Finance and Economics*, 6: 201–16.

Montiel, P. and C.M. Reinhart (1999) 'Do Capital Controls and Macroeconomic Policies Influence the Volume and Composition of Capital Flows? Evidence from the 1990s', *Journal of International Money and Finance*, 18: 619–35.

Montiel, P. and C.M. Reinhart (2001) 'The Dynamics of Capital Movements in Emerging Economies During the 1990s', in S. Griffith-Jones, M.F. Montes and A. Nasution (eds), *Short-term Capital Flows and Economic Crises*, Oxford: Oxford University Press for UNU-WIDER.

Obstfeld, M. and K. Rogoff (1996) *Foundations of International Macroeconomics*, London: IT Press.

Siegmann, A. (2003) 'Optimal Investment Policies for Defined Benefit Pension Funds', *Research Memoranda* 728/0308, Amsterdam: Netherlands Central Bank.

Taylor, M.P. and L. Sarno (1997) 'Capital Flows to Developing Countries: Long- and Short-Term Determinants', *World Bank Economic Review*, 11, 3: 451–70.

Tesar, L. and I. Werner (1995) 'Home Bias and High Turnover', *Journal of International Money and Finance*, 14, 4: 467–92.

17
Prolonged Use and Conditionality Failure: Investigating IMF Responsibility

Silvia Marchesi and Laura Sabani

Introduction

There exists a large body of evidence documenting an unsatisfactory record of implementation of IMF conditionality by borrowing countries.[1] A large proportion of IMF programmes are not successfully completed, with non-completion being not an indicator of graduation from the Fund but rather one of future referrals (or recidivism).[2] Specifically, the IMF has recently come under criticism for allowing some countries to establish long-term relationships, while, according to its original mandate, the Fund can only guarantee temporary assistance.

There has indeed been a natural evolution in the use of IMF assistance towards longer time frames (the original 18 months of a Stand-by Arrangement have lengthened to the three years of a Poverty Reduction and Growth Facility). However, such evolution has not changed the original structure of an IMF arrangement which still maintains fixed time limits. Nevertheless, the vast experience of countries has been to enter into a long-term relationship with the Fund by signing many consecutive agreements and thus making the time frames of IMF-supported programmes quite arbitrary.[3] Prolonged use has a significant effect on the revolving nature of IMF resources, which is measured by the average length of a lending cycle.[4] For example, Jeanne and Zettelmeyer (2001) find that for developing countries about 40 per cent of all the lending cycles initiated since the creation of the IMF were not completed by the year 2000 and that the average length of such incomplete cycles was 18 years.

A report published in 2002 by the IMF Independent Evaluation Office (IEO) deals specifically with the issue of prolonged use and provides a definition of prolonged use based on the concept of 'time under arrangements'.[5] A country is defined as being a prolonged user if it has been under an IMF arrangement for at least seven years out of ten. Using such definition, the report examines trends in prolonged use over the period 1971–2000. It emerges that prolonged use started to build up in the second half of the 1970s and accelerated sharply in the first half of the 1980s, due to the debt crisis. More specifically, 51 countries, out of the

128 countries that made use of IMF resources, meet the definition of prolonged user at some time during that period. In terms of the number of countries most of such expansion was in the use of concessional resources (i.e. by PRGF-eligible countries), but in terms of financial obligations, the expansion in prolonged use of general resources (i.e. mainly by middle-income countries) was greater. In addition, prolonged use is found to be persistent (i.e. countries are generally slow to 'graduate' from such use) and, in 2001, the arrangements with prolonged users represented about half of the total number of IMF programmes, with a total exposure of about half of the total outstanding obligation to the IMF.

In general, a prolonged use of IMF resources could be justified by thinking of economic adjustment as a multistage process that requires multiple IMF loans to be completed. However, empirical evidence does not support such an optimistic view, since the probability of 'graduation' from the IMF by a borrowing country does not appear to be positively related to the number of cumulated lending arrangements. Thus, prolonged use of IMF resources rather suggests a lack of effectiveness of IMF-supported programmes (i.e. poor programme implementation and flaws in programmes design).

In the literature, conditionality failures have generally been investigated by looking at the characteristics of the borrowing countries (the so-called 'demand side'). More recently, the possibility that an IMF-specific interest may influence the adoption of an IMF programme (and in turn its implementation) has also been considered (the so-called 'supply side'). Specifically, it has been argued that if the objective of conditional lending is to induce the borrowing country to carry out reforms (which otherwise would not be implemented), the threat of interrupting financial assistance, in the case of non-compliance, should be credible.[6] Nevertheless, several obstacles to the punishment of non-compliance have been identified by the literature: bureaucratic biases, political pressures, difficulties in monitoring and the so-called 'defensive lending' practice. In this chapter we propose a novel explanation, based on the contribution by Marchesi and Sabani (2005), according to which it is the repeated nature of IMF involvement, together with the fact that the Fund acts simultaneously as a lender and as a monitor (and as an advisor) of economic reforms, that weakens the credibility of warnings by the IMF and produces defensive lending.[7]

Our key proposal rests on the basis that since the IMF is not only a lender but also a monitor/advisor of economic adjustments, it is, at least partially, responsible for a borrowing country's bad performance. This is for at least two reasons: either because the Fund has prescribed the wrong reforms; or because it has not been able to detect, in its role as monitor, any deviations from the prescribed reforms early enough to get the country back on track. Therefore, the desire to avoid a loss of reputation as a good monitor/advisor might lead the Fund to exhibit some laxity in interrupting financial programmes (when a country is not meeting the agreed conditions) and such laxity will be exacerbated by the length of the relations between the country and the Fund. In fact, the longer the relationship with the borrowing country, the more disruptive for the IMF's reputation the decision not to refinance a country could be, since this outcome will have been influenced by many past monitoring (counselling) actions. Thus, we claim that prolonged use of IMF resources is not only a consequence of a lack of effectiveness of adjustment lending, but it might itself be a determinant of conditionality failure.

The chapter is organized as follows. The second section discusses the possible determinants of prolonged use, followed by a section that analyzes the effects of prolonged use on the nature and the extent of conditionality. Then we have a section that investigates conditionality failure by focusing on the so-called supply-side factors. There are then two sections analyzing the Fund's lending policy mindful of its reputation as a good monitor and as a good advisor, respectively, with the last section concluding with some policy implications.

Why do agreements continue?

In general, it is reasonable to think of the economic adjustment as a multistage process that requires multiple IMF loans to be completed. Borrowers' problems, in fact, often require structural reforms which could take years to produce positive effects. Under this interpretation, we would expect to see a gradual improvement and a borrowing country's 'graduation', at least after participation in a given number of adjustment lending programmes. However, there is some empirical evidence pointing to the opposite conclusion.[8]

Bird *et al.* (2004), examining IMF programmes between 1980 and 1996, find that repeated participation in IMF programmes is associated with: (i) larger current account deficits; (ii) lower levels of international reserves; (iii) fewer capital inflows; (iv) higher programme cancellation; (v) lower terms of trade; (vi) greater debt service ratios; and (vii) relatively more corrupt governments. According to Bird *et al.* recidivist nations seem to be caught in a vicious cycle: they start by entering Fund programmes out of necessity but then present a poor record of compliance, and thus a large proportion of IMF programmes are cancelled. However, with no penalty for past non-completion, such countries sooner or later turn again to the Fund.

Joyce (2005) analyzes in detail the time spans (spells) spent under IMF arrangements by a group of emerging countries over the period 1982–2000. He finds that, as the determinants of programmes duration are concerned, countries with lower per capita income, exports concentrated in primary goods, land-locked geographic status and autocratic regimes have longer spells. However, such evidence is not surprising, since prolonged use obviously reflects the persistence of economic difficulties. More interestingly, Joyce finds that the average length of each spell is almost three years (but a number of spells in the sample lasts for five years or longer) and that the probability that a spell would end in a given period first rises but then falls, as time passes.

Accordingly, Easterly (2005) finds that, among the top 20 recipients of adjustments loans (from both the IMF and the World Bank), in the period 1980–99, the probability of getting a new adjustment loan does not decrease with the number of loans already received (and actually it seems to increase after ten cumulative loans). These results are also confirmed by Knight and Santaella (1997) who, using a bi-variate probit model to estimate the approval of an IMF arrangement, for 91 developing countries over the period 1973–91, find that a dummy variable for past agreements increases significantly the probability to get another agreement.[9]

However, frequent use of loans by international financial institutions (IFI) and lack of graduation may actually take place for reasons controlled neither by the IMF (or the World Bank) nor by the borrowing countries. This could be the case of the countries subject to frequent external shocks, which, inducing a poor macro outcome, may prevent them from gaining independence from the IFI. Nevertheless, Easterly (2005), in his sample of intensive recipients of adjustment lending, does not find a clear association between macro shocks and prolonged use of IFI resources. In general, Easterly does not find any statistically significant difference in terms of economic performance (i.e. terms of trade growth and per capita growth) between the top 20 recipients of adjustment loans and the whole sample of developing countries, over the 1980s and the 1990s. This evidence is then in favour of the view that prolonged use reflects some shortcomings in the effectiveness of adjustment programmes (i.e. conditionality failure).

If poor programme implementation needs to be blamed for the lack of effectiveness of IMF-supported programmes and thereby for the prolonged use of IMF resources, the question then turns to how to explain the lack of selectivity by the IMF (and the World Bank) in rewarding compliance with the agreed conditions.[10] In principle, in fact, the Fund (and the World Bank) should not grant new loans to countries that have failed to deliver reforms in response to old ones. In the next section we will present some evidence on prolonged use and its effects on conditionality.

Prolonged use and its effects on conditionality

Some empirical studies have found that, controlling for country characteristics and economic performance, existing debt has a robust and positive impact on new IFI lending. For example, Marchesi and Missale (2004), estimating a dynamic panel of 52 low-income countries for the period 1982–99, find that the total amount of net transfers to HIPCs, as compared to non-HIPCs, increase with their debt level.[11] This evidence suggests that HIPCs have been receiving large amounts of resources due to their high levels of indebtedness.[12] Marchesi and Sabani (2005), estimating a dynamic panel of 53 middle-income countries for the period 1982–2001, show that a higher level of IMF debt significantly increases new IMF disbursements. This empirical evidence, together with that discussed in the previous section seems to suggest that the IFI incentives to punish bad policies (borrowing countries' failure to deliver reforms) decrease with the accumulated debt burden and with the number of loans already received.

In that respect, it actually seems that prolonged use has affected the extent and nature of conditionality, making the recipient countries more easily hide their policy slippages. The earlier mentioned IEO report (2002) presents some evidence in support of the idea that the persistence of IMF lending affects the extent and nature of conditionality. Its main conclusions are the following: (i) conditionality applied to prolonged users was on average less extensive and softer (fewer prior actions and performance criteria) than that applied to temporary users; (ii) there was a tendency for underestimation by the IMF on the technical and political limits of a country's implementation capacity (resulting in over-optimism about the feasibility and the effects of conditional reforms); (iii) there was not closer monitoring of performance under programmes with prolonged use (as one would have reasonably expected); (iv) IMF officials could generally exercise much more discretion with prolonged users than with temporary users in assessing compliance with the agreed conditions.

In conclusion, all these findings confirm the view that the problem of prolonged use (and recidivism) should be associated with some failure in inducing the governments of borrowing countries to implement policy changes. Specifically, it seems that the very fact of entering a long-term relationship with the IMF affects the nature of conditionality towards the adoption of softer and more qualitatively expressed conditions. The monitoring process itself seems to become less intensive, making it easier for policy slippages in recipient countries.

How can we explain this and what the mechanism behind it could be? Our conjecture is that the repeated nature of the IMF involvement, together with the fact that it acts simultaneously as a lender and as a monitor/counsellor of reforms, is responsible for such results. However, before explaining and justifying at length our idea (pp. 326–8), we now examine what other supply-side factors have been addressed by the literature so far to account for poor programme implementation.

Conditionality failure

When a government enters an IMF-supported programme, the Fund makes a given amount of foreign exchange available to the country for the duration of the agreement. The government can draw on these funds at scheduled intervals, provided that it satisfies the conditions specified in the arrangement. The multiple tranche system allows the IMF to deny access to subsequent disbursements if it does not observe compliance with the agreed conditions. For this agreement to work properly, it is essential that the Fund is able and willing to punish non-compliance, that is, the threat of early termination of financial assistance must be credible.[13]

The rather disappointing results of conditionality (as a means to induce reforms) have encouraged some authors to investigate on the motivations that could account for the lack of credibility of the termination warning. The main obstacles to punishment of non-compliance are identified by the literature in the existence of bureaucratic biases, political pressures difficulties in monitoring and defensive lending.

According to the international public choice approach (see, for instance, Vaubel 1986) the existence of a bureaucratic bias might lead the IMF to try to maximize its power in terms of budget size and influence in the world, without concern for its original mandate. The budget constraint the Fund faces is, in fact, a soft one. The more resources it uses, the more it can demand from its members through increased contributions. According to this view, the IMF would continue to grant new loans to protect its budget despite a lax reform effort.

To this argument it can be objected that the Fund must justify the use of its resources. However, there are several layers of Principal Agent problems that might account for a reduced IMF accountability to its members (see Vreeland 2003). Fund officials might report that policy changes are satisfactory although a programme has not been fully implemented. Moreover, they may attribute bad outcomes to adverse states of nature independently of a borrowing government's behaviour. Under these circumstances, the threat of interrupting disbursements (when conditions are not fulfilled) becomes not credible and loses its efficacy as an incentive to induce the government to keep on-track.

As reported by Rowlands (1995) the Fund has often been accused of being too much concerned with the interest of international lenders, especially after the 1982 debt crisis. External lenders (specifically the G7 governments) may exercise some political pressures on the IFI (especially the Fund) to stay involved with the countries they have important economic relations with. This is consistent with the evidence presented, among others, by Copelovitch (2004), who argues that IMF lending decisions are responsive to the interests of large industrial countries. However, according to Sturm *et al.* (2004), who estimate a panel model for 128 countries for the period 1972–98, while most economic variables are robustly related to the IMF lending activity, most political variables are non-significant. To the extent that political factors matter (especially elections), they seem more closely related to the conclusion of an agreement with the Fund than to the actual disbursement of an IMF loan.[14] For example, other political variables, like a country's relative size and its trade relations with the USA, do not appear to be significant.[15]

Moreover, a similar kind of pressure could also depend on the 'gatekeeper' role assigned to the IMF with respect to many other sources of official financing. For example Paris Club creditors have provided reschedules to developing countries conditionally on their adoption of an IMF programme.[16] Nevertheless, Marchesi and Sabani (2005) find that IMF disbursements significantly increase only with the lagged value of the IMF outstanding debt, while the impact of both bilateral and multilateral debt (and of the debt share held by private bondholders) is not significant, at least at conventional levels. Another important problem refers to the existence of difficulties in monitoring compliance with the required reforms (Cordella and Dell'Ariccia 2001). The policy reforms on which the IMF has progressively focused are more difficult to observe than traditional macro-variables (like, for instance, the rate of inflation and the exchange rate). The budgetary process can be very complex to monitor and, thus, governments might succeed in diverting resources to their most preferred use, without incurring in penalties.[17] Furthermore, the quality of monitoring might be undermined by a high IMF staff turnover that limits the accountability of mission chiefs and weakens their relationship with the recipient country's authorities. Such detrimental effects might be particularly relevant for prolonged users of IMF resources, due to the importance of track records and learning curves (see the IEO report, 2002). Moreover, in a risky economic environment (for example, due to supply conditions, international prices or world interest rates), the ability in monitoring compliance with conditionality would be strictly related to the IMF officials' ability to rapidly respond to unanticipated shocks through the necessary policies and targets adjustments. Finally, as an alternative explanation, some authors have attributed the prolonged use of Fund resources to IMF defensive lending, that is, to the practice of granting new loans to help countries pay off the old ones.[18]

This practice clearly disrupts recipient countries' incentives to comply with the agreed conditions, making the threat of being cut off from IMF financial assistance not credible. The rationale behind that practice rests on the fact that the lender would suffer from inflicting the suspension of disbursements, since that would trigger a macroeconomic crisis, with relative suspension of debt service payments. However, if the country does not adopt policy changes to ameliorate economic conditions, rolling over the debt simply postpones the default crisis. To understand the Fund's defensive lending practice we should then refer either to some 'political cost' borne by current IMF officials after a borrower's inability to pay has become public (as current officials have a shorter horizon than the institution they work for) or to the possibility that postponing default might come at a relatively lower pecuniary cost, due to some future debt relief programme (Ramcharan 2001; 2003).[19]

The political cost argument implicitly assumes that the IMF is accountable (at least to some extent) for a conditionality failure.[20] For example, the most powerful Fund members might refrain from increasing resources if its reputation is damaged.[21] What is not obvious, and thus needs to be explained, is the reason why the borrower's inability to pay can negatively affect the reputation of the IMF. Our conjecture rests on the dual role played by the Fund, which is at the same time a lender and a monitor/advisor of economic adjustments. Therefore, a borrower's inability to repay might be disruptive for the IMF's reputation as far as the latter can be, at least partially, responsible for a country's bad performance. This may happen for at least two reasons – either because the Fund has prescribed the wrong reforms, or because it has not been a good monitor. More specifically, it has not been able to detect deviations from the prescribed reform path and/or to get the country back on track by threat of immediately interrupting its financial assistance.

Therefore, it is reasonable to think that the IMF's 'prestige', as an institution, and with it its ability to maintain and to increase its budget, may depend on its the reputation of being either a good monitor or a good advisor of policy reforms. In the next section we will consider the case in which the Fund's reputation may be related to its ability as a monitor, while in the following one we will describe the case in which the Fund's reputation may depend on its ability as an advisor. Obviously the reputation of the Fund may be influenced by these two factors together (and eventually by some others); however, for simplicity, in this work we will present them separately.

Reputational concern as a monitor

In what follows, we formulate analytically our conjecture by sketching the reputational model of conditional lending as was proposed in Marchesi and Sabani (2005). In the model there are three agents: the borrowing country's government, the IMF and its stakeholders (global taxpayers) to whom the Fund is imperfectly accountable. The economy lasts for two periods. The government, at the beginning of each period, faces an 'adjustment option' that requires an indivisible investment. This structure captures the idea that the economic adjustment is a multistage process which requires multiple investments be completed. At the beginning of each period, the IMF is prepared to offer financial assistance in exchange for a precise set of policy reforms. The investment payoffs depend on the level of reforms implemented by the government.

We assume that the reforms indicated by the IMF maximize the end of period expected investment payoffs, but, by eliminating economic and other distortions, they also reduce the level of political and economic rents that the government can extract for its private gain.[22] Thus, conditional on receiving the loan, for the government it is never optimal to implement the level of reforms indicated by the Fund. Then, the optimal level of reforms will be implemented by the government only if the IMF is able to monitor efficiently and, in case of some reported deviations, it exercises, in a timely manner, the threat to interrupt current and future disbursements.

The long-term nature of the adjustment process gives the IMF more contractual power, since any first period deviation from the agreed conditions could be punished with the interruption of both current and future disbursements. Recognizing this, in our model we assume that, in the first period, if the government were actually facing the alternative between meeting the conditions and renouncing to present and future disbursements, it will always prefer to follow the adjustment path indicated by the Fund.[23] The structure of our model is complicated by the fact that the IMF can observe only imperfectly compliance with the agreed conditions. More specifically, we assume that the Fund can actually detect, without any uncertainty, whether or not the recipient country has respected its conditions only at the end of the programme. During the programme, instead, there exists some positive probability that policy slippage would not be immediately detected by Fund officials.[24] In this case, the government may conclude the first period neither respecting the agreed conditions nor incurring in a suspension. However, the IMF is able eventually to observe the reforms (not) accomplished and can render the borrowing country ineligible for the second agreement, if appropriate. If credible, such a threat could, per se, provide ex ante the government with enough incentives to meet the agreed conditions.

Nevertheless, we argue that this threat is not credible, since the interruption of the financial assistance, at the end of the first period, comes with some political cost to the Fund. Specifically, such political costs arise whenever the reputation of the Fund as a good monitor (of compliance with conditionality) is undermined.[25] In that respect we assume that there exists some uncertainty over the IMF's ability as a monitor. More specifically, the IMF can be of two types: either a good monitor or a bad monitor. If the IMF is a good monitor, it will discover departures from the optimal reform level early enough to put the country back on track, with probability ρ_g; if it is a bad monitor the probability would be ρ_b, with $\rho_g > \rho_b$.[26]

At the beginning of the first period, the IMF's type is unknown to everybody, but global taxpayers and the country's government attach a prior probability to the event that it is a good monitor. At the end of the first period, global taxpayers can observe the IMF decision to refinance or not refinance the country, but they cannot observe either the realized investment payoffs or the realized reforms. Thus, they can update their beliefs about the IMF ability as a monitor only by looking at the signal given by the refinancing decision. This generates incentives for the IMF to take action to protect its reputation as a good monitor by exploiting its informative advantage.

The IMF decision not to sign the second agreement conveys bad news for the Fund's reputation, since it indeed signals a failure of the Fund to detect policy slippages and exercise timely interruption threats. Therefore, at the end of the first period, when it comes to decide whether or not to sign a second agreement with the borrowing country, the Fund will not only look at the expected net present value (NPV) of the second loan, but also at the impact of such decision on its reputation. Then, the desire to avoid a loss of reputation as a monitor might lead the Fund to exhibit some laxity (relative to social optimum) in interrupting financial programmes which, in turn, may destroy government incentives to comply fully with conditionality.[27] Moreover, the greater the laxity, the higher the probability of financing a negative NPV investment in the second-period, since the expected outcome of the second-period adjustment is likely to depend on the reforms produced in the first period. In conclusion, persistence of bad outcomes appears to be strictly related to the long-term nature of the relationship between the IMF and the given country. Therefore, prolonged use of IMF resources may be one of the determinants of a borrowing country's poor economic performance.

Reputational concern as an advisor

In this section we present a possible extension of the Marchesi and Sabani (2005) model which considers the implications of the IMF being an advisor of economic reforms. When the uncertainty on the IMF's type does not concern the IMF ability to monitor a country's implementation of reforms, but rather its ability to design and suggest a set of reforms tailored to the specific characteristics of the borrowing country, our conclusion would remain the same. The IMF desire to hide its failure in identifying and suggesting the appropriate set of reforms will again distort its lending decisions towards greater laxity.

Let us suppose that the probability of success of the second-period adjustment option financed by the Fund is now a function of two arguments: the degree of effort exerted by the government in economic adjustment and the set of reforms suggested at the beginning of the first period by the IMF. Such a set of reforms could either be good, that is, targeted to the specific needs of the borrowing country, or bad, that is designed without taking into account the actual characteristics of the country. A good set of reforms not only increases the NPV of the second adjustment option, for each level of effort exerted, but increases also the marginal productivity of the effort produced.[28]

We assume that the IMF can be of two types: either a good advisor or a bad one. If the Fund is a good advisor, it will suggest a good set of reforms with probability θ_g, while if it is a bad advisor, this probability would become θ_b, with $\theta_g > \theta_b$. As before, we assume that the economic adjustment reduces the level of political and economic rents that can be extracted by the borrowing country's government for its private gain, but, differently from the previous section, we assume that the government's hostility to economic adjustment depends on its type which, at the beginning of the first loan, is unknown to the IMF. A government whose hostility towards adjustment is strong will exert a lower level of effort than a less hostile government. However, the quality of the reforms suggested by IMF affects positively the level of effort exerted by each type. Specifically, for each type, the more country-specific the conditions agreed with the IMF, the greater the effort.

We assume that, at the end of the first period (loan arrangement), the IMF will be able to judge whether or not the reforms suggested suit best the needs of the borrowing country and it will be also able to observe the government's type. Moreover, at this stage, the Fund decides whether or not to continue lending. Global taxpayers update their beliefs about the IMF quality as a good advisor by actually looking at the refinancing decision (the only event they can observe at the end of the first period). As before, the IMF wants to protect its reputation and so its willingness to keep on lending will depend not only on the expected NPV of the second loan, but also on the effects of the refinancing decision on its reputation. In this framework, if the suggested reforms are bad, the expected NPV is more likely to be negative, which in turn implies that the decision to stop lending is more likely when the suggested reforms are bad than when they are good. Therefore, the decision to stop lending conveys a worse signal for the Fund reputation than the decision to continue. Again, the desire to avoid a loss of reputation as an advisor might lead the Fund to exhibit a lack of selectivity in targeting financial assistance on those countries that would best utilize resources.

In conclusion, in both the models presented in this section and in the previous one, the length of the relationship between the IMF and the borrowing country plays a crucial role. It can be argued, in fact, that, when the IMF is a good monitor (or a good advisor), the probability to discover some deviations from the agreed conditions (or to design a package of reforms more tailored to a country's needs) increases with the number of years passed under arrangements, since as time passes the knowledge of the political and economic environment increases. On the contrary, if the IMF is a bad monitor (advisor) the probability to discover some deviations from the agreed conditions will be less dependent of the length of the relationship. Therefore, the decision of interrupt a programme becomes increasingly more disruptive for the IMF reputation as time passes and so prolonged use of IMF resources may exacerbate distortions in the IMF lending policy.[29]

Conclusions and policy implications

IMF conditionality specifies policies and structural reforms that borrowing countries must meet in order to obtain an IMF loan. In principle, the Fund can enable governments to implement economic reforms as a result of the leverage it exerts as a creditor. In practice the effectiveness of the conditional lending approach has been limited and numerous empirical studies have shown that a large proportion of Fund programmes last for too long, have not been successfully completed, and present a high degree of recidivism. In particular, prolonged use of Fund resources (regardless of its specific definition) has consistently expanded since the 1970s among both low-income and middle-income countries and the existing evidence overall suggests that it is linked with a lack of domestic reforms. A strand of the literature has explained such an unsatisfactory record of conditional lending, referring to the existence of bureaucratic and political biases and/or monitoring difficulties that might be responsible for the lack of credibility of IMF threats of interrupting financial assistance when a country is not complying with conditionality.

Our view is that such lack of credibility might be attributed to the dual role played by the Fund, which acts at the same time as a creditor and a monitor (advisor) of reforms. More specifically the IMF desire to hide its surveillance or counselling failures, in order to preserve its reputation, may actually distort its lending decisions towards greater laxity (relative to social optimum) in punishing non-compliance with economic reforms. Moreover, such distortionary incentives (towards excessive lending) may be exacerbated by the length of the relationship between a country and the IMF. In fact, the longer this relationship, the more informative (for the quality of the Fund monitoring and advising) the decision to interrupt a programme will be, since this outcome will have been influenced by many past monitoring actions.

An immediate policy implication of our analysis would be that, in order to eliminate distortions in the Fund lending policy, it would be better to separate its responsibility as a lender from that as a monitor (at least in the case of prolonged use). For example, the IMF could be responsible for designing appropriate policy conditions, monitoring and reporting, while, based on such reports, financial support could be decided by a separated intergovernmental body. Nevertheless, since Fund lending has so far been a precondition for many other official and, to some extent, private flows, it would be crucial that suitable alternatives to Fund lending were developed to serve as effective seal of approval in order to allow borrowing countries to keep their access to other sources of credit (IEO 2002).

An alternative proposal would envisage giving back to governments the responsibility for designing and implementing economic reforms. The surveillance function should be limited to the periodical evaluation of the attainment of objectives, rather than to the implementation of particular policy measures (Collier *et al.* 1997). In other words, substituting 'procedures conditionality' with 'target conditionality', the IMF would be less involved in managing reforms at a micro level and, in turn, it would be less responsible for observed disappointing results in the recipient countries. Outcome-based conditionality may provide a possible approach that minimizes IMF interference. Obviously, there are drawbacks pertaining to the difficulties in ascertaining how much of a disappointing result is due to a government's misbehaviour or to some negative shocks, therefore the efforts should be devoted to disentangle the consequences of bad policies from those of external shocks. Collier *et al.* suggest correcting for this bias by identifying important determinants beyond government control (for example, geographical factors and ethnolinguistic fractionalization).

Notes

1. For a review of this literature see, for example, Joyce (2005).
2. According to Mussa and Savastano (2000: 79–122) only 47 per cent of all IMF programmes have been successfully completed.
3. In particular, on this point, see Vreeland (2003).
4. Without subsequent programmes a lending cycle should be equal to the sum of the programme and the repayment period, that is a maximum of 13 years for either an Extended Fund Facility or a Poverty Reduction and Growth Facility and a minimum of 6.5 years for an 18-month Stand-by Arrangement.
5. However, a formal criterion to identify prolonged users has not yet been adopted by the IMF Executive Board, while an 'operational definition' of prolonged use would be a key step to investigate such phenomenon and develop a strategy to reduce its diffusion.
6. According to Drazen (2002: 36–67) there exists a conflict of interest between the Fund and its borrowers due to the influence of some private interests in the borrowing government's policy choices. Therefore, with no sanctions, the government will not implement reforms.
7. In a different context, this argument has been first applied by Boot and Thakor (1993) to sustain the view that the lender of last resort should not also be responsible for the surveillance of banks.
8. It is worth noting that very few studies have explicitly addressed issues related to prolonged use of IMF-supported programmes.
9. Besides, Conway (1994), estimating the probability of participating in an IMF programme for a sample of 74 developing countries over the period 1976–86, using a tobit model finds that the greater the percentage of IMF facility drawn down in the previous year the greater the duration of the current IMF programme.
10. Such lack of selectivity of both the IMF and the World Bank is confirmed by the results obtained in the case of foreign aid (see, for example, Burnside and Dollar 2000; Birdsall *et al.* 2002; Marchesi and Missale 2004).
11. Greater net transfers have taken the form of net loans from multilateral organizations and grants in exchange for loans from bilateral institutions.
12. On this point see also Easterly (2002) and Birdsall *et al.* (2002).
13. The effectiveness of this threat increases if the programme suspension undermines the country's long-term ability to negotiate new programmes with the Fund.
14. New governments are more likely to invest their political capital into an IMF-supported adjustment programme than governments later in their term because they are more likely to enjoy the outcome of their reforms. For the same reason, the Fund might judge new governments to be more reliable reformers (Sturm *et al.* 2004).
15. The relative size of a country may matter to the extent that the contagion risk of a large country's balance of payments deficit is higher (the 'too big to fail hypothesis').
16. Unlike official creditors, private creditors are less dependent on IMF programmes as a 'seal of approval'.
17. For example, conditions imposed on the composition of public expenditure require the monitoring of audited public accounts, which are seldom available on a sufficiently timely basis to implement legitimate penalties (Collier *et al.* 1997).

18. See, among others, Collier *et al.* (1997), Easterly (2002) and Ramcharan (2003).
19. However, we dismiss the role of such pecuniary costs since the IMF is a senior creditor.
20. This despite the fact that the attribution of responsibility of such failure (between the Fund and a country) may be blurred by the existence of asymmetric information.
21. The Fund can activate supplementary borrowing arrangements (through General Arrangements to Borrow and New Arrangements to Borrow) if it believes that its resources might fall short of members' needs.
22. On this point, among others, see Svensson (2000) and Drazen (2002).
23. In principle, leaving the IMF may not be particularly costly. However, if either official or private creditors around the world rely on the IMF seal of approval, then it may be very costly for a government to default. Obviously if the conditions to be implemented are particularly harsh, a country might still decide to exit from the IMF arrangement (see, for example, the case of Tanzania in the 1980s as reported in Vreeland 2003).
24. Alternatively, we could imagine that the policy slippage is detected but some political pressures prevent IMF officials from intervening.
25. Since the prestige of the Fund as an institution affects its ability to maintain and to increase its budget for such political costs, in our model, it enters the Fund objective function.
26. For example, the existence of uncertainty over the IMF monitoring ability could be explained by the uncertainty over the ability of executive directors to monitor the activity of staff officials.
27. If the IMF supervisory information was observable, the circumstance that the Fund may be self-interested would not cause any problem since it could be forced to take the right actions by its constituency.
28. The rationale behind this hypothesis rests on the fact that financial assistance becomes more productive in a good policy environment.
29. We overlook the possibility that fundamental breaks of the political and economic environment will make the IMF decisions less informative as its reputation is concerned.

References

Bird, G., M. Hussain and J.P. Joyce (2004) 'Many Happy Returns? Recidivism and the IMF', *Journal of International Money and Finance*, 23 2: 231–51.

Birdsall, N., S. Claessens and I. Diwan (2002) 'Policy Selectivity Foregone: Debt and Donor Behaviour in Africa', *CGD Working Paper* 17, Washington, DC: Center for Global Development.

Boot, W.A. and A.V. Thakor (1993) 'Self-Interested Bank Regulation', *American Economic Review*, 83: 206–12.

Burnside, C. and D. Dollar (2000) 'Aid, Policies and Growth', *American Economic Review*, 90: 847–86.

Collier, P., P. Guillaumont, S. Guillaumont and J.W. Gunning (1997) 'Redesigning Conditionality', *World Development*, 25: 1399–407.

Conway, P. (1994) 'IMF Lending Programmes Participation and Impact', *Journal of Development Economics*, 45: 365–91.

Copelovitch, M. (2004) 'Private Debt Composition and the Political Economy of IMF Lending', Mimeo, Cambridge, MA: Harvard University.

Cordella, T. and G. Dell'Ariccia (2001) 'Budget Support Versus Project Aid: A Theoretical Appraisal', mimeo, Washington, DC: IMF.

Drazen, A. (2002) 'Conditionality and Ownership in IMF Lending: A Political Economy Approach', *IMF Staff Papers* 49, Washington, DC: IMF.

Easterly, W. (2002) 'How Did Highly Indebted Poor Countries Become Highly Indebted? Reviewing Two Decades of Debt Relief', *World Development*, 30: 1677–96.

Easterly, W. (2005) 'What Did Structural Adjustment Adjust? The Association of Policies and Growth with Repeated IMF and World Bank Adjustment Loans', *Journal of Development Economics*, 76: 1–22.

Independent Evaluation Office (IEO) (2002) *Report on Prolonged Use of IMF Resources*, Washington, DC: IEO/IMF.

Jeanne, O. and J. Zettelmeyer (2001) 'International Bailouts, Moral Hazard and Conditionality', *Economic Policy*, 33: 409–32.

Joyce, J.P. (2005) 'Time Present and Time Past: A Duration Analysis of IMF Programme Spells', *Review of International Economics*, 13, 2: 283–97.

Knight, M. and J.A. Santaella (1997) 'Economic Determinants of IMF Financial Arrangements', *Journal of Development Economics*, 54: 405–36.

Marchesi, S. and A. Missale (2004) 'What Does Motivate Lending and Aid to the HIPCs?', *Centro Studi d'Agliano Development Working Paper* 189, Turin: Centro Studi d'Agliano.

Marchesi, S. and L. Sabani (2005) 'IMF Concern for Reputation and Conditional Lending Failure: Theory And Empirics', *FMG/LSE Working Paper* 535, London: London School of Economic.

Mussa, M. and M.A. Savastano (2000) 'The IMF Approach to Economic Stabilization', in B.S. Bernanke and J.J. Rotemberg (eds), *NBER Macroeconomics Annual 1999*, Cambridge, MA: MIT Press.

Ramcharan, R. (2001) 'Just Say No! (More Often): IMF Lending and Policy Reform', Mimeo.

Ramcharan, R. (2003) 'Reputation, Debt and Policy Conditionality', *IMF Working Paper* 192, Washington, DC: IMF.

Rowlands, D. (1995) 'Political and Economic Determinants of IMF Conditional Credit Agreements: 1973–1989', Mimeo, Ottawa: Norman Paterson School of International Affairs, Carleton University.

Sturm, J.E., H. Berger and J. de Haan (2004) 'Which Variables Explain Decisions on IMF Credit? An Extreme Bounds Analysis', *Economics and Politics*, 17, 5:177–213.

Svensson, J. (2000) 'When is Foreign Aid Policy Credible? Aid Dependence and Conditionality', *Journal of Development Economics*, 61: 61–80.

Vaubel, R. (1986) 'A Public Choice Approach to International Organizations', *Public Choice*, 51: 39–57.

Vreeland, J.R. (2003) *The IMF and Economic Development*, Cambridge: Cambridge University Press.

18
International Finance and the Developing World: The Next 20 Years

Tony Addison

Introduction

In August 1986, the year after UNU-WIDER began its work, the Institute hosted a conference to honour the memory of Carlos Díaz-Alejandro. Nearly 20 years on it is instructive to look over the resulting conference volume, *Debt, Stabilization and Development* (Calvo *et al.* 1989) to see how the world has, and has not, moved on. The book contains much discussion of whether a truly global market in capital has emerged, as well as the real effects of capital flows on developing countries – both areas of major debate today. Latin America's deepening debt crisis and the effects of the 'first generation' of reform programmes then underway across the developing world also featured. The terminology of 'emerging economies' was not yet common coin (the first retail fund for emerging markets did not list on the New York Stock Exchange until 1987), and the major global macroeconomic imbalance was between the USA and Japan (not China). Moreover, the acceleration in financial globalization via the new information technologies was only just beginning; Raj Kumar and Joseph Stiglitz (1989: 442) in their paper on sources of technological divergence between developed and developing economies write of 'greater talk about computers in Silicon Valley'.

Much has changed over 20 years. Funds investing in emerging market bonds and equities are taking in record amounts, and the pensions of Mr and Mrs Virtanen (Finland's Mr and Mrs Smith) now in part depend on the prospects for Chinese sovereign debt.[1] But much also remains the same, in particular Africa's plight. In the mid-1980s Africa was undergoing the first of many structural adjustment programmes, some of which worked and many of which failed dismally – resulting in the debt accumulation that has been one of the big concerns of recent years. UK finance minister Gordon Brown proclaims the need for a new 'Marshall Plan for Africa' but this call first went out in the 1980s.

In 1985 new events and crises were just around the corner: notably the Japanese financial bubble and subsequent collapse; economic transition and meltdown in the communist world; the Asian financial crisis of 1997–98 and the rapid integration of China into the global economy (resulting in trade tensions that have now come to the fore). These outcomes were largely unforeseen 20 years ago. So it may seem reckless to try and make predictions about the next 20 years. Nevertheless, speculation about the future is irresistible, not least to see how far one gets it wrong when we look back from the vantage point of 2025 – the year in which UNU-WIDER will celebrate its 40th anniversary.

International finance and the developing world is necessarily a very large subject, and therefore I confine myself to only some important aspects, leaving many others for discussion elsewhere – thus, on official aid flows see Addison *et al.* (2005); on new and innovative sources of development finance see Atkinson (2004); and on foreign direct investment see Asiedu (2006). The aspects that I do cover are as follows: the implications of ageing in the 'North' for investment in the 'South'; the expected growth in the financial services industry in emerging economies and the consequences for their capital flows; the impact of the present low levels of global interest rates on emerging market debt; and the impact of globalization in goods markets in lowering inflation expectations, and therefore global bond yields, and the implications of China's rise for this story. I close the chapter by noting the paradox that today we see ever larger amounts of capital flowing across the globe in search of superior investment returns, and yet the financing needs of the poorest countries (and the world's poorest people) remain largely unmet.

Ageing and global capital flows

An ageing world population is a certainty, barring some catastrophic health shock such as a global influenza pandemic, which would disproportionately affect the elderly. Fertility rates are falling almost everywhere and life expectancy is rising, with the exception of sub-Saharan Africa (SSA) countries with HIV/AIDS rates; people over the age of 65 will account for 16 per cent of the world's population by 2050, up from 7 per cent in 2000. These powerful demographic forces are now reshaping the global economy, not least in the area of finance where ageing influences cross-country savings rates (and therefore international flows of capital) as well as the rates of return that pension funds can expect (through the impact of ageing on economic growth).

Economic growth in the ageing societies of Europe and Japan will slow as workforces decline, unless labour productivity rises to compensate. Increased immigration (by no means certain) will be insufficient since an inconceivably large number of young immigrants are required to maintain the present ratio of workers to pensioners. The economies of Europe and Japan will therefore shrink relative to countries with younger populations, notably Brazil, India and the USA. Countries with young populations have a 'demographic window of opportunity' that gives them a potential advantage in the global economy, lasting until their present cohort of young workers retires. Investing retirement savings in these economies may therefore generate superior returns to those from investing at home, thereby pushing capital towards the former.

This is a seductive story and a popular one in the financial investment industry (not least in their sales pitch to investors) and for the North's retirees it is increasingly compelling since returns on annuities have fallen sharply (in the UK by almost two-thirds since 1990). This reflects rising life expectancy and a fall in yields, especially on government bonds which make up a large amount of pension fund assets (increasingly so after the equity market correction of 2000–03, which raised the deficits of company pension funds, leading them to reallocate from equities to bonds). In the UK case, the fall in yields on long-term gilts has been spectacular and real long-term interest rates are now around 1 per cent (their lowest level in 50 years). The fall in yields is self-reinforcing as pension funds are forced to bid up gilt prices (thereby reducing their yield) since their liabilities are calculated using a discount rate based on the long-gilt yield (and the present value of future liabilities rises as yields fall). The yield on US 30-year inflation-protected bonds, a key investment for US pension funding, is now below 2 per cent, and 10-year US treasury yields hover around 4 per cent. This makes the 8 per cent yield on a Brazilian 2040 note very attractive, to take just one example.

However, resolving the North's pension problem by investing in the youthful South is not without problems. Perhaps the most fundamental is that regions with the youngest populations face the greatest difficulties in accelerating growth, notably SSA and North Africa. This might provide an incentive for northern countries to increase official aid if aid raises growth (by financing infrastructure to stimulate higher rates of private investment in sectors employing young workers, for example). Investors then benefit from higher returns in equity markets, and find corporate debt more attractive. If aid helps to improve fiscal institutions and thereby raises the ability of poorer countries to manage their public finances, then their sovereign debt is more attractive to international investors. The associated improvement in macroeconomic stability would also reduce the exchange rate risk that foreign investors face in purchasing financial instruments, both private and public, denominated in local currencies. But nobody is yet making these arguments for aid in policy circles, and while there appears to be a positive relationship between aid and growth, there remains a very active debate about exactly how much more aid countries can absorb and effectively use (Killick 2005; Sachs 2005). Therefore, while we can expect to see more northern investor interest in the 'exotic' financial markets of the poorer South, this is likely to be a slow and somewhat tentative process, notwithstanding the benefits of diversification that these markets offer, an issue that I discuss shortly.

The countries that are most attractive to northern investors are those enjoying high growth, but many of these also have ageing populations, notably China, where retirees now outnumber new workers and there will be four retirees for every ten Chinese workers by 2030 (the ratio is presently 1:3). This implies a growing pool of domestic savings chasing the returns in domestic financial markets, and China's state pension fund is itself increasingly investing overseas.

Equally important, high growth does not convert automatically into higher returns for portfolio investors. China's stock market has fallen to its lowest point since 2000 despite annual GDP growth of close to 10 per cent. Natural-resource rents that flow overwhelmingly to state-owned oil companies account for much of the Middle East's present growth, not the private sector raising capital for investment via equity and debt markets (which would employ the region's very young population). And more generally, the returns to foreign investors depend upon foreign exchange risk (itself partly a function of a country's macroeconomic policy) as well as the quality of corporate governance, especially the protection of minority shareholder rights.

Investors must also put a sufficiently high proportion of their portfolio into the emerging market asset classes to benefit significantly (making allowance also for investment fees which are typically high). But investors hold more of their wealth in domestic assets than standard portfolio theory would predict (Lewis 1999), a 'home bias' that may now be starting to decline (see the next section) but one which remains strong nevertheless. Pension funds are also limited by law in the amount that they can invest in financial assets that are less than AAA investment-grade. Diversification towards emerging markets is traditionally thought to reduce the overall variance of a portfolio otherwise consisting of developed-country bonds and equities, but this may be less true in today's world of increasingly integrated capital markets, in which correlations between markets are declining. Nevertheless, diversification towards *smaller* stock markets in low-income countries may still reduce the overall standard deviation of a portfolio consisting of bonds, developed country equities and the larger emerging markets. Collins and Biekpe (2002) find that most African stock markets, with the exception of the larger markets of Egypt and South Africa, did not experience contagion during the 1997 Asian financial crisis, for example.

Finally, in the North it is the wealthy that have the greatest interest in emerging markets and obviously the greatest ability to invest and to take the risks implicit in the potentially high returns, not the poor who have the fewest pension assets, and generally the least investment knowledge. North–South capital flows are therefore unlikely to constitute any part of the solution to poverty among the elderly in the North, who will almost certainly continue to rely on their often meagre state pensions.

In summary, the story is more complex than that put out by the investment industry, which has its own (highly profitable) reasons for encouraging flows into its emerging market funds. With these caveats in mind, and for investors willing to take the plunge, the range of emerging market assets is widening, and this trend seems set to continue, with the following categories of particular interest:

- *Municipal bonds.* The need for infrastructure investment – in telecommunications, power and roads – in the developing world is considerable, amounting to US$465 billion annually, or 5.5 per cent of their GDP, from 2005–10 (Fay and Yepes 2003: 17). International emerging market bond funds now include municipal bonds, mainly from Latin America, and there must be scope for raising capital in this way for SSA's infrastructure, thereby reducing dependence on official aid (Leigland 1997).
- *Corporate bonds.* Firms in emerging economies have traditionally relied on retained profits and bank loans for investment finance, but issuing corporate debt could be attractive to international investors searching for yield. However,

international investors find the smallness and illiquidity of these markets unattractive. India's market is growing but remains small and fragmentary and afflicted by regulatory weakness, for example (Guha-Khasnobis and Kar 2005). Nevertheless, some middle-income countries have been able to interest global investors in their corporate debt markets.

- *Property.* Emerging market property is a potential asset class for the future, although international investor interest is confined to a small number of (mainly Asian) countries at present. There is a chance that mortgage loans from microfinance institutions (MFIs) could be bundled into securitized assets and sold internationally, since the connection between MFIs and formal financial institutions is at last increasing, at least in some countries (see the next section).

Southern financial services and capital flows

Financial services are growing rapidly in Brazil, China, India and Russia; by 2010 China's financial services sector will be as large as Italy's and will exceed Germany's by 2020 (Goldman Sachs 2003). Restructuring of domestic financial services featured in 'second-generation' reform programmes, with the privatization (either in whole or part) of state-owned banks including recapitalization by foreign banks in some cases (although a number of countries still limit foreign investment). This process has not been straightforward, banking crises have been unexpectedly frequent and the impact on domestic investment and growth receives mixed reviews.[2] Nevertheless, foreign investment in this sector looks set to accelerate, especially in Latin America[3] and in China which the big global banks see as a very attractive market.

Intense competition in mature financial markets and the fall in global interest rates have cut bank profit margins. Their profitability rests on borrowing short and lending long, but the compression of the spread between long-term and short-term interest rates (the flattening of the yield curve which we discuss further below) is forcing international banks to accelerate their search for new and growing markets. The interest rate spread between savings and lending rates is now less than 1 per cent in developed economies but remains up to 4–10 per cent in emerging economies. The latter is also falling as international banks enter the market, thereby deepening domestic financial systems, but banks then expect to profit from providing mortgages, mutual funds, insurance and credit cards, the demand for which is expected to rise with the growing middle class in emerging economies. Locally owned banks that succeed in becoming international players will also drive down transactions costs and expand the range of services. This growth will have some major consequences for capital flows, including:

- More finance for mergers and acquisitions at home and abroad by the most successful emerging market companies, which are turning themselves into international companies. The rapid expansion of India's Mittal Steel, now the world's largest steel company (and based in London and Rotterdam), is a foretaste of what will happen.

- Mutual funds and pension products, and their growth through increased investment abroad, a trend encouraged by a loosening of limits on their allocations to foreign assets (the Chilean case, for example).
- Growth in Islamic financial products, a US$200 billion market (these instruments do not pay interest, but are structured in such a way that the holder receives a rental income on the underlying assets). Bahrain, the Gulf States and Malaysia are selling Islamic financial services globally, and the middle-class in Africa (a region with more Muslims than Christians) is a small but expanding market.
- Increased competition is reducing the high transactions costs of making remittances; Western Union has cut its fee to US$10 on a US$200 transfer from the USA to Mexico. Remittances are growing rapidly as 'talent' becomes more mobile internationally (Solimano 2005). The World Bank estimates the annual value of remittances at US$95 billion but the true figure could be two or three times greater – it is difficult to guess how much flows through the *hawala* and other informal transfer mechanisms (Solimano 2004: 177–99).
- Greater connections from international capital markets to microfinance institutions (MFIs) eventually turning microfinance into a viable asset class for international investors. The first step is connecting MFIs to the domestic (formal) capital market. In 2004 Citigroup/Banamex helped Mexico's Compartamos (Latin America's biggest provided of microfinance) to raise the first slice of a US$45 billion (peso-denominated) bond from Mexican institutional investors. An IFC 34 per cent guarantee on the bonds helped them achieve an AA investment grade rating by Standard & Poor's. Tapping into global private equity also offers a direct route to international capital; Prisma Microfinance Inc. of Boston funds MFIs in Central America this way. Leveraging remittance flows by using them to back bonds to finance mortgages for house purchases by recipient families is another innovation that may become more important.
- Reduced transactions costs, and increased speed, in making cross-border philanthropic transfers to NGOs, humanitarian agencies and (increasingly) direct to individuals and communities. We can expect growth in flows of charitable donations from emerging economies with a rising middle class. Chinese individuals and companies donated some US$15 million for Asian countries hit by the 2004 tsunami disaster, for example.[4]

In summary, these are trends to watch for the future. Yet they are not without problems. Much depends on whether fast growth is sustained in the emerging economies, with China being critical to what happens next (see later discussion). Moreover, the increase in portfolio flows through increasingly sophisticated financial sectors will make it trickier for policy-makers to manage the macroeconomic effects of capital flows.[5] And a fundamental challenge is to encourage inflows to poorer countries (in part by deepening their domestic financial markets), and reducing the exclusion of the poor from formal financial markets (and therefore indirectly from access to international capital).

Global interest rates and capital flows

One big difference with the world of 20 years ago is the cost of money; in 1985 the US was just coming out of its adjustment to the round of sharp rate rises begun by Federal Reserve Chairman Paul Volcker in October 1979 (Cooper and Little 2000: 77–121). Fast forward to the present and the yield on the ten-year US Treasury note is around 4 per cent compared with 15 per cent back in the early 1980s. The real (inflation-adjusted) cost of money has fallen substantially. In the UK the long-term real rate is around 1 per cent, having varied between 2 and 4 per cent for much of the last 25 years.

From 2000–04 the US Federal Reserve (Fed) loosened monetary policy in response to the bursting of the tech-stock bubble (1996–2000) and the 9/11 terrorist attacks. The Federal funds rate, charged on overnight loans between banks, eventually reached 1 per cent in 2004, its lowest rate since the 1950s. The Fed went into reverse in June 2004 with the first increase in the Fed funds rate in four years, marking the start of 14 successive quarter-percentage point increases to 4.25 per cent as of January 2006. The Fed has signalled further increases, although the market consensus at the start of 2006 was for a pause after one more quarter-percentage point increase. However, while the Fed has raised short rates, the long end of the yield curve has actually fallen – thereby flattening the overall yield curve – and the yield on the ten-year US Treasury note is now below its level at the start of the Fed credit-tightening cycle. This is a 'puzzle' that is now exercising the market's best minds (see further discussion below). Bond yields are also at all-time lows in the six-year-old euro zone – the yield on ten-year German bonds is around 3.2 per cent – and long yields are close to 1 per cent in Japan, reflecting price deflation over the last decade.

With global monetary easing, the prices of all major assets – equities, bonds and property – are now substantially higher than two years ago, and emerging market equities and bonds are among the strongest performing asset classes. The J.P. Morgan Emerging Markets Bond Index Plus (EMBI+), which is the industry benchmark for US funds investing in emerging market debt, returned 8.01 per cent in the six-month period up to 28 February 2005, easily beating the paltry interest on any money market account. Large inflows from institutional and retail investors have occurred over the last five years, particularly pension funds as noted earlier, and this provides a level of market support that was largely absent in the past.

The risk premium on emerging market debt has also fallen with improvements in the public finances of emerging economies; this is partly a consequence of the commodity-market boom itself resulting from strong growth in China and India. In mid-2005, EMBI+ spreads over US treasuries were at their lowest level (338 basis points) since 1997 (just before Russia's sovereign default). Half of the countries in EMBI+ now have an investment grade credit rating, which is unprecedented in the history of emerging market debt.

What does the future hold? A rising Fed Funds rate is typically adverse for high-yield debt markets, emerging bond markets included. If you believe that 'push factors' (global capital supply) are more important than 'pull' factors (emerging market characteristics) in determining the flows into and out of emerging market debt – and there is increasing evidence that the former are more important than the latter[6] – then a rising Fed Funds rate does not bode well for the future. Moreover, the recent reversal in the dollar's fortunes (at least against the euro) reduces the relative attractiveness of non-dollar investments for both long-term US investors (to whom emerging markets have been sold as a way of playing the dollar's decline) and short-term investors engaged in the 'carry trade' (borrowing in US dollars to invest in non-dollar assets). Some market participants believe that the carry trade has created a major over-pricing of risky assets, emerging market debt included, as investors 'reach for yield'. This is consistent with a view that 'fair value' is only rarely seen in a market whose swings depend upon herd behaviour and momentum trading. The carry trade started to unwind in 2004 as the Fed raised rates although it has recently resumed along with the fall in US long yields.

The hedge-fund industry will play a central role in what happens next since it is often the market's marginal buyer (or seller); hedge funds now manage about US$1 trillion globally (double their 2000 level). Hedge funds as a whole were short on emerging market debt in the first half of 2005, betting against high-yield debt in general on the expectation of weakness as the Fed Fund rate increases. Spreads over US treasuries rose, although not by as much as the spreads on US high-yield corporate debt. However, short positions are now being closed as the decline in long yields resumes making the carry trade profitable again. The risks are, however, rising all the time since with the compression in spreads between high-yield debt and treasuries, hedge funds must increase their leverage to achieve superior returns, increasing their chances of a blow-up if spreads reverse their decline. One hedge-fund manager recently compared this to pushing down a spring 'you keep having to press it harder when it is already compressed and that is dangerous'.[7]

Long yields may rise independently of any action by the Federal Reserve if Asian central banks diversify significantly away from US treasuries, as many observers predict. However, for the moment the long-end is falling. For bears this is a temporary aberration indicating that the market has a misplaced belief that US growth will soften, thereby implying that the Federal Reserve will cease tightening after one or two more quarter-point rises. If the bears are right then US long yields will jump once the market realizes that it has underestimated the scale of Fed tightening; this will deliver a shock to emerging market bonds which will see a sharp rise in their spread over treasuries. In contrast, bulls see the downward trend in long yields continuing, the result of financial globalization and, perhaps, a reduction in the 'home bias' of investors over the last five years (see my earlier discussion). US yields, while low, are still higher than those in Europe and Japan, and hence attractive to international investors. As US yields fall, the level of demand for emerging market debt will rise further. This would then provide an excellent environment for increasing investor interest in the sovereign bonds of less well-known countries, especially the smaller countries of sub-Saharan Africa. How the bear–bull debate resolves itself will be critical to the fortunes of existing and newer borrowers in emerging market bonds over the next five or so years.

Given the very good run of emerging market debt, bears have looked for signs of trouble among the major borrowers. Brazil and Mexico loom large in investors' minds since they account for the largest weightings in EMBI+ (22.9 per cent and 19.6 per cent, respectively). Some believe that President da Silva, whose ruling party is now embroiled in a corruption scandal, will turn fiscally reckless in the run up to the 2006 elections, but this has yet to affect the Brazilian debt market. Likewise, both Moody's and Standard & Poor's have upgraded Mexico's sovereign debt rating. In 2005, Turkey's debt was expected to sell-off upon a 'no' vote in the French and Dutch referendums on the EU constitution – an outcome that is believed by many to reduce Turkey's chances of accession (thereby damaging the convergence of its interest rates with those of the EU). But the market rallied instead. Indeed, emerging market bonds may have stronger fundamentals than the high-yield corporate bonds of OECD countries. Mexico is the biggest BBB-rated credit in Lehman's investment-grade bond indices following the downgrade of General Motors and Ford to junk status in May 2005.[8] But it may simply be the case that country policies are less important as a market driver than global capital supply for, as Manuel Agosin (2005: 4) notes, countries with a very wide range of policy stances typically experience substantial capital inflows during periods of global capital surge.

Globalization in goods markets and capital flows

Despite some problems among the smaller borrowers (notably Bolivia in 2005) the emerging bond market class as whole looks robust in the near term. Nevertheless we can still find some grey clouds going forward if we look hard enough. A potentially serious threat for the whole asset class is what happens next in China. The 'China factor' is an important reason why the market for emerging market debt differs from that of ten years ago (and a factor that would have been inconceivable 20 years ago). And it has several interesting and interlinked dimensions.

First, China's high growth has raised world commodity prices and therefore GDP growth in commodity-producers, with the resulting buoyancy in tax revenues improving fiscal balances and sovereign credit ratings. This makes bond ratings vulnerable to any commodity-price shock resulting from slower Chinese growth. Any slackening of Chinese demand could be offset by rising demand from continental Europe and Japan, both of which are showing signs of recovery, but that recovery is itself partly driven by their rising exports to China (especially so in the Japanese case) and both regions face a longer-term growth slowdown as their societies age (see our earlier discussion). US growth remains perilously dependent upon its over-extended consumer, who remains vulnerable to any rise in mortgage rates from their present low levels (itself partly a product of Chinese purchases of US debt which contributed to lowering long-term interest rates upon which most US mortgage-financing is based). It is not inconceivable that governments in commodity-producing countries might offset the negative fiscal effect of a world commodity-price fall through better tax mobilization, but progress in this area has been generally slow (Brazil and Mexico) or entirely absent (Venezuela). Better domestic revenue mobilization remains one of their most urgent challenges, not least to dampen the scale of their adjustment to any future China shock.

Second, China is central to the story of low global inflation underpinning low interest rates. Many in the financial markets believe that China's low-cost manufacturing caps inflation in goods markets (while India's role in outsourcing contains service-sector inflation). This belief, which is not without foundation, has reduced inflation expectations and long bond yields. But rich countries must continue absorbing Chinese exports for low-inflation expectations to be maintained. Any major restraint on China's ability to export will undermine the low inflation story, and will ratchet up bond yields, thereby slowing global growth overall – and cutting away one of the foundations of the present inflow of capital into emerging bond markets. And any slowdown in growth will have a knock-on effect on the growth of the financial services industry in developing countries as well. Similarly, an upward revaluation in the renminbi, which the US is pressing the Chinese to undertake, will increase the cost to US consumers of imported Chinese goods (this is one of the paradoxes of US–Chinese relations).

Although China's performance certainly looks spectacular, it is in fact yet to recover the share of world output that it had in the late nineteenth century, during the first wave of globalization; Crafts (2004) estimates that China accounted for 12.5 per cent of global manufacturing output in 1880, dropping to a low of 2.3 per cent in 1950, and rising back to 7 per cent in 2000. As China's per capita income rises, so domestic demand growth will increasingly drive economic growth, but export growth will remain the main engine for the next decade at least. Access to an open trading system is therefore in China's paramount interest, but a surge in its exports of clothing and textiles following the expiry of quotas with the end of the Multi-Fibre Agreement at the start of 2005 stirred up a protectionist hornet's nest in Brussels and Washington, DC.

Notwithstanding these problems, we should not make too much of present difficulties. First, if the US and Europe go beyond modest protection against China into something much more substantial then they will undermine their own interests in a multilateral trading system. And second, the differences between China, the US and Europe reflect national interests within the ambit of a global market economy, and do not arise from a contest between fundamentally different economic systems – as they did 30 or 40 years ago when the Cold War was at its height. In that sense the politics of interstate relations which underlies economic relations today has a less calamitous downside than it did for most of the years after the Second World War.

Second, and perhaps a more lethal factor, China is one of Asia's big buyers of US treasuries, thereby reducing yields at the long end of the US curve and making the whole class of emerging market debt – which trades at a spread above treasuries – more attractive to buyers. Any large-scale reduction in China's purchases of treasuries would raise US long yields (unless offset by additional purchases by other Asian central banks) thereby reducing the relative attractiveness of high-yield debt in general, and emerging market debt in particular. A slowdown in Asia's purchases of US treasuries, including those by China, is inevitable in any case as the renminbi and Asia's other currencies appreciate against the dollar thereby reducing the region's very large current account surpluses (and requiring a commensurate reduction in the US current account deficit which is an unsustainable 6 per cent of GDP). A critical factor for the markets is whether this adjustment is orderly or not. If the former, then US long yields will move steadily upwards – which is what the Fed wants since it believes that US growth is now robust after the 9/11 shock and slowdown. The spreads of emerging market bonds over treasuries will then rise, but hopefully not too much to cause serious financing problems for Latin America and other borrowers. A disorderly adjustment would consist of a rapid sell-off in the US treasuries market (accelerated by hedge funds which would quickly take up short positions), a sharp jump in emerging market bond yields, and – in a worst-case scenario – a liquidity crunch, locking up high-yield debt markets in particular.

Since China's own sovereign debt is attractive to investors (the 'Virtanen' story with which I began the chapter), trouble in credit markets would hit China as well – perhaps therefore accelerating any initial slowdown in its growth. For this reason at least, China (and more broadly Asia) has an interest in an orderly and gradual adjustment of the present imbalances with the United States (IMF 2005). It is therefore highly unlikely that China would conduct a large and rapid sale of US treasuries, as some observers have speculated, and this is not a credible threat in US–China bilateral trade negotiations. There are, however, political 'wild cards' that could cause disorderly adjustment by pushing China into deep recession, resulting in a sell-off in emerging market debt. These include: the re-emergence of a strong domestic pro-democracy movement and a violent counter-reaction by the ruling Communist Party; a further deterioration in relations with Taiwan (with war being the worst-case scenario); and a deterioration in bilateral relations, both economic and political, with Japan. Since it is often 'unexpected' political events that initiate major global economic shocks, the tensions in the global politics of China's rise should not be discounted in any assessment of future international financial risks.

Conclusions

So what do we conclude from all this? We might say that speculation about the future is largely pointless; all kinds of forecasts can be developed, most of which will never come to pass and it is often the unnoticed trends, or completely unexpected events, that prove to be decisive. Nevertheless, we can discern some broad contours of the future in present trends.

The first set of these are the consequences that arise from financing the costs of ageing societies, notably Europe and Japan. This has powerful effects on international financial markets, and is one reasonably certain trend given the size of the retirement savings involved. But predicting which financial markets will benefit the most is much more difficult. The story in which ageing societies invest in the equity and bond markets of youthful developing countries could constitute the big picture for the next 20 years. As capital flows to developing countries are affected much more by risk rather than return (i.e. variance as opposed to mean) there is potentially a 'win-win' outcome for both North and South where northern investors get lower risk, and the South gets cheaper capital. If these capital flows are forthcoming then they will prove favourable to the expansion of southern markets for sovereign debt, equities, corporate debt and, eventually, municipal debt and property as asset classes for northern (and southern) investors. To work, however, this scenario requires that societies with young populations use the capital flow effectively to achieve higher growth, with this in turn translating itself into higher returns for foreign investors so that more capital is forthcoming. Foreign investors must also be sufficiently risk-taking to allocate a large enough share of their portfolio to the relevant asset categories to benefit significantly from any superior returns. This will entail considerable institution-building and innovation, including better corporate governance among southern companies (to protect shareholder rights), improved macroeconomic management to reduce exchange-rate and credit risks and to cope with the real-economy effects of the capital inflow (thereby ensuring that it enhances rather than damages economic development), and the increased use of derivative instruments to hedge some of the exchange-rate and political risk for international investors.

The second trend is the rapid growth now underway in the financial services industry, which on some predictions will account for 10 per cent of global GDP by 2020 – with much of the growth coming in the larger emerging economies (Goldman Sachs 2003). Deeper and more sophisticated domestic financial markets will draw in capital flows (attracting direct investment by international banks in joint ventures to provide financial services) as well as sending capital outwards (by offering domestic residents mutual funds that invest in foreign assets, in particular). This opens up new possibilities for connecting local demand for capital to the international capital market, including packaging microfinance loans into financial instruments that can then be sold to international investors (perhaps with some hedging of the currency risk) thereby enabling microfinance institutions to expand by diversifying from their present dependence on NGO and foundation funding. In summary, there is much potential but realizing these gains will not be easy. Fundamentally, the countries that most need external capital flow are the smaller and poorer countries but they have underdeveloped and illiquid capital markets and are often little known to investors who may by-pass them in favour of the bigger, better-known and deeper financial markets of Brazil, China and India. The smaller countries need more assistance to overcome information asymmetries and high transactions costs so that they can tap more effectively into international capital markets.

The third of our future trends comes from the recent and rapid growth in demand for emerging market debt, and the resulting compression in spreads over developed-market debt. There is considerable uncertainty over what happens next. Is the present market strength the result of ample global liquidity (with real interest-rates at historically very low levels) with the danger that as the interest-rate cycle turns, and liquidity contracts, emerging markets will turn down as they did in the past? Or have fundamentals in emerging markets improved sufficiently to attract continuing inflows even as US monetary policy tightens with, perhaps, the search for yield by investors from ageing societies putting some kind of floor under the market?

The fourth contour in the next 20 years of international finance relates to one of the biggest questions of all: will globalization, and specifically trade liberalization, continue or will it slow, or even stall and reverse? This is critical since globalization in goods markets (a massive expansion of low-cost producers) has been central to the formation of low expectations for future inflation – and therefore to the story of low and declining bond yields, to the benefit of borrowers in developed and emerging economies alike. Here the story can take many different future paths, depending very much on your chosen scenario as to how the relationship between Europe, the USA and Asia's rising economies, especially China, will work itself out.

To conclude: today we see a large volume of global savings moving through an increasingly integrated global capital market in search of investment opportunities, but finding low (and declining) returns. Asia continues to pour ever increasing amounts into low-yielding US treasuries, the counterpart to historically large US fiscal (and current-account) deficits. Yet running alongside this process are appeals for more official aid and debt relief for poorer and smaller countries, especially in SSA, which urgently need more external finance to meet their development and poverty-reduction goals. Twenty years from now, this may be seen as one of the starkest contrasts in the present system of international finance.

Notes

The author wishes to thank participants in the conference session for useful comments, especially Valpy FitzGerald and Anwar Nasution, as well as the comments of two anonymous referees.

1. In 2004, Finnish pension funds accounted for 7 per cent of the €4 billion of orders for a €1 billion Chinese government bond – their first significant purchase (Guerrera 2004).
2. For scepticism see Stiglitz (2002: 69).
3. See Guillén (2000).
4. Source: 'Japan, China Enter New Era of Giving', *Wall Street Journal*, 11 January 2005.
5. Which can sometimes be destabilizing; see Griffith-Jones *et al.* (2001).
6. See FitzGerald (Chapter 16 of this volume); Mody and Taylor (2002).
7. Quoted in 'Splish Splash', *Wall Street Journal*, 7 June 2005.
8. Recent progress under the heavily indebted poor countries (HIPC) initiative in relieving a portion of the debts owed to official creditors is also important to changing international investor perceptions and increasing the possibilities for these countries to fund their development expenditures via the sale of sovereign debt in international markets (Addison *et al.* 2004).

References

Addison, T., H. Hansen and F. Tarp (eds) (2004) *Debt Relief for Poor Countries*, Basingstoke: Palgrave Macmillan for UNU-WIDER.

Addison, T., G. Mavrotas and M. McGillivray (2005) 'Aid, Debt Relief, and New Sources of Finance for Meeting the Millennium Development Goals', *Journal of International Affairs*, 58, 2: 113–27.

Agosin, M.R. (2005) 'Capital Flows and Macroeconomic Policy in Emerging Economies', Mimeo, Washington, DC: Inter-American Development Bank.

Asiedu, E. (2006) 'Foreign Direct Investment in Africa: The Role of Natural Resources, Market Size, Government Policy, Institutions and Political Instability', *World Economy*, 29, 1: 63–77.

Atkinson, A.B. (ed.) (2004) *New Sources for Development Finance*, Oxford: Oxford University Press for UNU-WIDER.

Calvo, G., R. Findlay, P. Kouri and J. Braga de Macedo (eds) (1989) *Debt, Stabilization and Development*, Oxford: Basil Blackwell for UNU-WIDER.

Collins, D. and N. Biekpe (2002) 'Should Emerging Market Contagion Be a Fear for African Stock Markets?', Mimeo, Cape Town: University of Cape Town, School of Management Studies.

Cooper, R. and J.S. Little (2000) 'US Monetary Policy in an Integrating World: 1960 to 2000', in R.W. Kopcke and L.E. Browne (eds), *The Evolution of Monetary Policy and the Federal Reserve System Over the Past Thirty Years: A Conference in Honor of Frank E. Morris*, Boston: Federal Reserve Bank of Boston.

Crafts, N. (2004) 'The World Economy in the 1990s: A Long Run Perspective', *Working Papers in Economic History* 87/04, London: London School of Economics.

Fay, M. and T. Yepes (2003) 'Investing in Infrastructure: What is Needed from 2000 to 2010?', *Policy Research Working Paper* 3102, Washington, DC: World Bank.

Goldman Sachs (2003) 'Dreaming with the BRICs: The Path to 2050', *Global Economic Papers* 99, London: Goldman Sachs.

Griffith-Jones, S., M.F. Montes and A. Nasution (eds) (2001) *Short-Term Capital Flows and Economic Crises*, Oxford: Oxford University Press for UNU-WIDER.

Guerrera, F. (2004) 'On Asia: Keeping up with the Virtanens', *Financial Times*, 20 October.

Guha-Khasnobis, B. and S. Kar (2005) 'Corporate Debt Market in India – An Analytical Study of the Macroeconomic and Institutional Issues', Mimeo, Helsinki: UNU-WIDER.

Guillén, M. (2000) 'The Internationalization of Retail Banking: The Case of the Spanish Banks in Latin America', *Transnational Corporations*, 9, 3: 63–97.

IMF (2005) *Global Financial Stability Report: Market Developments and Issues*, Washington, DC: IMF.

Killick, T. (2005) 'Don't Throw Money at Africa', *IDS Bulletin*, 36, 3: 14–19.

Kumar, R. and J. Stiglitz (1989) 'Sources of Technological Divergence between Developed and Developing Economies', in G. Calvo, R. Findlay, P. Kouri and J. Braga de Macedo (eds), *Debt, Stabilization and Development*, Oxford: Basil Blackwell for UNU-WIDER.

Leigland, J. (1997) 'Accelerating Municipal Bond Market Development in Emerging Economies: An Assessment of Strategies and Progress', *Public Budgeting and Finance*, 17: 57–79.

Lewis, K. (1999) 'Trying to Explain Home Bias in Equities and Consumption', *Journal of Economic Literature*, 37, 2: 571–608.

Mody, A. and M.P. Taylor (2002) 'International Capital Crunches: The Time-Varying Role of Informational Asymmetries', *IMF Working Paper* 02/43, Washington, DC: IMF.

Sachs, J. (2005) *The End of Poverty: How We Can Make it Happen in Our Lifetime*, London: Penguin.

Solimano A. (2004) 'Remittances by Emigrants: Issues and Evidence', in A.B. Atkinson (ed.), *New Sources of Development Finance*, Oxford: Oxford University Press for UNU-WIDER.

Solimano, A. (2005) 'The International Mobility of Talent and its Impact on Global Development: An Overview', paper prepared for the UNU-WIDER project on the International Mobility of Talent.

Stiglitz, J. (2002) *Globalization and its Discontents*, London: Penguin Books.

Part VI
Growth and Poverty

19
Gender and Growth in Sub-Saharan Africa: Issues and Evidence

Mark Blackden, Sudharshan Canagarajah,
Stephan Klasen and David Lawson

Introduction

Since at least the mid-1970s, sub-Saharan Africa's growth performance has lagged behind all other developing regions, with large and rising income gaps compared with the rapidly growing economies in East and South Asia. This poor growth performance has translated into a similarly poor performance in terms of poverty reduction, with Africa having the highest poverty rates (incidence as well as depth using the international $1-a-day poverty line) and showing no progress in meeting Millennium Development Goal 1 (MDG1) since the early 1980s (Chen and Ravallion 2004). Africa also suffers from a low poverty elasticity of growth, largely due to its high inequality, which by now is among the highest in the developing world (World Bank 2005a).

The presumed sources of slow growth in African economies have been analyzed by many authors,[1] and range from the institutional legacy of colonialism, geographic challenges, trade and debt-related issues, high ethnic diversity, high incidence of conflict, demographic issues, weak institutions, considerable inequality, as well as poor economic policy choices. While these factors are clearly important contributors to Africa's poor economic prospects, we show that there is by now considerable evidence that gender inequality in various dimensions also plays a significant role in accounting for the poor growth performance in Africa, and can help us further our understanding of growth determinants.[2] These issues range from inequalities in education and formal sector employment to gender gaps in access to and control over important economic assets and productive inputs, and issues of governance. As we show below, there is considerable evidence that these gaps not only disadvantage women, and thus are inequitable, but reduce the growth potential in the region, and thus are partly responsible for the poor progress in poverty reduction in Africa.[3]

The study suggests that gender inequality plays a significant role in accounting for Africa's poor growth and poverty-reduction performance.[4] It argues that removing these inequalities would be an important precondition for addressing Africa's growth problems. To do so, this study focuses on the theoretical insights relating to gender and growth linkages and complements this with some recent empirical evidence. The next section of the study discusses the theoretical insights on gender and growth, highlighting the particular difficulties associated with gender-based analysis in a situation where market and household productive activities are often intertwined at the household level, an interdependence that is not fully captured in standard economic analyses. The third section provides some current evidence on the main gender issues that are particularly important for growth, including gender gaps in education, formal sector employment, access to assets and resources (particularly in agriculture) and gender gaps in time use. We then conclude with some policy-focused and research-oriented recommendations.

Theoretical linkages between gender and growth in sub-Saharan Africa

Growth theory suggests that economic growth depends on the accumulation of economic (including human) assets, and the return on these assets, which in turn depend on technological progress, the efficiency with which assets are being used, and the institutional frameworks of production. The different strands of the growth literature all agree on these factors but differ in the way these factors interact to generate sustainable growth. Gender issues will naturally come into play in the way all of these factors influence economic growth. As discussed below, there may be gender differences in the way human assets are being generated and accumulated, and gender issues may also play a role in the way physical assets (including land but also other physical capital) are being maintained and augmented. In addition, gender issues may play a role in influencing technological progress, as well as the efficiency with which assets are being used to produce incomes. Lastly, gender issues may influence institutions, both public and private, which can help or hinder the efficiency of resource use. The relevant literature in each of these factors will be discussed below.

Methodological constraints

It is important to highlight a few particular difficulties in analyzing these gender issues as they relate to economic growth. First, many gender differences relate to the way households decide on production and consumption matters.[5] As we discuss in the next section, the household plays a particularly important role as a producer of economic goods as well as human assets in Africa and, thus, a full understanding of the gender issues involved requires an analysis of household, and especially intra-household, issues. This is an area economics has historically shied away from, where our data are often quite patchy and the evidence is circumstantial.

Second, the importance of gender issues may not be as directly visible as some other issues affecting growth, due to the fact that a considerable share of the economic contribution of women is not included in national income aggregates and income-based poverty measures.[6] This has two important implications. First, the economic contribution of women to wellbeing and poverty (in a wider multidimensional perspective) is understated in conventional national income and poverty statistics. Similarly, the economic constraints women face in their productive activities and how they differ from those faced by men, often do not receive enough attention. Researchers interested in uncovering the gender dynamics of growth issues will have to move beyond direct influences of gender inequality on growth and include complex indirect influences. As shown below, indirect linkages might include issues such as the 'quantity' and 'quality' of children, the importance of time constraints for women's productive activities, and the impact of intra-household relations and resource control issues on women's willingness to invest in the improvement of land or in technical progress. Lastly, there are some issues that are traditionally viewed as non-economic but which can clearly have economic implications. Those include issues such as violence against women that affects their ability to produce, 'cultural' constraints on women's economic activities and issues of control over resources within households that may heavily influence household decision making about the allocation of resources for the accumulation of assets and/or the efficiency of asset use. These questions make it more difficult to identify clearly the role of gender issues in growth. But they make them no less important.

Theoretical insights

By now, there is a considerable theoretical literature suggesting that gender differences in asset accumulation and use can have significant growth effects. In particular, a number of models find that gender inequality in education and employment reduce economic growth. The main arguments from the literature, which are discussed in more detail in Klasen (1999; 2002) are briefly summarized below.

With respect to gender inequality in education, the theoretical literature suggests that such gender inequality reduces the average amount of human capital in a society and thus harms economic performance. It does so by artificially restricting the pool of talent from which to draw for education, thereby excluding highly qualified girls (and taking less qualified boys instead). Moreover, if there are declining marginal returns to education (and imperfect substitutability between males and females), restricting the education of girls to lower levels while educating boys at higher levels means that the *marginal* return to educating girls is higher than that of boys and thus would boost overall economic performance.[7]

A second argument relates to positive externalities of female education, that is positive effects that are not captured by the beneficiaries themselves (who, of course, also profit from higher education).[8] Promoting female education or earnings is known to reduce fertility levels reduce child mortality levels and promote the education of the next generation. Each factor in turn has a positive impact on economic growth. As shown in some models,[9] these effects can be large enough to ensure that some countries are trapped in a low-level equilibrium with large gender gaps in education or earnings, high fertility rates, low investment in each child and consequently low levels of per capita incomes.[10] This would be particularly relevant for low-income countries that have not entered the demographic transition – as applies to a significant number of countries in sub-Saharan Africa (SSA) – and which might be stuck in such a low-level poverty equilibrium, partly due to high gender inequality.

Related to this argument, some authors have emphasized that reducing gender gaps in education will help initiate the demographic transition that will, with some time lag, lead to a favourable age distribution in a population, known as the 'demographic gift', in which the share of working-age people is particularly high, compared to the declining cohorts of the young and not yet large cohorts of the elderly. This phase of the demographic gift can lead to higher savings and investment rates, and higher worker/capita ratios, all of which would boost per capita GDP (Bloom and Williamson 1998).

A third argument is that gender gaps in employment impose a similar distortion on the economy as do gender gaps in education. They artificially reduce the pool of talent from which employers can draw, thereby reducing the average ability of the workforce (Klasen and Lamanna 2003). In a related model by Esteve-Volart (2004), gender gaps in access to managerial positions and employment more generally distort the allocation of talent and the production and productivity of human capital, all of which serve to reduce economic growth.

Some authors have emphasized a fourth argument which also relates to education and employment inequalities.[11] They argue that low gender gaps in education and employment, combined with relatively large gender gaps in pay can be a source of competitive advantage in the promotion of export-oriented industries that draw heavily on female labour. These authors highlight the export-oriented growth strategies of East Asian economies where shrinking gender gaps in education and employment coincided with high gender pay gaps.[12]

A fifth argument relates to the importance of female employment for their bargaining power within families. There is a sizeable literature that demonstrates female employment and earnings increase their bargaining power in the home (Klasen and Wink 2002; World Bank 2001; Sen 1990). This not only benefits the women concerned, but their greater bargaining power has been shown to lead to greater investments in the health and education of their children, thus promoting human capital of the next generation and therefore improving the potential for economic growth (Thomas 1997; World Bank 2001).

A sixth argument relates to access to productive assets and inputs. In situations where women and men undertake different and/or separate productive activities (as is the case in agriculture in much of Africa but also in non-agricultural activities in many developing countries), differential access to productive assets and inputs constitutes a distortion in the sense that 'women's activities' are under-resourced and under-capitalized while 'male activities' are (comparatively) over-resourced and over-capitalized. Due to declining marginal returns and/or the loss associated with talented women being starved of economic resources, such a distortion reduces aggregate output (World Bank 2001; 2005a; Udry 1996). Such gender gaps might not only lead to static inefficiency but also reduce efficient investments in new technologies (Jones 1986; von Braun and Webb 1989) and the maintenance and improvement of assets, including particularly land.

A seventh argument relates to time constraints women face due particularly to high burdens associated with household tasks and large families. These constraints sharply reduce the ability of women to engage in market production, and thus their assets are not being used in ways that is captured by income growth and income poverty statistics.[13] This is partly a measurement issue where important wellbeing-related production is taking place within households that is not being counted in national accounts and thus in GDP growth. It is also an issue of an indirect growth linkage, as the ability of households to produce output and maintain and enhance assets importantly depends on this invisible and uncounted labour. Lastly, it is an issue related to the efficiency of asset use. To the extent that this labour, due to poor technology and infrastructure, exhibits very poor productivity levels, its growth would be lower even if this labour were fully captured in income statistics. Thus, it is not only a measurement issue but also an issue directly related to the efficiency of asset use, particularly the human assets of women.

An eighth argument relates to governance. There is a small but growing literature that has suggested that women are less prone to corruption and nepotism than men (World Bank 2001). Improving access to women to the workforce and decision-making bodies is therefore likely to improve governance in business and government. Similarly, there is a literature arguing that policies to achieve greater female political participation (such as quotas as in the case of India) can lead to the prioritization of investments of particular importance to women such as time-saving infrastructure and human capital, which in turn can promote economic growth (Duflo and Chatthopadhyay 2003; World Bank 2001). Thus, there are a large number of plausible theoretical arguments suggesting that gender gaps in education, employment, access to assets and inputs and time use can have a negative impact on economic growth. The relevance and economic importance of these arguments, however, is largely an empirical matter to which we turn presently.

Empirical findings

On the empirical side, there is now a considerable body of cross-country evidence that has shown gender inequality in education to reduce economic growth substantially.[14] While the point estimates of the size of the effects differ somewhat between studies, the results seem quite robust, as the studies use very different econometric approaches, time periods, country samples and model specifications. In particular, they all suggest that gender inequality in education accounts for a sizeable portion of the empirically observed growth differences between countries and regions.

Based on these empirical findings it is possible to estimate growth effects for countries that will not meet the education target for the MDG for gender equality. As shown by Abu-Ghaida and Klasen (2004) the estimated growth effects are quite substantial. There is also some cross-country and cross-regional evidence (although less robust at this stage)[15] that gender inequality in employment, both in terms of access to employment as well as type of employment (position in hierarchy and sectors, for instance) similarly reduces economic growth (Klasen 1999; Klasen and Lamanna 2003; Besley *et al.* 2004). There is also a wealth of micro-evidence that points out that gender inequalities in access to productive assets (such as land, fertilizer, seeds, credit, etc.) reduce the productivity of female producers and most often by more than the same inequality increases the productivity of male producers.[16]

In addition, there is overwhelming cross-country and micro-evidence that gender inequality in education leads to higher fertility, higher child mortality, higher undernutrition and lower educational investments[17] with the effects often being quite large. As shown by Abu-Ghaida and Klasen (2004), if countries were able to eliminate gender inequality in educational enrolments by 2005, they would reap considerable benefits in terms of these indicators. To the extent that these factors in turn influence economic growth, they are part of the reason why gender inequality in education reduces economic growth and thus increases poverty. Since these indicators are also development goals in their own right, promoting gender equality in education would reduce 'education poverty', 'health poverty' and 'nutrition poverty'. It would also be important to investigate to what extent the effects of gender inequality in education on these development outcomes are larger (or smaller) among the poor. But given the empirical findings that gender gaps in education are larger among the poor than the non-poor and that some of the effects of gender gaps in education (e.g. on fertility) are also larger among the poor than the non-poor, it is clear that policies to boost enrolments would particularly help poor women and thus make a direct contribution to poverty reduction in income and non-income dimensions.

Furthermore, there is a lot of evidence showing that women's bargaining power has a significantly positive impact on investments in children's education, health and nutrition (Thomas 1997; World Bank 2001; Lundberg *et al.* 1997; Murthi *et al.* 1995). Women's bargaining power is, in turn, heavily influenced by their employment status, their education and their access to unearned incomes; for instance, inheritances, remittances, state transfers (World Bank 2001; Sen 1990; Murthi *et al.* 1995; Klasen and Wink 2002; 2003). Improving the bargaining power of poor women would therefore lead not only to beneficial effects on the women themselves, but one would be able to reap considerable externalities in terms of improved outcomes for their families, with positive repercussions for economic growth.

Finally, there is some evidence that women's empowerment is associated with improved governance and reduced corruption, as women tend to have a lower propensity to engage in such behaviours (World Bank 2001; Swamy *et al.* 2001). This may be one of the reasons why gender gaps in education and employment are associated with lower growth.[18] There is also some evidence that greater female participation in political decision making at local levels can improve investments in priorities of women policy-makers, which in turn are likely to improve the contribution of women to economic growth (Duflo and Chattophadyay 2003).

Thus, the theoretical and empirical literature strongly suggests that improving gender equality in education, employment, access, to productive assets and in greater female bargaining power improves growth and other valuable development outcomes. In the education dimension, the findings are quite conclusive while in other dimensions (including employment, access to asset and inputs) the evidence is more sparse and certainly merits much closer attention in further research. We now assess the relevance of, and evidence for, these linkages for growth and poverty reduction in Africa, through an analysis of the most important gender gaps in Africa.

Gender gaps in education, employment, access to productive resources and agriculture in Africa

Both the general literature on gender and development (World Bank 2001) as well as specific works on Africa (World Bank 2000) have argued that reducing gender inequalities can be a powerful force for growth and poverty reduction in Africa. To assess how important the various gender issues are in the African context, it is useful to briefly review the evidence and most important gender gaps as they relate to education, employment and other issues such as agriculture and access to resources.

Gender and education

Table 19.1 shows that SSA is, along with South Asia, a region with the largest gender gap in education, both at the level of enrolment as well as at the level of attainment. The initial gaps are an inheritance from the colonial period where overall levels of education were low and gender gaps were considerable, although smaller than in South Asia (Klasen 2002). More worryingly, the absolute growth in education has been slower than in other regions so that the absolute levels of female attainment (or enrolments) in SSA are now below those of South Asia, which had not been the case previously. Thus, we are faced with a generalized education crisis in Africa. As women have had the most to gain from an expansion of education, the failure to accelerate the expansion of schooling has led to the low female attainments as well as large persistent gaps (see Abu-Ghaida and Klasen 2004). Important exceptions to this generally bleak picture include many countries of southern Africa (with the exception of Zimbabwe) as well as Uganda, where education has expanded considerably and gender gaps have fallen rapidly. Such expansion of education was typically accompanied by specific measures to reduce the costs of schooling (including, for example, free primary education in Uganda, Lesotho and Tanzania) and significant investments in the expansion of schooling infrastructure and teachers.

Combining the insights from the cross-country literature about the effects of gender gaps in education with the evidence on gender gaps in Africa, it is possible to estimate the amount of growth 'loss' associated with both the large initial gender gaps in education and the slow pace of reduction in these gaps.[19] Comparing Africa with East Asia and the Pacific, Klasen (2002) finds that some 0.6 percentage points in annual growth differences (of a total of 3.5 percentage points) between

Table 19.1 Enrolment rates and attainment by gender

Region	Primary gross enrolment rate				Secondary gross enrolment rate				Average years of attainment[b]			
	1975		1999		1975		1999		1970		1995	
	Females	Males	Females	Males	Females	Males	Females	Males	Females	Males	Females	Males
East Asia & Pacific	108	121	106	105	35	49	60	65	3.06	4.54	5.85	6.84
Europe & Central Asia		100	93	95			80	81	8.09	8.09	8.93	9.20
Latin America & Caribbean	97	99	130	133	34	35	87	80	3.52	4.14	5.58	5.91
Middle East & North Africa	64	99	91	99	24	44	67	72	1.39	2.75	4.21	5.74
South Asia	58	91	91	110	15	33	41	57	1.08	2.95	2.94	5.31
Sub-Saharan Africa[a]	45	66	73	85	6	13	23	28	1.56	2.60	2.82	3.98

Notes: [a] Latest available data on primary GERs are from 1998 and on secondary GERs from 1996. [b] Attainment data include schooling beyond secondary. Since data are from Barro and Lee (2001), the regional classification includes some countries with per capita incomes too high to be included in the World Bank's database (the one used for the GERs).

Sources: World Development Indicators central database and Barro and Lee (2001).

the two regions in 1960–92 can be accounted for by the higher *gender* gaps in Africa and the slower pace of reducing them. This is quite apart from the additional growth differences that arise from differences in initial overall education levels and the much slower growth in overall educational attainments.

Within Africa, growth differences can partly be attributed to considerable differences in levels and changes of gender gaps in education. We focus on Uganda here as a case study.[20] Table 19.2 shows that fully 1.3 percentage points of the growth differences between Uganda and Botswana can be accounted for by the much larger initial gender gaps in education in Uganda as well as the much slower pace of closing these gaps.

Since the mid-1980s, Uganda has been able to expand its education much faster than previously and has also reduced the gender gaps considerably. The female–male ratio of the expansion of schooling in the 1990s stood at 1.03, meaning that females expanded their schooling slightly faster than males. We also show how gender inequality since 1990 has affected growth based on the same growth regressions. Predictably, the effect is much smaller now, accounting for about 0.65 percentage points in the growth difference with Botswana, and 0.34 percentage points in the growth difference with East Asia. Interestingly, the effect of the female–male ratio of the growth of education is now negative suggesting that, compared with Botswana and East Asia, Uganda was closing its gender gap in education more quickly. But since Uganda had a much larger initial gender gap in 1990, the overall effect of gender inequality on growth held down growth, certainly compared with Botswana and East Asia.

Since Uganda's introduction of universal primary education (UPE) in 1997, educational enrolments have risen and gender gaps have closed, both at increasing rates. However, Uganda was still expected to miss the 2005 MDG on gender equity in education (due to remaining gaps at secondary level). Using results from Klasen (2002) and Knowles *et al.* (2002) and comparing the projected path of educational

Table 19.2 Estimating the effect of gender inequality in education on growth differences between Uganda and Botswana or East Asia

	1960–2000		1990–2000	
	Direct	Total	Direct	Total
Uganda versus Botswana				
Effect of gender inequality in 1960	0.45	1.14	0.29	0.73
Ratio of gender inequality in growth of education	0.13	0.18	–0.06	–0.08
Total	0.58	1.32	0.23	0.65
Uganda versus East Asia				
Effect of gender inequality in 1960	0.18	0.46	0.14	0.36
Ratio of gender inequality in growth of education	0.28	0.37	–0.02	–0.02
Total	0.46	0.84	0.12	0.34

Source: Based on Klasen and Lamanna (2003).

enrolments with a path that would allow Uganda to meet the MDG, Abu-Ghaida and Klasen (2004) estimated that failing to meet the MDG would lead to lower growth of 0.1–0.2 percentage points per year between 1995 and 2005, and less than 0.1 percentage points after 2005. This shows that sizeable growth costs can result from persistent gender gaps in education.[21]

As shown by Abu-Ghaida and Klasen (2004) and Klasen (2005b), many other African countries have not been nearly as successful in reducing gender gaps in enrolments as stipulated in the education-focused target of MDG3. In fact, of the 36 or so countries (with a population of at least 500,000) which have probabaly missed this MDG3 target (gender equality in primary and secondary enrolment rates in 2005), the majority (24) are from SSA.[22] As estimated by Abu-Ghaida and Klasen, the growth costs of missing this MDG3 target are considerable. For example, countries such as Togo are projected to suffer from 0.3 per cent lower growth between 1995 and 2005, and 0.5 per cent per year slower growth between 2005 and 2015 as a result of failing to reach the MDG3 target. Thus, failing to reach this target entails significant growth costs, but also delays progress in attaining other important MDGs. For example, as a result of failing to reach the target, Mozambique is projected to have 0.3 children per women more and Mali is projected to suffer from a 26/1000 higher under-five mortality rate in 2015.

Gender and employment

In contrast to some other regions, a distinguishing characteristic of SSA economies is that women have particularly high labour force participation rates, largely related to their high activity rates in agriculture. Female activity rates (percentage of women aged 15–64 that are economically active) as measured by the ILO are estimated to be around 67 per cent in Africa, far higher than in most other regions (except Eastern Europe and Central Asia). In contrast to other regions, however, these activity rates have fallen slightly over the past 40 years while they have risen strongly elsewhere (Klasen and Lamanna 2003).

One method of capturing the dynamics associated with the different economic contributions of men and women is through the 'gender intensity of production' in different sectors.[23] Adopting this methodology, and using ILO labour force data, Gueye has estimated the gender intensity of production for each country in SSA (Appendix Table 19.A1).[24] Although highly aggregated, and based on 1990 data comparable across countries, the estimates provide some indication of the respective contributions of men and women in African economies, and suggest a high degree of variability across countries and sectors. For example, men contribute two-thirds and women one-third to African GDP, with women's contribution ranging from a low of 26 per cent to a high of 52 per cent.[25] Bearing in mind that these estimates are based on national income accounting, and thus are likely not to fully capture (due to measurement issues) women's non-market production, these shares are very large, certainly when compared with other regions.

Issues relating to gender gaps in African employment are quite different from most other developing regions. The large contribution of women (see Appendix Table 19.A1) to measured GDP in Africa is largely driven by the substantial and often preponderant role they play in the agricultural sector. In some parts of agricultural production, women perform most of the tasks.[26] This important role of female labour in agricultural production implies that access to assets and inputs for their productive activities can have significant growth effects. This is particularly the case when women and men work on separate plots or separate tasks, where gender differences in access to inputs, technology and assets will affect the overall productivity of agriculture (see below).

In the industrial sector, women tend to play a much smaller role with some notable exceptions, such as the textile and garment industries in a few African states (for example, Lesotho, Mauritius and Madagascar). In the service sector, the shares vary greatly and represent a rather heterogeneous mix of public services, community and health services, as well as tourism and other services reflecting the diverse nature of services in African economies.

This important distinction between formal and informal sectors cannot be deduced from the data and other studies have to be considered, which show that the informal sector is particularly large in Africa, and uses a great deal of female labour (ILO 2002; Blunch *et al.* 2001). Excluding South Africa, the share of informal employment in non-agricultural employment is 78 per cent, rising to 83 per cent if agriculture is included. Self-employment represents 70 per cent of informal employment in SSA and 53 per cent of total non-agricultural employment. Outside agriculture, more than 60 per cent of women are in informal employment. In SSA, more than 84 per cent of women non-agricultural workers are informally employed compared with 63 per cent of men. Although women's participation rates are lower compared with men, they are important in street vending (90 per cent), home-based workers (80 per cent) and as home workers (80 per cent).[27]

Considering the overall economic contribution of the informal sector, we estimate the share of the informal sector in non-agricultural GDP in SSA to be 41 per cent. This compares with 29 per cent in LAC and 41 per cent in Asia. Country data suggest that the informal sector contributes 58 per cent to GDP in Ghana and 13 per cent in Mexico. In Tanzania, the informal sector contribution is estimated at 43 per cent. In Burkina Faso, of a 36 per cent overall GDP contribution, 29 per cent comes from women while 7 per cent is from men. In Kenya, out of the total 25 per cent, 11 per cent comes from women and 14 per cent from men, and in Mali 26 per cent from women and 14 per cent from men (Charmes 1998). Given the overall figures, the high participation of females in informal activities suggests that their representation in formal sector employment is, conversely, low. Data from the ILO suggest that formal sector employment rates in SSA are not any higher than in South Asia or the Middle East, and are much lower than in East Asia, Latin America, or Europe and Central Asia (Klasen and Lamanna 2003).

With respect to the economic impacts of this crowding of women in informal activities and their associated low share in formal sector employment, Klasen and Lamanna (2003) estimate the simultaneous impact of gender gaps in education and formal sector employment on economic growth in a panel framework. They find that both gender gaps in education and formal sector employment reduce economic growth. In fact, the (still preliminary) estimates suggest even larger growth costs for gender gaps in formal sector employment than in education. This is also corroborated by findings from South Asia, where gender gaps in employment are also particularly large (Esteve-Volart 2004).

To illustrate one example, based on the cross-country regressions mentioned above and 1992 census data on employment for Uganda from 1992, the growth difference accounted for by gender inequality in education and employment between East Asia and Uganda could amount to 0.6–0.7 per cent per year in the 1990s. If gender inequalities in non-agricultural and particularly formal sector employment persist, the costs of these gaps could mount considerably in future as the country will have to rely increasingly on non-agricultural employment.[28] Related to this is evidence on the impact of the under-utilized potential of women in non-farm employment more generally. Using household data for both Ghana and Uganda, Canagarajah *et al.* (2001) showed non-farm employment to be an important area of growth in SSA. In particular, they found that women's labour force participation had increased substantially within a period of five to six years in the 1990s, leading to lower poverty rates. Using poverty decompositions for both countries, they show that the contribution of growth to poverty reduction from this increased female employment in the non-farm sector is larger than the contribution from redistribution, findings consistent with many other countries.[29] Related analyses from Uganda show that women entrepreneurs face significant gender-based obstacles to establishing and operating their businesses, including access to finance, land and non-land assets, justice services and information. These in turn limit Uganda's capacity to expand such non-farm enterprises (Ellis *et al.* 2006).

It therefore appears that women are an under-utilized resource in non-farm formal sector employment. This is also related to the type of growth strategies that have been adopted by African countries. Evidence from East Asia as well as selected African countries (including Tunisia, Morocco, Lesotho and Mauritius) show that growth strategies that are based on export-oriented and labour-intensive light manufacturing is highly dependent on using female labour. In the countries that have adopted such a strategy, gender gaps in formal sector employment have become smaller and overall growth has been higher.[30] The potential to combine greater female employment in manufacturing with such an export-oriented growth strategy appears sizeable and merits much closer investigation.

Gender inequalities in agriculture

Given women's important role as agricultural producers, the conditions of production are of particular importance for both growth and poverty reduction in Africa. It is quite difficult to generate quantitative evidence on the efficiency effects of gender inequalities in access to land, inputs and control over resources. This is due to the fact that in many African countries (particularly in eastern and southern Africa) women and men collaborate on agricultural production by each providing certain inputs and, thus, it is very difficult to determine the efficiency of these inputs quantitatively. Or they produce different products where once again it is not easy to estimate the efficiency of production and thus the growth effects of existing gender gaps, although there is some evidence of the consequences of such gaps. For example, comparative evidence from Kenya suggests that men's gross value of output per hectare is 8 per cent higher than women's. However, if women had the same human capital endowments and used the same quantities of factor inputs as men, the value of their output would increase by 22 per cent. Hence, women's productivity appears well below its potential. Capturing this potential productivity gain by improving the circumstances of women farmers would substantially increase food production in SSA, thereby significantly reducing the level of food insecurity in the region. If these results from Kenya were to hold in SSA as a whole, simply raising the productivity of women to the same level as men could increase total production by 10–15 per cent.[31]

In places where women and men produced the same products on different plots, it is easier to see whether gender gaps affect efficiency. There is some evidence that gender gaps in input use significantly reduce overall efficiency of agricultural production. For example, studies by Udry (1996) and Udry *et al.* (1997) from Burkina Faso show that plots operated by women receive much less fertilizer and other inputs than those of men and if these inputs were equalized, aggregate output would rise by 10–15 per cent. Similar findings have been reported for other countries such as Zambia and Ghana (Blackden and Bhanu 1999; Goldstein and Udry 2002).

In addition to these static inefficiencies, there is considerable evidence about gender gaps in the adoption of new technologies. Such gender gaps have been visible for some time and it was usually assumed that they related to gender gaps in education, as well as gender bias in agricultural extension services. For example, Blumberg (1992) has demonstrated that where women are targeted for extension services they produce higher yields. However, while such factors are important, more recent evidence suggest that additional constraints relate particularly to women's time burdens and competing responsibilities as well as the critical question of who controls the proceeds of such investments in new technologies, including export-oriented cash crop production.[32]

Linkages with non-market work and the time burden

The different structural roles of men and women in the market economy (notably agriculture and the informal sector) are coupled with their equally different, and unbalanced, roles in the household economy. A further distinguishing characteristic of African economies is that the boundary between economic and household activity is less well drawn in Africa than in other regions (Gelb 2001). Women bear the brunt of domestic tasks – processing food crops, providing water and firewood, and caring for the elderly and the sick (especially important in the context of HIV/AIDS). In particular, the impact of HIV/AIDS is not limited to the 'visible' market economy, but has an equally, if not more, significant impact on the 'invisible' economy, yet this productive work is unrecorded and not included in the System of National Accounts (SNA). It is estimated that 66 per cent of female activities in developing countries are not captured by the SNA, compared with only 24 per cent of male activities (Elson and Evers 1997).

Considering African examples of time allocation statistics, for Cameroon, in the Centre province, men's total weekly labour averages 32 hours, while for women it is more than 64 hours. Even though much of this disparity results from differences in domestic labour hours (31 hours a week for women and four for men) a significant difference was also observed in agricultural labour hours: 26 a week for women and 12 for men (Henn 1988). Village transport surveys in Tanzania and Zambia also show that women spend nearly three times as much time in transport activities compared with men, and they transport about four times as much in volume (Malmberg-Calvo 1994; Barwell 1996). Moreover, fertility rates in Africa continue to be extremely high and have been reduced quite slowly in recent years, even in countries that have had considerable growth such as Uganda. Gender differences in time use are therefore exacerbated by very high fertility rates that continue to pose a disproportionate burden on women and prevent their greater participation in productive activities outside of the home. These unequal time burdens are not only an issue of equity, but also one of productivity. The high overall time burden, especially time spent on low-productivity household tasks (transport tasks associated with fuel and water collection, and food product processing and transformation) reduces the productivity of female labour and thus constrains their ability to contribute to growth and poverty reduction.[33]

Overall, therefore, the African situation appears to be large gender gaps in education and low overall female educational achievements, considerable gender gaps in formal sector employment and a predominance of women in the informal and agricultural sectors, where they face considerable gender-based differences in access to and control of land, modern inputs, time and other productive assets and resources.

Conclusions and policy implications

Notwithstanding extensive analysis and research, many of the conventionally accepted factors that determine growth and poverty reduction outcomes do not fully explain Africa's poor growth and poverty reduction performance. In this study, we outline the emerging findings about the importance of gender inequality and its relationship to growth in Africa. We have found that there is considerable evidence that gender gaps in education and formal sector employment reduce growth, that inequalities in access to land and productive inputs reduce agricultural productivity, investment and modernization, and that inequalities in time burdens, alongside the high demographic burden, all contribute to reducing women's ability to participate effectively in, and benefit equally from, growth and poverty reduction in Africa.

Some of the policy implications have been well recognized. There are efforts underway to improve female education and reduce gender gaps in many African countries, with some recent notable successes in some countries. Key to overcoming the education stagnation and the gender gaps have been significant investments in education sector, lifting of user fees for primary education and special programmes to target female education. Africa's high population growth and the disproportionate burden it places on women is also generally recognized, although there is much scope for improvement in ensuring better access to reproductive health and family planning services, and more could be done to promote smaller family sizes.

Unfortunately, there is much less progress on efforts to improve women's access to formal sector employment. As Africa will need to shift its workforce slowly from agriculture to the non-agricultural sector, improving employment opportunities for women will be critical. Indeed, women could play a key role in developing and implementing export-oriented growth strategies. Similarly, much remains to be done to improve equity in resource access and control in agriculture. In this area, there has been little progress and a gender-informed growth agenda would have to address improving women's greater land ownership and security of tenure and more equal access to modern inputs. Some of these changes might be supported by legislation and changes in agricultural policies. Others will depend on changes in intra-household relations, which are less amenable to government intervention although targeted support to female producers could play an important role here.

Lastly, it is critical that there be concurrent investment in areas which reduce women's excessive time burden. Here, time- and labour-saving infrastructure could play a role, especially in rural areas, including giving greater priority to water supply and sanitation, energy for household needs, access to appropriate means of transport commensurate with men's and women's different transport burdens, and investment in labour-saving technology in the area of food product transformation and processing. In addition, an acceleration of demographic change would contribute markedly to alleviating women's time burdens, as well as making MDG targets more attainable.

Apart from summarizing the main findings and its policy implications, it is important to lay out a forward-looking research agenda. While the evidence on the effects of gender gaps in education on growth is now quite substantial and robust, the impact of gender gaps in employment should receive much greater attention. Moreover, estimation of the efficiency costs of gender gaps in agriculture still relies on micro studies in specific settings, including often just purely qualitative results. It is necessary to investigate thoroughly the impact of gender gaps in access to land, modern inputs and technologies using advanced quantitative and econometric techniques to understand better these processes and design appropriate solutions.

We hope to have shown that gender is a critical economic issue for Africa, directly linked to growth and poverty reduction outcomes, and not a marginal social or women's issue concerned with equity. While much more remains to be done to show the particular ways gender gaps undermine Africa's growth potential, as well as policy measures needed to address them, what is already clear is that the linkages between gender inequality and growth in SSA deserve considerably more analysis and more policy attention.

Appendix

Table 19.A1 Estimates of the gender intensity of production by country and sector

Country	2000 Population (m)	1990 GDP US$ million	1990 Structure of economy (%)			Agriculture (shares M/F)		Industry (shares M/F)		Services (shares M/F)		Shares of GDP (%)	
			Agriculture	Industry	Services	M	F	M	F	M	F	M	F
ANGOLA	12.7	10,260.3	18	41	41	46.3	53.7	88.8	11.2	64.6	35.4	71.2	28.8
BENIN	6.3	1,845.0	36	13	51	50.8	49.2	76.5	23.5	49.4	50.6	53.4	46.6
BOTSWANA	1.6	3,765.8	5	56	39	69.3	30.7	73.3	26.7	43.9	56.1	61.7	38.3
BURKINA FASO	11.3	2,764.6	33	22	45	52.2	47.8	53.0	47.0	61.2	38.8	56.4	43.6
BURUNDI	6.8	1,132.1	56	19	25	47.7	52.3	80.6	19.4	91.2	8.8	64.9	35.1
CAMEROON	15.1	11,151.7	25	29	46	56.0	44.0	87.2	12.8	76.0	24.0	74.2	25.8
CAPE VERDE	0.4	338.7	14	21	65	58.7	41.3	78.8	21.2	50.3	49.7	57.5	42.5
C.A.R	3.6	1,487.5	48	20	33	–	–	–	–	–	–	–	–
CHAD	7.7	1,738.6	29	18	53	51.9	48.2	89.9	10.1	71.8	28.2	69.3	30.7
COMOROS	0.6	250.0	41	9	50	50.0	50.0	77.5	22.5	84.1	15.9	69.6	30.4
CONGO, D.R.	51.4	9,347.7	30	28	42	47.7	52.3	83.6	16.4	67.7	32.4	66.1	33.9
CONGO, REP.	2.9	2,798.7	13	41	46	38.8	61.2	88.4	11.6	68.4	31.6	72.7	27.3
CÔTE D'IVOIRE	16.0	10,796.0	33	23	44	61.5	38.6	81.0	19.1	76.7	23.3	72.6	27.4
EQUAT. GUINEA	0.5	132.1	61	11	28	56.3	43.7	86.2	13.9	85.7	14.3	67.8	32.2
ERITREA	4.1	–	–	–	–	49.5	50.5	81.3	18.8	57.1	42.9	–	–
ETHIOPIA	64.3	6,841.7	49	13	38	59.0	41.0	59.0	41.0	56.9	43.1	58.2	41.8
GABON	1.2	5,952.3	7	43	50	49.8	50.2	72.8	27.2	56.8	43.2	63.2	36.8
GAMBIA	1.3	316.9	29	13	58	49.6	50.4	88.0	12.0	74.0	26.0	68.8	31.2
GHANA	19.2	5,886.0	45	17	38	52.8	47.2	45.2	54.8	43.7	56.3	48.0	52.0
GUINEA	7.4	2,818.0	24	33	43	49.4	50.6	76.5	23.5	69.9	30.1	67.2	32.8
GUINEA-BISSAU	1.2	244.0	61	18	21	54.9	45.1	81.8	18.2	90.5	9.5	67.2	32.8
KENYA	30.1	8,533.2	29	19	52	51.5	48.5	73.0	27.0	49.7	50.3	54.6	45.4

LESOTHO	2.2	622.2	23	34	43	45.6	54.4	93.3	6.7	58.7	41.3	67.4	32.6
LIBERIA	3.1	–	–	–	–	54.8	45.2	93.4	6.6	71.8	28.2	–	–
MADAGASCAR	15.5	3,081.3	33	14	53	49.3	50.7	80.3	19.7	73.1	26.9	66.2	33.8
MALAWI	11.0	1,802.9	45	29	26	44.8	55.2	90.0	10.0	81.3	18.8	67.4	32.6
MALI	10.8	2,421.2	46	16	38	51.3	48.7	53.0	47.0	65.3	34.7	56.9	43.1
MAURITANIA	2.7	1,019.6	30	29	41	49.8	50.3	83.6	16.4	56.7	43.3	62.4	37.6
MAURITIUS	1.2	2,642.5	12	32	56	77.8	22.2	53.9	46.2	82.4	17.7	72.7	27.3
MOZAMBIQUE	17.6	2,512.1	37	18	45	44.1	55.9	94.2	5.8	84.4	15.6	71.3	28.7
NAMIBIA	1.7	2,529.6	11	35	54	50.7	49.3	72.4	27.6	70.2	29.8	68.8	31.2
NIGER	10.8	2,480.7	35	16	49	51.6	48.4	78.1	21.9	58.1	41.9	59.0	41.0
NIGERIA	126.9	28,472.5	33	41	26	64.5	35.5	84.8	15.2	63.2	36.8	72.5	27.5
RWANDA	8.5	2,584.4	33	25	42	47.7	52.3	86.2	13.8	80.6	19.4	71.2	28.8
SAO TOME, P.R.	0.1	57.6	28	18	55	–	–	–	–	–	–	–	–
SENEGAL	9.5	5,698.4	20	19	61	52.9	47.1	77.5	22.5	71.5	28.5	68.9	31.1
SEYCHELLES	0.1	368.6	5	16	79	–	–	–	–	–	–	–	–
SIERRA LEONE	5.0	896.8	47	20	33	56.8	43.2	90.7	9.3	66.7	33.3	66.9	33.1
SOMALIA	9.7	917.0	65	–	–	50.1	49.9	89.6	10.4	71.7	28.3	–	–
SOUTH AFRICA	42.8	111,997.0	5	40	55	73.2	26.9	82.7	17.3	48.5	51.5	63.4	36.6
SUDAN	29.7	1,316.7	–	–	–	67.3	32.7	24.4	15.6	82.5	13.5	–	–
SWAZILAND	1.0	859.9	14	43	43	–	–	–	–	–	–	–	–
TANZANIA	33.7	4,258.7	46	18	36	46.2	53.9	80.0	20.0	66.7	33.3	59.6	40.4
TOGO	4.7	1,628.4	34	23	43	60.4	39.6	72.0	28.0	53.2	46.8	60.0	40.0
UGANDA	22.1	4,304.5	57	11	32	49.9	50.1	79.1	20.9	56.5	43.5	55.3	44.7
ZAMBIA	10.1	3,288.4	21	49	30	49.0	51.0	83.6	16.4	61.4	38.6	69.7	30.3
ZIMBABWE	12.1	8,783.9	16	34	50	44.4	55.6	83.6	16.4	50.7	49.3	60.9	39.1
TOTAL/AVG	658.3	282,945.9	19.9	33.7	46.9	61.9	38.1	80.3	19.7	57.8	42.2	65.0	35.0

Sources: Calculations made by Aissatou Gueye (UNECA), while on secondment with the World Bank, May 2002. The principal data source is GenderStats on the World Bank's website, accessible at http://genderstats.worldbank.org/

Notes

We gratefully acknowledge constructive comments and suggestions from Tony Shorrocks and George Mavrotas, from two anonymous referees and from participants at the UNU-WIDER jubilee conference on the Future of Development Economics, June 2005, in Helsinki; and also from seminar participants at the University of Sussex, where earlier drafts of this chapter were presented.

1. See, for instance, Sachs and Warner (1997); Collier and Gunning (1999); Acemoglu *et al.* (2001); Easterly and Levine (1997); Mkandawire and Soludo (1999).
2. For example, Blackden and Bhanu (1999); World Bank (2001); Klasen (1999).
3. This study focuses on the growth effects of gender inequality. This is not to deny the importance of the equity implications and welfare implications of such inequalities. For a discussion, see Klasen (2004c; forthcoming).
4. While poverty reduction is not only affected by growth but also by distributional change, gender issues could affect poverty reduction also by affecting such distributional change. This is an issue discussed in more detail in Klasen (forthcoming) where it is shown that the impact of gender inequality on growth is much larger and more important for poverty reduction than the impact of gender inequality on distributional change.
5. In addition, economic options and incentives are different – that is, the choices people can make are going to be driven by non-economic control factors that are not uniform for men and women.
6. See UNDP (1995); Blackden and Bhanu (1999); Klasen (2005a; forthcoming).
7. See Knowles *et al.* (2002); World Bank (2001); Schultz (1993)
8. Note that in this study we are primarily concerned with gender *gaps* in education, and thus do not focus on absolute education levels which would, as is well known, also contribute to pro-poor growth.
9. See, for example, Lagerlöf (2003); Galor and Weil (1996); World Bank (2001).
10. Lagerlöf emphasizes gender gaps in education, while Galor and Weil concentrate on earnings gaps.
11. See, for example, Seguino (2000).
12. For a critical review of this argument and its empirical substantiation, see Klasen (1999; 2002; forthcoming). See also Seguino (2000).
13. UNDP (1995); Blackden and Bhanu (1999); Bardhan and Klasen (1998); World Bank (2005b); UPPAP (2002); Blackden and Wodon (2006).
14. See, for example, Dollar and Gatti (1999); Forbes (2000); Knowles *et al.* (2002); Klasen (2002); Yamarik and Ghosh (2003).
15. Investigations of the employment–growth nexus suffer from poor employment data that are often not comparable across countries, as well as potential endogeneity problems that are not easily addressed.
16. For surveys of this literature, see Blackden and Bhanu (1999); World Bank (2001); Bamberger *et al.* (2001); World Bank (2002).
17. Schultz (1997); Klasen (1999); Smith and Haddad (1999); World Bank (2001); Abu-Ghaida and Klasen (2004).
18. See, for example, Klasen and Lamanna (2003); Sauer (2001).
19. One should caution that these are point estimates that represent average effects of gender gaps in education. For an individual country (or region) the actual effect might be larger or smaller and, in any case, is sensitive to any measurement and specification errors in the underlying regressions.
20. See World Bank (2003a) for a related estimation in the context of Kenya. See also Klasen (2004a; 2004b).
21. The 2002/3 Ugandan National Household Survey (UNHS) suggests that Uganda is also closing the gender gap in secondary education, faster than anticipated, although gaps still remain and the second generation economic reforms need this higher skilled labour.
22. As the data for enrolments in 2005 will only be available later in 2006 or early 2007, the exact numbers of countries that have failed to meet the target is still not known and the information presented here is based on the most up-to-date projections.

23. The gender intensity of production relates the sex-specific employment shares with the overall structure of the economy to provide an assessment of what share of output is produced by males and females respectively. For details, see Elson and Evers (1997).
24. Aissatou Gueye, economist at UNECA, while on secondment at the World Bank in 2002.
25. It is probable that these estimates understate women's contribution to their economies, although they also do not take account of gender differences in productivity.
26. Data compiled by IFPRI indicate that African women perform about 90 per cent of the work of processing food crops, hoeing and weeding, 80 per cent of the work of food storage and transport from farm to village, and 60 per cent of the work of harvesting and marketing (Quisumbing *et al.* 1995). Time allocation data throughout SSA confirm women's predominant role in agricultural activities. In Zambia, for example, the preponderance of women's labour in agriculture is illustrated by time allocation studies which show women's greater labour contribution to crop production including, significantly, export crop production.
27. Home-based workers refers to those who carry out market work at home or adjacent premises, while home work refers to those who carry out work on a piece rate basis for businesses from home.
28. This receives further confirmation by estimates of returns to education. As shown by Mpuga (2003), employed women have higher returns to education than employed men Female returns to education appear to have been rising more than male returns in recent years suggesting great demand for higher female employment (Klasen 2004a).
29. Given that non-agricultural employment does not play such a quantitatively large role in Uganda at present (as a share of GDP or the labour force), the impact of gender inequalities in access to such employment is likely to be smaller than in regions with larger shares of non-agricultural employment (such as the Middle East and North Africa; see Klasen and Lamanna 2003). See also Barret *et al.* (2001); Cleaver and Donovan (1995).
30. Given the importance of trade for Africa's growth and poverty reduction prospects the different economic roles of men and women in SSA are especially significant in the area of trade expansion. See Seguino (2000); World Bank (2003b); Klasen (forthcoming).
31. See Saito *et al.* (1994). See also World Bank (1989; 2003a) and Horenstein (1989) on further evidence about consequences of gender gaps in Kenya on aggregate performance.
32. For example, Demery *et al.* (1993) show that time constraints reduce women's ability to invest in tea growing in Kenya. Jones (1986) shows that women in Senegal are reluctant to invest in rice as they do not control the proceeds from this production and are insufficiently compensated for their inputs (see also von Braun and Webb 1989). Lastly, Kasente *et al.* (2000) and Booth *et al.* (2003) suggest that women are reluctant to invest in export-oriented cash crop production as they would not control the proceeds and such investments would generate a particularly large and unaffordable time burden for them.
33. A more extensive analysis of 'time poverty' and its relationship to growth and consumption poverty can be found in Blackden and Wodon (2006).

References

Abu-Ghaida, D. and S. Klasen (2004) 'The Costs of Missing the Millenium Development Goals on Gender Equity', *World Development*, 32: 1075–107.

Acemoglu, D., S. Johnson and J.A. Robinson (2001) 'The Colonial Origins of Comparative Development: An Empirical Investigation', *American Economic Review*, 91, 5: 1369–401.

Bamberger, M., M. Blackden, L. Fort and V. Manoukian (eds) (2001) *Gender*, Poverty Reduction Strategy Paper Sourcebook, Washington, DC: World Bank.

Bardhan, K. and S. Klasen (1998) 'Women in Emerging Asia: Welfare, Employment, and Human Development', *Asian Development Review*, 16: 72–125.

Barret, C., T. Reardon and P. Webb (2001) 'Non-farm Income Diversification and Household Livelihood Strategies in Rural Africa: Concepts, Dynamics and Policy Implications', *Food Policy*, 26: 315–31.

Barro, R.J. and J. Lee (2001) 'Inequality Data on Educational Attainment: Updates and Implications', *Oxford Economic Papers*, 53, 3: 541–63.

Barwell, I. (1996) 'Transport and the Village: Findings from African Village-Level Travel and Transport Surveys and Related Studies', *World Bank Discussion Paper* 344, Africa Region Series, Washington, DC: World Bank.

Besley, T., R. Burgess and B. Esteve-Volart (2004) 'Operationalizing Pro-Poor Growth: India Case Study', Mimeo, London: DFID.

Blackden, C.M. and C. Bhanu (1999) 'Gender, Growth, and Poverty Reduction', *World Bank Technical Paper* 428, Special Programme of Assistance for Africa, 1998 Status Report on Poverty, Washington, DC: World Bank.

Blackden C.M. and Q. Wodon (eds) (2006) 'Gender, Time Use and Poverty in sub-Saharan Africa', *World Bank Working Paper* 73, Washington, DC: World Bank.

Bloom D. and J. Williamson (1998) 'Demographic Transition and Economic Miracles in Emerging Asia', *World Bank Economic Review*, 12: 419–55.

Blumberg, L.R. (1992) *African Women in Agriculture: Farmers, Students, Extension Agents, Chiefs*, Arkansas: Winrock International Institute for Agricultural Development.

Blunch, N.H., S. Canagarajah and D. Raju (2001) 'Informal Sector Revisited: A Synthesis Across Space and Time', *World Bank Social Protection Discussion Paper* 0119, Washington, DC: World Bank.

Booth, D., D. Kasente, G. Mavrotas, G. Mugambe and A. Muwonge (2003) 'The Strategic Exports Initiative in Uganda', Mimeo, Washington, DC: World Bank.

Canagarajah, S., C. Newman and R. Bhattamishra (2001) 'Non-Farm Income, Gender and Inequality: Evidence from Rural Ghana and Uganda', *Food Policy*, 26: 405–20.

Charmes, J. (1998) 'Informal Sector Poverty and Gender: A Review of Empirical Evidence', background paper for the *World Development Report 2001*, World Bank, Washington, DC.

Chen, S. and M. Ravallion (2004) 'How Have the World's Poorest Fared Since the Early 1980s?', *World Bank Policy Research Working Paper* 3341, Washington, DC: World Bank.

Cleaver, K. and W.G. Donovan (1995) 'Agriculture, Poverty and Policy Reform in SSA', *World Bank Technical Paper* 280, Washington, DC: World Bank.

Collier, P. and J.W. Gunning (1999) 'Explaining African Economic Performance', *Journal of Economic Literature*, 37, 1: 64–111.

Demery, L., M. Ferroni and C. Grootaert, with J. Wong-Valle (eds) (1993) *Understanding the Social Effects of Policy Reform*, Washington, DC: World Bank.

Dollar, D. and R. Gatti (1999) 'Gender Inequality, Income and Growth: Are Good Times Good for Women?', *World Bank Policy Research Working Paper* 1, Washington, DC: World Bank.

Duflo, E. and R. Chattophadyay (2003) 'Women as Policymakers', Mimeo, Cambridge, MA: MIT.

Easterly, W. and R. Levine (1997) 'Africa's Growth Tragedy: Policies and Ethnic Divisions', *Quarterly Journal of Economics*, 112, 4: 869–87.

Ellis, A., C. Manuel and C.M. Blackden (2006) *Gender and Economic Growth in Uganda: Unleashing the Power of Women*, Washington, DC: World Bank.

Elson, D. and B. Evers (1997) *Gender-Aware Country Economic Reports. Working Paper 2, Uganda*, prepared for DAC/WID Task Force on Programme Aid and Other Forms of Economic Policy-Related Assistance, Paris: OECD.

Esteve-Volart, B. (2004) 'Gender Discrimination and Growth: Theory and Evidence from India', *STICERD Discussion Paper* DEDPS42, London: LSE.

Forbes, K. (2000) 'A Reassessment of The Relationship Between Inequality And Growth', *American Economic Review*, 86: 374–87.

Galor, O. and D. Weil (1996) 'The Gender Gap, Fertility, and Growth', *American Economic Review*, 86: 374–87.

Gelb, A. (2001) 'Gender and Growth: Africa's Missed Potential', *Africa Region Findings* 197, Washington, DC: World Bank.

Goldstein, M. and C. Udry (2002) 'Gender, Land Rights, and Agriculture in Ghana', Mimeo, London: LSE.

Henn, J.K. (1988) 'Intra-Household Dynamics and State Policies as Constraints on Food Production: Results of a 1985 Agroeconomic Survey in Cameroon', in S.V. Poats,

M. Schmink and A. Spring (eds), *Gender Issues in Farming Systems Research and Extension*, Boulder, CO: Westview.

Horenstein, N.R. (1989) 'Women and Food Security in Kenya', *Policy Planning and Research Working Paper* 232, Washington, DC: World Bank.

ILO (2002) *Women and Men in the Informal Economy: A Statistical Picture*, Geneva: ILO.

Jones, C. (1986). 'Intrahousehold Bargaining in Response to the Introduction of New Crops: A Case Study from North Cameroon', in J.L. Moock (ed.), *Understanding Africa's Rural Households and Farming Systems*, Boulder, CO: Westview.

Kasente, D., M. Lockwood, J. Vivia and A. Whitehead (2000) 'Gender and the Expansion of Non-traditional Agricultural Exports in Uganda', *UNRISD Occasional Paper* 12, Geneva: UNRISD.

Klasen, S. (1999) 'Does Gender Inequality Reduce Growth and Development?', *World Bank Policy Research Department Working Paper* 7, Washington, DC: World Bank.

Klasen, S. (2002) 'Low Schooling for Girls, Slower Growth for All?', *World Bank Economic Review*, 16: 345–73.

Klasen, S. (2004a) 'Gender and Growth in Uganda: Some Preliminary Findings and Policy Issues', Mimeo, University of Göttingen.

Klasen, S. (2004b) 'Population Growth, (Per Capita) Economic Growth, and Poverty Reduction in Uganda: Theory and Evidence', Mimeo, Kampala: Ministry of Finance, Planning, and Economic Development.

Klasen, S. (2004c) 'Gender-Related Indicators of Wellbeing', *WIDER Discussion Paper* 2004/05, Helsinki: UNU-WIDER.

Klasen, S. (2005a) 'Economic Growth and Poverty Reduction: Measurement and Policy Issues', *OECD Development Centre Working Papers* 246, Paris: OECD.

Klasen, S. (2005b) 'Bridging the Gender Gap to Promote Economic and Social Development', *Journal of International Affairs*, 58, 2: 245–56.

Klasen, S. (forthcoming) 'Gender Inequality and Pro-Poor Growth', in L. Menkhoff (ed.), *Pro-Poor Growth*, Berlin: Duncker & Humboldt.

Klasen, S. and F. Lamanna (2003) 'The Impact of Gender Inequality in Education and Employment on Economic Growth in the Middle East and North Africa', background paper for *Gender and Development in the Middle East and North Africa*, World Bank, Washington, DC.

Klasen, S. and C. Wink (2002) 'A Turning-Point in Gender Bias in Mortality? An Update on the Number of Missing Women', *Population and Development Review*, 28: 285–312.

Klasen, S. and C. Wink (2003) 'Missing Women: Revisiting the Debate', *Feminist Economics*, 9: 263–99.

Knowles, S., P.K. Lorgelly and P.D. Owen (2002) 'Are Educational Gender Gaps a Break on Economic Development? Some Cross Country Empirical Evidence', *Oxford Economic Papers*, 54: 118–24.

Lagerlöf, N.P. (2003), 'Gender Equality and Long-Run Growth', *Journal of Economic Growth*, 8: 403–26.

Lundberg, S., R. Pollak and T. Wales (1997) 'Do Husbands and Wives Pool their Resources?', *Journal of Human Resources*, 32: 224–35.

Malmberg-Calvo, C. (1994) 'Case Study on the Role of Women in Rural Transport: Access of Women to Domestic Facilities', *Sub-Saharan Africa Transport Policy Program Working Paper* 11, Washington, DC: World Bank and Economic Commission for Africa.

Mkandawire, T. and C. Soludo (1999) *Our Continent, Our Future*, Asmara: Africa World Press.

Mpuga, P. (2003) 'Returns to Education and Credit Access by Gender in Uganda Based on the 1992, 1999, and 2002 Household Surveys', Mimeo, Kampala: World Bank.

Murthi, M., A.-C. Guio and J. Drèze (1995) 'Mortality, Fertility and Gender Bias in India: A District-Level Analysis', *Population and Development Review*, 21, 4: 745–82.

Quisumbing, A., L.R. Brown, H.S. Feldstein, L. Haddad and C. Peña (1995) 'Women: The Key to Food Security', *Food Policy Statements* 21, Washington, DC: International Food Policy Research Institute.

Sachs, J. and A. Warner (1997) 'Sources of Slow Growth in African Economies', *Journal of African Economies*, 6, 3: 335–76.

Saito, K., H. Mekonnen and D. Spurling (1994) 'Raising the Productivity of Women Farmers in sub-Saharan Africa', *World Bank Discussion Paper, Africa Technical Department Series* 230, Washington, DC: World Bank.

Sauer, C. (2001) 'Korrpution und Wirtschaftswachstum: der Beitrag der Gleichberechtigung', Mimeo, University of Munich.

Schultz, T.P. (1993) 'Returns to Women's Education', in E. King and A. Hill (eds), *Women's Education in Developing Countries*, Washington, DC: World Bank.

Schultz, T.P. (1997) 'Demand for Children in Low-Income Countries', in M. Rosenzweik and O. Stark (eds), *Handbook of Population and Family Economics*, Amsterdam: Elsevier.

Seguino, S. (2000) 'Gender Inequality and Economic Growth: A Cross-Country Analysis', *World Development*, 28: 1211–30.

Sen, A. (1990) 'Gender and Cooperative Conflicts', in I. Tinker (ed.), *Persistent Inequalities*, New York: Oxford University Press.

Smith, L. and L. Haddad (1999) 'Explaining Child Malnutrition in Developing Countries: A Cross-Country Analysis', *IFPRI Discussion Paper* 60, Washington, DC: International Food Policy Research Institute.

Swamy, A., S. Knack, Y. Lee and O. Azfar (2001) 'Gender and Corruption', *Journal of Development Economics*, 64, 1: 25–55.

Thomas, D. (1997) 'Incomes, Expenditures and Health Outcomes: Evidence on Intrahousehold Resource Allocation', in L. Haddad, J. Hoddinott and H. Alderman (eds), *Intrahousehold Resource Allocation in Developing Countries*, Baltimore: Johns Hopkins University Press.

Udry, C. (1996) 'Gender, Agricultural Production, and the Theory of the Household', *Journal of Political Economy*, 104: 551–69.

Udry, C., J. Hoddinott, H. Alderman and L. Haddad (1997) 'Gender Differentials in Farm Productivity: Implications for Household Efficiency and Agricultural Policy', *Food Policy*, 20, 5: 407–23.

UNDP (United Nations Development Programme) (1995) *Human Development Report: Gender and Human Development*, New York: Oxford University Press.

UPPAP (2002) *Ugandan Participatory Poverty Assessment II: National Report*, Kampala: MFPED.

von Braun, J. and R. Webb (1989) 'The Impact of New Crop Technologies on the Agricultural Division of Labour in a West African Setting', *Economic Development and Cultural Change*, 37: 513–34.

World Bank (1989) *Kenya, The Role of Women in Economic Development*, A World Bank Country Study, Washington, DC: World Bank.

World Bank (2000) *Can Africa Claim the 21st Century?*, report prepared jointly by the African Development Bank, African Economic Research Consortium, Global Coalition for Africa, Economic Commission for Africa and the World Bank, Washington, DC.

World Bank (2001) *Engendering Development: Through Gender Equality in Rights, Resources, and Voice*, A World Bank Policy Research Report, Washington, DC: World Bank.

World Bank (2002) *Education and HIV/AIDS: A Window of Hope*, Washington, DC: World Bank.

World Bank (2003a) *Kenya: A Policy Agenda to Restore Growth, World Bank Country Economic Memorandum Report* 25840-KE, Poverty Reduction and Economic Management, Africa Region, Washington, DC: World Bank.

World Bank (2003b) *Gender and Growth in the Middle East and North Africa*, Washington, DC: World Bank.

World Bank (2005a) *Pro-Poor Growth in the 1990s: Lessons and Insights from 14 Country Cases*, Washington, DC: World Bank.

World Bank (2005b) 'Uganda: From Periphery to Center: A Strategic Country Gender Assessment', *World Bank Report* 30136-UG, Washington, DC: World Bank.

Yamarik, S. and S. Ghosh. (2003) 'Is Female Education Productive? A Reassessment', Mimeo, Medford, MA: Tufts University.

20
Decomposing Growth: Do Low-income and HIPCs Differ from High-income Countries?

Pertti Haaparanta and Heli Virta

Introduction

Widespread and persisting international income differences have motivated ample research on the underlying factors. Aided by the developments in both growth theory and empirics, international differences in growth in per capita incomes or labour productivity have been decomposed in various fashions.[1] Hall and Jones, among others, find that many of the disparities are explained by differences in (labour-augmenting) technology instead of differences in factor availability. According to their interpretation, this reflects international differences in the quality of social infrastructure or, more generally, in institutions. Recent research has further strengthened the case for the role of institutions.[2] There is also evidence that geographical factors can account for poor performance (Sachs *et al.* 2004). Human capital may also be the deep determinant of economic growth, explaining also the institutional change (Glaeser *et al.* 2004).

One problem with these studies is that they cannot properly differentiate the impact of institutions: if the institutions affect for example the incentives to adopt new technology or divert resources to unproductive activities, one should have a measure both for the potential of the economy and the extent to which this potential is used. We take first steps to fill this gap: labour productivity can be augmented by accumulation of physical and human capital, improvements in technologies (technological change) and the extent to which these improvements are actually utilized (productive efficiency or catch-up). We decompose the change in labour productivity in 83 countries into these four categories with a special emphasis on low-income countries and among them on highly indebted countries.

This decomposition can shed light on the causes of international income differences. Artadi and Sala-í-Martín (2003) find that African problems can be traced to high price of capital goods, geographical factors, closedness to trade and too large public expenditures, as well as to conflicts. If geographical factors are very important by facilitating or delaying international trade and flow of information, one expects that the lack of technological catch-up plays a large role in the poor performance of geographically disadvantaged countries. Similarly, poor institutions can damage both the catch-up and accumulation of all types of capital and, hence, the various determinants of growth cannot be assigned uniquely to only one element in our decomposition. Yet, the decomposition gives some idea of the relative importance of the channels through which they have had an influence.

The decomposition helps also to understand the impacts of the debt crisis. High debt reduces incentives to invest, as the returns from investment must be used for servicing the debt creating the debt Laffer curve (Krugman 1988). At the same time, high indebtedness increases the bargaining power of the debtor countries vis-à-vis the creditors allowing them to escape from reforms necessary for long-run growth (Birdsall *et al.* 2003). The relative importance of these two channels can be assessed by looking at the relative contributions of factor accumulation and catch-up in the highly indebted countries.

The decomposition is based on constructing a world production possibility frontier using data envelopment analysis (DEA), as in our data it turns out that all the countries share the same technology. Productive efficiency is measured by the distance of a country's production from the world production possibility frontier.[3] We follow here Kumar and Russell (2002) with two crucial differences. While Kumar and Russell base their analysis on the basic Solow growth model framework, we use the Mankiw *et al.* (1992) framework, as the Solow model augmented with human capital accumulation fits the cross-country data very well.[4] We analyze data from 83 countries, which is a much larger dataset than in Kumar and Russell (2002) and Henderson and Russell (2004). We therefore get a much better focus on the low-income countries. Moreover, our data ranges from 1980–2000, while both Kumar and Russell and Henderson and Russell study the period 1965–90.

We find that developing countries, especially highly indebted poor countries (HIPC), have experienced large improvements in productive efficiency during the last two decades. This positive effect has been washed out by problems in capital accumulation with the result that the overall income distribution in these countries has remained stagnant. Also, production in these countries has shifted to sectors with below-average productivity growth and/or it has used old technology more efficiently. Thus, it is inaccurate to assign the stagnation to institutions providing bad incentives. Institutional factors should rather be viewed in association with other factors, such as lack of finance for basic infrastructure. The theory of debt overhang seems also to be more relevant than the theory emphasizing bad incentives to account for the stagnation in HIPC countries.

The change in world distribution of income has been driven also by technological change, not only by capital accumulation as in earlier periods (Kumar and Russell 2002). A natural interpretation is that the information and communication technology has shaped the international income distribution.

Analytical framework and data

Analytical framework

Production in year *t* in each country is given by the aggregate production function:

$$Y_t = F(E_t, L_t, H_t, K_t) \tag{20.1}$$

where E = efficiency (catch-up), which measures how far from the efficient world production frontier the production is, L = labour force, H = human capital stock and K = physical capital stock. Production is assumed to exhibit constant returns to scale with respect to L, H and K. This naturally gives average labour productivity as a function of efficiency and capital stocks per worker:

$$\frac{Y_t}{L_t} = F\left(E_t, 1, \frac{H_t}{L_t}, \frac{K_t}{L_t}\right) \tag{20.2}$$

The country-specific efficiency scores are calculated by data envelopment analysis,[5] which assigns a score of one to efficient countries situated at the world production frontier. Inefficient countries receive a score below one. Another option would have been to use some parametric frontier approach, such as stochastic frontier analysis. The main disadvantage of DEA is its deterministic nature and the resulting inability to distinguish between technical inefficiency and statistical noise. On the other hand, DEA does not require any functional specification for the relationship between inputs and outputs or for the inefficiency error term. Using it therefore means escaping various specification and estimation problems.[6] An additional benefit of a DEA decomposition is that it can catch at least some of the implications of factor-biased technological change. Caselli (2005) has argued that it can possibly explain much of the income differential between rich and poor countries.

The data

Countries

The availability of data between years 1980 and 2000 restricts the number of countries that can be included in the analysis to 83. Although developing economies tend to have measurement errors in statistics, it can be hoped that 'the strong signal from the diversity of the experience dominates the noise' (Barro 2000).

Output

Output is measured by GDP (constant 1995 US$) from the World Bank (2004) *World Development Indicators Online* (WDI).

Labour force

As it is not straightforward to choose a proxy for labour force in empirical analysis with both developed and developing nations, we use two different measures to assure the robustness of the results. First, the official labour force statistics from WDI are relatively accurate as to developed countries, but are likely to underestimate the size of the actual labour force in many developing economies, where the size of the informal economy is larger. As the citizens entering the labour market in developing economies are typically younger than in developed economies, a second possible proxy for labour force is the population aged between 15 and 64 years, also from WDI.[7]

Capital stock

Capital stock estimates originate from Ruotinen (2005), who uses the perpetual inventory method to generate them (see also Henry *et al.* 2003 and Caselli 2005). He uses WDI data on gross fixed capital formation (constant 1995 US$) for investment, and sets the depreciation rate at 10 per cent in accordance with Henry *et al.* (2003). The formulas for capital stocks are

$$K_{it} = (1 - \delta)K_{it-1} + I_{it-1} \text{ and}$$
$$K_{i0} = \frac{I_o}{(g^K + \delta)}$$

where K = the capital stock, δ = the depreciation rate, I = the gross fixed capital investment and g^K = the annual average growth rate of the investments. Subscript i indexes country and t indexes time.

Human capital stock

The total human capital stock H_{it} for country i at time t is often calculated as $H_{it} = S_{it} \times L_{it}$, where S_{it} and L_{it} indicate average years of educational attainment and the stock of individuals engaged in productive activity, respectively. This is also the approach we follow.

One of the most recent and widely used measures for E_{it} is that of Barro and Lee (2001).[8] In accordance with the nature of the labour market in developing countries, we use their series of average years of schooling (including primary, secondary and tertiary levels) for population over 15 years of age. It is also compatible with our second proxy for labour force, namely that of population aged between 15 and 64 years.

When constructing the dataset to be used at the efficiency analysis, the same proxy was used both as the labour force proxy and when calculating the total stock of human capital. Thus there were two datasets to begin with:

(1) Y (total GDP), L (total labour force), K (total capital stock), H (Barro and Lee average years of schooling for population over 15 years of age $\times$ total labour force)
(2) Y, L (population 15–64), K, H (Barro and Lee average years of schooling for population over 15 years of age $\times$ population 15–64).

Efficiency scores

Efficiency scores for labour productivity

Since we are particularly interested in changes in labour productivity, we concentrate on the case where inputs used to produce GDP per labour are physical and human capital per labour (equation (20.2)). The results for aggregate output are available upon request.

With official labour force statistics as the proxy for labour (Table 20.1), France and Sierra Leone[9] are the only countries that are efficient with an efficiency score

Table 20.1 Efficiency scores based on the use official labour force statistics: labour productivity

	1980	1985	1990	1995	2000
Algeria	0.50	0.43	0.39	0.38	0.42
Argentina	0.74	0.64	0.65	0.78	0.73
Australia	0.80	0.77	0.75	0.77	0.68
Austria	0.85	0.87	0.89	0.96	1.00
Bangladesh	0.34	0.38	0.42	0.53	0.61
Belgium	0.96	0.97	0.98	0.97	0.95
Bolivia	0.56	0.52	0.57	0.68	0.69
Botswana	0.68	0.76	0.73	0.60	0.59
Brazil	0.77	0.68	0.66	0.71	0.67
Cameroon	0.60	0.59	0.45	0.43	0.62
Canada	0.98	0.91	0.84	0.82	0.78
Chile	0.78	0.77	0.87	0.85	0.76
China	0.10	0.16	0.20	0.37	0.46
Colombia	0.80	0.72	0.78	0.73	0.73
Congo, Dem. Rep.	0.38	0.32	0.28	0.26	0.32
Costa Rica	0.87	0.82	0.84	0.80	0.83
Denmark	0.86	0.95	0.89	0.97	0.91
Dominican Rep.	0.71	0.64	0.57	0.58	0.72
Ecuador	0.63	0.62	0.67	0.69	0.75
Egypt, Arab Rep.	0.61	0.51	0.53	0.60	0.73
El Salvador	0.87	0.78	0.80	0.84	0.85
Finland	0.78	0.80	0.77	0.80	0.85
France	1.00	1.00	1.00	1.00	1.00
Gambia	0.87	0.67	0.61	0.59	0.73
Germany	0.78	0.79	0.84	0.85	0.80
Ghana	0.32	0.31	0.39	0.51	0.61
Greece	0.76	0.71	0.71	0.72	0.69
Guatemala	0.89	0.80	0.88	0.90	0.91
Guyana	0.16	0.16	0.18	0.26	0.35
Honduras	0.57	0.50	0.54	0.52	0.52
Hong Kong, China	0.82	0.77	0.83	0.82	0.68
Hungary	0.60	0.64	0.63	0.53	0.61
Iceland	0.90	0.87	0.87	0.87	0.83
India	0.23	0.27	0.33	0.44	0.55
Indonesia	0.43	0.45	0.53	0.57	0.52
Iran, Islamic Rep.	0.44	0.49	0.53	0.54	0.61

Continued

Table 20.1 Continued

	1980	1985	1990	1995	2000
Ireland	0.84	0.80	0.91	1.00	1.00
Israel	0.86	0.87	0.99	0.94	0.82
Italy	0.92	0.91	0.91	0.93	0.85
Jamaica	0.50	0.52	0.70	0.52	0.52
Japan	0.85	0.90	1.00	1.00	1.00
Jordan	0.63	0.57	0.46	0.47	0.53
Kenya	0.24	0.28	0.35	0.42	0.51
Korea, Rep.	0.77	0.77	0.75	0.66	0.60
Lesotho	0.23	0.24	0.28	0.25	0.26
Malawi	0.11	0.13	0.15	0.22	0.34
Malaysia	0.76	0.64	0.69	0.60	0.55
Mali	0.58	0.47	0.48	0.46	0.57
Mauritius	0.60	0.69	0.72	0.63	0.62
Mexico	0.85	0.75	0.72	0.62	0.71
Mozambique	0.53	0.38	0.46	0.53	0.57
Netherlands	0.81	0.83	0.85	0.89	0.89
New Zealand	0.80	0.81	0.75	0.80	0.72
Nicaragua	0.45	0.41	0.33	0.37	0.47
Niger	0.26	0.26	0.36	0.45	0.67
Norway	0.75	0.74	0.65	0.80	0.80
Pakistan	0.47	0.57	0.47	0.61	0.75
Panama	0.85	0.80	0.74	0.68	0.64
Papua New Guinea	0.50	0.45	0.43	0.56	0.65
Paraguay	0.73	0.61	0.61	0.58	0.59
Peru	0.81	0.74	0.62	0.66	0.64
Philippines	0.48	0.39	0.46	0.49	0.57
Portugal	0.84	0.79	0.84	0.76	0.64
Rwanda	0.52	0.46	0.42	0.35	0.58
Senegal	0.57	0.64	0.67	0.69	0.83
Sierra Leone	1.00	1.00	1.00	1.00	1.00
Singapore	0.82	0.66	0.78	0.86	0.94
South Africa	0.88	0.72	0.78	0.75	0.79
Spain	0.89	0.89	0.89	0.83	0.74
Sri Lanka	0.30	0.32	0.35	0.44	0.51
Swaziland	0.54	0.47	0.69	0.63	0.65
Sweden	0.97	1.00	0.97	0.92	0.90
Switzerland	1.00	1.00	0.99	0.96	0.97
Syrian Arab Rep.	0.32	0.28	0.30	0.41	0.48
Thailand	0.44	0.44	0.53	0.47	0.48
Togo	0.33	0.31	0.32	0.37	0.47
Tunisia	0.61	0.55	0.58	0.55	0.61
United Kingdom	0.92	0.94	0.94	0.94	0.84
United States	1.00	1.00	1.00	0.99	0.84
Uruguay	0.9998	0.80	1.00	1.00	1.00
Venezuela	0.61	0.56	0.66	0.65	0.68
Zambia	0.21	0.26	0.34	0.36	0.52
Zimbabwe	0.50	0.53	0.43	0.45	0.57

Source: The efficiency scores and decomposition of the labour productivity were obtained by OnFront Version 2.02. The scores were calculated with five-year intervals beginning from 1980 and ending with the year 2000.

of one over the whole period. The group of the least-efficient countries is composed of Malawi, Guyana, Lesotho and the Democratic Republic of the Congo. These have the lowest scores. China starts at the bottom of the list in 1980 and manages to climb only few positions by 2000. If the population aged between 15 and 64 years of age is used as the proxy for individuals engaged in productive activity (the results are available upon request), Sierra Leone and Switzerland are the only efficient countries every year. The other countries on the frontier, although not every year, include United States, Sweden, Uruguay, France, Denmark and Japan. The least efficient countries are the same as above. Thus, the results are not sensitive to the variable used to measure the labour input. Hence, in the following only the results based on dataset 1 are used.

Do high-income countries and developing economies share the same technological knowledge?[10]

The groups of high-income and developing countries may differ with respect to the availability of technology, invalidating the calculations above. We therefore use a method presented by Charnes *et al.* (1981) and discussed by Lovell (1994)[11] to take the categorical environmental variable into account: the observations are first divided into two mutually exclusive groups. After the efficiency scores have been calculated for each group separately, the scores are used to scale the individual outputs to the efficient frontier in the respective group. New efficiency scores are then calculated for the combined group of all countries so that the scaled GDP figures are used as the output.

The scaling of the countries to the efficient frontier in the country's group results in much smaller differences in the final efficiency scores.[12] The group of the most efficient countries comprises now of Austria, Belgium, France and Sierra Leone, closely tailed by Ireland, Spain and Switzerland, as well as a large number of other countries. At the other extreme, Brazil, Algeria, Argentina, Malaysia, South Africa, Venezuela, Tunisia, Iran and the Republic of Korea fare less well. These results imply that the assumption of equal access to the same technology is reasonable.

Productivity distributions: how has the world of 1980 changed into the world of 2000?

Average performance in country groups

We decompose labour productivity in a manner analogous to Kumar and Russell (2002). Unlike them, we incorporate changes in human capital in the spirit of Mankiw *et al.* (1992). The technical details of the decomposition are presented in Appendix 1, whereas this section concentrates on the empirical results. The decomposition results are in Table 20.2. The percentage change in labour productivity between 1980 and 2000 is displayed in column 2 (y%). Columns 3–6 display the effects that changes in efficiency (EC%), technology (TC%), physical capital (K%) and human capital (H%) have had on labour productivity development in each country.

Table 20.2 Decomposition of changes in labour productivity (L = official labour force statistics)

	y%	EC%	TC%	K%	H%
Algeria	−26.3	−16.1	10.3	−28.0	10.7
Argentina	−4.6	−1.0	9.2	−14.5	3.1
Australia	31.7	−15.7	19.2	29.9	1.0
Austria	45.2	17.9	6.6	5.9	9.1
Bangladesh	34.0	78.8	−44.1	16.5	15.0
Belgium	39.7	−0.4	9.1	18.4	8.6
Bolivia	−14.2	24.0	−31.8	−5.2	7.0
Botswana	137.2	−13.7	−2.6	145.7	14.9
Brazil	−8.9	−12.4	12.1	−13.4	7.1
Cameroon	−5.5	3.7	−24.2	6.8	12.7
Canada	28.1	−19.9	11.2	41.3	1.7
Chile	67.3	−3.6	−3.9	75.0	3.2
China	352.9	349.1	−56.9	98.5	18.0
Colombia	−6.8	−8.0	−8.9	7.0	3.9
Congo, Dem. Rep.	−62.1	−17.4	−55.4	−18.6	26.4
Costa Rica	9.5	−4.3	−1.0	12.4	2.9
Denmark	35.9	4.7	11.4	13.4	2.9
Dominican Rep.	30.1	1.7	−12.8	37.4	6.7
Ecuador	−23.3	18.6	−16.6	−23.4	1.3
Egypt, Arab Rep.	52.8	20.2	−19.1	24.2	26.6
El Salvador	−12.7	−3.0	−13.6	−7.1	12.1
Finland	53.8	8.3	13.1	8.6	15.7
France	37.0	0.0	7.8	14.0	11.5
Gambia	−0.4	−16.8	−40.0	33.3	49.8
Germany	39.0	3.1	10.5	14.9	6.2
Ghana	6.0	93.3	−51.4	6.0	6.5
Greece	11.0	−9.6	20.2	−1.1	3.3
Guatemala	−9.1	3.0	−6.1	−10.5	5.0
Guyana	−13.7	123.3	−7.3	−59.8	3.7
Honduras	−13.9	−9.1	−21.5	3.4	16.7
Hong Kong, China	103.6	−17.4	12.4	110.0	4.4
Hungary	29.0	0.4	−4.0	33.6	0.1
Iceland	26.3	−7.8	14.7	11.0	7.5
India	99.1	140.4	−53.0	39.8	26.1
Indonesia	64.6	22.6	−35.8	85.7	12.7
Iran, Islamic Rep.	16.5	37.4	2.4	−24.9	10.3
Ireland	122.4	18.8	22.9	42.4	6.9
Israel	29.1	−5.6	14.9	18.6	0.4
Italy	28.6	−7.8	13.1	13.6	8.5
Jamaica	−2.5	4.9	−4.5	−7.3	5.0
Japan	44.5	17.2	7.7	6.3	7.7
Jordan	−28.6	−15.6	−1.3	−21.2	8.9
Kenya	−11.1	111.9	−49.5	−24.8	10.5
Korea, Rep.	166.5	−22.5	1.4	218.5	6.5
Lesotho	60.8	15.9	−18.7	66.2	2.7
Malawi	9.4	208.5	−42.4	−43.1	8.2
Malaysia	94.8	−28.5	−1.8	163.1	5.4
Mali	1.2	−2.6	−7.8	1.7	10.7
Mauritius	96.0	3.1	−2.9	90.8	2.6

Continued

Table 20.2   Continued

	y%	EC%	TC%	K%	H%
Mexico	−8.2	−16.6	0.5	1.6	7.7
Mozambique	27.2	7.7	−45.6	82.8	18.8
Netherlands	26.9	9.9	6.1	2.2	6.5
New Zealand	9.2	−10.8	10.1	10.8	0.3
Nicaragua	−36.8	3.4	−26.6	−25.6	11.8
Niger	−34.8	160.2	−10.9	−75.7	15.7
Norway	55.2	6.5	8.3	3.8	29.7
Pakistan	53.3	59.6	−38.9	21.3	29.7
Panama	6.5	−24.9	−9.9	47.6	6.6
Papua New Guinea	9.2	30.7	−9.3	−17.9	12.1
Paraguay	−7.8	−19.6	−12.7	25.3	4.8
Peru	−24.9	−20.4	−9.1	−1.0	4.8
Philippines	−7.4	18.5	−34.4	9.1	9.2
Portugal	62.5	−24.0	23.3	53.5	13.0
Rwanda	−21.4	12.9	−54.8	23.9	24.3
Senegal	14.5	45.1	−32.5	10.2	6.0
Sierra Leone	−54.4	0.0	−97.3	1380.8	15.1
Singapore	137.7	14.4	16.4	55.4	14.8
South Africa	−19.9	−10.6	4.5	−20.0	7.2
Spain	35.5	−16.6	22.3	25.8	5.5
Sri Lanka	66.3	73.6	−44.1	56.2	9.8
Swaziland	31.8	20.1	−13.3	13.9	11.1
Sweden	31.9	−7.8	21.4	15.0	2.5
Switzerland	5.6	−2.9	6.1	1.8	0.7
Syrian Arab Rep.	−1.7	48.9	−11.4	−32.8	10.9
Thailand	117	8.0	−16.6	118.0	10.9
Togo	−27.6	42.9	−28.7	−36.9	12.6
Tunisia	30.3	0.8	2.2	15.9	9.2
United Kingdom	49.7	−9.0	15.9	39.0	2.1
United States	42.5	−16.2	15.5	46.8	0.2
Uruguay	1.8	0.0	−0.1	−2.0	3.9
Venezuela	−30.9	10.4	2.8	−40.9	3.0
Zambia	−32.3	140.8	−33.8	−62.4	13.0
Zimbabwe	−1.3	13.2	−32.9	−7.0	39.7

The *average* percentage changes between 1980 and 2000 for different country groups are collected in Table 20.3. Average productivity improvement in the world was mostly due to physical capital deepening, but this result is strongly affected by the presence of Sierra Leone in calculations.[13] Without Sierra Leone, the change in efficiency plays an equally important role. The averages reveal some interesting differences between the country groups. The average growth in output per worker, that is, labour productivity, exceeded 45 per cent in high-income countries, but remained below 20 per cent in developing economies. The effect of the change in efficiency is close to 30 per cent in developing economies, while the contribution of the component is negative (–2.8 per cent) in high-income countries. In contrast, the average effect from technological change, i.e. from the movement of the best practice frontier, has been positive at over 10 per cent in high-income

Table 20.3   Mean effects in different groups of countries

	The change in GDP per worker (%)	The contribution to the change in labour productivity of the change in			
		effciency	technology	physical capital	human capital
Mean, all countries	27.3	19.5	−9.8	35.5	10.0
excluding Sierra Leone	28.3	19.8	−8.8	19.1	10.0
Mean, high-income countries	45.3	−2.8	13.6	24.1	6.8
Mean, developing economies	19.5	29.2	−19.9	40.5	11.4
excluding Sierra Leone	20.8	29.7	−18.6	17.0	11.3
Mean, middle-income countries	28.4	15.3	−9.0	23.4	7.9
Mean, upper-middle-income countries	38.3	−8.9	0.3	49.8	5.3
Mean, lower-middle-income countries	22.4	30.0	−14.6	7.4	9.5
Mean, low-income countries	3.9	53.5	−39.3	70.5	17.5
excluding Sierra Leone	6.9	56.2	−36.4	5.0	17.6
Mean, not classified by debt	45.3	−2.8	13.6	24.1	6.8
Mean, less indebted countries	58.8	38.2	−17.0	40.8	11.0
Mean, moderately indebted countries	15.0	12.7	−17.6	22.0	11.0
Mean, severely indebted countries	−13.3	43.3	−26.2	66.3	12.3
excluding Sierra Leone	−10.7	46.0	−21.7	−15.9	12.1
Mean, HIPCs	−15.0	51.8	−36.7	66.5	15.0
excluding Sierra Leone	−12.7	54.8	−33.2	−10.8	15.0

Note: These are non-weighted arithmetic means. Country classifications presented in Appendix 2 are the World Bank classifications for the year 2000. These were chosen because the results can now be analyzed from the end-of-the-period point of view and because similar classifications are unavailable for the beginning of the period.

countries but is negative –20 per cent in developing economies. This is a major explanation for the divergence in average paths in output per worker.

How can one explain this technological implosion? One answer is that at the same time as these countries have improved their efficiency, their production structure has concentrated more in activities with relatively slow technological change. Second, some developing economies may be liquidity constrained, for example due to high debt, and cannot afford to buy the latest technologies but are, however, able to improve the efficiency at which they are using their old equipment.[14] The accumulation of physical capital seems to play an important role in sustaining average international income differentials. The contribution of human capital accumulation displays less variation although it has generally been a little higher in the developing economies. The striking observation is that improvements in efficiency seem to have been largest in the countries with either severe or low levels of debt.[15] The interpretation of this result will be given below.

The group average changes can be produced by large changes in just few countries. To begin with the analysis of changes in the entire distribution of labour productivity, we plot the growth rates of labour productivity and its components against the income per capita in 1980 in Figure 20.1. The first diagram gives the

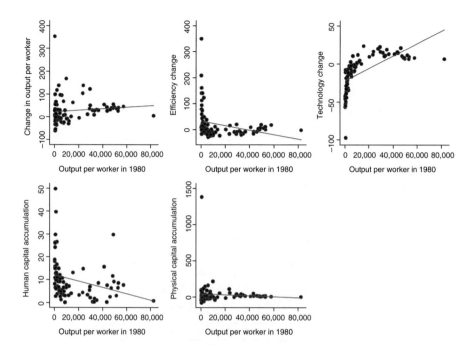

Figure 20.1　Percentage changes in output per worker, efficiency, technology, human capital and physical capital between 1980 and 2000

changes in output per worker over 1980–2000, the next ones changes in efficiency, technical change, human capital accumulation and physical capital accumulation. The figure also displays the trends (basically reproducing the same information as Table 20.3).

The dispersion among low-income countries is huge in comparison to high-income countries. Second, there is some non-linearity: the poorest countries have gained most from efficiency improvements, but the medium-income countries the least. This contrasts with Kumar and Russell (2002: figure 4b), who find that all countries benefited equally (little) from efficiency improvements.

Productivity distributions in country groups

We next examine the distribution dynamics of output per worker to get an idea of how individual countries and country groups performed, and how the distribution of labour productivity changed between 1980 and 2000. The distributions of labour productivity in these two years are in Figure 20.2 (the dotted line refers to the distribution in 2000 identified by c in the figure legend). These are kernel estimates of the distributions.

The usual story is that the world income per capita distribution has two peaks (Jones 1997), which was confirmed by Kumar and Russell (2002). Our results for the

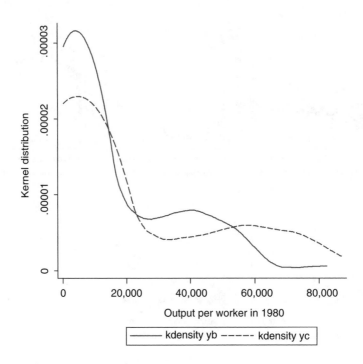

Figure 20.2   Distributions of output per worker, 1980 and 2000

year 1980 imply likewise a bimodal distribution, but the evidence for 2000 is weaker. This may naturally be partly due to differences in datasets, but one cannot rule out right away the possibility that the world is not as polarized as it used to be.

The kernel estimates of distributions of the efficiency scores (or catch-up measures) for years 1980 (label kdensity effb) and 2000 (label kdensity effc) are in Figure 20.3. The first panel depicts the efficiency scores calculated with the data comprising Sierra Leone, while the right-hand figure is based on a dataset without Sierra Leone. The figures imply that the same discussion holds for both cases. The density concentrated at the lowest efficiency scores is smaller in 2000 than in 1980. The second more striking feature is that the poorest countries, which had the lowest scores in 1980, have gained a lot in efficiency while rich countries have been losing.

To study how the labour productivity distribution of 1980 was transformed into the distribution of 2000, we analyze how the individual components of the decomposition (20.A6) presented in Appendix 1 change the distribution of 1980. We first show the transformation for all countries, then for developing economies, then for different income and debt classes within developing economies and, finally, for heavily indebted poor countries.[16] In Figure 20.4, the first diagram reproduces Figure 20.2. The second diagram shows the kernel estimate of

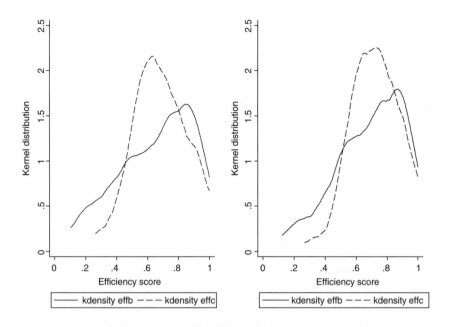

Figure 20.3 Distributions of efficiency index, 1980 and 2000 (with and without Sierra Leone)

the distribution in 2000 (depicted by the dash line) together with the estimate of distribution of

$$\frac{e_c}{e_b} y_b$$

where b = 1980 and c = 2000. Like in Kumar and Russell (2002), the latter and its equivalents will be called counterfactual distributions in the text below. The third diagram gives the impact of the cumulative changes in efficiency and technological change on 1980 labour productivity, the fourth the combined impact of efficiency, technological change and physical capital accumulation and the last diagram (producing the first) the combined impact of all the underlying changes, including human capital accumulation.[17] The order of presentation does not influence the results (transformations using other representative orders of presentation are given in Appendix 3).

All countries

The distributions of labour productivity in 1980 and in 2000 are statistically different. There is no single driver of the change in the distribution. Statistically,[18] the most significant driver of change has been technological change together with physical and human capital accumulation. Changes in efficiency have also contributed to the transformation of the labour productivity distribution by taking away the other peak from the distribution of 1980 (Figure 20.4).

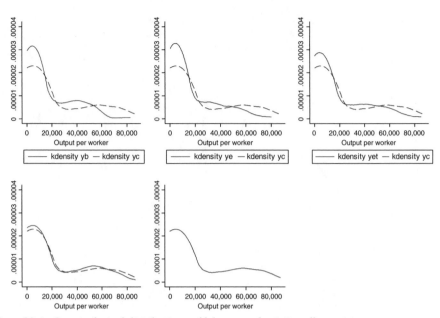

Figure 20.4 Counterfactual distributions of labour productivity: all countries

High-income countries

In high-income countries, the distribution has been altered jointly by technological change and physical capital accumulation.[19] This holds irrespective of the order in which the components are taken into account (Figure 20.A4 in Appendix 4). Statistically the distributions of labour productivity in 1980 and in 2000 are different.

Developing economies

Figure 20.5 displays the results for developing economies, the first diagram giving again the kernel estimates of the actual distributions. Statistically, the distributions of 1980 and 2000 are identical. Yet, there has been a significant improvement in efficiency, which has, jointly with human capital, increased developing country income (*ceteris paribus*). The positive effect has been nullified by technological change and lack of capital accumulation.

Is it possible to analyze the improvement in developing countries' efficiency (technological catch-up) in terms of the theories reviewed in the introduction? Geography cannot matter much, as the efficiency gain has been widespread (see Table 20.2). Similarly, it is hard to make a case for a change in institutions in this period as the single major factor causing the stagnation of developing country incomes. Such a result would have to be based on a more detailed analysis on the common (institutional) features of those countries that have gained in efficiency.

There thus seems to be a puzzle, which is even larger when we look at the debtor countries. The phenomenon is consistent with the Nelson-Phelps model, which

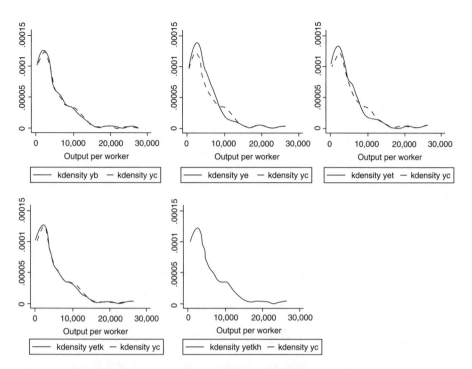

Figure 20.5 Counterfactual distributions of labour productivity: developing economies

implies the catch-up rate is an increasing function of human capital intensity. The model also helps to understand why the contribution of human capital, for given catch-up, seems to be small. In addition, finance constraints may explain the result.

Middle-income countries

In middle-income countries (see Figure 20.A5 in Appendix 4), the distributions of labour productivity in 1980 and 2000 are the same. The counterfactual 1980 distribution combining the effects of changes in efficiency and human and physical capital stocks differs significantly from the distribution of 2000.

Low-income countries

In low-income countries of Figure 20.6, changes in efficiency (jointly with human capital) and technology are statistically significant drivers of change, but netting each other out. Changes in efficiency improve incomes.

Debtor countries

In all three debtor country groups from severely indebted to less indebted countries, the actual 1980 distribution and all counterfactual distributions are statistically identical with the 2000 distribution (see also Figures 20.A6–A8). This

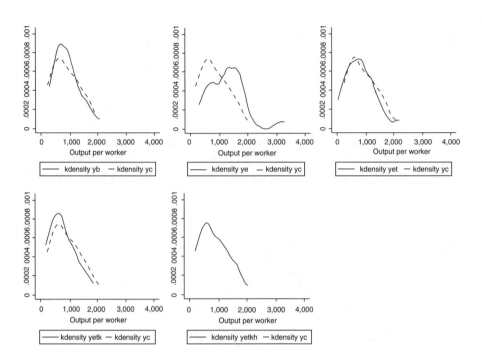

Figure 20.6   Counterfactual distributions of labour productivity: low-income countries (with Sierra Leone)

means that the component changes have been too small and too diverse, perhaps also in different directions, to have had a statistically significant impact.

HIPCs

Again, in the aggregate there has not been any statistically significant change in the distribution between 1980 and 2000 (Figure 20.7). Changes in productive efficiency have, however, had a large, statistically significant impact on the distribution of labour productivity in HIPCs: improvements in efficiency have tended to reduce the proportion of countries at low productivity levels and increased the proportion of countries at relatively high output per worker levels. Hence, efficiency improvements have tended to benefit the highly indebted countries. These benefits have been taken away by the technological implosion and contraction in physical capital accumulation.

The result[20] gives fairly strong support for the reasoning behind the debt Laffer curve: high indebtedness reduces incentives to invest in productive capital. Hansen (2004) finds also that high indebtedness reduces growth by reducing investment. Our data does not support the possibility that high indebtedness allows debtor countries to escape the necessary policy reforms. If the implication of the hypothesis is that the lack of reforms increases the waste of resources, then exactly the opposite has happened according to our data. Since most of the HIPCs

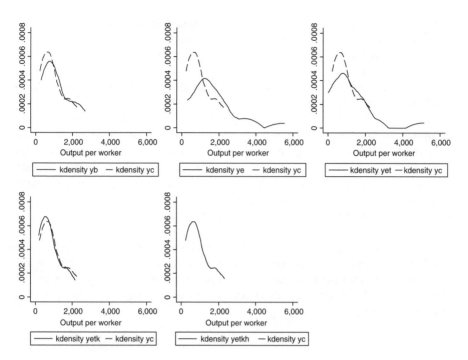

Figure 20.7   Counterfactual distributions of labour productivity: HIPCs

are in sub-Saharan Africa, the results are in line with Artadi and Sala-í-Martín (2003), who find that the high price of capital goods significantly reduces income there.

Conclusions

We studied the world distribution of output per worker between the years 1980 and 2000. We used data envelopment analysis to decompose the changes in the distribution of output per worker into changes in productive efficiency (which can be interpreted to measure the degree of technological catch-up), changes in best practice technology (technological change), accumulation of human capital and accumulation of physical capital. The most significant results are:

- The distribution of income in developing and HIPC countries has not changed between 1980 and 2000. This stagnation has been created by decline in capital accumulation, as at the same time improvements in production efficiency have been remarkable. In HIPCs, resources have been shifted to sectors with below-average productivity growth and/or production has been using old technology more efficiently, while at the same time investments in new technology have remained very low. This implies that one should not focus on institutions alone to explain stagnation, as institutional explanations usually emphasize the inefficiencies created by bad institutions. Instead, one should look for factors working together with institutional factors. The result also supports the reasoning behind the debt Laffer curve, as it implies that excessive debt creates a tax on investment. The analysis does not support the view that high indebtedness allows countries to escape reforms.

- The world distribution of output per worker since 1980 until 2000 has been altered *jointly* by technological change and accumulation of physical and human capital. Technological change together with changes in productive efficiency has had some effect, too. No single factor can explain the change since 1980s. This is in contrast with studies focusing on earlier periods: they have found the deepening of physical capital to be the major factor.
- Developed and developing countries share the same frontier technology.

A look at the distributions can thus clarify some of the issues related to the problems of development. To get further, it is necessary to model explicitly, for example, the determinants of efficiency. In the context of DEA this requires special care (for example, Simar and Wilson 2003), but the benefits may be large. This is left for future work.

Appendix 1

Decomposition of output/worker

We decompose labour productivity in a manner analogous to Kumar and Russell (2002) but incorporating also changes in human capital.[21] For any country for b(ase) and c(urrent) periods change in labour productivity can be decomposed into changes in efficiency and potential output:

$$\frac{y_c}{y_b} = \frac{e_c \times \bar{y}_c(k_c,h_c)}{e_b \times \bar{y}_b(k_b,h_b)} \qquad (20.A1)$$

where k_t, h_t are the physical capital and human capital stocks per capita for period t. Similarly, e_t is the efficiency score for period t. The potential output for the economy in period t is by definition. $\bar{y}_t(k_t,h_t)=y_t/e_t$. Change in potential output can be decomposed into changes in technology and inputs. The problem is that it matters in which order decompositions are made. One decomposition is:

$$\frac{y_c}{y_b} = \frac{e_c\bar{y}_c(k_c,h_c)\,\bar{y}_b(k_c,h_c)}{e_b\bar{y}_b(k_c,h_c)\,\bar{y}_b(k_b,h_b)} = \frac{e_c\bar{y}_c(k_c,h_c)\,\bar{y}_b(k_c,h_c)\,\bar{y}_b(k_c,h_b)}{e_b\bar{y}_b(k_c,h_c)\,\bar{y}_b(k_c,h_b)\,\bar{y}_b(k_b,h_b)} \qquad (20.A2)$$

The first ratio measures the change in efficiency, the second ratio the impact of technological change, the third the impact of human capital accumulation and the fourth the impact of physical capital accumulation. This is the other possible decomposition:

$$\frac{y_c}{y_b} = \frac{e_c \bar{y}_c(k_c,h_c)}{e_b} \frac{\bar{y}_b(k_c,h_c)}{\bar{y}_b(k_c,h_c)} \frac{\bar{y}_b(k_b,h_c)}{\bar{y}_b(k_b,h_b)} \qquad (20.A3)$$

The third ratio measures the impact of physical capital accumulation, and the last the impact of human capital accumulation. The problem is solved by taking the geometric average and weighing the changes equally:

$$\frac{y_c}{y_b} = \frac{e_c \bar{y}_c(k_c,h_c)}{e_b \bar{y}_b(k_c,h_c)} \left[\frac{\bar{y}_b(k_c,h_c)\,\bar{y}_b(k_b,h_c)}{\bar{y}_b(k_c,h_b)\,\bar{y}_b(k_b,h_b)} \right]^{\frac{1}{2}} \left[\frac{\bar{y}_b(k_c,h_c)\,\bar{y}_b(k_c,h_b)}{\bar{y}_b(k_b,h_c)\,\bar{y}_b(k_b,h_b)} \right]^{\frac{1}{2}} \qquad (20.A4)$$

The first ratio is again the change in efficiency, the second component is the technological change, the third measures the impact of human capital accumulation and the fourth the impact of physical capital accumulation.

In (20.A4) it still matters which capital stocks and techniques are used as the base, as the change can be decomposed as follows:

$$\frac{y_c}{y_b} = \frac{e_c \bar{y}_c(k_b,h_b)}{e_b \bar{y}_b(k_b,h_b)} \frac{\bar{y}_c(k_c,h_c)}{\bar{y}_c(k_c,h_b)} \frac{\bar{y}_c(k_c,h_b)}{\bar{y}_c(k_b,h_b)} \qquad (20.A5)$$

In addition, (20.A5) has the problem that the order in which the impacts of the capital accumulation is calculated matters. Putting all things together leads to the solution:

$$\frac{y_c}{y_b} = \frac{e_c}{e_b} \left[\frac{\bar{y}_c(k_c,h_c)\,\bar{y}_c(k_b,h_b)}{\bar{y}_b(k_c,h_c)\,\bar{y}_b(k_b,h_b)} \right]^{\frac{1}{2}} \left\{ \left[\frac{\bar{y}_b(k_c,h_c)\,\bar{y}_b(k_b,h_c)}{\bar{y}_b(k_c,h_b)\,\bar{y}_b(k_b,h_b)} \right]^{\frac{1}{2}} \left[\frac{\bar{y}_c(k_c,h_c)\bar{y}_c(k_b,h_c)}{\bar{y}_c(k_c,h_b)\bar{y}_c(k_b,h_b)} \right]^{\frac{1}{2}} \right\}^{\frac{1}{2}} \times \quad (20.A6)$$

$$\left\{ \left[\frac{\bar{y}_b(k_c,h_c)\,\bar{y}_b(k_c,h_b)}{\bar{y}_b(k_b,h_c)\,\bar{y}_b(k_b,h_b)} \right]^{\frac{1}{2}} \left[\frac{\bar{y}_c(k_c,h_c)\,\bar{y}_c(k_c,h_b)}{\bar{y}_c(k_b,h_c)\,\bar{y}_c(k_b,h_b)} \right]^{\frac{1}{2}} \right\}^{\frac{1}{2}}$$

where the first ratio measures the change in productive efficiency, the second technological change, the third the impact of human capital accumulation and the last the impact of physical capital accumulation.

Appendix 2

Table 20.A1 Country classifications for 2000

BY INCOME LEVEL

High income	Developing economies		
	Upper-middle income	Lower-middle income	Low income
Australia	Argentina	Algeria	Bangladesh
Austria	Botswana	Bolivia	Cameroon
Belgium	Brazil	China	Congo, Dem. Rep.
Canada	Chile	Colombia	Gambia
Denmark	Costa Rica	Dominican Republic	Ghana
Finland	Hungary	Ecuador	India
France	Korea, Rep.	Egypt, Arab Rep.	Indonesia
Germany	Malaysia	El Salvador	Kenya
Greece	Mauritius	Guatemala	Lesotho
Hong Kong, China	Mexico	Guyana	Malawi
Iceland	Panama	Honduras	Mali
Ireland	South Africa	Iran, Islamic Rep.	Mozambique
Israel	Uruguay	Jamaica	Nicaragua
Italy	Venezuela, RB	Jordan	Niger
Japan		Papua New Guinea	Pakistan
Netherlands		Paraguay	Rwanda
New Zealand		Peru	Senegal
Norway		Philippines	Sierra Leone
Portugal		Sri Lanka	Togo
Singapore		Swaziland	Zambia
Spain		Syrian Arab Republic	Zimbabwe
Sweden		Thailand	
Switzerland		Tunisia	
United Kingdom			
United States			

BY INDEBTEDNESS

Not Classified	Less indebted	Moderately indebted	Severely indebted	Highly indebted poor countries
Australia	Bangladesh	Algeria	Argentina	Bolivia
Austria	Botswana	Bolivia	Brazil	Cameroon
Belgium	China	Chile	Cameroon	Congo, Dem. Rep.
Canada	Costa Rica	Colombia	Congo, Dem. Rep.	Gambia
Denmark	Dominican	Gambia	Ecuador	Ghana
Finland	Republic	Ghana	Guyana	Guyana
France	Egypt, Arab Rep.	Honduras	Indonesia	Honduras
Germany	El Salvador	Hungary	Jordan	Kenya
Greece	Guatemala	Jamaica	Malawi	Malawi
Hong Kong,	India	Kenya	Nicaragua	Mali
China	Iran,	Malaysia	Niger	Mozambique
Iceland	Islamic Rep.	Mali	Pakistan	Nicaragua
	Korea, Rep.	Mauritius	Peru	Niger
Ireland	Lesotho	Mozambique	Rwanda	Rwanda
Israel	Mexico	Panama	Sierra Leone	Senegal
Italy	Paraguay	Papua	Syrian	Sierra Leone
Japan	South Africa	New Guinea	Arab Republic	Togo
Netherlands	Sri Lanka	Philippines	Zambia	Zambia
New Zealand	Swaziland	Senegal		

Table 20.A1 Continued

Not Classified	Less indebted	Moderately indebted	Severely indebted	Highly indebted poor countries
Norway		Thailand		
Portugal		Togo		
Singapore		Tunisia		
Spain		Uruguay		
Sweden		Venezuela, RB		
Switzerland		Zimbabwe		
United Kingdom				
United States				

Appendix 3

Decomposition of changes in world distribution of output per worker: alternative orderings

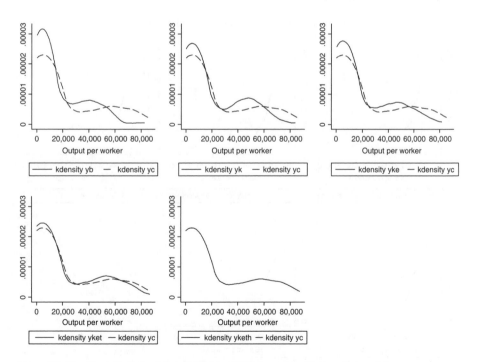

Figure 20.A1   Counterfactual distributions of labour productivity: all countries

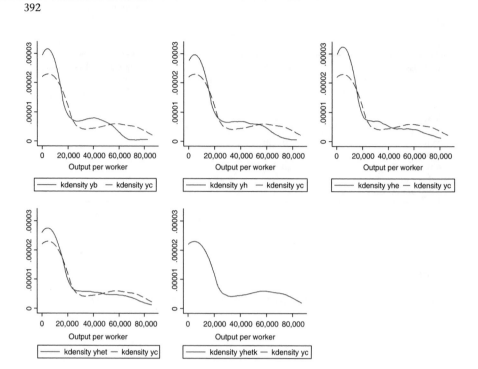

Figure 20.A2   Counterfactual distributions of labour productivity: all countries

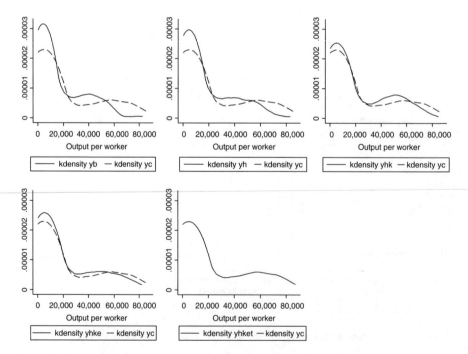

Figure 20.A3   Counterfactual distributions of labour productivity: all countries

Appendix 4

Decomposition of changes in the distribution of output per worker in different groups of countries

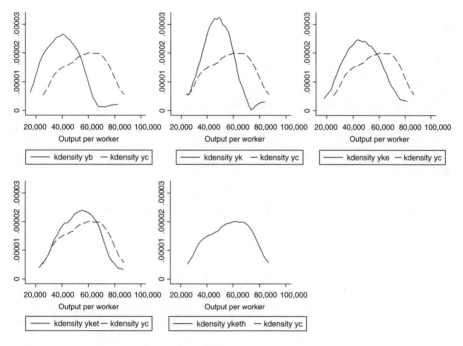

Figure 20.A4　Counterfactual distributions of labour productivity: high-income countries

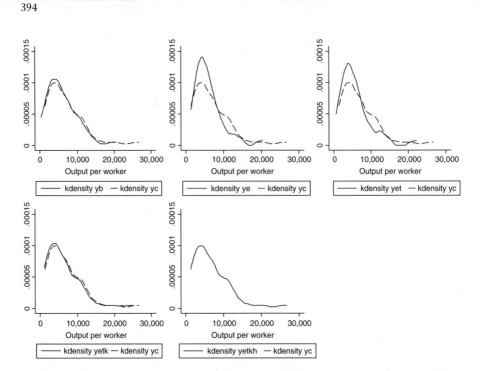

Figure 20.A5   Counterfactual distributions of labour productivity: middle-income countries

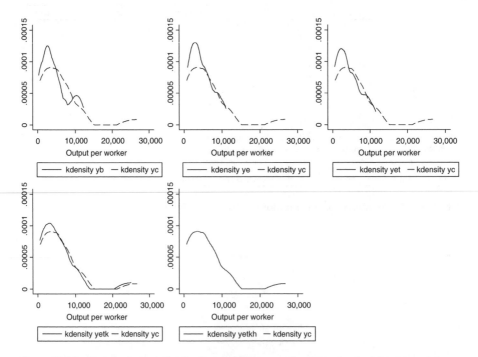

Figure 20.A6   Counterfactual distributions of labour productivity: less indebted countries

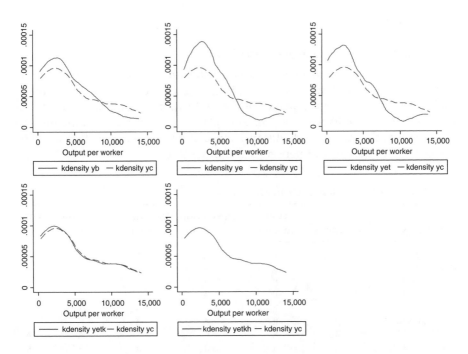

Figure 20.A7 Counterfactual distributions of labour productivity: moderately indebted countries

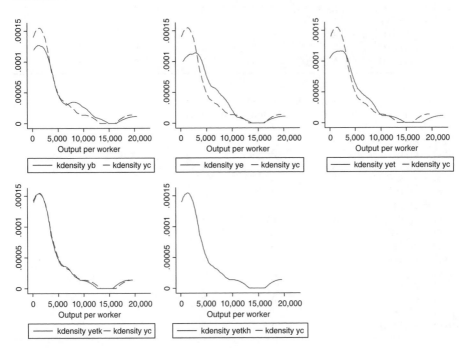

Figure 20.A8 Counterfactual distributions of labour productivity: severely indebted countries (with Sierra Leone)

Appendix 5

Statistical tests for the change in distribution

We used the bootstrap method to calculate the small sample distributions on which to base our tests. We resampled each country group 1,000 times. Table 20.A2 denotes the acceptance of the null hypothesis indicated in the left-most column, and R its rejection. For example in the HIPC case A in the first cell indicates that the null of no change in actual distribution between 1980 and 2000 is accepted. All tests are at 5 per cent significance level.

Table 20.A2   Test results for the change in distribution

Null hypothesis	All countries	High income	Developing economies	Low income	Middle income	HIPC
f(yc) = g(yb)	R	R	A	A	A	A
f(yc) = g(yE)	R	R	A	A	A	R
f(yc) = g(yT)	R	R	A	R	A	A
f(yc) = g(yK)	R	R	A	A	A	A
f(yc) = g(yH)	R	R	A	A	A	A
f(yc) = g(yET)	R	R	A	A	A	A
f(yc) = g(yEK)	R	R	A	A	A	A
f(yc) = g(yEH)	R	R	R	R	A	R
f(yc) = g(yTK)	A	A	A	R	A	A
f(yc) = g(yTH)	A	R	A	A	A	A
f(yc) = g(yKH)	R	R	A	A	A	A
f(yc) = g(yETK)	A	A	A	A	A	A
f(yc) = g(yETH)	A	R	A	A	A	A
f(yc) = g(yEKH)	R	A	R	R	R	R
f(yc) = g(yTKH)	A	A	A	A	A	A

Null hypothesis	Less indebted	Moderately indebted	Severely indebted
f(yc) = g(yb)	A	A	A
f(yc) = g(yE)	A	A	A
f(yc) = g(yT)	A	A	A
f(yc) = g(yK)	A	A	A
f(yc) = g(yH)	A	A	A
f(yc) = g(yET)	A	A	A
f(yc) = g(yEK)	A	A	A
f(yc) = g(yEH)	A	A	A
f(yc) = g(yTK)	A	A	A
f(yc) = g(yTH)	A	A	A
f(yc) = g(yKH)	A	A	A
f(yc) = g(yETK)	A	A	A
f(yc) = g(yETH)	A	A	A
f(yc) = g(yEKH)	A	A	A
f(yc) = g(yTKH)	A	A	A

Notes

This work is part of project no. 206014 financed by the Academy of Finland. Heli Virta thanks also the Yrjö Jahnsson Foundation for financial support. In addition, we would like to thank Merja Halme for advice in DEA, and the referees and participants both in the WIDER jubilee conference and the Nordic Conference in Development Economics, 2005.

1. See, for example, Hall and Jones (1999); Mankiw *et al.* (1992).
2. Pande and Udry (2005); Acemoglu *et al.* (2002); Rodrik (2003); and Collier and Gunning (1999) for Africa.
3. Recently Acemoglu *et al.* (2003) have proposed a model of growth in which the distance is determined endogenously. They apply the model to India. A classic model was built by Nelson and Phelps (1966).
4. This idea has been picked up also by Henderson and Russell (2004). They use the restriction that human and physical capital are substitutes while in our work such a restriction is not used. In our framework, human capital and physical capital can be complements. This seems to be the empirically relevant alternative given the evidence for capital–skill complementarity.
5. Färe *et al.* (1994) is a good reference for those interested in the use of the method in the context of economics, while Charnes *et al.* (1978; 1979) are more known in the management-science literature. Yet another source is Lovell (1994).
6. Murillo-Zamorano (2004) discusses the differences between parametric and non-parametric frontier methods in more detail.
7. It is promising that both proxies produce relatively similar results.
8. Cohen and Soto (2001) provide an alternative dataset for human capital based on some differences in sources and methodology. Correlation between their estimates and those of Barro and Lee (2001) is fairly high in levels, which implies that our overall results are not that dependent on the dataset chosen, even if the correlation of the human capital estimates is significantly lower in first difference.
9. Sierra Leone, with its exceptionally low capital per labour ratio, affects the scores of other low-income countries. In 1980, 54 countries, mostly developing economies, have Sierra Leone as their benchmark technology and in 2000, still 44 countries. Kumar and Russell (2002) find it possible that DEA might fail to identify the true production frontier especially at low capital–labour ratios. We check the sensitivity of results with a dataset without Sierra Leone.
10. In accordance with the World Bank convention, we use the term developing economies to denote low- and middle-income countries.
11. The method was originally developed for separating management efficiency from programme efficiency. See Charnes *et al.* (1981).
12. The results are available upon request.
13. If Sierra Leone, with its exceptionally low capital per labour ratio, is excluded from the data envelopment analysis, the efficiency scores of those lower-income countries that originally had Sierra Leone as a part of their reference technology improve. The most dramatic impacts are seen in the decompositions. Although the relative contributions of particularly efficiency change and capital accumulation may change somewhat drastically within a country, the signs of the contributions remain unchanged. These results are available upon request.
14. Henderson and Russell (2004) rule out the possibility of technological implosion. We did not want to follow them for the reasons just given.
15. The differences between debtor country groups are sensitive to the year on which the classification is based, because movements from one indebtedness group to another are not rare. The basic result of large efficiency improvements in debtor countries is not sensitive to this problem.

16. We use the test devised by Li (Pagan and Ullah 1999: 68–9, test statistic given by their equation 2.144) to test for the significance of the distribution change. The test is valid also when x and y are dependent. Test results are presented in Appendix 5.
17. Letter e in the legend of the next figures and diagrams refers to efficiency, t to technological change, h to the contribution of human capital and k to the contribution of physical capital.
18. See Table 20.A2 in Appendix 5.
19. Exactly, the Li test indicates that the distribution of labour productivity obtained from the distribution of 1980 by taking into account the changes in efficiency and physical capital stock is the same as the actual year 2000 distribution. For other combinations of underlying changes this does not hold.
20. To check the robustness of the results we have made the decompositions based on the efficiency scores calculated without Sierra Leone. With some minor exceptions all the results hold. The results are available upon request.
21. Our approach differs from Henderson and Russell (2004), who decompose the growth of labour productivity into the growth of output per efficiency unit of labour and the growth of human capital.

References

Acemoglu, D., S. Johnson and J. Robinson (2002) 'Reversal of Fortune: Geography and Institutions in the Making of the Modern World Income Distribution', *Quarterly Journal of Economicsx*, 117: 1369–401.

Acemoglu, D., P. Aghion and F. Zilibotti (2003) 'Distance to Frontier, Selection, and Economic Growth', Mimeo, University College London.

Artadi E. and X. Sala-i-Martín (2003) 'The Economic Tragedy of XXth Century: Growth in Africa', *NBER Working Paper* 9865, Cambridge, MA: National Bureau of Economic Research.

Barro, R.J. (2000) 'Inequality and Growth in a Panel of Countries', *Journal of Economic Growth*, 5, 1: 5–32.

Barro, R.J. and J. Lee (2001) 'International Data on Educational Attainment: Updates and Implications', *Oxford Economic Papers*, 53, 3: 541–63.

Birdsall, N., S. Claessens and I. Diwan (2003) 'Policy Selectivity Foregone: Debt and Donor Behavior in Africa', *World Bank Economic Review*, 17, 3: 409–35.

Caselli, F. (2005) 'Accounting for Cross-Country Income Differences', *CEP Discussion Paper* 667, London: Centre for Economic Policy Research.

Charnes, A., W.W. Cooper and E. Rhodes (1978) 'Measuring the Inefficiency of Decision Making Units', *European Journal of Operational Research*, 2, 6: 428–49.

Charnes, A., W.W. Cooper and E. Rhodes (1979) 'Measuring the Inefficiency of Decision Making Units', *European Journal of Operational Research*, 3, 4: 321–39.

Charnes, A., W.W. Cooper and E. Rhodes (1981) 'Evaluating Programme and Managerial Efficiency: An Application of Data Envelopment Analysis to Programme Follow Through', *Management Science*, 27, 6: 668–97.

Cohen, D. and M. Soto (2001) 'Growth and Human Capital: Good Data, Good Results', *CEPR Discussion Paper* 3025, London: Centre for Economic Policy Research.

Collier, P. and J. Gunning (1999) 'Explaining African Economic Performance', *Journal of Economic Literature*, 37, 1: 64–111.

Färe, R., S. Grosskopf and C.A.K. Lovell (1994) *Production Frontiers*, Cambridge: Cambridge University Press.

Glaeser, E., R. La Porta, F. Lopez-de-Silanes and A. Shleifer (2004) 'Do Institutions Cause Growth?', *NBER Working Paper* 10568, Cambridge, MA: National Bureau of Economic Research.

Hall, R.E. and C.I. Jones (1999) 'Why Do Some Countries Produce So Much More Output Per Worker Than Others?', *Quarterly Journal of Economics*, 114, 1: 83–116.

Hansen, H. (2004) 'The Impact of External Aid and Debt on Growth and Investment', in T. Addison, H. Hansen and F. Tarp (eds), *Debt Relief for Poor Countries*, New York: Palgrave Macmillan for UNU-WIDER.

Henderson, D. and R. Russell (2004) 'Human Capital and Convergence: A Production Function Approach', Mimeo, State University of New York, Albany.

Henry, M., R. Kneller and C. Milner (2003) 'Trade, Technology Transfer and National Efficiency in Developing Countries', *CREDIT Research Paper* 2003/50, Nottingham: Centre for Research in Economic Development and International Trade, University of Nottingham.

Jones, C.I. (1997) 'On the Evolution of the World Income Distribution', *Journal of Economic Perspectives*, 11, 3: 19–36.

Krugman, P. (1988) 'Financing vs. Forgiving a Debt Overhang', *Journal of Development Economics*, 29: 253–68.

Kumar, S. and R.R. Russell (2002) 'Technological Change, Technological Catch-up, and Capital Deepening: Relative Contributions to Growth and Convergence', *American Economic Review*, 92, 3: 527–48.

Li, Q. (1996) 'Non-parametric Testing of Closeness between Two Unknown Distribution Functions', *Econometric Reviews*, 15, 3: 261–74.

Lovell, C.A.K. (1994) 'Linear Programming Approaches to the Measurement and Analysis of Productive Efficiency', *Top*, 2, 2: 175–248.

Mankiw, N., D. Romer and D. Weil (1992) 'A Contribution to the Empirics of Economic Growth', *Quarterly Journal of Economics*, 107, 2: 407–37.

Murillo-Zamorano, L.R. (2004) 'Economic Efficiency and Frontier Techniques', *Journal of Economic Surveys*, 18, 1: 33–77.

Nelson, R. and E. Phelps (1966) 'Investment in Humans, Technological Diffusion, and Economic Growth', *American Economic Review*, 56, 1/2: 69–75.

Pagan, A. and A. Ullah (1999) *Non-parametric Econometrics*, Cambridge: Cambridge University Press.

Pande R. and C. Udry (2005) 'Institutions and Development: A View from Below', paper presented at the Econometric Society World Congress, August, London.

Rodrik, D. (ed.) (2003) *In Search of Prosperity*, New Jersey: Princeton University.

Ruotinen, J. (2005) 'Technological Diffusion and Trade in Services', Mimeo, Helsinki: Helsinki School of Economics.

Sachs J.D., J.W. MacArthur, G. Schmidt-Traub, M. Kruk, G. McCord, C. Bahadur and M. Faye (2004) 'Ending Africa's Poverty Trap', *Brookings Papers on Economic Activity* 1, Washington, DC: The Brookings Institution.

Simar L. and P. Wilson (2003) 'Estimation and Inference in Two-Stage, Semi-Parametric Models of Production Processes', *Institut de Statistique Discussion Paper* 0307, Louvain-la-Neuve: Université Catholique de Louvain.

World Bank (2002) *World Development Indicators*, Washington, DC: Oxford University Press for the World Bank.

World Bank (2004) *World Development Indicators Online*, retrieved in December 2004 from http://devdata.worldbank.org/dataonline/

21
Evaluating Targeting Efficiency of Government Programmes: International Comparisons

Nanak Kakwani and Hyun H. Son

Introduction

For about the last two decades, the consensus has been that economic growth is necessary but not, by itself, sufficient for the alleviation of poverty. Additional elements are required. First, poor households need to build up their asset base in order to participate in the growth process. Second, growth needs to be broad-based to reach all segments of society, including the poor. Third, short-term public assistance measures are required to protect vulnerable groups of society, because it takes time for the needy to benefit from the impact of a policy or strategy.

Implementing this agenda to reduce poverty requires methods or tools that can effectively reach poor households or individuals. This may be accomplished by public spending on items like universal education, which can reach wide sections of society, including the poor. Alternatively, it can be achieved through a direct transfer of resources to the poor. However, in practice, problems commonly arise because of scarcity of resources. With fixed budgets, governments are often forced to direct resources to specific groups of households or individuals. Targeting specific groups will achieve the maximum impact from a given budget or minimize the costs of achieving a given impact. This attraction is particularly strong for transfer programmes that constitute safety nets, because such transfers provide a benefit that is largely a private good for recipient households.

While targeting has its own merits, there are a number of methods that can provide resources to a particular group. The existing literature largely focuses on individual programmes, with comparative analyses tending to cover a single region or method of intervention (Grosh 1994; Braithwaite *et al.* 2000; Bigman and Fofack 2000; Rawlings *et al.* 2001). A partial approach of this kind is not helpful for making broader assessments about the effectiveness of different targeting methods. This chapter attempts to provide a general framework for evaluating the targeting efficiency of government welfare programmes and to draw lessons from developing country experiences that are relevant for policy making.

A government programme may be defined as pro-poor if it provides greater absolute benefits to the poor compared to the non-poor. Suppose there are two programmes, *A* and *B*, incurring the same cost. Then *A* will be more pro-poor than *B* if it leads to greater poverty reduction than *B*. Utilizing this definition, Kakwani and Son (2005) developed a new index called the 'Pro-Poor Policy' (ppp) index, which measures the pro-poorness of government programmes as well as of basic service delivery in education, health and infrastructure.

The ppp index is derived as the ratio of actual poverty reduction from a government programme to the poverty reduction that would have been achieved if every individual in society received exactly the same benefits from the programme. The ppp index provides a means of assessing the targeting efficiency of government programmes. Furthermore, Kakwani and Son (2005) developed two subtypes of ppp indices by socioeconomic groups, namely 'within-group' and 'total-group' ppp indices. While the within-group ppp index measures the pro-poorness of a programme within a group, the total-group ppp index captures the impact of operating a programme in a group on its pro-poorness at the national level. The argument is based on the premise that the targeting efficiency of a particular group should be judged on the basis of a total-group ppp index[1]. Using micro-data from household surveys, the proposed methodology is applied to Thailand, the Russian Federation, Vietnam and 15 African countries.

The chapter is organized as follows. The first section presents a brief non-technical description of the methodology proposed by Kakwani and Son (2005). It outlines the poverty measures used in the chapter; the definition of the ppp index; the values of the ppp index attainable under perfect targeting; and the ppp index by socioeconomic groups. More technical details are reported in Kakwani and Son (*Ibid.*). The following section presents empirical results for Thailand, Russia and Vietnam. The penultimate section provides empirical results for 15 African countries, and the final section summarizes the major findings.

Methodology

Poverty measure

We measure the pro-poorness of a government policy by measuring its impact on poverty. Policy *A* is more pro-poor than policy *B* if it achieves a greater reduction in aggregate poverty for a given cost. Aggregate poverty can be measured in a variety of ways. In this chapter, we focus on the Foster *et al.* (1984) class of additively separable poverty measures. These include the headcount ratio (the percentage of people living below a poverty threshold); the poverty gap ratio, capturing the depth of poverty; and the severity of poverty index. The evaluation of a poverty reduction policy depends on the choice of poverty measure. For instance, addressing the headcount ratio will require policies different than those for addressing the poverty gap or the severity of poverty index. The headcount ratio is a crude measure of poverty because it completely ignores the gaps in incomes from the poverty line and the distribution of income among the poor. The severity of poverty index has all the desirable properties.

Pro-poor policy index

Suppose that a welfare transfer from the government leads to an increase in recipients' income or consumption. Then there will be a reduction in poverty due to the increase in income. We define a government programme to be pro-poor if the poor receive greater absolute benefits than the non-poor. This means that a pro-poor government programme should achieve greater poverty reduction than a programme in which everyone receives exactly the same benefit. The ppp index is defined as the ratio of the actual poverty reduction from the programme to the poverty reduction that would have been achieved if every individual in the society received the average benefit from the programme. A programme is called pro-poor (or anti-poor) when the ppp index is greater (or less) than unity. The larger the value of the ppp index, the greater is the degree of pro-poorness of the programme.

To calculate the ppp index, a programme does not have to involve cash transfers. In fact, a large number of government programmes involve education, health and other social benefits which do not provide cash to individuals, but nevertheless contribute to their standard of living. Hence, it can be assumed that if a person uses a government service then they receive some notional cash. If all individuals who utilize a government service are assumed to receive the same notional cash benefits then we can calculate the ppp index.

Perfect targeting

The ppp index achieves its lowest value of zero if the government programme does not reduce any poverty at all, which will happen when all benefits go to the non-poor. This is considered to be the extreme situation of imperfect targeting. Conversely, perfect targeting may be defined as a situation where only the poor benefit, and all the benefits are proportional to the income shortfall from the poverty line. Kakwani and Son (2005) define two different values of the ppp index obtainable under perfect targeting, depending upon how the poverty line is defined. In one scenario every household has a different poverty line depending on household composition and the prices faced by that household. In our empirical study of Thailand, the official poverty line varies with households, whereas for Vietnam the poverty line is fixed for all households. In each case, the value of the ppp index under perfect targeting is defined differently.

In practice, it is not possible to achieve perfect targeting because it is difficult to obtain accurate information on household income or consumption. We generally resort to proxy targeting by geographical region or other socioeconomic characteristics of households. In this study, the targeting efficiency of a programme is judged on the basis of the value of the ppp index. The value of the ppp index under perfect targeting may be used as a benchmark to assess the targeting performance of government programmes. This methodology can also be used for ex ante formulation of new government programmes.

PPP index by socioeconomic groups

Taking the analysis a step further, a decomposition methodology is proposed to explain the ppp index in terms of two factors: the within-group ppp index and the total-group ppp index. Suppose there are k mutually exclusive socioeconomic groups. The within-group ppp index measures the degree of pro-poorness of a programme within the kth group. It does not tell us whether targeting the kth group will necessarily lead to a pro-poor outcome at the national level. Since our objective is to achieve the maximum reduction of poverty at the national level, we need to see the impact of targeting the kth group on national poverty. To capture this effect, another ppp index for the kth group is proposed, called the total-group ppp index.

The total-group ppp index shows that the pro-poor policy index for the whole country is the weighted average of the pro-poor policy indices for individual groups, with weights proportional to the share of benefits received by each group. To reduce poverty at national level, applying the government programme to some groups will be more efficient than to others. This efficiency can be captured by the value of the total-group ppp index; the larger the value of the total-group ppp index the more efficient is that group in reducing national poverty. On the whole, the methodology presented can help us to identify the efficient groups from the viewpoint of improving targeting efficiency.

Case studies I: Thailand, Russia and Vietnam

In this section, we apply our methodology to Thailand, Russia and Vietnam. The ppp index is applied to Thailand and Russia to capture the extent to which the welfare schemes of those governments benefit the poor. For Vietnam the ppp index reflects the degree to which basic services, including education and health, are used effectively by its population.

For all three countries, the data is taken from household surveys, and the analysis is based on per capita consumption. The surveys are nationwide and cover the periods 2000, 2002 and 1997–98 for Thailand, Russia and Vietnam, respectively. The poverty lines are country-specific. A single average national poverty line is used for Vietnam, but the Thai and Russian poverty lines differ across households because they take into account the different needs of household members by gender and age, as well as spatial variations in the cost of living.[2]

Welfare programmes in Thailand and Russia

Thailand

In recent years, the Thai government has implemented a few social welfare programmes, including social pensions for the elderly, low-income medical cards, health insurance cards and free school lunch programmes. These are means-tested and have been designed to target low-income groups. In this section, we use the ppp index to examine whether these welfare programmes have benefited poor people.

Table 21.1 presents the ppp index for Thailand's social welfare programmes.[3] As can be seen from the table, all four welfare programmes have a ppp index value

Table 21.1   Pro-poor policy index for welfare programmes in Thailand, 2000

Welfare schemes	Poverty gap ratio	Severity of poverty
Social pension for the elderly	1.68	1.54
Low-income medical cards	2.02	2.12
Health insurance cards	1.29	1.25
Free school lunches	2.02	2.06
Perfect targeting	6.77	10.31
Universal social pensions (for elderly over 65 years of age)	1.21	1.24

Source: Based on Thailand's *Household Socioeconomic Survey 2000* (National Statistics Office 2000).

greater than one. Hence, we may conclude that all four welfare programmes benefit the poor more than the non-poor. Overall, the poor have greater access to these government welfare programmes than the non-poor. Interestingly, the welfare programmes for low-income medical cards and free school lunches have higher ppp index values with respect to the severity of poverty measure. Since the severity of poverty measure gives greater weight to the ultra-poor, this indicates that the absolute benefits of low-income medical cards and free school lunches flow to the ultra-poor more than to the moderately poor.

We also calculated the ppp index for a hypothetical universal pension system. Suppose that every elderly person over 65 years of age receives a pension from the government. Is this scenario more pro-poor than the actual pension system? The ppp index indicates that although a universal pension scheme for the elderly is pro-poor – and is even more beneficial to the ultra-poor – the present pension system is far more pro-poor than the universal one. This implies that the current means-tested pension system yields more benefits to the poor than a universal pension system for those aged 65 years or more.[4]

Perfect targeting is the ideal policy for poverty reduction. In practice, it is not feasible to operate such a policy because: (i) the administrative cost is very high and (ii) it is difficult to obtain accurate information on individuals' income or consumption, particularly in countries with large informal sectors. If the government in Thailand had succeeded in implementing perfect targeting, the ppp index would have been 6.8 for the poverty gap and 10.3 for the severity of poverty measure. Thus, although pro-poor, the Thai welfare programmes have much lower values than the values that would have been obtained with perfect targeting. This suggests that there is scope for improving the targeting efficiency of the Thai welfare programmes.

In the previous section, we mentioned two types of ppp indices by groups: the within-group ppp index and the total-group ppp index. As stated, the former measures the pro-poorness of a programme within the *k*th group, whereas the latter captures the impact of operating a programme in the *k*th group on its pro-poorness at the national level. The results for Thailand are presented in Table 21.2. The total-group ppp index reveals that the welfare programmes are more pro-poor

Table 21.2 Pro-poor policy index by urban and rural areas in Thailand, 2000

	Total-group ppp index		Within-group ppp index	
Welfare schemes	urban	rural	urban	rural
	Poverty gap ratio			
Social pension for the elderly	1.13	1.76	4.41	1.31
Low-income medical cards	1.44	2.10	5.60	1.56
Health insurance cards	0.70	1.39	2.72	1.03
Free school lunches	0.81	2.21	3.15	1.64
	Severity of poverty			
Social pension for the elderly	1.18	1.60	5.42	1.17
Low-income medical cards	1.34	2.23	6.18	1.63
Health insurance cards	0.61	1.36	2.83	0.99
Free school lunches	0.73	2.27	3.37	1.66

Source: Based on Thailand's *Household Socioeconomic Survey* 2000 (National Statistics Office 2000).

in the rural areas than in the urban areas. In fact, healthcare cards and free school lunches are not pro-poor in the urban areas, indicating that the government expenditures on these programmes in the urban areas did not benefit the poor more than the non-poor. It is, however, interesting to note that the within-group ppp index shows that all programmes are more pro-poor in the urban areas than in the rural areas. Thus, the total-group and within-group indices present opposite results. The main reason for this is that welfare programmes in Thailand are better targeted within the urban areas than within the rural areas. Since the concentration of poor is higher in the rural areas, the impact of targeting the rural areas turns out to be more pro-poor at the national level. Thus, the two indices provide us with two different types of information about targeting. If our objective is to reduce poverty at the national level, then the efficiency of targeting a particular group should be judged on the basis of the total-group ppp index.

Russia

Russia has a well-developed social benefits system, of which old-age pension is the largest component. Table 21.3 shows that out of the total population of 143.3 million, 53.6 million (37.4 per cent) are receiving some kind of government benefit.[5] Thus, the Russian social benefits system is very large in terms of population coverage. The old-age pension is the largest welfare programme, with 26.32 million recipients. The second largest programme is child allowance, benefiting 17.42 million children. The disability pension is given to 3.19 million people.

The Russian government spends 46.8 billion roubles per month on welfare programmes (excluding administrative costs), of which 38.74 billion roubles pay for pensions. Expenditure on child allowances is only 1.45 billion roubles, which equates to only 83.1 roubles per month per child. As the incidence of poverty among children is very severe, the child allowance is too small to have a significant impact on poverty among children. Overall, the average benefit level is equal

Table 21.3 Russian welfare systems in 2002

Welfare benefits	Beneficiaries (million)	Percentage share	Cost per month (billion roubles)	Percentage share
Old-age pension	26.32	49.08	38.74	82.79
Disability pension	3.19	5.96	3.61	7.71
Loss of breadwinner pension	1.64	3.05	1.27	2.72
Social pension	0.27	0.5	0.26	0.56
Care for children under 18	0.84	1.57	0.41	0.88
Child allowance	17.42	32.49	1.45	3.09
Unemployment benefit	0.45	0.84	0.31	0.65
Other benefits	0.95	1.77	0.2	0.42
Scholarship	2.55	4.76	0.55	1.17
All benefits	53.6	100	46.89	100

Source: Based on Russian Family Budget Survey 2002.

Table 21.4 Pro-poor policy indices for Russian welfare system in 2002

Types of government benefits	Poverty gap ratio	Severity of poverty
Old-age pension	2.20	4.13
Disability pension	2.18	4.16
Loss of breadwinner pension	2.09	2.40
Social pension	2.22	2.80
Care for children under 18 months	1.78	1.87
Child (under 16 years) allowance	1.19	0.79
Unemployment benefits	2.22	3.80
Other benefits	1.74	2.75
Scholarship	0.90	0.62
All benefits	2.14	3.90
Perfect targeting	3.02	5.71

Source: Based on Russian Family Budget Survey 2002.

to 326.5 roubles per person per month. The average lower poverty line for Russia is 1055.9 roubles per person per month, so the government pays average benefits equal to one-third of the poverty line.[6]

To what extent do government benefits go to the poor compared to the non-poor in Russia? The ppp index values in Table 21.4 provide empirical estimates of the pro-poorness of each of the government welfare programmes that are currently implemented in Russia. As can be seen from the table, all benefits taken together have ppp values far greater than one. Thus, we may conclude that the welfare system in Russia tends to benefit the poor more than the non-poor. More importantly, the absolute benefits of the welfare system do indeed flow more to the ultra-poor than to the poor, as suggested by the higher value of ppp index (equal to 3.90) for the severity of poverty measure.[7] Table 21.4 also reveals that if the Russian government had implemented perfect targeting, the ppp index would have been 3.02 and 5.71 for the poverty gap ratio and the severity of poverty index, respectively. This suggests that although Russian welfare programmes are not perfectly targeted to the poor, the deviation from perfect targeting is not large.

Results for the severity of poverty index indicate that child allowances (given to those aged below 16 years) and scholarships are not particularly pro-poor. This is evident from the fact that the ppp indices of these two programmes fall far below unity for the severity of poverty measure, suggesting that the absolute benefits of these programmes do not flow to the ultra-poor. It further suggests that these programmes may require better targeting than the current system in order to favour those far below the poverty threshold.

Health services in Vietnam

Over the past decade or so, Vietnam has enjoyed a significant improvement in its standard of living as a result of its impressive performance in growth and poverty reduction. More importantly, growth has been pro-poor, benefiting the poor proportionally more than the non-poor (Kakwani and Son 2004). In this context, it is interesting to examine whether, along with a rising standard of living and pro-poor growth, poor people benefit from the provision of health services in Vietnam.

Table 21.5 presents the ppp index for utilization of various health facilities in Vietnam. The results show that only community health centres have a ppp index value greater than one. This suggests that the poor have greater access to community health centres than the non-poor and that community health centres play an important role in providing basic health services to the poor in Vietnam. Unfortunately, community health centres do not provide quality health services because they are generally poorly staffed and equipped. So the poor do not receive quality healthcare treatment.

Public hospitals in Vietnam provide higher quality care and are mainly used by individuals with health insurance. Utilization of government hospitals has a ppp

Table 21.5 Pro-poor policy index for health services in Vietnam, 1997–98 (poverty gap ratio)

Health facilities	Total-group ppp index			Within-group ppp index	
	Vietnam	urban	rural	urban	rural
	Poverty gap ratio				
Government hospitals	0.62	0.07	0.91	0.34	0.74
Community health centres	1.17	0.27	1.23	1.38	1.00
Regional polyclinics	0.84	0.42	0.98	2.14	0.79
Eastern medicine facilities	0.96	0.04	1.15	0.21	0.94
Pharmacies	0.96	0.26	1.16	1.29	0.94
Private doctors	0.79	0.12	0.98	0.59	0.80
Health insurance	0.50	0.08	0.79	0.40	0.64
Perfect targeting	2.86				

Note: The ppp index for the severity of poverty index was calculated but not presented in this chapter. Nevertheless, the results are similar to those for the poverty gap ratio.

Source: Based on Vietnam Living Standard Survey 1997–98.

index value far less than one, implying that public hospitals provide greater benefits to the non-poor than to the poor. Thus, the poor have less access to the quality health services provided by public hospitals.

It is not surprising that the provision of health insurance is not pro-poor because those covered by health insurance have access to government hospitals. Moreover, coverage under the health insurance programme is more extensive for better off individuals. Having health insurance is positively correlated with the individuals' income; while the coverage rate is 9.2 per cent in the bottom income quartile, 24.5 per cent have health insurance in the top income quartile.

The results presented in Table 21.5 indicate that pharmacy utilization is almost pro-poor (0.96 for the poverty gap ratio). It is reasonable to assume that more highly educated individuals – and hence presumably those more aware of the risks of self-medication – avoid pharmacy visits. Pharmacy utilization therefore appears to be an inferior good for the high-income group since rich individuals go to public hospitals for their healthcare. On the other hand, pharmacy visits are a normal good for poor households.

The total-group ppp index values in Table 21.5 also reveal that three health facilities – community health centres, pharmacies and Eastern medicine facilities – are more pro-poor in rural areas than in urban areas. This suggests that government subsidies on these health services in the rural areas do benefit poor people more than the non-poor. In addition, the within-group ppp index indicates that, within the urban sector, sick and injured individuals from poor households receive far fewer benefits from healthcare facilities such as government hospitals and Eastern medicine facilities. By comparison, in rural areas the poor benefit more from community health centres, Eastern medicine facilities and pharmacies.

Educational services in Vietnam

In this subsection, we apply our ppp index methodology to assess educational services in Vietnam. Our prime objective is to discover the extent to which public education at primary and secondary levels is pro-poor. We also attempt to find out whether free universal education will benefit the poor more than the non-poor.

Table 21.6 reveals that public primary education benefits the poor more than the non-poor, and is even more pro-poor for the ultra-poor. This conclusion is consistent with the fact that net primary school enrolment increased from 87–91 per cent over the period 1993–98 (Nguyen 2002). Changes in the allocation of public spending on education in the 1990s could have further favoured lower levels of education. The share of public spending on education going to the poor increased from 16.5 per cent in 1993 to 18.1 per cent in 1998 (*Ibid.*). Although public primary schools are pro-poor, other types of schools at the same level are very anti-poor. In other words, primary schools that are semi-public or sponsored by the private sector benefit better off children more than poor ones. This suggests that educational subsidies given to these types of schools are likely to benefit the non-poor more than the poor.

Table 21.6 also shows that lower secondary education in Vietnam is not pro-poor, as indicated by the ppp index. This finding emerges consistently, irrespective

Table 21.6 Pro-poor policy index for education service in Vietnam, 1997–98

School types	Primary	Lower secondary	Upper secondary
		Poverty gap ratio	
Public	1.29	0.79	0.37
Semi-public	0.55	0.15	0.23
Sponsored	0.63	0.51	0.00
		Severity of poverty	
Public	1.31	0.65	0.23
Semi-public	0.19	0.08	0.09
Sponsored	0.14	0.26	0.00

Note: The figures in the table do not separate the benefits of public and private expenditures going to individuals. However, they tell us to which services additional public subsidies should go.

Source: Based on Vietnam Living Standard Survey 1997–98.

of school type. At the lower secondary level, net enrolment rates more than doubled between 1993 and 1998, from 30–62 per cent. However, for the population as a whole, 38 per cent of children aged 11–14 years old were not enrolled in lower secondary school, while 66 per cent of the poorest children in this age range were not enrolled in primary school. The disparity in enrolment rates between the richest and poorest quintiles has been highly significant over the years.

As expected, the ppp index shows that upper secondary schools in Vietnam have far more children from better off households than from poor households. This is true for all types of schools at this level. No children from poor households were enrolled in the upper secondary level schools sponsored by the private sector. Over the period 1993–98, children from the poorest quintile experienced an increase in enrolment in upper secondary schools from 1–5 per cent, as compared to an increase from 21–64 per cent for the richest quintile (*Ibid.*).

We now use the ppp index to compare universal education with the current system. Table 21.7 shows that universal education at primary and lower secondary levels in Vietnam would provide more benefits to poor children than to the non-poor. The degree of pro-poorness of universal access to primary education among children aged six to ten years old is almost as high as actually achieved by the current education system. Similarly, if lower secondary education is made universal for children aged between 11 and 14 years, the outcome is pro-poor. This contrasts with the actual current situation. The ppp index is 0.79 for lower secondary education, compared to 1.08 if lower secondary education were universal. At higher levels, universal provision is not likely to deliver pro-poor outcomes, as indicated by a ppp index for upper secondary schooling of less than unity. Although, universal education at higher levels would not be pro-poor, it would encourage poor individuals aged between 15 and 17 to enrol for upper secondary schooling and hence obtain greater access to higher education compared to the current situation in Vietnam.

Table 21.7   Pro-poor policy index if universal education is provided in Vietnam

	Poverty gap ratio	Severity of poverty
Primary	1.28	1.33
Lower secondary	1.08	1.06
Upper secondary	0.91	0.85

Source: Based on Vietnam Living Standard Survey 1997–98.

Table 21.8   Pro-poor policy index for basic infrastructure service in Vietnam, 1997–98

Access to basic infrastructure services	Poverty gap ratio	Severity of poverty
Electricity	0.80	0.71
Piped and tap water	0.86	0.81
Collected waste	0.10	0.07
Sanitary toilets	0.10	0.05

Source: Based on Vietnam Living Standard Survey 1997–98.

Basic infrastructure services in Vietnam

Infrastructure services make significant contributions to people's wellbeing. Basic services, such as piped water and sanitation (for example, sewerage systems and flushing toilets), have a direct impact on health status and overall wellbeing. Access to other services, such as electricity and telephones, helps households increase their prospects for income generation. A number of studies reveal that household access to basic services has a high and negative correlation with poverty.

As shown in Table 21.8, the benefits generated from all types of basic services accrue to the non-poor more than to the poor in Vietnam. Poor households in general have much greater access to piped water and electricity than sanitary systems; the ppp index for water and electricity are 0.86 and 0.80, respectively, when measured by the poverty gap ratio, compared to only 0.10 for sanitary facilities. As suggested in Table 21.8, the benefits from sanitary services (waste collection and flushing toilets in this case) are highly skewed in favour of the non-poor. The benefits of all types of basic services are lower for the severity of poverty measure, suggesting that the ultra-poor have even less access to infrastructure services than the poor.

Case studies II: 15 African countries

This section makes use of household micro-datasets from 15 African countries obtained from the African Household Survey Data Bank of the World Bank. The countries and years of the survey are: Burundi 1998, Burkina Faso 1998, Ivory Coast 1998, Cameroon 1996, Ethiopia 2000, Ghana 1998, Guinea 1994, Gambia 1998, Kenya

1997, Madagascar 2001, Mozambique 1996, Malawi 1997, Nigeria 1996, Uganda 1999 and Zambia in 1998. National poverty lines for the 15 countries are obtained from various poverty assessment reports. These poverty lines were originally very crude and did not take account of the different needs of household members by age and gender. Moreover, the poverty lines were not adjusted for the economies of scale that exist in large households. To overcome these shortcomings, Kakwani and Subbarao (2005) made some modifications to the national poverty lines, taking into account the different needs of household members and economies of scale.

Targeting children: targeting versus universal

According to Coady *et al.* (2002), more than a quarter of targeted programmes in all developing countries had regressive benefit incidence. For instance, they found that the poorest 40 per cent received less than 40 per cent of poverty alleviation budget expenditures. Such ineffective targeting of poor households suggests that the overall impact of such spending on poverty has been smaller than it could have been. Moreover, the administrative cost of implementing any targeted programme is very high. Much of the budget is spent on simply getting the resources to poor families. Consequently, the cost per unit of income transferred can be substantial. Transfer programmes are administratively complex as they require resources to undertake targeting of transfers and to monitor the recipients' actions. In this context, one might argue for a scenario of universal transfers.

In this section, we estimate the ppp indices under a universal transfer programme for children aged between five and 16 years old. Under such a programme, every child in this age group is assumed to receive a fixed transfer irrespective poverty status. The results are presented in Figures 21.1 and 21.2 and Table 21.9. From Figures 21.1 and 21.2, we note that the ppp index values with perfect targeting are quite small for the 15 African countries compared to the ppp index values in Thailand, Russia and Vietnam. In fact, the ppp indices with perfect targeting differ little from the indices associated with universal transfers. This suggests that perfect targeting may not be needed in cases such as these 15 African countries, where poverty is extremely high.

Table 21.9 carries two important messages. First, the results indicate that universal transfers will provide more absolute benefits to children from poor families than those from non-poor families. Second, a universal transfer scheme is likely to bring about an even more pro-poor outcome if implemented in rural areas where most poor children live. One exception is in the case of Nigeria where, in contrast, poverty is widespread in both urban and rural areas.

One possible criticism is that we do not have an actual scenario which allows targeted transfers to be compared with universal transfers. Nevertheless, the main implication emerging from the ppp index is that if a transfer is given to every child aged between five and 16 years old, it is likely to provide more absolute benefits to poor children, particularly in rural areas. Furthermore, the analysis suggests that universal targeting of children may not be a bad policy option, particularly in rural areas. It may be more cost effective, as targeting only a small subgroup of children requires a high level of administrative costs to be devoted to identifying the poor.

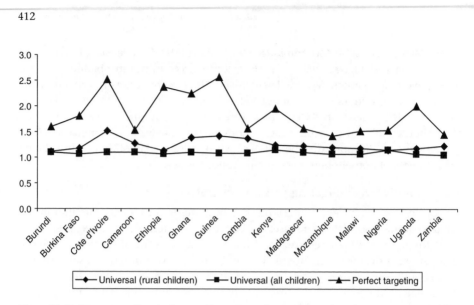

Figure 21.1 Pro-poor policy indices under universal transfers and perfect targeting (poverty gap ratio)

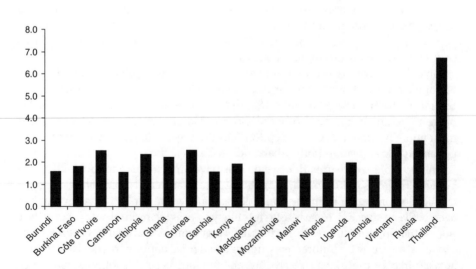

Figure 21.2 Pro-poor policy indices under perfect targeting for 18 countries (poverty gap ratio)

Table 21.9 Pro-poor policy index for universal transfers to rural and urban areas

Country	Poverty gap ratio				Severity of poverty			
	Universal targeting			Perfect targeting	Universal targeting			Perfect targeting
	rural	urban	total		rural	urban	total	
Burundi	1.12	0.28	1.09	1.59	1.16	0.23	1.12	2.11
Burkina Faso	1.18	0.43	1.07	1.81	1.21	0.38	1.08	2.53
Côte d'Ivoire	1.51	0.60	1.10	2.51	1.63	0.45	1.09	3.63
Cameroon	1.28	0.60	1.09	1.54	1.32	0.50	1.08	2.05
Ethiopia	1.13	0.73	1.07	2.37	1.14	0.74	1.09	3.42
Ghana	1.39	0.54	1.09	2.24	1.47	0.42	1.10	3.03
Guinea	1.42	0.37	1.08	2.56	1.47	0.31	1.10	3.40
Gambia	1.37	0.65	1.08	1.56	1.56	0.39	1.08	2.00
Kenya	1.25	0.29	1.14	1.95	1.27	0.18	1.16	2.53
Madagascar	1.22	0.65	1.09	1.57	1.29	0.57	1.13	1.95
Mozambique	1.19	0.62	1.07	1.42	1.24	0.59	1.11	1.77
Malawi	1.17	0.18	1.07	1.52	1.21	0.09	1.09	1.93
Nigeria	1.14	1.13	1.14	1.54	1.12	1.21	1.16	1.91
Uganda	1.17	0.25	1.06	2.00	1.20	0.19	1.08	2.75
Zambia	1.23	0.76	1.05	1.45	1.34	0.57	1.06	1.80

Conclusions

Kakawni and Son (2005) proposed a new index called the pro-poor policy (ppp) index. This index measures the pro-poorness of government welfare programmes and basic service delivery in education, health and infrastructure. It is an attempt to introduce a methodology for assessing the techniques of targeting in order to make them more effective.

The conclusion reached was that the targeting efficiency of a particular group should be judged on the basis of the total-group ppp index. If our objective is to reduce poverty, then social transfer programmes should be designed so that they lead to the maximum reduction in poverty under given resource constraints. To achieve this objective, perfect targeting is the ideal solution. Two prerequisites are necessary: the poor get all the benefits; and the benefits given to the poor are proportional to their income shortfalls from the poverty line. To implement such a programme, we must have detailed information of people's income or consumption expenditure. Such detailed information and the administrative ability to use it are, of course, not present in most developing countries. Therefore, policy-makers have to resort to a form of proxy targeting in which transfers are based on easily identifiable household characteristics. However, proxy targeting can never achieve complete targeting success. This study attempts to assess the targeting efficiency of government programmes by discovering how good proxy targeting is compared to perfect targeting. Government programmes may be defined as pro-poor if they provide greater benefits to the poor than to the non-poor.

Using micro household data, the methodology was applied to Thailand, Russia, Vietnam and 15 African countries. The major conclusions emerging from our empirical analysis can be synthesized as follows. First, all four welfare programmes implemented recently by the Thai government were found to be pro-poor. In particular, welfare programmes designed to help the very poor – including low-income medical cards and free school lunches – were shown to be highly pro-poor, benefiting the ultra-poor more than the poor. In addition, a universal pension for those over 65 years of age was found to be less pro-poor than the present old-age pension system. This suggests that the Thai government should continue with its present old-age pension scheme.

Second, the study found that the welfare system in Russia tends to benefit the poor more than the non-poor. Moreover, the absolute benefits of the welfare system flow more to the ultra-poor than to the poor, as suggested by the ppp index value for the severity of poverty index, which is higher than that for the poverty gap ratio. The study found the Russian welfare programmes to be reasonably well targeted, as is evident from the fact that the ppp indices of welfare programmes are quite close to (but still lower than) the index value expected with perfect targeting. The study also found that the child allowance and scholarship programmes are not pro-poor for the ultra-poor in particular. This suggests that these programmes may require better targeting than the current system in order to favour those living far below the poverty threshold.

Third, basic services – health and education – in Vietnam were found to be mostly anti-poor. Although government hospitals provide the highest quality of healthcare, the poor are much less likely to use them. This is not true for community health centres, which appear to provide more services to individuals from poor households. Unfortunately, community health centres do not provide quality health services because they are poorly staffed and equipped. Thus, on the whole, the poor in Vietnam have less access to quality healthcare. Public primary schools were found to be pro-poor – this was due partly to the increase in public spending on education for the poor in the 1990s. However, secondary education is not pro-poor. This suggests that Vietnam's universal education at primary and lower secondary levels could provide more benefits to students from poor households, although this is not true for higher levels of education.

Fourth, simulations of universal transfers to school-age children in 15 African countries indicate that universal transfers provide more absolute benefits to children from poor families than to those from non-poor families. In addition, a universal transfer scheme was found to be likely to have an even more pro-poor outcome if implemented in the rural areas, where most poor children reside. This finding is true for all the countries except Nigeria, where poverty is widespread in both urban and rural areas.

Finally, the study found that in the 15 African countries, the value of ppp index with perfect targeting was quite small compared to the index values for Thailand, Russia and Vietnam. The index value of perfect targeting for Thailand was far greater than for Russia and Vietnam. For the African countries the ppp indices under perfect targeting differed little from the indices corresponding to universal provision. Therefore, we conclude that perfect targeting is not necessary for cases such as these 15 African countries, where poverty is extremely high.

Notes

We would like to acknowledge helpful comments from an anonymous referee.

1. It is possible that a programme may be well targeted within group but may not be considered well targeted at the national level because of disparity in incomes between groups.
2. For a detailed discussion of Thailand and Russian poverty lines, see Kakwani (2003; 2004).
3. The ppp index was not calculated here for the headcount ratio because it required estimating the density function at the poverty line, which could not be done without making parametric assumptions. Moreover, the headcount ratio is a crude measure of poverty. Our focus is on the poverty gap ratio and the severity of poverty index, which are more satisfactory measures.
4. This analysis takes no account of the administrative costs involved in providing mean-tested pensions.
5. Some persons receive more than one benefit at the same time: the number is small and has been neglected here.
6. The poverty line in Russia is not constant across households, so we calculated the average poverty line across individuals in all households.
7. Note that the ppp index for all benefits is the weighted average of the ppp indices for all nine welfare programmes, with the weight proportional to the share of benefits accruing to people of each programme presented in the third column of Table 21.3.

References

Bigman, D. and H. Fofack (2000) 'Combining Census and Survey Data to Study Spatial Dimensions of Poverty: A Case Study of Ecuador', in *Geographical Targeting for Poverty Alleviation*, Washington, DC: World Bank.

Braithwaite, J., C. Grootaert and B. Milanovic (2000) *Poverty and Social Assistance in Transition Countries*, New York: St Martin's Press.

Coady, D., M. Grosh and J. Hoddinott (2002) *The Targeting of Transfers in Developing Countries: Review of Experiences and Lessons*, Social Safety Net Primer Series, Washington, DC: World Bank.

Foster, J., J. Greer and E. Thorbecke (1984) 'A Class of Decomposable Poverty Measures', *Econometrica* 52, 3: 761–66.

Grosh, M. (1994) *Administering Targeted Social Programmes in Latin America: From Platitudes to Practice*, Regional and Sectoral Studies, Washington, DC: World Bank.

Kakwani, N. (2003) 'Issues in Setting Absolute Poverty Lines', *Poverty and Social Development Paper*, 3, Manila: Asian Development Bank.

Kakwani, N. (2004) 'New Poverty Thresholds for Russia', Mimeo, Washington, DC: World Bank.

Kakwani, N. and H.H. Son (2004) 'Pro-Poor Growth: Asian Experience', *International Poverty Centre Working Paper* 1, Brasilia: International Poverty Centre, UNDP.

Kakwani, N. and H.H. Son (2005) 'On Assessing Pro-Poorness of Government Programmes: International Comparisons', *International Poverty Centre Working Paper* 8, Brasilia: International Poverty Centre, UNDP.

Kakwani, N. and K. Subbarao (2005) 'Ageing and Poverty in Africa and the Role of Social Pensions', Mimeo, Brasilia: International Poverty Centre, UNDP.

National Statistics Office (2000) *Household Socioeconomic Survey 2000*, Bangkok: National Statistics Office.

Nguyen, N.N. (2002) 'Trends in the Education Sector from 1993–1998', *Policy Research Working Paper* 2891, Washington, DC: World Bank.

Rawlings, L., L. Sherburne-Benz and J. Domelen (2001) *Evaluating Social Funds: A Cross-Country Analysis of Community Investments*, Washington, DC: World Bank.

22
Innovations, High-tech Trade and Industrial Development: Theory, Evidence and Policy

Lakhwinder Singh

Introduction

The knowledge base in the major economies has been growing at a fast pace. Investment in knowledge accounts for about 4.7 per cent of OECD-wide GDP and the high-knowledge-based economies invest between 5.2 and 6.5 per cent of GDP in knowledge development (OECD 2001). Developed and newly industrializing countries internationally trade goods and services that are knowledge-intensive. The industrial growth patterns and competitiveness of industries across countries and over time are closely related in the globalizing world. Two distinct patterns of industrial development are clearly noticeable: developed and newly industrializing countries moved faster towards producing and exporting goods and services that are knowledge intensive; a large number of countries could not catch up and their position in the fast globalizing world is being marginalized (Lall 2004). This pattern of industrial growth can be traced from the changing roles of innovative investment patterns in industry across countries and over time. The processes of globalization have affected different innovative activities differently and thus the rise/fall of innovative investment in some industries in some of the countries. Outsourcing of industrial R&D has shifted some of the innovative activities from developed to a few developing countries. The increasing role of foreign direct investment (FDI) and direct operation of multinational corporations in production of goods and services in the developing countries has significantly influenced development/underdevelopment of innovative capabilities. Developing countries under the new international economic order have substantially reduced the role of the state in innovative investment and have promoted the dependence on either private initiatives or on FDI. Therefore, it is legitimate to enquire about the changes in the pattern of industrial innovative investment on trade and industrial development that are occurring across countries and over time.

Asian countries (South East Asia, China and India) have shown dynamism, in terms of industrial development and contributing to global trade with high-tech exports, in the fast-globalizing world. East Asian economies followed a standard pattern of economic transformation and achieved more than a 9 per cent growth rate during the decades of the 1980s and 1990s in the twentieth century. The industrial sector is truly the engine of growth of these economies contrary to the service sector-led economic growth in the case of other economies. The industrial growth experience of East Asia remained highly controversial on two counts. One, capital accumulation versus technical progress: which of the factors has allowed East Asia to achieve a faster rate of industrial growth? Two, the role of the state in enacting suitable policies for industrial development or the market forces which led the East Asia to succeed in economic transformation as well as in the international market. Thus, Asian countries are most suitable to test new economic growth theory and draw lessons from successful public policy experience for other stagnant economies. This chapter is an attempt in that direction.

Knowledge accumulation and economic growth: theory and empirics

Technological knowledge accumulation is now being widely acknowledged and acclaimed as a source of economic growth. Differentials in the level and growth of income across countries and over time are being increasingly recognized due to knowledge accumulation differences. The evolution of the sources of economic growth can be seen through the development of the long-run theory of economic growth which has been developed after the Great Depression in the twentieth century in three waves (Ruttan 2001). The first wave was initiated by the work of Harrod (1939) and Domar (1946). Solow (1956; 1957) and Swan (1956) developed a model of long-run growth in neoclassical tradition that stimulated the second wave. More recently, the third wave was stimulated in the mid-1980s by the writings of Romer (1986) and Lucas (1988).

Modern theory of economic growth has recognized the dominant role of technological knowledge as a determinant of economic performance. The superior economic performance across countries and over time has been essentially attributed to the proportion of knowledge accumulation (Solow 1956; 1957). Knowledge accumulation and its growth have been attributed to be determined by the exogenous factors and seem to be the fundamental responsibility of the state. Thus, the agents of production are the receivers of new knowledge, which is external to their circumstances. Since knowledge has global public good property and is universally accessible, therefore, the tendency is towards convergence of productivity and overall economic growth. Contrary to this, the evolutionary growth theory has recognized the cost of acquiring new knowledge as well as benefits of accumulation of knowledge, which is path dependent. This signifies that knowledge accumulation and generation not only is endogenous but also assumes capability building. These capabilities ultimately allow economic agents of production to reap the benefits of being leaders in innovations that matter in the markets. Therefore, the prediction of the theory is that the level of development and growth is historically determined. Those countries and industries that invest more in knowledge accumulation and generation will stay ahead compared with others (Ruttan 2001).

New growth theory, which is popularly known as 'endogenous growth theory', not only recognized the importance of knowledge accumulation for economic growth but successfully modelled the commercially oriented innovative investment. Sources of knowledge generation were fundamentally endogenous and were driven by the commercial interest. An important characteristic of this kind of economic thinking is that knowledge accumulation and generation give birth to increasing returns to scale of an important scarce factor that is capital accumulation. However, knowledge accumulation in these kinds of models itself is susceptible to diminishing returns to scale (Romer 1986). Another property of endogenous knowledge accumulation is that it is non-rival and partially excludable and thus generates significant amount of externalities. It has been argued that knowledge is expensive to develop but is inexpensive to use which underlines the importance of scale effects. The value of knowledge increases with the increase in the size of the market (Romer 1993; 1997). Thus, the model predicts that those who invest more in knowledge generation and accumulation will grow at a faster rate and those who do not will continue to persist and stay backward.

An important implication of this kind of economic thinking is that knowledge exhibits public good property which is not completely appropriable through market transactions by the private agents of production. Thus, private agents of production have a tendency to underinvest and consequently underline the role of public policy to address this gap. The other important implication of Romer-Lucas stimulated endogenous growth literature is that there is incentive to enhance the quality of human and physical capital that has a capacity to raise permanently economic growth rate and level of per capita income. Thus, the activist technology policy pursued by the government to enhance quality of human and physical capital has a capacity to raise permanently not just the per capita income but the long-run rate of economic growth (Verspagen 1992).

Empirical literature, which draws inspiration from endogenous growth models, on knowledge generation and diffusion – both domestic and international – has grown recently by leaps and bounds. A seminal contribution to empirical literature that establishes the relationship between total factor productivity and stocks of measured knowledge has been made by Coe and Helpman (1995). The authors have selected OECD countries and Israel to verify empirically the relationship between superior economic performance and cumulated stock of technological knowledge. They have also established the interdependence, in terms of technological knowledge, among the developed countries and technological knowledge of the trading partner for smaller economies has been more important compared to that of the domestic knowledge. Trade has a capacity to transmit superior knowledge across national boundaries that matter for economic growth. However, the domestic knowledge in the large countries has recorded higher elasticity than that of the foreign knowledge. These results were confirmed while extending the scope of the study to include 77 developing countries in the sample (Coe *et al.* 1997). An important conclusion that emerged from the above mentioned study is that trade is the most important vehicle of knowledge diffusion across countries, and developing countries do benefit substantially from the innovations generated by the industrially advanced countries.

This revealing new evidence generated controversy and scepticism with regard to the validity of the evidence and thus resulted in a spurt in empirical literature on foreign knowledge spillovers (Keller 2004; Navaretti and Tarr 2000). The sceptics re-estimated after introducing the refinements in the Coe and Helpman estimates for the sample of OECD countries but endorsed the results more empathetically (Keller 1998; Lichtenberg and Potterie 1998). Contrary to this, Evenson and Singh (1997) in a sample of 11 Asian countries during the period 1970–93 found higher elasticity of domestic knowledge stock compared to foreign. However, East Asian countries did have higher impact of foreign knowledge transmitted through international trade. Somewhat similar empirical results were reported by Kim (2000) from the analysis of the East Asian countries during the period 1971–93. Transmission of technological knowledge to developing countries through trade literature has almost completely ignored the role of domestic technological capabilities which facilitates the adaptation of foreign knowledge barring a few.

FDI, at least in theory, has been widely recognized as the most important source of diffusion of technological knowledge across national boundaries. Flexible manufacturing systems have opened up ample opportunities, where a firm superior in technology can subcontract some of its operations to save costs and in the process can also transfer technical know-how to local firms. This is being done to maintain the required quality control of the processes of production of the local firm. Therefore, it was expected that substantial learning can occur and improve productivity of domestic firms. However, recent studies do not confirm the expected relationship between productivity growth and knowledge diffusion through FDI (Keller 2004; Hanson 2001; Gorg and Greenaway 2002). A more recent literature does report from micro-empirical studies some positive relationship for developed countries (Keller 2004). Domestic firms which have substantial technological capabilities are able to catch knowledge spillovers and raise productivity and those who do not have capabilities have negative productivity effects (Girma 2005; Siddharthan 2004). FDI at the most can supplement the domestic technological capabilities, but alone can not engineer innovations in the host country. Knowledge spillovers across countries and industries, as the major source of growth predicted by the endogenous growth literature, are fundamentally dependent on domestic technological capabilities and the stage of industrial development. As soon as a country's economic agents of production reach close to technology frontier, knowledge spillovers as a source of productivity growth cease to exist because knowledge at that level becomes more and more tacit (Stiglitz 2003; Singh 2004a).

Sources and indicators of innovations in the global economy

There are two main indicators of measurement of innovations: input and output. Research and development expenditure is the input measure of innovation. Patents registered, scientific research papers published in recognized international journals and high-tech trade are the output measures of innovations. These indicators that generate innovations and outcomes that can be realized through commercial operations are presented in Table 22.1. The generation of innovations has been widely acknowledged as dependent on the innovative investment in the global economy. Total R&D expenditure incurred in the global economy has increased from 409.8 billion PPP dollars in 1990, to 755.1 billion PPP dollars in 1999–2000. Industrially advanced countries expended 367.9 billion PPP dollars in 1990, which was nearly 90 per cent of the total global R&D expenditure. The expenditure on R&D increased to 596.7 billion PPP dollars in 1999–2000 but the relative share comes out to be 79 per cent of the global R&D. This clearly shows that, despite the absolute rise in the R&D expenditure of the developed countries, their share in relative terms has dwindled 11 percentage points during the last decade of the twentieth century. Developing countries, on the other hand, increased innovative efforts and raised their relative share from 10 per cent in 1990 to 21 per cent in the year 2000. This trend clearly shows reduction of concentration of innovative efforts in the still highly inequitable knowledge-based economy. The rise in the share of R&D of the developing countries in the global R&D is mainly due to the big push in innovative efforts of East Asian countries.

Table 22.1 clearly shows that the hub of innovative activities is North America, which has highest R&D intensity. The USA is the largest both in absolute level and in relative terms so far as innovative investment is concerned. The Asian continent is also emerging as a hub of both economic and innovative activities. R&D expenditure increased from US$94.2 billion in 1990 to US$235.6 billion in 2000, which is slightly more than a two-fold increase within a decade. Asian R&D expenditure increased faster compared to other regions and improved its relative position from third to second in the global reckoning. Asian countries accounted for 23 per cent of the global innovative investment expenditure in 1990, which increased to 30.9 per cent in 2000. Europe lagged behind because of decline in R&D expenditure in the East European countries. Two noteworthy facts here are: one, South East Asia and China substantially raised innovative investment expenditure and globally commercial/private sector stakes in innovative investment increased substantially; and two, R&D intensities either slightly declined or remained stagnant across regions except in North America, where it improved slightly.

The innovative efforts over a period of time have developed a system in which economic agents of production participate, learn to use and acquire knowledge. This process has not only given birth to a national system of innovation, but also nurtured economic agents of production to be pioneers in exploiting new opportunities and strongly built international comparative advantage. Therefore, there is a positive relationship between the innovative investment and the outcomes of

Table 22.1 Sources and indicators of innovations in developed and developing countries

Region/year	R&D expenditure (billion PPP$) 1990	R&D expenditure (billion PPP$) 1999/2000	Scientific and technical journal articles 1999	Technology and licence fees received (billion $) 2002	Patent application filed by residents in 2001	High-tech exports (billion $) 2000	FDI outflows (billion $) 2001
World total	409.8 (100.00)	755.1 (100.00)	528,627 (100.00)	79.61 (100.00)	939,267 (100.00)	998.00 (100.00)	630.30 (100.00)
Developed countries	367.9 (89.77)	596.7 (79.02)	451,877 (85.48)	78.21 (98.24)	855,902 (91.12)	881.00 (88.30)	470.10 (74.58)
Developing countries	42.0 (10.25)	158.4 (20.98)	76,750 (14.52)	1.40 (01.76)	83,365 (08.88)	117.00 (11.70)	115.20 (18.28)
North America	156.4 (38.16)	281.0 (37.21)	185,492 (35.09)	45.88 (57.63)	197,238 (21.00)	267.00 (26.75)	197.3 (31.30)
Latin America & Caribbean	11.3 (02.76)	21.3 (02.82)	12,018 (02.27)	0.41 (00.52)	7,383 (00.79)	27.00 (02.71)	69.10 (10.96)
Africa	5.2 (01.27)	5.8 (00.77)	3,612 (00.68)	0.06 (00.07)	207 (00.02)	2.62 (00.26)	8.5 (01.35)
Asia	94.2 (22.99)	235.6 (31.20)	22,824 (04.32)	0.17 (00.21)	30,722 (03.27)	130.08 (13.03)	36.5 (05.79)
Europe	138.8 (33.87)	202.9 (26.87)	122,017 (23.08)	10.96 (13.77)	128,297 (13.66)	–	236.6 (37.54)

Sources: UNESCO (2004); World Bank (2004); Singh (2004b).

innovations. Industrially advanced countries not only spend a higher proportion on R&D resources but also publish more than the 85 per cent of the global scientific papers published in scientific and technical journals. This clearly shows that national innovation system takes time to develop and the innovative outcomes lagged behind compared to the innovative investment.

Developing countries increased their share in innovative investment, however, the proportion of scientific and technical papers published in the journals remained substantially lower, that is, the share of R&D expenditure is 21 per cent and share of papers published is nearly 2 per cent in 1999. The share of North America and Europe for published scientific and technical papers in journals was 35 per cent and 23 per cent respectively in 1999. However, Asia published only 22,824 scientific and technical papers, which is about 4 per cent of the global figure (Table 22.1). This clearly brings out the concentration of production of new ideas in terms of scientific and technical papers in the developed countries. Thus, the contribution made by the developed countries towards the global pool of knowledge is amazingly high and the expansion of knowledge frontiers is largely conditioned by the evolution of the national innovation systems which is highly dependent on the history of innovative investment. It is expected that the contribution towards the expansion of new knowledge will be substantial from the Asian continent due to the speed at which resources devoted to innovative investment have increased in the recent past.

New scientific and technical knowledge that has commercial utility is being increasingly patented for producing goods and services to enhance comparative advantage of the nations. This indicator of innovation clearly shows the concentration of patent applications filed in the USA patent office by the developed countries. Out of total patent applications filed in 2001, the developed countries accounted for 91 per cent of global patent applications (Table 22.1). The concentration of innovations in developed countries further increases to 94.3 per cent if we take USA patents registered from 1977–2000 (Singh 2004b). However, the share of the developing countries in patenting of new ideas is not only meagre but the extent of the conversion of patent to commercial innovations may also be small. Even the conversion ratio of patent to innovations within the USA economy in 1982 was 57 per cent in Silicon Valley, 35 per cent in Boston and 0.3 per cent in Albany/Schenectady/Troy (New York), which clearly shows wide variations of patent to innovations conversion ratio across regions (Branscomb 2004). It is important to note here that patents have been largely concentrated in North America; Europe and Asian countries have filed just 3.27 per cent of the global patent applications for 2001.

The fundamental aim of commercially oriented innovations is to perpetuate and enhance international competitive advantage so that new innovations can be expanded and exploited globally. The theory of international trade leads us to expect an international division of labour that the leaders of innovations (developed countries) export high technology goods and services, and the laggards (developing countries) continue to export raw materials and low-skill-based goods and services in the international economy (Archibugi and Pietrobelli 2003). The empirical literature on knowledge growth and trade specialization has clearly established the relationship between innovations and international trade specialization (Malerba and Montobbio 2000).

High-technology trade has grown at a faster rate during the last quarter of the twentieth century. Total global high-tech trade in 2000 was US$998 billion, that is 20 per cent of manufactured goods and services traded internationally (World Bank 2003). It is important to note here that high-technology international trade is originating from the developed countries and is quite close to the prediction of the widely held wisdom of international trade theory. The share of high-tech trade of the developed countries in 2000 was 88.3 per cent of the total global high-tech international trade in manufactured goods. However, developing country high-tech-based international trade was of the order of US$117 billion in 2000, nearly 12 per cent of the global high-tech-based international trade in manufactured products. Since a substantial amount of inter- and intra-industry trade theory and empirical evidence suggests that international trade is governed by multinational corporations, it may be that the high-tech trade originating from developing countries could actually belong to innovative firms of developed countries producing in developing countries (Amable 2000; Urata 2001). North American countries are predominant as far as high-tech international trade is concerned and account for nearly 27 per cent globally. Newly industrialized countries have been improving their position in international high-tech trade and accounted for 13 per cent of the global figure in 2000 (Table 22.1). Growth experience of global international trade of manufactured goods and services reveals during 1985–2000 that developing countries recorded higher growth rates compared to developed countries (Table 22.2). The general pattern from the estimated growth rates of international trade reveals that high-tech exports increased at a faster rate compared to the resource-based medium- and low-technology-based exports. Exports of developing countries increased during 1985–2000 at a faster rate compared to developed countries.

FDI has been advocated as a panacea for the ills of the less developed countries. Apart from filling the gap of investment resources, FDI is also expected to bring in new management and technical innovations as well as new practices which help push up efficiency levels of domestic firms. Global FDI inflows decreased by 41 per cent in 2001, and were US$651 billion in 2002. The share of global FDI outflows originating from developed countries was nearly 75 per cent in 2001 (Table 22.1). European and North American countries contribute largely to the global FDI outflows. A noteworthy feature of global FDI inflows is that 72 per cent of the flows are being received by the developed countries themselves. Developing countries are receiving just 25 per cent of global FDI flows. Asia and the Pacific countries are receiving more than 51 per cent of developing countries FDI inflows. Among the Asian countries, China alone has been receiving 44 per cent of Asian and Pacific FDI inflows. This evidence clearly shows the high degree of concentration of FDI inflows in certain locations, and thus in general can be considered as a definite source that can fill the gap of developing economies' investment requirements. The relationship of FDI and innovations does not seem to hold as multinational

Table 22.2   Growth of high-tech and other manufactured exports across developed and developing countries (1985–2000)

Categories/regions	World	Developed countries	Developing countries
Resource-based	6.60	5.18	11.00
Low technology	8.85	6.86	11.69
Medium technology	8.45	7.57	13.36
High technology	13.19	11.13	19.21

Sources: Adapted from Lall (2004) and World Bank (2004).

corporations do not locate strategic R&D away from home locations. They do undertake some R&D in developing countries, but not much. In the mid-1990s R&D performed in developing country affiliates as reported by USA-based multinational corporations came to 8 per cent of total R&D of the affiliates; just 1 per cent of parent company R&D. The R&D expenditure incurred by multinational corporations (MNCs) away from home location at the most is adaptation of the existing products to the local conditions (UNCTAD 1999: 195–228; Evenson and Westphal 1995). Even the technological spillovers to local firms benefits only if the firms have enough technological capabilities to catch up the complex and tacit elements of technological knowledge. Otherwise the presence of FDI in developing countries adversely affects the technological performance of local firms (UNCTAD 1999; Siddharthan 2004).

Royalty payments received in terms of technology transfer is an important indicator of technology-generating countries. Global technology and licensing fees from technology transfer was nearly US$80 billion. The share of developing countries of the global revenue generated from technology and licensing fees in 2002 was more than 98 per cent. Thus, it shows a very high degree of concentration of revenue received. This implies that developed countries produce technologies, and developing countries are receivers of technological knowledge and know-how. On the whole, indicators, both input and output, of global innovations reveal a high degree of concentration of innovations in the developed countries.

Trends in industrial R&D expenditure across countries

Commercially oriented innovative investment has largely been done by the industrial sector of the countries with a view to securing profits from the markets, both domestic and international. The industrial research and development expenditure of the selected 17 countries for analysis (Table 22.3) has grown steadily over the period of 1977–2000 at rate of 3.87 per cent per annum. Total resources expended by these countries increased from PPP US$117.4 billion in 1977 to PPP US$289.6 billion in 2000. It is important to note here that more than 53 per cent of industrial expenditure was incurred by USA industry in 1977. US industrial R&D expenditure has steadily grown at 2.64 per cent per annum and absolute expenditure increased from US$62 billion in 1977 to US$118 billion in 2000. USA industries dominated the high-tech markets; however, the relative share of industrial R&D dwindled to 40.78 per cent in 2000.

Industrial R&D expenditure of three European countries recorded in Table 22.3 negative trends during the period 1977–2000. These are Ireland (−4.10 per cent), Italy (−1.43 per cent) and the UK (−0.55 per cent). Deceleration of industrial R&D expenditure has substantially reduced the relative shares and position of these

Table 22.3 Growth and structure of industrial R&D expenditure across countries

Country	1977 million PPP$ at 1995 prices	Rank	2000 million PPP$ at 1995 prices	Rank	Trend growth rate 1977–2000
USA	62,891 (53.54)	1	118,135 (40.78)	1	2.64
Japan	8,414 (07.16)	5	66,996 (23.13)	2	9.52
Australia	643 (00.55)	11	1,728 (00.60)	14	5.90
Canada	1,325 (01.13)	7	5,581 (01.93)	7	5.71
Denmark	298 (00.25)	15	1,196 (00.41)	15	6.66
Finland	286 (00.24)	16	2,461 (00.85)	13	8.78
France	9,870 (08.40)	3	16,322 (5.63)	4	2.30
Germany	8,484 (07.22)	4	32,688 (11.28)	3	5.09
Ireland	824 (00.70)	10	292 (00.10)	17	−4.10
Italy	8,282 (07.05)	6	5,315 (01.83)	8	−1.43
Netherlands	1,248 (1.06)	8	3,513 (01.21)	11	4.28
Norway	308 (00.26)	14	586 (00.20)	16	3.06
Spain	1,083 (00.92)	9	2,669 (00.92)	12	4.74
Sweden	199 (00.17)	17	5,127 (01.77)	9	6.54
UK	12,331 (10.50)	2	12,840 (04.43)	5	−0.55
India	607 (00.52)	12	4,828 (01.67)	10	7.82
South Korea	360 (00.31)	13	9,781 (03.38)	6	16.51
Total	117,451 (100.00)	–	289,657 (100.00)	–	3.87

Note: Figures in parentheses are percentages.

Sources: OECD (2002); Government of India (2003); KITA (2002).

three countries among the 17 countries during the period 1977–2000. Shift factors may have played an important role in reducing the industrial R&D expenditure of UK and Italy, that is, there appears to be a race to transform the economies from producers of industrial goods to knowledge-based economies. Thus, the substitution effect seems to have played dominant role, but relocating industrial activities to cheaper labour cost locations could be an explanation. Ireland has chosen to be dependent for industrial development on FDI. All other European countries have shown rising trends in their industrial R&D expenditures. It is significant to note that the European countries, who have expended smaller amounts of R&D in industry beginning with the initial period, have shown faster rates of industrial R&D expenditure during the period of study. This clearly shows a trend towards convergence across the European economies. Overall R&D expenditure has been empirically tested and an overall trend was found of convergence across European regions. However, private R&D expenditure has shown clearly wide dispersion across European economies (Martin *et al.* 2004).

Asian economies have surprisingly shown very high industrial R&D expenditure growth during the period 1977–2000. Japan's industrial R&D expenditure increased at a rate of 9.52 per cent per annum during the study period. Its relative position improved from fifth to second with shares jumping from 7.16 in 1977 to 23.13 in 2000. South Korea recorded the highest rate of growth in industrial R&D at 16.51 per cent per annum. This enabled the country's industrial R&D expenditure relative share to improve from a mere 0.31 per cent in 1977 to 3.38 per cent in 2000, jumping in rank from 13th to sixth position in the last quarter of the twentieth century. India's industrial R&D expenditure has grown at a rate of 7.82 per cent per annum and could marginally improve its relative share and position (Table 22.3). A noteworthy feature that emerges from the foregoing analysis is that the three Asian economies have shown substantial growth in industrial R&D expenditure.

So far as sources of industrial R&D expenditure are concerned, there is a trend towards a greater role of the private sector across countries and more so in the case of East Asian economies. The role of the private sector in India's industry has increased substantially. The share of private industrial R&D expenditure, which was nearly 55 per cent in 1980–81, has increased substantially during the period of fast globalization to 81 per cent. The real public sector R&D expenditure has decreased and recorded negative growth rate during the last decade of the twentieth century (Singh 2001). This tells about the role of state in downsizing the public sector economic activities, India's high-tech draw in substantial innovative investment amounting to nearly 70 per cent of the total industrial R&D expenditure for 1998–99 (Government of India 2003). Intensity of industrial R&D is substantially higher in the private sector high-tech industries compared with the public sector. However, defence-related industries have high R&D expenditure compared with civilian industries. Private sector industrial R&D is concentrated in the Maharashtra state (52 per cent) and Karnataka state is continuously able to corner a substantial proportion of public sector industrial R&D (36 per cent). The structure of India's industrial R&D expenditure is quite shallow and highly concentrated in a few industries and within two states.

The industrial R&D expenditure pattern has a bearing on industrial activities. During the last quarter of the twentieth century, a rapid rise in innovation investment caused a significant shift in the structure of industrial activities in the global economy. The industrial production and trade in high-tech activities has expanded at a faster rate compared with other manufacturing activities. High-tech industrial performance is highly correlated with high-tech R&D expenditure. Japan has the highest R&D expenditure in high-tech industrial activities. Japan and Korea are ranked first and seventh respectively among the 26 countries examined by Lall (2004), exporting high-tech products above US$5 billion in 1998. Other Asian countries that figure among the high-tech R&D expenditure per unit of exports are Taiwan (18th), China (19th), Singapore (21st), Malaysia (23rd), Hong Kong (24th), Thailand (25th) and the Philippines (26th). The rest of the ranks, in terms of high-tech R&D per unit of high-tech exports, were occupied by developed countries.

There are two distinct sets of countries which are engaged in high-tech manufacturing activities: (1) countries where the high-tech industrial R&D expenditure per unit of exports is being incurred by the domestic firms (Japan comes under this category); and (2) countries where the high-tech industrial R&D expenditure is dependent on transnational corporations for their high-tech industrial production and exports (Malaysia, Thailand and the Philippines come under this category). It is important to note here that there exists a strong positive relationship between domestic R&D expenditure and industrial performance. Lall (2004), using data of 75 countries for 1985 and 1998, has provided consistent and robust estimates from the econometric model for the relationship between the domestic R&D expenditure and industrial performance. UNCTAD (2005) has found a high degree of correlation between economic growth and domestic innovation capability index. This suggests that innovative investment that generates domestic innovation capabilities is a precondition for the transformation of industrial structure and sustained economic growth of a developing economy.

Sources and indicators of innovations across Asian countries

The differences in innovation investment are substantial across Asian countries. South Asian countries are far behind in innovative investment efforts compared with the East Asian Countries (Table 22.4). Indicators of technology development and the technological outcomes, which are presented in Table 22.4, clearly point out that Taiwan and South Korea have moved ahead. These countries systematically built domestic capabilities over the last quarter of the twentieth century. South Korea is highest investor in innovation activities, incurring 3.0 per cent of GNP on R&D. Next to Korea is Taiwan with a R&D intensity of 2.08. Taiwan is leading in technology development and is globally ranked number two in terms of technology index. Science and technology-based manufactured exports from Taiwan constitutes 39 per cent of total manufactured exports. Singapore is unique in terms of succeeding in technology development on a model dependent heavily

Table 22.4 Indicators of technology across South Asian and East Asian countries

Country	Share of R&D in GNP	High-tech exports as % of manufacturing exports 2002	Technology index rank 2002	FDI in million US$ 2002
Bangladesh	0.03 (2000)	0.00	79	47
India	0.60 (2000)	5.00	57	3030
Pakistan	0.92 (1987)	1.00	–	57
Sri Lanka	0.3	1.00	67	242
Indonesia	0.07 (2000)	16.00	65	−1513
Rep. of Korea	3.0 (2002)	35.00	18	1972
Malaysia	0.42 (2000)	59.00	26	3203
Singapore	1.84 (1999)	63.00	17	6097
Taiwan	2.08 (2000)	39.00	2	–
Thailand	0.16 (2001)	32.00	41	900
China	1.1 (2002)	23.00	63	49,308

Note: Figures in parentheses are the year of availability of R&D expenditure.

Sources: World Economic Forum (2003); UNDP (2004); World Bank (2004).

on FDI and is also able to combine domestic efforts to climb the technological ladder. Its investment in R&D is 1.84 per cent of GDP, and 76 per cent of the manufactured exports are high-tech. Its global technology development ranking is 17th. Malaysia is also quite successful in exporting high-tech manufactured goods and services which are solely dependent on FDI. However, domestic technological capabilities could not grow in the absence domestic innovative capabilities. Lately, China has raised substantially the investment in innovations and crossed the 1 per cent mark of GNP. The success of China in attracting FDI and international trade has been widely recognized; however, the country's global technological ranking based on technology index is 63.

Other East Asian countries are moving ahead in terms of raising technology as a factor in their respective economic development. Still, they lag behind as far as generating capabilities for development of technological knowledge is concerned. The international technological rankings of Malaysia, Thailand and Indonesia are quite low. Differential performance of East Asian countries in technology development clearly points out that there is no substitute for systematically building domestic technology development capabilities. FDI can perpetuate technological dependence and domestic agents of production continuously upgrade and adopt technologies developed elsewhere. This in the long run depletes resources and cripples capabilities to become leaders in innovations because technology import involves substantial costs. The fundamental lesson obvious from successful East Asian countries – South Korea and Taiwan – is that strategic state intervention in enhancing innovative investment along with a selective/restrictive role of foreign direct investment helps in building national innovation systems.

The East Asian success in technology development allows us to discern two distinct strategies. First, the international trade in high-tech products and industrial growth remained heavily dependent on FDI. The countries that followed this path are Malaysia, Thailand, Indonesia and the Philippines. Technological ranking and domestic efforts in these countries have remained quite weak. National innovation systems, which increase competitiveness of domestic firms, remain quite fragile because domestic governments have relied more on foreign capital for technology. Recently, these governments have realized that without building national innovation system, despite using foreign sources of innovations more judicially, technology development and sustainability of industrial growth is not possible. Therefore, efforts have been stepped up to provide incentives to domestic firms to be innovative with better management of technology transfer through policy to spur local innovations.

Second, South Korea and Taiwan from a very early stage have systematically started building their national innovation systems and have not relied purely on FDI. FDI was kept at arm's length, but domestic firms were nurtured and encouraged by the government to succeed in the international market. These economies developed early on high-quality human capital for simulative and adaptive learning capabilities for reverse engineering, creating a network of science and technological institutions that helped them understand the complex process of technological innovations. The later strategy for moving up the technology ladder has recently gained recognition of the role of technology policy in the fast pace of globalization.

South Asian countries are slowly moving ahead on the technological ladders. India has been recognized as the tenth largest spender in absolute-level innovation activities and is the most sought after place for location of R&D centres from the multinational corporations. When we look at hard data, India is ranked 57th according to technology development index among the 80 nations for which comparable science and technology statistics are available. India's share of R&D in GNP was just 0.6 in 2000. The decline in R&D intensity is attributed essentially to two factors. One, the faster rate of growth of national income during the 1990s. Two, the government's contribution in R&D spending declined/stagnated in the wake of controlling the fiscal deficit. However, the science and technology-based share of manufactured exports has increased continuously. The share of high-tech manufactured exports is 5 per cent. When we compare India's share of high-tech exports with East Asian countries the achievement is miniscule. Despite this, India is well recognized globally in the pharmaceutical as well as information and communication technology-based products and innovations.

The other major country in the South Asian region is Pakistan, which is a globally recognized nuclear power. From the civilian technology development point of view, its international recognition and contribution seems quite low. Pakistan's share of high-tech manufactured exports just 1 per cent. Another important indicator of technology development is the workforce engaged in R&D activities. Researchers engaged in R&D are 69 per population million, which is quite low compared with other South Asian countries (Sri Lanka and India employed 191 and 157 researchers per million respectively). FDI flow, which is considered important source of technology transfer, is quite low in general in South Asian countries. Pakistan received US$57 million in FDI in 2000, which again is low compared with Sri Lanka and India. R&D intensity is nearly 1 per cent of the GNP of Pakistan, which is much higher compared with other South Asian countries. Industrial enterprises in Pakistan incur hardly any formal research and development expenditure (Lall 2000).

State and innovations in the fast-changing global economy

East Asian economies surged ahead in the transformation process and succeeded in industrializing their economies as well as building innovation capabilities during the last quarter of the twentieth century. The emergence of East Asia as a hub of economic activity generated controversy with regard to whether governments or markets were the central factor in the successful economic transformation. However, the early attempt to describe the government's innovative role to enact interventionist policies, which led private agents of production to succeed in the fast pace of globalization, has been described as minority view (Wade 1990; Srinivasan 1995). It is important to note here that the 1997 East Asian crisis has changed the thinking among economists and international agencies with regard to the role of state in policy making and conducting development programmes. The 1997 crisis severely affected the stability of economic growth in general and innovative outcomes in particular of the region's economies, which has led to the renewal of the role of the state in terms of good governance.

Stern (2004) has recently emphasized that one important policy lesson which can be drawn from the five decades of development experience is that the state and markets complement each other. The *World Development Report* (World Bank 1998) clearly identified the role of the government in developing countries to develop capabilities to generate knowledge at home along with providing help to domestic agents of production to take advantage of the large global stock of knowledge. It is significant to note here that UNDP has gone ahead in terms of identifying knowledge gaps existing between developed and developing countries and articulated the arguments against the strict intellectual property rights regime enacted and implemented by the WTO. Furthermore, UNDP has not only suggested an innovative and fundamental role for the governments of the developing countries in generating capabilities that matter for knowledge development, but has also identified knowledge as a global public good and the role of the international community in reducing the knowledge gaps (UNDP 2001; Stiglitz 1999).

Apart from making suitable public innovation policies to strengthen national innovation systems, the governments of developing countries should also strive hard to seek co-operation among themselves as well as with the international institutions and agencies to negotiate in the WTO framework. Specifically, the negotiations should be with regard to MNC operations in their markets. They should also assess losses of domestic firms and seek compensation, using that to create capabilities to strengthen innovative infrastructure at home. The two-step strategy suggested above will go a long way to make capable domestic agents of production catch the spillover effects created by international capital and fill the knowledge gap for sustained economic growth.

Conclusions

The analysis of sources and indicators of innovations across countries and regions clearly shows some decrease in the concentration of innovations in the developed countries. East Asia has emerged as an innovative region of technology development, with numerous lessons for developing countries in general and South Asian countries in particular in a fast-globalizing world economy. The foremost lesson that should be learnt from the East Asian experience to succeed in the global economy is to reinvent the role of state to strengthen the national innovation institutional system. The developing countries are currently engaged in economic reforms to reduce the role of the state and provide more space for market forces, which essentially make the state scarce in economic activities. This strategy of making the state scarce in developing countries suffers from the drawback of substitutability of the state and the market and reduces the competitiveness of the domestic agents of production in the international economy. It is important to note here that intervention of the state in a fast-globalizing world economy is more difficult but at the same time is crucial and strategic. Therefore, there is a dire need to reinvent the role of government policy in crafting national innovation institutional arrangements for building and strengthening competitive advantage.

The East Asian economies have grown in an environment of import substitution and lax intellectual property regimes which are no longer available to developing economies. Intellectual property regimes enacted and imposed by the WTO have been restricting developing economies from putting into place national innovation systems with proven adverse effects on global innovations and more particularly least developed countries (Grossman and Lai 2004; Helpman 1993). Developing country markets are invaded by multinational corporations without contributing towards generating domestic innovation capabilities. The role of international institutions is to evolve policies that should decrease the knowledge gap through imposing conditions on multinational corporations to contribute in an equal measure the percentage of sales revenue expenditure on R&D in the host country as in the home country.

The reduction of fiscal deficits under the umbrella of reform programmes gives an easy option for developing country governments to cut down expenditure on institutions that are the backbone of economic development such as education, health and infrastructure. Further, curtailing support to the R&D institutions – public and private – has a capacity to weaken the institutions that, from a long-term perspective, have great importance for economic growth and welfare. The right combination of state and market that delivers long-run growth is the correct strategy, rather than going from one extreme to another, which in the past has introduced instability and blocked potential.

Note

The author is grateful to Matti Pohjola, Keun Lee, Germano Mwabu and K.J. Joseph for suggestions and enlightening discussions during the UNU-WIDER jubilee conference in Helsinki, 17–18 June 2005, which helped in carrying several refinements in the paper. Comments and suggestions of Robert E. Evenson of Yale University and two anonymous referees of the conference volume are duly acknowledged. However, the author is solely responsible for errors and omissions that remain.

References

Amable, B. (2000) 'International Specialization and Growth', *Structural Change and Economic Dynamics*, 11: 413–31.

Archibugi, D. and C. Pietrobelli (2003) 'The Globalization of Technology and Its Implications for Developing Countries: Windows of Opportunity or Further Burden?', *Technological Forecasting and Social Change*, 70: 861–83.

Branscomb, L. (2004) 'Where Do High-Tech Commercial Innovations Come From?', *Duke Law and Technology Review*, 5, 12.

Coe, D.T. and E. Helpman (1995) 'International R&D Spillovers', *European Economic Review*, 39: 859–87.

Coe, D.T., E. Helpman and A. Hoffmaister (1997) 'North-South R&D Spillovers', *Economic Journal*, 107: 134–49.

Domar, E. (1946) 'Capital Expansion, Rate of Growth and Employment', *Econometrica*, 14: 137–47.

Evenson, R.E. and L. Singh (1997) 'Economic Growth, International Technological Spillovers and Public Policy: Theory and Empirical Evidence from Asia', *Yale University Economic Growth Center Discussion Papers 777*, New Haven, CT: Yale University.

Evenson, R.E. and L.E. Westphal (1995) 'Technological Change and Technology Strategy', in J. Behrman and T.N. Srinivasan (eds), *Handbook of Development Economics* Vol. 3A, Amsterdam: Elsevier Science.

Girma, S. (2005) 'Absorptive Capacity and Productivity Spillovers from FDI: A Threshold Regression Analysis', *Oxford Bulletin of Economics and Statistics*, 67: 281–306.

Gorg, H. and D. Greenaway (2002) 'Much Ado About Nothing? Do Domestic Firms Really Benefit from Foreign Direct Investment?', Mimeo, Nottingham: University of Nottingham.

Government of India (2003) *Research and Development in Industry 2000–01*, New Delhi: Ministry of Science and Technology, Department of Science and Technology.

Grossman, G. and E.L.-C. Lai (2004) 'International Protection of Intellectual Property', *American Economic Review*, 94: 1635–53.

Hanson, G. (2001) 'Should Countries Promote Foreign Direct Investment', *G-24 Discussion Paper 9*, New York and Geneva: United Nations.

Harrod, R.F. (1939) 'An Essay in Dynamic Theory', *Economic Journal*, 49: 14–33.

Helpman, E. (1993) 'Innovation, Imitation and Intellectual Property Rights', *Econometrica*, 61: 1247–80.

Keller, W. (1998) 'Are International Technological Spillovers Trade Related? Analysing Spillovers Among Randomly Matched Trade Partners', *European Economic Review*, 42: 1469–81.

Keller, W. (2004) 'International Technology Diffusion', *Journal of Economic Literature*, 42: 752–82.

Kim, K. (2000) 'An Analysis of Sources of Growth in East Asian Economies and R&D Spillover Effects', *Journal of the Korean Economy*, 1: 83–107.

KITA (2002) *Major Indicators of Industrial Technology*, Seoul: Korea Industrial Technology Association.

Lall, S. (2000) 'Technological Change and Industrialization in the Asian Newly Industrializing Economies: Achievements and Challenges', in L. Kim and R.R. Nelson (eds), *Technology, Learning, and Innovation: Experience of Newly Industrializing Economies*, Cambridge: Cambridge University Press.

Lall, S. (2004) 'Industrial Success and Failure in a Globalizing World', *International Journal of Technology Management and Sustainable Development*, 3: 189–213.

Lichtenberg, F.L. and B.P. Potterie (1998) 'International R&D Spillovers: A Comment', *European Economic Review*, 42: 1483–91.

Lucas, R.E. (1988) 'On the Mechanics of Economic Development', *Journal of Monetary Economics*, 22, 1: 3–42.

Malerba, F. and F. Montobbio (2000) 'Knowledge Flows, Structure of Innovative Activity and International Specialization', *Centre for Research on Innovation and Internationalization Working Paper* 119, Milan: Università Bocconi.

Martin, C., C. Mulas-Granados and I. Sanz (2004) 'Spatial Distribution of R&D Expenditure and Patent Applications across EU Regions and its Impact on Economic Cohesion', *European Economy Group Working Paper* 32, Madrid: Facultad de Economicas, Universidad Complutense de Madrid.

Navaretti, G.B. and D.G. Tarr (2000) 'International Knowledge Flows and Economic Performance: A Review of Evidence', *World Bank Economic Review*, 14: 1–15.

OECD (2001) *STI Scoreboard: Creation and Diffusion of Knowledge*, Paris: OECD.

OECD (2002) *Research and Development Expenditure in Industry 1987–2000*, Paris: OECD.

Romer, P.M. (1986) 'Increasing Returns and Long-Run Growth', *Journal of Political Economy*, 94: 1002–37.

Romer, P.M. (1993) 'Ideas Gaps and Object Gaps in Economic Development', *Journal of Monetary Economics*, 32: 543–72.

Romer, P.M. (1997) 'Beyond Market Failure', in A.H. Teich, S.D. Nelson and C. McEnanoy (eds), *AAAS Science and Technology Policy Yearbook*, Washington, DC: American Association for the Advancement of Science.

Ruttan, V.W. (2001) *Technology, Growth, and Development: An Induced Innovation Perspective*, New York: Oxford University Press.

Siddharthan, N.S. (2004) 'Globalization: Productivity, Efficiency and Growth: An Overview', *Economic and Political Weekly*, 39: 420–2.

Singh, L. (2001) 'Public Policy and Expenditure on R&D in Industry', *Economic and Political Weekly*, 36: 2920–4.

Singh, L. (2004a) 'Domestic and International Knowledge Spillovers in Manufacturing Industries in South Korea', *Economic and Political Weekly*, 34: 498–505.

Singh, L. (2004b) 'Globalization, National Innovation Systems and Response of Public Policy', *International Journal of Technology Management and Sustainable Development*, 3: 215–31.

Solow, R.M. (1956) 'A Contribution to the Theory of Economic Growth', *Quarterly Journal of Economics* 70: 65–95.

Solow, R.M. (1957) 'Technical Progress and the Aggregate Production Function', *Review of Economics and Statistics*, 39: 312–20.

Srinivasan, T.N. (1995) 'Long-Run Growth Theories and Empirics: Anything New', in T. Ito and A.O. Krueger (eds), *Growth Theories in Light of East Asian Experience*, Chicago: University of Chicago Press.

Stern, N. (2004) 'Opportunities for India in a Changing World', in F. Bourguignon and B. Pleskovic (eds), *Accelerating Development, Annual World Bank Conference on Development Economics*, New York: Oxford University Press.

Stiglitz, J.E. (1999) 'Knowledge As a Global Public Good', in I. Kaul, I. Grunberg and M.A. Stern (eds), *Global Public Goods: International Co-operation in the 21st Century*, New York: Oxford University Press.

Stiglitz, J.E. (2003) 'Globalization, Technology, and Asian Development', *Asian Development Review*, 20: 1–18.

Swan, T.W. (1956) 'Economic Growth and Capital Accumulation', *Economic Record*, 32: 343–61.

UNCTAD (United Nations Conference on Trade and Development) (1999) *World Investment Report 1999: Foreign Direct Investment and the Challenge of Development*, New York and Geneva: United Nations.

UNCTAD (United Nations Conference on Trade and Development) (2005) *World Investment Report 2005: Transnational Corporations and the Internationalization of R&D*, New York and Geneva: United Nations.

UNDP (United Nations Development Programme) (2001) *Human Development Report*, New York: Oxford University Press for UNDP.

UNDP (United Nations Development Programme) (2004) *Human Development Report*, New Delhi: Oxford University Press.

UNESCO (2004) *UIS Bulletin on Science and Technology Statistics* 1 (April), UNESCO Institute of Statistics: Montreal.

Urata, U. (2001) 'Emergence of an FDI-Trade Nexus and Economic Growth in East Asia', in J.E. Stiglitz and S. Yusuf (eds), *Rethinking The East Asian Miracle*, Washington, DC: World Bank.

Verspagen, B. (1992) 'Endogenous Innovation in Neo-Classical Growth Models: A Survey', *Journal of Macroeconomics*, 14: 631–62.

Wade, R. (1990) *Governing the Market: Economic Theory and the Role of Government in East Asian Industrialization*, New Jersey: Princeton University Press.

World Bank (1998) *World Development Report*, New York: Oxford University Press for the World Bank.

World Bank (2003) *World Development Report*, New York: Oxford University Press for the World Bank.

World Bank (2004) *World Development Report*, New York: Oxford University Press for the World Bank.

World Economic Forum (2003) *The Global Competitiveness Report 2002–2003*, New York: Oxford University Press.

23
Manufacturing, Services and Premature Deindustrialization in Developing Countries: A Kaldorian Analysis

Sukti Dasgupta and Ajit Singh

Introduction

It is entirely befitting that this brief piece of Kaldorian empirics should be included in a volume dedicated to the memory of Lal Jayawardena. Lal regarded Nicholas Kaldor as his mentor and both shared an abiding interest in issues of economic policy. Kaldor was renowned as an apostle of industrialization. For both rich and poor countries alike, he regarded manufacturing as the engine of growth.[1] This chapter examines this central Kaldorian theme in relation to the recent experience of today's leading developing countries. In a number of these countries, certain long-term structural tendencies have become manifest, prima facie challenging Kaldor's theses. These tendencies, which will be documented more fully in subsequent sections, are as follows:

- Evidence of deindustrialization (the fall in the share of manufacturing employment or an absolute fall in such employment) in several developing countries at a much lower level of per capita income than observed historically in today's advanced countries during their period of industrialization.
- The related phenomenon of 'jobless growth' in the formal manufacturing sector both in slow-growing economies (as in Latin America) as well as more surprisingly in fast-growing economies (for instance, India).
- Evidence that manufacturing may no longer be as steadfast an engine of growth as has been the case in the past. Contrary to widespread past experience, in the last decade or so services have often grown at a faster long-term rate than manufacturing, as for example in India.

435

These phenomena are analytically interrelated, but all run contrary to the historical pattern of structural change observed in what are now developed countries. An important question is whether these new structural tendencies in developing countries should be viewed negatively or positively with respect to long-term industrialization and economic development in these countries.[2] Non-conformity with the past observed pattern could indicate that a country's industrial development will not progress very far. This is because the non-conforming structures may be unable to satisfy changes in consumer demand or the required changes in production technique or the institutional arrangements that normally occur during the process of industrialization. On the other hand, departures from the historical trajectory could suggest that there has been a fundamental break with past regularities, owing, perhaps, to the introduction of revolutionary new technology such as that of information and communications technology (ICT). This may lead to the service sector (particularly that related to ICT, telecommunications, business services and finance) replacing or complementing manufacturing as a new or as an additional engine of economic growth in emerging countries.[3]

The three phenomena of the last decade or so referred to above – namely, premature deindustrialization, jobless growth of manufacturing in the formal sector and faster growth of services than of manufacturing – are examined in this chapter both with respect to a large cross-section of developing countries and of states in the Indian economy.

This chapter is a sequel to Dasgupta and Singh (2005). In that study a preliminary analysis of these issues in a Kaldorian framework was carried out. This study takes the empirical analysis further in the following respects. First, in the main analysis it uses an extended dataset of 48 instead of 30 developing countries for the period 1990–2000. The larger dataset uses the maximum number of countries for which relevant data on sectoral employment is available. Second, this chapter provides a fuller analysis of manufacturing growth in the Indian economy in both the formal and informal sectors. Third, unlike the previous study, it examines inter-country differences in the manufacturing share of employment in developing countries.

Manufacturing as the engine of growth: the Kaldorian approach

Kaldor, in seminal contributions (1966; 1967), provided the intellectual basis for regarding manufacturing as the leading sector in economic growth. Here, Kaldor was following a long line of classical economic analysis, and was particularly influenced by Young (1928), who emphasized the overall macroeconomic spillover effects of the extension of manufacturing industry, the so-called macroeconomies of scale. Kaldor extended these ideas in the papers mentioned earlier and, importantly as an economic adviser to the British government in the late 1960s, proposed a selective employment tax to promote manufacturing in Britain. The underlying argument was that, for Britain to grow faster, manufacturing had to grow faster still and this required the transfer of labour from services to manufacturing. To encourage such a shift, a selective employment tax on services was introduced on Kaldor's recommendation.[4]

In Kaldor's opinion, the British economy was at a disadvantage in relation to its continental rivals because, as a result of its relatively earlier maturity, there was little surplus labour in agriculture that could be transferred to industry. Moreover, unlike in continental Europe, agricultural wages were nearer the average level of industrial wages. So that there was little incentive for labour to leave agriculture for industry.

Kaldor introduced the concept of dynamic economies of scale, such that the faster the growth of manufacturing output, the faster the growth of manufacturing productivity. He ascribed these dynamic economies to Arrow's (1962) notion of 'learning by doing' and argued that this occurred principally in industry and not in services or agriculture. Unlike the 'total factor productivity' concept of neoclassical economics, which is entirely based on the supply side, Kaldor's model considered both the demand and supply sides. As demand and supply conditions differ between sectors, Kaldor believed that it was not adequate to formulate a theory of economic growth based on a single product economy. His distinction between industry, agriculture and services may be summarized as follows. On the demand side, he suggested that the income elasticity of demand for manufacturing products was greater than that for agriculture, while being more or less similar to that of services. On the supply side, manufacturing was thought to have greater potential for productivity growth for the reasons outlined above. Notwithstanding the problem of the measurement of services production, the productivity growth of services tended to be considerably less than that of manufacturing.

On the basis of these stylized tendencies concerning demand and supply conditions in agriculture, manufacturing and services, Kaldor derived generalizations concerning the relationship between the growth of output, employment and productivity in different sectors of the economy. These generalizations are known as 'Kaldor's laws', which will be examined first on a preliminary informal basis in the next section. Pages 440–2, however, will provide an econometric examination of these laws using the dataset for 48 developing countries mentioned earlier.

In an early contribution Singh (1977) noted that for examining issues of industrialization and deindustrialization in an open economy it is not adequate to consider the characteristics of domestic economy alone. It is also essential to examine the interactions of the economy with the rest of world. In that context he drew attention to the crucial significance of the manufacturing sector for external balance. The case of a developed country like the UK, where the manufacturing sector is now quite small in terms of output and employment (each of which accounts for less than 20 per cent of total GDP or total employment) and which is also a leading exporter of knowledge-based services, provides a striking illustration of the continuing significance of manufacturing for the trade balance. Manufacturing still accounts for 60 per cent of the UK's foreign trade (exports and imports) and thus the importance of the sector for the whole economy cannot be exaggerated. However, for a developing country in the early stages of development, the contribution of agriculture to the balance of payments may be as, if not more, important as that of manufacturing. But as per capita income rises towards the level of middle-income countries, the role of manufacturing in maintaining external equilibrium becomes critical. This is because of the very high income elasticity of demand for manufactured products at these income levels, which means that, if this demand cannot be met from domestic sources, there will be an increasing burden of manufactured imports on the trade balance.

Growth of manufacturing and of GDP: preliminary analysis evidence

The relationship between the rate of growth of manufacturing and that of GDP is captured in Kaldor's first law that states that the faster the rate of growth of manufacturing in the economy, the faster will be its growth of GDP. Instead of simply being a correlation between two variables, Kaldor regarded the relationship as fundamentally a causal one, the causation running from the growth of manufacturing production to growth of GDP. In its stronger form, Kaldor's first law states that the greater the excess of manufacturing growth over GDP growth, the greater will be GDP growth. This implies that the growth of manufacturing would normally be much faster than the growth of GDP.

Table 23.1 provides interesting information on the behaviour of these two variables for the leading industrial countries. Between 1950 and 1973 manufacturing growth exceeded GDP growth for each of these countries. However, between 1973 and 1984, this was reversed for every one of the six countries. Such a comprehensive reversal across all leading industrial countries must indicate a major change in consumer preferences as countries and individuals become richer and as technology changes. It has been argued that, as per capita income increases beyond a certain point, the income elasticity of demand for services becomes greater than that for manufactures.[5] It is nevertheless much less likely that the rate of growth of demand for manufactures and services would vary a great deal. This is because,

Table 23.1 The excess of rate of growth of manufacturing over the rate of growth of GDP, leading OECD countries (annual percentage growth rates)

	1950–73	1973–84
UK	0.2	−2.4
France	1.3	−1.7
West Germany	1.1	−1.1
Italy	4.2	−0.5
US	0.8	−0.1
Japan	5.7	−1.3

Source: Matthews and Bowen (1988).

although in rich countries the income elasticity of demand for services may be greater than that for manufactures, this effect is counterbalanced to a greater or smaller degree by the fact that the prices of manufactures rise much more slowly or actually fall compared with those for a wide range of services. The underlying reason for the different price movements in these two sectors is that productivity growth in the manufacturing sector tends to be much faster than that for most services (Howes and Singh 2000).

Table 23.2 provides some basic information for developing countries in Asia and Latin America. The table indicates that in the ten Asian countries manufacturing production exceeded that of GDP in all countries except one in each of the three time periods; 1970–80, 1980–93 and 1993–2003.[6] However, in Latin America, during these three decades GDP growth exceeded manufacturing growth for an ever larger number of countries, so that by the third decade, 1993–2003, there was only one country, Mexico, for which GDP growth did not exceed manufacturing growth. As noted earlier, it is well established that at a high level of per capita income the share of manufacturing in GDP begins to fall, indicating faster growth of other sectors, particularly services. However, most recent literature, in line with the information given in Table 23.2 suggests that the turning point for the share

Table 23.2 Difference in the rate of growth of manufacturing versus rate of growth of GDP and the rate of growth of services versus the rate of growth of GDP, selected Asian and Latin American countries

	Difference in average annual growth rate (%)					
	Manufacturing vs GDP			**Services, etc. vs GDP**		
	1970–80	**1980–93**	**1993–2003**	**1970–80**	**1980–93**	**1993–2003**
Asia						
China	5.3	1.5	1.9	−0.2	1.5	−0.6
India	1.2	1.1	0.8	1.2	1.2	1.8
Indonesia	6.8	6.0	1.7	0.5	1.1	0.5
Korea	7.6	3.2	1.7	0.3	−0.8	0.1
Malaysia	3.8	4.1	1.4	1.2	−0.7	0.2
Pakistan	0.5	1.3	0.9	1.4	0.3	0.8
Philippines	0.1	−0.6	−0.3	−0.9	1.5	0.8
Sri Lanka	−2.2	2.7	1.1	1.6	−0.6	0.6
Thailand	3.4	2.6	2.1	−0.1	−0.5	−0.6
Latin America						
Argentina	−1.2	−0.4	−1.2	0.4	0.2	0.3
Bolivia	1.5	−	−0.1	3.1	−	0.3
Brazil	0.9	−1.9	−0.3	−0.3	1.2	−0.1
Chile	−2.6	−0.7	−1.6	1.1	0.3	0.0
Colombia	0.4	−0.2	−4.3	0.5	−0.3	2.4
Ecuador	1.0	−2.1	−0.6	−0.1	0.0	1.2
Mexico	0.7	0.5	0.1	0.0	0.0	−0.1
Peru	−	−	−0.6	−	−	−0.3
Venezuela	2.2	−0.8	−1.1	2.8	−0.5	1.0

Source: Compiled from World Bank (2004).

of manufacturing output and employment is now taking place at a much lower level of per capita income than hitherto (Rowthorn and Coutts 2004; Palma 2005; Pieper 2003). In the past this historical turning point occurred at a per capita of almost US$10,000 in current prices; it is now being estimated to take place at levels of income as low as US$3,000 in some countries.

The important question is whether the kind of premature deindustrialization outlined above is necessarily harmful to a country's long-term prospects. This question will be discussed more fully in the final section. However, we note here that it is, for example, perfectly possible to deindustrialize in terms of employment and yet not do so in terms of output. It is also pertinent to note that deindustrialization in either sense may not be a pathological condition if it is a normal response to changes in tastes and technology. Nevertheless, it is a worrying sign when so many developing countries at a low level of per capita income exhibit symptoms of deindustrialization in terms of output and employment (in the sense of their respective shares either remaining constant or falling). This would imply that much of the excess labour in agriculture in the reference countries will either remain in agriculture or will inevitably end up in low-productivity informal manufacturing and informal services.

Sectoral and GDP growth in Kaldorian analysis: the econometric approach

This section tests Kaldor's first law concerning the relationship between manufacturing growth and GDP growth. It also examines the analogous relationships for the other two sectors, agriculture and services. It then goes on to consider Kaldor's second and third laws while examining the determinants of productivity growth in Kaldorian terms. The empirical analysis here is carried out for 48 countries for the period 1990–2000.[7] This is the maximum number of developing countries for which we could obtain data for the main variables considered in this exercise. There is, however, no reason to believe that there is any serious sample selection problem here. The countries excluded are of all shapes and sizes, at all levels of income per capita – they simply have not reported the data for the variables used in the study. The results of the present study may be compared with those for the period 1980–90 and 1990–2000 reported in Dasgupta and Singh (2005) where a similar approach is followed, however it may be noted that the earlier study was based on a random sample of 30 developing countries, rather than the total sample with the available data considered here.

On Kaldor's first law, results of estimating the simple econometric equation for the period 1990–2000 normally used in this type of analysis are given below:[8]

Equation 1

$$gGDP = 0.022 + 0.473gManf.VA \qquad R^2 = 0.9833$$
$$(13.98) \quad (67.53) \qquad F_{Stat}(1, 46) = 2710.01$$

Diagnostic tests			Critical values
Functional form F(1, 44)	0.90	<	9.71
Normality JB Test ~ CHSQ (2)	0.79	<	5.99
Heteroscedasticity CHSQ (2)	0.17	<	3.84
No. of observations	48		

The estimated regression equation indicates a close association between manufacturing growth and GDP growth on a cross-section basis for the 1990s. The diagnostics in terms of functional form normality and heteroscedasticity are all satisfactory. It is also notable that the β-coefficient has a value of about 0.5, considerably less than one, which suggests that the greater the difference between manufacturing growth and GDP growth, the greater the GDP growth. In order to establish that manufacturing is the engine of growth, it is necessary to carry out a similar exercise to that above for the agriculture and service sectors as well and compare the respective outcomes. The results for agriculture are reported below.

Equation 2

$$gGDP = 0.167 + 1.421gAgr.VA \qquad R^2 = 0.6966$$
$$(2.31) \quad (10.44) \qquad F_{Stat}(1, 46) = 108.92$$

Diagnostic tests			Critical values
Functional form F(1, 44)	30.63	>	9.71
Normality JB Test ~ CHSQ (2)	14.33	>	5.99
Heteroscedasticity CHSQ (2)	11.89	>	3.84
No. of observations	48		

The estimated equation has a smaller R^2 compared with that of manufacturing value added. The relevant diagnostics are also poor for this equation as is evident above. Turning to the growth of services and the growth of GDP, equation 3 indicates a close relationship between these two variables. Growth of services accounts for 85 per cent of the inter-country variation for the period 1990–2000. The diagnostic tests are all satisfactory.

Equation 3

$$gGDP = 0.015 + 0.58gSer.VA \qquad R^2 = 0.9811$$
$$(8.53) \quad (48.85) \qquad F_{Stat}(1, 46) = 1576.34$$

Diagnostic tests			Critical values
Functional form F(1, 44)	7.12	<	251.0
Normality JB Test ~ CHSQ (2)	3.85	<	5.99
Heteroscedasticity CHSQ (2)	1.04	<	3.84
No. of observations	48		

It may, however, be noted that the value of β-coefficient in relation to services is much higher than that of corresponding β-coefficient related to manufacturing. In Kaldor's analysis, a strong positive correlation between GDP growth and sectoral output growth is necessary but not sufficient for that sector to be the 'engine of growth'.[9] It suggests that in terms of causal interpretation of the model, the difference between growth of services and growth of GDP is relatively less potent in causing inter-country variation in economic growth than that between manufacturing and GDP growth. In the Kaldorian analysis, it is customary to argue that the close relationship between many of the services and GDP growth is due to the fact that both variables are related to the growth of manufacturing. Service activities like retailing and transportation clearly depend on the expansion of manufacturing production. However, this consideration is much less applicable to a service activity such as software and computer programming or indeed to a general purpose technology such as ICT. Indeed, it will be more reasonable to suggest that expansion of manufacturing depends on the services linked with the ICT rather than the other way round. The scatter diagrams underlying equations 1–3 are given in the Appendix. In view of the special discussion of the Indian case in this paper, it may be useful to note that the observations for India lie close to the respective regression lines in each case, neither consistently above nor consistently below the line.

Finally, it will be useful to compare the results of the above analysis with those reported in Dasgutpa and Singh (2005). The main difference is that, with a bigger sample in the present analysis, the results are much more robust and the diagnostics are much more satisfactory than before.

Manufacturing, structural change and economic growth

In Kaldor's view of economic growth, the rate of growth of productivity in the economy as a whole depends on the expansion of the manufacturing sector, which not only leads to faster growth of productivity in manufacturing (due to the operation of Verdoorn's law), but also has spillover effects on the whole economy. It also, however, depends on the shrinkage of the decreasing returns, inefficient activities, such as agriculture or other non-manufacturing sectors. The release of labour and other resources from these to the dynamic manufacturing sector has a double gain for productivity growth in the economy as a whole: it increases productivity by releasing surplus labour from the non-dynamic sectors, and also by the expansion of the dynamic sectors. Both these effects are incorporated in the following regression equation, estimated on the datasets for 48 developing countries.

Equation 4

$$\text{gProductivity} = 0.0162 + 0.4984\text{gManf.VA} - 0.7054\text{gNonManf.Emp}$$

$$(3.71) \quad (22.62) \quad (10.93)$$

$$R^2 = 0.9701$$

$$F_{\text{Stat}}(1, 46) = 731.69$$

Diagnostic tests			Critical values
Functional form F(1, 44)	4.57	<	9.71
Normality JB Test ~ CHSQ (2)	167.2	>	5.99
Heteroscedasticity CHSQ (2)	0.06	<	3.84
No. of observations	48		

This was the equation used by Cripps and Tarling (1973) to examine Kaldor's engine of growth hypothesis. It performs well but the normality test is not met. It is interesting that if non-manufacturing is replaced by agricultural employment the results are much more robust and pass the diagnostic tests.

Equation 5

$$gProductivity = 0.003 + 0.4087gManf.VA - 0.286gAgri.Emp$$
$$(0.526) \quad (5.18) \qquad\qquad (8.96)$$

$$R^2 = 0.7641$$
$$F_{Stat}(1, 40) = 63.51$$

Diagnostic tests			Critical values
Functional form F(1, 38)	4.0	<	4.08
Normality JB Test ~ CHSQ (2)	1.25	<	5.99
Heteroscedasticity F(1, 40)	0.852	<	4.08

In order to examine the hypothesis that some service activities may help to make the service sector an additional engine of growth, the following equation makes productivity growth a function of the growth of services and agricultural employment. The estimated parameters of the equation and the relevant diagnostic tests are reported below.

Equation 6

$$gProductivity = -0.0207 + 0.9059gSer.VA - 0.276gAgri.Emp$$
$$(3.09) \quad (7.09) \qquad\qquad (10.04)$$

$$R^2 = 0.8259$$
$$F_{Stat}(1, 40) = 92.51$$

Diagnostic tests			Critical values
Functional form F(1, 38)	8.09	>	4.08
Normality JB Test ~ CHSQ (2)	6.53	>	5.99
Heteroscedasticity F(1, 40)	0.382	<	4.08

These results suggest that the service sector as a whole is much like manufacturing. Its expansion leads to a positive effect on the overall growth of productivity and it is the agricultural sector that is not dynamic. Even though the normality test is not strictly satisfied, it is a close approximation. This confirms the result, reported above, that the appropriate specification of the Kaldor structural change equation will nowadays work better for developing countries with the non-manufacturing sector being replaced by agriculture.

Inter-country variations in industrial employment

As the title indicates, this section reports on inter-country variations in industrial employment in developing economies. The analysis is made on a pooled time-series, cross-sectional basis, with the dependent variable being the share of industrial labour force in total employment. This investigation is conducted on a small subset of 14 developing countries for which the relevant data are available for the period 1986–2000. Apart from per capita income and the square of per capita income (to encompass the non-linear relationship between the share of industrial employment and per capita income which the theory predicts), the independent variables include gross fixed capital formation expressed as a percentage of GDP, trade openness (measured as exports plus imports as a percentage of GDP), a dummy for Latin America and also one for China.[10]

Table 23.3 provides the estimated regression equation results. The regression results are reasonably satisfactory. Although the regression equation explains only 14 per cent of the inter-firm variations in the share of industrial employment, all the independent variables have appropriate signs and are statistically significant at the 5 per cent level. The diagnostics are also generally satisfactory. The squared-term for per capita income has a negative sign (not unexpected in view of the range of per capita incomes of the sample countries), per capita income itself has the expected positive sign, is statistically significant and also economically very

Table 23.3 Explaining cross-country differences in share of manufacturing employment

Variable	Coefficients
Constant	−12.29
Log GDP	1.00 (2.50)
Log GDP^2	−0.02 (−2.47)
Fixed capital formation	0.004 (1.70)
Openness	0.001 (2.09)
Dummy for Latin America	0.082 (5.09)
Dummy for China	−0.059 (−1.16)
R^2	0.14
Ramsey RESET test Ho: model has no omitted variables	F (10, 180) = 2.56
No. of observations	196

Notes: Dependent variable = share of manufacturing in total employment. t-statistics in parenthesis.

Sources: Based on data from World Bank (2004); IMF Balance of Payments Statistics on http://www.imf.org/external/ bopage.

important. Other things being equal, the share of industry in employment does vary monotonically with per capita income until the turning point is reached. Industry, therefore, continues to be directly important as a source of employment and structural change for at least low- to middle-income countries.

The coefficient of the variable for gross fixed capital formation has a positive sign. This implies that the greater the capital investment in a country, which is generally biased towards manufacturing because gross capital formation takes place most in the manufacturing sector, the more does the employment structure shift towards manufacturing. The coefficient of the openness variable also has a positive sign implying that economies that are more open are also more likely to have relatively larger employment shares in manufacturing. However, in economic terms the size of the coefficient is quite small.

It is also interesting that the dummy variable for China is negative and for Latin American countries it is positive, other things being equal. The result for Latin America is highly statistically significant, indicating that Latin American share of manufacturing in total employment is greater than other countries, including specifically China. One interpretation of this result is that China is much more competitive than Latin American countries (even though China's coefficient is not statistically significant, its size in economic terms is quite large). The implication here is that the Chinese productivity growth is likely to be faster than that of Latin American countries because of its loss of labour force from the manufacturing sector. Another interpretation is that the Chinese began their reform programme with a lop-sided industrial sector and a much less developed service sector compared with other countries and what our results indicate is simply a correction. It is not possible for us to discriminate between these two interpretations but this could be a useful subject of further research.

Growth and employment in manufacturing: Indian states

To complement the earlier analysis on the nature of the relationship between sectoral and GDP growth in a large cross-section of developing countries, this section carries out a similar investigation for a cross-section of Indian states. It will be appreciated that, with a billion people overall, some of the Indian states like Uttar Pradesh (with population of more then a hundred million) are bigger in size than countries like Germany and France. However it is also important to note that the range of variation in per capita income for the Indian states is likely to be much smaller than the inter-country variation for the 48-country sample of developing countries employed on pages 440–4.

Since the late 1990s, the Indian economy has been growing quite impressively, but employment has failed to expand at a proportionate rate (GDP growth accelerated from 5.2 per cent between 1983–84 and 1993–94 to 6.7 per cent between 1993–94 and 1999–2000, while employment growth slowed from 2.7 per cent in the first period to 1.07 per cent in the latter period). The slow growth of employment has added to increased unemployment rates, especially among the youth.

Open unemployment rates increased from 5 per cent to 7.2 per cent in the respective periods, and youth unemployment was about 13 per cent in 1999/2000. The latest annual round of the National Sample Survey Organization (NSSO), based on a smaller sample size, estimates unemployment to be at 9.1 per cent in 2004.[11]

This fall in overall employment growth rates, however, has been mainly in agricultural, mining, electricity and community and social services sector – those that are numerically the larger employers. In manufacturing, employment growth increased during this period from 1.23 per cent in the first period to 2.58 in the second or post-reform period. However, the organized manufacturing sector has had almost no growth in employment during the post-reform period (0.87 per cent). Therefore the bulk of employment increase in manufacturing has been in the informal (or unregistered) manufacturing sector (2.95 per cent). Along with employment, GDP in the informal manufacturing sector also rose at 8.66 per cent. In contrast, GDP in the organized or formal manufacturing sector, which has had almost no employment growth, increased to 7.31 per cent. This implies high productivity gains for workers in the organized manufacturing industry especially.[12]

However, when Kaldor's law is tested for the Indian states for the registered (formal) and non-registered (informal) manufacturing sectors (results reported in Table 23.4) we find a positive and significant relation with the overall manufacturing sector, for the formal manufacturing sector (though for the formal manufacturing sector the coefficient is not significant at the 10 per cent level), as well as for the unregistered manufacturing sector. The Kaldor coefficient for manufacturing on a cross-section of states is 0.6, while that for formal manufacturing is 0.45 and informal manufacturing is 0.75. In fact, the relation between state GDP growth and unregistered manufacturing GDP growth is statistically more robust than that in the registered or formal sector.[13]

On the question of productivity too, its clear from Figures 23.A1–3 (in Appendix) that defined as per worker value addition, productivity in the

Table 23.4   Relationship between state GDP growth and growth in manufacturing sector

	All manufacturing	Formal manufacturing	Informal manufacturing
Constant	0.36 (4.205)	0.45 (6.05)	0.30 (5.62)
Coefficient	0.61 (2.684)	0.45 (1.754)	0.75 (3.92)
R^2	0.32	0.14	0.53
F test	7.204	3.078	15.441
F (Ramsey)	4.36	3.35	5.12
Ho: model has no omitted variables			
No. of observations	14	14	14

Notes: It is assumed that informal manufacturing is the same as unregistered manufacturing. Eqn. used is Growth (State GDP) = $a + b_1$ (Growth sectoral VA) + u_1

Source: Based on data in Government of India, Central Statistical Organisation, National Accounts Statistics.

manufacturing sector as whole has gone up in 2000–01 as compared to 1994–95 in most of the 14 states studied. Disaggregating the manufacturing sector by formal and informal, we find huge productivity gains in the formal manufacturing sector for most states, and positive gains, but relatively less in the informal manufacturing sectors at the state level, barring some exceptions such as the state of Gujarat and Karnataka. These two states have witnessed productivity gains in the informal manufacturing sector and productivity declines in the formal manufacturing sector.[14] In general, huge productivity gains in the formal sector are a mixed blessing as it implies no gain in employment despite the fast growth of manufacturing production. It is therefore fortunate that India has a dynamic informal manufacturing sector which is growing at a relatively fast pace even though its productivity growth, in general, is small or stagnant. This sector does the important job of maintaining an increasing employment while increasing production. The informal manufacturing sector accounts for 83 per cent of total employment in manufacturing. However, in the informal segment of manufacturing, full labour flexibility is the norm and labour protection does not exist. Therefore, while the quantity of employment generated in the informal manufacturing sector is very important, the often poor quality of employment in this segment of the manufacturing sector is a matter of concern.[15] Moreover, there is much heterogeneity in this sector – about 80 per cent of enterprises in informal manufacturing are 'own account enterprises', or enterprises run at the household level, and do not hire any workers (use only family labour), while there are those that hire workers and operate as an extension of the formal sector.

The results in Figures 23.A1–3 imply that growth in the manufacturing sector drives economic growth in the Indian states. However, the informal manufacturing sector, because of its relatively larger size and inefficient activities, needs to grow at fast rate to realize productivity gains that percolate to the workers. Moreover, since the informal manufacturing sector is a major employer, policies need to be devised to tap the dynamism in this sector so that it leads to both growth of employment and growth of productivity. Thus, notwithstanding the virtual jobless growth in formal manufacturing in India in the recent period, the statistically and economically significant relationship that exists between the growth of the manufacturing sector and growth of GDP at the state level for India indicates the importance of growth of formal and informal manufacturing and its linkages with all other sectors of the economy. It is also possible that the jobless growth in manufacturing is a once and for all effect of increased competition in the world markets as a consequence of entry by China, India itself, as well as other countries (Dasgupta and Singh 2005).[16]

Conclusions: premature deindustrialization and industrial policies

This paper has examined the role in developing countries of manufacturing and services using a Kaldorian framework. The results indicate that manufacturing continues to be a critical sector in economic development, but services overall, as well as many individual services, including those connected with ICT, also make a positive contribution in a number of developing countries such as India.[17] Because of a lack of data, we are unable to test separate hypotheses for individual services such as telecommunications, finance, ICT or tourism. Dasgupta and Singh (2005) provided some information on individual service sectors for the Indian economy. They found that apart from ICT-related services (back-office activities and software), many other services including those mentioned above have a faster rate of growth than either manufacturing or GDP. Services also improve the balance of payments.[18] They fulfil requirements of dynamic sectors in the Kaldor sense and could therefore be regarded as an additional engine of growth. In the specific case of India with the kind of primacy the country has achieved in ICT, the new engine might help India leapfrog in technological development to catch up with advanced countries.

We turn now to the question of premature deindustrialization in many countries in developing world. Although the fall in the share of manufacturing in total employment is occurring at a much lower level of per capita income than in the case of today's developed countries, the important point to note is that this is not necessarily a pathological phenomenon. In some developing countries it may be so, but in others it could be benign or advantageous. The question is both a conceptual and empirical one.

In a seminal contribution, Cairncross (1979) suggested that the best conceptualization of deindustrialization is what he called the 'Cambridge View', which he identified with that of Singh (1977). This argued that deindustrialization represents a pathological state when it stops the economy from being able to achieve its full potential of growth, employment and resource utilization. The Cambridge analysis had been developed in relationship to the weaknesses of British manufacturing in the 1970s and 1980s, but it has current application to the advanced developing world. There are two ideal types of deindustrialization that are occurring in the developing world. First there is the Indian kind, where manufacturing employment is not expanding in the formal sector but is growing at a respectably fast rate in the large informal sector. It is notable that manufacturing's share in Indian employment, including both the informal and formal sector, has not declined. Further, there has been a large expansion of manufacturing products, including those in the formal sector.

The second ideal type, which more likely suggests pathological deindustrialization, has occurred in several Latin American and African countries in the 1980s and 1990s. As a result of Washington Consensus policies of international financial institutions (IFIs), which Latin American as well as many African countries were obliged to follow in response to the debt crisis, there has indeed been considerable structural change in these countries. But Ocampo (2005a; b) and Shafaeddin (2005) have persuasively argued that this change has been of the wrong kind. Countries have begun to specialize according to their current comparative advantage instead of their long-term dynamic comparative advantage.

Furthermore, these economies have become more vulnerable to external economic shocks. UNCTAD's studies indicate that Latin American economies have now become balance of payments constrained at a much lower growth rate than before. As a consequence, the main Latin American countries are still not reverting to their long-term trend rate of growth under import-substitution industrialization which they experienced from 1950–80. Latin American deindustrialization exhibits all the signs of industrial failure, and the ability to develop modern services.

In conclusion, it must be reiterated that at the level of per capita incomes prevailing in the low- and middle-income developing countries, the income elasticity of demand for manufactures will continue to be very high. This suggests that countries such as India should use ICT to modernize other services as well as manufacturing, whose role must remain critical for a long time to come.[19] The experiences of the second category of countries during the last two decades raise in an acute form the question of industrial policy. These countries virtually abandoned industrial policies under the Washington Consensus. As suggested above, deindustrialization in these countries has all the hallmarks of being of a pathological kind since the long-term prospects for creating a modern manufacturing or service sector have worsened. These countries need to re-evaluate their approach to industrial policies. Instead of laissez faire and regarding industrial policies as a relic of the past, many of these countries need to adopt more creative and energetic but different industrial policies than they had done before. They also need to establish new institutions to support these policies.[20]

It is interesting in this overall context to note that institutional renewal of industrial policies in East Asia is far along the way with the focus being on government support of science and technology to knowledge-based industries and services. East Asia's mature high-tech industries and advanced services have benefited from a reformed type of industrial policy. Legal under the WTO, subsidies to high-tech businesses and services have taken the form of support to science and technology. The first-category countries, despite the benign character of their deindustrialization, should therefore continue with their industrial policies and adapt them to correspond to the changed economic circumstances. East Asia still provides an extremely useful role model for these countries.

Appendix

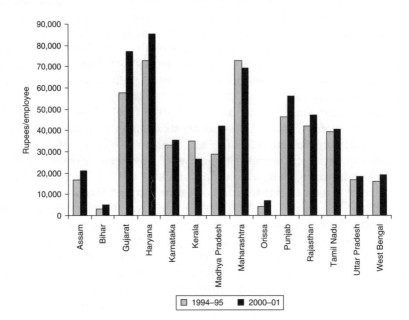

Figure 23.A1   Total manufacturing productivity

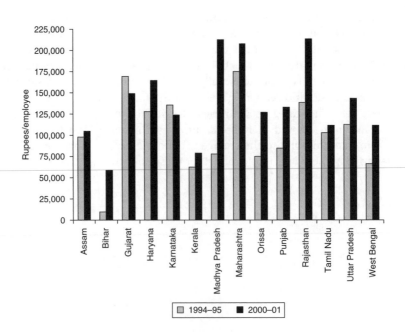

Figure 23.A2   Organized manufacturing productivity

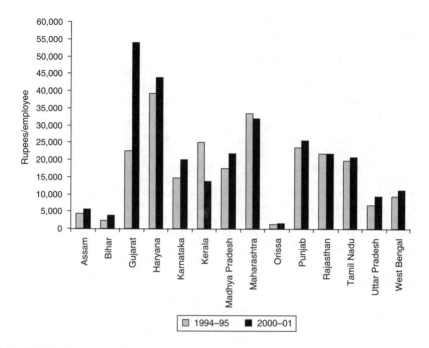

Figure 23.A3   Unorganized manufacturing productivity

Notes

The authors are extremely grateful to Alice Amsden for most helpful discussions on conceptual issues. The authors are also grateful to Kishore Dhavala and Rit Chandra for statistical assistance and to two anonymous referees for their comments. The views expressed here are those of the authors alone and should not be subscribed to the institutions they represent. The usual caveats apply.

1. For rich countries, the case for the primacy of manufacturing is best presented in Kaldor (1966); that for developing countries is put forward in Kaldor (1967).
2. Simon Kuznets derived generalizations concerning the structural changes that occurred in today's advanced countries during their process of industrialization. These generalizations were subsequently broadly confirmed in the more comprehensive analysis of Chenery *et al.* (1986) that contained data on both industrialized and industrializing countries.
3. Alternatively, the service sector embodying new technologies may be regarded as a means of technological leapfrogging for a developing country to catch up with advanced economies.
4. This is in striking contrast to the recent proposal by French President Chirac that the value added tax on restaurant meals should be reduced in order to encourage employment in the catering industry.
5. See, for example, Rowthorn and Ramaswamy (1999) and Thirlwall (2002).
6. The exceptions were Sri Lanka, 1970–80; the Philippines for each of the last two decades.
7. The countries are: Algeria, Argentina, Bangladesh, Barbados, Belize, Bolivia, Botswana, Brazil, Burkina Faso, Chile, China, Colombia, Costa Rica, Dominican Republic, Ecuador, Egypt, El Salvador, Ghana, Grenada, Guatemala, Honduras, India, Indonesia,

Jamaica, Kenya, Korea, Malaysia, Mauritius, Mexico, Namibia, Nepal, Nicaragua, Pakistan, Pananma, Paraguay, Peru, Philippines, Saint Lucia, Singapore, Sri Lanka, Suriname, Thailand, Trinidad and Tobago, Uruguay, Venezuela, Vietnam, Zambia. The number of countries studied in this section is limited to 48 because of data constraints, especially data on sectoral employment, for this period, which is required for the productivity analysis in the next section. Data on GDP is taken from World Bank (2004) *World Development Indicators*, and data on employment is taken from ILO (2004) *Key Indicators for the Labour Market*.

8. As noted in Dasgupta and Singh (2005) and Thirlwall (2002) Kaldor's propositions are empirically best examined in relation to cross-sectional data rather than in terms of time series or normal panel data analysis. The reason for this is that one needs to abstract from cyclical movements to arrive at the long-term relationship between the variables. The cyclical relationships between output employment growth and productivity growth are studied under Okun's law (1962: 98–104). It is important that the methodology used to examine Kaldor's laws should not conflate Okun's law with Kaldor's. A referee has rightly pointed out that a panel data analysis could have been done using ten-year averages of data so as to skirt the problem of cyclical changes. Further work could carry this suggestion forward. A fuller analysis would need to go beyond the panel data methodology as there are good reasons to believe that the hypothesis of slope coefficients being the same in different countries in unlikely to be true as has been emphasized in Pesaran and Smith (1995).

9. A reviewer has raised the point about why the obvious interpretation of the results in terms of the higher value of β-coefficient indicates a greater effect of the independent variable on the dependent variable. The reason for this apparently paradoxical conclusion is the causal model used by Kaldor where he regards manufacturing growth as causing, or, being essential to GDP growth. So the lower the value of the coefficient, the greater has to be the difference between GDP growth and manufacturing growth in order to achieve the same percentage increase in GDP growth.

10. Rowthorn and Ramaswamy (1999) use similar independent variables in a study of developed countries.

11. All figures calculated from the NSSO surveys 1987/88, 1993/94 and 1999/2000. The unemployment rate here is measured as 'current daily status'. For limitations of the reported unemployment rates in developing economies see Singh (2000). Data on employment and value added on registered manufacturing is from *Annual Survey of Industries*, and that on unregistered manufacturing from the NSSO Enterprise surveys.

12. Figures from Government of India (2002: 135).

13. The 14 states are Assam, Bihar, Gujarat, Haryana, Karnataka, Kerala, Madhya Pradesh, Maharashtra, Orissa, Punjab, Rajasthan, Tamil Nadu, Uttar Pradesh and West Bengal. Data for the formal sector has been taken from the *Annual Survey of Industries* and for the informal or unregistered manufacturing sector from the NSSO Enterprise surveys in 1994/95 and 2000/01.

14. Gujarat, which shows high productivity gains in the informal sector, witnessed job losses in the informal sector, whereas Karnataka witnessed moderate employment increases in the informal manufacturing sector along with productivity increases.

15. The NSSO data only gives numbers of workers, and does not distinguish between part time, full-time or contract workers.

16. The stagnant employment growth in the formal manufacturing sector has been attributed to rigid labour laws in India by some commentators. An alternative hypothesis is that these labour laws are ineffective except in the public sector and hence there have been significant job losses in sections of the formal manufacturing sector over the last few years in India. This is a controversial subject, which requires deeper analysis.

17. For other modern services that also are important as dynamic activities in the Kaldorian sense, see Dasgupta and Singh (2005). For Taiwan, see Amsden and Chu (2003).

18. In the Indian case, exports of software amount to 20 per cent of total Indian exports and expect to rise to 30 per cent in the next few years.
19. For a full analysis of these issues see Dasgupta and Singh (2005).
20. For fuller analysis of these issues see Singh (2005).

References

Amsden, A.H. and W. Chu (2003) *Beyond Late Development: Upgrading Policies*, Cambridge, MA: MIT Press.

Arrow, K.J. (1962) 'The Economic Implications of Learning By Doing', *Review of Economic Studies*, 29, 3: 155–73.

Cairncross, A. (1979) 'What is Deindustrialization?', in F. Blackaby (ed.), *Deindustrialization*, Oxford: Heinemann.

Chenery, H., S. Robinson and M. Syrquin (1986) *Industrialization and Growth: A Comparative Study*, New York: Oxford University Press.

Cripps, T.F. and J. Tarling (1973) *Growth in Advanced Capitalist Economies 1950–1970*, Cambridge: Cambridge University Press.

Dasgupta, S. and A. Singh (2005) 'Will Services Be the New Engine of Indian Economic Growth?', *Development and Change*, 36, 6: 1035–58.

Government of India (2002) *Report of the Special Group on Targeting Ten Million Employment Opportunities per Year*, New Delhi: Planning Commission.

Howes, C. and A. Singh (2000) *Competitiveness Matters: Industry and Economic Performance in the US*, Ann Arbor: University of Michigan Press.

ILO (2004) *Key Indicators for the Labour Market*, Geneva: ILO.

Kaldor, N. (1966) *Causes of the Slow Rate of Economic Growth of the United Kingdom*, Cambridge: Cambridge University Press.

Kaldor, N. (1967) *Strategic Factors in Economic Development*, Ithaca, NY: New York State School of Industrial and Labour Relations, Cornell University.

Kuznets, S. (1996) *Modern Economic Growth: Rate, Structure and Spread*, New Haven, CT: Yale University Press.

Matthews, R. and A. Bowen (1988) 'Keynsian and Other Explanations of Post-War Macroeconomic Trends', in W. Eltis and P. Sinclair (eds), *Keynes and Economic Policy: The Relevance of the General Theory After Fifty Years*, London: Macmillan.

Ocampo, J.A. (ed.) (2005a) *Beyond Reforms*, Palo Alto, CA: Stanford University Press.

Ocampo, J.A. (2005b) 'Latin America's Growth and Equity Frustrations During Structural Reforms', *Journal of Economic Perspectives*, 18, 2: 67–88.

Okun, A.M. (1962) 'Potential GNP: Its Measurement and Significance', *Proceedings of the Business and Economics Section*, Washington DC: American Statistical Association.

Palma, J.G. (2005) 'Four Sources of Deindustrialization and a New Concept of the Dutch Disease', in J. Ocampo (ed.), *Beyond Reforms*, Palo Alto, CA: Stanford University Press.

Pesaran, M.H. and R.P. Smith (1995) 'Estimating the Long-Run Relationships from Dynamic Heterogenous Panels', *Journal of Econometrics*, 68: 79–113.

Pieper, U. (2003) 'Sectoral Regularities of Productivity Growth in Developing Countries: A Kaldorian Interpretation', *Cambridge Journal of Economics*, 27: 831–50.

Rowthorn, R. and K. Coutts (2004) 'Deindustrialization and the Balance of Payments in Advanced Economies', *Cambridge Journal of Economics*, 28, 5: 767–90.

Rowthorn, R. and R. Ramaswamy (1999) 'Growth, Trade and Deindustrialization', *IMF Staff Papers*, 46, 1: 18–41, Washington, DC: IMF.

Shafaeddin, S.M. (2005) 'Trade Liberalization and Economic Reform in Developing Countries: Structural Change or Deindustrialization?', *UNCTAD Discussion Papers* 179, Geneva: UNCTAD.

Singh, A. (1977) 'UK Industry and the World Economy: A Case of De-industrialization?', *Cambridge Journal of Economics*, 1, 2: 113–36.

Singh, A. (2000). 'Global Economic Trends and Social Development', *UNRISD Occasional Papers* 9, Geneva: UNRISD.

Singh, A. (2005). 'The Past, Present and Future of Industrial Policy in India: Adapting to Changing Domestic and International Environment', paper presented at the New Delhi Industrial Policy Meeting, December.

Thirlwall, A.P. (2002) *The Nature of Economic Growth: An Alternative Framework for Understanding the Performance of Nations*, Cheltenham: Edward Elgar.

World Bank (2004) *World Development Indicators*, Washington, DC: Oxford University Press for the World Bank.

Young, A. (1928) 'Increasing Returns and Economic Progress', *Economic Journal*, 38, 152: 527–42.

Part VII
Development Strategies

24
Why Have All Development Strategies Failed in Latin America?

Guillermo Rozenwurcel

Introduction

The relevance of economic growth for social welfare cannot be underestimated. Even if the starting point is not rather different, as was the case for most economies before the industrial revolution, small differences in growth rates will generate in the long run quite divergent outcomes. Indeed, it is a fact that country differences in per capita incomes have been growing through time. Likewise, the gap between rich countries and the ones that remain poor has deepened.

Economic growth depends on capital accumulation, both physical and human, as well as on the evolution of total factor productivity (TFP). Several economic variables, such as present and expected profits, interest rates, investment risks, R&D and entrepreneurship, among others, do affect capital accumulation and TFP. However, social equity, including a fair income distribution, and the working of the institutional framework have been increasingly acknowledged as key determinants of economic growth, not only because they affect the non-idiosyncratic risks of investment, but also because they can promote or discourage entrepreneurship, innovation and technological progress.

The dismal long-run performance of Latin American (LATAM) economies since the end of the Second World War (despite differences in initial conditions and other country specificities) brings, nevertheless, an excellent opportunity to try to understand why economic growth and development can be so elusive. Consequently, the main purpose of the chapter is to establish the stylized facts of economic development in Latin America in the post-war time and to identify a few common factors underlying the rather poor outcomes achieved, no matter how different the development strategies implemented throughout this period were. To do so, the chapter is organized into four sections. The first briefly discusses the long-run economic performance of the region since the Great Depression from a comparative perspective. The second presents the stylized facts of the import substitution industrialization (ISI) period, trying to identify the main reasons of its failure. The third section does the same with the more recent period of market-friendly reforms. Finally, the last section concludes with some general remarks and a few comments on where LATAM countries stand now.

Different strategies, common weaknesses

There is little doubt that the long-run economic performance of LATAM countries in the past 70 years or so, especially in comparative terms, has been rather disappointing. While different countries experienced more or less extended periods of improving economic conditions and rapid expansion at different times, sustained growth proved unattainable for the region as a whole. Not only were LATAM countries ineffective in closing the income gap with the developed world (as a matter of fact the gap widened), they were also left far behind by several developing counties belonging to other regions of the world, which showed similar or even worse initial conditions than the ones prevailing in Latin America. In particular, the contrast with the 'Asian Tigers' is remarkably striking.[1] As illustrated in Figure 24.1, at the beginning of the 1960s the Tigers had on average a much lower per capita income than most LATAM countries. Nowadays, however, they show much better outcomes not only on per capita GDP, but also on income distribution and poverty indicators.

After the Great Depression in the early part of twentieth century and throughout the rest of the century, LATAM countries basically approached economic development following two successive and quite opposed strategies. The first approach was import substitution industrialization. While it initially appeared as a defensive response to the world crisis that put an end to the gold standard regime and reduced multilateral trade to minimum levels, industrialization based on import substitution and an interventionist state became a fully fledged strategy after the Second World War. The debt crisis of the early 1980s made the inherent

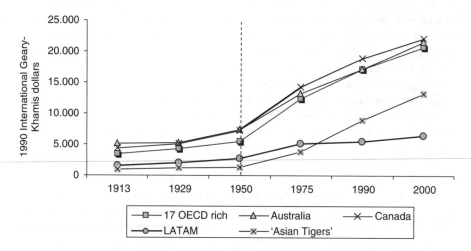

Figure 24.1   Per capita GDP (1913–2000)

Note: 17 OECD rich: Austria, Belgium, Denmark, Finland, France, Germany, Ireland, Italy, Japan, Netherlands, New Zealand, Norway, Spain, Sweden, Switzerland, United Kingdom and United States. LATAM: Argentina, Brazil, Chile, Colombia, Mexico, Peru, Uruguay and Venezuela. Asian Tigers: South Korea, Taiwan, Hong Kong, Singapore, Malaysia, Thailand and Indonesia.

Source: Based on Maddison (2003).

shortcomings of the LATAM version of the ISI strategy quite evident. As a result, in the second half of the decade an alternative approach gradually emerged. Its advocates stressed that this new approach, unlike the previous one, was market friendly and consistent with the ongoing process of globalization experienced by the world economy. Because of the support of the USA, the only remaining superpower after the fall of the Berlin Wall, as well as the international financial institutions (IFIs) based in Washington, DC, the market-friendly approach became known as the 'Washington Consensus'. In spite of the fact that the two approaches were founded on quite opposite premises, neither the ISI nor the Washington Consensus managed to deliver sustained economic development to LATAM countries.

After the Second World War, the Asian Tigers also adopted ISI led by an interventionist state, but from the mid-1960s or so they managed to gradually shift towards an outward-oriented development strategy based on fast export growth and a rather adequate balance between market forces and state intervention. This was made possible by a combination of factors. First, political stability, which enabled the adoption of sound macroeconomic policies, including fiscal discipline, and kept inflation rates at low levels. Second, a state strong enough to put into place not only effective incentives, including a competitive exchange rate and export promoting policies, but also heavy penalties on private firms when targets were not fulfilled. Third, a high domestic savings rate that helped sustain a significant investment effort without inducing external vulnerabilities. Needless to say, all such factors have been so far completely absent in Latin America. Moreover, the Asian Tigers combined fast growth with improving income distribution. Land reform and public investment in human capital, missing or weak in Latin America, played an important role in this regard.

The Chilean experience of the last 20 years is, to some extent, the regional exception that confirms the rule. In this period the country attained fast growth and was able to reduce poverty significantly (Figure 24.2). However, the high level

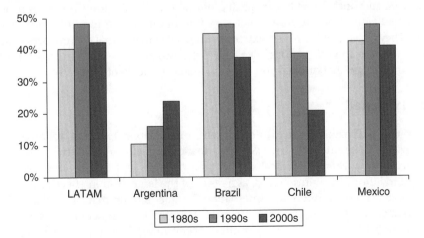

Figure 24.2 Population below the poverty line
Source: Based on ECLAC database on social indicators.

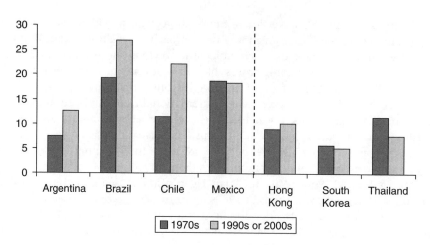

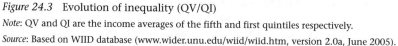

Figure 24.3   Evolution of inequality (QV/QI)

Note: QV and QI are the income averages of the fifth and first quintiles respectively.

Source: Based on WIID database (www.wider.unu.edu/wiid/wiid.htm, version 2.0a, June 2005).

of social inequality still needs to be sharply reduced and its productive structure has yet to overcome several weaknesses for Chile to join the club of countries undergoing sustained socioeconomic development (Figure 24.3).

In my view, two common factors are crucial to understand the successive failure of both the ISI and Washington Consensus approaches, despite their contrasts. On the one hand, the failure of the state to fulfil its role; indeed, governments were unable to deliver the required public policies and institutions, no matter how different they were under each of the two strategies. On the other hand, excessive protectionism under ISI and unrestrained liberalization during the Washington Consensus period prevented Latin America from achieving a fruitful integration into the world economy. They also made the region extremely vulnerable to external disturbances which were common to both periods, albeit for different reasons – terms of trade shocks until the late 1970s, both real and (mainly) financial shocks afterwards.

The ISI period

With the outbreak of the worldwide economic depression that followed the collapse in share prices on the USA stock market in October 1929, the world economic context changed radically. The sharp decline in USA economic activity spread to European countries and, as a result of the large drop in effective demand in the advanced economies, international trade fell dramatically, decreasing approximately 30 per cent during 1929–32. Meanwhile, many countries sought to ease their balance of payments difficulties by devaluing their respective currencies, thus undermining the gold standard. This, in turn, accentuated the decline in trade flows and triggered similar protectionist reactions in other countries. The approach of Latin American countries regarding their integration into the world economy was modified by this new scenario. The 'comparative advantages' paradigm, based on the exchange of raw materials for manufactured products, was no longer useful for peripheral countries. In the same way, the decline in the terms of trade imposed several problems in the external accounts of the balance of payments. The natural response of LATAM countries was to elevate import tariffs and to impose exchange controls in order to restore the equilibrium in the external accounts.

The new protectionist policies provided domestic industrial sectors with an opportunity for expansion. Nevertheless, this was not the result of a deliberate strategy aimed at fostering the countries' industrial development. Rather, it was basically the outcome of a defensive reaction adopted by governments in light of the new global economic scenario. Moreover, the outbreak of the Second World War in the late 1930s, with the natural protection it provided, implied an extra push to incipient industrialization. Nonetheless, after the end of the war import substitution industrialization was adopted as a deliberate policy option by many governments, not only in LATAM countries but also in East and Southeast Asia. During the early stages of the ISI strategy in Latin America, import substitution made fast progress in the so-called light industries, manufacturing consumer goods. In fact, their share in total imports declined sharply. However, the 'easy' phase of the ISI, far from substituting domestic production for aggregate imports, tended to replace imports of consumer goods with those of inputs and capital goods necessary to sustain the process of industrialization (Hirschman 1973). On the other hand, availability of the foreign exchange required to pay for these vital imports remained highly dependent on primary exports and, therefore, subject to the extreme volatility of the international prices of commodities. The outcome of this strategy was rather closed economies in which firms focused almost exclusively on protected domestic markets. In Figure 24.4 we can see the trade ratios of

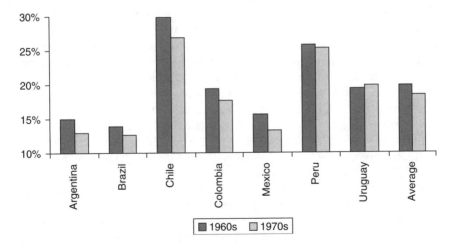

Figure 24.4   Trade openness (exports + imports/GDP)

Source: Based on ECLAC database.

LATAM countries for the 1960s and 1970s, when the ISI strategy was consolidated: they were not only low but, in most cases, showed a declining trend. Even Chile, the country with the highest ratio in the sample (around 30 per cent of GDP), was quite closed in international terms.

In many countries the adoption of the ISI strategy was the result of the hegemonic position of the military which, on repeated occasions, even ruled the countries for prolonged periods. In fact, the ideology prevailing in the region's armed forces considered industrialization as a necessary step towards 'economic independence' and national autonomy. An active role of the state was also thought crucial to further stimulate this process, particularly regarding the production of war material. As industrialization went on, however, it became more and more reliant on imports of intermediate inputs and capital goods. In a context of stagnant exports the natural consequence was recurrent balance of payments crises that imposed a stop-and-go pattern to the economic performance of LATAM countries. Import dependence and the stop-and-go nature of the business cycle became more evident in the larger economies of the region, where industrialization reached the so-called heavy industries. In these sectors, moreover, the optimal minimum scales of industrial plants are usually bigger and the costs of inefficiencies arising from operating below such levels are more severe. Although industrialization in the Asian Tigers was also initially based on import substitution, in the late 1960s and early 1970s its path started to diverge from the one followed by LATAM countries. Basically, the fact that the Tigers were not able to generate enough foreign currency through their exports of primary goods, as was the case of most LATAM economies, forced them to adopt export-oriented industrialization strategies (Oman and Wignaraja 1991).

Nevertheless, this change did not imply a weakening in the role played by the state in the allocation of resources. Basically, domestic markets remained protected and financing continued to be heavily subsidised. The main difference with LATAM countries was the capacity of the government to discipline domestic industries by means of export targets, government supervision and credible time limits to protectionist policies, in order to make their production more efficient and competitive in foreign markets.[2] In addition to this, the macroeconomic context was substantially different in both regions. Although state economic interventionism was a common feature of both experiences, in the case of the Asian Tigers this was combined with sound macroeconomic policies that resulted in robust public finances, low levels of inflation and less volatility. The combination of an adequate mix of policy incentives ('sticks and carrots') and a stable macro environment was key in order to provide the private firms the right business climate required for allocating their resources in productive activities and planning longer-term investments projects.

That was not the case in LATAM countries. Despite extreme protectionism and significant subsidies (both in terms of export drawbacks and financing with negative real interest rates), the industrial sector never became a mature and internationally competitive sector. A closed economic environment, the politically biased management of state-owned enterprises (SOEs) and the pervasiveness of unfair regulations favouring the interests of small but powerful groups, led to a context where rent-seeking behaviour tended to prevail over entrepreneurship (Krueger 1990). Moreover, political populism was the main resort by which governments in the region attempted to manage social conflicts and income distribution. Rent seeking and political populism caused the public sector to display chronic fiscal deficits which were basically financed by printing money. As a result, since the mid-1960s LATAM countries performed much worse than the Asian Tigers both in terms of inflation (Figure 24.5) and long-run economic growth (Figure 24.6).

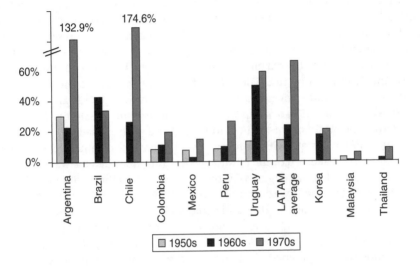

Figure 24.5   Average annual inflation rates
Source: Based on IMF statistics.

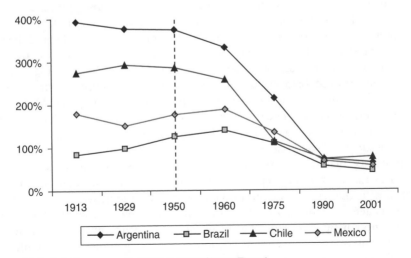

Figure 24.6   Relative per capita GDP (LATAM/Asian Tigers)
Source: Based on Maddison (2003).

The contrasting economic performance of Latin America and East Asia suggests that the ISI failure in most of Latin America has less to do with its alleged inherent weaknesses than with its inadequate implementation (Rodrik 2003). True enough, Latin America as a whole did grow faster between 1930 and 1975 than in any previous or subsequent period of its history. Furthermore, industrial exports began to expand in the mid-1960s in some of the largest LATAM economies.[3] Mexico and Brazil, in particular, did quite well throughout the period.[4] Moreover, in most countries economic growth was accompanied by significant progress on income distribution. These improvements, however, were almost exclusively based on direct subsidies, tax deductions and subsidized credit at negative real interest rates, mainly financed with the surpluses of the pay-as-you-go pension systems and the inflation tax. In sum, the ISI model implemented in LATAM countries proved unsustainable in the long run. Their limitations became more severe throughout the 1970s, as fiscal imbalances increased, inflation rates accelerated and economic activity tended to deteriorate *pari passu* with the worsening of external conditions arising from the oil shocks at the beginning and end of the decade.

External difficulties notwithstanding, two domestic elements are crucial to understand the breakdown of the ISI strategy in Latin America. One was the failure of the state to work as an engine of growth. The large inefficiencies of SOEs and the government's inability to appropriately combine the subsidies granted to private firms with suitable controls and penalties in case of their improper use, not only induced chronic fiscal deficits and short-run macro instability, but undermined overall productivity and long-run growth as well. Populist redistributive policies, moreover, heightened fiscal imbalances while, at the same time, impinged on the returns of the most productive economic sectors.

The second factor was the extremely inward orientation of industrialization induced by extended and protracted protectionism, which prevented LATAM economies from taking advantage of foreign markets as a disciplining device to gradually enhance the competitiveness of domestic firms. The indefinite postponement of the economy's opening to foreign competition kept domestic markets mostly in the hands of oligopolistic firms with fewer incentives to enhance productivity than to preserve their market shares by resorting to rent-seeking practices. Moreover, protectionist policies crystallized a structure of relative prices with a strong anti-export bias, particularly harming tradable sectors.

As the failure of the ISI strategy became more evident, there was a change in the conventional wisdom about what the developing countries should do in order to reach sustainable development. Nevertheless, the easy availability of financing in international markets, mainly as a consequence of the surpluses in OPEC countries, made it possible to postpone the inevitable economic adjustments.

At last, in the late 1970s, several LATAM countries launched programmes of economic reforms tending to reduce inflation, overcome external constraints and resume growth by increasing the openness of the economy and reducing the involvement of the state in the economy. The programmes implemented in Argentina, Chile and Uruguay were the more ambitious: they combined drastic trade and financial liberalization with severe cuts in public expenditures and a preannounced schedule of nominal exchange rate devaluation to curb price volatility. Inertial inflation arising from formal and informal practices of price indexation, however, resulted in the overvaluation of domestic currencies, large trade imbalances, an upsurge in foreign debt (both public and private) and, particularly in the case of Argentina, huge fiscal imbalances. The so-called Southern Cone liberalization attempts ended abruptly in the early 1980s, in the midst of simultaneous exchange rate and banking crises.

The rise in international interest rates as a consequence of the tightening in the monetary policy adopted by Paul Volcker, Chairman of the Federal Reserve, in the early 1980s, forced Mexico, where a somewhat similar process of liberalization-cum-real exchange rate appreciation had also been in place, to default on its external debt. Mexico's decision accentuated the already ongoing crisis in Argentina and triggered those in Uruguay and Chile. But it also deteriorated the external stance of the rest of LATAM countries, substantially increasing their foreign debt burden. The new international context of credit rationing and the subsequent attempts at closing the external and fiscal gaps particularly hit public and private investment, severely undermining the growth prospects across Latin America. The 1980s became known as the 'lost decade' for the region as a whole. Throughout that period per capita GDP decreased in all countries, with the only exception of Chile and Colombia.

The neoliberal view, then, already prevailing attributed the failure of the liberalization attempts of the late 1970s to the incomplete nature of their reforms. Therefore, under the increasing influence of this view on the region's elites and policy-makers, a second and broader wave of market-friendly structural reforms began to take shape in the late 1980s. The leverage achieved by the IFIs in LATAM countries as a result of their lending support and, consequently, their growing influence over their economic policies, also contributed to the dawning of this second wave. According to their advocates, the (relative) success of the Chilean experience, allegedly based on fully orthodox economic policies, was the example to be followed by the rest of Latin America. In the early 1990s, when the region regained access to international financial markets, the second round of market-friendly reforms, fuelled by large capital inflows, became unstoppable.

The Washington Consensus period

In the 30 years or so that spanned from the crumbling of the ISI strategy to the present, Latin American's economic decline dramatically intensified. Economic performance was among the worst in the world, exhibiting amazingly high macroeconomic volatility, recurrent and deep disruptions and a dismal record in terms of long-run growth (Figure 24.7) and income distribution. As was already mentioned, a first attempt at replacing the already useless ISI model by a market-based development strategy took place in the late 1970s and early 1980s. Twin fiscal imbalances in the public accounts and the balance of payments, an unsustainable growth in domestic and foreign indebtedness (both public and private) and the increasing fragility of domestic banking systems throughout the region were

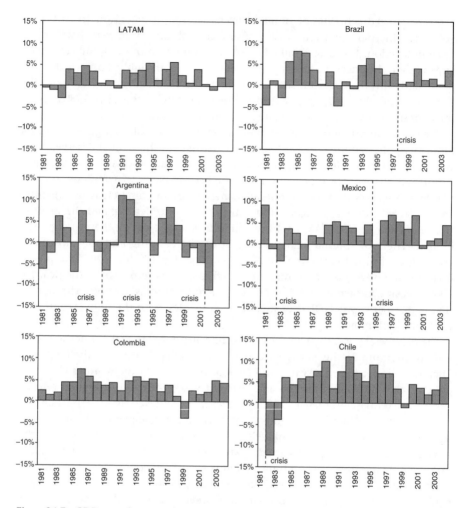

Figure 24.7   GDP growth
Sources: ECLAC and IMF statistics.

the main outcomes of this early attempt. The 1982 Mexican default and the ensuing debt crisis put an end to this process when voluntary financing to the region virtually disappeared. Most LATAM countries spent the 'lost decade' squeezing domestic absorption to transfer real resources abroad, while a feasible solution to the debt crisis was recurrently postponed.

The mainstream view among scholars and policy-makers blamed the half-hearted and incomplete nature of the reforms undertaken during the liberalization process of the late 1970s for its failure. The proper answer to the breakdown of the first attempt was therefore a second and broader wave of market-friendly structural reforms. This second round began to take shape in the late 1980s under the umbrella of the debt relief provided by the Brady Plan and gained momentum when the region recovered access to international financial markets in the early 1990s. Because of the support of the US government, as well as the Washington DC IFIs, the blueprint of the reform process became known as the Washington Consensus (Williamson 1990). The list of recommendations contained in the Washington Consensus blueprint was this time far more ambitious than the one that had guided the 1970s reforms. Outright trade and financial liberalization were once again at the core of the strategy. This time, however, widespread market deregulation and the privatization of SOEs made also part of the strategy. Moreover, to prevent financial liberalization from generating undesired volatility, the domestic banking system was to be strengthened by the adoption of stricter prudential regulations and, when possible, the lifting of barriers to foreign bank participation. To be sure, the scope and progress of the reform process varied from country to country depending on their initial economic conditions and other traits of their institutional and social environment, but the Washington Consensus ideas strongly influenced economic policies and performance throughout the region.

A stable macroeconomic environment was vital to carry out the proposed reforms. Therefore, fiscal discipline and sound money were two basic tenets of the Washington Consensus agenda. In this regard, the change in the institutional framework of monetary policy was seen as a major move in order to keep at bay political pressures, enlarge central bank autonomy and deprive politicians and bureaucrats from the conventional mechanism of printing money. The underlying idea was simple: if the government was denied access to central bank credit, it would then be forced to balance the budget by streamlining public expenditures and/or reforming the tax system and improving tax collection. The transitory funding required during the completion of fiscal reforms was to be provided by the privatization of loss-making public enterprises. In the same vein, the partial or full privatization of the pension system was aimed at consolidating the intertemporal solvency of the public sector.

In most cases, however, the idea did not work well. In practice, political populism was not that easy to eradicate. Politicians and public bureaucrats managed to substitute foreign indebtedness for central bank funding. Easy access to international financial markets allowed many governments in the region to circumvent fiscal discipline. For several countries the cost was the growth of unsustainable public indebtedness (Figure 24.8). As already mentioned, trade liberalization was one of the crucial pillars of the 1990s reform. Its main goals were to increase efficiency in resource allocation, eliminating the anti-export bias present in import tariffs, and to help fight inflation by imposing market discipline on domestic firms that had behaved as price-makers in rather imperfectly competitive environments for decades.

With only a few exceptions (Chile, Colombia), however, Latin American trade liberalization was not only fast and deep, but it was simultaneous to financial liberalization and exchange rate-based stabilization policies. In the context of pegged or quasi-pegged exchange rate regimes, massive foreign capital inflows strongly biased relative prices and profitability against tradable sectors and in favour of non-tradable goods and services.[5] Price increases in public utilities that came along

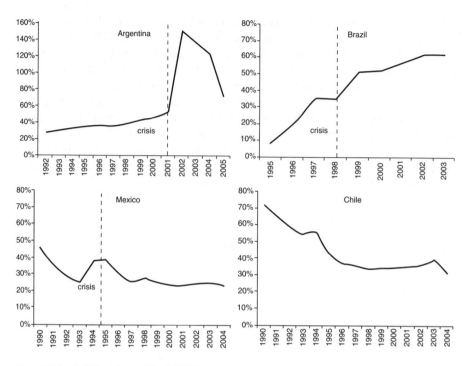

Figure 24.8   Public debt (as % of GDP)

with privatizations also worked in the same way. As a result of the peculiar combination of simultaneous trade and financial liberalization with overvalued real exchange rates, most Latin American countries experienced a significant deterioration in their trade balances and large deficits in their current accounts (Figures 24.9 and 24.10). The progressive rise in interest payments and dividend remittances tended to accentuate those deficits. Foreign direct investments, attracted by privatizations and some other business opportunities, covered part of the current imbalances, but the main bulk of the deficit had to be financed by public and private external indebtedness (Figure 24.10).

To be fair, the market-friendly strategy was initially successful in bringing down inflation. In several countries it also attracted significant flows of foreign direct investment (although privatizations were by far the main driver) and encouraged a more dynamic and diversified export performance. Basic infrastructure and the provision of public services did improve as well (Ocampo 2004). Nevertheless, without any kind of compensating policies to assist economic sectors in distress, the structural transformation that took place in LATAM economies had critical consequences on employment, income distribution and social welfare. Moreover, given the increasing external vulnerability and financial fragility of the region, when growing distress in international financial markets triggered sudden stops in capital inflows, they caused severe financial and currency crises in most Latin American countries, interrupting economic expansion abruptly and forcing

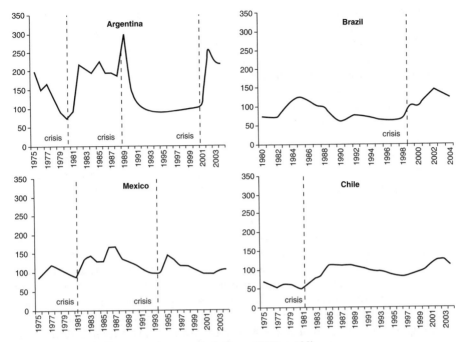

Figure 24.9 Real effective exchange rate (average 2000 = 100)

Source: Author's elaboration based on IMF statistics.

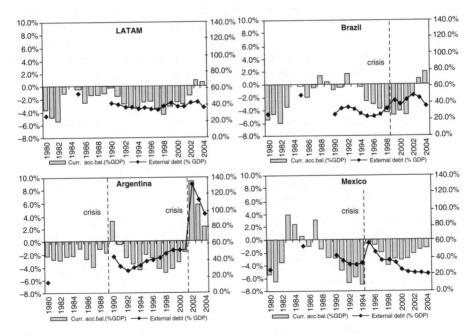

Figure 24.10 Current account balance and external debt (as % of GDP)

Sources: Author's elaboration based on ECLAC and IMF statistics.

several governments to renegotiate or even default their foreign financial obligations (Calvo 1998). Mexico (1994–95), Argentina (1995), Brazil (1998–99) and again Argentina (2001–02) probably experienced the largest crises, but only a few countries remained unaffected by this trend. As mentioned by Frenkel (2003), some common factors can be found in all the crises:

- pegged or quasi-pegged exchange rates regimes;
- overvalued real exchange rates;
- unrestrained capital movements;
- large capital inflows during economic expansions, both as a proportion of monetary aggregates and relative to the size of domestic financial markets; and
- weak supervision and inadequate regulations in the banking system.

In the appalling context of the Latin American economic performance of the last decades, Chile stands out as a remarkable exception. After the failure of its first liberalization attempt in the late 1970s, its economic achievements over the last 20 years, both in terms of growth and poverty reduction, were presented by the supporters of the Washington Consensus approach as evidence of the success of the market-friendly development strategy when properly implemented. In fact, however, the attempt to portray the Chilean experience as a success of the Washington Consensus approach is, to say the least, an oversimplification. To be sure, in line with Washington Consensus recommendations, Chile dramatically improved its fiscal and monetary stance. Also, it widely opened its economy to trade and extensively deregulated its real and financial domestic markets. Moreover, its privatization programme was one of the most ambitious in the developing world.

However, and despite its rhetoric, the Chilean economic policy complemented its orthodox approach with several measures that were not included in the Consensus blueprint. In particular, the country never privatized CODELCO, the public copper enterprise, a major source of foreign exchange and public revenues. It also combined its unilateral reduction of import tariffs with an active policy of export incentives and a successful strategy of bilateral trade negotiations aimed at diversifying its foreign markets. The other distinctive element of the Chilean economic policy since the late 1970 and until very recently was its clear commitment with the maintenance of a competitive real exchange rate. This goal was accomplished by adopting a crawling peg regime complemented, when necessary, with capital controls to discourage short-term inflows. It was only a few years ago that Chile decided to lift capital controls and switch to a flexible exchange rate regime. To conclude this brief comment on the Chilean case, it is worth stressing that, in sharp contrast with most of the LATAM countries, a strong institutional framework and an efficient public administration provided a strong backing to the effectiveness of economic policy.

Summing up, as happened during the ISI period, the two common elements that seriously undermined the overall outcome of the Washington Consensus experience were: (1) the failure of the state to play its required role, that in this case was to supervise properly and complement the role of markets; and (2) the inability to substitute a mature integration into the globalized world economy, properly balancing risks and opportunities, for the previous excessively inward orientation of the ISI period. The omnipresent public sector of the ISI period was replaced by a state that did not fulfil its most basic duties. The extreme protectionist policies of the past were replaced by completely unrestricted trade and financial liberalization.

The unproven notion that privatizations would automatically induce a dramatic improvement in systemic efficiency and productivity contributed to minimizing the attention paid to the way in which privatizations were carried out. In several cases this approach prevented the development of truly competitive markets in the privatized activities while, at the same time, made it easier for both public officials and private agents to engage in corrupt practices. Other basic regulations were also missing, including effective anti-trust regulation, consumer protection and adequate prudential supervision on banking and private pension funds. Moreover, the need to establish a social safety net to alleviate the inevitable social and economic hardships of the structural transformations was overtly neglected.

The reduced presence of the state in the regulation of economic activities, however, was not enough to curb the expansionary fiscal behaviour of the past. The idea that the complex political economy issues that shape public sector performance could be easily managed by limiting the government's access to central bank credit was at best naive. Beneath the surface, this approach failed to modify the deep determinants of public sector profligacy, which remained basically unchanged. As a matter of fact, the deeply ingrained populist practices of Latin American politicians and public bureaucrats were not eliminated by the reforms. Instead, when those politicians and bureaucrats found out that their old source of financing was no longer available, their immediate reaction was to look for a new one. The easy access to foreign financing prevailing in the international capital markets until the late 1990s solved their problem: the issuance of public debt substituted for the inflation tax.

Indeed, despite the allegedly neoliberal inspiration of the reforms, in this area the policy course followed in most LATAM countries throughout the 1990s could be best characterized as neopopulist. Quite paradoxically, by disregarding the role of the state in a market economy and reducing public sector reform to the privatization of public firms, the Washington Consensus rhetoric helped preserve the status quo in the workings of the public sector.

The second element that contributed to shaping the final outcome of Washington Consensus reforms has to do with the relationship established between stabilization policies on the one hand, and trade and financial liberalization on the other. Stabilization policies mainly chose the exchange rate as nominal anchor. Simultaneously, with the full support of multilateral institutions and the establishment of industrialized countries, the USA in the first place, Latin America embarked on a process of outright trade and financial liberalization. As mentioned before, the speed and depth of trade liberalization deepened the overvaluation of the domestic currency associated with the use of the exchange rate as nominal anchor. The combination of overvaluation and liberalization dramatically altered relative prices and triggered a sharp transformation on the real side of the economy. At the same time, the sudden change in relative prices generated a competitiveness gap that helped to raise the current account imbalance. External adjustment was postponed because a growing foreign indebtedness provided the funds required to finance the persistent current account deficits. As a result, Latin American economies became not only less competitive but also more vulnerable to the volatility of world financial markets (Rozenwurcel 2003).

The risks posed by the mix of a stabilization policy based on a pegged exchange rate and a simultaneous trade and financial liberalization were hardly unknown in the region. The Southern Cone's dismal experience with trade and financial liberalization in the 1970s had been extensively discussed in the sequencing literature of the 1980s. The need to carefully consider the timing of stabilization and liberalization in the goods and financial markets was one of the main lessons arising from that discussion (Fanelli *et al.* 1992). Therefore, one can only conclude that policy mistakes were not the only reason behind the inconsistent implementation of stabilization and liberalization. The interests of powerful economic players that benefited from the new scenario despite its social costs certainly played a significant role in the process. There is nothing surprising in this fact. What is less understandable is the support given to this process by the multilateral institutions and other participants in the Washington Consensus.

Where does Latin America stand now?

After the Great Depression and throughout the rest of the twentieth century, LATAM countries have basically approached economic development following two successive and quite opposed strategies. The first one was import substitution industrialization. The second was the so-called Washington Consensus approach. While the two views were founded on quite opposite premises, neither the ISI nor the Washington Consensus managed to deliver sustained economic development to LATAM countries. External difficulties notwithstanding, two domestic elements are crucial to understand the breakdown of the ISI strategy in Latin America. One was the failure of the state to work as an engine of growth. This was so because of the large inefficiencies of SOEs, the government's inability to appropriately combine sticks and carrots in its relationships with private firms, and the use of populist policies as the main redistributive device. All this not only induced chronic fiscal deficits and short-run macro-instability, but undermined overall productivity and long-run growth as well. The second factor was the extremely inward orientation of industrialization induced by extended and protracted protectionism, which prevented LATAM economies from taking advantage of foreign markets as a disciplining mechanism to gradually enhance the competitiveness of domestic firms.

The strong social coalition supporting the status quo, including industrial firms, benefiting from captive domestic markets and public subsidies, industrial workers, favoured by low prices of food staples and utilities, and public bureaucrats taking advantage of the power given by the discretionary channelling of public funds, prevented the progressive transformation of ISI into an export-led industrialization strategy as was the case in East Asia. A first attempt at replacing the ISI model by a market-based development strategy took place in the late 1970s and early 1980s. The 1982 Mexican default and the ensuing debt crisis abruptly put an end to this process when voluntary financing to the region virtually disappeared. The neoliberal view, then already prevailing, attributed the failure of the liberalization attempts of the late 1970s to the incomplete nature of their reforms. According to this view, the proper answer to the breakdown of the first attempt was therefore a second and broader wave of market-friendly structural reforms. This second round began to take shape in the late 1980s and gained momentum in the 1990s.

The structural transformation that took place in LATAM economies under the Washington Consensus did not deliver its promises either. Not only was their long-run growth performance even worse than under ISI, but huge wealth and income inequalities accompanied their poor growth record. Moreover, the increasing external vulnerability and financial fragility of the region resulted in severe financial and currency crises in several Latin American countries. As happened with the ISI strategy, the two common elements that seriously undermined the overall outcome of the Washington Consensus experience were, first, the failure of the state to play its required role, that in this case was to supervise properly and complement the role of markets and, second, the inability to substitute a mature integration into the globalized world economy, properly balancing risks and opportunities, for the previous excessively inward orientation of the ISI period. Nevertheless, practically all countries in Latin America have experienced a significant recovery in the last couple of years. In 2004, in a context of remarkable macro stability, the region as a whole grew almost 6 per cent, the highest rate in the last 25 years (see Figure 24.7), and it is expected that growth will be around 4 per cent. If this performance materializes, the regional per capita GDP would increase 10 per cent between 2004 and 2006.

While it is true that growth resumption has been favoured by positive external conditions, it is also true that LATAM countries seem to have learned a few lessons. In fact, thanks to more flexible exchange rate regimes, growth in the region has been fuelled by significant increases in exports. Instead of generating current account deficits, therefore, this time economic expansion has been accompanied by current account surpluses. Moreover, governments are taking advantage of this favourable situation to improve their fiscal stance and reduce public indebtedness ratios. Foreign debt ratios are also declining and country risk premia are close to their historical lows.

Will this new scenario become sustainable? In order for this to take place LATAM countries have yet to consolidate the newly acquired macro stability, increase their investment ratios and dramatically reduce poverty and improve social equity. While current international conditions are positive, several uncertainties are present and it would be foolish to bet on the indefinite permanence of current trends. Therefore, the region has still to find its own way to take advantage of the opportunities created by economic globalization (adding value to its exports and diversifying their composition and destination, or attracting FDI towards dynamic sectors among other initiatives), while at the same time protecting itself from its negative effects. In this regard, designing effective countercyclical macroeconomic policies, as well as capital-flow regulations (particularly considering the role of these flows on LATAM's business countries) is crucial. Moreover, LATAM countries need to find their own mix of market incentives and state intervention consistent with economic development under their specific circumstances. The fact that the emergence of dynamic economic activities is not necessarily an endogenous outcome of liberalized markets alone needs to be acknowledged. Rather to replace the private initiative, public policies should aim at fostering linkages between the most dynamic firms and sectors and the rest of the economy.

Finally, social objectives should be mainstreamed into economic policy. The benefits of economic growth will not trickle down spontaneously to the less favoured groups in society. Besides fostering democracy, institutional development and the quality of their political systems, LATAM counties will have to build proper safety nets and put into place efficient redistributive policies in order to achieve this goal.

Notes

The research assistance of Rodrigo Pena and Gastón Rossi is gratefully acknowledged, as well as the comments of participants at the Helsinki conference and two anonymous referees. Remaining mistakes are of course my sole responsibility.

1. The Asian Tigers include the following countries: South Korea, Taiwan, Hong Kong, Singapore, Malaysia, Thailand and Indonesia.
2. As a picturesque example of the disciplinary power of the state in East Asia, we can mention the case of Park's dictatorship in Korea. Shortly after taking power, he imprisoned the principal businessmen of his country, accusing them of having illegally enriched themselves during the previous regime. Even though they were set free shortly afterwards, this only occurred after these businessmen committed themselves to carrying out specific investments requested by Park. See Rodrik (1995); also Amsden (1996).
3. In any case, already in the mid-1980s, the share of manufactured exports in the total remained much lower in Latin America (25.1 per cent in 1985) than in East Asia (51.7 per cent in the same year). See Narula (2002).
4. Indeed, Brazil was among the fastest-growing economies in the world.
5. The policy mix involved accepting a high risk, to the extent that trade liberalization demands a higher real equilibrium exchange rate, while unrestricted capital flows and the fixing of an overvalued nominal exchange rate in countries that are structurally net capital importers tend to keep the real exchange rate below its equilibrium level.

References

Amsden, A.H. (1996) 'Un enfoque estratégico para el Crecimiento Económico y la Intervención Estatal en los Países de Industrialización Tardía', *Pensamiento Iberoamericano*, 29: 107–56.

Calvo, G. (1998) 'Capital Flows and Capital-Market Crises: The Simple Economics of Sudden Stops', *Journal of Applied Economics*, 1, 1: 35–54.

Fanelli, J., R. Frenkel and G. Rozenwurcel (1992) 'Growth and Structural Reform, Where We Stand', in A. Zini Jr (ed.), *The Market and the State in Economic Development in the 1990s*, Amsterdam: North Holland.

Frenkel, R. (2003) 'Globalización y crisis financieras en América Latina', *Revista de la CEPAL*, 80: 41–54, Santiago de Chile.

Hirschman, A. (1973) 'La economía política de la industrialización a través de la sustitución de importaciones en América Latina', in *Desarrollo y América Latina*, Mexico City: Fondo de Cultura Económica.

Krueger, A. (1990) 'Government Failures in Development', *Journal of Economic Perspectives*, 4, 3: 9–23.

Maddison, A. (2003) *The World Economy: Historical Statistics*, Paris: Development Centre, OECD.

Narula, R. (2002) 'Switching from Import Substitution to the "New Economic Model" in Latin America: a Case of Not Learning from Asia', *LAEBA Working Paper* 4, Washington DC: Latin America/Caribbean and Asia/Pacific Economics and Business Association, Inter-American Development Bank.

Ocampo, J.A. (2004) 'Latin America's Growth and Equity Frustrations During Structural Reforms', *Journal of Economic Perspectives*, 18, 2: 67–88.

Oman, C. and G. Wignaraja (1991) *The Post-War Evolution of Development Thinking*, London: Macmillan.

Rodrik, D. (1995) 'Getting Interventions Right: How South Korea and Taiwan Grew Rich', *NBER Working Paper* 4964, Cambridge, MA: National Bureau of Economic Research.

Rodrik, D. (2003) 'What Do We Learn from Country Narratives?', in D. Rodrik (ed.), *In Search of Prosperity*, New Jersey: Princeton University Press.

Rozenwurcel, G. (2003) 'The Collapse of the Currency Board and the Hard Way Back to Normality in Argentina', at www.networkideas.org/featart/featart_Argentina.htm

Williamson, J. (1990) 'What Washington Means by Policy Reform', in J. Williamson, (ed.), *Latin American Adjustment: How Much Has Happened?*, Washington, DC: Institute for International Economics.

25
Development in Chile 1990–2005: Lessons from a Positive Experience

Álvaro García Hurtado

Introduction

In December 1989, a democratic president was elected in Chile. The 16-year Pinochet dictatorship had been defeated by a national vote. The Concertación had a simple but widely supported strategic vision – democracy and equitable growth. On three accounts the defeated authoritarian regime had shown a very poor outcome: it had interrupted a long democratic tradition; there had been very little growth (3 per cent per year between 1974 and 1989 amounting to 1.5 per cent in per capita terms); and income had become more concentrated resulting in an increase in poverty (amounting to 38.6 per cent of the population in 1990).[1]

During the past 16 years the Concertación government has carried through deep and simultaneous changes in the economic, social and political dimension. Some of the economic reforms, like opening up the economy, were built on changes made by the authoritarian regime. But the Concertación strategy assumed that simultaneous reforms should reinforce each other in promoting democratization and growth with equity. Throughout these 16 years there has been a permanent, coherent and fruitful effort from the government to advance in this strategic direction.

The political scenario in which this reform process took place was a complicated one, because most legal reforms require high majorities in Parliament where the right-wing opposition parties are over-represented (due to the electoral system inherited from Pinochet). Whenever political agreements were reached, they occurred in Congress and always on specific issues, never on a national vision. There never has been an explicit agreement around the vision that involves all social and political stakeholders of Chile. This has implied very lengthy and repetitive discussion, particularly on the ways to finance the reforms. This fact, as will be seen, has retarded and weakened the effects of the reforms particularly in the equity objective.

All in all, the implementation of the Concertación vision shows positive results. Increasing competitiveness was the way chosen to promote growth. Competitiveness was sought through macroeconomic reforms to stabilize and continue opening the economy, complemented by microeconomic reforms to increase efficiency and productivity. Their outcome has been positive. Chile in the last

20 years has averaged an annual per capita growth rate of 4.2 per cent. According to the IMF database, Chile ranks ninth among the fastest-growing economies in this period. The majority of the countries that are ahead of Chile have a much lower income per capita and thus are less affected by convergence.

Chile also experienced a sharp reduction in poverty. According to Mideplan (2004), total poverty decreased from 38.6 per cent in 1990 to 18.8 per cent in 2003; while the incidence of extreme poverty decreased from 12.9 per cent to 4.7 per cent in the same period. Chile had the most rapid decrease in poverty in Latin America and is the only country that has reached the poverty Millennium Development Goal.

Also very important reforms were completed to strengthen democratic governance. The most important, were the constitutional reforms finally approved by Congress in June 2005 which eliminate the most important non-democratic institutions that had been put in place by the Pinochet regime. Before that, important institutional changes were implemented, particularly in the economic area. These changes, according to the World Bank, placed Chile among the 15 countries with better institutional quality.[2]

These outcomes place Chile among the more successful developing countries. But Chile also has important current problems. As will be seen, there is still low value added and diversification of exports, low investment in R&D and human capital; insufficient support to small- and medium-sized enterprises (SMEs); problems of coverage in social areas; health, pre-school education and pensions; also a very unequal income distribution with a relatively low tax burden; and an electoral system that over-represents the minority. This study will analyze the instruments (competitiveness, social reforms and institutional change) used to reach the three pillars of the Chilean development strategy – growth, equity and democratic governance – as well as the remaining challenges.

Growth and competitiveness

Strong macro fundamentals and open trade

From the very beginning the democratic governments aimed at reducing inflation and continue opening the economy. Reaching strong macro fundamentals was the instrument to promote investment, considered the main restriction to economic growth. Opening the economy was the instrument to turn exports into the engine of growth. Investment and exports were the two main economic pillars of the growth strategy.

During the military regime, tariffs were reduced in a very significant manner. From an average tariff of over 100 per cent they were reduced to a flat one of 15 per cent. Democratic governments continued the unilateral reduction of import duties (to its present level of a flat 6 per cent) and initiated the negotiations of free trade agreements (FTAs) as a complementary way of opening the economy. Chile has now signed FTAs with all American countries (except Cuba), the European Union, China and some other countries in Asia and Oceania. These FTAs cover 65 per cent of the world's population and about 80 per cent of

Chilean trade. Additionally, it is presently negotiating trade agreements with Japan and India.

The FTAs not only continued to open the economy (the effective tariff after the agreements is below 2 per cent) but also changed the economic features of the country. Chile grew from being a small economy (15 million inhabitants with an income per capita PPP (2005) of U$10,981) into an export-producing country where domestic firms could trade on the larger global market with quite advantageous conditions. This feature was an additional source of attraction for foreign direct investment (FDI).

Simultaneously, an effort was made to strengthen fiscal accounts and reduce inflation that was increasing at the time of the democratic transition (yearly inflation at the end of 1989 was 25.6 per cent). Although in 1989 there was a surplus in the fiscal accounts, it was financed by a large sum of non-permanent government revenues that came from privatizations and an unusually high price of copper. Thus, a tax reform was proposed and approved to make compatible fiscal balance with the necessary increase in social expenditure to promote equity.

The Concertación governments have kept a permanent surplus in fiscal accounts with the only exemption of the years of the Asian crisis that had a large effect on the price of copper, which in turn has a large impact on government revenues. Because of this, in 2000 a new fiscal rule was established. This implied maintaining a structural surplus of 1 per cent of GNP on the fiscal accounts, which has been strictly kept. The structural surplus calculates the budget considering the revenues that would exist with a tendential rate of growth, which is very significantly affected by the price of copper. Thus, when the price of copper is down, the rule enables a deficit. This happened in 2000–03 (where it reached a maximum of 1 per cent of GNP). But when the price of copper is above its tendency it forces a surplus, as we have now (in 2004 fiscal accounts had a surplus of 2.2 per cent of GNP). This ensures countercyclical government spending, as well as a tendency towards larger government savings (that in the future could be used to cover deficits in the private pension system). This fiscal innovation is a very attractive tool for all developing countries whose export structure is very intensive in commodities that experience sharp and frequent changes in prices with its consequent cyclical effect on growth and fiscal accounts.

A strict fiscal policy plus an autonomous central bank (since 1990) with inflation targeting (2–4 per cent) drastically decreased inflation to its present and within the target level (1999–2004 averaged 2.6 per cent). At the same time it has been permanently reducing the country's risk, up to its present level (August 2005) of 52 basic points of Chilean sovereign debt over the US treasury bonds, which places Chile among the three lower country risks in emerging markets. This creates a very significant difference in the cost of capital relative to other Latin American countries (average 300 basic points) and contributes to explaining the larger increase in investment and growth.

Microeconomic efficiency

In order to increase competitiveness, since the early 1990s an effort has been made to improve microeconomic efficiency in four main policy areas: infrastructure, human capital, productive development (R&D and support to SMEs) and strength-ening economic institutions (mostly regulatory and anti-trust). In 2001, with much the same purpose, a 'pro-growth agenda' was agreed between government and busi-ness. This agenda was geared towards improving transparency and efficiency in the public sector, overcoming market failures and stimulating private participation in the provision of public goods. Public policies in this area were horizontal, that is the benefits were open to all sectors of the economy. As well as pro-competition, given a market distortion, a first attempt was to stimulate competition and if this was not successful, regulate the market with a framework that emulated competition.

Promoting private investment in infrastructure and public goods was aimed to improve the global connectivity of the Chilean economy. The private sector was incorporated in the provision of public utilities, as well as in all kinds of infra-structure. In order to do this, new regulatory bodies were created that enabled the participation of the private sector and/or authorized the privatization of existing infrastructure. Particular emphasis was placed in promoting and/or emulating competition in each sector, as a means of transferring the gains of productivity to consumers and users of public utilities and infrastructure.

In the last decade, 62 projects for over U$7 billion have been granted as conces-sions to the private sector to build and operate highways, ports, airports, trains, buses, prisons and hospitals. Additionally, the privatization of the telecommuni-cation and water and sewage services brought enormous investments with the consequent improvement in efficiency (tariffs) and quality. The electricity sector was already privatized, but there was an important change in its regulatory bodies and very significant amounts of FDI in it. The outcome of these changes is very positive. Chile has a 100 per cent digitalized telecommunication system, it is con-nected to three international fibre optics networks, and ranks among the first 15 in all transportation and communication variables of the IMD competitiveness report.[3] This is an important achievement considering that in the early 1990s infrastructure was one of the least-competitive sectors of the Chilean economy according to the same report.

Investment in human capital was also a very high priority. Since 1990 public expenditure in education has more than tripled, increasing its participation from 2.5–4 per cent of GNP. According to UNESCO, Chile's total expenditure in educa-tion amounts to 7.3 per cent of GNP, which favourably compares to the 5.4 per cent of OECD countries. Simultaneously an important effort was made to increase investment in training of the labour force (it increased over 100 per cent). Although the increase in investment enabled a large improvement in the coverage of these services, it still has a long way to go in terms of quality. For example, Chile is reaching 100 per cent coverage of secondary education, but it is lagging behind in pre-school coverage and in quality, it ranks 37 for education systems and 55 in pupil/teacher ratios. Access to training programmes for workers, although increas-ing at a fast pace, is very limited for SMEs and nonexistent for self-employed workers, which are precisely the sectors with lower productivity.

The increase in coverage of education was particularly high in universities (more than double), reaching 37.5 per cent of the population, which still compares unfavourably to the 65 per cent figure for developed countries. A good example of the social and economic impact of this progress is that presently 70 per cent of all university students are the first members of their families to reach this educational level; a very significant change that will transform the quality of life for these families and productivity in the country. The total impact of the very large increase in investment in human capital is still to be felt in terms of equitable growth.

From the very beginning the Concertación government aimed at reaching what was called the second phase of the export model, one more intensive in value added. For this purpose public research funds were created to stimulate R&D in the private sector and to strengthen the link with universities. As well as a programme to support productivity growth and market penetration for SMEs, mostly through stimulating its association. Although existing evaluations of these programmes show very positive results, their size did not enable them to have a very large impact. Their limited funds plus the 'horizontal' criteria (to avoid 'picking the winners') in the definition of public R&D policy attempted against real progress. Moving towards a cluster approach around the existing export sectors could take the Chilean economy faster to an export structure more intensive in value added. As will be seen, R&D is still a competitive disadvantage for the Chilean economy and SMEs have kept the 75 per cent productivity gap they had with large firms. The final goal of moving into the second phase of export growth was not reached either.

Chile also invested in modernizing economic institutions to increase transparency and efficiency. Since 1990 it has completed a reform of the entire judicial system. It has transformed all regulatory institutions and its legislation, it has created a fair competition tribunal and an independent tax tribunal. It has new legislation and institutions on consumer protection, industrial property rights and international commercial arbitration. It also legislated on corporate governance and venture capital industry. It has improved the legislation on private pension funds and incorporated voluntary savings in it.

The positive impact of these transformations can be appreciated in several international reports. The IMD (2004) *Competitiveness Report* ranks Chile first in central bank policies and second in pro-business country and management of public finances, sixth in financial institutions transparency and eighth in government efficiency. The Economist Intelligence Unit ranks Chile 15th in its offshore environment ranking and says that, 'Chile outshines its neighbours, luring investment with educated workers and strong IT skills ... Chile is the strongest performing Latin American country.' Transparency International ranks Chile 20th (out 145 countries) in its level of corruption.

Exports and investment the two engines of growth and competitiveness

The macro- and microeconomic reforms were geared towards increasing competitiveness and making exports and investment the two engines of growth. The strategy succeeded on all of these accounts. Competitiveness, as measured by the international reports, has been increasing. The 2005 IMD report places Chile in the 19th place under New Zealand and above Japan. Many studies show that Chile is the best place to do business in Latin America. For example, the Kearney off-shore location index places Chile ninth in the world and underlines that it 'offers the best business environment and infrastructure in the region'. The strategy was effective in promoting investment and exports, both variables grew faster than GNP. While investment averaged 22 per cent of GNP in 1987–89, it increased to 32 per cent in the period 1995–98. The cooling effect on Chilean growth brought on by the Asian crisis decreased the investment rate, but it is already increasing its participation in GNP again.

As expected by policy-makers in Chile, foreign direct investment was crucial to increase total investment. While before 1990 FDI did not reach 0.7 per cent of GNP, in 1990–91 it more than doubled, reaching 1.4 per cent of GNP. In 1997–99 it increased to 7.5 per cent and in 2004 it was 7.1 per cent of GNP. Thus, over 60 per cent of the increase in investment is explained by the increase in FDI. Chile is second, after Ireland, in its reception of FDI relative to GNP and it doubles the average of developing countries. It is important to notice that democracy brought a large increase in FDI (more than double), although the legislation that governed foreign investment was the same as that under the authoritarian regime. Democracy seems to make a difference for FDI.

Annual exports grew 9.7 per cent in the decade before 1997, while GNPs grew 7 per cent per year. In 1998–2003 exports grew 6.3 per cent per year, while GNP growth was 3.1 per cent. External shocks (in this case the effect of the Asian crisis) have a very large effect in Chile, decreasing exports and terms of trade. The price of exports grew 6.2 per cent annually in the first period and −3.6 per cent per year in the second, which explains 1.5 percentage points of reduction in the growth rate. In spite of the fall in terms of trade, exports were permanently an engine for growth and, in 2004, accounted for one-third of GNP.

This results shows that Chile successfully identified engines for rapid growth, as well as instruments to promote exports and investment, but there are a few clouds on the horizon that need to be dealt with. As seen, Chile's growth is very sensitive to international cycles and this is so because its structure of exports is still too concentrated on commodities that experience sharp changes in terms of trade. Up till now Chile still shows little value added in its main exports; this is due to a relatively low investment in R&D and to the need for further progress in labour productivity.

Pending challenges in Chile's growth strategy

Chile has suffered a kind of 'Dutch Disease'. The very large and simultaneous growth in exports and FDI appreciated the real exchange rate. Between 1990 and 1998 the Chilean peso permanently revalued accumulating a change of 45 per cent. After the Asian crisis, with its negative impact on exports and terms of trade, the peso devalued, but this process was reversed in 2002, as soon as the price of copper started increasing again. Mining exports represent 40 per cent of total exports in Chile and when the price of copper is very high, as in 2004–05, they come up to about 50 per cent.

Although non-traditional exports have grown, still the structure of exports is dominated by low-value-added exports. If the World Bank's definition of 'dominated exports' is considered,[4] Chile, relative to Latin America, has kept a high participation of exports that do not induce technological change. Landerretche *et al.* (2004) show that dominated exports accounted for a large amount of total exports between 1986 and 2001 (from 93 per cent they decreased to 89 per cent); while in Latin America and the Caribbean in the same period they decreased from 82 to 55 per cent.

This is partially due and also explains why R&D remains at very low levels in Chile. R&D represents 0.6 per cent of GNP, while in the OECD countries it is 2.6 per cent. The way this investment is financed also differs drastically – in Chile it is 80 per cent public, in OECD countries is 80 per cent private. In other words the private sector in Chile is making a very marginal effort to incorporate more value added into exports. This is probably related to the uncertainty that generates the permanent changes in the real value of the exchange rate and its tendency towards appreciation, making more secure and less expensive the export of raw materials.

There is already an agreed way of increasing investment in R&D in Chile. Parliament has approved a royalty to the extraction of copper and its entire proceeds will go to finance 'innovation for competitiveness'. Its amount should at least double the present level of investment and help overcome the most important missing link in the country's growth strategy. This structure of exports, in turn, has a large social impact through the labour market. Although employment, as will be seen, is the most important explanatory variable in reducing poverty; exports made no contribution in this respect. As a matter of fact, total employment in tradable goods plus construction (this latter sector grew very significantly in the first decade) remained practically constant in about 2 million employees between 1990 and 2003, while employment in non-tradable goods permanently increased from 2.5–3.4 million employees. A large proportion of this latter employment was in low-quality/productivity jobs in the informal sector, SMEs or the personal service sector, which contributed to deteriorate income distribution and did not promote competitiveness in the economy as a whole.

Although the unemployment rate in general was not very high (it increased to 10–11 per cent around the year 2000), the participation rate of 57 per cent (42 per cent for women) is the lowest in Latin America. Labour participation is particularly low among poor families and is very elastic to growth in employment opportunities (it increased in the first half of the 1990s). The dependency ratio is 4.7 for the poorest 20 per cent and 2.6 for the wealthiest 20 per cent. Thus, if more employment could be generated in the export sector, more members of poor families would look and find a job, making an important addition to family income. The same is true if a larger effort is made to support the modernization of SMEs and, thus, increase the quality of the jobs they generate. Exports with more value added and/or more competitive SMEs would also reduce the depth and duration of external shocks and, through that, increase the average growth rate of the economy. New high-quality jobs could be crucial to reduce the incidence of poverty and to move towards a more equitable distribution of income. Real support to SMEs is a pending challenge for equitable growth.

Reduction of poverty and inequality

High growth enabled Chile to close in 30 per cent its per capita gap with developed countries and to significantly reduce the incidence of poverty, even more for extreme poverty. But, during 1990–2003, there was no change in a very regressive income distribution structure. In this period the Gini coefficient fluctuated between 0.58 and 0.57 and the relationship between the income level of the wealthiest and poorest 20 per cent of the population was 14 in 1990 and 14.3 in 2003.[5]

Chile and Brazil were the two Latin American countries with better results in terms of poverty reduction, but their relationship to economic growth is very different. Brazil reduced its incidence of poverty from 41.4 in 1990 to 29.9 in 2001, but it did not grow (per capita GNP grew 0 per cent in the 1990s and 0.1 per cent in 2000–03); while Chile grew quite substantially (4.1 per cent per capita per year in the 1990s and 2.1 per cent in 2000–03).[6] Although Brazilian and Chilean outcomes are quite impressive, Attanasio and Székely (2001) show that about 85 per cent of the poverty reduction in Chile is due to economic growth, while in Brazil 70 per cent of the decrease can be explained by income distribution.

In Chile poverty was mostly reduced because of productivity growth (5 per cent per year between 1990 and 2000), which was transferred to higher wages. The minimum wage, that receives a large proportion of the poor, increased 70.1 per cent in real terms between 1990 and 2004. As average productivity and wages increased at the same pace, the functional distribution of income did not change. But higher wages increased 20 per cent more than the lower ones, this differential in the growth of wages is an important explanation for the regressive personal income distribution.

Throughout this period, the ratio between reduction of poverty and growth of GNP constantly varied. It went from 3.9 percentage points of growth for 1 percentage point reduction of poverty in the period of faster growth (1996–98), to 1.8 in the period of lower growth but higher expenditure on targeted employment programmes. This is a good example of the potential effect of public transfers on income distribution and reduction of poverty, if they have a significant amount of resources. With redistribution Chile could have done better in reducing poverty. If it had had permanently the growth/reduction of poverty ratio of 1999–2000 it would have eliminated extreme poverty and almost all the rest of poverty as well.

Inequality and the labour market

High inequality in Chile, and its permanence through time, is mostly a reflection of what happens in the labour market. The poorest 20 per cent have very precarious jobs: low productivity and, mostly, informal (53 per cent of the employed have a permanent job and 40.3 per cent do not have a labour contract). They also have higher unemployment rates (they represent 41.6 per cent of all the unemployed) and higher dependency ratios (twice as large as the average).

One of the largest problems, in terms of inequality, is the permanence of informal employment.[7] This was 36.9 per cent of total employment in 1990 and 37.6 per cent in 2000. Informal jobs have only 25 per cent of the average productivity of the formal ones and, thus, pay much less. The incidence of poverty among their workers is 26 per cent, while in formal jobs is 8.5 per cent, also informal workers are less educated (8.6 versus 12.2 years in formal employees). Only 50 per cent of informal workers have a formal contract (and thus access to social benefits), while 86.5 per cent of formal workers have such a contract.

The permanence of low productivity and informal jobs partially explains why although low-income workers increased employment in the decade 1990–2000 at a faster speed than high-income workers (2.6 per cent versus 1.7 per cent per annum); their per capita family income increased less (4.4 per cent versus 5.4 per cent per year). Their productivity and wages grow at a lower pace (3.3 per cent versus 4.7 per cent per year) and 61.5 per cent of all the high-quality jobs created in the decade were captured by workers of high-income families.[8] Although income from labour increased rapidly, its distribution became more unequal. Thus, the labour market in this period was a source of inequality and, at the same time, because of its dynamism, the main explanation for the reduction of poverty.

Precarious employment is the source of poverty and inequality in Chile. The government tried to support productivity growth in SMEs but with very limited funds (in the years 2002–04 these programmes added an amount of U\$25 million per annum) and had little impact. Increasing productive employment for the poor; is the most effective tool to overcome poverty and reduce inequalities, as well as coherent with growth. This poses two challenges. The first is increasing productivity (training) of the poor; the second, more important in the short run, is increasing the productivity of the working place. In other words, increase the access to capital for SMEs, where the majority of the poor work.

Social reforms in Chile, income distribution and tax burden

During the Concertación government, Chile significantly increased its level of social expenditure and reformed its policies. Between 1990–2005 social investment more than doubled in real terms, its priority was reflected in its increased participation in GNP from 12.9–16.4 per cent, as well as from 60–72 per cent in government expenditure. This increase in the volume of social expenditure had an important distributive impact, particularly in the period of greater unemployment, where special employment programmes for the poor were implemented. The portion of social expenditure that can be distributed among income groups implied that income of poor families increased by 17 per cent between 1990 and 1996, by 46 per cent in 1998–2000 and by 30 per cent throughout the period.[9] Its redistributive effect can be appreciated by comparing the relationship between the average income of the wealthiest and the poorest 20 per cent of the population. This, as mentioned, was 14.3 in 2003 for autonomous income (return to labour and capital), but it decreases to 7.6 when social expenditure is incorporated and total income is considered. Thus, social expenditure has an important equalizing effect in Chile and has compensated the inequities created in the labour market, maintaining a stable income distribution.

It is not possible, in this short review, to analyze the important changes that took place in each social policy. The most important effort, from 1990 onwards, was on the educational sector and geared towards improving equitable access and quality to all levels of education. Education is the most important factor behind inequality in Chile, explaining between 9 and 40 per cent of it, depending on sample, definition of income, method, year and cohort used. No other factors such as region, gender, occupation explain as much as education (Palma 2005). The reforms underway should, in the long run, affect both growth and distribution but it is too early to find quantitative results. Evaluations of these programmes show that progress is underway, although there still is ample room for greater quality in education, as well as to increase coverage at the pre-school level (which has a large distributive effect).

In 2000 an unemployment insurance scheme was created. This system had some solidarity, although benefits are related to private financing, like the private pension system which the Concertación government inherited and have not changed in a substantial manner. The unemployment insurance does not cover workers with unstable or informal employments, which constitute the majority of the jobs of the poor. Also a health reform project has been implemented since 2002. The original project had a solidarity component incorporated, but was not approved by Congress.

The pension system is the most important pending social reform to increase equity. The system is based on individual private accounts and thus reproduces the existing inequities in the labour market and excludes workers with no labour contract. Coverage of the system increased from 57–61 per cent between 1991 and 2003 (still lower than the 62 per cent the old system had, but the highest in Latin America). The unprotected workers are mostly poor, mainly women and with no or few qualifications. Besides that, the return for savings is higher for higher-income workers (between 1981 and 2003 it was 8.3 per cent per year for non-poor families and 6.4 per cent for the poor ones). In addition, monthly savings have not been deposited (by the employer) for an important number of, especially low-income, workers. All this implies that if the system were to continue as it is, about 50 per cent of the labour force (the poorest) will depend on the state for their pensions. The present level of public pensions does not ensure that these people will be above the poverty line. Solving this situation, depends on the availability of public funds, specially because the annual deficit of the private system between 1999 and 2003 amounted to 5.9 per cent of GNP that was also covered by public savings.[10]

Thus, equitable growth in Chile depends very strongly on furthering social reforms and policies. As seen, all social policies have well-functioning and correctly targeted programmes whose benefits could increase with additional resources. Also the government has reallocated resources in favour of these programmes, as well as increased their efficiency; further efforts along this line although positive will have marginal effects. Greater coverage and/or quality of social programmes require larger funding. In all of these areas increasing solidarity towards poor families exclusively depends on the availability of public funding. Engel *et al.* (1997) show that the structure of the tax system is quite indifferent from a distributive point of view – what counts is the level and targeting of public expenditure. The Gini coefficient could be reduced by 5 percentage points with an increase in the level of taxes (keeping the present structure of expenditure), even if the structure of the tax system turns more regressive. What really counts is government social expenditure.

The discussion on the level of taxes has been a permanent issue throughout the Concertación government. Three tax reforms have been approved after a pro-longed and difficult discussion in Congress, but the tax burden has slightly decreased. The tax burden was 18.06 per cent of GNP in 1993 and 16.29 per cent ten years later (2003). Although all tax reforms were geared to increase taxes (mostly value added tax) and/or reduce evasion, the trade agreements that Chile signed plus the unilateral reduction of tariffs implied a permanent decrease in the tax burden. Between 1993 and 2003 foreign duties decreased its contribution to total taxes from 2.3 per cent of GNP to 0.75 per cent, about the same amount by which the tax burden decreased. In 2005 the net tax burden has increased to 17.9 per cent of GNP (because of reduction in tax evasion), lower than in devel-oped countries (G7 is 26.3 per cent and other OECD are 29.5 per cent of GNP). The fact that there has not been an explicit agreement on the tax burden in Chile has turned this discussion into a permanently unresolved political issue.

Whichever course of action is taken to reach a more equitable distribution of income, the underlying discussion in Chile will be the same one: the tax burden. Given that the electoral system in Chile forces an equal representation in Parliament for the opposition, it seems unlikely that the political composition of Parliament will change creating new conditions for an agreement on a larger tax burden. An important way out of this dilemma could be to incorporate new actors into the political dialogue. Until now social actors – with the exemption of the business community – have had a very weak voice in this discussion and thus all interests have not been adequately represented. A national dialogue, on such a crucial strategic issue, is advisable to reach an agreement that is clearly necessary to advance in equity and also to end a discussion that introduces economic insta-bility. Greater participation of social actors interested in promoting equity should strengthen the political viability of a permanent agreement on the tax burden that increases financing of social policies.

Institutions for good democratic governance

Chile made a successful effort to implement reforms that produced simultaneous economic, social and political changes. Unlike the rest of Latin America, with these reforms Chile grew steadily at a much higher rate than in the past and also reduced poverty. Corbo *et al.* (2005), based on a cross-sectional econometric model, show that Chile's better performance is explained by the reforms that lead to stronger macro fundamentals and, most importantly, better institutions. The study proves that if all Latin American countries could have had the post-reform institutions that Chile has, their average rate of growth of GNP per capita would have been 1.6 per cent higher per year, and Chile grew 2.4 per cent more than the rest. Now, if quality of institutions could have been similar to the ones of Finland, growth per capita would have been 2.3 per cent higher. Building and strengthening economic institutions explains more than half of the difference in Chile's growth vis-à-vis the rest of Latin America.

Institution building is also related to the reduction of poverty. The three countries with lower incidence of poverty in Latin America (Uruguay, Chile and Costa Rica) are also the three with stronger institutions (according to Kaufmann *et al.* 2003). Brazil is fourth in poverty and fifth in institutions. The two most successful countries in reducing poverty in Latin America followed different strategies during the 1990s but both had in common institutional reforms. Chile placed its emphasis in financial and economic institutions with a positive response in terms of economic growth. Brazil emphasized reform in income transfers with a positive outcome in terms of income distribution. Both routes had a positive effect on poverty.

The relationship between equitable growth and institutions is also present in Rodrik's (1999) findings that show that Latin American countries recuperate growth, after external shocks, at a lower pace than the rest of the world because of their weak institutions. Particularly, because of the inability of these institutions to deal with the distributional impacts that external shocks generate. This inability generates political and economic instability, prolonging the effect of the shocks.

When it comes to political institutions, there still is a discussion in Chile about its transition to democracy. Some argue that it was completed at the beginning of the 1990s when Chile proved it could live under democratic rules and deal with the human rights problems that took place under the Pinochet regime. Others argue that it just concluded with the approval (June 2005) of the amendments to the Constitution that eliminated the non-democratic institutions inherited from the Pinochet regime. Finally, there are some who say that there is still one pending issue, the electoral system, which although taken out of the Constitution is still undemocratic. What is clear is that Chile has been able to deal with its problems under democratic rule and improve the quality of its institutions in a democratic manner.

It is also clear that institutions could still be perfected from a democratic point of view. The real test for democracy is the way it is perceived by the population and its degree of democratic participation. In Chile, support for democracy has grown from 54 per cent in 1996 to 57 per cent in 2004; in the same period in Latin America it decreased from 61 to 53 per cent of the population.[11] But half of those who support democracy believe that it has big problems and that the worst problem is poverty and inequality. Most people (70 per cent in Chile) also believe that governments are run for and by the wealthy and powerful. Also 41 per cent of the population does not participate in democratic elections and only 53 per cent of the people with the right to vote feel it is important to do it. Democracy still needs to be strengthened.

Democracy and equitable growth are strongly related. García (2003) shows a positive correlation between income distribution and support to democracy in

Latin America, the stronger inequality the less satisfaction with democracy. There is also a relationship between the economic cycle and support to democracy. In Chile, 1997 was the last year of a prolonged period of growth: democracy support was at its peak (61 per cent) as it also was satisfaction with it (37 per cent); the opposite took place on 2001 (lowest point of the cycle and where democracy had 45 per cent of support and 23 per cent of satisfaction). Reduction of poverty also had a positive effect on the political arena; Chile (as well as Brazil, Uruguay and Costa Rica) has strongly supported democratic government. The Chilean president, although completing his mandate, is among the most approved of in Latin America (65 per cent).

Confidence in institutions is also related to inequity. Equal rights or access is the most important variable (47 per cent) to define the level of confidence in an institution, the second reason (28 per cent) is that they fulfil promises. Prevailing inequality in Chile reduced confidence in the market economy; 36 per cent of the population (the highest in Latin America) express satisfaction with the market economy, while 51 per cent are unsatisfied. Lack of confidence also affects other institutions, governments, the judicial system, Congress and political parties (in that order) were conceived as the least reliable institutions because they are perceived as unequal in ensuring rights and opportunities (their level of confidence varied between 14 and 25 per cent).

The lack of support for democracy and confidence in institutions, as a result of prevailing inequality, in turn, can have an economic impact. The last report of Business Monitor International,[12] that evaluates country risk, places Chile at number 20 out of 127 countries analyzed. But while Chile is number seven in present political stability, it comes down to 27 in future political stability.

Surprisingly enough, dealing with the weakness of institutions related to distributional issues was not an important aspect, or was definitely not present, in the reform package of the 1990s in most countries in Latin America. In Chile there were three frustrated efforts to create a tripartite dialogue institution that could deal with the egalitarian development agenda: none of them survives now. There also were partial reforms in the labour code, social security and the tax system, all crucial from a distributional point of view. Building or strengthening institutions able to deal with distributional issues is an ongoing challenge in Chile and Latin America.

As mentioned, to advance in equality, it is particularly important to reach a widespread agreement on the tax burden. A good starting point, already used in the last tax reform, is to continue reducing tax evasion, which could simultaneously increase government revenues and allow for rationalizing the system, including tax cuts. The possibility of a further reduction in tax evasion is proven by the fact that the wealthiest 10 per cent of Chileans get 41.2 per cent of total income and their marginal income tax rate is 40 per cent but the total revenue of this tax is only 4.1 per cent of GNP. If the wealthiest 10 per cent were to pay 40 per cent of their marginal income and the economy would continue to grow at 6 per cent a year; the additional amount of income tax collected in four years would enable a doubling of income by the poorest 40 per cent, eliminating poverty in Chile.

Conclusion: a national strategic vision on the equity agenda

Chile has followed a well-defined and successful development strategy for a prolonged period of time. It has done better than any other time in its history, better than all other Latin American countries and has partially closed the gap with developed countries. Although there was progress in all three main goals of the strategy, it lagged behind in the equity objectives. Remaining inequality, in turn, has weakened the confidence in democratic institutions. Strong institutions, on the other hand, are a good part of the explanation of why Chile did so well.

Many of the changes that Chile made during the last 16 years provide a positive experience for other Latin American countries. This is the case of the successful and innovative fiscal rule that reduces the depth of the cycle in countries where commodity exports play an important role. Another important lesson has been the priority given to social reform, in terms of the allocation of public funds and the reduction of tax evasion as a means of financing these reforms. Microeconomic changes, in the areas of regulation, transparency and public efficiency have also proven important to promote competitiveness. A crucial tool for the competitive objective has been the private concession of public infrastructures that increased total investment in this area. Chile has several good practices to show to other Latin American countries.

Although Chile's development outcome has been positive, the challenge to progress simultaneously on growth, distribution and democratization remains valid. These objectives seem highly probable to combine, according to econometric evidence. Cornia (2004) shows that high inequality (Gini coefficient over 0.45) limits economic growth. Thus, redistribution should foster growth, especially if it is done through investment in increasing productivity of the poor. Marshall (2004) shows that closing productivity gaps with developed countries would enable Chile to increase its average rate of growth by 2 per cent. Greater equity on the other hand will strengthen trust in democratic institutions which, in turn, also strengthens growth perspectives making possible the realization of a virtuous circle between growth, distribution and democratization.

After 16 years the strategic vision raised by the Concertación government has proven to be realistic and it has been adopted by all political parties; undoubtedly a very important political success of the governmental coalition. The presidential campaign that has recently taken place (elections in December 2005) has assigned first priority to equity and distribution. But recent experience shows that political agreements in an electoral period do not necessarily imply that opposition parties will later support governmental actions to implement them. This is particularly true for the most controversial instruments, such as the tax and labour reform, where the opposition has voted against them or forced a political agreement that minimizes their effects. The fact that electoral agreements are implicit (there is no explicit commitment on specific actions to be implemented) and do not involve social partners weakens its national representation and its possibilities of realization.

The road to progress in equity and redistribution is well known in Chile. Inequality is mostly explained by the precarious working conditions of the poor: unemployment, underemployment, informal employment and low investment in human capital. Thus, redistribution can be done directly through an increase in existing social programmes (that are efficient and well targeted) or indirectly through increasing productivity of poor workers at a faster pace than average (which requires training, support to SMEs and compliance with labour standards). More public resources are required to finance the road to equitable growth.

Increasing the tax burden has been the major difficulty and the crucial stepping stone towards greater equality. The fact that it has not been done has reduced the pace of progress towards equality, and also has permanently kept in the political agenda a source of conflict and economic instability. These political difficulties remain present and will probably continue in the future because political actors have divergent interests once a government–opposition relationship is established.

Given the widespread political support to Concertación's strategic vision and its positive but incomplete outcome, it is necessary to create an explicit national agreement that involves political and social actors on an equity agenda; that is, on the content and priority of the social reforms to be implemented, the account-ability procedures and the required tax burden to ensure their implementation. This strategic agreement should also strengthen the voice of the social partners that benefit from redistribution and democratization and that, until now, have had little presence in decision making. The social partners would provide more stable conditions for the implementation of the equity agenda. Creating an insti-tution that involves all stakeholders and agrees on a socioeconomic agenda has been crucial in most countries that have combined growth and distribution as well as greater social participation in the democratic process.[13]

A formal social pact that explicitly agrees on a strategic vision, its priorities, expected outcomes and financing sources is an important missing link in Chile's successful development strategy.

Notes

1. All data references in this text that do not have a source can be found in the Monthly Bulletin of the Central Bank of Chile. A compilation of this information, up to year 2000, can be found in Banco Central de Chile (2001).
2. See Kaufmann *et al.* (2003). The institutions are those related to voice and accountability, political stability, government effectiveness, regulatory quality, rule of law, control of corruption and economic freedom ranking.
3. IMD (2004). This ranked Chile 26th out of 60 countries analyzed.
4. 'Dominated' are those exports where innovation is induced by the companies that provide capital goods. Thus, its growth does not induce technological development in the domestic economy and the incorporation of value added into exports. Commodities lose terms of trade relative to goods and services intensive in value added. See Bell and Pavitt (1992).
5. All information on poverty and income distribution comes from the CASEN survey pub-lished by Mideplan (2004).

6. Data on poverty in Latin America comes from ECLAC (2005).
7. Informal employment is understood as ILO does: workers in firms with five or fewer employees and self-employed workers that are not professional, technicians or provide domestic services.
8. For a more detailed analysis see Infante and Sunkel (2005).
9. See Mideplan (2004). It is important to notice that there is no international convention on how to compute government social expenditure in household surveys but their inclusion, as can be seen for the case of Chile, can make a large difference in terms of income distribution and the incidence of poverty.
10. For a more detailed analysis of these figures, see Arenas de Mesa (2005).
11. Information on democracy and social support comes from 'Latinbarometro 2004, Una década de mediciones', Corporación Latinbarómetro, Santiago Chile, 13 August 2004. See wwww.latinbarometro.org
12. See www.businessmonitor.com
13. See IDEA *et al.* (2005).

References

Arenas de Mesa, A. (2005) 'El sistema de Pensiones en Chile en OIT', *El sistema de pensiones en Chile en el contexto mundial y de América latina: Evaluación y desafíos*, Santiago: Organización Internacional del Trabajo (OIT).

Attanasio, O. and M. Székely (2001) 'Going Beyond Income: Redefining Poverty in Latin America', in O. Attanasio and M Székely (eds), *A Portrait of the Poor: An Asset-Based Approach*, Baltimore: Johns Hopkins University Press.

Banco Central de Chile (2001) *Indicadores económicos y Sociales de Chile, 1960–2000*, Santiago: Banco Central de Chile.

Bell, M. and K. Pavitt, (1992) 'Accumulating Technological Capacity in Developing Countries', paper presented at the World Bank Annual Conference on Economic Development, World Bank, Washington, DC.

Corbo, V., L. Hernandez and F. Parro (2005) 'Institutions, Economic Policies and Growth: Lessons from the Chilean Experience', *Central Bank of Chile Working Paper* 317, Santiago: Banco Central de Chile.

Cornia, G.A. (ed.) (2004) *Inequality, Growth, and Poverty in an Era of Liberalization and Globalization*, Oxford and New York: Oxford University Press for UNU-WIDER.

ECLAC (2005) *Panorama Social de América Latina, 2004*, Santiago: ECLAC.

Engel, E., A. Galetovic and C. Raddatz (1997) 'Taxes and Income Distribution in Chile: Some Unpleasant Redistributional Arithmetic', Mimeo, Santiago: Department of Industrial Engineering, Universidad de Chile.

García, A. (2003) 'The Social Dimension of Globalization in Latin America', *ILO Working Paper* 23, Geneva: ILO.

IDEA, World Bank and ECLAC (2005) *National Visions Matter: Lessons of Success*, proceedings of a public-private sector development forum, 25–7 July, Santiago, Chile.

IMD (2004). *Competitiveness Report*, Lausanne: IMD.

Infante, R. and G. Sunkel (2005) *Chile, Trabajo Decente y Calidad de Vida Familiar, 1990–2000*, Santiago: Organización Internacional del Trabajo.

Kaufmann, D., A. Kraay and M. Mastruzzi (2003) 'Governance Matters III: Governance Indicators for 1996–2002', Washington, DC: World Bank.

Landerretche, O., M. Lanzarotti and C. Ominami (2004) 'El Desarrollo Económico de Chile en la Encrucijada: o Cómo las Viejas Controversias Impiden Abordar los Nuevos Problemas', *Revista Foro*, 34, Santiago: Fundación Chile 21.

Marshall, J. (2004) 'Cómo Superar el 5%? Políticas e Instituciones', *Revista Foro*, 39, Santiago: Fundación Chile 21.

Mideplan (2004) Serie CASEN 2003, Volumen 1 'Pobreza, Distribución del Ingreso e impacto distributivo del Gasto Social', Santiago, Chile.

Palma, A. (2005) 'Income Inequality in Chile: A Summary of Experiences and Explanations', unpublished manuscript, Department of Economics, Gothenburg University.

Rodrik D. (1999). 'Where Did All The Growth Go? External Shocks, Social Conflict, Growth Collapse', *Journal of Economic Growth*, 4, 4: 385–412.

26

Three Decades of Rural Development Projects in Asia, Latin America and Africa: Learning from Successes and Failures

Annelies Zoomers

Introduction: the changing policy context

For many years, rural development has been one of the priority goals of Dutch development co-operation. Rural development projects were seen as important drivers of development, as they provided the inputs for industrial development and increased export earnings, and contributed to food security. Stagnating agricultural production, environmental degradation and the concentration of poverty in the countryside were considered obstacles to further national development. Consequently, large investments were made in agricultural research and extension services, water management, natural resource management and integrated rural development.

Since the mid-1990s, it was increasingly acknowledged that isolated projects would not result in sustainable results, unless they were embedded in a sound macroeconomic situation and a supportive policy environment (Schulpen 2001; DGIS 2003a). The often mentioned negative consequences of the project-based approach include the patchwork management of development assistance, inadequate local ownership, the overloading of local capacity to co-ordinate donor relationships and the lack of sustainability and institutional development, all of which result in a waste of development resources (Euforic 2004; Grinspun 2001; Foster *et al.* 2000: 31; Mayhew 2002). Against a backdrop of increasing aid fatigue and heightened concern about development performance and results, aid agencies began to move resources from project funding to sector-wide approaches (SWAps), which required donors to pool their funds and make development intervention part of the receiving countries' 'normal' government policy. Instead of carrying out development projects, donors nowadays come together to pool their funds rather than supporting separate programmes. Donors and recipient governments jointly agree on targets and strategies for allocating the pooled funds and implementing defined priority projects (DGIS 2003b).

An example of a donor that moved from project funding to the SWAps is the Netherlands' Directorate-General for International Co-operation (DGIS). The DGIS forms part of the Dutch foreign ministry and is responsible for development co-operation policy which is based on an annual budget of 0.8 per cent of the Netherlands' GNP (in line with internationally agreed standards). The DGIS decided to introduce the sectoral approach in 1999, '[t]o boost the effectiveness and sustainability of Dutch aid'. This has meant reducing both the number of countries receiving aid and the number of beneficiary sectors within recipient countries. This sectoral approach is not an end in itself but a process by which sector-based assistance can be lent more effectively. 'It is a way of integrating aid into the sectoral policies of recipient countries' (DGIS 2000: 3).

The Netherlands has selected 36 partner countries on the basis of 'good governance' and provided budget support and assistance to sector-wide pro-grammes. The DGIS is giving emphasis to working with other donors to devise a more cohesive aid package and ultimately to move towards sectoral budget aid. These efforts are largely guided by the key policy aims of poverty reduction, gen-der equality and women's empowerment, environmental protection, good gover-nance and institutional development, which are collectively expressed by the Dutch acronym 'GAVIM'. Priority is given to policy fields that contribute to the achievement of the Millennium Development Goals, with half of the budget going to Africa (*Ibid.*).

While making attempts to implement the SWAps, the DGIS decided to carry out a field evaluation of rural development projects realized in the period 1975–2005, in order to learn from earlier experiences and see how the lessons could be used to improve the implementation of the new programme-oriented strategy. They took a representative sample of 46 projects in the field of water management, natural resource management, agricultural extension and integrated rural development[1] and asked separate teams to use a similar format in making an assessment of the results, and identify the underlying success and failure factors.[2] Successes and malfunctions were expressed in terms of relevance, efficiency, effectiveness, sustainability and impact of project interventions,[3] while also taking into account the orientation of projects on poverty, gender, institutional development, gover-nance and environment (the GAVIM-goals, prioritized by DGIS).

This study is an attempt to learn from experience, that is, making an aggregate-level assessment of the factors contributing to the success or failure of development projects in contributing to sustainable development. Insofar as lessons are drawn from development projects, emphasis is often put on the reasons for failure: Projects will not contribute to sustainable results, due to the limited scale of inter-vention (islands of wealth), the lack of ownership, and the lack of connection between the micro and macro level (Foster 2000: 41; Mayhew 2002). Little is known about why similarly designed projects, with similar aims, produce differ-ential results in different settings. Making a distinction between the successful projects and failures on the basis of DAC and GAVIM performance, what types of factors explain the different results; what can we learn to make future policy more effective?

- To facilitate an aggregate-level assessment of the factors contributing to the success or failure of the projects, we compiled a database on the basis of the 46 evaluation reports containing the following information.
- Background to the context of the projects at country level and, if possible, at the level of the intervention area (HDI, life expectancy, literacy rate, GDP, macro-structural reform, political situation, ecological problems and climate).
- Basic project characteristics, namely duration, budget, type of activities, mission or goal, donor collaboration, etc.
- Project results (as formulated in the evaluation reports), namely the indicators used, and the assessment of critical success and failure factors as mentioned in the report; also the scores on the GAVIM goals and the DAC indicators.

This study first presents a summary of the characteristics of the 46 projects under review, followed by a description of the DAC and GAVIM results. An attempt is then made to establish patterns of factors that contribute to the success or failure of development projects. Finally, it identifies a number of hidden problems that are often neglected in policy debates. I will show that DAC and GAVIM criteria help in understanding what type of factors play a role in the success or failure of projects; the outcome will finally depend on more general factors such as how projects are strategically linked in broader policies, their local embeddedness (i.e. how to respond to or anticipate complexities), and whether they are in line with the short- and long-term strategies of the people who are supposed to benefit from the project interventions. These dimensions are often not sufficiently taken into account in current discussions about learning in development co-operation.

General characteristics of the projects under review

Since the 1980s, DGIS has been actively trying rural development by implementing development projects in various fields, notably agricultural research (AR), water management (WM), natural resource management (NRM) and integrated rural development (IRD). The DGIS has implemented these projects in a large number of countries that were usually confronted by adverse economic, political and environmental circumstances (Table 26.1). Using the HDI ranking as an indicator for the socioeconomic situation, we see that many projects were carried out in the poorest countries (Mozambique, Mali, Burkina Faso, Ethiopia), although there were also interventions in relatively richer countries (Ecuador, Philippines, Costa Rica). Most countries were in a post-conflict or even war situation (Ethiopia, Mozambique, Nicaragua, El Salvador); experienced a lot of political turbulence during the period of project implementation (Pakistan, Philippines, Mali, Kenya, Nepal, India) and/or had to deal with adverse climatic/environmental conditions, namely a combination of hurricanes and earthquakes (Bangladesh, Nepal,

Table 26.1   Selection of the projects included in the sample, per country and per continent

	Agricultural research (AR)	Water management (WM)	Natural resource management (NRM)	Integrated rural development (IRD)	Total	HDI rank
Pakistan	1	–	2	2	5	138
India	–	2	1	1	4	124
Bangladesh	–	4	–	–	4	145
Nepal	–	2	–	–	2	142
Philippines	–	1	–	–	1	77
Asia	1	6	6	3	16 (35%)	
Burkina Faso	–	–	–	4	4	169
Ethiopia	–	–	–	4	4	168
Mali	2	–	–	–	2	167
Kenya	1	–	1	–	2	134
Egypt	–	2	–	–	2	115
Benin	1	–	–	–	1	158
Cape Verde	–	–	–	1	1	100
Mozambique	1	–	–	–	1	170
Africa	5	2	1	9	17 (37%)	
Bolivia	2	1	–	2	5	114
Nicaragua	–	–	2	2	4	118
Honduras	–	–	–	1	1	116
Costa Rica	–	–	1	–	1	43
El Salvador	–	–	1	–	1	104
Ecuador	–	–	–	1	1	93
L. America	2	1	4	6	13 (28%)	–
	8 (17%)	9 (19%)	11 (24%)	18 (40%)	46 (100%)	

Sources: Database containing information from 46 evaluation reports (see Appendix) and UNDP (2004).

Mozambique, Honduras, El Salvador), drought (Burkina Faso, Ethiopia, Mali), or a combination of hurricanes, droughts and floods (Kenya, Nicaragua).

Of the projects under review, most of the AR and IRD projects were carried out in Africa (for example, Mali, Kenya, Benin, Mozambique, Burkina Faso, Ethiopia). WM projects were mainly concentrated in Asia (for example, Bangladesh, India), while the NRM projects, although more dispersed, were mostly found in Central America (for example, Nicaragua, Costa Rica, El Salvador) and Asia (for example, Pakistan, Nepal, India, Philippines). Even though it is difficult to make a strict distinction between the different categories,[4] the goals and scope of activities (described later in Table 26.2) can be summarized as follows.

Agricultural research projects

Most of the AR projects under review were initiated in an attempt to fill the vacuum in agricultural research that was created during the neoliberal period when many of the national research institutes and the extension services were closed down, and no further investments were made in agricultural development. Many are national projects with dispersed intervention areas, and the major concern is to deal with the problem of low agricultural returns.

In many projects, attempts were made to introduce farming-system research (to replace the 'old-fashioned' crop-related research), and much emphasis was put on developing new packages more suitable for the poor and with more concern for environmental factors. Initially, many AR projects paid little attention to economic aspects and often had a top-down orientation. In the course of time, along with the tendency to give more priority to extension (rather than research), more attention was paid to linking up with the target group and introducing a more participatory approach. Institutional linkages were rather weak, even though the gap between policy making and research was often seen as a bottleneck.

Water management projects

Water management has been on the DGIS agenda for some time, and was often presented as a necessary ingredient for agricultural modernization. Interestingly, whereas many donors (and the DGIS) had refrained from intervening in politically sensitive issues, such as land reform, large sums of money have been invested in the construction of irrigation systems, the feasibility of which was expressed in cost–benefit relations. Little mention was made of the political dimensions of the water project, namely the distribution of water.

As regards the WM projects under review, it is important to distinguish between irrigation projects (which help farmers to improve production/solve salination problems) and flood-control projects (which help farmers to prevent flooding). In these two types of projects, infrastructure plays a more important role than it does in the other projects, but in the course of time important changes have taken place: instead of infrastructure/production goals, more attention is paid to the environment. Whereas most WM projects initially had direct links with the national level (line ministries), in the course of time more attention was given to the local level (watershed management, integrated water management). Social aspects and environment were increasingly considered important as a direct consequence of shifting development agendas.

Integrated rural development projects

Integrated rural development projects were very popular in the 1980s as the best instrument for alleviating the situation of the rural poor in the most marginalized areas of the developing world (Livingstone 1979; Zoomers and Geurten 1991). Growing disillusionment with technocratic and bureaucratic approaches to rural development (green revolution, agricultural colonization, land reform, etc.) resulted in the conclusion that it was not appropriate to attack single constraints through top-down planning and narrow sector programmes. It was recognized that rural development comprises the interaction of a large number of interrelated activities, and most IRD projects are relatively broad. Attention is paid to agriculture, but also to roads, irrigation, schooling, sanitation, credit and/or small-scale industrialization. 'IRD involves all the things that can most improve the living conditions of the rural masses' (Gebregziabher 1975, cited in Zoomers and Geurten 1991: 195).

The IRD projects under review were often carried out in marginal and isolated regions, concentrated in dry desert areas with problems of famine and ecological degradation. Projects aim at supporting subsistence farmers in guaranteeing food security, usually in combination with a wide range of other activities. Most IRD projects use a bottom-up approach, aimed at simultaneous development of different activities in accordance with local needs and circumstances. Many IRD projects developed in isolation from national policy (IRD being too broad to be covered by a single ministry).

Natural resource management projects

Many of the NRM projects were introduced in the early 1990s, in response to a call by the United Nations Conference on Environment and Development (UNCED) to pay more attention to environmental sustainability. Although environmental problems (erosion, overgrazing, climate change, etc.) affect large parts of the developing world, all NRM projects reviewed have a direct link with forest resources, and were located in subtropical rainforests, often in old colonization areas.[5] Whereas earlier DGIS interventions had been aimed at helping governments to carry out colonization projects (settlement of colonists), most NRM projects focused on reducing deforestation and environmental degradation, while helping small colonist farmers to improve forest management.[6] Many of the NRM projects underwent changes during their lifetime; the focus shifted from tree planting to forest management. Later, many of these projects broadened their scope, and paid more attention to the economic dimensions and/or social aspects (including gender) while introducing a more participatory approach; there was some shift from nature to economic activities and people. Because of the institutional weakness in the field of natural resources (no specialized ministries), many of these projects were rather isolated in the beginning; but in the course of time – along with decentralization policies in the countries involved – the projects developed closer relationships with the local government.

There is some differentiation between AR and WM projects (more 'technical' and specialized) on the one hand, and IRD and NRM projects (more 'social' and broader) on the other.[7] The IRD and NRM projects also have in common that they are usually carried out in the more marginal, most deprived areas, are often isolated from state interventions and/or have to deal with emergency situations. This is in contrast to the WM and AR projects, which are usually based on specialized knowledge and are aimed at helping crop farmers to improve production in areas with relatively more potential; WM and AR projects are often aimed at increasing production, and NRM and IRD projects at environmental and livelihood improvement (Table 26.2).

Most of the projects have relatively small areas of interventions: 38 projects only covered one single municipality, a district, or a watershed (with a limited target population); only eight projects (AR) were national projects with scattered intervention areas. In our sample, but also in other cases, there are no examples of projects working together within the same project area.[8] DGIS-funded projects are in general mostly dispersed, and there is little or no geographic clustering.

Table 26.2 Characterization of the projects

	Field of activities	Dominant goal	Type of problem	Type of target group	Location (also Table 26.1)
40% (N = 18) IRD (> 5 activities) with tendency to become more restricted	IRD-related range of activities	Disaster prevention and food security Livelihood improvement Institutional strengthening	Famine and marginalization Ecological degradation	Subsistence farmers, marginalized, support related to food crops	Often in dry-desert areas of sub-Saharan Africa
24% (N = 11) NRM (2–5 activities) with tendency to become broader	Range of activities related to agro-forestry/social forestry	Environmental goals, combined with livelihood improvement, settlement, land distribution	Deforestation and 'cattleization' Environmental problems	Crop producers, diversified, often in combination with migration, support related to agro-forestry	Mainly in old colonization areas; forest frontiers of Central America
19% (N = 9) WM (< 2 activities) relatively specialized	Watershed management, irrigation and flood control, often with infrastructure development	Agricultural production, livelihood improvement, settlement, land distribution Institutional strengthenning	Waterlogging and salination Flooding and groundwater problems	Crop producers, diversified and specialized, support related to WM and irrigation	Mainly in Asian watersheds
17% (N = 8) AR (< 2 activities) relatively specialized	Farming systems research and crop development, often related to dry land farming	Agricultural production Institutional strengthening	Low agricultural returns support, related to cotton, soya, potatoes, rice	Crop producers. Diversified, crop-specific	Dispersed, often national projects crop-specific

Source: Database containing information from 46 evaluation reports (see Annexe).

There are considerable differences in geographical characteristics of the project areas (Table 26.3): 22 per cent of the projects were carried out in the savannahs of the Sahel and 11 per cent in the high mountains of the Andes; 37 per cent of the projects focused on deforested areas in the tropics/subtropics, while 22 per cent were carried out in watersheds and/or on flood plains; in 8 per cent of the cases the project area was not specified. In the project documents little information is usually available about the characteristics of the target group: 23 per cent of the projects focused on subsistence farmers; the rest speak about 'smallholders' (that is, a very diverse group of people). It is striking, however, that little or no attention is given to other groups such as fishers, cattle herders, landless people, or non-sedentary groups (nomads), even though these often form a considerable part of the rural population, also within the project areas.

A noticeable characteristic of the projects under review is their long duration. The average duration of the projects under review was 10.7 years (range: 3–25 years); almost 50 per cent lasted between eight and 11 years, which was often not foreseen in the original design. Many of the projects experienced a chain of extensions. The project team stayed longer than planned, in response to disappointing results or to problems related to transferring the results to counterpart organizations. In spite of being extended several times, 52 per cent of the projects ended without a clear exit strategy; 20 per cent ended 'unexpectedly' as a direct consequence of changing donor policy (including projects that were stopped with the introduction of the SWAp policy).

During the lifetime of the projects, important transformations took place in 80 per cent of the cases. These transformations concerned the aims of the project (65 per cent of cases, for example, shifting, from environmental to social goals); the approach (50 per cent; e.g. with more participation, more attention to gender relations), the delimitation of the project area (35 per cent; often a reduction for reasons of efficiency); changes in counterpart organizations (52 per cent), and/or in donor structure and funding situation (13 per cent). Most of the DGIS projects were carried out bilaterally, without the involvement of other donors.[9] Almost all

Table 26.3   Type of intervention area

	AR	WM	NRM	IRD	Total (%)
Deforested area in lowland/tropical/subtropical areas	–	–	10	7	17 (37)
Desert area and Savannah (Sahel)	3	–	–	7	10 (22)
High mountain areas (Andes)	1	1	–	3	5 (11)
Flood plains and irrigated areas	1	8	1	–	10 (22)
No specific project area	3	–	–	1	4 (8)

Source: Database containing information from 46 evaluation reports (see Appendix).

DGIS projects were traditional in the sense that 83 per cent were directed by expatriates, usually under the guidance of a specialized Dutch consultancy firm or development organization. Salary costs (project staff and missions) form the bulk of the budget, although there were considerable differences between the different projects. In WM, for example, large sums were spent on infrastructure, whereas in IRD much was also spent on credit programmes, sanitation and/or education. There was considerable diversity in the project budgets.[10]

As regards the extent to which the projects worked in isolation and/or had links with the government and/or non-governmental organizations (NGOs), there is a clear difference between AR and WM projects on the one hand (direct contact with line ministries, central level) and IRD and NRM projects on the other (networking mainly with NGOs and community organizations, local level). The 'vertical integration' of most projects was very weak. It is only during the final period (along with the introduction of the SWAps) that projects became incorporated into the policy structure – projects started to link up with ministries, and this had positive implications for their capacity to influence mainstream policy.

Assessing the project results: successes or failures?

DAC and GAVIM evaluation criteria

Reviewing the characteristics of the Dutch development projects, we see a reflection of the various deficiencies that are often mentioned in the literature (Euforic 2004; Grinspun 2001; Foster *et al.* 2000; Mayhew 2002). Fragmentation, lack of ownership and a lack of sustainability appear as important bottlenecks – but instead of further focusing on the weakness of the individual projects, I make an aggregate-level analysis of why some projects become a success and others end up as failures.

In order to make a distinction between the projects on the basis of failure or success, we first made an assessment on the basis of the DAC evaluation criteria (see Box 26.1) and the GAVIM goals (see Box 26.2) both adopted by DGIS as guidelines for field evaluations in the early 1990s. The DAC criteria give an impression of the relevance, effectiveness, efficiency, impact and sustainability of the individual project results (OECD-DAC 1991). The GAVIM criteria help to assess whether the projects gave sufficient priority to dimensions such as poverty, environment, gender, governance and institutional development. These dimensions are considered important by DGIS for achieving positive results (DGIS 2003a; Schulpen 2001). For the purpose of this evaluation, the consultants were asked to give scores for each of these dimensions for every project (here used as an input for further analysis). An assessment was made of the 46 projects in terms of DAC and GAVIM scores, using different ratings (1 = very positive; 2 = positive; 3 = negative; 4 = very negative).[11] A low DAC rating indicates a project's success, namely it was relevant, effective, efficient, had a good impact and led to sustainable results. A low GAVIM rating indicates that sufficient priority was given to goals such as poverty alleviation, environment, gender and so forth. Higher DAC scores indicate a negative performance, and a high GAVIM rating shows that insufficient attention was paid to the GAVIM dimensions.

Box 26.1:   DAC criteria for project evaluation

Relevance: The extent to which the aid activity is suited to the priorities and policies of the target group, recipient, and donor: Are the objectives valid? Are the activities and outputs consistent with the overall goal and with the attainment of the objectives? Are the activities and outputs of the programme consistent with the intended impacts and effects?

Effectiveness: A measure of the extent to which an aid activity attains its objectives. Were the objectives achieved? What were the major factors influencing achievement/ non-achievement?

Efficiency: Measures the outputs, both qualitative and quantitative, in relation to the inputs. Were the activities cost-efficient? Were the objectives achieved on time? Was the project implemented in the most efficient way compared to the alternatives?

Impact: The positive and negative changes produced by a development intervention, directly or indirectly, intended or unintended. What has happened as a result of the project? What real differences have the activities made to the beneficiaries? How many people have been affected?

Sustainability: This is concerned with measuring whether the benefits of an activity are likely to continue after donor funding has been withdrawn. Projects need to be environmentally as well as financially sustainable. What happened to the benefits of the project after funding ceased? What were the major factors that influence the achievement or non-achievement of sustainability of the programme or project?

Source: OECD-DAC (1991).

Box 26.2:   GAVIM criteria for project evaluation

The Dutch acronym 'GAVIM' spells out the key policy aims and themes targeted by Dutch Development Co-operation. *Poverty reduction, gender equality and women's empowerment, protection of the environment, natural resources and nature conservation* are the core themes. *Good governance* was recently added, and because these aims can be achieved only through a process of broad institutional development, *institutional development* became the fifth theme. Moreover, good governance and institutional development are prerequisites for effective and sustainable development co-operation.

These GAVIM goals provide a key reference framework for annual plans and macroeconomic programmes and are used as a reference framework when analyzing the sectors to be assisted and when deciding on methods and objectives, not just to help meet the stated goals but also to boost the effectiveness and sustainability of aid. The emphasis on GAVIM is based on international agreements reached at conferences like United Nations Summit on Environment and Development (UNCED) in Rio de Janeiro, the Cairo World Population conference, the social summit in Copenhagen, the Beijing World Conference on Women and the Habitat Conference in Istanbul. The GAVIM policy goals are also brought together in the form of international development targets in the OECD's *Shaping the 21st Century* (OECD-DAC 1996).

Source: Working Document GAVIM and the Sectoral Approach (source from www.minbuza.nl).

Table 26.4 shows that the best DAC results were achieved in terms of relevance and effectiveness (1.73 and 2.24, respectively); the results for sustainability, impact and efficiency are less favourable (2.73, 2.51 and 2.38). With respect to the GAVIM goals (Table 26.5), the scores for environment, gender and poverty are relatively favourable (2.14, 2.17 and 2.19), while those for institutional development and governance are less favourable (2.40, 2.55).

The best GAVIM results were achieved by the IRD projects (in spite of relatively negative scores for governance and institutional development); this positive picture is supported by a rather positive DAC score for relevance (but negative scores for effectiveness, impact and sustainability). AR projects have relatively positive results for DAC (relevance and effectiveness), in spite of showing a rather negative score for sustainability; these projects also show rather positive GAVIM scores for institutional development and governance (but negative for gender, environment and poverty).

Table 26.4 Mean DAC scores in different types of projects

DAC	Efficiency	Effectiveness	Impact	Relevance	Sustainability	DAC total
AR	2.19	1.94	2.13	2.00	2.81	11.06 (10–12.5)
WM	2.28	2.28	2.22	1.94	2.44	11.17 (9.5–15)
NRM	2.67	2.50	2.86	1.81	2.86	12.78 (9–18)
IRD	2.36	2.21	2.62	1.44	2.77	11.36 (6–17)
Total	2.38	2.24	2.51	1.73	2.73	11.58 (6–18)

Source: Database containing information from 46 evaluation reports (see Appendix).

Table 26.5 Mean GAVIM scores in different types of projects

GAVIM	Governance	Poverty	Gender	Environment	Institutional development	GAVIM total
AR	2.00	2.38	2.69	2.43	1.88	9.36 (7–11)
WM	2.50	2.21	2.40	2.00	2.19	9.17 (8–10.5)
NRM	2.61	2.59	2.36	2.32	2.86	10.14 (7–13)
IRD	2.75	1.82	1.74	1.93	2.44	7.91 (5–10.5)
Total	2.55	2.19	2.17	2.14	2.40	8.96

Source: Database containing information from 46 evaluation reports (see Appendix).

WM projects have scores for environment (GAVIM) and relevance (DAC), but negative GAVIM scores for governance and gender. The NRM projects were the least successful projects: they have negative scores for efficiency, effectiveness, impact and sustainability (DAC), and negative ratings for all GAVIM goals (Tables 26.4 and 26.5). As for the different regions, Tables 26.6 and 26.7 show that the projects in Africa achieved relatively favourable GAVIM scores (poverty and environment) and DAC scores (relevance). At the other extreme, projects in Central and South America have negative GAVIM scores for governance and institutional development, as well as negative DAC scores for impact and sustainability (in combination with a relatively favourable score for relevance).

Successes versus failures

For the purpose of this study, we divided the projects into two groups: namely the successful projects (i.e. projects with DAC *and* GAVIM scores of less than 11 and eight, respectively) and the unsuccessful projects (projects with DAC and GAVIM scores higher than or equal to 11 and eight) (see Table 26.8). These cut-off points

Table 26.6   Mean DAC scores in different continents

DAC	Efficiency	Effectiveness	Impact	Relevance	Sustainability	DAC total
Asia	2.35	2.06	2.31	1.88	2.56	11.27 (6–15)
Sub-Saharan Africa	2.19	2.09	2.44	1.59	2.66	10.94 (9–13.5)
Central/South America	2.68	2.65	2.85	1.73	3.04	12.87 (9–18)
Total	2.38	2.24	2.51	1.73	2.73	11.58

Source: Database containing information from 46 evaluation reports (see Appendix).

Table 26.7   Mean GAVIM scores in different continents

GAVIM	Governance	Poverty	Gender	Environment	Institutional development	GAVIM total
Asia	2.56	2.34	2.36	2.23	2.29	9.46 (5–13)
Sub-Saharan Africa	2.43	1.93	2.07	1.92	2.13	7.96 (6–11)
Central/South America	2.75	2.27	2.08	2.23	2.85	9.42 (7–11.5)
Total	2.55	2.19	2.17	2.14	2.40	8.96

Source: Database containing information from 46 evaluation reports (see Appendix).

Table 26.8 Ten most successful and 16 least successful projects on the basis of mean DAC-GAVIM scores

	Most successful projects				Least successful projects		
Name of project	Country	Type of project	DAC + GAVIM	Name of project	Country	Type of project	DAC + GAVIM
ERP	Pakistan	NRM-institutional development	16	SARC-TSARDD	Philippines	NRM-IRD	22.5
PDI/Z-PDL/Z	Burkina Faso	IRD	17	CHOROTEG	Costa Rica	NRM-IRD	22.5
BAREAP	Ethiopia	IRD	16	PRODES	Nicaragua	IRD-NRM	24.5
GIRPDP	Ethiopia	IRD	16.5	PROCODEFOR	Nicaragua	NRM-IRD	24
LEMPIRA	Honduras	IRD	17.5	PSB/PB	Burkina Faso	IRD	22
ADTDP	India	IRD	11	Chuquisaca Centro	Bolivia	IRD-NRM	20
SUPAK	Ethiopia	IRD-institutional development	16	Fortalecimient org.	Bolivia	IRD-Inst.Dev	23.5
MALAKA	Pakistan	NRM	18	Servicio postcosecha	Ecuador	IRD-Inst.Dev	26
CDSP	Bangladesh	WM/IRD	19	NRAP-ISWASRI	Pakistan	AR	23.5
BENGAL TERAI	India	WM/IRD	18	Bundelkhand	India	NRM/WM	27
				Mechi Hill	Nepal	NRM-IRD	26
				PIE Monte	Nicaragua	NRM	29
				RAMR-PARP	Benin	AR	21.5
				SRP	Bangladesh	WM	21.5
				CPP	Bangladesh	WM	21.5
				HOPP	India	WM	25

Source: Database containing information from 46 evaluation reports (see Appendix).

were chosen because they allowed us to make a selection of the top 20–30 per cent of the most and least successful projects (reflected by consistent patterns of extreme negative and positive scores, respectively). Projects with mixed results were not taken into consideration.[12]

The most successful projects (a group of ten) have positive DAC scores for relevance (1.45), efficiency (1.85) and effectiveness (1.90), and favourable GAVIM scores for environment (1.67), gender (1.75) and poverty (1.80). At the other extreme, the failures (16 projects) have negative DAC scores for sustainability (3.16), impact (2.90), efficiency (2.90) and effectiveness (2.63), and unfavourable GAVIM scores for governance (2.81) and institutional development (2.70). As for the characteristics of the more successful projects, there is some concentration of IRD projects carried out in relatively marginal and isolated areas in poor countries (three in Ethiopia, one each in Burkina Faso, Honduras and India): successful projects were relatively strong in helping subsistence farmers to improve their food security situation, in contributing to disaster prevention and in working with the poorer groups of subsistence farmers; other successful projects were in Pakistan (2 × NRM) and in India and Bangladesh (2 × WM).

At the other extreme (the failures), there is some over-representation of NRM projects carried out in the colonization areas of Central America (three in Nicaragua and one in Costa Rica) that were aimed at solving the problems of deforestation and/or overgrazing (introduction of cattle); most involved working with farmers with diversified livelihoods (farming combined with migration, partly as an exit strategy). Other failed NRM projects were in Nepal, India and the Philippines. Also the IRD projects carried out in Nicaragua, Ecuador, Bolivia (2 ×) and Burkina Faso were not a success; other failures were found in India and Bangladesh (3 × WM) and in Benin and Pakistan (2 × AR). The best results were thus found in the most deprived regions in Africa; this is mainly reflected by the higher scores for poverty (GAVIM) and relevance (DAC). The most negative results were in the colonization projects in Central and South America.

Even though DAC and GAVIM criteria help to get a global picture of projects' successes versus failures, there are several limitations in the use of such indicators. A negative evaluation in terms of DAC or GAVIM will not necessarily mean that the original project goals were not achieved: in many cases, DAC or GAVIM criteria are used *ex post facto* for purposes of evaluation, while in the original project document no mention was made of aspects such as gender or environment. Also the opposite is true; a positive evaluation in terms of DAC and GAVIM will not necessary mean that the project was in line with the livelihood priorities of the population (or was appreciated by the population). Projects aimed at improving farm income might be called a success in terms of DAC criteria or GAVIM goals, but this view is not necessarily shared by the majority of the population who might have had a preference for other, non-agricultural, activities (Reardon *et al.* 2001). There might have been better, more effective solutions or a shorter road to poverty alleviation. In many cases, the scores are not so much a reflection of the performances of the project, but much more a reflection of the complexity of context: GAVIM and DAC criteria tend to evidence more favourable results in settings that are subject to climatic disaster or political upheaval, given that the scores for poverty (GAVIM) or relevance (DAC) will show more striking, positive results. At the same time, however, improvements in the local situation will not necessarily be a proof of the 'success' of the project; improvements may be nothing to do with the project, but with political peace or stability, or recovery after a war or a natural disaster. In addition, it is myopic to make an assessment of the success or failure of projects without taking into account cost–benefit aspects of project implementation. Although natural-resource management projects might have generated less positive results than other projects, how much money was spent and who benefited? Low-cost failures cannot be automatically compared with high-cost failures. It is important to take such dimensions into account when referring to DAC and GAVIM scores in evaluations.

Searching for an explanation

An important aim of this study was to make an aggregate-level assessment of the factors contributing to the success or failure of a project. To do so, an investigation was made into what patterns could be identified regarding the factors affecting the success or failure of activities, and the extent to which these factors are region- or theme-specific. There are a number of interesting correlations between DAC and GAVIM scores and other variables available in the data material that give an indication of the kind of factors that explain the success or failure of project interventions.

First, there is correlation between DAC and GAVIM scores, even though they measure different things (the correlation between the total DAC and GAVIM score amounts to 572**). There is a strong correlation between the effectiveness of projects (DAC) and the GAVIM score for governance (710**); there is also correlation between the total DAC score with GAVIM scores for governance (626**), institutional development (505**) and poverty (427**); there is less correlation with GAVIM scores for environment (351*) and gender (no correlation). Other correlations were found for the total GAVIM score and the DAC scores for efficiency (550**) and effectiveness (403**), impact (395*) and sustainability (376*); no correlation was found with the DAC score for relevance. In spite of measuring different dimensions, DAC and GAVIM scores often point in similar directions and seem to be mutually linked.

Second, there are significant correlations between the GAVIM and/or DAC scores and a number of project characteristics; Table 26.9. The most *relevant* projects are well focused (422**) and sufficiently large (DGIS-contribution; −398**). The *impact* of a project seems to depend mainly on the degree of vertical integration and/or the availability of micro–macro linkages (406**), as well as on the level of investments (not too large; 349*) and the degree of flexibility (allowing for timely adaptations without losing their focus; 310*), and are relatively small and inexpensive (DGIS-contribution; 349*). The *effectiveness* of projects is mainly related to the context (HDI score; −310*). Finally, *efficiency* is linked with the availability of systems for monitoring and evaluation (−393* and −386*, respectively).

Table 26.9   Analysis of correlations

	Significant at the 0.01 level (**)	Significant at the 0.05 level (*)
The project context:		
HDI scores (and underlying variables)		GAVIMtotal (−339)
		GAVIMinstitdev (−336)
		DACeffectiveness (−310)
Project characteristics:		
Networking/ (horizontal linkages with NGOs, local government etc.)	GAVIMtot (−413)	GAVIMgender (−370)
		GAVIMenvironment (−365)
Integration micro-macro/ (vertical linkages with regional and national levels)	DACimpact (406)	GAVIMgovernance (508)
		DACrelevance (−353)
Stability-flexibility/ process approach/ (changes during project life)	GAVIMgovernance (585)	DACtotal (313)
		DACimpact (310)
		DACsustainability (305)
Project focus/range of activities/ (broad versus specialized)	DACrelevance (422)	GAVIMpoverty (−322)
Monitoring and evaluation/ (yes versus no)		DACefficiency (−393)
		DACtotal (−386)
DGIS contribution/ (high versus low budget)	DACrelevance (−398)	DACimpact (349)

Source: Database containing information from 46 evaluation reports (see Appendix).

The achievement of GAVIM goals seem to be related to the horizontal linkages/ networking capacity (−413**, −370*, −365*), and a sufficient degree of stability-flexibility (585**), as well as to the project focus (not too specialized; −322*). Also the degree of vertical integration (micro–macro; 508*) and the context (HDI: −339* and 336*) are important for the GAVIM scores. Projects active in networking show a good performance on *gender* and *environment*. Projects carried out in complex situations show positive results for *institutional development*. Stable and well-focused projects with a sufficient degree of vertical integration show positive scores for *governance*. And broader projects (no specialization) have the best *poverty* scores. The correlation between the HDI rank and the DAC and GAVIM scores confirms the earlier conclusion that in more problematic situations (with lower levels of human development according to the HDI), the DAC and GAVIM scores are more positive than in countries with lower rankings. This picture of patterns of factors explaining the success or failure of projects is confirmed by a more detailed analysis of the critical success and failure factors mentioned in the different evaluation reports. The following list reflects the kind of factors identified (Table 26.10):

- *Target group orientation* (mentioned 60 times in the evaluation reports). Successful projects are said to have a homogeneous and clearly defined target group, with sufficient attention paid to empowerment and tangible benefits.

- *Institutional characteristics and organizational setup* (mentioned 56 times). Successful projects are locally embedded: they involve all the crucial actors and counterparts with a sufficient level of involvement of the grassroots level (bottom up). Staff quality and continuity are also very important.
- The *policy context* (mentioned 54 times). In successful projects often there is consistency between project goals and national policy with a minimum of donor-driven changes.
- The *sociopolitical circumstances* (mentioned 14 times), *economic environment/ infrastructure* (23 times) and *ecology* (16 times). Project results are often negatively influenced by the unfavourable macroeconomic conditions and pricing, and by a poor ecological situation.
- *Project design, planning and implementation* (mentioned 52 times) play an important role; successful projects show consistency between goal and activities, and have appropriate technologies. It is also important to have a process approach with a sufficient degree of flexibility.
- The *human resources and project team organization* (mentioned 22 times). Successful projects have a professional staff with sufficient continuity (staff turnover is often a problem).

More specifically, the most important determinants of success or of failure are the consistency between project goals and national policy (E, mentioned 35 times; 19 times as a reason for failure; 16 times as a reason for successes), the conceptual setup and/or lack of consistency (B, mentioned 27 times; 21: failure, 6: success), the local embeddedness/involvement of the crucial actors or counterparts (D, mentioned 26 times; 16: failure, 10: success), target group orientation (C, mentioned 25 times; 16: success, 9: failure) and empowerment activities (C, mentioned 22 times; 12: failure, 10: success).

More specifically, success was mainly attributed to: Having a clear target group focus and paying sufficient attention to empowerment (C); local ownership and the involvement of crucial actors/counterparts (D); consistency between project goals and national policy (E); and having a process approach/sufficient flexibility in project implementation (B). The failure of projects was mainly explained in terms of inappropriate project design and lack of consistency (B), an unfavourable policy environment (E) and/or other unfavourable external circumstances (F, H, G) and lack of continuity of staff/high staff turnover (A).

The hidden dimensions: priorities for learning

The above indicates that the DGIS projects have changed considerably over the last period, and that many projects are wrongly described as static and fragmented. Many projects show rather positive results, even though performance depends very much on the local circumstances (target group, available actors etc.). The performance of projects will very much depend on the project design, the institutional landscape, human capacities, etc. At the same time, however, the move from projects to SWAps seems a step in the right direction. This new policy context will offer better opportunities to apply more co-ordinated, multisectoral

Table 26.10 Critical success and failure factors

Success factors (+)	Critical factors for success +	Critical factors for failure −	Total
A. *Human resources of project team/internal organization: 22*			
composition of team/expertise		4	4
professionalism of team	1	4	5
continuity of team/staff turnover		9	9
organizational capacity	1	3	4
B. *Project design, planning and implementation: 52*			
process approach at project level	9		9
conceptual setup/consistency	6	21	27
appropriateness of technologies	7	7	14
monitoring and evaluation	1	1	2
C. *Target group orientation: 60*			
target group focus	16	9	25
activities aimed at strengthening target group	10	12	22
tangible benefits for target group	8	4	12
process approach at target group level	1		1
D. *Institutional characteristics/organizational setup: 56*			
local ownership	7	10	17
local embeddedness/involvement of crucial actors/counterparts	10	16	26
professionalism of the (local) counterpart		8	8
tangible benefits in terms of institutional strengthening	2	3	5
E. *Policy environment: 54*			
consistency between project goals and national policy	16	19	35
donor policies/donor co-ordination	4	15	19
F. *Sociopolitical environment: 14*			
heterogeneity of target group	2	6	8
civil unrest/political conflicts		5	5
human rights/civil rights/democratisation		1	1
G. *Economic environment and infrastructure: 23*			
poverty of the target group		7	7
macroeconomic conditions/pricing	1	11	12
availability of supportive institutions/infrastructure		4	4
H. *Ecology: 16*			
availability of natural resources/ environmental	1	9	10
climatological conditions/drought and natural disasters		6	6

Source: Database containing information from 46 evaluation reports (see Appendix).

approaches, with more ownership and a better degree of vertical integration. In some cases change is the result of DGIS reacting to external changes and in other cases is a result of lessons learned. In many cases there is not a strict separation between the project and programme approach. Many projects during their lifetime moved into the direction of a SWAp (became more focused, adopted a process approach, were active in networking, strengthened 'local' ownership etc.).

In the current debate about how to improve the performance of development co-operation, much emphasis is given to the subject of organizational learning – the lack of solid knowledge about the impact of 'aid' is nowadays mentioned as problematic, having a negative impact for the effectiveness of aid (Grinspun 2001). According to Carlsson and Wohlgemuth (2000: 7), learning in development co-operation is difficult due to five factors that seem to be particularly prominent: political constraints; the unequal nature of aid relationship; problems internal to the organization of the aid agency; organization and capacity of the recipient; and sources of knowledge and quality of information. In order to improve the learning experiences of the stakeholders active in development co-operation ('do we learn from our experiences and do we feed that knowledge back into improved practices?'), much will depend on the availability of data collections systems.[13] Much priority is given to social analysis: improving feedback and communication practices to promote an evaluation culture and to implement country programmes and joint evaluations; and to promote partnerships in evaluations, design and implement performance measurement systems (OECD-DAC 1998: 2; Bamberger and Hewitt 1986).

Even though these kinds of transformations will be important inputs for learning, we would like to raise a number of 'hidden' issues that are often neglected in the current debate, and which need to be solved in order to improve the performance of development co-operation.

A strategic mission?

An important bottleneck to successful development policy is the lack of a clear mission. Many DGIS projects focused on supporting agriculture, without establishing whether this was in line with the livelihood strategies of the people (who often invested in exit strategies) and/or assessing the long-term viability at the macro level. While the DGIS supported neoliberal policies, it financed a large number of projects in the field of rural development (helping the poor to survive neoliberalism). Development projects helped to keep people on the land, but there was no vision about whether this would help people in their attempts to escape from poverty. The DGIS worked in AR, WM, NRM and IRD; interventions were mainly related to agriculture, neglecting such other activities as migration, cattle ranching and fishery. Little attention was paid to the landless groups, including nomadic people. There was not much strategic thinking about target groups, and there was no priority given to particular project areas. In the decades under review, rural development policy was rather fragmented (with separate AR, WM, NRM and IRD projects); each project had its own project area: there are no examples of combined efforts where different projects focused on the same project area. Each project had its own goals and its own area of intervention; co-ordination often involved different sections of the ministry (DGIS) and various sector specialists working at the embassies.

Consistency between goals and activities?

Looking at the goals and activities of the various projects, it is striking that project aims are usually very vague, and it is not so clear why priority was given to a particular strategy (instead of alternative ways to achieve poverty alleviation). In addition, during the final decade the consistency between goals and activities even deteriorated due to the multiplication of evaluation criteria (for example, GAVIM etc.), among other things. Many projects in the 1990s moved away from their original project goals, without adjusting the strategy as to how they wanted to contribute to poverty alleviation. Projects which, according to their mission statement, were mainly aimed at 'helping farmers to improve their income situation' focus on activities such as tree planting or institutional development even though this will probably not be the shortest way to poverty alleviation. Projects aimed at supporting the rural poor to escape from poverty (still) focus on introducing new crop varieties or improving irrigation as a strategy for agricultural development. There are no interventions related to migration even though this would have helped people to accumulate capital in a much easier way. There was often no systematic search for the best solution given the whole range of opportunities and the aspirations of the population.

Neglecting the problematic context?

In project documents, little attention is usually given to the context, or more specifically the reality that most of the projects concentrate in areas where floods, hurricanes etc., are part of normal life (people will have to deal with such situations, even though they are calculated as a risk). The projects under review were carried out in post-conflict regions, or in areas hit by natural disasters, but in almost all the project documents targets are set on the basis of the 'lucky' situation (no disasters as the 0-situation). In evaluations, the war situation, conflicts, or the incidence of drought or flood, are mentioned as reasons for not achieving the expected results, which is often the reason for prolongation. In areas of development co-operation work, situations of war, drought and hurricanes are insufficiently seen as 'normalities'; project goals are formulated in terms of poverty alleviation, even in circumstances where priority should be given to earlier goals (such as political stabilization). Given the complexity of the project situation, it is striking that so little attention is paid in most projects to disaster prevention. Every time a new hurricane occurs donor funds are spent on reconstruction as if it were mere bad luck and not as part of the normal life situation.[14] Many projects have negative results as a direct consequence of setting unrealistic goals. It is important to mention the problematic context in a more explicit way, and to see how interventions could help people to anticipate future emergencies better (preventing problems, instead of solving them).

Final reflections

In order improve the performance of development co-operation, it is important to take into account the various lessons that can be drawn from the analysis of DAC and GAVIM scores (the importance of target group orientation, vertical integration, and so on). At the same time, however, these kinds of evaluation criteria are restricted in the sense of not giving sufficient attention to the context (successes and failures being a reflection of the external situation), and do not necessarily give an indication of the ability of projects to respond to the needs of the population: many of the projects under review originally did not have GAVIM goals, and the use of GAVIM scores *ex post facto* for evaluation purposes does not say much about real successes or failures. More attention should be given to how to make development co-operation more strategic and strengthening the link with the local context.

Development co-operation should preferably target broader development programmes (SWAps) instead of isolated projects – the success will finally depend on the kind of projects that will be implemented. Rather than suggesting a contrast between the 'isolated' projects and the 'broader' SWAps, it is clear that it is a continuum. Many projects during their lifetime adopted SWAp elements and it is not realistic to expect that programmes will per se produce better results than projects. The success of sectoral programmes will finally depend on the kind of projects being implemented in the context of the SWAp; the outcome will very much depend on the degree to which projects fit the local context and local trends, and the underlying strategy. In the current discussion about how to generate significant and sustainable outcomes too much attention is given to 'procedures' and 'tangible results' and too little to the contents and significance. Modern SWAps (aimed at infrastructure development) will often search for tangible results (how many kilometres of road improvement) without discussing that many roads will most probably be flooded or destroyed by severe weather. Sectoral programmes (for example, aimed at educational reform) often lack strategic goals, such as stopping out-migration. In the current debate, much value is given to the subject of organizational learning in development co-operation. Aid effectiveness is expected to improve if aid agencies, and their counterparts on the receiving end, devote more attention to the collection of information.[15] Large investments are made in monitoring systems and the design of project performance systems which will allow visible and tangible results.

However, *learning* is not a matter of data collection or measurement of output indicators, but a matter of better *understanding* the dynamics of daily life. Rather than spending much time on having internal discussions about organizational learning between institutions, more priority should be given to having regular meetings with the common people in the countryside. Grass-roots participation and dialogue are important elements of bringing development interventions better in line with the livelihood priorities of the population. In order to improve the performance of development co-operation it is important that interventions keep track (are interventions still in line with local priorities and trends?). This is much more important than measuring output (are results in line with the project goal?) which is wrongly presented as a priority in monitoring and evaluation practices.

Appendix

List of reviewed projects

Natural resource management

Country	Name of project
Philippines	SARC-TSARDD
Pakistan	ERP (Environmental Rehabilitation Project) in Malakand Division Malakand Social Forestry Project
Costa Rica	Agroforestry Project Chorotega Consolidación del Uso Adecuado de los Recursos Forestales en Comunidades Rurales de la Región de Chorotega y Pacífico Central
El Salvador	Sustainable Agriculture on Sloping Lands (Agricultura Sostenible en Zonas de Ladera)
Nicaragua	Conservation and Sustainable Forest Development project (PROCODEFOR) Pie de Monte Reforestation Project Jalapa
Kenya	Kenya Woodfuel Agro-Forestry Programme
India	Bundelkhand Integrated Water Resources Management Project
Nepal	Mechi Hill Development Programme Mahottari Natural Resource Management Project

Agricultural research

Country	Name of project
Bolivia	Optimización de la Fijación Biológica de Nitrógeno para la Agricultura en Bolivia, 'Rhizobiología' Seed potato project (PROSEMPA)
Mozambique	Consolidation of the household food security and nutrition information network for policy formulation and development planning
Pakistan	Netherlands Research Assistance Project (NRAP) at the International Waterlogging and Salinity Research Institute (IWASRI)
Mali	Division de Recherche des Systèmes de Production Rurale Projet Riz Irrigué
Benin	Projet Recherche Appliquée en Milieu Réel (RAMR/PARP)
Kenya	National Agricultural Research Programme Kenya

Water management

Country	Name of project
Bolivia	Mink'a Potosi (Mink'a III)
India	Operational Pilot Project for Reclamation of Waterlogged and Saline Lands (HOPP)

	North Bengal Terai Development Project (NB-Terai)
Bangladesh	System Rehabilitation Project (SRP)
	Early Implementation Project (EIP)
	Char Development and Settlement Project (CDSP)
	Compartimentalization Pilot Project (CPP)
Egypt	Drainage Executive Management Project (DEMP)
	Fayoum Water Management Project (FWMP)

Integrated rural development

Country	Name of project
Philippines	SARC-TSARDD Sustainable Agrarian Reform Communities in the Philippines – Technical Support to Agrarian Reform and Rural Development
Nicaragua	Rural Development Project in the area of Nueva Guinea, Muelle de los Bueyes y El Rama
	Apoyo al Desarrollo Humano Sostenible de la Comunidades Indígenas y Campesinas de la Zona Norte de la Región Autónoma Atlántico Sur (PRORAAS II)
Burkina Faso	Integrated Development Programme of the provinces Sanguié and Boulkiemdé (PDISAB)
	Programming and Implementation of Integrated Development in Kaya (PEDI-Kaya)
	Burkinabè Sahel Programme (PSB/PB)
	Zoundwéogo Integrated Rural Development Programme (PDI/Z, now PDL/Z)
Bolivia	Sub-regional Development of Chuquisaca Centro, Management of Natural Resources
	Fortalecimiento de organizaciones económicas de base (Strengthening of economic base organizations)
Ethiopia	Bugna Integrated Rural Development Programme (BIRDP)
	Gidan Integrated Rural Development Programme (GIRDP)
	Meket Integrated Rural development programme (MIRDP)
	Sustainable Poverty Alleviation in Kafa Zone (SUPAK)
Cape Verde	Programme de Apoio ao Desenvolvimento Santo Antao (PADESA, Support to the Development of Santo Antao)
Ecuador	Centros de referencia para la oferta de servicios poscosecha (Reference centres for post-harvest services)
Honduras	Desarrollo Rural del Sur de Lempira, Phase II (Rural Development of South Lempira)
India	Andhra Pradesh Tribal Development Project (APTDP – IN/90/023)
Pakistan	Animal Husbandry In-service Training Institute, Phase III (AHITI) Provincial Administrated Tribal Areas Integrated Agricultural Development Project (PATA)

Notes

An earlier version of this study was published in the *International Development Planning Review*.

1. This selection was made by the DGIS staff, based on project goals, location, duration and budget size. The selected projects represent almost 50 per cent of the total budget spent on agricultural research and extension services, water management, natural resource management and integrated rural development (1975–2005), and covers about 25 per cent of the total number of projects. The sample is restricted to project support (i.e. not including programme and/or budget support). No further details are available for reasons of confidentiality, but the sample contains the more important projects in terms of budget and duration. The representativeness issue did not consider, however, when projects were instigated (1975–2005), and there is some over-representation of the more recent projects.
2. This study is based on these 46 reports. The author participated in a consultancy assigned to analyze patterns explaining the success and failure of projects; see, for the final reports, van Dijk *et al.* (2005).
3. For instance, the official Development Assistance Committee (DAC) evaluation criteria.
4. In making a classification of the projects, it is important to realize that there is a lot of overlap of goals. Seven projects fall between IRD and NRM projects; four projects classified as WM have the characteristics of IRD projects; and five projects classified as IRD were mainly focused on institutional development (which is not mentioned as one of the administrative categories). Project classifications are often arbitrary.
5. In the 1970s and 1980s, governments, and especially Latin American governments, often supported by international donor organizations, carried out a policy of agricultural colonization. The expansion of the crop farming area was seen as an appropriate strategy for economic growth; in addition it would provide landless workers with new land, thus solving the social problems in the countryside. Some years after their initial cultivation, however, many colonization areas started to show severe problems: forest areas were not very suitable for permanent cultivation and, in many of these zones, land conflict appeared between different groups (cattle herders, agro-industries, indigenous groups, colonists, lumber enterprises, etc.).
6. It is striking that relatively little attention is given by DGIS to environmental problems in other types of areas, such as deserts, mountains, etc. NRM interventions show a strong bias in favour of forest areas.
7. Initially, IRD projects were broad but they became more focused; NRM projects started with an environmental focus, but the scope widened in the course of time.
8. All the projects were aimed at different regions (i.e. no overlap in area of intervention between WM-NRM-AR-IRD projects. All seem to have had their own target area, with the exception of the Malakan Division (Pakistan) and the Bluefield region (Nicaragua).
9. Exceptions are projects where co-financing took place with the UN World Food Programme, UNDP, International Fund for Agricultural Development, EU and the World Bank.
10. NRM and AR projects were relatively low cost, as opposed to the IRD and WM projects.
11. The rating process, presented here as very straightforward, was in practice very complex and rather subjective. We took the ratings given by the different teams, but had to make adaptations based on differences in interpretation (each team having their own reference framework) but also the lack of consistency between the teams. By making an assessment of the ratings in comparison with the contents of the reports, the author tried to eliminate subjectivities and make the information more comparable. The ratings give some indication of the performance of the projects and are used as a starting point of further analysis.
12. We only looked at the projects showing extreme scores; and did not take into account the projects with 'opposite' DAC and GAVIM scores. This decision was made to reduce subjectivities and inconsistencies (see Note 11). We decided to select 26 cases with the clearest and most consistent results, and used this as an input for further analysis.
13. Only 13 per cent of the reviewed projects had some kind of monitoring system. To the extent that information is available about the DGIS projects, this mainly consists of simple output variables (e.g. number of people trained, improvements realized, settlements helped, hectares under irrigation, trees planted, roads improved, etc.), but there was no systematic collection of information about the impact.

14. Only in the case of WM (flood control) and IRD (food security) is there some reflection on how the project could help people to cope better with such misfortunes.
15. 'In the ideal learning situation there is a substantial amount of information created on both sides. This information is often scattered among different sources, which does not make it easy to access it and obtain a good overview. The information needs to be aggregated and synthesized in order to provide a comprehensible and available picture of the current situation' (Carlsson and Wohlgemuth 2000: 9).

References

Bamberger, M. and E. Hewitt (1986) 'Monitoring and Evaluating Urban Development Programmes. A Handbook for Program Managers and Researchers', *World Bank Technical Paper* 53, Washington, DC: World Bank.

Carlsson, J. and L. Wohlgemuth (eds) (2000) *Learning in Development Co-operation*, Stockholm: Almqvist & Wiksell International.

DGIS (2000) 'Working Document GAVIM and the Sectoral Approach', Mimeo (www. minbuza.nl) The Hague: Ministry of Foreign Affairs.

DGIS (2003a) 'Aan elkaar verplicht. Ontwikkelingssamenwerking op weg naar 2015' (www.minbuza.nl), Den Haag: Ministerie voor Buitenlandse Zaken (DGIS).

DGIS (2003b) 'Sectorale Benadering, Organiserend Principe Voor De Bilaterale Ontwikkelingssamenwerking', *Groeidocument* 2, Den Haag: Ministerie voor Buitenlandse Zaken (DGIS), Steungroep Sectorale Benadering.

Euforic (2004) Europe's Forum on International Co-operation (www.euforic.org).

Foster, M. (2000) 'New Approaches to Development Co-operation: What Can We Learn From Experience with Implementing Sector-Wide Approaches?', *ODI Working Paper* 140, London: Overseas Development Institute, Centre for Aid and Public Expenditure.

Foster M., A. Brown and F. Naschold (2000) 'What's Different About Agricultural SWAps?', paper presented at DFID Natural Resources Advisers Conference, 10–14 July, Centre for Aid and Public Expenditure (CAPE), London.

Gebregziabher, B. (1975) *Integrated Development in Rural Ethiopia*, Bloomington, IN: International Development Center.

Grinspun, A. (2001) *Choices for the Poor: Lessons From National Poverty Strategies*, New York: UNDP.

Livingstone, I. (1979) 'On the Concept of Integrated Rural Development Planning in Less Developed Countries', *Journal of Agricultural Economics* XXX: 49–53.

Mayhew, S. (2002) 'Donor Dealings: The Impact of International Donor Aid on Sexual and Reproductive Health Services', *International Family Planning Perspectives*, 28, 4: 220–4.

OECD-DAC (1991) *DAC Principles for Evaluation of Development Assistance*, Paris: OECD-Development Assistance Committee.

OECD-DAC (1996) *Shaping The 21st Century: The Contribution Of Development Co-operation*, Paris: OECD-Development Assistance Committee.

OECD-DAC (1998) *Review of the DAC Principles for Evaluation of Development Assistance*, Paris: OECD-Development Assistance Committee.

Reardon, T., J. Berdegué and G. Escobar (2001) 'Rural Non-farm Employment and Incomes in Latin America: Overview and Policy Implications', *World Development* 29, 3: 395–409.

Schulpen, L. (ed.) (2001) *Hulp In Ontwikkeling: Bouwstenen Voor De Toekomst Van Internationale Samenwerking*, Assen: van Gorcum.

UNDP (United Nations Development Programme) (2004) *Human Development Report*, New York: Oxford University Press for UNDP.

van Dijk, J.W.M., D.F. Bryceson, P. Howard, J. Oorthuizen and A. Zoomers (2005) 'Rural Development Project Performance: A Review of 46 Evaluation Studies of DGIS-funded Projects in the Themes Agricultural Research, Natural Resource Management, Water Management and Area Development and the Implications for the Sector Wide Approach', Consultancy Report for DGIS DDE/NB on behalf of CERES Research School for Resource Studies for Development, Utrecht.

Zoomers, E.B. and G. Geurten (1991) 'A Decade of Integrated Rural Development Planning: An Assessment of PRODERM Experiences in Cusco, Peru', *Journal of Economic and Social Geography*, 82, 3: 195–205.

27
Development Strategy, Viability and Economic Institutions: The Case of China

Justin Yifu Lin, Mingxing Liu, Shiyuan Pan and Pengfei Zhang

Introduction

In recent years, many economists believe that least developed countries (LDCs) failed to catch up with the developed countries because of bad institutions with weak protection for property rights and ineffective constraints on power holders (Acemoglu *et al.* 2004). At the same time, how to understand government behaviour becomes the most important issue for research on institutions. Both policy reformers and researchers from a very diverse set of perspectives have tried to understand how government intervention and regulation occur and how they can subsequently shape the macro incentive structure that firms in an LDC face.

Although the economists and policy-makers have hotly debated the merits of government behaviours and their relationship with the formation of institutions, such issues can be roughly framed within the context of the so-called 'helping hand' (Pigou 1938) versus the 'grabbing hand' taxonomy in the literature. An alternative strand of the grabbing hand view (Shleifer and Vishny 1994) holds that the government interventions are pursued for the benefits of politicians and bureaucrats. For example, politicians use regulations to favour friendly firms and other political constituencies, and thereby obtain benefits such as campaign contributions and votes.[1]

Suppose that government regulations in the LDCs could arise from the grabbing hand of government or political elites. The unsolved question in the literature is how to understand the evolution of institutional structure under government interventions. In the LDCs, the institutional structure shaped by government interventions is quite complicated. We wonder what the incentives are for political leaders to design such complicated systems, because the increased expropriation costs and political control due to the complexity of institutions would diminish the gains of grabbing. Corruptions induced by the special interest groups might not be a good answer for this question either, because the benefited groups are often taxed or suppressed alongside with the protections/subsidies. Actually, many interventions do not have obvious beneficiary groups.

Beyond the views from the helping and grabbing hand categories, there are also other theories suggesting that government regulations and controls over firms in the developing countries might root in the high cost of collecting public funds and the poor taxation system. For example, Gordon and Li (2005a; b) argued that the financial disintermediation and informal economy might make tax enforcement difficult, and politicians have to design the distorted structure of taxation and red tape towards industry. Or, as the administrative weakness is exaggerated, government is likely to control the production capacity directly by state ownership (Esfahani 2000). Such existing viewpoints definitely reveal some intrinsic features of government behaviours in LDCs, but the characteristics of institutional structure are still partially captured. Actually, the regulatory policies adopted in LDCs are much more complicated than their theoretical settings. In addition, the researchers also offer few insights into the motivations of politicians to collect the public funds overburdening the economy.

This chapter will explore the politically determined development objectives and the intrinsic logic of government intervention policies with the comprehensive implications for institutional building in LDCs. We argue that the distorted institutional structure in China and many LDCs after the Second World War can be largely explained by government adoption of inappropriate development strategies. Motivated by nation building, most LDCs, including the socialist countries, adopted a CAD (comparative advantage defying) strategy to accelerate the growth of capital-intensive, advanced sectors in their countries. Many firms in the priority sectors of CAD strategy were non-viable in open, competitive markets because they did not have comparative advantage in the priority sectors. Therefore, to maximize resource mobilization for building up the priority sectors and to support non-viable firms in those sectors, a regulatory system had to be established. According to Lin *et al.* (1996; 1999; 2003), such a system was characterized by the trinity of a macro-policy environment of distorted prices for products and essential factors of production (for example, trained personnel, funds, technologies, resources, etc.), highly centralized planned resource allocation and a micro-management mechanism in which firms had no decision-making powers.

First, if government wants to implement a CAD strategy and promote the status of capital-intensive industry, it must either distort artificially the relative prices of factors and products, or subsidize the heavy industry sector by collecting taxes from the light industry sector. Owing to information asymmetry, costs for the heavy explicit tax collection are prohibitively high. The government then has to resort to artificially distorting relative prices of input factors and products, for example, depressed interest rate, exchange rates and prices of popular goods, prerequisite for the prioritized development of the heavy industries. Second, when the price of a product or a factor is artificially set below its equilibrium price, the demand will be stimulated and the supply will be suppressed. Implementing the planned resource allocation system was the objective demand to solve the contradiction that gross demand exceeds gross supply under the distorted macro-policy environment and to guarantee resources go to prioritizing industries. Third, the planning system makes the imbalance of returns between the light and heavy industries, which drives the firms transfer of resources to non-prioritized industries. Alternatively, with the missing competition and the distorted prices, the profitability of an enterprise is not determined by its performance. If the firm were given autonomy, due to the information asymmetries between the government (the principal) and the firm manager (the agent), managers and workers would inevitably prey upon its profit and assets. To avoid the investment arbitrage and the erosion of profits and state assets, the state has to deprive enterprises of autonomy.

We will statistically measure the evolution of the development strategy of government and the economic institutions in China from 1950s to 1980s, including the deviation of industry structure from the fundamentals, the distorted relative prices both for the agricultural and industrial products and endowment factors, scope of material allocation by state, and the extent of state ownership of industrial firms. It shows that this trinity system of government controls does exist concurrently with CAD strategy.

CAD strategy and viability

After the Opium War of 1840, China, once an influential nation, began to decline. Chinese political leaders and intellectuals devoted their lives to the ideals of a strong nation and a prosperous people. In 1949, the founding of the People's Republic marked a new era of China's history. According to China's development level and the knowledge available to its leaders at that time, industrialization was virtually synonymous with economic development and the goal of eliminating poverty and backwardness. The ambitious government leaders believed that to defend the newly established socialist system, and to keep pace and even overtake Western industrial countries, rapid industrial development, especially the establishment of heavy industry, were essential.[2]

Learning mainly from the Soviet experiences, the Chinese government began to formulate and implement the first Five-year Plan that gave priority to heavy industrial development from 1953. In the first Five-year Plan, heavy industrial development was put in a strategic position. The central and backbone projects of industrial construction in the first Five-year Plan were the 156 key projects designed with aid from the Soviet Union. During the first five-year period, investment in heavy industrial infrastructure accounted for 85 per cent of total industrial infrastructure and 72.9 per cent of total investment in agricultural and industrial infrastructure.

However, the development strategy of prioritizing heavy industries was inconsistent with China's endowment structure. During the initial period of China's economic development, capital was in very short supply, hence market interest rates were naturally high while labour was rather cheap. The cost of developing capital-intensive heavy industries was extremely high and such industries would have no competitiveness in an open and free competitive market economy (see Lin and Tan 1999). If resources had been allocated by the market mechanism, investment would not have flowed to heavy industry sectors. Rather, industrialization with light industry would have occurred, which would have been contradictory to the goal of implementing the heavy industry-oriented development strategy. To support the non-viable firms, institutional arrangements were made, and the barriers to heavy industry development were lowered artificially. Then, the catch-up strategy, the distorted macro-policy environment, the planned resource allocation system and the rigid micro-management institutions would be left intact.

To illustrate how the viability problem may arise, assume there is a simple economy that possesses two given factor endowments, capital and labour, and produces only one good. Each point on the isoquant shown in Figure 27.1 represents a technology of production or a combination of capital and labour required to produce a given amount of a certain product. The technology represented by A is more labour intensive than that of B. C_1, C_2 and C_3 are the isocost lines. The slope of an isocost line represents the relative prices of capital and labour. In an economy where capital is relatively expensive and labour is relatively inexpensive, as represented by isocost lines C_2 and C_3, the adoption of technology A to produce the given amount of output will cost the least. When the relative price of labour increases, as represented by the isocost lines by C_1, production will cost the least if technology B is adopted.

In a free, open, and competitive market economy, a firm will be viable only if it adopts the least-cost technology in its production. In Figure 27.1, if the relative prices of capital and labour can be presented by C_2, the adoption of technology A costs the least. Market competition will make firms that adopt technologies other than A non-viable. On the other hand, the relative prices of capital and labour are determined by the relative abundance/scarcity of capital and labour in the economy's factor endowments. Therefore, the viability of a firm depends on

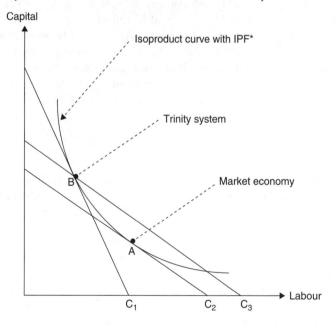

Figure 27.1 Viability and economic institution

Note: IPF = institutional possibility frontier.

whether its choice of technology is on the least-cost lines determined by the factor endowments of the economy. Most importantly, we need to clearly define the indicators measuring development strategy. According to Lin (2003), we construct a technological choice index (TCI) based on the capital intensity of the manufacturing sector to measure a country's choice of development strategy and in turn the quality of policy and institutional environment of that country:

$$TCI_{it}^1 = \left(\frac{MK_{it}/ML_{it}}{K_{it}/L_{it}} \right) \tag{27.1}$$

where MK_{it} / ML_{it} is the capital–labour ratio of the manufacturing sector, and K_{it} / L_{it} is the capital–labour ratio of the ith economy in year t. This index not only reflects how much the government's preference for developing capital-intensive industries is, but also can be used to measure how much the economy is distorted by the government. Given the development stage of a country, the higher this index is, the more an economy is distorted. Lin (2003) found this index well explained the economic growth in a cross-country empirical analysis. An alternative measurement for development strategy is defined as

$$TCI_{it}^2 = \frac{AVM_{it}/GDP_{it}}{LM_{it}/L_{it}} \tag{27.2}$$

where AVM_{it} is the added value of manufacturing industries of the ith country in year t; GDP_{it} is the GDP of the ith country in year t; LM_{it} is the labour in the manufacturing industry and L_{it} is the total labour of ith country in year t.[3] If a government adopts a CAD strategy to promote its capital-intensive industries, this index is expected to be larger than otherwise. This is because a country that adopts a CAD strategy in its manufacturing industries will be more capital intensive and absorb less labour *ceteris paribus*. So, two measures have the similar nature in statistics. Figure 27.2 shows the basic description about the TCI 1 and 2 for China from 1952–2002.[4]

The trinity system in China

To maximize the resource mobilization for the capital-intensive-oriented industrialization, a planned system had to be established. The logic for the trinity of intervention policies characterizing the CAD strategy is as follows:

(1) A macro-policy environment with depressed interest rate, exchange rate and prices of popular goods was prerequisite for prioritized development of heavy industry.
(2) Implementing the planned resource allocation system was the objective demand to solve the contradiction that gross demand exceeded gross supply under the distorted macro-policy environment and to guarantee resources went to heavy industries.

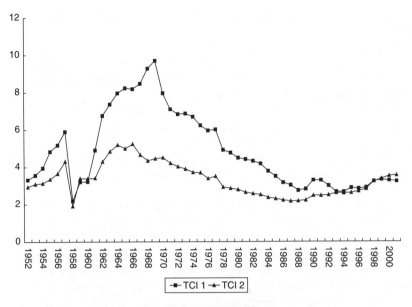

Figure 27.2   TCI 1 and TCI 2 in China (1952–2002)

(3) The micro-management institution without any autonomy was implemented in order to prevent enterprises from corroding profits and state assets taking advantage of their operation rights. In the rural areas, the People's Commune system was to guarantee state monopoly of procurement and marketing of agricultural produces.

Due to this huge scale, the government had to collect heavy explicit taxes from the economic sectors that were generating a surplus and create direct financial subsidies for the non-viable industries. But such a surplus would have come only from the small and scattered agricultural sector, making tax collection difficult and costly. The key to supporting the non-viable firms was to reject market mechanisms completely by artificially distorting the relative prices of factors and products. The cost of developing heavy industries had to be decreased artificially, while resource mobilization – including the supply of cheap labour, funds, raw materials, imported equipment and technology – had to be improved. As a result, a macro-policy environment was needed to allocate resources in a way that would encourage the development of heavy industries. Such a policy environment includes various components:

(1) The most important condition needed for fast, low-cost growth of heavy industry is low-price capital, so a low interest rate policy and other financial repression policies were adopted by the government.
(2) To ensure that key projects could import the critical equipment at low prices, the Chinese government had to interfere in the formulation of the foreign

exchange rate by artificially overvaluing home currency and by instituting a low exchange rate policy.

(3) Following the policies for reducing capital costs, the government suppressed the cost of labour and other inputs (so-called 'a policy of low nominal wages and low prices for energy and raw materials') in order to enhance the potential for surplus accumulation of heavy industry.

(4) The low-wage policy held down the purchasing power of urban residents. The solution for sustaining worker welfare was to set low prices for agricultural products and essential goods and services. Because large-scale industries were concentrated in urban areas, the low-cost policy was targeted towards urban populations, and rural populations did not benefit from it.

Due to the policy of low prices for agricultural products and other essential goods and services, a large proportion of the costs of heavy industry development were transferred to traditional economic sectors such as agriculture. In Figure 27.3 we compare the price level of grain in the rural informal market with government procurement prices to indicate how the relative price of the agriculture was suppressed under the traditional macro-policy environment from the 1950s–80s.

A macro-policy environment that distorts prices of products and production factors thus causes a serious imbalance between the supply and the demand of funds, foreign exchange, raw materials, agricultural products and other basic necessities. If the market had been allowed to direct resource allocation, the policy of suppressing prices could not have ensured that these resources would flow to

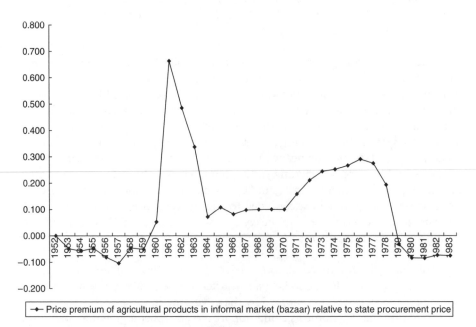

Figure 27.3   Price premium of agricultural products in China (1952–83)

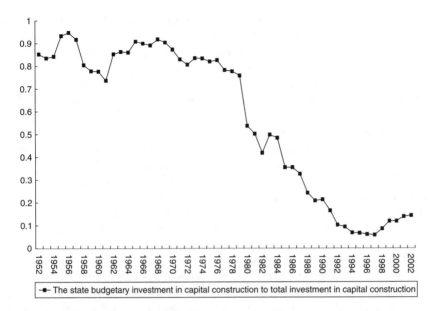

Figure 27.4 Share of budgetary appropriation in investment on capital construction in China (1952–2002)

strategic sectors. To replace the role of the market in allocating resources and also to ensure that materials and resources in short supply would be allocated to prioritized industries, the government had to create a new set of institutions.

The planned administrative means can be summarized as follows. The first step was to establish a financial administration institution. Between 1949 and 1952, China gradually completed the primary nationalization of banks. In 1953, the People's Bank of China established credit plan managerial bureaus at various levels of its underling banks to work out and implement overall credit and loan plans. Within the bank, a corresponding credit fund internal control system with unified revenue and expenditure management was imposed. The second step was to establish a management system for foreign trade and exchange. The state made a unified arrangement for imports and exports by imposing a monopoly over foreign trade and a highly controlled regulatory system over foreign trade and exchange. The third step was to establish a monopoly system to manage the allocation of materials and the procurement and marketing of agricultural products. Based on these administrative means, most of resource allocation was controlled by government. From Figure 27.4, we can find a large proportion of capital construction investment in China was allocated by the fiscal budget directly before economic reform.

To manage the planning system, China established the State Planning Commission in 1953, whose function was to allocate important materials across the country. The commission classified the materials into three categories: (1) materials under the unified allocation of the state; (2) materials under allocation by state industrial ministries and commissions under the state council; and (3) materials under the allocation of the local administration. Table 27.1 shows the basic figures for the materials of the first two categories from the 1950s–80s. From 1953–57 the number of different types of industrial products under direct distribution by the government increased rapidly. The types of materials under unified distribution increased from 227 to 532. But, after the economic reform, the direct allocation by the state of materials dramatically decreased in 1980s.

There was a strong demand for light industry goods because of insufficient market supply; at the same time, the technological structure of light industries catered well to the comparative advantages of the Chinese economy. With the state focused on developing heavy industry, investment in the suppressed industries would tend to yield high returns. Because the profit-oriented private enterprises would allocate their resources to the sectors that yielded the highest returns, the state had to nationalize private enterprises. Figure 27.5 shows that government made a big push for the nationalization movement towards the industrial firms in 1950s.

Because of information asymmetry, monitoring costs to state-owned enterprises (SOEs) for the state was prohibitively high. In particular, since prices were distorted by macro policy, profits and losses ceased to reflect management's performance. When competition was eliminated after private enterprises were artificially

Table 27.1   Number of types of materials under government control in China (1950–88)

Year	Under the unified state distribution system	Under the mandatory plans of corresponding departments in state council
1950	8	
1951	33	
1952	55	
1953	112	115
1954	121	140
1955	162	139
1956	234	151
1957	231	301
1958	93	336
1959	67	218
1960	75	342
1961	87	416
1962	153	345
1963	256	260
1964	370	222
1965	370	222
1966	326	253
1972	49	168
1973	50	567
1975	52	565
1978	53	636
1979	210	581
1981	256	581
1988	27	45

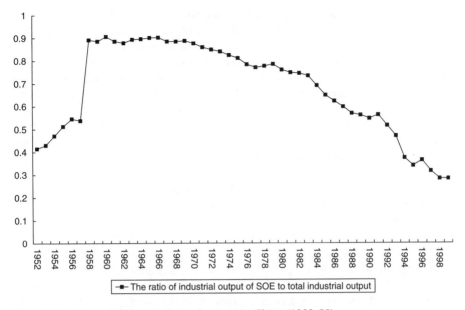

Figure 27.5   Share of SOEs in industrial output in China (1952–98)

destroyed, and the allocation of goods and resources was carried out only by the state, profits and losses for enterprises in an industry ceased to be a function of their market competitiveness. Under these conditions, it was impossible for SOEs with autonomy in production and management to avoid encroaching on the surplus. As a result, on the basis of an ownership arrangement, the state chose to deprive SOEs of any autonomy. All production materials used by SOEs were supplied by the government, and all their output was sold to and allocated by the state. And, it was imperative to establish a compulsory production plan system and a unified revenue and expenditure system.

Accompanying the nationalization of industry, the collectivization of agriculture through the People's Commune System was also accelerated, which was an important step towards realizing the state monopoly policy of procurement of agricultural products at a low price. If the state wishes to increase the quantity of agricultural product procurement, it must exercise direct control over agricultural production. Collectivization should be an institutional arrangement by which the government can upgrade its direct control over agricultural production.[5]

Here, we trace the formation of the trinity system in accord with the enforcement of CAD strategy in China. Obviously, a highly centralized trinity system inevitably undermined the incentives of local agents. To facilitate the implementation of central targets, some measures were adopted for local government and SOEs in the pre-1978 reforms, which included (1) eliminating the central government's over-concentration of power by decentralizing administrative authority and responsibility; and (2) eliminating unequal distribution of benefits among regions and sectors by adjusting their administrative authority and responsibility.

As a special case, in early 1960s, the central government decentralized the autonomy to the farmers in order to recover the agricultural production from the Great Famine. However, the decentralization under a trinity system was not able to solve the inefficiency problem since it could neither improve micro-efficiency through market discipline, nor change the heavy industry development strategy inconsistent with China's comparative advantage. These reforms had not touched on the basic framework of the trinity system. Under the soft budget constraints faced by local government and SOEs, a cycle of decentralization leading to disorder, disorder leading to centralization, centralization leading to stagnation and stagnation leading to decentralization was inevitable. In terms of this centralization cycle, the trinity system supporting the CAD strategy was not a stable institution.

The economic reform that began in 1978 signified Chinese leaders' search for a new path of economic development. The basic framework of trinity system and CAD strategy was no longer off limits; this enabled reform to penetrate all levels of the economic system. During this thorough and increasingly powerful reform compulsory plans were gradually replaced by indicative plans, and the planned allocation mechanism was replaced by a market mechanism. The new economic system gradually took shape. Our empirical measures could roughly capture the formation and collapse of trinity system. Comparing Figures 27.2–27.5 and Table 27.1, a co-movement trend can be found for the indicators measuring the economic institution and development strategy in China's history. The measures peaked in the 1960s, and decreased gradually in 1970s, which means the changing structure of economic institution can be explained by the choice of development strategy.

Conclusion

According to Lin's various studies, many developing countries, including those socialist countries such as Russia, East Europe Countries and China, and even many Latin American countries and India, that adopted an import substitution strategy after the Second World War were actually adopting a forward-moving development strategy. However, for most LDCs, capital was in short supply; hence the market interest rate was naturally high, while the cost of labour was low. Developing capital-intensive heavy industries was thus extremely costly, and such industries could not hope to be viable in an open, free market economy. Thus, the government had to distort the economic institution, and nationalize the resources, so as to sustain the non-viable industry. From this perspective, our study sheds light on the inherent laws for a variety of regulatory policies and intervention syndromes in LDCs in an integrated framework, which can be summarized as a trinity system including the macro-policy environment, highly centralized planned resource allocation system and dependent micro-management institution. This point is in contrast with the existing theories of political economy, the so-called helping hand versus grabbing hand taxonomy. That means that heavily regulations on the economy in LDCs might not be due to the corruption of politicians or manipulation of interest group, but the CAD strategy by government.

Although we illustrate the above argument only by the empirical evidence of China, the formation of the trinity system as a result of the adoption of a CAD strategy should not be unique to China or particular to the socialist system. Therefore, the formation, consequences and reform process of China's traditional economic institution have valuable implications for other socialist economies and developing countries that adopted the development strategies similar to China's. In short, the liberalization reforms will depend on the final removal of the viability problem that exists in many firms in the priority sectors under the previously adopted CAD strategy.

Notes

We are grateful to conference and seminar participants at UNU-WIDER, Peking University and AEA meetings for helpful comments. Two anonymous referees provided very useful suggestions.

1. Djankov *et al.* (2002), who provided an empirical test on theories of the grabbing hand, say, the barrier for business entry might arise from corrupt bureaucrats.
2. The development strategy is exogenously determined by political considerations. In fact, in addition to China and socialist countries, many non-socialist developing nations, notably those in South Asia and Latin America, made similar choices, and their economic systems had many features in common with the Chinese system. For the discussion on the historical causes of CAD strategy, see Lin *et al.* (2003: chapter 2).
3. The industry data on the output, the fixed capital stock and labour was collected from various issues of *China Industry Statistical Yearbook*, and the total value of fixed capital stock was devaluated by the index of fixed-asset investment price taken from the various issues of *China Statistical Yearbook*. The national data on the output, the fixed capital formation and labour was collected from *China Compendium of Statistics 1949–2004* and various issues of the *China Statistical Yearbook*. The capital stock at national level was calculated by the perpetual-stock method.
4. Two indicators measuring CAD strategy miss capturing the policy change and distortion during the Great Leap Movement. The government produced the poor-quality iron and steel by using backyard furnaces and millions of farmers were forced to join in with iron and steel manufacturing instead of harvesting the crops. The number of industry workers increased from 14.02 million in 1957 to 44.16 million in 1958 and decreased to 28.79 million in 1959. That is, although the government launched a political movement for a faster-paced industrialization, the technology level for industrial production was low. However, capital–labour ratio measures the embodied technology level in the production, while TCI means the deviation of technology adoption in the industry from the fundamentals. Then, by these measures, the CAD strategy reached the peak in accord with the 'Three Line Construction' in the late 1960s, other than the 'Great Leap Movement'.
5. An example is the Great Leap Forward Movement in economic construction launched in 1958, which proposed that China might surpass the United Kingdom's level of economic development and catch up to that of the United States in ten years. Heavy industries were emphasized, especially iron and steel. Several preposterously high indicators of industrial development were fabricated. At the same time, the nationalization movement and policies for planning control were also pushed. Because of the inappropriate ratio of accumulation and the shortage of consumption funds, and also because agricultural production could not meet increasing needs, the government had to increase compulsory procurement quotas. In 1958, grain production increased by 2.55 per cent, but the quantity procured rose by 22.3 per cent. At the same time, agricultural collectivization was suddenly accelerated to ensure the low-price procurement of agricultural products. As is well known, its consequences were disastrous.

References

Acemoglu, D., S. Johnson and J. Robinson (2004) 'Institutions as the Fundamental Cause of Long-Run Growth', in P. Aghion and S. Durlauf (eds), *Handbook of Economic Growth*, Amsterdam: North Holland.

Djankov, S., R. LaPorta, F. Lopez-de-Silanes and A. Shleifer (2002) 'Regulation of Entry', *Quarterly Journal of Economics*, 117, 1: 1–37.

Esfahani, H.S. (2000) 'Institutions and Government Controls', *Journal of Development Economics*, 63: 197–229.

Gordon, R. and W. Li (2005a) 'Tax Structure in Developing Countries: Many Puzzles and a Possible Explanation', *NBER Working Paper* 11267, Cambridge, MA: National Bureau of Economic Research.

Gordon, R. and W. Li (2005b) 'Financial, Taxation, and Regulatory Structures in Developing Countries', Mimeo.

Lin, J.Y. (2003) 'Development Strategy, Viability and Economic Convergence', *Economic Development and Cultural Change*, 53, 2: 277–308.

Lin, J.Y. and G. Tan. (1999) 'Policy Burdens, Accountability, and the Soft Budget Constraint', *American Economic Review: Papers and Proceedings*, 89, 2: 426–31.

Lin, J.Y., F. Cai and Z. Li (2003) *The China Miracle: Development Strategy and Economic Reform*, Hong Kong: Chinese University Press.

Pigou, A. (1938) *The Economics of Welfare*, London: Macmillan.

Shleifer, A. and R.W. Vishny (1994) 'Politicians and Firms', *Quarterly Journal of Economics*, 109: 995–1025.

28
Institutions, Policies and Economic Development

Grzegorz W. Kolodko

Introduction

When it seems that everything or nearly everything has been said about the prerequisites and prospects of economic growth[1] it is worthwhile to revisit certain aspects of this phenomenon, which is of vital importance for the functioning and development of society. All the more so in view of the conflicting opinions on the matter: while some authors appear quite optimistic, hopefully not without justification, others tend towards pessimism, on rational grounds, too.[2] We are especially interested in growth factors and the causes of disparities between the potential and actual growth rates. In this connection, I wish to take up some issues pertaining to the interaction between, on the one hand, the structure and functioning of market economy institutions and, on the other, the policy followed within their framework and the efficiency of its instruments, focusing on the implications for long-term output dynamics. A great many reflections spring to mind in this context, at least some of which merit a closer look.

Particularly, the investigation focuses on Poland. The case of Poland – the largest economy (the GDP of almost PPP$500 billion in 2006) and most populated (38.2 million inhabitants) country in East Central Europe – is remarkable, yet the progress accomplished over last 15 years has been quite different in particular periods of time. And the case is still more interesting since Poland was a pioneer of transition to a market system among the former socialist centrally planned economies. No doubt, the Polish lessons are relevant not only for countries in the region, but for developing economies generally.[3] So, it is indeed illuminating to consider the prevailing economic and political conditions in Poland and East Central Europe for other emerging market economies and developing countries.

Inevitable growth

Above a certain level of maturity, economic mechanisms make long-term growth inevitable. The exceptions only prove the rule here, although the most persistent of these (nowadays mainly in some poor countries of sub-Saharan Africa) inflict great hardships upon the affected populations. The main reason behind the self-sustaining nature of growth is an objective desire on the part of producers to maximize profits and on the part of consumers to lead a better life. These goals are unattainable in the long run through the redistribution of a stagnant national income. The increase of manufacturers' profits, along with the improvement of the living standards, can only be driven by output growth.

Importantly, the politicians in power should actively seek to promote growth, or else their authority will wither away in the long run, at least in democratic countries. In non-democratic ones, too, for even though it may be possible to stay in power longer in their environment, the ultimate fall becomes all the more dramatic and in the ensuing interregnum, the country is plunged into even greater chaos, with disastrous consequences for the level of economic activity, as we have witnessed recently in Zaire, Haiti or Venezuela.

Seen against this background, the experience of post-socialist transforming economies has been relatively encouraging. It shows that power can be gained (or lost, as has been the case in Poland) at constitutionally prescribed intervals through a democratic election, but also (as in Georgia in late 2003 and early 2004) as a result of a strong political pressure exerted by rioters in the streets (who, interestingly, won the support of the democratic part of the international community). Even so, it is possible that a government may really thirst for economic growth and yet fail to pursue an effective policy to attain this goal.

Another inauspicious scenario can materialize when the economic policy – in its fiscal, monetary, industrial and trade dimensions – followed by a government or by an independent central bank is intentionally oriented towards other top-priority goals, to the detriment of economic dynamics, which is seen as a matter of secondary importance only. Such a policy may sometimes be justified, in particular, when maintaining or restoring financial and economic equilibrium is at stake. But on other occasions, as was demonstrated in Poland in 1998–2001, and even more dramatically in 1989–92, such a policy confuses the instruments of economic policy with its aims (Kolodko 2000a; Stiglitz 2002). To be sure, and quite predictably, the proponents and advocates of such policies are of quite a different opinion (IMF 2000: 127–201).

Incidentally, the question of identifying means and ends in the context of development processes deserves further serious debate. From a purely economic standpoint, it should be obvious that the goal is socioeconomic development, part of which is economic growth per se. Such categories and processes as budget, inflation, privatization, rates of exchange, interest rates, taxes, etc. are merely instruments facilitating the attainment of this supreme goal. Confusing these two things in economic policy is quite costly, as the Poles have had a chance to learn over the past 15 years, although, luckily, on a smaller scale than some other countries in the region. In a broader context, bearing in mind that freedom and democracy are autonomous values, dilemmas arise around the question of what should be subservient and subordinate to what. Sen (2000: 10) appears to be free from doubt on that score as he declares that 'freedoms are not only the primary ends of development, they are also among its principal means'. This is the right approach, for it emphasizes the positive feedback between freedom and development. The problem is that this synergy only manifests itself in the long-term or even very long-term perspective. Once again, one needs to be very patient. However, as the biological clock is ticking away, not everyone will be able to enjoy the fruits of their patience.

Is it then possible, or, differently put, is it worthwhile to subordinate freedom and democracy to the requirements of an efficient economic policy and rapid output growth, which brings about an outcome of vast importance: an improvement in the living standards? This seems to be the prevailing approach, for instance, in China and Vietnam, where sensible development policies have been pursued for many years, in the context of rather limited democratic arrangements, but not so in Uzbekistan or Turkmenistan, where such policies have been lacking. Or is it, perhaps, better to cherish freedom and democracy, even if they stand in the way of implementing an effective pro-growth policy? This has been the case in Poland, among other places, where the institutional weakness of a young political democracy and civil society hampers the pursuit of a sensible pro-growth policy and affects the functionality of the painstakingly constructed institutions of market economy.

I believe that it is not enough to win majority support for one's views: these need to be the right views in the first place. But the reverse is also true: in a democracy, being right is not enough – one needs majority support besides. And political practice shows unequivocally that what is right on substantive grounds may not come across to the majority and win its understanding and approval. Not least because an influential, opinion-making minority can make use of various democratic institutions, such as the media, to impose their priorities on others. This is the paradoxical case of a democratically endorsed, yet erroneous policy. Such a policy has to be continued until the majority comes round to the right way of thinking or, conversely, those who are right become a majority. Once again, this requires not only knowledge and culture, but also time and patience. And the latter is likely to run out with some people or at certain times.

The main problems of interest for us are the rate of economic growth, the structure of the increments of global output and their absorption over time, as well as the distribution of growth effects among various social, occupational and income groups, and their allocation to various types of goals. When analyzing these problems, one must not abstract away from the regional aspect of income creation and distribution. The policy of GDP (re)distribution in time and space (construed in social as well as geographical terms) is more likely to stir up controversy than the issue of output dynamics itself. In some cases more social and economic problems arise in times of relatively faster growth, because it is accompanied by increased redistribution. As a result, grievances about perceived inequitable division of the fruits of growth are more acute than at a time of weaker economic dynamics.

Undoubtedly, this syndrome can be observed in present-day Poland, as the rate of growth has accelerated again. For even if GDP increases at 4–5 per cent a year, a significant part of society (possibly even a majority) still fails to benefit from this growth. Worse still, there are groups of households and entrepreneurs who experience a continuing, painful drop in real incomes. For them, the growth of output, which has already attained substantial proportions, signifies a 'loss'. This generates resentment which not only prevents reaching the level of social contentment that would be attainable assuming a different distribution of income, but also affects growth in the long run (Tanzi *et al.* 1999; Kolodko 2000b). Thus, an inequitable distribution of income (or, more precisely, of the effects of its real increase) is harmful not only from a social point of view, but also for purely pragmatic reasons, for such a policy hinders efficiency and growth, so after a while it turns against its former beneficiaries. Interestingly, the latter often fail to understand this, also in Poland, as is attested to by the never-ending controversies over tax rates applicable to the relatively richer sectors of society.

Expectations and realities

Global experience shows that the expected growth rate is usually higher than that actually achieved. It is enough just to compare the annually published International Monetary Fund economic outlooks and their forecast, which quite often, even after half a year, is downward revised and less optimistic than at the earlier date. To be sure, there had been a lot of exaggerated optimistic expectations at the onset of post-socialist transition in Poland, Russia and elsewhere among the transition economies (Kolodko 2002). In Poland the transitional recession – according to the government plans, approved by the IMF – was supposed not to exceed 3.2 per cent and last no more than one year. Indeed, it lasted three years (from mid-1989 until mid-1992) and the GDP shrunk by almost 20 per cent (EBRD 1996; Kolodko 1993).

This gives rise afterwards to never-ending scholarly and political debates, as well as increasing social frustration. It almost looks like an inherent feature, shared not only by politicians (who are especially prone to exhibit it) and economists (that is to say, most of them), but also by entire societies at low to medium levels of economic development. The reason may be that politicians and economists tend to persuade societies ex ante they can attain certain goals, and then blame ex post their failure to achieve it, alternately, on others (politicians and economists) or acts of God (such as too high or too low oil prices, the Russian or Argentinean crisis, too high or too low exchange rates, etc.). Only the most highly developed countries have been cured of this peculiar malaise of excessive optimism, although, perhaps, not forever, not everywhere and not fully.

Thus nearly everyone expects a higher growth rate than they deserve in view of their perseverance (or lack thereof), organization and management quality, institutional (im)maturity and foresight. In particular, this symptom has been observed, from the very outset, in post-socialist transforming economies, where expectations about the scale and rate of production and consumption growth far exceeded the rather disappointing, as it was later to turn out, reality. This also applies to Poland, even though its aggregate growth over the past 15 years of transformation – for all its enormous variability over time – has been larger than in any other country in Central and Eastern Europe (CEE) and the Commonwealth of Independent States (CIS); see Figure 28.1. Apparently only China has avoided

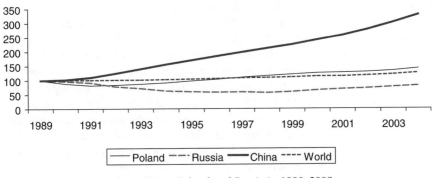

Figure 28.1 GDP growth in China, Poland and Russia in 1990–2003
Note: 1989 = 100.
Source: World Bank (2004).

this kind of disillusionment, as it manages to have doubled its GDP every decade thanks to an incredibly rapid growth, and discontentment may only stem from the distribution of the effects of this growth and certain extra economic factors affecting the ways Chinese society functions (Lin *et al.* 2003).

Of course, the period of fundamental systemic changes related to the very essence of the post-socialist transformation has its specificity. It has involved many processes and phenomena which were extremely difficult to predict and accurately forecast. This may explain, but only to some extent, the enormous gap between the highly optimistic declarations and expectations on the one hand and reality on the other. Regrettably, this phenomenon has not as yet been studied in detail, but one can assume, not only on intuitive basis, that the societies of Central Eastern European and post-Soviet countries expected to achieve, after a decade and a half of transformation, twice as high a national income as they actually recorded – roughly equivalent, on average, to its level of 1989.[4] This leads to the question about the error margin in today's assumptions. Do the 'elites' and societies still expect more (and how much more?) economic growth in the next 15 years than they will actually manage to accomplish? Surely, we still see excessive optimism, especially in countries integrating or striving to integrate with the European Union, but much more realism is being observed, too. One learns from experience.

The foundations of growth

Any attempt to answer the question about the sources of much-needed growth at the current phase of structural transformation should take into account two main factors. The first is a steady improvement of allocative efficiency, resulting from better utilization of resources (in comparison with the period preceding the trans-formation and its early stage, marked by a lot of friction). This requires constant efforts to stimulate creative enterprise, appropriate resource utilization at micro-economic level, and measures to improve the quality of corporate governance.

Poland has achieved a great deal in this field and continues to make progress, as shown by the constant increase of labour productivity (Figure 28.2). In recent years – since 1998 when strong budgetary and monetary measures were taken to cool down the economy – it has been the only source of output growth. For output *has* been increasing all the time, although at varying rates, accompanied by decreasing employment figures and concomitant growth in unemployment. Opposite tendencies emerged only for brief spells, especially in 2003, when unemployment began to decrease thanks to the one-off intervention consisting of the cancellation of debts owed by more than 60,000 small and medium-size enterprises, and GDP dynamics increased significantly from 0.8 per cent in the second quarter of 2002 to 3.8 per cent a year later.[5] Then, unfortunately, unemployment rose again by more than one percentage point and reached, following a different calculation method than before, 20.6 per cent in February 2004. This is one of the differences between transition economies in the midst of profound structural and institutional changes and highly developed economies. In the latter, a GDP growth rate of just 1–2 per cent is enough to stimulate employment and reduce joblessness, whereas in our region, without special anti-unemployment measures (an area where not enough proactive steps are taken despite the repeated political declarations), employment does not begin to go up until GDP growth approaches 4 per cent.

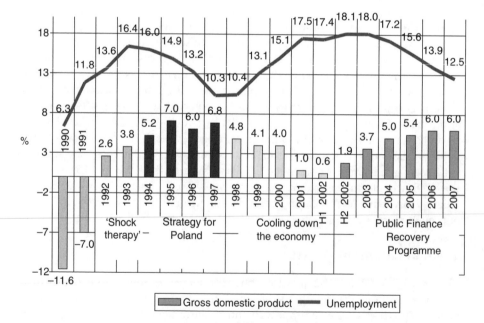

Figure 28.2 The rate of GDP growth/fall and unemployment rate in Poland (1990–2007)

Note: The indicators shown above are based on the old methodology of unemployment calculation, which underestimates the results by about two percentage points in comparison with the current method.

Sources: 1990–2003, Central Statistical Office (GUS); 2004–07 projection, after PNFR (2003).

Incidentally, this 'side effect' of the hitherto transformation efforts – massive unemployment afflicting Poland – is by far the most harmful outcome of the mis-guided economic policy: the overshot stabilization programme at the beginning of the previous decade and the overcooling of the economy towards its end. The inept 'proactive' anti-unemployment policy in the past few years is also to blame. Surely, the market transformation would hardly have gained the approval of the public, had it been announced 15 years ago that after nearly generation-long endeavours, almost one in every five of us would be out of job and frequently – which is the most distressing thing – without prospects of finding one. This is inevitably a frustrating situation, bearing in mind that long-term unemployment is the main cause of poverty. As much as 69 per cent of the population of the EU accession countries believe unemployment to be the main factor responsible for poverty and social exclusion, whereas in the 'old' EU states this indicator stands at 50 per cent.[6]

The other growth factor is a renewed (after a period of sharp decline caused by the transformational shock and recession) propensity to save and to accumulate capital (Figure 28.3). An increased accumulation capacity in the economy is necessary in the long run to maintain a high-growth dynamics, especially in a situation when many simple reserves opened up by the new economic system are exhausted as the transformation proceeds. It is necessary not only to encour-age domestic savings, but also to attract – in the open economic environment – foreign savings in the form of portfolio capital and, especially, foreign direct investment. These create a new production capacity which often boosts the competitiveness of the economy and its export potential, thus facilitating export-driven economic growth. Of course, this form of expansion depends even more crucially on other factors, especially the rates of exchange and trade policy in all its aspects, but the role of foreign direct investment as a significant factor in the formation of capital and modern production capacity must not be overlooked. The fact that we expect nowadays an increased propensity to save does not imply that this indicator was low under the previous system. Far from it, it was very high indeed, at times even excessive. Planned economy was char-acterized by a very high rate of accumulation and investment, except that these resulted from forced saving, in contrast with the mechanisms of voluntary saving triggered by market economy. Savings were made then, partly due to necessity faced by insufficient supply in a shortage economy. Today Poland's citizens *choose* to save, where possible, for the future. However, the transition from planned to market economy should not be equated with an increased propensity to save combined with a lower marginal propensity to consume in the long run. What is needed nowadays, in a developing market environment, is increased efficiency in the use of whatever savings we are able to make on the nationwide scale.

Over the last decade and a half, we should have learned something in this respect. At times when economic policy – both at macro level, oriented towards stimulating savings and controlling macro-scale growth proportions, and at micro level, stimu-lating improvement in corporate governance and competitiveness – was essentially

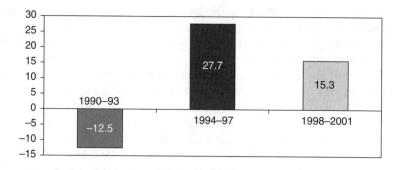

Figure 28.3   GDP growth in Poland in subsequent four-year periods, 1990–2001
Source: Central Statistical Office (GUS), Warsaw.

correct, growth rate was markedly higher. Similar opportunities (and threats) will
also exist in the future. Today no one is in a position to plot even an approximate
GDP growth curve in Poland until, say, 2030. Whatever its shape, however, this
curve will periodically depart, alternately upwards and downwards, from an averaged trend line – if for no other reason then because of the fluctuations typical of the
business cycle. But whether this average growth rate will be closer to 6 per cent,
which would be a great success, or to a mere 3 per cent, which would be a failure,
will depend on the quality of development policy. In the recent past, when a better
policy was followed, GDP growth was likewise higher, and vice versa.

In the long run, the allocative efficiency of the capital employed should continually increase, whereas the rate of capital formation may and should increase only
within the limits set by the consumption barrier. Therefore, within the time span
of a couple of years, certainly not more than a decade or two, the only available
way to increase growth will be to improve efficiency, without increasing in any
way the relative burden imposed on the national income by accumulation, that
is, without further increasing the share of investment in absorbed GDP. Only then
we will have entered the phase of truly intensive growth (to borrow terminology
from a different era), in contrast with extensive growth, which still prevails.

Institution building and learning

Both the collapse in the early 1990s and the great transitional depression that followed proved beyond any doubt that the one-sided orientation towards liberalization (of prices, trade, business entry and exit) and privatization, neglecting
the importance of institution building – that is the rules of the market-economy
game – for the efficient functioning and development of market economy, came at
a heavy price for all (well, nearly all) of us. Such a recipe is certainly not sufficient
to create a dynamic, expanding market economy.[7] Worse still, lost output is unre-
coverable, while social costs in terms of massive unemployment and exclusion
are enormous.

Today, however, no one calls into question the role of institutions any more; just the opposite – it has been heavily emphasized for the last couple of years, even by the former advocates of a naive, neoliberal approach subscribing to the unrealistic notion that the mythical invisible hand of the market would now replace the old institutions, which were rightly being eliminated, such as state ownership, central planning, administrative controls on prices, inconvertible currency or subsidies. In most cases it is not that simple: the old institutions must indeed be dismantled or die away, but new ones must emerge in their place. The latter is a tedious process, requiring constant involvement of the state – itself one of the most essential institutions in the process of fundamental change.[8]

The popularity of the term *institutions* towards the end of the first 15 years of transformation is comparable to that of *liberalization* and *stabilization* at the beginning of this period, or other buzzwords, such as *privatization* and *deregulation* slightly later. Nowadays, terms such as *institutions, institution building, institutional structure of the market* or *institutional order* are household words in many languages, not only English, but also Russian or Chinese. Luckily, in Polish, too. A review of the relevant literature worldwide, including the weighty publications of such institutions as the World Bank or, especially, the International Monetary Fund, would reveal a striking contrast between the absence of these notions from earlier works, published in the early 1990s, and their very frequent use nowadays.[9]

What, then, are institutions? In a narrower sense, institutions comprise the rules of the economic game – in this case, the market game – made up by the law and organizations that enforce compliance with these rules on the part of all economic entities, using incentives, rewards and penalties (carrots and sticks). The quantifier *all* used in this context includes the government and non-governmental organizations, enterprises from the vanishing state sector and expanding private sector, internal and external agencies operating in an open-market economy, financial and capital-market intermediaries, as well as households. Incidentally, it should be noted that some confusion arises due to the fact that the word 'institution' is quite often used in the economic jargon in the sense of an organization or structure – one speaks, for instance, of financial institutions or state institutions – whereas the institutions that we discuss here organize, control and shape economic processes to ensure their sufficiently smooth progress, with due respect to the interests of all the partners in the social reproduction process; just like traffic regulations, which govern the use of public roads, apply to pedestrians, drivers and the police alike, to streets and parking spaces, by day and by night. A car or scooter may be privately owned, but its use, in view of its external effects, is a matter of not only personal, but also public concern. Therefore, it must be subjected to some restrictions and regulated in ways the actors understand and are obliged to respect in the public interest, as well as for their own good. To continue this simile, institutions include both a speed limit and a ticket for breaking this limit, as well as a delinquency fee for its late payment; likewise, institutions comprise traffic regulations and the applicable enforcement measures.

By the same token, market institutions include both a contract between entrepreneurs and arbitration or court proceedings; both the price of a commodity or service, agreed upon between the buyer and the vendor, and the right to make a complaint about a faulty product, as well as consumer organizations which strengthen the market position of buyers vis-à-vis manufacturers and vendors. To sum up, institutions comprise:

1. the procedures and rules of conduct sanctioned by the law or by custom;
2. the applicable laws and regulations, promulgated in order to protect the interests of market entities;
3. the organizations and administrative/political structures that serve the needs of various market entities – from the government and central bank to capital-market agencies and anti-monopoly authorities (expected to compel economic entities to follow specific norms defined by the applicable laws *in the interest* of the entire socioeconomic system) to commercial banks and commodity exchanges;
4. lastly to extend the scope of our definition, institutions in the broad sense of the term also include market culture and mentality. In this perspective, institutions are not only built, promulgated or decreed, but also understood and learned. Besides, it is (or should be) obvious that this learning process, even if very actively pursued, must be gradual and lengthy. Also in the case of the unique, unprecedented process of reunification of Germany, the fourth institutional dimension, 'learning the market', had to be protracted and could not follow a shock formula, because no single political act would have effected a radical transformation of a culture and mentality rooted in the socialist system and planned economy into their capitalist, market-based counterparts.

To be able to follow the rules of the market game, one needs an adequate knowledge, which may not always be acquired from textbooks or from other actors, but must be learned by experience. One also has to form specific habits and characteristics, which were often unnecessary or poorly developed under the previous system. Now the old habits – so to speak, the 'old, non-market culture' – becomes a liability from which one has to be freed, in particular, by successively learning market economy. It is an instance of learning by doing, which takes time. It is, thus, a lasting process which, however, requires much less time to complete in those countries where market reforms had reached an advanced stage already by 1989 in comparison with those which embarked on a systemic transformation with institutions that followed more closely the socialist orthodoxy. This explains to some extent why the transitional recession was much shorter in Poland and Hungary than, for example, in Romania and Ukraine. I believe we still tend to underrate the cultural component of institution building and its importance for growth processes, while hastily assuming that adjustment in this field proceeds fast enough. Unfortunately, it does not.

In 1871, by Lake Tanganyika in Burundi, Henry Stanley uttered the famous line 'Dr Livingstone, I presume?' on meeting another great explorer of the mysteries of Africa. Stanley was accompanied on his expedition by a group of native bearers.

After a rest period, he ordered them to rise and get on the way, but the men were reluctant. When Stanley urged them to hurry they replied, 'We indeed hurry, but our souls can't catch up with us, so we need to wait for them a little longer.' Our attitudes are similar. We have to be goaded into action and, on the other hand, still need to wait for our souls to catch up.

It thus turns out that the changes of mentality in response to the challenges of systemic transformation – which is not restricted to the economic sphere, but also has its political, social and cultural dimensions – come about slowly. Intellectuals and enlightened economists, as well as forward-thinking political leaders (who like to solve rather than create problems), want these changes to be instituted as soon as possible in the newly emerging economic order and its actors, including economic entities and people who need to follow the new rules in the face of hard budget constraints and tough global competition. But these actors are like the souls of Stanley's bearers. They walk, or rather linger, behind their more knowledgeable guides, who are supposed to be able to find their way in the *terra incognita* of an emerging market economy and to persevere in pursuit of successive targets in the never-ending journey. After some delay, these new arrangements become accommodated by broader social groups which, like Stanley's men, are not exactly the vanguard on this difficult mission to chart the future, penetrate it in depth and, perhaps, find there a better world. Instead, they hamper the badly needed progress en route. Everything takes time to ripen and needs to reach maturity at its own pace and time.

As early as the mid-1990s, Anders Åslund (1995) concluded that Russia had already become a market economy, except that the people failed to understand it, to which I replied (and I still subscribe to this view) that if the people fail to grasp the nature and mechanisms of market economy with sufficient clarity and, therefore, disapprove of the current policy – applauded though it may be by technocratically minded economists – then this is hardly a market economy yet: just an economy in the process of market transition. In this sense, the systemic transformation is still underway in Poland and other countries of the region, although we have already joined the European Union, because the EU applies different assessment criteria and may have viewed our progress on the way towards market economy with excessive optimism. Such delays – partly organizational and partly cultural, or more broadly, civilizational in nature, hindering the attainment of a 'critical mass' by the market culture, which is a sine qua non of rapid growth – are a liability. Apart from the paucity of hard infrastructure and financial capital, they are the main factor limiting the pace of economic growth. To a large extent, these delays account for the existence and size of the gap between the theoretically attainable growth rate and the actual development path. However, if this is indeed the case, which it is, it should be seen as a manifestation of an excessively optimistic assessment of the actual potential to achieve a high growth rate under given institutional circumstances.

A policy will fail to put the existing social, human, financial and fixed capital to a better use, when *institutional capital* is in short supply. Therefore, a dual approach is needed. On the one hand, we should endeavour at all times to keep the evolution of institutions on the desired path – which includes their setup, structure, maturation and learning – while, on the other hand, we need to wait patiently 'for the souls to mature', facilitating this process in the meantime by sensible persuasion, so as to keep pressing ahead. No amount of rushing people to move faster and (political) lambasting will do any good. Worse still, such measures may provoke an increasing opposition against the direction and pace of change, thus fomenting protest and strengthening the propensity to rebel. This is what we observe these days in all post-socialist transition economies, even though the scale of these developments understandably differs across countries.

It is quite obvious that the institutional form of the Polish economy has been determined in general outline by the strategic orientation towards integration with the European Union. Our institutions will, thus, become gradually assimilated to those of the EU, reproducing in the process all the faults of the latter's institutional structure. Many of these are revealed by a comparison with the more efficient and more highly competitive institutional infrastructure of the US economy. For it appears that the US economy owes its higher production and consumption levels and markedly faster growth in the last decade mainly to the higher efficiency of its institutions, rather than to a superior national economic policy. American institutions are less bureaucratic than their EU counterparts, and so they provide a more favourable environment for business development and increased competitiveness of enterprises. This leads to some conclusions on how the EU should modify its institutions and policies – now also applicable to Poland as an EU member state.

Better off, worse off?

The social reception of the economic benefits accruing to the systemic transformation and the economic growth that has accompanied it for some time – since mid-1992 in Poland, but only since 1999 in Ukraine – has been cautious at best (European Commission 2004a). Large sectors of society in post-socialist countries have been less optimistic, or more pessimistic, in their assessment of reality then their so-called political elites, including publicly involved, opinion-making economists.

The comparison of the quality of life as perceived by society in various countries and the corresponding satisfaction (or dissatisfaction) levels yields fascinating results. Taking into account nine dimensions – home, family life, neighbourhood, health, social life, personal security, work, income and health service – it turns out that among the incumbent EU members (EU-15), the highest satisfaction levels are observed in Denmark and Austria, respectively, at 91 per cent and 89 per cent. The least satisfied with the quality of their lives are the inhabitants of Italy (72 per cent) and Portugal (71 per cent). The most significant factors in these assessments are satisfaction with home, family and social life and the neighbourhood. Among the new EU-members (EU-10), the most satisfied societies are those of Slovenia (81 per cent) – surpassing several incumbents: Great Britain, Germany, Spain, Italy and Portugal – and the Czech Republic (70 per cent).

Closing the ranking list are Lithuania (59 per cent) and Latvia (55 per cent). Interestingly, Poland scores right behind Slovenia and the Czech Republic with a satisfaction level of 64 per cent (Figure 28.4). In post-socialist transforming countries, the relatively lower satisfaction level has to do with strictly economic factors – such as working conditions, earnings and access to medical services – which has some implications for the long-term development policy. In Poland, the average indicator of 64 per cent reflects the relatively high levels of satisfaction with family life, home and social life (respectively, 85 per cent, 84 per cent and 80 per cent) and limited contentment with work, earnings and the health system (respectively, 46 per cent, 33 per cent and 32 per cent). This is a striking asymmetry: the quality of life is lowest where the living standards are determined by politics and relatively high in those places where politics cannot essentially do too much harm, as people are generally left to themselves, their families, neighbours and friends. It follows – once again – that it is necessary and worthwhile to foster rapid economic growth, since this area leaves the most room for improvement.

It is both interesting and sad that of all nations of the enlarged European Union (EU-25), the Poles, when asked about the causes of their difficult situation, are the most likely to mention *social injustice*. As much as 53 per cent of the Poles blame on it their difficult material and social situation, as compared with the EU-15 average of 35 per cent. The fewest complaints in this respect among EU-10 come from the Czechs (31 per cent) and among EU-15 from the Danes (13 per cent). Equally interesting, though not so much sad as baffling, is the fact that only 13 per cent of the Poles attribute their failures and difficult material situation to laziness and lack of will power, in contrast with the Portuguese, who are much more given to

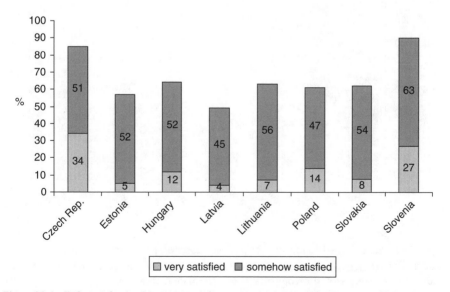

Figure 28.4 'Life satisfaction' in post-socialist countries joining the European Union
Source: European Commission (2004a).

self- criticism (31 per cent). The only societies among the EU-25 who show an even greater reserve in this respect are the Lithuanians (8 per cent) are the Estonians (10 per cent).

In this context, one should wonder how to apply the old maxim that every cloud has a silver lining. How do we turn dejected and pessimistic moods into yet another growth driver? If society perceives its situation as worse than a fair and impartial analysis of the economic and social indicators would suggest, it is all the more necessary to move forward even faster. Assuming this is possible – and studies on potentially attainable growth rates (Kolodko 2002; IMF 2003) indicate that indeed it is – it then becomes all the more worthwhile to subordinate the policy to this imperative. We already know that institutions are vital, but so is policy. It should also be obvious that even top-quality institutions (which are still a long way off in our case) do not automatically guarantee a good policy. One should be able to make creative use of both. Countries that have managed to do this – alas, few in numbers – have also advanced further than others in their development. Significant differences exist in development levels attained in the first years of the 21st century, also within the enlarged European Union and between the EU and other most highly developed countries of the world. Let us remember that per capita GDP in the United States now exceeds the EU-15 average by more than 40 per cent. Thus, if per capita GDP in Poland amounts at present to some 38 per cent of the EU-15 average, this translates into a mere 27 per cent of the USA standard.

Given such an enormous gap in output levels and living standards between the new European Union members and rich countries, every fraction of a percentage

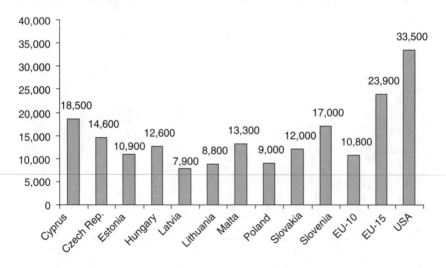

Figure 28.5 Per capita GDP, adjusted for purchasing power parity (in PPS units)

Note: The PPS (Purchasing Power Standard) is a unit representing an identical basket of goods and services in each of the countries being compared, regardless of price differentials. Approximately, 1 PPS equals 1 euro. The estimates shown are for 2002.

Source: European Commission (2004b).

point and every quarter of a year when GDP is even marginally higher matter on the scale of economic growth (Figure 28.5). After all, a long period is the sum of short episodes, and the output increments attained are the greater, in absolute terms, the higher the starting level was. Accordingly, the overshot stabilization programme and overcooling of the economy have not only cost us dearly in the past (Poland's current GDP is an estimated 20 per cent below what would have been attainable without those policy errors), but also encumber the future, just like the positive effects of faster growth in some past periods will continue to be felt in years to come. To see this, it is enough to realize that, starting from today's level of about US$10,000 (in purchasing power parity terms), per capita GDP will have to rise in 15 and 25 years, respectively, to US$15,580 and US$20,940 at an average growth rate of 3 per cent, a year, US$18,000 and US$26,660 at 4 per cent and as much as US$20,790 and US$33,860 if the economy expands by 5 per cent a year. If the growth rate fluctuates around the last-mentioned value for a time span of a whole generation, or about 25 years, even a difference of one per thousand matters, as it translates into an extra US$400 of income after a quarter of a century. The stakes, therefore, are high.

The grey sector in politics

As has been said, institutions are vital, and so is policy; institutions are not a substitute for it, but they facilitate or hamper its efficient implementation from the point of view of economic dynamics. We construe policy, in this context, in various ways, concentrating in most cases on its overt, public aspects. However, just like the economy has its grey sector (so-called shadow economy), hard to observe and control, so a grey sector exists in politics (shadow politics). It has been even less studied than its economic counterpart. The reason is that the scientific community and so-called independent media are all but paralyzed with fear when it comes to a systematic investigation of 'grey politics'. And yet many decisions, sometimes of key importance for economic growth, are taken in the grey sector and only then transferred to the sphere of overt policy at officially recorded cabinet meetings, sessions of the Parliament and its committees, or proceedings of the independent central bank and its monetary policy council.

The actual decisions are taken after informal discussions that take into account political arrangements and the position of various interest groups, whereas official politics serves only as a formal and public instrument to implement settlements made elsewhere. Elaborating on the simile between politics and economics, one can venture to say that the proportion of decisions made de facto in the political grey sector to those that are taken entirely through official channels is higher than the ratio of unrecorded and untaxed grey-sector turnover to registered economic transactions. Any analysis and evaluation of current policies should take into account this phenomenon, particularly in connection with recommendations on desired policy directions. It is fairly obvious that the scope for grey-sector politics depends on the maturity of the institutions of a democratic state and civil society on the one hand, and the market economy on the other.

What, then, is economic policy? It should be seen as an ability to solve mass-scale social problems on economic grounds. To put it differently, it is a capacity to engage in a specific kind of game with all the actors involved in the liberalized market economy. In the context of the present discussion, it is a game which should lead to expanded macroeconomic reproduction. Its object is to maintain the highest growth rate possible and distribute its effects in an equitable, that is, socially acceptable, manner. For it is social sentiment, rather than the judgement of some economists or political leaders, that decides what is equitable and what is not. Ultimately, decisions on such matters must be taken in the Parliament, through the adoption of laws, budget acts and other arrangements relating to the tax system, financial transfers and social policy.

However, such public decisions are often secondary to decisions taken in private in government offices or party caucuses, since many persons involved view politics differently: as a matter of *who supports whom against whom and for what kind of money*. On such an interpretation, it is likewise a game, but one of a negative and often harmful character, oriented towards destroying political enemies and advancing particularistic interests of one's own and one's political clientele. In other words, politics, and especially the better part of grey-sector politics, does not have to be subordinated to the common good and public interest, and hence does not have to promote economic growth. Sometimes it may even impede it.

One might ask why the growth rate in Poland plunged form 7.5 per cent in the second quarter of 1997 to a stagnant 0.2 per cent in the fourth quarter of 2001. After all, it was hardly a consequence of external shocks. Neither was it a case of institutional retrogression, for the maturation process in this area went on uninterrupted. Privatization and liberalization were continued; openness to the global economy was increasing; integration with the European Union was in progress. But the state was being weakened and the economic policy was being misdirected through a harmful combination of liberal and populist ideas.

Furthermore, the power struggle aspect of politics is present at all times. Some attempt to stay in power, others to gain power, usually affecting in the process the dynamics of the economy by obstructing decisions that foster development and hindering growth-promoting structural reforms. In this approach to politics, the yardstick is the 'effectiveness' of a policy from the point of view of its proponents' interests, which translate in many cases into weakening authority, rather than enhancing growth tendencies. This inevitably leads to relatively slower growth, despite the successive strengthening of market institutions, mainly in the course of the ongoing adjustment of the Polish economy to the requirements of the *acquis communautaire* of the European Union.

Assessments, warnings, suggestions

The answer to the initial question about the origin of the gap between the potential (that is, supposedly attainable) and actual growth rate is, thus, at the same time trivial and penetrating: the discrepancy results from the shortcomings of the economic policy which purportedly could have been followed in the existing structural, institutional and cultural configuration. One might, therefore, ask 'if it could have been followed, why was it not?' But perhaps that very configuration not only hindered, but simply prevented the pursuit of a policy that would boost growth rate to its theoretical maximum? This is seemingly an easy question, especially in the context of two divergent and quite interesting opinions which are repeatedly voiced in the ongoing discourse.

On the one hand, the reviewers and critics of the actual policy – scholars, theorists, commentators, individual and institutional experts and advisors of all kinds, analysts, opposition politicians – claim as a rule that you can do better and achieve more. In particular, they point out that output volume and the scope of services provided could increase faster than they do in reality. On the other hand, those who implement this policy – the government, central administrative authorities in charge of the economy, the central bank, political supporters of the ruling coalition, regional and local administrators – believe faster growth to be out of reach for the time being and, if anything, only make predictions (bona fide or otherwise) of its increase in a longer or shorter perspective.

Whereas the passive commentators (reviewers and critics) generally agree that a different, faster (or potential, to stick to our terminology) growth path is available – at least until some of them switch roles and take charge of actually running the economic policy – the opinions of the active participants are divided. Some believe it is possible to attain higher growth dynamics already in a short-term perspective, while others disagree. Worst of all, members of the active group are usually unable to attain sufficient consensus (a full consensus is always out of the question) as to the recommended course and methods of action. Interestingly, this is observed in all countries, including those which boast the most modern and sophisticated economic structure and the most mature market institutions – among others, the United States (Stiglitz 2003). This time, however, it is not just a question of conflicting views (which, after all, vary even more widely among the passive critics, who invariably attack those in power, from the left, from the right, or sometimes also from commonsensical positions): the main problem is that the measures they take often lack co-ordination, while the compromises they reach are devoid of creative content. The very term 'economic policy' gives rise to numerous issues that require constant deliberation.

First, there is the question of policy, which, in order to yield good and beneficial results, needs to be based on a vision and yet free from illusions. Without a vision, a policy (or a politician) is incomplete, halfhearted and decidedly unconvincing. It is like a journey without a destination or like aimless rambling which, enjoyable though it may be at times, fails to lead from A to B, as a policy should. A long-term vision should be at the same time ambitious and realistic, acting as a signpost showing society the right development path and the way to fulfil its aspirations. It should stimulate such aspirations while keeping them within reasonable limits, so that they can in time be attained. If the lack of such a vision is covered up by the illusions of 'beneficial shocks' or 'civilizational leaps' in the sphere of declarations, and a foreshortened political perspective in the face of a coming election in actual practice, growth prospects are hardly encouraging.

Second, there is the question of economy – which means that the policy should be based on a theory that accounts for the workings of the economy and for its growth. A bad theory can only serve as a foundation of a bad policy. We have recently witnessed this in Poland, in the years of shock without therapy at the beginning of the previous decade and of needless cooling towards its end. By contrast, a good policy can only be formulated and pursued on the basis of a good economic theory, although such a theory is in itself not enough to accomplish this. But it certainly is indispensable.

There was a time when running the economy was far easier than today and one could, in a sense, get away with an uninformed economic policy, resorting to trial and error or in vivo experimentation. After all, a thousand years ago the world population amounted to just about 310 million. By now, however, mankind has become more than 20 times more numerous. The implementation of an economic policy – that is, exerting a deliberate and purposeful influence on participants in the economic market game in order to attain the goals of development: fuller satisfaction of society's needs as consumers thanks to more competitive enterprises, and an efficient state catering for individual and corporate actors – is nowadays an incredibly complex task which requires an enormous knowledge. Such a knowledge must be based not only on practical experience, but first and foremost on a good economic theory, which is, unfortunately, not always available. It is long since Michal Kalecki observed that, contrary to popular belief, politicians do listen to economists but only to those of the previous generation. Yet even modern-generation economists have at their disposal only some elements of an economic theory, some empirical findings and fragmentary discussions. This situation is especially acutely felt under the conditions of the post-socialist transformation.

But the main problem is that economic views, all too often contradictory, are even more numerous than good ideas and could serve to pave many a road to hell. Politics, therefore, is constantly faced with dilemmas: whom to take heed of and whom to ignore? Which ideas to build upon and which to reject? Which to deem erroneous, and which correct? And how are we to know it, in the first place? Accordingly, the risk of errors is enormous and further aggravated by the fact that many politicians who pretend to be in the know are, in fact, ignorant, and even those who do have some knowledge often make mistakes anyway. For such is the peculiarity of economics that even those conversant with this discipline, to a greater or lesser degree, are still prone to error in policy decisions and choices. Moreover, the desire for dialogue and compromise, flexibility and openness, justified though it is in many cases, is often confused with the need for methodological and factual correctness and academic rigour. Average values are useful in statistics, but not in development economics or growth theory. An efficient policy cannot be a result of 'averaging', with some elements taken from one scientific approach and some from another, mixing monetarism with a neo-Keynesian approach, new institutional economics with the Swedish school, socialism with capitalism – with a sole view to satisfying the possibly broadest spectrum of disputants.

Of particularly destructive character in our post-socialist realities are the attempts to combine leftist ideas in an intentionally social-democratic spirit with elements of neoliberal economics, taken out of the context of a theory which applies to the vastly different world of highly developed capitalism.[10] What is interesting is that this tendency was equally pronounced in the coalition government formed by the Solidarity Electoral Action and Freedom Union (AWS–UW) in 1998–2001, and in that run by the Democratic Left Alliance and the Polish Peasant Party (SLD–PSL) in 2001–05. It was certainly a consequence of the fact that the policies of all these parties have been more often guided by their respective ideologies than by economic theory in the strict sense of the term. Regrettably, such a bizarre hybrid of left-wing populism and right-wing liberal market fundamentalism continues nowadays to weaken the economic fabric. It stands in the way of attaining the potential growth rate and, most important of all, prevents the painstakingly restored economic dynamics from being sustained in a long-term perspective.

Third, the abundance of views is matched by the multitude of interests at stake. The configuration of conflicting interests should be watched with even greater care than the meanders of theory, in order to find out why certain views, but not others, gain the upper hand. For in actual fact, it is differing interests, rather than views, that matter. In the end, some interests prevail, not some views. In this context, interests are primary and views secondary. The latter are often simply bought and sold, using a whole gamut of instruments of lobbying, political marketing, persuasion, pressure, or simply intellectual corruption. Under such circumstances, views are adjusted to fit the relevant pseudo-science (inspired de facto by political considerations and having very little to do with genuine learning).

In recent years, the best example has been provided by the lobbying in favour of a linear tax – an idea that is both theoretically erroneous and harmful in actual practice. It is intrinsically wrong in the context of both domestic capital formation, which it is ostensibly (but only seemingly) intended to foster, and does not provide for a socially advantageous redistribution of income. Incidentally, these two aspects are inseparable, as moving to a linear tax *always* entails a transfer of some net income from the poorer to the richer, which inevitably produces – in a society at an early phase of capital accumulation – a *drop* rather than an *increase* in the macro-scale propensity to save. This has been convincingly demonstrated by the past 15 years of transformation, when the increasing spread of incomes has usually been accompanied by a diminishing, and not growing, propensity to save. Such a transfer of income in the Polish conditions would further markedly aggravate the trade imbalance by stimulating additional imports of costly, domestically unavailable goods and outward capital transfers. In the end, the national economy might be left with less rather than more resources. Such was the experience of Russia in recent years. Flat taxation is not only inequitable – which need not be a legitimate issue for every economist and politician – but first and foremost it has a destabilizing effect and destroys efficiency, which must not be overlooked by those economists and economic policy-makers who are keen on ensuring sustained growth.

Fourth, the efficient implementation of good economic policy concepts requires determined political leadership. The decision-makers must know what they want; we must really know 'what we are fighting for and where we are headed'. Without such knowledge, one gets stuck and treads water, which is not to say that those who are stuck and tread water do not struggle as hard as they can. But in that case even a good theory will not help, as there is a shortage of people who know how to use it. Correct answers are of little avail, either, if the political decision-makers often do not even know what the questions are.

Political leadership can be analyzed at various levels. In a political democracy and a budding civil society, it is mainly the question of well-organized, efficient political parties, whose workings are open to public scrutiny, and of their leaders. From this point of view, the situation in Poland is highly inauspicious and, paradoxically, it is deteriorating instead of improving. This spells trouble for the future, not only from the point of view of potentially attainable growth rate. But even if the analyses and assessments were restricted to this single aspect, they would show clearly that the actual growth rate in the next couple of years, or perhaps even a decade or more, will be lower than potentially attainable without this extra-economic constraint. This is a factor which unlike, say, computers or oil, cannot be imported. It has to be *learned* in the historic process of evolution and development, by building appropriate institutions and forging a new and different political culture.

Fifth, politics is the art of co-ordination. The multi-threaded nature of economic activity necessitates handling a great many matters simultaneously. Of course, some of them are more important or more urgent than others. Incidentally, the ability to find out what really *is* important and urgent and to tell fundamental and strategic issues from trivial everyday matters is a special gift that not all politicians possess. Politics, on the one hand, can be compared to managing a huge company or organization where multiple difficult decisions have to be taken at a moment's notice – sometimes in a crisis situation – often on the basis of incomplete infor-mation and under noisy pressure from the outside. On the other hand, it is a strategic activity that requires latitude, perspective and reflection. It also calls for a creative interaction with the less noisy parts of the environment – one's intellec-tual backers and experts, foreign partners representing the global economy, and, most importantly of all, social partners. If we succeed in achieving some measure of co-ordination among all these components, eliminating 'information noise' and friction in the decision-making mechanisms, the machine is working: decisions do not contradict one another, positive feedback channels are activated, obstacles that hamper the desired processes are removed and, in time, the expected results begin to show in the real and financial spheres, in respect of pro-duction, distribution and consumption. In short, the economy is growing.

Sixth and last, politics in all areas, including the economy, is the art of compro-mise. It is necessary at all times to keep searching for a creative consensus that reconciles the necessary with the possible, accommodates the contradictory interests of society in various time scales (as in the classic accumulation vs con-sumption dilemma), resolves conflicts between short- and long-term interests of specific social, occupational and income groups, between the needs of the state and the regions, between taxpayers and the recipients of budget funds, between consumers and producers. There exist many more levels on which economic interests diverge. The point is that unless conflict-prone situations are defused using appropriate policy instruments, full-fledged conflicts threaten to develop. And then a compromise usually becomes even harder to reach. Moreover, a compromise needs to be positive, in the sense that – unlike a negative one, accepted out of necessity, but inconvenient to all parties – it should make everyone (or nearly everyone) satisfied to approximately the same degree with the settlement achieved. Such a compromise serves as a foundation on which one can try to build some reasonable long-term arrangements.

Lessons from Poland's transition for emerging markets

Unfortunately, too many compromises in Poland – covering issues from tax rates to the financing of highway construction to the calculation of old-age benefits – are makeshift, superficial and precarious affairs. This, far from balancing the dynamic socioeconomic relationships, prevents the economic policy from taking a more far-sighted perspective. A myopic, hand-to-mouth policy will never foster rapid growth: it is a task which requires a long-term approach. In Poland, unless the *Public Finance Recovery Programme* (PNFR 2003) is implemented in sufficient measure – which, most unfortunately, appears unlikely – a hand-to-mouth policy will continue to dominate. So far, this syndrome was overcome only once – and merely for a couple of years – in the course of the implementation of a long-term socioeconomic development programme linked with profound structural reforms and measures fostering market-economy institutions, known as the Strategy for Poland and pursued between 1994 and 1997.[11]

It is, thus, possible to conduct a good economic policy under any structural, institutional and cultural circumstances, because the definition of a 'good' policy implicitly contains the assumption that it must fit the existing conditions – in a manner of speaking, it should be compatible with them. Of course, for the very same reason, a policy may be suboptimal or downright bad. History shows that the latter is, alas, far more frequent and, therefore, it is easier to quote numerous sorry outcomes, rather than spectacular successes, of economic policies. This is also true of post-socialist transforming economies, Poland included, particularly during certain periods in the past 15 years.

This explains why the attempts to transplant into the post-socialist realities a policy that may even have succeeded to some extent under different circumstances were doomed to failure – through the lack of compatibility. Such was the case with the adoption of recipes based on the so-called Washington Consensus in Poland and Russia in the early 1990s.[12] Even if some political conception did work in practice, for instance, in Chile, it could have been totally inappropriate for Poland, and vice versa. Contrary to appearances, the reasons in both cases are not at all different, as they boil down in the end to the inadequacy of the proposed policy *instruments* for the existing *institutions*. It is like having a church organist play a virtuoso violin cadenza: it can be played, if only just barely, but hardly bears listening to. In this context we may even conclude – and the paradox here is only superficial – that, for instance, Uganda has had a better economic policy in recent years than not only Zimbabwe, but also Germany. For a policy should never be assessed 'in the abstract', but only under concrete circumstances, here and now, and always in terms of its effectiveness.

Of course, the assertion that it is possible to conduct a better policy (more compatible with its determinants) in less favourable circumstances as well as a less appropriate one in a more advantageous environment should be seen as relative to the passage of time. That is to say that the external conditions should be seen as an objective *given* in a short time span only; in the long run, the structural, institutional and cultural conditions for growth and development are created, shaped and modified by the policy itself. Being an object of policy, they provide feedback affecting its efficiency. And even if John Maynard Keynes (1924) was right saying that 'in the long run, we are all dead', before it happens, we have quite some time left to create and develop appropriate institutions by way of improving the law and bringing order to the rules of the competitive market game, to optimize the operation of the central and local government administration, and to promote the formation of non-governmental organizations that stimulate enterprise and the rise of a civil society (World Bank 2004). This too is politics, except that it is conducted on a different time scale and pertains to different matters.

Thus, if our short-term policy is constrained by the existing institutional conditions, in the long run, we mould these institutions into a factor strongly promoting output growth and socioeconomic development. But such a policy calls for knowledge and skills of a different type than those required by the (admittedly difficult) tasks of adjusting tax and interest rates to encourage capital formation, applying the mechanisms of exchange rates and obligatory reserves to maintain a dynamic monetary equilibrium, or using public procurement and budget outlays as a means to improve the economic climate.

It appears then that Keynes was right – although not quite, because societies do not die even in the long-term perspective, development processes never cease, and as we have built upon the legacy of previous generations, it is only appropriate that we bequeath to our descendants something beyond mounting problems. And for the here and now, it may also be that those of us are right who believe that it is possible to attain economic success in the process and, moreover, know a thing or two about ways to achieve it.

Notes

1. See Helpman (2004); Rodrik (2005).
2. See Kolodko (2002); Sachs (2005); Podkaminer (2004).
3. See Kolodko (2004).
4. See EBRD (2003).
5. See Kolodko (2003).
6. See European Commission (2004a).
7. See North (1997).
8. See Kolodko (2000a); Kornai (2001).
9. See World Bank (2002); IMF (2003).
10. See North (2002).

11. See Kolodko and Nuti (1997); Stiglitz (2002); Baka (2004).
12. See Kolodko (1999); Stiglitz (1998).

References

Åslund, A. (1995) *How Russia Became a Market Economy*, Washington, DC: The Brookings Institution.
Baka, W. (2004) 'Economic Ideas of the "Round Table" After Fifteen Years. Lessons for the Future', *TIGER Research Paper* 54, Warsaw: Transformation, Integration and Globalization Economic Research at the Leon Kozminski Academy of Entrepreneurship and Management.
EBRD (1996) *Transition Report*, London: European Bank for Reconstruction and Development.
EBRD (2003) *Transition Report*, London: European Bank for Reconstruction and Development.
European Commission (2004a) *Perception of Living Conditions in an Enlarged Europe*, Luxembourg and Dublin: European Foundation for the Improvement of Living and Working Conditions.
European Commission (2004b) *Panorama of the European Union*, Brussels: European Commission.
Helpman, E. (2004) *The Mystery of Economic Growth*, Cambridge, MA: Belknap Press.
IMF (2000) *World Economic Outlook*, Washington, DC: IMF.
IMF (2003) *World Economic Outlook: Growth and Institutions*, Washington, DC: IMF.
Keynes, J.M. (1924) *A Tract on Monetary Reform*, London: Macmillan.
Kolodko, G.W. (1993) 'From Recession to Growth in Post-Communist Economies', *Communist and Post-Communist Studies*, 2 (June): 123–43.
Kolodko, G.W. (1999) 'Ten Years of Postsocialist Transition: the Lessons for Policy Reforms', *Policy Research Working Paper* 2095, Washington, DC: World Bank.
Kolodko, G.W. (2000a) *From Shock to Therapy. Political Economy of Postsocialist Transformation*, Oxford and New York: Oxford University Press for UNU-WIDER.
Kolodko, G.W. (2000b) *Post-Communist Transition. The Thorny Road*, Rochester, NY: University of Rochester Press.
Kolodko, G.W. (2002) *Globalization and Catching-up in Transition Economies*, Rochester, NY: University of Rochester Press.
Kolodko, G.W. (2003) *Structural Reform and Economic Growth in 2002–2003. The Opening and Closing Balance*, Warsaw: Transformation, Integration and Globalization Economic Research, Leon Kozminski Academy of Entrepreneurship and Management.
Kolodko, G.W (2004) *The Polish Miracle. Lessons for the Emerging Markets*, Aldershot: Ashgate.
Kolodko, G.W. and D.M. Nuti (1997) 'The Polish Alternative. Old Myths, Hard Facts and New Strategies in the Successful Transformation of the Polish Economy', *Research for Action* 33, Helsinki: UNU-WIDER.
Kornai, J. (2001) 'The Role of the State in a Post-socialist Economy', *Distinguished Lectures* 6, Warsaw: Leon Kozminski Academy of Entrepreneurship and Management.
Lin, J.Y., F. Cai and Z. Li (2003) *The China Miracle. Development Strategy and Economic Reform*, Hong Kong: Chinese University Press.
North, D.C. (1997) 'The Contribution of the New Institutional Economics to an Understanding of the Transition Problem', *WIDER Annual Lecture* 1, Helsinki: UNU-WIDER. Reprinted (2005) *WIDER Perspectives on Global Development*, Basingstoke: Palgrave Macmillan for UNU-WIDER.
North, D.C. (2002) 'Understanding Economic Change and Economic Growth', *Distinguished Lectures Series* 7, Warsaw: Leon Kozminski Academy of Entrepreneurship and Management.
PNFR (2003) *Public Finance Recovery Programme*, Warsaw: Rada Ministrów.

Podkaminer, L. (2004) 'Is Rapid, Long-Term Economic Growth in Poland Likely?', *TIGER Working Paper* 55, Warsaw: Transformation, Integration and Globalization Economic Research at the Leon Kozminski Academy of Entrepreneurship and Management.

Rodrik, D. (2005) 'Rethinking Growth Strategies', in *WIDER Perspectives on Global Development*, Basingstoke: Palgrave Macmillan for UNU-WIDER.

Sachs, J.D. (2005) *The End of Poverty: Economic Possibilities for our Time*, New York: Penguin.

Sen, A. (2000) *Development as Freedom*, New York: Alfred A. Knopf.

Stiglitz, J.E. (1998) 'More Instruments and Broader Goals: Moving towards the Post-Washington Consensus', *WIDER Annual Lecture* 2, Helsinki: UNU-WIDER. Reprinted (2005) *WIDER Perspectives on Global Development*, Basingstoke: Palgrave Macmillan for UNU-WIDER.

Stiglitz, J.E. (2002) *Globalization and Its Discontents*, New York and London: W.W. Norton & Company.

Stiglitz, J.E. (2003) *The Roaring Nineties. A New History of the World's Most Prosperous Decade*, New York and London: W.W. Norton & Company.

Tanzi, V., K.-Y. Chu and S. Gupta (eds) (1999) *Economic Policy and Equity*, Washington, DC: IMF.

World Bank (2002) *Building Institutions for Markets. World Development Report 2002*, Washington, DC: World Bank.

World Bank (2004) *A Better Investment Climate for Everyone. World Development Report 2005*, Washington, DC: World Bank.

29
Patterns of Rent Extraction and Deployment in Developing Countries: Implications for Governance, Economic Policy and Performance

Richard M. Auty

The context

Attempts to model the political economy of the developing countries' transition to high-income democracies proliferate, despite scepticism that the process is too complex and idiosyncratic to generalize (Haggard (1990: 3–4). Many economists (Barro 1996; 1999; Feng and Zak 1999) and political scientists (Lipset 1959; Jackman 1973; Burkhart and Lewis-Beck 1994) support a consensus view that per capita income is positively associated with political accountability – rising income 'causes' government to improve.

The consensus has not gone unchallenged, however. For example, Kaufmann and Kraay (2002) suggest that the causal direction may be the reverse of the consensus. Zak and Feng (2003) report that transitions to democracy can occur if economic growth falters. Elsewhere, Przeworski *et al.* (2000) claim that rising per capita income does not change the likelihood of transition to democracy although it does reduce the probability of regression. They explain this by the fact that the gains from a shift to democracy attenuate at high-income levels due to the declining marginal utility of the redistribution gains, whereas the losses from any associated destruction of capital stock (due to violence) strengthen with rising incomes. However, two recent studies (Boix and Stokes 2003; Epstein *et al.* 2004) convincingly challenge Przeworski *et al.* (2000).

The explanations proffered for these contested outcomes are rather parsimonious. For instance, Barro (1999) notes the 'surprising' lack of a theory that might inform the debate. This chapter draws upon recent theoretical and empirical literature to help fill this gap and also to reconcile the contesting views. It reflects early work on a planned research programme into how the political state in developing countries is affected by differences in the scale of the economic rent and how the rent is extracted and deployed. The chapter therefore presents themes for further research rather than definitive findings.

Three basic categories of rent are commonly identified in developing countries, namely natural resource rent, contrived rent (or government monopoly rent) and geopolitical rent (reflecting the revenues that states extract from the global community through strategic alliances, humanitarian concerns or terror threats). All three rents are relatively high because most developing countries still depend on their primary sectors (which boosts the relative importance of natural-resource rent); they often receive sizeable amounts of external aid (geopolitical rent) and they tend to have fallible institutions (rule of law, property rights, legislative assemblies and bureaucracies), which tendency increases both the temptation to extract contrived rent and the risk of its suboptimal deployment. Within specific developing countries each of the three rents can measure up to tens of per cent of GDP and in aggregate they not atypically range from 15–50 per cent of GDP (and more during commodity price surges like the 1974–78 and 1979–81 oil booms). Rent on such a scale attracts competition from political and economic agents and its capture can severely distort the political economy at the expense of broad-based welfare.

This chapter derives a dynamic political economy model from two rent-driven stylized facts economic models, namely the competitive industrialization model (CIM), which is associated with low rents and the staple trap model (STM) linked to high rents. These rent-driven economic models suggests that the smaller the rent relative to GDP and the more diffusely it is spread across economic agents, the greater the probability of engendering a developmental political state[1] (Table 29.1) that competitively diversifies the economy to sustain rapid growth in per capita GDP (PCGDP) (Auty and Gelb 2001: 126–44). This economic trajectory incrementally strengthens three sanctions against anti-social governance (political accountability, social capital and the rule of law) to foster endogenous democratization.

The CIM prediction of a developmental political state is rooted in the observation that limited rent-seeking opportunities in resource-poor countries concentrate government efforts on wealth creation through the provision of public goods and the maintenance of efficiency incentives. If government income depends wholly on taxation of productive activity rather than drawing also upon rent extraction, the political state retains strong incentives to pursue policies that encourage economic inputs to be deployed efficiently. Consequently, the economy adheres to its comparative advantage, which for a resource-poor country initially lies in competitive industrialization,[2] which promotes endogenous democratization. The corollary is that the larger the rent relative to GDP and the more concentrated it is on a handful of economic agents, the greater the probability of engendering a non-developmental political state that presides over a growth collapse (the STM development trajectory) and represses political accountability. However, a growth collapse may trigger an abrupt switch to democracy where

Table 29.1 A typology of political states based on aims and autonomy

Autonomy + type	Aims	Basic type	Markets role	Country examples
Autonomous predator	Maximize rent siphoning	Military elite	Soft constraint	Nigeria 1966–79 + 1983–99, Ghana 1970–83
		Central planning	Soft constraint	Algeria, Turkmenistan, USSR
Autonomous benevolent	Maximize social welfare	Growth with equity	Hard constraint	Chile 1975–89, Hong Kong, Korea, Taiwan
		Paternalistic monarchy	Relaxed constraint	Brunei, Kuwait, Saudi Arabia, UAE
Factional oligarchy	Maximize rent siphoning	Landed/industrial captures policy	Soft constraint	Argentina, Brazil, Mexico, Bolivia
		Public officials capture policy	Soft constraint	Azerbaijan, India, Kazakhstan, Russia, Uzbekistan
		Ethnic alliance captures policy	Soft constraint	Kenya, Sudan, pre-1993 South Africa
Factional democracy	Maximize social welfare	Consensual: Growth + equity	Hard constraint	Malaysia, Botswana
		Polarized: equity > growth	Relaxed constraint	Costa Rica, Sri Lanka

Source: Based on Lal (1995).

exogenous factors are favourable. This exogenous democratization trajectory is therefore likely to be erratic and unstable.

This chapter focuses upon the elaboration of the political component of the political economy models. It begins in the next section by establishing a six-fold classification of political states linked to differences in the scale and deployment of the rent. The typology identifies parallel low-rent and high-rent variants of the basic stylized transition from an autocratic state to a democracy via an oligarchy. The section following explains the link between the CIM development trajectory and endogenous democratization, followed by a section linking exogenous democratization to the high-rent STM trajectory. Then I report simple preliminary tests of the predictions of the endogenous and exogenous democratization models; the penultimate section briefly illustrates some policy implications, while the final section summarizes the findings and suggests a research agenda.

A rent-based typology of political states

This section elaborates a rent-driven typology of political states from the typologies of Lal (1995: 310–27), Olson (2000a), Auty (2001) and Eifert *et al.* (2003). Olson's (2000a) evolutionary typology provides a useful starting point. His basic premise is that the incentive for a government to provide public goods (and thereby reduce transaction costs and strengthen investment incentives) increases as the political state encompasses the interests of a wider fraction of society. Olson's four basic categories of political state assume a progressive improvement in governance moving from the roving bandit state (conceived as a pillaging warlord) to a democracy, via two intermediate stages, namely the stationary bandit state (an autocrat) and the oligarchic state.

More specifically, whereas the roving bandit plunders a region and moves on to the next region, the stationary bandit has a longer time horizon due to the need to ensure a sustained income stream from the region of residence, which is the region being exploited. The stationary bandit therefore maximizes his income by providing some public goods that facilitate exchange (such as law and order, income-related taxation and essential infrastructure) and leaving producers with sufficient revenue to retain an incentive to increase output. An oligarchy reflects the capture of the political state by a political group that administers patronage in a more collegiate manner than either form of autocratic state. It will tax less than a stationary bandit does and will also invest more in public goods. This is because, unlike either bandit state, the elite in an oligarchy is a producer of goods as well as a consumer of rent so it benefits directly from incentives to boost output and it is also less dependent for its income upon siphoning off rents. In other words, an oligarchy has wider encompassing interests than a stationary bandit state does. Finally, a democracy embraces even wider interests and therefore promotes conditions still more conducive to broad-based wealth creation.

Olson's system can be usefully elaborated into a six-category typology (Table 29.2) by recognizing low-rent and high-rent variants of the three basic types of political state (autocracy, oligarchy and democracy). The typology identifies two paths from autocracy to democracy: one is likely to nurture developmental governments under the incentives conferred by low rents and the other is a high-rent path linked to more predatory governments. The six-fold typology can be further extended to enhance its flexibility by recognizing subgroups of the basic types, and some examples are given below. However, the main purpose of the remainder of this section is to explain the principal features of the six political states in Table 29.2.

Olson assumes the stationary bandit state will be benevolent and, relative to the roving bandit this may be true, but empirical evidence suggests it is useful to acknowledge how differences in rents affect the conduct of stationary bandit states. For example, Olson's stationary bandit category includes rent-poor South Korea between 1963 and 1987 along with rent-rich Azerbaijan and Turkmenistan. Yet whereas the South Korean elite was careful to enrich itself without allowing rent seeking to damage GDP growth and welfare gains (Khan and Jomo 2000), both rent-rich Caspian Basin governments conferred wealth in the 1990s on an autocracy even as basic services deteriorated and poverty increased. If stationary bandit states are likely to be benevolent in rent-poor countries and predatory in rent-rich ones, it is useful to formally identify benevolent and predatory variations of the autocratic state (Table 29.2). In this context, Olson's roving bandit state may be regarded as an

Table 29.2 Evolution of political accountability under political states with differing autonomy and aims

Autonomy of state	Basic aims of state	Critical features	Rent pattern	Strength of sanction — Political accountability	Against anti-social — Social capital	Governance — Rule of law
Developmental						
Benevolent autocratic nation builder	Secure rapid GDP growth to sustain compact elite + build social unity	Low rent; external threat; poor have low opportunity cost	Low rent siphoning: efficient diffuse rent raising + dispersal	Weak; but predation curbed by priority for social unity	Bonding social capital dominant; slow expansion of bridging + linking	Nominal; elite dispense justice, at times arbitrarily
Diffuse factional oligarchy	Expand elite to deter policy capture and sustain rapid GDP growth	Low rent; intra-elite (land/ethnic/army) rivals; rapid equal GDP growth	Low diffuse rent extraction for public goods + (skewed) wealth creation	Moderate: growing parliament power vs executive	Competitive urbanization builds autonomous linking + bridging social capital	Strengthening legal protection; common law fairer > civil law
Consensual factional democracy	Growth then equity via providing basic social entitlements	Low rent; middle-class growth saps elite + shrinks poor	Diffuse extraction + dispersal for growth > redistribution	High: independent parliament + second chamber	Autonomous linking + bridging social capital; risk of Olson effects	Legal independence cuts transaction costs + risk
Non-Developmental						
Predatory autocratic dictator	Maximize elite rent siphoning, through force if necessary	High rent; violent predation; staple trap trajectory	Point rent extraction by elite slows GDP growth	None: power held by violence, which only elite contest	Weak: intense elite rivalry; weak bond social capital of poor vs elite	None: elite controls by force; poor rely on custom
Concentrated factional oligarchy	Dominant faction captures policy to sustain rent + power	High rent; unequal asset share; staple trap trajectory	Point extraction but some public goods benefit mainly elite	Minimal; puppet legislature run by oligarchy	Dependent on elite; repressed civic associations	Skewed to favour elite > poor
Polarized factional democracy	Capture policy to benefit tribal clients even if slows long-term GDP growth	Democracy polarized on tribal lines; retarded GDP growth	Rent extraction + skewed distribution to tribal clients > GDP growth	Fragile: Parliament liable to wild policy swings + some dictator risk	Polarized civic associations feed polarized democracy	Judiciary subject to capture + biased to tribal clients

Note: Moving down the table, political accountability strengthens incrementally and endogenously under developmental political states (associated with low rent). It is retarded for non-developmental political states, but after a growth collapse exogenous democratization can occur abruptly if neighbourhood effects are accommodated.

extreme variant of the predatory autocracy, one of several extensions to the typology that enhance its flexibility. Saudi Arabia provides an example of an extreme variant of the benevolent autocracy, which is paternalistic, as identified by Auty (2001) and Eifert *et al.* (2003: 89). The latter also recognize a reformist autocracy (benevolent autocracy in Table 29.2) and predatory autocracy (the same in Table 29.2).

It is similarly useful to distinguish more than one form of oligarchy because a *low-rent* oligarchy is likely to rely more on wealth creation and less on rent siphoning than a high-rent oligarchy is. In addition, a low-rent oligarchy will increasingly comprise industrialists rather than landowners because the low-rent CIM development trajectory diversifies early into manufacturing (as explained in the next section). According to Acemoglu and Robinson (2005) industrialists are likely to form a diffusing oligarchy, a category recognized in Table 29.2 (second row). This is because industrialists rely more heavily on co-operation from an urban work-force to sustain their wealth than landowners do and also the assets of factory owners tend to be more concentrated and vulnerable. A diffuse oligarchy is also likely to exhibit sufficient plurality to impose checks and balances on what any subgroup can gain from policy capture. Moreover, an oligarchy with a diffuse structure has within it the seeds of its own dissolution because the political jockeying it entails is likely to encourage the co-option of outsider groups, most likely factions of the middle class, so that the political system is one that increasingly shifts towards a democratic political state. Nineteenth-century Britain provides an illustration of a diffusing oligarchy.[3] In contrast, a high-rent oligarchy can use the rent to sustain its monopoly and by force if necessary, whether the collegiate group comprises landowners, the military or a dominant ethnic group.

Finally, it is useful to distinguish between polarized and consensual democracies (respectively, the 'factional' and 'mature' democracies of Eifert *et al.* 2003: 89). The STM explains why high rents polarize income distribution and society, and stimulate the formation of political coalitions against income redistribution. Such a polarized democracy struggles to sustain economic growth because elections bring abrupt and large changes in policy, which undermine the coherence of economic policy and diminish investor confidence. Jamaica, Mauritius and Malaysia provide interesting examples.[4] In contrast, low-rent economies are less likely to have a highly skewed income distribution, while in addition economic success builds a consensus in favour of an economic policy that promotes wealth creation over redistribution (row 3, Table 29.2). Consequently, policy differences between political parties within a consensual democracy are modest so that elections do not bring abrupt changes and economic policy is more coherent. The next section explains why low-rent political states are likely to evolve incrementally towards a consensual democracy, in marked contrast to high-rent political states.

The endogenous democratization model

This section explains endogenous democratization by linking the CIM development trajectory to three sanctions against anti-social governance (political accountability, social capital and legal institutions).

Low-rent growth: the competitive industrialization model

The CIM model explains why low rents limit the period of dependence on primary product exports and nurture early industrialization (at a relatively low per capita income), which is both labour intensive and competitive and triggers beneficial economic and social circles (Auty 2001). Focusing on the virtuous economic circle, early industrialization also entails early urbanization, which speeds passage through the demographic cycle, lowering the rate of population growth. This improves the worker/dependant ratio and raises the rate of saving and investment in GDP (Appendix Figure 29.A1). It also rapidly absorbs surplus rural labour so that labour costs rise and propel diversification into capital- and skill-intensive industry. This competitive diversification of the economy in turn sustains investment efficiency and strengthens the resilience of the economy, so that the CIM achieves rapid and sustained PCGDP growth.

As for the virtuous social circle, income distribution is equitable because the early elimination of surplus labour puts a floor under the wages of the poor and the rapid accumulation of human capital caps the skill premium. In addition, competitive urbanization (as opposed to dependent urbanization under high-rent growth) is associated with the rapid accumulation of market-enhancing social capital. In this way, the competitive industrialization trajectory rapidly accumulates produced capital (Auty and Kiiski 2001: 19–35), human capital (Birdsall *et al.* 2001: 57–75) and social capital (Woolcock *et al.* 2001). The competitive industrialization trajectory sharply raises the genuine saving coefficient, implying that the trajectory is strongly sustainable (Hamilton 2001: 36–56). Per capita incomes can double every ten years so that the transition from poverty to a mature economy can occur in fewer than two generations compared with more than five generations for the developing countries on average (according to Syrquin 1986: 232).

CIM trajectory, sanctions versus anti-social governance and endogenous democratization

The CIM trajectory strengthens political accountability for two main reasons. First, competitive industrialization rapidly restructures the economy away from its initial dependence on the primary sector so that the relative importance of natural resource rents declines early (*Ibid.*), creating pressure to diversify tax revenue away from commodity and export taxes towards sales, income and profits taxes. This trend intensifies pressure for greater political accountability regarding how public revenue is raised and allocated. Lizzeri and Persico (2004) describe just such a self-reinforcing interaction for nineteenth century Britain.

Second, along with the swift relative decline of the primary sector, the proliferation of competitive manufacturing shrinks the scope for state intervention and rent seeking, effectively de-politicizing the economy (Ranis and Mahmood 1992). For example, Åslund (2000: 399–424) reports an inverse relationship between increasing reform (i.e. greater competition) and the scale of rent seeking in the Russian Federation. After initially stalling, Russian reform briefly restarted during 1994–95 and this shrank both rents and inflation but when reform stalled a second time rent-seeking opportunities re-expanded. Li *et al.* (2000: 284) set out the basic insight with reference to China: 'All government bureaucrats seek rents and are reluctant to give up their power. However, without a monopoly, rents can be guaranteed only by improving the efficiency of their firms.' They show how growing competition between firms in adjacent administrative areas exerted pressure on local governments to strengthen efficiency incentives so that the governments can escape onerous charges from loss-making firms. The local governments achieved this by establishing profit-sensitive co-operatives like town and village enterprises (TVEs) in place of state-owned enterprises (SOEs) or by allowing entry of new private firms. Consistent with this thesis, privatization of state assets in China proceeded fastest where competition was most intense, as with simple undifferentiated products or where transport costs fell sharply, as in the southeast coastal provinces. It also proceeded faster at lower tiers of government where the absence of scale economies facilitated entry by new firms and officials had least administrative and legal leverage to protect firms.

The second sanction against anti-social governance, social capital, may continue to be effective where political accountability regresses, as recently shown in Georgia. The World Bank (1997: 81) defines social capital as the group knowledge and trust backed up by sanctions that facilitate economic exchange by reducing uncertainty and risk. In economic terms social capital manifests itself in variations in transaction costs between regions and countries (Djankov *et al.* 2003). In sociological terms the two principal components within social capital are civic spirit and civic associations. Civic spirit is defined as the reluctance of individuals within society to take advantage of private misfortune or public administrative error. Civic associations are horizontal networks such as membership of societies for politics, professions, environment, arts, sport and trade unions that build trust.

Evidence is emerging that the rate of social capital formation traces an S-shaped curve with rising per capita income, accumulating slowly at first before accelerating through mid-income levels as urbanization peaks and then decelerating at high-income levels. At low-income levels transaction costs are high because many markets are missing due to the low density of *economic* activity and absence of the physical infrastructure that facilitates exchange.[5] In these circumstances, most transactions occur over short (i.e. local) distances (Woolcock and Narayan 2000) and are facilitated by bonding social capital because it provides individuals with insurance against risk, although the community as a whole is not protected from unforeseen shocks. However, bonding social capital can stifle innovative and entrepreneurial activity, thereby impeding development at low-income levels (Stiglitz 1995: 48–81). This is because bonding social capital often requires any gains accruing to an individual, whether from luck or unusual diligence, to be shared among the group, hampering wealth accumulation and thereby depressing individual incentives to innovate.

As development proceeds, however, urbanization allows individuals to reduce their dependence on local groups by extending social links beyond the individual village or town through regional associations. Such *linking* social capital provides an alternative means of risk reduction to bonding social capital but imposes fewer redistributive claims than bonding social capital. Moreover, expanding spatial horizons also allow scale thresholds to be crossed to create viable markets and increase the division of labour. Social capital therefore accumulates fastest in low-rent countries because urbanization occurs earlier than in resource-rich countries, and is characterized by atomized transactions negotiated out of mutual self-interest, as opposed to the dependent social capital associated with rent-driven urbanization. Consequently, low-rent countries accelerate both the emergence of an integrated settlement hierarchy (of villages nesting in the hinterlands of towns, which in turn nest in those of cities) that promotes competitive markets and the formation of a resilient linking social capital.

At high-income levels, however, the rate of social capital formation may deceler-ate or even regress because institutions and pressure groups become so specialized and powerful as to *raise* transaction costs (Killick 1995) by pursuing single-issue interests at the expense of the broader social interest, which is more diffuse and less vigorously defended. These 'Olson effects' are particularly associated with countries that enjoy prolonged periods of stability like the USSR prior to the late 1980s (Olson 2000b 119–37) and the legacy can persist (Jones Luong 2002).

Finally, formal legal institutions increase in importance as economic develop-ment proceeds, relative to social capital because; 'large anonymous markets are more effective than [informal] networks because the "best" buyer or seller may not be part of the network' (Serageldin and Grooteart 2000: 213). Such markets require the creation of effective institutions, notably a legal system and property rights. Clague *et al.* (1997: 67–90) concur, and argue that: 'societal differences in property rights and contract enforcement mechanisms are an important part of the expla-nation of why some countries prosper while others do not'.

There is evidence that increasing competition (and decreasing rent dependence) with rising PCGDP along the CIM trajectory strengthens demands from businesses to improve property rights and the rule of law. For example, SOE managers in China demanded strengthened legal guarantees for transactions and property rights as they assumed more responsibility for becoming self-funding (Li *et al.* 2000). The process acquired a self-sustaining momentum as competitive markets proliferated.

The exogenous democratization model

I now examine the link between the STM development trajectory and sanctions against anti-social governance, but first I summarize the main features of the STM.

High-rent growth: the staple trap model

In the resource-rich developing countries, the presence of resource rents, which typically ranged between 13–21 per cent of GDP in the mid-1990s (Table 29.3), increases the attraction for governments of capturing and distributing the rents and thereby diverts effort away from promoting wealth creation. It also extends the period of reliance on primary product exports, which delays competitive industrialization (Lal and Myint 1998). Under a non-developmental political state the virtuous economic and social circles of early labour-intensive industrialization

Table 29.3 Share of rents in GDP 1994 and GDP growth 1985–97, by natural resource endowment

Resource endowment	PCGDP growth 1985–97 (%)	Total rent (% GDP)	Pasture and cropland rent (% GDP)	Mineral rent (% GDP)
Resource poor[1,2]				
Large	4.7	10.56	7.34	3.22
Small	2.4	9.86	5.41	4.45
Resource rich				
Large	1.9	12.65	5.83	6.86
Small, non-mineral	0.9	15.42	12.89	2.53
Small, hard mineral	−0.4	17.51	9.62	7.89
Small, oil exporter	−0.7	21.22	2.18	19.04
All countries		15.03	8.78	6.25

Notes: 1. Resource poor = 1970 cropland/head < 0.3 hectares, mineral economies draw > 40% of exports from mining. 2. Large = 1970 GDP > US$billion.

Source: Auty and Gelb (2001: 131).

are omitted so that competitive diversification of the economy is aborted and incomes polarize. The resulting staple trap development trajectory accumulates human capital and social capital more slowly and erratically than the competitive industrialization trajectory. A caveat is in order, however, where governments of resource-rich countries are motivated to generate wealth in order to placate a large low-income rural constituency, as for example in Malaysia and Indonesia. In such circumstances, the political state may remain developmental so that competitive industrialization is merely retarded, rather than aborted (Auty and Gelb 2001).

More usually, however, the incentive to boost rural welfare has been rare in resource-abundant countries in recent decades, so that the capture of natural resource rents has more typically deflected the political state from nurturing wealth creation and into predation. Moreover, the longer reliance on primary product exports under a predatory political state does not merely retard *competitive* industrialization, but rather postpones it indefinitely. This is because in the absence of rapid labour-intensive industrialization, surplus rural labour persists and prompts the government to use the rents to create employment directly and inefficiently instead of indirectly by nurturing efficient wealth creation. Consequently, diversification occurs into an over-expanded government bureaucracy and protected industry, which is not only inefficient but also, ironically, capital intensive (*Ibid.*).

Far from achieving competitive diversification, the staple trap trajectory renders an increasingly large sector of the economy dependent on subsidies from the rent. This expanding parasitic sector absorbs a greater share of resources so that the economy-wide efficiency of investment is depressed and GDP growth slows. Yet the rent recipients form a powerful vested interest and block economic reform. Therefore, as the rents shrink relative to GDP, either because of ongoing structural change or falling prices for the leading commodity, a non-developmental government finds it politically attractive to sustain transfers to the parasitic sector by extracting the returns to capital as well as the rent from the commodity sector. But this depresses incentives in the primary sector and erodes its competitiveness. This is the essence of the staple trap model: a predatory political state uses rent to subsidize employment and thereby aborts competitive diversification so the economy is increasingly vulnerable to shocks and a growth collapse (Appendix Figure 29.A2).

STM and sanctions against anti-social governance

Ross (2001) notes that oil-rich governments have the highest rents among the developing countries, which they have used to reduce taxation, which in turn weakens demands for representation and democratic accountability. As the GDP growth rate decelerates along the staple trap trajectory, competition for the rent stream intensifies so that, far from depoliticizing the economy, the staple trap trajectory increases government intervention. Krueger (1993: 61–73) attests that the resulting system of overt and covert levies and subsidies becomes too complex for either policy-makers or economic agents to understand the cause and effect relationship. In addition, the diversification of public finances stalls and 'taxation' may extract a sizeable fraction of the return to capital and labour in the primary sector to meet the demands of the parasitic sector when these demands outstrip the rent-generating capacity of the primary sector. This is especially likely in the presence of natural-resource extraction that is characterized by high sunk costs (Mcmillan 1997). Far from strengthening, therefore, political accountability regresses as the collision between the expanding patronage system that hitherto sustained the authority of the government and shrinking rents renders the political state brittle so that it concentrates rent on key supporters and resorts to repression to maintain its control.

Social capital formed under rent dependence, as with the parasitic urban sector that is characteristic of most rent-rich countries (Gelb *et al.* 1991), is likely to prove distinctly less effective as a sanction against anti-social governance compared with the more autonomous civic associations produced by competitive urbanization. A second cause of atrophying social capital under dependent urbanization is the fact that a growth collapse reduces per capita income and thereby increases corruption and rent seeking (Treisman 2002). The fact that most developing countries are rent-rich may explain why Barro (1999) finds little evidence that (dependent) urbanization is more strongly associated with voice and political accountability than rusticity.

Corruption also weakens institutions like the rule of law. This is partly because a growth collapse depresses public sector revenues and is associated with declining real wages in the public sector. The resulting under-remuneration provides an incentive for public officials at all levels of government to augment their incomes by abusing the government monopoly of public service provision. Atomized corruption therefore undermines the integrity of the legal system and sharply raises transaction costs (Mauro 1995). In the absence of effective formal institutions, able people may find rent seeking much more lucrative than work in legitimate channels. Social sanctions such as shaming also appear to be ineffective in such circumstances so corruption plays a central role in corroding social capital.

It therefore seems plausible that all three sanctions against anti-social gover-nance will stagnate or regress along the STM trajectory as PCGDP growth deceler-ates and governments dependent on dispensing rent to maintain their authority resort to repression. However, a growth collapse may abruptly trigger democracy, if exogenous factors are conducive. One such favourable external factor is the con-ditional provision of geopolitical rent by high-income democracies, which is most likely to occur after a growth collapse and this is also when it is at its most effec-tive (Mayer and Mourmourus 2002). Relative location, in the form of a regional neighbourhood effect, is a second exogenous determinant of political evolution according to the political science literature. For instance, O'Loughlin *et al.* (1998) document global regional fluxes between democratic and autocratic regimes since 1946, which point to a strong regional demonstration effect. They link this to shared contextual constraints:

> At the meso-level [global regional level], certain types of regionally clustered states are more susceptible to democratization than other regions due to 'snow-balling' or contagion effects from neighbours. The internal conditions in neigh-bouring states are typically similar and they provide similar impetus toward regime transition. (*Ibid.*: 549)

De Soysa (2003) finds further evidence to support the spatial diffusion of democracy, based on the regression of institutional, economic and social factors on the Polity III index of democracy. He shows that levels of PCGDP and urbanization are positively associated with democracy, whereas negative associations arise for growth collapses, oil dependence and Muslim religion. The addition of regional dummies deflates the importance of PCGDP as a determinant of democracy, however, and strengthens regional conformity. It therefore seems likely that democracy diffuses geographically and survives where neighbours are not hostile to it. The exogenous democratization path may therefore explain the fact that the shift towards democracy has historically often required external pressure to come to fruition (*Ibid.*: 552). For example, Whitehead (1986) finds very few instances of democratization that can be attributed to purely endogenous factors. He con-cludes that outsiders have heavily influenced the vast majority of democratization episodes, but he makes no attempt to qualify the generalization according to growth experience or resource endowment.

In summary, the link between exogenous democratization and growth collapses in rent-rich countries, which can occur at almost any income level, yields a less predictable and more erratic pattern of political evolution for high-rent countries compared with low-rent countries. It also suggests that there is more likelihood that high-rent countries may regress or that, at least, a prolonged period of consolidation of democracy may characterize such rent countries, especially at lower income levels. Such an outcome is consistent with the recent finding of Epstein *et al.* (2004), who usefully identify a category of 'consolidating democracies' as a neglected subgroup of political state among developing countries.

Simple tests of the model predictions

This section reports some very preliminary tests of the political economy models. Table 29.4, drawn from a paper by Woolcock *et al.* (2001), provides a rough and ready test of the evolution of political accountability. It uses a country's export dependence as a proxy for its natural-resource endowment, so that low-rent developing countries are identified as exporters of manufactured goods. Table 29.4 (main column 1) confirms that political liberty is significantly higher among manufacturing exporting (low-rent) countries. The differences are not large, however, given the full range of that particular scale and the fact that, as a group, the low-rent countries have a higher PCGDP than the high-rent countries. These doubts about the endogenous democratization model's predicted strengthening of political accountability with increasing PCGDP are reinforced by a second test, based on the World Bank (2002) perceptions index of voice and accountability (Table 29.5). Moreover, the correlation coefficient for PCGDP and voice and accountability is not significant for the resource-poor countries (Table 29.6). It is also relatively weak for the resource-rich countries, but this is not inconsistent with the exogenous growth model.

Column 3 in Table 29.4 tests the social capital thesis using a social development indicator, which is based on a factor analysis of a range of variables determined by Adelman and Morris (1967). The index suggests that social capital does accumulate faster in those developing countries that export manufactured goods (i.e. low-rent countries) than in rent-rich countries, in line with the competitive industrialization model. The social development index is by far and away highest for the low-rent countries.

Regression analysis for PCGDP and voice confirms the absence of the predicted significant relationship among the resource-poor countries (Table 29.7), but the scatter plot helps show why (Appendix Figure 29.A3). The voice indices of all three Chinese territories are significantly below the expected levels, given their PCGDP

Table 29.4 Exports, socioeconomic linkages, social capital and political institutions

	Total	Political liberties	N	Civil liberties	N	Social development index	N	Bureaucratic quality	N	Rule of law	N
All countries	90	3.06	88	3.19	88	−0.07	62	2.26	80	2.19	80
(minimum, maximum)		(1, 7)		(1, 7)		(−1.86, 1.59)		(0, 6)		(0, 6)	
Manufactured goods	9	3.63	8	3.19	8	0.23	5	3.75	8	3.88	8
Resource: diffuse	18	2.94	18	3.31	18	0.17	12	2.06	17	1.94	17
Resource: point source	45	3.09	44	3.17	44	−0.14	31	2.24	40	2.08	40
Resource: mixed (coffee and cocoa)	18	2.83	18	3.14	18	−0.25	14	1.73	15	1.87	15

Notes: The first row lists the means of five indicators of social and political institutions and their available subsample sizes (among the larger sample of 90 countries); the second row lists the minima and maxima or the indicators. The other rows are the means and subsample sizes of the indicators among four classifications of socioeconomic linkages. In all cases, higher values indicate a more desirable social or political outcome.

Source: Based on Woolcock *et al.* (2001: 86).

Table 29.5   Quality of institutions 2001, by natural resource endowment

Resource endowment	PCGDP 2000 (US$ PPP)	Voice and accountability	Control of corruption	Rule of law	Average institution index
All countries	4740	−0.24	−0.33	−0.32	−0.30
Resource poor	7060	−0.13	−0.16	−0.21	−0.17
Resource rich	3970	−0.28	−0.40	−0.38	−0.35

Note: Institutional quality ranges from 2.5 high to −2.5 low.

Sources: Auty and Gelb (2001: 131) and World Bank (2002).

and if they are excluded from the regression, the R^2 quadruples to 0.59 and becomes significant. The fact that South Korea, as well as Hong Kong and Singapore, among the higher income resource-poor countries also has a lower voice index than is predicted by the adjusted trend line suggests that political accountability may lag in high-growth low-rent countries, even when they espouse democracy. One possible reason for this is that historically justified expectations of continued sustained rises in welfare ease pressure for more political accountability. Finally, among the resource-rich countries, the R^2 for voice and PCGDP is significant but only 0.22 (Table 29.7), indicating that, as expected with exogenous democratization, voice has little connection to PCGDP. However, the scatter about the trend line narrows at higher income levels for these countries.

Corruption affords a second (proxy) index of the social capital endowment, being higher where social capital is weaker (Treisman 2002). Table 29.5 shows that the resource-poor countries have less corruption, measured by the World Bank (2002) index of graft than the resource-rich countries. The correlation coefficient for graft and PCI in Table 29.6 confirms a significantly stronger inverse relationship between per capita GDP and corruption for the low-rent countries compared with high-rent countries. Finally, consistent with the endogenous democratization model, regressing graft upon PCGDP provides a strongly significant and high R^2 of 0.831 for the low-rent countries compared with 0.368 for the high-rent countries, which as expected exhibit much more variation around the trend line (Appendix Figure 29.A4).

Finally, the index for rule of law in Table 29.4 (column 5) suggests that exporters of manufactured goods (low-rent countries) enjoy markedly stronger rule of law than the three resource-rich groups. In addition, Table 29.5 shows that low-rent countries have stronger legal institutions than low-rent countries. The correlation coefficients in Table 29.6 for this same relationship reinforce this pattern: the correlation coefficient for low-rent countries is strongly significant ($p = 0.000$) and 0.897 compared with 0.683 for the high-rent countries. Finally, the R^2 for the regression of law on PCI is strongly significant in each category of rent endowment and a very high 0.804 for the low-rent countries compared with only 0.467 for the high-rent group (Table 29.7 and Appendix Figure 29.A5).

Summarizing, in the cases of social capital and law, but not political accountability, the data support the prediction of the endogenous democratization model

Table 29.6 Correlations, PCI (US$ PPP) and voice, graft and law, by natural resource endowment

Resource endowment	Voice	Graft	Rule of law	PCGDP 2000 (US$ PPP)
Resource poor				
PPP$ Pearson correlation	0.385	0.912**	0.897**	1
Significance (two-tailed)	0.141	0.000	0.000	–
N	16	16	16	16
Voice Pearson correlation	1	0.417	0.451	0.385
Significance (two-tailed)	–	0.108	0.079	0.141
N	16	16	18	16
Graft Pearson correlation	0.417	1	0.936**	0.912**
Significance (two-tailed)	0.108	–	0.000	0.000
N	16	16	16	16
Law Pearson correlation	0.451	0.936**	1	0.897**
Significance (two-tailed)	0.079	0.000	–	0.000
N	48	16	16	16
Resource rich				
PPP$ Pearson correlation	0.469**	0.607**	0.683**	1
Significance (two-tailed)	0.001	0.000	0.000	–
N	46	46	48	48
Voice Pearson correlation	1	0.612**	0.577**	0.469**
Significance (two-tailed)	–	0.000	0.000	0.001
N	49	47	49	46
Graft Pearson correlation	0.612**	1	0.742**	0.607**
Significance (two-tailed)	0.000	–	0.000	0.000
N	47	47	47	46
Law Pearson correlation	0.577**	0.742**	1	0.683**
Significance (two-tailed)	0.00	0.000	–	0.000
N	49	47	49	48

Notes: Institutional quality ranges from 2.5 high to −2.5 low. **Significant with a two-tail test.

Source: World Bank (2002).

Table 29.7 Regression of voice, graft and law on PCGDP (US$ PPP)

Dependent variable	R^2	Significance
Low rent		
Voice	0.148	0.141
Graft	0.831	0.000
Law	0.804	0.000
High rent		
Voice	0.220	0.001
Graft	0.368	0.000
Law	0.467	0.000

Source: World Bank (2002).

that sanctions against anti-social governance strengthen with rising PCGDP for low-rent countries. The low reading for political accountability is strongly affected by limited freedom in all three Chinese-speaking low-rent territories, but even when these territories are removed it remains significantly weaker than the other two sanctions. This lag may reflect the readiness of citizens in developmental states to trade off political freedom for sustained growth in PCGDP.

Some policy implications

The development of a strategy for reforming the *political economy* of collapsed high-rent countries will provide an example of the policy implications of the models developed here. Although successful economic reform can reinforce democratic consolidation by triggering rapid GDP growth, the reform of collapsed high-rent economies over the past two decades has proved disappointing, with growth often two-thirds or half the targeted rate, so that PCGDP growth rates were often negative (Table 29.3). Within the reform packages, programmes for economic stabilization have been more successful than those for economic restructuring. However, slow or negative PCGDP growth undermines stabilization efforts, trapping economies in a slow-growth trajectory that also undermines the political consolidation of reforming regimes. A principal cause of failed restructuring is opposition from vested (rent-capturing) interests that stand to lose from reform, which either block reform or capture the policy and bend it to their advantage (Auty 2002).

In the face of blocked reform, geopolitical and/or natural resource rents might be directed towards supporting a dual-track reform programme. The essence of the dual track reform strategy is to grow a dynamic market sector in early reform zones (ERZs) equipped from the very outset with post-reform (world-class) infrastructure, economic incentives and institutions. The dynamic market sector not only creates conditions conducive to rapid GDP growth, but just as importantly it also builds a pro-reform political constituency while initially leaving the rest of the economy (termed the 'lagging sector') and its anti-reform political interest groups, to be reformed gradually. This dual-track reform strategy has been systematically applied by China since the 1980s. But other successful structural reformers have stumbled upon a variant of the strategy by encouraging competitive export zones, like Malaysia and Mauritius in the 1970s, or by permitting highly efficient domestic enterprises to capture the bulk of the rents provided by 'infant' industry policies, as in Indonesia (Flatters and Jenkins 1986). Ireland also pursued a variant of this policy when it nurtured a dynamic market sector from the late 1980s, which saw FDI quadruple (to 2.8 per cent of GDP annually) and grew to produce half the country's manufactured exports within a decade (Gorg and Ruane 2000). As it emerges from incubation the dynamic market sector strengthens in terms of its capacity to absorb under-employed workers from the lagging sector and generate foreign exchange and tax revenues.

The Irish economy was similar in size to that of Algeria in the late 1980s (Auty 2002), implying that a dynamic market sector may take a decade to reach a scale sufficient to favourably impact the lagging sector of a middle-sized developing country. Such a time period is not dissimilar from the period during which competitive manufacturing sectors in Malaysia and Indonesia grew before being required to assume the role of growth locomotive when oil prices collapsed in 1985. This suggests that a highly rent-rich country like Algeria might use a fraction of its rents to support this incubation period not by subsidies but by correcting market failure though the provision of modern infrastructure and maintenance of an enabling macro-economic environment. In other countries, geopolitical rent might be targeted to similar effect.

Meanwhile, reform of the lagging sector can proceed more cautiously until the dynamic sector's economic and political impacts render its acceleration feasible. The long-term objective of reform of the lagging sector is to align it with conditions in the ERZs in terms of infrastructure, incentives and institutional quality. More immediately some modest restructuring can be achieved by encouraging private construction firms within the lagging sector to substitute employment for that erstwhile provided by the state-backed parasitic subsector so that the government can focus its social expenditure on those least able to fend for themselves (*Ibid.* 2002).

Bolder policy initiatives might be feasible in the wake of a growth collapse, using geopolitical rent to strengthen government incentives to support pro-poor policies. For example, geopolitical rent might be provided on condition that commodity rent is distributed equitably among the population in the form of an annual dividend, as currently carried out in Alaska, and recently proposed for Iran (World Bank 2002). This diffuse deployment of the rent should both improve economic efficiency (Baldwin 1956; Bevan *et al.* 1987) and help consolidate a developmental political state.

Conclusions

In connection with the initial stages of designing a research programme, this chapter has presented some initial speculations regarding the manner in which economic rent affects the evolution of the political state in developing countries. The political economy models described here imply that low-rent countries have superior prospects for democratization as well as for economic growth compared to high-rent countries. The models are motivated by the insight that the lower and more diffuse the rents the greater the likelihood that the political state will be developmental and sustain rapid PCGDP growth that strengthens sanctions against anti-social governance.

The chapter identifies two basic routes to democracy. The first route, endogenous democratization, is associated with high-growth, low-rent countries and tends to be incremental and stable. Simple tests suggest that two of the three basic sanctions against anti-social governance (social capital and rule of law) do strengthen with rapidly rising PCGDP in low-rent countries. Political accountability lags the model predictions, however, and this may reflect the tradeoff by citizens of sustained rising welfare for less political freedom.

High-rent countries are more likely to experience exogenous democratization. The exogenous factors can be systematic (like geopolitical rent and relative location) or idiosyncratic (like leadership change). High-rent countries are likely to trace the staple trap development trajectory, which corrodes all sanctions against anti-social governance, and the more so the higher and more concentrated the rents. Consequently, countries with rents that are unusually high relative to GDP and concentrated like the oil-exporting countries are especially vulnerable. However, a growth collapse creates scope for democratization, which can occur at almost any level of PCGDP and may regress and/or require a prolonged period of consolidation. Moreover, the significance attached to exogenous factors in the process of recovery from a growth collapse (which is in any case likely to be protracted and take more than a generation, given the deterioration of all forms of capital ahead of such a collapse) suggests that geopolitical rent is as an important instrument for consolidating shifts towards developmental regimes and for discouraging regression.

These speculations motivate a proposed research programme that is planned to proceed in three stages. The first stage will involve in-depth country case studies designed to tighten and refine the evolutionary typology of political states by, for example, adding more detail regarding political relations within each category. Stage two will test the capacity of the typology to explain current measures of the quality of governance in developing countries, providing further scope to hone up the basic typology and fine-tune the rent-based models that drive it. Finally, the dynamic component of the models will be strengthened with time series data, using early sociopolitical datasets, such as that of Adelman and Morris (1967) for the early 1960s to construct the required indices of the initial political economy conditions.

Appendix

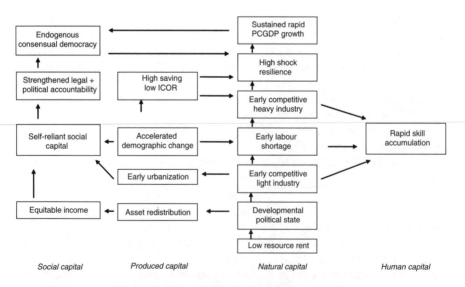

Figure 29.A1   Low rent and the competitive industrialization model

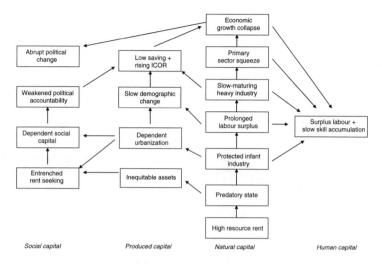

Figure 29.A2 High rent and the staple trap model

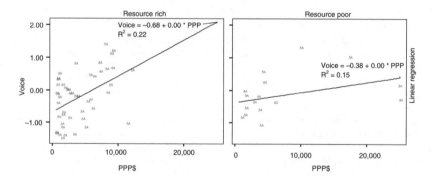

Figure 29.A3 Relationship between PCGDP (PPP $US 2000) and voice

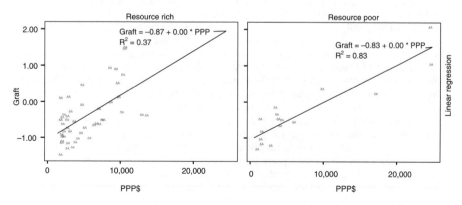

Figure 29.A4 Relationship between PCGDP (PPP $US 2000) and graft

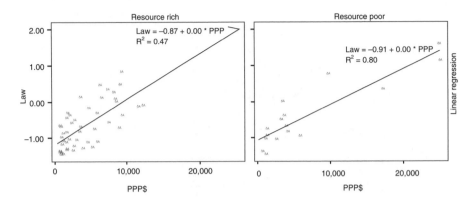

Figure 29.A5   Relationship between PCGDP (PPP $US 2000) and law

Notes

An earlier version of this paper was presented at the World Bank PREM meeting in April 2004, and the author has benefited from the helpful comments of the three discussants (Alan Gelb, Robert Bates and William Asher), as well as other seminar participants.

1. A developmental political state is defined here, after Lal (1995), as one that has sufficient autonomy to pursue a coherent economic policy and the aim of raising social welfare, and it may be autocratic.

2. Industry tended to be the motor for economic transition during the nineteenth and twentieth centuries, but it is increasingly recognized that some services may perform that role, so the specific product is less important than the lead sector's capacity to accumulate rapidly all forms of capital by flexibly recombining inputs in response to the changes in the relative prices of factors of production as development proceeds.

3. Lizzeri and Persico (2004) argue that concern for the inadequate provision of urban public goods was the dominant factor behind an incremental widening of the franchise. During the early decades of the nineteenth century, rising urban mortality fuelled demands to redirect public funds from the pork barrel patronage of an autocratic government towards improving public goods, notably urban sanitation. Lizzeri and Persico (*Ibid.*) demonstrate that the 1832 electoral reform triggered this process, which did not increase its share of GDP but rather shifted it towards local government and urban public goods provision. The redirection of public funds continued for a century and the periodic widening of the franchise incrementally transformed a diffusing oligarchy into a democracy.

4. For instance, in post-independence Jamaica, the two leading political parties polarized the electorate because each party built a political coalition either to promote major wealth redistribution or to protect the status quo. The 1972 election triggered an abrupt swing in economic policy that promoted rapid redistribution, deterred investment and led to a spectacular growth collapse in the late 1970s. Mauritius provides a second example. Its political state exhibited a similar polarization to Jamaica prior to the 1970s when sugar plantations dominated the economy. Thereafter a shortage of land installed competitive labour-intensive industrialization as the economic motor, ushering in a phase of consensual democracy in which each party backed wealth creation over redistribution (Findlay and Wellisz 1993). Malaysia provides an interesting anomaly where the adverse effects of polarization were recognized and avoided through an agreement that redistribution towards the low-income Malay majority should not be at the expense of the wealth-generating capacity of the large Chinese minority.

5. Rural India in the 1960s provides examples of market failure. The basic unit of socioeconomic organization, the village, was too small to support competitive banking, crop markets and an all-weather road (Johnson 1970). In the absence of these facilities, little progress could be made in specializing in high-productivity crops, the response required to boost incomes where land is becoming scarce and labour relatively abundant. Meanwhile, real interest rates might reach triple figures (*Ibid.*) and a location more than 4 kilometres from an all-weather road rendered transport costs too high to allow villages to adopt green revolution technologies (Owen 1967).

References

Acemoglu, D. and J.A. Robinson (2005) *Economic Origins of Dictatorship and Democracy*, Cambridge, MA: MIT Press.

Adelman, I. and C.T. Morris (1967) *Society, Politics and Economic Development*, Baltimore: Johns Hopkins University Press.

Åslund, A. (2000) 'Why Has Russia's Economic Transformation Been So Arduous?', in B. Pleskovic and J.E. Stiglitz (eds), *Annual World Bank Conference on Development Economics 1999*, Washington, DC: World Bank.

Auty, R.M (2001). *Resource Abundance and Economic Development*, Oxford: Oxford University Press for UNU-WIDER.

Auty, R.M. (2002) 'Integrating Industrialising Oil-Exporting Countries into the Global Economy: Egypt and Algeria', Mimeo, MNSIF, MENA, Washington, DC: World Bank.

Auty, R.M. and A.H. Gelb (2001) 'Political Economy of Resource-Abundant States', in R.M. Auty (ed.), *Resource Abundance and Economic Development*, Oxford: Oxford University Press for UNU-WIDER.

Auty, R.M. and S. Kiiski (2001) 'Natural Resources, Capital Accumulation and Welfare', in R.M. Auty (ed.), *Resource Abundance and Economic Development*, Oxford: Oxford University Press for UNU-WIDER.

Baldwin, R.E. (1956) 'Patterns of Development in Newly Settled Regions', *Manchester School of Social and Economic Studies*, 24: 161–79.

Barro, R. (1996) 'Democracy and Growth', *Journal of Economic Growth*, 1: 1–27.

Barro, R. (1999) 'Determinants of Democracy', *Journal of Political Economy*, 107, 6: 158–83.

Bevan, D.I., P. Collier and J.W. Gunning (1987) 'Consequences of a Commodity Boom in a Controlled Economy: Accumulation and Redistribution in Kenya', *World Bank Economic Review*, 1: 489–513.

Birdsall, N., T. Pinckney and R. Sabot (2001) 'Natural Resources, Human Capital and Growth', in R.M. Auty (ed.), *Resource Abundance and Economic Development*, Oxford: Oxford University Press for UNU-WIDER.

Boix, C. and S.C. Stokes (2003) 'Endogenous Democratization', *World Politics*, 55, 3: 517–45.

Burkhart, R.E. and M.S. Lewis-Beck (1994) 'Comparative Democracy: The Economic Development Thesis', *American Political Science Review*, 88: 903–10.

Clague, C., P. Keefer, K. Knack and M. Olson (1997) 'Institutions and Economic Performance: Property Rights and Contract Enforcement, in C. Clague (ed.), *Institutions and Economic Development*, Baltimore: Johns Hopkins University Press.

De Soysa, I. (2003) 'Why George W. Bush May Become Champion of Democracy', Mimeo, Bonn: ZEF.

Djankov, S., E. Glaeser, R. La Porta, F. Lopez-de-Silanes and A. Shleifer (2003) 'The New Comparative Economics', *Journal of Comparative Economics*, 31: 595–619.

Eifert, B., A.H. Gelb and N.B. Tallroth (2003) 'The Political Economy of Fiscal Policy and Economic Management in Oil-Exporting Countries', in J.M. Davis, R. Ossowski and A. Fedelino (eds), *Fiscal Policy Formulation and Implementation in Oil-Producing Countries*, Washington, DC: IMF.

Epstein, D.L., R. Bates, J. Goldstone, I. Kristensen and S. O'Halloran (2004) 'Democratic Transitions', *CID Working Paper* 101, Cambridge, MA: Centre for International Development.

Feng, Y. and P.J. Zak (1999) 'Determinants of Demographic Transitions', *Journal of Conflict Resolution*, 43: 162–77.

Findlay, R. and S. Wellisz (1993) *The Political Economy of Poverty, Equity and Growth: Five Small Open Economies*, New York: Oxford University Press.

Flatters, F. and G. Jenkins (1986) 'Trade Policy in Indonesia', Mimeo, Cambridge, MA: Harvard Institute for International Development.

Gelb, A.H., J. Knight and R. Sabot (1991) 'Public Sector Employment, Rent Seeking and Economic Growth', *Economic Journal*, 101: 1186–99.

Gorg, H. and F. Ruane (2000) 'European Integration and Periphery: Lessons From Irish Experience', *World Economy*, 23, 3: 405–21.

Haggard, S. (1990) *Pathways from the Periphery: The Politics of Growth in the Newly Industrializing Countries*, Ithaca, NY: Cornell University Press.

Hamilton, K. (2001) 'The Sustainability of Extractive Industries', in R.M. Auty (ed.), *Resource Abundance and Economic Development*, Oxford: Oxford University Press for UNU-WIDER.

Jackman, R.W. (1973) 'On the Relationship of Economic Development to Political Performance', *American Journal of Political Science*, 17: 611–21.

Johnson, E.A.J. (1970) *The Organization and Use of Space in the Developing Countries*, Cambridge, MA: Harvard University Press.

Jones Luong, P. (2002) *Institutional Change and Political Continuity in Post-Soviet Central Asia: Power, Perceptions and Pacts*, Cambridge: Cambridge University Press.

Kaufmann, D. and A. Kraay (2002) 'Growth Without Governance', *World Bank Working Paper* 2928, Washington, DC: World Bank.

Khan, M.H. and K.S. Jomo (eds) (2000) *Rents, Rent-Seeking and Economic Development*, Cambridge: Cambridge University Press.

Killick, T. (1995) *The Flexible Economy*, London: Routledge.

Krueger, A.O. (1993) *The Political Economy of Agricultural Pricing Policy: A Synthesis of the Political Economy in Developing Countries*, Baltimore: Johns Hopkins University Press.

Lal, D. (1995) 'Why Growth Rates Differ: The Political Economy of Social Capability in 21 Developing Countries', in B.H. Koo and D.H. Perkins (eds), *Social Capability and Long-run Economic Growth*, Basingstoke: Macmillan.

Lal, D. and H. Myint (1999) *The Political Economy of Poverty, Equity and Growth: A Comparative Study*, Oxford: Clarendon Press.

Li, S., S. Li and W. Zhang (2000) 'The Road to Capitalism: Competition and Institutional Change in China', *Journal of Comparative Economics*, 28: 269–92.

Lipset, S.M. (1959) 'Some Social Requisites of Democracy: Economic Development and Political Legitimacy', *American Political Science Review*, 53: 69–105.

Lizzeri, A. and N. Persico (2004) 'Why Did the Elites Extend the Suffrage? Democracy and the Scope of Government With Application to Britain's Age of Reform', *Quarterly Journal of Economics*, 119: 707–65.

Mauro, P. (1995) 'Corruption and Growth', *Quarterly Journal of Economics*, 90: 681–712.

Mayer, W. and A. Mourmouras (2002) 'Vested Interests in a Positive Theory of IFI Conditionality', *IMF Working Paper* 02/73, Washington, DC: IMF.

Mcmillan, M. (1997) 'A Dynamic Theory of Primary Export Taxation: Evidence from sub-Saharan Africa', Mimeo, New York: Columbia University.

O'Loughlin, J., M.D. Ward, C.L. Lofdahl, J.S. Cohen, D.S. Brown, D. Reilly, K.S. Gleditsch and M. Shin (1998) 'The Diffusion of Democracy 1946–94', *Annals Association of American Geographers*, 88, 4: 545–74.

Olson, M. (2000a) *Power and Prosperity: Outgrowing Communist and Capitalist Dictatorships*, New York: Basic Books.

Olson, M. (2000b) 'Dictatorship, Democracy and Development', in M. Olson and S. Kahkonen (eds), *A Not-so-Dismal Science: A Broader View of Economies and Societies*, Oxford: Oxford University Press.

Owen, W. (1967) *Distance and Development*, Washington, DC: The Brookings Institution.

Przeworski, A., M.E. Alvarez, J.A. Cheibub and F. Limongi (2000) *Democracy and Development: Political Institutions and Well-Being in the World 1950–1990*, Cambridge: Cambridge University Press.

Ranis, G. and S. Mahmood (1992) *The Political Economy of Development Policy Change*, Oxford: Blackwell.

Ross, M. (2001) 'Does Oil Hinder Democracy?', *World Politics*, 53, 3: 325–61.

Serageldin, I. and C. Grootaert (2000) 'Defining Social Capital: An Integrating View', in R. Picciotto and E. Wiesner (eds), *Evaluation and Development: The Institutional Dimension*, New Brunswick: Transaction.

Stiglitz, J.E. (1995) 'Social Absorption Capability And Innovation', in B.H. Koo and D.H. Perkins (eds), *Social Capability and Long-Term Economic Growth*, Basingstoke: Macmillan.

Syrquin, M. (1986) 'Productivity Growth and Factor Reallocation', in H. Chenery, S. Robinson and M. Syrquin (eds), *Industrialization and Growth: A Comparative Study*, New York: Oxford University Press.

Treisman, D. (2002) 'Post-Communist Corruption', Mimeo, Los Angeles: Department of Political Science, UCLA.

Whitehead, L. (1986) 'International Aspects of Democratization', in G. O'Donnell, P.C. Schmitter and L. Whitehead (eds), *Transitions From Authoritarian Rule: Comparative Perspectives*, Baltimore: Johns Hopkins University Press.

Woolcock, M. and D. Narayan (2000) 'Social Capital: Implications for Development Theory, Research and Policy', *World Bank Research Observer*, 15, 2: 225–49.

Woolcock, M., L. Pritchett and J. Isham (2001) 'The Social Foundations of Poor Economic Growth in Resource-Rich Countries', in R.M. Auty (ed.), *Resource Abundance and Economic Development*, Oxford: Oxford University Press for UNU-WIDER.

World Bank (1997) 'Expanding the Measure of Wealth', *Environmentally Sustainable Development Studies and Monograph Series* 17, Washington, DC: World Bank.

World Bank (2002) *Estimates of Governance Quality*, Washington, DC: World Bank.

Zak, P.J. and Y. Feng (2003) 'A Dynamic Theory of the Transition to Democracy', *Journal of Economic Behavior and Organization*, 52: 1–25.

30

Credit Co-operatives in Locally Financed Economic Development: Using Energy Efficiency as a Lever

Robert J. McIntyre

Overview

Outside dynamic and often prosperous-looking capital cities, most of the transition economies have not yet achieved broad-based and sustainable growth. A misguided chain of assumptions – that the small enterprise sector would by itself create successful economic growth; that individual private ownership was the only viable form; and that local banking services are best provided by large, usually foreign-owned, national units – have together wasted much time (see McIntyre 2003). The major questions of large enterprise–small enterprise ecology and small and medium-sized enterprise (SME) financing, which are central to systems-level success, have been left largely unaddresed.

Earlier UNU-WIDER research shows that success of a 'productive' SME sector requires both active financial and non-financial support services at the local level and the survival, or revival, or development of a healthy large enterprise sector. This chapter focuses on the failure to develop institutions capable of supporting economic development with localized saving-investment cycles. This leaves a crucial gap, in no way addressed by either country-level macro programmes that deal with 'development finance', or by donor-driven 'microcredit' schemes of Grameen and other types operating at a lower (local) level. The latter seldom if ever evolve into financial institutions able to sustain themselves on the basis of purely local resources, do not operate on a sufficient scale to trigger dynamic local-level economic growth, and are ultimately artificial manifestations of concessional or charitable aid.

The advantages of credit co-operatives in mobilizing and financing local economic development contrast with the disadvantages of both conventional

578

microcredit and the most recent neoliberal fashion of so-called 'new wave financial institutions'. Both precedent (discussed below) and the structural logic of their situations suggest that this is a promising space for the development of a localized financial system based on credit co-operatives which elsewhere have overcome the SME credit famine and stimulated local saving-investment cycles.

Transition without sustainable propagation mechanisms

Most of these economies require but do not dispose of coherent local-level developmental policies, supported by national-level policy that allows room for constructive local initiative and a variety of ownership forms. Local and regional governments have a central role in stimulating growth of various types of business activity. The 'local developmental state' growth model implies a directly para-entrepreneurial role for local government (even including equity ownership), which is likely to be at least in part followed. In most of the transition economies this will require creation of some kind of local finance system. The natural synergy between savings/credit co-operatives and production units with co-operative or partial employee ownership is evident in Nordic and other experience. Local government para-entrepreneurship and credit co-operatives are two among very few cases where 'advanced country experience' is directly relevant in much of the former Soviet Union and East Europe, but have still not been applied after 15 years of 'transition'.

It is important to link the mechanism to finance the foundation and expansion of small enterprises, based on localized saving-investment cycles, with measures to support local production in the face of the pressure of internationalization of the market. With the arrival in developing markets of large, well-financed foreign producers and distributors, even potentially promising local production capacities may be destroyed before finding their feet. Local producers may expire as a result of short-run 'predatory' tactics (penetration pricing, loss leaders, bribery of distributors or retailers, etc.) or loss of market access. Full-information approaches to labelling and non-tariff preferences for locally produced goods are possible local-level policy responses. It is especially important to maintain consumer access to locally produced goods when new distribution channels emerge. Locally rooted financial capacity is essential if this 'buffering' is to have sustainable developmental effects.

One particularly promising local government strategy is to combine the credit co-operative, local social sector and anti-poverty funding and energy efficiency in a virtuous circle. In many parts of the former Soviet Union (FSU), especially outside the capital cities, urban populations remain dependent on centralized hot water and space heat systems in which there has been little attention to upgrading main thermal distribution systems and no systematic attention to improving efficiency at the block and building level. Energy efficiency is therefore a sector where local-level financing of small-scale local-level investment offers great potential to simultaneously stimulate SME growth, reduce energy waste and (by reducing the diversion of local social service budgets to pay for higher and rising energy costs) preserve funds for local health, education and welfare programmes. This combination is appropriate to most previously centrally planned economies and some other parts of the world as well.

Modest results at best for SMEs and local economic development, outside capital cities, in transition

Despite the tendency to think of and present the SME as an alternative to the former state-owned enterprise (SOE), except for the face-to-face retail and service delivery sector, little can be expected from the SME without either: (a) active support efforts at the local level; or (b) the survival or development of a healthy large-enterprise sector which the SME can utilize as supplier, customer and provider of various social and technical externalities. If ways can be found to encourage the formation of purpose-built alliances and subcontracting relationships, positive and mutually reinforcing interactions can be expected to emerge.

Earlier research stresses the importance of developing productive local small enterprise systems that go beyond retail and traditional services and the centrality of locally rooted financial support mechanisms if there is to be any success in filling the still gaping (directly productive) small enterprise 'black hole' (McIntyre and Dallago 2003). The SME sector needs the large-enterprise sector as a source of inputs, a market for its output and also (unexpectedly) as source of individual entrepreneurial leadership. This points to the need to create a synergistic relationship between the SME and the large enterprise sectors, not thinking of a zero-sum environment where success of the small can only be secured by destroying or disassembling the large. While the issues of the survival of larger entities (where they indeed exist) involve inherently national-level considerations, they also require correlate local-level initiatives.

Many examples of the merits of diverse organizational forms, policy approaches and financial mechanisms

There are real SME-stimulation alternatives based on actual developmental experience, taking the form of the *local developmental state* (Johnson 1982). This model has been pervasive in successful post-Second World War cases, from Germany, Austria and Italy to Japan, Taiwan, South Korea and, most recently, China, but has been conspicuously absent from policy advice or practice in the transition economies after 1989. Bateman (2000; 2003) points out that virtually everywhere, national-level success in rebuilding and modernizing after the Second World War was heavily dependent on SME support measures, carried out as part of a national development strategy, but executed by local-level governments. And often provincial- or city-level banking entities have played an important role, either as government-owned entities or as co-operatives with strong government support and quasi-public duties. This experience should be well known, but is oddly invisible outside their home countries, even when the action bodies themselves (Raffeisenbank, various Landesbanken, RaboBank, Okopankki, etc.) are familiar participants in international financial markets.

TVEs are a new illustration of the local developmental state

One of the most interesting aspects of dynamic Chinese development after 1978 is the emergence of unorthodox ownership and governance approaches that form a distinctive 'mixed property' system. Barriers of culture, development level and political culture have made it convenient to not think carefully about the challenging and complex micro- and mezzo-level lessons of the Chinese experience, briefly discussed here.

The township and village enterprise (TVE) part of the system is in active, rapid evolution towards unclear future forms (Granick 1990; Sun 1997; Sun *et al.* 1999; Chi and Chou 2003). The remarkable success of Chinese local authorities as facilitators and direct entrepreneurs (para-entrepreneurial activity) perfectly illustrates the local developmental state conception (Johnson 1982) and is extremely important to other transition economies. The often excessive lending enthusiasm (and corruption) of many banks owned by various local government authorities should not deflect attention from the extent to which ownership, banking and quasi-planning of export-oriented development have been locally orchestrated.

Local authorities in some Central Eastern Europe (CEE) and Commonwealth of Independent States (CIS) economies face structural conditions that are similar in important ways (they bear effective responsibility for some local production and distribution, often have nearly identical ownership/partial ownership/effective ownership rights in some local goods- and service-producing entities in the face of the collapse of the economic leadership role of the central state and must deal with a stagnant local economy). Even in countries where privatization and market reforms have gone quite far, some structural carryovers from the planned economy remain. Local-level governments in transition economies are likely to remain economic actors on a scale generally greater than in long-time market economies, so getting better developmental effects from this activity is a vital task.

A key lesson of Chinese experience is that the original core TVE[1] should be considered as a promising partial or subsystem model[2] for other countries. Within this complex small town and rural mixed system there are strong elements of municipal socialism in which 'social' but non-nationalized property ownership plays an important role (Weitzman and Xu 1994). In what are essentially closed co-operatives, local government may either play only a supervisory and facilitative role or act directly as full or partial owner. The classificatory logic used by the World Bank treats all these variations as private sector development (no matter who owns it, if it is not the national government, the entity is considered 'private'), making this vital experience statistically invisible to most non-specialists.

Chinese institutional reforms and mixtures thus have unexpected local-level relevance elsewhere, especially once it is noted how strongly these new structures resemble the multi-owner partnership form that is widely successful in advanced market economies. Stiglitz (1999) and others (Nolan 1995; McIntyre 1998; Stiglitz and Ellerman 2000; Ellerman 2005) propose wide application of this aspect of the Chinese experience in other transition countries. How Chinese ownership will develop in the future is an open question, but many small- and medium-sized local SOEs facing or experiencing comprehensive reform and loss of national subsidies are likely to end up under township and local government control, taking the joint stock co-operative form with some degree of employee ownership. When TVEs move from full local government ownership to joint-stock co-operative form (with mixed local government and employee share ownership) they are indeed and example of what Stiglitz (1999; 2000) advocates as 'privatization to stakeholders'. A similar category of employee-owned enterprises (*narodnaya predpreyatiya*) was established by 1998 Russian legislation and has interesting, but as yet unutilized, potential. It is structurally similar to Chinese joint-stock co-operatives and may eventually be able to include local government as partial equity owner (McIntyre 2001).

A combination these features could be useful in local-level revitalization efforts elsewhere, even though enormous regional differences in incomes and living standards and sharply increased inequality within regions pose a great threat to the continued success of this mixed model in China itself (Riskin 2001).

Finnish co-operatives and development policy

The Finnish co-operative tradition provides another useful point of reference. For over a century, Finland has used co-operatively owned local-level financial institutions as part of a national-level economic development strategy (Kuisma *et al.* 1999). In 2005 one-third of all Finnish deposits and loans involve *Okopankki*, the capstone co-operative bank. The Finnish example is a provocative addition to debates about SME financing and suggests new tools to support market-based economic growth under sparsely settled, peripheral conditions found in much of the FSU and parts of CEE (Skurnik and Vihriälä 1999).

Finland has been astute and vigorous in pursuing complex and subtle industrial and developmental policies, while simultaneous appearing to the outside world to be practising free market rectitude. The banking sector is a case in point, where the success of the co-operative banking system traces back to tsarist period government (Grand Duchy of Finland) deposits (to overcome the initial trust and scale problems) and forming local banks into regional alliances under a national confederation, creating scale economies and assuring political visibility. Parallel to and with the support of co-operative banks, a wide array of production and marketing co-operatives arose. A century later they retain a large share (meat 71 per cent; dairy 96 per cent; eggs 60 per cent; forest owners 34 per cent; livestock breeding 100 per cent; retail trade 41 per cent; banking 34 per cent; insurance 8 per cent) of the contemporary Finnish market (Skurnik 2002). This type of active use of policy to create institutions is not unique to Nordic countries, but is especially strong there. As *The European Observatory for SMEs* notes, across the EU

> Many banking/credit/insurance co-operatives and mutuals have their roots in the co-operation of SMEs and the objective of providing auxiliary services to

these enterprises. Co-operation is an important strategy for SMEs to strengthen their market position against larger competitors. In crafts, retail, trade, transport and some production, co-operative members are almost exclusively SMEs. ... [M]any [co-operatives] have been founded by and for SMEs and are, on the whole, SMEs themselves. (European Commission 1996: 351–2)

In many countries co-operatives operate in legal categories that are not explicitly 'co-operative'. This leads the *Observatory* to note that it is unexpectedly hard to judge the scale of operation by productive co-operative SMEs in the EU. Thus, it is difficult to say how large the co-operative sector 'should be' by simple comparisons to other countries. It is nonetheless clear that combining co-operative saving and lending institutions with production, processing and service co-operatives makes good sense in many transition economies. The hundreds of new wave co-operatives formed during the severe Finnish recession of the early 1990s are similarly promising. Many are technology and technical service companies, in the form of 'multi-branch work co-operatives' and 'single-branch expert co-operatives'. The linkage between these new co-operative forms and co-operative banking is both logical and straightforward.

National or local government engagement is generally required to start such savings and lending institutions, but is criticized as constituting an unproductive subsidy or unfair competition to commercial banks. On theoretical and historical–empirical grounds, Bateman (2000) has attacked the idea that market interest rates, combined with banking conventions about acceptable risk, answer all necessary questions about what is wise and developmentally viable in thinking about small enterprise support policies. Studies appraising differential SME access to finance within the EU reach the same conclusion:

> The financial structure of an enterprise seems to depend more on the financial system and the financial habits of the country in which it operates than on any other characteristics of enterprises such as size, sector, age and even profitability. Moreover, the smaller the enterprise, the greater are the international differences in financial structure. (European Commission 2000: 19)

It is useful to consider the implications of these findings for the SME aspect of local economic development policy in transition countries, especially in light of the felt policy imperatives within the EU:

> The efforts aimed at meeting the Maastricht criteria have substantially narrowed the room EU countries' governments used to have for manoeuvres in the field of SME policy. *This has not reduced the necessity to adopt new stimulating measures especially for SMEs and, in some case, has led governments to widen the scope of their enterprise policy. (Ibid.*: 249–50, emphasis supplied)

This suggests that Finnish-style use of national policy to create conditions in which local-level saving, financial services, production, marketing, wholesale buying and other co-operatives take root, is directly relevant to solution of the puzzling failure of productive SMEs to play a significant role during the first decade of transition. The vast literature on the 'efficiency of worker-managed enterprises' brings former Yugoslavia to mind here, perhaps carrying with it doubts about the viability and efficiency of real co-operatives. Addressing exactly this concern, Hansmann (1996; 1999) and Stiglitz (2000) offer a bracing reinterpretation of the net efficiency advantages of co-operatives in light of new developments in agency and information theory dear to the hearts of all neoclassical economists.

Co-operative core bank plus business consultancy in Spain

While the Finnish (and other Nordic countries) co-operative approach to local-level enterprise finance and production reinforces the local developmental state conception and illustrates a highly successful solution to the pervasive SME finance famine, relationships like this can be found all over the world. An example is the role of the Lankide Aurrezzkia Bank in the famous Mondragón system of locally owned co-operatives in Spain, all of which were, and many of which remain SMEs. The core bank provides borrowers with technical and management guidance when needed and sometimes even moves employees between juridical distinct co-operatives in *keiretsu* style (Shuman 1998).

The French-Canadian Mouvement des Caisses Desjardins and the Caisses Populaires/Caisses D'Économie

Another example is Credit Desjardins and the associated Casises Populaires and Caisses D'Économie that form the largest element in the financial system of Quebec province, Canada. The co-operative development in Quebec was independent and in many ways unique, but has some rough similarities to the Finnish path. The Credit Desjardins movement began in the late 1890s after the formation of a government commission to study the causes of poverty and degradation in Quebec. The commission came to unexpectedly specific conclusions about the need to create local-level financing sources for decentralized development. This process occurred in the presence of knowledge about such developments in continental Europe and the UK, but it developed its own self-contained set of rules and structural approaches.

In Quebec the progression from small-scale testing of the ideas to rapid social acceptance occurred with extraordinary speed and large developmental effects. Credit co-operative development in the USA proceeded by direct copying of Quebec approaches, rules and regulations, led by the Massachusetts legislature in 1908. The Boston department store magnate and philanthropist Joseph Filene stimulated this development. Filene followed the serendipitous path of first observing British-inspired co-operatives in India, drawing immediate conclusion about their appropriateness at home, and then finding a fully developed system growing rapidly 'next door' with a complete set of laws, by-laws and institutional structures, that required little more than translation.

The special contemporary interest in the Credit Desjardins approach comes from the rapid spread of this same style of organization in Russia, first in the south and now elsewhere in Russia under a development assistance programme financed by the Canadian International Development Agency (CIDA) and operated by the Développement international Desjardins (DiD) branch of the Credit Desjardins organization. This programme emulates, with culturally appropriate amendments, the approaches that were successful under structurally similar and extremely unpromising circumstances in Quebec and Finland, among others. LegaCoop (Lega Nazionale delle Co-operative e Mutue, in Italy), RaboBank (Netherlands) and Raiffeisenbank (Austria), all co-operative banks, are further illustrations of the viability in the financial sector of divergent ownership, management and organizational arrangements.

Asymmetric opening: market access and other necessary protections for SMEs

The major problems of SME development – an inadequate institutional/organizational context, lack of product-market access for small-scale producers and most critically finance – are made worse by rapid, uncontrolled and asymmetric market opening that has occurred in all transition economies except for China, Vietnam and Slovenia. A recent UNCTAD (2002) study suggests that the process of opening up even well-established market economies has strong negative effects on the SME sector. The results could be even more negative in those (many) transition countries where an era of normal growth is yet to occur, magnifying vulnerability to outsiders. This reflects a mixture of the effects of initial domestic demand repression and the early arrival of more mature foreign competitors in all economic sectors. With the arrival in developing markets of large, well-financed foreign producers and distributors, even potentially promising local production capacities may be destroyed before finding their feet. Local producers may expire as a result of short-run predatory tactics (penetration pricing, loss leaders, bribery/blackmail of distributors or retailers, etc.) or loss of market access.

A central but often invisible aspect of the survival or growth of productive SMEs is the ability to expose their products to the processes of consumer choice. It is especially important to maintain consumer access to locally produced goods when new distribution channels emerge. Only a short period of exclusion from the market is enough to kill off otherwise viable and promising local production capacities. It is important to link financing of small enterprises based on localized savings and investment cycles with measures to support local production in the face of the pressure of internationalization of the market. 'Full-information' approaches to labelling and non-tariff preferences for locally produced goods are possible policy responses.

Small-scale credit is obviously central to any successful cumulative SME development, but conventional microcredit approaches are not development-functional in the middle income, urbanized settings that characterize the bulk of the CIS and CEE. Based largely on grant funds and building no viable locally owned institutions able to grow and evolve to a scale adequate to finance serious small enterprise development, they are at best viewed as a poverty palliative. Even in agricultural areas their long-term value is suspect because microcredit propagators often work to prevent the rise of alternative self-supporting credit institutions, such as real credit co-operatives. The enthusiasm with which various donors and multinational institutions view the microcredit approach is not justified by their efficacy. Similarly doomed to failure is the recent enthusiasm for so-called 'new wave microfinance institutions' – commercially oriented, competing, independent, financially self-sustaining lending bodies to deliver financial services to the poor and disadvantaged. This 'new wave' model quickly became a major local-level strand of the neoliberal development conception worldwide and

> has also attracted substantial political support and donor agency funding in the context of the reconstruction of southeast Europe in the wake of the Yugoslav civil war which ended in late 1995 and, more recently, in the aftermath of the Kosovo conflict of 1999 ... In some countries, such as Bosnia, the 'new wave' MFI model has effectively been the centre-piece of the international donor community's support for local economic development and poverty reduction. (Bateman 2003)

Like earlier misguided efforts to 'commercialize' business support services in transition economies, these new entities will almost automatically diverge from and ultimately abandon pursuit of the positive externalities that are the essence of successful local development efforts in all market economy environments:

> It appears that the short-term benefits of this approach are largely wiped out by the negative effects of the associated economic policies that accompany it, including accelerated de-industrialization, rising trade deficits, declining state legitimacy and capacity, and the destruction of social capital. (*Ibid.*)

Dynamic economic growth that works for the poor regions and the poor nationally requires credit co-operatives and other forms of locally owned banking institutions tasked with serving local small enterprise interests. Locally-owned banks and local small enterprise systems in various countries function successfully on 'social capital' that is very costly for large banks that have no inherent local development mission or mandate to acquire (Dallago 2003: 78–97). It does not make sense for them to provide the type of patient, step-by-step credit and other financial service support that firms of a nascent small-enterprise sector require.

Concern over the concrete local development effects is intensified when all or most local banks are absorbed by international banking companies. Once under foreign ownership local banks are very unlikely to devote significant resources to support foundation or growth of SMEs in areas where poverty is concentrated. The indebtedness and low profitability of the large banks that did retain their independence strengthened their inherited attitude of avoiding risky financing, requiring high collateral and charging high interest rates. In whatever form, the consolidation, restructuring and privatization of large banks prevented the establishment and development of financial institutions for SMEs in most transition countries. The 2003 WIDER study (McIntyre and Dallago 2003) concluded that these features of the credit market discouraged expansion and modernization but apparently not the foundation of SMEs.

Contingent policy advice or a (discredited) cookbook?

The point of these examples was to provide the basis for reflection on the following questions: why are reform/reorganization approaches so often suggested/ imposed on transition countries in a 'cookbook' fashion? And why do the institutions proposed seldom reflect the variety that rules in existing successful market economies, but instead focus on institutional variants of distinctly Anglo-American origin (which even for those countries reflect an introductory textbook simplification rather than the actual variety of forms extant there). The same point is to be made regarding fiscal policy (USA and one or more large EU states) and monetary policy (USA), where behavioural norms 'at home' diverge sharply from the restrictionist prescriptions offered to others. Exact parallels are also evident in all departments of social welfare policy.

While there is no simple answer as to what the recipients of advice and suggestions should do to reduce the damage caused by narrow and unrealistic recommendations, one approach could be to simply demand the discussion of alternatives in the certainty that there are some. A particularly useful point of reference is the research department of the World Bank that regularly produces (in Washington) results that can be used to challenge the policy advice delivered (from Washington) through the channel of the World Bank country office (Ellerman 2005). As the fashionable management analysis of Christensen and Raynor (2003) points out, management (and management reform) and policy (and policy reform) are inherently contingent processes, not amenable to one-size-fits-all solutions. What will work in a situation depends on careful analysis of the micro-, mezzo- and macro-level internally, as well as the external features of the concrete situation. This leads us back to conclusions about specific SME policies.

Conclusions

A successful SME sector that goes beyond neighbourhood-level services and retail distribution (the latter often doomed in any case) requires both active support services at the local level and the survival, revival or development of a healthy large-enterprise sector as supplier of inputs, output market, provider of various social and technical externalities, and also (unexpectedly) as source of individual entrepreneurial leadership. Systems success is more a question of quality than quantity, particularly concerning the interconnection of all the elements that form the economic system. SMEs are a crucial element, but policies that target the SME sector without paying attention to these surrounding conditions are unlikely to have substantial and long-lasting positive effects. Efforts to provide direct assistance to the SME sector often become mired in corruption, have high overhead costs and ultimately serve other-than-announced programme interests (Bateman 2000).

Local and regional governments have a central role in stimulating growth of various types of business activity. This includes creation of a local finance system based on credit co-operatives to overcome the SME credit famine and stimulate local saving-investment cycles, as well as directly para-entrepreneurial functions (including equity ownership), all generally consistent with the model of the local developmental state. The natural synergy between savings/credit co-operatives and production units with co-operative or partial employee ownership is evident in Nordic and other experience and is especially relevant in transition or post-transition economies. Even in countries where privatization and market reforms have gone quite far, some structural carryovers from the planned economy remain. Local-level governments in transition economies are likely to remain economic actors on a scale generally greater than in long-time market economies. Incomplete privatization often leaves local government with some de facto ownership rights, raising the possibility of development of something like the (early reform period) core-TVEs in China. At the enterprise level, various forms of full and partial employee ownership are appropriate, not excluding the local government as a possible equity co-owner. Pressures to reorganize units that provide municipal services into quasi-corporate ESCOs (Energy Service Companies), TSCOs and so on offer similar opportunities.

Notes

This chapter further develops work done in the UNU-WIDER research project Small and Medium-Size Enterprises in Transition Economies, between 1998 and 2003. A feasibility study conducted in Russia between 2003 and 2006 by Local Development in Transition (funded in part by the Ford Foundation grant 1245–2309), formed the basis for some of the research presented here, providing empirical examples and elucidating the conditions for success of credit co-operatives in this developmental role.

1. Many existing TVEs changed legal form during the 1990s, becoming *joint stock co-operatives* or *joint stock partnerships* (Sun *et al.* 1999). This is sometimes little more than a name change, but large TVEs are thereby structurally prepared for the future possibility of becoming autonomous publicly traded entities. At the same time there was a sharp movement by purely private entities to take on this same legal form.
2. This is a partial model in the sense of constituting one of the organization types that could be included in a system, but not in being a universal model for all components of that system.

References

Bateman, M. (2000) 'Neoliberalism, SME Development and the Role of Business Support Centres in the Transition Economies of Central and Eastern Europe', *Small Business Economics*, 14, 4: 275–98.

Bateman, M. (2003) 'New Wave Micro-finance Institutions in South-East Europe: Towards a More Realistic Assessment of Impact', *Small Enterprise Development*, 16, 3: 176–91.

Chi, R. and N.-T. Chou (2003) 'Small Enterprise Development: Evidence for China', *Small Enterprise Development*, 14, 2: 48–55.

Christensen, C. and M.E. Raynor (2003) *The Innovator's Solution: Creating and Sustaining Successful Growth*, Cambridge, MA: Harvard Business School Press.

Dallago, B. (2003) 'SME Development in Hungary: Legacy, Transition and Policy', in R. McIntyre and B. Dallago (eds), *Small and Medium Enterprises in Transitional Economies*, Basingstoke: Palgrave Macmillan for UNU-WIDER.

Ellerman, D. (2005) *Helping People Help Themselves: From the World Bank to an Alternative Philosophy of Development Assistance*, Ann Arbor: University of Michigan Press.

European Commission (1996) *The European Observatory for SMEs: 4ᵗʰ Report*, Luxembourg: Office of Official Publications.

European Commission (2000) *The European Observatory for SMEs: 6ᵗʰ Report*, Luxembourg: Office of Official Publications.

Granick, D. (1990) *Chinese State Enterprises: A Regional Property Rights Analysis*, Chicago: University of Chicago Press.

Hansmann, H. (1996) *Ownership of Enterprise*, Cambridge, MA: Belkuap Press of Harvard University Press.

Hansmann, H. (1999) 'Co-operative Firms in Theory and Practice', *Finnish Journal of Business Economics*, 44, 4: 387–403.

Johnson, C. (1982) *MITI and the Japanese Miracle*, Stanford: Stanford University Press.

Kuisma, M., A. Henttinen, S. Karhu and M. Pohls (1999) *The Pellervo Story*, Helsinki: Pellervo Confederation of Finnish Co-operatives.

McIntyre, R. (1998) 'Regional Stabilization Policy under Transitional Period Conditions in Russia: Price Controls, Regional Trade Barriers and Other Local-level Measures', *Europe-Asia Studies*, 50, 5: 959–71.

McIntyre, R. (2001) 'The Community as Actor in and Incubator of Economic and Social Revival', *Local Development in Transition Policy Papers* 2, New York: LDiT.

McIntyre, R. (2003) 'Waiting for Development: FDI, the Informal Sector and Poverty Reduction Policy', paper prepared for Eastern European Investment Summit, October, Bucharest.

McIntyre, R. and B. Dallago (eds) (2003) *Small and Medium Enterprises in Transitional Economies*, Basingstoke: Palgrave Macmillan for UNU-WIDER.

Nolan, P. (1995) *China's Rise, Russia's Fall: Politics, Economics and Planning in the Transition from Stalinism*, New York: St Martin's Press.

Riskin, C. (2001) 'Decentralization in China's Transition', *Local Development in Transition Policy Papers* 4, New York: LDiT.

Shuman, M.H. (1998) *Going Local: Creating Self-Reliant Communities in a Global Age*, New York: Free Press.

Skurnik, S. (2002) 'Role of Co-operative Entrepreneurship and Firms in Organising Economic Activities: Past, Present and Future', *Finnish Journal of Business Economics*, 51, 1: 103–24.

Skurnik, S. and V. Vihriälä (1999) 'Role of Co-operative Entrepreneurship in the Modern Market Environment: Introduction and Summary', *Finnish Journal of Business Economics*, 44, 4: 375–83.

Stiglitz, J.E. (1999) 'Whither Reform? Ten Years of the Transition', paper presented at the Annual Bank Conference on Development Economics, April, World Bank, Washington, DC.

Stiglitz, J.E. (2000) *Democratic Development as the Fruits of Labor*, Boston: Industrial Relations Research Association.

Stiglitz, J.E. and D. Ellerman (2000) 'New Bridges Across the Chasm: Macro- and Micro-Strategies for Russia', Mimeo, Washington, DC: World Bank.

Sun, L. (1997) 'Emergence of Unorthodox Ownership and Governance Structures in East Asia: An Alternative Transition Path', *Research for Action* 38, Helsinki: UNU-WIDER.

Sun, L., with E. Gu and R. McIntyre (1999) 'The Evolutionary Dynamics of China's Small and Medium Enterprises in the 1990s', *World Development Studies* 14, Helsinki: UNU-WIDER.

UNCTAD (United Nations Conference on Trade and Development) (2002) *The Least Developed Countries Report 2002: Escaping the Poverty Trap*, Geneva: UNCTAD.

Weitzman, M. and C. Xu (1994) 'Chinese Township-Village Enterprises as Vaguely Defined Collectives', *Journal of Comparative Economics*, 18, 2: 121–45.

Part VIII

Development Economics in Prospect

31
Development through Globalization?

Deepak Nayyar

Introduction

Globalization, which gathered momentum during the last quarter of the twentieth century, has created unparalleled opportunities and posed unprecedented challenges for development. Yet, the virtual ideology of our times has transformed globalization from a descriptive word into a prescriptive word. But the reality that has unfolded so far belies the expectations of the ideologues. The exclusion of countries and of people from globalization, which is partly attributable to the logic of markets, is a fact of life. Even so, there is a strong belief and an influential view that globalization is the road to development during the first quarter of the twenty-first century.[1] In a volume that seeks to think ahead about the future of development economics, development through globalization is an appropriate theme. It is even more appropriate, perhaps, with a question mark at the end.

The object of this chapter is to reflect on development in prospect, not retrospect, situated in the wider international context of globalization. In doing so, it shall, of course, address the question posed in the title. The main object, however, is to focus on the correctives that would have to be introduced and the rethinking that would have to be done, given the reality of globalization, if development is to bring about an improvement in the living conditions of people, ordinary people.

Globalization as a mantra for development

Recent years have witnessed the formulation of an intellectual rationale for globalization that is almost prescriptive. It is perceived as a means of ensuring not only efficiency and equity but also growth and development in the world economy. The analytical foundations of this world view are provided by the neoliberal model. Orthodox neoclassical economics suggests that intervention in markets is inefficient. Neoliberal political economy argues that governments are incapable of intervening efficiently. The essence of the neoliberal model, then, can be stated as follows. First, the government should be rolled back wherever possible so that it approximates to the ideal of a minimalist state. Second, the market is not only a substitute for the state but also the preferred alternative because it performs better.

593

Third, resource allocation and resource utilization must be based on market prices which should conform as closely as possible to international prices. Fourth, national political objectives, domestic economic concerns or even national boundaries should not act as constraints. In this world, domestic economic concerns mesh with, or are subsumed in, the maximization of international economic welfare and national political objectives melt away in the bargain.

The ideologues believe that globalization led to rapid industrialization and economic convergence in the world economy during the late nineteenth century. In their view, the promise of the emerging global capitalist system was wasted for more than half a century, to begin with by three decades of conflict and autarchy that followed the First World War and subsequently, for another three decades, by the socialist path and a statist worldview. The conclusion drawn is that globalization, now as much as then, promises economic prosperity for countries that join the system and economic deprivation for countries that do not.[2] It needs to be stressed that this prescriptive view of globalization is contested and controversial.[3] Yet, for those who have this strong belief, globalization is the road to development in the first quarter of the twenty-first century.[4]

Interestingly enough, the development experience of the world economy in the last quarter of the twentieth century is invoked as supporting evidence, not only by advocates but also by critics of this prescription. In caricature form, these conflicting perceptions are almost polar opposites of each other. The pro-globalization advocates argue that it led to faster growth, that it reduced poverty and that it brought about a decrease in inequality. The anti-globalization critics argue that it led to slower but more volatile growth, that it increased poverty in most parts of the world and that there was an increase in inequality. Of course, such a broad-brush picture of conflicting perceptions abstracts from the nuances and the qualifications. But it highlights the impasse in a debate that borders on a dialogue of the deaf.

Yet, there is a little dispute about some important dimensions of reality. In conventional terms, the world has made enormous economic progress during the second half of the twentieth century. Over the past 50 years, world GDP multiplied almost twelve-fold while per capita income more than trebled. The growth has been impressive even in the developing world, particularly when compared with underdevelopment and stagnation in the colonial era during the first half of the twentieth century. But such aggregates conceal more than they reveal. In fact, development has been uneven within and between countries. The pattern of development has been such that it has led to an increase in the economic distance between the industrialized world and much of the developing world. It has also led to an increase in the economic distance between the newly industrializing countries at one end and the least developed countries at the other. At the same time, economic disparities between regions and between people within countries have registered a significant increase.

Uneven development is not without consequences for people. Poverty, inequality and deprivation persist. And there is poverty everywhere. One-eighth of the people in industrial societies are affected by, or live in, poverty. Almost one-third of the people in the developing world live in poverty and experience absolute deprivation in so far as they cannot meet their basic human needs. As many as 830 million people suffer from malnutrition, while 1.2 billion people do not have access to clean water and 2.7 billion people do not have adequate sanitation facilities. More than 250 million children who should be in school are not. Nearly 300 million women are not expected to survive to the age of 40. And 850 million adults remain illiterate. Most of them are in developing countries. But, in a functional sense, the number of illiterate people in industrial societies at 100 million is also large.[5]

In other words, many parts of the world and a significant proportion of its people are largely excluded from development. This may be attributable to the logic of markets, which give to those who have and take away from those who have not, as the process of cumulative causation leads to market-driven virtuous or vicious circles. This may be the outcome of patterns of development where economic growth is uneven between regions and the distribution of its benefits is unequal between people, so that the outcome is growing affluence for some combined with persistent poverty for many. This may be the consequence of strategies of development as a similar economic performance in the aggregate could lead to egalitarian development in one situation and growth which by-passes the majority of the people in another situation.

Consequences, constraints and choices

In retrospect, it is apparent that globalization has been associated with simultaneous, yet asymmetrical, consequences for countries and for people. There is an inclusion for some and an exclusion, or marginalization, for many. There is affluence for some and poverty for many. There are some winners and many losers. Joan Robinson once said, 'There is only one thing that is worse than being exploited by capitalists. And that is not being exploited by capitalists.' Much the same can be said about markets and globalization which may not ensure prosperity for everyone but may, in fact, exclude a significant proportion of people.

It would seem that globalization has created two worlds that co-exist in space even if they are far apart in wellbeing. For some, in a world more interconnected than ever before, globalization has opened door to many benefits. Open economies and open societies are conducive to innovation, entrepreneurship and wealth creation. Better communications, it is said, have enhanced awareness of rights and identities, just as they have enabled social movements to mobilize opinion. For many, the fundamental problems of poverty, unemployment and inequality persist. Of course, these problems existed even earlier. But globalization may have accentuated exclusion and deprivation, for it has dislocated traditional livelihoods and local communities. It also threatens environmental sustainability and cultural diversity. Better communications, it is said, have enhanced awareness of widening disparities. Everybody sees the world through the optic of their lives. Therefore, perceptions about globalization depend on who you are, what you do and where you live. Some focus on the benefits and the opportunities. Others focus on the costs and the dangers. Both are right in terms of what they see. But both are wrong in terms of what they do not see.

On balance, it is clear that there is exclusion of countries and of people.[6] Too many people in poor countries, particularly in rural areas or in the informal sector, are marginalized if not excluded. Too few share in the benefits. Too many have no voice in its design or influence on its course. There is a growing polarization between the winners and the losers. The gap between rich and poor countries, between rich and poor in the world's population and between rich and poor people within countries, has widened. These mounting imbalances in the world are ethically unacceptable and politically unsustainable.[7]

But that is not all. Globalization has diminished the policy space so essential for countries that are latecomers to development. Indeed, the space for, and autonomy to formulate policies in the pursuit of national development objectives is significantly reduced. This is so for two reasons: unfair rules of the game in the world economy and consequences of integration into international financial markets. In a world of unequal partners, it is not surprising that the rules of the game are asymmetrical in terms of construct and inequitable in terms of outcome. The strong have the power to make the rules and the authority to implement the rules. In contrast, the weak can neither set nor invoke the rules. The problem, however, takes different forms.[8]

First, there are different rules in different spheres. The rules of the game for the international trading system, being progressively set in the WTO, provide the most obvious example. There are striking asymmetries. National boundaries should not matter for trade flows and capital flows but should be clearly demarcated for technology flows and labour flows. It follows that developing countries would provide access to their markets without a corresponding access to technology and would accept capital mobility without a corresponding provision for labour mobility. This implies more openness in some spheres but less openness in other spheres. The contrast between the free movement of capital and the unfree movement of labour across national boundaries lies at the heart of the inequality in the rules of the game.

Second, there are rules for some but not for others. In the WTO, for instance, major trading countries resort to a unilateral exercise of power, ignoring the rules, because small countries do not have the economic strength even if they have the legal right to retaliate. The conditions imposed by the IMF and the World Bank, however, provide the more familiar example. There are no rules for surplus countries, or even deficit countries, in the industrialized world, which do not borrow from the multilateral financial institutions. But the IMF and the World Bank set rules for borrowers in the developing world and in the transition economies. The conditionality is meant in principle to ensure repayment, but in practice it imposes conditions to serve the interests of international banks which lend to the same countries. The Bretton Woods institutions, then, act as watchdogs for moneylenders in international capital markets. This has been so for some time. But there is more to it now. IMF programmes of stabilization and World Bank programmes of structural adjustment seek to harmonize policies and institutions across countries, which is in consonance with the needs of globalization.

Third, the agenda for new rules is partisan, but the unsaid is just as important as the said. The attempt to create a multilateral agreement on investment in the WTO, which seeks free access and national treatment for foreign investors, with provisions to enforce commitments and obligations to foreign investors, provides the most obvious example. Surely, these rights of foreign investors must be matched by some obligations. Thus, a discipline on restrictive business practices of transnational corporations, the importance of conformity with anti-trust laws in home countries, or a level playing field for domestic firms in host countries, should also be in the picture. The process of globalization is already reducing the autonomy of developing countries in the formulation of economic policies in their pursuit of development. These unfair rules also encroach on the policy space so essential for national development.

The existing (and prospective) rules of the WTO regime allow few exceptions and provide little flexibility to countries that are latecomers to industrialization. In comparison, there was more room for manoeuvre in the erstwhile GATT, inter alia, because of special and differential treatment for developing countries. The new regime is much stricter in terms of the law and the implementation. The rules on trade in the new regime make the selective protection or strategic promotion of domestic firms vis-à-vis foreign competition much more difficult. The tight system for the protection of intellectual property rights could pre-empt or stifle the development of domestic technological capabilities. The possible multilateral agreement on investment, should it materialize, would almost certainly reduce the possibilities of strategic bargaining with transnational firms. Similarly, commitments on structural reform, an integral part of stabilization and adjustment programmes with the IMF and the World Bank, inevitably prescribe industrial deregulation, privatization, trade liberalization and financial deregulation. In sum, the new regime appears rule-based but the rules are not uniform. And it is not clear how or why this is better than discretion. For, taken together, such rules and conditions are bound to curb the use of industrial policy, technology policy, trade policy and financial policy as strategic forms of intervention to foster industrialization.[9]

At the same time, the consequences of integration into international capital markets also reduce degrees of freedom. Exchange rates can no longer be used as a strategic device to provide an entry into world markets for manufactured goods, just as the interest rates can no longer be used as a strategic instrument for guiding the allocation of scarce investible resources in a market economy. What is more, countries that are integrated into the international financial system are constrained in using an autonomous management of demand to maintain levels of output and employment. Expansionary fiscal and monetary policies – large government deficits to stimulate aggregate demand or low interest rates to encourage domestic investment – can no longer be used because of an overwhelming fear that such measures could lead to speculative capital flight and a run on the national currency.[10]

In sum, the existing global rules encroach upon essential policy space. And the problem is compounded by the rapid, sometimes premature, integration into international financial markets. Therefore, latecomers to industrialization would find it difficult to emulate the East Asian success stories. Indeed, the industrialized countries had much more freedom and space in policy formulation at comparable stages of their industrialization.[11] There is an obvious question that arises. What are the options or choices in this situation for countries that are latecomers to development? First, it is essential to use the available policy space for national development, given the international context. Second, it is important to create more policy space by reshaping the rules of the game in the world economy. In the national context, therefore, it is necessary to redesign strategies by introducing correctives, and to rethink development by incorporating different perspectives, that would make for egalitarian economic development and a more broad-based social development. In the international context, even if difficult, it is necessary to reshape the rules of the game and contemplate some governance of globalization.

Conception of development

Before considering these possibilities, it is both necessary and desirable to reflect on the essential meaning of development. For this purpose, a short digression is worthwhile. The reason is that the agenda on development in terms of both theory and policy has, unfortunately, narrowed with the passage of time. So has its meaning and the object of its focus. Hence, there is a need to reflect on the meaning and rethink the focus. There is a vast literature on economic development which is rich in terms of range and depth. Yet, there is not enough clarity about the meaning of development. There are many different views. And perspectives have changed over time.

In the early 1950s, conventional thinking identified development with growth in GDP or GDP per capita. The earlier literature emphasized economic growth and capital accumulation at a macro level. The contemporary literature emphasizes economic efficiency and productivity increases at a macro level. Industrialization has always been seen as an essential attribute of development. The emphasis has simply shifted from the pace of industrialization to the efficiency of industrialization. The underlying presumption is that economic growth and economic efficiency are not only necessary but also sufficient for bringing about an improvement in the living conditions of people. From time to time, dissenting voices question conventional wisdom to suggest other indicators of development but these were largely ignored by mainstream economics. And, even 50 years later, economic growth or increases in per capita remain the most important measure of development.

The early 1970s witnessed the emergence of a literature that suggested other indicators of development such as a reduction in poverty, inequality and unemployment, which would capture changes in the quality of life.[12] This thinking moved further. Development, it was argued, must bring about an improvement in the living conditions of people. It should, therefore, ensure the provision of basic human needs for all – not just food and clothing but also shelter, healthcare and education.[13] It was stressed that this simple but powerful proposition is often forgotten in the conventional concerns of economics. Such thinking culminated in writings on, and an index of, human development.[14]

In the late 1990s, Amartya Sen provided the broadest possible conception of development as freedom: a process of expanding real freedoms that people enjoy for their economic wellbeing, social opportunities and political rights.[15] Such freedoms are not just constitutive as the primary ends of development. Such freedoms are also instrumental as the principal means of attaining development. What is more, there are strong interconnections that link different freedoms with one another. Political freedoms help promote economic security. Social opportunities facilitate economic participation. Economic wellbeing supports social facilities and reinforces political rights. In this manner, freedoms of different kinds strengthen one another. The purpose of development, after all, is to create a milieu that enables people, ordinary people, to lead a good life. Development must, therefore, provide all men and women the rights, the opportunities and the capabilities they need to exercise their own choices for a decent life.

The significance of this abstraction about or conceptualization of development is not lost on everyone. But it is the tangible or the measurable that remains dominant in terms of wide use and popular understanding. Per capita income is only an arithmetic mean. Social indicators are also statistical averages. And neither captures the wellbeing of the poor. Even the human development index is not quite an exception. The quantifiable is obviously important. But it should not shape our thinking about development. In fact, it does. Consequently, the focus is misplaced. It needs to be corrected. And the correction has several dimensions. It is essential to make a distinction between means and ends. Economic growth and economic efficiency, or for that matter industrialization, are means. It is development which is an end. Much of the focus in the literature on development is on economies. But aggregates often conceal more than they reveal. Thus, it is important to shift the focus from countries to people. However, people are not just beneficiaries. It is only if people are centre-stage in the process of development, as the main actors, that development can empower people to participate in the decisions that shape their lives. The significance of this proposition is highlighted by the medieval distinction between agents and patients, which is invoked by Sen. He argues that the freedom-centred understanding of economics and of the process of development is very much an agent-oriented view. This is because individuals with adequate social opportunities can effectively shape their own destiny and help each other. They must not be seen primarily as patients, or passive recipients, of the benefits of cunning development programmes.[16]

Redesigning strategies: introducing correctives

The introduction of correctives in the design of strategies for development is easier said than done. Even so, some essential correctives emerge from an understanding of theory and a study of experience that recognizes not only the diversity but also the complexity of development. In this reflection, it is necessary to recognize the limitations of orthodox economic theory and policy prescriptions even if these represent influential thinking about development at the present juncture. It is just as necessary to learn lessons from the history of development experience embedded in both successes and failures without neglecting specificities in time and space.

The first limitation of orthodoxy is its unquestioned faith in the market mechanism. It fails to recognize that there is no magic in the market. Indeed, market failures are not quite an exception but are closer to being the rule. The strong belief in the market mechanism is based on the proposition that market forces, or the invisible hand, achieve a competitive equilibrium. The fundamental theorems of welfare economics establish that this is an efficient state and a desirable state.[17] In spite of analytical elegance of these theorems, such faith is not quite warranted. The scepticism extends much beyond the critics. Consider, for example, the following quotations from three distinguished economic theorists: Frank Hahn, Amartya Sen and Joseph Stiglitz:

> It showed that it is logically possible to describe a world where greedy and rational people responding only to price signals take actions which are mutually compatible. The theory does not describe the invisible hand in motion but displays it with its task accomplished ... The importance of this intellectual achievement is that it provides a benchmark ... Now one of the mysteries which future historians of thought will surely wish to unravel is how it came about that the Arrow-Debreu model came to be taken descriptively; that is as sufficient in itself for the study and control of actual economies. (Hahn 1984: 308).

> The intellectual climate has changed quite dramatically over the last few decades, and the tables are now turned. The virtues of the market mechanism are now standardly assumed to be so pervasive that qualifications seem unimportant ... The need for critical scrutiny of standard preconceptions and politico-economic attitudes has never been stronger. Today's prejudices (in favour of the pure market mechanism) need to be investigated and, I would argue, partly rejected. (Sen 1999: 111–12).

> ... the reason the invisible hand is invisible is partly because it's simply not there. (Stiglitz)[18]

There are, in fact, many reasons why these results, which highlight the virtues of the market, may not hold.[19] First, there may be externalities in production or consumption which would lead to market failure. The original solution to this problem was appropriate taxes and subsidies to be introduced by the government. But this went out of fashion with the Coase Theorem, which returned the market to its pedestal.[20] Second, in such a world, markets may not deliver efficient and desirable outcomes if transaction costs are too high or if there is no government that can assign and protect property rights. Third, markets may not function, as textbooks would have us believe, in situations where an enforcement of contracts is difficult or not possible. And this is a common occurrence in developing countries which are significantly different from industrial societies in this sphere. Fourth, markets may cease to function as expected if there is an uncertainty about quality. In other words, doing business in markets is difficult where goods or services are of poor quality and where quality cannot be discerned by consumers before purchase.[21] Fifth, it would seem that the market mechanism needs support to function as it is meant to. The need for such support spans a wide range from taxes-cum-subsidies in the presence of externalities, and laws to enforce contracts or property rights, to certification and regulation in a world of asymmetric information. Even with such support, markets are prone to corrupt practices whenever agents engaged by institutions to enforce regulations or laws are more interested in their own welfare rather than in achieving the goals set for them by institutions established to regulate markets.[22]

The second limitation of orthodoxy is the belief that getting-prices-right is enough. Such thinking makes an elementary, but commonplace, error in the design of policies. It confuses *comparison* (of equilibrium positions) with *change* (from one equilibrium position to another). In the real world, economic policy must be concerned not merely with comparison but with how to direct the process of change. Thus, for example, even if a reduction in protection can, in principle, lead to a more cost-efficient economy the transition path is by no means clear. And the process of change should not be confused with the ultimate destination of an economy that is competitive in the world market (Bhaduri and Nayyar 1996; Nayyar 1997).

The third limitation of orthodoxy is the presumption that policy regimes that are necessary are also sufficient.[23] The management of incentives motivated by the object of minimizing costs and maximizing efficiency at a micro level is based on a set of policies that is intended to increase competition between firms in the marketplace. Domestic competition is sought to be provided through deregulation in investment decisions, in the financial sector and in labour markets. Foreign competition is sought to be provided through openness in trade, investment and technology flows. It must, however, be recognized that there is nothing automatic about competition. Policy regimes can allow things to happen but cannot cause things to happen. The creation of competitive markets that enforce efficiency may, in fact, require strategic intervention through industrial policy, trade policy and financial policy, just as it may require the creation of institutions.

The fourth limitation of orthodoxy is its stress on government failures and its neglect of market failures. However, both market failure and government failure are facts of life. For neither markets nor governments are, or can ever be, perfect. Indeed, markets are invariably imperfect and governments are without exception fallible. The juxtaposition of government failure and market failure in an either-or mode, as if there was a choice to be made, is misleading. It is important to introduce correctives against both market failure and government failure. In such a perspective, the state and the market are complements rather than substitutes. What is more, the relationship between the state and the market cannot be defined once-and-for-all in any dogmatic manner but must change over time in an adaptive manner as circumstances change.[24] In this context, it is important to remember that markets are good servants but bad masters. What is more, efficient markets need effective states.

Development experience during the second half of the twentieth century also suggests important correctives for redesigning strategies. There are some important lessons that can be learned from mistakes and failures of the past.[25] The first lesson to emerge from experience is that competition in the market is desirable. Such competition is essential between domestic firms, between domestic firms and foreign firms, as also between the public sector and the private sector. Industrial deregulation that removes barriers to entry for new firms and limits on the growth in the existing firms leads to competition between domestic firms. Trade liberalization that reduces restrictions or tariffs on imports leads to competition between domestic and foreign firms. The dismantling of public sector monopolies leads to competition between the public sector and the private sector. It is such competition between firms, in price and in quality, that creates efficiency among producers and provides a choice for consumers.

The second lesson to emerge from experience is that prudent macro management of the economy is both necessary and desirable. Soft options, such as borrowing by the government only postpone the day of reckoning. Borrowing to support consumption almost always leads to a fiscal crisis. The problem may be compounded by a reliance on external resources to finance development. And if such borrowing is used to support consumption, a debt crisis is almost inevitable. Even so, it is necessary to recognize the fallacies of deficit fetishism. It must be stressed that the size of the fiscal deficit or the amount of borrowings are symptoms and not the disease. The real issue is the use to which the government borrowing is put in relation to the cost of borrowing by the government. Thus, government borrowing is always sustainable if it is used to finance investment and if the rate of return on such investment is greater than the interest rate payable.

The third lesson to emerge from experience is that excessive and inappropriate state intervention is counter-productive. It is, of course, important to learn from mistakes but it is just as important to avoid over-correction in learning from mistakes, because there are dangers implicit in over-reaction. Clearly, there are things that markets can and should do. However, there are some things that only governments can do. If governments do these badly, it is not possible to dispense with governments or replace them with markets. Governments must be made to perform better. It is, therefore, necessary to reformulate the questions about the economic role of the state.[26] The real question is no longer about the size of the state (how big?) or the degree of state intervention (how much?). The question is now about the nature of state intervention (what sort?) and the quality of the performance of the state (how good?).

The fourth lesson to emerge from experience, in the more recent past, is that the speed and the sequence of change matter. For one, the speed of change must be calibrated so that it can be absorbed by the economy. For another, the sequence of change must be planned with reference to an order of priorities. The significance of speed and sequence emerges clearly in the sphere of trade policy reform and even more clearly from the experience with capital account liberalization. In both, whether speed or sequence, deregulation and openness must be compatible with initial conditions and must be consistent with each other.

Clearly, it is important to learn from failures. Recognition of where things went wrong translates easily into correctives. But it is just as important to learn from successes. And there are two important lessons that emerge from development experience in countries that are success stories. First, there are specificities in time and space which must be recognized and cannot be ignored. Obviously, one size does not fit all. Second, latecomers to industrialization during the twentieth century, to begin with in Europe, and subsequently in Asia, that succeeded adopted strategies of development that not only varied across countries over time but also differed significantly from orthodox policy prescriptions now in fashion.[27]

Last but not least, there are some forgotten essentials that should form an integral part of any attempt at redesigning strategies of development. First, it is not quite recognized that economic growth is necessary but not sufficient to bring about a reduction in poverty. It cannot suffice to say that the outcomes of economic policies should be moderated by social policies. The dichotomy between economic and social policies is inadequate just as the dichotomy between economic and social development is inappropriate. In fact, no such distinction is made in industrialized countries. And the experience of industrialized world suggests that there is a clear need for an integration, rather than separation, of economic and social policies. Thus, it is important to create institutional mechanisms that mediate between economic growth and social development.

Second, it is often forgotten that the wellbeing of humankind is the essence of development. Thus, distributional outcomes are important. So are employment and livelihoods. Structural reforms associated with economic liberalization have important implications for employment creation and income opportunities. For one, insofar as such reforms increase the average productivity of labour, through the use of capital-intensive or labour-saving technologies, or through a restructuring of firms, which increases efficiency, it reduces the contribution of any given rate of economic growth to employment growth. For another, insofar as trade liberalization enforces closures rather than efficiency at a micro level, or switches demand away from home-produced goods to foreign goods at a macro level, it has an adverse effect on output, hence employment, which is magnified through the multiplier effect. This has important consequences in the medium term. There is a contraction of employment in some sectors without a compensatory expansion of employment in other sectors. And, as employment elasticities of output decline, employment creation slows down. It need hardly be stressed that employment creation is the only sustainable means of reducing poverty. Moreover, employment is also essential for the wellbeing and dignity of people.

Rethinking development: different perspectives

The discourse on theory and policy in development has become narrower with the passing of time. Some rethinking on development is essential. It must incorporate different perspectives. A systematic, let alone complete, analysis of such alternatives would mean too much of a digression. Even so, it is necessary to stress the following as an integral part of any rethinking on development: the importance of initial conditions, the significance of institutions, the relevance of politics in economics and the critical role of good governance.

It is obvious that initial conditions are important determinants of development. It should also be recognized that initial conditions can and should be changed to foster development. This is an unambiguous lesson that emerges from economic history.[28] In countries that are latecomers to industrialization, state intervention creates conditions for the development of industrial capitalism through the spread of education in society, the creation of a physical infrastructure and the introduction of institutional change. This role has always been recognized. The building of managerial capabilities in individuals and technological capabilities in firms is also an important, even if less recognized, dimension of initial conditions, for such capabilities determine technical efficiency in the short run and competitiveness in the long run. This has been recognized for some time. The present juncture, however, is characterized by a widespread disillusionment with the economic role of the state and a strong belief in the magic of the market. Hence, orthodoxy neglects the importance of initial conditions. There is an irony in this situation. In the context of globalization, such a role for the state is more necessary than ever before. Indeed, creating the initial conditions is essential for maximizing the benefits and minimizing the costs of integration with the world economy.

The debate on development is, in large part, about policies. The time has come to move beyond policies to institutions. The recent recognition of the importance of institutions, even if late, is welcome.[29] Yet, the understanding of institutions in the profession of economics is, to say the least, limited. Economists have treated institutions as a black box in much the same way as they treated technology for some time. What is more, orthodox economics has sought to harmonize the role as also the form of institutions across the world irrespective of space and time. This is a serious mistake, since one size does not fit all. There are specificities in space. Institutions are local and cannot be transplanted out of context. There are specificities in time. Institutions need time to evolve and cannot be created by a magic wand. The blueprints for economic liberalization over the past 25 years have simply not recognized this reality.

The meaning of institutions is not always clear. At one level, institutions refer to the rules of the game. These rules can be formal, as in constitutions, laws or statutes. These rules can also be informal, as in norms, conventions or practices. At another level, institutions refer to organizations or entities that are not players. The role of the state is crucial in almost every dimension of institutions. In an economy, the state seeks to govern the market through rules or laws. It does so by setting rules of the game for players in the market. In particular, it creates frameworks for regulating markets. But it also creates institutions, whether organizations or entities, to monitor the functioning of markets. The development of such institutions, which cannot always develop on their own, may need some proactive help from the state, as catalyst if not leader. Of course, there are institutions that may develop through markets, as in standards or for safety, but these depend on social norms.

In a market economy, social norms are perhaps as important as laws or organizations in the world of institutions.[30] Clearly, there is a world beyond 'methodological individualism' that reduces all social and economic interaction simply to the self-interest of the individual. This proposition is nicely illustrated by Adam Smith's intellectual journey from the *Theory of Moral Sentiments* to the *Wealth of Nations*. The notion of society came to be embedded in a wider range of human moral sentiments. This was Smith's composite notion of 'sympathy'. Such sympathy was not just altruism. It was a complex range of co-existing, often conflicting, human motives that culminated in social norms such as trust in exchange, respect for contracts or reciprocity in behaviour. Some of these may also have been the outcome of longer-term enlightened self-interest. In this world, exchange and production in markets is sustained by underlying, unwritten, social norms. Indeed, without such social norms, no market economy can function. Unfortunately, social norms, so essential for institutions, are no longer part of conventional academic discourse, which exaggerates the efficiency of an abstract market mechanism based on an invented auctioneer and neglects the role of the state in preserving or reinforcing these norms.

The literature does not make any clear distinction between forms and functions of institutions. There is, also, little understanding of processes of change in existing institutions or in evolution of new institutions. Much remains to be done so as to improve understanding of institutions and of institutional change in the process of development, which could be the difference between success and failure at development. Such understanding needs not only theory but also history. However, the theory must be non-ideological just as the history must be non-selective.

In every society, economy and polity are closely intertwined. It is the interaction of economics and politics that shapes outcome for people. Therefore, it is essential to explore the interplay between economics and politics in the process of development.[31] There is, then, need for a political economy that extends beyond econometric analysis at a micro level, even if it is the fashion of our times. This is easier said than done. But a beginning could be made by exploring the relationship between markets and democracy, democracy and development, and development and empowerment.

The essence of the tension between the economics of markets and politics of democracy must be recognized. In a market economy, people vote with their money in the marketplace. But a political democracy works on the basis of one-person-one-vote. The distribution of votes, unlike the distribution of incomes or assets, is equal. One adult has one vote in politics even though a rich man has more votes than a poor man, in terms of purchasing power, in the market. This tension may be compounded by a related asymmetry between economy and polity. The people who are excluded by the economics of markets are included by the politics of democracy. The rich dominate a market economy in terms of purchasing power. But the poor have a strong voice in a political democracy in terms of votes. Hence, exclusion and inclusion are asymmetrical in economics and politics. In reconciling the market economy and political democracy, successive generations of economic thinkers and political philosophers have stressed the role of the state in this process of mediation. The reason is important even if it is not obvious. Governments are accountable to their people whereas markets are not. In a democracy, however, governments are elected by the people. But even where they are not, the state needs legitimation from the people, most of whom are not rich or are poor.[32]

The relationship between democracy and development is also complex. But it is important to reject the view that latecomers to development cannot afford the luxury of democracy. Indeed, thinking ahead, it is clear that democracy is going to be conducive to the process of development. The reason is straightforward. The essential attributes of democracy, transparency and accountability, provide the means for combining sensible economics with feasible politics.[33] The economic priorities of the people will be reflected more and more in the political agenda of parties if there is a transparency in the system. The agenda of political parties will be reflected more and more in the reality of economic development if there is accountability in the system. Once this two-way process gathers momentum, transparency and accountability will create a commitment to long-term objectives of development in the context of a political democracy where governments are bound to change through elections over time.

The problem is that democracy, while conducive and necessary, is not sufficient to actually produce development. We know that from experience. Development may or may not be provided from above by benevolent governments. It must be claimed from below by people as citizens from governments that are accountable. The empowerment of people, then, is an integral part of any process of change that leads to development. A political democracy, even if it is slow, provides a sure path for two reasons. It increases political consciousness among voters to judge political parties for their performance. At the same time, it increases partici-pation in the political process when it leads to mobilization on some issues. This highlights the significance of Sen's conception of development as freedom. Expanding freedoms for people at large constitute development. But the same expanding freedoms, which empower people, are instruments that drive the process of change in development.

Governance is critical in the process of development. The real issue is not about more or less government. It is about the quality of government performance. This has two dimensions. The first dimension is more obvious. It is about redefining the economic role of the state in a changed national and international context. In the earlier stages of development, the primary role is to create initial conditions. In the later stages of development, the role is neither that of a promoter nor that of a catalyst. It is somewhat different and spans a range: functional intervention to correct for market failure, institutional intervention to govern the market, or the strategic intervention to guide the market (Nayyar 1997; see also Bhaduri and Nayyar 1996). In this era of markets and globalization, surprisingly enough, the role of the state is more critical than ever before and extends beyond correcting for market failures or regulating domestic markets. It is about creating the initial con-ditions to capture the benefits from globalization, about managing the process of integration into the world economy in terms of pace and sequence, about provid-ing social protection and safeguarding the vulnerable in the process of change and about ensuring that economic growth creates employment and livelihoods for people.[34] In sum, governments need to regulate and complement markets so as to make them people-friendly. Thus, the role of the state in the process of development will continue to be made for some time to come, even as the scope of the market increases through liberalization in the wider context of globalization.

The second dimension, good governance, is less obvious. It is, however, more concrete and less abstract. Governance is largely about rules and institutions that regulate the public realm in civil society. A democratic system seeks to provide for equal participation of the rich and the poor, or the strong and the weak, individuals as citizens in political processes. And good governance is a process characterized by communication and consultation, through which disputes are resolved, consensus is built and performance is reviewed on a continuous basis. The basis for good governance is a democratic political system that ensures representative and honest governments responsive to the needs of people. This involves more than simply free and fair elections. It implies a respect for economic, social and political rights of citizens. The rule of law is a foundation. An equitable legal framework, applied consistently to everyone, defends people from the abuse of power by state and non-state actors. It empowers people to assert their rights. The need for good governance extends to economic, social and political institutions required for the functioning of market economy and political democracy. A vibrant civil society, empowered by freedom of association and expression which can voice diversity in views, is just as important for good governance insofar as it provides checks and balances when governments do not act as they should. In sum, good governance, where governments are accountable to citizens and people are centre-stage in the process of development, is essential for creating capabilities, providing opportunities and ensuring rights for ordinary people. Governance capabilities matter. Indeed, the quality of governance is an important determinant of success or failure at development.[35] The moral of the story is not less government but good governance.

International context: governing globalization

It is clear that, during the first quarter of the twenty-first century, development outcomes would be shaped, at least in part, by the international context. It is also clear that unfair rules of the game in the contemporary world economy would encroach on policy space so essential for development. This situation needs to be corrected. The correctives should endeavour to make existing rules less unfair, introduce new rules where necessary and recognize that even fair rules may not suffice. But this endeavour cannot succeed without more democratic structures of governance in the world economy. In this process, interestingly enough, the role of nation-states would be critical. In reshaping unfair rules, it need hardly be said that the nature of the solution depends upon the nature of the problem. Where there are different rules in different spheres, it is necessary to make the rules symmetrical across spheres. Where there are rules for some but not for others, it is necessary to ensure that the rules are uniformly applicable to all. Where the agenda for new rules is partisan, it is imperative to redress the balance in the agenda.[36]

There is a clear need for greater symmetry in the rules of multilateral trading system embodied in the WTO. If developing countries provide access to their markets, it should be matched with some corresponding access to technology. If there is almost complete freedom for capital mobility, the draconian restrictions on labour mobility should at least be reduced. The enforcement of rules is also asymmetrical. In the Bretton Woods institutions, enforcement is possible through conditionality. Such conditionality, however, is applicable only to developing countries or transition economies that borrow from the IMF or the World Bank. In the WTO, enforcement is possible through retaliation. But most developing countries do not have the economic strength, even if they have the legal right, to retaliate. The reality, then, is that the countries that are poor or weak conform to the rules, whereas countries that are rich or strong can flout the rules. And the hegemonic powers, often, simply ignore the rules. The enforcement of rules for the rich and the powerful is, therefore, essential. In addition, the agenda for the new rules needs careful scrutiny for it is shaped by the interests of industrialized countries while the needs of development are largely neglected. For instance, if the proposed multilateral agreement on investment is so concerned about the rights of transnational corporations, some attention should also be paid to their possible obligations. In any case, such an agreement should not be lodged in the WTO. The issue of labour standards, of course, is simply not in the domain of the WTO.

But that is not all. There are some spheres where there are no rules, such as international financial markets or cross-border movements of people, which are not even on the agenda. The time has come to introduce some rules that govern speculative financial flows constituted mostly by short-term capital movements, sensitive to exchange rates and interest rates, in search of capital gains. It is also perhaps necessary to think about a new international financial architecture in which a World Financial Authority would manage systemic risk associated with international financial liberalization, co-ordinate national action against market-failure or abuse, and act as a regulator in international financial markets.[37] Similarly, it is worth contemplating a multilateral framework for consular practices and immigration laws that would govern cross-border movements of people, akin to multilateral frameworks that exist, or are sought to be created, for the governance of national laws, or rules, about the movement of goods, services, technology, investment and information across national boundaries.[38] The essential object should be to create a transparent and non-discriminatory system, based on rules rather than discretion, for people who wish to move, temporarily or permanently, across borders.

Rules that are fair are necessary but not sufficient. For a game is not simply about rules. It is also about players. And if one of the teams or one of the players does not have adequate training or preparation, it will simply be crushed by the other. In other words, the rules must be such that newcomers or latecomers to the game, for example developing countries, are provided with the time and the space to learn so that they can become competitive players rather than push-over opponents. In this context, it is important to stress that, for countries at vastly different levels of development, there should be some flexibility, instead of complete rigidity, in the application of uniform rules. Indeed, uniform rules for unequal partners can only produce unequal outcomes. Thus, we should be concerned with the desirability of the outcomes and not with the procedural uniformity of rules. It is, in principle, possible to formulate general rules where application is a function of country-specific or time-specific circumstances, without resorting to exceptions. It implies a set of multilateral rules in which every country has the same rights but the obligations are a function of its level or stage of development. In other words, rights and obligations should not be strictly symmetrical across countries. And there is a clear need for positive discrimination or affirmative action in favour of countries that are latecomers to development.

The reshaping of rules is easier said than done. Much would depend upon structures of governance. The existing arrangements for global governance are characterized by a large democratic deficit.[39] In terms of representation, the existing system is less than democratic. For one thing, representation is unequal, in part because of unequal weights in representation in institutions such as the IMF and the World Bank, and in part because of exclusion from representation in arrangements such as the P5 or the G7 or even the OECD. For another, representation is incomplete insofar as it is confined mostly to governments, with little that could be described as participation by civil society or corporate entities, let alone people or citizens. In terms of decision making, the existing system is even less democratic. Where some countries have more votes than others and yet other countries have no votes, the system is obviously undemocratic. Even the principle of one-country-one-vote, however, does not ensure a democratic mode. Much also depends on how decisions are made. The right of veto in the Security Council of the UN is explicitly undemocratic. But decision making by consensus, as in the WTO, can also be undemocratic if there is bilateral arm twisting or a consensus is hammered out among a small subset of powerful players, while most countries are silent spectators that are in the end a part of the apparent consensus.

It is difficult to imagine more democratic structures of governance in a world of such disparities, economic and political, between countries. But democracy is not simply about majority rule. It is as much about the protection of rights of minorities. The essential corrective, then, is to create institutional mechanisms that give poor countries and poor people a voice in the process of global governance. Even if they cannot shape decisions, they have a right to be heard. In addition, wherever existing rules constrain autonomy or choices in the pursuit of development, there is a need for the equivalent of an escape clause. Such a provision to opt out of obligations embedded in international rules, without having to forsake rights, could provide countries that are latecomers to development with the requisite degrees of freedom in their national pursuit of development objectives. It is important to recognize that, in democratic situations, *exit* has as much significance as *voice*.

In the international context, where the distribution of economic and political power is so unequal, the nation-state is, perhaps, the only institutional medium through which poor countries or poor people can attempt to influence or shape rules and institutions in a world of unequal partners. This is because only nation-states have the authority to set international rules. Groups of countries with mutual interests are more likely to be heard than single countries by themselves. There will always be some conflict of interest but there will always be areas where it is possible to find common cause and accept tradeoffs. In principle, it is possible to contemplate co-operation among nation-states to create rules and norms for the market that transcend national boundaries, just as the nation-state created rules and norms for the market within national boundaries. In practice, however, a recognition of the benefits of such co-operation might not be motivation enough. Co-operation among nation-states is far more likely to materialize, much like stable coalitions, if and when the costs of non-co-operation cross the threshold of tolerance. In either case, the nation-state is the most important player in the game. Therefore, it is not possible to imagine good governance in the world without nation-states, just as it is not possible to have good governance in countries without governments.

Conclusion

In considering the prospects for development during the first quarter of the twenty-first century, it is time to reflect on a new agenda for development. In this reflection, the concern for efficiency must be balanced with a concern for equity, just as the concern for economic growth must be balanced with a concern for social progress. It is also time to evolve a new consensus on development, in which the focus is on people rather than economies. Such a consensus must be built on a sense of proportion which does not re-open old ideological battles in terms of either-or choices, and on a depth of understanding which recognizes the complexity and the diversity of development. This thinking should not be limited to the sphere of economics. It must extend to the realm of politics. For substantive democracy, which creates a political accountability of governments to the people, must be an integral part of the new agenda for, and the new consensus on development. In such a world, ensuring decent living conditions for people, ordinary people, would naturally emerge as a fundamental objective. Development must, therefore, provide all men and women the rights, the opportunities and the capabilities to expand their freedoms and exercise their own choices for their wellbeing. In this process, people would be participants rather than beneficiaries. The distinction between ends and means would remain critical. And, in the pursuit of development, the importance of public action cannot be stressed enough. It must be an integral part of development strategies, which should not be forgotten in the enthusiasm for markets and globalization.

Notes

I am grateful to Amit Bhaduri, Ha-Joon Chang and Lance Taylor for helpful discussion. I would also like to thank Andrea Cornia, Gustav Ranis and Frances Stewart for valuable comments.

1. See, for example, Sachs and Warner (1995), who were among the first exponents of this view. This prescriptive view of globalization is also set out, at some length, by Bhagwati (2004); Wolf (2004).
2. See, in particular, Sachs and Warner (1995). For a very different, contrasting, historical perspective on globalization and development, see Nayyar (2006).
3. In an interesting critique, Samuelson (2004) questions the analytical basis and the theoretical foundations of this prescriptive view. For a critical perspective on the implications

of globalization for development, see Stiglitz (2002); Nayyar (2003a); Kaplinsky (2005). See also Soros (1998); Baker *et al.* (1998).

4. Sachs and Warner (1995); Bhagwati (2004); Wolf (2004).
5. The evidence cited in this paragraph is obtained from UNDP, *Human Development Report* (various issues), and World Commission on the Social Dimension of Globalization (2004).
6. For a detailed discussion, as also evidence, see Nayyar (2003a; 2006).
7. This proposition is set out, as also explained, in the report of the World Commission on the Social Dimension of Globalization (2004).
8. For a more complete discussion on rules of the game, see Nayyar (2002a; 2003a).
9. It must be recognized that such state intervention was crucial for development in the success stories among late industrializers during the second half of the twentieth century. For a convincing exposition of this view, see Amsden (1989); Wade (1990); Chang (1996).
10. For an analysis of this issue, see Nayyar (2002b).
11. See Bairoch (1993); Chang (2002a); Maddison (1995).
12. See, for example, Baster (1972); Seers (1972); Morris (1979).
13. See Streeten (1981); Stewart (1985).
14. There is an extensive literature on the subject. For a discussion on the conceptual foundations, see Sen (1989) and ul Haque (1995). For an analysis of issues related to methodology and measurement, see Anand and Sen (1994).
15. See Sen (1999).
16. For a lucid analysis, see Sen (1999).
17. For a detailed examination of the fundamental theorems of welfare economics, see Arrow (1950).
18. Joseph Stiglitz during interview on WBAI Radio, 15 August 2002, New York.
19. For a succinct discussion on why these results may not hold, see Mukherji (2005).
20. See Coase (1960). It is worth noting that Richard Coase was awarded the Nobel Prize in Economics, for this contribution, in 1991.
21. This proposition was developed by Akerlof (1970) in a seminal contribution.
22. See, for instance, Banerjee (1997).
23. See Nayyar (1997); Stiglitz (1998).
24. For an analysis of the relationship between the state and the market, from this perspective, see Bhaduri and Nayyar (1996).
25. The discussion on lessons in the following paragraphs draws upon Nayyar (2004).
26. For a discussion on the economic role of the state, see Stiglitz (1989); Killick (1990). See also Lall (1990); Shapiro and Taylor (1990).
27. See Amsden (1989); Lall (1990); Wade (1990); Chang (2002a).
28. For a fascinating historical analysis of the development experience of latecomers to industrialization, see Amsden (2001); Chang (2002a).
29. See for example, North (1990); Chang (2002b).
30. For a lucid discussion on the importance of social norms in market economies, with particular reference to Adam Smith, see Bhaduri (2002).
31. This is stressed by North (2001) in a short essay on understanding development.
32. The discussion in this paragraph draws upon Nayyar (2003b).
33. For a more detailed discussion, see Bhaduri and Nayyar (1996).
34. See World Commission on the Social Dimension of Globalization (2004).
35. A striking illustration of this proposition is provided by the wide diversity in economic performance across states in India, despite common policies, similar institutions and the economic union. There are even more striking examples that emerge from a comparison of economic performance across countries in the developing world.
36. The following discussion on the rules of the game in the world economy draws upon earlier work of the author (Nayyar 2002a; 2003a).
37. For a discussion on the rationale for, and contours of, such a World Financial Authority, see Eatwell and Taylor (2000).

38. For a discussion on the rationale for such a multilateral framework to govern cross-border movements of people, see Nayyar (2002c). The World Commission on the Social Dimension of Globalization (2004) makes a similar proposal.
39. The democratic deficit is analyzed, at some length, in Nayyar (2002a).

References

Akerlof, G.A. (1970) 'The Market for Lemons: Quality Uncertainty and the Market Mechanism', *Quarterly Journal of Economics*, 84, 3: 488–500.

Amsden, A.H. (1989) *Asia's Next Giant: South Korea and Late Industrialization*, New York: Oxford University Press.

Amsden, A.H. (2001) *The Rise of the Rest: Challenges to the West from Late Industrializing Economies*, New York: Oxford University Press.

Anand, S. and A. Sen (1994) 'Human Development Index: Methodology and Measurement', *HDRO Occasional Paper* 12, New York: UNDP.

Arrow, K.J. (1950) 'An Extension of the Basic Theorems of Classical Welfare Economics', in J. Neyman (ed.), *Proceedings of the Second Berkeley Symposium in Mathematical Statistics and Probability*, Berkeley, CA: University of California Press.

Bairoch, P. (1993) *Economics and World History: Myths and Paradoxes*, Chicago, IL: University of Chicago Press.

Baker, D., G. Epstein and R. Pollin (eds) (1998) *Globalization and Progressive Economic Policy*, Cambridge: Cambridge University Press.

Banerjee, A.V. (1997) 'A Theory of Misgovernance', *Quarterly Journal of Economics*, 112, 4: 1289–332.

Baster, N. (1972) 'Development Indicators', *Journal of Development Studies*, 8, 3: 1–20.

Bhaduri, A. (2002) 'Nationalism and Economic Policy in an Era of Globalization', in D. Nayyar (ed.), *Governing Globalization: Issues and Institutions*, Oxford: Oxford University Press for UNU-WIDER.

Bhaduri, A. and D. Nayyar (1996) *The Intelligent Person's Guide to Liberalization*, New Delhi: Penguin.

Bhagwati, J. (2004) *In Defence of Globalization*, Oxford: Oxford University Press.

Chang, H.-J. (1996) *The Political Economy of Industrial Policy*, London: Macmillan.

Chang, H.-J. (2002a) *Kicking Away the Ladder: Development Strategy in Historical Perspective*, London: Anthem Press.

Chang, H.-J. (2002b) 'Breaking the Mould: An Institutionalist Political Economy Alternative to the Neoliberal Theory of the Market and the State', *Cambridge Journal of Economics*, 26, 5: 539–59.

Coase, R. (1960) 'The Problem of Social Cost', *Journal of Law and Economics*, 3: 1–44.

Eatwell, J. and L. Taylor (2000) *Global Finance at Risk: The Case of International Regulation*, New York: The New Press.

Hahn, F. (1984) *Equilibrium and Macroeconomics*, Oxford: Basil Blackwell.

Kaplinsky, R. (2005) *Globalization, Poverty and Inequality*, Cambridge: Polity Press.

Killick, T. (1990) *A Reaction Too Far: Economic Theory and the Role of the State in Developing Countries*, London: Overseas Development Institute.

Lall, S. (1990) *Building Industrial Competitiveness in Developing Countries*, Paris: Development Centre, OECD.

Maddison, A. (1995) *Monitoring the World Economy: 1820–1992*, Paris: Development Centre, OECD.

Morris, M.D. (1979) *Measuring the Conditions of the World's Poor*, Oxford: Pergamon Press.

Mukherji, A. (2005) 'Development Economics and Governance: A Theoretical Perspective', Mimeo, New Delhi: Centre for Economic Studies and Planning, Jawaharlal Nehru University.

Nayyar, D (1997). 'Themes in Trade and Industrialization', in D. Nayyar (ed.), *Trade and Industrialization*, Delhi: Oxford University Press.

Nayyar, D. (2002a) 'The Existing System and the Missing Institutions', in D. Nayyar (ed.), *Governing Globalization: Issues and Institutions*, Oxford: Oxford University Press for UNU-WIDER.

Nayyar, D. (2002b) 'Capital Controls and the World Financial Authority: What Can We Learn from the Indian Experience', in J. Eatwell and L. Taylor (eds), *International Capital Markets: Systems in Transition*, New York: Oxford University Press.

Nayyar, D. (2002c) 'Cross-Border Movements of People', in D. Nayyar (ed.), *Governing Globalization: Issues and Institutions*, Oxford: Oxford University Press for UNU-WIDER.

Nayyar, D. (2003a) 'Globalization and Development Strategies', in J. Toye (ed.), *Trade and Development*, Cheltenham: Edward Elgar.

Nayyar, D. (2003b) 'The Political Economy of Exclusion and Inclusion: Democracy, Markets and People', in A.K. Dutt and J. Ros (eds), *Development Economics and Structuralist Macroeconomics: Essays in Honour of Lance Taylor*, Cheltenham: Edward Elgar.

Nayyar, D. (2004) 'Economic Reforms in India: Understanding the Process and Learning from Experience', *International Journal of Development Issues*, 3, 2: 31–55.

Nayyar, D. (2006) 'Globalization, History and Development: A Tale of Two Centuries', *Cambridge Journal of Economics*, 30, 1: 137–59.

North, D.C. (1990) *Institutions, Institutional Change and Economic Performance*, Cambridge, and New York: Cambridge University Press.

North, D.C. (2001) 'Needed: A Theory of Change', in G.M. Meier and J.E. Stiglitz (eds), *Frontiers of Development Economics*, Washington, DC: World Bank.

Sachs, J. and A. Warner (1995) 'Economic Reforms and the Process of Global Integration', *Brookings Papers on Economic Activity*, 1: 1–118.

Samuelson, P.A. (2004) 'Where Ricardo and Mill Rebut and Confirm Arguments of Mainstream Economists Supporting Globalization', *Journal of Economic Perspectives*, 18, 3, 135–46.

Seers, D. (1972) 'What Are We Trying to Measure?', *Journal of Development Studies*, 8, 3: 21–36.

Sen, A.K. (1989) 'Development as Capability Expansion', *Journal of Development Planning*, 19: 41–58.

Sen, A.K. (1999) *Development as Freedom*, New York: Alfred E. Knopf.

Shapiro, H. and L. Taylor (1990) 'The State and Industrial Strategy', *World Development* 18, 6: 861–78.

Soros, G. (1998) *The Crisis of Global Capitalism: Open Society Endangered*, London and New York: Little Brown.

Stewart, F. (1985) *Planning to Meet Basic Needs*, London: Macmillan.

Stiglitz, J.E. (1989) 'On the Economic Role of the State', in A. Heertje (ed.), *Economic Role of the State*, Oxford: Basil Blackwell.

Stiglitz, J.E. (1998) 'More Instruments and Broader Goals: Moving Toward the Post-Washington Consensus', *WIDER Annual Lecture* 2, Helsinki: UNU-WIDER. Reprinted (2005) *WIDER Perspectives on Global Development*, Basingstoke: Palgrave Macmillan for UNU-WIDER.

Stiglitz, J.E. (2002) *Globalization and its Discontents*, London: Allen Lane.

Streeten, P. (1981) *First Things First: Meeting Basic Human Needs in Developing Countries*, Oxford: Oxford University Press.

ul Haque, M. (1995) *Reflections on Human Development*, New York: Oxford University Press.

UNDP (United Nations Development Programme) (various issues) *Human Development Report*, New York: Oxford University Press for UNDP.

Wade, R. (1990) *Governing the Market: Economic Theory and the Role of Government in East Asian Industrialization*, New Jersey: Princeton University Press.

Wolf, M. (2004) *Why Globalization Works*, New Haven, CT, and London: Yale University Press.

World Commission on the Social Dimension of Globalization (2004) *A Fair Globalization: Creating Opportunities for All*, Geneva: ILO.

32
Do We Need a New 'Great Transformation'? Is One Likely?

Frances Stewart

> Undoubtedly, our age will be credited with having seen the end of the self-regulating market. (Polanyi 1944: 148)

> It appeared then [in 1995] that that the idea of an integrated world economy, founded on market relationships, had been reborn after a long collectivist hiatus. (Wolf 2004: xvii)

Introduction

In his path-breaking book *The Great Transformation: The Political and Economic Origins of our Times*,[1] Polanyi analyzed what he called the Great Transformation in Europe in the nineteenth and twentieth centuries. Indeed, he actually describes a 'double movement': one from the pre-market, pre-industrial system to the market-dominated industrialization of the nineteenth century. The second – which was what he termed the Great Transformation – consisted in the succession of changes that were provoked by the predominance of the market model. When he wrote the book, in 1944, it seemed that this second transformation was here to stay. Yet, there has been a huge resurgence of the market since the 1970s – many of the changes which Polanyi described have been rolled back, especially in developing countries. Indeed, in developing countries, it appears that the situation may be back to one resembling the pre-transformation situation of nineteenth-century Europe. This chapter considers the types of change documented by Polanyi for Europe in contemporary developing countries, and in the light of these explores, first whether a new Great Transformation is needed, and second whether, in a Polanyi-style reaction to the market model, such a transformation is likely.

Polanyi's basic argument was that the market model involved such excesses and distortions that a reaction was inevitable. Is this still true today? And are the political processes similar to those of nineteenth- and twentieth-century Europe, or have changes in the nature of capitalism in general, and constraints imposed by globalization on developing countries, in particular, made an effective reaction (or a new Great Transformation) impossible?

Polanyi's Great Transformation

To understand the Great Transformation, or series of reactions to the pure market system reinstating regulation, one has first to explore the origins of this market system. While markets may exist in some form in most, if not all, societies, they frequently do so in a subordinate role which is not what Polanyi meant by a market economy. What Polanyi defines as a market economy is a self-regulating system 'directed by market prices and nothing but market prices' (Polanyi: 45). In such a fully fledged, self-regulating market system:

> the control of the economic system by the market is of overwhelming conse-
> quence to the whole organization of society: it means no less than the running
> of society as an adjunct to the market. Instead of economy being embedded in
> social relations, social relations are embedded in the market. (*Ibid.*: 60)

Markets dominate where (a) each individual is motivated primarily by economic gain for him/herself; and (b) there are no (or few) regulations preventing the free flow of resources to where gains are maximized. Polanyi argues that neither of these conditions obtained either historically or in pre-modernized societies,[2] so that 'Though the institution of the market was fairly common since the later Stone Age, its role was no more than incidental to economic life' (*Ibid.*: 45).

Drawing on the famous anthropological works available to him (Mead, Lewis, Malinowski, Thurnwald) he claims that all anthropological research shows that economic (or maximizing) motives were subordinate to social relationships. 'man's economy as a rule is submerged in his social relationships. He does not act so as to safeguard his individual interest in the possession of material goods; he acts so as to safeguard his social standing, his social assets' (*Ibid.*: 48). In these societies, transactions were motivated by principles of reciprocity and of redistribution, while what he defined as *householding*, following Aristotle (subsistence production in modern terms), provided the third principle of economic production.

The subordinate role of private economic gains as a motive is one characteristic of non-market economies. Another is the pervasive regulation of transactions, including land, labour, financial capital and goods that obtained in pre-nineteenth-century Europe, as well as elsewhere. Internal as well as external trade was subject to strict regulations, often administered by guilds. Tolls and prohibitions restricted trade between towns. Though many of these were abolished as a result of mercantilist pressures in the sixteenth and seventeenth centuries, they were replaced by extended government regulation. Equally, land was embedded in social relations and controlled politically and socially, rather than through the market (*Ibid.*: 73). Labour was subject to numerous regulations and controls, including those governing the relations of master, journeyman and apprentice, by guild, custom and statute. Moreover, in England, the Act of Settlement of 1662 had imposed severe restrictions on labour mobility, since it gave to each parish the responsibility and duty to provide for their own destitutes. In general, 'The economic system was submerged in general social relations; markets were merely an accessory feature of an institutional setting controlled and regulated more than ever by social authority' (*Ibid.*: 70).

The manifold regulations slowed down the growth of industry; and under pressure from the new entrepreneurial class, and with the support of economists, including Smith, Ricardo and Bentham, who argued that the self-regulating market would promote efficiency and growth, the main elements of regulation were abolished as the nineteenth century progressed. The restrictions on labour mobility were loosened in 1795, temporarily to be replaced by the unworkable Speenhamland system (which essentially entitled every worker to a quite generous minimum income, irrespective of their work situation or earnings, discouraging work and imposing burdens on the rates). This was abolished in 1834 (by the reformed House of Commons, which now included representatives of the emerging industrial entrepreneurial class), leaving only minimal and demeaning support for the destitute via workhouses. Combined with the Combination Laws of 1799 and 1800 which banned workers' combinations, this marked the beginning of a competitive labour market.[3] Restrictions on land transfers were likewise abolished.[4] With the repeal of the Corn Laws in 1846, the UK came close to a purely market economy. In Polanyi's terms, labour, land and money had become 'fictitious' commodities – fictitious because they were not produced in the same way as normal commodities and their price and use had implications way beyond that of the typical commodity, determining a family's survival (in the case of wages), and environment and place, in the case of land.[5] Yet, according to Bentham,[6] in a view that is echoed by many advocating the introduction of 'modern' property rights reforms in developing countries, 'The condition most favourable to the prosperity of agriculture exists when there are no entails, no inalienable endowments, no common lands, no rights or redemptions, no tithes' (quoted in *Ibid.*: 189).

The social consequences of these reforms, in the short to medium term, were appalling in terms of poverty, squalor and indignities. Workers were forced to work very lengthy days in dangerous conditions; child labour abounded; and health, sanitation and housing were all of abysmal standards.[7] The business cycle saw sharp fluctuations in activity culminating in the Great Depression of the 1920s and 1930s. These extreme consequences led to reactions which limited market freedoms. Two types of reaction occurred: piecemeal reform in Britain and some other countries in Western Europe; and massive changes in the whole organization of society and the economy in the cases of Marxist and fascist societies.

In Britain, reforms emerged as a result of a combination of pressures: liberal observers campaigned to correct gross abuses – including Robert Owen who initiated the co-operative movement; the Chartist movement, which fought for political rights (without success in the short run); and the growth of the trade union movement. Factory acts followed that regulated hours and conditions and banned child labour. The extension of the franchise to the (male) urban skilled working class in 1867, and then to skilled and semi-skilled agricultural labourers and miners in 1887, increased political pressure to improve working conditions. These reforms were soon followed by the expansion of education to much of the working class and by further legislation regulating factory conditions. The twentieth century saw more social interventions (with Lloyd George's reforms, including unemployment insurance and pensions), the end of the gold standard and the reintroduction of tariffs in reaction to the massive unemployment of the 1920s and 1930s. During the Second World War, planning and controls basically replaced the market. Polanyi was writing at the peak of regulations over the market in the UK. However, state interventions in the economy continued over the subsequent 30 years or so: Keynesian interventions dominated macro policy, while a comprehensive welfare state was established, following the recommendations of the Beveridge Report. Other features that constrained the role of the market included a strong role for trade unions, national wage bargaining, industrial and agricultural subsidies, a large state sector, tariffs on imports and limitations on currency convertibility. This was the Great Transformation – from an almost unadulterated market system to a strongly controlled one (with an even greater transformation in this direction in the cases of fascism and socialism). At the time Polanyi was writing neither Keynesian macro policy, nor industrial nationalization, nor the comprehensive welfare state had been introduced. Yet all fit so well into his Great Transformation that they serve to strengthen the case he was making. According to Polanyi this Great Transformation was the inevitable consequence of adopting a pure market economy because of its harsh and unacceptable human and environmental consequences:

> Our thesis is that the idea of a self-adjusting market implied a stark utopia. Such an institution could not exist for any length of time without annihilating the human and natural substance of society ... Inevitably, society took measures to protect itself, but whatever measures it took impaired the self-regulation of the market, disorganized industrial life, and thus endangered society in yet another way. (p. 3)

In the last part of this quotation, Polanyi hints that the situation brought about by the Great Transformation may not be a stable one. And, as is now well recognized, the heavily regulated society Polanyi described lasted only about 30 years and was followed by a swing back towards a market economy. Regulations and interventions were at their peak in the 1940s in the UK, just when Polanyi was writing. But a 'bonfire of controls' soon followed, as wartime price controls and licensing were dismantled. In the subsequent decades, there was gradual liberalization, with lowered trade restrictions and a slow move towards convertible currency. However, the sharp policy reversal occurred in the Thatcherite era of the 1980s, in a political move to the right which was due in part to the way the previous interventionist system had, as noted by Polanyi in the above quotation, 'disorganized industrial life and thus endangered society in yet another way'. Keynesian macro policies were generally discredited and disavowed in theory, though not always in practice. Britain led the way in privatizing previously nationalized industries and in limiting the powers of the trade unions. The private sector began to make headway even in the provision of public services. The market once again dominated society, albeit a much regulated market, constrained on most fronts by myriad regulations relating to employment conditions, market structure, trading conditions, etc. Moreover, in most developed countries extensive measures of social protection were maintained.

Polanyi and developing countries

Insofar as Polanyi himself considered what we now term 'developing countries' in his book on the Great Transformation he did so as the subject of study by anthropologists, pointing out, as already noted, that in these societies the market played a subordinate role only, and that neither land nor labour were treated as commodities, to be bought and sold on an unregulated market.[8] Rather both had important social functions, and social relationships largely determined their allocation and use. According to Polanyi, exchange took place according to the principles of reciprocity and redistribution, the latter involving hierarchical and centralized modes. Since the developing countries provided just a backdrop in Polanyi's book – a model with which to contrast European developments – what follows is my own attempt to describe developments in Polanyist terms.

To summarize a hugely complex and differentiated situation, the colonial period saw a mixture of 'traditional' relationships outside the market, and forced markets, introduced by the colonists. The colonial period did not see the introduction of an extensive unregulated market to the extent that occurred in nineteenth-century Europe because large swathes of most economies remained outside the market. Political independence (for most developing countries occurring between 1945 and 1970, though, of course, in Latin America it was much earlier) happened at a time when planning, public ownership and market regulation was dominant in Europe. This was also the era of apparently thriving socialism in the Soviet empire. The interventionist philosophy resonated with the objectives, politics and philosophy of the newly independent countries, and of Latin American governments, which had already started to initiate active industrial policies in reaction to the fall in commodity prices in the 1930s.

For most post-colonial countries in the 1950s, the overriding reality was underdevelopment, characterized by low incomes, a predominantly agrarian structure with a large subsistence subsector and heavy dependence on the industrialized countries for all modern inputs. Governments of the newly independent countries had two related economic objectives: to become economically as well as politically independent; and to raise their incomes to the levels of the developed countries. In a famous statement President Truman declared that:

> We must embark on a bold new program for making the benefits of our scientific advances and industrial progress available for the improvement and growth of underdeveloped areas. The old imperialism is dead – exploitation for foreign profit has no place in our plans. What we must envisage is a program of development based on the concepts of democratic fair dealing.[9]

The desirability of development planning was widely accepted, by developed country observers[10] as well as developing country theoreticians and practitioners. Development plans were introduced by Mahalanobis in India, Prebisch in Latin America and visiting economists in many African economies (Killick 1983). The state was given a major role in determining economic priorities via price and import controls, investment planning and sometimes as a producer, with the adoption of a strategy of import-substituting industrialization. Formal sector labour markets were subject to regulations, including minimum wages. And trade unions were recognized as important players. Thus, developing countries virtually skipped Polanyi's unregulated market phase, moving straight into a situation of extensive regulation and a large public sector, with markets, again, playing a subordinate role.

The policies adopted were in some ways remarkably successful. Savings and investment rates rose dramatically from the mid-1950s and growth accelerated in most countries, and some countries, notably in East Asia, experienced spectacular growth rates. Social indicators, such as infant mortality and literacy rates, also improved, although other developments were less welcome. Population growth accelerated, and growth in employment lagged behind output. Unemployment and underemployment emerged as serious problems; and the absolute numbers of people falling below the poverty line increased. A dualistic pattern of development continued, with a small relatively privileged modern sector leaving the rest of the economy with low incomes and investment.[11] Moreover, the economic independence sought proved elusive, as dependence on developed countries for capital and technology increased.

The situation changed in the early 1980s, following the abrupt switch to monetarism in Britain and the US. Interest rates rose and there was world recession, with a sharp worsening in commodity prices. Most developing countries – who had borrowed heavily in the 1970s to finance current account deficits resulting from oil price rises – found themselves in an unsustainable financial position and were forced to request assistance from the international financial institutions (IFIs). These institutions used the opportunity to enforce a series of pro-market reforms on the borrowing countries (a package which came to be known as the 'Washington Consensus'). These reforms together led to a virtually complete retreat from interventionism and the institution of something approaching the 'self-regulating market'.

The following reforms were widely enacted:[12]

- conversion of quotas into tariffs and reduction of tariffs
- abolition of industrial licensing
- privatization
- reduced/eliminated restrictions on foreign ownership of assets and supplies of components
- reduction/abolition of minimum wage
- reduced role of trade unions

- move towards budget balance
- reduced 'financial repression' with abolition of directed credit and market determination of interest rates.

In many countries, in addition, there was:

- a move towards convertibility of currencies
- capital account liberalization
- an increased market role in the provision of government services
- the introduction of Western-style property rights with respect to land
- and similarly, with respect to intellectual property.

The changes paralleled changes introduced in developed countries roughly at the same time, but far exceeded them as developed countries confronted much less harsh economic conditions, were not dependent on the IFIs and could therefore follow independent policies. Moreover, as democracies, they were unable to adopt policies against the interests of the majority, while some of the well-established interest groups were extremely powerful. Thus, the US and EU retained agricultural subsidies that would not have been permitted by the IFIs in developing countries. The US has periodically run huge budget deficits, which, similarly would be unacceptable to the IFIs; in continental Europe the labour movement retains considerable power to regulate the labour market, resisting efforts to make it 'more flexible' and, despite privatization, the state continues to account for 40 per cent or more of most European economies. Most importantly, in Europe, the state continues to guarantee reasonable minimum standards of living and of public services for all citizens.

In developing countries, the pro-market changes were more radical and systematic, albeit at uneven pace, varying with the degree of local autonomy. The large and powerful countries – China and India – were able to choose the pace and degree of liberalization, whereas small African countries generally had to take the medicine in one go, with Latin American countries in an intermediate position. Moreover, whereas in most developed countries the impact on livelihoods was cushioned by elaborate social security systems and the newly privatized industries were circumscribed by more or less effective regulation, in developing countries, social security systems were much more limited in scope and the regulatory system much more tenuous. However, while interventionism had been extensive in virtually all developing countries, it generally only directly affected a minority of the population – those in the so-called formal sector. The majority of the population in most developing countries were in unregulated or weakly regulated sectors, including those in the non-agricultural informal sector and most people working in agriculture. Social security systems, such as they were, also mostly only related to this relatively privileged minority, as did the trade unions. So the unravelling of interventions and reduced social security that went with the reforms for the most part only affected the minority in the formal sector directly, albeit the others were affected via knock-on affects, as, for example, the newly unemployed joined the informal sector, swelling numbers and depressing incomes.

Interpreting and analyzing these changes in Polanyist terms, we can see that in developing countries they might be best interpreted as being parallel to the move to the market in Europe in the nineteenth century, with the abolition of regulations being akin to the unravelling of the various guild and statutory regulations of pre-nineteenth-century Europe. It was not so much, therefore, the reintroduction of a market for labour or land, or money, but the introduction of these markets in more or less pure form for the first time. And as in Europe in the nineteenth century, the changes were not accompanied by mechanisms to protect people from the harshest affects. Only after nearly a decade of tough reforms with evidence of sharply rising poverty levels, did the IFIs recommend some rather weak mechanisms to protect the poor in developing countries. In this there is a contrast with Europe of the late twentieth century, where existing protective mechanisms – although they did not prevent rising inequality – have prevented poverty rising in absolute terms.

There are some other important differences in the developing country switch to the market from the changes in nineteenth-century Europe. First, in Europe the changes reflected the ideas of major domestic philosophers and were introduced as a result of domestic pressures. In contrast, in contemporary developing countries, the 'liberal' pro-market philosophy almost all came from outside; including Milton Friedman (US), Ian Little (UK), Maurice Scott (UK), Tibor Scitovsky (US), Bela Balassa (US), Anne Krueger (US), with Deepak Lal and Jagdish Bhagwati (from India, but educated in the UK) almost the sole developing country representatives of the initial push towards marketization. And while it was the emerging industrial classes who forced the pace of reform in the UK in the nineteenth century, it was the IFIs, themselves ruled by and largely representing the interests of the developed countries, which forced the pace in developing countries. In neither nineteenth-century Europe, nor contemporary developing countries, were the changes introduced through democratic institutions. In Europe, they predated democracy, and were largely reversed once democratic institutions were instituted. The second pro-market transformation in Europe (in the late twentieth century) did occur in democracies, but this time, as noted, it was surrounded by regulations and social protection mechanisms. Most developing countries adopting pro-market changes were not democratic, as the extensive democratization of the 1990s mainly followed the reforms (and in part may have been a reaction to them). In any case, it was the IFIs – sometimes with the support of local elites – who initiated the changes, although some of the local elite undoubtedly benefited from some reforms, such as privatization. Few countries had any sort of democratic debate on the measures. Where there was debate (as in Nigeria in 1986), the proposed reforms were rejected.

Another big difference from nineteenth-century Europe was the importance of globalization in the late twentieth century, and particularly global corporations. In the nineteenth century, the UK, if not the rest of Europe, could largely ignore global forces and determine its policy autonomously in what it considered to be its own best interests.[13] This is not an option for developing countries today, whose high dependence on aid, trade and overseas investment makes global considerations paramount. The huge influence of the IFIs has already been noted. But even countries which do not depend on them must consider the impact of their policies on trade and capital flows. In general, such global influences reinforced (and lay behind) the IFIs promotion of market mechanisms. The new global economy also makes a fundamental difference, as compared with Europe of the nineteenth and twentieth centuries, in constraining the possibilities of a new Great Transformation, as we shall discuss below.

A further difference arises from the nature of politics in developing countries; whereas politics in Europe historically tended to be class based – perhaps because of the relative homogeneity of populations – contemporary developing country politics tend to be patrimonial and/or political support and divisions follow ethnic or religious differences (Horowitz 1985; UNRISD 2005).

Consequences of the switch to the market for developing countries[14]

The pro-side argues, in brief, that growth accelerated, poverty declined and inequality fell during the era of pro-market reforms and enhanced global integration. The anti-side argues that while growth accelerated in the two Asian giants (China and India) it has slowed down in Africa and Latin America; poverty numbers showed little fall and the Millennium Development Goals will not be met in large numbers of countries (UNDP 2005). The pro-side argues that world income distribution has improved since 1980 when country incomes are weighted by population (Boltho and Toniolo 1999). The anti-side points to a worsening of inequality in the majority of countries and a widening in absolute gaps between the richest and poorest countries (Wolf 2004: ch. 9; Cornia 2004). In addition, national instability and personal insecurity has risen with higher fluctuations in national incomes as capital swings in and out which is reflected in rising personal insecurity, particularly as social security systems are cut back.

There were huge differences in impact in different parts of the world which are not reflected in these aggregates. Out of 104 low and middle HDI countries, the majority (64) had per capita growth rates of less than 1 per cent from 1975–2002, and 41 had falling per capita incomes (UNDP 2005). For the most part, the performance in Africa was extremely weak on all fronts. In Latin America, growth was virtually non-existent over a 20-year period and inequality and poverty rose. Yet in most of Asia, and notably India and China, there was a marked acceleration in growth, and, despite rising inequality, poverty ratios and (more controversially) numbers fell. But the anti-globalization team would argue that India and China controlled the market and did not accept it in pure form – hence their success. And the pro-team argue that if only it had been accepted in pure form everywhere, the results would be even better. 'The world needs more globalization, not less' (Wolf 2004: 320), echoing the arguments of some observers of nineteenth-century Europe.[15]

Yet, everywhere it is agreed that there remains unacceptable poverty. And while the market provides employment, incomes and private health and education for some, in virtually all developing countries it leaves out many more. In most

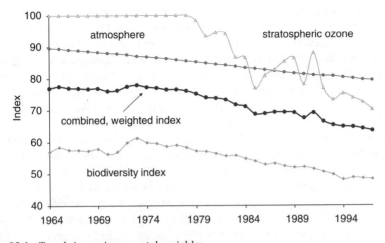

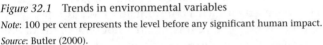

Figure 32.1 Trends in environmental variables

Note: 100 per cent represents the level before any significant human impact.

Source: Butler (2000).

places, the market is virtually unregulated, and conditions of work frequently parallel those of nineteenth-century Europe, with long hours, unhealthy and unsafe conditions, employment of children and young women, crowded and unsanitary housing and pitiful wages. Moreover, the global attack on trade unions has weakened workers' ability to protect themselves and downward pressure on government expenditure has weakened governments' ability to do so.

The devastating environmental consequences of current patterns of growth seems to be difficult to question (Figure 32.1). In the nineteenth century there were local environmental consequences not dissimilar to those experienced by developing counties today, but the global hazards – particularly that of global warming as a result of CO_2 emissions – is unprecedented.[16] This, as well as local environmental problems, is another consequence of an unregulated market world economy. Even the most enthusiastic globalizers argue that 'the management of the environment requires well targeted measures' (Wolf 2004: 194).

Apart from the magnitude of the environmental threat, the balance is not dissimilar from assessments of the market in the nineteenth century. There too a comparison with the previous situation was by no means ambiguously negative – growth had occurred at an unprecedented rate; some had gained significantly; and over the long run there was the prospect of an escape from the harsh conditions. But the downside was large, hence the reactions and the Great Transformation. In today's developing world much the same can be said: so do we need, and can we expect, a new Great Transformation?

The need for a new Great Transformation

The basic characteristic of the first Great Transformation was to pull back control over people's lives from being solely the product of impersonal market forces to being in society's care, so that the market might serve society rather than society be subservient to the market. In order to achieve this political and organizational changes were necessary – basically an organized working class and democratic reforms. The measures taken included those directed at improving working conditions, regulating firms, assuming power over macroeconomic policy, extending social protection and social services, and reintroducing restrictions on international trade. Any new Great Transformation would not necessarily include all the same elements – indeed it would be surprising if exactly the same ones were relevant today. But it would be based on the same objective; to make the market serve society rather than conversely, and it would be directed at 'the protection of man, nature and productive organization ... to rehabilitate the lives of men and their environment' (Polanyi: 225). In view of the insecure and impoverished lives that so many live in developing countries today, and the severe damage to the environment that the current system is producing, it seems difficult to argue against the objective of securing changes in such a direction. Indeed, given the global nature of the market today, the need for such a transformation would appear even greater than in the nineteenth century, since it is a matter not only of the disempowerment of all those (the vast majority) with few or no assets, but also the disempowerment of whole countries and even continents.

While, as noted, actual measures most appropriate to achieving this fundamental objective are likely to differ from some of those in the earlier period and, indeed, between regions or countries, some (broadly defined) are likely to be shared across time and space. Each country needs to decide for itself what changes are needed – indeed this is part of having the market serve society. But common characteristics are likely to be:

- Regulation of conditions of work, not only in the formal sector but in the economy as a whole.
- Reasonable minimal income guarantees for all – to be determined, of course, in the light of the resource availability of the particular country. Where this does not permit a survival standard, aid resources may be called upon.
- Assurance of universal provision of basic social services.
- Regulation of the market to avoid monopolistic (or other) exploitation.
- Regulation of the economy to ensure environmental protection.
- Regulation of capital markets and of fiscal and monetary policy to avoid excess fluctuations in activity.

Is a new Great Transformation underway?

The original Great Transformation occurred through myriad activities in response to the harsh conditions of the market,

> The purpose of the intervention was to rehabilitate the lives of men and their environment, to give them some security of status, intervention necessarily aimed at reducing the flexibility of wages and the mobility of labour, giving

stability to incomes, continuity to production, introducing public control of natural resources and the management of currencies in order to avoid the unsettling changes in the price level. (Polanyi: 225)

Among the forces supporting interventions of this kind, the most important in the UK were the emergence of the trade union movement, together with the extension of the franchise and the political changes that followed, as well as changes in the intellectual climate (epitomized by Keynesian economics); elsewhere the communist and fascist revolutions were responses to these self-same harsh conditions. Above all, the changes followed because people *combined* to bring about changes that would control or even replace the market. As de Tocqueville (1966: 666) wrote, 'In democratic countries knowledge of how to combine is the mother of all forms of knowledge; on its progress depends that of all others.' The question then is whether we can expect, or indeed can already detect, similar changes in developing countries. There are some signs that indeed we can, but also evidence of severe constraints on their potential effectiveness.

Democratization has made considerable progress among developing countries over recent decades. Between 1974 and 1999 multiparty electoral systems were introduced in 113 countries (UNDP 2000: 38). This provides a permissive environment for transformation, particularly since the numerical majority have below average incomes and are disproportionately lacking in social protection. However, whether this translates into extensive social change and market regulation depends on the nature of democracy and, particularly, political parties. In many countries, political parties are not ideological but organized behind personalities, family, ethnicity or religion, and use these ties together with patronage and corrupt practices to gain or retain power. But populist leaders have emerged with democratic transition and have tried to introduce some transforming policies. Examples include Nelson Mandela in South Africa, Lula da Silva in Brazil, Hugo Chavez in Venezuela and Evo Morales in Bolivia. In principle, one would expect democracy in poor countries eventually to generate transforming policies. Indeed, there is some econometric evidence that democratic regimes are more redistributive than non-democratic (Silva Leander 2005). But there are some important constraints on governments in developing countries, including countries with democratic systems, which will be discussed later.

A second force making for transformation is the growth of non-governmental organizations (NGOs) and community organizations, both international and national. There has been a rapid growth in their numbers over recent decades (Salamon and Anheier 1999). In India, at least 1 million non-profit organizations have been counted (Sen 1998); in Brazil, federal government records include over 200,000 (Salamon and Anheier 1999); in Thailand, 15,000 were recorded by one observer (Pongsapich 1998). Of course, the category includes very different types of organization. Many are 'efficiency'-type groups,[17] basically providing services where the market fails and complementing rather than challenging the market. But these may soften its harshest impacts. Others are 'pro bono' groups, delivering goods and services to the most impoverished, again supporting but also softening the market. The third category are groups with 'claims' functions; these aim to improve the position of their members by challenging rules and regulations and demanding greater shares of output. This third group includes, for example, associations of landless, worker associations of various types and also advocacy groups formed to alter regulations in ways that favour the deprived. In practice, many groups have more than one of these three functions. Where formed among or for the deprived, all three types of group tend to improve the social and economic operation of the market but only the third type fully contributes to a Great Transformation, in the sense of being directed at changing the rules.

A survey of local organizations in the early 1980s found about two-thirds were primarily devoted to production/efficiency issues, and one-third to advancing group interests (Esman and Uphoff 1984).[18] NGOs receiving government or international support tend to be entirely in the first two categories (production and/or pro bono).[19] NGOs undoubtedly do contribute to a transformation, but generally their impact is limited for various reasons. One reason is that their total coverage is mostly quite limited.[20] Moreover, in general, the poor are particularly handicapped in forming such groups because of lack of education, finance and networks (Thorp *et al.* 2005), and many of the NGOs purportedly intended to assist the poor in practice do not, either because their real agendas are rather different or because they are ineffective. Thus, a study of NGOs in Africa argues that local NGOs lack effective power: 'this absence of NGO power has undermined development across the continent' (Michael 2004: 105). Moreover, new models of organization (the 'New Public Administration')[21] have been imposed on many local NGOs organization (in the name of transparency, accountability and efficiency), which have tended to undermine their effectiveness in reaching the poor (Lorgen 2002; Mawdsley *et al.* 2002).

A more general critique of the role of NGOs as a mechanism for challenging dominant power structures is the Marxist/Gramsci view that what civil society organizations essentially do is to support the hegemonic power – they may challenge aspects of this power, 'But there is also no doubt that such sacrifices and such a compromise cannot touch the essential' (Gramsci 1971: 161). 'In this paradigm, civil society is understood as the arena in which the state perpetuates its power through hegemonic rather than coercive means' (Brown 2004: 20; see also Femia 2001). In general, NGOs do not attack the fundamental causes of poverty (land distribution, technology, terms of trade). For example, a review of NGOs in Egypt concluded that

> The mission of the majority of Egyptian NGOs is not to alter the structural inequalities in society, but rather to attempt to 'alleviate' the suffering of the poor and render their lives more bearable. By doing so, NGOs are actually postponing any real lasting solutions to deeply embedded problems of the poor and exploited in society. (Abdelrahman 2004: 196–7)

The spectacular growth of international NGOs (INGOs),[22] sometimes known as 'global civil society' (GSC), may also challenge the model of market dominance at a global level. A breakdown of GSC according to their function, however, shows that INGOs devoted to 'economic development and infrastructure' (efficiency functions as defined above) account for the largest number (around 9,500), followed by 'research' at over 8,000 (presumably leading to advocacy), then social services, health and education also around 8,000 (which would be classified as efficiency and pro bono) with 'politics' at a little over 1,000 and showing a small decline, 1990–2000. Like NGOs, the total impact of INGOs is limited. For example, they initiated the growing fair trade movement but it still accounts for only a very small fraction of total trade; just 2 per cent of the coffee market in 2002 (and this is an industry where it has probably made most progress). The total value of fair trade was estimated at GB£500 million; only 0.03 per cent of 2002 value of developing country merchandise exports.[23]

INGO advocacy is directed at global rules and may contribute to a transformation at this level.[24] INGO campaigns can take credit for the introduction of the developing country debt relief (HIPC), which has alleviated some of the financial problems of the poorest countries, but in no way contributed to structural transformation as can be seen by the content of the Poverty Reduction Strategy Papers (PRSPs) with which HIPC is associated, to be discussed further below.

Another international source of transformation is the growing movement for corporate social responsibility (CSR). Campaigns in the North have put pressure on multinational companies to operate in a 'responsible' way. Responsibility is interpreted as not using child labour, providing reasonable conditions for workers, sometimes including provision of social services for workers and for the locality where the companies operate, and being environmentally responsible.[25] Schemes include company codes of conduct, multi-stakeholder initiatives and public–private partnerships. These have changed the operations of particular companies, but the impact is spotty, typically confined to particular companies operations and not to the economy at large. They often sideline trade unions and do not extend to the informal sector. Some companies clearly use CSR for public relations, while continuing with deleterious activities (for example, British American Tobacco, see ASH 2002). As Utting (2004: 1) notes, 'There is a danger ... of codes as being seen as something more than they really are, and being used to deflect criticism, reduce the demand for external regulation and undermine the position of trade unions.' Nevertheless, among foreign companies, some participation in CSR has become fairly extensive. Multi-stakeholder initiatives of various kinds were estimated to cover about 53,000 companies in 2004, of which over 90 per cent mostly related to certification schemes. The estimated number of TNCs plus affiliates in 2002 was 934,000 (data from Utting 2004). Only about 4,000 TNCs produce reports on their social or environmental performance (IDS 2005). Public–private partnerships have also been growing, encouraged at a global level by the United Nations. However, regulation seems to be weak: 'the lack of attention to criteria and procedures for selecting and screening corporate partners, and to monitoring and compliance mechanisms, are downsides to the rapid proliferation of PPPs [public–private partnerships]' (Utting 2004: 2). These initiatives are mostly fairly recent. With a strong input into monitoring from communities and NGOs and the development of government regulatory mechanisms, including the development of appropriate standards for the whole economy and mechanisms for monitoring and complaints and penalties, CSR could make a contribution to a new transformation, albeit confined to the sectors controlled by multinational corporations.

Taken together, these non-governmental organizations, national and international, do make a contribution but a limited one, largely because that is the nature of voluntary non-governmental activity. Their ambiguous impact – partly carrying out official policy and partly challenging it – again reflects the ambiguity in Gramsci, who, while seeing them as largely instrumentalized by prevailing powers, also saw them as a source of dissent: civil society is 'the space where the subaltern classes can challenge the power of the state' (Abdelrahman 2004: 22). In line with this ambiguity, such organizations may achieve a minor transformation, but not a great one.

In the North, the Great Transformation essentially occurred as a result of *government*, not non-governmental action, even though NGO pressure was highly influential over government action. There is a parallel with nineteenth-century Britain: Owen's Lanarkshire experiment (a 'socially responsible' factory) and the co-operative movement he supported did make a contribution, as did the Workers' Education Association and many charitable institutions that dispensed support for the poor of various kinds, but the Great Transformation had to await government action. While there was a paternalistic element to some action by leaders such as Disraeli, appalled at the condition of the poor, most reforms were due to political pressures coming from political parties and their supporters. Hence, we need to return to the question of how much we can expect to come from this source in contemporary developing countries.

Constraints on a new Great Transformation

In countries where the market is basically succeeding, in the sense that it is generating relatively stable growth and expansion of employment and incomes, political parties may be expected broadly to support the extension of the market, intervening only at the edges. But in countries where the market seems be failing, associated with high and sometimes rising levels of poverty and stagnant and sometimes falling incomes, one would expect a more robust political challenge. This seems particularly probable where there are democratic institutions – the situation, as noted, in most developing countries today. Yet everywhere the political and economic situation seems to constrain any political challenge to the market to a much greater extent than it did in Europe and the USA in the late nineteenth and early twentieth century. Moreover, the way politics is organized in most developing countries also militates against radical change. Constraints arise from the growth of the multinational corporation and other global institutions, as well as the increasing importance of the global economy for most developing countries, which together severely limit countries' freedom of action.

It is often pointed out that globalization is not a new phenomenon, but was equally in evidence pre-1914 (Hirst 1997). However, a major difference today is the presence of MNCs and multinational institutions which present more severe constraints to independent and market-challenging action than was the case in

Europe when the Great Transformation occurred. The constraints are partly external and economic, partly internal and political.

First, there are multinational institutions – the IFIs and the WTO in particular – whose rules and influence all promote pro-market policies. Their impact on developing country policy is extensive. Policy-based lending represents 10–20 per cent of total World Bank lending and one-third of commitments. In one way or other adjustment conditions affect virtually every borrowing country – that is, almost every developing country. About half the conditions (1999–2004) involve a strong pro-market component (those relating to trade, economic management, agriculture and infrastructure and finance and the private sector), while the rest relate to the social sector and infrastructure and public sector management (also often involving market reforms). In the 1980s, the conditions involving direct market elements accounted for a substantially higher proportion (at 70 per cent) (data from World Bank 2005).

The IMF's traditional focus is on macroeconomic stabilization, but what they term 'structural' conditions have become of increasing importance. These are 'comprehensive programs that include policies of the scope and character required to correct structural imbalances in production, trade and prices'.[26] Structural policies cover a wide range of reforms relating to tariffs and pricing policy, subsidies, privatization, as well as some institutional reforms. The thrust of the reforms, like those of the adjustment lending of the World Bank, is towards a greater role for the market (although not every one could be classified in this way – some involve improving administration, for example). By the mid-1990s almost all arrangements had some structural arrangements, while the number of structural conditions per arrangement also grew (IMF 2001: 9). Conditions relate predominantly to the exchange system, the trade regime, pricing and marketing, public enterprise reform, privatization (accounting for the largest proportion of conditions) and the financial sector (IMF 2001: 24). While World Bank lending is virtually universal, IMF conditions only come into play among countries that have a financial crisis and need IMF support. Hence, the conditions have been mainly felt in Africa, Latin America and the transition countries. However, after the East Asian financial crisis of 1997 structural conditionality extended to East Asian countries. In Indonesia this involved reforms across the board; in Korea, reforms were mainly in relation to the financial sector and some 'systemic reforms'; and in Thailand the reforms extended to privatization, the financial sector and 'systemic reforms'.

Despite claims that the IFIs wish to promote country 'ownership', no country wishing to receive support from the international institutions can undertake any major challenges to the market organization of their economies – indeed, quite the reverse, as there is a continual push for a greater role for the market. While the desirability of tackling poverty is universally accepted, actual policies to achieve this are severely constrained by this market context, together with requirements for budget balance. The PRSPs are a good example of this. They are the main mechanism by which the World Bank, IMF and donor community have been promoting poverty reduction and engineering country 'ownership' of programmes: yet they all accept orthodox pro-market macro and meso policies, making only minor changes in resource allocation at the local level (Table 32.1).

Table 32.1 Some policy reforms contained in PRSPs[a]

Reforms	Albania	Azerbaijan	Benin	Bolivia	Burkina Faso	Cambodia	Cameroon	Chad	Ethiopia	Ghana	Guyana	Honduras	Kyrgyzstan
Economic management													
Reliance on macroeconomic stability for poverty reduction	x	x	x	x	x	x	x	x	x	x		x	x
Trade policy (tariff reduction/ export promotion)	x		x	x	x	x			x	x	x	x	x
Monetary restraint	x	x	x	x		x	x	x	x	x		x	x
Exchange rate policy	x	x	x	x	x	x	x	x	x	x	x	x	x
Fiscal restraint	x	x	x	x	x	x	x	x	x	x	x	x	x
Tax and customs reforms	x	x			x		x		x			x	x
Price control/wage policies	x	x											
User fees	x	x				x		x	x	x			x
Sectoral policies	x	x	x		x	x	x	x	x			x	x
Financial sector reform													
Financial institutions	x	x	x			x	x	x	x	x		x	x
Financial intermediation policies	x	x					x	x	x	x		x	x
Private sector development													
Privatization	x	x	x		x	x	x		x	x		x	x
Price liberalization	x	x					x						
Legal and judicial reform	x		x	x	x	x	x	x	x	x	x	x	x
Land tenure laws	x		x	x	x		x		x		x	x	x

Reforms	Malawi	Mali	Mauritania	Mozambique	Nicaragua	Niger	Rwanda	Senegal	Sri Lanka	Tajikistan	Tanzania	Uganda	Yemen	Zambia
Economic management														
Reliance on macroeconomic														
stability for poverty reduction	x	x	x	x	x	x	x	x	x	x	x	x	x	x
Trade policy (tariff reduction/														
export promotion)		x	x	x	x	x	x	x	x	x	x	x	x	x
Monetary restraint	x	x	x	x	x	x	x	x	x	x	x	x	x	x
Exchange rate policy			x	x					x	x	x	x	x	x
Fiscal restraint	x	x	x	x	x	x	x	x	x	x	x	x	x	x
Tax and customs reforms	x	x	x	x	x	x		x	x	x	x	x	x	
Price control/wage policies			x										x	
User fees			x			x			x				x	
Sectoral policies	x	x	x	x	x	x	x	x	x		x	x	x	x
Financial sector reform														
Financial institutions		x	x			x	x	x	x	x		x	x	
Financial intermediation														
policies	x	x	x	x		x	x	x	x	x	x	x	x	
Private sector development														
Privatization		x	x	x	x	x	x	x	x	x	x	x	x	x
Price liberalization		x							x	x				x
Legal and judicial reform	x	x	x	x	x	x	x	x	x	x	x	x	x	x
Land tenure laws	x	x	x	x	x	x	x	x	x	x	x	x	x	x

Note: a. The reforms also include public sector governance and management and social sector reforms, but these are not detailed here for space reasons.
Source: The full table is in Stewart and Wang (2005: 447–74).

The WTO is another global institution devoted to promoting free market resource allocations – though with notable exceptions. Trade reforms are all towards freer trade, even though progress in areas of particular interest to developing countries, especially agriculture, is slow. However, the WTO does not cover the movement of labour, and many countries are increasing restrictions on international labour mobility, particularly in relation to unskilled labour. Insofar as the WTO supports and extends intellectual property rights, this too goes against free trade and resource allocational efficiency since it prices a commodity far in excess of its marginal cost.

Multinational corporations are the other global institutions which constrain moves towards a transformation. They do so partly by putting pressure on democratic institutions, through lobbying, financing of political parties, and corrupt practices, and partly by threatening to remove their investments if a country introduces policies which might be costly for them. Crouch (2000: 2) has analyzed what he terms 'post-democracy' in developed countries, which is a system in which political outcomes stem from business pressures:

> Under this model, while elections certainly exist and can change governments, public electoral debate is a tightly controlled spectacle, managed by rival teams of professionals expert in the techniques of persuasion, and considering a small range of issue selected by those teams. The mass of citizens plays a passive quiescent, even apathetic part, responding only to the signals given them. Behind this spectacle of the electoral game politics is really shaped by private interaction between elected governments and elites which overwhelmingly represent business interests.

Crouch (*Ibid.*: 15–16) argues that the globalization of business interests (together with the fragmentation of the working population) shifts political advantage away from those 'seeking to reduce inequalities of wealth and power in favour of those wishing to return them to levels of the pre-democratic past'.[27] And, as a consequence,

> The welfare state is gradually becoming residualised as something for the deserving poor rather than a range of universal rights of citizenship; trade unions exist on the margins of society; the role of the state as policeman and incarcerator returns to prominence; the wealth gap between rich and poor grows; taxation becomes less redistributive.

Confronted by such powerful forces, can we expect the fragile new democracies of developing countries to do better? Will they move straight from pre-democracy to post-democracy, by-passing what Crouch calls 'the democratic moment'? Crouch points to the fragmentation of social classes in contemporary developed countries, which prevents unity of interests, such as obtained among the working class in Europe at earlier times.[28] Such fragmentation is also in evidence in developing countries – the interests of the agricultural sector generally differ from that of the industrial or services sectors; the landless from small and large landowners; unskilled industrial workers from skilled, professional and managerial workers; and women from men. This fragmentation is similar to that of Europe in the early industrial revolution and may explain the weakness of political parties representing working classes and progressive ideas. Moreover, it is overlaid, in a way that was much less true of Europe in the nineteenth century, by ethnic and religious divisions. Indeed, Horowitz (1985) has argued that in the many ethnically (or religiously) divided societies, political parties tend to mobilize along ethnic rather than class lines. Work at the Centre for Research on Inequality, Human Security and Ethnicy (CRISE) has confirmed the strong ethnic/religious dimensions to politics in the countries studied and the weak element of ideological class-based politics.[29]

Yet, as industrialization proceeds, we may expect a more homogeneous working-class population to emerge in many countries – as an increasing proportion of the working population are employed in the formal non-agricultural sector. More ideological and class-based political parties (and governments) may develop as institutions evolve that represent, argue for and unite such interests. Such institutions would not develop from NGOs, nor INGOs, even of an advocacy variety, nor social movements, because these tend to be single-issue organizations and to divide rather than unite different groups. In developed countries, the growth of trade unions spearheaded such a movement (and was largely responsible for the Great Transformation). In contemporary developing countries, however, trade unions tend to be weak and divided, co-opted by governments and covering only a minority of workers, undermined wherever possible by the IFIs, MNCs and the elite,[30] and lacking leadership because the most intelligent and entrepreneurial people move up the educational ladder and away from working-class occupations. Twenty-first century technology requires a greater variety of skills and generates high and growing wage differentials between the skilled and unskilled which also reduces the unity of purpose of employees. To the extent that 'post-Fordism' prevails, it lends itself to post-democracy.

Nonetheless, there are some signs that workers are acquiring some power in the more developed developing countries; that political parties are becoming more ideological; and that where the progressive parties do gain political power, moves occur in the direction of a transformation – South Korea and Brazil are examples. But where governments broadly representing alternative perspectives do emerge, their achievements are heavily circumscribed by the international context; as can be seen in the developments in these two countries, and elsewhere, for example, in India, South Africa and Venezuela. Like developed countries today, the transformatory achievements of such governments seem likely to be somewhat marginal – a small transformation, not a great one. Moreover, the tragedy is that alternative politics only seem to gain ground at late stages of development (as in Europe) and not in the poorer countries when the economy's operations are most harsh and such a change is most needed.

Devastating events can be another source of transformation. In Europe it was the Great Depression and the Second World War. Today environmental disasters most likely eventually force a pullback. The environmental shortcomings of the unregulated market (already pointed to by Polanyi) in time will affect the world's elite as well as the poor and may therefore eventually – probably too late to offset the worst consequences of global warming – be a trigger for major transformatory action.

Conclusion

This chapter has explored whether Polanyi's arguments – put forward in 1944 with respect to Europe – apply to contemporary developing countries. Polanyi showed how the harsh consequences of the unregulated market led to a counter-movement (a Great Transformation) to regulate and humanize the market, so that society controlled the market rather than vice-versa. This control over the market lasted about 40 years, but then a counter-revolution set in, once more giving a central role to the market throughout the world and again leading to inequality and insecurity, along with accelerated growth in some places but stagnation in others. This reflected the 'double movement' that Polanyi analyzed – the swing of the pendulum that occurs as the adverse consequences of movement in one direction lead to political reaction and consequently a reversal of the previous position. In developed countries, the renewed role for the market was accompanied by quite effective regulation and measures of social protection, but this has not been the case in most developing countries. In developing countries especially, therefore, the harsh consequences of the market make a new great transformation desirable, but the possibilities of change are severely constrained by global forces, especially international institutions that were not present in the first Great Transformation – the IFIs, the WTO and the huge powers of MNCs – which pose severe constraints even on democratic politics. For developed and developing countries alike, the environmental consequences of the global market necessitate a major turn around. Yet here too, powerful business interests are preventing any serious change.

This chapter has covered a huge amount of ground rather superficially. Hence it represents a research agenda, rather than a finished product. Certain areas seem particularly in need of further research:

- What is the strength of movements for political change in particular countries around the world?
- Are the trade unions as weak as depicted here? And ideological parties broadly absent?
- Are there cases where the majority workers in the informal and agricultural sector have succeeded in uniting and advancing their interests by so doing?
- How extensive and effective is the impact of the various CSR initiatives?
- Can single-issue movements achieve major change?
- Can institutions for change be strengthened by international unity?
- Have some countries managed to break the constraints apparently imposed by the global institutions and the global economy, and secure changes towards a transformation?

Notes

I am grateful to Graham Brown, Yvan Guichaoua and F.G. Block for comments on an earlier version of this study.

1. All page references to Polanyi refer to the 1944 book.
2. He quotes Aristotle as arguing that production for gain was not 'natural to man', although the fact that Aristotle found it necessary to state this suggests that production for gain was to some extent prevalent in his time.
3. Workers' combinations developed, nonetheless, and the Act was repealed in 1824 in the belief that if legalized they would be less threatening. In fact, they burgeoned and in 1825 a new Combination Act was enacted which permitted trade unions to form but limited their right to strike (Briggs 1979: 212).
4. By the Prescriptions Act, the Inheritance Act, the Fines and Recovery Act, the Real Property Act and the general Enclosures Act of 1801, as well as subsequent legislation.
5. 'The economic function is but one of many vital functions of land. It invests man's life with stability; it is the site of his habituation; it is a condition of his physical safety; it is the landscape and the seasons' (Polanyi 1944: 187).
6. *Jeremy Bentham's Economic Writings* (1952–54) critical edition based on his printed works and unprinted manuscripts, by W. Stark. Published for the Royal Economic Society, Allen & Unwin, London.
7. Engels (1845) was among the first to record the conditions of the English working class in detail. Later in the nineteenth century, Rowntree (1901) started his pioneering investigation into poverty. Among many more recent accounts see, for example, Thompson (1964); Brown (1990); Huck (1995).
8. He treated the topic more systematically in Polanyi (1957).
9. Inaugural Address, 20 January 1949, Washington, DC.
10. For example, Fei and Ranis, by no means anti-market economists, stated that 'The need for development planning is well recognised' (Fei and Ranis 1964: 199).
11. The ILO summarized the position, 'It has become increasingly evident ... that rapid growth at the national level does not automatically reduce poverty or inequality or provide sufficient productive employment' (ILO 1976: 15).
12. For evidence of the advance of these policies in Latin America and Africa see, for example, Williamson (1990); World Bank and UNDP (1989); Dean *et al.* (1994).
13. It is often pointed out that globalization was high pre-First World War, fell after the war and then resumed its upward growth. For example, foreign assets over GDP were estimated at 18.6 per cent in 1900, falling to 4.9 per cent in 1945 and rising to 17.7 per cent in 1980. However, in 1870 it was only 6.9 per cent and by 1995, the ratio had risen to 56.8 per cent, which supports the view that global forces were much more important towards the end of the twentieth century than in the mid-nineteenth century (data from Crafts 2000).
14. There is a huge literature on the consequences of marketization and globalization, with highly divergent opinions. This is reflected in the titles of recent works if we take globalization as broadly synonymous with pro-market reforms. On the one hand, Martin Wolf (2004) has written *Why Globalization Works*, described by the *Economist* as 'the definitive treatment of the subject', while Jagdish Bhagwati (2004) has written a very similar book entitled *In Defence of Globalization*. In contrast, Joe Stiglitz's (2002) book on the same subject is entitled *Globalization and its Discontents*, while George Soros (himself a major actor in advancing globalization) has produced a book entitled *The Crisis of Global Capitalism: Open Society Endangered* (1998).
15. 'Liberal writers like Spencer (1940), Sumner (1963), von Mises (1978) and Lippmann (1938), offer an account of the double movement substantially similar to our own, but they put an entirely different interpretation on it. In their view all protectionism was a mistake due to impatience, greed and short-sightedness, *but for which the market would have resolved its difficulties*' (Polanyi 1944: 148, italics added).

16. These too were predicted by Polanyi (1944: 193), who argued that the consequences of the unregulated market might extend to 'even the climate of the country which might suffer from the denudation of forests, from erosions and dust bowls, all of which ultimately depend on the factor land, yet none of which respond to the supply and demand mechanism of the market'.
17. This is the categorization adopted by Heyer *et al.* (2002).
18. Pro bono type organizations were not included.
19. See, for example, the activities recorded in a survey of NGOs in Uganda; Barr *et al.* (2005).
20. There are a few well-known exceptions; for example total microcredit provision in Bangladesh is estimated to extend to over 13 million people; the health and nutrition programmes of BRAC in Bangladesh are estimated to cover over 30 million people. But even these appear to have a rather small impact on poverty, as indicated by the so-called macro–micro paradox of Bangladesh – that despite such extensive and effective NGOs, poverty remains high (White 1992).
21. See Greenwood *et al.* (2002); Frederickson (1980).
22. Kaldor *et al.* (2004).
23. Estimate from D. Carvajal, 'Third world gets help to help itself', *International Herald Tribune*, 7 December 2005.
24. For example Oxfam's trade reports. Jubilee 2000's campaign for debt relief.
25. The movement has generated 'codes of conduct, improvements in occupational health and safety, environmental management systems, social and environmental reporting, support for community projects and philanthropy' (Utting 2004: 1); see also IDS (2005).
26. Decision of the Executive Board in 1974 when establishing the extended fund facility (EFF) quoted by IMF (2001: 3).
27. Similar arguments are advanced by Foot (2005) who goes further than Crouch, stating that 'The system of society favoured by the rich across the world, capitalism, is in its essence and in its daily dealing with human beings wholly hostile to democracy. In all its manifestations it is hierarchical and bureaucratic' (p. 428). 'Capitalism and democracy are always in conflict and the history of all capitalist states that have conceded universal suffrage has been, in part, a history of that conflict' (p. 429). See also Brittan (1975), who identified a clash between market capitalism and liberal democracy and predicted the victory of the former over the latter.
28. 'Nevertheless, when every caution has been made, the outstanding fact of the period between 1790 and 1830 is the formation of the "working-class". This is revealed, first in the growth of class consciousness: the consciousness of an identity of interests as between all these diverse groups of working people and as against the interests of all other classes. And second in the growth of corresponding forms of political and industrial organization. By 1932 there were strongly based and self-conscious working-class institutions – trade unions, friendly societies, educational and religious movements, political organizations, periodicals – working-class intellectual traditions, working-class community patterns, and a working-class structure of feeling' (Thompson 1964: 168, 212–3).
29. See, for example, Akindes (2006); Brown (2005); Caumartin (2006).
30. For example, in the early 1990s the Malaysian government indicated that it would not allow the unionization of the electronics sector because it would frighten foreign investors (since then, in-house unions have been allowed but still no sector-wide union); Brown (2004); cites *Business Times*, 4 September 1992 'Some investors against nationwide union'.

References

Abdelrahman, M. (2004) *Civil Society Exposed: The Politics of NGOs in Egypt*, London: Tauris Academic Studies.

Akindes, F. (2006) 'Mobilization of Identity, Horizontal Inequality and Sociohistory of Political Violence in Côte d'Ivoire', *CRISE Working Paper* 4, Oxford: Centre for Research on Inequality, Human Security and Ethnicity.

ASH (Action on Smoking and Health) (2002) 'British American Tobacco – The Other Report to Society', www.ash.org.uk/html/conduct/html/reporttosociety

Barr, A., M. Fafchamps and T. Owens (2005) 'The Governance of Non-Governmental Organizations in Uganda', *World Development*, 33, 4: 657–79.

Bhagwati, J. (2004) *In Defence of Globalization*, Oxford: Oxford University Press.

Boltho, A. and G. Toniolo (1999) 'The Assessment: The Twentieth Century Achievements, Failures, Lessons', *Oxford Review of Economic Policy*, 15, 4: 1–17.

Briggs, A. (1979) *The Age of Improvement: 1783–1867*, London: Longman.

Brittan, S. (1975) 'The Economic Contradictions of Democracy', *British Journal of Political Science*, 5, 2: 129–59.

Brown, J.C. (1990) 'The Condition of England and the Standard of Living of Cotton Textile Workers in the Northwest, 1906–1850', *Journal of Economic History*, 50, 3: 591–614.

Brown, G. (2004) 'Civil Society and Social Movements in an Ethnically Divided Society: The Case of Malaysia, 1981–2001', PhD thesis, Nottingham University.

Brown, G. (2005) 'The Formation and Management of Political Identities: Indonesia and Malaysia Compared', *CRISE Working Paper* 10, Oxford: Centre for Research on Inequality, Human Security and Ethnicity.

Butler, C. (2000) 'Inequality, Global Change and the Sustainability of Civilisation', *Global Change and Human Health*, 1, 2: 156–72.

Caumartin, C. (2006) 'Racism, Violence and Inequalities: An Overview of the Guatemalan Case', *CRISE Working Paper* 11, Oxford: Centre for Research on Inequality, Human Security and Ethnicity.

Cornia, G.A. (ed.) (2004) *Inequality, Growth, and Poverty in an Era of Liberalization and Globalization*, Oxford and New York: Oxford University Press for UNU-WIDER.

Crafts, N. (2000) 'Globalization and Growth in the Twentieth Century', *IMF Working Paper 00/44*, Washington, DC: IMF.

Crouch, C. (2000) *Coping With Post-Democracy*, London: Fabian Society.

Dean, J., S. Desai and J. Riedel (1994) 'Trade Policy Reform in Developing Countries Since 1985: A Review of the Evidence', *World Bank Discussion Paper* 267, Washington, DC: World Bank.

de Tocqueville, A. (1966) *The Ancient Regime and the French Revolution*, London: Collins Fontana.

Engels, F. (1920) *The Condition of the Working-Class in England in 1844*, London: Allen.

Esman, M.J. and N.T. Uphoff (1984) *Local Organizations: Intermediaries in Rural Development*, Ithaca: Cornell University Press.

Fei, J.C.H. and G. Ranis (1964) *Development of the Labor Surplus Economy: Theory and Policy*, Homewood, IL: Irwin.

Femia, J. (2001) *Against the Masses: Varieties of Anti-Democratic Thought Since the French Revolution*, Oxford: Oxford University Press.

Foot, P. (2005) *How it Was Won: And How it Was Undermined*, London: Penguin Viking.

Frederickson, H.G. (1980) *New Public Administration*, Tuscaloosa, AL: University of Alabama Press.

Gramsci, A. (1971) *Selections from the Prison Notebooks of Antonio Gramsci*, edited and translated by Q. Hoare and G. Nowell-Smith, London: Lawrence & Wishart.

Greenwood, J.R., D.J. Wilson and R. Pyper (2002) *New Public Administration in Britain*, London: Routledge.

Heyer, J., F. Stewart and R. Thorp (2002) *Group Behaviour and Development: Is the Market Destroying Co-operation?*, Oxford: Oxford University Press for UNU-WIDER.

Hirst, P. (1997) 'The Global Economy: Myths and Realities', *International Affairs*, 73, 3: 409–25.

Horowitz, D. (1985) *Ethnic Groups in Conflict*, Berkeley: University of California Press.

Huck, P. (1995) 'Infant Morality and Living Standards of English Workers during the Industrial Revolution', *Journal of Economic History*, 55, 3: 528–50.

IDS (2005) *ID21 Insights* 54, 'Making Business Work for Development: Rethinking Corporate Social Responsibility', Brighton: Institute of Development Studies, University of Sussex.

ILO (1976) *Employment, Growth and Basic Needs: A One-World Problem*, Geneva: International Labour Organisation.

IMF (2001) 'Structural Conditionality in Fund-Supported Programs', prepared by the Policy Development and Review Department, http://www.imf.org/external/np/pdr/cond/2001/eng/struct/index.htm

Kaldor, M., H.K. Anheier and M. Glasius (2004) *Global Civil Society 2004/5*, London: Sage.

Killick, T. (1983) 'Development Planning in Africa: Experiences, Weaknesses and Prescriptions', *Development Policy Review*.

Lippmann, W. (1938) *The Good Society*, London: Allen and Unwin.

Lorgen, C. (2002) 'The Case of Indigenous NGOs in Uganda's Health Sector', in J. Heyer, F. Stewart and R. Thorp (eds), *Group Behaviour and Development*, Oxford: Oxford University Press for UNU-WIDER.

Mawdsley, E., J. Townsend, G. Porter and P. Oakley (2002) *Knowledge, Power and Development Agendas: NGOs North and South*, Oxford: Intrac.

Michael, S. (2004) *Undermining Development: The Absence of Power Among Local NGOs in Africa*, Abingdon and Bloomington, IN: James Currey and Indiana University Press.

Polanyi, K. (1944) *The Great Transformation: The Political and Economic Origins of Our Times*, Boston, MA: Beacon Press.

Polanyi, K. (1957) *Trade and Market in the Early Empires; Economies in History and Theory*, Glencoe, IL: Free Press.

Pongsapich, A. (1998) 'The Non-Profit Sector in Thailand', in H. Anheier and L. Salamon (eds), *The Non-Profit Sector in the Developing World*, Manchester: Manchester University Press.

Rowntree, B.S. (1901) *Poverty: A Study of Town Life*, London: Macmillan.

Salamon, L. and H. Anheier (1999) 'The Third World's Third Sector in Comparative Perspective', in D. Lewis (ed.), *International Perspectives on Voluntary Action*, London: Earthscan.

Sen, S. (1998) 'The Non-Profit Sector in India', in H. Anheier and L. Salamon (eds), *The Non-Profit Sector in the Developing World*, Manchester: Manchester University Press.

Silva Leander, S. (2005) 'Democracy, Development and Inequality; Reflections on a Chilean Puzzle', PhD thesis, Oxford University.

Soros, G. (1998) *The Crisis of Global Capitalism: Open Society Endangered*, London and New York: Little Brown.

Spencer, H. (1940) *The Man versus the State*, Caldwell, ID: Caxton.

Stewart, F. and M. Wang (2005) 'Poverty Reduction Strategy Papers Within the Human Rights Perspective', P. Alston and M. Robinson (eds), *Human Rights and Development*, Oxford: Oxford University Press.

Stiglitz, J. (2002) *Globalization and its Discontents*, New York: W.W. Norton & Co.

Sumner, W.G. (1963) *Social Darwinism: Selected Essays of William Graham Sumner*, Englewood Cliffs, NJ: Prentice Hall.

Thompson, E.P. (1964) *The Making of the English Working-Class*, New York: Pantheon Books.

Thorp, R., F. Stewart and A. Heyer (2005) 'When and How Far is Group Formation a Route Out of Chronic Poverty?', *World Development*, 33, 6: 907–20.

UNDP (United Nations Development Programme) (various years) *Human Development Report*, New York: Oxford University Press for UNDP.

UNRISD (2005) 'Ethnic Inequalities and Public Sector Governance', report of the UNRISD-Latvian Ministry of Social Integration-UNDP Joint International Conference, 25–7 March 2004, Riga.

Utting, P. (2004) 'Corporate Social Responsibility and Business Regulation', *UNRISD Research and Policy Brief* 1, Geneva: UNRISD.

von Mises, L. (1978) *Liberalism: A Socio-economic Exposition*, Kansas City: Sheed Andrews and McMeel.

White, S. (1992) *Arguing with Crocodiles: Gender and Class in Bangladesh*, London: Zed Books.

Williamson, J. (1990) *The Progress of Policy Reform in Latin America*, Washington, DC: Institute for International Economics.

Wolf, M. (2004) *Why Globalization Works*, New Haven CT, and London: Yale University Press.

World Bank (2005) 'World Bank Conditionality Review: Conditionality and Policy-Based Lending', http:sitereources.worldbank.org/projects/resources/conditionalityTrends Presentation12705. pdf

World Bank and UNDP (1989) *Africa's Adjustment and Growth in the 1980s*, Washington, DC: World Bank.

33
Absorptive Capacity and Achieving the MDGs

François Bourguignon and Mark Sundberg

Introduction

The recent discussion about the need to scale-up official development assistance (ODA) in order to make significant progress towards the MDGs has highlighted the concept of 'absorptive capacity'. On one side are advocates of a general scaling up who rely on calculations of the amount of additional annual aid per capita needed in the next ten years to reach the MDGs. On the other side are advocates of 'aid effectiveness' cautioning against too much aid being delivered beyond the actual 'absorptive capacity' of a country. Absorptive capacity refers loosely to the ability to use additional aid without pronounced inefficiency of public spending and without induced adverse effects, for instance the 'Dutch Disease', or the crowding out of domestic saving.[1]

In 2005 a decision was taken by the international development community to scale-up aid, the objective being to roughly double the volume of development assistance to Africa by 2010, and increase aid to other countries by around US$25 billion annually. This is an important and overdue decision, but it has not made the issue of 'absorptive capacity' less relevant. Should this aid materialize as promised, care will need to be taken to ensure that it is properly used by recipient countries in order to maximize its efficient use towards attaining the MDGs. This will require managing additional aid-financed public spending and addressing absorptive capacity at a given point of time and, at the same time, ensuring that this absorptive capacity progressively strengthens to be commensurate with available aid flows in order to reach the MDGs. Absorptive capacity has indeed much to do with the timing and sequencing of ODA disbursements. Rapid scaling up of assistance in a country with very limited capacity to train and hire skilled labour, build new infrastructure, or manage large-scale public programmes may result in bottlenecks that result in rising unit costs, and falling quality of service delivery. In extreme cases it could conceivably lead to impaired growth potential with adverse medium-term consequences, for example if country competitiveness is undermined or public revenue efforts are adversely impacted.

To date, there has been very little systematic effort either to define the key drivers of absorptive capacity or to measure country ability to absorb scaled up foreign assistance. Empirical assessment must be country-specific since countries differ widely in their structural and institutional characteristics, and because absorptive capacity is essentially a dynamic concept that depends on the entire time path of an economy. Binding limitations today may be addressed over time through appropriate planning and investment strategies. In some instances the constraints to absorptive capacity may indeed be quite limiting, and indicate that a credible programme to fully reach the MDGs by 2015 is unlikely. This is particularly true in unstable or fragile stages, and indicates that alternative delivery tools may be needed, and that more modest targets are to be envisaged. In other countries, given an adequate strategic framework and sufficient external assistance, absorptive capacity may not be a barrier to rapid scaling up of assistance.

This chapter addresses absorptive capacity in low-income countries from both a theoretical and empirical perspective. It first seeks to clarify what is meant in economic terms by 'aid effectiveness' and 'absorptive capacity', arguing that there are several potentially binding constraints to absorptive capacity that pose risks in any economy at any point of time for scaling assistance up too rapidly. The chapter then briefly presents a framework for undertaking country-specific analysis and taking explicitly into account absorptive capacity. This framework relates the macroeconomic environment and economic growth on the one hand, and sector-specific micro-constraints affecting implementation of the social MDGs on the other. It presents the rudimentary elements of the modelling framework used here to examine absorptive capacity and illustrates the framework with a simple application to the case of Ethiopia. The chapter concludes with a brief discussion of the main findings and implications for designing MDG-based assistance strategies consistent with absorptive capacity and its dynamics.

Definition and role of absorptive capacity

Concern is often raised about the ability of low-income countries to absorb large amounts of aid due to insufficient structural and institutional capacity. The literature on aid and growth usually considers that a country has reached its *absorptive capacity limit* for foreign aid when the rate of return on further increments of aid falls to some minimum acceptable level (for example, see Radelet 2003: 136).[2] There is ample evidence that many low-income countries suffer from capacity constraints and that the potential benefits from additional aid may often be constrained by weak capacity, frequently failing to meet intended objectives. Several empirical cross-country studies (Collier and Dollar 2002; Hansen and Tarp 2001; Radelet *et al.* 2004) show that after a certain level additional aid to GDP has little effect on growth. This 'saturation point' is a function of different proxies for absorptive capacity arising from macroeconomic, institutional, infrastructure, human capital, or sociocultural constraints (World Bank 2004). There has been an extensive literature in particular on the policy environment, which has emphasized that countries with 'good policies and institutions' can absorb larger amounts of aid before diminishing returns set in.[3] In countries with low capacity the saturation point arrives much sooner, and additional amounts of aid are unlikely to be very productive.

This conclusion is intuitive and appealing, even though it is derived from cross-country analysis which is of little help when examining the case of a particular country. Moreover, the literature is not very clear on the causes of the complex phenomenon of declining returns. In effect, there is little insight in the literature provided from country-specific examples of capacity constraints and when or how they inhibit absorptive capacity and aid effectiveness. To clarify concepts, it is helpful to distinguish between these broad factors affecting aid effectiveness over time, and absorptive capacity at a given point in time. Figure 33.1 helps define formally the related concepts of aid effectiveness and that of absorptive capacity. 'Aid effectiveness' refers to the total economic and social return to aid at a given point in time.

The return to aid has many dimensions. In Figure 33.1 it is associated with the rate of growth of GDP. But other dimensions, for instance poverty, the various other MDGs, or even summary measures of the welfare effects of aid, could have been used. This return will vary depending on several initial conditions – institutions, endowments, policy environment, etc. – working in isolation or together. It is an increasing function of the amount of aid that is made available. Aid effectiveness is the height of this 'return to aid' curve. It represents 'what aid can buy' in the recipient economy at a given level of aid and given existing physical and institutional constraints. 'Absorptive capacity' refers to the *marginal rate of return* to aid, which is reasonably taken to decline as the amount of aid increases.[4] At a given point in time, the physical capacity of the economy to produce new infrastructure is limited. At some stage, providing more aid to expand infrastructure will result in less and less new infrastructure being installed and more and more distortions in the economy coming from the increase in aggregate demand. Absorptive capacity sets limits on the productive potential of aid, and as constraints become binding the returns to additional aid falls – or in other words, the unit cost of additional public goods and services, will rise. This distinction between aid effectiveness and absorption capacity is depicted in Figure 33.1.

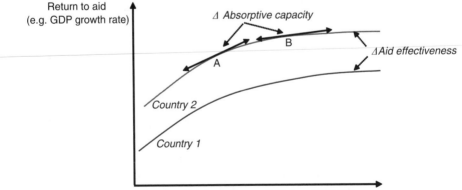

Figure 33.1   Aid effectiveness and absorptive capacity

Aid effectiveness can be characterized as the difference between the top and bottom curves, representing the return to aid in two different countries. Country 2 is able to utilize aid more effectively than Country 1 at any given level of aid (relative to the size of its economy) due to a combination of endowments, institutions and policies.

'Capacity' on the other hand, refers to the declining return to aid in each country as the total amount of aid is increased, that is the slope of the return to aid curve. As constraints on capacity become binding – skilled labour costs rise, physical infrastructure cannot meet demands, administration is overwhelmed – the *incremental* returns to aid fall. The limit of absorptive capacity is reached when the marginal rate of return falls below some minimal acceptable level. This may be at a point such as B, where a relatively low rate of return is still considered acceptable, or it may be at a point like A, representing a higher positive marginal rate of return relative to some opportunity cost of funds. In countries with lower overall aid effectiveness, such as Country 1, the total returns to aid will be lower. However, the absorptive capacity – the marginal return for a given aid/GDP ratio given by the slope of the curve – may be higher or lower than in the country with higher aid effectiveness. The two curves showing the total returns to aid can also be thought of as the same country at two points in time. This underscores the fact that aid effectiveness and absorptive capacity are dynamic processes linked to the underlying forces of economic development and change over time. Development targets which today are difficult to reach at any level of aid due to absorptive capacity constraints, may be possible to reach over time as capacity is built and the returns to aid increase.

The adoption of international development goals, the MDGs, affects the debate over intertemporal aid allocation in some basic ways. First, the MDGs are targets that have been adopted for all low-income countries, with differing levels of aid effectiveness. Allocating aid to only those countries with the highest level of aid effectiveness may help to meet *global* targets, but would not advance the MDG cause in countries with lower aid effectiveness and deeper development challenges. Second, the MDG targets are clearly defined by their end-point in 2015. This concretely raises the question of how to allocate resources optimally to reach these targets over the coming decade.

Several potential constraints to expanding service delivery and accelerating growth help determine the shape of the returns to aid curve – both its position and its shape. There are three broad categories: quantitative, macroeconomic and institutional:

- *Quantitative* constraints refer to key inputs to production of the MDGs, such as skilled workers (teachers, healthcare workers), required for delivery of core MDG-related services. Scarcity of physical capital and infrastructure (schools, roads, power, etc.) are also important factors in this category.
- *Macroeconomic* constraints refer to the effects of aid flows on the economy – when they are fully absorbed and spent. In particular, too much aid inflow is likely to distort domestic prices, in favour of non-tradable goods, assuming a limited capacity of that sector to respond to increased demand. This is turn

reduces the purchasing power of aid in terms of domestic goods and crowds out domestic resources from their initial use. It may also lower the competitiveness of the economy on foreign markets. Of course, central banks may try to mitigate these effects. Also, public investment may be used to unlock productivity growth and may neutralize adverse effects of aid on competitiveness. But this can only be done progressively, and absorptive capacity will be increase only after some time.

- *Institutional* constraints refer to the governance environment broadly, both in terms of narrow resource management capacities (budget management, accounting, procurement, etc.), checks and balances institutions affecting the overall investment climate (regulatory, judicial, legislative) and the quality of service delivery to frontline users. The institutional and governance environment determines the extent to which resource leakage and corruption divert resources as aid is scaled up.

A general framework for measuring absorptive capacity

Identifying the constraints for scaling up aid with a view at reaching the MDGs is complex and requires an analytic framework that can capture the main macroeconomic and microeconomic aspects surrounding attainment of the MDGs. This framework must be dynamic so as to take into account possible changes in absorptive capacity, and in particular the effects of public investment and capacity building, the financial and non-financial requirements to reach the MDGs, and the whole path of public services and outcomes consistent with these goals. There presumably are many different time paths that lead to the MDGs at a given time horizon. Comparing them is crucial to determine the least cost in terms of both domestic and foreign resources to reach that goal. This requires in particular considering relevant opportunity costs of all domestic resources being used and policies being implemented. In standard project cost-benefit analysis this is relatively straightforward, but in the case of economy-wide interventions with multiple objectives, there are several complications that make measurement difficult.

One such issue is the cross-effects of investment in one MDG-related activity on the whole economy and other MDG outcomes. For instance, investment in water and sanitation (MDG7) can quickly improve health outcomes; investment in school and toilet facilities for girls and training female staff can improve gender balance and primary completion rates; improved roads and connectivity will reduce unit costs of supplying other public services, particularly to remote regions.[5] Identifying an optimal path will therefore depend on identifying these cross-effects and ensuring appropriate sequencing of investments. Another consideration is constraints from the demand side. If demand for public services is weak, due to poor-quality services, uncertainty over returns, sociocultural factors (such as a gender bias against girls), or costly tradeoffs (such as the opportunity costs of education which arise from forgone child incomes), then there will be limits on public service uptake.

Comparing different paths leading to the MDGs over time requires some common measure of the benefits generated. There is no clear way to measure social welfare in the context of the MDGs. This would require aggregating across the different MDG targets (primary completion, maternal health, access to sanitation, poverty incidence, etc.) whereas an important feature of the MDGs is precisely the non-substitution view behind such a multidimensional objective. It is not clear how to compare one path with, for example, better education outcomes at the beginning of the period under analysis but worse sanitation outcomes with its converse, nor what appropriate discount rates should apply to social returns.

Approaching these complex issues requires a framework which incorporates the major productive assets in the economy, production processes both in the private and public sector, and policy instruments. Figure 33.2 illustrates the general architecture of such an integrated approach. The schema of interconnected boxes shows the core elements that need to be integrated conceptually and analytically. Starting from the left of Figure 33.2, the key factors that determine the state of the economy during a unit period and are inherited from the past are identified: (i) *physical* assets, not only plants and equipment, but MDG capital – schools, clinics, etc.; (ii) *human* assets, including labour by skills, possibly in specific occupations – nurses, doctors, etc.; (iii) *environmental* assets including clean water and sanitation (MDG7); (iv) *governance* assets, including institutions, and accountability mechanisms relevant to the efficiency of service delivery; and finally (v) intermediate inputs.

The middle boxes in Figure 33.2 represent the general equilibrium of the economy during the current period. The outcome of economic activity is represented by levels of output (GDP) including in the public sector, and the distribution of income within the population. These outcomes jointly determine results on the MDG front, both for income MDG (i.e. poverty) and non-income goals. Of course, the equilibrium of the economy is also governed by the macroeconomic framework

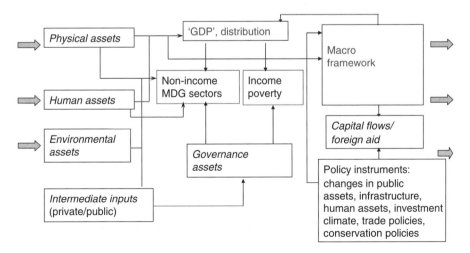

Figure 33.2 The general architecture of an integrative approach

and by public policies, which are shown on the right side, and represent the key policy space that influences outcomes on the MDG and non-MDG fronts. At the same time policies and the equilibrium of the economy determine the changes taking place in the various assets, appearing on the left-hand side of the diagram. This framework not only informs on the current state of the economy but also on its dynamics through these changes; this is the meaning of the arrows at both the right and left side of the chart.

Having such an analytic tool that integrates the key elements of assets, production and policy can help guide policy and prioritize across alternative interventions. Consider some simple examples. If as a result of additional aid inflows a country reallocates spending towards providing public services to achieve the MDGs, this will clearly have implications for other public services and for the rest of the economy. Shifting domestic resources towards the social sectors will impact on available resources in the private sector or in the public sector for infrastructure investment, administration, or for operations and maintenance of public assets. Likewise, public hiring of skilled labour to fill critical vacancies in social sectors leads to reducing labour from other activities, including the private sector, and will raise real wages and possibly lower private growth and income poverty reduction.

Some of these issues are very difficult to address in empirical work, while others can be approximated to generate insights into the main policy challenges. To understand these issues more concretely and clarify their relevance, the previous general framework must be made capable of taking country-specific context and constraints into account. The next section briefly sets out a modelling framework to examine MDG country targets.

A model for simulating MDG-oriented policies and measuring absorptive capacity

MAMS (for 'Maquette for MDG Simulation') is a model built along the preceding lines with a focus on the capacity constraints and tradeoffs to achieve the MDGs. MAMS is a dynamic computable general equilibrium (CGE) model, the main originality of which is to incorporate a module that covers those MDGs most amenable to economic modelling: poverty, health, education, water and sanitation. Unlike many other CGE models, MAMS thus relies on a thorough representation of the allocation and the outcome of public spending. As noted in the Introduction, the rationale for the use of a model of this type is that the pursuit of MDG strategies has strong interactions with the whole economy via markets for foreign exchange, factors (especially labour), goods and services, with feedback effects that may significantly alter the findings of more narrow sectoral analyses. For example, the amount of real health or education services that a dollar in aid can purchase may change significantly in light of changes in exchange rates, prices and wages whereas the latter may significantly affect the rate of growth of the economy and the rate of poverty reduction. In addition, existing relationships between different MDGs (for example, health and education) may influence the expansion in real services that is required – improvements in water and sanitation may reduce the expansion in health services that is required to reach health MDGs.

In the application described in the following section, the model is applied to an Ethiopian database and solved for the period 2002–15.[6] More specifically, building on the recent literature and sector studies on health and education outcomes, MAMS considers the following MDGs: (MDG1) halving, between 1990 and 2015, the headcount poverty rate; (MDG2) achieve universal primary education (100 per cent completion rate by 2015); (MDG4) reducing by two-thirds the under-five mortality rate (U5MR) by 2015; (MDG5) reducing by three-quarters the maternal mortality rate; and (MDG7) reducing by half the number of people without access to safe water and basic sanitation. The model has relatively detailed treatment of government activities related to these MDGs. Government consumption, investment and capital stocks are disaggregated by function into three education sectors (primary, secondary, tertiary), three health sectors, one sector for water and sanitation, public infrastructure and other government activities. The major government revenue sources are taxes (direct and indirect), foreign borrowing and foreign grants. The non-government economy is represented by a single activity. The primary factors of production are divided into public capital, private capital and three types of labour (unskilled, skilled and highly skilled). GDP growth is a function of growth in the stocks of labour and capital and productivity growth. The composition and overall growth of the labour force depends on the evolution of the education sector, whereas capital stock growth depends on investments. Productivity growth is also endogenous and is represented by the effects of changes in the stock of public capital in infrastructure on private production.

The core MDG module specifies how changes in the different MDG indicators are determined. It is parameterized on the basis of detailed sector studies on Ethiopia. In the module the government has an annual primary education budget covering teacher salaries, recurrent operations and maintenance costs, and capital investment (for example, in new classrooms). Recurrent expenditures and the capital stock in primary education together determine the supply side.[7] Demand for primary schooling and pupil behaviour – the population share that enrols in the first grade, graduation shares among the enrolled and the shares of the graduates that choose to continue to the next grade – depend on the quality of education (pupil–teacher and pupil–capital ratios), income incentives (using current wages as a proxy, the expected relative income gain from climbing one step on the salary ladder), the U5MR (a proxy for the health status of the school population), household consumption per capita and the level of public infrastructure services – proxying for roads and ease of access to schools. Supply and demand equilibrate through the number of pupils in the educational system and the quality of education. With fixed supply capacity, more demand means more children enrolled in primary and a decline in quality, which in turn reduces the excess demand. This specification of sector demand and supply also captures lags between educational investment and outcomes, which is one strength of the approach. Based on sector studies, the lags between increased enrolments and outcomes at different education levels are related to the number of years required for completion, and actual completion rates.

The specification of health services draws on a World Bank health sector strategy report for Ethiopia. It also relies on a supply–demand framework. Improvement in U5MR and maternal mortality rates (MDG4 and MDG5) are determined by the level of health services per capita (public and private services), per capita consumption, the population shares with access to improved water and sanitation services (MDG7) and infrastructure in general – for example, the role of rural roads in improving health outcomes with given healthcare supply. The package of health services that achieves MDG4 and MDG5 also includes HIV/AIDS prevention services sufficient to halt its spread (part of MDG6). For water and sanitation, the population shares with access to improved services are modelled as functions of per capita household consumption and provision of government water and sanitation services.

The provision of the additional government services needed to reach the MDGs clearly requires additional resources – capital, labour and intermediate inputs – that become unavailable to the rest of the economy. The effects of a programme depend on how it is financed – from foreign sources, domestic taxes (which reduce consumption), or domestic borrowing (which crowds out private investment). Even with 100 per cent foreign grant financing for additional services, which minimizes domestic resource costs, the rest of the economy is affected through two main channels – labour markets and relative prices. At one point of time, expanding provision of health or education services increases demand for teachers and doctors, reducing the number of skilled workers available in other sectors and therefore the output in those sectors. Increased school enrolment also reduces the size of the overall labour force (since it removes a larger part of the school-age population from the labour force), though in the medium run it adds to the share of skilled labour in the labour force.

Two forces drive changes in relative commodity prices. First, domestic demand switches towards MDG-related government services with impacts on production costs and prices throughout the economy. Second, increased aid flows lead to an appreciation of the real exchange rate, manifested in increased prices of non-traded relative to traded outputs. These manifestations of the Dutch Disease can bring about long-lasting changes in the structure of production, which is diverted from exports and competition with imports.

The limitations on absorptive capacity are captured through three main channels: the two channels just mentioned, through labour market and through changes in the real exchange rate (relative price of the domestic good and international prices); a third channel through potential infrastructure bottlenecks, particularly in transport and energy. Large investments in education services, for example, will tend to reduce further absorptive capacity as skilled labour is diverted to education, as the relative price of non-tradables rises (for example, real wages are bid up reflecting the Dutch Disease effect) and as infrastructure bottlenecks reduce the efficiency of public service delivery. Moreover, the impact will not be limited to the education sector but affects costs throughout the economy, including other public services and the private sector. Policy-makers thus face important tradeoffs: increased investment in public service delivery is essential for improved MDG outcomes, but beyond some point the unit costs begin to rise, along with indirect costs to other sectors. The challenge is to keep costs down while also targeting social outcomes over time. Building absorptive capacity is clearly a central element to this process.

There are also important complementarities across spending on different MDGs, in our modelling framework represented by cross-elasticities, where progress for one MDG may contribute to progress for other MDGs. For example, progress in the provision of improved water and sanitation services has a positive impact on health outcomes. In addition, in education the provision of education services (primary, secondary and higher) helps to expand the skilled workforce needed to both increase productivity of the private sector, and work in publicly funded schools and clinics.

Building absorptive capacity to reach the MDGs: an illustration

The discussion in this section is based on scenarios that have been roughly calibrated to the country case of Ethiopia.[8] However the results are also of broad relevance to other poor countries with limited weak absorptive capacity. The scenarios serve to illustrate some of the key aspects of absorptive capacity, and the tradeoffs facing policy-makers. The starting point for considering capacity constraints to reach the MDGs is to consider a business-as-usual ('base') case, under which Ethiopia continues to receive external assistance at the current level and to perform along current trends.[9] For most of the MDGs, including income poverty, primary school completion and water and sanitation, Ethiopia is expected to fall far short of the MDG targets in this scenario. In contrast, two other cases are shown that correspond to, first, accelerated investment in core infrastructure considered key to improving economic growth (denoted as 'base-infra' in the figures that follow) and, second, additional expenditures to reach each of the five education, health and sanitary MDGs being modelled (denoted 'full MDG'). In each of these cases the additional financing is assumed to come from external grants, requirements for which are shown in Figure 33.3.

Ethiopia's basic infrastructure requirements are separately shown from investments needed to reach the five social MDG targets since these investment streams are quite distinct, and increasing core infrastructure spending is considered critical to accelerating growth, a necessary input into the first MDG (income poverty). These investments include the basic transport system, expanding power generation and distribution, to link the urban, peri-urban and rural economies, and investing in large-scale water management and irrigation systems to improve agricultural productivity.[10] It is assumed that a gestation lag of five years is necessary for this expanded infrastructure to generate an increase in the productivity of the private sector. This is the reason why the need for external financing appearing in Figure 33.3 for this scenario falls to a level close to the base case after this initial period, after adding more than US$10 per capita of external financing.[11]

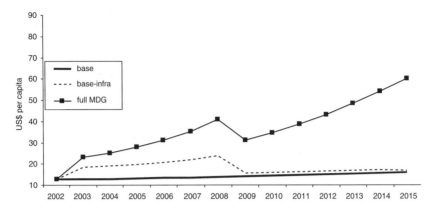

Figure 33.3   Foreign grant financing (US$ per capita)

The third scenario combines external financing requirements for infrastructure with the amounts needed to fulfil the five MDG social services. This is the main scenario that illustrates the impact of full external grant financing to achieve both the income poverty and reach the social MDGs. The combined external financing requirements, rise to around US$60 per capita by the end of the period, or approximately 33 per cent of GDP as compared with current aid levels of 16 per cent. This undoubtedly represents a huge absolute and relative increase in the development assistance received by Ethiopia.

The results suggest that under a set of specific conditions it is possible to achieve the MDGs by 2015. Several key conditions pertain however: a *predictable* flow of external grant financing increasing at a rather fast speed; flexible financing that can be used for current or capital expenditure needs; grant financing received is actually 'absorbed and spent',[12] actual delivery of the services for which expenditures have been provided; and so forth. The progress towards select MDGs is shown in Figures 33.4 and 33.5, and reveals the different contributions made by these investments in basic infrastructure and direct investment in the MDGs. The contribution of investment in basic infrastructure, which helps accelerate the growth rate relative to the base case by around 1.5 per cent annually, is very important for achieving MDG1 – halving the incidence of poverty from its 1990 level of 36 per cent of the population (using the national poverty line). Spending on MDG-related sectors also helps to increase growth and household consumption levels, mainly by raising the supply of skilled labour and through employment generated by higher public investment.[13] In the full MDG scenario (full-MDG), where both sets of investments are taken together, the incidence of extreme poverty is roughly halved from 1990 levels to around 19 per cent.

Completion rates for primary education increase from 35 per cent in 2002 to 100 per cent by 2015. Likewise, the U5MR and maternal mortality rate also fall to levels that just reach the MDG targets. The path along which these targets are achieved is not always smooth. The dip seen in the first five years for primary

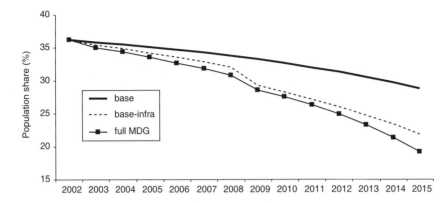

Figure 33.4   MDG1: population living on $1 (PPP) per day or less (%)

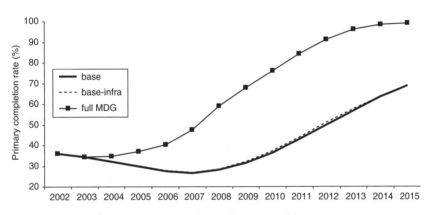

Figure 33.5   MDG2: net primary school completion rate (%)

school completion with the base and base-infra scenarios reflects the rapid expansion of demand for schooling and enrolment. Without a corresponding increase in the supply of educational services, this increase in enrolment contributes to a drop in the quality of schooling and therefore in completion rates. This process stops when public expenditures in education catch up with demand. Three types of capacity constraints particularly affect aid absorption: infrastructure constraints, skilled labour constraints and macroeconomic constraints. These help illustrate the importance of sequentially addressing absorptive capacity over time to reach the MDGs.

Infrastructure constraints

As infrastructure networks are developed (roads, energy, irrigation and telecoms), producers and consumers are better integrated into national and international markets, expanding opportunities and capturing network effects that can serve to accelerate growth. Investment in infrastructure also reduces the indirect costs of doing business (through improving, for example, the reliability of power, transport logistics, or reliable product-to-market timing) and associated losses that depress firm productivity.[14] Capturing these gains requires a sufficient level of, and sequencing of, public or private investment in infrastructure to reach the threshold where economy-wide network effects can begin to support higher productivity. Without such productivity gains, additional aid aimed at reaching the MDGs would be less effective since it would buy much less of those domestic services needed for the MDGs. This is an argument to give some priority to these productivity-enhancing investments even though they may not be directly related to the achievement of the MDGs.

Other infrastructure investments are associated with service delivery to reach the MDGs rather than enhancing the productivity of the private sector. Investment in schools, clinics and training facilities, and water and sanitation facilities is clearly required to meet the primary education, health, water and sanitation MDG targets. Physical facilities need to expand in parallel with outlays on personnel and other recurrent expenditures to avoid deterioration in the quality of services, declining demand and failure to reach targeted outcomes.

Skilled labour constraints

The requirements for accelerating primary school completion rates help to illustrate the importance of skilled labour constraints. Between 2002 and 2015 over 100,000 trained teachers will need to be brought into Ethiopia's educational system to achieve the target of 100 per cent primary school completion and to maintain education quality standards necessary to ensure there is demand for education services.[15] This requires investment in teacher training facilities and expanding the number of higher education graduates to meet the requirements for skilled teachers. In the short run, skilled labour can be hired from other sectors, in particular the private sector, but at the cost of both higher wages and some loss in output as labour exits the private sector. Accelerating this process serves to push up unit costs, which is reflected in rising costs in the model as capacity limits are reached.

Figure 33.6 shows the path of real wages, and hence the pressure on skilled labour, under three scenarios: the base case; the full-MDG case examined earlier; and the case with aid frontloaded to allow increased hiring of teachers and accelerate achievement of the enrolment rates to meet the primary completion target. As more funds are spent on hiring skilled labour for education, real wages increase significantly, and unit costs consequently rise as available skilled labour is limited, and must be bid away from other sectors. In the full-MDG scenario, the private sector loses labour to the public sector and wages for skilled labour rise across all sectors initially, before levelling off when the expanded schooling system starts producing an increasing number of skilled workers. The loss of labour and higher real wages also causes private growth to contract. In the frontloading scenario, total grants and MDG-related expenditures are sharply elevated for two years and

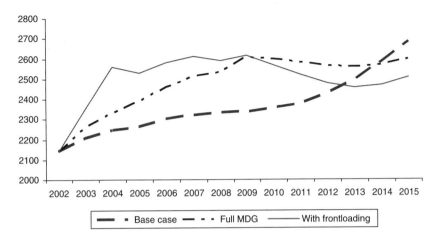

Figure 33.6   Real wages of workers with secondary school education (Birr)

then subside to rates required to reach the MDGs. Real wages spike to almost 25 per cent above their initial value in the first two years, sharply raising unit costs of achieving the MDGs and slowing the rate of growth. Investment in teacher training and other secondary and higher education programmes helps expand the supply of skilled labour with a lag, and wage pressures hence begin to moderate. By the middle of the projection period the real wage path moderates and begins to decline.

The comparison of these two real wage paths shows the importance of the timing of investments in teacher training capacity. In Figure 33.6, it would seem that the frontloading scenario leads to a cost of skilled labour larger than with the investment profile implicit in the full-MDG scenario when looking at the algebraic sum of the areas between the two curves. However, things are different when the gap between the two curves is weighed by the number of skilled workers.

There are plausible conditions under which the market clearing wage for skilled labour suggested by the model may underestimate what would be necessary to generate sufficient supply. Skilled labour may be attracted abroad by higher wages, a chronic problem for many developing countries, new graduates may not be of sufficient quality, or there may not be adequate incentives for skilled workers to relocate to remote areas of the country. Under these circumstances skilled wages would have to rise more sharply in order to recruit and retain adequate teachers, generating higher unit costs.

Macroeconomic constraints

A major concern across the scenarios for meeting the MDGs is the impact of scaled-up aid flows on domestic demand, relative prices and the real exchange rate. Aid flows permit a much larger trade deficit, but to the extent that they are not spent exclusively on imports they place upward pressure on prices in the non-traded

sector and on the real exchange rate, reducing competitiveness and resources flowing to traded goods and services. These issues are well recognized.[16] As stressed in
Bevan (2005), the extent to which aid flows are associated with the problem of real
exchange rate appreciation depends largely on the relative impact on demand and
supply in the non-tradables sector.[17] The supply response, depending on the effects
of aid on productivity across sectors, largely determines the depth and duration of
adverse effects following the surge in aid.

In the case of Ethiopia, all scenarios show exchange rate appreciation, rising real
wage rates, and a deterioration in the trade balance as imports surge and export
performance deteriorates. Differences in the level of external financing and the
way in which aid is used determine the impact on the exchange rate, real wages
and trade performance. Figure 33.7 shows the path of real exports through 2015.
Dutch Disease effects are clearly a serious concern in the medium term with the
full-MDG scenario and the surge that it generates in aid flows. The aid induced
appreciation of the exchange rate and the drop in net exports are severe. Exports
fall from around 14 per cent of GDP to 8 per cent by 2015, and the real exchange
rate appreciates by close to 20 per cent. However, the impact on real GDP growth,
which is essentially driven by factor supplies and infrastructure led productivity
gains, is quite limited.[18] This result is to be contrasted with what happens in the
'base-infra' scenario, where the GDP export share is slightly above that observed in
the base scenario at the end of the period.

Public spending on infrastructure and MDG services differ in their effects on the
supply side and in their import intensities. Infrastructure spending has a positive
but lagged impact on productivity, whereas spending on MDG services has only a
very modest impact on productivity in the short run, but affects supply through
adding to the stock of skilled labour. Infrastructure spending initially causes some
exchange rate appreciation until productivity improvements raise growth GDP,

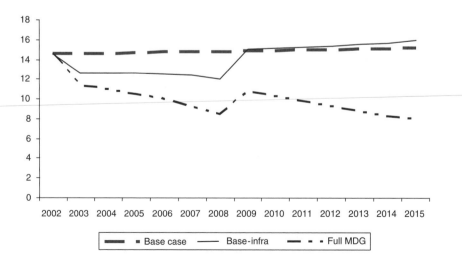

Figure 33.7   Real exports as a share of GDP, 2002–15

incomes and demand. The import intensity of basic infrastructure in Ethiopia, a country with limited domestic capacity for manufacturing inputs, is also high. This helps reduce the impact of infrastructure spending on relative prices, and hence reduces the adverse impact on competitiveness.

By contrast, investment in provision of MDG-related social services takes much longer to impact on productivity (through a healthier, better-educated workforce), and in the near term places greater pressure on the real exchange rate. In the case of aid spent on MDG-related services, and in the absence of higher investment in basic infrastructure, the real exchange rate appreciates by about 30 per cent and exports decline to less than half their initial share of GDP by 2015. Note that appreciation of the real exchange rate also reduces the purchasing power of foreign grants – unit costs rise and it requires larger aid flows to reach the MDG targets. This comparison confirms the importance of the sequencing of public spending in scenarios of aid scaling up. Reaching the MDGs requires increasing the absorptive capacity of the economy, which in turn requires increases in productivity and eliminating bottlenecks in factor markets, most notably in the skilled labour market.

Overall absorptive capacity constraints

Linking this back to the earlier discussion about aid effectiveness and absorptive capacity (Figure 33.1), constraints posed by skilled labour supply, macro balances and infrastructure capacity determine the returns to aid as the levels of total aid increase. Figure 33.8 shows the 'returns to aid', as the amount of aid used towards the MDGs is increased. Returns are measured here in 2005 and 2011 for the education sector, based on the percentage of primary school completion achieved (MDG2). The bottom curve illustrates the return to investment in education that faces the economy initially (in 2005). As grants are used to bring more teachers into the school system and expand education services, primary completion rates rise but at a declining rate. The declining rate of return is due to both rising costs (higher wage payments to attract skilled labour) and to declining quality levels, which reduce demand. Schools cannot be built rapidly enough, and teacher–classroom ratios decline.

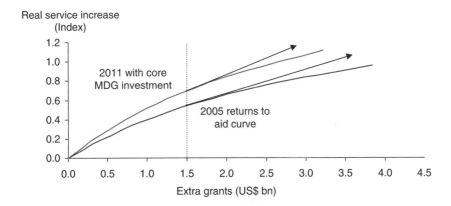

Figure 33.8 Aid effectiveness and capacity constraints

The top curve in Figure 33.8 shows the same return to aid profile five years later, when public investment in higher education and teacher training is already helping to moderate wages, school construction has expanded and improvements in infrastructure are serving to raise productivity and reduce unit costs of services. The returns to aid are higher, meaning that aid effectiveness has increased. Also, for any level of aid, it is the case that the slope of the return to aid curve has increased, meaning that *absorptive capacity has increased.*[19] Greater increases in primary school completion rates per additional dollar invested, for example, can be attained in 2011 than is the case in 2005.

Sequencing investments

The preceding has shown the importance of correctly sequencing investments to address capacity constraints over time to reduce total costs. The simulation with core infrastructure investment underscores this point: a threshold level of core infrastructure must be in place before productivity gains can be fully realized. Frontloading investment in infrastructure is required to capture these gains early on. Delaying core infrastructure investment and focusing on social services will delay gains in productivity, with implications for the rate of overall growth, household incomes and public revenues, as well as for the productivity of public service delivery and the effectiveness of aid.

Investment prioritization across MDG service sectors depends on lags in the production process and cross-sector externalities. Since skilled labour is developed with a lag, and since skilled labour is a critical input to expanding the supply of all the MDG services, this argues for early investment in education. Placing priority on the sectoral sequencing of public services that *generate positive externalities* also helps to lower the investment cost of other MDGs. Both the access to improved water and education levels are important elements of reducing under-five mortality. Hence, investment in developing and maintaining potable water supplies, as well as maternal education, should precede or move in parallel with other child health-related investments. If this sequencing is reversed (that is, placing initial priority on non-education-related MDGs, followed by investment in water, education and finally basic infrastructure services), it would result in higher total costs of meeting the MDGs, or, if resources are constrained, it would lead to a shortfall in meeting the MDG targets.

Frontloading

Excessive frontloading of aid, it was argued above, places pressure on real wages, slows growth and raises the overall cost of achieving the MDGs. The discussion of sequencing also suggests that *inadequate* frontloading of some investments, such as infrastructure, can impose costs through delaying the potential productivity gains and exploiting externalities. At the limit, investing too late in training or infrastructure makes reaching the MDGs impossible. Taken together this suggests that there is an optimal level of frontloading that minimizes costs over time. An intuitive argument suggests that absorptive capacity is the main criterion in minimizing this cost. Clearly, if the absorptive capacity of aid is not constant over time, the total cost of reaching the MDGs could be lowered by reallocation aid from the periods where the absorptive capacity is low to periods where it is high. The problem is that such a simple argument, borrowed from elementary optimization theory, would work if the returns from aid could be measured by a scalar. In the context of the MDGs, where no substitution is allowed across goals, this is clearly not the case. Yet, a simple experiment shows that the preceding intuition is correct and that there is something like an optimal sequencing of public spending on the MDGs and therefore optimal sequencing of aid flows.

To explore the question of optimal frontloading further, Figure 33.9 shows the present discounted value of grants required to reach the MDGs as the share of expenditures 'frontloaded' is varied – with the relative composition of these expenditures across MDGs maintained constant. Two five-year periods are considered, varying the share of total outlays between the two periods.[20] The resulting 'U-curve' shows how the present value of total costs falls as the share frontloaded increases from very low levels, costs are minimized at around 20 per cent, and thereafter rise at an accelerating rate as capacity constraints become binding – labour costs rise, exchange rate appreciation reduces the purchasing value of aid and congestion costs rise from infrastructure bottlenecks. In the extreme, at some point around 70 per cent frontloading, costs become effectively infinite and reaching the MDGs is not possible.

It is important to be cautious in interpreting this result, however. First, while it suggests that total costs are minimized at around 20 per cent of outlays taking place in the first half of the period, it is important to stress that the calculation has not taken into account the welfare outcomes along the different paths towards reaching the MDGs. As more resources are frontloaded, social service outcomes improve *earlier*, and social welfare consequently improves. The MDG focus leads to ignoring variations in social welfare along the path towards the MDGs. Second, the underlying exchange rate and wage dynamics differ along the curve, with consequences for competitiveness of traded goods and for wage differentials, the effects of which may appear after the MDG horizon. Consideration of scaling up

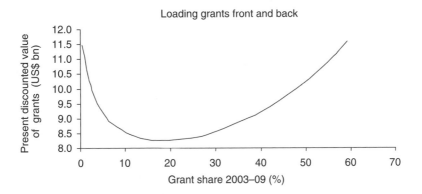

Figure 33.9   Total costs and frontloading of expenditure shares

and frontloading aid clearly needs to consider the impact on welfare and the consequences for growth and MDG outcomes post-2015.

Governance and institutional reforms

The model does not address the critical question of how underlying institutional capacity and governance can be improved. The broad range of issues that this encompasses are frequently part of poverty reduction strategies and tackled in policy-based lending by institutions like the World Bank – improving public expenditure management, strengthening oversight mechanisms, strengthening the business climate and so on. Taken together, governance and institutional reforms can be thought of as measures to improve the efficiency of public resource utilization. In terms of the model, they affect the underlying productivity of public activities and reduce unit costs of achieving the MDGs – falling teacher absenteeism, reduced waiting times for processing legal cases, licensing, and regulatory issues, less leakage in the use of central government resources for delivery of services to end-users. Simple reforms can sometimes have major consequences.[21]

Consider the effect of introducing governance and institutional reforms in the form of improvement in the underlying efficiency of public services at the rate of 2 per cent compounded annually, and independent of the rate of public investment (this assumption is used in the World Bank, for example, to guide annual budget parameters). Introducing this to the model and recalculating the U-curve in Figure 33.10 suggests several effects that emerge from this. First, the productivity gain in public services significantly reduces the cost of achieving the MDGs along all points of the curve and 'flattens' the curve, reducing the total variation in costs. The total cost of achieving the MDGs by 2015 in present value terms falls by around one-third.

Second, the new point of cost minimization leans slightly towards greater frontloading contrary to the expectation that it would shift towards the left (less frontloading as productivity levels are higher and unit costs are lower during the

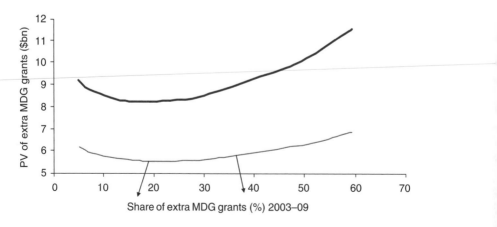

Figure 33.10   Frontloading with enhanced governance and institutions

second period). The ambiguity in this outcome arises from two underlying effects that push in opposite directions. Increasing future productivity of public spending pushes towards more frontloading in order to benefit from productivity gains longer. On the other hand, there is a change in relative prices between periods. The decline in the cost of investment over time pushes towards delaying public investment. In the present case, the first effect seems to be stronger than the second. One important implication of this analysis is that anticipated incremental gains in underlying governance or productivity should not be a reason to delay public expenditures towards capacity building and service delivery. Even if there are underlying efficiency gains that reduce costs over time, this does not constitute a reason to delay investment in the MDGs, but rather suggests that future gains in absorptive capacity due to increasing productivity in public services must be capitalized on by investing early.

Conclusions

The capacity of low-income counties to absorb and effectively use large aid flows in support of the MDGs is a central concern in the debate over international financing of MDG efforts. Direct estimates of the financing necessary to achieve the MDGs imply very large increases in aid flows at the level of the individual recipient countries. A basic question being asked relates to the absorptive capacity of low-income countries as higher levels of aid will become available to advance the MDG agenda.

We have shown in this chapter that absorptive capacity should not be seen as a rigid characteristic of recipient countries that would depend only on the quality of its governance institutions. In a strict economic sense, absorptive capacity, defined as the marginal return to aid, is a dynamic concept that depends on the timing and sequencing of public spending. Rapid scaling up of aid in a country with very limited capacity to train and hire skilled labour, build new infrastructure, manage new and large-scale public programmes, or maintain macro stability may lead to bottlenecks, rising unit costs and falling quality of service delivery. Taken to extremes it could also lead to impaired growth potential with adverse medium-term consequences. In such a country, mobilizing international aid in support of the MDGs should therefore move in tandem with efforts to identify a suitable time profile of aid flows in recipient countries which balances the need to quickly accelerate progress towards achieving the MDG outcomes through expanded and improved public service delivery, with constraints on absorptive capacity and the way to progressively weaken these constraints.

This has implications for the sectoral composition and sequencing of public spending and aid disbursements for meeting the MDGs. Country-specific plans are required to identify key constraints, identify bottlenecks to growth, clarify potential externalities and formulate strategic plans to build capacity. This requires in-depth and country-specific analysis to determine the appropriate sequencing of public investment for each country. To provide some empirical basis to address these questions the chapter employs a modelling approach (MAMS) that combines a relatively standard and highly aggregated CGE model with an MDG module that links MDG performance to the functioning of social sectors and the way different public services (in health, education, water, sanitation and public infrastructure) are provided. The model has been applied to Ethiopia to help illustrate the main messages. It focuses on three main constraints to aid absorption – skilled labour, infrastructure and macroeconomic constraints.

Four main conclusions can be drawn from the simulations undertaken with this model:

- First, careful sequencing of public investment is important for minimizing the total cost of reaching the MDGs. From the outset priority investment is needed in basic infrastructure to generate the basis for higher productivity growth and net-work effects improving linkages across and within regions and sectors. Among the MDG services, accelerating education spending is a priority since skilled labour can only be produced with a lag and is restricting absorptive capacity.
- Second, the macroeconomic impact of large aid flows on the tradables sector (the Dutch Disease) can be serious, resulting in a significant decline in the share of exports in the economy, at least in the short run. The threat to future growth will depend in large measure on the supply response in the economy, and the impact of aid and development strategies in spurring accelerated productivity growth in both the traded and non-traded sectors.
- Third, large-scale frontloading of aid disbursements (other than infrastructure) is costly as it pushes against absorptive capacity constraints, intensifies the premium on skilled wages, bids labour away from the private sector (depressing growth) and augments short-term Dutch Disease effects. In the case of Ethiopia, the model suggests that the cost-minimizing MDG strategy involves a steep upward profile of public spending and aid disbursements. It is not clear, how-ever, how much this result is country-specific.
- Fourth, improvements in the underlying governance and institutional struc-tures help to secure broad productivity improvements in public service delivery, and should underpin development strategies. Their cumulative effect can sig-nificantly reduce overall costs of achieving the MDGs and secure long-term pro-ductivity gains. However, it is not necessarily because very much progress is anticipated in the future that aid should be delayed. It might be optimal to increase early public investment precisely to take full advantage of the ongoing and future gains in public sector productivity.

Two last remarks should help draw some lessons from the preceding exercise for the allocation and the management of aid. First, the chapter focused on the allo-cation of the aid directed towards a specific country across sectors and over time. It did not tackle the issue of the allocation of aid across countries. Of course, this is where the notion of comparative aid effectiveness introduced in Figure 33.1 should play a role. After taking into account country-specificity in aggregating returns from aid across countries, an optimal allocation clearly tends to equalize marginal returns, or 'absorptive capacities' across countries. If not enough aid is available, absorptive capacities will not be equalized and some countries will not receive adequate aid. The argument in this chapter suggests that such reasoning might be incorrect if applied in a static way. Absorptive capacity is a dynamic concept and the optimal allocation of aid should be based on both perceived absorptive capacity today but also anticipated capacities in the future as defined by an explicit MDG strategy. Poverty Reduction Strategy Papers could be playing this role nowadays.

Second, the argument in this chapter is based on framework with no uncertainty, where donors have perfect knowledge of the MDG strategy of recipient countries and recipient countries reveal their true strategy based on the anticipation of fully certain future aid flows. Clearly, the optimal strategy of recipient countries depends very much on the confidence they have that donors will hold on their commitments. Likewise, the commitment of the donors depends on the confidence they have that recipient countries will hold on the strategy they have announced. Such a situation may lead to some low-equilibrium of the type found in the well-known Prisoner's Dilemma, with none of the players trusting their partner. The argument in this chapter corresponds to the high equilibrium but leaves aside the issue of how donors and recipients can co-ordinate on that equilibrium, which is today the core of the international debate on aid effectiveness.

Notes

1. The major publications in 2005 on scaling up all have some discussion of absorptive capacity, including the Commission for Africa Report 'Our Common Interest'; the Global Monitoring Report 2005 'The Millennium Development Goals: From Consensus to Momentum'; the Millennium Project Report, 'Investing in Development', and the UN report 'In Larger Freedom: Towards Development, Security, and Human Rights For All'. The September 2005 edition of the IMF publication, *Finance & Development*, included several articles relevant to this debate on 'Making Aid Work'. De Renzio (2005) summarizes the issues surrounding scaling up and absorption.
2. The literature on aid effectiveness discusses two types of complications that can arise if flows of foreign aid are large: macroeconomic and structural complications. Whereas in the case of macroeconomic problems, it is the quantity of aid and its allocation between the tradeable and non-tradeable sectors that matter, in the case of absorptive capacity, the issue is the quality of spending. See the detailed discussion in World Bank (2002).
3. For discussions of this perspective on aid effectiveness, see World Bank (2004), Heller and Gupta (2002a) and Goldin *et al.* (2002). Recent papers that take issue with the result that effectiveness depends on policy and institutional quality include Hansen and Tarp (2001) and Easterly *et al.* (2003). The link between country conditions and aid effectiveness is borne out by case studies of individual countries, as well as evidence on project-level returns (for example, see the studies in Devarajan *et al.* 2001). The importance of institutional capacity has been emphasized, for example, in Kanbur *et al.* (1999), Heller and Gupta (2002b) and Bulir and Lane (2002).
4. In other words, the aid effectiveness curve is taken to be concave. Note that it is not necessarily increasing everywhere, though. Some authors assume that increasing aid beyond some limit may be detrimental to the recipient economy at some stage. See, for instance, Hansen and Tarp (2001).
5. Recent research in Nepal suggests that spending on agricultural research and extension, followed by rural roads, can have the greatest marginal impact on poverty reduction (Fan *et al.* 2004)

6. The model is presented in detail in Bourguignon *et al.* (2004). Preliminary applications to Ethiopia are discussed in Lofgren and Diaz-Bonilla (2005), Bourguinon and Sundberg (2006) and Sundberg and Lofgren (2006). More work is presently done in the case of Ethiopia and MAMS is now being applied to a variety of countries in Africa and Latin America.

7. Private supply of education services has not been separately included since this is relatively small in Ethiopia, but this could be elaborated for countries where it is important.

8. Presented in Bourguignon *et al.* (2004).

9. External grants expand at an annual rate of 1.5 per cent from their 2002 level, while foreign loans remain at their 2002 level. Government services and GDP all grow at around a 4 per cent annual rate, similar to the long-run growth trend.

10. Discussed in World Bank (2005). Three priorities identified for growth are: (1) public investment to support urban–rural linkages; (2) reduce risks to agricultural producers through investing in improved water management, social safety nets and security of land tenure; and (3) improve the investment climate and reduce risk facing private agents.

11. This five-year lag in the effect of infrastructure investment also explains the change in the slopes of most curves shown below around 2008–09.

12. See Aiyar *et al.* (2006) for a discussion of aid surges and absorption versus switching. Such an immediate and complete use of aid flows would not necessarily occur if exogenous macroeconomic shocks were introduced in the initial framework.

13. An additional factor is through the exchange rate effect of appreciation of the currency helping to increase average real purchasing power.

14. Recent work by Eifert *et al.* (2005) on African economies highlights productivity costs associated with the quality of infrastructure services.

15. This is based on Education for All: Fast Track Initiative standards, which implies moving from the current 75:1 pupil–teacher ratio to a targeted level of 40:1.

16. Heller and Gupta (2002a) provide a clear overview of the issues and cite several country studies.

17. How aid is initially used, whether it is used to finance public investment (is spent) and whether it increases net imports (is absorbed), will also have a major short-term impact. It is assumed here that all aid is spent and has an impact on net imports, and we ignore these short-term issues.

18. Things would be different if growth were somewhat related to the share of exports in GDP, as is sometimes argued in the literature on growth and trade-openness.

19. Although this requires further verification and improvement in the precision of the calculations, it would seem that this property still holds when the comparison is made for aid/GDP rather than aid maintained constant.

20. Because the model has been parameterized around 2002, the actual simulation periods correspond to 2003–09 and 2009–15.

21. For an in depth discussion of governance, institutional capacity and service delivery, see World Bank (2003). One example often cited is the Ugandan newspaper campaign to boost schools' and parents' ability to monitor local officials' handling of school grants. Through greater public awareness, 'capture' or leakage of budget resources fell from 80 to 20 per cent between 1995 and 2001 (Reinikka and Svensson 2004).

References

Aiyar, S., A. Berg, M. Hussain, A. Mahone and S. Roache (2006) 'High Aid Inflows: The Case of Ghana', in P. Isard, L. Lipschitz, A. Mourmouras and B. Yontcheva (eds), *The Macroeconomic Management of Foreign Aid: Opportunities and Pitfalls*, Washington, DC: IMF.

Bevan, D. (2005) 'An Analytical Overview of Aid Absorption: Recognizing and Avoiding Macroeconomic Hazards', paper for the Seminar on Foreign Aid and Macroeconomic Management, 14–15 March, Maputo.

Bourguignon, F. and M. Sundberg (2006) 'Constraints to Achieving the MDGs with Scaled-Up Aid', *UN DESA Working Paper* 15, New York: United Nations.

Bourguignon, F., M. Bussolo, L. Pereira da Silva, H. Timmer and D. van der Mensbrugghe (2004) 'MAMS: Maquette for MDG Simulations', Mimeo, Washington, DC: World Bank.

Bulir, A. and T. Lane (2002) 'Aid and Fiscal Management', *IMF Policy Development and Review Department Working Paper* 02/112, Washington, DC: IMF.

Collier, P. and D. Dollar (2002) 'Aid Allocation and Poverty Reduction', *European Economic Review*, 46, 8: 1475–500.

de Renzio, P. (2005) 'Scaling Up Versus Absorptive Capacity: Challenges and Opportunities for Reaching the MDGs in Africa', *ODI Briefing Papers* May, London: Overseas Development Institute.

Devarajan, S., D. Dollar and T. Holmgren (eds) (2001) *Aid and Reform in Africa: Lessons from Ten Case Studies*, Washington, DC: World Bank.

Easterly, W., R. Levine and D. Roodman (2003) 'New Data, New Doubts: A Comment on Burnside and Dollar's "Aid, Policies, and Growth (2000)" ', Mimeo, New York: New York University.

Eifert, B., A. Gelb and V. Ramachandran (2005) 'Business Environment and Comparative Advantage in Africa: Evidence from the Investment Climate Data', *Center for Global Development Working Paper* 56, Washington, DC: Center for Global Development.

Fan, S., X. Zhang and N. Rao (2004) 'Public Expenditure, Growth, and Poverty Reduction in Rural Uganda', *IFPRI Development Strategy and Governance Division Discussion Paper* 4, Washington, DC: International Food Policy Research Institute.

Goldin, I., H. Rogers and N. Stern (2002) 'The Role and Effectiveness of Development Assistance: Lessons from World Bank Experience', in *The Case for Aid*, Washington, DC: World Bank.

Hansen, H. and F. Tarp (2001) 'Aid and Growth Regressions', *Journal of Development Economics*, 64, 2: 547–70.

Heller, P. and S. Gupta (2002a) 'More Aid: Making it Work for the Poor', *World Economics*, 3, 4: 131–46, Washington, DC: IMF.

Heller, P. and S. Gupta (2002b) 'Challenges in Expanding Development Assistance', *IMF Discussion Paper* PDP/02/5, Washington, DC: IMF.

Kanbur, R., T. Sandler and K. Morrisson (1999) *The Future of Development Assistance: Common Pools and International Public Goods*, Washington, DC: Overseas Development Council.

Lofgren, H. and C. Diaz-Bonilla (2005) 'Economy-wide Simulations of Ethiopian MDG Strategies', Mimeo, Washington, DC: World Bank.

Radelet, S. (2003) *Challenging Foreign Aid. A Policymaker's Guide to the Millennium Challenge Account*, Washington, DC: Center for Global Development.

Radelet, S., M.A. Clemens and R. Bhavnani (2004) 'Counting Chickens When They Hatch: The Short-Term of Aid on Growth', *Center for Global Development Working Paper* 44, Washington, DC: Center for Global Development.

Reinikka, R. and J. Svensson (2004) 'The Power of Information: Evidence from a Newspaper Campaign to Reduce Capture', *World Bank Policy Research Department Working Paper* 3239, Washington, DC: World Bank.

Sundberg, M. and H. Lofgren (2006) 'Absorptive Capacity and Achieving the MDGs: The Case of Ethiopia', in P. Isard, L. Lipschitz, A. Mourmouras and B. Yontcheva (eds), *The Macroeconomic Management of Foreign Aid: Opportunities and Pitfalls*, Washington, DC: IMF.

World Bank (2002) *Macroeconomic and Structural Policy Implications of Increased Aid. A Guidance Note for Bank Staff*, Washington, DC: World Bank.

World Bank (2003) *World Development Report: Making Services Work for Poor People*, Washington, DC: Oxford University Press for World Bank.

World Bank (2004) 'Aid Effectiveness and Financing Modalities', paper prepared for Development Committee Meeting, 2 October, Washington, DC: World Bank.

World Bank (2005) 'Ethiopia: A Strategy to Balance and Stimulate Growth', *Country Economic Memorandums* 29383-ET, Washington, DC: World Bank.

34
Applying Behavioural Economics to International Development Policy

C. Leigh Anderson and Kostas Stamoulis

Introduction

Many development policies and programmes are premised on a traditional economic model of rationality to predict how individuals will respond to changes in incentives. Despite the emphasis of these programmes on poverty reduction, economists and the development community in general are still unable to understand fully how the poor make decisions, especially under uncertainty and over time. We do not understand why, for example, individuals do not regularly adopt subsidized technologies, such as ventilated cooking stoves to reduce health risks. Even when cultural norms and other constraints are considered, our models do not explain why a massive HIV/AIDS information campaign does not encourage individuals to regularly use condoms. Individuals avail themselves less than predicted in health programmes, participate less than expected in market opportunities, under- or over-insure themselves and make short-run decisions that are inconsistent with their long-run welfare. The rise and fall of different descriptive models and paradigms of poor-household behaviour can partly be attributed to this limited understanding. We believe that some more helpful answers may lie within behavioural economics, that these insights are particularly important for poor populations, and that they can improve the future design, implementation and subsequent effectiveness of development programmes.

Behavioural economics is an approach that rigorously combines the insights of psychology and economics to try to understand better and predict human decision making. Empirical evidence is helping us learn, for example, how cognitive limitations, fairness, loss aversion, framing of choices, variable discount rates and the qualitative dimensions of risk – such as proximity and control – affect decision making. The regularity of many of these anomalies suggests that these behaviours are anomalous only to our traditional models, but that they may otherwise be the norm.

The accumulated evidence is largely from the USA and Europe, with little comparable work from developing or transition countries. Most of the work has been laboratory based, with far fewer observations from the field. The motivation for trying to understand the preponderance and nature of similar behavioural anomalies in less developed countries stems from our prior that they are at least as prevalent, and that they will more acutely affect policy outcomes because there are fewer formal institutions to temper their effects. This prior stems from three developing country characteristics: the greater incidence of poverty and food insecurity, larger rural populations and the dearth of well-functioning markets.

We begin by discussing what we mean by behavioural anomalies and with a brief review of some USA and Western European experiments. We draw heavily on earlier experimental summaries, and in particular, Kahneman (2003), Thaler (1991) and Rabin (1996). After that, using original field data collected with stated and revealed preference surveys in Vietnam and Russia, we examine discount rate patterns, risk attitudes and decision heuristics. Our final section briefly summarizes why we believe these ideas are particularly important for international development, and what some of the obstacles are to change.

What are behavioural anomalies and behavioural economics?

Over the past 25 years economists have been increasingly focusing on the behaviours of individuals that deviate from what would be predicted from our standard model of rational maximization. The focus is not on behaviours driven by social and other institutional factors that have been neglected (or not properly captured) in economic models. Of interest are psychological factors that although susceptible to, or shaped by, the institutional environment, differ for other reasons among individuals living in identical circumstances.

Behavioural economics is an effort to understand how systematic these deviations are and to adjust our models accordingly. Our standard economic model posits choice as being the outcome of an individual maximizing stable, well-behaved preferences, $U(x)$, over a set of goods and services, subject to a set of measurable constraints such as income or prices. In this chapter we examine four potential model misspecifications that we believe are particularly problematic if they arise in poverty alleviation policies and programmes. The first is the common discounted utility model (DU), because of how fundamental intertemporal choices are to growth, borrowing, investment and all sustainability issues where costs and benefits are spread over time. The second is the dominant expected utility model (EU), because the poor, particularly those who live in rural areas and rely on agriculture, face considerable risks and generally have fewer formal institutions to manage those risks. The third is the disregard by the prevailing economic model for reference levels and fairness, because any intervention changes the status quo. Our fourth concern is with the method behind the model, and the assumption that 'Every decision is thoroughly contemplated, perfectly calculated and easily executed' (Mullainathan forthcoming). Instead, we look at decision heuristics, because information to inform decisions is particularly complex in many developing and transition economies and scarce in rural environments – see Kreps (1990) and Rubinstein (1998), among others, for a technical exposition on which traditional behavioural axioms are violated by observed anomalies.

Decision making over time

Discount rates affect investments in education and health, use of the environment, borrowing and saving, and all choices where something has to be given up in the present for a return in the future. Since Paul Samuelson's seminal article in 1937, intertemporal choices have been most commonly modelled with discount rates that are invariant to the period in which the choice occurs. The assumption is that individuals have constant discount rates, that is, they will make the same tradeoffs within any period regardless of the proximity of that tradeoff. This suggests that the short-run discount rate we experience in postponing immediate consumption is the same as the long-run discount rate we use in planning future tradeoffs (Harris and Laibson 2001).

Yet, as Rabin (2002: 669) writes, 'Common sense, millennia of folk wisdom, and hundreds of psychological experiments all support present-biased preferences.' For most of us, the cost of foregoing something today for tomorrow is higher than the cost of agreeing to give up something ten days from now for a return on the eleventh day. Many economists believe that intertemporal choices are better represented by a hyperbolic or quasi-hyperbolic discount function than the more commonly employed exponential function (Rabin 1996; 2002; Laibson 1997; Loewenstein and Elster 1992; Loewenstein and Prelec 1992; Ainslie 1991). The evidence suggests that discount rates do vary with time, and that short-run discount rates, experienced at the moment, are higher than the long-run discount rates we project forward into our planning horizon. Hence people with time varying discount rates, if they lack perfect self-control, may pursue short-run actions that they had previously calculated were not in their best long-run interest – they may consume their savings, fail to stick to a debt repayment schedule, skip school or healthcare visits, or choose environmentally unsustainable production methods.

Decision making under uncertainty

The traditional model of individual choice under uncertainty represents preferences by an expected utility function, the shortcomings of which have been well documented (Allais 1953; Kahneman *et al.* 1982; Machina 1987). Experiments instead support prospect theory, with a value function defined over changes in one's position rather than wealth, and which is assumed concave over gains, convex over losses and more steeply sloped over losses than gains (Kahneman and Tversky 1979). These features better account for the impact of losses and gains and loss aversion – individuals being risk averse over gains but risk seeking over losses. Unlike basic utility theory, research suggests that losses hurt more than commensurate-sized gains help – in several cases with losses being weighed more than twice as heavily as gains (Knetsch 1995). Prospect theory seems especially relevant for developing countries and rural economies where income levels can be highly variable.

The subjective weighting function of prospect theory reflects three characteristics of observations on decision making: the overweighting of small probabilities and underweighting of large ones; decreasing relative sensitivity that discounts probabilities further from one proportionately less than probabilities closer to one (subproportionality); and increasing absolute sensitivity towards the end-points of probabilities equal to zero and one (subadditivity) (Prelec 2001: 86).

In addition to magnitude, the qualitative dimensions of risky outcomes have been shown to affect risk perceptions. The characteristics that shape decision making about risk include magnitude, reversibility, control, familiarity, proximity and distribution of impacts, among others (Slovic *et al.* 1979; Pate 1983; NRC 1996). The risk perception literature shows that individuals systematically overestimate the size of risks that are small (the Allais paradox), unfamiliar, involuntary and uncertain (the Ellsberg paradox). By contrast individuals underestimate the size of risks that are more certain, larger, familiar, or in some sense voluntary.

The true form of U(x): reference levels and fairness

Most of us understand that behaviour is motivated by considerations other than pure self-interest. What we understand less well is how, and when, to weight these motivations. If self-interest is narrowly considered as increasing material wealth, for example, how much wealth will one forego to satisfy fairness, revenge or altruism? And when are the motives governed by more complex issues such as reciprocity? For example, studies suggest that people are more likely to contribute to public goods when they believe others are also doing this, even though from an efficiency perspective there are diminishing social benefits to each additional person contributing. Pure altruism would suggest that one should give more when others give less (Rabin 1996: 13).

Repeated experiments suggest that individuals are willing to suffer monetary losses to punish opponents for outcomes that they perceive as unfair (see for example, Rabin 1996, and Camerer and Thaler 1995). They may either judge the resulting distribution or the intent of the distribution as unfair (Bereby-Meyer and Niederle 2005). In USA experiments, individuals will refuse allocations that deviate much from 50:50 if their refusal means that both players receive nothing. That is, they are willing to give up their smaller share to prevent the other player from receiving their larger one. Interestingly, in the results of a study of ultimatum games in 15 small-scale societies there was a positive correlation between offers to share more equitably and degrees of market integration and co-operation (Henrich *et al.* 2005). Under what conditions and forms of economic organization, if any, can we regularly predict that satisfying the desire to retaliate will outweigh the desire to increase wealth?

Kahneman *et al.* (1986) conducted several experiments to assess how fairness might be a constraint on profit seeking in the market. Consider the different percentage of the approximately 125 respondents who considered a company decision to be unfair under the circumstances in Q1 and Q2:

Q1. A company is making a small profit. It is located in a community experiencing a recession with substantial unemployment but no inflation. There are many workers anxious to work at the company. The company decides to decrease wages and salaries 7 per cent this year. Sixty-two per cent considered this unfair.

Q2. A company is making a small profit. It is located in a community with sub-stantial unemployment and inflation of 12 per cent. There are many workers anxious to work at the company. The company decides to increase salaries only 5 per cent this year. Twenty-two per cent considered this unfair.

From their experiments they proposed the principle of reference transactions and dual entitlement: that buyers feel entitled to the terms of some reference transac-tion and firms to some reference profit, without necessarily knowing profit levels at the reference transaction. Transactors found it largely unacceptable for firms to raise prices and appropriate surplus from demand increases, but acceptable for firms to pass on cost increases. This included price or wage changes in response to com-modity shortages or labour surpluses. If these views of fairness affect individuals' decisions on where, and with whom, to exchange, or constrain profit seeking by vendors in the market, then we should expect that people will respond differently than traditionally predicted to policies that regulate or liberalize markets.

Reference levels apply to wealth as well as prices. Considerable evidence suggests that individuals are sensitive not only to absolute wealth levels, but also to changes in their relative wealth. The baseline could be their own past wealth, such that it is the increase or decrease in their wealth that matters as much as the final level. Or it could be changes in the wealth of a neighbour, friend, or other indi-vidual they are apt to compare themselves to. Thus, for example, an individual could feel worse off from the good fortune of their neighbour or from a colleague getting a pay raise, despite no change in their absolute wealth levels.

Many of these ideas on relative wellbeing stem from the literature around happi-ness. Beginning with Easterlin (1996), several studies have shown that although on average individuals in wealthier countries are happier than their poorer country counterparts, average happiness levels do not rise as countries grow wealthier. One hypothesis is that as average wealth levels rise, individuals do not necessarily feel relatively better off. Graham (2004) explores some of these ideas in the context of globalization, growth and inequality for developing countries. She cites results from Gurr (1970), who after studying conflict-related deaths in over a hundred countries, cites relative, not absolute, deprivation as 'the basic, instigating condition for participants in collective violence' (Graham 2004: 5).

Clearly, the extent to which it is relative income that affects welfare must be of some concern to development economists. First, judgements of fairness may underlie individual responses to all mechanisms that allocate scarce resources. Depending on the principles underlying how programme resources are allocated – maximizing social welfare, helping the most needy, or helping everyone equally – judgements of fairness may affect programme participation. Ignoring perceptions of fairness may affect interventions designed to make markets work for the poor – including increasing access to and allocating resources through vouch-ers, subsidies and other market-based mechanisms. Second, the goal of economic growth presumes wellbeing rises with absolute income and is neutral with respect to inequality, but that rising inequality may affect the pace of growth. This evidence suggests that the concern with inequality should rest directly with its effect on wellbeing, not just the long-run growth process. For the very poor, however, changes in absolute income may still be the most important for wellbeing. McBride (2001) estimates for a developed country sample that relative income effects are smaller at lower income levels.

Loss aversion and mental accounting

Loss aversion may contribute to two other phenomena called the status quo bias and the endowment effect. Experiments suggest that individuals tend to prefer the status quo to changes that involve losses in some dimension, even when these losses are coupled with gains in another direction. In other words, actions that are, on net, revenue neutral or even revenue enhancing may be welfare decreasing if they involve losses. And either because of the status quo bias or inertia, default options dominate choices. A study of insurance in Pennsylvania and New Jersey found that with full coverage as the default option in Pennsylvania the take-up rate was 79 per cent. With limited coverage as the default option in New Jersey, only 30 per cent of drivers choose full coverage (Johnson *et al.* 1993). We should expect project recipients to be willing to take bigger gambles to maintain the status quo than to acquire it in the first place, and that default options will dominate choice for reasons other than traditional welfare maximization.

The increased value attributable to possession or property rights, commonly called the endowment effect, was documented in a series of experiments with University of Victoria undergraduate students. In one experiment, respondents were divided into three classes. One class was given a choice between a mug of value $4.95 and a chocolate bar of approximate value $6.00. Students were not told the purchase price of the items. Students in the first class were given a choice between the two items and 56 per cent chose the mug over the chocolate, giving us a sense of a distribution of preferences. Students in the second class were first given the mug, and then five minutes later given the opportunity to trade for the chocolate – 89 per cent chose to keep their mug. Students in the third class were initially given the chocolate and then the offer to trade for a mug. This time, 90 per cent chose to keep their chocolate. (Kahneman *et al.* 1990).

Evidence suggests that individuals have mental accounting systems that influence decision making in ways not predicted by traditional economic theory. Thaler has documented numerous examples, including how individuals are more likely to spend 'windfall' winnings on luxury items than equivalent-sized salary increases. People often give gifts that recipients value but would not purchase for themselves. Many individuals seem to have mental accounts for different expenses, such as entertainment and education. Consider Thaler's example revealing the discrepancy in choices over buying a theatre ticket that have the same net impact on wealth:

> Q1. Imagine that you have decided to see a play where admission is $10 per ticket. As you enter the theatre you discover that you have lost a $10 bill. Would you still pay $10 for a ticket to the play? Yes: 88 per cent. No: 12 per cent.

Q2. Imagine that you have decided to see a play and paid the admission price of $10 per ticket. As you enter the theatre you discover that you have lost your ticket. The seat was not marked and the ticket cannot be recovered. Would you pay $10 for another ticket? Yes: 46 per cent. No: 54 per cent.

The bundling and sequencing of monetary gains and losses also matter. With equivalent cash outcomes, people are happier winning two small prizes ($50, $25) than one large prize ($75); paying one large penalty (−$150) than two small penalties (−$100, −$50); paying one large penalty and winning one small one (−$200, $25) than paying one medium sized penalty (−$175); and winning one small prize ($20) than winning one large prize and paying one medium penalty ($100, −$80) (Thaler 1991: 55). Experiments in health indicate that with the same net outcome, people prefer improving sequences to declining sequences and that the duration of a sequence of events is less important than the experience of the final frame (Chapman 2003).

Economists have long argued that money is the best gift because it can be redeemed on whatever the recipient wants, and that the most efficient redistribution is via lump sum transfers to the poor. These examples suggest that how money is received, and what it is mentally earmarked for, matter both in terms of the recipients' welfare and their decision on how to use the resources. These findings have implications for debates over, for example, the effects of vouchers versus cash, earmarking funds, and segregating gains and bundling losses. Loss aversion, the endowment effect and mental accounting may explain current challenges to how we conceptualize opportunity and sunk costs – people often behave as though opportunity costs matter less than out-of-pocket expenses.

Systematic errors in maximizing U(x): decision heuristics

The expected utility model is particularly inappropriate for complex and infrequent decisions, where evidence supports a bounded rationality model. Individuals often resort to decision heuristics that can produce behaviour that appears imperfectly rational. Decision heuristics refer to the simple rules of thumb that individuals use to make decisions either in the absence of full information or when they are unable or unwilling to process all the information that is available. Some common heuristics are representativeness, availability, anchoring and affect.

When people use the representativeness heuristic, their judgement of the probability that one event or person originates from or belongs to another class is based on how the events or people resemble each other. The representativeness heuristic judges such a frequency by comparing the similarity of the case with the image or stereotype of the class, often to the exclusion of prior probabilities, base-rate frequencies, sample size, regression to the mean and other factors that should affect judgements of probability (Tversky and Kahneman 1974). For example, people tend to overestimate how often a small group will closely resemble the parent population. The bias occurs when frequency and similarity are not well correlated. As an example from Thaler (1991: 153, originally from Tversky and Kahneman 1983):

Consider a regular six-sided die with four green faces and two red faces. The die will be rolled 20 times and the sequence of greens (G) and reds (R) will be recorded. You are asked to select one sequence, from a set of three, and you will win $25 if the sequence you choose appears on successive rolls of the die. Please check the sequence of greens and reds on which you prefer to bet:

A. RGRRR

B. GRGRRR

C. GRRRRR

Since A is a subset of B, it must be more probable than B. But B may appear more representative of a probable sequence because of the two Gs. In this experiment, 63 per cent of respondents chose B, and 35 per cent chose A.

The availability heuristic leads individuals to overestimate probabilities of recent or vivid events. It arises when people estimate the frequency of a class by the ease of recalling specific instances in that class. People also use anchoring heuristics, where arbitrary amounts become the bases for forming numerical estimates of uncertain quantities. One example is an experiment asking subjects to state the percentage of African countries in the United Nations after being given an arbitrary starting point (based on a ball thrown on a spinning wheel with numbers from 1 to 100). The median estimates of membership were 25 per cent for groups with ten as a starting point and 45 per cent for groups that received 65 as a starting point (Tversky and Kahneman 1974).

The affect heuristic, recently proposed by Slovic and others (2002), describes the bias estimating probabilities that results from an individual's like or dislike of an outcome. They argue that the affect heuristic can affect one's evaluation of costs and benefits and even the predicted economic performance of various industries (Kahneman 2003: 1463).

Finally, choices between alternatives can also be affected by the context of the event and the way in which a risk is framed (Kahneman and Tversky 1979). For example, McNeil *et al.* (1982) framed a hypothetical choice about lung cancer treatments from surgery in two ways; as either a 68 per cent chance of survival or a 32 per cent chance of not surviving. With a 68 per cent chance of survival, 44 per cent of respondents chose surgery over radiation. Framed as a 32 per cent chance of not surviving, the number dropped to 18 per cent.

Developing country studies

Our goal is to understand the prevalence and nature of anomalies in developing country contexts in the field (as opposed to the laboratory), and to compare decisions across policy domains. Examining behavioural anomalies first requires designing and implementing stated and revealed preference surveys for eliciting and measuring characteristics that affect individual decision making. Stated preference methods involve asking for responses (by choosing, ranking, or providing an open-ended answer) to sets of hypothetical scenarios, defined by underlying attributes. For example, to elicit a discount rate, a stated preference experiment might ask a respondent to choose between an immediate lump sum payment and a series of constant payments over a number of years (Cameron and Gerdes 2002) or to provide an amount of money that would equate lump sum payments to be received at different times (Anderson *et al.* 2004).

Revealed preference questions measure actual behaviours. For example, to study risk attitudes, a stated preference question may ask a respondent to indicate their preference for a different set of hypothetical gambles with a coin toss, the return that would make a certain outcome equivalent to a gamble, or how important they believe risk taking is for certain outcomes like financial success. Conversely, revealed preference surveys would look at actual choices that reveal risk tolerance, for example, at how the individual has diversified their income sources or other portfolios. Binswanger (1980) looked at the relationship between stated preference and actual behaviour.

Common concerns with stated preference surveys are validity and learning. Sceptics worry that especially without remuneration respondents will put little effort into responding. In a review of over 70 experiments, however, Camerer and Hogarth (1999) conclude that overall there is no effect on mean performance though response variance declines with financial incentives. Performance of some specific tasks, including complex ones, does improve with remuneration. The authors note (p. 7), however, 'that no replicated study has made rationality violations disappear purely by raising incentives'. Though learning may occur in repeated experiments, experimenters have found that amateurs and experts in the field tend to perform similarly.

The vast majority of the methodological work on stated preference surveys has been in developed counties. Elements of these instruments can be adapted for use in developing countries, but experience suggests that great care is necessary at both the survey design and data analysis phase to control for the different context (Cameron and Gerdes 2002; Corso *et al.* 2001). For example, Kuechler (1998) has argued that a country's recognition of freedom of speech and culture of individualism will affect survey responses. Certainly in Russia and Vietnam one can imagine that many individuals still fear answering questions or offering opinions that might deviate from official expectations. In this section we briefly describe some ongoing work: discount rates in Vietnam and Russia; risk perceptions in Russia; and decision heuristics by level of policy-maker in Vietnam. Full details on these experiments can be found in Thaler (1981), Benzion *et al.* (1989), Anderson *et al.* (2004) and Anderson *et al.* (2006).

Example 1: intertemporal choices in Vietnam and Russia

There is a considerable literature on time preference and discount rates – the rate at which individuals trade off future for present consumption. One type of experiment to reveal discount rate patterns compares discount rates calculated from respondents comparing smaller, earlier rewards (or penalties) to larger, later rewards (or penalties). In 1981, Richard Thaler asked University of Oregon students to state the amount of money they would require either to postpone a fine or expedite the receipt of lottery winnings, assuming no risk. Thaler asked the question for lottery winnings of $15, $250 and $3,000 and three-month, one-year, and three-year delays. Several years later, Benzion *et al.* (1989) conducted a similar study with students at the University of Haifa and the Technion-Israel Institute of Technology. Their questionnaire asked for intertemporal choices over four scenarios of postponing or expediting a receipt or payment, time delays and sizes of cash flow. The Israel study used dollar amounts of $40, $200, $1,000 and $5,000 and time delays of five months, one, two and four years.

For both the USA and Israel we show their results in Table 34.1 for the scenario that most closely corresponds to the Vietnam and Russia experiment. The first and fifth column represent the different cash flows in the USA and Israel, with the different time delays for repayment across the top row. The discount rates inferred from their dollar responses appear in the cells; median rates for the USA and mean rates for Israel.

In both the USA and Israel, the results suggest that discount rates are not constant, and that they decrease as the size of the cash flow increases. That is, the smaller the postponed fine or delayed receipt, the higher the discount rate. Discount rates also vary inversely with the period of time until repayment or receipt. The discount rate of 277 for $15 in three months is the highest in the US, and the discount rate of 53.5 for $40 in five months is the highest in Israel. The Vietnam and Russia studies were undertaken more than ten years later. In 2000, interviewers from Vietnam's Institute of Sociology randomly sampled individuals from two communes near Hanoi city: the urban Quynh Mai and the more rural Thach Ban. In 2002 we replicated the Vietnam study with a random sample from in and around two southern Siberian cities.

We sought to replicate the USA and Israel questions as closely as possible, but we encountered several difficulties during pre-tests. First, respondents had strong feelings about receipts or payments from public institutions – often either extreme distrust or extreme allegiance. Non-governmental organizations (NGOs) elicited less emotion. Second, respondents had some difficulty with the idea of hypothetical tradeoffs. Third, the discount rate for respondents in Vietnam and Russia fell to almost zero after three months; respondents were unable or unwilling to differentiate among longer time periods. Finally, we could not use comparable monetary amounts, even adjusted for purchasing power parity. Respondents in Vietnam were unable or unwilling to differentiate among large amounts beyond about half their annual income.

Table 34.1 Inferred discount rates, USA (median) and Israel (mean)

Original amount, USA	Later amount paid in			Original amount, Israel	Later amount paid in			
	3 months	1 year	3 years		5 months	1 year	2 years	4 years
$15	277	139	63	$40	53.5	33.0	26.5	20.6
$250	73	34	23	$200	32.1	23.6	21.0	15.7
$3,000	62	29	23	$1,000	31.0	21.9	16.6	16.3
				$5,000	26.1	19.2	14.9	13.6
N = 20				N = 204				

Sources: Thaler (1981) and Benzion *et al.* (1989).

Ultimately in Vietnam we asked respondents to imagine that they had the opportunity to receive a loan from a NGO and that they had the choice of paying back the loan immediately or postponing the payment to a later date, at which time they would have to pay back a larger amount. The questions used sums of Vietnamese dong (VND), 100,000, 1,000,000 and 4,000,000, and time periods of one day, three months and one year. At the time of the study, US$1 was worth about VND 14,500, so the survey amounts were worth about $7, $70 and $276.

Russian respondents were asked to imagine that they had just received a loan with the choice of paying it back immediately or postponing repayment to a later date, at which time they would have to pay back a larger amount. We used sums of Russian roubles, 1,500, 6,000 and 30,000, for the same Vietnam time periods of one day, three months and one year. At the time of the survey, US$1 was worth about 30 roubles, so survey amounts were worth about $50, $200 and $1,000.

Table 34.2 reports the results for Vietnam and Russia. We report median rates for the Russian (and USA) study, where the size of the inferred discount rates and the standard deviation of responses was much larger, and mean rates for Vietnam (and Israel). Thaler speculates that this large deviation may be due to the hypothetical nature of the study or the age of the respondents. There are, however, cases of similar results in studies without hypothetical questions Hausman (1979), and Benzion *et al.* (1989) compute considerably lower rates with a similarly young sample. Nonetheless, as Thaler points out, what matters is the relative, not the absolute levels.

Table 34.2 again reports the varying dollar amounts for the two studies in columns one and five, the time periods across the top rows and the discount rates in the cells within. Our results suggest that despite field and experimental differences and despite the vastly different demographics and circumstances of the respondents, the discount rate patterns are all inconsistent with assumptions of time invariant discount rates. The variance within the discount rates in each study all suggest the same conclusion: respondents' discount rates are not constant over time, but rather vary inversely with time and the size of the cash flow, and in contradiction to the standard DU model, which would predict the same rate for one day, one month and one year.

Our surveys also collected some basic information on respondents. Living rurally was a strong indicator of higher discount rates, which may partially reflect risk. Consistent with other studies, we found discount rates decreased with age and were negatively associated with income (Davies and Lea 1995; Anderson and Nevitte 2006). Irving Fisher (1930: 73) asserted that 'a small income, other things being equal, tends to produce a high rate of impatience'. Lawrence (1991: 54) found similar evidence of this in the United States. Her results may imply that impatience leads to poverty, as individuals with high rates of time preference choose jobs with low and flat pay scales rather than ones that pay well only after a period of training or education. Alternatively, poverty breeds impatience from living at or near subsistence. Relative, rather than absolute, income may also matter in ways we have not picked up. Even within a poor, rural commune in Vietnam, for example, members will distinguish between who is 'poor' and who is not.

Table 34.2   Inferred discount rates, Vietnam (mean) and Russia (median)

Original amount, Vietnam	Later amount paid in			Original amount, Russia	Later amount paid in		
	1 day	1 month	1 year		1 day	1 month	1 year
$7	66.9	2.5	1.5	$50	102.4	3.2	1.3
$70	33.5	0.9	0.7	$200	56.2	2.4	1.1
$276	18.3	0.7	0.6	$1,000	55.8	1.8	0.9
N = 232				N = 417			

Source: Anderson and Cullen (2005).

Example 2: risk perceptions in Russia

Our Russian data were collected during a three-month period in the summer of 2000. Russian-speaking USA graduate students teamed with Russian graduate students to survey approximately 500 residents of Novosibirsk oblast and Irkutsk oblast in southwestern Siberia.

Novosibirsk grew to prominence during the Second World War when, for security reasons, the Kremlin decided to relocate its military-industrial complex and the Academy of Sciences there. With over 2 million inhabitants, Novosibirsk is Russia's third largest city after Moscow and St Petersburg. The city hosts the arts, industry, 13 institutes of higher education including its 'Academgorodok' university campus, and the seat of regional government (Carver 2003: 9). Irkutsk lies further to the east, near Lake Baikal, and has a history dating from the mid-1600s as a trading juncture between China and Russia's south. In the mid-1800s, the exile of several intellectual radicals to Irkutsk associated Siberia with labour camps and prisons. In 1898, the trans-Siberian railway added to its importance as a trading post. It is populated with small businesses, traders and its 650,000 inhabitants are more ethnically mixed than Novosibirsk.

The survey contained multiple stated preference questions that were intended to measure risk and related psychological parameters: three coin-toss questions, nine discounting questions, two risk and optimism attitudinal questions and six questions on uncertain outcomes intended to represent qualitative dimensions of risk. We report only a few preliminary results here. The coin-toss questions took the usual form, with even odds for flipping heads or tails. Situation 1 and 2 involved simple prospects: a sure positive outcome for option one versus gambling for a positive payoff in option two. Situation 3 was a binary prospect, offering two gambles, both with a possible loss. Payoffs in roubles, the percentage of responses for option one (%) and total sample size (N) are in Table 34.3. At the time, US$1 = 30 roubles. Sixty-two per cent of respondents chose the riskless option in a fair gamble (option 1 in situation 1). More people were willing to gamble when the expected value of the gamble was less than the sure bet, as in situation 2. But in situation 2 the amounts are small, even in Siberia 300 roubles ($10) is not a lot of money. Hence we expect that the small magnitude of the gamble is affecting this result, that is, people are more willing to give up a sure 300 roubles to gamble

Table 34.3   The expected values of the options in the three scenarios

	Option 1	%	Option 2	N
Situation 1	10,000	62	EV = 0.5(20,000) + 0.5(0) = 20,000	948
Situation 2	300	52	EV = 0.5(450) + 0.5(0) = 225	914
Situation 3	EV = 0.5(900) − 0.5(30) = 435	76	EV = 0.5(6000) − 0.5(4500) = 750	890

Source: Anderson and Cullen (2005).

with smaller amounts (Rabin 1998). The results in situation 3 are consistent with loss aversion. People are willing to gamble for a much lower expected value in order to avoid a potentially large loss.

The question on the qualitative dimensions of uncertain outcomes was primarily intended to assess if risk perceptions varied by experience, that is, if small business owners perceived certain risks differently than non-small business owners. Arguably some of these outcomes, such as mafia involvement, taxes and debt, represent other dimensions that have been found to affect risk perceptions, such as proximity, control, dread and familiarity. The survey asked respondents to indicate which, of a number of listed reasons, they thought might lead someone to not be interested in borrowing. Responses were coded from a zero for strongly agree, to a three for strongly disagree. The OLS results (equally weak but easier to interpret than an ordered probit estimation) appear in Table 34.4. The dependent variable is the degree to which respondents disagreed with proposed reasons for individuals not wanting to borrow money to start a business, hence the higher the response of the individual the more likely they disagreed. Income was excluded because of our concerns with its validity and we acknowledge the possibility that small business ownership is endogenous, biasing the estimates.

In general, age is a predictor of risk attitudes: the older one is, the more likely they are to believe that concerns about the mafia, legal system, or interest rate would deter someone from small business ownership. Mafia is more of a concern in Irkutsk, debt is less (despite earlier results that discount rates are significantly higher). Gender is only significant in the case of concern over taxes, and internet access in the case of the mafia. Small business owners see these risks differently from the population as a whole. They are more likely to find taxes and interest rates too high, and less likely to view mafia involvement as a deterrent. These results are preliminary, but suggest that loss aversion matters and that familiarity affects subjective risk perceptions.

Example 3: fairness and decision heuristics in Vietnam

To understand systematic and recurrent biases in resource allocation and programme design requires taking these experiments a step further. It requires identifying regular differences in patterns of bounded rationality along the policy chain: between the policy-makers, programme/project designers and programme/project recipients. Policy-makers convey broad ideas, directions and priorities, and

Table 34.4 Perceptions of the qualitative dimensions of risky outcomes

Dependent variable	Taxes too high	Mafia is a problem	Worried about debt	No trust in legal system	Interest rate too high
Constant	0.553***	0.989***	0.679***	1.28***	0.985***
Age	9.74E-05	−0.007**	0.001	−0.011***	−0.006**
Gender, male = 1	0.314***	0.103	0.059	0.093	0.105
Education	0.042*	0.041	0.030	−0.016	0.009
City of interview Irkutsk = 1	−0.053	0.272**	−0.149*	−0.032	0.089
Internet access yes = 1 no = 0	0.027	0.122	0.155*	0.010	0.037
Small business owner yes = 1	−0.174**	0.253**	0.004	−0.020	−0.151*
N = 610	$R^2 = 0.03$	$R^2 = 0.05$	$R^2 = 0.01$	$R^2 = 0.03$	$R^2 = 0.03$

Note: *** significant at 1%; ** significant at 5%; * significant at 10%.

Source: Anderson and Cullen (2005).

thereby a flow of resources to intermediary groups – government agencies, quasi or non-governmental organizations, or members of the private sector – for programme design and implementation. These intermediaries convert policy statements into a set of rules that represent the incentives – constraints and opportunities – faced by recipients. Hence, decisions at each level allocate resources and frame the decisions for the group that follow.

Kahneman (2003) describes two modes of thinking: intuition and reasoning. Effort and association are two characteristics that distinguish these processes: intuition is effortless and associative, while reasoning is slow, effortful and rule-governed. We posit that the amount of effort one chooses to expend making a decision is a function of the responsibility they bear and experience they have over decision making and the outcome, and the expected net value of the outcome. The expected net value of the outcome depends on the decision-makers' risk attitudes, and their expectations about the benefits relative to the effort, time and other resource costs of making the decision. These costs are affected by their access to information, both internal (through association) and external (through exposure). Benefits depend on the probability of the outcome occurring and the qualitative dimensions of risky outcomes: how much control they perceive over it, their familiarity with it, and its regularity, proximity and reversibility. If this theory holds, then the degree to which one expends effort and the type of decision heuristics they use is expected to vary by experience, responsibility and risk perceptions. For most developing and transition countries, these characteristics can be expected to differ significantly between the policy-makers and programme recipients. These parameters are also assumed to depend on the decision-making domain. For example, one may be very conservative in financial decisions, but reveal a high risk tolerance in health decisions or a strong willingness to experiment with a variety of seeds. These domain sensitivities may split according to decision-making roles, which are often segregated by age and gender.

To explore these ideas in Vietnam, we asked the same set of behavioural questions to 40 relatively poor farmers (mean monthly income = 842,062 VND, or approximately $53) and to 40 middle- and high-level professionals involved in policy making (mean monthly income = 4,210,213 VND, or approximately $265). We refer to this latter group as policy-makers, though their direct involvement varies. Respondents were asked a series of questions designed to reflect cognitive effort and views on fairness. We report on some preliminary results. First, farmers and policy-makers would allocate development funds in quite different proportions, with farmers allocating much more to healthcare and policy-makers to the financial sector. Both favoured vouchers as a form of aid, but farmers were more in favour of unconditional money transfers than policy-makers were. Policy-makers would allocate more money to subsidized seed, while farmers would allocate relatively more to subsidized medicine and subsidized credit.

Following on the work of Kahneman *et al.* (1986), respondents were asked how fair they considered interest rate changes in response to an increase in demand versus an increase in costs of the lenders. On average, both groups considered it more fair for savings and co-operatives to raise rates than for moneylenders to do so. This distinction, perhaps driven more by views about the lenders than by behavioural issues, is more pronounced than differences according to whether the increases are demand versus cost driven. One interesting finding is that policy-makers were significantly more inclined to give an answer and state whether they thought the increases were acceptable or unfair. Almost half of the farmer sample responded that they did not know, compared to approximately 10 per cent of policy-makers.

Respondents were given a series of questions first suggested by Frederick *et al.* (2002, reported in Kahneman 2003) such as: medicine and a vaccination cost VND 110,000 in total. The medicine costs 100,000 more than the vaccination. How much does the vaccination cost? In Frederick's experiments, 50 per cent or fewer university students gave a correct response to this question. In our sample, the percentages of correct and incorrect responses are given in Table 34.5. The questions differed slightly in their wording, though the algorithm for determining the answer is the same in all cases.

Table 34.5 shows that for each decision a much higher percentage of policy-makers answered correctly. For example, 70 per cent of policy-makers compared to 5 per cent of farmers in the question that substituted socks and shoes for medicine and a vaccine. The questions appeared in the survey in the same order as in the table. Given the common algorithm, the variation by domain is surprising. In all cases, policy-makers also took at least a minute longer (significant at 10 per cent) to answer.

Table 34.5   Per cent answering correctly

Decision	Socks and shoes	Medicines and vaccines	Chicken and rice	Interest and loan fees
% correct farmers	5	0	25	0
% correct policy-makers	70	60	90	45

Source: Anderson *et al.* (2006).

We then asked respondents to make choices among outcomes with multiple attributes: a medicine for diarrhoea, a modern variety seed and a loan officer for a local savings co-operative. In the case of the seed, for example, they were given the rankings out of 10 for three varieties:

Variety 1 – 4, 5, 9
Variety 2 – 6, 6, 6
Variety 3 – 10, 10, 0

The 4, 5 and 9 refer to the ranking out of 10 for each of three desirable attributes (taste, pest resistance and drought resistance), but respondents were told that it was unknown which ranking went with which attribute. In all domains the farmers were more likely than policy-makers to choose the option where a single element and a subset of attributes scored the highest, but where one attribute scored 0 (variety 3 in this case). We interpreted the option with a zero as the riskiest, but in two batteries of risk questions – one with lotteries and one asking to identify their own risk preferences – farmers were significantly more risk adverse than the policy-makers. This suggests that something other than risk preferences may be driving the decision heuristic on option choice. Policy-makers were significantly more likely to choose the option where every attribute scored equally (variety 2 in this case), and in all cases but one it was their first choice. The one exception was in the seed question where their first choice was the last choice of farmers. This is arguably the domain where direct experience differs most between policy-makers and recipients.

In many cases the differences emerging between farmers and policy-makers is striking. It is premature to know whether and how these results derive from differences in cognitive processes and, if so, what is behind this – exposure, experience, a sense of control, responsibility, etc. But it is not, we believe, premature to recognize that if systematic differences are revealed in these behavioural experiments that they may lead to a disconnect between the resource allocations and policy designs of policy-makers and programme recipients.

Why does this matter for international development policy?

Three developing country characteristics suggest that behavioural anomalies may be even less anomalous (i.e. they may be much closer to the norm) than observed in the USA and Europe. These characteristics are:

1. greater incidence of poverty and food insecurity;
2. lower incidence of well-functioning markets, combined with greater price and output variability common to rural agricultural markets and aggravated by the occurrence of extreme events such as natural disasters and war; and
3. greater rural proportion of the population and the concentration of poverty in rural areas.

The poor may disproportionately represent populations for whom traditional behavioural assertions are inappropriate if anomalies arise from threshold effects around base levels such as minimum subsistence income. And more individuals in developing countries live in poverty, with few assets, and are food insecure. The 2004 gross national income per capita was US$510 for low-income countries compared to US$32,040 for high-income countries (World Bank 2005; the gap narrows using figures adjusted for purchasing power parity (PPP) to US$2,290 and US$30,980).

Critics of behavioural economics argue that the anomalies of imperfect rationality can be ignored because the actions of a few that deviate from utility or profit maximization will be eliminated by arbitrage and competition in well-functioning markets. But much of the exchange that occurs in developing and transition economies takes place in small, personal, informal and poorly functioning markets, such that any anomalous behaviour is more likely to influence resource allocation. Schneider and Klinglmair (2004) estimate the average size of shadow economies as a percentage of official GDP to be 18 per cent for OECD countries, 38 per cent for transition countries and 41 per cent for developing countries.

Price variability is common to developing country markets and chronic in agricultural commodity, input and labour markets. Variability is due to factors such as lack of credit, migration, inadequate infrastructure such as roads, irrigation and storage facilities, and erratic input supply. It is exacerbated by droughts, floods, pestilence, war and civil strife. If fairness motives influence decision making in response to price changes, then we would predict, on average, that resource allocation would be particularly affected in the more volatile markets of developing countries. Living rurally has also been a strong predictor of differences in time preference and risk tolerance, even when income is controlled for. These results may stem from the relatively high transaction costs faced by rural dwellers compared to their urban counterparts. In particular, the high cost of exchanging information, and thereby contextualizing and verifying it, may result in fewer, more homogeneous, and less reliable or valid sources.

More individuals in developing countries live in rural areas, with South America being more urbanized than other regions. More than half of the population of most African countries live rurally. Two-thirds to three-quarters of the population live rurally in the largest countries in Asia (UNDP 2002). In the wealthier countries of North America and Europe, these numbers tend to be reversed. Rural populations also tend to be poorer and have access to fewer formal institutions and markets that might offer opportunities to insure against present consumption biases and perceived risks. Kinship and other informal means of solidarity tend to break down in periods of extreme hardship.

Transition economies vary widely in terms of rural living and poverty, but they share some characteristics such as limited market experience, a history of controlled information and growing levels of inequality. In Russia, for instance, there is evidence that individuals measure their wellbeing relative to reference points, either their own baseline, or relative to others (Easterlin 1996; McBride 2001; Graham *et al.* 2004). For seven consecutive years after the 'fall of the wall' GDP per capita annual growth declined, and current levels remain below 1989 levels. The Gini coefficient for Russia in 2000 was 45.62, high by OECD country standards, higher than estimates of 29 in 1992, and most certainly higher than estimates prior to 1989 (Graham 2004: 6). Hence we can expect that some individuals, at least relative to their income pre-transition, perceive themselves as being worse off than previously.

Individuals in transition economies are facing vast changes in how scarce resources are allocated; prices and a market system are replacing time and personal networks. There is some evidence that suggests market experience is important to the distribution of rents and overcoming the endowment effect, but that with 'sufficient' experience learning occurs and competitive market outcomes can be expected (Camerer 1987; List 2003; 2004a; 2004b). The pace and extent of this learning, however, can be expected to vary with age and experience with the former regime.

It becomes rather obvious from the observations above that, in the context of developing and transition economies, policy based on standard economic model predictions may fail to achieve its objectives. This seems to be consistent with the evidence regarding the rather limited effectiveness of development assistance in producing the expected results both in terms of growth and poverty reduction. This poor performance has led to changes in the prevailing paradigms for development policy and the search for the proper balance between 'state-led' and 'market-led' solutions. We are suggesting that this distinction may in fact be artificial or, in any case, not the most important one. Rather, development policy frameworks may have missed salient points of people's behaviour which determine the success (or lack thereof) of the policies themselves.

How might behavioural economics contribute?

There are hundreds of models of decision making that more accurately describe behaviour in a particular context relative to strict rational maximization. But efficient policy requires less *ad hoc* behavioural models. Preserving the ability to generalize may come from retaining the rigour of the current model where its predictions have been regularly confirmed, and making changes only where behaviours systematically deviate for certain populations or in certain domains.

For example, the findings of time-varying discount rates appear to be fairly robust across at least four cultures (Anderson *et al.* 2004). And experiments suggest that many of the poor are sophisticates who seek self-commitment mechanisms (Ashraf *et al.* 2006). Gugerty (2004) provides evidence from Kenya that women join rotating savings and credit associations because they help to provide a self-commitment mechanism. Yet much microfinance literature and practice still rests on the traditional assumption that individuals can only be made better off with access to credit since they can always chose not to avail themselves of it. A behavioural perspective would recognize that even with good intent, the initial borrowing and payback plan of individuals can change. As it stands, offering credit without acknowledging imperfect self-control, and hence without the appropriate institutional incentives, such as voluntary and mandatory savings, assumes away a possible source of repayment difficulties.

Empirically documenting regular deviations from standard rationality is the first step to identifying where the payoffs from modifying the model, and hence the policy design, may be worthwhile. Experiments that reveal individuals are willing to suffer economic losses for reasons of fairness and revenge may help to explain why simply improving market or programme access for individuals does not guarantee participation. Interventions that affect the qualitative dimensions of risky outcomes, such as technologies that increase a farmer's sense of control even if they do not affect the magnitude of the risk, may alter the decision to adopt. Considering the endowment effect in the design of land reform programmes may narrow the gap between buying and selling prices. When property rights are incomplete, the endowment effect might also explain an individual's willingness to expend more than the value of the right through violence, law suits, etc., in order to secure what they believe is already theirs (Mullainathan 2005).

Ravi Kanbur's (2003: 2) observation that 'the development journals are by and large stuck in the rational choice paradigm', is as Knetsch notes ironically, predicted by the findings of behavioural economics (1995: 75). But the problem may run deeper than the status quo bias to which Knetsch refers and may include uncomfortable compromises to consumer sovereignty, 'ought we allow people to behave imprudently?' (Strotz 1956: 179). Camerer *et al.* (2003) have suggested 'asymmetric paternalism', regulations that would create large benefits for those who are not fully rational but impose little or no harm on those who are. But it is not always clear how to move from experimental findings to policy recommendations. Sample sizes are often small due to the complexity of the survey instruments, and not random, which limits our ability to generalize. And without more theoretical guidance, the empirical strategy is often more inductive than deductive, and more opportunistic than strategic.

In his 1993 Nobel Prize speech, Douglass North argued that explaining the performance of economies through time required a better understanding of institutions and cognition (North 1994). International development policy now reflects a growing understanding of the role of institutions, but despite Nobel prizes to Herbert Simon, Vernon Smith and the psychologist Daniel Kahneman, what we know about cognition has yet to regularly penetrate our analysis. Yet our research suggests that for the future of development policy, despite the challenges, getting the institutions right requires understanding patterns of imperfect rationality.

Note

The authors would like to thank the Center for Studies in Demography and Ecology at the University of Washington, the Agricultural and Development Economics Division at the United Nations Food and Agriculture Organization (FAO) and the US Department of State for the funding that made these experiments possible. The authors would also like to extend their thanks to the participants at a seminar in FAO for useful comments and suggestions.

References

Ainslie, G. (1991) 'Derivation of "Rational" Economic Behaviour from Hyperbolic Discount Curves', *AEA Papers and Proceedings*, 81: 334–40.

Allais, M. (1953) 'Le comportement de l'homme rationnel devant le risque, critique des postulats et axiomes de lécole Americaine', *Econometrica*, 21: 503–46.

Anderson, C.L. and A. Cullen (2005) 'The Qualitative Dimensions of Risky Outcomes and Decision Making in Russia', Mimeo.

Anderson, C.L., A. Cullen and K. Stamoulis (2006) 'Decision Making Along the Policy Chain in Vietnam', Mimeo.

Anderson C.L., M. Dietz, A. Gordon and M. Klawitter (2004) 'Discount Rates in Vietnam', *Economic Development and Cultural Change*, 52, 4: 110–34.

Anderson, C.L. and N. Nevitte (2006) 'Teach Your Children Well: Changing Values of Thrift and Saving', *Journal of Economic Psychology*, 27, 1: 247–61.

Ashraf, N., D.S. Karlan and W. Yin (2006) 'Tying Odysseus to the Mast: Evidence from a Commitment Savings Product in the Philippines', *Quarterly Journal of Economics*, 121, 2: 635–72.

Benzion, U., A. Rapoport and J. Yagil (1989) 'Discount Rates Inferred from Decisions: An Experimental Study', *Management Science*, 35: 270–84.

Bereby-Meyer, Y. and M. Niederle (2005) 'Fairness and Bargaining', *Journal of Economic Behaviour and Organization*, 56: 173–86.

Binswanger, H. (1980) 'Attitudes Toward Risk: Experimental Measurement in Rural India', *American Agricultural Economics Association*, 62: 395–406.

Camerer, C.F. (1987) 'Do Biases in Probability Judgement Matter in Markets? Experimental Evidence', *American Economic Review*, 77, 5: 981–97.

Camerer, C. and R. Hogarth (1999) 'The Effects of Financial Incentives in Economics Experiments: A Review and Capital-Labour-Production Framework', *Journal of Risk and Uncertainty*, 19: 7–42.

Camerer, C.F. and R.H. Thaler (1995) 'Ultimatums, Dictators, and Manners', *Journal of Economic Perspectives*, 9, 2: 209–19.

Camerer, C., S. Issacharoff, G. Loewenstein, T. O'Donoghue and M. Rabin (2003) 'Regulation for Conservatives: Behavioural Economics and the Case for "Asymmetric Paternalism" ', *University of Pennsylvania Law Review*, 151: 1211–54.

Cameron, T.A. and G.R. Gerdes (2002) 'Eliciting-Specific Discount Rates', unpublished manuscript.

Carver, J.W. (2003) 'Cross-Cultural Data Production: The Case of Russia', Mimeo, University of Washington: Evans School of Public Affairs.

Chapman, G.B. (2003) 'Discounting of Health Outcomes, in Time and Decision', in G. Loewenstein, D. Read and R.F. Baumeister (eds), *Time and Decision*, New York: Russell Sage Foundation.

Corso, P.S., J.K. Hammitt and J.D. Graham (2001) 'Valuing Mortality-Risk Reduction: Using Visual Aids to Improve the Validity of Contingent Valuation', *Journal of Risk and Uncertainty*, 23, 2: 165–84.

Davies, E. and S.E.G. Lea (1995) 'Student Attitudes to Student Debt', *Journal of Economic Psychology*, 16: 663–79.

Easterlin, R.A. (1996) *Growth Triumphant: The Twenty-first Century in Historical Perspective*, Ann Arbor: University of Michigan Press.

Fisher, I. (1930) *The Theory of Interest*, London: Macmillan.

Frederick, S., G. Loewenstein and T. O'Donoghue (2002) 'Time Discounting and Time Preference: A Critical Review', *Journal of Economic Literature*, XL: 351–401.

Graham, C. (2004) 'Can Happiness Research Contribute to Development Economics?', Mimeo, Washington, DC: The Brookings Institution.

Graham, C., A. Eggers and S. Sukhtankar (2004) 'Does Happiness Pay? An Exploration Based on Panel Data from Russia', *Journal of Economic Behaviour and Organization*, 55: 319–42.

Gugerty, M.K. (2004) 'You Can't Save Alone: Commitment in Rotating Savings and Credit Associations in Kenya', Mimeo, Seattle: University of Washington.

Gurr, T.R. (1970) *Why Men Rebel*, New Jersey: Princeton University Press.

Harris, C. and D. Laibson (2001) 'Hyperbolic Discounting and Consumption', forthcoming in 8th World Congress of the Econometric Society.

Hausman, J. (1979) 'Individual Discount Rates and the Purchase and Utilization of Energy Using Durables', *Bell Journal of Economics*, 10, 1: 33–54.

Henrich, J., R. Boyd, S. Bowles, C. Camerer, E. Fehr, H. Gintis, R. McElreath, M. Alvard, A. Barr, J. Ensminger, N.S. Henrich, K. Hill, F. Gil-White, M. Gurven, F.W. Marlowe, J.Q. Patton and D. Tracer (2005) 'Economic Man in Cross-Cultural Perspective: Behavioural Experiments in 15 Small-Scale Societies', *Behavioural and Brain Sciences*, 28: 795–855.

Johnson, E.J., J. Hershey, J. Meszaros and H. Kunreuther (1993) 'Framing, Probability Distortions, and Insurance Decisions', *Journal of Risk and Uncertainty*, 7, 1: 35–51.

Kahneman, D. (2003) 'Maps of Bounded Rationality: Psychology for Behavioural Economics', *American Economic Review*, 93, 5: 1449–75.

Kahneman, D. and A. Tversky (1979) 'Prospect Theory: An Analysis of Decision Under Risk', *Econometrica*, 47: 263–91.

Kahneman, D., J. Knetsch and R.H. Thaler (1986) 'Fairness as a Constraint on Profit Seeking: Entitlements in the Market', *American Economic Review*, 76, 4: 728–41.

Kahneman, D., J. Knetsch and R.H. Thaler (1990) 'Experimental Effects of the Endowment Effect and the Coase Theorem', *Journal of Political Economy*, 98, 6: 1325–48.

Kahneman, D., P. Slovic and A. Tversky (eds) (1982) *Judgement under Uncertainty: Heuristics and Biases*, Cambridge: Cambridge University Press.

Kanbur, R. (2003) 'Behavioural Development Economics', notes from the conference on Economics for an Imperfect World.

Knetsch, J.L. (1995) 'Assumptions, Behavioural Findings, and Policy Analysis', *Journal of Policy Analysis and Management*, 14, 1: 68–78.

Kreps, D.M. (1990) *A Course in Microeconomic Theory*, New Jersey: Princeton University Press.

Kuechler, M. (1998) 'The Survey Method', *American Behavioural Scientist*, 42, 2: 178–200.

Laibson, D. (1997) 'Golden Eggs and Hyperbolic Discounting', *Quarterly Journal of Economics*, 112, 2: 443–78.

Lawrence, E. (1991) 'Poverty and the Rate of Time Preference: Evidence from Panel Data', *Journal of Political Economy*, 99: 54–77.

List, J. (2003) 'Does Market Experience Eliminate Market Anomalies?', *Quarterly Journal of Economics*, 118, 1: 41–71.

List, J. (2004a) 'Neoclassical Theory Versus Prospect Theory: Evidence from the Marketplace', *Econometrica*, 72, 2: 615–25.

List, J. (2004b) 'Testing Neoclassical Competitive Theory in Multi-Lateral Decentralized Markets', *Journal of Political Economy*, 112: 1131–56.

Loewenstein, G. and J. Elster (1992) *Choice Over Time*, New York: Russell Sage Foundation.

Loewenstein, G. and D. Prelec (1992) 'Anomalies in Intertemporal Choice: Evidence and Interpretation', *Quarterly Journal of Economics*, 107: 573–97.

Machina, M.J. (1987) 'Choice Under Uncertainty: Problems Solved and Unsolved', *Journal of Economic Perspectives*, 1: 121–54.

McBride, M. (2001) 'Relative-Income Effects on Subjective Wellbeing in the Cross-Section', *Journal of Economic Behaviour and Organization*, 45: 251–78.

McNeil, B.J., S.G. Pauker, H.C. Sox and A. Tversky (1982) 'On the Elicitation of Preferences for Alternative Therapies', *New England Journal of Medicine*, 306, 21: 1259–62.

Mullainathan, S. (2005) 'Development Economics through the Lens of Psychology', *Annual Bank Conference in Development Economics*, in F. Bourguigon and B. Pleskovic (eds), Washington, DC: World Bank.

North, D.C. (1994) 'Economic Performance Through Time', *American Economic Review*, 84, 3: 359–68.

Pate, E. (1983) 'Acceptable Decision Processes and Acceptable Risks in Public Sector Regulations', *IEEE Transactions on Systems, Man, and Cybernetics* SMC-13: 113–24.

Prelec, D. (2001) 'Compound Invariant Weighting Functions in Prospect Theory', in D. Kahneman and A. Tversky (eds), *Choices, Values, and Frames*, New York: Russell Sage Foundation.

Rabin, M. (1996) 'Psychology and Economics', Mimeo.

Rabin, M. (1998) 'Psychology and Economics', *Journal of Economic Literature*, 36, 1: 11–46.

Rabin, M. (2002) 'A Perspective on Psychology and Economics', *European Economic Review*, 46: 657–85.

Rubinstein, A. (1998) *Modeling Bounded Rationality*, Cambridge, MA: MIT Press.

Samuelson, P. (1937) 'A Note on Measurement of Utility', *Review of Economic Studies*, 4: 155–61.

Schneider, F. and R. Klinglmair (2004) 'Shadow Economies around the World: What Do We Know?', *Institute for the Study of Labour (IZA) Discussion Paper* 1043, Bonn: IZA.

Slovic, P., B. Fischoff and S. Lichtenstein (1979) 'Rating the Risks', *Environment*, 21: 14–20, 36–9.

Slovic, P., M. Finucane, E. Peters and D.G. MacGregor (2002) 'The Affect Heuristic', in T. Gilovich, D. Griffin and D. Kahneman (eds), *Heuristics and Biases: The Psychology of Intuitive Thought*, New York: Cambridge University Press.

Strotz, R. (1956) 'Myopia and Inconsistency in Dynamic Utility Maximization', *Review of Economic Studies*, 23: 177.

Thaler, R. (1981) 'Some Empirical Evidence on Dynamic Inconsistency', *Economic Letters*, 8: 201–7.

Thaler, R.H. (1991) *Quasi Rational Economics*, New York: Russell Sage Foundation.

Tversky, A. and D. Kahneman (1974) 'Judgment Under Uncertainty: Heuristics and Biases', *Science*, 185: 1124–31.

Tversky, A. and D. Kahneman (1983) 'Extensional Versus Intuitive Reasoning: The Conjunction Fallacy in Probability Judgement', *Psychological Review*, 90: 293–315.

UNDP (United Nations Development Programme) (2002) *Human Development Report*, New York: Oxford University Press for UNDP.

World Bank (2005) *World Development Indicators*, Washington, DC: Oxford University Press for World Bank.

35

The Human Dimensions of the Global Development Process in the Early Part of the Twenty-first Century: Critical Trends and New Challenges

Mihály Simai

Introduction

> To allow the market mechanism to be the sole director of the fate of human beings and their environment, indeed, even of the amount and use of purchasing power, would result in the demolition of society ... Robbed on the protective covering of cultural institutions, human beings would perish from the effects of social exposure; they would die as the victims of acute social dislocation through vice, perversion, crime and starvation. Nature would be reduced to its elements, neighbourhoods and landscapes defiled, rivers polluted, military safety jeopardized, the power to produce food and raw materials destroyed. (Polanyi 1957; quoted in Leys 2001: 4)

Development may be measured in economic aggregates and the achievements of the different countries can be reflected in GDP statistics, but the human dimensions are of central importance, both as objectives and as input factors. This truism has been often forgotten in the international debates about the global changes and challenges. It is particularly important in the twenty-first century to include human dimensions in the analysis of changes which are influencing the global development process in this new era. In fact, all aspects of development, progress or decline are related to human actions and influence the life of human beings. Some of these changes have, however, more direct influence on it, while others may be more indirect. The process itself is embedded in a global social, political, cultural and economic environment with interdependencies and feedback between these processes.

Human beings are both the key actors and they are also directly affected by those comprehensive and complex global changes, which may be characterized as transformations in many key areas of the evolving world order. The new forces of history have phased out many of the long-, medium- and short-term political and socioeconomic processes that had earlier influenced the world.[1] New regulating forces, 'drivers' have emerged to replace, or to interact powerfully with, old forces.[2] These changes have been evolving in a number of critical areas – in global politics, economics, social structures, population trends, technology, environment and governance. Most of the changes are rooted in the global heritage of the twentieth century and are interconnected with the new evolving factors and forces in different parts of the world. New interrelationships have developed between various global processes. These forces and interrelationships are playing a critical role of forming the international system into a more complex and diverse structure.

The coincidence of major changes is rare in human history. The last stage of the twentieth century and the first decades of the present one comprise therefore a historically more or less unprecedented environment. The new era represents important challenges also for social sciences.[3] Alternative interpretations are offered and alternative solutions are proposed. The coincidence of these transformations created also new conditions for the global development process and particularly for its human dimensions.[4] It has been increasingly recognized, however, that the changes did not and will not have a common meaning for the different actors of the international system and many of their long-term consequences – both in positive and negative terms – may greatly differ, not only for the developed and for the developing countries, but also within the North and the South.

The development process has been characterized by several scholars and politicians as 'the global drama' of the twentieth century,[5] written by billions of individuals, the story of their hopes, efforts, successes, frustrations and failures.[6] The 'first act' of this drama has been considered as a 'golden age' by many people. It ended by the collapse of the efforts for the establishment of a new international economic order. The second act was dominated by the ideas and practices of the market revolution and the Washington Consensus. The directors and the actors changed too, both in the developed and in the developing countries. In most of the developing countries, the new generations of political leaders had quite different political experiences and intellectual background, than their predecessors, the leaders of the national revolutions for independence. People and societies all over the world have become more directly exposed to the forces of the world market. Due to the extent and character of the changes, one may ask the question, is the new era which started with the collapse of the socialist regimes and the dismembering of the Soviet Union a 'third act' in the drama, or the beginning of a new play? Probably it is. There are new actors and, while many of the old actors write the scenario, their increasingly diverse interests, values, ideas and actions make the outcomes much more unpredictable and uncertain.

The purpose of this chapter is to search for tentative answers to the question of how the changes shape the framework of the global development process and particularly its human dimensions in the new era. Will it be more or less conducive for the development process than the past 40–50 years have been? It is of course impossible to offer a comprehensive global picture of those actors and describe the challenges of the evolving era. What we can offer in this chapter is much more modest, to look at some of the main drivers of the changing global environment influencing development. These drivers include the global political processes, the forces of globalization acting in the restored universality of the world system of capitalism. Two other forces of change are discussed in this chapter and their interrelations with the political transformations and the globalization process – the influence of the demographic polarization and the forces of the new technological era. The transition to a knowledge-based society is particularly important from the perspective of human development.

The global development process in itself is of course an important dimension of the main global challenges of the twenty-first century. It is an important warning for the new century that in spite of the great progress achieved since the beginnings of decolonization, only two countries (South Korea and Singapore) joined the high-income states according the World Bank definition, and only two countries could escape the 'least developed' segment. Downward mobility has been more general than upward mobility. We have to answer, first of all, a fundamentally important question: will the new era, characterized by a politically univocal, hierarchical global political structure, be more conducive for the development process, that the bipolar world of the Cold War era?

Will the evolving global political order be more or less conducive for the development process?

The emergence of the Third World in the second half of the twentieth century has been the consequence of those major, global political transformations which resulted in the bipolarity and had important global consequences for the functioning of the given world order. The 1990s marked the conclusion of the period of great empires. Its precise terminus was the collapse of the Soviet Union, which was the territorial successor of the Russian Empire. The process of imperial collapse began with the Spanish, the Ottoman Empire followed suit, as did the British, the French, and so on until the cessation of the Russian Empire. A historical period, which lasted close to 500 years, has ended.

The political changes included the collapse of some of the main pillars of the Versailles–Washington peace regime, an imperial order, established after the First World War, and of the Yalta–Potsdam peace regime established after the Second World War. The collapse of the colonial empires including of the Soviet Union resulted in a great number of new states and new political and economic power structure. The hierarchical political unipolarity may last for quite some time as the result of these changes the traditional concept of the Third World as a non-aligned part of the world lost its meaning as an organizing concept of geopolitics.[7]

Non-alignment has, by and large, lost its old meaning and cohesive force and with that an important political component of the southern solidarity became substantially weaker if not completely lost. The developing world has also lost a large part of its bargaining power. With the disintegration of the bipolar system of the global power structure, the South is not needed any more as an ally or proxy in different East–West conflicts. It is not just the development demagogy of the Cold War that lost its political ground; there is also dwindling political support for development as a key issue on the international agenda. The major powers of the world are in the process of redefining their international policies and attitudes in a number of areas related also to the global development process. According to some experts, a neo-Third Worldism is emerging, characterized in a number of countries by indigenous, reactionary populism and a strong inclination towards cultural insularism.[8]

The global economy developed into a multipolar system. Three main economic concentrations emerged: the American, the European and the Asian. In the structure of the global economy the different development gaps between the rich and the poor states became even wider, this is particularly painful for the small, mini and micro states in the developing world, which have small markets, weak economic capacity and very little hope of modern development without well-functioning regional co-operation and more meaningful international support.

The political changes had also a major influence on the multilateral, intergovernmental institutions, the UN and the specialized agencies, the Bretton Woods institutions and others, which have been playing an important role in shaping the ideas of the development process, in the introduction of deliberate development policies and particularly in advocating the human dimensions of the process. The market revolution of the 1980s reduced the importance of development issues in the work and on the agenda of multilateral institutions. The Cold War tensions and the global arms race have been considered in the past in these organizations as major constraints and obstacles for their most effective contribution to the development process. It was expected by many experts that in the post-Cold War era, there would be a peace dividend, which will be distributed in a multilateral framework and accelerate global development. These expectations have not been realized so far. After the Cold War, national priorities changed and the states assigned a much higher priority to their own national (and frequently parochial) economic interests, than in the past. During the Millennium Assembly and its follow-ups, there have been a lot of political discussions, but much less political readiness for meaningful actions accelerating the global development process. The outcome of the September 2005 summit has not been a new breakthrough either.[9]

Another important change in global politics has been the disappearance of the 'bloc discipline' without a democratic replacement for the management of conflicts. A critical issue which dominated the second half of the twentieth century, how to constrain or discipline the behaviour of states, thus making states predictable reliable partners, will remain even more important in the world of the twenty-first century in the absence of the bloc discipline and with the new attitudes of the main powers. Global governance will require strong norms, enforcing authority and established codes of conduct in a global arena of constant change and full of unsolved old problems and new challenges. The international organizations will have to be better equipped in order to confront sources of international instability and manage risks that may otherwise result in global crises. The process of the political fragmentation is far from being over and it is jeopardizing many multi-ethnic states. In the developing world regional power centres are emerging, which may be interested at some stage to create a network of client states around them. It is still a very much open question how this process will develop. What is apparent, however, that as the number of states grows, so does the diversity of the global political system in terms of interests, values, intentions and political, military and economic potentials.

The number of unstable states, some of which are characterized as 'failed states', is growing; they have become sources of global risk through their own domestic instability resulting in civil wars, regional hostilities and human tragedies. Hundreds of thousands of people have been massacred in different civil wars in Africa. Together with the evolving grave social problems, many regions are increasingly destabilized. It is evident that these civil wars and local conflicts are not only detrimental for the development process, because of the material losses, but they are the sources of human suffering, resulting in masses of refugees, destroying rural communities. These changes may be resulting in the disintegration of many existing states and are in sharp contrast with the process of globalization which in both its theoretical understandings and practical consequences has been considered as the centrally important factor in the ongoing global transformation process.[10]

The influence of globalization, fragmentation and the 'restored' universality of the global capitalist system

The history of modern internationalization started with the industrial revolution and its different stages resulted in the growing interconnectedness of countries. In the early part of the twenty-first century this is sustained by the expanded global flows of information, technology, capital, goods, services and people throughout the world. But the future of globalization is not fixed. States and non-state actors – including both private companies and NGOs – will struggle to shape its contours. Some aspects of globalization, such as the growing global interconnectedness stemming from the information technology (IT) revolution, almost certainly will be irreversible. Yet it is also possible that the process of globalization could be slowed or even stopped, just as the era of globalization in the late nineteenth and early twentieth centuries was reversed by catastrophic war and global depression.

Globalization, by definition is interrelated with all aspects of global changes, including the development process and particularly its human dimensions. There are many erroneous and correct definitions of 'globalization'. I consider globalization a qualitatively higher level of internationalization with pervasive influence on the national economies, societies, politics, culture and other areas of human life. As for the consequences of the process, I also share the views of the late Pope John Paul II, that

> Globalization, a priori, is neither good nor bad. It will be what people make of it. No system is an end in itself, and it is necessary to insist that globalization, like any other system, must be at the service of the human person; it must serve solidarity and the common good.

Globalization may be considered as a process resulting in the widening, deepening and accelerating of worldwide interconnectedness in all aspects of social life, from the cultural to the criminal, the financial to the spiritual. Globalization can be also characterized as the new global age of market integration – open trade, global financial flows, driven by transnational corporations (TNCs). With a multifaceted notion of globalization, some aspects of it, for example the worldwide criminal networks, the global spread of illegal drug trade, prostitution, the faster spread of epidemics and other adverse consequences of the process should be blocked and eliminated. Other aspects of kinds of globalization, such as the global spread of honouring human rights and democratic norms, should be promoted. Most kinds of globalization, such as open trade, foreign direct investments and multinationals, are a mixed blessing. The extent to which these sorts of globalization enhance, secure, or restore human capabilities will depend on context and especially on how national policies adapt to the new demands, to what extent can they protect the losers.

For the majority of developing countries, it is very difficult to reconstitute themselves in a world order dominated by market forces and powerful global and regional actors and shaped by economic, political (regulatory), cultural institutions. Even in this age of globalization, the long-term goal of good national and global development must be to secure an adequate level of basic capabilities for everyone in the world, regardless of nationality, ethnicity, age, gender, or sexual preference. There is a grave danger that the forces of international competition divert their resources and capabilities away from more urgent development priorities such as education, public health, industrial capacity and social cohesion. This may also undermine nascent democratic institutions by removing the choice of development strategy from public debates.

Globalization, even during the existence of the two systems, was going on mainly within the capitalist part of the world, where liberalization was supported by the economically advanced states, the large financial institutions and industrial corporations. The human consequences of globalization have been influenced by the interests of the main actors of the system. With the collapse of the main pillars of the etatist-socialist system, capitalism became again global. It is important to question, particularly from the perspectives of the global development process, whether this system will be driven by the interests for expansion of markets and profits. Will it be leading to increasing levels of human insecurity, inequality in income, resources and opportunities? Or will it result a better world? The answers are not easy.

It is important to note that the global capitalist system of the twenty-first century differs in many respects from the capitalism whose universal character was broken in 1917. By the beginnings of the twenty-first century, the 'core' of the global market system in itself is more diverse than it was in the nineteenth and early twentieth centuries. There are no 'territorial empires' oppressing hundreds of millions of people. There are also different models of the market system: the American regulated liberal free market system, the different configurations of the social market economies of Europe, the co-operative model in Japan and in other Asian countries; and of course the hybrids which characterize mainly the developing world and most of the former socialist countries. The different models or reincarnations of the capitalist system are the results of a number of factors – historical traditions, social forces, the character and level of economic development, etc. The decades of co-existence with the socialist system, the internal political and social struggles influenced also the emergence and functioning of the different systemic models, by promoting different reforms. The systemic models in many developing countries have been shaped under the influence of the former colonial structure, the patterns of the socialist countries, the institutional pressures of the global market and evolving domestic factors. It is an interesting and by and large open question to what extent global capitalism will be able to manage the inherited and new challenges of the twenty-first century and particularly the development process.

In this context, the question, which was asked by Francis Fukuyama and some of his followers about the end of history, is not completely irrelevant for our subject (Fukuyama 1989: 16). Fukuyama published his work in 1989, before the collapse of the socialist system. One important statement of Fukuyama had been that the ideological competition, which according to him started with the French revolution about the main questions of the social progress, was over by the recognition that the capitalist market economy and the liberal democracy represent the future horizon. This formation has no alternative. There is no higher level of social development.

The restoration of the universal character of global capitalism at the last stage of the twentieth century served as the justification of his thesis. The protagonists of the market system formulated the promises of capitalism for the people mainly in three areas in the past: the constant improvement of material welfare, which was considered as an unprecedented process in human history; the freedom of the individuals; and that under the circumstances of prosperity and freedom, the individuals will be able to satisfy their hopes (Bell and Kristol 1971: 14–15).

The capabilities and readiness of capitalism to fulfil its historical promises on a global scale have been questioned time and again by different political and social thinkers and movements. In the light of many old and new problems of humankind, it is a fundamental question again to what extent will the evolving global market system solve or at least moderate them. It is not just the instruments and the capabilities that must be analyzed but also the interests and the collective will. Can the system be humanized and transformed towards the acceptance of ethical norms in its functioning in the age of globalization?

It has become already increasingly apparent that the social influence of the globalization process, and its main drivers, cut across the traditional social classes, which traditionally characterized capitalist development. In a simplified way, three main groups of the world population can be defined as emerging because of globalization. The first is the *globalized* segment of society. This is a diverse group, topped by the 'super-rich' of the world. The richest 225 people in the world have a combined wealth equal to the annual income of 47 per cent of the world's people. Two-thirds of these super-rich are the citizens of the industrial countries, while the remainder come from the Third World and the former socialist countries (UNDP 1998: 30). The most important and influential section of the group is the one that commands the hierarchies of the major institutions that have a fundamental influence on the political, economic and military processes of globalization, through their role in decision making. These people are also powerful enough to implement their decisions, due to their wealth, executive position or both. They are not solitary actors, but surrounded by specialists, advisers, consultants, scholars and institutions, and by the influential personalities in the media. Their power derives from a number of factors: personal wealth, the size of the human, financial and material resources over which they dispose, and the political and military influence of these decisions on various countries. Gustav Speth, the former administrator of the UNDP, wrote, 'An emerging global elite, mostly urban-based and interconnected in a variety of ways, is amassing great wealth and power, while over half of humanity is left out.'[11] The global profiteers and speculators often mentioned by the critics of globalization comprise only a small part of the 'global power elite' in the various societies.[12] Beyond the owners and managers of the 60,000–65,000 TNCs, there are 100–120 large international banks, auditing and consultancy firms, whose core executives also belong to the globalized group of society. According to UN statistics, the transnationals employ globally about 90 million people. Many of these work in sweatshops and cannot be considered as parts of the globalized society, but the small and medium-sized entrepreneurs who are their subcontractors belong to this group.

The global political elite are diverse and hierarchical. The role of the executive and legislative elite of the US, Japan, the main European countries, Russia and China are particularly important. Indicators such as presence in the General Assembly Hall during the speeches by heads of state at the UN Millennium Summit reflected well how the world 'evaluated' the leading politicians of different countries, in terms of global hierarchies. Apart from the top elected and appointed part of the political elite, the globalized group can also be considered to contain the majority of leading members of the civil service, the top military personnel and the academic community, as well as media figures and leading personalities in 'global' religious denominations. Naturally, the benefits are also shared by family members of these people. This segment can be estimated to include 15–20 per cent of the population in the industrial countries and much less in the developing world. Of course, there are great differences in income, power and influence among them. Some of them share common interests in the globalization process. They also share a number of common values and convictions, and even use a common language. They form the most mobile part of their society. They project an image and concept of success measured in power and financial gains. There is also a poorer part of the group, whose livelihoods nonetheless depend on the success of the globalized sectors, so that they share certain interests in this context.

At the opposite social extreme stand a much greater number of people. They are mainly losers. These people are not simply excluded from the globalization process and marginalized by it, but often (and increasingly) exposed to the global mass consumption and mass culture ideology, to a greater extent than the globalized group. They include the vast majority of the agricultural population, although the agricultural sector and agricultural population are also divided. Only a small minority is engaged in industrial-scale agriculture. The vast majority, including the masses of rural poor, belongs to the informal economy. However, there are some interactions between the two types of agriculture. The tens of millions who have been squeezed out of agriculture by the technological and economic changes in agriculture can only find an alternative livelihood by migrating to urban areas.

The large, diverse *non-globalized* group in society consists of the unskilled, most small entrepreneurs (especially the 'barefoot capitalists' of the informal sector), the urban poor, the unemployed, various ethnic minorities and the victims of social exclusion. Many people in this group are functionally illiterate, even in the industrial countries. According to an OECD classification, the proportion of functionally illiterate comprises 20–40 per cent of the population in its member states.[13] The proportion of this group is much higher in the developing countries. Those excluded include the 'proletarians' of the professional world, such as primary schoolteachers. Statistical estimates suggest that the group excluded from the globalization process may comprise about 50 per cent of the world population.

The third group consists of those between the two previous groups or on the frontiers of them. This group is exposed to the opportunities and losses connected with the globalization process, and tends to split. The well-educated and wealthier part will probably join the first group, as the knowledge-based economies open up new opportunities for them. The remainder will progressively experience the full disadvantages of the globalization process.[14]

One of the big dilemmas for social scientists examining the social consequences of globalization is to decide whether it will push humanity into stormy, turbulent waters. Can the process be managed in such a way as to reduce its detrimental effects and extend its opportunities to much larger numbers of people? These are not theoretical issues. They are closely related to such practical problems as the global organization of production and the social responsibility and accountability of the business sector. Also an important practical issue is the functioning of government, particularly in such areas as controlling market forces and the adverse consequences of global competition.

It was the late John Paul II, who in his Encyclical Letter, entitled *Centesimus Annus*, in 1991 raised these questions first, after the collapse of the Soviet bloc:

> The crisis of Marxism does not rid the world of the situation of injustice and oppression ... The Marxist solution has failed, but the realities of marginalization

and exploitation remain in the world, especially the Third World as does the reality of human alienation ... Vast multitudes are still living in conditions of great material and moral poverty ... Indeed there is a risk that a radical capitalist ideology could spread which refuses even to consider these problems ... and which blindly entrusts their solution to the free development of market forces.[15]

It is interesting to add that one of the active actors of the global market system, George Soros, has also arrived at similar conclusions. In one of his recent books *The Crisis of Global Capitalism* he characterized market fundamentalism, as a cruel, predatory system, which, however, can be modified and humanized (Soros 1998).

In the early decades of the twenty-first century the global order is developing with uneven spatial spread and sectoral intensity in technology, economics, finance, trade and culture. While most of the recent trends practically at all levels of human existence from human reproduction to global cultural co-operation are also put under the 'umbrella' of globalization, the global changes enshrine a great number of relations between different actors and trajectories in a wide variety of fields. Some of these relations are integrative; others can lead to further disintegration and fragmentation. These processes are not necessarily developing as contradictory ones, which are crowding out each other.

The influence of globalization on the development process has been the subject of heated debates. Some authors put the emphasis on the erosion of independent policy-making capacity in economic, social, cultural and technological areas, mainly due to the liberalization of markets and the unchecked power of the big players of the global system in capital and technology flows, in setting the rules and norms of the international economy.[16] Other authors and experts emphasize that globalization can contribute decisively to the eradication of poverty and the construction of a more equal world. In order to do that, however, the process has to be managed correctly and the right balance between market forces and government intervention has to be reached. In a recent book by Wolf (2004), the author compared 24 more globalized and 49 less globalized developing countries and arrived to the conclusion that the per capita GDP growth rates of the globalized countries has been faster between 1980 and 2000, and they have been more successful in reducing poverty, increasing employment, etc.

In my view, comprehensive empirical research work undertaken so far on the influence of globalization on the development process and particularly on its human dimensions is still not sufficiently widespread and complex for a convincing answer and there may not be an unambiguous statement on the issue. The alternatives are also missing in the analysis. Would a disintegrating world be better for the developing countries? How real are the possibilities for the humanization of the globalization process under the prevailing conditions?

The influence of globalizing economic forces on the different societies depends on many internal and external factors. The growing dependence of economic growth on exports of the developing countries has been well researched and documented. There have been also important studies on liberalization, which is one of the important prerequisites of globalization. Liberalization has resulted in greater inequalities in primary incomes in countries with weak competitive power.[17] According to an empirical study extended to a few countries, wage differentials between skilled and unskilled workers have increased (Ben-David 2000). Since the 1990s, the close co-operation of previous decades had weakened, and there could be serious negative consequences for world peace and development. The global economic turmoil of the last century's final years warns that there are serious threats to the health and stability of the global economy. One of the most vulnerable aspects of the post-Cold War world order is the poor public understanding of the functioning of the market system, and of how capitalism creates wealth. Arguments that open markets are very beneficial and that trade protection can be very costly are frequently overwhelmed by popular misconceptions and self-serving demands for protection against 'cheap' imports from China and other developing countries and 'unfair' trading partners.

In the new century, issues arising from economic globalization confront national societies and the international community. Earlier expectations at the end of the Cold War that economic globalization would lead to a world of open and prosperous economies, political democracy and international co-operation failed. A powerful negative reaction to globalization arose in both developed and in the developing countries. Rejections of globalization and its alleged negative consequences became especially strident within the USA, Western Europe and some industrializing economies. In many developing countries globalization has been blamed for everything from growing income inequality to chronic high levels of unemployment and even to the oppression of women. Certainly the future of the international economic and political system will be strongly affected by the relative success or failure of the proponents and opponents of globalization.

Many measures will be required to moderate the uneven consequences of globalization to increase human security and also to improve the ability of the countries to provide goods and services for the poor. This will require revisiting some of the policy prescriptions that have constituted the bulk of transformative reform these recent years. Domestic political issues related to the role of the state, the civil society and the character of governance in the developing countries moved also into the international limelight, under the slogan of improving the quality of governance. In principle, the globalization process created also better conditions for the more equitable distribution of global public goods, the spread of human rights and the global spread of democratization. All these are basically value-loaded and not just a set of better techniques. It includes national and outside pressures for the greater accountability of the local elite in the developing countries. It has also facilitated the greater articulation of conflicting interests, but often without promoting tolerance and institutional guarantees for the different minorities, ethnic or religious groups. It is evident however, that the sustainability of democratization requires also commitments from the international community and the implementation of those, which have been anticipated in the Millennium Programme.

Can the present system be managed in such a way resulting in the reduction of the negative effects of globalization, and make those opportunities that are offered by it available to a much larger number of people? This is not just a theoretical issue. It is closely related to such practical problems as the global organization of production and social responsibility and accountability of the governments and the business sector. The functioning of the governments, particularly in such areas as the harnessing the market forces, and adverse consequences of global competition are also important practical issues. The social consequences of globalization particularly in the context of labour conditions and standards, the prohibition of child labour and the use of prisoners in export industries became also important questions for the research work of international organizations.

The global distribution challenge and the development process

The increasing gap between winners and losers and its relation to the consequences of the globalization process is, however, only one aspect of the realities. It is related to a number of different economic and social problems and also to systemic factors. It was the late John Paul II, in 1991, who raised these questions first, after the collapse of the Soviet bloc.[18]

The Millennium Development Goals, adopted in 2000 by the participants on the Millennium Assembly, and the follow up summit in 2005, reflected the global consensus, that progress towards a more equitable society, reduction of human poverty in the developing world must be a central goal of global and national development policies in the twenty-first century.

The interpretation of the two main dimensions of inequality – inequality *between* and *within* countries – requires an understanding of the economic and social conditions in a complex way and the sources of differences between the main developing regions. International inequalities, the different gaps between rich and poor states, have been in the forefront of the international debates. The Secretary General of the UN in his Report to the Millennium Assembly rightly stated that the twentieth century ended without liberating humankind from dramatic inequality. The gap of incomes widened dramatically between the developed and less developed states. According to economic historians the difference in income levels between the poorest and the richest country was 1:3 in 1820, and 1:78 at the end of the twentieth century. UNDP studies suggest that the richest 20 per cent of the world consumed about two-thirds of all the goods and services while 60 per cent of the world's population receives less than 20 per cent during the last decade of the twentieth century (UNDP 1999: figure 1.6). There are other publications, according to which the gap is smaller, but they also recognize the widening tendency.[19] The historical roots of inequalities between countries are in most cases connected with colonialism and the unequal nature of the geo-economic conditions. The most recent tendencies are not only the consequences of domestic political shocks, civil wars, bad governance or systemic transformations, but also of the adverse consequences of global economic changes. The differences increased also within the developing world. The profound structural changes, which took place in their economies and societies, reflected the fact that the capabilities of many developing countries to cope with difficult economic and social problems improved. Those changes, however, were far from universal. The speed and scope of the changes of the different components, sectors and regions differed and asymmetries increased. The division between the neediest and the speediest in economic performance has made the developing world more diverse.

The inequalities within the countries have been also growing in most countries during the past ten to 20 years.[20] There are six main sources of inequalities:

(1) the distribution of incomes;
(2) the distribution of assets;
(3) distribution of opportunities for work and employment;
(4) distribution of social services and benefits, particularly education and health;
(5) distribution of political power, notably access to information and participation in political processes;
(6) gender inequality and social exclusion – their combined effects make the reduction of inequalities particularly difficult and explain the necessity of deliberate policies with complex measures for their implementation.

Inequality has increased within most countries.[21] On the basis of the available data, one can estimate a 'media' Gini coefficient for the African developing countries on global scale. This is approximately 44, which is higher than in many other developing regions. In China the Gini coefficient was 0.26 in 1984, 0.33 in 1995 and 0.37 in 2000. In Pakistan, the Gini coefficient is estimated to have risen from 0.37 to 0.41 during the 1990s. Income distribution in Latin America, a region traditionally characterized by high levels of income inequality, became more unequal during the 1980s and the 1990s. Inequality has risen not only between the groups at the two extremes of the income ladder – the rich have become richer and the poor have become poorer, in relative terms and in some cases in absolute terms – but also in a number of countries inequality has also increased between the richest and the middle income groups. The growing income inequality is partly explained by a major shift from labour to capital and its remuneration: the share of capital income in the total income has increased significantly in many countries.

The redistribution of assets within the countries is not a realistic option in the dominating global market system. The redistribution of incomes would require more progressive taxation. In order to empower people, countries should increase spending in education and assure a democratic access to credit and other productive resources. None of these measures, however, will be effective unless there is a concurrent, dramatic restructuring of many public programmes, and measures promoting employment by putting emphasis in the promotion of labour-intensive industries are introduced. The upgrading of the large informal sector and increasing the productivity of small-scale agriculture must be also important components of development policies.

Policies related to the reduction of inequalities would require also a broader perspective in the understanding of its roots in the inherent characteristics, the potentials and limitations of the market system and of the globalization process not only in general terms, but also in the given regions and countries. Is the present global system interested in and capable of, for example, returning to the full employment commitments of 1945? Under what conditions is possible to eliminate poverty in the global market system? Is social justice an acceptable idea and practice for the main actors and protagonists of the system?

While the answer to those questions would require a more profound analysis of the realities of the twenty-first century, one can anticipate that the progress towards a more equitable society and reduction of human poverty in the developing world is highly improbable if the inequality in the distribution of initial assets and final income is not substantially reduced. In order to do that, countries should make an effort to make taxation more progressive, provide income transfers, increase spending in education and assure a democratic access to credit and other productive resources, as mentioned.

One must refer an important reality in the context of the 'distribution challenge': markets, in the final analysis are social constructs, they are made of people. Market economies are particular social arrangements, constantly changing and evolving systems and instruments to serve changing human needs. Human needs in all of their dimensions at the same time are most directly related to global population trends and to the growth, spatial distribution, age structure, education, employment and welfare of the people of the world.

The transforming global population trends: a new era in the human dimension of development

Forty years ago, in 1965, the World Population Conference of the UN underlined for the first time the necessity of longitudinal analysis of demographic changes in development planning. The growth and quality of the population, its global and national distribution, the causes and consequences of poverty and inequality, the patterns of production and consumption and the environmental problems have remained since then central issues in the work of national institutions, international organizations and in the different disciplines dealing with development studies. In the 1960s several experts predicted an approaching disaster, due to a global population explosion.[22] Global population in 2005 was 6.4 billion, growing by about 76 million persons per year. By 2050, according to the projection of the UN, the world will add some 2.5 billion people, an amount equal to the world's total population in 1950. There is also a more or less general agreement between demographers that the world is approaching to the conclusion of a close to 200-year epoch in population trends, characterized by the acceleration in the increase of the population on the globe. Growth has slowed since it peaked in the mid-1990s at around 82 million annually. The average family size has declined from six children per woman in 1960, to around three today as family planning has become more accessible and widely used. Projections suggest total population will start to level off by the middle of this century, as fertility drops to replacement level or lower. But some countries will reach that point much later than others. There are two very important consequences of these demographic trends. One of them is a demographic polarization. In the developed parts of the world the population is declining and ageing. This trend is particularly important in Europe and in Japan, less in the US. The populations of Europe and Japan are now declining and the pace of decline is projected to double by 2010–15.

More than half of all children will be born in five countries – India, China, Pakistan, Indonesia and Nigeria.[23] The probability that 96 per cent of the projected growth will be in developing countries is a key challenge for the global development process. There are difficult questions requiring practical policy answers. How should the increasing number of young people in the developing world be made an asset in development, rather than an additional constraint? To what extent are the developing countries prepared to provide additional food, education and health services for their growing population? How can the developing countries create employment opportunities or acceptable sources of living for an additional 1 billion people in the coming decades? The latter is a particularly important challenge.

In the majority of the developing countries, such an increase of the number and share of people in the working age groups will be an increase in the supply of labour, much above the potential growth of possibilities to provide sustainable livelihood, particularly of employment in the modern sectors of the economy. One important consequence of the changing population dynamics is the pressure for migration. The demographic polarization may in itself increase both the pull and push factors. Such social problems as poverty, high population density, income disparities, lack of job openings, limited opportunities, unequal distribution of land, uneven agricultural development may be important push factors in a number of countries, stimulating large-scale migration of people both within the countries and on an international level. International migration of labour is a very limited option. Internal migration implies mainly the movement of people to urban settlements. People will have to be employed within a national economic framework. The individual governments must formulate and implement their employment policies in response to the domestic political, social and economic pressures and conditions (even though the domestic policies may have important international implications).

Transition to a predominantly urban world, which is another important component of the demographic transformation, may offer better opportunities for health, education and employment, but it may become a source of unprecedented problems for many developing countries. Not only will the majority of these countries live in urban agglomerations, but unprecedented large cities (mega cities) are emerging, concentrating 10–30 million people. From among the 23 largest cities of the world, with populations over 10 million, 21 will be in the developing countries. In 1975 about half of the inhabitants of the cities on the globe lived in the developing world. By 2025 about 77 per cent of city dwellers will live in the developing countries. In these countries the cities will have a dual structure This duality will be expressed in the cohabitation of ultramodern districts and slums, the 'citadels of the rich' and at the same time the 'ghettos of the poor' According to the projections of the UN, by 2050 there may be close to 3 billion slum dwellers on the globe.

All these indicate that such issues as family planning will remain a very important part of national and global population policies. Since the first global population conference in the mid-1950s, there has been major progress in family planning. The following global population conferences promoted the integration into national development strategies such population problems as the implication of the maternal health, the empowerment of women, the reduction of child mortality, the achievement of universal primary education, the specific tasks related to the changing age structure. There are, however, many unmet and new needs in the scope of family planning, in the reduction of infant, child and maternal mortality. The better harmonization of different policies and measures related to population dynamics require qualitative changes of many institutions on different levels of governance: in the local communities, in the framework of governments, on the level of the regions and of the global community. The tasks emerging in the harmonization of urbanization, population problems and development policies will be particularly important and difficult. Most of the socioeconomic problems related to urbanization have been, of course, fairly extensively researched. Still, the management of migration, the increase of employment and labour absorption capabilities, the upgrading of the growing urban informal sector, the problems of housing, the progress of infrastructure and general urban services in the slums, the specific consequences of stratification within the urban population, polarization between rural and urban areas, the specific problems of mega cities, the management of large agglomerations and the environmental problems in the cities, comprise just some important items on the long list of research and actions. Much more research will be needed also about the problems of youth and children, conflicts related to the different roots and consequences of social struggles, communal relations, ethnic, religious problems. The influence of the ongoing technological transformation on the population, education and health, and particularly on the economic changes in the developing countries will be one of the key issues in the global system of the twenty-first century.

The emerging knowledge-based world economy and the development process

The debate on the role of science and technology in development has a long history. Since the last third of the twentieth century high technology has become a primary factor in international competition, as a measure of progress and as an important goal for many countries. In its developmental dimensions three key issues have been raised: how to increase the technological capabilities of the developing countries, how to increase the role of knowledge in societies and how to disseminate the imported technology. Each of these issues has been dependent on the human dimensions of technological changes. The era, which started in the latter stages of the last century, is increasingly characterized as the transition to the 'knowledge-based economy' or society. In the debates, concerning the new challenges related to the new technological era, there are three main approaches to the new interrelations between technology and development. There are those who consider knowledge as quantitatively and qualitatively a more important factor in economic growth than ever before. Developing countries should therefore devote much more effort and funds for education and research. There is another view, according to which knowledge as a commodity has become more important than in the past in the competitiveness of the firms, and the essence of the knowledge-based economy is the knowledge market, which is based on the information revolution. This market is dominated by developed countries and TNCs. Developing countries must improve their competitive position, mainly by developing such an environment, which facilitates the growth of national entrepreneurship in competitive high-tech industries, and promote FDI. The third approach is emphasizing the double role of science and technology for people: the positive and potentially negative consequences and, in this context, the active role of the state and the civil society. For the developing countries it is necessary to be able to select and develop an efficient national system of R&D and innovations that is more relevant for their specific needs, instead of copying the West.

It is important to note that the developing world made important progress during the second half of the twentieth century. While there are still 'technological deserts', the techno-economic map of the world has been substantially redrawn by the beginning of the twenty-first century. The global spread of the key technologies has been much faster than earlier. About ten to 12 developing countries – China, India, Indonesia, Thailand, Egypt, Brazil, Argentina, Chile, Venezuela, Mexico and others – could establish more favourable conditions for the faster improvement of their technological and industrial capabilities by the faster development of the educational system, the active participation in the international networks of science education, information and production. Enrolment in higher education in the developing countries in general was more than 30 times higher in 2000 than in 1950. The industrial output of the developing countries in 2004 is many times higher than it was in the middle of the twentieth century and it includes modern, competitive high-tech industries. The combined GDP of the developing countries increased more than six times and in per capita terms close to three times between 1950 and 2004. The share of the South in global value added in manufacturing industries increased from less than 5 per cent in 1953 to about 23 per cent by 2000. Industry became the leading sector in the economy of many developing countries. While the dependence on the exports of primary products is still strong in many developing countries, the share of commodities in their exports has been declining. Economic growth for most of the developing countries has become much more dependent of international trade and FDI than in the past and new patterns of interdependence emerged. The northern markets in the new trade matrix became even more important for the South, but the importance of the southern markets increased dramatically for the North.[24]

The significance of South–South trade increased also, particularly within regions. Those developing countries that introduced and consequently followed export-oriented strategies not only discovered but also created complementarities among them. The share of the South in commodity processing and trade increased too.[25] All these changes have increased the global importance of multilateral trade negotiations for both the developing and the developed countries. The fact, that development strategies in practically all the developing countries shifted from import substitution to export orientation was a consequence of the recognition that in the age of globalization, national isolation may be counterproductive as guiding idea of development policy.[26] In an increasingly export-oriented South, the interrelationship between trade, scientific, technological and industrial development is also changing. Increasing global competitiveness through diversification, technological upgrading of the economy and new global linkages are becoming more important than in the past. The evolving new global linkages include the rapidly changing structure of relations with the TNCs. While a certain number of TNCs are still in the traditional commodity sector, the international firms contributed to the industrial restructuring of many developing countries through the establishment of new industries, particularly car manufacturing, petrochemicals, machinery, electronics, etc., and to the modernization of traditional industries, like textiles, and food processing.[27]

In the 1970s some of the international organizations, particularly UNIDO have developed different schemes for the deliberate global 'redeployment' of industries. They anticipated that migration of traditional branches of manufacturing to the South would accompany the new specialization of the North on high-tech manufacturing and services. This redeployment has been going on, but without any global plan. It has been guided by market forces and mainly by the system of the transnational corporations. Some of the developing countries created also favourable human and institutional conditions for the establishment of modern high-tech industries. The evolving new global division of labour in the early twenty-first century is based more on competitive than on comparative advantages. On this basis one can anticipate that by 2025 about half of the world's manufacturing output may come from the developing world of today.

Transition to the knowledge-based economy is, however, still a long-term, complex and uneven process everywhere, but particularly in the developing countries. Education in general, and science education in particular, is of utmost importance for transition to a knowledge-based society. The share of those people who are employed in high-tech sectors in the developing countries is still very low. Among the factors resulting in the uneven character of the changes has been a particular form of international migration. International migration is a complex phenomenon and can have many diverse causes. Historically, many nations have benefited from migration. However, when the migration is of highly educated and skilled people who go from poorer to richer countries, there is the so-called 'brain drain'. The smaller developing countries send usually a higher proportion of their highly skilled people to the developed part of the world. The proportion is usually smaller in the larger countries. The migration of scientists is the result of poor working conditions, lack of resources, scarcity of jobs, unstable institutional and governmental support for science and technology, as well as lack of incentives to scientists and science students, etc. Those countries that have fewer scientists per capita and badly need to increase their numbers are also the ones that are 'exporting' them to the richer countries. Brain drain, which so severely affects some of the less developed countries, can only be reversed by changing the above mentioned conditions. International co-operation must be more supportive in counteracting or mitigating the negative effects of such migration.

Improving agriculture is another very important consequence of the progress towards the knowledge-based economy and society, beyond progress in the development of modern industries. The better understanding and the efficient management of ecological problems and the creation of more favourable conditions for the social and environmental sustainability of development is also closely related to the ongoing technological changes.

Environmental challenges and the human aspects of sustainable development issues

Introducing the concept of sustainability constituted a major change in the theoretical and practical approach to the development process. The accumulation of environmental problems of the globe is, of course, a major challenge for the whole of humanity. The achievement of environmental sustainability is the bedrock of any future global human economic and social development. Meeting even the most basic needs of a stabilized population which, by 2050, will be at least 50 per cent larger than in 2005 implies greater production and consumption of goods and services, increased demand for land, energy and materials, and intensified pressures on the environment and living resources. Unsustainable consumption and production patterns, coupled with rapid population growth may result in environmental tragedies in many developing countries. Can the transition to a stable human population also be a transition to sustainability, in which the people living on earth over the next half century meet their needs while nurturing and restoring the planet's life support systems? On the basis of the recent experiences, the answer may be negative. On the other hand, scientific and technological progress resulted in most of the instruments for achieving sustainability within two or three generations. The diverging interests of countries, the different political approaches and economic priorities in consumption and production, the lack of financial resources and organizational capabilities are, however, shaping a less promising picture.

The history of the developing world is full of eco-catastrophes. Droughts and floods, scarcities of water, creeping desertification, earthquakes and landslides, are not unknown. Still these problems have been more of local or regional nature. The poor countries in the past have been more the victims of environmental degradation, before becoming the sources of it. In the twenty-first century they may be also important contributors by clearing large areas of the forests, transforming pasturelands to deserts, polluting soil and water, and contribution to global warming at an increasing scale. The problems caused by water scarcity by 2025 may hit 2–3 billion people. It is very important to avoid this perspective as much as possible by strengthening the environmental sustainability of the development process. The developing countries have many specific problems. As the developed industrial countries generate about 80 per cent of total global pollution, developing countries often remark that they do not want to sacrifice their development, thus mitigating some environmental damage in order to manage the problems caused by the industrialized countries. Some of the more radical experts or political figures of the South even accuse the North of environmental imperialism and insist that environmental issues cannot be dealt with in isolation from general global socioeconomic inequalities. The policies of the developing countries in the use of energy, for example, are more oriented towards promoting industrial development that is relatively cheap and which uses subsidized energy. While the divisiveness over priorities predominantly occurs between North and South, there are great differences between the different developing regions in the size and increase of population, the character of settlements, the accumulated damages caused by the development patterns, and the effectiveness of policies, dealing with environmental issues. There are important differences between developing countries in resource management, for example, in water or oil prices, or in the commercial utilization of tropical forests.

There are specific rural problems. In many developing countries there is a downward spiral of environmental degradation. For the poor and hungry people the key issue is survival. They often destroy their immediate environment in order to increase the available land, overgraze grasslands resulting in desertification and unsustainable conditions for agriculture and deteriorating conditions for biodiversity. They move then to the already overcrowded cities in order to find employment, where they become even more vulnerable to natural and man-made disasters. Cities face serious environmental challenges even in the developed countries. These are, however, dwarfed by the environmental difficulties of the cities in the developing world, where urbanization has greater influence also on the environment of neighbouring settlements. Waste disposal is also a greater problem in the developing countries. The interrelations of the urbanization process with water supplies are also an important and difficult issue. The use of water within the cities results in a faster increase in the total water consumption, and also results in greater and more concentrated sources of water pollution. The super-urbanization of the coming years indicates demand for new approaches to water management. It is important to note that about 60 per cent of poor people in the developing world (some 600 million people) live in highly vulnerable areas: arid or semi-arid lands, steep slopes and poorly serviced urban land. The rural poor generally suffer from ill health due to under-nutrition or malnutrition. Their health is also affected by various forms of pollution, mainly by water pollution, indoor air pollution and direct exposure to agricultural chemicals.

The harmonization of international actions and the co-ordination of the work of the different intergovernmental organizations in the area of environment have proven to be more difficult than expected. During the 1990s, much work was done in formulating and clarifying the concept of sustainable development and its implications for theoretical issues and research on economic growth also in the developing countries. The concept of sustainable development implied the greater emphasis on the quality of economic growth than its quantity in two dimensions of welfare – economic and social. The social dimensions of sustainability in their broader formulation enshrine the necessity of eradicating poverty, providing employment, improving human health conditions, education, managing the demographic problems, reducing inequalities and participation in more effective decision making. The interaction between the environmental and social dimensions, the operationalization of the concept of intergenerational equity has proven to be even more difficult in the developing countries.

Conclusions for global and national development policies

Practically all areas of the transformations dealt with in this chapter influence the development process and its human dimensions and consequences. Some of the influences are more detrimental, like the increase of political risks and uncertainties, factors leading to failed states, tensions, civil wars, terrorism. Other changes are more positive like the transition to knowledge-based economy, which may accelerate the development process and may improve the capabilities of humankind to avoid future ecological disasters. The most pervasive factors, the globalization process and the restoration of the universal global capitalist system, may have both positive and negative consequences. There will be many winners as global capitalism refashions almost every aspect of domestic and international economic affairs. There will also be many losers, at least over the short term, as international competition intensifies and as businesses and workers lose the secure niches that they enjoyed in the past. Economic globalization in the universal capitalist system presents both threats and challenges for the wellbeing of people everywhere. If individuals and societies are to adjust intelligently to the challenge of global capitalism, it is imperative that they understand the principal forces transforming international economic and political affairs.

Many future problems and their consequences are related to demographic changes, to demographic polarization, the changing structure of the population, to the patterns and rates of economic growth and employment, and to the process of urbanization. The common denominator between them is that their management needs co-ordinated international, preferably multilateral, actions and radical improvement of the quality of national governance. These can help to avoid adverse human consequences and at the same time use the opportunity for the spread of democratization and the transition to knowledge-based economy and society. There are differences between the influences of the various changes. The 'clockwork of history' has been moving at a different rate within global politics than within the world economy, and there have also been important variations in the depth and character of political changes. In the light of the evolving new problems, there is an increasing demand for greater predictability, reliability and accountability of policies in a complex system governed by increasingly divergent interests and divided by growing economic competition. In this increasingly undisciplined environment, the collective management of different regimes could become much more difficult. Old and new sources of risks and instability may overwhelm the opportunities for constructive action in the absence of significant, deliberate and new collective efforts to engage in such opportunities.

There are great differences also between the developing countries in their capabilities to deal with different new challenges and their consequences. This is due to several factors: uneven economic strengths, structural differences, information and communication gaps, economic and political mismanagement, etc. It has always been difficult to manage changes and to avoid or at least to moderate the adverse consequences of them. Some countries have proven to be more successful, others could not avoid political turmoil, economic collapses and massive human cost. In this new era of cumulative transformations, the tasks are much more difficult and the capabilities of the countries to deal with them are more diverse. Beyond the country- and region-specific aspects of adaptation there are some general tasks, which require multilateral actions.

First, global challenges require an internationally oriented domestic policy that goes far beyond the traditional domestic responsibilities of governments. This will not be possible without the better harmonization of diverse values, interests, intentions and without more effective assistance for the weaker countries. In the evolving global power relations the growing complexity in itself is a major source of uncertainties which require the strengthening of global security in a multidimensional framework. Increasing interdependence requires at a minimum that each country give more consideration to the consequences of its actions on others. Second, multilateral solutions can only work if they do not undermine national self-responsibility – they should be shaped accordingly. In the international system the improvement of the quality of co-operation and particularly of development partnership is a critically important issue. Third, the market has undoubtedly proven itself as the best co-ordinating mechanism between free agents. Some degree of competition is healthy for the world economy. There is no doubt, however, that market forces need control and orientation. That is why we need an international regulatory framework for globalization, with recognized rules and effective institutions. Fourth, the impact of globalization on the economic and social development is resulting in winners and losers. The separation of people into winners and losers; a language reflecting the centrality of competition in the market system appears to have connotations beyond economics and distribution of work opportunities, income and assets. The winners comprise on global level a small minority. The losers are much more numerous and diverse – most of them less educated and less skilled, most rural populations, many peoples living in remote regions and small towns and also those belonging to certain ethnic groups. The social dimensions of the main challenges, particularly of globalization, have to be given more consideration in national policies and in international co-operation. Fifth, there are also important tasks for developing more relevant theories.

The state-centred bureaucratic models of development were not able to give satisfactory response to the pressure of global markets and to the needs of more efficient resource allocation within countries. The dominating market theories, related mainly to the neoliberal school of thought, due to their limitations, particularly in comprehending the intensity and the scope of the changes and the role of different external forces and non-economic factors and with their short-term approaches, were not able to give appropriate responses to the new social and economic challenges. The demand for a new thinking on development became widespread, and some scholars emphasized the need for a new development paradigm. Institutional economics became particularly popular among the different theories. There is an Islamic approach, which is spreading in some parts of the world, and neo-Marxism is also gaining popularity. There are also important methodological requirements. Much more empirical research is needed for the support of national policies, for creating and using more information on the main trends and interactions in the changing society, influencing growth, income distribution, structural changes, etc. Such issues, as the elaboration of the conditions of sustainable economic and social development, or the interrelations between the technological transformation, and the socioeconomic aspects of the development process, require broadly based interdisciplinary research. An important methodological but also theoretical issue is the need to study much more thoroughly the history of ideas and theories on or related to the development process, and also the role of different international and national institutions in their global spread. This would facilitate better understanding for not only the changing intellectual background of development thinking, but also the sources of soundness or deficiencies and inevitable limitations in the different theoretical approaches and models.

Notes

Many thanks to Don Puchala of the University of South Carolina and to Jerome Glenn, Director of the Millennium Project of the American Council of UNU for their stimulating comments, and to Lorraine Telfer-Taivainen of UNU-WIDER for the valuable editorial and technical assistance.

1. The world order concept is particularly useful for the analysis of the international framework of the development process and its human dimensions in both its broader and narrower understanding. In the broader meaning, world order can be defined as the totality of globally valid norms, rules and international codes of conduct designed for, and generally observed by, states and transnational actors in the international public policy-making process. More narrowly, world order is the entirety of legally binding norms and institutions that regulate interstate relations. This definition is not dissimilar to the formulations offered by a relatively large number of scholars.

2. These regulating forces are many, and include the 'invisible hands' of global markets; social and technoeconomic factors, such as the socioeconomic conditions that determine how technology is used; government attitudes and policies towards technoeconomic problems; the international power structure dominated by the economic and political interests of major powers; the character and intensity of international co-operation; and the management and regulatory practices of international institutions and co-operation regimes, etc.

3. The implications of these transformations for global governance have been analyzed in Simai (1994).

4. According to the *Webster Encyclopaedic Dictionary*, 'development' means: to bring out capabilities or possibilities or to bring to a more advanced or effective state. In social sciences, it was first economics that introduced it as an attribute of a new discipline; development economics. In its broadest understanding, development meant primarily a task, to change backward, static societies, in order to achieve dynamism and capacity for sustained and sufficiently high rate of economic growth. The concept has been related to the dynamism of transformation (modernization) of the developing countries. Development has been considered as a complex and multidimensional transformation process, carried out by people who are either active agents or objects of the process, with different goals and expectations. It has been recognized from the very beginning of development studies, that the different groups in the society had different possibilities to influence the goals and the outcomes. It is not only the economic and social structure; the technological foundations, the human settlements, the way of life and the quality of life also are transforming the people.

5. Mainly after the famous work of Myrdal (1968), *Asian Drama*.

6. The history of the twentieth century is one of the characteristic examples for the conflicting aspects of the 'human dimensions' of changes. It has been the era of nationalism and of internationalism under different flags and ideologies, using peaceful or violent instruments. It was the century of decolonization, the disintegration of the great empires. The century has included some of the worst dictatorships of human history and the unprecedented broadening of freedom and democracy. Revolutions and counter-revolutions, world wars, national liberation wars, religious, class, ideological and ethnic conflicts paved the bumpy road towards the third millennium. Civil society do-gooders preaching human solidarity, narrow-minded dogmatic and violent fundamentalists, movements with members that were declared as terrorists and later became leaders of their new countries, political leaders who were responsible the mass murder of millions and are still considered as their heroes by certain groups, global organizations of criminals and many other strange, violent or non-violent groups were among its main actors. Ninety per cent of those scholars who lived and worked in human history have been shaping and developing the rapid progress of science and technology, embodied in new products, processes, consumer goods and horrible weapon systems. A radical improvement in the quality of life of many millions, mass poverty and misery, expectations, disappointment and despair of billions are all parts of the controversial heritage of the century behind us.

7. *Third World Quarterly*, in a special issue (2004: 25, 1) analyzed the character and the consequences of the political and ideological consequences of abandoning the concept.

8. See Hadiz (2004: 56).

9. Manmohan Singh, India's Prime Minister, was right in his statement during the Summit: 'we find that the international community is generous in setting goals, but parsimonious in pursuing them'. There was no clear or new commitment and timetable for the implementation of measures adopted by previous strategic conferences or summits and no clear future commitment were made. The summit left mainly question marks concerning the will and ability to fulfil the Millennium Development Goals.

10. Some social scientists consider globalization, with its pervasive, multidimensional and multilevel consequences, as a new paradigm that will replace the traditional approach of analyzing social processes in national framework. I do not intend to discuss the paradigm theory, popular though it has become in some schools of social scientific thought. Scholars are generally inclined to use a central hypothesis in their research like the trunk of a tree, on which they can develop the branches and flowers of their arguments. The social sciences have never been able to build on a single central factor. Societies are complex systems influenced by several factors and the interactions between them.

11. *The New York Times*, 15 July 1996: 55.

12. Mills (1956: 269–97) provides an authoritative account of the American ruling elite. It could still offer an interesting starting point for analyzing the global power elite, which is an important task awaiting sociologists.

13. See Foreman (1999).
14. See Drucker (1994).
15. *Centesimus Annus* Encyclical Letter, 1 May 1991: 82–3. USA Catholic Conference, Publication No. 436–8, Washington, DC.
16. See, for example, Khor (2000).
17. See Berg and Taylor (2000).
18. *Centesimus Annus* Encyclical Letter, 1 May 1991: 82–3. USA Catholic Conference, Publication No. 436–8, Washington, DC.
19. Milanovic (2005), in his recent book, wrote that the incomes of the richest countries, which were 16 times higher than those of the poorest countries in the 1960s, grew to be 35 times higher by the end of the century.
20. An important study undertaken by the United Nations Secretariat, DESA-Division for Social Policy and Development in the framework of the UN International Forum for Social Development programme on Equity, Inequalities and Interdependence, underlined that interpreting inequality within the countries requires an understanding of the economic and social conditions and processes in a complex way and the sources of differences between the main developing regions of the word. The papers will be published in 2006.
21. See above.
22. Since the release of *The Population Bomb* in 1968, Ehrlich has been one of the most frequently cited 'experts' on environmental issues by the media, despite the fact that his predictions on the fate of the planet, more often than not, have been wrong. In the book Ehrlich predicted that hundreds of millions of people would die of starvation during the 1970s because the earth's inhabitants would multiply at a faster rate than the world's ability to supply food. Six years later, in *The End of Affluence*, a book he co-authored with his wife Anne, Ehrlich increased his death toll estimate suggesting that a billion or more could die from starvation by the mid-1980s. By 1985, Ehrlich predicted, the world would enter a genuine era of scarcity. Ehrlich's predicted famines never materialized. Indeed, the death toll from famines steadily declined over the 25-year period. Though world population has grown by more 50 per cent since 1968, food production has grown at an even faster rate due to technological advances.
23. UNFPA (2004: 106–8). Practically all developing countries surveyed in the report incorporated some population policy measures in their development and poverty reduction strategies. The use of modern contraception has risen to 61 per cent of the couples by 2004, compared to 55 per cent in 1994. Efforts to fight HIV/AIDS have been stepped up. Still more than 350 million couples still do not have access to family planning services.
24. In 2002 the merchandise exports of the developing countries was already close to one-third. In 1990 it was about 25 per cent. Their share in trade of services increased from 18 per cent in 1990 to 23 per cent in 2002. In 2003 for the first time the USA imported more goods from developing than from developed countries. South–South trade accounts for about 40 per cent of developing countries exports (UNCTAD 2004).
25. By 2003 close to 50 per cent of the exports of non-fuel commodities of the South went to other developing countries. The figure for fuel exports was about 40 per cent (UNCTAD 2005).
26. Import substitution strategies, which were considered as the counterpoint to export orientation, had many different roots. They were the consequences of the beliefs that independent nationhood and economic decolonization implies protectionism and autarchy. The demonstration effect of successful past development patterns based on inward-looking import substituting strategy: Germany, the Soviet Union and others, also encouraged import substitution strategies. The rise of export orientation also has other roots than globalization. The failures of import substitution, the pressure of the international financial institutions and the demonstration effects of Japan and South East Asia are also among the causes.

27. At the beginning of the twenty-first century, traditional commodities made up 15 per cent of developing country exports, down from 24 per cent in 1990. Foodstuffs made up about 9 per cent, agricultural raw materials for industry 2 per cent, ores and metals 4 per cent. The share of fuels were 21 per cent (UNDP 2003).

References

Bell, D. and I. Kristol (1971) *Capitalism Today*, New York: Mentor Books.

Ben-David, D. (2000) *Trade, Growth and Disparity among Nations*, Geneva: WTO.

Berg, J. and L. Taylor (2000) 'External Liberalization, Economic Performance and Social Policy', *Center for Economic Policy Analysis Working Papers* 2000–02, New York: New School for Social Research.

Drucker, P. (1994) 'Knowledge Work and Knowledge Society: The Social Transformation of this Century', The 1994 Edwin L. Godkin Lecture, Cambridge, MA: J.F. Kennedy School of Government, Harvard University.

Foreman, M. (ed.) (1999) *AIDS and Men: Taking Risks or Responsibility*, London: Zed Books.

Fukuyama, F. (1989) 'The End of History', *The National Interest*, Summer: 3–18.

Hadiz, V.R. (2004) 'The Rise of Neo-Third Worldism', *Third World Quarterly*, 25, 1: 56.

Khor, M. (2000) 'Globalization and the South: Some Critical Issues', *UNCTAD Discussion Papers* 147, Geneva: UNCTAD.

Leys, C. (2001) *Market-Driven Politics: Neoliberal Democracy and the Public Interest*, London: Verso Books.

Milanovic, B. (2005) *The World Apart: Measuring International and Global Inequality*, New Jersey: Princeton University Press.

Mills, C.W. (1956) *The Power Elite*, Oxford: Oxford University Press.

Myrdal, G. (1968) *Asian Drama: An Inquiry into the Poverty of Nations*, London: Penguin.

Simai, M. (1994) *The Future of Global Governance, Managing Risk and Change in the International System*, Washington, DC: USIP Press.

Soros, G. (1998) *The Crisis of Global Capitalism: Open Society Endangered*, London and New York: Little, Brown.

UNCTAD (United Nations Conference on Trade and Development) (2004) *World Investment Report*, Geneva: UNCTAD.

UNCTAD (United Nations Conference on Trade and Development) (2005). *Some Key Issues in South-South Trade and Economic Co-operation*, Geneva: UNCTAD.

UNDP (United Nations Development Programme) (1998) *Human Development Report*, New York: Oxford University Press for UNDP.

UNDP (United Nations Development Programme) (1999) *Human Development Report*, New York: Oxford University Press for UNDP.

UNDP (United Nations Development Programme) (2003) *Human Development Report*, New York: Oxford University Press for UNDP.

UNFPA (2004) *The State of the World Population 2004*, New York: UNFPA.

Wolf, M. (2004) *Why Globalization Works*, New Haven, CT, and London: Yale University Press.

36
Development Questions for 25 Years
Lance Taylor

Recent development

Looking at recent history, a first point that stands out is that there has been a massive divergence of growth rates in the last decades. Figure 36.1 shows income ratios of poor to rich countries in purchasing power parity (PPP) terms for selected regions in the second half of the last century, based on data from Maddison (2001). The East Asian 'Tigers' are the only group showing a sustained increase over most of the period, with modest catching-up on the part of other Asian regions (including China since the 1980s, and more recently India) in the last 25 years. Elsewhere, ratios declined, most notably for the Middle East and the formerly socialist countries after 1975. The diagram is disturbing especially because the downward paths of the ratios in several instances are due to stagnation or a decrease in the absolute value of GDP per capita of the follower countries. For example, Africa's GDP per capita decreased from a high of 1,433 Geary-Khamis dollars[1] in 1977 to 1,217 in 1998. The Middle East fell to 4,053 Geary-Khamis dollars in 1998 from 4,716 in 1977. Lastly, the former USSR lost ground in record time, from 7,078 dollars per capita in 1989 to 3,893 in 1998.[2]

It is also notable that sustained growth among 'successful' countries was accompanied by structural change, an aspect of the whole process of development that has basically been ignored for the past 20 years. Tables 36.1 and 36.2 provide numerical illustrations, with implications for development theory. The former gives a decomposition of labour productivity growth for the Tigers and Southeast Asia between tradable and non-tradable sectors, with the overall total as a weighted average at the far right.[3] The total incorporates own-rates of productivity growth (weighted by output shares) for all sectors and 'reallocation effects', which are positive for sectors with relatively low average productivity (often non-tradables) in which employment falls or for high-productivity sectors (tradables) in which employment rises.

In the Tiger region, weighted own-rates of productivity growth in both sectors are high and reallocation effects generally positive. In Southeast Asia on the other hand, non-tradable productivity growth lags the rate in tradables (the finding for most countries) and reallocation effects are often negative. This sort of contrast

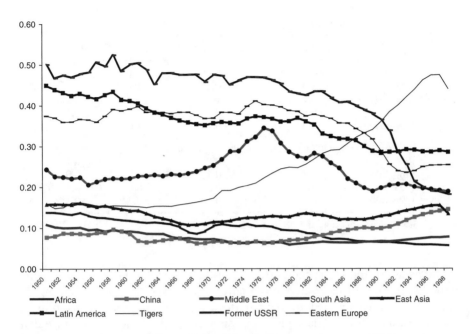

Figure 36.1 Catching up: GDP per capita of developing countries versus OECD

Table 36.1 Labour productivity decompositions

	Tradables		Non-tradables		Productivity
	Sector's productivity %	Reallocation effect %	Sector's productivity %	Reallocation effect %	Total %
Tiger region: Korea, Malaysia, Singapore, Taiwan					
1980–85	2.2	0.1	1.3	0.5	4.1
1986–90	2.0	−0.1	3.5	0.3	5.7
1991–95	2.5	0.1	2.5	0.3	5.3
1996–2000	1.8	0.0	1.8	0.0	3.6
Southeast Asia region: Indonesia, Philippines, Thailand, Vietnam					
1980–85	0.5	−0.6	−0.7	1.9	1.0
1986–90	1.1	−1.0	3.0	0.8	3.9
1991–95	3.1	0.2	0.9	1.5	5.7
1996–2000	0.1	−0.3	−0.7	0.5	−0.4

Sources: www.icsead.org and UN databases.

underlines how different economies perform differently at a disaggregated level, which undoubtedly helps determine their performance overall. Table 36.2 decomposes growth rates of the economy-wide employment/population ratio (far right) into an average of growth rates of the ratio by sectors weighted by employment shares. As it turns out, the ratio of a sector's own-employment to population will rise if the growth rate of its output per capita exceeds its growth rate of labour productivity.

Table 36.2   Population–employment decompositions

	Agriculture %	Manufacturing %	Others %	Total %
Tiger region: Korea, Malaysia, Singapore, Taiwan				
1980–85	−1.3	0.2	1.7	0.6
1986–90	−0.7	1.1	1.8	2.2
1991–95	−0.8	−0.3	2.1	1.0
1996–2000	−0.3	−0.2	1.0	0.5
Southeast Asia region: Indonesia, Philippines, Thailand, Vietnam				
1980–85	−0.4	0.0	0.5	0.1
1986–90	−0.3	0.1	0.2	0.0
1991–95	−1.2	0.2	0.6	−0.5
1996–2000	−0.3	0.1	0.2	−0.1

Sources: www.icsead.org and UN databases.

The panel for the Tigers shows that agriculture consistently shed labour while 'other' (tertiary) sectors created jobs. Manufacturing was job-creating during the 1980s but shifted to shedding labour (to a lesser degree than agriculture) in the 1990s. In Southeast Asia, agriculture was a far less dynamic labour source than in the Tigers and the other sectors were less effective at creating jobs so the overall employment/population ratio was quite stable.

Decompositions such those in Tables 36.1 and 36.2 can readily be constructed to analyze disaggregated effects of external shocks, import substitution and export promotion policies and so on. Work along these lines ceased to be popular two decades ago but that does not mean it is useless. In one final illustration of structural change, Figure 36.2 gives net borrowing flows (incomes minus expenditures) over time for the government, private and rest of the world sectors in the Tiger region (normalized by GDP). As an accounting identity, borrowings must sum to zero:

(private investment − saving) + (public spending − taxes) +
(exports − imports) = 0

with a positive entry indicating that a sector is a net contributor to effective demand.

In the Tigers, public sector spending as a share of GDP has been close to zero, so that private and foreign net lending and borrowing levels look like twins. There was an external deficit in the early 1980s, with a reversal signalled by the Plaza accord in 1985. A surplus period followed until the early 1990s, then a deficit which ended as the region switched to a strong trade surplus after the 1997 crisis. The private sector pattern is broadly the same, with signs reversed. Of course, the diagram does not establish which 'twin' is driving the other, but it does point to linkages to be explored. Again, patterns across countries differ. The Tigers illustrate flexible adjustment in the face of external and internal shifts. Elsewhere, one or

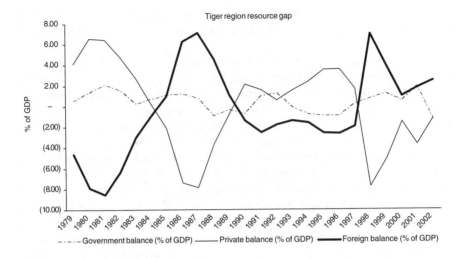

Figure 36.2 Effective demand decompositions

another sector may consistently lead demand, as has the government for several decades in India. What one does *not* see in general are opposite-signed co-movements of the fiscal and foreign deficits. That is, the traditional 'twin deficits' of orthodox open economy macroeconomics do not often appear. They have been at the core of IMF stabilization packages for 50 years. Small wonder that the programmes very often fail.

These decompositions are also useful in tracing though the implications of a major policy shift that has occurred worldwide since the 1980s – a move on the part of most countries to deregulate or liberalize their external current and capital accounts along with domestic labour and financial markets. They have also privatized public enterprises, de-emphasized industrial policy interventions, and allowed a greater private sector role in general. The results have been mixed (Taylor 2006).

As Figure 36.1 illustrates, growth performances deteriorated in many parts of the world. The success cases – the Tigers, China and, more recently, India – are scarcely paragons of neoliberalism. Liberalization has often been accompanied by a peculiar combination of 'macro prices', strong real exchange rates and high interest rates in particular. Together with current account deregulation, the shift in prices seemed to stimulate productivity growth and hold down demand in tradable sectors, which consistently shed jobs. Along the lines of Table 36.2, any employment creation that occurred took place in agriculture and non-tradable sectors, often at lower pay levels than in tradables. Import 'leakage' coefficients tended to rise and saving rates to decline in the wake of liberalization, leading to the net borrowing pattern illustrated in Figure 36.2 for the Tiger countries in the 1990s prior to the crisis. Not just in Asia, such shifts have been brusquely reversed as external accounts deteriorated. In somewhat related fashion, privatization and financial deregulation were followed by financial crises (sometimes repeated) in many countries.

Other supply-side policies seemed to have a range of results. Take the effort to stimulate human capital accumulation. A useful indicator is average years of schooling. After the 1970s, its growth rates were broadly similar in the Tigers, Latin America and sub-Saharan Africa. Levels differed, being roughly nine, six and three years respectively in 2000. It may be that a certain *level* of human capital is required to support development, but faster *growth* of this 'produced means of production' is clearly not closely associated across regions with higher growth rates of output per capita. Distributive impacts of all these changes also were mixed. High-quality jobs were lost in tradable sectors but in some cases employment opened up in non-tradables benefiting the poor. The functional distribution often shifted against labour and in favour of profits and (especially) interest earnings associated with newly deregulated financial sectors. Turkey and Brazil are striking examples of economies in which a distributive shift towards the financial sector has been accompanied by skewed macro prices, overall instability and unimpressive growth over the medium run.

Some more ancient history

It makes sense to place these relatively recent observations against a longer historical background, with a focus on the role of the state. Following Chang (2002) we can briefly consider how macro and micro 'policy' was formed when currently prosperous countries were growing rapidly.

In the USA throughout the nineteenth century, for example, investment in infrastructure like the Erie Canal and the railways was aggressively supported by several levels of government, with subsidies to the private sector often channelled via Wall Street which always took care to cream off a generous portion of the funding (Shapiro and Taylor 1990). The period between the Civil War and the 1890s was, of course, incredibly corrupt, with robber barons practically ruling the land under a succession of permissive Republican administrations in Washington. Even after the partial private regulation or 'Morganization' of finance in the 1890s and the subsequent reformist pressure from the Populists and Progressives, the system was at best partly democratic and economically opaque. All of this went on behind towering tariff walls, in a bank-based financial system without a central bank, embellished by patchy property rights and a corrupt judiciary.

Similar periods of state-sponsored developmentalism took place elsewhere: Sweden between the 1930s and 1980s, where a long string of Social Democratic governments actively collaborated with private industrial groups, notably the Wallenberg empire; Japan, Korea and Taiwan long had close state/private collaboration, which has been chronicled by many scholars (Alice Amsden and Robert Wade were the pioneers); Brazil was ultimately less successful but had an extremely high growth rate between 1950 and 1980 under state control. And as noted in connection with Figure 36.1, China and India are more recent success cases with rather tightly regulated market systems.

Thinking about development

Liberalization was of course heavily promoted by the Bretton Woods institutions under the famous aegis of the 'Washington Consensus'. One new strand in development thinking is related to liberalization's motley and often unfavourable outcomes. It is the study of 'governance' or how 'institutions' condition the development process. This line of thought easily boils down to 'blame the victim'. To put the two institutions' accusation in a childish vein: 'We gave you all those great policies. They haven't worked. Which means you have bad institutions. So it is your fault.'

Now, of course, the Bank and the Fund do not normally rant, but they have engaged in a great deal of discourse about how developing and transition economies should pull up their institutional socks along neoliberal lines, a view that is thoroughly ahistorical as discussed above. Other ideas are more worth developing. We can begin with notions relevant to the growth process as such. One important point, strongly enunciated by Nayyar (Chapter 31, this volume), is that policy-makers in developing countries have had their hands tied by the liberalization process in the areas of macroeconomics and industrial policy among others.

An idea tracing back to Adam Smith and recently restated by Reinert (2005) is that the economy can usefully be viewed as a combination of dynamic increasing returns sectors and more plodding constant or decreasing returns activities. The goal is to stimulate the former while shifting resources (especially labour) from the latter. Tables 36.1 and 36.2 illustrate how the Tigers succeeded at this task. The question is how to design policies that will facilitate similar processes elsewhere. As illustrated in Figure 36.3, Kaldor (1978) has always been a fertile source of thought about such an endeavour. Indeed, charting institutional changes that could open up degrees of freedom for the pursuit of developmentalist policies looks like a more fruitful approach than abstractly theorizing about institutions and trying to quantify their impacts along purely neoclassical lines. Some examples: does the open economy 'trilemma' really bind? That is, can independent monetary/fiscal policies, exchange rate programming, and open capital markets all be combined? In the land of textbooks it is straightforward to show that they can be, or in other words that the Mundell-Fleming 'duality' between a floating exchange rate and control of the money supply does not exist. A central bank in principle has enough tools at its disposal to control monetary aggregates regardless of the forces determining the exchange rate.[4]

In practice, however, arbitrary changes in monetary and exchange rate policies may be attacked by markets. Along Nayyar's lines, the question then becomes one of how other policies may be deployed to widen boundaries on feasible manoeuvres. Frenkel and Taylor (2005) argue that under appropriate circumstances a weak exchange rate can be desirable for developmentalist reasons. The 'circumstances' include a productive sector that is responsive to price signals, a monetary authority willing and able to maintain a weak rate for an extended period of time (perhaps supported by capital market and other interventions), and political willingness to bear the (conceivably high) initial costs of devaluation including potential

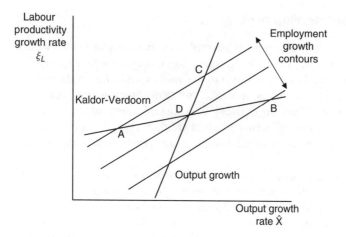

Figure 36.3 Joint determination of output, labour productivity and employment growth rates

inflation and output contraction. Getting away from the recent obsession with using the exchange rate for 'inflation targeting' could be a useful step towards making it a more developmentally useful policy tool.

In the area of industrial/commercial policy, the impact of the WTO has been to rule out interventions involving tariffs and trade while up to a point different forms of subsidies (witness Airbus versus Boeing) are still considered kosher. How can developing and transition economies operate effectively in this new environment? The Smith-Reinert prescription to stimulate increasing returns sectors did not cease to apply when the WTO was born. The question is how to implement it under present circumstances.

At the macro level, the question implicit in Table 36.2 is also relevant: how can economies avoid the 'jobless growth' that has been characteristic of the liberalization period? Evidently, productivity growth must be positive for per capita incomes to rise but demand growth must be stronger for employment to be created. It remains to be seen in many countries whether they will be able to programme rapid growth in demand under a regime of liberalized international capital markets. And how are these markets themselves to be regulated? This question became internationally prominent after the round of crises in the late 1990s. It could return again.

One way to summarize some of these ideas is in terms of differential growth rates of labour productivity, which have historically been the most important force behind diverging income levels across countries. Following Ocampo (2001) and ultimately Kaldor (1978), productivity growth in the medium run can be viewed as the outcome of two positive feedback loops building up from basic input factors such as the accumulation of physical and human capital, jumps in productivity resulting from successful industrial and trade policy, and the exploitation of technological backwardness. As will be seen, this system has strong implications for employment growth as well.

The first loop is from output and/or capital stock growth to labour productivity growth, as emphasized by Verdoorn (1949) and Kaldor. These authors insisted that industrial expansion (or, more generally, expansion of tradable or increasing returns sectors) is the key factor in transmitting technological advance. The second loop runs from labour productivity growth to output growth. Potential channels include stimulation of investment demand and relaxation of foreign exchange shortages via more rapidly growing production for exports. Finally, the growth rate of employment is equal to the difference between the growth rates of output and productivity. Following Rada and Taylor (2004), this observation means that one can plot 'employment growth contours' with slopes of 45 degrees in a diagram with the output growth rate ($\hat{X}$) on the horizontal axis and the labour productivity growth rate (ξ_L) on the vertical. Each line shows combinations of the two rates that hold the employment growth rate ($\hat{L} = \hat{X} - \xi_L$) constant. Employment growth is more rapid along contours further to the SE. As in Kaldor's (1978) original diagram (sketched verbally but not actually drawn in this chapter), Figure 36.3 also contains illustrative schedules for a 'Kaldor-Verdoorn' technical progress function (the first loop mentioned above) and 'output growth' (second loop).

The dominant tradition in growth theory is to make $\hat{X}$ endogenous by combining a predetermined growth rate of employment with a technical progress function, in effect dropping the output growth relationship. For example, if employment grows at the rate corresponding to the contour passing through point A, then its intersection with the Kaldor-Verdoorn schedule determines $\hat{X}$. If employment growth were faster, say along the contour passing through point B, then $\hat{X}$ would increase as well. However, under the standard assumptions its response elasticity would be *less than one*, so that output growth per employee is *lower* at C than A. This finding has important implications for the interpretation of mainstream growth methodology.[5] A second way to make the schedules in the diagram consistent with one another is to ignore the technical progress function while combining a predetermined employment growth rate with the output growth function as at point C. The productivity growth rate becomes 'endogenous' and unrelated to the Kaldor-Verdoorn schedule, precisely in the sense of New Growth Theory.[6]

A third approach to Figure 36.3 is to combine Kaldor-Verdoorn and output growth schedules, letting employment growth be determined along one of its contour lines as at point D. In a developing country context, one might reasonably take effective demand or available foreign resources as binding restrictions on $\hat{X}$.[7] With such a growth rate 'closure', effects on employment of shifts in the two schedules become of interest. The employment growth rate is higher for combinations of values of $\hat{X}$ and ξ_L lying below the contour running through D than at the point itself, and lower for combinations above. Faster overall productivity growth in the sense of an upward shift of the Kaldor-Verdoorn schedule would reduce $\hat{L}$ due to 'labour shedding'; an outward shift in the output growth schedule (for example, due to more rapidly growing aggregate demand and/or more availability of foreign exchange possibly) would speed up job creation.

Insofar as increased employment growth is a policy objective, it may or may not transpire depending on how the schedules shift. As we have seen, external liberalization in many developing countries in the 1980s and 1990s was associated with faster productivity than demand growth (especially in traded goods sectors), leading to reductions in $\hat{L}$. A combination of active industrial and exchange rate policies could possibly speed output growth enough to offset the job losses that liberalization has provoked.

Finally, a few thoughts about microeconomics. Stein (2005) points out the major complaint to be made about recent work is that economists have been spending far too much time using increasingly sophisticated techniques to examine data that are available, rather than thinking about how diverse economies really function in practice (which could suggest new ways to generate useful information). In other words, the profession suffers from the 'looking under the lamp post' syndrome. Even worse, the axiomatic nature of neoclassical economics has meant that data are used for 'verification' of theories, not their falsification. It is no surprise that the mainstream has such a paucity of new ideas to offer the developing world. Indeed, the major academic topics date back for decades: endless themes and variations around human capital; ever finer detail on the measurement of poverty with scant consideration of the socioeconomic forces that permit it to continue to exist; imperfect information models that 40 years ago seemed to be a mildly illuminating way to look at phenomena like sharecropping but which have little new to offer today; and the North/Coase musings about property rights that underlie much of the governance/institutional literature mentioned above. A more recent, seemingly more relevant literature based on field evidence in what the sociologist Peter Evans (2005) calls the 'institutional turn' usually turns out to be ersatz political science or sociology couched in phraseology that economists can understand.

As noted above, the institutional literature has been used by the Bank and Fund to justify the failures of their market-friendly policies. At the same time, many recent micro models support the old development economists' view that poor countries are rife with market-failures which can only be overcome by proactive policy intervention. The Bretton Woods institutions seem to want the theory to run both ways.

Where to go from here

As an institute devoted to development economics research, UNU-WIDER can and should play a major role in exploring the issues pointed out above – the analysis of structural change; a serious study of institutions and the role of the state, ideally from the perspectives of the 'old' institutional economics of Veblen, Myrdal and Galbraith and Hobsbawm's (certainly *not* North's) brand of economic history; and the construction of policy-relevant micro and macro models of developing and transition economies which can withstand academic scrutiny but which are not driven by academic fads. Lal Jayawardena, the inaugural director of UNU-WIDER, tried to push the institute in these directions. I hope it will continue to realize his vision for a long time to come.

Notes

This chapter is a revised version of a talk presented at a panel discussion on Prospects for Development at the UNU-WIDER Conference on WIDER Thinking Ahead: The Future of Development Economics, held in Helsinki on 17–18 June 2005. Support from the Ford Foundation and the United Nations Department of Economic and Social Affairs, and suggestions by Codrina Rada and Helen Shapiro, are gratefully acknowledged.

1. Geary-Khamis dollars for the year 1990 are Maddison's preferred benchmark numeraire for computing PPP income levels.
2. Needless to say, Figure 36.1 runs completely counter to the ahistorical optimism of mainstream authors such as Lucas (2000). His model resembles a horserace with a staggered start. Each successive group of poor countries leaves the gate some time after its immediate predecessor and then appropriates existing technology to run faster than all the rest to catch up. Because the USSR must now be reckoned a failure, over almost 200 years Japan and possibly the Tigers are the only observed successes among new entrants to the race.
3. Rada and Taylor (2005) present the formal details of the decomposition procedures discussed herein as well as empirical results for 12 regions.
4. For the gory textbook details see chapter 10 in Taylor (2004). Frenkel and Taylor (2005) present a more institutionally nuanced discussion.
5. For example, slower population growth will be associated with faster income growth per capita, a deduction from the model often used to support population control programmes. The fact that countries with negative population growth are not racing towards greater prosperity belies this particular notion.
6. For example, the well-known 'AK' model includes predetermined values of the national saving rate (s) and the output/capital ratio (u). Their product determines the output growth rate, $\hat{X} = su$.
7. Demand-driven growth models are presented in Rada and Taylor (2004). External constraints can be modelled in a gap model framework (Taylor 1994), taking into account foreign aid, capital movements and shifts in the terms of trade. Using a counterfactual methodology, Taylor and Rada (2003) show that output growth rates in the late twentieth century in sub-Saharan Africa and Latin America might have been substantially higher if the debt crisis and adverse terms of trade shocks had not happened.

References

Chang, H.-J. (2002) *Kicking Away the Ladder: Development Strategy in Historical Perspective*, London: Anthem Press.

Evans, P. (2005) 'Extending the "Institutional" Turn: Property, Politics and Development Trajectories', paper presented at the UNU-WIDER workshop on Institutions and Economic Development, 18–19 April, Helsinki.

Frenkel, R. and L. Taylor (2005) 'Real Exchange Rate, Monetary Policy, and Employment', paper prepared for the High-Level UN Development Conference on the Millennium Development Goals, 14–15 March, New York.

Kaldor, N. (1978) 'Causes of the Slow Rate of Growth of the United Kingdom', in N. Kaldor, *Further Essays on Economic Theory*, London: Duckworth.

Lucas, R.E., Jr (2000) 'Some Macroeconomics for the 21st Century', *Journal of Economic Perspectives* 14: 159–68.

Maddison, A. (2001) *The World Economy: A Millennial Perspective*, Paris: Development Centre, OECD.

Ocampo, J.A. (2001) 'Structural Dynamics and Economic Development', Mimeo, Santiago: ECLAC.

Rada, C. and L. Taylor (2004) 'Empty Sources of Growth Accounting, and Empirical Replacements à la Kaldor with Some Beef', New York: Schwartz Center for Economic Policy Analysis, New School for Social Research.

Rada, C. and L. Taylor (2005) 'Growth and Development in the Late 20th Century: The Great Divergence', Mimeo, New York: UN Department of Economic and Social Affairs.

Reinert, E.S. (2005) 'Development and Social Goals: Balancing Aid and Development to Prevent "Welfare Colonialism" ', paper prepared for the High-Level UN Development Conference on the Millennium Development Goals, 14–15 March, New York.

Shapiro, H. and L. Taylor (1990) 'The State and Industrial Strategy', *World Development*, 18, 6: 861–78.

Stein, H. (2005) 'Building on Lost Foundations: The Institutional Matrix and Socio-Economic Development', Mimeo, Ann Arbor: Center for Afroamerican and African Studies and Department of Epidemiology, School of Public Health, University of Michigan.

Taylor, L. (1994) 'Gap Models', *Journal of Development Economics*, 45: 17–34.

Taylor, L. (2004) *Reconstructing Macroeconomics: Structuralist Proposals and Critiques of the Mainstream*, Cambridge, MA: Harvard University Press.

Taylor, L. (ed.) (2006) *Economic Liberalization in Asia, Post-Socialist Europe, and Brazil*, New York: Oxford University Press.

Taylor, L. and C. Rada (2003) 'Would Better Terms of Trade and Capital Inflows Have Improved Economic Performance in Latin America and Africa in the 1970s through the 1990s?', Mimeo, New York: Schwartz Center for Economic Policy Analysis, New School for Social Research.

Verdoorn, P.J. (1949) 'Fattori che Regolano lo Sviluppo della Produttivita del Lavoro', *L'Industria*, 1: 3–10.

Index of Names

Notes: f = figure; n = note; t = table; **bold** = extended discussion or heading emphasized in main text.

Subject Index